The Sporting News
PRO FOOTBALL REGISTER

2000 EDITION

Editors/Pro Football Register
BRENDAN ROBERTS
DAVID WALTON

Editorial Director, Books
Steve Meyerhoff

Layout
Christen Sager, Terry Shea

Prepress
Michael Behrens, Dave Brickey, Russ Carr
Matt Kindt, Bob Parajon

Editorial Contributors
Joe Klaas, Joe Nonnenkamp,
Chris Paul, Josh Smith

CONTENTS

EXPLANATION OF ABBREVIATIONS AND TERMS

LEAGUES: AFL: American Football League. **Ar.FL., Arena Football:** Arena Football League. **CFL:** Canadian Football League. **CoFL:** Continental Football League. **NFL:** National Football League. **NFLE:** NFL Europe League. **USFL:** United States Football League. **WFL:** World Football League. **W.L.:** World League. **WLAF:** World League of American Football.

TEAMS: Birm.: Birmingham. **Jack., Jax.:** Jacksonville. **L.A. Raiders:** Los Angeles Raiders. **L.A. Rams:** Los Angeles Rams. **New Eng.:** New England. **N.Y. Giants:** New York Giants. **N.Y. Jets:** New York Jets. **N.Y./N.J.:** New York/New Jersey. **San Ant.:** San Antonio. **San Fran.:** San Francisco. **Sask.:** Saskatchewan. **StL.:** St. Louis.

STATISTICS: Att.: Attempts. **Avg.:** Average. **Blk.:** Blocked punts. **Cmp.:** Completions. **FGA:** Field goals attempted. **FGM:** Field goals made. **50+:** Field goals of 50 yards or longer. **F., Fum.:** Fumbles. **G:** Games. **In. 20:** Punts inside 20-yard line. **Int.:** Interceptions. **Lg.:** Longest made field goal. **L:** Lost. **Net avg.:** Net punting average. **No.:** Number. **Rat.:** Passer rating. **Pct.:** Percentage. **Pts.:** Points scored. **T:** Tied. **TD:** Touchdowns. **2-pt.:** Two-point conversions. **W:** Won. **XPA:** Extra points attempted. **XPM:** Extra points made.**Yds.:** Yards.

POSITIONS: C: Center. **CB:** Cornerback. **DB:** Defensive back. **DE:** Defensive end. **DT:** Defensive tackle. **FB:** Fullback. **G:** Guard. **K:** Kicker. **LB:** Linebacker. **OL:** Offensive lineman. **OT:** Offensive tackle. **P:** Punter. **QB:** Quarterback. **RB:** Running back. **S:** Safety. **TE:** Tight end. **WR:** Wide receiver.

SINGLE GAME HIGHS (regular season): If a player reached a single game high on numerous occasions—had one rushing touchdown in a game, for example—the most recent occurrence is listed.

EXPLANATION OF AWARDS

AWARDS: Butkus Award: Nation's top college linebacker. **Chuck Bednarik Award:** Nation's top defensive player. **Davey O'Brien Award:** Nation's top college quarterback. **Doak Walker Award:** Nation's top college junior or senior running back. **Fred Biletnikoff Award:** Nation's top college wide receiver. **Harlon Hill Trophy:** Nation's top college Division II player. **Heisman Trophy:** Nation's top college player. **Jim Thorpe Award:** Nation's top college defensive back. **Lombardi Award:** Nation's top college lineman. **Lou Groza Award:** Nation's top college kicker. **Maxwell Award:** Nation's top college player. **Outland Trophy:** Nation's top college interior lineman. **Walter Payton Award:** Nation's top college Division I-AA player.

ON THE COVER: Eddie George. (Large photo by Bob Leverone/THE SPORTING NEWS, action photo by Dilip Vishwanat THE SPORTING NEWS.)

Copyright © 2000 by The Sporting News, a division of Vulcan Print Media; 10176 Corporate Square Dr., Suite 200, St. Louis, MO 63132. All rights reserved. Printed in the U.S.A.

No part of the Pro Football Register may be reproduced or transmitted in any form or by any means, electronic or mechanical, including photocopy, recording or any information storage and retrieval system now known or to be invented, without permission in writing from the publisher, except by a reviewer who wishes to quote brief passages in connection with a review written for inclusion in a magazine, newspaper or broadcast.

ISBN: 0-89204-636-8   10 9 8 7 6 5 4 3 2 1

VETERAN PLAYERS

Please note for statistical comparisons: In 1982, only nine of 16 games were played due to the cancellation of games because of a player's strike. In 1987, only 15 of 16 games were played due to the cancellation of games in the third week because of a player's strike. Most NFL players also missed games scheduled in the fourth, fifth and sixth weeks.

Sacks became an official NFL statistic in 1982.

Two-point conversions became an official NFL statistic in 1994.

* Indicates league leader.	† Indicates tied for league lead.	... Statistics unavailable, unofficial, or mathematically
‡ Indicates NFC leader.	§ Indicates AFC leader.	impossible to calculate.
∞ Indicates tied for NFC lead.	▲ Indicates tied for AFC lead.	

ABDUL-JABBAR, KARIM   RB

PERSONAL: Born June 28, 1974, in Los Angeles. ... 5-10/205. ... Formerly known as Sharmon Shah.
HIGH SCHOOL: Dorsey (Los Angeles).
COLLEGE: UCLA.
TRANSACTIONS/CAREER NOTES: Selected after junior season by Miami Dolphins in third round (80th pick overall) of 1996 NFL draft. ... Signed by Dolphins (July 18, 1996). ... Granted free agency (February 12, 1999). ... Re-signed by Dolphins (April 13, 1999). ... Traded by Dolphins to Cleveland Browns for sixth-round pick (DT Earnest Grant) in 2000 draft and conditional fifth-round pick in 2001 draft (October 19, 1999). ... Granted unconditional free agency (February 11, 2000).
HONORS: Named running back on THE SPORTING NEWS college All-America second team (1995).
PRO STATISTICS: 1998—Recovered one fumble. 1999—Recovered one fumble.
SINGLE GAME HIGHS (regular season): Attempts—33 (September 20, 1998, vs. Pittsburgh); yards—152 (December 22, 1996, vs. New York Jets); and rushing touchdowns—3 (November 23, 1997, vs. New England).
STATISTICAL PLATEAUS: 100-yard rushing games: 1996 (4), 1997 (2), 1998 (3). Total: 9.

| | | | RUSHING | | | | RECEIVING | | | | TOTALS | | | |
Year Team	G	GS	Att.	Yds.	Avg.	TD	No.	Yds.	Avg.	TD	TD	2pt.	Pts.	Fum.
1996—Miami NFL	16	14	307	1116	3.6	11	23	139	6.0	0	11	0	66	4
1997—Miami NFL	16	14	283	892	3.2	†15	29	261	9.0	1	*16	0	†96	3
1998—Miami NFL	15	15	270	960	3.6	6	21	102	4.9	0	6	0	36	2
1999—Miami NFL	3	3	28	95	3.4	1	4	25	6.3	0	1	0	6	0
—Cleveland NFL	10	6	115	350	3.0	0	13	59	4.5	1	1	0	6	0
Pro totals (4 years)	60	52	1003	3413	3.4	33	90	586	6.5	2	35	0	210	9

ABDULLAH, RABIH   RB   BUCCANEERS

PERSONAL: Born April 27, 1975, in Martinsville, Va. ... 6-1/227. ... Name pronounced RAH-bee ab-DUE-lah.
HIGH SCHOOL: Barham Clark (Roselle, N.J.).
COLLEGE: Lehigh.
TRANSACTIONS/CAREER NOTES: Signed as non-drafted free agent by Tampa Bay Buccaneers (April 20, 1998). ... Inactive for all 16 games (1998). ... On injured reserve with thumb injury (December 28, 1999-remainder of season).
PLAYING EXPERIENCE: Tampa Bay NFL, 1999. ... Games/Games started: 1999 (15/1).
PRO STATISTICS: 1999—Rushed five times for 12 yards and caught two passes for 11 yards.
SINGLE GAME HIGHS (regular season): Attempts—4 (December 19, 1999, vs. Oakland); yards—12 (December 19, 1999, vs. Oakland); and rushing touchdowns—0.

ABDULLAH, RAHIM   LB   BROWNS

PERSONAL: Born March 22, 1976, in Jacksonville. ... 6-5/233. ... Full name: Rahim Fahim Abdullah. ... Name pronounced ra-HEEM ab-DUE-lah.
HIGH SCHOOL: Fletcher (Neptune Beach, Fla.).
COLLEGE: Clemson.
TRANSACTIONS/CAREER NOTES: Selected after junior season by Cleveland Browns in second round (45th pick overall) of 1999 NFL draft. ... Signed by Browns (July 22, 1999).
PLAYING EXPERIENCE: Cleveland NFL, 1999. ... Games/Games started: 1999 (16/13).
PRO STATISTICS: 1999—Intercepted one pass for no yards.

ABRAHAM, DONNIE   CB   BUCCANEERS

PERSONAL: Born October 8, 1973, in Orangeburg, S.C. ... 5-10/192. ... Full name: Nathaniel Donnell Abraham.
HIGH SCHOOL: Orangeburg (S.C.)-Wilkinson.
COLLEGE: East Tennessee State (degree in business management, 1995).
TRANSACTIONS/CAREER NOTES: Selected by Tampa Bay Buccaneers in third round (71st pick overall) of 1996 NFL draft. ... Signed by Buccaneers (July 13, 1996).
CHAMPIONSHIP GAME EXPERIENCE: Played in NFC championship game (1999 season).
PRO STATISTICS: 1996—Recovered two fumbles for three yards. 1997—Recovered one fumble for two yards. 1998—Recovered two fumbles. 1999—Credited with two sacks.

| | | | INTERCEPTIONS | | | |
Year Team	G	GS	No.	Yds.	Avg.	TD
1996—Tampa Bay NFL	16	12	5	27	5.4	0
1997—Tampa Bay NFL	16	16	5	16	3.2	0

1998—Tampa Bay NFL	13	13	1	3	3.0	0
1999—Tampa Bay NFL	16	16	†7	115	16.4	†2
Pro totals (4 years)	61	57	18	161	8.9	2

ABRAMS, KEVIN — CB — LIONS

PERSONAL: Born February 28, 1974, in Tampa. ... 5-8/170. ... Full name: Kevin R. Abrams.
HIGH SCHOOL: Hillsborough (Tampa).
COLLEGE: Syracuse.
TRANSACTIONS/CAREER NOTES: Selected by Detroit Lions in second round (54th pick overall) of 1997 NFL draft. ... Signed by Lions (July 14, 1997). ... On physically unable to perform list with foot injury (September 5-October 30, 1999). ... On injured reserve with toe injury (December 3, 1999-remainder of season).
HONORS: Named defensive back on THE SPORTING NEWS college All-America first team (1995).
PRO STATISTICS: 1997—Intercepted one pass for 29 yards. 1998—Returned two punts for 12 yards and recovered one fumble for seven yards.

Year Team	G	GS	SACKS
1997—Detroit NFL	15	4	2.0
1998—Detroit NFL	16	7	3.0
1999—Detroit NFL	1	0	0.0
Pro totals (3 years)	32	11	5.0

ACKERMAN, TOM — C/G — SAINTS

PERSONAL: Born September 6, 1972, in Bellingham, Wash. ... 6-3/298. ... Full name: Thomas Michael Ackerman.
HIGH SCHOOL: Nooksack (Wash.) Valley.
COLLEGE: Eastern Washington.
TRANSACTIONS/CAREER NOTES: Selected by New Orleans Saints in fifth round (145th pick overall) of 1996 NFL draft. ... Signed by Saints (July 14, 1996). ... Granted free agency (February 12, 1999). ... Re-signed by Saints (April 14, 1999). ... Granted unconditional free agency (February 11, 2000). ... Re-signed by Saints (February 15, 2000).
PLAYING EXPERIENCE: New Orleans NFL, 1996-1999. ... Games/Games started: 1996 (2/0), 1997 (14/0), 1998 (15/10), 1999 (16/8). Total: 47/18.

ADAMS, FLOZELL — OT — COWBOYS

PERSONAL: Born May 18, 1975, in Chicago. ... 6-7/335. ... Full name: Flozell Jootin Adams. ... Cousin of Hersey Hawkins, guard, Chicago Bulls.
HIGH SCHOOL: Proviso West (Hillside, Ill.).
COLLEGE: Michigan State.
TRANSACTIONS/CAREER NOTES: Selected by Dallas Cowboys in second round (38th pick overall) of 1998 NFL draft. ... Signed by Cowboys (July 17, 1998).
PLAYING EXPERIENCE: Dallas NFL, 1998 and 1999. ... Games/Games started: 1998 (16/12), 1999 (16/16). Total: 32/28.
HONORS: Named offensive tackle on THE SPORTING NEWS college All-America third team (1997).
PRO STATISTICS: 1998—Recovered one fumble. 1999—Recovered one fumble.

ADAMS, SAM — DT — RAVENS

PERSONAL: Born June 13, 1973, in Houston. ... 6-3/297. ... Full name: Sam Aaron Adams. ... Son of Sam Adams Sr., guard with New England Patriots (1972-80) and New Orleans Saints (1981).
HIGH SCHOOL: Cypress Creek (Houston).
COLLEGE: Texas A&M.
TRANSACTIONS/CAREER NOTES: Selected after junior season by Seattle Seahawks in first round (eighth pick overall) of 1994 NFL draft. ... Signed by Seahawks (July 30, 1994). ... Granted unconditional free agency (February 11, 2000). ... Signed by Baltimore Ravens (April 17, 2000).
HONORS: Named defensive lineman on THE SPORTING NEWS college All-America first team (1993).
PRO STATISTICS: 1996—Recovered one fumble for two yards. 1998—Intercepted one pass for 25 yards and a touchdown and recovered one fumble. 1999—Recovered one fumble.

Year Team	G	GS	SACKS
1994—Seattle NFL	12	7	4.0
1995—Seattle NFL	16	5	3.5
1996—Seattle NFL	16	15	5.5
1997—Seattle NFL	16	16	7.0
1998—Seattle NFL	16	11	2.0
1999—Seattle NFL	13	13	1.0
Pro totals (6 years)	89	67	23.0

AGNEW, RAY — DT — RAMS

PERSONAL: Born December 9, 1967, in Winston-Salem, N.C. ... 6-3/285. ... Full name: Raymond Mitchell Agnew.
HIGH SCHOOL: Carver (Winston-Salem, N.C.).
COLLEGE: North Carolina State.
TRANSACTIONS/CAREER NOTES: Selected by New England Patriots in first round (10th pick overall) of 1990 NFL draft. ... Signed by Patriots (July 19, 1990). ... On injured reserve with knee injury (December 29, 1990-remainder of season). ... Granted unconditional free agency (February 17, 1995). ... Signed by New York Giants (March 10, 1995). ... Released by Giants (June 4, 1997). ... Signed by Carolina Panthers

(June 12, 1997). ... Released by Panthers (August 19, 1997). ... Signed by Giants (August 21, 1997). ... Granted unconditional free agency (February 13, 1998). ... Signed by St. Louis Rams (March 5, 1998).

CHAMPIONSHIP GAME EXPERIENCE: Played in NFC championship game (1999 season). ... Member of Super Bowl championship team (1999 season).

PRO STATISTICS: 1990—Recovered one fumble. 1992—Recovered one fumble. 1995—Recovered one fumble. 1996—Intercepted one pass for 34 yards and a touchdown. 1997—Recovered one fumble. 1998—Intercepted one pass for no yards and recovered one fumble.

Year Team	G	GS	SACKS
1990—New England NFL	12	9	2.5
1991—New England NFL	13	10	2.0
1992—New England NFL	14	14	1.0
1993—New England NFL	16	1	1.5
1994—New England NFL	11	3	0.5
1995—New York Giants NFL	16	15	1.0
1996—New York Giants NFL	13	2	0.5
1997—New York Giants NFL	15	0	2.0
1998—St. Louis NFL	16	12	5.0
1999—St. Louis NFL	16	16	2.5
Pro totals (10 years)	142	82	18.5

AGUIAR, LOUIE   P

PERSONAL: Born June 30, 1966, in Livermore, Calif. ... 6-2/218. ... Full name: Louis Raymond Aguiar. ... Name pronounced AG-ee-ar.
HIGH SCHOOL: Granada (Livermore, Calif.).
JUNIOR COLLEGE: Chabot College (Calif.).
COLLEGE: Utah State.
TRANSACTIONS/CAREER NOTES: Signed as non-drafted free agent by Buffalo Bills (May 8, 1989). ... Released by Bills (August 14, 1989). ... Re-signed by Bills (March 27, 1990). ... Released by Bills (August 7, 1990). ... Signed by WLAF (January 8, 1991). ... Selected by Barcelona Dragons in first round (first punter) of 1991 WLAF positional draft. ... Signed by New York Jets (June 14, 1991). ... Granted free agency (February 17, 1994). ... Signed by Kansas City Chiefs (April 1994). ... Granted unconditional free agency (February 14, 1997). ... Re-signed by Chiefs (April 18, 1997). ... Released by Chiefs (September 5, 1999). ... Signed by Green Bay Packers (September 15, 1999). ... Granted free agency (February 11, 2000).
PRO STATISTICS: NFL: 1991—Made one of two field goal attempts (23 yards), rushed once for 18 yards and recovered one fumble. 1993—Rushed three times for minus 27 yards, attempted two passes without a completion and an interception, fumbled twice and recovered one fumble for minus 10 yards. 1997—Rushed twice for 11 yards and completed only pass attempt for 35 yards. 1998—Recovered one fumble.

				PUNTING			
Year Team	G	No.	Yds.	Avg.	Net avg.	In. 20	Blk.
1991—Barcelona W.L.	10	49	2029	41.4	33.7	15	1
—New York Jets NFL	16	64	2521	39.4	34.6	14	0
1992—New York Jets NFL	16	73	2993	41.0	37.6	21	0
1993—New York Jets NFL	16	73	2806	38.4	34.3	21	0
1994—Kansas City NFL	16	85	3582	42.1	34.5	15	0
1995—Kansas City NFL	16	91	3990	43.8	36.5	†29	0
1996—Kansas City NFL	16	88	3667	41.7	33.7	25	0
1997—Kansas City NFL	16	82	3465	42.3	38.2	▲28	0
1998—Kansas City NFL	16	75	3226	43.0	34.4	20	1
1999—Green Bay NFL	15	75	2954	39.4	33.9	20	0
W.L. totals (1 year)	10	49	2029	41.4	33.7	15	1
NFL totals (9 years)	143	706	29204	41.4	35.3	193	1
Pro totals (10 years)	153	755	31233	41.4	35.2	208	2

AHANOTU, CHIDI   DE   BUCCANEERS

PERSONAL: Born October 11, 1970, in Modesto, Calif. ... 6-2/285. ... Full name: Chidi Obioma Ahanotu. ... Name pronounced CHEE-dee a-HA-noe-too.
HIGH SCHOOL: Berkeley (Calif.).
COLLEGE: California (degree in physical education).
TRANSACTIONS/CAREER NOTES: Selected by Tampa Bay Buccaneers in sixth round (145th pick overall) of 1993 NFL draft. ... Signed by Buccaneers (July 9, 1993). ... Granted free agency (February 16, 1996). ... Re-signed by Buccaneers (February 20, 1996). ... On injured reserve with shoulder injury (October 27, 1998-remainder of season). ... Designated by Buccaneers as franchise player (February 12, 1999). ... Re-signed by Buccaneers (July 30, 1999).
CHAMPIONSHIP GAME EXPERIENCE: Played in NFC championship game (1999 season).
PRO STATISTICS: 1996—Recovered one fumble. 1997—Recovered two fumbles.

Year Team	G	GS	SACKS
1993—Tampa Bay NFL	16	10	1.5
1994—Tampa Bay NFL	16	16	1.0
1995—Tampa Bay NFL	16	15	3.0
1996—Tampa Bay NFL	13	13	5.5
1997—Tampa Bay NFL	16	15	10.0
1998—Tampa Bay NFL	4	4	0.0
1999—Tampa Bay NFL	16	15	6.5
Pro totals (7 years)	97	88	27.5

AIKMAN, TROY   QB   COWBOYS

PERSONAL: Born November 21, 1966, in West Covina, Calif. ... 6-4/220. ... Full name: Troy Kenneth Aikman.
HIGH SCHOOL: Henryetta (Okla.).
COLLEGE: Oklahoma, then UCLA.

A

TRANSACTIONS/CAREER NOTES: Selected by Dallas Cowboys in first round (first pick overall) of 1989 NFL draft. ... Signed by Cowboys (April 20, 1989). ... On injured reserve with shoulder injury (December 28, 1990-remainder of season).
CHAMPIONSHIP GAME EXPERIENCE: Played in NFC championship game (1992-1995 seasons). ... Member of Super Bowl championship team (1992, 1993 and 1995 seasons).
HONORS: Named quarterback on THE SPORTING NEWS college All-America second team (1987). ... Davey O'Brien Award winner (1988). ... Named quarterback on THE SPORTING NEWS college All-America first team (1988). ... Played in Pro Bowl (1991, 1992 and 1994 seasons). ... Named Most Valuable Player of Super Bowl XXVII (1992 season). ... Named quarterback on THE SPORTING NEWS NFL All-Pro team (1993). ... Named to play in Pro Bowl (1993 season); replaced by Bobby Hebert due to injury. ... Named to play in Pro Bowl (1995 season); replaced by Warren Moon due to injury. ... Named to play in Pro Bowl (1996 season); replaced by Gus Frerotte due to injury.
POST SEASON RECORDS: Holds Super Bowl career record for highest percentage of passes completed (minimum 40 attempts)—70.0. ... Holds NFL postseason single-game record for longest pass completion to Alvin Harper)—94 yards (January 8, 1995, vs. Green Bay).
PRO STATISTICS: 1989—Caught one pass for minus 13 yards, fumbled six times and recovered three fumbles. 1990—Fumbled five times and recovered one fumble. 1991—Caught one pass for minus six yards and fumbled four times. 1992—Fumbled four times and recovered one fumble. 1993—Fumbled seven times and recovered three fumbles for minus three yards. 1994—Fumbled twice and recovered two fumbles. 1995—Fumbled five times and recovered two fumbles for minus 15 yards. 1996—Fumbled six times and recovered two fumbles for minus eight yards. 1997—Fumbled six times for minus five yards. 1998—Fumbled three times for minus 20 yards. 1999—Fumbled eight times and recovered two fumbles for minus 12 yards.
SINGLE GAME HIGHS (regular season): Attempts—57 (November 26, 1998, vs. Minnesota); completions—34 (November 26, 1998, vs. Minnesota); yards—455 (November 26, 1998, vs. Minnesota); and touchdown passes—5 (September 12, 1999, vs. Washington).
STATISTICAL PLATEAUS: 300-yard passing games: 1989 (1), 1990 (1), 1991 (1), 1993 (1), 1994 (1), 1995 (2), 1996 (1), 1997 (2), 1998 (1), 1999 (1). Total: 12.
MISCELLANEOUS: Regular-season record as starting NFL quarterback: 90-64 (.584). ... Postseason record as starting NFL quarterback: 11-4 (.733). ... Holds Dallas Cowboys all-time record for most yards passing (31,310) and most touchdown passes (158).

					PASSING						RUSHING				TOTALS		
Year Team	G	GS	Att.	Cmp.	Pct.	Yds.	TD	Int.	Avg.	Rat.	Att.	Yds.	Avg.	TD	TD	2pt.	Pts.
1989—Dallas NFL	11	11	293	155	52.9	1749	9	18	5.97	55.7	38	302	7.9	0	0	0	0
1990—Dallas NFL	15	15	399	226	56.6	2579	11	∞18	6.46	66.6	40	172	4.3	1	1	0	6
1991—Dallas NFL	12	12	363	237	‡65.3	2754	11	10	7.59	86.7	16	5	0.3	1	1	0	6
1992—Dallas NFL	16	16	473	∞302	63.8	3445	23	14	7.28	89.5	37	105	2.8	1	1	0	6
1993—Dallas NFL	14	14	392	271	*69.1	3100	15	6	7.91	99.0	32	125	3.9	0	0	0	0
1994—Dallas NFL	14	14	361	233	64.5	2676	13	12	7.41	84.9	30	62	2.1	1	1	0	6
1995—Dallas NFL	16	16	432	280	64.8	3304	16	7	7.65	93.6	21	32	1.5	1	1	0	6
1996—Dallas NFL	15	15	465	296	63.7	3126	12	13	6.72	80.1	35	42	1.2	1	1	0	6
1997—Dallas NFL	16	16	‡518	292	56.4	3283	19	12	6.34	78.0	25	79	3.2	0	0	0	0
1998—Dallas NFL	11	11	315	187	59.4	2330	12	5	7.40	88.5	22	69	3.1	2	2	0	12
1999—Dallas NFL	14	14	442	263	59.5	2964	17	12	6.71	81.1	21	10	0.5	1	1	0	6
Pro totals (11 years)	154	154	4453	2742	61.6	31310	158	127	7.03	82.6	317	1003	3.2	9	9	0	54

AKERS, DAVID — K — EAGLES

PERSONAL: Born December 9, 1974, in Lexington, Ky. ... 5-10/180. ... Full name: David Roy Akers. ... Name pronounced A-kers.
HIGH SCHOOL: Tates Creek (Lexington, Ky.).
COLLEGE: Louisville.
TRANSACTIONS/CAREER NOTES: Signed as non-drafted free agent by Carolina Panthers (April 19, 1997). ... Released by Panthers (August 17, 1997). ... Signed by Atlanta Falcons (April 28, 1998). ... Released by Falcons (July 7, 1998). ... Re-signed by Falcons (July 21, 1998). ... Released by Falcons (August 24, 1998). ... Signed by Washington Redskins to practice squad (September 1, 1998). ... Activated (September 15, 1998). ... Released by Redskins (September 22, 1998). ... Signed by Philadelphia Eagles (January 11, 1999). ... Assigned by Eagles to Berlin Thunder in 1999 NFL Europe enhancement allocation program (February 22, 1999).

		KICKING						
Year Team	G	XPM	XPA	FGM	FGA	Lg.	50+	Pts.
1998—Washington NFL	1	2	2	0	2	0	0-0	2
1999—Berlin NFLE	...	3	3	10	15	0	2-5	33
—Philadelphia NFL	16	2	2	3	6	∞53	1-3	11
NFL Europe totals (1 year)	...	3	3	10	15	0	2-5	33
NFL totals (2 years)	17	4	4	3	8	53	1-3	13
Pro totals (3 years)	...	7	7	13	23	53	3-0	46

AKINS, CHRIS — S — COWBOYS

PERSONAL: Born November 29, 1976, in Little Rock, Ark. ... 5-11/195. ... Full name: Christopher Drew Akins. ... Second cousin of Jackie Harris, tight end, Dallas Cowboys. ... Name pronounced A-kenz.
HIGH SCHOOL: Little Rock (Ark.) Hall.
COLLEGE: Arkansas, then Arkansas-Pine Bluff.
TRANSACTIONS/CAREER NOTES: Selected by Green Bay Packers in seventh round (212th pick overall) of 1999 NFL draft. ... Signed by Packers (June 1, 1999). ... Released by Packers (September 5, 1999). ... Re-signed by Packers to practice squad (September 14, 1999). ... Signed by Dallas Cowboys off Packers practice squad (October 27, 1999). ... Assigned by Cowboys to Rhein Fire in 2000 NFL Europe enhancement allocation program (February 18, 2000).
PLAYING EXPERIENCE: Dallas NFL, 1999. ... Games/Games started: 1999 (9/0).

ALBRIGHT, ETHAN — OL — BILLS

PERSONAL: Born May 1, 1971, in Greensboro, N.C. ... 6-5/278. ... Full name: Lawrence Ethan Albright.
HIGH SCHOOL: Grimsley (Greensboro, N.C.).
COLLEGE: North Carolina.
TRANSACTIONS/CAREER NOTES: Signed as non-drafted free agent by Miami Dolphins (April 28, 1994). ... Released by Dolphins (August 22, 1994). ... Re-signed by Dolphins to practice squad (August 29, 1994). ... Released by Dolphins (September 14, 1994). ... Re-signed by

Dolphins to practice squad (September 28, 1994). ... Released by Dolphins (November 2, 1994). ... Re-signed by Dolphins (February 16, 1995). ... On injured reserve with knee injury (November 15, 1995-remainder of season). ... Released by Dolphins (August 20, 1996). ... Signed by Buffalo Bills (August 26, 1996). ... Granted free agency (February 13, 1998). ... Re-signed by Bills (April 15, 1998). ... Granted unconditional free agency (February 12, 1999). ... Re-signed by Bills (April 1, 1999).
PLAYING EXPERIENCE: Miami NFL, 1995; Buffalo NFL, 1996-1999. ... Games/Games started: 1995 (10/0), 1996 (16/0), 1997 (16/0), 1998 (16/0), 1999 (16/0). Total: 74/0.
PRO STATISTICS: 1998—Recovered one fumble. 1999—Fumbled once for minus eight yards.

ALDRIDGE, ALLEN LB LIONS

PERSONAL: Born May 30, 1972, in Houston. ... 6-1/254. ... Full name: Allen Ray Aldridge. ... Son of Allen Aldridge, defensive end with Houston Oilers (1971-72) and Cleveland Browns (1974).
HIGH SCHOOL: Willowridge (Sugar Land, Texas).
COLLEGE: Houston.
TRANSACTIONS/CAREER NOTES: Selected by Denver Broncos in second round (51st pick overall) of 1994 NFL draft. ... Signed by Broncos (July 12, 1994). ... Granted free agency (February 14, 1997). ... Re-signed by Broncos (April 15, 1997). ... Granted unconditional free agency (February 13, 1998). ... Signed by Detroit Lions (February 14, 1998).
CHAMPIONSHIP GAME EXPERIENCE: Played in AFC championship game (1997 season). ... Member of Super Bowl championship team (1997 season).
PRO STATISTICS: 1995—Recovered one fumble. 1998—Recovered one fumble. 1999—Fumbled once and recovered one fumble for eight yards and a touchdown.

Year Team	G	GS	SACKS
1994—Denver NFL	16	2	0.0
1995—Denver NFL	16	12	1.5
1996—Denver NFL	16	16	0.0
1997—Denver NFL	16	15	0.0
1998—Detroit NFL	16	15	3.0
1999—Detroit NFL	16	14	3.0
Pro totals (6 years)	96	74	7.5

ALEAGA, INK LB

PERSONAL: Born April 4, 1973, in Honolulu. ... 6-1/251. ... Name pronounced ah-lee-AH-ga.
HIGH SCHOOL: Maryknoll (Honolulu).
COLLEGE: Washington.
TRANSACTIONS/CAREER NOTES: Signed as non-drafted free agent by New Orleans Saints (April 25, 1997). ... Released by Saints (August 24, 1997). ... Re-signed by Saints to practice squad (August 25, 1997). ... Activated (October 17, 1997). ... On injured reserve with knee injury (December 3, 1999-remainder of season). ... Granted free agency (February 11, 2000).
PLAYING EXPERIENCE: New Orleans NFL, 1997-1999. ... Games/Games started: 1997 (3/1), 1998 (15/3), 1999 (8/2). Total: 26/6.
PRO STATISTICS: 1998—Credited with one sack.

ALEXANDER, BRENT S STEELERS

PERSONAL: Born July 10, 1971, in Gallatin, Tenn. ... 5-11/196. ... Full name: Ronald Brent Alexander.
HIGH SCHOOL: Gallatin (Tenn.).
COLLEGE: Tennessee State.
TRANSACTIONS/CAREER NOTES: Signed as non-drafted free agent by Arizona Cardinals (April 28, 1994). ... Granted unconditional free agency (February 13, 1998). ... Signed by Carolina Panthers (March 20, 1998). ... Released by Panthers (April 18, 2000). ... Signed by Pittsburgh Steelers (May 30, 2000).
PRO STATISTICS: 1995—Credited with $1/2$ sack and recovered one fumble. 1998—Recovered one fumble for 12 yards.

Year Team	G	GS	INTERCEPTIONS No.	Yds.	Avg.	TD
1994—Arizona NFL	16	7	0	0	0.0	0
1995—Arizona NFL	16	13	2	14	7.0	0
1996—Arizona NFL	16	15	2	3	1.5	0
1997—Arizona NFL	16	15	0	0	0.0	0
1998—Carolina NFL	16	16	0	0	0.0	0
1999—Carolina NFL	16	16	2	18	9.0	0
Pro totals (6 years)	96	82	6	35	5.8	0

ALEXANDER, DERRICK DE BROWNS

PERSONAL: Born November 13, 1973, in Jacksonville. ... 6-4/286.
HIGH SCHOOL: Raines (Jacksonville).
COLLEGE: Florida State.
TRANSACTIONS/CAREER NOTES: Selected after junior season by Minnesota Vikings in first round (11th pick overall) of 1995 NFL draft. ... Signed by Vikings (August 16, 1995). ... Granted unconditional free agency (February 12, 1999). ... Signed by Cleveland Browns (April 17, 1999). ... On physically unable to perform list with knee injury (July 27-August 11, 1999).
CHAMPIONSHIP GAME EXPERIENCE: Played in NFC championship game (1998 season).
HONORS: Named defensive lineman on THE SPORTING NEWS college All-America second team (1994).
PRO STATISTICS: 1995—Recovered one fumble. 1996—Recovered one fumble for three yards. 1997—Recovered one fumble.

Year Team	G	GS	SACKS
1995—Minnesota NFL	15	12	2.0
1996—Minnesota NFL	12	9	3.5
1997—Minnesota NFL	14	14	4.5
1998—Baltimore NFL	16	16	7.5
1999—Cleveland NFL	16	16	2.5
Pro totals (5 years)	**73**	**67**	**20.0**

ALEXANDER, DERRICK   WR   CHIEFS

PERSONAL: Born November 6, 1971, in Detroit. ... 6-2/210. ... Full name: Derrick Scott Alexander.
HIGH SCHOOL: Benedictine (Detroit).
COLLEGE: Michigan (degree in sports management).
TRANSACTIONS/CAREER NOTES: Selected by Cleveland Browns in first round (29th pick overall) of 1994 NFL draft. ... Signed by Browns (August 3, 1994). ... Browns franchise moved to Baltimore and renamed Ravens for 1996 season (March 11, 1996). ... Granted unconditional free agency (February 13, 1998). ... Signed by Kansas City Chiefs (March 2, 1998).
PRO STATISTICS: 1995—Fumbled three times and recovered one fumble. 1997—Fumbled once.
SINGLE GAME HIGHS (regular season): Receptions—8 (November 21, 1999, vs. Seattle); yards—198 (December 1, 1996, vs. Pittsburgh); and touchdown receptions—2 (November 29, 1998, vs. Arizona).
STATISTICAL PLATEAUS: 100-yard receiving games: 1994 (3), 1996 (3), 1997 (3), 1998 (2), 1999 (4). Total: 15.
MISCELLANEOUS: Shares Baltimore Ravens all-time records for most touchdowns (18) and touchdown receptions (18).

			RUSHING				RECEIVING				PUNT RETURNS				KICKOFF RETURNS				TOTALS		
Year Team	G	GS	Att.	Yds.	Avg.	TD	No.	Yds.	Avg.	TD	No.	Yds.	Avg.	TD	No.	Yds.	Avg.	TD	TD	2pt.	Pts.
1994—Cleveland NFL	14	12	4	38	9.5	0	48	828	17.3	2	0	0	0.0	0	0	0	0.0	0	2	1	14
1995—Cleveland NFL	14	2	1	29	29.0	0	15	216	14.4	0	9	122	13.6	†1	21	419	20.0	0	1	0	6
1996—Baltimore NFL	15	14	3	0	0.0	0	62	1099	17.7	9	1	15	15.0	0	1	13	13.0	0	9	1	56
1997—Baltimore NFL	15	13	1	0	0.0	0	65	1009	15.5	9	1	34	34.0	0	0	0	0.0	0	9	0	54
1998—Kansas City NFL	15	14	0	0	0.0	0	54	992	18.4	4	0	0	0.0	0	0	0	0.0	0	4	0	24
1999—Kansas City NFL	16	15	2	82	41.0	1	54	832	15.4	2	0	0	0.0	0	0	0	0.0	0	3	0	18
Pro totals (6 years)	**89**	**70**	**11**	**149**	**13.5**	**1**	**298**	**4976**	**16.7**	**26**	**11**	**171**	**15.5**	**1**	**22**	**432**	**19.6**	**0**	**28**	**2**	**172**

ALEXANDER, STEPHEN   TE   REDSKINS

PERSONAL: Born November 7, 1975, in Chickasha, Okla. ... 6-4/246.
HIGH SCHOOL: Chickasha (Okla.).
COLLEGE: Oklahoma.
TRANSACTIONS/CAREER NOTES: Selected by Washington Redskins in second round (48th pick overall) of 1998 NFL draft. ... Signed by Redskins (July 13, 1998).
SINGLE GAME HIGHS (regular season): Receptions—7 (December 13, 1998, vs. Carolina); yards—86 (September 19, 1999, vs. New York Giants); and touchdown receptions—2 (September 19, 1999, vs. New York Giants).

			RECEIVING				TOTALS			
Year Team	G	GS	No.	Yds.	Avg.	TD	TD	2pt.	Pts.	Fum.
1998—Washington NFL	15	5	37	383	10.4	4	4	0	24	2
1999—Washington NFL	15	15	29	324	11.2	3	3	0	18	0
Pro totals (2 years)	**30**	**20**	**66**	**707**	**10.7**	**7**	**7**	**0**	**42**	**2**

ALFORD, BRIAN   WR   GIANTS

PERSONAL: Born June 7, 1975, in Oak Park, Mich. ... 6-1/190. ... Full name: Brian Wayne Alford.
HIGH SCHOOL: Oak Park (Mich.).
COLLEGE: Purdue.
TRANSACTIONS/CAREER NOTES: Selected by New York Giants in third round (70th pick overall) of 1998 NFL draft. ... Signed by Giants (July 24, 1998).
PLAYING EXPERIENCE: New York Giants NFL, 1998 and 1999. ... Games/Games started: 1998 (2/0), 1999 (2/0). Total: 4/0.
HONORS: Named wide receiver on THE SPORTING NEWS college All-America third team (1997).
PRO STATISTICS: 1998—Caught one pass for 11 yards. 1999—Caught one pass for seven yards and a touchdown.
SINGLE GAME HIGHS (regular season): Receptions—1 (January 2, 2000, vs. Dallas); yards—11 (December 20, 1998, vs. Kansas City); and touchdown receptions—1 (January 2, 2000, vs. Dallas).

ALLEN, ERIC   DB   RAIDERS

PERSONAL: Born November 22, 1965, in San Diego. ... 5-10/185. ... Full name: Eric Andre Allen.
HIGH SCHOOL: Point Loma (San Diego).
COLLEGE: Arizona State (degree in broadcasting, 1988).
TRANSACTIONS/CAREER NOTES: Selected by Philadelphia Eagles in second round (30th pick overall) of 1988 NFL draft. ... Signed by Eagles (July 19, 1988). ... Granted free agency (February 1, 1992). ... Re-signed by Eagles (September 2, 1992). ... Granted roster exemption (September 2-4, 1992). ... Designated by Eagles as transition player (February 25, 1993). ... Tendered offer sheet by New Orleans Saints (March 20, 1995). ... Eagles declined to match offer (March 27, 1995). ... Traded by Saints to Oakland Raiders for fourth-round pick (DB Fred Weary) in 1998 draft (March 5, 1998). ... On injured reserve with knee injury (November 18, 1998-remainder of season).
HONORS: Played in Pro Bowl (1989 and 1991-1995 seasons).
RECORDS: Shares NFL single-season record for most touchdowns by interception—4 (1993). ... Shares NFL single-game record for most touchdowns by interception—2 (December 26, 1993, vs. New Orleans).

PRO STATISTICS: 1989—Fumbled once for seven yards. 1990—Returned one kickoff for two yards and recovered one fumble. 1991—Recovered one fumble. 1992—Recovered two fumbles. 1993—Credited with two sacks. 1994—Recovered one fumble for 30 yards. 1999—Recovered one fumble.

MISCELLANEOUS: Shares Philadelphia Eagles all-time record for most interceptions (34).

				INTERCEPTIONS		
Year Team	G	GS	No.	Yds.	Avg.	TD
1988—Philadelphia NFL	16	16	5	76	15.2	0
1989—Philadelphia NFL	15	15	‡8	38	4.8	0
1990—Philadelphia NFL	16	15	3	37	12.3	1
1991—Philadelphia NFL	16	16	5	20	4.0	0
1992—Philadelphia NFL	16	16	4	49	12.3	0
1993—Philadelphia NFL	16	16	6	*201	33.5	*4
1994—Philadelphia NFL	16	16	3	61	20.3	0
1995—New Orleans NFL	16	16	2	28	14.0	0
1996—New Orleans NFL	16	16	1	33	33.0	0
1997—New Orleans NFL	16	16	2	27	13.5	0
1998—Oakland NFL	10	10	5	59	11.8	0
1999—Oakland NFL	16	16	3	33	11.0	0
Pro totals (12 years)	185	184	47	662	14.1	5

ALLEN, JAMES — RB — BEARS

PERSONAL: Born March 28, 1975, in Wynnewood, Okla. ... 5-10/215.
HIGH SCHOOL: Wynnewood (Okla.).
COLLEGE: Oklahoma.
TRANSACTIONS/CAREER NOTES: Signed as non-drafted free agent by Tennessee Oilers (May 14, 1997). ... Released by Oilers (August 20, 1997). ... Signed by Philadelphia Eagles to practice squad (August 27, 1997). ... Released by Eagles (September 2, 1997). ... Re-signed by Eagles to practice squad (September 10, 1997). ... Signed by Chicago Bears off Eagles practice squad (December 9, 1997). ... Inactive for two games (1997). ... Released by Bears (August 25, 1998). ... Re-signed by Bears to practice squad (August 31, 1998). ... Activated (October 13, 1998).
PRO STATISTICS: 1998—Recovered two fumbles.
SINGLE GAME HIGHS (regular season): Attempts—23 (December 20, 1998, vs. Baltimore); yards—163 (December 20, 1998, vs. Baltimore); and rushing touchdowns—1 (December 20, 1998, vs. Baltimore).
STATISTICAL PLATEAUS: 100-yard rushing games: 1998 (1).

			RUSHING				RECEIVING				TOTALS			
Year Team	G	GS	Att.	Yds.	Avg.	TD	No.	Yds.	Avg.	TD	TD	2pt.	Pts.	Fum.
1997—Chicago NFL					Did not play.									
1998—Chicago NFL	6	2	58	270	4.7	1	8	77	9.6	1	2	0	12	1
1999—Chicago NFL	12	3	32	119	3.7	0	9	91	10.1	0	0	0	0	0
Pro totals (2 years)	18	5	90	389	4.3	1	17	168	9.9	1	2	0	12	1

ALLEN, LARRY — G — COWBOYS

PERSONAL: Born November 27, 1971, in Los Angeles. ... 6-3/326. ... Full name: Larry Christopher Allen.
HIGH SCHOOL: Vintage (Napa, Calif.).
JUNIOR COLLEGE: Butte College (Calif.).
COLLEGE: Sonoma State (Calif.).
TRANSACTIONS/CAREER NOTES: Selected by Dallas Cowboys in second round (46th pick overall) of 1994 NFL draft. ... Signed by Cowboys (July 16, 1994).
PLAYING EXPERIENCE: Dallas NFL, 1994-1999. ... Games/Games started: 1994 (16/10), 1995 (16/16), 1996 (16/16), 1997 (16/16), 1998 (16/16), 1999 (11/11). Total: 91/85.
CHAMPIONSHIP GAME EXPERIENCE: Played in NFC championship game (1994 and 1995 seasons). ... Member of Super Bowl championship team (1995 season).
HONORS: Named guard on The Sporting News NFL All-Pro team (1995-97 and 1999). ... Played in Pro Bowl (1995-1998 seasons). ... Named to play in Pro Bowl (1999 season); replaced by Adam Timmerman due to injury. ... Named offensive tackle on The Sporting News NFL All-Pro team (1998).
PRO STATISTICS: 1995—Recovered one fumble.

ALLEN, TAJE — CB — RAMS

PERSONAL: Born November 6, 1973, in Lubbock, Texas. ... 5-10/185. ... Full name: Taje LaQuane Allen.
HIGH SCHOOL: Estacado (Lubbock, Texas).
COLLEGE: Texas.
TRANSACTIONS/CAREER NOTES: Selected by St. Louis Rams in fifth round (158th pick overall) of 1997 NFL draft. ... Signed by Rams (July 3, 1997). ... Granted free agency (February 11, 2000).
PLAYING EXPERIENCE: St. Louis NFL, 1997-1999. ... Games/Games started: 1997 (14/1), 1998 (16/0), 1999 (16/2). Total: 46/3.
CHAMPIONSHIP GAME EXPERIENCE: Played in NFC championship game (1999 season). ... Member of Super Bowl championship team (1999 season); did not play.
PRO STATISTICS: 1999—Intercepted two passes for 76 yards and credited with 1/2 sack.

ALLEN, TERRY — RB

PERSONAL: Born February 21, 1968, in Commerce, Ga. ... 5-10/208. ... Full name: Terry Thomas Allen Jr.
HIGH SCHOOL: Banks County (Homer, Ga.).

COLLEGE: Clemson.

TRANSACTIONS/CAREER NOTES: Selected after junior season by Minnesota Vikings in ninth round (241st pick overall) of 1990 NFL draft. ... Signed by Vikings (July 2, 1990). ... On injured reserve with knee injury (August 28, 1990-entire season). ... On injured reserve with knee injury (August 23, 1993-entire season). ... Released by Vikings (May 8, 1995). ... Signed by Washington Redskins (June 15, 1995). ... Granted free agency (February 16, 1996). ... Re-signed by Redskins (July 17, 1996). ... Granted unconditional free agency (February 14, 1997). ... Re-signed by Redskins (February 26, 1997). ... Released by Redskins (April 19, 1999). ... Signed by New England Patriots (August 27, 1999). ... Released by Patriots (February 14, 2000).

HONORS: Played in Pro Bowl (1996 season).

PRO STATISTICS: 1991—Returned one kickoff for 14 yards and recovered one fumble. 1992—Recovered two fumbles. 1994—Recovered two fumbles for four yards. 1995—Recovered one fumble. 1997—Recovered one fumble. 1998—Recovered one fumble. 1999—Recovered one fumble.

SINGLE GAME HIGHS (regular season): Attempts—36 (September 28, 1997, vs. Jacksonville); yards—172 (December 20, 1992, vs. Pittsburgh); and rushing touchdowns—3 (December 22, 1996, vs. Dallas).

STATISTICAL PLATEAUS: 100-yard rushing games: 1991 (1), 1992 (3), 1994 (3), 1995 (4), 1996 (5), 1997 (3), 1999 (2). Total: 21. ... 100-yard receiving games: 1992 (1).

				RUSHING				RECEIVING				TOTALS		
Year Team	G	GS	Att.	Yds.	Avg.	TD	No.	Yds.	Avg.	TD	TD	2pt.	Pts.	Fum.
1990—Minnesota NFL							Did not play.							
1991—Minnesota NFL	15	6	120	563	‡4.7	2	6	49	8.2	1	3	0	18	4
1992—Minnesota NFL	16	16	266	1201	4.5	13	49	478	9.8	2	15	0	90	9
1993—Minnesota NFL							Did not play.							
1994—Minnesota NFL	16	16	255	1031	4.0	8	17	148	8.7	0	8	1	50	3
1995—Washington NFL	16	16	338	1309	3.9	10	31	232	7.5	1	11	0	66	6
1996—Washington NFL	16	16	347	1353	3.9	*21	32	194	6.1	0	*21	0	126	4
1997—Washington NFL	10	10	210	724	3.4	4	20	172	8.6	1	5	0	30	2
1998—Washington NFL	10	10	148	700	4.7	2	17	128	7.5	0	2	0	12	4
1999—New England NFL	16	13	254	896	3.5	8	14	125	8.9	1	9	0	54	8
Pro totals (8 years)	115	103	1938	7777	4.0	68	186	1526	8.2	6	74	1	446	40

ALLRED, JOHN — TE — BEARS

PERSONAL: Born September 9, 1974, in Del Mar, Calif. ... 6-4/249.

HIGH SCHOOL: Torrey Pines (Encinitas, Calif.).

COLLEGE: Southern California.

TRANSACTIONS/CAREER NOTES: Selected by Chicago Bears in second round (38th pick overall) of 1997 NFL draft. ... Signed by Bears (July 14, 1997). ... Granted free agency (February 11, 2000). ... Re-signed by Bears (April 20, 2000).

PRO STATISTICS: 1997—Returned two kickoffs for 21 yards.

SINGLE GAME HIGHS (regular season): Receptions—2 (December 26, 1999, vs. St. Louis); yards—34 (December 26, 1999, vs. St. Louis); and touchdown receptions—1 (September 12, 1999, vs. Kansas City).

			RECEIVING				TOTALS		
Year Team	G	GS	No.	Yds.	Avg.	TD	TD	2pt.	Pts.	Fum.
1997—Chicago NFL	15	4	8	70	8.8	0	0	0	0	0
1998—Chicago NFL	3	0	0	0	0.0	0	0	0	0	0
1999—Chicago NFL	16	5	13	102	7.8	1	1	0	6	0
Pro totals (3 years)	34	9	21	172	8.2	1	1	0	6	0

ALSTOTT, MIKE — FB — BUCCANEERS

PERSONAL: Born December 21, 1973, in Joliet, Ill. ... 6-1/248. ... Full name: Michael Joseph Alstott.

HIGH SCHOOL: Joliet (Ill.) Catholic.

COLLEGE: Purdue (degree in business, 1995).

TRANSACTIONS/CAREER NOTES: Selected by Tampa Bay Buccaneers in second round (35th pick overall) of 1996 NFL draft. ... Signed by Buccaneers (July 21, 1996).

CHAMPIONSHIP GAME EXPERIENCE: Played in NFC championship game (1999 season).

HONORS: Played in Pro Bowl (1997-1999 seasons).

PRO STATISTICS: 1996—Returned one kickoff for 14 yards. 1997—Returned one kickoff for no yards. 1998—Attempted one pass without a completion and returned one kickoff for eight yards. 1999—Returned one kickoff for 19 yards.

SINGLE GAME HIGHS (regular season): Attempts—25 (November 7, 1999, vs. New Orleans); yards—131 (September 26, 1999, vs. Denver); and rushing touchdowns—3 (December 27, 1998, vs. Cincinnati).

STATISTICAL PLATEAUS: 100-yard rushing games: 1998 (2), 1999 (2). Total: 4.

			RUSHING				RECEIVING				TOTALS		
Year Team	G	GS	Att.	Yds.	Avg.	TD	No.	Yds.	Avg.	TD	TD	2pt.	Pts.	Fum.
1996—Tampa Bay NFL	16	16	96	377	3.9	3	65	557	8.6	3	6	0	36	4
1997—Tampa Bay NFL	15	15	176	665	3.8	7	23	178	7.7	3	10	0	60	5
1998—Tampa Bay NFL	16	16	215	846	3.9	8	22	152	6.9	1	9	0	54	5
1999—Tampa Bay NFL	16	16	242	949	3.9	7	27	239	8.9	2	9	0	54	6
Pro totals (4 years)	63	63	729	2837	3.9	25	137	1126	8.2	9	34	0	204	20

AMBROSE, ASHLEY — CB — FALCONS

PERSONAL: Born September 17, 1970, in New Orleans. ... 5-10/185. ... Full name: Ashley Avery Ambrose.

HIGH SCHOOL: Fortier (New Orleans).

COLLEGE: Mississippi Valley State (degree in industrial technology).

TRANSACTIONS/CAREER NOTES: Selected by Indianapolis Colts in second round (29th pick overall) of 1992 NFL draft. ... Signed by Colts (August 11, 1992). ... On injured reserve with leg injury (September 14-October 29, 1992); on practice squad (October 21-29, 1992). ...

Granted free agency (February 17, 1995). ... Re-signed by Colts (April 29, 1995). ... Granted unconditional free agency (February 16, 1996). ... Signed by Cincinnati Bengals (February 25, 1996). ... Granted unconditional free agency (February 12, 1999). ... Signed by New Orleans Saints (July 13, 1999). ... Granted unconditional free agency (February 11, 2000). ... Signed by Atlanta Falcons (February 12, 2000).

CHAMPIONSHIP GAME EXPERIENCE: Played in AFC championship game (1995 season).

HONORS: Played in Pro Bowl (1996 season).

PRO STATISTICS: 1992—Returned eight kickoffs for 126 yards. 1994—Recovered one fumble. 1997—Credited with one sack and recovered two fumbles. 1999—Recovered two fumbles for 29 yards.

			INTERCEPTIONS			
Year Team	G	GS	No.	Yds.	Avg.	TD
1992—Indianapolis NFL	10	2	0	0	0.0	0
1993—Indianapolis NFL	14	6	0	0	0.0	0
1994—Indianapolis NFL	16	4	2	50	25.0	0
1995—Indianapolis NFL	16	0	3	12	4.0	0
1996—Cincinnati NFL	16	16	8	63	7.9	1
1997—Cincinnati NFL	16	16	3	56	18.7	0
1998—Cincinnati NFL	15	15	2	0	0.0	0
1999—New Orleans NFL	16	16	6	27	4.5	0
Pro totals (8 years)	119	75	24	208	8.7	1

ANDERS, KIMBLE — RB — CHIEFS

PERSONAL: Born September 10, 1966, in Galveston, Texas. ... 5-11/226. ... Full name: Kimble Lynard Anders.

HIGH SCHOOL: Ball (Galveston, Texas).

COLLEGE: Houston.

TRANSACTIONS/CAREER NOTES: Signed as non-drafted free agent by Pittsburgh Steelers (April 25, 1990). ... Released by Steelers (September 3, 1990). ... Signed by Kansas City Chiefs (March 13, 1991). ... On injured reserve with hand injury (September 15, 1991-remainder of season). ... On injured reserve with knee injury (September 12-October 17, 1992); on practice squad (October 7-17, 1992). ... Granted unconditional free agency (February 16, 1996). ... Re-signed by Chiefs (April 1, 1996). ... On injured reserve with Achilles' tendon injury (September 20, 1999-remainder of season).

CHAMPIONSHIP GAME EXPERIENCE: Played in AFC championship game (1993 season).

HONORS: Played in Pro Bowl (1995-1997 seasons).

PRO STATISTICS: 1994—Recovered two fumbles. 1997—Recovered one fumble. 1998—Recovered one fumble.

SINGLE GAME HIGHS (regular season): Attempts—22 (September 19, 1999, vs. Denver); yards—142 (September 19, 1999, vs. Denver); and rushing touchdowns—1 (September 13, 1998, vs. Jacksonville).

STATISTICAL PLATEAUS: 100-yard rushing games: 1999 (1).

			RUSHING				RECEIVING				KICKOFF RETURNS				TOTALS			
Year Team	G	GS	Att.	Yds.	Avg.	TD	No.	Yds.	Avg.	TD	No.	Yds.	Avg.	TD	TD	2pt.	Pts.	Fum.
1991—Kansas City NFL	2	0	0	0	0.0	0	2	30	15.0	0	0	0	0.0	0	0	0	0	0
1992—Kansas City NFL	11	2	1	1	1.0	0	5	65	13.0	0	1	20	20.0	0	0	0	0	1
1993—Kansas City NFL	16	13	75	291	3.9	0	40	326	8.2	1	1	47	47.0	0	1	0	6	1
1994—Kansas City NFL	16	13	62	231	3.7	2	67	525	7.8	1	2	36	18.0	0	3	0	18	1
1995—Kansas City NFL	16	13	58	398	6.9	2	55	349	6.3	1	0	0	0.0	0	3	0	18	1
1996—Kansas City NFL	16	15	54	201	3.7	2	60	529	8.8	2	2	37	18.5	0	4	0	24	0
1997—Kansas City NFL	15	14	79	397	5.0	0	59	453	7.7	2	1	0	0.0	0	2	0	12	3
1998—Kansas City NFL	16	15	58	230	4.0	1	64	462	7.2	2	1	16	16.0	0	3	0	18	6
1999—Kansas City NFL	2	2	32	181	5.7	0	2	14	7.0	0	0	0	0.0	0	0	0	0	1
Pro totals (9 years)	110	87	419	1930	4.6	7	354	2753	7.8	9	8	156	19.5	0	16	0	96	14

ANDERSEN, JASON — C — PATRIOTS

PERSONAL: Born September 3, 1975, in Hayward, Calif. ... 6-6/295. ... Full name: Jason Allen Andersen.

HIGH SCHOOL: Piedmont (Calif.).

COLLEGE: Brigham Young.

TRANSACTIONS/CAREER NOTES: Selected by New England Patriots in seventh round (211th pick overall) of 1998 NFL draft. ... Signed by Patriots (June 18, 1998). ... Active for seven games (1998); did not play.

PLAYING EXPERIENCE: New England NFL, 1999. ... Games/Games started: 1999 (9/0).

ANDERSEN, MORTEN — K — FALCONS

PERSONAL: Born August 19, 1960, in Copenhagen, Denmark. ... 6-2/225.

HIGH SCHOOL: Ben Davis (Indianapolis).

COLLEGE: Michigan State (degrees in communications and German).

TRANSACTIONS/CAREER NOTES: Selected by New Orleans Saints in fourth round (86th pick overall) of 1982 NFL draft. ... On injured reserve with sprained ankle (September 15-November 20, 1982). ... Designated by Saints as transition player (February 25, 1993). ... Released by Saints (July 19, 1995). ... Signed by Atlanta Falcons (July 21, 1995).

CHAMPIONSHIP GAME EXPERIENCE: Played in NFC championship game (1998 season). ... Played in Super Bowl XXXIII (1998 season).

HONORS: Named kicker on THE SPORTING NEWS college All-America first team (1981). ... Named kicker on THE SPORTING NEWS NFL All-Pro team (1985-1987 and 1995). ... Played in Pro Bowl (1985-1988, 1990, 1992 and 1995 seasons).

RECORDS: Holds NFL career records for most seasons with 100 or more points—12 (1985-89, 1991-95, 1997 and 1998); for most consecutive games scoring—254 (December 11, 1983-present); and for most made field goals of 50 or more yards—35. ... Holds NFL single-season record for most field goals of 50 or more yards—8 (1995). ... Holds NFL single-game record for most made field goals of 50 or more yards—3 (December 11, 1983, at Philadelphia).

		KICKING						
Year Team	G	XPM	XPA	FGM	FGA	Lg.	50+	Pts.
1982—New Orleans NFL	8	6	6	2	5	45	0-1	12

	G	XPM	XPA	FGM	FGA	Lg.	50+	Pts.
1983—New Orleans NFL	16	37	38	18	24	52	3-4	91
1984—New Orleans NFL	16	34	34	20	27	53	2-3	94
1985—New Orleans NFL	16	27	29	31	35	§55	3-4	120
1986—New Orleans NFL	16	30	30	26	30	53	2-5	108
1987—New Orleans NFL	12	37	37	*28	*36	52	2-6	121
1988—New Orleans NFL	16	32	33	26	36	51	1-4	110
1989—New Orleans NFL	16	44	45	20	29	49	0-4	104
1990—New Orleans NFL	16	29	29	21	27	52	3-4	92
1991—New Orleans NFL	16	38	38	25	32	*60	2-4	113
1992—New Orleans NFL	16	33	34	29	34	52	3-3	∞120
1993—New Orleans NFL	16	33	33	28	35	56	1-5	117
1994—New Orleans NFL	16	32	32	28	†39	48	0-6	116
1995—Atlanta NFL	16	29	30	‡31	37	*59	8-9	122
1996—Atlanta NFL	16	31	31	22	29	∞54	1-5	97
1997—Atlanta NFL	16	35	35	23	27	∞55	2-3	104
1998—Atlanta NFL	16	51	52	23	28	53	2-2	120
1999—Atlanta NFL	16	34	34	15	21	49	0-1	79
Pro totals (18 years)	276	592	600	416	531	60	35-73	1840

ANDERSON, GARY   K   VIKINGS

PERSONAL: Born July 16, 1959, in Parys, Orange Free State, South Africa. ... 5-11/170. ... Full name: Gary Allan Anderson. ... Son of Rev. Douglas Anderson, former professional soccer player in England.
HIGH SCHOOL: Brettonwood (Durban, South Africa).
COLLEGE: Syracuse (degree in management and accounting, 1982).
TRANSACTIONS/CAREER NOTES: Selected by Buffalo Bills in seventh round (171st pick overall) of 1982 NFL draft. ... Signed by Bills for 1982 season. ... Claimed on waivers by Pittsburgh Steelers (September 7, 1982). ... Designated by Steelers as transition player (February 15, 1994). ... On reserve/did not report list (August 23-25, 1994). ... Free agency status changed by Steelers from transition to unconditional (February 17, 1995). ... Signed by Philadelphia Eagles (July 23, 1995). ... Released by Eagles (April 22, 1997). ... Signed by San Francisco 49ers (June 11, 1997). ... Granted unconditional free agency (February 13, 1998). ... Signed by Minnesota Vikings (February 20, 1998).
CHAMPIONSHIP GAME EXPERIENCE: Played in AFC championship game (1984 and 1994 seasons). ... Played in NFC championship game (1997 and 1998 seasons).
HONORS: Played in Pro Bowl (1983, 1985, 1993 and 1998 seasons). ... Named kicker on THE SPORTING NEWS NFL All-Pro team (1998).
RECORDS: Holds NFL career record for most field goals made—439; and most consecutive field goals made—40. ... Holds NFL single-season records for most PATs made without a miss—59 (1998); and most points scored without a touchdown—164 (1998). ... Shares NFL single-season record for highest field-goal percentage—100.0 (1998).
POST SEASON RECORDS: Holds NFL postseason career record for most made field goals—26. ... Holds NFL postseason record for most consecutive made field goals—16 (1989-95).
PRO STATISTICS: 1994—Rushed once for three yards.

				KICKING				
Year Team	G	XPM	XPA	FGM	FGA	Lg.	50+	Pts.
1982—Pittsburgh NFL	9	22	22	10	12	48	0-1	52
1983—Pittsburgh NFL	16	38	39	27	31	49	0-0	§119
1984—Pittsburgh NFL	16	45	45	▲24	32	55	2-3	§117
1985—Pittsburgh NFL	16	40	40	*33	*42	52	1-4	§139
1986—Pittsburgh NFL	16	32	32	21	32	45	0-3	95
1987—Pittsburgh NFL	12	21	21	22	27	52	2-2	87
1988—Pittsburgh NFL	16	34	35	28	36	52	1-2	118
1989—Pittsburgh NFL	16	28	28	21	30	49	0-0	91
1990—Pittsburgh NFL	16	32	32	20	25	48	0-2	92
1991—Pittsburgh NFL	16	31	31	23	33	54	1-6	100
1992—Pittsburgh NFL	16	29	31	28	36	49	0-2	113
1993—Pittsburgh NFL	16	32	32	28	30	46	0-0	*116
1994—Pittsburgh NFL	16	32	32	24	29	50	1-2	104
1995—Philadelphia NFL	16	32	33	22	30	43	0-3	98
1996—Philadelphia NFL	16	40	40	25	29	46	0-0	115
1997—San Francisco NFL	16	38	38	29	36	51	1-3	125
1998—Minnesota NFL	16	*59	*59	‡35	∞35	53	2-2	*164
1999—Minnesota NFL	16	46	46	19	30	44	0-2	103
Pro totals (18 years)	277	631	636	439	555	55	11-37	1948

ANDERSON, JAMAL   RB   FALCONS

PERSONAL: Born September 30, 1972, in Woodland Hills, Calif. ... 5-11/235. ... Full name: Jamal Sharif Anderson.
HIGH SCHOOL: El Camino Real (Woodland Hills, Calif.).
JUNIOR COLLEGE: Moorpark (Calif.) Junior College.
COLLEGE: Utah.
TRANSACTIONS/CAREER NOTES: Selected by Atlanta Falcons in seventh round (201st pick overall) of 1994 NFL draft. ... Signed by Falcons (June 21, 1994). ... On injured reserve with knee injury (September 22, 1999-remainder of season).
CHAMPIONSHIP GAME EXPERIENCE: Played in NFC championship game (1998 season). ... Played in Super Bowl XXXIII (1998 season).
HONORS: Named running back on THE SPORTING NEWS NFL All-Pro team (1998). ... Played in Pro Bowl (1998 season).
RECORDS: Holds NFL single-season record for most rushing attempts—410 (1998).
PRO STATISTICS: 1996—Recovered one fumble. 1997—Attempted four passes with one completion for 27 yards and one touchdown and a interception and recovered one fumble. 1998—Attempted two passes without a completion and recovered one fumble.
SINGLE GAME HIGHS (regular season): Attempts—33 (December 21, 1997, vs. Arizona); yards—188 (November 29, 1998, vs. St. Louis); and rushing touchdowns—3 (October 6, 1996, vs. Detroit).
STATISTICAL PLATEAUS: 100-yard rushing games: 1996 (3), 1997 (2), 1998 (12). Total: 17.

Year Team	G	GS	RUSHING Att.	Yds.	Avg.	TD	RECEIVING No.	Yds.	Avg.	TD	KICKOFF RETURNS No.	Yds.	Avg.	TD	TOTALS TD	2pt.	Pts.	Fum.
1994—Atlanta NFL	3	0	2	-1	-0.5	0	0	0	0.0	0	1	11	11.0	0	0	0	0	0
1995—Atlanta NFL	16	0	39	161	4.1	1	4	42	10.5	0	24	541	22.5	0	1	0	6	0
1996—Atlanta NFL	16	12	232	1055	4.5	5	49	473	9.7	1	4	80	20.0	0	6	0	36	4
1997—Atlanta NFL	16	15	290	1002	3.5	7	29	284	9.8	3	0	0	0.0	0	10	0	60	4
1998—Atlanta NFL	16	16	*410	‡1846	4.5	‡14	27	319	11.8	2	0	0	0.0	0	16	1	98	5
1999—Atlanta NFL	2	2	19	59	3.1	0	2	34	17.0	0	0	0	0.0	0	0	0	0	0
Pro totals (6 years)	69	45	992	4122	4.2	27	111	1152	10.4	6	29	632	21.8	0	33	1	200	13

ANDERSON, KEN   DT   BEARS

PERSONAL: Born October 4, 1975, in Shreveport, La. ... 6-3/310.
HIGH SCHOOL: Captain Shreve (Shreveport, La.).
COLLEGE: Arkansas.
TRANSACTIONS/CAREER NOTES: Signed as non-drafted free agent by Chicago Bears (April 19, 1998). ... On injured reserve with ankle injury (August 25, 1998-entire season). ... Assigned by Bears to Frankfurt Galaxy in 2000 NFL Europe enhancement allocation program (February 18, 2000).
PLAYING EXPERIENCE: Chicago NFL, 1999. ... Games/Games started: 1999 (2/0).

ANDERSON, RICHIE   RB   JETS

PERSONAL: Born September 13, 1971, in Sandy Spring, Md. ... 6-2/230. ... Full name: Richard Darnoll Anderson II.
HIGH SCHOOL: Sherwood (Sandy Spring, Md.).
COLLEGE: Penn State.
TRANSACTIONS/CAREER NOTES: Selected after junior season by New York Jets in sixth round (144th pick overall) of 1993 NFL draft. ... Signed by Jets (June 10, 1993). ... On injured reserve with ankle injury (December 31, 1993-remainder of season). ... On injured reserve with ankle injury (November 30, 1995-remainder of season).
CHAMPIONSHIP GAME EXPERIENCE: Member of Jets for AFC championship game (1998 season); did not play.
PRO STATISTICS: 1993—Recovered one fumble. 1994—Recovered one fumble. 1995—Attempted one pass without a completion. 1996—Recovered one fumble. 1997—Recovered one fumble.
SINGLE GAME HIGHS (regular season): Attempts—9 (November 13, 1994, vs. Green Bay); yards—74 (November 13, 1994, vs. Green Bay); and rushing touchdowns—1 (October 27, 1996, vs. Arizona).

Year Team	G	GS	RUSHING Att.	Yds.	Avg.	TD	RECEIVING No.	Yds.	Avg.	TD	KICKOFF RETURNS No.	Yds.	Avg.	TD	TOTALS TD	2pt.	Pts.	Fum.
1993—New York Jets NFL	7	0	0	0	0.0	0	0	0	0.0	0	4	66	16.5	0	0	0	0	1
1994—New York Jets NFL	13	5	43	207	4.8	1	25	212	8.5	1	3	43	14.3	0	2	0	12	1
1995—New York Jets NFL	10	0	5	17	3.4	0	5	26	5.2	0	0	0	0.0	0	0	0	0	2
1996—New York Jets NFL	16	13	47	150	3.2	1	44	385	8.8	0	0	0	0.0	0	1	0	6	0
1997—New York Jets NFL	16	3	21	70	3.3	0	26	150	5.8	1	0	0	0.0	0	1	0	6	2
1998—New York Jets NFL	8	2	1	2	2.0	0	3	12	4.0	0	0	0	0.0	0	0	0	0	0
1999—New York Jets NFL	16	9	16	84	5.3	0	29	302	10.4	3	0	0	0.0	0	3	0	18	0
Pro totals (7 years)	86	32	133	530	4.0	2	132	1087	8.2	5	7	109	15.6	0	7	0	42	6

ANDERSON, WILLIE   OT   BENGALS

PERSONAL: Born July 11, 1975, in Mobile, Ala. ... 6-5/340. ... Full name: Willie Aaron Anderson.
HIGH SCHOOL: Vigor (Prichard, Ala.).
COLLEGE: Auburn.
TRANSACTIONS/CAREER NOTES: Selected after junior season by Cincinnati Bengals in first round (10th pick overall) of 1996 NFL draft. ... Signed by Bengals (August 5, 1996).
PLAYING EXPERIENCE: Cincinnati NFL, 1996-1999. ... Games/Games started: 1996 (16/10), 1997 (16/16), 1998 (16/16), 1999 (14/14). Total: 62/56.
PRO STATISTICS: 1998—Recovered one fumble. 1999—Recovered one fumble.

ANDRUZZI, JOE   G   PACKERS

PERSONAL: Born August 23, 1975, in Brooklyn, N.Y. ... 6-3/310. ... Full name: Joseph Dominick Andruzzi. ... Name pronounced ann-DROOZ-ee.
HIGH SCHOOL: Tottenville (Staten Island, N.Y.).
COLLEGE: Southern Connecticut State.
TRANSACTIONS/CAREER NOTES: Signed as non-drafted free agent by Green Bay Packers (April 25, 1997). ... Inactive for all 16 games (1997). ... Assigned by Packers to Scottish Claymores in 1998 NFL Europe enhancement allocations program (February 18, 1998). ... On injured reserve with knee injury (November 23, 1999-remainder of season).
PLAYING EXPERIENCE: Scottish NFLE, 1998; Green Bay NFL, 1998 and 1999. ... Games/Games started: NFLE 1998 (10/10), NFL 1998 (15/1), 1999 (8/3). Total NFLE: 10/10. Total NFL: 23/4. Total Pro: 33/14.
CHAMPIONSHIP GAME EXPERIENCE: Member of Packers for NFC championship game (1997 season); inactive. ... Member of Packers for Super Bowl XXXII (1997 season); inactive.
PRO STATISTICS: 1998—Recovered one fumble.

ANTHONY, REIDEL   WR   BUCCANEERS

PERSONAL: Born October 20, 1976, in South Bay, Fla. ... 5-11/180. ... Full name: Reidel Clarence Anthony. ... Name pronounced REE-dell.
HIGH SCHOOL: Glades Central (Belle Glade, Fla.).

COLLEGE: Florida.

TRANSACTIONS/CAREER NOTES: Selected after junior season by Tampa Bay Buccaneers in first round (16th pick overall) of 1997 NFL draft. ... Signed by Buccaneers (July 20, 1997).

CHAMPIONSHIP GAME EXPERIENCE: Member of Buccaneers for NFC championship game (1999 season); inactive.

HONORS: Named wide receiver on THE SPORTING NEWS college All-America first team (1996).

PRO STATISTICS: 1998—Recovered one fumble.

SINGLE GAME HIGHS (regular season): Receptions—7 (October 3, 1999, vs. Minnesota); yards—126 (November 15, 1998, vs. Jacksonville); and touchdown receptions—2 (November 15, 1998, vs. Jacksonville).

STATISTICAL PLATEAUS: 100-yard receiving games: 1998 (1).

			RUSHING				RECEIVING				KICKOFF RETURNS				TOTALS			
Year Team	G	GS	Att.	Yds.	Avg.	TD	No.	Yds.	Avg.	TD	No.	Yds.	Avg.	TD	TD	2pt.	Pts.	Fum.
1997—Tampa Bay NFL..........	16	12	5	84	16.8	0	35	448	12.8	4	25	592	23.7	0	4	0	24	0
1998—Tampa Bay NFL..........	15	13	4	43	10.8	0	51	708	13.9	4	46	1118	24.3	0	7	1	44	0
1999—Tampa Bay NFL..........	13	7	1	2	2.0	0	30	296	9.9	1	21	434	20.7	0	1	0	6	1
Pro totals (3 years)................	44	32	10	129	12.9	0	116	1452	12.5	12	92	2144	23.3	0	12	1	74	1

ARAGUZ, LEO P RAIDERS

PERSONAL: Born January 18, 1970, in Pharr, Texas. ... 5-11/190. ... Full name: Leobardo Jaime Araguz. ... Name pronounced ara-GOOSE.

HIGH SCHOOL: Harlingen (Texas).

COLLEGE: Stephen F. Austin State.

TRANSACTIONS/CAREER NOTES: Signed as non-drafted free agent by Miami Dolphins (March 28, 1994). ... Released by Dolphins prior to 1994 season. ... Signed by San Diego Chargers (1995). ... Released by Chargers prior to 1995 season. ... Signed by Rhein Fire of the World League for 1996 season. ... Signed by Oakland Raiders (December 4, 1996).

RECORDS: Holds NFL single-game record for most punts—16 (October 11, 1998, vs. San Diego).

PRO STATISTICS: 1996—Rushed once for no yards and recovered one fumble. 1997—Rushed once for no yards, fumbled once and recovered one fumble for minus 21 yards. 1998—Rushed once for minus 12 yards and completed only pass attempt for minus one yard.

		PUNTING					
Year Team	G	No.	Yds.	Avg.	Net avg.	In. 20	Blk.
1996—Rhein W.L.	...	41	1735	42.3	37.8	17	0
—Oakland NFL.....................................	3	13	534	41.1	34.5	4	0
1997—Oakland NFL....................................	16	§93	§4189	‡45.0	*39.1	▲28	0
1998—Oakland NFL....................................	16	§98	§4256	43.4	33.4	29	0
1999—Oakland NFL....................................	16	76	3045	40.1	32.3	25	1
W.L. totals (1 year)....................................	...	41	1735	42.3	37.8	17	0
NFL totals (4 years)	51	280	12024	42.9	35.0	86	1
Pro totals (5 years)	...	321	13759	42.9	35.4	103	1

ARCHAMBEAU, LESTER DE BRONCOS

PERSONAL: Born June 27, 1967, in Montville, N.J. ... 6-5/275. ... Full name: Lester Milward Archambeau. ... Name pronounced AR-shambow.

HIGH SCHOOL: Montville (N.J.).

COLLEGE: Stanford (degree in industrial engineering).

TRANSACTIONS/CAREER NOTES: Selected by Green Bay Packers in seventh round (186th pick overall) of 1990 NFL draft. ... Signed by Packers (July 22, 1990). ... On injured reserve with back injury (October 6, 1990-remainder of season). ... Granted free agency (February 1, 1992). ... Re-signed by Packers (August 12, 1992). ... Traded by Packers to Atlanta Falcons for WR James Milling (June 3, 1993). ... Granted unconditional free agency (February 17, 1994). ... Re-signed by Falcons (March 7, 1994). ... Granted unconditional free agency (February 14, 1997). ... Re-signed by Falcons (March 3, 1997). ... Granted unconditional free agency (February 11, 2000). ... Signed by Denver Broncos (February 23, 2000).

CHAMPIONSHIP GAME EXPERIENCE: Played in NFC championship game (1998 season). ... Played in Super Bowl XXXIII (1998 season).

PRO STATISTICS: 1995—Recovered one fumble. 1997—Intercepted one pass for no yards and recovered three fumbles. 1998—Recovered two fumbles.

Year Team	G	GS	SACKS
1990—Green Bay NFL...	4	0	0.0
1991—Green Bay NFL...	16	0	4.5
1992—Green Bay NFL...	16	0	1.0
1993—Atlanta NFL..	15	11	0.0
1994—Atlanta NFL..	16	12	2.0
1995—Atlanta NFL..	16	7	3.0
1996—Atlanta NFL..	15	15	2.0
1997—Atlanta NFL..	16	16	8.5
1998—Atlanta NFL..	15	15	10.0
1999—Atlanta NFL..	15	15	5.5
Pro totals (10 years)...	144	91	36.5

ARMOUR, JO JUAN S BENGALS

PERSONAL: Born July 10, 1976, in Toledo, Ohio. ... 5-11/220. ... Name pronounced JOE-wan.

HIGH SCHOOL: Central Catholic (Toledo, Ohio).

COLLEGE: Miami of Ohio.

TRANSACTIONS/CAREER NOTES: Selected by Oakland Raiders in seventh round (224th pick overall) of 1999 NFL draft. ... Signed by Raiders (July 24, 1999). ... Claimed on waivers by Jacksonville Jaguars (September 7, 1999). ... Inactive for two games with Jaguars (1999). ... Claimed on waivers by Cincinnati Bengals (September 21, 1999). ... Released by Bengals (October 15, 1999). ... Re-signed by Bengals to practice squad (October 16, 1999). ... Activated (December 16, 1999).

PLAYING EXPERIENCE: Cincinnati NFL, 1999. ... Games/Games started: 1999 (2/0).

HONORS: Named outside linebacker on THE SPORTING NEWS college All-America second team (1997).

ARMOUR, JUSTIN   WR

PERSONAL: Born January 1, 1973, in Colorado Springs, Colo. ... 6-4/209. ... Full name: Justin Hugh Armour.
HIGH SCHOOL: Manitou Springs (Colo.).
COLLEGE: Stanford.
TRANSACTIONS/CAREER NOTES: Selected by Buffalo Bills in fourth round (113th pick overall) of 1995 NFL draft. ... Signed by Bills (June 27, 1995). ... Inactive for 11 games (1996). ... On injured reserve with foot injury (November 22, 1996-remainder of season). ... Released by Bills (August 24, 1997). ... Signed by Philadelphia Eagles (September 23, 1997). ... Released by Eagles (September 27, 1997). ... Re-signed by Eagles (September 29, 1997). ... Released by Eagles (November 4, 1997). ... Signed by San Francisco 49ers (December 29, 1997). ... Released by 49ers after 1997 season. ... Signed by Denver Broncos (February 24, 1998). ... Selected by Cleveland Browns from Broncos in NFL expansion draft (February 9, 1999). ... Released by Browns (May 24, 1999). ... Signed by Baltimore Ravens (June 24, 1999). ... Granted unconditional free agency (February 11, 2000).
CHAMPIONSHIP GAME EXPERIENCE: Member of 49ers for NFC championship game (1997 season); inactive. ... Member of Broncos for AFC championship game (1998 season); inactive. ... Member of Super Bowl championship team (1998 season); inactive.
PRO STATISTICS: 1995—Rushed four times for minus five yards, attempted one pass without a completion, fumbled once and recovered two fumbles.
SINGLE GAME HIGHS (regular season): Receptions—6 (October 21, 1999, vs. Kansas City); yards—76 (September 12, 1999, vs. St. Louis); and touchdown receptions—1 (December 19, 1999, vs. New Orleans).

			RECEIVING				TOTALS			
Year Team	G	GS	No.	Yds.	Avg.	TD	TD	2pt.	Pts.	Fum.
1995—Buffalo NFL	15	9	26	300	11.5	3	3	0	18	1
1996—Buffalo NFL						Did not play.				
1997—Philadelphia NFL	1	0	0	0	0.0	0	0	0	0	0
1998—Denver NFL	7	0	1	23	23.0	0	0	0	0	0
1999—Baltimore NFL	15	7	37	538	14.5	4	4	0	24	0
Pro totals (4 years)	38	16	64	861	13.5	7	7	0	42	1

ARMSTEAD, JESSIE   LB   GIANTS

PERSONAL: Born October 26, 1970, in Dallas. ... 6-1/240. ... Full name: Jessie W. Armstead.
HIGH SCHOOL: David W. Carter (Dallas).
COLLEGE: Miami, Fla. (degree in criminal justice, 1992).
TRANSACTIONS/CAREER NOTES: Selected by New York Giants in eighth round (207th pick overall) of 1993 NFL draft. ... Signed by Giants (July 19, 1993).
HONORS: Named outside linebacker on THE SPORTING NEWS NFL All-Pro team (1997). ... Played in Pro Bowl (1997-1999 seasons).
PRO STATISTICS: 1995—Recovered one fumble. 1996—Fumbled once and recovered two fumbles. 1997—Recovered one fumble.

			INTERCEPTIONS				SACKS
Year Team	G	GS	No.	Yds.	Avg.	TD	No.
1993—New York Giants NFL	16	0	1	0	0.0	0	0.0
1994—New York Giants NFL	16	0	1	0	0.0	0	3.0
1995—New York Giants NFL	16	2	1	58	58.0	1	0.5
1996—New York Giants NFL	16	16	2	23	11.5	0	3.0
1997—New York Giants NFL	16	16	2	57	28.5	1	3.5
1998—New York Giants NFL	16	16	2	4	2.0	0	5.0
1999—New York Giants NFL	16	16	2	35	17.5	0	9.0
Pro totals (7 years)	112	66	11	177	16.1	2	24.0

ARMSTRONG, BRUCE   OT

PERSONAL: Born September 7, 1965, in Miami. ... 6-4/295. ... Full name: Bruce Charles Armstrong.
HIGH SCHOOL: Miami Central.
COLLEGE: Louisville.
TRANSACTIONS/CAREER NOTES: Selected by New England Patriots in first round (23rd pick overall) of 1987 NFL draft. ... Signed by Patriots (July 23, 1987). ... On injured reserve with knee injury (November 2, 1992-remainder of season). ... On physically unable to perform list with knee injury (July 16-27, 1993). ... Granted unconditional free agency (February 13, 1998). ... Re-signed by Patriots (February 13, 1998). ... Released by Patriots (February 10, 2000).
PLAYING EXPERIENCE: New England NFL, 1987-1999. ... Games: 1987 (12/12), 1988 (16/16), 1989 (16/16), 1990 (16/16), 1991 (16/16), 1992 (8/8), 1993 (16/16), 1994 (16/16), 1995 (16/16), 1996 (16/16), 1997 (16/16), 1998 (16/16), 1999 (16/16). Total: 196/196.
CHAMPIONSHIP GAME EXPERIENCE: Played in AFC championship game (1996 season). ... Played in Super Bowl XXXI (1996 season).
HONORS: Named offensive tackle on THE SPORTING NEWS NFL All-Pro team (1988). ... Played in Pro Bowl (1990, 1991 and 1994-1997 seasons).
PRO STATISTICS: 1990—Recovered two fumbles for four yards. 1992—Recovered one fumble. 1993—Recovered one fumble for one yard. 1995—Recovered one fumble. 1998—Recovered three fumbles. 1999—Recovered one fumble.

ARMSTRONG, TRACE   DE   DOLPHINS

PERSONAL: Born October 5, 1965, in Bethesda, Md. ... 6-4/270. ... Full name: Raymond Lester Armstrong.
HIGH SCHOOL: John Carroll (Birmingham, Ala.).
COLLEGE: Arizona State, then Florida (degree in psychology, 1989).
TRANSACTIONS/CAREER NOTES: Selected by Chicago Bears in first round (12th pick overall) of 1989 NFL draft. ... Signed by Bears (August 18, 1989). ... On injured reserve with knee injury (September 24-November 3, 1991). ... Granted free agency (March 1, 1993). ... Re-signed by Bears (March 14, 1993). ... Traded by Bears to Miami Dolphins for second- (P Todd Sauerbrun) and third-round (G Evan Pilgrim) picks in 1995 draft (April 4, 1995).
HONORS: Named defensive lineman on THE SPORTING NEWS college All-America first team (1988).

PRO STATISTICS: 1989—Recovered one fumble. 1990—Recovered two fumbles. 1992—Recovered one fumble. 1993—Recovered three fumbles for three yards. 1995—Recovered one fumble. 1996—Recovered two fumbles. 1997—Recovered three fumbles. 1998—Recovered one fumble for two yards.

Year Team	G	GS	SACKS
1989—Chicago NFL	15	14	5.0
1990—Chicago NFL	16	16	10.0
1991—Chicago NFL	12	12	1.5
1992—Chicago NFL	14	14	6.5
1993—Chicago NFL	16	16	11.5
1994—Chicago NFL	15	15	7.5
1995—Miami NFL	15	0	4.5
1996—Miami NFL	16	9	12.0
1997—Miami NFL	16	16	5.5
1998—Miami NFL	16	0	10.5
1999—Miami NFL	16	2	7.5
Pro totals (11 years)	167	114	82.0

ARNOLD, JAHINE — WR

PERSONAL: Born June 19, 1973, in Cupertino, Calif. ... 6-0/180. ... Full name: Jahine Amid Arnold. ... Name pronounced JAH-heen.
HIGH SCHOOL: Homestead (Cupertino, Calif.).
JUNIOR COLLEGE: De Anza College (Calif.).
COLLEGE: Fresno State.
TRANSACTIONS/CAREER NOTES: Selected by Pittsburgh Steelers in fourth round (132nd pick overall) of 1996 NFL draft. ... Signed by Steelers (July 16, 1996). ... On injured reserve with knee injury (August 19, 1997-entire season). ... On injured reserve with finger injury (November 20, 1998-remainder of season). ... Granted free agency (February 12, 1999). ... Re-signed by Steelers (April 6, 1999). ... Traded by Steelers to Green Bay Packers for past considerations (April 6, 1999). ... On injured reserve with knee injury (October 20, 1999-remainder of season). ... Granted unconditional free agency (February 11, 2000).
PRO STATISTICS: 1996—Rushed once for minus three yards and returned two punts for six yards. 1998—Returned four punts for 19 yards.
SINGLE GAME HIGHS (regular season): Receptions—2 (December 22, 1996, vs. Carolina); yards—26 (October 7, 1996, vs. Kansas City); and touchdown receptions—0.

			RECEIVING				KICKOFF RETURNS				TOTALS			
Year Team	G	GS	No.	Yds.	Avg.	TD	No.	Yds.	Avg.	TD	TD	2pt.	Pts.	Fum.
1996—Pittsburgh NFL	9	0	6	76	12.7	0	19	425	22.4	0	0	0	0	1
1997—Pittsburgh NFL							Did not play.							
1998—Pittsburgh NFL	2	0	0	0	0.0	0	3	78	26.0	0	0	0	0	0
1999—Green Bay NFL	1	0	0	0	0.0	0	0	0	0.0	0	0	0	0	0
Pro totals (3 years)	12	0	6	76	12.7	0	22	503	22.9	0	0	0	0	1

ARTMORE, RODNEY — S

PERSONAL: Born June 14, 1974, in Galveston, Texas. ... 6-0/210. ... Full name: Rodney Dwayne Artmore.
HIGH SCHOOL: Ball (Galveston, Texas).
JUNIOR COLLEGE: Garden City (Kan.) Community College.
COLLEGE: Baylor.
TRANSACTIONS/CAREER NOTES: Signed as non-drafted free agent by Green Bay Packers to practice squad (December 31, 1998). ... On injured reserve with hamstring injury (December 20, 1999-remainder of season). ... Released by Packers (February 11, 2000).
PLAYING EXPERIENCE: Green Bay NFL, 1999. ... Games/Games started: 1999 (5/0).

ASHMORE, DARRYL — G/OT — RAIDERS

PERSONAL: Born November 1, 1969, in Peoria, Ill. ... 6-7/310. ... Full name: Darryl Allan Ashmore.
HIGH SCHOOL: Peoria (Ill.) Central.
COLLEGE: Northwestern (degree in business).
TRANSACTIONS/CAREER NOTES: Selected by Los Angeles Rams in seventh round (171st pick overall) of 1992 NFL draft. ... Signed by Rams (July 13, 1992). ... On injured reserve with knee injury (September 3-October 7, 1992). ... On practice squad (October 7, 1992-remainder of season). ... Granted free agency (February 17, 1995). ... Rams franchise moved to St. Louis (April 12, 1995). ... Re-signed by Rams (July 20, 1995). ... Released by Rams (October 14, 1996). ... Signed by Washington Redskins (October 26, 1996). ... Granted unconditional free agency (February 14, 1997). ... Re-signed by Redskins (May 9, 1997). ... Granted unconditional free agency (February 13, 1998). ... Signed by Oakland Raiders (April 25, 1998). ... Granted unconditional free agency (February 11, 2000). ... Re-signed by Raiders (February 22, 2000).
PLAYING EXPERIENCE: Los Angeles Rams NFL, 1993 and 1994; St. Louis NFL, 1995; St. Louis (6)-Washington (5) NFL, 1996; Washington NFL, 1997; Oakland NFL, 1998 and 1999. ... Games/Games started: 1993 (9/7), 1994 (11/3), 1995 (16/15), 1996 (St.L-6/0; Wash.-5/0; Total: 11/0), 1997 (11/2), 1998 (15/4), 1999 (16/2). Total: 89/33.
PRO STATISTICS: 1998—Recovered one fumble for one yard and a touchdown. 1999—Returned one kickoff for no yards.

ATKINS, JAMES — OL

PERSONAL: Born January 28, 1970, in Amite, La. ... 6-6/306.
HIGH SCHOOL: Woodland (Amite, La.).
COLLEGE: Southwestern Louisiana.
TRANSACTIONS/CAREER NOTES: Signed as non-drafted free agent by Houston Oilers (May 26, 1993). ... Released by Oilers (August 31, 1993). ... Signed by Seattle Seahawks to practice squad (October 11, 1993). ... Released by Seahawks (February 27, 1998). ... Signed by Baltimore Ravens (March 25, 1998). ... Granted unconditional free agency (February 11, 2000).
PLAYING EXPERIENCE: Seattle NFL, 1994-1997; Baltimore NFL, 1998 and 1999. ... Games/Games started: 1994 (4/2), 1995 (16/16), 1996 (16/16), 1997 (13/3), 1998 (9/6), 1999 (2/1). Total: 60/44.
PRO STATISTICS: 1995—Recovered one fumble. 1996—Recovered two fumbles. 1997—Recovered one fumble. 1998—Caught one pass for no yards.

ATKINS, LARRY   S   CHIEFS

PERSONAL: Born July 21, 1975, in Santa Monica, Calif. ... 6-3/230. ... Full name: Larry Tabay Atkins III.
HIGH SCHOOL: Venice (Los Angeles).
COLLEGE: UCLA.
TRANSACTIONS/CAREER NOTES: Selected by Kansas City Chiefs in third round (84th pick overall) of 1999 NFL draft. ... Signed by Chiefs (July 15, 1999).
PLAYING EXPERIENCE: Kansas City NFL, 1999. ... Games/Games started: 1999 (9/0).
HONORS: Named free safety on THE SPORTING NEWS college All-America second team (1998).

ATWATER, STEVE   S

PERSONAL: Born October 28, 1966, in Chicago. ... 6-3/217. ... Full name: Stephen Dennis Atwater. ... Cousin of Mark Ingram, wide receiver with four NFL teams (1987-96).
HIGH SCHOOL: Lutheran North (St. Louis).
COLLEGE: Arkansas (degree in business administration, 1989).
TRANSACTIONS/CAREER NOTES: Selected by Denver Broncos in first round (20th pick overall) of 1989 NFL draft. ... Signed by Broncos (August 1, 1989). ... Designated by Broncos as transition player (February 25, 1993). ... Designated by Broncos as franchise player (February 15, 1995). ... Released by Broncos (February 17, 1999). ... Signed by New York Jets (March 2, 1999). ... Released by Jets (February 2, 2000).
CHAMPIONSHIP GAME EXPERIENCE: Played in AFC championship game (1989, 1991, 1997 and 1998 seasons). ... Played in Super Bowl XXIV (1989 season). ... Member of Super Bowl championship team (1997 and 1998 seasons).
HONORS: Named defensive back on THE SPORTING NEWS college All-America second team (1988). ... Played in Pro Bowl (1990-1995 and 1998 seasons). ... Named free safety on THE SPORTING NEWS NFL All-Pro team (1992). ... Named to play in Pro Bowl (1996 season); replaced by Eric Turner due to injury.
PRO STATISTICS: 1989—Recovered one fumble for 29 yards. 1990—Returned one kickoff for no yards. 1991—Recovered one fumble. 1992—Recovered two fumbles for one yard. 1994—Recovered two fumbles for 17 yards. 1996—Fumbled once. 1997—Recovered two fumbles.

			INTERCEPTIONS				SACKS
Year Team	G	GS	No.	Yds.	Avg.	TD	No.
1989—Denver NFL	16	16	3	34	11.3	0	0.0
1990—Denver NFL	15	15	2	32	16.0	0	1.0
1991—Denver NFL	16	16	5	104	20.8	0	1.0
1992—Denver NFL	15	15	2	22	11.0	0	1.0
1993—Denver NFL	16	16	2	81	40.5	0	1.0
1994—Denver NFL	14	14	1	24	24.0	0	0.0
1995—Denver NFL	16	16	3	54	18.0	0	0.0
1996—Denver NFL	16	16	3	11	3.7	0	0.0
1997—Denver NFL	15	15	2	42	21.0	1	1.0
1998—Denver NFL	16	16	1	4	4.0	0	0.0
1999—New York Jets NFL	12	11	0	0	0.0	0	0.0
Pro totals (11 years)	167	166	24	408	17.0	1	5.0

AUSTIN, BILLY   DB   COLTS

PERSONAL: Born March 8, 1975, in Washington, D.C. ... 5-10/195.
HIGH SCHOOL: Kempner (Sugar Land, Texas).
COLLEGE: New Mexico.
TRANSACTIONS/CAREER NOTES: Signed as non-drafted free agent by St. Louis Rams (April 20, 1998). ... Released by Rams (July 8, 1998). ... Re-signed by Rams (July 21, 1998). ... Released by Rams (August 24, 1998). ... Signed by Indianapolis Colts to practice squad (September 9, 1998). ... Activated (December 16, 1998).
PLAYING EXPERIENCE: Indianapolis NFL, 1998 and 1999. ... Games/Games started: 1998 (1/0), 1999 (16/0). Total: 17/0.
PRO STATISTICS: 1999—Returned one kickoff for no yards and recovered one fumble.

AUSTIN, RAY   S   BEARS

PERSONAL: Born December 21, 1974, in Greensboro, N.C. ... 5-11/204. ... Full name: Raymond Demont Austin.
HIGH SCHOOL: Leilehua (Hawaii), then Eisenhower (Lawton, Okla.).
COLLEGE: Tennessee.
TRANSACTIONS/CAREER NOTES: Selected by New York Jets in fifth round (145th pick overall) of 1997 NFL draft. ... Signed by Jets (June 15, 1997). ... Claimed on waivers by Chicago Bears (August 31, 1998). ... Granted free agency (February 11, 2000). ... Re-signed by Bears (April 6, 2000).
PLAYING EXPERIENCE: New York Jets NFL, 1997; Chicago NFL, 1998 and 1999. ... Games/Games started: 1997 (16/0), 1998 (12/0), 1999 (15/0). Total: 43/0.

AVERY, JOHN   RB   BRONCOS

PERSONAL: Born January 11, 1976, in Richmond, Va. ... 5-9/190. ... Full name: John Edward Avery III.
HIGH SCHOOL: Asheville (N.C.).
JUNIOR COLLEGE: Northwest Mississippi Community College.
COLLEGE: Mississippi.
TRANSACTIONS/CAREER NOTES: Selected by Miami Dolphins in first round (29th pick overall) of 1998 NFL draft. ... Signed by Dolphins (July 17, 1998). ... Traded by Dolphins to Denver Broncos for WR Marcus Nash (September 21, 1999).
PRO STATISTICS: 1998—Recovered two fumbles.

SINGLE GAME HIGHS (regular season): Attempts—21 (November 8, 1998, vs. Indianapolis); yards—99 (November 8, 1998, vs. Seattle); and rushing touchdowns—1 (November 8, 1998, vs. Indianapolis).

Year Team	G	GS	RUSHING				RECEIVING				KICKOFF RETURNS				TOTALS			
			Att.	Yds.	Avg.	TD	No.	Yds.	Avg.	TD	No.	Yds.	Avg.	TD	TD	2pt.	Pts.	Fum.
1998—Miami NFL	16	0	143	503	3.5	2	10	67	6.7	1	43	1085	25.2	0	3	0	18	5
1999—Miami NFL	1	0	0	0	0.0	0	0	0	0.0	0	2	55	27.5	0	0	0	0	0
—Denver NFL	6	0	5	21	4.2	0	4	24	6.0	0	7	137	19.6	0	0	0	0	0
Pro totals (2 years)	23	0	148	524	3.5	2	14	91	6.5	1	52	1277	24.6	0	3	0	18	5

AYANBADEJO, OBAFEMI　　FB　　RAVENS

PERSONAL: Born March 5, 1975, in Chicago. ... 6-2/235. ... Name pronounced oh-BUH-fem-me eye-an-buh-DAY-ho.
HIGH SCHOOL: Santa Cruz (Calif.).
JUNIOR COLLEGE: Cabrillo College (Calif.).
COLLEGE: San Diego State.
TRANSACTIONS/CAREER NOTES: Signed as non-drafted free agent by Minnesota Vikings (April 25, 1997). ... Released by Vikings (August 18, 1997). ... Re-signed by Vikings (February 6, 1998). ... Assigned by Vikings to England Monarchs in 1998 NFL Europe enhancement allocation program (February 17, 1998). ... Released by Vikings (August 24, 1998). ... Re-signed by Vikings to practice squad (August 31, 1998). ... Activated (December 1, 1998). ... Released by Vikings (December 23, 1998). ... Re-signed by Vikings to practice squad (December 24, 1998). ... Released by Vikings (September 21, 1999). ... Signed by Baltimore Ravens (September 27, 1999).
PLAYING EXPERIENCE: England Monarchs NFLE, 1998; Minnesota NFL, 1998; Minnesota (2)-Baltimore (12) NFL, 1999. ... Games/Games started: NFLE 1998 (games played unavailable), NFL 1998 (1/0), 1999 (Min.-2/0; Balt.-12/0; Total: 14/0). Total NFL: 15/0.
PRO STATISTICS: NFLE: 1998—Caught two passes for 28 yards. NFL: 1999—Caught one pass for two yards.

AZUMAH, JERRY　　CB　　BEARS

PERSONAL: Born September 1, 1977, in Worcester, Mass. ... 5-10/195. ... Name pronounced ah-ZOO-muh.
HIGH SCHOOL: St. Peter-Marian (Worcester, Mass.).
COLLEGE: New Hampshire.
TRANSACTIONS/CAREER NOTES: Selected by Chicago Bears in fifth round (147th pick overall) of 1999 NFL draft. ... Signed by Bears (June 8, 1999).
PLAYING EXPERIENCE: Chicago NFL, 1999. ... Games/Games started: 1999 (16/2).
HONORS: Walter Payton Award winner (1998).

BADGER, BRAD　　G　　VIKINGS

PERSONAL: Born January 11, 1975, in Corvallis, Ore. ... 6-4/298.
HIGH SCHOOL: Corvallis (Ore.).
COLLEGE: Stanford.
TRANSACTIONS/CAREER NOTES: Selected by Washington Redskins in fifth round (162nd pick overall) of 1997 NFL draft. ... Signed by Redskins (May 5, 1997). ... Granted free agency (February 11, 2000). ... Tendered offer sheet by Minnesota Vikings (April 10, 2000). ... Redskins declined to match offer (April 11, 2000).
PLAYING EXPERIENCE: Washington NFL, 1997-1999. ... Games/Games started: 1997 (12/2), 1998 (16/16), 1999 (14/4). Total: 42/22.

BAILEY, AARON　　WR/KR　　PATRIOTS

PERSONAL: Born October 24, 1971, in Ann Arbor, Mich. ... 5-10/185. ... Full name: Aaron Duane Bailey.
HIGH SCHOOL: Pioneer (Ann Arbor, Mich.).
COLLEGE: College of DuPage (Ill.), then Louisville.
TRANSACTIONS/CAREER NOTES: Signed as non-drafted free agent by Indianapolis Colts (May 5, 1994). ... Released by Colts (April 12, 1999). ... Signed by New England Patriots (March 9, 2000).
CHAMPIONSHIP GAME EXPERIENCE: Played in AFC championship game (1995 season).
PRO STATISTICS: 1995—Rushed once for 34 yards and recovered one fumble. 1996—Recovered one fumble. 1997—Rushed three times for 20 yards and recovered one fumble. 1998—Recovered one fumble.
SINGLE GAME HIGHS (regular season): Receptions—7 (September 21, 1997, vs. Buffalo); yards—96 (September 21, 1997, vs. Buffalo); and touchdown receptions—1 (November 30, 1997, vs. New England).

Year Team	G	GS	RECEIVING				PUNT RETURNS				KICKOFF RETURNS				TOTALS			
			No.	Yds.	Avg.	TD	No.	Yds.	Avg.	TD	No.	Yds.	Avg.	TD	TD	2pt.	Pts.	Fum.
1994—Indianapolis NFL	13	0	2	30	15.0	0	0	0	0.0	0	0	0	0.0	0	0	0	0	0
1995—Indianapolis NFL	15	3	21	379	18.0	3	0	0	0.0	0	21	495	23.6	1	4	0	24	0
1996—Indianapolis NFL	14	2	18	302	16.8	0	0	0	0.0	0	43	1041	24.2	▲1	1	0	6	3
1997—Indianapolis NFL	13	4	26	329	12.7	3	1	19	19.0	0	55	1206	21.9	0	3	0	18	2
1998—Indianapolis NFL	9	0	0	0	0.0	0	19	176	9.3	0	34	759	22.3	0	0	0	0	2
1999—									Did not play.									
Pro totals (5 years)	64	9	67	1040	15.5	6	20	195	9.8	0	153	3501	22.9	2	8	0	48	7

BAILEY, CHAMP　　CB　　REDSKINS

PERSONAL: Born June 22, 1978 ... 6-1/184. ... Full name: Roland Champ Bailey.
HIGH SCHOOL: Charlton County (Folkson, Ga.).
COLLEGE: Georgia.
TRANSACTIONS/CAREER NOTES: Selected after junior season by Washington Redskins in first round (seventh pick overall) of 1999 NFL draft. ... Signed by Redskins (July 24, 1999).

| | | | INTERCEPTIONS | | | | SACKS |
Year Team	G	GS	No.	Yds.	Avg.	TD	No.
1999—Washington NFL	16	16	5	55	11.0	1	1.0

BAILEY, KARSTEN   WR   SEAHAWKS

PERSONAL: Born April 26, 1977, in Newnan, Ga. ... 5-10/201. ... Full name: Karsten Mario Bailey.
HIGH SCHOOL: East Coweta (Sharpsburg, Ga.).
COLLEGE: Auburn.
TRANSACTIONS/CAREER NOTES: Selected by Seattle Seahawks in third round (82nd pick overall) of 1999 NFL draft. ... Signed by Seahawks (July 29, 1999).
PLAYING EXPERIENCE: Seattle NFL, 1999. ... Games/Games started: 1999 (2/0).

B

BAILEY, ROBERT   CB   RAVENS

PERSONAL: Born September 3, 1968, in Barbados. ... 5-10/182. ... Full name: Robert Martin Luther Bailey.
HIGH SCHOOL: Miami Southridge Senior.
COLLEGE: Miami, Fla. (degree in science).
TRANSACTIONS/CAREER NOTES: Selected by Los Angeles Rams in fourth round (107th pick overall) of 1991 NFL draft. ... Signed by Rams (July 17, 1991). ... On injured reserve with broken hand (August 27-October 11, 1991). ... On injured reserve with finger injury (November 19, 1991-remainder of season). ... On injured reserve with knee injury (December 11, 1993-remainder of season). ... Granted free agency (February 17, 1994). ... Re-signed by Rams (June 10, 1994). ... Released by Rams (August 22, 1995). ... Signed by Washington Redskins (September 11, 1995). ... Released by Redskins (October 17, 1995). ... Signed by Dallas Cowboys (October 19, 1995). ... Granted unconditional free agency (February 16, 1996). ... Signed by Miami Dolphins (March 7, 1996). ... Released by Dolphins (March 20, 1997). ... Signed by Detroit Lions (April 24, 1997). ... Released by Lions (June 20, 1997). ... Re-signed by Lions (July 22, 1997). ... Granted unconditional free agency (February 13, 1998). ... Re-signed by Lions (March 6, 1998). ... Granted unconditional free agency (February 11, 2000). ... Signed by Baltimore Ravens (March 16, 2000).
CHAMPIONSHIP GAME EXPERIENCE: Played in NFC championship game (1995 season). ... Member of Super Bowl championship team (1995 season).
RECORDS: Holds NFL record for longest punt return—103 yards, touchdown (October 23, 1994, at New Orleans).
PRO STATISTICS: 1994—Returned one punt for 103 yards and a touchdown and recovered one fumble. 1996—Credited with one sack. 1997—Credited with two sacks. 1999—Credited with two sacks.

| | | | INTERCEPTIONS | | | |
Year Team	G	GS	No.	Yds.	Avg.	TD
1991—Los Angeles Rams NFL..	6	0	0	0	0.0	0
1992—Los Angeles Rams NFL..	16	6	3	61	20.3	1
1993—Los Angeles Rams NFL..	9	3	2	41	20.5	0
1994—Los Angeles Rams NFL..	16	2	0	0	0.0	0
1995—Washington NFL	4	0	0	0	0.0	0
—Dallas NFL..	9	0	0	0	0.0	0
1996—Miami NFL...	14	0	0	0	0.0	0
1997—Detroit NFL..	15	0	1	0	0.0	0
1998—Detroit NFL..	16	0	0	0	0.0	0
1999—Detroit NFL..	16	11	2	39	19.5	0
Pro totals (9 years)	121	22	8	141	17.6	1

BAKER, EUGENE   WR   FALCONS

PERSONAL: Born March 18, 1976, in Monroeville, Pa. ... 6-0/177.
HIGH SCHOOL: Shady Side Academy (Monroeville, Pa.).
COLLEGE: Kent.
TRANSACTIONS/CAREER NOTES: Selected by Atlanta Falcons in fifth round (164th pick overall) of 1999 NFL draft. ... Signed by Falcons (July 7, 1999). ... Released by Falcons (September 5, 1999). ... Re-signed by Falcons to practice squad (September 7, 1999). ... Activated (December 13, 1999).
PLAYING EXPERIENCE: Atlanta NFL, 1999. ... Games/Games started: 1999 (3/1).
PRO STATISTICS: 1999—Caught seven passes for 118 yards.
SINGLE GAME HIGHS (regular season): Receptions—5 (December 19, 1999, vs. Tennessee); yards—66 (December 19, 1999, vs. Tennessee); and touchdown receptions—0.

BAKER, JON   K

PERSONAL: Born August 13, 1972, in Orange, Calif. ... 6-1/170. ... Full name: Jonathon David Baker.
HIGH SCHOOL: Foothill (Bakersfield, Calif.).
JUNIOR COLLEGE: Bakersfield (Calif.) Community College.
COLLEGE: Arizona State.
TRANSACTIONS/CAREER NOTES: Signed as non-drafted free agent by Dallas Cowboys (April 27, 1995). ... Released by Cowboys (September 19, 1995). ... Signed by San Francisco 49ers (May 16, 1996). ... Released by 49ers (July 19, 1996). ... Re-signed by 49ers (April 2, 1997). ... Released by 49ers (August 15, 1997). ... Selected by Scottish Claymores in 1998 NFL Europe draft (February 17, 1998). ... Signed by Miami Dolphins (February 18, 1998). ... Released by Dolphins (July 22, 1998). ... Signed by Kansas City Chiefs (December 21, 1999). ... Granted free agency (February 11, 2000).
PLAYING EXPERIENCE: Dallas NFL, 1995; Scottish NFLE, 1998; Kansas City NFL, 1999. ... Games/Games started: 1995 (3/0), 1998 (games played unavailable), 1999 (2/0). Total NFL: 5/0.
PRO STATISTICS: 1998—Converted six of seven field goals for 18 points.

BALL, JERRY   DT   VIKINGS

PERSONAL: Born December 15, 1964, in Beaumont, Texas. ... 6-1/330. ... Full name: Jerry Lee Ball. ... Nephew of Mel Farr Sr., running back with Detroit Lions (1967-73); cousin of Mel Farr Jr., running back with Los Angeles Rams (1989) and Sacramento Surge of World League (1991); and cousin of Mike Farr, wide receiver with Detroit Lions (1990-92).
HIGH SCHOOL: Westbrook (Texas).
COLLEGE: Southern Methodist.
TRANSACTIONS/CAREER NOTES: Selected by Detroit Lions in third round (63rd pick overall) of 1987 NFL draft. ... Signed by Lions (July 6, 1987). ... On injured reserve with knee injury (December 12, 1991-remainder of season). ... On injured reserve with ankle injury (December 13, 1992-remainder of season). ... Traded by Lions to Cleveland Browns for third-round pick (LB Antonio London) in 1993 draft (April 23, 1993). ... Granted unconditional free agency (February 17, 1994). ... Signed by Los Angeles Raiders (June 21, 1994). ... Raiders franchise moved to Oakland (July 21, 1995). ... Released by Raiders (February 14, 1997). ... Signed by Minnesota Vikings (September 24, 1997). ... Granted unconditional free agency (February 12, 1999). ... Signed by Browns (April 28, 1999). ... Traded by Browns to Vikings for DE Stalin Colinet (September 28, 1999).
CHAMPIONSHIP GAME EXPERIENCE: Played in NFC championship game (1998 season).
HONORS: Played in Pro Bowl (1989 and 1990 seasons). ... Named to play in Pro Bowl (1991 season); replaced by Henry Thomas due to injury.
PRO STATISTICS: 1987—Returned two kickoffs for 23 yards. 1989—Recovered three fumbles. 1991—Credited with a safety. 1992—Recovered three fumbles for 21 yards and a touchdown. 1994—Recovered one fumble. 1995—Recovered one fumble. 1996—Intercepted one pass for 66 yards and a touchdown and recovered one fumble. 1997—Recovered two fumbles. 1998—Recovered one fumble.

Year Team	G	GS	SACKS
1987—Detroit NFL	12	12	1.0
1988—Detroit NFL	16	16	2.0
1989—Detroit NFL	16	16	9.0
1990—Detroit NFL	15	16	2.0
1991—Detroit NFL	13	13	2.0
1992—Detroit NFL	12	12	2.5
1993—Cleveland NFL	16	7	3.0
1994—Los Angeles Raiders NFL	16	14	3.0
1995—Oakland NFL	15	15	3.0
1996—Oakland NFL	16	0	3.0
1997—Minnesota NFL	12	6	0.0
1998—Minnesota NFL	16	16	0.0
1999—Cleveland NFL	3	3	1.0
—Minnesota NFL	13	10	1.0
Pro totals (13 years)	191	156	32.5

BANKS, ANTONIO   CB   VIKINGS

PERSONAL: Born March 12, 1973, in Ivor, Va. ... 5-10/195. ... Full name: Antonio Dontral Banks.
HIGH SCHOOL: Warwick (Newport News, Va.).
COLLEGE: Virginia Tech.
TRANSACTIONS/CAREER NOTES: Selected by Minnesota Vikings in fourth round (113th pick overall) of 1997 NFL draft. ... Signed by Vikings (June 9, 1997). ... On injured reserve with foot injury (August 18, 1997-entire season). ... Assigned by Vikings to Amsterdam Admirals in 1998 NFL Europe enhancement allocation program (February 18, 1998). ... Released by Vikings (August 30, 1998). ... Signed by Winnipeg Blue Bombers of CFL (September 24, 1998). ... Released by Blue Bombers (October 21, 1998). ... Signed by Vikings to practice squad (November 10, 1998). ... Activated (December 3, 1998). ... Released by Vikings (September 21, 1999). ... Re-signed by Vikings (November 24, 1999). ... Assigned by Vikings to Amsterdam Admirals in 2000 NFL Europe enhancement allocation program (February 18, 2000).
PLAYING EXPERIENCE: Amsterdam Admirals NFLE, 1998; Winnipeg Blue Bombers CFL, 1998; Minnesota NFL, 1998 and 1999. ... Games/Games started: NFLE 1998 (games played unavailable), CFL 1998 (4/-games started unavailable), NFL 1998 (4/0), 1999 (6/1). Total NFL: 10/1.
CHAMPIONSHIP GAME EXPERIENCE: Played in NFC championship game (1998 season).
PRO STATISTICS: NFLE: 1998—Credited with three sacks. CFL: 1998—Intercepted one pass and recovered one fumble for seven yards and a touchdown. NFL: 1999—Recovered one fumble.

BANKS, CHRIS   G   BRONCOS

PERSONAL: Born April 4, 1973, in Lexington, Mo. ... 6-1/300. ... Full name: Warren Christopher Banks.
HIGH SCHOOL: Lexington (Mo.).
COLLEGE: Kansas.
TRANSACTIONS/CAREER NOTES: Selected by Denver Broncos in seventh round (226th pick overall) of 1996 NFL draft. ... Signed by Broncos (July 16, 1996). ... On injured reserve with knee injury (August 25-September 6, 1996). ... Released by Broncos (September 6, 1996). ... Re-signed by Broncos (January 29, 1997). ... Assigned by Broncos to Barcelona Dragons in 1997 World League enhancement allocation program (February 19, 1997). ... Released by Broncos (August 24, 1997). ... Re-signed by Broncos to practice squad (August 25, 1997). ... Released by Broncos (January 26, 1998). ... Re-signed by Broncos to practice squad (January 30, 1998).
PLAYING EXPERIENCE: Barcelona W.L., 1997; Denver NFL, 1998 and 1999. ... Games/Games started: W.L. 1997 (games played unavailable), 1998 (4/0), 1999 (16/1). Total NFL: 20/1.
CHAMPIONSHIP GAME EXPERIENCE: Member of Broncos for AFC championship game (1998 season); inactive. ... Member of Super Bowl championship team (1998 season); inactive.

BANKS, TAVIAN   RB   JAGUARS

PERSONAL: Born February 17, 1974, in Davenport, Iowa. ... 5-10/208. ... Full name: Tavian Remond Banks. ... Name pronounced TAY-vee-un.
HIGH SCHOOL: Bettendorf (Iowa).
COLLEGE: Iowa (degree in sports management, 1997).
TRANSACTIONS/CAREER NOTES: Selected by Jacksonville Jaguars in fourth round (101st pick overall) of 1998 NFL draft. ... Signed by Jaguars (May 26, 1998). ... On injured reserve with knee injury (November 10, 1999-remainder of season).

PRO STATISTICS: 1998—Recovered one fumble.
SINGLE GAME HIGHS (regular season): Attempts—9 (October 12, 1998, vs. Miami); yards—75 (October 12, 1998, vs. Miami); and rushing touchdowns—1 (October 18, 1998, vs. Buffalo).

			RUSHING				RECEIVING				KICKOFF RETURNS				TOTALS		
Year Team	G	GS	Att.	Yds.	Avg.	TD	No.	Yds.	Avg.	TD	No.	Yds.	Avg.	TD	TD	2pt.	Pts. Fum.
1998—Jacksonville NFL	6	1	26	140	5.4	1	4	20	5.0	0	5	133	26.6	0	1	0	6 2
1999—Jacksonville NFL	8	1	23	82	3.6	0	14	137	9.8	0	5	78	15.6	0	0	0	0 0
Pro totals (2 years)	14	2	49	222	4.5	1	18	157	8.7	0	10	211	21.1	0	1	0	6 2

BANKS, TONY   QB   RAVENS

B

PERSONAL: Born April 5, 1973, in San Diego. ... 6-4/225. ... Full name: Anthony Lamar Banks. ... Cousin of Chip Banks, linebacker with Cleveland Browns (1982-86), San Diego Chargers (1987) and Indianapolis Colts (1989-92).
HIGH SCHOOL: Herbert Hoover (San Diego).
JUNIOR COLLEGE: San Diego Mesa College.
COLLEGE: Michigan State.
TRANSACTIONS/CAREER NOTES: Selected by St. Louis Rams in second round (42nd pick overall) of 1996 NFL draft. ... Signed by Rams (July 15, 1996). ... On injured reserve list with knee injury (December 14, 1998-remainder of season). ... Granted free agency (February 12, 1999). ... Re-signed by Rams (April 17, 1999). ... Traded by Rams to Baltimore Ravens for fifth-round pick (G Cameron Spikes) in 1999 draft and seventh-round pick (traded to Chicago) in 2000 draft (April 17, 1999). ... Granted unconditional free agency (February 11, 2000). ... Re-signed by Ravens (February 17, 2000).
RECORDS: Holds NFL single-season record for most fumbles—21 (1996).
PRO STATISTICS: 1996—Led league with 21 fumbles and recovered four fumbles for minus 17 yards. 1997—Tied for NFC lead with 15 fumbles and recovered three fumbles for minus 27 yards. 1998—Fumbled 10 times and recovered eight fumbles for minus 23 yards. 1999—Fumbled 11 times and recovered two fumbles.
SINGLE GAME HIGHS (regular season): Attempts—49 (September 28, 1997, vs. Oakland); completions—29 (September 6, 1998, vs. New Orleans); yards—401 (November 2, 1997, vs. Atlanta); and touchdown passes—4 (December 5, 1999, vs. Tennessee).
STATISTICAL PLATEAUS: 300-yard passing games: 1996 (2), 1997 (1), 1999 (1). Total: 4.
MISCELLANEOUS: Regular-season record as starting NFL quarterback: 20-33 (.377).

					PASSING							RUSHING				TOTALS	
Year Team	G	GS	Att.	Cmp.	Pct.	Yds.	TD	Int.	Avg.	Rat.	Att.	Yds.	Avg.	TD	TD	2pt.	Pts.
1996—St. Louis NFL	14	13	368	192	52.2	2544	15	15	6.91	71.0	61	212	3.5	0	0	1	2
1997—St. Louis NFL	16	16	487	252	51.7	3254	14	13	6.68	71.5	47	186	4.0	1	1	0	6
1998—St. Louis NFL	14	14	408	241	59.1	2535	7	14	6.21	68.6	40	156	3.9	3	3	1	20
1999—Baltimore NFL	12	10	320	169	52.8	2136	17	8	6.68	81.2	24	93	3.9	0	0	0	0
Pro totals (4 years)	56	53	1583	854	53.9	10469	53	50	6.61	72.6	172	647	3.8	4	4	2	28

RECORD AS BASEBALL PLAYER

TRANSACTIONS/CAREER NOTES: Threw right, batted right. ... Selected by Minnesota Twins organization in 10th round of free-agent draft (June 3, 1991).

						BATTING									FIELDING		
Year Team (League)	Pos.	G	AB	R	H	2B	3B	HR	RBI	Avg.	BB	SO	SB	PO	A	E	Avg.
1991—GC Twins (GCL)......	DH	17	57	7	13	3	0	0	1	.228	4	16	2	...	...	...	...

BANKSTON, MICHAEL   DE   BENGALS

PERSONAL: Born March 12, 1970, in East Bernard, Texas. ... 6-5/285.
HIGH SCHOOL: East Bernard (Texas).
COLLEGE: Sam Houston State.
TRANSACTIONS/CAREER NOTES: Selected by Phoenix Cardinals in fourth round (100th pick overall) of 1992 NFL draft. ... Signed by Cardinals (July 20, 1992). ... Cardinals franchise renamed Arizona Cardinals for 1994 season. ... Granted unconditional free agency (February 14, 1997). ... Re-signed by Cardinals (April 2, 1997). ... Granted free agency (February 13, 1998). ... Tendered offer sheet by Cincinnati Bengals (February 13, 1998). ... Cardinals declined to match offer (February 14, 1998).
PRO STATISTICS: 1993—Recovered five fumbles for 16 yards. 1994—Recovered one fumble for two yards. 1995—Intercepted one pass for 28 yards and fumbled once. 1996—Recovered one fumble. 1998—Recovered one fumble for five yards.

Year Team	G	GS	SACKS
1992—Phoenix NFL..	16	6	2.0
1993—Phoenix NFL..	16	12	3.0
1994—Arizona NFL..	16	16	7.0
1995—Arizona NFL..	16	16	2.0
1996—Arizona NFL..	16	16	0.5
1997—Arizona NFL..	16	16	2.0
1998—Cincinnati NFL..	16	16	4.5
1999—Cincinnati NFL..	16	9	6.0
Pro totals (8 years)..	128	107	27.0

BANTA, BRADFORD   TE   COLTS

PERSONAL: Born December 14, 1970, in Baton Rouge, La. ... 6-6/255. ... Full name: Dennis Bradford Banta.
HIGH SCHOOL: University (Baton Rouge, La.).
COLLEGE: Southern California.
TRANSACTIONS/CAREER NOTES: Selected by Indianapolis Colts in fourth round (106th pick overall) of 1994 NFL draft. ... Signed by Colts (July 22, 1994). ... Granted free agency (February 14, 1997). ... Re-signed by Colts (May 14, 1997). ... Granted unconditional free agency (February 11, 2000). ... Re-signed by Colts (March 9, 2000).

PLAYING EXPERIENCE: Indianapolis NFL, 1994-1999. ... Games/Games started: 1994 (16/0), 1995 (16/2), 1996 (13/0), 1997 (15/0), 1998 (16/0), 1999 (16/0). Total: 92/2.
CHAMPIONSHIP GAME EXPERIENCE: Played in AFC championship game (1995 season).
PRO STATISTICS: 1995—Caught one pass for six yards. 1998—Caught one pass for seven yards and recovered one fumble.
SINGLE GAME HIGHS (regular season): Receptions—1 (November 1, 1998, vs. New England); yards—7 (November 1, 1998, vs. New England); and touchdown receptions—0.

BARBER, KANTROY　　　FB

PERSONAL: Born October 4, 1973, in Miami. ... 6-1/245. ... Son of Rudy Barber, linebacker with Miami Dolphins (1968).
HIGH SCHOOL: Carol City (Miami).
COLLEGE: Colorado, then West Virginia.
TRANSACTIONS/CAREER NOTES: Selected by New England Patriots in fourth round (124th pick overall) of 1996 NFL draft. ... Signed by Patriots (July 18, 1996). ... Inactive for six games (1996). ... On injured reserve with shoulder injury (October 15, 1996-remainder of season). ... Claimed on waivers by Carolina Panthers (August 25, 1997). ... Inactive for six games (1997). ... Released by Panthers (October 16, 1997). ... Signed by Tampa Bay Buccaneers (February 10, 1998). ... Released by Buccaneers (August 25, 1998). ... Signed by Buffalo Bills to practice squad (October 1, 1998). ... Signed by Indianapolis Colts off Bills practice squad (November 9, 1998). ... Released by Colts (December 16, 1998). ... Re-signed by Colts to practice squad (December 17, 1998). ... Signed by Miami Dolphins off Colts practice squad (December 29, 1998). ... Released by Dolphins (September 5, 1999). ... Re-signed by Dolphins to practice squad (September 7, 1999). ... Activated (October 19, 1999). ... On injured reserve with neck injury (November 29, 1999-remainder of season). ... Released by Dolphins (February 17, 2000).
PLAYING EXPERIENCE: Miami NFL,1999. ... Games/Games started: 1999 (2/0).

BARBER, MICHAEL　　　LB

PERSONAL: Born November 9, 1971, in Edgemore, S.C. ... 6-0/246.
HIGH SCHOOL: Lewisville (Richburg, S.C.).
COLLEGE: Clemson.
TRANSACTIONS/CAREER NOTES: Signed as non-drafted free agent by Seattle Seahawks (April 26, 1995). ... Granted free agency (February 13, 1998). ... Re-signed by Seahawks (May 13, 1998). ... Claimed on waivers by Indianapolis Colts (August 31, 1998). ... Released by Colts (February 8, 2000).
PLAYING EXPERIENCE: Seattle NFL, 1995-1997; Indianapolis NFL, 1998 and 1999. ... Games/Games started: 1995 (2/0), 1996 (13/7), 1997 (8/2), 1998 (12/6), 1999 (16/16). Total: 51/31.
PRO STATISTICS: 1996—Returned one kickoff for 12 yards and recovered one fumble. 1997—Recovered one fumble. 1998—Intercepted one pass for no yards and credited with two sacks. 1999—Recovered one fumble.

BARBER, RONDE　　　CB　　　BUCCANEERS

PERSONAL: Born April 7, 1975, in Montgomery County, Va. ... 5-10/184. ... Full name: Jamael Oronde Barber. ... Twin brother of Tiki Barber, running back, New York Giants. ... Name pronounced RON-day.
HIGH SCHOOL: Cave Spring (Roanoke, Va.).
COLLEGE: Virginia (degree in commerce, 1996).
TRANSACTIONS/CAREER NOTES: Selected after junior season by Tampa Bay Buccaneers in third round (66th pick overall) of 1997 NFL draft. ... Signed by Buccaneers (July 18, 1997). ... Granted free agency (February 11, 2000).
CHAMPIONSHIP GAME EXPERIENCE: Played in NFC championship game (1999 season).
PRO STATISTICS: 1998—Returned one punt for 23 yards and a touchdown.

| | | | INTERCEPTIONS | | | | SACKS |
Year　Team	G	GS	No.	Yds.	Avg.	TD	No.
1997—Tampa Bay NFL	1	0	0	0	0.0	0	0.0
1998—Tampa Bay NFL	16	9	2	67	33.5	0	3.0
1999—Tampa Bay NFL	16	15	2	60	30.0	0	1.0
Pro totals (3 years)	33	24	4	127	31.8	0	4.0

BARBER, SHAWN　　　LB　　　REDSKINS

PERSONAL: Born January 14, 1975, in Richmond, Va. ... 6-2/224.
HIGH SCHOOL: Hermitage (Richmond, Va.).
COLLEGE: Richmond.
TRANSACTIONS/CAREER NOTES: Selected by Washington Redskins in fourth round (113th pick overall) of 1998 NFL draft. ... Signed by Redskins (May 13, 1998).
PRO STATISTICS: 1999—Credited with one sack.

| | | | INTERCEPTIONS | | | |
Year　Team	G	GS	No.	Yds.	Avg.	TD
1998—Washington NFL	16	1	1	0	0.0	0
1999—Washington NFL	16	16	2	70	35.0	1
Pro totals (2 years)	32	17	3	70	23.3	1

BARBER, TIKI　　　RB　　　GIANTS

PERSONAL: Born April 7, 1975, in Roanoke, Va. ... 5-10/200. ... Full name: Atiim Kiambu Barber. ... Twin brother of Ronde Barber, cornerback, Tampa Bay Buccaneers. ... Name pronounced TEE-kee.
HIGH SCHOOL: Cave Spring (Roanoke, Va.).
COLLEGE: Virginia.

TRANSACTIONS/CAREER NOTES: Selected by New York Giants in second round (36th pick overall) of 1997 NFL draft. ... Signed by Giants for 1997 season. ... Granted free agency (February 11, 2000).

PRO STATISTICS: 1997—Fumbled three times. 1998—Fumbled once. 1999—Fumbled five times and recovered five fumbles.

SINGLE GAME HIGHS (regular season): Attempts—21 (December 7, 1997, vs. Philadelphia); yards—114 (December 7, 1997, vs. Philadelphia); and rushing touchdowns—1 (September 14, 1997, vs. Baltimore).

STATISTICAL PLATEAUS: 100-yard rushing games: 1997 (1). ... 100-yard receiving games: 1999 (1).

			RUSHING				RECEIVING				PUNT RETURNS				KICKOFF RETURNS				TOTALS		
Year Team	G	GS	Att.	Yds.	Avg.	TD	No.	Yds.	Avg.	TD	No.	Yds.	Avg.	TD	No.	Yds.	Avg.	TD	TD	2pt.	Pts.
1997—N.Y. Giants NFL...	12	6	136	511	3.8	3	34	299	8.8	1	0	0	0.0	0	0	0	0.0	0	4	1	26
1998—N.Y. Giants NFL...	16	4	52	166	3.2	0	42	348	8.3	3	0	0	0.0	0	14	250	17.9	0	3	0	18
1999—N.Y. Giants NFL...	16	1	62	258	4.2	0	66	609	9.2	2	∞44	‡506	11.5	∞1	12	266	22.2	0	3	0	18
Pro totals (3 years)........	44	11	250	935	3.7	3	142	1256	8.8	6	44	506	11.5	1	26	516	19.8	0	10	1	62

BARKER, BRYAN   P   JAGUARS   B

PERSONAL: Born June 28, 1964, in Jacksonville Beach, Fla. ... 6-2/199. ... Full name: Bryan Christopher Barker.

HIGH SCHOOL: Miramonte (Orinda, Calif.).

COLLEGE: Santa Clara (degree in economics).

TRANSACTIONS/CAREER NOTES: Signed as non-drafted free agent by Denver Broncos (May 1988). ... Released by Broncos (July 19, 1988). ... Signed by Seattle Seahawks (1989). ... Released by Seahawks (August 30, 1989). ... Signed by Kansas City Chiefs (May 1, 1990). ... Released by Chiefs (August 28, 1990). ... Re-signed by Chiefs (September 26, 1990). ... Granted unconditional free agency (February 1-April 1, 1991). ... Re-signed by Chiefs for 1991 season. ... Granted unconditional free agency (February 1-April 1, 1992). ... Re-signed by Chiefs for 1992 season. ... Released by Chiefs (1994). ... Signed by Minnesota Vikings (May 18, 1994). ... Released by Vikings (August 30, 1994). ... Signed by Philadelphia Eagles (October 11, 1994). ... Granted unconditional free agency (February 17, 1995). ... Signed by Jacksonville Jaguars (March 7, 1995).

CHAMPIONSHIP GAME EXPERIENCE: Played in AFC championship game (1993, 1996 and 1999 seasons).

HONORS: Played in Pro Bowl (1997 season).

PRO STATISTICS: 1997—Rushed once for no yards, attempted one pass with a completion for 22 yards and fumbled once for minus 19 yards. 1999—Rushed once for six yards.

			PUNTING			
Year Team	G	No.	Yds.	Avg.	Net avg.	In. 20	Blk.
1990—Kansas City NFL..................................	13	64	2479	38.7	33.3	16	0
1991—Kansas City NFL..................................	16	57	2303	40.4	35.0	14	0
1992—Kansas City NFL..................................	15	75	3245	43.3	35.2	16	1
1993—Kansas City NFL..................................	16	76	3240	42.6	35.3	19	1
1994—Philadelphia NFL	11	66	2696	40.8	‡36.2	20	0
1995—Jacksonville NFL................................	16	82	3591	43.8	*38.6	19	0
1996—Jacksonville NFL................................	16	69	3016	43.7	35.6	16	0
1997—Jacksonville NFL................................	16	66	2964	44.9	38.8	27	0
1998—Jacksonville NFL................................	16	85	3824	45.0	38.5	28	0
1999—Jacksonville NFL................................	16	78	3260	41.8	36.9	32	0
Pro totals (10 years).................................	151	718	30618	42.6	36.5	207	2

BARKER, ROY   DE

PERSONAL: Born February 24, 1969, in New York. ... 6-5/290.

HIGH SCHOOL: Central Islip (N.Y.).

COLLEGE: North Carolina (degree in speech communications, 1991).

TRANSACTIONS/CAREER NOTES: Selected by Minnesota Vikings in fourth round (98th pick overall) of 1992 NFL draft. ... Signed by Vikings (July 16, 1992). ... On injured reserve with knee injury (September 1-30, 1992). ... Granted unconditional free agency (February 16, 1996). ... Signed by San Francisco 49ers (February 28, 1996). ... Traded by 49ers with TE Irv Smith to Cleveland Browns for past considerations (February 12, 1999). ... Claimed on waivers by Green Bay Packers (December 21, 1999). ... Released by Packers (December 27, 1999).

CHAMPIONSHIP GAME EXPERIENCE: Played in NFC championship game (1997 season).

PRO STATISTICS: 1993—Recovered one fumble. 1994—Recovered one fumble. 1995—Intercepted one pass for minus two yards. 1998—Intercepted one pass for minus four yards. 1999—Intercepted one pass for 14 yards.

Year Team	G	GS	SACKS
1992—Minnesota NFL	8	0	0.0
1993—Minnesota NFL	16	16	6.0
1994—Minnesota NFL	16	15	3.5
1995—Minnesota NFL	16	16	3.0
1996—San Francisco NFL..	16	16	12.5
1997—San Francisco NFL..	13	12	5.5
1998—San Francisco NFL..	16	16	12.0
1999—Cleveland NFL..	12	3	2.0
—Green Bay NFL..	1	0	0.0
Pro totals (8 years)..	114	94	44.5

BARLOW, REGGIE   WR/PR/KR   JAGUARS

PERSONAL: Born January 22, 1973, in Montgomery, Ala. ... 6-0/186. ... Full name: Reggie Devon Barlow.

HIGH SCHOOL: Lanier (Montgomery, Ala.).

COLLEGE: Alabama State.

TRANSACTIONS/CAREER NOTES: Selected by Jacksonville Jaguars in fourth round (110th pick overall) of 1996 NFL draft. ... Signed by Jaguars (May 28, 1996). ... Granted free agency (February 12, 1999). ... Re-signed by Jaguars (March 23, 1999).

CHAMPIONSHIP GAME EXPERIENCE: Played in AFC championship game (1996 and 1999 seasons).

PRO STATISTICS: 1997—Recovered one fumble. 1998—Recovered one fumble. 1999—Recovered one fumble.

SINGLE GAME HIGHS (regular season): Receptions—4 (December 2, 1999, vs. Pittsburgh); yards—50 (October 12, 1998, vs. Miami); and touchdown receptions—0.

			RECEIVING				PUNT RETURNS				KICKOFF RETURNS				TOTALS			
Year—Team	G	GS	No.	Yds.	Avg.	TD	No.	Yds.	Avg.	TD	No.	Yds.	Avg.	TD	TD	2pt.	Pts.	Fum.
1996—Jacksonville NFL	7	0	0	0	0.0	0	0	0	0.0	0	0	0	0.0	0	0	0	0	0
1997—Jacksonville NFL	16	0	5	74	14.8	0	36	412	11.4	0	10	267	26.7	▲1	2	0	12	2
1998—Jacksonville NFL	16	2	11	168	15.3	0	43	*555	§12.9	1	30	747	24.9	0	1	0	6	1
1999—Jacksonville NFL	14	2	16	202	12.6	0	38	414	10.9	1	19	396	20.8	0	1	0	6	4
Pro totals (4 years)	53	4	32	444	13.9	0	117	1381	11.8	2	59	1410	23.9	1	4	0	24	7

BARNDT, TOM DT BENGALS

PERSONAL: Born March 14, 1972, in Mentor, Ohio. ... 6-3/293. ... Full name: Thomas Allen Barndt.
HIGH SCHOOL: Mentor (Ohio).
COLLEGE: Pittsburgh.
TRANSACTIONS/CAREER NOTES: Selected by Kansas City Chiefs in sixth round (207th pick overall) of 1995 NFL draft. ... Signed by Chiefs for the 1995 season. ... Released by Chiefs (August 27, 1995). ... Re-signed by Chiefs to practice squad (August 29, 1995). ... Assigned by Chiefs to Scottish Claymores in 1996 World League enhancement allocation program (February 19, 1996). ... Granted free agency (February 12, 1999). ... Re-signed by Chiefs (June 16, 1999). ... Granted unconditional free agency (February 11, 2000). ... Signed by Cincinnati Bengals (February 18, 2000).
PRO STATISTICS: 1998—Recovered two fumbles. 1999—Recovered one fumble.

Year—Team	G	GS	SACKS
1995—Kansas City NFL	Did not play.		
1996—Scottish W.L.	...	...	0.0
—Kansas City NFL	13	0	0.0
1997—Kansas City NFL	16	1	2.0
1998—Kansas City NFL	16	16	3.5
1999—Kansas City NFL	16	13	2.5
Pro totals (4 years)	61	30	8.0

BARNES, LIONEL DE RAMS

PERSONAL: Born April 19, 1976, in New Orleans. ... 6-4/264. ... Full name: Lionel Barnes Jr.
HIGH SCHOOL: Lakenheath American (Suffolk, England).
JUNIOR COLLEGE: Barton County Community College, Kan. (did not play football).
COLLEGE: Northeast Louisiana.
TRANSACTIONS/CAREER NOTES: Selected by St. Louis Rams in sixth round (176th pick overall) of 1999 NFL draft. ... Signed by Rams (July 19, 1999).
PLAYING EXPERIENCE: St. Louis NFL, 1999. ... Games/Games started: 1999 (3/0).
CHAMPIONSHIP GAME EXPERIENCE: Member of Rams for NFC championship game (1999 season); inactive. ... Member of Super Bowl championship team (1999 season); inactive.

BARNES, PAT QB

PERSONAL: Born February 23, 1975, in Arlington Heights, Ill. ... 6-3/215. ... Full name: Patrick Barnes.
HIGH SCHOOL: Trabuco Hills (Calif.).
COLLEGE: California.
TRANSACTIONS/CAREER NOTES: Selected by Kansas City Chiefs in fourth round (110th pick overall) of 1997 NFL draft. ... Signed by Chiefs (May 8, 1997). ... Active for one game (1997); did not play. ... Released by Chiefs (August 25, 1998). ... Signed by Washington Redskins to practice squad (September 9, 1998). ... Released by Redskins (September 15, 1998). ... Signed by Oakland Raiders to practice squad (September 30, 1998). ... Activated (October 7, 1998); did not play. ... Released by Raiders (October 12, 1998). ... Re-signed by Raiders to practice squad (October 14, 1998). ... Activated (October 21, 1998); did not play. ... Released by Raiders (October 27, 1998). ... Re-signed by Raiders to practice squad (October 28, 1998). ... Activated (December 5, 1998); did not play. ... Assigned by Raiders to Frankfurt Galaxy in 1999 NFL Europe enhancement allocation program (February 22, 1999). ... Released by Raiders (September 4, 1999). ... Signed by San Francisco 49ers (October 1, 1999). ... Released by 49ers (October 5, 1999). ... Re-signed by 49ers (October 8, 1999). ... Released by 49ers (October 12, 1999). ... Re-signed by 49ers (October 19, 1999). ... Granted free agency (February 11, 2000).

			PASSING								RUSHING				TOTALS		
Year—Team	G	GS	Att.	Cmp.	Pct.	Yds.	TD	Int.	Avg.	Rat.	Att.	Yds.	Avg.	TD	TD	2pt.	Pts.
1997—Kansas City NFL							Did not play.										
1998—Oakland NFL							Did not play.										
1999—Frankfurt NFLE	10	...	164	94	57.3	1468	12	8	8.95	91.2	22	107	4.9	1	1	0	6
—San Francisco NFL	1	0	0	0	0.0	0	0	0	0.0	...	0	0	0.0	0	0	0	0
NFL Europe totals (1 year)	10	...	164	94	57.3	1468	12	8	8.95	91.2	22	107	4.9	1	1	0	6
NFL totals (1 year)	1	0	0	0	0.0	0	0	0	0.0		0	0	0.0	0	0	0	0
Pro totals (2 years)	11	...	164	94	57.3	1468	12	8	8.95	91.2	22	107	4.9	1	1	0	6

BARNHARDT, TOMMY P REDSKINS

PERSONAL: Born June 11, 1963, in China Grove, N.C. ... 6-2/228. ... Full name: Tommy Ray Barnhardt.
HIGH SCHOOL: South Rowan (China Grove, N.C.).
COLLEGE: East Carolina, then North Carolina (degree in industrial relations, 1986).
TRANSACTIONS/CAREER NOTES: Selected by Baltimore Stars in 1986 USFL territorial draft. ... Selected by Tampa Bay Buccaneers in ninth round (223rd pick overall) of 1986 NFL draft. ... Signed by Buccaneers (July 16, 1986). ... Released by Buccaneers (August 25, 1986). ... Re-signed by Buccaneers (February 6, 1987). ... Released by Buccaneers (August 5, 1987). ... Signed as replacement player by New Orleans Saints (September 23, 1987). ... Released by Saints (November 3, 1987). ... Signed by Chicago Bears (December 16, 1987). ... Released by

Bears (August 24, 1988). ... Signed by Washington Redskins (September 9, 1988). ... On injured reserve with pulled quadricep (October 11, 1988-remainder of season). ... Granted unconditional free agency (February 1-April 1, 1989). ... Re-signed by Redskins (May 11, 1989). ... Released by Redskins (June 27, 1989). ... Signed by Detroit Lions (July 20, 1989). ... Released by Lions (August 30, 1989). ... Signed by Saints (October 11, 1989). ... Granted unconditional free agency (February 1-April 1, 1992). ... Re-signed by Saints for 1992 season. ... Granted unconditional free agency (March 1, 1993). ... Re-signed by Saints (July 15, 1993). ... Granted unconditional free agency (February 17, 1995). ... Signed by Carolina Panthers (March 2, 1995). ... Released by Panthers (May 7, 1996). ... Signed by Buccaneers (May 13, 1996). ... On injured reserve with broken collarbone (October 9, 1997-remainder of season). ... Granted unconditional free agency (February 12, 1999). ... Signed by Saints (June 28, 1999). ... Released by Saints (April 6, 2000). ... Signed by Washington Redskins (May 8, 2000).

PRO STATISTICS: 1987—Rushed once for minus 13 yards. 1991—Rushed once for no yards. 1992—Rushed four times for minus two yards and fumbled twice for minus 16 yards. 1993—Rushed once for 18 yards and completed only pass attempt for seven yards. 1994—Rushed once for 21 yards and attempted one pass without a completion. 1996—Rushed twice for 27 yards. 1997—Completed only pass attempt for 25 yards. 1999—Rushed once for four yards, fumbled once and recovered one fumble.

				PUNTING			
Year Team	G	No.	Yds.	Avg.	Net avg.	In. 20	Blk.
1987—New Orleans NFL	3	11	483	43.9	0	4	0
—Chicago NFL	2	6	236	39.3	35.2	2	0
1988—Washington NFL	4	15	628	41.9	34.2	1	0
1989—New Orleans NFL	11	55	2179	39.6	35.0	17	0
1990—New Orleans NFL	16	70	2990	42.7	36.2	20	1
1991—New Orleans NFL	16	86	*3743	43.5	35.2	20	1
1992—New Orleans NFL	16	67	2947	44.0	37.7	19	0
1993—New Orleans NFL	16	77	3356	43.6	37.5	26	0
1994—New Orleans NFL	16	67	2920	43.6	33.5	14	0
1995—Carolina NFL	16	‡95	‡3906	41.1	35.2	27	0
1996—Tampa Bay NFL	16	70	3015	43.1	37.7	24	1
1997—Tampa Bay NFL	6	29	1304	45.0	39.1	12	0
1998—Tampa Bay NFL	16	81	3340	41.2	35.3	19	0
1999—New Orleans NFL	16	82	3262	39.8	35.1	14	0
Pro totals (13 years)	170	811	34309	42.3	35.4	219	3

BARROW, MIKE　　　　　LB　　　　　GIANTS

PERSONAL: Born April 19, 1970, in Homestead, Fla. ... 6-2/236. ... Full name: Micheal Colvin Barrow.
HIGH SCHOOL: Homestead (Fla.) Senior.
COLLEGE: Miami, Fla. (degree in accounting, 1992).
TRANSACTIONS/CAREER NOTES: Selected by Houston Oilers in second round (47th pick overall) of 1993 NFL draft. ... Signed by Oilers (July 30, 1993). ... Granted free agency (February 16, 1996). ... Re-signed by Oilers (August 9, 1996). ... Granted unconditional free agency (February 14, 1997). ... Signed by Carolina Panthers (February 20, 1997). ... Released by Panthers (February 22, 2000). ... Signed by New York Giants (March 2, 2000).
HONORS: Named linebacker on THE SPORTING NEWS college All-America first team (1992).
PRO STATISTICS: 1995—Recovered one fumble. 1996—Recovered one fumble. 1997—Recovered two fumbles. 1998—Intercepted one pass for 10 yards and recovered two fumbles. 1999—Recovered one fumble.

Year Team	G	GS	SACKS
1993—Houston NFL	16	0	1.0
1994—Houston NFL	16	16	2.5
1995—Houston NFL	13	12	3.0
1996—Houston NFL	16	16	6.0
1997—Carolina NFL	16	16	8.5
1998—Carolina NFL	16	16	4.0
1999—Carolina NFL	16	16	4.0
Pro totals (7 years)	109	92	29.0

BARTHOLOMEW, BRENT　　　　　P　　　　　BEARS

PERSONAL: Born October 22, 1976, in Birmingham, Ala. ... 6-2/220. ... Full name: Brent Robert Bartholomew.
HIGH SCHOOL: Apopka (Fla.).
COLLEGE: Ohio State.
TRANSACTIONS/CAREER NOTES: Selected by Miami Dolphins in sixth round (192nd pick overall) of 1999 NFL draft. ... Signed by Dolphins (July 27, 1999). ... On injured reserve with knee injury (September 27, 1999-remainder of season). ... Traded by Dolphins to Chicago Bears for seventh-round pick (DB Jeff Harris) in 2000 draft and seventh-round pick in 2001 draft (April 16, 2000).

				PUNTING			
Year Team	G	No.	Yds.	Avg.	Net avg.	In. 20	Blk.
1999—Miami NFL	2	7	308	44.0	32.6	1	0

BARTON, ERIC　　　　　LB　　　　　RAIDERS

PERSONAL: Born September 29, 1977, in Alexandria, Va. ... 6-2/245.
HIGH SCHOOL: Thomas A. Edison (Alexandria, Va.).
COLLEGE: Maryland.
TRANSACTIONS/CAREER NOTES: Selected by Oakland Raiders in fifth round (146th pick overall) of 1999 NFL draft. ...Signed by Raiders for 1999 season.

Year Team	G	GS	Sacks
1999—Oakland NFL	16	3	3.0

BARTRUM, MIKE   TE   EAGLES

PERSONAL: Born June 23, 1970, in Galliapolis, Ohio. ... 6-4/245. ... Full name: Michael Weldon Bartrum.
HIGH SCHOOL: Meigs (Pomeroy, Ohio).
COLLEGE: Marshall (degree in education).
TRANSACTIONS/CAREER NOTES: Signed as non-drafted free agent by Kansas City Chiefs (May 5, 1993). ... Released by Chiefs (August 30, 1993). ... Re-signed by Chiefs to practice squad (August 31, 1993). ... Activated (October 27, 1993). ... Released by Chiefs (August 23, 1994). ... Signed by Green Bay Packers (January 20, 1995). ... On injured reserve with broken arm (October 11, 1995-remainder of season). ... Traded by Packers with DE Walter Scott to New England Patriots for past considerations (August 25, 1996). ... On injured reserve with forearm injury (November 12, 1997-remainder of season). ... Granted unconditional free agency (February 13, 1998). ... Re-signed by Patriots (April 7, 1998). ... Released by Patriots (April 10, 2000). ... Signed by Philadelphia Eagles (April 17, 2000).
PLAYING EXPERIENCE: Kansas City NFL, 1993; Green Bay NFL, 1995; New England NFL, 1996-1999. ... Games/Games started: 1993 (3/0), 1995 (4/0), 1996 (16/0), 1997 (9/0), 1998 (16/0), 1999 (16/0). Total: 64/0.
CHAMPIONSHIP GAME EXPERIENCE: Member of Chiefs for AFC championship game (1993 season); inactive. ... Played in AFC championship game (1996 season). ... Played in Super Bowl XXXI (1996 season).
PRO STATISTICS: 1996—Caught one pass for one yard and a touchdown. 1999—Caught one pass for one yard and a touchdown and fumbled once for minus seven yards.
SINGLE GAME HIGHS (regular season): Receptions—1 (January 2, 2000, vs. Baltimore); yards—1 (January 2, 2000, vs. Baltimore); and touchdown receptions—1 (January 2, 2000, vs. Baltimore).

BASNIGHT, MICHAEL   RB   BENGALS

PERSONAL: Born September 3, 1977, in Norfolk, Va. ... 6-1/230.
HIGH SCHOOL: Booker T. Washington (Norfolk, Va.).
COLLEGE: North Carolina A&T.
TRANSACTIONS/CAREER NOTES: Signed as non-drafted free agent by Cincinnati Bengals (April 28, 1999). ... Released by Bengals (September 5, 1999). ... Re-signed by Bengals to practice squad (September 6, 1999). ... Activated (September 29, 1999).
PRO STATISTICS: 1999—Recovered one fumble.
SINGLE GAME HIGHS (regular season): Attempts—12 (December 12, 1999, vs. Cleveland); yards—86 (January 2, 2000, Jacksonville); and rushing touchdowns—0.

Year Team	G	GS	Att.	Yds.	Avg.	TD	No.	Yds.	Avg.	TD	TD	2pt.	Pts.	Fum.
1999—Cincinnati NFL	13	1	62	308	5.0	0	16	172	10.8	0	0	0	0	1

(columns: RUSHING: Att. Yds. Avg. TD; RECEIVING: No. Yds. Avg. TD; TOTALS: TD 2pt. Pts. Fum.)

BASS, ANTHONY   DB   VIKINGS

PERSONAL: Born March 27, 1975, in St. Alban, W.Va. ... 6-1/200.
HIGH SCHOOL: South Charleston (W.Va.).
COLLEGE: Bethune-Cookman.
TRANSACTIONS/CAREER NOTES: Signed as non-drafted free agent by Minnesota Vikings (April 23, 1998). ... Released by Vikings (August 24, 1998). ... Signed by Green Bay Packers to practice squad (September 9, 1998). ... Released by Packers (September 12, 1998). ... Signed by Vikings to practice squad (September 17, 1998). ... Activated (November 10, 1998).
PLAYING EXPERIENCE: Minnesota NFL, 1998 and 1999. ... Games/Games started: 1998 (3/0), 1999 (14/3). Total: 17/3.
CHAMPIONSHIP GAME EXPERIENCE: Played in NFC championship game (1998 season).
PRO STATISTICS: 1999—Intercepted one pass for four yards.

BATCH, CHARLIE   QB   LIONS

PERSONAL: Born December 5, 1974, in Homestead, Pa. ... 6-2/220. ... Full name: Charles D'Donte Batch.
HIGH SCHOOL: Steel Valley (Munhall, Pa.).
COLLEGE: Eastern Michigan (degree in business, 1997).
TRANSACTIONS/CAREER NOTES: Selected by Detroit Lions in second round (60th pick overall) of 1998 NFL draft. ... Signed by Lions (July 19, 1998). ... On injured reserve with back injury (December 24, 1998-remainder of season).
RECORDS: Holds NFL rookie-season record for lowest interception percentage—1.98.
PRO STATISTICS: 1998—Fumbled twice. 1999—Fumbled four times.
SINGLE GAME HIGHS (regular season): Attempts—40 (December 25, 1999, vs. Denver); completions—21 (December 25, 1999, vs. Denver); yards—268 (October 4, 1998, vs. Chicago); and touchdown passes—3 (September 12, 1999, vs. Seattle).
MISCELLANEOUS: Regular-season record as starting NFL quarterback: 11-11 (.500).

Year Team	G	GS	Att.	Cmp.	Pct.	Yds.	TD	Int.	Avg.	Rat.	Att.	Yds.	Avg.	TD	TD	2pt.	Pts.
1998—Detroit NFL	12	12	303	173	57.1	2178	11	6	7.19	83.5	41	229	5.6	1	1	0	6
1999—Detroit NFL	11	10	270	151	55.9	1957	13	7	7.25	84.1	28	87	3.1	2	2	0	12
Pro totals (2 years)	23	22	573	324	56.5	4135	24	13	7.22	83.8	69	316	4.6	3	3	0	18

(columns: PASSING: Att. Cmp. Pct. Yds. TD Int. Avg. Rat.; RUSHING: Att. Yds. Avg. TD; TOTALS: TD 2pt. Pts.)

BATES, D'WAYNE   WR   BEARS

PERSONAL: Born December 4, 1975, in Aiken, S.C. ... 6-2/215. ... Full name: D'Wayne Lavoris Bates.
HIGH SCHOOL: Silver Bluff (Aiken, S.C.).
COLLEGE: Northwestern.

B

TRANSACTIONS/CAREER NOTES: Selected by Chicago Bears in third round (71st pick overall) of 1999 NFL draft. ... Signed by Bears (July 22, 1999).
PLAYING EXPERIENCE: Chicago NFL, 1999. ... Games/Games started: 1999 (7/1).
PRO STATISTICS: 1999—Caught two passes for 19 yards.
SINGLE GAME HIGHS (regular season): Receptions—1 (November 7, 1999, vs. Green Bay); yards—11 (October 31, 1999, vs. Washington); and touchdown receptions—2 (November 29, 1998, vs. Arizona).
MISCELLANEOUS: Selected by Toronto Blue Jays organization in 53rd round of free-agent draft (June 2, 1994); did not sign.

BATES, MARIO — RB — CARDINALS

PERSONAL: Born January 16, 1973, in Tucson, Ariz. ... 6-2/237. ... Full name: Mario Doniel Bates. ... Brother of Michael Bates, running back/kick returner, Carolina Panthers.
HIGH SCHOOL: Amphitheater (Tucson, Ariz.).
COLLEGE: Arizona State.
TRANSACTIONS/CAREER NOTES: Selected after junior season by New Orleans Saints in second round (44th pick overall) of 1994 NFL draft. ... Signed by Saints (July 6, 1994). ... Granted free agency (February 14, 1997). ... Re-signed by Saints (June 12, 1997). ... Granted unconditional free agency (February 13, 1998). ... Signed by Arizona Cardinals (March 6, 1998).
PRO STATISTICS: 1994—Recovered one fumble. 1995—Recovered one fumble. 1997—Attempted one pass with a completion for 21 yards and a touchdown. 1999—Recovered one fumble.
SINGLE GAME HIGHS (regular season): Attempts—32 (December 15, 1996, vs. New York Giants); yards—162 (September 21, 1997, vs. Detroit); and rushing touchdowns—3 (December 4, 1994, vs. Los Angeles Rams).
STATISTICAL PLATEAUS: 100-yard rushing games: 1994 (1), 1995 (3), 1996 (1), 1997 (1). Total: 6.

			RUSHING				RECEIVING				KICKOFF RETURNS				TOTALS			
Year Team	G	GS	Att.	Yds.	Avg.	TD	No.	Yds.	Avg.	TD	No.	Yds.	Avg.	TD	TD	2pt.	Pts.	Fum.
1994—New Orleans NFL.....	11	7	151	579	3.8	6	8	62	7.8	0	1	20	20.0	0	6	0	36	3
1995—New Orleans NFL.....	16	16	244	951	3.9	7	18	114	6.3	0	0	0	0.0	0	7	0	42	2
1996—New Orleans NFL.....	14	10	164	584	3.6	4	13	44	3.4	0	0	0	0.0	0	4	0	24	4
1997—New Orleans NFL.....	12	7	119	440	3.7	4	5	42	8.4	0	0	0	0.0	0	4	0	24	2
1998—Arizona NFL	16	1	60	165	2.8	6	1	14	14.0	0	0	0	0.0	0	6	0	36	0
1999—Arizona NFL	16	2	72	202	2.8	9	5	34	6.8	0	52	1231	23.7	0	9	0	54	2
Pro totals (6 years)...........	85	43	810	2921	3.6	36	50	310	6.2	0	53	1251	23.6	0	36	0	216	13

BATES, MICHAEL — RB/KR — PANTHERS

PERSONAL: Born December 19, 1969, in Tucson, Ariz. ... 5-10/189. ... Full name: Michael Dion Bates. ... Brother of Mario Bates, running back, Arizona Cardinals.
HIGH SCHOOL: Amphitheater (Tucson, Ariz.).
COLLEGE: Arizona.
TRANSACTIONS/CAREER NOTES: Selected after sophomore season by Seattle Seahawks in sixth round (151st pick overall) of 1992 NFL draft. ... Missed 1992 season due to contract dispute. ... Signed by Seahawks (March 7, 1993). ... Claimed on waivers by Carolina Panthers (August 28, 1995). ... Traded by Panthers to Cleveland Browns for LB Travis Hill (August 29, 1995). ... Granted unconditional free agency (February 16, 1996). ... Signed by Panthers (March 12, 1996). ... Granted unconditional free agency (February 13, 1998). ... Re-signed by Panthers (March 4, 1998).
CHAMPIONSHIP GAME EXPERIENCE: Played in NFC championship game (1996 season).
HONORS: Named kick returner on THE SPORTING NEWS NFL All-Pro team (1996 and 1997). ... Played in Pro Bowl (1996-1999 seasons).
PRO STATISTICS: 1993—Rushed twice for 12 yards and recovered two fumbles for three yards. 1994—Rushed twice for minus four yards. 1997—Returned one punt for eight yards and recovered two fumbles. 1999—Rushed three times for 12 yards.
SINGLE GAME HIGHS (regular season): Attempts—2 (November 7, 1999, vs. Philadelphia); yards—14 (November 7, 1999, vs. Philadelphia); and rushing touchdowns—0.
MISCELLANEOUS: Won bronze medal in 200-meter dash in 1992 Summer Olympics.

			RECEIVING				KICKOFF RETURNS				TOTALS			
Year Team	G	GS	No.	Yds.	Avg.	TD	No.	Yds.	Avg.	TD	TD	2pt.	Pts.	Fum.
1992—Seattle NFL...................................					Did not play.										
1993—Seattle NFL...................................	16	1	1	6	6.0	0	30	603	20.1	0	0	0	0	1
1994—Seattle NFL...................................	15	0	5	112	22.4	1	26	508	19.5	0	1	0	6	3
1995—Cleveland NFL...............................	13	0	0	0	0.0	0	9	176	19.6	0	0	0	0	0
1996—Carolina NFL.................................	14	0	0	0	0.0	0	33	998	*30.2	1	1	0	6	2
1997—Carolina NFL.................................	16	0	0	0	0.0	0	47	1281	*27.3	0	0	0	0	4
1998—Carolina NFL.................................	14	0	0	0	0.0	0	59	1480	25.1	1	1	0	6	1
1999—Carolina NFL.................................	16	0	1	2	2.0	0	52	1287	24.8	†2	2	0	12	1
Pro totals (7 years)................................	104	1	7	120	17.1	1	256	6333	24.7	4	5	0	30	12

BATTAGLIA, MARCO — TE — BENGALS

PERSONAL: Born January 25, 1973, in Howard Beach, N.Y. ... 6-3/252. ... Name pronounced buh-TAG-lee-uh.
HIGH SCHOOL: St. Francis (Fresh Meadows, N.Y.).
COLLEGE: Rutgers.
TRANSACTIONS/CAREER NOTES: Selected by Cincinnati Bengals in second round (39th pick overall) of 1996 NFL draft. ... Signed by Bengals (July 15, 1996). ... Granted free agency (February 12, 1999). ... Re-signed by Bengals (May 25, 1999).
HONORS: Named tight end on THE SPORTING NEWS college All-America first team (1995).
PRO STATISTICS: 1996—Returned one kickoff for eight yards and recovered one fumble. 1997—Recovered two fumbles. 1998—Returned one kickoff for five yards and recovered three fumbles.
SINGLE GAME HIGHS (regular season): Receptions—3 (November 7, 1999, vs. Seattle); yards—42 (December 21, 1997, vs. Baltimore); and touchdown receptions—1 (November 1, 1998, vs. Denver).

Year Team	G	GS	RECEIVING				TOTALS			
			No.	Yds.	Avg.	TD	TD	2pt.	Pts.	Fum.
1996—Cincinnati NFL	16	0	8	79	9.9	0	0	0	0	0
1997—Cincinnati NFL	16	0	12	149	12.4	1	1	0	6	2
1998—Cincinnati NFL	16	0	10	47	4.7	1	1	0	6	1
1999—Cincinnati NFL	16	0	14	153	10.9	0	0	0	0	0
Pro totals (4 years)	64	0	44	428	9.7	2	2	0	12	3

BAXTER, FRED   TE   JETS

PERSONAL: Born June 14, 1971, in Brundidge, Ala. ... 6-3/265. ... Full name: Frederick Denard Baxter.
HIGH SCHOOL: Pike County (Brundidge, Ala.).
COLLEGE: Auburn.
TRANSACTIONS/CAREER NOTES: Selected by New York Jets in fifth round (115th pick overall) of 1993 NFL draft. ... Signed by Jets (July 13, 1993).
CHAMPIONSHIP GAME EXPERIENCE: Played in AFC championship game (1998 season).
PRO STATISTICS: 1994—Returned one kickoff for 20 yards and recovered one fumble. 1995—Returned six kickoffs for 36 yards and recovered two fumbles for eight yards. 1997—Returned one kickoff for no yards. 1998—Returned one kickoff for eight yards and recovered one fumble. 1999—Recovered one fumble.
SINGLE GAME HIGHS (regular season): Receptions—6 (September 17, 1995, vs. Jacksonville); yards—99 (September 17, 1995, vs. Jacksonville); and touchdown receptions—1 (November 15, 1999, vs. New England).

Year Team	G	GS	RECEIVING				TOTALS			
			No.	Yds.	Avg.	TD	TD	2pt.	Pts.	Fum.
1993—New York Jets NFL	7	0	3	48	16.0	1	1	0	6	0
1994—New York Jets NFL	11	1	3	11	3.7	1	1	0	6	0
1995—New York Jets NFL	15	3	18	222	12.3	1	1	0	6	1
1996—New York Jets NFL	16	4	7	114	16.3	0	0	0	0	1
1997—New York Jets NFL	16	9	27	276	10.2	3	3	0	18	1
1998—New York Jets NFL	14	1	3	50	16.7	0	0	0	0	0
1999—New York Jets NFL	14	8	8	66	8.3	2	2	0	12	0
Pro totals (7 years)	93	26	69	787	11.4	8	8	0	48	3

BEASLEY, AARON   CB   JAGUARS

PERSONAL: Born July 7, 1973, in Pottstown, Pa. ... 6-0/195. ... Full name: Aaron Bruce Beasley.
HIGH SCHOOL: Pottstown (Pa.), then Valley Forge Military Academy (Wayne, Pa.).
COLLEGE: West Virginia.
TRANSACTIONS/CAREER NOTES: Selected by Jacksonville Jaguars in third round (63rd pick overall) of 1996 NFL draft. ... Signed by Jaguars (May 24, 1996). ... Granted free agency (February 12, 1999). ... Re-signed by Jaguars (March 3, 1999). ... Granted unconditional free agency (February 11, 2000). ... Re-signed by Jaguars (February 11, 2000).
CHAMPIONSHIP GAME EXPERIENCE: Played in AFC championship game (1996 and 1999 seasons).
PRO STATISTICS: 1998—Recovered one fumble for 90 yards and a touchdown and ran 30 yards on a lateral from punt return.
MISCELLANEOUS: Holds Jacksonville Jaguars all-time record for most interceptions (11).

Year Team	G	GS	INTERCEPTIONS				SACKS
			No.	Yds.	Avg.	TD	No.
1996—Jacksonville NFL	9	7	1	0	0.0	0	1.0
1997—Jacksonville NFL	9	7	1	5	5.0	0	0.0
1998—Jacksonville NFL	16	15	3	35	11.7	0	0.0
1999—Jacksonville NFL	16	16	6	*200	§33.3	†2	1.5
Pro totals (4 years)	50	45	11	240	21.8	2	2.5

BEASLEY, FRED   FB   49ERS

PERSONAL: Born September 18, 1974, in Montgomery, Ala. ... 6-0/235. ... Full name: Frederick Jerome Beasley.
HIGH SCHOOL: Robert E. Lee (Montgomery, Ala.).
COLLEGE: Auburn.
TRANSACTIONS/CAREER NOTES: Selected by San Francisco 49ers in sixth round (180th pick overall) of 1998 NFL draft. ... Signed by 49ers (July 18, 1998).
PRO STATISTICS: 1999—Recovered two fumbles.
SINGLE GAME HIGHS (regular season): Attempts—12 (December 26, 1999, vs. Washington); yards—65 (December 26, 1999, vs. Washington); and rushing touchdowns—2 (December 12, 1999, vs. Atlanta).

Year Team	G	GS	RUSHING				RECEIVING				TOTALS			
			Att.	Yds.	Avg.	TD	No.	Yds.	Avg.	TD	TD	2pt.	Pts.	Fum.
1998—San Francisco NFL	16	0	0	0	0.0	0	1	11	11.0	0	0	0	0	0
1999—San Francisco NFL	13	11	58	276	4.8	4	32	282	8.8	0	4	0	24	2
Pro totals (2 years)	29	11	58	276	4.8	4	33	293	8.9	0	4	0	24	2

BECH, BRETT   WR

PERSONAL: Born August 20, 1971, in Slidell, La. ... 6-1/201. ... Full name: Brett Lamar Bech.
HIGH SCHOOL: Slidell (La.).
COLLEGE: Louisiana State.
TRANSACTIONS/CAREER NOTES: Signed as non-drafted free agent by Jacksonville Jaguars (April 24, 1995). ... Released by Jaguars (June 7, 1995). ... Signed by San Antonio Texans of CFL (July 1995). ... Signed by New Orleans Saints to practice squad (November 13, 1996). ...

Activated (December 19, 1996); did not play. ... Released by Saints (August 24, 1997). ... Re-signed by Saints to practice squad (August 25, 1997). ... Activated (September 27, 1997). ... On injured reserve with hand and shoulder injuries (December 12, 1997-remainder of season). ... On injured reserve with abdominal injury (December 1, 1999-remainder of season). ... Granted free agency (February 11, 2000).
PRO STATISTICS: 1997—Recovered one fumble.
SINGLE GAME HIGHS (regular season): Receptions—4 (December 27, 1998, vs. Buffalo); yards—113 (December 27, 1998, vs. Buffalo); and touchdown receptions—2 (December 27, 1998, vs. Buffalo).
STATISTICAL PLATEAUS: 100-yard receiving games: 1998 (1).

			RECEIVING				KICKOFF RETURNS				TOTALS		
Year Team	G	GS	No.	Yds.	Avg.	TD	No.	Yds.	Avg.	TD	TD	2pt.	Pts.	Fum.
1995—San Antonio CFL	5	...	0	0	0.0	0	0	0	0.0	0	0	0	0	0
1996—New Orleans NFL							Did not play.							
1997—New Orleans NFL	10	0	3	50	16.7	0	3	47	15.7	0	0	0	0	0
1998—New Orleans NFL	16	0	14	264	18.9	3	1	20	20.0	0	3	0	18	0
1999—New Orleans NFL	8	0	4	65	16.3	1	1	12	12.0	0	1	†1	8	0
CFL totals (1 year)	5	...	0	0	0.0	0	0	0	0.0	0	0	0	0	0
NFL totals (3 years)	34	0	21	379	18.0	4	5	79	15.8	0	4	1	26	0
Pro totals (4 years)	39	...	21	379	18.0	4	5	79	15.8	0	4	1	26	0

BEEDE, FRANK G SEAHAWKS

PERSONAL: Born May 1, 1973, in Antioch, Calif. ... 6-4/296. ... Name pronounced BEE-dee.
HIGH SCHOOL: Antioch (Calif.).
COLLEGE: Panhandle State (Okla.).
TRANSACTIONS/CAREER NOTES: Signed as non-drafted free agent by Seattle Seahawks (April 22, 1996). ... On injured reserve with knee injury (August 25, 1998-entire season). ... Granted free agency (February 12, 1999). ... Re-signed by Seahawks (April 7, 1999). ... Granted unconditional free agency (February 11, 2000). ... Re-signed by Seahawks (April 25, 2000).
PLAYING EXPERIENCE: Seattle NFL, 1996, 1997 and 1999. ... Games/Games started: 1996 (14/2), 1997 (16/6), 1999 (10/0). Total: 40/8.
PRO STATISTICS: 1997—Returned one kick for no yards and fumbled once.

BELL, MYRON S

PERSONAL: Born September 15, 1971, in Toledo, Ohio. ... 5-11/203. ... Full name: Myron Corey Bell.
HIGH SCHOOL: Macomber-Whitney (Toledo, Ohio).
COLLEGE: Michigan State.
TRANSACTIONS/CAREER NOTES: Selected by Pittsburgh Steelers in fifth round (140th pick overall) of 1994 NFL draft. ... Signed by Steelers (July 18, 1994). ... Granted free agency (February 14, 1997). ... Re-signed by Steelers (April 15, 1997). ... Granted unconditional free agency (February 13, 1998). ... Signed by Cincinnati Bengals (June 26, 1998). ... Granted unconditional free agency (February 11, 2000).
CHAMPIONSHIP GAME EXPERIENCE: Played in AFC championship game (1994, 1995 and 1997 seasons). ... Played in Super Bowl XXX (1995 season).
PRO STATISTICS: 1995—Recovered one fumble. 1996—Recovered two fumbles. 1997—Recovered one fumble.

			INTERCEPTIONS				SACKS
Year Team	G	GS	No.	Yds.	Avg.	TD	No.
1994—Pittsburgh NFL	15	0	0	0	0.0	0	0.0
1995—Pittsburgh NFL	16	9	2	4	2.0	0	0.0
1996—Pittsburgh NFL	16	4	0	0	0.0	0	2.0
1997—Pittsburgh NFL	16	8	1	10	10.0	0	1.5
1998—Cincinnati NFL	16	2	0	0	0.0	0	1.0
1999—Cincinnati NFL	16	16	1	5	5.0	0	2.0
Pro totals (6 years)	95	39	4	19	4.8	0	6.5

BELL, SHONN TE 49ERS

PERSONAL: Born October 25, 1974, in Waynesboro, Va. ... 6-5/257. ... Full name: Jamara Riashonn Bell.
HIGH SCHOOL: Stuarts Draft (Va.).
COLLEGE: Clinch Valley College (Va.).
TRANSACTIONS/CAREER NOTES: Signed as non-drafted free agent by Houston Oilers (April 23, 1996). ... Released by Oilers (August 12, 1996). ... Signed by San Francisco 49ers (June 12, 1998). ... Released by 49ers (August 25, 1998). ... Re-signed by 49ers (January 21, 1999). ... Assigned by 49ers to Scottish Claymores in 1999 NFL Europe enhancement allocation program (February 22, 1999). ... On injured reserve with shoulder injury (October 26, 1999-remainder of season).
PLAYING EXPERIENCE: Scottish NFLE, 1999; San Francisco NFL, 1999. ... Games/Games started: NFLE 1999 (games played unavailable), NFL 1999 (2/0).

BELL, TYRONE CB PACKERS

PERSONAL: Born October 20, 1974, in West Point, Miss. ... 6-2/210. ... Full name: Tyrone Edward Bell.
HIGH SCHOOL: West Point (Miss.).
COLLEGE: North Alabama.
TRANSACTIONS/CAREER NOTES: Selected by San Diego Chargers in sixth round (178th pick overall) of 1999 NFL draft. ... Signed by Chargers (July 22, 1999). ... Released by Chargers (August 30, 1999). ... Signed by Green Bay Packers to practice squad (September 9, 1999). ... Activated (December 24, 1999).
PLAYING EXPERIENCE: Green Bay NFL, 1999. ... Games/Games started: 1999 (1/0).

B

BELLAMY, JAY   S   SEAHAWKS

PERSONAL: Born July 8, 1972, in Perth Amboy, N.J. ... 5-11/199. ... Full name: John Lee Bellamy. ... Name pronounced BELL-a-me.
HIGH SCHOOL: Matawan Regional (Aberdeen, N.J.).
COLLEGE: Rutgers.
TRANSACTIONS/CAREER NOTES: Signed as non-drafted free agent by Seattle Seahawks (April 27, 1994). ... On injured reserve with shoulder injury (November 11, 1994-remainder of season).
PRO STATISTICS: 1997—Credited with two sacks. 1998—Credited with one sack and recovered two fumbles. 1999—Recovered one fumble.

			INTERCEPTIONS			
Year Team	G	GS	No.	Yds.	Avg.	TD
1994—Seattle NFL	3	0	0	0	0.0	0
1995—Seattle NFL	14	0	0	0	0.0	0
1996—Seattle NFL	16	0	3	18	6.0	0
1997—Seattle NFL	16	7	1	13	13.0	0
1998—Seattle NFL	16	16	3	40	13.3	0
1999—Seattle NFL	16	16	4	4	1.0	0
Pro totals (6 years)	81	39	11	75	6.8	0

BELSER, JASON   DB   COLTS

PERSONAL: Born May 28, 1970, in Kansas City, Mo. ... 5-9/196. ... Full name: Jason Daks Belser. ... Son of Caeser Belser, defensive back with Kansas City Chiefs (1968-71) and linebacker with San Francisco 49ers (1974). ... Name pronounced BELL-sir.
HIGH SCHOOL: Raytown (Mo.) South.
COLLEGE: Oklahoma.
TRANSACTIONS/CAREER NOTES: Selected by Indianapolis Colts in eighth round (197th pick overall) of 1992 NFL draft. ... Signed by Colts (July 22, 1992). ... Granted free agency (February 17, 1995). ... Tendered offer sheet by Carolina Panthers (April 17, 1995). ... Offer matched by Colts (April 19, 1995).
CHAMPIONSHIP GAME EXPERIENCE: Played in AFC championship game (1995 season).
PRO STATISTICS: 1992—Fumbled once and recovered two fumbles. 1993—Recovered three fumbles. 1995—Returned one kickoff for 15 yards and recovered two fumbles. 1996—Recovered one fumble. 1998—Returned one punt for 53 yards and recovered one fumble.

			INTERCEPTIONS				SACKS
Year Team	G	GS	No.	Yds.	Avg.	TD	No.
1992—Indianapolis NFL	16	2	3	27	9.0	0	0.0
1993—Indianapolis NFL	16	16	1	14	14.0	0	0.0
1994—Indianapolis NFL	13	12	1	31	31.0	0	0.0
1995—Indianapolis NFL	16	16	1	0	0.0	0	0.0
1996—Indianapolis NFL	16	16	4	81	20.3	†2	1.0
1997—Indianapolis NFL	16	16	2	121	60.5	1	1.0
1998—Indianapolis NFL	16	16	1	19	19.0	0	1.0
1999—Indianapolis NFL	16	16	0	0	0.0	0	1.0
Pro totals (8 years)	125	110	13	293	22.5	3	4.0

BENNETT, CORNELIUS   LB   COLTS

PERSONAL: Born August 25, 1965, in Birmingham, Ala. ... 6-3/240. ... Full name: Cornelius O'landa Bennett.
HIGH SCHOOL: Ensley (Birmingham, Ala.).
COLLEGE: Alabama.
TRANSACTIONS/CAREER NOTES: Selected by Indianapolis Colts in first round (second pick overall) of 1987 NFL draft. ... Placed on reserve/unsigned list (August 31-October 30, 1987). ... Rights traded by Colts to Buffalo Bills in exchange for Bills trading first-round pick (RB Gaston Green) in 1988 draft, first-(RB Cleveland Gary) and second-round (CB Darryl Henley) picks in 1989 draft and RB Greg Bell to Los Angeles Rams (October 31, 1987); Rams also traded RB Eric Dickerson to Colts for first-(WR Aaron Cox) and second-round (LB Fred Strickland) picks in 1988 draft, second-round pick (LB Frank Stams) in 1989 draft and RB Owen Gill. ... Signed by Bills (October 31, 1987). ... Granted roster exemption (October 31-November 7, 1987). ... Granted free agency (February 1, 1992). ... Re-signed by Bills (August 31, 1992). ... Designated by Bills as franchise player (February 15, 1995). ... Granted unconditional free agency (February 16, 1996). ... Signed by Atlanta Falcons (March 1, 1996). ... Released by Falcons (February 17, 1999). ... Signed by Indianapolis Colts (March 1, 1999).
CHAMPIONSHIP GAME EXPERIENCE: Played in AFC championship game (1988 and 1990-1993 seasons). ... Played in Super Bowl XXV (1990 season), Super Bowl XXVI (1991 season), Super Bowl XXVII (1992 season), Super Bowl XXVIII (1993 season) and Super Bowl XXXIII (1998 season). ... Played in NFC championship game (1998 season).
HONORS: Named linebacker on THE SPORTING NEWS college All-America first team (1984-1986). ... Lombardi Award winner (1986). ... Named outside linebacker on THE SPORTING NEWS NFL All-Pro team (1988). ... Played in Pro Bowl (1988 and 1990-1993 seasons).
PRO STATISTICS: 1988—Recovered three fumbles. 1989—Recovered two fumbles for five yards. 1990—Returned blocked field-goal attempt 80 yards for a touchdown and recovered two fumbles. 1991—Recovered two fumbles for nine yards and one touchdown. 1992—Recovered three fumbles. 1993—Recovered two fumbles for 40 yards and fumbled once. 1994—Recovered three fumbles for 14 yards. 1995—Recovered two fumbles. 1996—Recovered two fumbles. 1997—Recovered one fumble. 1998—Recovered two fumbles for 10 yards. 1999—Recovered two fumbles.

			INTERCEPTIONS				SACKS
Year Team	G	GS	No.	Yds.	Avg.	TD	No.
1987—Buffalo NFL	8	7	0	0	0.0	0	8.5
1988—Buffalo NFL	16	16	2	30	15.0	0	9.5
1989—Buffalo NFL	12	12	2	5	2.5	0	5.5
1990—Buffalo NFL	16	16	0	0	0.0	0	4.0
1991—Buffalo NFL	16	16	0	0	0.0	0	9.0
1992—Buffalo NFL	15	15	0	0	0.0	0	4.0
1993—Buffalo NFL	16	16	1	5	5.0	0	5.0
1994—Buffalo NFL	16	16	0	0	0.0	0	5.0
1995—Buffalo NFL	14	14	1	69	69.0	▲1	2.0

1996—Atlanta NFL	13	13	1	3	3.0	0	3.0
1997—Atlanta NFL	16	16	0	0	0.0	0	7.0
1998—Atlanta NFL	16	16	0	0	0.0	0	1.0
1999—Indianapolis NFL	16	16	0	0	0.0	0	5.0
Pro totals (13 years)	190	189	7	112	16.0	1	68.5

BENNETT, DARREN   P   CHARGERS

PERSONAL: Born January 9, 1965, in Sydney, Australia. ... 6-5/235. ... Full name: Darren Leslie Bennett.
HIGH SCHOOL: Applecross (Perth, Western Australia).
COLLEGE: None.
TRANSACTIONS/CAREER NOTES: Played Australian Rules Football (1987-1993). ... Signed as non-drafted free agent by San Diego Chargers (April 14, 1994). ... Released by Chargers (August 28, 1994). ... Re-signed by Chargers to practice squad (August 29, 1994). ... Assigned by Chargers to Amsterdam Admirals in 1995 World League enhancement allocation program (February 20, 1995). ... Granted unconditional free agency (February 11, 2000). ... Re-signed by Chargers (March 7, 2000).
HONORS: Named punter on THE SPORTING NEWS NFL All-Pro team (1995). ... Played in Pro Bowl (1995 season).
PRO STATISTICS: 1998—Fumbled once and recovered one fumble.

				PUNTING			
Year Team	G	No.	Yds.	Avg.	Net avg.	In. 20	Blk.
1994—San Diego NFL				Did not play.			
1995—Amsterdam W.L.	10	60	2296	38.3	35.1	24	1
—San Diego NFL	16	72	3221	44.7	36.6	28	0
1996—San Diego NFL	16	87	3967	45.6	37.2	23	0
1997—San Diego NFL	16	89	3972	44.6	37.7	26	1
1998—San Diego NFL	16	95	4174	43.9	36.8	27	0
1999—San Diego NFL	16	89	3910	43.9	*38.7	32	0
W.L. totals (1 year)	10	60	2296	38.3	35.1	24	1
NFL totals (5 years)	80	432	19244	44.5	37.4	136	1
Pro totals (6 years)	90	492	21540	43.8	37.1	160	2

BENNETT, DONNELL   FB   CHIEFS

PERSONAL: Born September 14, 1972, in Fort Lauderdale, Fla. ... 6-0/245.
HIGH SCHOOL: Cardinal Gibbons (Fort Lauderdale, Fla.).
COLLEGE: Miami (Fla.).
TRANSACTIONS/CAREER NOTES: Selected after junior season by Kansas City Chiefs in second round (58th pick overall) of 1994 NFL draft. ... Signed by Chiefs (May 6, 1994). ... On injured reserve with knee injury (December 20, 1994-remainder of season). ... On physically unable to perform list with knee injury (August 22-October 31, 1995). ... Granted free agency (February 14, 1997). ... Re-signed by Chiefs (April 22, 1997).
PRO STATISTICS: 1994—Returned one kickoff for 12 yards and recovered one fumble. 1999—Returned three kickoffs for 51 yards.
SINGLE GAME HIGHS (regular season): Attempts—30 (September 20, 1998, vs. San Diego); yards—115 (September 6, 1998, vs, Oakland); and rushing touchdowns—3 (September 27, 1998, vs. Philadelphia).
STATISTICAL PLATEAUS: 100-yard rushing games: 1998 (1).

			RUSHING				RECEIVING				TOTALS			
Year Team	G	GS	Att.	Yds.	Avg.	TD	No.	Yds.	Avg.	TD	TD	2pt.	Pts.	Fum.
1994—Kansas City NFL	15	0	46	178	3.9	2	7	53	7.6	0	2	0	12	2
1995—Kansas City NFL	3	1	7	11	1.6	0	1	12	12.0	0	0	0	0	0
1996—Kansas City NFL	16	0	36	166	4.6	0	8	21	2.6	0	0	0	0	0
1997—Kansas City NFL	14	1	94	369	3.9	1	7	5	0.7	0	1	0	6	0
1998—Kansas City NFL	16	10	148	527	3.6	5	16	91	5.7	1	6	0	36	4
1999—Kansas City NFL	15	1	161	627	3.9	8	10	41	4.1	0	8	0	48	1
Pro totals (6 years)	79	13	492	1878	3.8	16	49	223	4.6	1	17	0	102	7

BENNETT, EDGAR   RB

PERSONAL: Born February 15, 1969, in Jacksonville. ... 6-0/218. ... Full name: Edgar Bennett III.
HIGH SCHOOL: Robert E. Lee Senior (Jacksonville).
COLLEGE: Florida State.
TRANSACTIONS/CAREER NOTES: Selected by Green Bay Packers in fourth round (103rd pick overall) of 1992 NFL draft. ... Signed by Packers (July 22, 1992). ... Granted free agency (February 17, 1995). ... Re-signed by Packers (May 5, 1995). ... On injured reserve with knee injury (August 18, 1997-entire season). ... Granted unconditional free agency (February 13, 1998). ... Signed by Chicago Bears (February 20, 1998). ... Released by Bears (February 7, 2000).
CHAMPIONSHIP GAME EXPERIENCE: Played in NFC championship game (1995 and 1996 seasons). ... Member of Super Bowl championship team (1996 season).
PRO STATISTICS: 1992—Returned five kickoffs for 104 yards. 1993—Recovered one fumble. 1994—Recovered one fumble. 1995—Recovered one fumble. 1996—Recovered one fumble. 1998—Attempted two passes with one completion for 18 yards and a touchdown and recovered one fumble. 1999—Returned three kickoffs for 53 yards.
SINGLE GAME HIGHS (regular season): Attempts—30 (September 11, 1995, vs. Chicago); yards—121 (October 29, 1995, vs. Detroit); and rushing touchdowns—2 (October 31, 1994, vs. Chicago).
STATISTICAL PLATEAUS: 100-yard rushing games: 1992 (1), 1994 (3), 1995 (1), 1996 (1). Total: 6. ... 100-yard receiving games: 1994 (1).

			RUSHING				RECEIVING				TOTALS			
Year Team	G	GS	Att.	Yds.	Avg.	TD	No.	Yds.	Avg.	TD	TD	2pt.	Pts.	Fum.
1992—Green Bay NFL	16	2	61	214	3.5	0	13	93	7.2	0	0	0	0	2
1993—Green Bay NFL	16	14	159	550	3.5	9	59	457	7.7	1	10	0	60	0
1994—Green Bay NFL	16	15	178	623	3.5	5	78	546	7.0	4	9	0	54	1
1995—Green Bay NFL	16	16	316	1067	3.4	3	61	648	10.6	4	7	0	42	2

B

Year Team	G	GS	Att	Yds	Avg	TD	No	Yds	Avg	TD	2pt	Pts.	Fum.
1996—Green Bay NFL	16	15	222	899	4.0	2	31	176	5.7	1	3	‡2	22	2
1997—Green Bay NFL								Did not play.						
1998—Chicago NFL	16	13	173	611	3.5	2	28	209	7.5	0	2	0	12	2
1999—Chicago NFL	16	2	6	28	4.7	0	14	116	8.3	0	0	0	0	1
Pro totals (7 years)	112	77	1115	3992	3.6	21	284	2245	7.9	10	31	2	190	10

BENNETT, SEAN RB GIANTS

PERSONAL: Born November 9, 1975, in Evansville, Ind. ... 6-1/230. ... Full name: William Sean Bennett.
HIGH SCHOOL: Harrison (Evansville, Ind.).
COLLEGE: Illinois (did not play football), then Evansville, then Northwestern.
TRANSACTIONS/CAREER NOTES: Selected by New York Giants in fourth round (112th pick overall) of 1999 NFL draft. ... Signed by Giants (July 27, 1999).
SINGLE GAME HIGHS (regular season): Attempts—13 (September 12, 1999, vs. Tampa Bay); yards—45 (September 19, 1999, vs. Washington); and rushing touchdowns—1 (November 28, 1999, vs. Arizona).

			RUSHING				RECEIVING				TOTALS		
Year Team	G	GS	Att.	Yds.	Avg.	TD	No.	Yds.	Avg.	TD	TD	2pt.	Pts.	Fum.
1999—New York Giants NFL	9	2	29	126	4.3	1	4	27	6.8	0	1	0	6	0

BENNETT, TOMMY S

PERSONAL: Born February 19, 1973, in Las Vegas, Nev. ... 6-2/212.
HIGH SCHOOL: Samuel F.B. Morse (San Diego).
COLLEGE: UCLA.
TRANSACTIONS/CAREER NOTES: Signed as a non-drafted free agent by Arizona Cardinals (April 23, 1996). ... Granted free agency (February 12, 1999). ... Re-signed by Cardinals (June 16, 1999). ... Granted unconditional free agency (February 11, 2000).
PRO STATISTICS: 1997—Recovered blocked punt in end zone for a touchdown. 1999—Recovered one fumble.

			INTERCEPTIONS				TOTALS		
Year Team	G	GS	No.	Yds.	Avg.	TD	TD	2pt.	Pts.	Fum.
1996—Arizona NFL	16	1	0	0	0.0	0	0	0	0	0
1997—Arizona NFL	13	7	1	0	0.0	0	1	0	6	0
1998—Arizona NFL	16	16	2	100	50.0	1	1	0	6	0
1999—Arizona NFL	15	15	1	13	13.0	0	0	0	0	0
Pro totals (4 years)	60	39	4	113	28.3	1	2	0	12	0

BENTLEY, SCOTT K

PERSONAL: Born April 10, 1974, in Dallas. ... 6-0/203.
HIGH SCHOOL: Aurora (Colo.).
COLLEGE: Florida State.
TRANSACTIONS/CAREER NOTES: Signed as non-drafted free agent by Arizona Cardinals (April 21, 1997). ... Released by Cardinals (August 19, 1997). ... Signed by Denver Broncos to practice squad (October 1, 1997). ... Activated (October 6, 1997). ... Released by Broncos (October 7, 1997). ... Signed by Atlanta Falcons to practice squad (December 2, 1997). ... Activated (December 14, 1997). ... Granted free agency (February 13, 1998). ... Signed by Denver Broncos to practice squad (October 7, 1998). ... Released by Broncos (October 13, 1998). ... Signed by Tampa Bay Buccaneers (April 7, 1999). ... Claimed on waivers by Baltimore Ravens (April 21, 1999). ... Released by Ravens (September 4, 1999). ... Signed by Kansas City Chiefs (November 10, 1999). ... Released by Chiefs (November 22, 1999).

				KICKING				
Year Team	G	XPM	XPA	FGM	FGA	Lg.	50+	Pts.
1997—Denver NFL	1	4	4	2	3	33	0-0	10
—Atlanta NFL	2	0	0	0	0	0	0-0	0
1998—				Did not play.				
1999—Kansas City NFL	2	0	0	0	0	0	0-0	0
Pro totals (2 years)	5	4	4	2	3	33	0-0	10

BERGER, MITCH P VIKINGS

PERSONAL: Born June 24, 1972, in Kamloops, B.C. ... 6-4/221.
HIGH SCHOOL: North Delta (Vancouver).
JUNIOR COLLEGE: Tyler (Texas) Junior College.
COLLEGE: Colorado.
TRANSACTIONS/CAREER NOTES: Selected by Philadelphia Eagles in sixth round (193rd pick overall) of 1994 NFL draft. ... Signed by Eagles (July 11, 1994). ... Released by Eagles (October 10, 1994). ... Signed by Cincinnati Bengals to practice squad (October 13, 1994). ... Released by Bengals (November 30, 1994). ... Signed by Chicago Bears (March 7, 1995). ... Released by Bears (May 4, 1995). ... Signed by Indianapolis Colts (May 16, 1995). ... Claimed on waivers by Green Bay Packers (August 24, 1995). ... Released by Packers (August 27, 1995). ... Signed by Bears (November 7, 1995). ... Released by Bears (November 13, 1995). ... Signed by Minnesota Vikings (April 19, 1996). ... Granted unconditional free agency (February 11, 2000). ... Re-signed by Vikings (February 16, 2000).
CHAMPIONSHIP GAME EXPERIENCE: Played in NFC championship game (1998 season).
HONORS: Named punter on THE SPORTING NEWS NFL All-Pro team (1999). ... Played in Pro Bowl (1999 season).
PRO STATISTICS: 1997—Rushed once for no yards and fumbled once for minus nine yards. 1999—Recovered one fumble.

				PUNTING			
Year Team	G	No.	Yds.	Avg.	Net avg.	In. 20	Blk.
1994—Philadelphia NFL	5	25	951	38.0	31.3	8	0
1995—				Did not play.			
1996—Minnesota NFL	16	88	3616	41.1	32.3	26	2

1997—Minnesota NFL	14	73	3133	42.9	34.1	22	0
1998—Minnesota NFL	16	55	2458	44.7	37.0	17	0
1999—Minnesota NFL	16	61	2769	‡45.4	‡38.4	18	0
Pro totals (5 years)	67	302	12927	42.8	34.7	91	2

BERRY, BERT — LB

PERSONAL: Born August 15, 1975, in Houston. ... 6-2/248. ... Full name: Bertrand Demond Berry.
HIGH SCHOOL: Humble (Texas).
COLLEGE: Notre Dame.
TRANSACTIONS/CAREER NOTES: Selected by Indianapolis Colts in third round (86th pick overall) of 1997 NFL draft. ... Signed by Colts (July 9, 1997). ... Granted free agency (February 11, 2000).

Year Team	G	GS	SACKS
1997—Indianapolis NFL	10	1	0.0
1998—Indianapolis NFL	16	12	4.0
1999—Indianapolis NFL	16	0	1.0
Pro totals (3 years)	42	13	5.0

BETTIS, JEROME — RB — STEELERS

PERSONAL: Born February 16, 1972, in Detroit. ... 5-11/250. ... Full name: Jerome Abram Bettis. ... Nickname: The Bus.
HIGH SCHOOL: Mackenzie (Detroit).
COLLEGE: Notre Dame.
TRANSACTIONS/CAREER NOTES: Selected after junior season by Los Angeles Rams in first round (10th pick overall) of 1993 NFL draft. ... Signed by Rams (July 22, 1993). ... Rams franchise moved to St. Louis (April 12, 1995). ... Traded by Rams with third-round pick (LB Steven Conley) in 1996 draft to Pittsburgh Steelers for second-round pick (TE Ernie Conwell) in 1996 draft and fourth-round pick (traded to Miami) in 1997 draft (April 20, 1996). ... Granted unconditional free agency (February 14, 1997). ... Re-signed by Steelers (February 17, 1997).
CHAMPIONSHIP GAME EXPERIENCE: Played in AFC championship game (1997 season).
HONORS: Named NFL Rookie of the Year by THE SPORTING NEWS (1993). ... Played in Pro Bowl (1993, 1994, 1996 and 1997 seasons).
PRO STATISTICS: 1994—Recovered three fumbles. 1995—Recovered two fumbles. 1996—Recovered two fumbles. 1997—Recovered one fumble. 1999—Completed only pass attempt for 21 yards and a touchdown and recovered three fumbles for one yard.
SINGLE GAME HIGHS (regular season): Attempts—39 (January 2, 1994, vs. Chicago); yards—212 (December 12, 1993, vs. New Orleans); and rushing touchdowns—3 (November 30, 1997, vs. Arizona).
STATISTICAL PLATEAUS: 100-yard rushing games: 1993 (7), 1994 (4), 1996 (10), 1997 (10), 1998 (6), 1999 (2). Total: 39.

			RUSHING				RECEIVING				TOTALS			
Year Team	G	GS	Att.	Yds.	Avg.	TD	No.	Yds.	Avg.	TD	TD	2pt.	Pts.	Fum.
1993—Los Angeles Rams NFL	16	12	‡294	1429	4.9	7	26	244	9.4	0	7	0	42	4
1994—Los Angeles Rams NFL	16	16	319	1025	3.2	3	31	293	9.5	1	4	∞2	28	5
1995—St. Louis NFL	15	13	183	637	3.5	3	18	106	5.9	0	3	0	18	4
1996—Pittsburgh NFL	16	12	320	1431	4.5	11	22	122	5.5	0	11	0	66	7
1997—Pittsburgh NFL	15	15	*375	1665	4.4	7	15	110	7.3	2	9	0	54	6
1998—Pittsburgh NFL	15	15	316	1185	3.8	3	16	90	5.6	0	3	0	18	2
1999—Pittsburgh NFL	16	16	299	1091	3.6	7	21	110	5.2	0	7	0	42	2
Pro totals (7 years)	109	99	2106	8463	4.0	41	149	1075	7.2	3	44	2	268	30

BEUERLEIN, STEVE — QB — PANTHERS

PERSONAL: Born March 7, 1965, in Hollywood, Calif. ... 6-3/220. ... Full name: Stephen Taylor Beuerlein. ... Name pronounced BURR-line.
HIGH SCHOOL: Servite (Anaheim, Calif.).
COLLEGE: Notre Dame (degree in American studies, 1987).
TRANSACTIONS/CAREER NOTES: Selected by Los Angeles Raiders in fourth round (110th pick overall) of 1987 NFL draft. ... Signed by Raiders (July 24, 1987). ... On injured reserve with elbow and shoulder injuries (September 7, 1987-entire season). ... Granted free agency (February 1, 1990). ... Re-signed by Raiders (September 3, 1990). ... Granted roster exemption (September 3-16, 1990). ... Inactive for all 16 games (1990). ... Granted free agency (February 1, 1991). ... Re-signed by Raiders (July 8, 1991). ... Traded by Raiders to Dallas Cowboys for fourth-round pick (traded to Indianapolis) in 1992 draft (August 25, 1991). ... Granted unconditional free agency (March 1, 1993). ... Signed by Phoenix Cardinals (April 21, 1993). ... Cardinals franchise renamed Arizona Cardinals for 1994 season. ... Selected by Jacksonville Jaguars from Cardinals in NFL expansion draft (February 15, 1995). ... Granted free agency (February 16, 1996). ... Signed by Carolina Panthers (April 10, 1996).
CHAMPIONSHIP GAME EXPERIENCE: Member of Raiders for AFC championship game (1990 season); inactive. ... Played in NFC championship game (1992 season). ... Member of Super Bowl championship team (1992 season). ... Member of Panthers for NFC championship game (1996 season); did not play.
HONORS: Played in Pro Bowl (1999 season).
PRO STATISTICS: 1988—Caught one pass for 21 yards, fumbled six times and recovered two fumbles for minus one yard. 1989—Fumbled six times and recovered three fumbles for minus eight yards. 1993—Fumbled eight times and recovered two fumbles. 1994—Fumbled eight times and recovered three fumbles for minus 13 yards. 1995—Fumbled three times. 1996—Fumbled nine times and recovered two fumbles for minus seven yards. 1997—Fumbled once. 1998—Fumbled 13 times and recovered five fumbles for minus 19 yards. 1999—Tied for NFC lead with 12 fumbles for minus four yards.
SINGLE GAME HIGHS (regular season): Attempts—53 (December 19, 1993, vs. Seattle); completions—34 (December 19, 1993, vs. Seattle); yards—431 (December 19, 1993, vs. Seattle); and touchdown passes—5 (January 2, 2000, vs. New Orleans).
STATISTICAL PLATEAUS: 300-yard passing games: 1988 (1), 1993 (2), 1999 (5). Total: 8.
MISCELLANEOUS: Regular-season record as starting NFL quarterback: 38-43 (.469). ... Postseason record as starting NFL quarterback: 1-1 (.500). ... Holds Carolina Panthers all-time records for most passing yards (8,960) and touchdown passes (67).

			PASSING								RUSHING				TOTALS		
Year Team	G	GS	Att.	Cmp.	Pct.	Yds.	TD	Int.	Avg.	Rat.	Att.	Yds.	Avg.	TD	TD	2pt.	Pts.
1987—L.A. Raiders NFL						Did not play.											
1988—L.A. Raiders NFL	10	8	238	105	44.1	1643	8	7	6.90	66.6	30	35	1.2	0	0	0	0

Year—Team																
1989—L.A. Raiders NFL.........	10	7	217	108	49.8	1677	13	9	7.73	78.4	16	39	2.4	0	0	0	0
1990—L.A. Raiders NFL.........						Did not play.											
1991—Dallas NFL..................	8	4	137	68	49.6	909	5	2	6.64	77.2	7	-14	-2.0	0	0	0	0
1992—Dallas NFL..................	16	0	18	12	66.7	152	0	1	8.44	69.7	4	-7	-1.8	0	0	0	0
1993—Phoenix NFL................	16	14	418	258	61.7	3164	18	17	7.57	82.5	22	45	2.0	0	0	0	0
1994—Arizona NFL	9	7	255	130	51.0	1545	5	9	6.06	61.6	22	39	1.8	1	1	0	6
1995—Jacksonville NFL........	7	6	142	71	50.0	952	4	7	6.70	60.5	5	32	6.4	0	0	0	0
1996—Carolina NFL	8	4	123	69	56.1	879	8	2	7.15	93.5	12	17	1.4	0	0	0	0
1997—Carolina NFL	7	3	153	89	58.2	1032	6	3	6.75	83.6	4	32	8.0	0	0	0	0
1998—Carolina NFL	12	12	343	216	63.0	2613	17	12	7.62	88.2	22	26	1.2	0	0	0	0
1999—Carolina NFL	16	16	571	*343	60.1	*4436	36	15	7.77	94.6	27	124	4.6	2	2	0	12
Pro totals (11 years).............	119	81	2615	1469	56.2	19002	120	84	7.27	81.1	171	368	2.2	3	3	0	18

B

BEVERLY, ERIC — C — LIONS

PERSONAL: Born March 28, 1974, in Cleveland. ... 6-3/294. ... Full name: Eric Raymonde Beverly.
HIGH SCHOOL: Bedford Heights (Ohio).
COLLEGE: Miami of Ohio.
TRANSACTIONS/CAREER NOTES: Signed as non-drafted free agent by Detroit Lions (April 24, 1997). ... Released by Lions (August 24, 1997). ... Re-signed by Lions to practice squad (August 26, 1997). ... Activated (December 20, 1997). ... Active for one game (1997); did not play.
PLAYING EXPERIENCE: Detroit NFL, 1998 and 1999. ... Games/Games started: 1998 (16/0), 1999 (16/2). Total: 32/2.

BIAKABUTUKA, TSHIMANGA — RB — PANTHERS

PERSONAL: Born January 24, 1974, in Kinsasha, Zaire. ... 6-0/215. ... Name pronounced tee-MON-guh bee-ock-a-ba-TWO-kah. ... Nickname: Tim.
HIGH SCHOOL: John Jacques Rosseau (Longueuil, Que.), then Vanier College (Montreal).
COLLEGE: Michigan.
TRANSACTIONS/CAREER NOTES: Selected after junior season by Carolina Panthers in first round (eighth pick overall) of 1996 NFL draft. ... Signed by Panthers (August 16, 1996). ... On injured reserve with knee injury (October 1, 1996-remainder of season).
SINGLE GAME HIGHS (regular season): Attempts—31 (November 28, 1999, vs. Atlanta); yards—142 (October 3, 1999, vs. Washington); and rushing touchdowns—3 (October 3, 1999, vs. Washington).
STATISTICAL PLATEAUS: 100-yard rushing games: 1997 (1), 1998 (2), 1999 (2). Total: 5.

			RUSHING				RECEIVING				TOTALS			
Year Team	G	GS	Att.	Yds.	Avg.	TD	No.	Yds.	Avg.	TD	TD	2pt.	Pts.	Fum.
1996—Carolina NFL	4	4	71	229	3.2	0	0	0	0.0	0	0	0	0	0
1997—Carolina NFL	8	2	75	299	4.0	2	0	0	0.0	0	2	0	12	1
1998—Carolina NFL	11	3	101	427	4.2	3	8	138	17.3	1	4	0	24	1
1999—Carolina NFL	11	11	138	718	5.2	6	23	189	8.2	0	6	0	36	3
Pro totals (4 years)...................................	34	20	385	1673	4.3	11	31	327	10.5	1	12	0	72	5

BIDWELL, JOSH — P — PACKERS

PERSONAL: Born March 13, 1976, in Roseburg, Ore. ... 6-3/225. ... Full name: Joshua John Bidwell.
HIGH SCHOOL: Douglas (Winston, Ore.).
COLLEGE: Oregon (degree in English).
TRANSACTIONS/CAREER NOTES: Selected by Green Bay Packers in fourth round (133rd pick overall) of 1999 NFL draft. ... Signed by Packers (July 27, 1999). ... On non-football illness list with cancer (September 5, 1999-entire season).
HONORS: Named punter on THE SPORTING NEWS college All-America second team (1998).

BIEKERT, GREG — LB — RAIDERS

PERSONAL: Born March 14, 1969, in Iowa City, Iowa. ... 6-2/255. ... Name pronounced BEEK-ert.
HIGH SCHOOL: Longmont (Colo.).
COLLEGE: Colorado (degree in marketing, 1992).
TRANSACTIONS/CAREER NOTES: Selected by Los Angeles Raiders in seventh round (181st pick overall) of 1993 NFL draft. ... Signed by Raiders (July 13, 1993). ... Raiders franchise moved to Oakland (July 21, 1995).
PRO STATISTICS: 1994—Intercepted one pass for 11 yards. 1996—Recovered one fumble. 1997—Returned one kickoff for 16 yards. 1998—Recovered one fumble. 1999—Intercepted two passes for 57 yards.

Year Team	G	GS	SACKS
1993—Los Angeles Raiders NFL	16	0	0.0
1994—Los Angeles Raiders NFL	16	14	1.5
1995—Oakland NFL	16	14	1.0
1996—Oakland NFL	16	15	0.0
1997—Oakland NFL	16	16	2.5
1998—Oakland NFL	16	16	3.0
1999—Oakland NFL	16	16	2.0
Pro totals (7 years)...	112	91	10.0

BIENIEMY, ERIC — RB

PERSONAL: Born August 15, 1969, in New Orleans. ... 5-9/205. ... Full name: Eric Bieniemy Jr. ... Name pronounced bee-EN-uh-me.
HIGH SCHOOL: Bishop Amat (La Puente, Calif.).
COLLEGE: Colorado.

TRANSACTIONS/CAREER NOTES: Selected by San Diego Chargers in second round (39th pick overall) of 1991 NFL draft. ... Signed by Chargers (July 19, 1991). ... Granted free agency (February 17, 1994). ... Re-signed by Chargers (June 6, 1994). ... Granted unconditional free agency (February 17, 1995). ... Signed by Cincinnati Bengals (March 27, 1995). ... Granted unconditional free agency (February 12, 1999). ... Signed by Philadelphia Eagles (May 7, 1999). ... Granted unconditional free agency (February 11, 2000).
CHAMPIONSHIP GAME EXPERIENCE: Played in AFC championship game (1994 season). ... Played in Super Bowl XXIX (1994 season).
HONORS: Named running back on THE SPORTING NEWS college All-America first team (1990).
PRO STATISTICS: 1992—Fumbled four times and recovered one fumble. 1993—Fumbled once. 1994—Fumbled once and recovered one fumble. 1995—Attempted two passes without a completion, fumbled once and recovered one fumble. 1996—Fumbled once. 1997—Fumbled twice. 1998—Fumbled once.
SINGLE GAME HIGHS (regular season): Attempts—19 (November 12, 1995, vs. Houston); yards—65 (September 10, 1995, vs. Jacksonville); and rushing touchdowns—1 (November 14, 1999, vs. Washington).

Year Team	G	GS	RUSHING				RECEIVING				PUNT RETURNS				KICKOFF RETURNS				TOTALS		
			Att.	Yds.	Avg.	TD	No.	Yds.	Avg.	TD	No.	Yds.	Avg.	TD	No.	Yds.	Avg.	TD	TD	2pt.	Pts.
1991—San Diego NFL....	15	0	3	17	5.7	0	0	0	0.0	0	0	0	0.0	0	0	0	0.0	0	0	0	0
1992—San Diego NFL....	15	0	74	264	3.6	3	5	49	9.8	0	30	229	7.6	0	15	257	17.1	0	3	0	18
1993—San Diego NFL....	16	0	33	135	4.1	1	1	0	0.0	0	0	0	0.0	0	7	110	15.7	0	1	0	6
1994—San Diego NFL....	16	0	73	295	4.0	0	5	48	9.6	0	0	0	0.0	0	0	0	0.0	0	0	0	0
1995—Cincinnati NFL.....	16	1	98	381	3.9	3	43	424	9.9	0	7	47	6.7	0	8	168	21.0	0	3	0	18
1996—Cincinnati NFL.....	16	0	56	269	4.8	2	32	272	8.5	0	0	0	0.0	0	0	0	0.0	0	2	0	12
1997—Cincinnati NFL.....	16	0	21	97	4.6	1	31	249	8.0	0	0	0	0.0	0	34	789	23.2	▲1	2	0	12
1998—Cincinnati NFL.....	16	0	17	56	3.3	0	27	153	5.7	0	0	0	0.0	0	5	87	17.4	0	0	0	0
1999—Philadelphia NFL..	16	0	12	75	6.3	1	2	28	14.0	0	0	0	0.0	0	10	210	21.0	0	1	0	6
Pro totals (9 years)........	142	1	387	1589	4.1	11	146	1223	8.4	0	37	276	7.5	0	79	1621	20.5	1	12	0	72

BILLUPS, TERRY   CB

PERSONAL: Born February 9, 1975, in Weisboden, Germany ... 5-9/179. ... Full name: Terry Michael Billups.
HIGH SCHOOL: Oak Ridge (Orlando).
COLLEGE: North Carolina.
TRANSACTIONS/CAREER NOTES: Signed as non-drafted free agent by New England Patriots (April 19, 1998). ... Released by Patriots (August 25, 1998). ... Re-signed by Patriots to practice squad (August 31, 1998). ... Released by Patriots (September 10, 1998). ... Signed by Miami Dolphins to practice squad (September 15, 1998). ... Released by Dolphins (September 30, 1998). ... Signed by Dallas Cowboys to practice squad (October 5, 1998). ... Activated (November 24, 1998). ... Released by Cowboys (December 7, 1998). ... Re-signed by Cowboys to practice squad (December 9, 1998). ... Assigned by Cowboys to Scottish Claymores in 1999 NFL Europe enhancement allocation program (February 22, 1999). ... Released by Cowboys (August 31, 1999). ... Signed by Patriots (December 15, 1999). ... Released by Patriots (March 13, 2000).
PLAYING EXPERIENCE: Dallas NFL, 1998; Scottish NFLE, 1999; New England NFL, 1999. ... Games/Games started: 1998 (1/0), NFLE 1999 (games played unavailable), 1999 NFL (2/1). Total NFL: 3/1.

BINN, DAVID   C   CHARGERS

PERSONAL: Born February 6, 1972, in San Mateo, Calif. ... 6-3/245. ... Full name: David Aaron Binn.
HIGH SCHOOL: San Mateo (Calif.).
COLLEGE: California (degree in ecology and the social system, 1993).
TRANSACTIONS/CAREER NOTES: Signed as non-drafted free agent by San Diego Chargers (April 28, 1994). ... Granted unconditional free agency (February 13, 1998). ... Re-signed by Chargers (February 25, 1998). ... Granted unconditional free agency (February 11, 2000). ... Re-signed by Chargers (February 11, 2000).
PLAYING EXPERIENCE: San Diego NFL, 1994-1999. ... Games/Games started: 1994 (16/0), 1995 (16/0), 1996 (16/0), 1997 (16/0), 1998 (15/0), 1999 (16/0). Total: 95/0.
CHAMPIONSHIP GAME EXPERIENCE: Played in AFC championship game (1994 season). ... Played in Super Bowl XXIX (1994 season).
PRO STATISTICS: 1999—Fumbled once for minus 36 yards.

BIRK, MATT   C   VIKINGS

PERSONAL: Born July 23, 1976, in St. Paul, Minn. ... 6-4/304. ... Full name: Matthew Robert Birk.
HIGH SCHOOL: Cretin-Derham Hall (St. Paul, Minn.).
COLLEGE: Harvard (degree in economics, 1998).
TRANSACTIONS/CAREER NOTES: Selected by Minnesota Vikings in sixth round (173rd pick overall) of 1998 NFL draft. ... Signed by Vikings (June 24, 1998).
PLAYING EXPERIENCE: Minnesota NFL, 1998 and 1999. ... Games/Games started: 1998 (7/0), 1999 (15/0). Total: 22/0.
CHAMPIONSHIP GAME EXPERIENCE: Member of Vikings for NFC championship game (1998 season); did not play.

BISHOP, BLAINE   S   TITANS

PERSONAL: Born July 24, 1970, in Indianapolis. ... 5-9/203. ... Full name: Blaine Elwood Bishop.
HIGH SCHOOL: Cathedral (Indianapolis).
COLLEGE: Saint Joseph's College (Ind.), then Ball State (degree in insurance, 1993).
TRANSACTIONS/CAREER NOTES: Selected by Houston Oilers in eighth round (214th pick overall) of 1993 NFL draft. ... Signed by Oilers (July 16, 1993). ... Granted free agency (February 16, 1996). ... Re-signed by Oilers (June 17, 1996). ... Designated by Oilers as franchise player (February 14, 1997). ... Oilers franchise moved to Tennessee for 1997 season. ... Re-signed by Oilers (August 27, 1997). ... Oilers franchise renamed Tennessee Titans for 1999 season (December 26, 1998).
CHAMPIONSHIP GAME EXPERIENCE: Played in AFC championship game (1999 season). ... Played in Super Bowl XXXIV (1999 season).
HONORS: Played in Pro Bowl (1995 and 1997 seasons). ... Named to play in Pro Bowl (1996 season); replaced by Tyrone Braxton due to injury.

PRO STATISTICS: 1993—Fumbled once and recovered one fumble. 1994—Returned two kickoffs for 18 yards and recovered one fumble. 1995—Recovered four fumbles for six yards. 1997—Recovered two fumbles. 1998—Recovered one fumble. 1999—Recovered two fumbles.

| Year Team | G | GS | INTERCEPTIONS | | | | SACKS |
			No.	Yds.	Avg.	TD	No.
1993—Houston NFL	16	2	1	1	1.0	0	1.0
1994—Houston NFL	16	13	1	21	21.0	0	1.5
1995—Houston NFL	16	16	1	62	62.0	▲1	1.5
1996—Houston NFL	15	15	1	6	6.0	0	0.0
1997—Tennessee NFL	14	14	0	0	0.0	0	1.5
1998—Tennessee NFL	13	13	1	13	13.0	0	3.0
1999—Tennessee NFL	15	15	0	0	0.0	0	2.5
Pro totals (7 years)	105	88	5	103	20.6	1	11.0

BISHOP, GREG G FALCONS

PERSONAL: Born May 2, 1971, in Stockton, Calif. ... 6-5/315. ... Full name: Gregory Lawrence Bishop.
HIGH SCHOOL: Lodi (Calif.).
COLLEGE: Pacific.
TRANSACTIONS/CAREER NOTES: Selected by New York Giants in fourth round (93rd pick overall) of 1993 NFL draft. ... Signed by Giants (July 19, 1993). ... Granted unconditional free agency (February 12, 1999). ... Signed by Atlanta Falcons (March 24, 1999). ... Announced retirement (March 23, 2000).
PLAYING EXPERIENCE: New York Giants NFL, 1993-1998; Atlanta NFL, 1999. ... Games/Games started: 1993 (8/0), 1994 (16/1), 1995 (16/16), 1996 (16/16), 1997 (16/16), 1998 (16/16), 1999 (13/2). Total: 101/67.
PRO STATISTICS: 1994—Recovered two fumbles. 1995—Recovered one fumble. 1996—Recovered one fumble. 1997—Recovered one fumble.

BISHOP, MICHAEL QB PATRIOTS

PERSONAL: Born May 15, 1976, in Galveston, Texas. ... 6-2/217. ... Full name: Michael Paul Bishop.
HIGH SCHOOL: Willis (Texas).
JUNIOR COLLEGE: Blinn College (Texas).
COLLEGE: Kansas State.
TRANSACTIONS/CAREER NOTES: Selected by New England Patriots in seventh round (227th pick overall) of 1999 NFL draft. ... Signed by Patriots (June 25, 1999). ... Active for one game (1999); did not play.
HONORS: Davey O'Brien Award winner (1998). ... Named quarterback on THE SPORTING NEWS college All-America first team (1998).

BJORNSON, ERIC TE PATRIOTS

PERSONAL: Born December 15, 1971, in San Francisco. ... 6-4/236. ... Name pronounced be-YORN-son.
HIGH SCHOOL: Bishop O'Dowd (Oakland).
COLLEGE: Washington.
TRANSACTIONS/CAREER NOTES: Selected by Dallas Cowboys in fourth round (110th pick overall) of 1995 NFL draft. ... Signed by Cowboys (July 18, 1995). ... Granted free agency (February 13, 1998). ... Re-signed by Cowboys (July 13, 1998). ... Granted unconditional free agency (February 11, 2000). ... Signed by New England Patriots (February 26, 2000).
CHAMPIONSHIP GAME EXPERIENCE: Played in NFC championship game (1995 season). ... Member of Super Bowl championship team (1995 season).
PRO STATISTICS: 1998—Rushed once for seven yards and a touchdown. 1999—Rushed once for 20 yards and a touchdown.
SINGLE GAME HIGHS (regular season): Receptions—8 (November 10, 1996, vs. San Francisco); yards—71 (October 5, 1997, vs. New York Giants); and touchdown receptions—1 (November 8, 1998, vs. Nedw York Giants).

| Year Team | G | GS | RECEIVING | | | | TOTALS | | | |
			No.	Yds.	Avg.	TD	TD	2pt.	Pts.	Fum.
1995—Dallas NFL	14	1	7	53	7.6	0	0	0	0	0
1996—Dallas NFL	14	10	48	388	8.1	3	3	1	20	1
1997—Dallas NFL	14	14	47	442	9.4	0	0	1	2	2
1998—Dallas NFL	16	4	15	218	14.5	1	2	0	12	0
1999—Dallas NFL	16	6	10	131	13.1	0	1	0	6	0
Pro totals (5 years)	74	35	127	1232	9.7	4	6	2	40	3

BLACKMON, ROOSEVELT CB BENGALS

PERSONAL: Born September 10, 1974, in Pahokee, Fla. ... 6-1/185. ... Full name: Roosevelt Blackmon III.
HIGH SCHOOL: Glades Central (Belle Glade, Fla.).
COLLEGE: Morris Brown College (Ga.).
TRANSACTIONS/CAREER NOTES: Selected by Green Bay Packers in fourth round (121st pick overall) of 1998 NFL draft. ... Signed by Packers (July 17, 1998). ... Claimed on waivers by Cincinnati Bengals (October 1, 1998). ... On injured reserve with ankle injury (December 24, 1999-remainder of season).
PLAYING EXPERIENCE: Green Bay (3)-Cincinnati (12) NFL, 1998; Cincinnati NFL, 1999. ... Games/Games started: 1998 (G.B.-3/0; Cin.-12/0; Total: 15/0), 1999 (5/3). Total: 20/3.
PRO STATISTICS: 1999—Intercepted one pass for no yards.

BLACKSHEAR, JEFF G CHIEFS

PERSONAL: Born March 29, 1969, in Fort Pierce, Fla. ... 6-6/323. ... Full name: Jeffrey Leon Blackshear.
HIGH SCHOOL: Westwood Christian (Miami).

JUNIOR COLLEGE: Northwest Mississippi Junior College.
COLLEGE: Northeast Louisiana.
TRANSACTIONS/CAREER NOTES: Selected by Seattle Seahawks in eighth round (197th pick overall) of 1993 NFL draft. ... Signed by Seahawks (July 15, 1993). ... Traded by Seahawks to Cleveland Browns for fourth-round pick (traded to Atlanta) in 1997 draft (March 12, 1996). ... Browns franchise moved to Baltimore and renamed Ravens for 1996 season (March 11, 1996). ... Granted unconditional free agency (February 14, 1997). ... Re-signed by Ravens (March 13, 1997). ... Released by Ravens (February 23, 2000). ... Signed by Kansas City Chiefs (May 4, 2000).
PLAYING EXPERIENCE: Seattle NFL, 1993 and 1994; Cleveland NFL, 1995; Baltimore NFL, 1996-1999. ... Games/Games started: 1993 (15/2), 1994 (16/16), 1995 (16/3), 1996 (16/12), 1997 (16/16), 1998 (16/16), 1999 (16/16). Total: 111/81.

BLACKWELL, WILL   WR   STEELERS

PERSONAL: Born July 6, 1975, in Texarkana, Texas. ... 6-0/190. ... Full name: William Herman Blackwell Jr.
HIGH SCHOOL: Skyline (Oakland).
COLLEGE: San Diego State.
TRANSACTIONS/CAREER NOTES: Selected after junior season by Pittsburgh Steelers in second round (53rd pick overall) of 1997 NFL draft. ... Signed by Steelers (July 15, 1997). ... On injured reserve with foot injury (December 6, 1999-remainder of season). ... Granted free agency (February 11, 2000). ... Re-signed by Steelers (March 17, 2000).
CHAMPIONSHIP GAME EXPERIENCE: Played in AFC championship game (1997 season).
PRO STATISTICS: 1997—Recovered two fumbles.
SINGLE GAME HIGHS (regular season): Receptions—4 (November 21, 1999, vs. Tennessee); yards—68 (September 28, 1997, vs. Tennessee); and touchdown receptions—1 (November 26, 1998, vs. Detroit).

			RECEIVING				PUNT RETURNS				KICKOFF RETURNS				TOTALS			
Year Team	G	GS	No.	Yds.	Avg.	TD	No.	Yds.	Avg.	TD	No.	Yds.	Avg.	TD	TD	2pt.	Pts.	Fum.
1997—Pittsburgh NFL............	14	0	12	168	14.0	1	23	149	6.5	0	32	791	24.7	▲1	2	0	12	3
1998—Pittsburgh NFL............	16	2	32	297	9.3	1	4	22	5.5	0	20	382	19.1	0	1	1	8	1
1999—Pittsburgh NFL............	11	1	20	186	9.3	0	1	39	39.0	0	14	282	20.1	0	0	0	0	1
Pro totals (3 years)	41	3	64	651	10.2	2	28	210	7.5	0	66	1455	22.0	1	3	1	20	5

BLAISE, KERLIN   G   LIONS

PERSONAL: Born December 25, 1974, in Orlando, Fla. ... 6-5/323.
HIGH SCHOOL: Maynard Evans (Orlando, Fla.).
COLLEGE: Miami (Fla.).
TRANSACTIONS/CAREER NOTES: Signed as non-drafted free agent by Detroit Lions (April 24, 1998). ... Released by Lions (August 30, 1998). ... Re-signed by Lions to practice squad (September 1, 1998). ... Activated (October 27, 1998); did not play. ... On injured reserve with knee injury (December 1, 1998-remainder of season).
PLAYING EXPERIENCE: Detroit NFL, 1999. ... Games/Games started: 1999 (16/4).

BLAKE, JEFF   QB   SAINTS

PERSONAL: Born December 4, 1970, in Daytona Beach, Fla. ... 6-0/210. ... Son of Emory Blake, running back with Toronto Argonauts of CFL (1974).
HIGH SCHOOL: Seminole (Sanford, Fla.).
COLLEGE: East Carolina.
TRANSACTIONS/CAREER NOTES: Selected by New York Jets in sixth round (166th pick overall) of 1992 NFL draft. ... Signed by Jets (July 14, 1992). ... Inactive for all 16 games (1993). ... Claimed on waivers by Cincinnati Bengals (August 29, 1994). ... Granted free agency (February 17, 1995). ... Re-signed by Bengals (May 8, 1995). ... On injured reserve with wrist injury (December 24, 1998-remainder of season). ... Granted unconditional free agency (February 11, 2000). ... Signed by New Orleans Saints (February 11, 2000).
HONORS: Played in Pro Bowl (1995 season).
PRO STATISTICS: 1992—Fumbled once. 1994—Fumbled six times. 1995—Fumbled 10 times for minus seven yards. 1996—Fumbled seven times and recovered one fumble for minus five yards. 1997—Fumbled seven times. 1998—Fumbled once. 1999—Fumbled 12 times and recovered seven fumbles for minus 28 yards.
SINGLE GAME HIGHS (regular season): Attempts—46 (December 17, 1995, vs. Cleveland); completions—31 (November 6, 1994, vs. Seattle); yards—387 (November 6, 1994, vs. Seattle); and touchdown passes—4 (December 5, 1999, vs. San Francisco).
STATISTICAL PLATEAUS: 300-yard passing games: 1994 (2), 1995 (1), 1996 (2), 1997 (1), 1998 (1), 1999 (1). Total: 8.
MISCELLANEOUS: Regular-season record as starting NFL quarterback: 25-41 (.379).

			PASSING								RUSHING				TOTALS		
Year Team	G	GS	Att.	Cmp.	Pct.	Yds.	TD	Int.	Avg.	Rat.	Att.	Yds.	Avg.	TD	TD	2pt.	Pts.
1992—New York Jets NFL......	3	0	9	4	44.4	40	0	1	4.44	18.1	2	-2	-1.0	0	0	0	0
1993—New York Jets NFL......							Did not play.										
1994—Cincinnati NFL............	10	9	306	156	51.0	2154	14	9	7.04	76.9	37	204	5.5	1	1	1	8
1995—Cincinnati NFL............	16	16	567	§326	57.5	3822	§28	17	6.74	82.1	53	309	5.8	2	2	1	14
1996—Cincinnati NFL............	16	16	549	308	56.1	3624	24	14	6.60	80.3	72	317	4.4	2	2	0	12
1997—Cincinnati NFL............	11	11	317	184	58.0	2125	8	7	6.70	77.6	45	234	5.2	3	3	0	18
1998—Cincinnati NFL............	9	2	93	51	54.8	739	3	3	7.95	78.2	15	103	6.9	0	0	0	0
1999—Cincinnati NFL............	14	12	389	215	55.3	2670	16	12	6.86	77.6	63	332	5.3	2	2	0	12
Pro totals (7 years)	79	66	2230	1244	55.8	15174	93	63	6.80	79.1	287	1497	5.2	10	10	2	64

BLANCHARD, CARY   K   CARDINALS

PERSONAL: Born November 5, 1968, in Fort Worth, Texas. ... 6-1/232. ... Full name: Robert Cary Blanchard.
HIGH SCHOOL: L.D. Bell (Hurst, Texas).
COLLEGE: Oklahoma State.

TRANSACTIONS/CAREER NOTES: Signed as non-drafted free agent by Dallas Cowboys (April 25, 1991). ... Released by Cowboys (August 4, 1991). ... Signed by Sacramento Surge of World League (1992). ... Signed by New Orleans Saints (July 7, 1992). ... Released by Saints (August 31, 1992). ... Re-signed by Saints to practice squad (September 7, 1992). ... Activated (September 14, 1992). ... Active for one game with Saints (1992); did not play. ... Claimed on waivers by New York Jets (September 29, 1992). ... Released by Jets (June 24, 1994). ... Signed by Minnesota Vikings (July 12, 1994). ... Released by Vikings (August 28, 1994). ... Signed by Saints (April 18, 1995). ... Released by Saints (August 27, 1995). ... Signed by Indianapolis Colts (October 3, 1995). ... Released by Colts (August 30, 1998). ... Signed by Washington Redskins (September 22, 1998). ... Granted unconditional free agency (February 12, 1999). ... Re-signed by Redskins (April 20, 1999). ... Released by Redskins (August 30, 1999). ... Signed by New York Giants (October 20, 1999). ... Granted unconditional free agency (February 11, 2000). ... Signed by Arizona Cardinals (February 28, 2000).

CHAMPIONSHIP GAME EXPERIENCE: Played in AFC championship game (1995 season).

HONORS: Named kicker on THE SPORTING NEWS NFL All-Pro team (1996). ... Played in Pro Bowl (1996 season).

PRO STATISTICS: 1998—Punted three times for 113 yards.

					KICKING				
Year Team	G	XPM	XPA	FGM	FGA	Lg.	50+	Pts.
1992—Sacramento W.L.	4	17	17	5	8	42	0-0	32
—New York Jets NFL	11	17	17	16	22	47	0-1	65
1993—New York Jets NFL	16	31	31	17	26	45	0-2	82
1994—				Did not play.				
1995—Indianapolis NFL	12	25	25	19	24	50	1-1	82
1996—Indianapolis NFL	16	27	27	§36	§40	52	5-5	§135
1997—Indianapolis NFL	16	21	21	§32	†41	50	1-3	117
1998—Washington NFL	13	30	31	11	17	54	1-2	63
1999—New York Giants NFL	10	19	19	18	21	48	0-0	73
W.L. totals (1 year)	4	17	17	5	8	42	0-0	32
NFL totals (7 years)	94	170	171	149	191	54	8-14	617
Pro totals (8 years)	98	187	188	154	199	54	8-0	649

BLEDSOE, DREW — QB — PATRIOTS

PERSONAL: Born February 14, 1972, in Ellensburg, Wash. ... 6-5/233.

HIGH SCHOOL: Walla Walla (Wash.).

COLLEGE: Washington State.

TRANSACTIONS/CAREER NOTES: Selected after junior season by New England Patriots in first round (first pick overall) of 1993 NFL draft. ... Signed by Patriots (July 6, 1993).

CHAMPIONSHIP GAME EXPERIENCE: Played in AFC championship game (1996 season). ... Played in Super Bowl XXXI (1996 season).

HONORS: Played in Pro Bowl (1994, 1996 and 1997 seasons).

RECORDS: Holds NFL single-season record for most passes attempted—691 (1994). ... Holds NFL single-game records for most passes completed—45; most passes attempted—70; and most passes attempted without an interception—70 (November 13, 1994, vs. Minnesota).

POST SEASON RECORDS: Shares Super Bowl single-game record for most passes intercepted—4 (January 26, 1997, vs. Green Bay).

PRO STATISTICS: 1993—Fumbled eight times and recovered five fumbles for minus 23 yards. 1994—Fumbled nine times and recovered three fumbles for minus five yards. 1995—Caught one pass for minus nine yards, fumbled 11 times and recovered one fumble for minus eight yards. 1996—Fumbled nine times and recovered one fumble for minus two yards. 1997—Fumbled four times and recovered three fumbles for minus four yards. 1998—Fumbled nine times and recovered four fumbles for minus 10 yards. 1999—Fumbled eight times and recovered six fumbles for minus 13 yards.

SINGLE GAME HIGHS (regular season): Attempts—70 (November 13, 1994, vs. Minnesota); completions—45 (November 13, 1994, vs. Minnesota); yards—426 (November 13, 1994, vs. Minnesota); and touchdown passes—4 (October 31, 1999, vs. Arizona).

STATISTICAL PLATEAUS: 300-yard passing games: 1993 (1), 1994 (6), 1995 (2), 1996 (4), 1997 (3), 1998 (4), 1999 (5). Total: 25.

MISCELLANEOUS: Regular-season record as starting NFL quarterback: 58-47 (.552). ... Postseason record as starting NFL quarterback: 3-3 (.500).

			PASSING							RUSHING				TOTALS		
Year Team	G	GS	Att.	Cmp.	Pct.	Yds.	TD	Int.	Avg.	Rat.	Att.	Yds.	Avg.	TD	TD	2pt.	Pts.
1993—New England NFL	13	12	429	214	49.9	2494	15	15	5.81	65.0	32	82	2.6	0	0	0	0
1994—New England NFL	16	16	*691	*400	57.9	*4555	25	*27	6.59	73.6	44	40	0.9	0	0	0	0
1995—New England NFL	15	15	*636	323	50.8	3507	13	16	5.51	63.7	20	28	1.4	0	0	0	0
1996—New England NFL	16	16	*623	*373	59.9	4086	27	15	6.56	83.7	24	27	1.1	0	0	0	0
1997—New England NFL	16	16	522	314	60.2	3706	28	15	7.10	87.7	28	55	2.0	0	0	0	0
1998—New England NFL	14	14	481	263	54.7	3633	20	14	7.55	80.9	28	44	1.6	0	0	0	0
1999—New England NFL	16	16	§539	305	56.6	3985	19	§21	7.39	75.6	42	101	2.4	0	0	0	0
Pro totals (7 years)	106	105	3921	2192	55.9	25966	147	123	6.62	75.7	218	377	1.7	0	0	0	0

BLEVINS, TONY — DB — COLTS

PERSONAL: Born January 29, 1975, in Rockford, Ill. ... 6-0/165.

HIGH SCHOOL: Rockhurst (Kansas City, Mo.).

COLLEGE: Kansas.

TRANSACTIONS/CAREER NOTES: Signed as non-drafted free agent by San Francisco 49ers (April 24, 1998). ... Released by 49ers (August 25, 1998). ... Re-signed by 49ers to practice squad (September 1, 1998). ... Activated (September 26, 1998). ... Released by 49ers (September 29, 1998). ... Re-signed by 49ers to practice squad (October 1, 1998). ... Activated (October 7, 1998). ... Claimed on waivers by Indianapolis Colts (October 30, 1998).

PLAYING EXPERIENCE: San Francisco (2)-Indianapolis (3) NFL, 1998, Indianapolis NFL, 1999. ... Games/Games started: 1998 (S.F.-2/0; Ind.-3/0; Total: 5/0), 1999 (15/0). Total: 20/0.

PRO STATISTICS: 1999—Intercepted two passes for 115 yards and one touchdown, credited with one sack and recovered two fumbles for two yards.

BLOEDORN, GREG   C   SEAHAWKS

PERSONAL: Born November 15, 1972, in Elmhurst, Ill. ... 6-6/278. ... Name pronounced BLAY-dorn.
HIGH SCHOOL: Glenbard South (Glen Ellyn, Ill.).
COLLEGE: Cornell (degree in economics, 1995).
TRANSACTIONS/CAREER NOTES: Signed as non-drafted free agent by Seattle Seahawks (April 25, 1996). ... Released by Seahawks (August 13, 1996). ... Re-signed by Seahawks to practice squad (September 11, 1996). ... Released by Seahawks (August 26, 1997). ... Re-signed by Seahawks to practice squad (August 27, 1997). ... Activated (October 31, 1997). ... Released by Seahawks (November 4, 1997). ... Re-signed by Seahawks to practice squad (November 5, 1997). ... Activated (November 21, 1997). ... Released by Seahawks (November 24, 1997). ... Re-signed by Seahawks to practice squad (November 25, 1997). ... Activated (November 28, 1997). ... Assigned by Seahawks to England Monarchs in 1998 NFL Europe enhancement allocation program (February 18, 1998). ... Released by Seahawks (August 30, 1998). ... Re-signed by Seahawks (November 18, 1998). ... Active for five games (1998); did not play.
PLAYING EXPERIENCE: Seattle NFL, 1997 and 1999; England NFLE, 1998. ... Games/Games started: 1997 (3/0), 1998 (games played unavailable), 1999 (9/0). Total NFL: 12/0.
PRO STATISTICS: 1999—Recovered one fumble for minus six yards.

BLY, DRE'   CB   RAMS

PERSONAL: Born May 22, 1977, in Chesapeake, Va. ... 5-9/185. ... Full name: Donald Andre Bly.
HIGH SCHOOL: Western Branch (Chesapeake, Va.).
COLLEGE: North Carolina (degree in exercise and sports science).
TRANSACTIONS/CAREER NOTES: Selected after junior season by St. Louis Rams in second round (41st pick overall) of 1999 NFL draft. ... Signed by Rams (July 16, 1999).
CHAMPIONSHIP GAME EXPERIENCE: Played in NFC championship game (1999 season). ... Member of Super Bowl championship team (1999 season).
HONORS: Named cornerback on THE SPORTING NEWS college All-America first team (1996). ... Named cornerback on THE SPORTING NEWS college All-America third team (1997).
PRO STATISTICS: 1999—Returned one kickoff for one yard.

			INTERCEPTIONS			
Year Team	G	GS	No.	Yds.	Avg.	TD
1999—St. Louis NFL	16	2	3	53	17.7	1

BOBO, ORLANDO   G   RAVENS

PERSONAL: Born February 9, 1974, in Westpoint, Miss. ... 6-3/300.
HIGH SCHOOL: Westpoint (Miss.).
JUNIOR COLLEGE: East Mississippi Community College.
COLLEGE: Northeast Louisiana.
TRANSACTIONS/CAREER NOTES: Signed as non-drafted free agent by Minnesota Vikings (April 26, 1996). ... Released by Vikings (August 20, 1996). ... Re-signed by Vikings to practice squad (August 26, 1996). ... Released by Vikings (August 27, 1997). ... Re-signed by Vikings to practice squad (August 29, 1997). ... Activated (September 12, 1997). ... On injured reserve with leg injury (October 27, 1998-remainder of season). ... Selected by Cleveland Browns from Vikings in NFL expansion draft (February 9, 1999). ... Granted free agency (February 11, 2000). ... Signed by Baltimore Ravens (April 7, 2000).
PLAYING EXPERIENCE: Minnesota NFL, 1997 and 1998; Cleveland NFL, 1999. ... Games/Games started: 1997 (5/0), 1998 (4/0), 1999 (9/1). Total: 18/1.
PRO STATISTICS: 1999—Caught one pass for three yards.

BOCK, JOHN   G   DOLPHINS

PERSONAL: Born February 11, 1971, in Chicago. ... 6-3/295. ... Full name: John Matthew Bock. ... Nephew of Wayne Bock, tackle with Chicago Cardinals (1957).
HIGH SCHOOL: Crystal Lake (Ill.).
COLLEGE: Louisville, then Indiana State (degree in sociology).
TRANSACTIONS/CAREER NOTES: Signed as non-drafted free agent by Buffalo Bills (May 7, 1994). ... Released by Bills (August 22, 1994). ... Selected by Amsterdam Admirals in 1995 World League draft. ... Signed by New York Jets (June 22, 1995). ... Released by Jets (August 29, 1996). ... Signed by Miami Dolphins (October 16, 1996). ... Granted unconditional free agency (February 12, 1999). ... Re-signed by Dolphins (March 23, 1999). ... On injured reserve with knee injury (November 2, 1999-remainder of season). ... Granted unconditional free agency (February 11, 2000). ... Re-signed by Dolphins (March 2, 2000).
PLAYING EXPERIENCE: Amsterdam W.L., 1995; New York Jets NFL, 1995; Miami NFL, 1996-1999. ... Games/Games started: W.L. 1995 (10/10), NFL 1995 (10/7), 1996 (2/0), 1997 (14/3), 1998 (16/6), 1999 (7/0). Total W.L.: 10/10. Total NFL: 49/16. Total Pro: 59/26.
PRO STATISTICS: 1995—Fumbled once for minus one yard.

BOLDEN, JURAN   CB

PERSONAL: Born June 27, 1974, in Tampa. ... 6-2/201. ... Cousin of K.D. Williams, linebacker, New Orleans Saints.
HIGH SCHOOL: Hillsborough (Tampa).
JUNIOR COLLEGE: Mississippi Delta Community College.
TRANSACTIONS/CAREER NOTES: Signed by Winnipeg Blue Bombers of CFL (April 1995). ... Selected by Atlanta Falcons in fourth round (127th pick overall) of 1996 NFL draft. ... Signed by Falcons (July 20, 1996). ... On injured reserve with knee injury (December 9, 1996-remainder of season). ... Claimed on waivers by Green Bay Packers (September 30, 1998). ... Claimed on waivers by Carolina Panthers (October 27, 1998). ... Released by Panthers (February 12, 1999). ... Signed by Kansas City Chiefs (April 19, 1999). ... Released by Chiefs (September 5, 1999). ... Re-signed by Chiefs (September 21, 1999). ... Released by Chiefs (December 21, 1999). ... Signed by Winnipeg Blue Bombers of CFL (June 8, 2000).

PLAYING EXPERIENCE: Winnipeg CFL, 1995; Atlanta NFL, 1996 and 1997; Atlanta (3)-Green Bay (3)-Carolina (6) NFL, 1998, Kansas City NFL, 1999. ... Games/Games started: 1995 (9/9), 1996 (9/0), 1997 (14/1), 1998 (Atl.-3/0; G.B.-3/0; Car.-6/0; Total: 12/0), 1999 (7/0). Total CFL: 9/9. Total NFL: 42/1. Total Pro: 51/10.

PRO STATISTICS: CFL: 1995—Intercepted six passes for 28 yards and returned one kickoff for two yards. NFL: 1997—Returned five kick-offs for 106 yards. 1998—Recovered one fumble.

BONHAM, SHANE — DT

PERSONAL: Born October 18, 1970, in Fairbanks, Alaska. ... 6-2/286. ... Full name: Steven Shane Bonham.
HIGH SCHOOL: Lathrop (Fairbanks, Alaska).
COLLEGE: Air Force, then Tennessee.
TRANSACTIONS/CAREER NOTES: Selected by Detroit Lions in third round (93rd pick overall) of 1994 NFL draft. ... Signed by Lions (July 21, 1994). ... Granted free agency (February 14, 1997). ... Re-signed by Lions (May 22, 1997). ... Granted unconditional free agency (February 13, 1998). ... Signed by San Francisco 49ers (April 21, 1998). ... Released by 49ers (September 5, 1999). ... Re-signed by 49ers (October 12, 1999). ... Released by 49ers (November 9, 1999). ... Signed by Indianapolis Colts (November 24, 1999). ... Granted unconditional free agency (February 11, 2000).

Year Team	G	GS	SACKS
1994—Detroit NFL	15	1	0.0
1995—Detroit NFL	15	0	1.0
1996—Detroit NFL	15	2	2.0
1997—Detroit NFL	16	0	1.0
1998—San Francisco NFL	8	0	0.0
1999—San Francisco NFL	3	0	0.0
—Indianapolis NFL	3	0	0.0
Pro totals (6 years)	75	3	4.0

BONIOL, CHRIS — K

PERSONAL: Born December 9, 1971, in Alexandria, La. ... 5-11/167. ... Name pronounced BONE-yol.
HIGH SCHOOL: Alexandria (La.).
COLLEGE: Louisiana Tech.
TRANSACTIONS/CAREER NOTES: Signed as non-drafted free agent by Dallas Cowboys (April 28, 1994). ... Granted free agency (February 14, 1997). ... Tendered offer sheet by Philadelphia Eagles (March 7, 1997). ... Cowboys declined to match offer (March 14, 1997). ... Claimed on waivers by Cleveland Browns (August 21, 1999). ... Released by Browns (September 3, 1999). ... Signed by Chicago Bears (October 13, 1999). ... Released by Bears (December 27, 1999).
CHAMPIONSHIP GAME EXPERIENCE: Played in NFC championship game (1994 and 1995 season). ... Member of Super Bowl championship team (1995 season).
RECORDS: Shares NFL single-game record for most field goals—7 (November 18, 1996, vs. Green Bay).
PRO STATISTICS: 1995—Punted twice for 77 yards.

Year Team	G	KICKING						
		XPM	XPA	FGM	FGA	Lg.	50+	Pts.
1994—Dallas NFL	16	48	48	22	29	47	0-1	114
1995—Dallas NFL	16	46	†48	27	28	45	0-0	127
1996—Dallas NFL	16	24	25	32	36	52	1-2	120
1997—Philadelphia NFL	16	33	33	22	31	49	0-1	99
1998—Philadelphia NFL	16	15	17	14	21	50	1-1	57
1999—Chicago NFL	10	17	18	11	18	46	0-1	50
Pro totals (6 years)	90	183	189	128	163	52	2-6	567

BONO, STEVE — QB

PERSONAL: Born May 11, 1962, in Norristown, Pa. ... 6-4/212. ... Full name: Steven Christopher Bono.
HIGH SCHOOL: Norristown (Pa.).
COLLEGE: UCLA.
TRANSACTIONS/CAREER NOTES: Selected by Memphis Showboats in 1985 USFL territorial draft. ... Selected by Minnesota Vikings in sixth round (142nd pick overall) of 1985 NFL draft. ... Signed by Vikings (July 10, 1985). ... Released by Vikings (October 4, 1986). ... Re-signed by Vikings (November 19, 1986). ... Released by Vikings (December 9, 1986). ... Signed by Pittsburgh Steelers (March 25, 1987). ... Released by Steelers (September 7, 1987). ... Re-signed as replacement player by Steelers (September 24, 1987). ... Released by Steelers (April 13, 1989). ... Signed by San Francisco 49ers (June 13, 1989). ... Active for seven games (1990); did not play. ... Granted free agency (February 1, 1991). ... Re-signed by 49ers (1991). ... Granted unconditional free agency (March 1, 1993). ... Re-signed by 49ers (April 7, 1993). ... Released by 49ers (April 29, 1994). ... Re-signed by 49ers (May 2, 1994). ... Traded by 49ers to Kansas City Chiefs for fourth-round pick (traded to Cleveland) in 1995 draft (May 2, 1994). ... Released by Chiefs (June 12, 1997). ... Signed by Green Bay Packers (June 20, 1997). ... Traded by Packers to St. Louis Rams for future considerations (April 6, 1998). ... Granted unconditional free agency (February 12, 1999). ... Signed by Carolina Panthers (March 19, 1999). ... Released by Panthers (February 10, 2000).
CHAMPIONSHIP GAME EXPERIENCE: Member of 49ers for NFC championship game (1989 and 1990 seasons); inactive. ... Member of Super Bowl championship team (1989 season). ... Played in NFC championship game (1992 and 1993 seasons). ... Member of Packers for NFC championship game (1997 season); did not play. ... Member of Packers for Super Bowl XXXII (1997 season); did not play.
HONORS: Played in Pro Bowl (1995 season).
PRO STATISTICS: 1987—Caught one pass for two yards, fumbled five times and recovered three fumbles. 1991—Fumbled seven times for minus eight yards. 1992—Fumbled twice and recovered one fumble for minus three yards. 1995—Fumbled 10 times and recovered one fumble for minus five yards. 1996—Fumbled five times. 1997—Fumbled once. 1998—Fumbled four times for minus 11 yards.
SINGLE GAME HIGHS (regular season): Attempts—55 (December 12, 1994, vs. Miami); completions—33 (December 12, 1994, vs. Miami); yards—347 (December 1, 1991, vs. New Orleans); and touchdown passes—3 (December 27, 1998, vs. San Francisco).
STATISTICAL PLATEAUS: 300-yard passing games: 1991 (2), 1994 (2), 1995 (1). Total: 5.
MISCELLANEOUS: Regular-season record as starting NFL quarterback: 28-14 (.667). ... Postseason record as starting NFL quarterback: 0-1.

| | | | PASSING | | | | | | | | RUSHING | | | | TOTALS | | |
Year Team	G	GS	Att.	Cmp.	Pct.	Yds.	TD	Int.	Avg.	Rat.	Att.	Yds.	Avg.	TD	TD	2pt.	Pts.
1985—Minnesota NFL	1	0	10	1	10.0	5	0	0	0.50	39.6	0	0	0.0	0	0	0	0
1986—Minnesota NFL	1	0	1	1	100.0	3	0	0	3.00	79.2	0	0	0.0	0	0	0	0
1987—Pittsburgh NFL	3	3	74	34	45.9	438	5	2	5.92	76.3	8	27	3.4	1	1	0	6
1988—Pittsburgh NFL	2	0	35	10	28.6	110	1	2	3.14	25.9	0	0	0.0	0	0	0	0
1989—San Francisco NFL	1	0	5	4	80.0	62	1	0	12.40	157.9	0	0	0.0	0	0	0	0
1990—San Francisco NFL						Did not play.											
1991—San Francisco NFL	9	6	237	141	59.5	1617	11	4	6.82	88.5	17	46	2.7	0	0	0	0
1992—San Francisco NFL	16	0	56	36	64.3	463	2	2	8.27	87.1	15	23	1.5	0	0	0	0
1993—San Francisco NFL	8	0	61	39	63.9	416	0	1	6.82	76.9	12	14	1.2	1	1	0	6
1994—Kansas City NFL	7	2	117	66	56.4	796	4	4	6.80	74.6	4	-1	-0.3	0	0	0	0
1995—Kansas City NFL	16	16	520	293	56.3	3121	21	10	6.00	79.5	28	113	4.0	5	5	0	30
1996—Kansas City NFL	13	13	438	235	53.7	2572	12	13	5.87	68.0	26	27	1.0	0	0	0	0
1997—Green Bay NFL	2	0	10	5	50.0	29	0	0	2.90	56.3	3	-3	-1.0	0	0	0	0
1998—St. Louis NFL	6	2	136	69	50.7	807	5	4	5.93	69.1	10	13	1.3	0	0	1	2
1999—Carolina NFL	2	0	1	0	0.0	0	0	0	0.0	39.6	2	-2	-1.0	0	0	0	0
Pro totals (14 years)	87	42	1701	934	54.9	10439	62	42	6.14	75.3	125	257	2.1	7	7	1	44

BOOKER, MARTY — WR — BEARS

PERSONAL: Born July 31, 1976, in Marrero, La. ... 5-11/215.
HIGH SCHOOL: Jonesboro-Hodge (Jonesboro, La.).
COLLEGE: Northeastern Louisiana.
TRANSACTIONS/CAREER NOTES: Selected by Chicago Bears in third round (78th pick overall) of 1999 NFL draft. ... Signed by Bears (July 22, 1999).
PRO STATISTICS: 1999—Rushed once for eight yards.
SINGLE GAME HIGHS (regular season): Receptions—7 (November 14, 1999, vs. Minnesota); yards—134 (November 14, 1999, vs. Minnesota); and touchdown receptions—2 (November 14, 1999, vs. Minnesota).
STATISTICAL PLATEAUS: 100-yard receiving games: 1999 (1).

| | | | RECEIVING | | | | TOTALS | | | |
Year Team	G	GS	No.	Yds.	Avg.	TD	TD	2pt.	Pts.	Fum.
1999—Chicago NFL	9	4	19	219	11.5	3	3	0	18	0

BOOKER, MICHAEL — CB — FALCONS

PERSONAL: Born April 27, 1975, in Oceanside, Calif. ... 6-2/200. ... Full name: Michael Allen Booker.
HIGH SCHOOL: El Camino (Calif.).
COLLEGE: Nebraska.
TRANSACTIONS/CAREER NOTES: Selected by Atlanta Falcons in first round (11th pick overall) of 1997 NFL draft. ... Signed by Falcons (July 16, 1997).
CHAMPIONSHIP GAME EXPERIENCE: Played in NFC championship game (1998 season). ... Played in Super Bowl XXXIII (1998 season).
PRO STATISTICS: 1998—Fumbled once and recovered one fumble for five yards.

| | | | INTERCEPTIONS | | | |
Year Team	G	GS	No.	Yds.	Avg.	TD
1997—Atlanta NFL	15	2	3	16	5.3	0
1998—Atlanta NFL	14	6	1	27	27.0	0
1999—Atlanta NFL	13	1	2	10	5.0	0
Pro totals (3 years)	42	9	6	53	8.8	0

BOOKER, VAUGHN — DE — BENGALS

PERSONAL: Born February 24, 1968, in Cincinnati. ... 6-5/300. ... Full name: Vaughn Jamel Booker.
HIGH SCHOOL: Taft (Cincinnati).
COLLEGE: Cincinnati.
TRANSACTIONS/CAREER NOTES: Signed by Winnipeg Blue Bombers of CFL (June 1992). ... Granted free agency after 1993 season. ... Signed as non-drafted free agent by Kansas City Chiefs (May 2, 1994). ... Traded by Chiefs to Green Bay Packers for DT Darius Holland (May 13, 1998). ... Granted unconditional free agency (February 11, 2000). ... Signed by Cincinnati Bengals (February 16, 2000).
PRO STATISTICS: CFL: 1992—Recovered four fumbles and returned one kickoff for three yards. NFL: 1994—Recovered two fumbles for six yards and returned two kickoffs for 10 yards. 1995—Recovered one fumble for 14 yards and a touchdown. 1996—Recovered one fumble. 1997—Recovered one fumble.
MISCELLANEOUS: Served in U.S. Army (1988-90).

Year Team	G	GS	SACKS
1992—Winnipeg CFL	15	...	2.0
1993—Winnipeg CFL	9	...	4.0
1994—Kansas City NFL	13	0	0.0
1995—Kansas City NFL	16	10	1.5
1996—Kansas City NFL	14	12	1.0
1997—Kansas City NFL	13	13	4.0
1998—Green Bay NFL	16	4	3.0
1999—Green Bay NFL	14	14	3.5
CFL totals (2 years)	24	...	6.0
NFL totals (6 years)	86	53	13.0
Pro totals (8 years)	110	...	19.0

BOOSE, DORIAN   DE   JETS

PERSONAL: Born January 29, 1974, in Frankfurt, West Germany. ... 6-5/292. ... Full name: Dorian Alexander Boose.
HIGH SCHOOL: Henry Foss (Tacoma, Wash.).
JUNIOR COLLEGE: Walla Walla (Wash.) Community College.
COLLEGE: Washington State.
TRANSACTIONS/CAREER NOTES: Selected by New York Jets in second round (56th pick overall) of 1998 NFL draft. ... Signed by Jets (July 8, 1998).
PLAYING EXPERIENCE: New York Jets NFL, 1998 and 1999. ... Games/Games started: 1998 (12/0), 1999 (12/0). Total: 24/0.
CHAMPIONSHIP GAME EXPERIENCE: Member of Jets for AFC championship game (1998 season); inactive.
PRO STATISTICS: 1999—Recovered one fumble.

B

BORDANO, CHRIS   LB   COWBOYS

PERSONAL: Born December 30, 1974, in San Antonio. ... 6-1/241.
HIGH SCHOOL: Southwest (San Antonio).
COLLEGE: Southern Methodist.
TRANSACTIONS/CAREER NOTES: Selected by New Orleans Saints in sixth round (161st pick overall) of 1998 NFL draft. ... Signed by Saints (June 11, 1998). ... Traded by Saints to Dallas Cowboys for CB Kevin Mathis (April 26, 2000).
PLAYING EXPERIENCE: New Orleans NFL, 1998 and 1999. ... Games/Games started: 1998 (16/6), 1999 (15/12). Total: 31/18.
PRO STATISTICS: 1998—Credited with one sack.

BOSELLI, TONY   OT   JAGUARS

PERSONAL: Born April 17, 1972, in Boulder, Colo. ... 6-7/319. ... Full name: Don Anthony Boselli Jr.
HIGH SCHOOL: Fairview (Boulder, Colo.).
COLLEGE: Southern California (degree in business administration, 1995).
TRANSACTIONS/CAREER NOTES: Selected by Jacksonville Jaguars in first round (second pick overall) of 1995 NFL draft. ... Signed by Jaguars (June 1, 1995). ... On injured reserve with knee injury (January 4, 2000-remainder of playoffs).
PLAYING EXPERIENCE: Jacksonville NFL, 1995-1999. ... Games/Games started: 1995 (13/12), 1996 (16/16), 1997 (12/12), 1998 (15/15), 1999 (16/16). Total: 72/71.
CHAMPIONSHIP GAME EXPERIENCE: Played in AFC championship game (1996 season).
HONORS: Named offensive lineman on THE SPORTING NEWS college All-America first team (1994). ... Played in Pro Bowl (1996-1998 seasons). ... Named offensive tackle on THE SPORTING NEWS NFL All-Pro team (1997-99). ... Named to play in Pro Bowl (1999 season); replaced by Walter Jones due to injury.
PRO STATISTICS: 1996—Recovered one fumble. 1998—Recovered one fumble for two yards. 1999—Recoverd three fumbles.

BOSTIC, JAMES   RB

PERSONAL: Born March 13, 1972, in Fort Lauderdale, Fla. ... 5-11/225. ... Full name: James Edward Bostic.
HIGH SCHOOL: Dillard (Fort Lauderdale, Fla.).
COLLEGE: Auburn.
TRANSACTIONS/CAREER NOTES: Selected after junior season by Los Angeles Rams in third round (83rd pick overall) of 1994 NFL draft. ... Signed by Rams (July 6, 1994). ... Active for 10 games (1994); did not play. ... On injured reserve with wrist injury (November 16, 1994-remainder of season). ... Rams franchise moved to St. Louis (April 12, 1995). ... Released by Rams (August 27, 1995). ... Signed by Green Bay Packers (January 10, 1996). ... On injured reserve with knee injury (August 20, 1996-entire season). ... Released by Packers (June 24, 1997). ... Signed by Kansas City Chiefs (April 7, 1998). ... Released by Chiefs (August 30, 1998). ... Signed by Miami Dolphins to practice squad (September 9, 1998). ... Released by Dolphins (September 30, 1998). ... Signed by Philadelphia Eagles to practice squad (October 7, 1998). ... Activated (November 27, 1998). ... Released by Eagles (November 16, 1999).
PLAYING EXPERIENCE: Philadelphia NFL, 1998 and 1999. ... Games/Games started: 1998 (2/0), 1999 (9/0). Total: 11/0.
PRO STATISTICS: 1999—Rushed five times for 19 yards, caught five passes for eight yards and fumbled twice.
SINGLE GAME HIGHS (regular season): Attempts—2 (November 7, 1999, vs. Carolina); yards—8 (November 7, 1999, vs. Carolina); and rushing touchdowns—0.

BOSTIC, JASON   CB   EAGLES

PERSONAL: Born June 30, 1976, in Lauderhill, Fla. ... 5-9/181. ... Full name: Jason Devon Bostic.
HIGH SCHOOL: Cardinal Gibbons (Lauderhill, Fla.).
COLLEGE: Georgia Tech.
TRANSACTIONS/CAREER NOTES: Signed as non-drafted free agent by Philadelphia Eagles (April 19, 1999). ... Released by Eagles (September 5, 1999). ... Re-signed by Eagles to practice squad (September 8, 1999). ... Activated (December 27, 1999).
PLAYING EXPERIENCE: Philadelphia NFL, 1999. ... Games/Games started: 1999 (1/0).

BOSTON, DAVID   WR   CARDINALS

PERSONAL: Born August 19, 1978, in Humble, Texas. ... 6-2/210.
HIGH SCHOOL: Humble (Texas).
COLLEGE: Ohio State.
TRANSACTIONS/CAREER NOTES: Selected after junior season by Arizona Cardinals in first round (eighth pick overall) of 1999 NFL draft. ... Signed by Cardinals (August 2, 1999).
HONORS: Named wide receiver on THE SPORTING NEWS college All-America second team (1998).

PRO STATISTICS: 1999—Recovered one fumble.
SINGLE GAME HIGHS (regular season): Receptions—8 (October 10, 1999, vs. New York Giants); yards—101 (October 10, 1999, vs. New York Giants); and touchdown receptions—1 (December 5, 1999, vs. Philadelphia).
STATISTICAL PLATEAUS: 100-yard receiving games: 1999 (1).

				RUSHING				RECEIVING				PUNT RETURNS				TOTALS	
Year Team	G	GS	Att.	Yds.	Avg.	TD	No.	Yds.	Avg.	TD	No.	Yds.	Avg.	TD	TD	2pt.	Pts. Fum.
1999—Arizona NFL	16	8	5	0	0.0	0	40	473	11.8	2	7	62	8.9	0	2	0	12 2

BOULWARE, PETER　　　LB　　　RAVENS

PERSONAL: Born December 18, 1974, in Columbia, S.C. ... 6-4/255. ... Full name: Peter Nicholas Boulware. ... Name pronounced BOWL-ware.
HIGH SCHOOL: Spring Valley (Columbia, S.C.).
COLLEGE: Florida State (degree in management information systems, 1997).
TRANSACTIONS/CAREER NOTES: Selected after junior season by Baltimore Ravens in first round (fourth pick overall) of 1997 NFL draft. ... Signed by Ravens (August 16, 1997).
HONORS: Named defensive end on The Sporting News college All-America first team (1996). ... Played in Pro Bowl (1998 and 1999 seasons).
PRO STATISTICS: 1998—Recovered one fumble.

Year Team	G	GS	SACKS
1997—Baltimore NFL..	16	16	11.5
1998—Baltimore NFL..	16	16	8.5
1999—Baltimore NFL..	16	11	10.0
Pro totals (3 years)..	48	43	30.0

BOUTTE, MARC　　　DT

PERSONAL: Born July 26, 1969, in Lake Charles, La. ... 6-4/307. ... Full name: Marc Anthony Boutte. ... Name pronounced boo-TAY.
HIGH SCHOOL: William Oscar Boston (Lake Charles, La.).
COLLEGE: Louisiana State.
TRANSACTIONS/CAREER NOTES: Selected by Los Angeles Rams in third round (57th pick overall) of 1992 NFL draft. ... Signed by Rams (July 13, 1992). ... Claimed on waivers by Washington Redskins (August 29, 1994). ... Granted free agency (February 17, 1995). ... Re-signed by Redskins (April 21, 1995). ... Granted unconditional free agency (February 16, 1996). ... Re-signed by Redskins (February 17, 1996). ... On injured reserve with knee injury (October 13, 1996-remainder of season). ... Granted unconditional free agency (February 11, 2000).
PRO STATISTICS: 1993—Recovered one fumble. 1995—Recovered one fumble. 1996—Intercepted one pass for no yards. 1997—Intercepted one pass for 10 yards. 1998—Credited with a safety.

Year Team	G	GS	SACKS
1992—Los Angeles Rams NFL	16	15	1.0
1993—Los Angeles Rams NFL	16	16	1.0
1994—Washington NFL..	9	3	0.0
1995—Washington NFL..	16	16	2.0
1996—Washington NFL..	10	10	0.0
1997—Washington NFL..	16	13	2.0
1998—Washington NFL..	13	1	2.0
1999—Washington NFL..	6	0	1.0
Pro totals (8 years)..	102	74	9.0

BOWDEN, JOE　　　LB　　　COWBOYS

PERSONAL: Born February 25, 1970, in Dallas. ... 5-11/235. ... Full name: Joseph Tarrod Bowden.
HIGH SCHOOL: North Mesquite (Mesquite, Texas).
COLLEGE: Oklahoma.
TRANSACTIONS/CAREER NOTES: Selected by Houston Oilers in fifth round (133rd pick overall) of 1992 NFL draft. ... Signed by Oilers (July 16, 1992). ... Granted free agency (February 17, 1995). ... Re-signed by Oilers (June 6, 1995). ... Granted unconditional free agency (February 16, 1996). ... Re-signed by Oilers (March 4, 1996). ... Oilers franchise moved to Tennessee for 1997 season. ... Oilers franchise renamed Tennessee Titans for 1999 season (December 26, 1998). ... Granted unconditional free agency (February 11, 2000). ... Signed by Dallas Cowboys (May 4, 2000).
CHAMPIONSHIP GAME EXPERIENCE: Played in AFC championship game (1999 season). ... Played in Super Bowl XXXIV (1999 season).
PRO STATISTICS: 1993—Recovered one fumble. 1995—Returned one kickoff for six yards and recovered one fumble. 1997—Recovered one fumble. 1998—Intercepted one pass for one yard and a touchdown and recovered two fumbles for 17 yards and one touchdown. 1999—Intercepted one pass for 29 yards and recovered three fumbles for 11 yards.

Year Team	G	GS	SACKS
1992—Houston NFL	14	0	0.0
1993—Houston NFL	16	6	1.0
1994—Houston NFL	14	1	0.0
1995—Houston NFL	16	14	1.0
1996—Houston NFL	16	16	3.0
1997—Tennessee NFL	16	16	2.5
1998—Tennessee NFL	16	16	1.5
1999—Tennessee NFL	15	15	3.5
Pro totals (8 years)..	123	84	12.5

BOWENS, DAVID　　　DE　　　PACKERS

PERSONAL: Born July 3, 1977, in Denver. ... 6-2/255. ... Full name: David Walter Bowens.
HIGH SCHOOL: St. Mary's (Orchard Lake, Mich.).
COLLEGE: Michigan, then Western Illinois.

TRANSACTIONS/CAREER NOTES: Selected after junior season by Denver Broncos in fifth round (158th pick overall) of 1999 NFL draft. ... Signed by Broncos (July 22, 1999). ... Traded by Broncos to Green Bay Packers for undisclosed draft pick (February 24, 2000).
PRO STATISTICS: 1999—Recovered one fumble.

Year Team	G	GS	SACKS
1999—Denver NFL	16	0	1.0

BOWENS, TIM — DT — DOLPHINS

PERSONAL: Born February 7, 1973, in Okolona, Miss. ... 6-4/315. ... Full name: Timothy L. Bowens.
HIGH SCHOOL: Okolona (Miss.).
JUNIOR COLLEGE: Itawamba Community College (Miss.).
COLLEGE: Mississippi.
TRANSACTIONS/CAREER NOTES: Selected after junior season by Miami Dolphins in first round (20th pick overall) of 1994 NFL draft. ... Signed by Dolphins (June 2, 1994). ... Designated by Dolphins as franchise player (February 13, 1998). ... Re-signed by Dolphins (August 21, 1998). ... On injured reserve with torn biceps muscle (January 3, 1999-remainder of playoffs).
HONORS: Named to play in Pro Bowl (1998 season); replaced by Cortez Kennedy due to injury.
PRO STATISTICS: 1994—Recovered one fumble. 1995—Recovered two fumbles. 1996—Recovered one fumble. 1997—Recovered one fumble in end zone for a touchdown.

Year Team	G	GS	SACKS
1994—Miami NFL	16	15	3.0
1995—Miami NFL	16	16	2.0
1996—Miami NFL	16	16	3.0
1997—Miami NFL	16	16	5.0
1998—Miami NFL	16	16	0.0
1999—Miami NFL	16	15	1.5
Pro totals (6 years)	96	94	14.5

BOWIE, LARRY — FB

PERSONAL: Born March 21, 1973, in Anniston, Ala. ... 6-0/249.
HIGH SCHOOL: Anniston (Ala.).
COLLEGE: Northeast Oklahoma A&M, then Georgia.
TRANSACTIONS/CAREER NOTES: Signed as non-drafted free agent by Washington Redskins (May 1, 1996). ... On injured reserve with leg injury (October 6, 1998-remainder of season). ... Released by Redskins (June 1, 2000).
PRO STATISTICS: 1997—Returned one kickoff for 15 yards and recovered one fumble. 1999—Returned one kickoff for no yards and recovered one fumble.
SINGLE GAME HIGHS (regular season): Attempts—6 (December 7, 1997, vs. Arizona); yards—23 (December 21, 1997, vs. Philadelphia); and rushing touchdowns—1 (December 21, 1997, vs. Philadelphia).

Year Team	G	GS	RUSHING Att.	Yds.	Avg.	TD	RECEIVING No.	Yds.	Avg.	TD	TOTALS TD	2pt.	Pts.	Fum.
1996—Washington NFL	3	0	0	0	0.0	0	3	17	5.7	0	0	0	0	0
1997—Washington NFL	15	13	28	100	3.6	2	34	388	11.4	2	4	0	24	2
1998—Washington NFL	5	4	4	8	2.0	0	7	53	7.6	1	1	0	6	0
1999—Washington NFL	2	0	0	0	0.0	0	0	0	0.0	0	0	0	0	1
Pro totals (4 years)	25	17	32	108	3.4	2	44	458	10.4	3	5	0	30	3

BOWNES, FABIEN — WR — SEAHAWKS

PERSONAL: Born February 29, 1972, in Aurora, Ill. ... 5-11/192. ... Name pronounced FAY-bee-en BOW-ens.
HIGH SCHOOL: Waubonsie Valley (Aurora, Ill.).
COLLEGE: Western Illinois.
TRANSACTIONS/CAREER NOTES: Signed as non-drafted free agent by Chicago Bears (April 27, 1995). ... Released by Bears (August 27, 1995). ... Re-signed by Bears to practice squad (August 29, 1995). ... Activated (December 14, 1995). ... Released by Bears (August 19, 1996). ... Re-signed by Bears to practice squad (October 15, 1996). ... Claimed on waivers by Seattle Seahawks (September 6, 1999). ... Granted free agency (February 11, 2000). ... Re-signed by Seahawks (May 1, 2000).
PRO STATISTICS: 1997—Recovered one fumble. 1999—Rushed once for minus 14 yards.
SINGLE GAME HIGHS (regular season): Receptions—4 (November 2, 1997, vs. Washington); yards—56 (September 27, 1998, vs. Minnesota); and touchdown receptions—1 (September 19, 1999, vs. Chicago).

Year Team	G	GS	RECEIVING No.	Yds.	Avg.	TD	KICKOFF RETURNS No.	Yds.	Avg.	TD	TOTALS TD	2pt.	Pts.	Fum.
1995—Chicago NFL	1	0	0	0	0.0	0	0	0	0.0	0	0	0	0	0
1996—Chicago NFL							Did not play.							
1997—Chicago NFL	16	0	12	146	12.2	0	19	396	20.8	0	0	0	0	0
1998—Chicago NFL	16	0	5	69	13.8	1	1	19	19.0	0	1	0	6	0
1999—Seattle NFL	15	0	4	68	17.0	1	2	40	20.0	0	1	0	6	0
Pro totals (4 years)	48	0	21	283	13.5	2	22	455	20.7	0	2	0	12	0

BOYD, STEPHEN — LB — LIONS

PERSONAL: Born August 22, 1972, in Valley Stream, N.Y. ... 6-0/242. ... Full name: Stephen Gerard Boyd.
HIGH SCHOOL: Valley Stream (N.Y.).
COLLEGE: Boston College (degree in human development).
TRANSACTIONS/CAREER NOTES: Selected by Detroit Lions in fifth round (141st pick overall) of 1995 NFL draft. ... Signed by Lions (July 19, 1995). ... Granted free agency (February 13, 1998). ... Re-signed by Lions (April 17, 1998). ... On injured reserve with shoulder injury

(December 23, 1998-remainder of season). ... Granted unconditional free agency (February 12, 1999). ... Re-signed by Lions (February 23, 1999).
PLAYING EXPERIENCE: Detroit NFL, 1995-1999. ... Games/Games started: 1995 (16/0), 1996 (8/5), 1997 (16/16), 1998 (13/13), 1999 (14/14). Total: 67/48.
HONORS: Named linebacker on THE SPORTING NEWS college All-America first team (1994). ... Played in Pro Bowl (1999 season).
RECORDS: Shares NFL single-game record for most opponents' fumbles recovered—3 (October 4, 1998, vs. Chicago).
PRO STATISTICS: 1997—Intercepted one pass for four yards and recovered one fumble for 42 yards and a touchdown. 1998—Credited with four sacks and recovered four fumbles for one yard. 1999—Intercepted one pass for 18 yards.

BOYER, BRANT — LB — JAGUARS

PERSONAL: Born June 27, 1971, in Ogden, Utah. ... 6-1/232. ... Full name: Brant T. Boyer.
HIGH SCHOOL: North Summit (Coalville, Utah).
JUNIOR COLLEGE: Snow College (Utah).
COLLEGE: Arizona.
TRANSACTIONS/CAREER NOTES: Selected by Miami Dolphins in sixth round (177th pick overall) of 1994 NFL draft. ... Signed by Dolphins (July 11, 1994). ... Released by Dolphins (September 21, 1994). ... Re-signed by Dolphins to practice squad (September 22, 1994). ... Activated (October 5, 1994). ... Selected by Jacksonville Jaguars from Dolphins in NFL expansion draft (February 15, 1995). ... Released by Jaguars (August 27, 1995). ... Re-signed by Jaguars (December 13, 1995). ... Released by Jaguars (August 25, 1996). ... Re-signed by Jaguars (September 24, 1996). ... Released by Jaguars (September 25, 1996). ... Re-signed by Jaguars (September 27, 1996). ... Granted free agency (February 13, 1998). ... Re-signed by Jaguars (March 18, 1998). ... On injured reserve with neck injury (December 2, 1998-remainder of season). ... Granted unconditional free agency (February 12, 1999). ... Re-signed by Jaguars (March 15, 1999).
PLAYING EXPERIENCE: Miami NFL, 1994; Jacksonville NFL, 1995-1999. ... Games/Games started: 1994 (14/0), 1995 (2/0), 1996 (12/0), 1997 (16/2), 1998 (11/0), 1999 (15/0). Total: 70/2.
CHAMPIONSHIP GAME EXPERIENCE: Played in AFC championship game (1996 and 1999 seasons).
PRO STATISTICS: 1997—Credited with 1$^1/_2$ sacks. 1998—Credited with one sack. 1999—Intercepted one pass for five yards and credited with four sacks.

BRACKENS, TONY — DE — JAGUARS

PERSONAL: Born December 26, 1974, in Fairfield, Texas. ... 6-4/257. ... Full name: Tony Lynn Brackens Jr.
HIGH SCHOOL: Fairfield (Texas).
COLLEGE: Texas.
TRANSACTIONS/CAREER NOTES: Selected after junior season by Jacksonville Jaguars in second round (33rd pick overall) of 1996 NFL draft. ... Signed by Jaguars (May 28, 1996). ... Designated by Jaguars as franchise player (February 11, 2000).
CHAMPIONSHIP GAME EXPERIENCE: Played in AFC championship game (1996 and 1999 seasons).
HONORS: Named defensive lineman on THE SPORTING NEWS college All-America first team (1995). ... Played in Pro Bowl (1999 season).
PRO STATISTICS: 1996—Intercepted one pass for 27 yards and recovered three fumbles. 1997—Recovered one fumble. 1998—Recovered three fumbles for eight yards. 1999—Intercepted two passes for 16 yards and one touchdown and recovered two fumbles for six yards.
MISCELLANEOUS: Holds Jacksonville Jaguars all-time record for most sacks (29.5).

Year Team	G	GS	SACKS
1996—Jacksonville NFL	16	1	7.0
1997—Jacksonville NFL	15	3	7.0
1998—Jacksonville NFL	12	8	3.5
1999—Jacksonville NFL	16	15	12.0
Pro totals (4 years)	59	27	29.5

BRADFORD, COREY — WR — PACKERS

PERSONAL: Born December 8, 1975, in Baton Rouge, La. ... 6-1/205. ... Full name: Corey Lamon Bradford.
HIGH SCHOOL: Clinton (La.).
JUNIOR COLLEGE: Hinds Community College (Miss.).
COLLEGE: Jackson State.
TRANSACTIONS/CAREER NOTES: Selected by Green Bay Packers in fifth round (150th pick overall) of 1998 NFL draft. ... Signed by Packers (July 17, 1998).
PRO STATISTICS: 1998—Returned two kickoffs for 33 yards.
SINGLE GAME HIGHS (regular season): Receptions—6 (November 21, 1999, vs. Detroit); yards—106 (November 1, 1999, vs. Seattle); and touchdown receptions—1 (November 29, 1999, vs. San Francisco).
STATISTICAL PLATEAUS: 100-yard receiving games: 1999 (1).

Year Team	G	GS	RECEIVING No.	Yds.	Avg.	TD	TOTALS TD	2pt.	Pts.	Fum.
1998—Green Bay NFL	8	0	3	27	9.0	0	0	0	0	1
1999—Green Bay NFL	16	2	37	637	17.2	5	5	†1	32	1
Pro totals (2 years)	24	2	40	664	16.6	5	5	1	32	2

BRADFORD, RONNIE — CB — FALCONS

PERSONAL: Born October 1, 1970, in Minot, N.D. ... 5-10/198. ... Full name: Ronald L. Bradford.
HIGH SCHOOL: Adams City (Commerce City, Colo.).
COLLEGE: Colorado.
TRANSACTIONS/CAREER NOTES: Selected by Miami Dolphins in fourth round (105th pick overall) of 1993 NFL draft. ... Signed by Dolphins (July 14, 1993). ... Released by Dolphins (August 24, 1993). ... Signed by Denver Broncos to practice squad (September 1, 1993). ... Activated (October 12, 1993). ... On injured reserve with knee injury (September 28, 1995-remainder of season). ... Released by Broncos (August 25,

1996). ... Signed by Arizona Cardinals (August 27, 1996). ... Granted unconditional free agency (February 14, 1997). ... Signed by Atlanta Falcons (April 11, 1997). ... Granted unconditional free agency (February 12, 1999). ... Re-signed by Falcons (March 11, 1999).

CHAMPIONSHIP GAME EXPERIENCE: Played in NFC championship game (1998 season). ... Played in Super Bowl XXXIII (1998 season).

PRO STATISTICS: 1993—Returned one punt for no yards and fumbled once. 1994—Credited with one sack and recovered two fumbles. 1996—Recovered one fumble. 1998—Credited with a safety and recovered one fumble.

			INTERCEPTIONS				TOTALS			
Year Team	G	GS	No.	Yds.	Avg.	TD	TD	2pt.	Pts.	Fum.
1993—Denver NFL	10	3	1	0	0.0	0	0	0	0	1
1994—Denver NFL	12	0	0	0	0.0	0	0	0	0	0
1995—Denver NFL	4	0	0	0	0.0	0	0	0	0	0
1996—Arizona NFL	15	11	1	0	0.0	0	0	0	0	0
1997—Atlanta NFL	16	15	4	9	2.3	0	0	0	0	0
1998—Atlanta NFL	14	10	3	11	3.7	1	1	0	8	0
1999—Atlanta NFL	16	16	0	0	0.0	0	0	0	0	0
Pro totals (7 years)	87	55	9	20	2.2	1	1	0	8	1

B

BRADLEY, MELVIN — LB — CARDINALS

PERSONAL: Born August 15, 1976, in Barton, Ark. ... 6-2/271.
HIGH SCHOOL: Barton (Ark.).
COLLEGE: Arkansas.
TRANSACTIONS/CAREER NOTES: Selected by Arizona Cardinals in sixth round (202nd pick overall) of 1999 NFL draft. ... Signed by Cardinals for 1999 season. ... Released by Cardinals (September 5, 1999). ... Re-signed by Cardinals to practice squad (September 7, 1999). ... Activated (December 15, 1999). ... Assigned by Cardinals to Rhein Fire in 2000 NFL Europe enhancement allocation program (February 18, 2000).
PLAYING EXPERIENCE: Arizona NFL, 1999. ... Games/Games started: 1999 (1/0).

BRADY, JEFF — LB

PERSONAL: Born November 9, 1968, in Cincinnati. ... 6-1/243. ... Full name: Jeffrey Thomas Brady.
HIGH SCHOOL: Newport (Ky.) Central Catholic.
COLLEGE: Kentucky (degree in telecommunications, 1990).
TRANSACTIONS/CAREER NOTES: Selected by Pittsburgh Steelers in 12th round (323rd pick overall) of 1991 NFL draft. ... Signed by Steelers (July 10, 1991). ... Granted unconditional free agency (February 1, 1992). ... Signed by Green Bay Packers (March 30, 1992). ... On injured reserve with knee injury (September 26-November 21, 1992). ... Claimed on waivers by Los Angeles Rams (August 31, 1993). ... Released by Rams (October 20, 1993). ... Signed by San Diego Chargers (October 25, 1993). ... Granted free agency (February 17, 1994). ... Signed by Tampa Bay Buccaneers (May 4, 1994). ... Granted unconditional free agency (February 17, 1995). ... Signed by Minnesota Vikings (April 13, 1995). ... Granted unconditional free agency (February 16, 1996). ... Re-signed by Vikings (February 28, 1996). ... Granted unconditional free agency (February 14, 1997). ... Re-signed by Vikings (March 1, 1997). ... On injured reserve with hamstring injury (December 30, 1997-remainder of playoffs). ... Released by Vikings (February 13, 1998). ... Signed by Carolina Panthers (March 31, 1998). ... Granted unconditional free agency (February 12, 1999). ... Signed by Indianapolis Colts (June 15, 1999). ... On injured reserve with knee injury (October 28, 1999-remainder of season). ... Granted unconditional free agency (February 11, 2000).
PRO STATISTICS: 1993—Recovered one fumble. 1995—Recovered two fumbles. 1996—Recovered three fumbles. 1997—Recovered three fumbles for 30 yards and one touchdown. 1998—Returned one kickoff for eight yards, fumbled once and recovered one fumble.

			INTERCEPTIONS				SACKS
Year Team	G	GS	No.	Yds.	Avg.	TD	No.
1991—Pittsburgh NFL	16	0	0	0	0.0	0	0.0
1992—Green Bay NFL	8	0	0	0	0.0	0	0.0
1993—Los Angeles Rams NFL	6	0	0	0	0.0	0	0.0
—San Diego NFL	3	0	0	0	0.0	0	0.0
1994—Tampa Bay NFL	16	0	0	0	0.0	0	0.0
1995—Minnesota NFL	16	7	2	7	3.5	0	3.0
1996—Minnesota NFL	16	16	3	20	6.7	0	1.5
1997—Minnesota NFL	15	14	0	0	0.0	0	0.0
1998—Carolina NFL	16	16	4	85	21.3	0	4.0
1999—Indianapolis NFL	3	0	0	0	0.0	0	0.0
Pro totals (9 years)	115	53	9	112	12.4	0	8.5

BRADY, KYLE — TE — JAGUARS

PERSONAL: Born January 14, 1972, in New Cumberland, Pa. ... 6-6/274. ... Full name: Kyle James Brady.
HIGH SCHOOL: Cedar Cliff (Camp Hill, Pa.).
COLLEGE: Penn State.
TRANSACTIONS/CAREER NOTES: Selected by New York Jets in first round (ninth pick overall) of 1995 NFL draft. ... Signed by Jets (July 17, 1995). ... Designated by Jets as transition player (February 12, 1999). ... Tendered offer sheet by Jacksonville Jaguars (February 16, 1999). ... Jets declined to match offer (February 18, 1999).
CHAMPIONSHIP GAME EXPERIENCE: Played in AFC championship game (1998 and 1999 seasons).
HONORS: Named tight end on The Sporting News college All-America second team (1994).
PRO STATISTICS: 1995—Returned two kickoffs for 25 yards. 1996—Returned two kickoffs for 26 yards. 1998—Returned one kickoff for 20 yards.
SINGLE GAME HIGHS (regular season): Receptions—5 (October 11, 1999, vs. New York Jets); yards—65 (November 28, 1999, vs. Baltimore); and touchdown receptions—2 (October 19, 1998, vs. New England).

			RECEIVING				TOTALS			
Year Team	G	GS	No.	Yds.	Avg.	TD	TD	2pt.	Pts.	Fum.
1995—New York Jets NFL	15	11	26	252	9.7	2	2	0	12	0
1996—New York Jets NFL	16	16	15	144	9.6	1	1	1	8	1

1997—New York Jets NFL	16	14	22	238	10.8	2	2	0	12	1
1998—New York Jets NFL	16	16	30	315	10.5	5	5	0	30	1
1999—Jacksonville NFL	13	12	32	346	10.8	1	1	†1	8	0
Pro totals (5 years)	76	69	125	1295	10.4	11	11	2	70	3

BRAHAM, RICH — C — BENGALS

PERSONAL: Born November 6, 1970, in Morgantown, W.Va. ... 6-4/305. ... Name pronounced BRAY-um.
HIGH SCHOOL: University (Morgantown, W.Va.).
COLLEGE: West Virginia (degree in finance).
TRANSACTIONS/CAREER NOTES: Selected by Arizona Cardinals in third round (76th pick overall) of 1994 NFL draft. ... Signed by Cardinals (July 30, 1994). ... Claimed on waivers by Cincinnati Bengals (November 18, 1994). ... On injured reserve with ankle injury (August 29, 1995-entire season). ... Granted free agency (February 14, 1997). ... Tendered offer sheet by New England Patriots (April 8, 1997). ... Offer matched by Bengals (April 15, 1997). ... On injured reserve with knee injury (December 3, 1998-remainder of season).
PLAYING EXPERIENCE: Cincinnati NFL, 1994 and 1996-1999. ... Games/Games started: 1994 (3/0), 1996 (16/16), 1997 (16/16), 1998 (12/12), 1999 (16/16). Total: 63/60.
HONORS: Named offensive lineman on THE SPORTING NEWS college All-America second team (1993).
PRO STATISTICS: 1999—Recovered one fumble.

BRANCH, CALVIN — S — RAIDERS

PERSONAL: Born May 8, 1974, in Lexington, Ky. ... 5-11/195. ... Full name: Calvin Stanley Branch.
HIGH SCHOOL: Klein (Spring, Texas).
COLLEGE: Iowa State, then Colorado State.
TRANSACTIONS/CAREER NOTES: Selected by Oakland Raiders in sixth round (172nd pick overall) of 1997 NFL draft. ... Signed by Raiders (July 21, 1997). ... Assigned by Raiders to Barcelona Dragons in 1999 NFL Europe enhancement allocation program (February 22, 1999).
PLAYING EXPERIENCE: Oakland NFL, 1997-1999; Barcelona Dragons NFLE, 1999. ... Games/Games started: 1997 (6/0), 1998 (16/0), NFLE 1999 (games played unavailable), NFL 1999 (16/1). Total NFL: 38/1.
PRO STATISTICS: 1998—Returned five kickoffs for 70 yards, fumbled once and recovered one fumble. 1999—Returned six kickoffs for 96 yards.

BRANDENBURG, DAN — LB — EAGLES

PERSONAL: Born February 16, 1973, in Rensselaer, Ind. ... 6-2/255. ... Full name: Daniel James Brandenburg.
HIGH SCHOOL: Rensselaer (Ind.) Central.
COLLEGE: Indiana State.
TRANSACTIONS/CAREER NOTES: Selected by Buffalo Bills in seventh round (237th pick overall) of 1996 NFL draft. ... Signed by Bills (July 9, 1996). ... Released by Bills (August 20, 1996). ... Re-signed by Bills to practice squad (August 26, 1996). ... Activated (November 22, 1996); did not play. ... Granted unconditional free agency (February 11, 2000). ... Signed by Philadelphia Eagles (March 3, 2000).
PLAYING EXPERIENCE: Buffalo NFL, 1997-1999. ... Games/Games started: 1997 (12/0), 1998 (16/1), 1999 (14/0). Total: 42/1.
PRO STATISTICS: 1997—Recovered one fumble.

BRATZKE, CHAD — DE — COLTS

PERSONAL: Born September 15, 1971, in Brandon, Fla. ... 6-5/275. ... Full name: Chad Allen Bratzke. ... Name pronounced BRAT-ski.
HIGH SCHOOL: Bloomingdale (Valcro, Fla.).
COLLEGE: Eastern Kentucky.
TRANSACTIONS/CAREER NOTES: Selected by New York Giants in fifth round (155th pick overall) of 1994 NFL draft. ... Signed by Giants (July 17, 1994). ... On injured reserve with knee injury (November 12, 1997-remainder of season). ... Granted unconditional free agency (February 12, 1999). ... Signed by Indianapolis Colts (March 1, 1999).
PRO STATISTICS: 1996—Recovered two fumbles. 1997—Recovered two fumbles. 1998—Recovered one fumble. 1999—Fumbled once and recovered one fumble for three yards.

Year Team	G	GS	SACKS
1994—New York Giants NFL	2	0	0.0
1995—New York Giants NFL	6	0	0.0
1996—New York Giants NFL	16	16	5.0
1997—New York Giants NFL	10	10	3.5
1998—New York Giants NFL	16	16	11.0
1999—Indianapolis NFL	16	16	12.0
Pro totals (6 years)	66	58	31.5

BRAXTON, TYRONE — S

PERSONAL: Born December 17, 1964, in Madison, Wis. ... 5-11/190. ... Full name: Tyrone Scott Braxton. ... Related to Jim Braxton, fullback with Buffalo Bills (1971-78) and Miami Dolphins (1978).
HIGH SCHOOL: James Madison Memorial (Madison, Wis.).
COLLEGE: North Dakota State.
TRANSACTIONS/CAREER NOTES: Selected by Denver Broncos in 12th round (334th pick overall) of 1987 NFL draft. ... Signed by Broncos (July 18, 1987). ... On injured reserve with shoulder injury (September 1-December 18, 1987). ... On injured reserve with knee injury (September 25, 1990-remainder of season). ... Granted unconditional free agency (February 17, 1994). ... Signed by Miami Dolphins (May 13, 1994). ... Released by Dolphins (April 20, 1995). ... Signed by Broncos (May 5, 1995). ... Granted unconditional free agency (February 16, 1996). ... Re-signed by Broncos (March 1, 1996). ... Annouced retirement effective at end of season (December 29, 1999). ... Granted unconditional free agency (February 11, 2000).

B

CHAMPIONSHIP GAME EXPERIENCE: Played in AFC championship game (1987, 1989, 1991, 1997 and 1998 seasons). ... Played in Super Bowl XXII (1987 season) and Super Bowl XXIV (1989 season). ... Member of Super Bowl championship team (1997 and 1998 seasons).
HONORS: Played in Pro Bowl (1996 season).
PRO STATISTICS: 1988—Recovered one fumble. 1989—Recovered two fumbles for 35 yards. 1991—Fumbled once and recovered one fumble. 1993—Recovered two fumbles for six yards. 1994—Returned one kickoff for 34 yards. 1996—Recovered one fumble for 20 yards. 1997—Recovered three fumbles for 45 yards.

				INTERCEPTIONS				SACKS
Year Team	G	GS	No.	Yds.	Avg.	TD		No.
1987—Denver NFL	2	0	0	0	0.0	0		0.0
1988—Denver NFL	16	0	2	6	3.0	0		1.0
1989—Denver NFL	16	16	6	103	17.2	1		0.0
1990—Denver NFL	3	2	1	10	10.0	0		0.0
1991—Denver NFL	16	15	4	55	13.8	1		1.0
1992—Denver NFL	16	14	2	54	27.0	0		0.0
1993—Denver NFL	16	16	3	37	12.3	0		0.0
1994—Miami NFL	16	0	2	3	1.5	0		0.0
1995—Denver NFL	16	16	2	36	18.0	0		0.0
1996—Denver NFL	16	16	†9	128	14.2	1		0.0
1997—Denver NFL	16	16	4	113	28.3	1		0.5
1998—Denver NFL	16	6	1	72	72.0	0		0.0
1999—Denver NFL	16	15	0	0	0.0	0		1.0
Pro totals (13 years)	181	132	36	617	17.1	4		3.5

BRAZZELL, CHRIS — WR — COWBOYS

PERSONAL: Born May 22, 1976, in Fort Worth, Texas. ... 6-2/193. ... Name pronounced BRA-zel.
HIGH SCHOOL: Alice (Texas).
JUNIOR COLLEGE: Blinn College (Texas).
COLLEGE: Angelo State (Texas).
TRANSACTIONS/CAREER NOTES: Selected by New York Jets in sixth round (174th pick overall) of 1998 NFL draft. ... Signed by Jets (May 29, 1998). ... Released by Jets (August 30, 1998). ... Re-signed by Jets to practice squad (August 31, 1998). ... Claimed on waivers by Dallas Cowboys (September 6, 1999). ... Released by Cowboys (October 14, 1999). ... Re-signed by Cowboys to practice squad (October 16, 1999). ... Activated (December 10, 1999).
PLAYING EXPERIENCE: Dallas NFL, 1999. ... Games/Games started: 1999 (5/0).
PRO STATISTICS: 1999—Caught five passes for 114 yards.
SINGLE GAME HIGHS (regular season): Receptions—2 (December 19, 1999, vs. New York Jets); yards—62 (December 19, 1999, vs. New York Jets); and touchdown receptions—0.

BRICE, WILL — P — EAGLES

PERSONAL: Born October 24, 1974, in Lancaster, S.C. ... 6-4/220. ... Full name: William Jamison Brice.
HIGH SCHOOL: Lancaster (S.C.).
COLLEGE: Virginia.
TRANSACTIONS/CAREER NOTES: Signed as non-drafted free agent by St. Louis Rams (April 29, 1997). ... Released by Rams (October 12, 1997). ... Signed by New York Giants (February 18, 1998). ... Assigned by Giants to Amsterdam Admirals in 1998 NFL Europe enhancement allocation program (February 18, 1998). ... Released by Giants (August 22, 1998). ... Signed by Green Bay Packers (March 25, 1999). ... Released by Packers (August 25, 1999). ... Signed by Cincinnati Bengals (September 3, 1999). ... Released by Bengals (November 23, 1999). ... Signed by Philadelphia Eagles (April 28, 2000).
PRO STATISTICS: 1999—Recovered one fumble.

				PUNTING			
Year Team	G	No.	Yds.	Avg.	Net avg.	In. 20	Blk.
1997—St. Louis NFL	6	41	1713	41.8	30.5	6	1
1998—Amsterdam NFLE	...	40	1478	37.0	32.5	14	1
1999—Cincinnati NFL	11	60	2475	41.3	32.1	12	†2
NFL Europe totals (1 year)	...	40	1478	37.0	32.5	14	1
NFL totals (2 years)	17	101	4188	41.5	31.5	18	3
Pro totals (3 years)	...	141	5666	40.2	31.7	32	4

BRIEN, DOUG — K — SAINTS

PERSONAL: Born November 24, 1970, in Bloomfield, N.J. ... 6-0/180. ... Full name: Douglas Robert Zachariah Brien.
HIGH SCHOOL: De La Salle Catholic (Concord, Calif.).
COLLEGE: California (degree in political economies).
TRANSACTIONS/CAREER NOTES: Selected by San Francisco 49ers in third round (85th pick overall) of 1994 NFL draft. ... Signed by 49ers (July 27, 1994). ... Released by 49ers (October 16, 1995). ... Signed by New Orleans Saints (October 31, 1995). ... Granted free agency (February 14, 1997). ... Re-signed by Saints (July 17, 1997).
CHAMPIONSHIP GAME EXPERIENCE: Played in NFC championship game (1994 season). ... Member of Super Bowl championship team (1994 season).
POST SEASON RECORDS: Shares Super Bowl single-game record for most extra points—7 (January 29, 1995, vs. San Diego).
PRO STATISTICS: 1998—Punted twice for 72 yards. 1999—Punted once for 20 yards.

				KICKING					
Year Team	G	XPM	XPA	FGM	FGA	Lg.	50+	Pts.
1994—San Francisco NFL	16	*60	*62	15	20	48	0-1	105
1995—San Francisco NFL	6	19	19	7	12	51	1-1	40
—New Orleans NFL	8	16	16	12	17	47	0-1	52

1996—New Orleans NFL	16	18	18	21	25	‡54	3-4	81
1997—New Orleans NFL	16	22	22	23	27	53	4-5	91
1998—New Orleans NFL	16	31	31	20	22	56	4-6	91
1999—New Orleans NFL	16	20	21	24	29	52	2-2	92
Pro totals (6 years)	94	186	189	122	152	56	14-20	552

BRIGANCE, O.J.　　　LB

PERSONAL: Born September 29, 1969, in Houston. ... 6-0/236. ... Full name: Orenthial James Brigance.
HIGH SCHOOL: Willowridge (Sugar Land, Texas).
COLLEGE: Rice (degree in managerial studies).
TRANSACTIONS/CAREER NOTES: Signed by B.C. Lions of CFL (May 1991). ... Granted free agency (February 1994). ... Signed by Baltimore Stallions of CFL (April 1994). ... Granted free agency (February 16, 1996). ... Signed as non-drafted free agent by Miami Dolphins (May 17, 1996). ... Granted free agency (February 12, 1999). ... Re-signed by Dolphins (May 20, 1999). ... On physically unable to perform list with back injury (July 30-August 25, 1999). ... Granted unconditional free agency (February 11, 2000).
PRO STATISTICS: CFL: 1991—Intercepted one pass for seven yards. 1992—Returned five kickoffs for 40 yards and recovered three fumbles. 1993—Recovered one fumble for 27 yards. 1994—Recovered two fumbles. 1995—Intercepted one pass for 13 yards and recovered three fumbles for 10 yards. NFL: 1997—Recovered one fumble.

Year　Team	G	GS	SACKS
1991—British Columbia CFL	18	...	2.0
1992—British Columbia CFL	18	...	0.0
1993—British Columbia CFL	18	...	20.0
1994—Baltimore CFL	18	...	6.0
1995—Baltimore CFL	18	...	7.0
1996—Miami NFL	12	0	0.0
1997—Miami NFL	16	0	0.0
1998—Miami NFL	16	0	0.0
1999—Miami NFL	16	0	0.0
CFL totals (5 years)	90	...	35.0
NFL totals (4 years)	60	0	0.0
Pro totals (9 years)	150	...	35.0

BRIGHAM, JEREMY　　　TE　　　RAIDERS

PERSONAL: Born March 22, 1975, in Boston. ... 6-6/255.
HIGH SCHOOL: Saguara (Scottsdale, Ariz.).
COLLEGE: Washington.
TRANSACTIONS/CAREER NOTES: Selected by Oakland Raiders in fifth round (127th pick overall) of 1998 NFL draft. ... Signed by Raiders (July 18, 1998).
PLAYING EXPERIENCE: Oakland NFL, 1998 and 1999. ... Games/Games started: 1998 (2/0), 1999 (16/2). Total: 18/2.
PRO STATISTICS: 1999—Caught eight passes for 108 yards.
SINGLE GAME HIGHS (regular season): Receptions—2 (September 26, 1999, vs. Chicago); yards—39 (September 19, 1999, vs. Minnesota); and touchdown receptions—0.

BRISBY, VINCENT　　　WR　　　PATRIOTS

PERSONAL: Born January 25, 1971, in Houston. ... 6-3/193. ... Full name: Vincent Cole Brisby.
HIGH SCHOOL: Washington-Marion Magnet (Lake Charles, La.).
COLLEGE: Northeast Louisiana (degree in business administration, 1993).
TRANSACTIONS/CAREER NOTES: Selected by New England Patriots in second round (56th pick overall) of 1993 NFL draft. ... Signed by Patriots (July 30, 1993). ... Granted free agency (February 16, 1996). ... Re-signed by Patriots (May 31, 1996). ... On injured reserve with broken finger and hamstring injury (November 21, 1998-remainder of season).
CHAMPIONSHIP GAME EXPERIENCE: Played in AFC championship game (1996 season). ... Played in Super Bowl XXXI (1996 season).
PRO STATISTICS: 1993—Recovered one fumble.
SINGLE GAME HIGHS (regular season): Receptions—9 (October 1, 1995, vs. Atlanta); yards—161 (October 1, 1995, vs. Atlanta); and touchdown receptions—2 (December 18, 1994, vs. Buffalo).
STATISTICAL PLATEAUS: 100-yard receiving games: 1994 (2), 1995 (3). Total: 5.

			RECEIVING				TOTALS			
Year　Team	G	GS	No.	Yds.	Avg.	TD	TD	2pt.	Pts.	Fum.
1993—New England NFL	16	12	45	626	13.9	2	2	0	12	1
1994—New England NFL	14	11	58	904	15.6	5	5	0	30	1
1995—New England NFL	16	16	66	974	14.8	3	3	0	18	0
1996—New England NFL	3	0	0	0	0.0	0	0	0	0	0
1997—New England NFL	16	4	23	276	12.0	2	2	0	12	0
1998—New England NFL	6	1	7	96	13.7	2	2	0	12	0
1999—New England NFL	12	1	18	266	14.8	0	0	0	0	0
Pro totals (7 years)	83	45	217	3142	14.5	14	14	0	84	2

BRISTER, BUBBY　　　QB　　　VIKINGS

PERSONAL: Born August 15, 1962, in Alexandria, La. ... 6-3/205. ... Full name: Walter Andrew Brister III.
HIGH SCHOOL: Neville (Monroe, La.).
COLLEGE: Tulane, then Northeast Louisiana.
TRANSACTIONS/CAREER NOTES: Selected by Pittsburgh Steelers in third round (67th pick overall) of 1986 NFL draft. ... Selected by New Jersey Generals in 11th round (80th pick overall) of 1986 USFL draft; did not sign. ... Signed by Steelers (July 25, 1986). ... Granted free

agency (February 1, 1992). ... Re-signed by Steelers (June 16, 1992). ... Released by Steelers (June 4, 1993). ... Signed by Philadelphia Eagles (July 19, 1993). ... Granted unconditional free agency (February 17, 1994). ... Re-signed by Eagles (April 6, 1994). ... Granted unconditional free agency (February 17, 1995). ... Released by New York Jets (March 17, 1995). ... Released by Jets (February 29, 1996). ... Signed by Denver Broncos (April 7, 1997). ... Released by Broncos (March 29, 2000). ... Signed by Minnesota Vikings (April 5, 2000).

CHAMPIONSHIP GAME EXPERIENCE: Member of Broncos for AFC championship game (1997 season); did not play. ... Member of Super Bowl championship team (1997 season); did not play. ... Member of Broncos for AFC championship game (1998 season); did not play. ... Member of Super Bowl championship team (1998 season).

PRO STATISTICS: 1986—Fumbled once. 1988—Recovered two fumbles. 1989—Caught one pass for minus 10 yards, fumbled eight times and recovered one fumble. 1990—Fumbled nine times. 1991—Fumbled four times and recovered two fumbles. 1992—Fumbled twice and recovered two fumbles for minus two yards. 1993—Fumbled three times. 1995—Caught one pass for two yards, fumbled four times and recovered three fumbles for minus nine yards. 1998—Fumbled twice and recovered one fumble for minus one yard.

SINGLE GAME HIGHS (regular season): Attempts—48 (December 12, 1993, vs. Buffalo); completions—28 (December 12, 1993, vs. Buffalo); yards—353 (October 14, 1990, vs. Denver); and touchdown passes—4 (October 4, 1998, vs. Philadelphia).

STATISTICAL PLATEAUS: 300-yard passing games: 1988 (2), 1993 (1), 1994 (1). Total: 4.

MISCELLANEOUS: Regular-season record as starting NFL quarterback: 37-38 (.493). ... Postseason record as starting NFL quarterback: 1-1 (.500).

Year Team	G	GS	Att.	Cmp.	Pct.	Yds.	TD	Int.	Avg.	Rat.	Att.	Yds.	Avg.	TD	TD	2pt.	Pts.
					PASSING							RUSHING				TOTALS	
1986—Pittsburgh NFL........	2	2	60	21	35.0	291	0	2	4.85	37.6	6	10	1.7	1	1	0	6
1987—Pittsburgh NFL........	2	0	12	4	33.3	20	0	3	1.67	2.8	0	0	0.0	0	0	0	0
1988—Pittsburgh NFL........	13	13	370	175	47.3	2634	11	14	7.12	65.3	45	209	4.6	6	6	0	36
1989—Pittsburgh NFL........	14	14	342	187	54.7	2365	9	10	6.92	73.1	27	25	0.9	0	0	0	0
1990—Pittsburgh NFL........	16	16	387	223	57.6	2725	20	14	7.04	81.6	25	64	2.6	0	0	0	0
1991—Pittsburgh NFL........	8	8	190	103	54.2	1350	9	9	7.11	72.9	11	17	1.5	0	0	0	0
1992—Pittsburgh NFL........	6	4	116	63	54.3	719	2	5	6.20	61.0	10	16	1.6	0	0	0	0
1993—Philadelphia NFL	10	8	309	181	58.6	1905	14	5	6.17	84.9	20	39	2.0	0	0	0	0
1994—Philadelphia NFL	7	2	76	51	67.1	507	2	1	6.67	89.1	1	7	7.0	0	0	0	0
1995—New York Jets NFL ...	9	4	170	93	54.7	726	4	8	4.27	53.7	16	18	1.1	0	0	0	0
1997—Denver NFL	1	0	9	6	66.7	48	0	0	5.33	79.9	4	2	0.5	0	0	0	0
1998—Denver NFL	7	4	131	78	59.5	986	10	3	7.53	99.0	19	102	5.4	1	1	0	6
1999—Denver NFL	2	0	20	12	60.0	87	0	3	4.35	30.6	2	17	8.5	0	0	0	0
Pro totals (13 years)..........	97	75	2192	1197	54.6	14363	81	77	6.55	72.6	186	526	2.8	8	8	0	48

RECORD AS BASEBALL PLAYER

TRANSACTIONS/CAREER NOTES: Threw right, batted right. ... Selected by Detroit Tigers organization in fourth round of free-agent draft (June 8, 1981). ... On suspended list (June 22, 1982-entire season). ... Placed on restricted list (October 7, 1982).

Year Team (League)	Pos.	G	AB	R	H	2B	3B	HR	RBI	Avg.	BB	SO	SB	PO	A	E	Avg.
						BATTING									FIELDING		
1981—Bristol (Appal.)	OF-SS	39	111	12	20	7	0	0	10	.180	16	27	5	46	11	9	.864
1982—................................						Did not play.											

BROCKERMEYER, BLAKE   OT   BEARS

PERSONAL: Born April 11, 1973, in Fort Worth, Texas. ... 6-4/312. ... Full name: Blake Weeks Brockermeyer.
HIGH SCHOOL: Arlington Heights (Texas).
COLLEGE: Texas.
TRANSACTIONS/CAREER NOTES: Selected after junior season by Carolina Panthers in first round (29th pick overall) of 1995 NFL draft. ... Signed by Panthers (July 14, 1995). ... Granted unconditional free agency (February 12, 1999). ... Signed by Chicago Bears (February 27, 1999).
PLAYING EXPERIENCE: Carolina NFL, 1995-1998; Chicago NFL, 1999. ... Games/Games started: 1995 (16/16), 1996 (12/12), 1997 (16/13), 1998 (14/14), 1999 (15/15). Total: 73/70.
CHAMPIONSHIP GAME EXPERIENCE: Played in NFC championship game (1996 season).
HONORS: Named offensive lineman on THE SPORTING NEWS college All-America first team (1994).
PRO STATISTICS: 1998—Recovered two fumbles.

BROMELL, LORENZO   DE   DOLPHINS

PERSONAL: Born September 23, 1975, in Georgetown, S.C. ... 6-6/270. ... Full name: Lorenzo Alexis Bromell.
HIGH SCHOOL: Choppee (Georgetown, S.C.).
JUNIOR COLLEGE: Georgia Military College.
COLLEGE: Clemson.
TRANSACTIONS/CAREER NOTES: Selected by Miami Dolphins in fourth round (102nd pick overall) of 1998 draft. ... Signed by Dolphins (July 10, 1998).
PRO STATISTICS: 1998—Recovered one fumble.

Year Team	G	GS	SACKS
1998—Miami NFL...	14	0	8.0
1999—Miami NFL...	15	1	5.0
Pro totals (2 years)	29	1	13.0

BRONSON, ZACK   S   49ERS

PERSONAL: Born January 28, 1974, in Jasper, Texas. ... 6-1/195. ... Full name: Robert Bronson.
HIGH SCHOOL: Jasper (Texas).
COLLEGE: McNeese State.

TRANSACTIONS/CAREER NOTES: Signed as non-drafted free agent by San Francisco 49ers (May 2, 1997). ... On injured reserve with foot injury (December 29, 1999-remainder of season). ... Granted free agency (February 11, 2000).
CHAMPIONSHIP GAME EXPERIENCE: Played in NFC championship game (1997 season).
PRO STATISTICS: 1997—Recovered one fumble for three yards.

			INTERCEPTIONS			
Year Team	G	GS	No.	Yds.	Avg.	TD
1997—San Francisco NFL	16	0	1	22	22.0	0
1998—San Francisco NFL	11	0	4	34	8.5	0
1999—San Francisco NFL	15	2	0	0	0.0	0
Pro totals (3 years)	42	2	5	56	11.2	0

BROOKING, KEITH — LB — FALCONS

PERSONAL: Born October 30, 1975, in Senoia, Ga. ... 6-2/245. ... Full name: Keith Howard Brooking.
HIGH SCHOOL: East Coweta (Sharpsburg, Ga.).
COLLEGE: Georgia Tech.
TRANSACTIONS/CAREER NOTES: Selected by Atlanta Falcons in first round (12th pick overall) of 1998 NFL draft. ... Signed by Falcons (June 29, 1998).
PLAYING EXPERIENCE: Atlanta NFL, 1998 and 1999. ... Games/Games started: 1998 (15/0), 1999 (13/13). Total: 28/13.
CHAMPIONSHIP GAME EXPERIENCE: Played in NFC championship game (1998 season). ... Played in Super Bowl XXXIII (1998 season).
PRO STATISTICS: 1998—Intercepted one pass for 12 yards. 1999—Credited with two sacks.

BROOKS, AARON — QB — PACKERS

PERSONAL: Born March 24, 1976, in Newport News, Va. ... 6-4/205. ... Full name: Aaron Lafette Brooks.
HIGH SCHOOL: Homer L. Ferguson (Newport News, Va.).
COLLEGE: Virginia (degree in anthropology).
TRANSACTIONS/CAREER NOTES: Selected by Green Bay Packers in fourth round (131st pick overall) of 1999 NFL draft. ... Signed by Packers (July 27, 1999).
PLAYING EXPERIENCE: Green Bay NFL, 1999. ... Games/Games started: 1999 (1/0).

BROOKS, BARRETT — OT — LIONS

PERSONAL: Born May 5, 1972, in St. Louis. ... 6-4/326.
HIGH SCHOOL: McCluer North (Florissant, Mo.).
COLLEGE: Kansas State.
TRANSACTIONS/CAREER NOTES: Selected by Philadelphia Eagles in second round (58th pick overall) of 1995 NFL draft. ... Signed by Eagles (July 19, 1995). ... Granted free agency (February 13, 1998). ... Re-signed by Eagles (April 21, 1998). ... Granted unconditional free agency (February 12, 1999). ... Signed by Detroit Lions (April 12, 1999).
PLAYING EXPERIENCE: Philadelphia NFL, 1995-1998; Detroit NFL, 1999. ... Games/Games started: 1995 (16/16), 1996 (16/15), 1997 (16/14), 1998 (16/1), 1999 (16/12). Total: 80/58.
PRO STATISTICS: 1996—Returned one kickoff for no yards and recovered one fumble. 1997—Recovered two fumbles. 1998—Returned one kickoff for seven yards.

BROOKS, BOBBY — LB — RAIDERS

PERSONAL: Born March 3, 1976, in Vallejo, Calif. ... 6-2/235.
HIGH SCHOOL: Hogan (Vallejo, Calif.).
COLLEGE: Fresno State.
TRANSACTIONS/CAREER NOTES: Signed as non-drafted free agent by Oakland Raiders (April 1999). ... Released by Raiders (September 5, 1999). ... Re-signed by Raiders to practice squad (October 20, 1999). ... Activated (December 1999).
PLAYING EXPERIENCE: Oakland NFL, 1999 ... Games/Games started: 1999 (1/0).

BROOKS, DERRICK — LB — BUCCANEERS

PERSONAL: Born April 18, 1973, in Pensacola, Fla. ... 6-0/235. ... Full name: Derrick Dewan Brooks.
HIGH SCHOOL: Booker T. Washington (Pensacola, Fla.).
COLLEGE: Florida State (degree in communications, 1994).
TRANSACTIONS/CAREER NOTES: Selected by Tampa Bay Buccaneers in first round (28th pick overall) of 1995 NFL draft. ... Signed by Buccaneers (May 3, 1995).
CHAMPIONSHIP GAME EXPERIENCE: Played in NFC championship game (1999 season).
HONORS: Named linebacker on The Sporting News college All-America first team (1993 and 1994). ... Played in Pro Bowl (1997-1999 seasons). ... Named linebacker on The Sporting News NFL All-Pro team (1999).
PRO STATISTICS: 1997—Fumbled once and recovered one fumble. 1999—Recovered two fumbles for four yards.

			INTERCEPTIONS				SACKS
Year Team	G	GS	No.	Yds.	Avg.	TD	No.
1995—Tampa Bay NFL	16	13	0	0	0.0	0	1.0
1996—Tampa Bay NFL	16	16	1	6	6.0	0	0.0
1997—Tampa Bay NFL	16	16	2	13	6.5	0	1.5
1998—Tampa Bay NFL	16	16	1	25	25.0	0	0.0
1999—Tampa Bay NFL	16	16	4	61	15.3	0	2.0
Pro totals (5 years)	80	77	8	105	13.1	0	4.5

BROOKS, MACEY   WR   BEARS

PERSONAL: Born February 2, 1975, in Hampton, Va. ... 6-5/215. ... Full name: Barry Macey Brooks.
HIGH SCHOOL: Kecoughtan (Hampton, Va.).
COLLEGE: James Madison.
TRANSACTIONS/CAREER NOTES: Selected by Dallas Cowboys in fourth round (127th pick overall) of 1997 NFL draft. ... Signed by Cowboys (July 14, 1997). ... On injured reserve with arm injury (August 27, 1997-entire season). ... Released by Cowboys (August 30, 1998). ... Signed by Chicago Bears to practice squad (September 1, 1998). ... Activated (October 7, 1998); did not play. ... On injured reserve with knee injury (November 10, 1999-remainder of season). ... Granted free agency (February 11, 2000). ... Re-signed by Bears (April 17, 2000).
PLAYING EXPERIENCE: Chicago NFL, 1999. ... Games/Games started: 1999 (9/2).
PRO STATISTICS: 1999—Rushed once for seven yards, caught 14 passes for 160 yards and recovered one fumble.
SINGLE GAME HIGHS (regular season): Receptions—3 (October 24, 1999, vs. Tampa Bay); yards—51 (September 26, 1999, vs. Oakland); and touchdown receptions—0.
MISCELLANEOUS: Selected by San Francisco Giants organization in second round of free-agent draft (June 2, 1993); did not sign. ... Selected by Kansas City Royals organization in 55th round of free-agent draft (June 4, 1996); did not sign.

BROUGHTON, LUTHER   TE   EAGLES

PERSONAL: Born November 30, 1974, in Charleston, S.C. ... 6-2/248. ... Full name: Luther Rashard Broughton Jr.
HIGH SCHOOL: Cainhoy (Huger, S.C.).
COLLEGE: Furman.
TRANSACTIONS/CAREER NOTES: Selected by Philadelphia Eagles in fifth round (155th pick overall) of 1997 NFL draft. ... Signed by Eagles (July 15, 1997). ... Active for one game with Eagles (1997); did not play. ... Released by Eagles (November 5, 1997). ... Re-signed by Eagles to practice squad (November 5, 1997). ... Signed by Carolina Panthers from Eagles practice squad (December 15, 1997). ... Inactive for one game with Panthers (1997). ... Traded by Panthers to Philadelphia Eagles for undisclosed draft pick (September 5, 1999). ... Granted free agency (February 11, 2000). ... Re-signed by Eagles (April 10, 2000).
PRO STATISTICS: 1998—Recovered one fumble. 1999—Returned one kickoff for five yards and recovered one fumble.
SINGLE GAME HIGHS (regular season): Receptions—4 (November 21, 1999, vs. Indianapolis); yards—78 (December 20, 1998, vs. St. Louis); and touchdown receptions—2 (November 28, 1999, vs. Washington).

| | | | RECEIVING | | | | TOTALS | | | |
Year Team	G	GS	No.	Yds.	Avg.	TD	TD	2pt.	Pts.	Fum.
1997—Philadelphia NFL						Did not play.				
1998—Carolina NFL	16	4	6	142	23.7	1	1	0	6	1
1999—Philadelphia NFL	16	3	26	295	11.3	4	4	0	24	0
Pro totals (2 years)	32	7	32	437	13.7	5	5	0	30	1

BROWN, ANTHONY   OT   STEELERS

PERSONAL: Born November 6, 1972, in Okinawa, Japan. ... 6-5/315.
HIGH SCHOOL: American (Wurzburg, West Germany).
COLLEGE: Utah.
TRANSACTIONS/CAREER NOTES: Signed as non-drafted free agent by Cincinnati Bengals (April 26, 1995). ... Granted free agency (February 13, 1998). ... Re-signed by Bengals (April 13, 1998). ... Granted unconditional free agency (February 12, 1999). ... Signed by Pittsburgh Steelers (April 23, 1999).
PLAYING EXPERIENCE: Cincinnati NFL, 1995-1998; Pittsburgh NFL, 1999. ... Games/Games started: 1995 (7/1), 1996 (7/0), 1997 (6/0), 1998 (16/5), 1999 (16/11). Total: 52/17.

BROWN, CHAD   LB   SEAHAWKS

PERSONAL: Born July 12, 1970, in Altadena, Calif. ... 6-2/240. ... Full name: Chadwick Everett Brown.
HIGH SCHOOL: John Muir (Pasadena, Calif.).
COLLEGE: Colorado (degree in marketing, 1992).
TRANSACTIONS/CAREER NOTES: Selected by Pittsburgh Steelers in second round (44th pick overall) of 1993 NFL draft. ... Signed by Steelers (July 26, 1993). ... Granted unconditional free agency (February 14, 1997). ... Signed by Seattle Seahawks (February 15, 1997).
CHAMPIONSHIP GAME EXPERIENCE: Played in AFC championship game (1994 and 1995 seasons). ... Played in Super Bowl XXX (1995 season).
HONORS: Named linebacker on THE SPORTING NEWS NFL All-Pro team (1996 and 1998). ... Played in Pro Bowl (1996, 1998 and 1999 seasons).
PRO STATISTICS: 1996—Fumbled once and recovered two fumbles. 1997—Recovered four fumbles for 68 yards and two touchdowns. 1998—Recovered one fumble. 1999—Recovered one fumble.

| | | | INTERCEPTIONS | | | | SACKS |
Year Team	G	GS	No.	Yds.	Avg.	TD	No.
1993—Pittsburgh NFL	16	9	0	0	0.0	0	3.0
1994—Pittsburgh NFL	16	16	1	9	9.0	0	8.5
1995—Pittsburgh NFL	10	10	0	0	0.0	0	5.5
1996—Pittsburgh NFL	14	14	2	20	10.0	0	13.0
1997—Seattle NFL	15	15	0	0	0.0	0	6.5
1998—Seattle NFL	16	16	1	11	11.0	0	7.5
1999—Seattle NFL	15	15	0	0	0.0	0	5.5
Pro totals (7 years)	102	95	4	40	10.0	0	49.5

BROWN, CORNELL — LB — RAVENS

PERSONAL: Born March 15, 1975, in Englewood, N.J. ... 6-0/240. ... Full name: Cornell Desmond Brown. ... Brother of Ruben Brown, guard, Buffalo Bills.
HIGH SCHOOL: E.C. Glass (Lynchburg, Va.).
COLLEGE: Virginia Tech.
TRANSACTIONS/CAREER NOTES: Selected by Baltimore Ravens in sixth round (194th pick overall) of 1997 NFL draft. ... Signed by Ravens (July 10, 1997). ... Granted free agency (February 11, 2000). ... Re-signed by Ravens (April 25, 2000)
PLAYING EXPERIENCE: Baltimore NFL, 1997-1999. ... Games/Games started: 1997 (16/1), 1998 (16/1), 1999 (16/5). Total: 48/7.
HONORS: Named defensive lineman on THE SPORTING NEWS college All-America first team (1995).
PRO STATISTICS: 1997—Intercepted one pass for 21 yards and credited with ½ sack. 1999—Credited with one sack.

BROWN, CORWIN — S — LIONS

B

PERSONAL: Born April 25, 1970, in Chicago. ... 6-1/205. ... Full name: Corwin Alan Brown.
HIGH SCHOOL: Percy L. Julian (Chicago).
COLLEGE: Michigan (degree in English).
TRANSACTIONS/CAREER NOTES: Selected by New England Patriots in fourth round (110th pick overall) of 1993 NFL draft. ... Signed by Patriots (July 16, 1993). ... Granted free agency (February 16, 1996). ... Re-signed by Patriots (February 27, 1996). ... Released by Patriots (August 24, 1997). ... Signed by New York Jets (August 25, 1997). ... Released by Jets (September 5, 1999). ... Signed by Detroit Lions (October 4, 1999). ... Granted unconditional free agency (February 11, 2000). ... Re-signed by Lions (April 25, 2000).
PLAYING EXPERIENCE: New England NFL, 1993-1996; New York Jets NFL, 1997 and 1998; Detroit NFL, 1999. ... Games/Games started: 1993 (15/12), 1994 (16/0), 1995 (16/2), 1996 (14/0), 1997 (16/0), 1998 (16/1), 1999 (13/1). Total: 106/16.
CHAMPIONSHIP GAME EXPERIENCE: Played in AFC championship game (1996 and 1998 seasons). ... Played in Super Bowl XXXI (1996 season).
PRO STATISTICS: 1993—Recovered one fumble. 1995—Recovered one fumble. 1996—Recovered one fumble for 42 yards and a touchdown. 1997—Caught one pass for 26 yards. 1998—Intercepted one pass for no yards and recovered one fumble for 16 yards.

BROWN, CYRON — DE — BRONCOS

PERSONAL: Born June 28, 1975, in Chicago ... 6-5/275. ... Full name: Cyron DeAndre Brown. ... Name pronounced SY-ron.
HIGH SCHOOL: Lane Tech (Chicago).
COLLEGE: Illinois, then Western Illinois.
TRANSACTIONS/CAREER NOTES: Signed as non-drafted free agent by Denver Broncos (May 1, 1998). ... On suspended list for violating league substance abuse policy (October 29-November 22, 1999).
PLAYING EXPERIENCE: Denver NFL, 1998 and 1999. ... Games/Games started: 1998 (4/0), 1999 (7/0). Total: 11/0.
CHAMPIONSHIP GAME EXPERIENCE: Member of Broncos for AFC championship game (1998 season); inactive. ... Member of Super Bowl championship team (1998 season); inactive.

BROWN, DAVE — QB — CARDINALS

PERSONAL: Born February 25, 1970, in Summit, N.J. ... 6-6/225. ... Full name: David Michael Brown.
HIGH SCHOOL: Westfield (N.J.).
COLLEGE: Duke (degrees in history and political science, 1992).
TRANSACTIONS/CAREER NOTES: Selected by New York Giants in first round of 1992 NFL supplemental draft. ... Signed by Giants (August 12, 1992). ... On injured reserve with thumb injury (December 18, 1992-remainder of season). ... Granted unconditional free agency (February 16, 1996). ... Re-signed by Giants (May 3, 1996). ... Released by Giants (February 20, 1998). ... Signed by Arizona Cardinals (April 29, 1998). ... Granted unconditional free agency (February 11, 2000). ... Re-signed by Cardinals (February 23, 2000).
PRO STATISTICS: 1994—Punted twice for 57 yards, fumbled 11 times and recovered four fumbles for minus 15 yards. 1995—Punted once for 15 yards, fumbled 10 times and recovered two fumbles for minus eight yards. 1996—Fumbled nine times and recovered one fumble for minus three yards. 1997—Fumbled once. 1999—Fumbled four times and recovered one fumble.
SINGLE GAME HIGHS (regular season): Attempts—50 (September 17, 1995, vs. Green Bay); completions—28 (September 14, 1997, vs. Baltimore); yards—299 (November 5, 1995, vs. Seattle); and touchdown passes—2 (September 28, 1997, vs. New Orleans).
MISCELLANEOUS: Regular-season record as starting NFL quarterback: 26-32 (.448).

Year Team	G	GS	Att.	Cmp.	Pct.	Yds.	TD	Int.	Avg.	Rat.	Att.	Yds.	Avg.	TD	TD	2pt.	Pts.
					PASSING							RUSHING				TOTALS	
1992—N.Y. Giants NFL	2	0	7	4	57.1	21	0	0	3.00	62.2	2	-1	-0.5	0	0	0	0
1993—N.Y. Giants NFL	1	0	0	0	0.0	0	0	0	0.0	...	3	-4	-1.3	0	0	0	0
1994—N.Y. Giants NFL	15	15	350	201	57.4	2536	12	16	7.25	72.5	60	196	3.3	2	2	0	12
1995—N.Y. Giants NFL	16	16	456	254	55.7	2814	11	10	6.17	73.1	45	228	5.1	4	4	0	24
1996—N.Y. Giants NFL	16	16	398	214	53.8	2412	12	20	6.06	61.3	50	170	3.4	0	0	0	0
1997—N.Y. Giants NFL	8	6	180	93	51.7	1023	5	3	5.68	71.1	17	29	1.7	1	1	0	6
1998—Arizona NFL	1	0	5	2	40.0	31	0	0	6.20	61.3	1	2	2.0	0	0	0	0
1999—Arizona NFL	8	5	169	84	49.7	944	2	6	5.59	55.9	13	49	3.8	0	0	0	0
Pro totals (8 years)	67	58	1565	852	54.4	9781	42	55	6.25	67.8	191	669	3.5	7	7	0	42

BROWN, DEREK — TE — CARDINALS

PERSONAL: Born March 31, 1970, in Fairfax, Va. ... 6-6/271. ... Full name: Derek Vernon Brown.
HIGH SCHOOL: Merritt Island (Fla.).
COLLEGE: Notre Dame.
TRANSACTIONS/CAREER NOTES: Selected by New York Giants in first round (14th pick overall) of 1992 NFL draft. ... Signed by Giants (July 29, 1992). ... Selected by Jacksonville Jaguars from Giants in NFL expansion draft (February 15, 1995). ... Inactive for six games (1995). ...

On injured reserve with rib injury (October 10, 1995-remainder of season). ... Granted unconditional free agency (February 14, 1997). ... Re-signed by Jaguars (February 26, 1997). ... Granted unconditional free agency (February 13, 1998). ... Signed by Oakland Raiders (May 13, 1998). ... Granted unconditional free agency (February 12, 1999). ... Signed by Arizona Cardinals (July 1, 1999). ... Granted unconditional free agency (February 11, 2000). ... Re-signed by Cardinals (April 28, 2000)

CHAMPIONSHIP GAME EXPERIENCE: Played in AFC championship game (1996 season).

PRO STATISTICS: 1994—Returned one kickoff for one yard and recovered one fumble. 1998—Recovered one fumble.

SINGLE GAME HIGHS (regular season): Receptions—3 (November 22, 1998, vs. Denver); yards—38 (November 22, 1998, vs. Denver); and touchdown receptions—1 (October 19, 1997, vs. Dallas).

				RECEIVING			TOTALS			
Year Team	G	GS	No.	Yds.	Avg.	TD	TD	2pt.	Pts.	Fum.
1992—New York Giants NFL	16	7	4	31	7.8	0	0	0	0	0
1993—New York Giants NFL	16	0	7	56	8.0	0	0	0	0	0
1994—New York Giants NFL	13	0	0	0	0.0	0	0	0	0	0
1995—Jacksonville NFL						Did not play.				
1996—Jacksonville NFL	16	14	17	141	8.3	0	0	0	0	0
1997—Jacksonville NFL	13	7	8	84	10.5	1	1	0	6	0
1998—Oakland NFL	16	4	7	89	12.7	0	0	0	0	0
1999—Arizona NFL	15	0	0	0	0.0	0	0	0	0	0
Pro totals (7 years)	105	32	43	401	9.3	1	1	0	6	0

BROWN, DOUG   DT   REDSKINS

PERSONAL: Born September 29, 1974, in New Westminster, B.C. ... 6-7/290.
HIGH SCHOOL: Port Moody (B.C.) Senior Secondary.
COLLEGE: Simon Fraser (B.C.).
TRANSACTIONS/CAREER NOTES: Signed as non-drafted free agent by Buffalo Bills (May 20, 1997). ... Released by Bills (August 24, 1997). ... Re-signed by Bills to practice squad (August 26, 1997). ... Granted free agency after 1997 season. ... Signed by Washington Redskins (February 17, 1998).
PLAYING EXPERIENCE: Washington NFL, 1998 and 1999. ... Games/Games started: 1998 (10/8), 1999 (10/0). Total: 20/8.
PRO STATISTICS: 1999—Recovered one fumble.

BROWN, ERIC   S   BRONCOS

PERSONAL: Born March 20, 1975, in San Antonio. ... 6-0/210. ... Full name: Eric Jon Brown.
HIGH SCHOOL: Judson (Converse, Texas).
JUNIOR COLLEGE: Blinn College (Texas).
COLLEGE: Mississippi State.
TRANSACTIONS/CAREER NOTES: Selected by Denver Broncos in second round (61st pick overall) of 1998 NFL draft. ... Signed by Broncos (July 16, 1998). ... On injured reserve with knee injury (November 19, 1999-remainder of season).
PLAYING EXPERIENCE: Denver NFL, 1998 and 1999. ... Games/Games started: 1998 (11/10), 1999 (10/10). Total: 21/20.
CHAMPIONSHIP GAME EXPERIENCE: Member of Broncos for AFC championship game (1998 season); inactive. ... Member of Super Bowl championship team (1998 season); inactive.
PRO STATISTICS: 1998—Recovered one fumble. 1999—Intercepted one pass for 13 yards, credited with $1\frac{1}{2}$ sacks, fumbled twice and recovered one fumble.

BROWN, ERNIE   DL   STEELERS

PERSONAL: Born March 14, 1971, in Pittsburgh. ... 6-3/295. ... Full name: Ernie Davis Brown.
HIGH SCHOOL: North Catholic (Pittsburgh).
COLLEGE: Syracuse.
TRANSACTIONS/CAREER NOTES: Signed as non-drafted free agent by Detroit Lions (April 29, 1994). ... Released by Lions (August 24, 1994). ... Signed by Sasketchewan Roughriders of CFL (February 22, 1996). ... Released by Roughriders (September 7, 1996). ... Signed by Calgary Stampeders of CFL (September 11, 1996). ... Released by Stampeders (October 25, 1997). ... Signed by Roughriders (May 12, 1998). ... Signed by Pittsburgh Steelers (February 3, 1999). ... Released by Steelers (September 5, 1999). ... Re-signed by Steelers to practice squad (September 6, 1999). ... Activated (December 14, 1999). ... Assigned by Steelers to Rhein Fire in 2000 NFL Europe enhancement allocation program (February 18, 2000).

Year Team	G	GS	SACKS
1996—Saskatchewan CFL	3	...	0.0
—Calgary CFL	6	...	1.0
1997—Calgary CFL	15	...	2.0
1998—Saskatchewan CFL	14	...	7.0
1999—Pittsburgh NFL	3	0	0.0
CFL totals (3 years)	38	...	10.0
NFL totals (1 year)	3	0	0.0
Pro totals (4 years)	41	...	10.0

BROWN, FAKHIR   CB   CHARGERS

PERSONAL: Born September 21, 1977, in Detroit. ... 5-11/192. ... Full name: Fakhir Hamin Brown. ... Name pronounced fah-KEAR.
HIGH SCHOOL: Mansfield (La.).
COLLEGE: Grambling State.
TRANSACTIONS/CAREER NOTES: Signed by Toronto Argonauts of CFL (April 6, 1998). ... Signed as non-drafted free agent by San Diego Chargers (April 20, 1999). ... Released by Chargers (September 4, 1999). ... Re-signed by Chargers to practice squad (September 7, 1999). ... Activated (October 9, 1999). ... Released by Chragers (October 15, 1999). ... Re-signed by Chargers to practice squad (October 16, 1999). ... Activated (October 22, 1999).

B

PLAYING EXPERIENCE: Toronto CFL, 1998; San Diego NFL, 1999. ... Games/Games started: 1998 (6/games started unavailable), 1999 (9/3).
PRO STATISTICS: CFL: 1998—Intercepted one pass for no yards.

BROWN, GARY   RB

PERSONAL: Born July 1, 1969, in Williamsport, Pa. ... 5-11/230. ... Full name: Gary Leroy Brown.
HIGH SCHOOL: Williamsport (Pa.) Area.
COLLEGE: Penn State.
TRANSACTIONS/CAREER NOTES: Selected by Houston Oilers in eighth round (214th pick overall) of 1991 NFL draft. ... Signed by Oilers (July 15, 1991). ... Granted free agency (February 17, 1994). ... Re-signed by Oilers (July 15, 1994). ... Released by Oilers (April 19, 1996). ... Signed by San Diego Chargers (February 24, 1997). ... Granted unconditional free agency (February 13, 1998). ... Signed by New York Giants (April 21, 1998). ... On non-football injury list with knee injury (July 31, 1999-September 12, 1999). ... On injured reserve with knee injury (October 26, 1999-remainder of season). ... Released by Giants (February 11, 2000).
PRO STATISTICS: 1992—Recovered one fumble. 1993—Recovered two fumbles for four yards. 1995—Recovered one fumble. 1998—Recovered one fumble.
SINGLE GAME HIGHS (regular season): Attempts—36 (October 5, 1997, vs. Oakland); yards—194 (November 21, 1993, vs. Cleveland); and rushing touchdowns—2 (September 11, 1994, vs. Dallas).
STATISTICAL PLATEAUS: 100-yard rushing games: 1993 (5), 1995 (1), 1997 (2), 1998 (6). Total: 14.

			RUSHING				RECEIVING				KICKOFF RETURNS				TOTALS			
Year Team	G	GS	Att.	Yds.	Avg.	TD	No.	Yds.	Avg.	TD	No.	Yds.	Avg.	TD	TD	2pt.	Pts.	Fum.
1991—Houston NFL	11	0	8	85	10.6	1	2	1	0.5	0	3	30	10.0	0	1	0	6	0
1992—Houston NFL	16	0	19	87	4.6	1	1	5	5.0	0	1	15	15.0	0	1	0	6	0
1993—Houston NFL	16	8	195	1002	§5.1	6	21	240	11.4	2	2	29	14.5	0	8	0	48	4
1994—Houston NFL	12	8	169	648	3.8	4	18	194	10.8	1	0	0	0.0	0	5	0	30	6
1995—Houston NFL	9	4	86	293	3.4	0	6	16	2.7	0	0	0	0.0	0	0	0	0	2
1997—San Diego NFL	15	14	253	945	3.7	4	21	137	6.5	0	0	0	0.0	0	4	0	24	2
1998—New York Giants NFL	16	11	247	1063	4.3	5	13	36	2.8	0	0	0	0.0	0	5	0	30	1
1999—New York Giants NFL	3	2	55	177	3.2	0	2	2	1.0	0	0	0	0.0	0	0	0	0	1
Pro totals (8 years)	98	47	1032	4300	4.2	21	84	631	7.5	3	6	74	12.3	0	24	0	144	16

BROWN, GILBERT   DT

PERSONAL: Born February 22, 1971, in Detroit. ... 6-2/345. ... Full name: Gilbert Jesse Brown.
HIGH SCHOOL: Mackenzie (Detroit).
COLLEGE: Kansas.
TRANSACTIONS/CAREER NOTES: Selected by Minnesota Vikings in third round (79th pick overall) of 1993 NFL draft. ... Signed by Vikings (July 16, 1993). ... Claimed on waivers by Green Bay Packers (August 31, 1993). ... On injured reserve with knee injury (December 6, 1994-remainder of season). ... Granted unconditional free agency (February 14, 1997). ... Re-signed by Packers (February 18, 1997). ... Granted unconditional free agency (February 11, 2000).
CHAMPIONSHIP GAME EXPERIENCE: Played in NFC championship game (1995-97 seasons). ... Member of Super Bowl championship team (1996 season). ... Played in Super Bowl XXXII (1997 season).

Year Team	G	GS	SACKS
1993—Green Bay NFL	2	0	0.0
1994—Green Bay NFL	13	1	3.0
1995—Greeh Bay NFL	13	7	0.0
1996—Green Bay NFL	16	16	1.0
1997—Green Bay NFL	12	12	3.0
1998—Green Bay NFL	16	16	0.0
1999—Green Bay NFL	16	15	0.0
Pro totals (7 years)	88	67	7.0

BROWN, J.B.   CB

PERSONAL: Born January 5, 1967, in Washington, D.C. ... 6-0/191. ... Full name: James Harold Brown.
HIGH SCHOOL: DeMatha Catholic (Hyattsville, Md.).
COLLEGE: Maryland.
TRANSACTIONS/CAREER NOTES: Selected by Miami Dolphins in 12th round (315th pick overall) of 1989 NFL draft. ... Signed by Dolphins (July 16, 1989). ... Granted free agency (February 1, 1991). ... Re-signed by Dolphins to practice squad (August 29, 1991). ... Activated (September 7, 1991). ... Granted free agency (March 1, 1993). ... Re-signed by Dolphins (July 21, 1993). ... Released by Dolphins (February 3, 1997). ... Signed by Pittsburgh Steelers (February 7, 1997). ... Traded by Steelers to Arizona Cardinals for seventh-round pick (K Kris Brown) in 1999 draft (August 25, 1998). ... Released by Cardinals after 1998 season. ... Signed by Detroit Lions (July 20, 1999). ... Granted unconditional free agency (February 11, 2000).
CHAMPIONSHIP GAME EXPERIENCE: Played in AFC championship game (1992 and 1997 seasons).
PRO STATISTICS: 1990—Credited with one sack. 1992—Recovered one fumble. 1993—Fumbled once. 1995—Fumbled once and recovered two fumbles. 1998—Recovered one fumble.

			INTERCEPTIONS			
Year Team	G	GS	No.	Yds.	Avg.	TD
1989—Miami NFL	16	0	0	0	0.0	0
1990—Miami NFL	16	16	0	0	0.0	0
1991—Miami NFL	15	11	1	0	0.0	0
1992—Miami NFL	16	16	4	119	29.8	1
1993—Miami NFL	16	16	5	43	8.6	0
1994—Miami NFL	16	16	3	82	27.3	0
1995—Miami NFL	13	12	2	20	10.0	0
1996—Miami NFL	14	1	1	29	29.0	0
1997—Pittsburgh NFL	13	0	0	0	0.0	0

B

1998—Arizona NFL	15	6	0	0	0.0	0
1999—Detroit NFL	13	3	0	0	0.0	0
Pro totals (11 years)	163	97	16	293	18.3	1

BROWN, JAMES OT DOLPHINS

PERSONAL: Born November 30, 1970, in Philadelphia. ... 6-6/325. ... Full name: James Lamont Brown.
HIGH SCHOOL: Mastbaum Area Vo-Tech (Philadelphia).
COLLEGE: Virginia State.
TRANSACTIONS/CAREER NOTES: Selected by Dallas Cowboys in third round (82nd pick overall) of 1992 NFL draft. ... Signed by Cowboys (July 15, 1992). ... Released by Cowboys (August 17, 1992). ... Signed by Indianapolis Colts (August 19, 1992). ... Released by Colts (August 31, 1992). ... Signed by New York Jets to practice squad (September 2, 1992). ... Traded by Jets to Miami Dolphins for fifth-round pick (DB Raymond Austin) in 1997 draft (March 4, 1996). ... Granted unconditional free agency (February 13, 1998). ... Re-signed by Dolphins (March 3, 1998).
PLAYING EXPERIENCE: New York Jets NFL, 1993-1995; Miami NFL, 1996-1999. ... Games/Games started: 1993 (14/1), 1994 (16/6), 1995 (14/12), 1996 (16/16), 1997 (16/16), 1998 (16/16), 1999 (15/14). Total: 107/81.
PRO STATISTICS: 1994—Recovered one fumble.

BROWN, JAMIE OT

PERSONAL: Born April 24, 1972, in Miami. ... 6-8/318. ... Full name: Jamie Shepard Brown. ... Brother-in-law of Michael Irvin, wide receiver, Dallas Cowboys.
HIGH SCHOOL: Miami Killian.
COLLEGE: Florida A&M.
TRANSACTIONS/CAREER NOTES: Selected by Denver Broncos in fourth round (121st pick overall) of 1995 NFL draft. ... Signed by Broncos (May 25, 1995). ... On injured reserve with foot injury (November 29, 1995-remainder of season). ... Granted free agency (February 13, 1998). ... Re-signed by Broncos (April 15, 1998). ... Traded by Broncos to San Francisco 49ers for second-round pick (DE Montae Reagor) in 1999 draft (April 15, 1998). ... On reserve/suspended list (August 25-September 15, 1998). ... Released by 49ers (February 9, 1999). ... Signed by Washington Redskins (March 18, 1999). ... Granted unconditional free agency (February 11, 2000).
PLAYING EXPERIENCE: Denver NFL, 1995-1997; San Francisco NFL, 1998; Washington NFL, 1999. ... Games/Games started: 1995 (6/0), 1996 (12/2), 1997 (11/2), 1998 (8/5), 1999 (1/0). Total: 38/9.
CHAMPIONSHIP GAME EXPERIENCE: Member of Broncos for AFC championship game (1997 season); inactive. ... Member of Super Bowl championship team (1997 season); inactive.

BROWN, KRIS K STEELERS

PERSONAL: Born December 23, 1976, in Southlake, Texas. ... 5-10/204.
HIGH SCHOOL: Carroll (Southlake, Texas).
COLLEGE: Nebraska.
TRANSACTIONS/CAREER NOTES: Selected by Pittsburgh Steelers in seventh round (228th pick overall) of 1999 NFL draft. ... Signed by Steelers (June 29, 1999).

				KICKING				
Year Team	G	XPM	XPA	FGM	FGA	Lg.	50+	Pts.
1999—Pittsburgh NFL	16	30	31	25	29	51	1-1	105

BROWN, LANCE DB STEELERS

PERSONAL: Born February 2, 1972, in Jacksonville. ... 6-2/203.
HIGH SCHOOL: Terry Parker (Jacksonville).
COLLEGE: Indiana.
TRANSACTIONS/CAREER NOTES: Selected by Pittsburgh Steelers in fifth round (161st pick overall) of 1995 NFL draft. ... Signed by Steelers (July 18, 1995). ... Claimed on waivers by Arizona Cardinals (September 25, 1995). ... Released by Cardinals (September 10, 1996). ... Signed by New York Jets to practice squad (November 19, 1996). ... Released by Jets (August 7, 1997). ... Signed by Steelers (February 13, 1998). ... Granted unconditional free agency (February 11, 2000). ... Re-signed by Steelers (April 10, 2000).
PLAYING EXPERIENCE: Arizona NFL, 1995 and 1996; Pittsburgh NFL, 1998 and 1999. ... Games/Games started: 1995 (11/5), 1996 (1/0), 1998 (16/0), 1999 (16/0). Total: 44/5.
PRO STATISTICS: 1995—Recovered one fumble. 1998—Recovered two fumbles for one yard. 1999—Credited with one sack.

BROWN, LARRY TE TITANS

PERSONAL: Born September 1, 1976, in Atlanta. ... 6-4/280. ... Full name: Larry Lovette Brown.
HIGH SCHOOL: Alonzo A. Crim (Decatur, Ga.).
COLLEGE: Georgia.
TRANSACTIONS/CAREER NOTES: Signed as non-drafted free agent by San Diego Chargers (April 20, 1999). ... Released by Chargers (July 22, 1999). ... Signed by Tennessee Titans (August 2, 1999). ... Released by Titans (September 15, 1999). ... Re-signed by Titans to practice squad (September 16, 1999). ... Activated (September 29, 1999).
PLAYING EXPERIENCE: Tennessee NFL, 1999. ... Games/Games started: 1999 (9/0).
CHAMPIONSHIP GAME EXPERIENCE: Member of Titans for AFC championship game (1999 season); inactive. ... Played in Super Bowl XXXIV (1999 season).

BROWN, LOMAS — OT — GIANTS

PERSONAL: Born March 30, 1963, in Miami. ... 6-4/290. ... Full name: Lomas Brown Jr. ... Cousin of Joe Taylor, defensive back with Chicago Bears (1967-74); cousin of Guy McIntyre, guard with San Francisco 49ers (1984-93), Green Bay Packers (1994) and Philadelphia Eagles (1995 and 1996); and cousin of Eric Curry, defensive end, Jacksonville Jaguars.
HIGH SCHOOL: Miami Springs Senior.
COLLEGE: Florida (degree in public recreation, 1996).
TRANSACTIONS/CAREER NOTES: Selected by Orlando Renegades in second round (18th pick overall) of 1985 USFL draft. ... Selected by Detroit Lions in first round (sixth pick overall) of 1985 NFL draft. ... Signed by Lions (August 9, 1985). ... Designated by Lions as franchise player (February 25, 1993). ... Granted roster exemption (September 1-3, 1993). ... Designated by Lions as franchise player (February 15, 1995). ... Re-signed by Lions (September 7, 1995). ... Granted unconditional free agency (February 16, 1996). ... Signed by Arizona Cardinals (February 28, 1996). ... Granted unconditional free agency (February 12, 1999). ... Signed by Cleveland Browns (March 9, 1999). ... On injured reserve with knee injury (December 14, 1999-remainder of season). ... Released by Browns (February 8, 2000). ... Signed by New York Giants (February 22, 2000).
PLAYING EXPERIENCE: Detroit NFL, 1985-1995; Arizona NFL, 1996-1998; Cleveland NFL, 1999. ... Games/Games started: 1985 (16/16), 1986 (16/16), 1987 (11/11), 1988 (16/16), 1989 (16/16), 1990 (16/16), 1991 (15/15), 1992 (16/16), 1993 (11/11), 1994 (16/16), 1995 (15/14), 1996 (16/16), 1997 (14/14), 1998 (16/16), 1999 (10/10). Total: 220/219.
CHAMPIONSHIP GAME EXPERIENCE: Played in NFC championship game (1991 season).
HONORS: Named tackle on THE SPORTING NEWS college All-America first team (1984). ... Played in Pro Bowl (1990-1996 seasons). ... Named offensive tackle on THE SPORTING NEWS NFL All-Pro team (1992).
PRO STATISTICS: 1989—Rushed once for three yards and recovered one fumble. 1991—Recovered one fumble.

B

BROWN, NA — WR — EAGLES

PERSONAL: Born February 22, 1977, in Reidsville, N.C. ... 6-0/187. ... Full name: Na Orlando Brown. ... Name pronounced NAY.
HIGH SCHOOL: Reidsville (N.C.).
COLLEGE: North Carolina.
TRANSACTIONS/CAREER NOTES: Selected by Philadelphia Eagles in fourth round (130th pick overall) of 1999 NFL draft. ... Signed by Eagles (July 28, 1999).
SINGLE GAME HIGHS (regular season): Receptions—4 (December 5, 1999, vs. Arizona); yards—60 (December 19, 1999, vs. New England); and touchdown receptions—1 (December 12, 1999, vs. Dallas).

Year Team	G	GS	RECEIVING				TOTALS			
			No.	Yds.	Avg.	TD	TD	2pt.	Pts.	Fum.
1999—Philadelphia NFL	12	5	18	188	10.4	1	1	0	6	0

BROWN, OMAR — S — FALCONS

PERSONAL: Born March 28, 1975, in York, Pa. ... 5-10/200. ... Full name: Omar L. Brown.
HIGH SCHOOL: William Penn (York, Pa.).
COLLEGE: North Carolina.
TRANSACTIONS/CAREER NOTES: Selected by Atlanta Falcons in fourth round (103rd pick overall) of 1998 NFL draft. ... Signed by Falcons (July 2, 1998).
PLAYING EXPERIENCE: Atlanta NFL, 1998 and 1999. ... Games/Games started: 1998 (2/0), 1999 (13/0). Total: 15/0.
CHAMPIONSHIP GAME EXPERIENCE: Member of Falcons for NFC championship game (1998 season); inactive. ... Member of Falcons for Super Bowl XXXIII (1998 season); inactive.

BROWN, ORLANDO — OT — BROWNS

PERSONAL: Born December 20, 1970, in Washington, D.C. ... 6-7/350. ... Full name: Orlando Claude Brown.
HIGH SCHOOL: Howard D. Woodson (Washington, D.C.).
COLLEGE: Central State (Ohio), then South Carolina State.
TRANSACTIONS/CAREER NOTES: Signed as non-drafted free agent by Cleveland Browns (May 13, 1993). ... On injured reserve with shoulder injury (August 30, 1993-entire season). ... Browns franchise moved to Baltimore and renamed Ravens for 1996 season (March 11, 1996). ... Granted unconditional free agency (February 12, 1999). ... Signed by Browns (February 17, 1999). ... On suspended list for abusing an official (December 22, 1999-remainder of season).
PLAYING EXPERIENCE: Cleveland NFL, 1994, 1995 and 1999; Baltimore NFL, 1996-1998. ... Games/Games started: 1994 (14/8), 1995 (16/16), 1996 (16/16), 1997 (16/16), 1998 (13/13), 1999 (15/15). Total: 90/84.
PRO STATISTICS: 1995—Recovered one fumble.

BROWN, RAY — G — 49ERS

PERSONAL: Born December 12, 1962, in Marion, Ark. ... 6-5/318. ... Full name: Leonard Ray Brown Jr.
HIGH SCHOOL: Marion (Ark.).
COLLEGE: Memphis State, then Arizona State, then Arkansas State.
TRANSACTIONS/CAREER NOTES: Selected by St. Louis Cardinals in eighth round (201st pick overall) of 1986 NFL draft. ... Signed by Cardinals (July 14, 1986). ... On injured reserve with knee injury (October 17-November 21, 1986). ... Released by Cardinals (September 7, 1987). ... Re-signed by Cardinals as replacement player (September 25, 1987). ... On injured reserve with finger injury (November 12-December 12, 1987). ... Cardinals franchise moved to Phoenix (March 15, 1988). ... Granted unconditional free agency (February 1, 1989). ... Signed by Washington Redskins (March 10, 1989). ... On injured reserve with knee injury (September 5-November 4, 1989). ... On injured reserve with knee injury (September 4, 1990-January 4, 1991). ... Granted unconditional free agency (February 1-April 1, 1991). ... Re-signed by Redskins for 1991 season. ... On injured reserve with elbow injury (August 27, 1991-entire season). ... Granted unconditional free agency (February 16, 1996). ... Signed by San Francisco 49ers (March 1, 1996).

PLAYING EXPERIENCE: St. Louis NFL, 1986 and 1987; Phoenix NFL, 1988; Washington NFL, 1989, 1992-1995; San Francisco NFL, 1996-1999. ... Games/Games started: 1986 (11/4), 1987 (7/3), 1988 (15/1), 1989 (7/0), 1992 (16/8), 1993 (16/14), 1994 (16/16), 1995 (16/16), 1996 (16/16), 1997 (15/15), 1998 (16/16), 1999 (16/16). Total: 167/125.
CHAMPIONSHIP GAME EXPERIENCE: Played in NFC championship game (1997 season).
PRO STATISTICS: 1999—Recovered two fumbles.

BROWN, REGGIE — FB — SEAHAWKS

PERSONAL: Born June 26, 1973, in Highland Park, Mich. ... 6-0/244. ... Full name: Regilyn Brown.
HIGH SCHOOL: Henry Ford (Detroit).
JUNIOR COLLEGE: College of the Desert (Calif.).
COLLEGE: Fresno State.
TRANSACTIONS/CAREER NOTES: Selected by Seattle Seahawks in third round (91st pick overall) of 1996 NFL draft. ... Signed by Seahawks (July 17, 1996). ... On injured reserve with knee injury (October 23, 1996-remainder of season). ... On injured reserve with knee injury (December 17, 1997-remainder of season). ... Granted free agency (February 12, 1999). ... Re-signed by Seahawks (April 14, 1999). ... Granted unconditional free agency (February 11, 2000). ... Re-signed by Seahawks (May 19, 2000).
SINGLE GAME HIGHS (regular season): Attempts—4 (October 17, 1999, vs. San Diego); yards—9 (September 26, 1999, vs. Pittsburgh); and rushing touchdowns—0.

			RUSHING				RECEIVING				KICKOFF RETURNS				TOTALS		
Year Team	G	GS	Att.	Yds.	Avg.	TD	No.	Yds.	Avg.	TD	No.	Yds.	Avg.	TD	TD	2pt.	Pts. Fum.
1996—Seattle NFL	7	0	0	0	0.0	0	0	0	0.0	0	4	51	12.8	0	0	0	0 0
1997—Seattle NFL	11	0	0	0	0.0	0	0	0	0.0	0	1	16	16.0	0	0	0	0 0
1998—Seattle NFL	15	1	1	2	2.0	0	0	0	0.0	0	4	44	11.0	0	0	0	0 0
1999—Seattle NFL	16	8	14	38	2.7	0	34	228	6.7	1	0	0	0.0	0	1	0	6 1
Pro totals (4 years)	49	9	15	40	2.7	0	34	228	6.7	1	9	111	12.3	0	1	0	6 1

BROWN, RUBEN — G — BILLS

PERSONAL: Born February 13, 1972, in Englewood, N.J. ... 6-3/304. ... Full name: Ruben Pernell Brown. ... Brother of Cornell Brown, line-backer, Baltimore Ravens.
HIGH SCHOOL: E.C. Glass (Lynchburg, Va.).
COLLEGE: Pittsburgh.
TRANSACTIONS/CAREER NOTES: Selected by Buffalo Bills in first round (14th pick overall) of 1995 NFL draft. ... Signed by Bills (June 20, 1995). ... Granted unconditional free agency (February 11, 2000). ... Re-signed by Bills (March 31, 2000).
PLAYING EXPERIENCE: Buffalo NFL, 1995-1999. ... Games/Games started: 1995 (16/16), 1996 (14/14), 1997 (16/16), 1998 (13/13), 1999 (14/14). Total: 73/73.
HONORS: Named offensive lineman on The Sporting News college All-America second team (1994). ... Played in Pro Bowl (1996-1999 seasons).
PRO STATISTICS: 1997—Recovered one fumble.

BROWN, TIM — WR — RAIDERS

PERSONAL: Born July 22, 1966, in Dallas. ... 6-0/195. ... Full name: Timothy Donell Brown.
HIGH SCHOOL: Woodrow Wilson (Dallas).
COLLEGE: Notre Dame (degree in sociology).
TRANSACTIONS/CAREER NOTES: Selected by Los Angeles Raiders in first round (sixth pick overall) of 1988 NFL draft. ... Signed by Raiders (July 14, 1988). ... On injured reserve with knee injury (September 12, 1989-remainder of season). ... Granted free agency (February 1, 1992). ... Re-signed by Raiders (August 13, 1992). ... Designated by Raiders as transition player (February 25, 1993). ... Tendered offer sheet by Denver Broncos (March 11, 1994). ... Offer matched by Raiders (March 16, 1994). ... Raiders franchise moved to Oakland (July 21, 1995).
CHAMPIONSHIP GAME EXPERIENCE: Played in AFC championship game (1990 season).
HONORS: Named wide receiver on The Sporting News college All-America first team (1986 and 1987). ... Heisman Trophy winner (1987). ... Named College Football Player of the Year by The Sporting News (1987). ... Named kick returner on The Sporting News NFL All-Pro team (1988). ... Played in Pro Bowl (1988, 1991 and 1993-1997 seasons). ... Named wide receiver on The Sporting News NFL All-Pro team (1997). ... Named to play in Pro Bowl (1999 season); replaced by Terry Glenn due to injury.
RECORDS: Holds NFL rookie-season record for most combined yards gained—2,317 (1988).
PRO STATISTICS: 1988—Fumbled five times and recovered one fumble for seven yards. 1989—Fumbled once. 1990—Fumbled three times. 1991—Fumbled once. 1992—Fumbled six times and recovered one fumble. 1993—Fumbled once. 1994—Fumbled three times. 1995—Recovered one fumble for three yards. 1996—Fumbled three times and recovered one fumble. 1997—Fumbled once. 1998—Fumbled three times and recovered two fumbles.
SINGLE GAME HIGHS (regular season): Receptions—14 (December 21, 1997, vs. Jacksonville); yards—190 (October 24, 1999, vs. New York Jets); and touchdown receptions—3 (August 31, 1997, vs. Tennessee).
STATISTICAL PLATEAUS: 100-yard receiving games: 1988 (1), 1991 (1), 1992 (1), 1993 (4), 1994 (4), 1995 (6), 1996 (2), 1997 (7), 1998 (3), 1999 (6). Total: 35.
MISCELLANEOUS: Holds Raiders franchise all-time record for most receptions (770) and most yards receiving (10,944).

			RUSHING				RECEIVING				PUNT RETURNS				KICKOFF RETURNS				TOTALS		
Year Team	G	GS	Att.	Yds.	Avg.	TD	No.	Yds.	Avg.	TD	No.	Yds.	Avg.	TD	No.	Yds.	Avg.	TD	TD	2pt.	Pts.
1988—L.A. Raiders NFL	16	9	14	50	3.6	1	43	725	16.9	5	§49	§444	9.1	0	†41	*1098	*26.8	†1	7	0	42
1989—L.A. Raiders NFL	1	1	0	0	0.0	0	1	8	8.0	0	4	43	10.8	0	3	63	21.0	0	0	0	0
1990—L.A. Raiders NFL	16	0	0	0	0.0	0	18	265	14.7	3	34	295	8.7	0	0	0	0.0	0	3	0	18
1991—L.A. Raiders NFL	16	1	5	16	3.2	0	36	554	15.4	5	29	§330	11.4	▲1	1	29	29.0	0	6	0	36
1992—L.A. Raiders NFL	15	12	3	-4	-1.3	0	49	693	14.1	7	37	383	10.4	0	2	14	7.0	0	7	0	42
1993—L.A. Raiders NFL	16	16	2	7	3.5	0	80	§1180	14.8	7	40	§465	11.6	1	0	0	0.0	0	8	0	48
1994—L.A. Raiders NFL	16	16	0	0	0.0	0	89	§1309	14.7	9	40	*487	12.2	0	0	0	0.0	0	9	0	54
1995—Oakland NFL	16	16	0	0	0.0	0	89	§1342	15.1	10	36	364	10.1	0	0	0	0.0	0	10	0	60
1996—Oakland NFL	16	16	6	35	5.8	0	90	1104	12.3	9	32	272	8.5	0	1	24	24.0	0	9	0	54
1997—Oakland NFL	16	16	5	19	3.8	0	†104	§1408	13.5	5	0	0	0.0	0	1	7	7.0	0	5	1	32

1998—Oakland NFL........	16	16	1	-7	-7.0	0	81	1012	12.5	9	3	23	7.7	0	0	0	0.0	0	9	0	54
1999—Oakland NFL........	16	16	1	4	4.0	0	90	1344	14.9	6	0	0	0.0	0	0	0	0.0	0	6	0	36
Pro totals (12 years)......	176	135	37	120	3.2	1	770	10944	14.2	75	304	3106	10.2	2	49	1235	25.2	1	79	1	476

BROWN, TROY   WR   PATRIOTS

PERSONAL: Born July 2, 1971, in Barnwell, S.C. ... 5-10/190. ... Full name: Troy Fitzgerald Brown.
HIGH SCHOOL: Blackville (S.C.)-Hilda.
JUNIOR COLLEGE: Lees-McRae College (N.C.).
COLLEGE: Marshall.
TRANSACTIONS/CAREER NOTES: Selected by New England Patriots in eighth round (198th pick overall) of 1993 NFL draft. ... Signed by Patriots (July 16, 1993). ... On injured reserve with quadriceps injury (December 31, 1993-remainder of season). ... Released by Patriots (August 28, 1994). ... Re-signed by Patriots (October 19, 1994). ... Granted unconditional free agency (February 14, 1997). ... Re-signed by Patriots (March 10, 1997). ... Granted unconditional free agency (February 11, 2000). ... Re-signed by Patriots (February 26, 2000).
CHAMPIONSHIP GAME EXPERIENCE: Played in AFC championship game (1996 season). ... Member of Patriots for Super Bowl XXXI (1996 season); inactive.
PRO STATISTICS: 1993—Recovered one fumble. 1994—Recovered two fumbles. 1995—Recovered one fumble for 75 yards and a touchdown. 1997—Rushed once for minus 18 yards. 1999—Attempted one pass without a completion and recovered two fumbles.
SINGLE GAME HIGHS (regular season): Receptions—7 (December 21, 1996, vs. New York Giants); yards—125 (October 19, 1997, vs. New York Jets); and touchdown receptions—1 (November 15, 1999, vs. New York Jets).
STATISTICAL PLATEAUS: 100-yard receiving games: 1997 (2), 1999 (1). Total: 3.

			RECEIVING				PUNT RETURNS				KICKOFF RETURNS				TOTALS			
Year Team	G	GS	No.	Yds.	Avg.	TD	No.	Yds.	Avg.	TD	No.	Yds.	Avg.	TD	TD	2pt.	Pts.	Fum.
1993—New England NFL.......	12	0	2	22	11.0	0	25	224	9.0	0	15	243	16.2	0	0	0	0	2
1994—New England NFL.......	9	0	0	0	0.0	0	24	202	8.4	0	1	14	14.0	0	0	0	0	2
1995—New England NFL.......	16	0	14	159	11.4	0	0	0	0.0	0	31	672	21.7	0	1	0	6	1
1996—New England NFL.......	16	0	21	222	10.6	0	0	0	0.0	0	29	634	21.9	0	0	0	0	0
1997—New England NFL.......	16	6	41	607	14.8	6	0	0	0.0	0	0	0	0.0	0	6	0	36	0
1998—New England NFL.......	10	0	23	346	15.0	1	17	225	13.2	0	0	0	0.0	0	1	0	6	0
1999—New England NFL.......	13	1	36	471	13.1	1	38	405	10.7	0	8	271	33.9	0	1	0	6	1
Pro totals (7 years)...............	92	7	137	1827	13.3	8	104	1056	10.2	0	84	1834	21.8	0	9	0	54	6

BROWN, WILBERT   G   CHARGERS

PERSONAL: Born May 9, 1977, in Texarkana, Texas. ... 6-2/310. ... Full name: Wilbert Lemon Brown. ... Cousin of Curtis Enis, running back, Chicago Bears.
HIGH SCHOOL: Hooks (Texas).
COLLEGE: Houston.
TRANSACTIONS/CAREER NOTES: Signed as non-drafted free agent by San Diego Chargers (April 20, 1999). ... Released by Chargers (September 4, 1999). ... Re-signed by Chargers to practice squad (September 6, 1999). ... Released by Chargers (September 14, 1999). ... Re-signed by Chargers to practice squad (September 21, 1999). ... Activated (December 4, 1999).
PLAYING EXPERIENCE: San Diego NFL, 1999. ... Games/Games started: 1999 (5/0).

BROWNING, JOHN   DE   CHIEFS

PERSONAL: Born September 30, 1973, in Miami. ... 6-4/305.
HIGH SCHOOL: North Miami (Fla.).
COLLEGE: West Virginia.
TRANSACTIONS/CAREER NOTES: Selected by Kansas City Chiefs in third round (68th pick overall) of 1996 NFL draft. ... Signed by Chiefs (July 24, 1996). ... On injured reserve with Achilles' tendon injury (September 1, 1999-entire season). ... Granted unconditional free agency (February 11, 2000). ... Re-signed by Chiefs (February 11, 2000).
PRO STATISTICS: 1997—Recovered one fumble.

Year Team	G	GS	SACKS
1996—Kansas City NFL	13	2	2.0
1997—Kansas City NFL	14	13	4.0
1998—Kansas City NFL	8	8	0.0
1999—Kansas City NFL	Did not play.		
Pro totals (3 years)...	35	23	6.0

BRUCE, ISAAC   WR   RAMS

PERSONAL: Born November 10, 1972, in Fort Lauderdale, Fla. ... 6-0/188. ... Full name: Isaac Isidore Bruce. ... Cousin of Derrick Moore, running back with Detroit Lions (1993 and 1994) and Carolina Panthers (1995).
HIGH SCHOOL: Dillard (Fort Lauderdale, Fla.).
JUNIOR COLLEGE: West Los Angeles Junior College, then Santa Monica (Calif.) Junior College.
COLLEGE: Memphis State.
TRANSACTIONS/CAREER NOTES: Selected by Los Angeles Rams in second round (33rd pick overall) of 1994 NFL draft. ... Signed by Rams (July 13, 1994). ... On injured reserve with sprained right knee (December 9, 1994-remainder of season). ... Rams franchise moved to St. Louis (April 12, 1995). ... On injured reserve with hamstring injury (December 9, 1998-remainder of season).
CHAMPIONSHIP GAME EXPERIENCE: Played in NFC championship game (1999 season). ... Member of Super Bowl championship team (1999 season).
HONORS: Named wide receiver on THE SPORTING NEWS NFL All-Pro team (1999). ... Played in Pro Bowl (1996 and 1999 season).
PRO STATISTICS: 1995—Ran 52 yards with lateral from punt return and recovered one fumble. 1996—Attempted two passes with one completion for 15 yards and one interception.

SINGLE GAME HIGHS (regular season): Receptions—15 (December 24, 1995, vs. Miami); yards—233 (November 2, 1997, vs. Atlanta); and touchdown receptions—4 (October 10, 1999, vs. San Francisco).

STATISTICAL PLATEAUS: 100-yard receiving games: 1995 (9), 1996 (4), 1997 (2), 1998 (2), 1999 (4). Total: 21.

				RUSHING				RECEIVING				TOTALS		
Year Team	G	GS	Att.	Yds.	Avg.	TD	No.	Yds.	Avg.	TD	TD	2pt.	Pts.	Fum.
1994—Los Angeles Rams NFL	12	0	1	2	2.0	0	21	272	13.0	3	3	0	18	0
1995—St. Louis NFL	16	16	3	17	5.7	0	119	1781	15.0	13	13	1	80	2
1996—St. Louis NFL	16	16	1	4	4.0	0	84	*1338	15.9	7	7	0	42	1
1997—St. Louis NFL	12	12	0	0	0.0	0	56	815	14.6	5	5	0	30	1
1998—St. Louis NFL	5	5	1	30	30.0	0	32	457	14.3	1	1	0	6	0
1999—St. Louis NFL	16	16	5	32	6.4	0	77	1165	15.1	12	12	†1	74	0
Pro totals (6 years)	77	65	11	85	7.7	0	389	5828	15.0	41	41	2	250	4

B

BRUENER, MARK　　　　TE　　　　STEELERS

PERSONAL: Born September 16, 1972, in Olympia, Wash. ... 6-4/261. ... Full name: Mark Frederick Bruener. ... Name pronounced BREW-ner.

HIGH SCHOOL: Aberdeen (Wash.).

COLLEGE: Washington (degree in economics).

TRANSACTIONS/CAREER NOTES: Selected by Pittsburgh Steelers in first round (27th pick overall) of 1995 NFL draft. ... Signed by Steelers (July 25, 1995). ... On injured reserve with knee injury (November 29, 1996-remainder of season).

CHAMPIONSHIP GAME EXPERIENCE: Played in AFC championship game (1995 and 1997 seasons). ... Played in Super Bowl XXX (1995 season).

PRO STATISTICS: 1995—Returned two kickoffs for 19 yards. 1998—Lost seven yards with lateral from kickoff return. 1999—Recovered two fumbles for four yards.

SINGLE GAME HIGHS (regular season): Receptions—5 (December 13, 1997, vs. New England); yards—51 (November 28, 1999, vs. Cincinnati); and touchdown receptions—1 (November 22, 1998, vs. Jacksonville).

			RECEIVING				TOTALS		
Year Team	G	GS	No.	Yds.	Avg.	TD	TD	2pt.	Pts.	Fum.
1995—Pittsburgh NFL	16	13	26	238	9.2	3	3	0	18	0
1996—Pittsburgh NFL	12	12	12	141	11.8	0	0	1	2	0
1997—Pittsburgh NFL	16	16	18	117	6.5	6	6	0	36	1
1998—Pittsburgh NFL	16	16	19	157	8.3	2	2	0	12	0
1999—Pittsburgh NFL	14	14	18	176	9.8	0	0	0	0	0
Pro totals (5 years)	74	71	93	829	8.9	11	11	1	68	1

BRUNELL, MARK　　　　QB　　　　JAGUARS

PERSONAL: Born September 17, 1970, in Los Angeles. ... 6-1/216. ... Full name: Mark Allen Brunell.

HIGH SCHOOL: St. Joseph (Santa Maria, Calif.).

COLLEGE: Washington (degree in history).

TRANSACTIONS/CAREER NOTES: Selected by Green Bay Packers in fifth round (118th pick overall) of 1993 NFL draft. ... Signed by Packers (July 1, 1993). ... Traded by Packers to Jacksonville Jaguars for third- (FB William Henderson) and fifth-round (RB Travis Jervey) picks in 1995 draft (April 21, 1995).

CHAMPIONSHIP GAME EXPERIENCE: Played in AFC championship game (1996 and 1999 seasons).

HONORS: Played in Pro Bowl (1996, 1997 and 1999 seasons). ... Named Outstanding Player of Pro Bowl (1996 season).

PRO STATISTICS: 1994—Fumbled once. 1995—Fumbled five times and recovered three fumbles. 1996—Led AFC with 14 fumbles and recovered five fumbles for minus 14 yards. 1997—Fumbled four times for minus five yards. 1998—Fumbled three times and recovered two fumbles for minus one yard. 1999—Fumbled six times and recovered three fumbles for minus two yards.

SINGLE GAME HIGHS (regular season): Attempts—52 (October 20, 1996, vs. St. Louis); completions—37 (October 20, 1996, vs. St. Louis); yards—432 (September 22, 1996, vs. New England); and touchdown passes—4 (November 29, 1998, vs. Cincinnati).

STATISTICAL PLATEAUS: 300-yard passing games: 1995 (2), 1996 (6), 1997 (3), 1998 (2), 1999 (3). Total: 16.

MISCELLANEOUS: Regular-season record as starting NFL quarterback: 44-24 (.667). ... Postseason record as starting NFL quarterback: 4-4 (.500). ... Holds Jacksonville Jaguars all-time record for most yards passing (15,477) and most touchdown passes (86).

			PASSING							RUSHING				TOTALS		
Year Team	G	GS	Att.	Cmp.	Pct.	Yds.	TD	Int.	Avg.	Rat.	Att.	Yds.	Avg.	TD	TD	2pt.	Pts.
1993—Green Bay NFL						Did not play.											
1994—Green Bay NFL	2	0	27	12	44.4	95	0	0	3.52	53.8	6	7	1.2	1	1	0	6
1995—Jacksonville NFL	13	10	346	201	58.1	2168	15	7	6.27	82.6	67	480	7.2	4	4	0	24
1996—Jacksonville NFL	16	16	557	353	§63.4	*4367	19	§20	*7.84	84.0	80	396	5.0	3	3	2	22
1997—Jacksonville NFL	14	14	435	264	60.7	3281	18	7	§7.54	§91.2	48	257	5.4	2	2	0	12
1998—Jacksonville NFL	13	13	354	208	58.8	2601	20	9	7.35	89.9	49	192	3.9	0	0	0	0
1999—Jacksonville NFL	15	15	441	259	58.7	3060	14	9	6.94	82.0	47	208	4.4	1	1	†1	8
Pro totals (6 years)	73	68	2160	1297	60.0	15572	86	52	7.21	85.4	297	1540	5.2	11	11	3	72

BRUSCHI, TEDY　　　　LB　　　　PATRIOTS

PERSONAL: Born June 9, 1973, in San Francisco. ... 6-1/245. ... Full name: Tedy Lacap Bruschi. ... Stepson of Ronald Sandys, former professional tennis player. ... Name pronounced BREW-ski.

HIGH SCHOOL: Roseville (Calif.).

COLLEGE: Arizona (degree in communications).

TRANSACTIONS/CAREER NOTES: Selected by New England Patriots in third round (86th pick overall) of 1996 NFL draft. ... Signed by Patriots (July 17, 1996). ... Granted free agency (February 12, 1999). ... Re-signed by Patriots (June 1, 1999). ... Granted unconditional free agency (February 11, 2000). ... Re-signed by Patriots (March 22, 2000).

CHAMPIONSHIP GAME EXPERIENCE: Played in AFC championship game (1996 season). ... Played in Super Bowl XXXI (1996 season).

HONORS: Named defensive lineman on THE SPORTING NEWS college All-America first team (1994 and 1995).

PRO STATISTICS: 1996—Returned blocked punt four yards for a touchdown. 1997—Recovered two fumbles. 1998—Returned one kickoff for four yards. 1999—Intercepted one pass for one yard and recovered one fumble.

Year Team	G	GS	SACKS
1996—New England NFL	16	0	4.0
1997—New England NFL	16	1	4.0
1998—New England NFL	16	7	2.0
1999—New England NFL	14	14	2.0
Pro totals (4 years)	62	22	12.0

BRYANT, FERNANDO　　　　CB　　　　JAGUARS

PERSONAL: Born March 26, 1977, in Albany, Ga. ... 5-10/174. ... Full name: Fernando Antoneiyo Bryant. ... Nephew of Don Griffin, cornerback with San Francisco 49ers (1986-93), Cleveland Browns (1994 and 1995) and Philadelphia Eagles (1996); and nephew of James Griffin, defensive back with Cincinnati Bengals (1983-85) and Detroit Lions (1986-89).
HIGH SCHOOL: Riverdale (Murfreesboro, Tenn.).
COLLEGE: Alabama.
TRANSACTIONS/CAREER NOTES: Selected by Jacksonville Jaguars in first round (26th pick overall) of 1999 NFL draft. ... Signed by Jaguars (August 9, 1999).
CHAMPIONSHIP GAME EXPERIENCE: Played in AFC championship game (1999 season).
PRO STATISTICS: 1999—Recovered three fumbles for 27 yards.

			INTERCEPTIONS			
Year Team	G	GS	No.	Yds.	Avg.	TD
1999—Jacksonville NFL	16	16	2	0	0.0	0

BRYANT, JUNIOR　　　　DT　　　　49ERS

PERSONAL: Born January 16, 1971, in Omaha, Neb. ... 6-4/278. ... Full name: Edward E. Bryant.
HIGH SCHOOL: Creighton Prep (Omaha, Neb.).
COLLEGE: Notre Dame.
TRANSACTIONS/CAREER NOTES: Signed as non-drafted free agent by San Francisco 49ers (May 3, 1993). ... Released by 49ers (August 30, 1993). ... Re-signed by 49ers to practice squad (August 31, 1993). ... Released by 49ers (August 27, 1994). ... Re-signed by 49ers to practice squad (August 31, 1994). ... Granted unconditional free agency (February 11, 2000). ... Re-signed by 49ers (February 17, 2000).
CHAMPIONSHIP GAME EXPERIENCE: Played in NFC championship game (1997 season).
PRO STATISTICS: 1996—Recovered one fumble. 1999—Recovered one fumble in end zone for a touchdown.

Year Team	G	GS	SACKS
1993—San Francisco NFL	Did not play.		
1994—San Francisco NFL	Did not play.		
1995—San Francisco NFL	16	4	1.0
1996—San Francisco NFL	16	1	0.5
1997—San Francisco NFL	16	3	2.5
1998—San Francisco NFL	16	16	5.0
1999—San Francisco NFL	16	16	4.5
Pro totals (5 years)	80	40	13.5

BRYANT, TONY　　　　DE　　　　RAIDERS

PERSONAL: Born September 3, 1976, in Marathon, Fla. ... 6-6/275.
HIGH SCHOOL: Marathon (Fla.).
JUNIOR COLLEGE: Copiah-Lincoln Junior College (Miss.).
COLLEGE: Florida State.
TRANSACTIONS/CAREER NOTES: Selected by Oakland Raiders in second round (40th pick overall) of 1999 NFL draft. ... Signed by Raiders (July 22, 1999).

Year Team	G	GS	SACKS
1999—Oakland NFL	10	0	4.5

BRYSON, SHAWN　　　　RB　　　　BILLS

PERSONAL: Born August 26, 1976, in Franklin, N.C. ... 6-4/249. ... Full name: Adrian Shawn Bryson.
HIGH SCHOOL: Franklin (N.C.).
COLLEGE: Tennessee.
TRANSACTIONS/CAREER NOTES: Selected by Buffalo Bills in third round (86th pick overall) of 1999 NFL draft. ... Signed by Bills (July 27, 1999). ... On injured reserve with knee injury (August 30, 1999-entire season).

BRZEZINSKI, DOUG　　　　G　　　　EAGLES

PERSONAL: Born March 11, 1976, in Livonia, Mich. ... 6-4/305. ... Full name: Douglas Gregory Brzezinski. ... Name pronounced bruh-ZHIN-skee.
HIGH SCHOOL: Detroit Catholic Central.
COLLEGE: Boston College.
TRANSACTIONS/CAREER NOTES: Selected by Philadelphia Eagles in third round (64th pick overall) of 1999 NFL draft. ... Signed by Eagles (July 28, 1999).
PLAYING EXPERIENCE: Philadelphia NFL, 1999. ... Games/Games started: 1999 (16/16).
HONORS: Named offensive guard on THE SPORTING NEWS college All-America first team (1998).

BUCHANAN, RAY   CB   FALCONS

PERSONAL: Born September 29, 1971, in Chicago. ... 5-9/186. ... Full name: Raymond Louis Buchanan.
HIGH SCHOOL: Proviso East (Maywood, Ill.).
COLLEGE: Louisville.
TRANSACTIONS/CAREER NOTES: Selected by Indianapolis Colts in third round (65th pick overall) of 1993 NFL draft. ... Signed by Colts (July 26, 1993). ... Designated by Colts as transition player (February 13, 1997). ... Tendered offer sheet by Atlanta Falcons (February 25, 1997). ... Colts declined to match offer (March 3, 1997).
CHAMPIONSHIP GAME EXPERIENCE: Played in AFC championship game (1995 season). ... Played in NFC championship game (1998 season). ... Played in Super Bowl XXXIII (1998 season).
HONORS: Played in Pro Bowl (1998 season).
PRO STATISTICS: 1994—Credited with one sack and recovered one fumble. 1995—Returned one kickoff for 22 yards, credited with one sack and recovered two fumbles. 1996—Returned one kickoff for 20 yards. 1997—Ran 37 yards with lateral from punt return. 1999—Credited with one sack.

			INTERCEPTIONS				PUNT RETURNS				TOTALS		
Year Team	G	GS	No.	Yds.	Avg.	TD	No.	Yds.	Avg.	TD	TD	2pt.	Pts.	Fum.
1993—Indianapolis NFL	16	5	4	45	11.3	0	0	0	0.0	0	0	0	0	0
1994—Indianapolis NFL	16	16	8	221	27.6	†3	0	0	0.0	0	3	0	18	0
1995—Indianapolis NFL	16	16	2	60	30.0	0	16	113	7.1	0	0	0	0	1
1996—Indianapolis NFL	13	13	2	32	16.0	0	12	201	16.8	0	0	0	0	0
1997—Atlanta NFL	16	16	5	49	9.8	0	0	37	0.0	0	0	0	0	0
1998—Atlanta NFL	16	16	7	102	14.6	0	1	4	4.0	0	0	0	0	0
1999—Atlanta NFL	16	16	4	81	20.3	1	0	0	0.0	0	1	0	6	0
Pro totals (7 years)	109	98	32	590	18.4	4	29	355	12.2	0	4	0	24	1

BUCKEY, JEFF   OT

PERSONAL: Born August 7, 1974, in Bakersfield, Calif. ... 6-5/305. ... Full name: Jeffery Michael Buckey.
HIGH SCHOOL: Bakersfield (Calif.).
COLLEGE: Stanford (degree in economics).
TRANSACTIONS/CAREER NOTES: Selected by Miami Dolphins in seventh round (230th pick overall) of 1996 NFL draft. ... Signed by Dolphins for 1996 season. ... On injured reserve with back injury (November 11, 1998-remainder of season). ... Selected by Cleveland Browns from Dolphins in NFL expansion draft (February 9, 1999). ... Granted free agency (February 12, 1999). ... Re-signed by Browns (June 3, 1999). ... Released by Browns (August 23, 1999). ... Signed by San Francisco 49ers (October 20, 1999). ... Granted unconditional free agency (February 11, 2000).
PLAYING EXPERIENCE: Miami NFL, 1996-1998; San Francisco NFL, 1999. ... Games/Games started: 1996 (15/1), 1997 (16/12), 1998 (7/0), 1999 (7/0). Totals: 45/13.

BUCKLEY, CURTIS   CB   REDSKINS

PERSONAL: Born September 25, 1970, in Oakdale, Calif. ... 6-0/182. ... Full name: Curtis LaDonn Buckley.
HIGH SCHOOL: Silsbee (Texas).
JUNIOR COLLEGE: Kilgore (Texas) College.
COLLEGE: East Texas State.
TRANSACTIONS/CAREER NOTES: Signed as non-drafted free agent by Tampa Bay Buccaneers (May 3, 1993). ... Released by Buccaneers (August 30, 1993). ... Re-signed by Buccaneers (August 31, 1993). ... Released by Buccaneers (September 7, 1993). ... Re-signed by Buccaneers to practice squad (September 9, 1993). ... Activated (November 5, 1993). ... Released by Buccaneers (August 30, 1994). ... Re-signed by Buccaneers (September 7, 1994). ... Released by Buccaneers (September 30, 1994). ... Granted free agency (February 16, 1996). ... Tendered offer sheet by San Francisco 49ers (February 21, 1996). ... Buccaneers declined to match offer (February 28, 1996). ... Claimed on waivers by New York Giants (November 13, 1998). ... Released by Giants (June 14, 1999). ... Signed by Washington Redskins (November 16, 1999). ... Granted unconditional free agency (February 11, 2000). ... Re-signed by Redskins (February 29, 2000).
CHAMPIONSHIP GAME EXPERIENCE: Played in NFC championship game (1997 season).
PRO STATISTICS: 1994—Recovered two fumbles. 1996—Recovered two fumbles. 1997—Recovered one fumble.

			KICKOFF RETURNS				TOTALS		
Year Team	G	GS	No.	Yds.	Avg.	TD	TD	2pt.	Pts.	Fum.
1993—Tampa Bay NFL	10	2	0	0	0.0	0	0	0	0	0
1994—Tampa Bay NFL	13	0	8	177	22.1	0	0	0	0	1
1995—Tampa Bay NFL	15	0	2	29	14.5	0	0	0	0	0
1996—San Francisco NFL	15	0	0	0	0.0	0	0	0	0	0
1997—San Francisco NFL	15	0	0	0	0.0	0	0	0	0	0
1998—San Francisco NFL	8	0	0	0	0.0	0	0	0	0	0
—New York Giants NFL	6	0	0	0	0.0	0	0	0	0	0
1999—Washington NFL	7	0	0	0	0.0	0	0	0	0	0
Pro totals (7 years)	89	2	10	206	20.6	0	0	0	0	1

BUCKLEY, MARCUS   LB   FALCONS

PERSONAL: Born February 3, 1971, in Fort Worth, Texas. ... 6-3/240. ... Full name: Marcus Wayne Buckley.
HIGH SCHOOL: Eastern Hills (Fort Worth, Texas).
COLLEGE: Texas A&M.
TRANSACTIONS/CAREER NOTES: Selected by New York Giants in third round (66th pick overall) of 1993 NFL draft. ... Signed by Giants (July 23, 1993). ... Granted free agency (February 16, 1996). ... Re-signed by Giants (April 15, 1996). ... Granted unconditional free agency (February 13, 1998). ... Re-signed by Giants (February 19, 1998). ... Released by Giants (February 10, 2000). ... Signed by Atlanta Falcons (March 8, 2000).

PLAYING EXPERIENCE: New York Giants NFL, 1993-1999. ... Games/Games started: 1993 (16/2), 1994 (16/1), 1995 (16/5), 1996 (15/2), 1997 (12/3), 1998 (14/12), 1999 (12/0). Total: 101/25.

HONORS: Named linebacker on THE SPORTING NEWS college All-America first team (1992).

PRO STATISTICS: 1993—Recovered one fumble. 1995—Recovered one fumble. 1997—Recovered one fumble. 1998—Intercepted one pass for no yards, credited with 1$^1/_2$ sacks and recovered one fumble.

BUCKLEY, TERRELL — CB

PERSONAL: Born June 7, 1971, in Pascagoula, Miss. ... 5-10/180. ... Full name: Douglas Terrell Buckley.
HIGH SCHOOL: Pascagoula (Miss.).
COLLEGE: Florida State.
TRANSACTIONS/CAREER NOTES: Selected after junior season by Green Bay Packers in first round (fifth pick overall) of 1992 NFL draft. ... Signed by Packers (September 11, 1992). ... Granted roster exemption for one game (September 1992). ... Traded by Packers to Miami Dolphins for past considerations (April 3, 1995). ... Granted unconditional free agency (February 11, 2000).
HONORS: Named defensive back on THE SPORTING NEWS college All-America second team (1990). ... Jim Thorpe Award winner (1991). ... Named defensive back on THE SPORTING NEWS college All-America first team (1991).
PRO STATISTICS: 1992—Recovered four fumbles. 1994—Recovered one fumble. 1995—Returned one kickoff for 16 yards. 1996—Returned one kickoff for 48 yards and recovered two fumbles. 1997—Recovered two fumbles for 23 yards and one touchdown. 1998—Recovered two fumbles. 1999—Credited with one sack.

			INTERCEPTIONS				PUNT RETURNS				TOTALS		
Year Team	G	GS	No.	Yds.	Avg.	TD	No.	Yds.	Avg.	TD	TD	2pt.	Pts.	Fum.
1992—Green Bay NFL	14	12	3	33	11.0	1	21	211	10.0	1	2	0	12	7
1993—Green Bay NFL	16	16	2	31	15.5	0	11	76	6.9	0	0	0	0	1
1994—Green Bay NFL	16	16	5	38	7.6	0	0	0	0.0	0	0	0	0	0
1995—Miami NFL	16	4	1	0	0.0	0	0	0	0.0	0	0	0	0	0
1996—Miami NFL	16	16	6	*164	27.3	1	3	24	8.0	0	1	0	6	1
1997—Miami NFL	16	16	4	26	6.5	0	4	58	14.5	0	1	0	6	0
1998—Miami NFL	16	16	8	157	19.6	1	29	354	12.2	0	1	0	6	1
1999—Miami NFL	16	11	3	3	1.0	0	8	13	1.6	0	0	0	0	1
Pro totals (8 years)	126	107	32	452	14.1	3	76	736	9.7	1	5	0	30	11

BUCKNER, BRENTSON — DE

PERSONAL: Born September 30, 1971, in Columbus, Ga. ... 6-2/305. ... Full name: Brentson Andre Buckner. ... Name pronounced BRENT-son.
HIGH SCHOOL: Carver (Columbus, Ga.).
COLLEGE: Clemson (degree in English, 1993).
TRANSACTIONS/CAREER NOTES: Selected by Pittsburgh Steelers in second round (50th pick overall) of 1994 NFL Draft. ... Signed by Steelers (July 23, 1994). ... Traded by Steelers to Kansas City Chiefs for seventh-round pick (traded to San Diego) in 1997 draft (April 4, 1997). ... Claimed on waivers by Cincinnati Bengals (August 25, 1997). ... Granted unconditional free agency (February 13, 1998). ... Signed by San Francisco 49ers (May 26, 1998). ... On physically unable to perform list with pulled quadricep muscle (July 17-August 15, 1998). ... Granted unconditional free agency (February 12, 1999). ... Re-signed by 49ers (April 7, 1999). ... Granted unconditional free agency (February 11, 2000).
CHAMPIONSHIP GAME EXPERIENCE: Played in AFC championship game (1994 and 1995 seasons). ... Played in Super Bowl XXX (1995 season).
PRO STATISTICS: 1994—Recovered one fumble. 1995—Recovered one fumble for 46 yards and a touchdown. 1996—Fumbled once and recovered one fumble for 13 yards. 1998—Recovered one fumble.

Year Team	G	GS	SACKS
1994—Pittsburgh NFL	13	5	2.0
1995—Pittsburgh NFL	16	16	3.0
1996—Pittsburgh NFL	15	14	3.0
1997—Cincinnati NFL	14	5	0.0
1998—San Francisco NFL	13	0	0.5
1999—San Francisco NFL	16	5	1.0
Pro totals (6 years)	87	45	9.5

BUNDREN, JIM — C — BROWNS

PERSONAL: Born October 6, 1974, in Pontiac, Mich. ... 6-3/303. ... Full name: Jim G. Bundren.
HIGH SCHOOL: Alexis I. Dupont (Greenville, Del.), then Valley Forge Military Academy (Wayne, Pa.).
COLLEGE: Clemson.
TRANSACTIONS/CAREER NOTES: Selected by Miami Dolphins in seventh round (210th pick overall) of 1998 NFL draft. ... Signed by Dolphins (July 15, 1998). ... Claimed on waivers by New York Jets (September 1, 1998). ... Inactive for all 16 games (1998). ... Selected by Cleveland Browns from Jets in NFL expansion draft (February 9, 1999).
PLAYING EXPERIENCE: Cleveland NFL, 1999. ... Games/Games started: 1999 (16/1).
CHAMPIONSHIP GAME EXPERIENCE: Member of Jets for AFC championship game (1998 season); inactive.
HONORS: Named offensive tackle on THE SPORTING NEWS college All-America third team (1997).

BURKE, THOMAS — DE — CARDINALS

PERSONAL: Born October 12, 1976, in Poplar, Wis. ... 6-3/261.
HIGH SCHOOL: Northwestern (Maple, Wis.).
COLLEGE: Wisconsin.
TRANSACTIONS/CAREER NOTES: Selected by Arizona Cardinals in third round (83rd pick overall) of 1999 NFL draft. ... Signed by Cardinals (June 18, 1999).

HONORS: Named defensive end on THE SPORTING NEWS college All-America first team (1998).

Year Team	G	GS	SACKS
1999—Arizona NFL	16	3	2.5

BURNETT, ROB — DE — RAVENS

PERSONAL: Born August 27, 1967, in Livingston, N.J. ... 6-4/270. ... Full name: Robert Barry Burnett.
HIGH SCHOOL: Newfield (Selden, N.Y.).
COLLEGE: Syracuse (degree in economics).
TRANSACTIONS/CAREER NOTES: Selected by Cleveland Browns in fifth round (129th pick overall) of 1990 NFL draft. ... Signed by Browns (July 22, 1990). ... Granted free agency (March 1, 1993). ... Re-signed by Browns (June 11, 1993). ... Browns franchise moved to Baltimore and renamed Ravens for 1996 season (March 11, 1996). ... Granted unconditional free agency (February 11, 2000). ... Re-signed by Ravens (February 17, 2000).
HONORS: Played in Pro Bowl (1994 season).
PRO STATISTICS: 1991—Recovered one fumble for nine yards. 1992—Recovered two fumbles. 1993—Recovered two fumbles. 1994—Recovered one fumble. 1995—Recovered one fumble. 1997—Recovered one fumble. 1998—Credited with a safety and recovered one fumble.

Year Team	G	GS	SACKS
1990—Cleveland NFL	16	6	2.0
1991—Cleveland NFL	13	8	3.0
1992—Cleveland NFL	16	16	9.0
1993—Cleveland NFL	16	16	9.0
1994—Cleveland NFL	16	16	10.0
1995—Cleveland NFL	16	16	7.5
1996—Baltimore NFL	6	6	3.0
1997—Baltimore NFL	15	15	4.0
1998—Baltimore NFL	16	16	2.5
1999—Baltimore NFL	16	16	6.5
Pro totals (10 years)	146	131	56.5

BURNS, KEITH — LB — BEARS

PERSONAL: Born May 16, 1972, in Greelyville, S.C. ... 6-2/245. ... Full name: Keith Bernard Burns.
HIGH SCHOOL: T. C. Williams (Alexandria, Va.).
JUNIOR COLLEGE: Navarro College (Texas).
COLLEGE: Oklahoma State.
TRANSACTIONS/CAREER NOTES: Selected by Denver Broncos in seventh round (210th pick overall) of 1994 NFL draft. ... Signed by Broncos (July 12, 1994). ... Granted free agency (February 14, 1997). ... Re-signed by Broncos (June 30, 1997). ... Granted unconditional free agency (February 12, 1999). ... Signed by Chicago Bears (April 6, 1999).
PLAYING EXPERIENCE: Denver NFL, 1994-1998; Chicago NFL, 1999. ... Games/Games started: 1994 (11/1), 1995 (16/0), 1996 (16/0), 1997 (16/0), 1998 (16/0), 1999 (15/0). Total: 90/1.
CHAMPIONSHIP GAME EXPERIENCE: Played in AFC championship game (1997 and 1998 seasons). ... Member of Super Bowl championship team (1997 and 1998 seasons).
PRO STATISTICS: 1995—Credited with 1½ sacks, returned one kickoff for five yards and recovered two fumbles. 1997—Returned four kickoffs for 45 yards. 1998—Returned two kickoffs for 17 yards, fumbled once and recovered one fumble. 1999—Intercepted one pass for 15 yards and recovered one fumble.

BURRIS, JEFF — DB — COLTS

PERSONAL: Born June 7, 1972, in Rock Hill, S.C. ... 6-0/190. ... Full name: Jeffrey Lamar Burris.
HIGH SCHOOL: Northwestern (Rock Hill, S.C.).
COLLEGE: Notre Dame.
TRANSACTIONS/CAREER NOTES: Selected by Buffalo Bills in first round (27th pick overall) of 1994 NFL draft. ... Signed by Bills (July 18, 1994). ... On injured reserve with knee injury (November 20, 1995-remainder of season). ... Granted unconditional free agency (February 13, 1998). ... Signed by Indianapolis Colts (February 18, 1998).
HONORS: Named defensive back on THE SPORTING NEWS college All-America second team (1993).
PRO STATISTICS: 1994—Recovered one fumble. 1996—Recovered one fumble. 1997—Returned one kickoff for 10 yards and recovered one fumble. 1999—Credited with two sacks.

			INTERCEPTIONS				PUNT RETURNS				TOTALS			
Year Team	G	GS	No.	Yds.	Avg.	TD	No.	Yds.	Avg.	TD	TD	2pt.	Pts.	Fum.
1994—Buffalo NFL	16	0	2	24	12.0	0	32	332	10.4	0	0	0	0	2
1995—Buffalo NFL	9	9	1	19	19.0	0	20	229	11.5	0	0	0	0	0
1996—Buffalo NFL	15	15	1	28	28.0	0	27	286	10.6	0	0	0	0	1
1997—Buffalo NFL	14	14	2	19	9.5	0	21	198	9.4	0	0	0	0	3
1998—Indianapolis NFL	14	14	1	0	0.0	0	0	0	0.0	0	0	0	0	0
1999—Indianapolis NFL	16	16	2	83	41.5	0	0	0	0.0	0	0	0	0	0
Pro totals (6 years)	84	68	9	173	19.2	0	100	1045	10.5	0	0	0	0	6

BURROUGH, JOHN — DE — VIKINGS

PERSONAL: Born May 17, 1972, in Laramie, Wyo. ... 6-5/276.
HIGH SCHOOL: Pinedale (Wyo.).
COLLEGE: Wyoming.

TRANSACTIONS/CAREER NOTES: Selected by Atlanta Falcons in seventh round (245th pick overall) of 1995 NFL draft. ... Signed by Falcons (June 30, 1995). ... Granted free agency (February 13, 1998). ... Re-signed by Falcons (April 1, 1998). ... Granted unconditional free agency (February 12, 1999). ... Signed by Minnesota Vikings (February 17, 1999).
PLAYING EXPERIENCE: Atlanta NFL, 1995-1998; Minnesota NFL, 1999. ... Games/Games started: 1995 (16/0), 1996 (16/1), 1997 (16/1), 1998 (16/3), 1999 (10/3). Total: 74/8.
CHAMPIONSHIP GAME EXPERIENCE: Played in NFC championship game (1998 season). ... Played in Super Bowl XXXIII (1998 season).
PRO STATISTICS: 1997—Returned one kickoff for six yards and credited with one sack. 1998—Credited with 1/2 sack and recovered one fumble. 1999—Returned one kickoff for nine yards and credited with one sack.

BURTON, SHANE   DT/DE   JETS

PERSONAL: Born January 18, 1974, in Logan, W.Va. ... 6-6/305. ... Full name: Franklin Shane Burton.
HIGH SCHOOL: Bandys (Catawba, N.C.).
COLLEGE: Tennessee.
TRANSACTIONS/CAREER NOTES: Selected by Miami Dolphins in fifth round (150th pick overall) of 1996 NFL draft. ... Signed by Dolphins (June 18, 1996). ... Granted free agency (February 12, 1999). ... Re-signed by Dolphins (April 13, 1999). ... Claimed on waivers by Chicago Bears (August 24, 1999). ... Granted unconditional free agency (February 11, 2000). ... Signed by New York Jets (March 20, 2000).
PRO STATISTICS: 1996—Recovered one fumble. 1997—Recovered one fumble. 1998—Recovered one fumble. 1999—Intercepted one pass for 37 yards.

Year Team	G	GS	SACKS
1996—Miami NFL	16	8	3.0
1997—Miami NFL	16	4	4.0
1998—Miami NFL	15	0	2.0
1999—Chicago NFL	15	0	3.0
Pro totals (4 years)	62	12	12.0

BUSH, DEVIN   S   RAMS

PERSONAL: Born July 3, 1973, in Miami. ... 6-0/210.
HIGH SCHOOL: Hialeah (Fla.) Miami Lakes.
COLLEGE: Florida State.
TRANSACTIONS/CAREER NOTES: Selected after junior season by Atlanta Falcons in first round (26th pick overall) of 1995 NFL draft. ... Signed by Falcons (August 8, 1995). ... Granted unconditional free agency (February 12, 1999). ... Signed by St. Louis Rams (February 18, 1999).
CHAMPIONSHIP GAME EXPERIENCE: Member of Falcons for NFC championship game (1998 season); inactive. ... Played in Super Bowl XXXIII (1998 season). ... Played in NFC championship game (1999 season). ... Member of Super Bowl championship team (1999 season).
PRO STATISTICS: 1995—Recovered one fumble. 1996—Recovered one fumble. 1997—Recovered one fumble. 1999—Recovered two fumbles for 31 yards.

Year Team	G	GS	No.	Yds.	Avg.	TD
			INTERCEPTIONS			
1995—Atlanta NFL	11	5	1	0	0.0	0
1996—Atlanta NFL	16	15	1	2	2.0	0
1997—Atlanta NFL	16	16	1	4	4.0	0
1998—Atlanta NFL	13	0	0	0	0.0	0
1999—St. Louis NFL	16	7	2	45	22.5	1
Pro totals (5 years)	72	43	5	51	10.2	1

BUSH, LEW   LB   CHIEFS

PERSONAL: Born December 2, 1969, in Atlanta. ... 6-2/245. ... Full name: Lewis Fitzgerald Bush.
HIGH SCHOOL: Washington (Tacoma, Wash.).
COLLEGE: Washington State.
TRANSACTIONS/CAREER NOTES: Selected by San Diego Chargers in fourth round (99th pick overall) of 1993 NFL draft. ... Signed by Chargers (July 9, 1993). ... Granted free agency (February 16, 1996). ... Re-signed by Chargers (June 14, 1996). ... Granted unconditional free agency (February 14, 1997). ... Re-signed by Chargers (May 13, 1997). ... On injured reserve with knee injury (December 26, 1998-remainder of season). ... Released by Chargers (March 1, 2000). ... Signed by Kansas City Chiefs (March 4, 2000).
PLAYING EXPERIENCE: San Diego NFL, 1993-1999. ... Games/Games started: 1993 (16/0), 1994 (16/0), 1995 (16/15), 1996 (16/16), 1997 (14/13), 1998 (10/10), 1999 (16/14). Total: 104/68.
CHAMPIONSHIP GAME EXPERIENCE: Played in AFC championship game (1994 season). ... Played in Super Bowl XXIX (1994 season).
PRO STATISTICS: 1994—Recovered one fumble. 1995—Intercepted one pass and recovered two fumbles. 1996—Credited with one sack and recovered two fumbles. 1998—Credited with one sack. 1999—Credited with one sack and recovered one fumble.

BUSH, STEVE   TE/FB   BENGALS

PERSONAL: Born July 4, 1974, in Phoenix. ... 6-3/258. ... Full name: Steven Jack Bush.
HIGH SCHOOL: Paradise Valley (Phoenix).
COLLEGE: Arizona State.
TRANSACTIONS/CAREER NOTES: Signed as non-drafted free agent by Cincinnati Bengals (April 25, 1997). ... Granted free agency (February 11, 2000). ... Re-signed by Bengals (April 25, 2000).
PLAYING EXPERIENCE: Cincinnati NFL, 1997-1999. ... Games/Games started: 1997 (16/0), 1998 (12/2), 1999 (13/0). Total: 41/2.
PRO STATISTICS: 1998—Caught four passes for 39 yards. 1999—Caught one pass for four yards.
SINGLE GAME HIGHS (regular season): Receptions—1 (October 10, 1999, vs. Cleveland); yards—18 (November 22, 1998, vs. Baltimore); and touchdown receptions—0.

BUTLER, LEROY　　　　　　　　　　S　　　　　　　　　PACKERS

PERSONAL: Born July 19, 1968, in Jacksonville. ... 6-0/203. ... Full name: LeRoy Butler III. ... Name pronounced luh-ROY.
HIGH SCHOOL: Robert E. Lee Senior (Jacksonville).
COLLEGE: Florida State.
TRANSACTIONS/CAREER NOTES: Selected by Green Bay Packers in second round (48th pick overall) of 1990 NFL draft. ... Signed by Packers (July 25, 1990). ... On suspended list (December 9, 1992). ... Designated by Packers as transition player (February 15, 1994).
CHAMPIONSHIP GAME EXPERIENCE: Played in NFC championship game (1995-1997 seasons). ... Member of Super Bowl championship team (1996 season). ... Played in Super Bowl XXXII (1997 season).
HONORS: Named strong safety on THE SPORTING NEWS NFL All-Pro team (1993 and 1996-1998). ... Played in Pro Bowl (1993 and 1996-1998 seasons).
PRO STATISTICS: 1991—Recovered one fumble. 1992—Recovered one fumble for 17 yards. 1993—Ran 25 yards with lateral from fumble recovery for a touchdown. 1996—Recovered two fumbles for two yards. 1997—Recovered one fumble. 1998—Recovered two fumbles for 32 yards and one touchdown. 1999—Recovered one fumble.

				INTERCEPTIONS			SACKS
Year　Team	G	GS	No.	Yds.	Avg.	TD	No.
1990—Green Bay NFL	16	0	3	42	14.0	0	0.0
1991—Green Bay NFL	16	16	3	6	2.0	0	0.0
1992—Green Bay NFL	15	15	1	0	0.0	0	0.0
1993—Green Bay NFL	16	16	6	131	21.8	0	1.0
1994—Green Bay NFL	13	13	3	68	22.7	0	1.0
1995—Green Bay NFL	16	16	5	105	21.0	0	1.0
1996—Green Bay NFL	16	16	5	149	29.8	1	6.5
1997—Green Bay NFL	16	16	5	4	0.8	0	3.0
1998—Green Bay NFL	16	16	3	3	1.0	0	4.0
1999—Green Bay NFL	16	16	2	0	0.0	0	1.0
Pro totals (10 years)	156	140	36	508	14.1	1	17.5

BYNUM, KENNY　　　　　　　　RB　　　　　　　　CHARGERS

PERSONAL: Born May 29, 1974, in Gainesville, Fla. ... 5-11/191. ... Full name: Kenneth Bernard Bynum.
HIGH SCHOOL: Gainesville (Fla.).
COLLEGE: South Carolina State.
TRANSACTIONS/CAREER NOTES: Selected by San Diego Chargers in fifth round (138th pick overall) of 1997 NFL draft. ... Signed by Chargers (June 16, 1997). ... Assigned by Chargers to Rhein Fire in 1999 NFL Europe enhancement allocation program (February 22, 1999). ... Granted free agency (February 11, 2000).
PRO STATISTICS: 1998—Recovered two fumbles. 1999—Recovered three fumbles.
SINGLE GAME HIGHS (regular season): Attempts—17 (December 5, 1999, vs. Cleveland); yards—64 (November 23, 1997, vs. San Francisco); and rushing touchdowns—1 (December 5, 1999, vs. Cleveland).

			RUSHING				RECEIVING				KICKOFF RETURNS				TOTALS			
Year　Team	G	GS	Att.	Yds.	Avg.	TD	No.	Yds.	Avg.	TD	No.	Yds.	Avg.	TD	TD	2pt.	Pts.	Fum.
1997—San Diego NFL	13	0	30	97	3.2	0	2	4	2.0	0	38	814	21.4	0	0	0	0	0
1998—San Diego NFL	10	0	11	23	2.1	0	4	27	6.8	0	19	345	18.2	0	0	0	0	3
1999—Rhein NFLE	...	...	194	960	4.9	5	10	86	8.6	1	0	0	0.0	0	6	0	36	0
—San Diego NFL	16	5	92	287	3.1	1	16	209	13.1	2	37	781	21.1	0	3	0	18	3
NFL Europe totals (1 year)	...	...	194	960	4.9	5	10	86	8.6	1	0	0	0.0	0	6	0	36	0
NFL totals (3 years)	39	5	133	407	3.1	1	22	240	10.9	2	94	1940	20.6	0	3	0	18	6
Pro totals (4 years)	...	...	327	1367	4.2	6	32	326	10.2	3	94	1940	20.6	0	9	0	54	6

BYRD, ISAAC　　　　　　　　WR　　　　　　　　TITANS

PERSONAL: Born November 16, 1974, in St. Louis. ... 6-1/188. ... Full name: Isaac Byrd III. ... Brother of Israel Byrd, defensive back with New Orleans Saints (1994 and 1995).
HIGH SCHOOL: Parkway Central (Chesterfield, Mo.).
COLLEGE: Kansas.
TRANSACTIONS/CAREER NOTES: Selected by Kansas City Chiefs in sixth round (195th pick overall) of 1997 NFL draft. ... Signed by Chiefs (May 6, 1997). ... Released by Chiefs (August 23, 1997). ... Re-signed by Chiefs to practice squad (August 25, 1997). ... Signed by Tennessee Oilers off Chiefs practice squad (November 7, 1997). ... Oilers franchise renamed Tennessee Titans for 1999 season (December 26, 1998). ... Granted free agency (February 11, 2000).
CHAMPIONSHIP GAME EXPERIENCE: Played in AFC championship game (1999 season). ... Played in Super Bowl XXXIV (1999 season).
PRO STATISTICS: 1998—Recovered one fumble. 1999—Returned two punts for eight yards and returned two kickoffs for 16 yards.
SINGLE GAME HIGHS (regular season): Receptions—5 (October 18, 1998, vs. Cincinnati); yards—84 (December 19, 1999, vs. Atlanta); and touchdown receptions—1 (December 26, 1999, vs. Jacksonville).

			RECEIVING				TOTALS			
Year　Team	G	GS	No.	Yds.	Avg.	TD	TD	2pt.	Pts.	Fum.
1997—Tennessee NFL	2	0	0	0	0.0	0	0	0	0	0
1998—Tennessee NFL	4	3	6	71	11.8	0	0	0	0	0
1999—Tennessee NFL	12	6	14	261	18.6	2	2	0	12	1
Pro totals (3 years)	18	9	20	332	16.6	2	2	0	12	1

RECORD AS BASEBALL PLAYER

TRANSACTIONS/CAREER NOTES: Batted right, threw right. ... Selected by San Diego Padres organization in 24th round of free-agent draft (June 3, 1993); did not sign. ... Selected by St. Louis Cardinals organization in 11th round of free agent draft (June 2, 1996).

					BATTING									FIELDING			
Year　Team (League)	Pos.	G	AB	R	H	2B	3B	HR	RBI	Avg.	BB	SO	SB	PO	A	E	Avg.
1996—Johnson City (Appal.)	OF	24	94	16	26	6	1	2	15	.277	8	19	5	37	1	1	.974

CADREZ, GLENN — LB — BRONCOS

PERSONAL: Born January 2, 1970, in El Centro, Calif. ... 6-3/240. ... Full name: Glenn E. Cadrez. ... Name pronounced ku-DREZ.
HIGH SCHOOL: El Centro Central Union (El Centro, Calif.).
JUNIOR COLLEGE: Chaffey College (Calif.).
COLLEGE: Houston.
TRANSACTIONS/CAREER NOTES: Selected by New York Jets in sixth round (154th pick overall) of 1992 NFL draft. ... Signed by Jets (July 13, 1992). ... Released by Jets (September 19, 1995). ... Signed by Denver Broncos (September 27, 1995).
CHAMPIONSHIP GAME EXPERIENCE: Played in AFC championship game (1997 and 1998 seasons). ... Member of Super Bowl championship team (1997 and 1998 seasons).
PRO STATISTICS: 1992—Recovered one fumble. 1994—Returned one kickoff for 10 yards and recovered one fumble. 1995—Recovered one fumble. 1996—Recovered one fumble. 1998—Intercepted two passes for 11 yards. 1999—Recovered four fumbles for 74 yards and one touchdown.

Year Team	G	GS	SACKS
1992—New York Jets NFL	16	0	0.0
1993—New York Jets NFL	16	0	0.0
1994—New York Jets NFL	16	0	0.0
1995—New York Jets NFL	1	0	0.0
—Denver NFL	10	7	2.0
1996—Denver NFL	16	0	0.0
1997—Denver NFL	16	0	0.0
1998—Denver NFL	16	15	4.0
1999—Denver NFL	16	15	7.0
Pro totals (8 years)	123	37	13.0

CALDWELL, MIKE — LB — EAGLES

PERSONAL: Born August 31, 1971, in Oak Ridge, Tenn. ... 6-2/237. ... Full name: Mike Isiah Caldwell. ... Nickname: Zeke.
HIGH SCHOOL: Oak Ridge (Tenn.).
COLLEGE: Middle Tennessee State (degree in business administration, 1996).
TRANSACTIONS/CAREER NOTES: Selected by Cleveland Browns in third round (83rd pick overall) of 1993 NFL draft. ... Signed by Browns (July 14, 1993). ... Granted free agency (February 16, 1996). ... Browns franchise moved to Baltimore and renamed Ravens for 1996 season (March 11, 1996). ... Re-signed by Ravens for 1996 season. ... Granted unconditional free agency (February 14, 1997). ... Signed by Arizona Cardinals (July 16, 1997). ... Granted unconditional free agency (February 13, 1998). ... Signed by Philadelphia Eagles (April 9, 1998).
PRO STATISTICS: 1993—Recovered one fumble. 1994—Returned one punt for two yards. 1999—Recovered one fumble.

Year Team	G	GS	INTERCEPTIONS No.	Yds.	Avg.	TD	SACKS No.
1993—Cleveland NFL	15	1	0	0	0.0	0	0.0
1994—Cleveland NFL	16	1	1	0	0.0	0	0.0
1995—Cleveland NFL	16	6	2	24	12.0	▲1	0.0
1996—Baltimore NFL	9	9	1	45	45.0	1	4.5
1997—Arizona NFL	16	0	1	5	5.0	0	2.0
1998—Philadelphia NFL	16	8	1	33	33.0	0	1.0
1999—Philadelphia NFL	14	2	1	12	12.0	0	1.0
Pro totals (7 years)	102	27	7	119	17.0	2	8.5

CALLOWAY, CHRIS — WR

PERSONAL: Born March 29, 1968, in Chicago. ... 5-10/182. ... Full name: Christopher Fitzpatrick Calloway.
HIGH SCHOOL: Mount Carmel (Chicago).
COLLEGE: Michigan (degree in communications and film, 1990).
TRANSACTIONS/CAREER NOTES: Selected by Pittsburgh Steelers in fourth round (97th pick overall) of 1990 NFL draft. ... Signed by Steelers (July 18, 1990). ... On injured reserve with knee injury (November 25, 1991-remainder of season). ... Granted unconditional free agency (February 1, 1992). ... Signed by New York Giants (April 1, 1992). ... Granted unconditional free agency (February 17, 1994). ... Re-signed by Giants (July 18, 1994). ... Granted unconditional free agency (February 16, 1996). ... Re-signed by Giants (April 2, 1996). ... Released by Giants (February 17, 1999). ... Signed by Atlanta Falcons (March 3, 1999). ... Released by Falcons (May 23, 2000).
PRO STATISTICS: 1991—Recovered one fumble. 1992—Returned two kickoffs for 29 yards. 1993—Returned six kickoffs for 89 yards and recovered one fumble. 1996—Recovered one fumble for seven yards.
SINGLE GAME HIGHS (regular season): Receptions—9 (October 20, 1996, vs. Washington); yards—145 (October 19, 1997, vs. Detroit); and touchdown receptions—2 (December 27, 1998, vs. Philadelphia).
STATISTICAL PLATEAUS: 100-yard receiving games: 1995 (1), 1996 (1), 1997 (1). Total: 3.

Year Team	G	GS	RUSHING Att.	Yds.	Avg.	TD	RECEIVING No.	Yds.	Avg.	TD	TOTALS TD	2pt.	Pts.	Fum.
1990—Pittsburgh NFL	16	2	0	0	0.0	0	10	124	12.4	1	1	0	6	0
1991—Pittsburgh NFL	12	0	0	0	0.0	0	15	254	16.9	1	1	0	6	0
1992—New York Giants NFL	16	1	0	0	0.0	0	27	335	12.4	1	1	0	6	0
1993—New York Giants NFL	16	9	0	0	0.0	0	35	513	14.7	3	3	0	18	0
1994—New York Giants NFL	16	14	8	77	9.6	0	43	666	15.5	2	2	0	12	1
1995—New York Giants NFL	16	15	2	-9	-4.5	0	56	796	14.2	3	3	0	18	0
1996—New York Giants NFL	16	15	1	2	2.0	0	53	739	13.9	4	4	0	24	1
1997—New York Giants NFL	16	16	1	-1	-1.0	0	58	849	14.6	8	8	0	48	0
1998—New York Giants NFL	16	16	0	0	0.0	0	62	812	13.1	6	6	0	36	1
1999—Atlanta NFL	11	6	0	0	0.0	0	22	314	14.3	1	1	0	6	0
Pro totals (10 years)	151	94	12	69	5.8	0	381	5402	14.2	30	30	0	180	3

C

CAMPBELL, DAN   TE   GIANTS

PERSONAL: Born April 13, 1976, in Glen Rose, Texas. ... 6-5/265. ... Full name: Daniel Allen Campbell.
HIGH SCHOOL: Glen Rose (Texas).
COLLEGE: Texas A&M.
TRANSACTIONS/CAREER NOTES: Selected by New York Giants in third round (79th pick overall) of 1999 NFL draft. ... Signed by Giants (July 29, 1999).
PLAYING EXPERIENCE: New York Giants NFL, 1999. ... Games/Games started: 1999 (12/1).

CAMPBELL, LAMAR   CB   LIONS

PERSONAL: Born August 29, 1976, in Chester, Pa. ... 5-11/183.
HIGH SCHOOL: Strath Haven (Wallingford, Pa.).
COLLEGE: Wisconsin.
TRANSACTIONS/CAREER NOTES: Signed as non-drafted free agent by Detroit Lions (April 24, 1998).
PLAYING EXPERIENCE: Detroit NFL, 1998 and 1999. ... Games/Games started: 1998 (12/0), 1999 (15/2). Total: 27/2.

CAMPBELL, MARK   TE   BROWNS

PERSONAL: Born December 6, 1975, in Clawson, Mich. ... 6-6/253.
HIGH SCHOOL: Bishop Foley (Madison Heights, Mich.).
COLLEGE: Michigan.
TRANSACTIONS/CAREER NOTES: Signed as non-drafted free agent by Cleveland Browns (April 23, 1999). ... On injured reserve with ankle injury (December 14, 1999-remainder of season).
PRO STATISTICS: 1999—Recovered two fumbles.
SINGLE GAME HIGHS (regular season): Receptions—2 (December 12, 1999, vs. Cincinnati); yards—33 (December 12, 1999, vs. Cincinnati); and touchdown receptions—0.

			RECEIVING				KICKOFF RETURNS				TOTALS		
Year Team	G	GS	No.	Yds.	Avg.	TD	No.	Yds.	Avg.	TD	TD	2pt.	Pts.	Fum.
1999—Cleveland NFL	14	4	9	131	14.6	0	3	28	9.3	0	0	0	0	0

CAMPBELL, MATT   G   PANTHERS

PERSONAL: Born July 14, 1972, in North Augusta, S.C. ... 6-4/300. ... Full name: Mathew Thomas Campbell.
HIGH SCHOOL: North Augusta (S.C.).
COLLEGE: South Carolina.
TRANSACTIONS/CAREER NOTES: Signed as non-drafted free agent by New Orleans Saints (April 28, 1994). ... Released by Saints (August 23, 1994). ... Re-signed by Saints to practice squad (August 30, 1994). ... Released by Saints (September 20, 1994). ... Signed by Carolina Panthers (December 15, 1994). ... Granted free agency (February 13, 1998). ... Tendered offer sheet by Miami Dolphins (February 20, 1998). ... Offer matched by Panthers (February 27, 1998).
PLAYING EXPERIENCE: Carolina NFL, 1995-1999. ... Games/Games started: 1995 (10/1), 1996 (9/8), 1997 (16/14), 1998 (10/10), 1999 (10/10). Total: 55/33.
CHAMPIONSHIP GAME EXPERIENCE: Played in NFC championship game (1996 season).
PRO STATISTICS: 1995—Caught three passes for 32 yards and fumbled once.
MISCELLANEOUS: Played tight end during 1995 season.

CANNIDA, JAMES   DT   BUCCANEERS

PERSONAL: Born January 3, 1975, in Savannah, Ga. ... 6-2/291. ... Full name: James Thomas Cannida II.
HIGH SCHOOL: American (Fremont, Calif.).
COLLEGE: Nevada-Reno.
TRANSACTIONS/CAREER NOTES: Selected by Tampa Bay Buccaneers in sixth round (175th pick overall) of 1998 NFL draft. ... Signed by Buccaneers (June 4, 1998).
PLAYING EXPERIENCE: Tampa Bay NFL, 1998 and 1999. ... Games/Games started: 1998 (10/0), 1999 (2/1). Total: 12/1.
CHAMPIONSHIP GAME EXPERIENCE: Member of Buccaneers for NFC championship game (1999 season); inactive.

CANTY, CHRIS   CB   SEAHAWKS

PERSONAL: Born March 30, 1976, in Long Beach, Calif. ... 5-9/185. ... Full name: Christopher Shawn Patrick Canty.
HIGH SCHOOL: Eastern (Voorhees, N.J.).
COLLEGE: Kansas State.
TRANSACTIONS/CAREER NOTES: Selected after junior season by New England Patriots in first round (29th pick overall) of 1997 NFL draft. ... Signed by Patriots (July 17, 1997). ... Released by Patriots (June 7, 1999). ... Signed by Chicago Bears (July 21, 1999). ... Claimed on waivers by Seattle Seahawks (September 6, 1999). ... Granted free agency (February 11, 2000). ... Re-signed by Seahawks (April 17, 2000).
HONORS: Named defensive back on THE SPORTING NEWS college All-America first team (1995). ... Named cornerback on THE SPORTING NEWS college All-America first team (1996).
PRO STATISTICS: 1997—Recovered two fumbles for nine yards.

			INTERCEPTIONS				SACKS	PUNT RETURNS				KICKOFF RETURNS				TOTALS			
Year Team	G	GS	No.	Yds.	Avg.	TD	No.	No.	Yds.	Avg.	TD	No.	Yds.	Avg.	TD	TD	2pt.	Pts.	Fum.
1997—New England NFL	16	1	0	0	0.0	0	2.0	0	0	0.0	0	4	115	28.8	0	0	0	0	0
1998—New England NFL	16	9	1	12	12.0	0	1.0	16	170	10.6	0	11	198	18.0	0	0	0	0	2

1999—Seattle NFL	14	1	3	26	8.7	0	0.0	0	0	0.0	0	0	0	0.0	0	0 0 0 0
Pro totals (3 years)	46	11	4	38	9.5	0	3.0	16	170	10.6	0	15	313	20.9	0	0 0 0 2

CARNEY, JOHN — K — CHARGERS

PERSONAL: Born April 20, 1964, in Hartford, Conn. ... 5-11/170. ... Full name: John Michael Carney.
HIGH SCHOOL: Cardinal Newman (West Palm Beach, Fla.).
COLLEGE: Notre Dame (degree in marketing, 1987).
TRANSACTIONS/CAREER NOTES: Signed as non-drafted free agent by Cincinnati Bengals (May 1, 1987). ... Released by Bengals (August 10, 1987). ... Signed as replacement player by Tampa Bay Buccaneers (September 24, 1987). ... Released by Buccaneers (October 14, 1987). ... Re-signed by Buccaneers (April 5, 1988). ... Released by Buccaneers (August 23, 1988). ... Re-signed by Buccaneers (November 22, 1988). ... Granted unconditional free agency (February 1-April 1, 1989). ... Re-signed by Buccaneers (April 13, 1989). ... Released by Buccaneers (September 5, 1989). ... Re-signed by Buccaneers (December 13, 1989). ... Granted unconditional free agency (February 1, 1990). ... Signed by San Diego Chargers (April 1, 1990). ... Released by Chargers (August 28, 1990). ... Signed by Los Angeles Rams (September 21, 1990). ... Released by Rams (September 26, 1990). ... Signed by Chargers (October 3, 1990). ... Granted free agency (February 1, 1992). ... Re-signed by Chargers (July 27, 1992). ... Granted free agency (March 1, 1993). ... Re-signed by Chargers (June 9, 1993). ... Granted unconditional free agency (February 17, 1994). ... Re-signed by Chargers (April 6, 1994). ... On injured reserve with knee injury (November 15, 1997-remainder of season).
CHAMPIONSHIP GAME EXPERIENCE: Played in AFC championship game (1994 season). ... Played in Super Bowl XXIX (1994 season).
HONORS: Named kicker on THE SPORTING NEWS NFL All-Pro team (1994). ... Played in Pro Bowl (1994 season).
RECORDS: Holds NFL career record for highest field-goal percentage—81.67.
PRO STATISTICS: 1993—Punted four times for 155 yards. 1999—Recovered one fumble.

		KICKING							
Year Team	G	XPM	XPA	FGM	FGA	Lg.	50+	Pts.
1988—Tampa Bay NFL	4	6	6	2	5	29	0-0	12
1989—Tampa Bay NFL	1	0	0	0	0	0	0-0	0
1990—Los Angeles Rams NFL	1	0	0	0	0	0	0-0	0
—San Diego NFL	12	27	28	19	21	43	0-1	84
1991—San Diego NFL	16	31	31	19	29	54	2-4	88
1992—San Diego NFL	16	35	35	26	32	50	1-3	113
1993—San Diego NFL	16	31	33	31	40	51	2-3	124
1994—San Diego NFL	16	33	33	†34	§38	50	2-2	*135
1995—San Diego NFL	16	32	33	21	26	45	0-2	95
1996—San Diego NFL	16	31	31	29	36	53	3-3	118
1997—San Diego NFL	4	5	5	7	7	41	0-0	26
1998—San Diego NFL	16	19	19	26	30	54	2-3	97
1999—San Diego NFL	16	22	23	31	36	50	1-1	115
Pro totals (12 years)	150	272	277	245	300	54	13-22	1007

CARPENTER, KEION — S — BILLS

PERSONAL: Born October 31, 1977, in Baltimore. ... 5-11/205. ... Full name: Keion Eric Carpenter.
HIGH SCHOOL: Woodlawn (Baltimore).
COLLEGE: Virginia Tech.
TRANSACTIONS/CAREER NOTES: Signed as non-drafted free agent by Buffalo Bills (April 19, 1999).
PLAYING EXPERIENCE: Buffalo NFL, 1999. ... Games/Games started: 1999 (10/0).

CARPENTER, RON — S

PERSONAL: Born January 20, 1970, in Cincinnati. ... 6-1/188.
HIGH SCHOOL: Princeton (Cincinnati).
COLLEGE: Miami of Ohio.
TRANSACTIONS/CAREER NOTES: Signed as non-drafted free agent by Minnesota Vikings (May 1, 1993). ... Claimed on waivers by Cincinnati Bengals (November 3, 1993). ... Released by Bengals (July 29, 1994). ... Signed by Minnesota Vikings (August 2, 1994). ... Released by Vikings (August 22, 1994). ... Selected by Amsterdam Admirals in fifth round (27th pick overall) of 1995 World League Draft. ... Signed by New York Jets (June 28, 1995). ... Released by Jets (September 18, 1996). ... Signed by St. Louis Rams (July 16, 1997). ... Released by Rams (August 24, 1997). ... Played for New York Cityhawks of Arena Football League (1998). ... Signed by Rams (November 17, 1998). ... Released by Rams (September 4, 1999). ... Re-signed by Rams (September 13, 1999). ... Granted unconditional free agency (February 11, 2000).
CHAMPIONSHIP GAME EXPERIENCE: Member of Rams for NFC championship game (1999 season); inactive. ... Member of Super Bowl championship team (1999 season); inactive.

			INTERCEPTIONS				KICKOFF RETURNS				TOTALS			
Year Team	G	GS	No.	Yds.	Avg.	TD	No.	Yds.	Avg.	TD	TD	2pt.	Pts.	Fum.
1993—Minnesota NFL	7	0	0	0	0.0	0	0	0	0.0	0	0	0	0	0
—Cincinnati NFL	6	0	0	0	0.0	0	0	0	0.0	0	0	0	0	0
1994—							Did not play.							
1995—Amsterdam W.L.	...	...	7	93	13.3	1	7	219	31.3	0	1	0	6	0
—New York Jets NFL	13	4	0	0	0.0	0	20	553	*27.7	0	0	0	0	2
1996—New York Jets NFL	2	0	0	0	0.0	0	6	107	17.8	0	0	0	0	0
1997—Amsterdam W.L.	...	...	2	45	22.5	0	23	580	25.2	0	0	0	0	0
1998—St. Louis NFL	6	0	0	0	0.0	0	0	0	0.0	0	0	0	0	0
1999—St. Louis NFL	11	0	0	0	0.0	0	16	406	25.4	0	0	0	0	0
W.L. totals (2 years)	...	...	9	138	15.3	1	30	799	26.6	0	1	0	6	0
NFL totals (5 years)	45	4	0	0	0.0	0	42	1066	25.4	0	0	0	0	2
Pro totals (7 years)	...	...	9	138	15.3	1	72	1865	25.9	0	1	0	6	2

CARRIER, MARK   S   REDSKINS

PERSONAL: Born April 28, 1968, in Lake Charles, La. ... 6-1/190. ... Full name: Mark Anthony Carrier III. ... Related to Mark Carrier, wide receiver with Tampa Bay Buccaneers (1987-92), Cleveland Browns (1993 and 1994) and Carolina Panthers (1995-98).
HIGH SCHOOL: Polytechnic (Pasadena, Calif.).
COLLEGE: Southern California (degree in communications).
TRANSACTIONS/CAREER NOTES: Selected after junior season by Chicago Bears in first round (sixth pick overall) of 1990 NFL draft. ... Signed by Bears (April 22, 1990). ... Designated by Bears as transition player (February 25, 1993). ... Released by Bears (June 1, 1997). ... Signed by Detroit Lions (June 20, 1997). ... Granted unconditional free agency (February 11, 2000). ... Signed by Washington Redskins (February 17, 2000).
HONORS: Named defensive back on THE SPORTING NEWS college All-America second team (1988). ... Jim Thorpe Award winner (1989). ... Named defensive back on THE SPORTING NEWS college All-America first team (1989). ... Played in Pro Bowl (1990, 1991 and 1993 seasons). ... Named free safety on THE SPORTING NEWS NFL All-Pro team (1991).
PRO STATISTICS: 1990—Recovered two fumbles for 16 yards. 1991—Recovered one fumble for two yards. 1992—Recovered two fumbles. 1995—Recovered one fumble. 1996—Recovered one fumble. 1997—Returned one punt for no yards and fumbled once. 1998—Fumbled once. 1999—Recovered one fumble for six yards.

			INTERCEPTIONS			
Year Team	G	GS	No.	Yds.	Avg.	TD
1990—Chicago NFL	16	16	*10	39	3.9	0
1991—Chicago NFL	16	16	2	54	27.0	0
1992—Chicago NFL	16	14	0	0	0.0	0
1993—Chicago NFL	16	16	4	94	23.5	1
1994—Chicago NFL	16	15	2	10	5.0	0
1995—Chicago NFL	16	15	0	0	0.0	0
1996—Chicago NFL	13	13	2	0	0.0	0
1997—Detroit NFL	16	16	5	94	18.8	0
1998—Detroit NFL	13	13	3	33	11.0	0
1999—Detroit NFL	15	15	3	16	5.3	0
Pro totals (10 years)	153	149	31	340	11.0	1

CARRUTH, RAE   WR

PERSONAL: Born January 20, 1974, in Sacramento. ... 5-11/195. ... Full name: Rae Lamar Carruth. ... Name pronounced KA-ruth.
HIGH SCHOOL: Valley (Sacramento).
COLLEGE: Colorado.
TRANSACTIONS/CAREER NOTES: Selected by Carolina Panthers in first round (27th pick overall) of 1997 NFL draft. ... Signed by Panthers (July 18, 1997). ... On injured reserve with foot injury (November 28, 1998-remainder of season). ... Suspended by NFL for personal reasons (December 16, 1999-present). ... Released by Panthers (December 17, 1999).
HONORS: Named wide receiver on THE SPORTING NEWS college All-America first team (1996).
SINGLE GAME HIGHS (regular season): Receptions—8 (September 21, 1997, vs. Kansas City); yards—110 (September 21, 1997, vs. Kansas City); and touchdown receptions—1 (December 20, 1997, vs. St. Louis).
STATISTICAL PLATEAUS: 100-yard receiving games: 1997 (2).

			RUSHING				RECEIVING				TOTALS			
Year Team	G	GS	Att.	Yds.	Avg.	TD	No.	Yds.	Avg.	TD	TD	2pt.	Pts.	Fum.
1997—Carolina NFL	15	14	6	23	3.8	0	44	545	12.4	4	4	0	24	2
1998—Carolina NFL	2	1	0	0	0.0	0	4	59	14.8	0	0	0	0	0
1999—Carolina NFL	5	5	1	4	4.0	0	14	200	14.3	0	0	0	0	0
Pro totals (3 years)	22	20	7	27	3.9	0	62	804	13.0	4	4	0	24	2

CARSWELL, DWAYNE   TE   BRONCOS

PERSONAL: Born January 18, 1972, in Jacksonville. ... 6-3/260.
HIGH SCHOOL: University Christian (Jacksonville).
COLLEGE: Liberty (Va.).
TRANSACTIONS/CAREER NOTES: Signed as non-drafted free agent by Denver Broncos (May 2, 1994). ... Released by Broncos (August 26, 1994). ... Re-signed by Broncos to practice squad (August 30, 1994). ... Activated (November 25, 1994).
CHAMPIONSHIP GAME EXPERIENCE: Played in AFC championship game (1997 and 1998 seasons). ... Member of Super Bowl championship team (1997 and 1998 seasons).
PRO STATISTICS: 1994—Returned one kickoff for no yards and recovered one fumble. 1997—Recovered one fumble.
SINGLE GAME HIGHS (regular season): Receptions—6 (December 25, 1999, vs. Detroit); yards—47 (September 14, 1997, vs. St. Louis); and touchdown receptions—1 (December 25, 1999, vs. Detroit).

			RECEIVING				TOTALS			
Year Team	G	GS	No.	Yds.	Avg.	TD	TD	2pt.	Pts.	Fum.
1994—Denver NFL	4	0	0	0	0.0	0	0	0	0	0
1995—Denver NFL	9	2	3	37	12.3	0	0	0	0	0
1996—Denver NFL	16	2	15	85	5.7	0	0	0	0	0
1997—Denver NFL	16	3	12	96	8.0	1	1	0	6	0
1998—Denver NFL	16	1	4	51	12.8	0	0	0	0	0
1999—Denver NFL	16	11	24	201	8.4	2	2	0	12	0
Pro totals (6 years)	77	19	58	470	8.1	3	3	0	18	0

CARTER, CHRIS   S   PATRIOTS

PERSONAL: Born September 27, 1974, in Tyler, Texas. ... 6-2/209. ... Full name: Christopher Cary Carter. ... Cousin of Joe Carter, first baseman/outfielder with five major league baseball teams (1984-98).

C

HIGH SCHOOL: John Tyler (Tyler, Texas).
COLLEGE: Texas.
TRANSACTIONS/CAREER NOTES: Selected by New England Patriots in third round (89th pick overall) of 1997 NFL draft. ... Signed by Patriots (July 15, 1997). ... Granted free agency (February 11, 2000).
PLAYING EXPERIENCE: New England NFL, 1997-1999. ... Games/Games started: 1997 (16/0), 1998 (16/0), 1999 (15/15). Total: 47/15.
PRO STATISTICS: 1998—Credited with one sack. 1999—Intercepted three passes for 13 yards, credited with one sack and recovered two fumbles.

CARTER, CRIS   WR   VIKINGS

PERSONAL: Born November 25, 1965, in Troy, Ohio. ... 6-3/220. ... Full name: Christopher D. Carter. ... Brother of Butch Carter, head coach, Toronto Raptors.
HIGH SCHOOL: Middletown (Ohio).
COLLEGE: Ohio State.
TRANSACTIONS/CAREER NOTES: Selected by Philadelphia Eagles in fourth round of 1987 NFL supplemental draft (September 4, 1987). ... Signed by Eagles (September 17, 1987). ... Granted roster exemption (September 17-October 26, 1987). ... Claimed on waivers by Minnesota Vikings (September 4, 1990). ... Granted free agency (February 1, 1991). ... Re-signed by Vikings (July 9, 1991). ... Granted free agency (February 1, 1992). ... Re-signed by Vikings (July 26, 1992). ... On injured reserve with broken collarbone (December 4-30, 1992).
CHAMPIONSHIP GAME EXPERIENCE: Played in NFC championship game (1998 season).
HONORS: Played in Pro Bowl (1993-1999 seasons). ... Named wide receiver on THE SPORTING NEWS NFL All-Pro team (1994).
PRO STATISTICS: 1987—Attempted one pass without a completion and returned 12 kickoffs for 241 yards. 1988—Recovered one fumble in end zone for a touchdown. 1989—Recovered one fumble. 1993—Recovered one fumble. 1996—Returned one kickoff for three yards and recovered one fumble.
SINGLE GAME HIGHS (regular season): Receptions—14 (October 2, 1994, vs. Arizona); yards—167 (October 2, 1994, vs. Arizona); and touchdown receptions—3 (November 14, 1999, vs. Chicago).
STATISTICAL PLATEAUS: 100-yard receiving games: 1988 (1), 1989 (1), 1990 (2), 1991 (4), 1992 (1), 1993 (3), 1994 (5), 1995 (5), 1996 (1), 1997 (4), 1998 (3), 1999 (5). Total: 35.
MISCELLANEOUS: Holds Minnesota Vikings all-time records for most receptions (835), most yards receiving (10,238), most touchdowns (95) and most touchdown receptions (95).

			RUSHING				RECEIVING				TOTALS			
Year Team	G	GS	Att.	Yds.	Avg.	TD	No.	Yds.	Avg.	TD	TD	2pt.	Pts.	Fum.
1987—Philadelphia NFL	9	0	0	0	0.0	0	5	84	16.8	2	2	0	12	0
1988—Philadelphia NFL	16	16	1	1	1.0	0	39	761	19.5	6	7	0	42	0
1989—Philadelphia NFL	16	15	2	16	8.0	0	45	605	13.4	11	11	0	66	1
1990—Minnesota NFL	16	5	2	6	3.0	0	27	413	15.3	3	3	0	18	0
1991—Minnesota NFL	16	16	0	0	0.0	0	72	962	13.4	5	5	0	30	1
1992—Minnesota NFL	12	12	5	15	3.0	0	53	681	12.8	6	6	0	36	1
1993—Minnesota NFL	16	16	0	0	0.0	0	86	1071	12.5	9	9	0	54	0
1994—Minnesota NFL	16	16	0	0	0.0	0	*122	1256	10.3	7	7	2	46	4
1995—Minnesota NFL	16	16	1	0	0.0	0	122	1371	11.2	†17	17	0	102	0
1996—Minnesota NFL	16	16	0	0	0.0	0	96	1163	12.1	10	10	0	60	1
1997—Minnesota NFL	16	16	0	0	0.0	0	89	1069	12.0	*13	13	3	84	3
1998—Minnesota NFL	16	16	1	-1	-1.0	0	78	1011	13.0	12	12	0	72	0
1999—Minnesota NFL	16	16	0	0	0.0	0	90	1241	13.8	*13	13	0	78	0
Pro totals (13 years)	197	176	12	37	3.1	0	924	11688	12.6	114	115	5	700	11

CARTER, DALE   CB   BRONCOS

PERSONAL: Born November 28, 1969, in Covington, Ga. ... 6-1/188. ... Full name: Dale Lavelle Carter. ... Brother of Jake Reed, wide receiver, New Orleans Saints.
HIGH SCHOOL: Newton County (Covington, Ga.).
JUNIOR COLLEGE: Ellsworth (Iowa) Community College.
COLLEGE: Tennessee.
TRANSACTIONS/CAREER NOTES: Selected by Kansas City Chiefs in first round (20th pick overall) of 1992 NFL draft. ... Signed by Chiefs (June 2, 1992). ... Designated by Chiefs as transition player (February 25, 1993). ... On injured reserve with broken arm (January 7, 1994-remainder of 1993 playoffs). ... Tendered offer sheet by Minnesota Vikings (July 12, 1996). ... Offer matched by Chiefs (July 19, 1996). ... Granted unconditional free agency (February 12, 1999). ... Signed by Denver Broncos (February 19, 1999). ... Suspended by NFL for violating league substance abuse policy (April 25, 2000-present).
HONORS: Named kick returner on THE SPORTING NEWS college All-America first team (1990). ... Named defensive back on THE SPORTING NEWS college All-America first team (1991). ... Played in Pro Bowl (1994, 1995 and 1997 seasons). ... Named cornerback on THE SPORTING NEWS NFL All-Pro team (1996). ... Named to play in Pro Bowl (1996 season); replaced by Terry McDaniel due to injury.
PRO STATISTICS: 1992—Recovered two fumbles. 1993—Rushed once for two yards and recovered two fumbles. 1994—Recovered one fumble. 1995—Recovered two fumbles. 1996—Rushed once for three yards, caught six passes for 89 yards and a touchdown and recovered two fumbles for seven yards.

			INTERCEPTIONS				PUNT RETURNS				KICKOFF RETURNS				TOTALS			
Year Team	G	GS	No.	Yds.	Avg.	TD	No.	Yds.	Avg.	TD	No.	Yds.	Avg.	TD	TD	2pt.	Pts.	Fum.
1992—Kansas City NFL	16	9	7	65	9.3	0	38	398	10.5	†2	11	190	17.3	0	3	0	18	7
1993—Kansas City NFL	15	11	1	0	0.0	0	27	247	9.1	0	0	0	0.0	0	0	0	0	4
1994—Kansas City NFL	16	16	2	24	12.0	0	16	124	7.8	0	0	0	0.0	0	0	0	0	1
1995—Kansas City NFL	16	14	4	45	11.3	0	0	0	0.0	0	0	0	0.0	0	0	0	0	0
1996—Kansas City NFL	14	14	3	17	5.7	0	2	18	9.0	0	0	0	0.0	0	1	0	6	1
1997—Kansas City NFL	16	15	2	9	4.5	0	0	0	0.0	0	0	0	0.0	0	0	0	0	0
1998—Kansas City NFL	11	9	2	23	11.5	0	0	0	0.0	0	0	0	0.0	0	0	0	0	0
1999—Denver NFL	14	14	2	48	24.0	0	0	0	0.0	0	0	0	0.0	0	0	0	0	0
Pro totals (8 years)	118	102	23	231	10.0	1	83	787	9.5	2	11	190	17.3	0	4	0	24	13

CARTER, KEVIN DE RAMS

PERSONAL: Born September 21, 1973, in Miami. ... 6-5/280. ... Full name: Kevin Louis Carter. ... Brother of Bernard Carter, linebacker with Jacksonville Jaguars (1995).
HIGH SCHOOL: Lincoln (Tallahassee, Fla.).
COLLEGE: Florida.
TRANSACTIONS/CAREER NOTES: Selected by St. Louis Rams in first round (sixth pick overall) of 1995 NFL draft. ... Signed by Rams (July 17, 1995).
CHAMPIONSHIP GAME EXPERIENCE: Played in NFC championship game (1999 season). ... Member of Super Bowl championship team (1999 season).
HONORS: Named defensive lineman on The Sporting News college All-America first team (1994). ... Named defensive end on The Sporting News NFL All-Pro team (1999). ... Played in Pro Bowl (1999 season).
PRO STATISTICS: 1995—Recovered one fumble. 1996—Recovered two fumbles. 1997—Recovered two fumbles for five yards. 1999—Recovered two fumbles.

Year Team	G	GS	SACKS
1995—St. Louis NFL	16	16	6.0
1996—St. Louis NFL	16	16	9.5
1997—St. Louis NFL	16	16	7.5
1998—St. Louis NFL	16	16	12.0
1999—St. Louis NFL	16	16	*17.0
Pro totals (5 years)	80	80	52.0

CARTER, KI-JANA RB

PERSONAL: Born September 12, 1973, in Westerville, Ohio. ... 5-10/222. ... Full name: Kenneth Leonard Carter. ... Name pronounced KEE-john-uh.
HIGH SCHOOL: Westerville (Ohio) North.
COLLEGE: Penn State.
TRANSACTIONS/CAREER NOTES: Selected after junior season by Cincinnati Bengals in first round (first pick overall) of 1995 NFL draft. ... Signed by Bengals (July 19, 1995). ... On injured reserve with knee injury (August 22, 1995-entire season). ... On injured reserve with wrist injury (September 7, 1998-remainder of season). ... On injured reserve with knee injury (September 29, 1999-remainder of season). ... Released by Bengals (June 1, 2000).
HONORS: Named running back on The Sporting News college All-America first team (1994).
PRO STATISTICS: 1996—Recovered two fumbles for minus eight yards. 1997—Attempted one pass without a completion, returned one kickoff for nine yards and recovered two fumbles.
SINGLE GAME HIGHS (regular season): Attempts—19 (August 31, 1997, vs. Arizona); yards—104 (September 21, 1997, vs. Denver); and rushing touchdowns—2 (August 31, 1997, vs. Arizona).
STATISTICAL PLATEAUS: 100-yard rushing games: 1997 (1).

Year Team	G	GS	RUSHING				RECEIVING				TOTALS			
			Att.	Yds.	Avg.	TD	No.	Yds.	Avg.	TD	TD	2pt.	Pts.	Fum.
1995—Cincinnati NFL							Did not play.							
1996—Cincinnati NFL	16	4	91	264	2.9	8	22	169	7.7	1	9	0	54	2
1997—Cincinnati NFL	15	10	128	464	3.6	7	21	157	7.5	0	7	0	42	3
1998—Cincinnati NFL	1	0	2	4	2.0	0	6	25	4.2	0	0	0	0	0
1999—Cincinnati NFL	3	0	6	15	2.5	1	3	24	8.0	0	1	0	6	0
Pro totals (4 years)	35	14	227	747	3.3	16	52	375	7.2	1	17	0	102	5

CARTER, MARTY S FALCONS

PERSONAL: Born December 17, 1969, in La Grange, Ga. ... 6-1/210. ... Full name: Marty LaVincent Carter.
HIGH SCHOOL: La Grange (Ga.).
COLLEGE: Middle Tennessee State.
TRANSACTIONS/CAREER NOTES: Selected by Tampa Bay Buccaneers in eighth round (207th pick overall) of 1991 NFL draft. ... Signed by Buccaneers (July 19, 1991). ... Granted unconditional free agency (February 17, 1995). ... Signed by Chicago Bears (March 3, 1995). ... Granted unconditional free agency (February 12, 1999). ... Signed by Atlanta Falcons (March 12, 1999). ... On injured reserve with knee injury (November 30, 1999-remainder of season).
PRO STATISTICS: 1993—Recovered two fumbles. 1994—Caught one pass for 21 yards and returned one kickoff for no yards. 1995—Recovered one fumble. 1998—Recovered two fumbles. 1999—Recovered one fumble.

Year Team	G	GS	INTERCEPTIONS				SACKS
			No.	Yds.	Avg.	TD	No.
1991—Tampa Bay NFL	14	11	1	5	5.0	0	0.0
1992—Tampa Bay NFL	16	16	3	1	0.3	0	2.0
1993—Tampa Bay NFL	16	14	1	0	0.0	0	0.0
1994—Tampa Bay NFL	16	14	0	0	0.0	0	1.0
1995—Chicago NFL	16	16	2	20	10.0	0	0.0
1996—Chicago NFL	16	16	3	34	11.3	0	0.0
1997—Chicago NFL	15	15	1	14	14.0	0	1.0
1998—Chicago NFL	16	16	0	0	0.0	0	0.0
1999—Atlanta NFL	11	11	1	4	4.0	0	0.0
Pro totals (9 years)	136	129	12	78	6.5	0	4.0

CARTER, TOM CB BENGALS

PERSONAL: Born September 5, 1972, in St. Petersburg, Fla. ... 6-0/190. ... Full name: Thomas Carter III.
HIGH SCHOOL: Lakeland (Fla.).
COLLEGE: Notre Dame (degree in finance, 1996).

TRANSACTIONS/CAREER NOTES: Selected after junior season by Washington Redskins in first round (17th pick overall) of 1993 NFL draft. ... Signed by Redskins for 1993 season. ... Designated by Redskins as transition player (February 15, 1994). ... Designated by Redskins as transition player (February 12, 1997). ... Tendered offer sheet by Chicago Bears (March 31, 1997). ... Redskins declined to match offer (April 7, 1997). ... On injured reserve with broken collarbone (September 30, 1998-remainder of season). ... Claimed on waivers by Cincinnati Bengals (December 14, 1999).

PRO STATISTICS: 1999—Recovered one fumble for 21 yards.

				INTERCEPTIONS		
Year Team	G	GS	No.	Yds.	Avg.	TD
1993—Washington NFL	14	11	6	54	9.0	0
1994—Washington NFL	16	16	3	58	19.3	0
1995—Washington NFL	16	16	4	116	29.0	1
1996—Washington NFL	16	16	5	24	4.8	0
1997—Chicago NFL	16	16	3	12	4.0	0
1998—Chicago NFL	4	4	2	20	10.0	0
1999—Chicago NFL	12	6	1	36	36.0	0
—Cincinnati NFL	2	2	1	0	0.0	0
Pro totals (7 years)	96	87	25	320	12.8	1

CARTER, TONY   FB   PATRIOTS

PERSONAL: Born August 23, 1972, in Columbus, Ohio. ... 6-0/232. ... Full name: Antonio Marcus Carter.
HIGH SCHOOL: South (Columbus, Ohio).
COLLEGE: Minnesota.
TRANSACTIONS/CAREER NOTES: Signed as non-drafted free agent by Chicago Bears (April 28, 1994). ... Granted unconditional free agency (February 13, 1998). ... Signed by New England Patriots (February 25, 1998).
PRO STATISTICS: 1996—Recovered one fumble. 1997—Recovered one fumble. 1999—Recovered one fumble.
SINGLE GAME HIGHS (regular season): Attempts—6 (October 13, 1996, vs. New Orleans); yards—37 (October 13, 1996, vs. New Orleans); and rushing touchdowns—0.

			RUSHING				RECEIVING				KICKOFF RETURNS				TOTALS			
Year Team	G	GS	Att.	Yds.	Avg.	TD	No.	Yds.	Avg.	TD	No.	Yds.	Avg.	TD	TD	2pt.	Pts.	Fum.
1994—Chicago NFL	14	0	0	0	0.0	0	1	24	24.0	0	6	99	16.5	0	0	0	0	0
1995—Chicago NFL	16	11	10	34	3.4	0	40	329	8.2	1	3	24	8.0	0	1	0	6	1
1996—Chicago NFL	16	11	11	43	3.9	0	41	233	5.7	0	0	0	0.0	0	0	0	0	1
1997—Chicago NFL	16	10	9	56	6.2	0	24	152	6.3	0	2	34	17.0	0	0	0	0	0
1998—New England NFL	11	7	2	3	1.5	0	18	166	9.2	0	0	0	0.0	0	0	0	0	0
1999—New England NFL	16	14	6	26	4.3	0	20	108	5.4	0	0	0	0.0	0	0	0	0	0
Pro totals (6 years)	89	53	38	162	4.3	0	144	1012	7.0	1	11	157	14.3	0	1	0	6	2

CARTY, JOHNDALE   S   FALCONS

PERSONAL: Born August 27, 1977, in Miami. ... 6-0/202.
HIGH SCHOOL: Hialeah (Fla.) Miami Lakes.
COLLEGE: Utah State.
TRANSACTIONS/CAREER NOTES: Selected by Atlanta Falcons in fourth round (126th pick overall) of 1999 NFL draft. ... Signed by Falcons (July 8, 1999).
PLAYING EXPERIENCE: Atlanta NFL, 1999. ... Games/Games started: 1999 (14/0).

CASCADDEN, CHAD   LB

PERSONAL: Born May 14, 1972, in Two Rivers, Wis. ... 6-1/240. ... Name pronounced cas-CAD-den.
HIGH SCHOOL: Chippewa Falls (Wis.).
COLLEGE: Wisconsin (degree in kinesiology).
TRANSACTIONS/CAREER NOTES: Signed as non-drafted free agent by New York Jets (April 28, 1995). ... Released by Jets (August 27, 1995). ... Re-signed by Jets to practice squad (August 29, 1995). ... Activated (September 19, 1995). ... Granted free agency (February 13, 1998). ... Tendered offer sheet by St. Louis Rams (April 6, 1998). ... Offer matched by Jets (April 13, 1998). ... On injured reserve with knee injury (October 6, 1999-remainder of season). ... Released by Jets (March 2, 2000).
CHAMPIONSHIP GAME EXPERIENCE: Played in AFC championship game (1998 season).
PRO STATISTICS: 1996—Recovered one fumble. 1997—Recovered one fumble. 1998—Recovered two fumbles for 23 yards and one touchdown.

Year Team	G	GS	SACKS
1995—New York Jets NFL	12	0	0.0
1996—New York Jets NFL	16	8	3.0
1997—New York Jets NFL	15	0	0.0
1998—New York Jets NFL	13	4	5.0
1999—New York Jets NFL	4	0	0.0
Pro totals (5 years)	60	12	8.0

CASE, STONEY   QB

PERSONAL: Born July 7, 1972, in Odessa, Texas. ... 6-3/201. ... Full name: Stoney Jarrod Case.
HIGH SCHOOL: Permian (Odessa, Texas).
COLLEGE: New Mexico (degree in biology, 1995).
TRANSACTIONS/CAREER NOTES: Selected by Arizona Cardinals in third round (80th pick overall) of 1995 NFL draft. ... Signed by Cardinals for 1995 season. ... Inactive for all 16 games (1996). ... Assigned by Cardinals to Barcelona Dragons in 1997 World League enhancement allocation program (February 19, 1997). ... Granted free agency (February 13, 1998). ... Re-signed by Cardinals (April 28, 1998). ... Granted

C

unconditional free agency (February 12, 1999). ... Signed by Indianapolis Colts (March 4, 1999). ... Released by Colts (August 11, 1999). ... Signed by Baltimore Ravens (August 17, 1999). ... Granted unconditional free agency (February 11, 2000).

PRO STATISTICS: 1997—Fumbled three times. 1999—Fumbled twice and recovered two fumbles for minus three yards.

SINGLE GAME HIGHS (regular season): Attempts—37 (October 21, 1999, vs. Kansas City); completions—18 (October 12, 1997, vs. New York Giants); yards—222 (October 12, 1997, vs. New York Giants); and touchdown passes—2 (October 3, 1999, vs. Atlanta).

MISCELLANEOUS: Regular-season record as starting NFL quarterback: 2-3 (.400).

Year Team	G	GS	PASSING Att.	Cmp.	Pct.	Yds.	TD	Int.	Avg.	Rat.	RUSHING Att.	Yds.	Avg.	TD	TOTALS TD	2pt.	Pts.
1995—Arizona NFL	2	0	2	1	50.0	19	0	1	9.50	43.8	1	4	4.0	0	0	0	0
1996—Arizona NFL								Did not play.									
1997—Arizona NFL	3	1	55	29	52.7	316	0	2	5.75	54.8	7	8	1.1	1	1	0	6
1998—Arizona NFL	1	0	0	0	0.0	0	0	0	0.0	...	0	0	0.0	0	0	0	0
1999—Baltimore NFL	10	4	170	77	45.3	988	3	8	5.81	50.3	36	141	3.9	3	3	0	18
Pro totals (4 years)	16	5	227	107	47.1	1323	3	11	5.83	49.9	44	153	3.5	4	4	0	24

CENTERS, LARRY   RB   REDSKINS

PERSONAL: Born June 1, 1968, in Tatum, Texas. ... 6-0/225. ... Full name: Larry E. Centers.

HIGH SCHOOL: Tatum (Texas).

COLLEGE: Stephen F. Austin State.

TRANSACTIONS/CAREER NOTES: Selected by Phoenix Cardinals in fifth round (115th pick overall) of 1990 NFL draft. ... Signed by Cardinals (July 23, 1990). ... On injured reserve with broken foot (September 11-October 30, 1991). ... Granted free agency (February 1, 1992). ... Re-signed by Cardinals (July 23, 1992). ... Granted unconditional free agency (February 17, 1994). ... Re-signed by Cardinals (March 15, 1994). ... Cardinals franchise renamed Arizona Cardinals for 1994 season. ... Granted unconditional free agency (February 14, 1997). ... Re-signed by Cardinals (March 14, 1997). ... Released by Cardinals (June 18, 1999). ... Signed by Washington Redskins (July 6, 1999).

HONORS: Played in Pro Bowl (1995 and 1996 seasons).

PRO STATISTICS: 1991—Returned five punts for 30 yards and recovered two fumbles. 1993—Recovered two fumbles. 1994—Recovered two fumbles for 27 yards. 1995—Had only pass attempt intercepted and recovered one fumble. 1996—Recovered one fumble. 1999—Recovered one fumble.

SINGLE GAME HIGHS (regular season): Attempts—15 (September 4, 1994, vs. Los Angeles Rams); yards—62 (November 26, 1995, vs. Atlanta); and rushing touchdowns—2 (December 4, 1994, vs. Houston).

STATISTICAL PLATEAUS: 100-yard receiving games: 1995 (2), 1996 (1). Total: 3.

MISCELLANEOUS: Holds Cardinals franchise all-time record for most receptions (535).

Year Team	G	GS	RUSHING Att.	Yds.	Avg.	TD	RECEIVING No.	Yds.	Avg.	TD	KICKOFF RETURNS No.	Yds.	Avg.	TD	TOTALS TD	2pt.	Pts.	Fum.
1990—Phoenix NFL	6	0	0	0	0.0	0	0	0	0.0	0	16	272	17.0	0	0	0	0	1
1991—Phoenix NFL	9	2	14	44	3.1	0	19	176	9.3	0	16	330	20.6	0	0	0	0	4
1992—Phoenix NFL	16	1	37	139	3.8	0	50	417	8.3	2	0	0	0.0	0	2	0	12	1
1993—Phoenix NFL	16	9	25	152	6.1	0	66	603	9.1	3	0	0	0.0	0	3	0	18	1
1994—Arizona NFL	16	5	115	336	2.9	5	77	647	8.4	2	0	0	0.0	0	7	0	42	2
1995—Arizona NFL	16	10	78	254	3.3	2	101	962	9.5	2	1	15	15.0	0	4	0	24	2
1996—Arizona NFL	16	14	116	425	3.7	2	99	766	7.7	7	0	0	0.0	0	9	0	54	1
1997—Arizona NFL	15	14	101	276	2.7	1	54	409	7.6	1	0	0	0.0	0	2	0	12	1
1998—Arizona NFL	16	12	31	110	3.5	0	69	559	8.1	2	0	0	0.0	0	2	0	12	1
1999—Washington NFL	16	12	13	51	3.9	0	69	544	7.9	3	0	0	0.0	0	3	0	18	2
Pro totals (10 years)	142	79	530	1787	3.4	10	604	5083	8.4	22	33	617	18.7	0	32	0	192	16

CHAMBERLAIN, BYRON   TE   BRONCOS

PERSONAL: Born October 17, 1971, in Honolulu. ... 6-1/242.

HIGH SCHOOL: Eastern Hills (Fort Worth, Texas).

COLLEGE: Missouri, then Wayne State (Neb.).

TRANSACTIONS/CAREER NOTES: Selected by Denver Broncos in seventh round (222nd pick overall) of 1995 NFL draft. ... Signed by Broncos (August 27, 1995). ... Released by Broncos (August 27, 1995). ... Re-signed by Broncos to practice squad (August 28, 1995). ... Activated (November 24, 1995). ... Assigned by Broncos to Rhein Fire in 1996 World League enhancement allocation program (February 19, 1996).

CHAMPIONSHIP GAME EXPERIENCE: Played in AFC championship game (1997 and 1998 seasons). ... Member of Super Bowl championship team (1997 season); did not play. ... Member of Super Bowl championship team (1998 season).

PRO STATISTICS: W.L.: 1996—Rushed once for four yards and returned one kickoff for eight yards. NFL: 1996—Returned three kickoffs for 49 yards. 1997—Returned one kickoff for 13 yards.

SINGLE GAME HIGHS (regular season): Receptions—5 (October 31, 1999, vs. Minnesota); yards—123 (October 17, 1999, vs. Green Bay); and touchdown receptions—1 (December 13, 1999, vs. Jacksonville).

STATISTICAL PLATEAUS: 100-yard receiving games: 1999 (1).

Year Team	G	GS	RECEIVING No.	Yds.	Avg.	TD	TOTALS TD	2pt.	Pts.	Fum.
1995—Denver NFL	5	0	1	11	11.0	0	0	0	0	0
1996—Rhein W.L.	10	10	58	685	11.8	8	8	0	48	0
—Denver NFL	11	0	12	129	10.8	0	0	0	0	1
1997—Denver NFL	10	0	2	18	9.0	0	0	0	0	1
1998—Denver NFL	16	0	3	35	11.7	0	0	0	0	0
1999—Denver NFL	16	0	32	488	15.3	2	2	0	12	0
W.L. totals (1 year)	10	10	58	685	11.8	8	8	0	48	0
NFL totals (5 years)	58	0	50	681	13.6	2	2	0	12	2
Pro totals (6 years)	68	10	108	1366	12.6	10	10	0	60	2

CHAMBLIN, COREY CB JAGUARS

PERSONAL: Born May 29, 1977, in Birmingham, Ala. ... 5-10/188. ... Full name: Corey Jermaine Chamblin.
HIGH SCHOOL: Ensley (Birmingham, Ala.).
COLLEGE: Tennessee Tech.
TRANSACTIONS/CAREER NOTES: Signed as non-drafted free agent by Baltimore Ravens (April 23, 1999). ... Released by Ravens (September 5, 1999). ... Signed by Jacksonville Jaguars to practice squad (September 7, 1999). ... Activated (September 20, 1999).
PLAYING EXPERIENCE: Jacksonville NFL, 1999. ... Games/Games started: 1999 (11/0).
PRO STATISTICS: 1999—Returned one kickoff for six yards.

CHANCEY, ROBERT RB CHARGERS

PERSONAL: Born September 7, 1972, in Macon, Ala. ... 6-0/252. ... Full name: Robert Dewayne Chancey. ... Name pronounced CHAN-see.
HIGH SCHOOL: Stanhope Elmore (Millbrook, Ala.).
COLLEGE: None.
TRANSACTIONS/CAREER NOTES: Signed as non-drafted free agent by San Diego Chargers (April 7, 1997). ... Released by Chargers (August 24, 1997). ... Re-signed by Chargers to practice squad (August 25, 1997). ... Activated (November 4, 1997). ... Released by Chargers (July 23, 1998). ... Signed by Chicago Bears (July 26, 1998). ... Released by Bears (September 5, 1999). ... Signed by Dallas Cowboys (October 5, 1999). ... Granted free agency (February 11, 2000). ... Signed by San Diego Chargers (February 28, 2000).
PRO STATISTICS: 1998—Returned two kickoffs for 18 yards.
SINGLE GAME HIGHS (regular season): Attempts—14 (November 14, 1999, vs. Green Bay); yards—57 (November 14, 1999, vs. Green Bay) and rushing touchdowns—1 (December 20, 1998, vs. Baltimore).

				RUSHING				RECEIVING				TOTALS		
Year Team	G	GS	Att.	Yds.	Avg.	TD	No.	Yds.	Avg.	TD	TD	2pt.	Pts.	Fum.
1997—San Diego NFL	6	0	0	0	0.0	0	0	0	0.0	0	0	0	0	0
1998—Chicago NFL	16	1	29	122	4.2	2	11	102	9.3	0	2	0	12	2
1999—Dallas NFL	3	0	14	57	4.1	0	0	0	0.0	0	0	0	0	0
Pro totals (3 years)	25	1	43	179	4.2	2	11	102	9.3	0	2	0	12	2

RECORD AS BASEBALL PLAYER

TRANSACTIONS/CAREER NOTES: Selected by Baltimore Orioles organization in sixth round of free-agent draft (June 1, 1992). ... Released by Gulf Coast Orioles, Orioles organization (September 30, 1993). ... Signed by Pittsfield, New York Mets organization (April 15, 1996). ... On Pittsfield temporarily inactive list (May 10-June 10, 1996). ... Released by Kingsport, Mets organization (July 1, 1996).
STATISTICAL NOTES: Led Gulf Coast League outfielders with seven errors (1992).

							BATTING							FIELDING		
Year Team (League)	Pos.	G	AB	R	H	2B	3B	HR	RBI	Avg.	BB	SO	SB	PO	A	E	Avg.
1992—GC Orioles (GCL)	OF	43	141	22	41	3	3	1	23	.291	7	50	13	70	5	7	.915
1993—GC Orioles (GCL)	OF	29	84	7	12	3	0	0	3	.143	4	39	3	31	3	6	.850
1996—Kingsport (Appal.)	OF	6	19	4	5	0	0	1	3	.263	2	5	1	7	0	1	.875

CHANDLER, CHRIS QB FALCONS

PERSONAL: Born October 12, 1965, in Everett, Wash. ... 6-4/226. ... Full name: Christopher Mark Chandler. ... Brother of Greg Chandler, catcher with San Francisco Giants organization (1978); and son-in-law of John Brodie, quarterback with San Francisco 49ers (1957-73).
HIGH SCHOOL: Everett (Wash.).
COLLEGE: Washington (degree in economics, 1988).
TRANSACTIONS/CAREER NOTES: Selected by Indianapolis Colts in third round (76th pick overall) of 1988 NFL draft. ... Signed by Colts (July 23, 1988). ... On injured reserve with knee injury (October 3, 1989-remainder of season). ... Traded by Colts to Tampa Bay Buccaneers for first round pick (LB Quentin Coryatt) in 1992 draft (August 7, 1990). ... Claimed on waivers by Phoenix Cardinals (November 6, 1991). ... Granted unconditional free agency (February 17, 1994). ... Signed by Los Angeles Rams (May 6, 1994). ... Granted unconditional free agency (February 17, 1995). ... Signed by Houston Oilers (March 10, 1995). ... Traded by Oilers to Atlanta Falcons for fourth- (WR Derrick Mason) and sixth-round (traded to New Orleans) picks in 1997 draft (February 24, 1997).
CHAMPIONSHIP GAME EXPERIENCE: Played in NFC championship game (1998 season). ... Played in Super Bowl XXXIII (1998 season).
HONORS: Played in Pro Bowl (1997 and 1998 seasons).
PRO STATISTICS: 1988—Fumbled eight times and recovered five fumbles for minus six yards. 1990—Fumbled five times and recovered one fumble for minus two yards. 1991—Fumbled six times and recovered two fumbles for minus seven yards. 1992—Fumbled nine times and recovered two fumbles for minus 11 yards. 1993—Fumbled twice. 1994—Fumbled three times. 1995—Tied for AFC lead with 12 fumbles and recovered five fumbles for minus nine yards. 1996—Fumbled eight times and recovered three fumbles for minus four yards. 1997—Fumbled nine times and recovered three fumbles for minus 18 yards. 1998—Caught one pass for 22 yards, fumbled six times and recovered five fumbles for minus nine yards. 1999—Fumbled seven times and recovered four fumbles for minus 14 yards.
SINGLE GAME HIGHS (regular season): Attempts—47 (October 1, 1995, vs. Jacksonville); completions—28 (September 20, 1992, vs. Dallas); yards—383 (September 20, 1992, vs. Dallas); and touchdown passes—4 (November 28, 1999, vs. Carolina).
STATISTICAL PLATEAUS: 300-yard passing games: 1992 (1), 1995 (1), 1998 (1), 1999 (2). Total: 5.
MISCELLANEOUS: Regular-season record as starting NFL quarterback: 52-58 (.473). ... Postseason record as starting NFL quarterback: 2-1 (.667).

				PASSING							RUSHING				TOTALS		
Year Team	G	GS	Att.	Cmp.	Pct.	Yds.	TD	Int.	Avg.	Rat.	Att.	Yds.	Avg.	TD	TD	2pt.	Pts.
1988—Indianapolis NFL	15	13	233	129	55.4	1619	8	12	6.95	67.2	46	139	3.0	3	3	0	18
1989—Indianapolis NFL	3	3	80	39	48.8	537	2	3	6.71	63.4	7	57	8.1	1	1	0	6
1990—Tampa Bay NFL	7	3	83	42	50.6	464	1	6	5.59	41.4	13	71	5.5	1	1	0	6
1991—Tampa Bay NFL	6	3	104	53	51.0	557	4	8	5.36	47.6	18	79	4.4	0	1	0	6
—Phoenix NFL	3	2	50	25	50.0	289	1	2	5.78	57.8	8	32	4.0	0	0	0	0
1992—Phoenix NFL	15	13	413	245	59.3	2832	15	15	6.86	77.1	36	149	4.1	1	1	0	6
1993—Phoenix NFL	4	2	103	52	50.5	471	3	2	4.57	64.8	3	2	0.7	0	0	0	0
1994—L.A. Rams NFL	12	6	176	108	61.4	1352	7	2	7.68	93.8	18	61	3.4	1	1	0	6
1995—Houston NFL	13	13	356	225	63.2	2460	17	10	6.91	87.8	28	58	2.1	2	2	1	14

Year—Team																
1996—Houston NFL	12	12	320	184	57.5	2099	16	11	6.56	79.7	28	113	4.0	0	0	0	0
1997—Atlanta NFL	14	14	342	202	59.1	2692	20	7	7.87	95.1	43	158	3.7	0	0	0	0
1998—Atlanta NFL	14	14	327	190	58.1	3154	25	12	*9.65	100.9	36	121	3.4	2	2	0	12
1999—Atlanta NFL	12	12	307	174	56.7	2339	16	11	7.62	83.5	16	57	3.6	1	1	0	6
Pro totals (12 years)	130	110	2894	1668	57.6	20865	135	101	7.21	81.2	300	1097	3.7	12	12	1	74

CHANOINE, ROGER — OT — BROWNS

PERSONAL: Born August 11, 1976, in Newark, N.J. ... 6-4/295. ... Full name: Roger Chanoine Jr. ... Name pronounced SHAN-wah.
HIGH SCHOOL: Linden (N.J.).
COLLEGE: Temple.
TRANSACTIONS/CAREER NOTES: Signed as non-drafted free agent by St. Louis Rams (April 20, 1998). ... On injured reserve with ankle injury (August 25, 1998-entire season). ... Released by Rams (August 30, 1999). ... Signed by Cleveland Browns to practice squad (September 7, 1999). ... Activated (December 8, 1999).
PLAYING EXPERIENCE: Cleveland NFL, 1999. ... Games/Games started: 1999 (1/0).

CHASE, MARTIN — DT — RAVENS

PERSONAL: Born December 19, 1974, in Lawton, Okla. ... 6-2/310. ... Full name: Cecil Martin Chase.
HIGH SCHOOL: Eisenhower (Lawton, Okla.).
COLLEGE: Oklahoma.
TRANSACTIONS/CAREER NOTES: Selected by Baltimore Ravens in fifth round (124th pick overall) of 1998 NFL draft. ... Signed by Ravens (July 17, 1998). ... On injured reserve with ankle injury (August 25, 1998-entire season). ... Assigned by Ravens to Frankfurt Galaxy in 2000 NFL Europe enhancement allocation program (February 18, 2000).
PLAYING EXPERIENCE: Baltimore NFL, 1999. ... Games/Games started: 1999 (3/0).

C

CHAVOUS, COREY — CB — CARDINALS

PERSONAL: Born January 15, 1976, in Aiken, S.C. ... 6-1/200. ... Cousin of Fred Vinson, cornerback, Seattle Seahawks. ... Name pronounced CHAY-vus.
HIGH SCHOOL: Silver Bluff (Aiken, S.C.).
COLLEGE: Vanderbilt.
TRANSACTIONS/CAREER NOTES: Selected by Arizona Cardinals in second round (33rd pick overall) of 1998 NFL draft. ... Signed by Cardinals (July 23, 1998).
PRO STATISTICS: 1998—Recovered one fumble.

			INTERCEPTIONS		
Year Team	G	GS	No.	Yds.	Avg.	TD
1998—Arizona NFL	16	5	2	0	0.0	0
1999—Arizona NFL	15	4	1	1	1.0	0
Pro totals (2 years)	31	9	3	1	0.3	0

CHERRY, Je'ROD — S — RAIDERS

PERSONAL: Born May 30, 1973, in Charlotte. ... 6-1/205. ... Full name: Je'Rod L. Cherry. ... Name pronounced juh-ROD.
HIGH SCHOOL: Berkeley (Calif.).
COLLEGE: California (degree in political science, 1995).
TRANSACTIONS/CAREER NOTES: Selected by New Orleans Saints in second round (40th pick overall) of 1996 NFL draft. ... Signed by Saints (July 3, 1996). ... Granted free agency (February 12, 1999). ... Re-signed by Saints (July 21, 1999). ... Granted unconditional free agency (February 11, 2000). ... Signed by Oakland Raiders (February 19, 2000).
PLAYING EXPERIENCE: New Orleans NFL, 1996-1999. ... Games/Games started: 1996 (13/0), 1997 (16/0), 1998 (14/0), 1999 (16/0). Total: 59/0.
PRO STATISTICS: 1996—Recovered one fumble. 1998—Credited with two sacks.

CHESTER, LARRY — DT — COLTS

PERSONAL: Born October 17, 1975, in Hammond, La. ... 6-2/310.
HIGH SCHOOL: Hammond (La.).
JUNIOR COLLEGE: Southwest Mississippi Junior College.
COLLEGE: Temple.
TRANSACTIONS/CAREER NOTES: Signed as non-drafted free agent by Indianapolis Colts (April 24, 1998). ... Released by Colts (August 31, 1998). ... Re-signed by Colts to practice squad (September 2, 1998). ... Activated (September 11, 1998).
PRO STATISTICS: 1999—Recovered one fumble.

Year Team	G	GS	SACKS
1998—Indianapolis NFL	14	2	3.0
1999—Indianapolis NFL	16	8	1.0
Pro totals (2 years)	30	10	4.0

CHIAVERINI, DARRIN — WR — BROWNS

PERSONAL: Born October 12, 1977, in Orange County, Calif. ... 6-2/210. ... Name pronounced SHEVV-er-re-nee.
HIGH SCHOOL: Corona (Calif.).
COLLEGE: Colorado.

TRANSACTIONS/CAREER NOTES: Selected by Cleveland Browns in fifth round (148th pick overall) of 1999 NFL draft. ... Signed by Browns (July 22, 1999).
PRO STATISTICS: 1999—Returned two kickoffs for 35 yards and recovered one fumble.
SINGLE GAME HIGHS (regular season): Receptions—10 (December 19, 1999, vs. Jacksonville); yards—108 (December 19, 1999, vs. Jacksonville); and touchdown receptions—1 (December 26, 1999, vs. Indianapolis).
STATISTICAL PLATEAUS: 100-yard receiving games: 1999 (1).

				RECEIVING			TOTALS			
Year Team	G	GS	No.	Yds.	Avg.	TD	TD	2pt.	Pts.	Fum.
1999—Cleveland NFL	16	8	44	487	11.1	4	4	0	24	0

CHILDRESS, O.J. LB GIANTS

PERSONAL: Born December 6, 1975, in Hermitage, Tenn. ... 6-1/245. ... Full name: Orin J. Childress.
HIGH SCHOOL: McGavock (Nashville).
COLLEGE: Clemson.
TRANSACTIONS/CAREER NOTES: Selected by New York Giants in seventh round (231st pick overall) of 1999 NFL draft. ... Signed by Giants (July 29, 1999). ... Released by Giants (September 5, 1999). ... Re-signed by Giants to practice squad (September 6, 1999). ... Activated (November 27, 1999). ... Assigned by Giants to Amsterdam Admirals in 2000 NFL Europe enhancement allocation program (February 18, 2000).
PLAYING EXPERIENCE: New York Giants NFL, 1999. ... Games/Games started: 1999 (4/0).

CHMURA, MARK TE

C

PERSONAL: Born February 22, 1969, in Deerfield, Mass. ... 6-5/255. ... Full name: Mark William Chmura. ... Name pronounced cha-MER-ah.
HIGH SCHOOL: Frontier Regional (South Deerfield, Mass.).
COLLEGE: Boston College.
TRANSACTIONS/CAREER NOTES: Selected by Green Bay Packers in sixth round (157th pick overall) of 1992 NFL draft. ... Signed by Packers (July 22, 1992). ... On injured reserve with back injury (August 24, 1992-entire season). ... On injured reserve with neck injury (September 25, 1999-remainder of season). ... Released by Packers (June 5, 2000).
CHAMPIONSHIP GAME EXPERIENCE: Played in NFC championship game (1995-97 seasons). ... Member of Super Bowl championship team (1996 season). ... Played in Super Bowl XXXII (1997 season).
HONORS: Named tight end on THE SPORTING NEWS college All-America second team (1991). ... Played in Pro Bowl (1995, 1997 and 1998 seasons).
POST SEASON RECORDS: Shares Super Bowl and NFL postseason career and single-game records for most two-point conversions—1 (January 26, 1997, vs. New England).
PRO STATISTICS: 1993—Returned one kickoff for no yards and recovered one fumble.
SINGLE GAME HIGHS (regular season): Receptions—7 (December 3, 1995, vs. Cincinnati); yards—109 (December 3, 1995, vs. Cincinnati); and touchdown receptions—2 (December 7, 1998, vs. Tampa Bay).
STATISTICAL PLATEAUS: 100-yard receiving games: 1995 (2).

				RECEIVING			TOTALS			
Year Team	G	GS	No.	Yds.	Avg.	TD	TD	2pt.	Pts.	Fum.
1992—Green Bay NFL					Did not play.					
1993—Green Bay NFL	14	0	2	13	6.5	0	0	0	0	1
1994—Green Bay NFL	14	4	14	165	11.8	0	0	0	0	0
1995—Green Bay NFL	16	15	54	679	12.6	7	7	1	44	0
1996—Green Bay NFL	13	13	28	370	13.2	0	0	0	0	0
1997—Green Bay NFL	15	14	38	417	11.0	6	6	0	36	1
1998—Green Bay NFL	15	14	47	554	11.8	4	4	0	24	1
1999—Green Bay NFL	2	2	5	55	11.0	0	0	0	0	0
Pro totals (7 years)	89	62	188	2253	12.0	17	17	1	104	3

CHREBET, WAYNE WR JETS

PERSONAL: Born August 14, 1973, in Garfield, N.J. ... 5-10/188. ... Name pronounced kra-BET.
HIGH SCHOOL: Garfield (N.J.).
COLLEGE: Hofstra.
TRANSACTIONS/CAREER NOTES: Signed as non-drafted free agent by New York Jets (April 25, 1995).
CHAMPIONSHIP GAME EXPERIENCE: Played in AFC championship game (1998 season).
PRO STATISTICS: 1995—Rushed once for one yard. 1996—Recovered two fumbles. 1997—Returned one kickoff for five yards.
SINGLE GAME HIGHS (regular season): Receptions—12 (October 13, 1996, vs. Jacksonville); yards—162 (October 13, 1996, vs. Jacksonville); and touchdown receptions—2 (December 5, 1999, vs. New York Giants).
STATISTICAL PLATEAUS: 100-yard receiving games: 1996 (1), 1997 (1), 1998 (5), 1999 (1). Total: 8.

				RECEIVING			PUNT RETURNS				TOTALS		
Year Team	G	GS	No.	Yds.	Avg.	TD	No.	Yds.	Avg.	TD	TD	2pt.	Pts. Fum.
1995—New York Jets NFL	16	16	66	726	11.0	4	0	0	0.0	0	4	0	24 1
1996—New York Jets NFL	16	9	84	909	10.8	3	28	139	5.0	0	3	0	18 5
1997—New York Jets NFL	16	1	58	799	13.8	3	0	0	0.0	0	3	0	18 0
1998—New York Jets NFL	16	15	75	1083	14.4	8	0	0	0.0	0	8	0	48 0
1999—New York Jets NFL	11	11	48	631	13.1	3	0	0	0.0	0	3	0	18 0
Pro totals (5 years)	75	52	331	4148	12.5	21	28	139	5.0	0	21	0	126 6

CHRISTIAN, BOB FB FALCONS

PERSONAL: Born November 14, 1968, in St. Louis. ... 5-11/232. ... Full name: Robert Douglas Christian.
HIGH SCHOOL: McCluer North (Florissant, Mo.).

COLLEGE: Northwestern.
TRANSACTIONS/CAREER NOTES: Selected by Atlanta Falcons in 12th round (310th pick overall) of 1991 NFL draft. ... Signed by Falcons (July 18, 1991). ... Released by Falcons (August 20, 1991). ... Selected by London Monarchs in 16th round (175th pick overall) of 1992 World League draft. ... Signed by San Diego Chargers (July 10, 1992). ... Released by Chargers (August 25, 1992). ... Signed by Chicago Bears to practice squad (September 8, 1992). ... Activated (December 18, 1992). ... On injured reserve with knee injury (December 2, 1994-remainder of season). ... Selected by Carolina Panthers from Bears in NFL expansion draft (February 15, 1995). ... Granted free agency (February 16, 1996). ... Re-signed by Panthers (July 19, 1996). ... On injured reserve with shoulder injury (August 25, 1996-entire season). ... Granted unconditional free agency (February 14, 1997). ... Signed by Falcons (March 6, 1997). ... On injured reserve with knee injury (December 15, 1998-remainder of season).
PRO STATISTICS: 1995—Recovered one fumble. 1997—Recovered one fumble. 1998—Recovered two fumbles.
SINGLE GAME HIGHS (regular season): Attempts—9 (December 26, 1999, vs. Arizona); yards—54 (December 26, 1998, vs. Arizona); and rushing touchdowns—2 (December 26, 1999, vs. Arizona).

			RUSHING				RECEIVING				TOTALS			
Year Team	G	GS	Att.	Yds.	Avg.	TD	No.	Yds.	Avg.	TD	TD	2pt.	Pts.	Fum.
1992—Chicago NFL	2	0	0	0	0.0	0	0	0	0.0	0	0	0	0	0
1993—Chicago NFL	14	1	8	19	2.4	0	16	160	10.0	0	0	0	0	0
1994—Chicago NFL	12	0	7	29	4.1	0	2	30	15.0	0	0	0	0	0
1995—Carolina NFL	14	12	41	158	3.9	0	29	255	8.8	1	1	1	8	1
1996—Carolina NFL							Did not play.							
1997—Atlanta NFL	16	12	7	8	1.1	0	22	154	7.0	1	1	0	6	3
1998—Atlanta NFL	14	11	8	21	2.6	2	19	214	11.3	1	3	0	18	1
1999—Atlanta NFL	16	14	38	174	4.6	5	40	354	8.9	2	7	0	42	1
Pro totals (7 years)	88	50	109	409	3.8	7	128	1167	9.1	5	12	1	74	6

C

CHRISTIE, STEVE — K — BILLS

PERSONAL: Born November 13, 1967, in Oakville, Ont. ... 6-0/190. ... Full name: Geoffrey Stephen Christie.
HIGH SCHOOL: Trafalgar (Oakville, Ont.).
COLLEGE: William & Mary.
TRANSACTIONS/CAREER NOTES: Signed as non-drafted free agent by Tampa Bay Buccaneers (May 8, 1990). ... Granted unconditional free agency (February 1, 1992). ... Signed by Buffalo Bills (February 5, 1992).
CHAMPIONSHIP GAME EXPERIENCE: Played in AFC championship game (1992 and 1993 seasons). ... Played in Super Bowl XXVII (1992 season) and Super Bowl XXVIII (1993 season).
POST SEASON RECORDS: Holds Super Bowl single-game record for longest field goal—54 yards (January 30, 1994, vs. Dallas). ... Shares NFL postseason single-game record for most field goals made—5; and most field goals attempted—6 (January 17, 1993, at Miami).
PRO STATISTICS: 1994—Recovered one fumble. 1999—Recovered one fumble.

				KICKING				
Year Team	G	XPM	XPA	FGM	FGA	Lg.	50+	Pts.
1990—Tampa Bay NFL	16	27	27	23	27	54	2-2	96
1991—Tampa Bay NFL	16	22	22	15	20	49	0-0	67
1992—Buffalo NFL	16	§43	§44	24	30	†54	3-5	115
1993—Buffalo NFL	16	36	37	23	32	*59	1-6	105
1994—Buffalo NFL	16	§38	§38	24	28	52	2-2	110
1995—Buffalo NFL	16	33	35	31	40	51	2-5	126
1996—Buffalo NFL	16	33	33	24	29	48	0-1	105
1997—Buffalo NFL	16	21	21	24	30	†55	1-2	93
1998—Buffalo NFL	16	41	41	33	*41	52	1-3	§140
1999—Buffalo NFL	16	33	33	25	34	52	3-3	108
Pro totals (10 years)	160	327	331	246	311	59	15-29	1065

CHRISTY, JEFF — C — BUCCANEERS

PERSONAL: Born February 3, 1969, in Natrona Heights, Pa. ... 6-2/285. ... Full name: Jeffrey Allen Christy. ... Brother of Greg Christy, offensive tackle with Buffalo Bills (1985).
HIGH SCHOOL: Freeport (Pa.) Area.
COLLEGE: Pittsburgh.
TRANSACTIONS/CAREER NOTES: Selected by Phoenix Cardinals in fourth round (91st pick overall) of 1992 NFL draft. ... Signed by Cardinals (July 21, 1992). ... Released by Cardinals (August 31, 1992). ... Signed by Minnesota Vikings (March 16, 1993). ... On injured reserve with ankle injury (November 26, 1997-remainder of season). ... Granted unconditional free agency (February 11, 2000). ... Signed by Tampa Bay Buccaneers (February 15, 2000).
PLAYING EXPERIENCE: Minnesota NFL, 1993-1999. ... Games/Games started: 1993 (9/0), 1994 (16/16), 1995 (16/16), 1996 (16/16), 1997 (12/12), 1998 (16/16), 1999 (16/16). Total: 101/92.
CHAMPIONSHIP GAME EXPERIENCE: Played in NFC championship game (1998 season).
HONORS: Played in Pro Bowl (1998 and 1999 seasons).

CHRYPLEWICZ, PETE — TE — LIONS

PERSONAL: Born April 27, 1974, in Detroit. ... 6-5/261. ... Full name: Peter Gerald Chryplewicz. ... Name pronounced crip-LEV-itch.
HIGH SCHOOL: Stevenson (Sterling Heights, Mich.).
COLLEGE: Notre Dame (degree in business administration, 1996).
TRANSACTIONS/CAREER NOTES: Selected by Detroit Lions in fifth round (135th pick overall) of 1997 NFL draft. ... Signed by Lions (July 10, 1997). ... On injured reserve with knee injury (December 8, 1999-remainder of season). ... Granted free agency (February 11, 2000). ... Re-signed by Lions (March 22, 2000).
SINGLE GAME HIGHS (regular season): Receptions—2 (November 7, 1999, vs. St. Louis); yards—23 (September 21, 1997, vs. New Orleans); and touchdown receptions—1 (October 15, 1998, vs. Green Bay).

| | | | RECEIVING | | | | TOTALS | | | |
Year Team	G	GS	No.	Yds.	Avg.	TD	TD	2pt.	Pts.	Fum.
1997—Detroit NFL	10	0	3	27	9.0	1	1	0	6	0
1998—Detroit NFL	16	2	4	20	5.0	2	2	0	12	1
1999—Detroit NFL	11	1	2	18	9.0	0	0	0	0	0
Pro totals (3 years)	37	3	9	65	7.2	3	3	0	18	1

CLAIBORNE, CHRIS   LB   LIONS

PERSONAL: Born July 26, 1978, in Riverdale, Calif. ... 6-3/255.
HIGH SCHOOL: John W. North (Riverside, Calif.).
COLLEGE: Southern California.
TRANSACTIONS/CAREER NOTES: Selected after junior season by Detroit Lions in first round (ninth pick overall) of 1999 NFL draft. ... Signed by Lions (July 24, 1999).
HONORS: Butkus Award winner (1998). ... Named inside linebacker on THE SPORTING NEWS college All-America first team (1998).
PRO STATISTICS: 1999—Recovered three fumbles for 27 yards.

Year Team	G	GS	SACKS
1999—Detroit NFL	15	13	1.5

CLARK, DESMOND   TE   BRONCOS

PERSONAL: Born April 20, 1977, in Bartow, Fla. ... 6-3/255. ... Full name: Desmond Darice Clark.
HIGH SCHOOL: Kathleen (Lakeland, Fla.).
COLLEGE: Wake Forest.
TRANSACTIONS/CAREER NOTES: Selected by Denver Broncos in sixth round (179th pick overall) of 1999 NFL draft. ... Signed by Broncos (June 14, 1999).
PLAYING EXPERIENCE: Denver NFL, 1999. ... Games/Games started: 1999 (9/0).
PRO STATISTICS: 1999—Caught one pass for five yards.
SINGLE GAME HIGHS (regular season): Receptions—1 (October 17, 1999, vs. Green Bay); yards—5 (October 17, 1999, vs. Green Bay); and touchdown receptions—0.

C

CLARK, GREG   TE   49ERS

PERSONAL: Born April 7, 1972, in Centerville, Utah. ... 6-4/251. ... Full name: Gregory Jay Clark.
HIGH SCHOOL: Viewmont (Bountiful, Utah).
JUNIOR COLLEGE: Ricks College (Idaho).
COLLEGE: Stanford (degree in psychology, 1996).
TRANSACTIONS/CAREER NOTES: Selected by San Francisco 49ers in third round (77th pick overall) of 1997 NFL draft. ... Signed by 49ers (July 17, 1997). ... Granted free agency (February 11, 2000).
CHAMPIONSHIP GAME EXPERIENCE: Played in NFC championship game (1997 season).
POST SEASON RECORDS: Shares NFL postseason career record for most two-point conversions—1.
SINGLE GAME HIGHS (regular season): Receptions—5 (December 18, 1999, vs. Carolina); yards—46 (December 26, 1999, vs. Washington); and touchdown receptions—1 (October 11, 1998, vs. New Orleans).

| | | | RECEIVING | | | | TOTALS | | | |
Year Team	G	GS	No.	Yds.	Avg.	TD	TD	2pt.	Pts.	Fum.
1997—San Francisco NFL	15	4	8	96	12.0	1	1	0	6	0
1998—San Francisco NFL	13	8	12	124	10.3	1	1	1	8	0
1999—San Francisco NFL	12	11	34	347	10.2	0	0	0	0	1
Pro totals (3 years)	40	23	54	567	10.5	2	2	1	14	1

CLARK, JON   OT   CARDINALS

PERSONAL: Born April 11, 1973, in Philadelphia. ... 6-7/346.
HIGH SCHOOL: John Bartram (Philadelphia).
COLLEGE: Temple.
TRANSACTIONS/CAREER NOTES: Selected by Chicago Bears in sixth round (187th pick overall) of 1996 NFL draft. ... Signed by Bears (July 11, 1996). ... Released by Bears (October 7, 1997). ... Signed by New York Jets (December 8, 1997). ... Released by Jets (December 12, 1997). ... Signed by Arizona Cardinals (February 18, 1998). ... Released by Cardinals (September 12, 1998). ... Re-signed by Cardinals to practice squad (September 16, 1998). ... Activated (November 19, 1998). ... Released by Cardinals (October 17, 1999). ... Re-signed by Cardinals to practice squad (October 19, 1999).
PLAYING EXPERIENCE: Chicago NFL, 1996 and 1997; Arizona NFL, 1998 and 1999. ... Games/Games started: 1996 (1/0), 1997 (1/0), 1998 (6/0), 1999 (2/0). Total: 10/0.

CLARK, RICO   DB

PERSONAL: Born June 6, 1974, in Atlanta. ... 5-10/181. ... Full name: Rico Cornell Clark.
HIGH SCHOOL: Lakeside (Atlanta).
COLLEGE: Louisville.
TRANSACTIONS/CAREER NOTES: Signed as non-drafted free agent by Indianapolis Colts (April 27, 1997). ... Released by Colts (August 18, 1997). ... Re-signed by Colts to practice squad (August 25, 1997). ... Released by Colts (October 8, 1997). ... Re-signed by Colts to practice squad (November 4, 1997). ... Activated (November 25, 1997). ... Claimed on waivers by Cincinnati Bengals (September 6, 1999). ... Released by Bengals (December 14, 1999). ... Signed by New England Patriots (December 29, 1999). ... Granted free agency (February 11, 2000).
PRO STATISTICS: 1998—Returned three kickoffs for 38 yards.

Year Team		G	GS	No.	Yds.	Avg.	TD
				INTERCEPTIONS			
1997—Indianapolis NFL		4	2	1	14	14.0	0
1998—Indianapolis NFL		16	0	1	30	30.0	0
1999—Cincinnati NFL		8	1	0	0	0.0	0
—New England NFL		1	0	0	0	0.0	0
Pro totals (3 years)		29	3	2	44	22.0	0

CLARKE, PHIL — LB — SAINTS

PERSONAL: Born January 9, 1977, in Miami. ... 6-0/241.
HIGH SCHOOL: South Miami.
COLLEGE: Pittsburgh.
TRANSACTIONS/CAREER NOTES: Signed as non-drafted free agent by New Orleans Saints (May 17, 1999). ... Released by Saints (September 5, 1999). ... Re-signed by Saints to practice squad (September 6, 1999). ... Activated (November 10, 1999).
PLAYING EXPERIENCE: New Orleans NFL, 1999. ... Games/Games started: 1999 (8/3).

CLAY, WILLIE — S

C

PERSONAL: Born September 5, 1970, in Pittsburgh. ... 5-10/200. ... Full name: Willie James Clay.
HIGH SCHOOL: Linsly (Wheeling, W.Va.).
COLLEGE: Georgia Tech.
TRANSACTIONS/CAREER NOTES: Selected by Detroit Lions in eighth round (221st pick overall) of 1992 NFL draft. ... Signed by Lions (July 25, 1992). ... Released by Lions (September 4, 1992). ... Re-signed by Lions to practice squad (September 8, 1992). ... Activated (November 20, 1992). ... Granted free agency (February 17, 1995). ... Re-signed by Lions (May 16, 1995). ... Granted unconditional free agency (February 16, 1996). ... Signed by New England Patriots (March 14, 1996). ... Released by Patriots (July 28, 1999). ... Signed by New Orleans Saints (August 11, 1999). ... Granted unconditional free agency (February 11, 2000).
CHAMPIONSHIP GAME EXPERIENCE: Played in AFC championship game (1996 season). ... Played in Super Bowl XXXI (1996 season).
HONORS: Named defensive back on THE SPORTING NEWS college All-America second team (1991).
PRO STATISTICS: 1993—Credited with one sack, returned two kickoffs for 34 yards and recovered two fumbles for 54 yards and two touchdowns. 1996—Recovered one fumble for 17 yards. 1997—Recovered two fumbles. 1998—Recovered one fumble for three yards.

Year Team		G	GS	No.	Yds.	Avg.	TD
				INTERCEPTIONS			
1992—Detroit NFL		6	0	0	0	0.0	0
1993—Detroit NFL		16	1	0	0	0.0	0
1994—Detroit NFL		16	16	3	54	18.0	1
1995—Detroit NFL		16	16	8	*173	21.6	0
1996—New England NFL		16	16	4	50	12.5	0
1997—New England NFL		16	16	6	109	18.2	1
1998—New England NFL		16	16	3	19	6.3	0
1999—New Orleans NFL		16	9	3	32	10.7	0
Pro totals (8 years)		118	90	27	437	16.2	2

CLEELAND, CAM — TE — SAINTS

PERSONAL: Born April 15, 1975, in Sedro Woolley, Wash. ... 6-4/272. ... Full name: Cameron Cleeland. ... Nephew of Phil Misley, pitcher in Milwaukee Braves organization (1956-58).
HIGH SCHOOL: Sedro Woolley (Wash.).
COLLEGE: Washington.
TRANSACTIONS/CAREER NOTES: Selected by New Orleans Saints in second round (40th pick overall) of 1998 NFL draft. ... Signed by Saints (June 9, 1998).
PRO STATISTICS: 1998—Recovered two fumbles for seven yards.
SINGLE GAME HIGHS (regular season): Receptions—10 (December 27, 1998, vs. Buffalo); yards—112 (December 27, 1998, vs. Buffalo); and touchdown receptions—1 (December 12, 1999, vs. New Orleans).
STATISTICAL PLATEAUS: 100-yard receiving games: 1998 (1).

Year Team		G	GS	No.	Yds.	Avg.	TD	TD	2pt.	Pts.	Fum.
				RECEIVING					**TOTALS**		
1998—New Orleans NFL		16	16	54	684	12.7	6	6	0	36	1
1999—New Orleans NFL		11	8	26	325	12.5	1	1	†1	8	1
Pro totals (2 years)		27	24	80	1009	12.6	7	7	1	44	2

CLEMENT, ANTHONY — OT — CARDINALS

PERSONAL: Born April 10, 1976, in Lafayette, La. ... 6-8/355.
HIGH SCHOOL: Cecilia (La.).
COLLEGE: Southwestern Louisiana.
TRANSACTIONS/CAREER NOTES: Selected by Arizona Cardinals in second round (36th pick overall) of 1998 NFL draft. ... Signed by Cardinals (June 16, 1998). ... On injured reserve with back injury (November 17, 1998-remainder of season).
PLAYING EXPERIENCE: Arizona NFL, 1998 and 1999. ... Games/Games started: 1998 (1/0), 1999 (16/14). Total: 17/14.

CLEMONS, CHARLIE — LB — SAINTS

PERSONAL: Born July 4, 1972, in Griffin, Ga. ... 6-2/250. ... Full name: Charlie Fitzgerald Clemons.

HIGH SCHOOL: Griffin (Ga.).
JUNIOR COLLEGE: Northeast Oklahoma Junior College.
COLLEGE: Georgia (degree in recreation and leisure studies, 1993).
TRANSACTIONS/CAREER NOTES: Signed by Winnipeg Blue Bombers of CFL (May 1994). ... Transferred to Ottawa Rough Riders of CFL (August 1995). ... Transferred back to Blue Bombers (January 1996). ... Signed as non-drafted free agent by St. Louis Rams (February 19, 1997). ... On injured reserve with hamstring injury (November 24, 1997-remainder of season). ... Granted free agency (February 11, 2000). ... Tendered offer sheet by New Orleans Saints (February 16, 2000). ... Rams declined to match offer (February 22, 2000).
CHAMPIONSHIP GAME EXPERIENCE: Played in NFC championship game (1999 season). ... Member of Super Bowl championship team (1999 season).
PRO STATISTICS: CFL: 1994—Recovered one fumble. 1995—Returned one kickoff for 10 yards. NFL: 1998—Returned one kickoff for no yards. 1999—Intercepted one pass for no yards and recovered one fumble.

Year Team	G	GS	SACKS
1994—Winnipeg CFL	7	...	0.0
1995—Winnipeg CFL	6	...	3.0
—Ottawa CFL	7	...	3.0
1996—Winnipeg CFL	14	...	6.0
1997—St. Louis NFL	5	0	0.0
1998—St. Louis NFL	16	0	2.0
1999—St. Louis NFL	16	0	3.0
CFL totals (3 years)	34	...	12.0
NFL totals (3 years)	37	0	5.0
Pro totals (6 years)	71	...	17.0

CLEMONS, DUANE   DE   CHIEFS

PERSONAL: Born May 23, 1974, in Riverside, Calif. ... 6-5/272.
HIGH SCHOOL: John W. North (Riverside, Calif.).
COLLEGE: California (degree in ethnic studies, 1993).
TRANSACTIONS/CAREER NOTES: Selected after junior season by Minnesota Vikings in first round (16th pick overall) of 1996 NFL draft. ... Signed by Vikings (July 25, 1996). ... Granted unconditional free agency (February 11, 2000). ... Signed by Kansas City Chiefs (April 4, 2000).
CHAMPIONSHIP GAME EXPERIENCE: Played in NFC championship game (1998 season).
PRO STATISTICS: 1996—Recovered one fumble for eight yards. 1997—Recovered one fumble. 1999—Recovered four fumbles.

Year Team	G	GS	SACKS
1996—Minnesota NFL	13	0	0.0
1997—Minnesota NFL	13	3	7.0
1998—Minnesota NFL	16	4	2.5
1999—Minnesota NFL	16	9	9.0
Pro totals (4 years)	58	16	18.5

CLINE, TONY   TE

PERSONAL: Born November 24, 1971, in Davis, Calif. ... 6-4/247. ... Full name: Anthony Francis Cline. ... Son of Tony Cline, defensive lineman with Oakland Raiders (1970-75) and San Francisco 49ers (1976).
HIGH SCHOOL: Davis (Calif.).
COLLEGE: Stanford.
TRANSACTIONS/CAREER NOTES: Selected by Buffalo Bills in fourth round (131st pick overall) of 1995 NFL draft. ... Signed by Bills (July 10, 1995). ... Granted free agency (February 13, 1998). ... Signed by Oakland Raiders (April 20, 1998). ... Released by Raiders (July 24, 1998). ... Signed by San Francisco 49ers (August 14, 1999). ... Released by 49ers (December 14, 1999). ... Signed by Pittsburgh Steelers (December 15, 1999). ... Granted unconditional free agency (February 11, 2000).
PRO STATISTICS: 1995—Returned one kickoff for 11 yards. 1997—Returned one kickoff for no yards.
SINGLE GAME HIGHS (regular season): Receptions—6 (September 1, 1996, vs. New York Giants); yards—41 (September 1, 1996, vs. New York Giants); and touchdown receptions—1 (December 22, 1996, vs. Kansas City).

			RECEIVING				TOTALS			
Year Team	G	GS	No.	Yds.	Avg.	TD	TD	2pt.	Pts.	Fum.
1995—Buffalo NFL	16	1	8	64	8.0	0	0	0	0	0
1996—Buffalo NFL	16	7	19	117	6.2	1	1	0	6	0
1997—Buffalo NFL	10	1	1	29	29.0	0	0	0	0	0
1998—					Did not play.					
1999—San Francisco NFL	8	0	4	45	11.3	0	0	0	0	0
—Pittsburgh NFL	2	0	0	0	0.0	0	0	0	0	0
Pro totals (4 years)	52	9	32	255	8.0	1	1	0	6	0

CLOUD, MIKE   RB   CHIEFS

PERSONAL: Born July 1, 1975, in Charleston, S.C. ... 5-10/205. ... Full name: Michael Alexander Cloud.
HIGH SCHOOL: Portsmouth (R.I.).
COLLEGE: Boston College.
TRANSACTIONS/CAREER NOTES: Selected by Kansas City Chiefs in second round (54th pick overall) of 1999 NFL draft. ... Signed by Chiefs (July 30, 1999).
PRO STATISTICS: 1999—Returned two kickoffs for 28 yards.
SINGLE GAME HIGHS (regular season): Attempts—11 (November 28, 1999, vs. Oakland); yards—58 (November 28, 1999, vs. Oakland); and rushing touchdowns—0.

			RUSHING				RECEIVING				TOTALS			
Year Team	G	GS	Att.	Yds.	Avg.	TD	No.	Yds.	Avg.	TD	TD	2pt.	Pts.	Fum.
1999—Kansas City NFL	11	0	35	128	3.7	0	3	25	8.3	0	0	0	0	0

C

COADY, RICH　　　　　　　　S　　　　　　　　RAMS

PERSONAL: Born January 26, 1976, in Dallas. ... 6-0/203. ... Full name: Richard Joseph Coady IV. ... Son of Rich Coady, tight end/center with Chicago Bears (1970-74).
HIGH SCHOOL: J.J. Pearce (Richardson, Texas).
COLLEGE: Texas A&M.
TRANSACTIONS/CAREER NOTES: Selected by St. Louis Rams in third round (68th pick overall) of 1999 NFL draft. ... Signed by Rams (July 16, 1999).
PLAYING EXPERIENCE: St. Louis NFL, 1999. ... Games/Games started: 1999 (16/0).
CHAMPIONSHIP GAME EXPERIENCE: Played in NFC championship game (1999 season). ... Member of Super Bowl championship team (1999 season).

COAKLEY, DEXTER　　　　　　　LB　　　　　　　COWBOYS

PERSONAL: Born October 20, 1972, in Charleston, S.C. ... 5-10/228. ... Full name: William Dexter Coakley.
HIGH SCHOOL: Wando (Mt. Pleasant, S.C.), then Fork Union (Va.) Military Academy.
COLLEGE: Appalachian State.
TRANSACTIONS/CAREER NOTES: Selected by Dallas Cowboys in third round (65th pick overall) of 1997 NFL draft. ... Signed by Cowboys (July 14, 1997). ... Granted free agency (February 11, 2000). ... Re-signed by Cowboys (April 28, 2000).
HONORS: Played in Pro Bowl (1999 season).
PRO STATISTICS: 1997—Recovered one fumble for 16 yards and a touchdown. 1998—Recovered one fumble. 1999—Returned one kickoff for three yards.

			INTERCEPTIONS				SACKS
Year　Team	G	GS	No.	Yds.	Avg.	TD	No.
1997—Dallas NFL	16	16	1	6	6.0	0	2.5
1998—Dallas NFL	16	16	1	18	18.0	0	2.0
1999—Dallas NFL	16	16	4	119	29.8	1	1.0
Pro totals (3 years)	48	48	6	143	23.8	1	5.5

COATES, BEN　　　　　　　　TE

PERSONAL: Born August 16, 1969, in Greenwood, S.C. ... 6-5/245. ... Full name: Ben Terrence Coates.
HIGH SCHOOL: Greenwood (S.C.).
COLLEGE: Livingstone College, N.C. (degree in sports management).
TRANSACTIONS/CAREER NOTES: Selected after junior season by New England Patriots in fifth round (124th pick overall) of 1991 NFL draft. ... Signed by Patriots (April 25, 1991). ... Granted free agency (February 17, 1994). ... Re-signed by Patriots (April 2, 1994). ... Released by Patriots (February 9, 2000).
CHAMPIONSHIP GAME EXPERIENCE: Played in AFC championship game (1996 season). ... Played in Super Bowl XXXI (1996 season).
HONORS: Named tight end on THE SPORTING NEWS NFL All-Pro team (1994 and 1995). ... Played in Pro Bowl (1994-1998 seasons).
RECORDS: Holds NFL single-season record for most receptions by tight end—96 (1994).
PRO STATISTICS: 1991—Rushed once for minus six yards and returned one kickoff for six yards. 1992—Rushed once for two yards. 1994—Rushed once for no yards and recovered two fumbles. 1997—Returned one kickoff for 20 yards.
SINGLE GAME HIGHS (regular season): Receptions—12 (November 27, 1994, vs. Indianapolis); yards—161 (September 4, 1994, vs. Miami); and touchdown receptions—3 (November 26, 1995, vs. Buffalo).
STATISTICAL PLATEAUS: 100-yard receiving games: 1993 (1), 1994 (5), 1995 (1), 1996 (1), 1998 (1). Total: 9.

			RECEIVING				TOTALS			
Year　Team	G	GS	No.	Yds.	Avg.	TD	TD	2pt.	Pts.	Fum.
1991—New England NFL	16	2	10	95	9.5	1	1	0	6	0
1992—New England NFL	16	2	20	171	8.6	3	3	0	18	1
1993—New England NFL	16	10	53	659	12.4	8	8	0	48	0
1994—New England NFL	16	16	§96	1174	12.2	7	7	0	42	2
1995—New England NFL	16	15	84	915	10.9	6	6	0	36	4
1996—New England NFL	16	15	62	682	11.0	9	9	1	56	1
1997—New England NFL	16	16	66	737	11.2	8	8	0	48	0
1998—New England NFL	14	14	67	668	10.0	6	6	0	36	0
1999—New England NFL	16	15	32	370	11.6	2	2	0	12	0
Pro totals (9 years)	142	105	490	5471	11.2	50	50	1	302	8

COCHRAN, ANTONIO　　　　　　DE　　　　　　SEAHAWKS

PERSONAL: Born June 21, 1976, in Montezuma, Ga. ... 6-4/297. ... Full name: Antonio Desez Cochran.
HIGH SCHOOL: Macon County (Montezuma, Ga.).
JUNIOR COLLEGE: Middle Georgia College.
COLLEGE: Georgia.
TRANSACTIONS/CAREER NOTES: Selected by Seattle Seahawks in fourth round (115th pick overall) of 1999 NFL draft. ... Signed by Seahawks (July 27, 1999).
PLAYING EXPERIENCE: Seattle NFL, 1999. ... Games/Games started: 1999 (4/0).

CODY, MAC　　　　　　　　WR　　　　　　CARDINALS

PERSONAL: Born August 7, 1972, in St. Louis. ... 5-11/182. ... Full name: Maclin Cody.
HIGH SCHOOL: Vashon (St. Louis).
COLLEGE: Memphis State.

TRANSACTIONS/CAREER NOTES: Signed as non-drafted free agent by Indianapolis Colts (April 1994). ... Released by Colts (August 1994). ... Signed by Winnipeg Blue Bombers of CFL (September 1994). ... Released by Blue Bombers (September 1994). ... Signed by Ottawa Roughriders of CFL (September 1994). ... Released by Roughriders (September 29, 1994). ... Signed by Birmingham Barracudas of CFL (May 1995). ... Selected by Hamilton Tiger-Cats of CFL in 1996 U.S. Team Dispersal Draft. ... Played with Orlando Predators of Arena League (1997). ... Signed by Montreal Alouettes of CFL (May 22, 1998). ... Signed by St. Louis Rams (February 25, 1999). ... Claimed on waivers by Arizona Cardinals (September 5, 1999).

PRO STATISTICS: CFL: 1996—Rushed once for one yard. NFL: 1999—Recovered one fumble.

SINGLE GAME HIGHS (regular season): Receptions—2 (December 5, 1999, vs. Philadelphia); yards—19 (December 5, 1999, vs. Philadelphia); and touchdown receptions—1 (January 2, 2000, vs. Green Bay).

Year Team	G	GS	RECEIVING				PUNT RETURNS				KICKOFF RETURNS				TOTALS			
			No.	Yds.	Avg.	TD	No.	Yds.	Avg.	TD	No.	Yds.	Avg.	TD	TD	2pt.	Pts.	Fum.
1994—Ottawa CFL	2	...	0	0	0.0	0	13	100	7.7	0	13	276	21.2	0	0	0	0	0
1995—Birmingham CFL	15	...	31	452	14.6	3	26	278	10.7	0	18	334	18.6	0	3	0	18	0
1996—Hamilton CFL	17	...	80	1426	17.8	11	17	123	7.2	0	20	333	16.7	0	11	0	66	0
1997—Orlando Arena Football									Statistics unavailable.									
1998—Montreal CFL	12	...	33	479	14.5	5	7	30	4.3	0	6	115	19.2	0	5	0	30	0
1999—Arizona NFL	13	0	6	60	10.0	1	32	373	‡11.7	0	4	76	19.0	0	1	0	6	2
CFL totals (4 years)	46	...	144	2357	16.4	19	63	531	8.4	0	57	1058	18.6	0	19	0	118	0
NFL totals (1 year)	13	0	6	60	10.0	1	32	373	11.7	0	4	76	19.0	0	1	0	6	2
Pro totals (5 years)	59	...	150	2417	16.1	20	95	904	9.5	0	61	1134	18.6	0	20	0	124	2

COGHILL, GEORGE — S — BRONCOS

C

PERSONAL: Born March 30, 1970, in Fredericksburg, Va. ... 6-0/210.
HIGH SCHOOL: James Madison (Vienna, Va.).
COLLEGE: Wake Forest.
TRANSACTIONS/CAREER NOTES: Signed as non-drafted free agent by New Orleans Saints (April 27, 1993). ... On injured reserve with knee injury (August 12, 1993-entire season). ... Released by Saints (August 22, 1994). ... Played for Scottish Claymores of World League (1995-1997). ... Signed by Denver Broncos (July 16, 1997). ... Released by Broncos (August 24, 1997). ... Re-signed by Broncos to practice squad (August 25, 1997). ... Released by Broncos (January 26, 1998). ... Re-signed by Broncos (January 28, 1998).
PLAYING EXPERIENCE: Scottish Claymores W.L., 1995-1997; Denver NFL, 1998 and 1999. ... Games/Games started: 1995 (games played unavailable), 1996 (-), 1997 (-), 1998 (9/0), 1999 (13/5). Total NFL: 22/5.
CHAMPIONSHIP GAME EXPERIENCE: Played in AFC championship game (1998 season). ... Member of Super Bowl championship team (1998 season).
PRO STATISTICS: 1998—Intercepted one pass for 20 yards and returned three punts for 20 yards. 1999—Intercepted one pass for no yards and returned three punts for 25 yards.

COLEMAN, BEN — G/OT

PERSONAL: Born May 18, 1971, in South Hill, Va. ... 6-5/327. ... Full name: Benjamin Leon Coleman.
HIGH SCHOOL: Park View Senior (South Hill, Va.).
COLLEGE: Wake Forest.
TRANSACTIONS/CAREER NOTES: Selected by Phoenix Cardinals in second round (32nd pick overall) of 1993 NFL draft. ... Signed by Cardinals (July 6, 1993). ... Cardinals franchise renamed Arizona Cardinals for 1994 season. ... Claimed on waivers by Jacksonville Jaguars (September 27, 1995). ... Granted free agency (February 16, 1996). ... Re-signed by Jaguars (June 6, 1996). ... Granted unconditional free agency (February 14, 1997). ... Re-signed by Jaguars (March 3, 1997). ... Granted unconditional free agency (February 11, 2000).
PLAYING EXPERIENCE: Phoenix NFL, 1993; Arizona NFL, 1994; Arizona (3)-Jacksonville (10) NFL, 1995; Jacksonville NFL, 1996-1999. ... Games/Games started: 1993 (12/0), 1994 (15/13), 1995 (Ariz.-3/0; Jack.-10/5; Total: 13/5), 1996 (16/16), 1997 (16/16), 1998 (16/16), 1999 (16/12). Total: 104/78.
CHAMPIONSHIP GAME EXPERIENCE: Played in AFC championship game (1996 and 1999 seasons).
PRO STATISTICS: 1995—Recovered one fumble.

COLEMAN, MARCO — DE — REDSKINS

PERSONAL: Born December 18, 1969, in Dayton, Ohio. ... 6-3/267. ... Full name: Marco Darnell Coleman.
HIGH SCHOOL: Patterson Co-op (Dayton, Ohio).
COLLEGE: Georgia Tech.
TRANSACTIONS/CAREER NOTES: Selected after junior season by Miami Dolphins in first round (12th pick overall) of 1992 NFL draft. ... Signed by Dolphins (August 1, 1992). ... Designated by Dolphins as transition player (February 25, 1993). ... Tendered offer sheet by San Diego Chargers (February 28, 1996). ... Dolphins declined to match offer (March 7, 1996). ... Granted unconditional free agency (February 12, 1999). ... Signed by Washington Redskins (June 3, 1999). ... Granted unconditional free agency (February 11, 2000). ... Re-signed by Redskins (February 29, 2000).
CHAMPIONSHIP GAME EXPERIENCE: Played in AFC championship game (1992 season).
HONORS: Named linebacker on THE SPORTING NEWS college All-America second team (1991).
PRO STATISTICS: 1997—Intercepted one pass for two yards. 1998—Recovered two fumbles. 1999—Recovered one fumble for 42 yards and a touchdown.

Year Team	G	GS	SACKS
1992—Miami NFL	16	15	6.0
1993—Miami NFL	15	15	5.5
1994—Miami NFL	16	16	6.0
1995—Miami NFL	16	16	6.5
1996—San Diego NFL	16	15	4.0
1997—San Diego NFL	16	16	2.0
1998—San Diego NFL	16	16	3.5
1999—Washington NFL	16	16	6.5
Pro totals (8 years)	127	125	40.0

COLEMAN, MARCUS　　　　　　CB　　　　　　　JETS

PERSONAL: Born May 24, 1974, in Dallas. ... 6-2/210.
HIGH SCHOOL: Lake Highlands (Dallas).
COLLEGE: Texas Tech.
TRANSACTIONS/CAREER NOTES: Selected by New York Jets in fifth round (133rd pick overall) of 1996 NFL draft. ... Signed by Jets (July 11, 1996). ... Granted unconditional free agency (February 11, 2000). ... Re-signed by Jets (February 14, 2000).
CHAMPIONSHIP GAME EXPERIENCE: Played in AFC championship game (1998 season).
PRO STATISTICS: 1997—Recovered one fumble. 1999—Recovered one fumble.

				INTERCEPTIONS		
Year　Team	G	GS	No.	Yds.	Avg.	TD
1996—New York Jets NFL	13	4	1	23	23.0	0
1997—New York Jets NFL	16	2	1	24	24.0	0
1998—New York Jets NFL	14	0	0	0	0.0	0
1999—New York Jets NFL	16	10	6	165	27.5	1
Pro totals (4 years)	59	16	8	212	26.5	1

COLEMAN, RODERICK　　　　DE　　　　　　RAIDERS

PERSONAL: Born August 16, 1976, in Philadelphia. ... 6-2/265.
HIGH SCHOOL: Simon Gratz (Philadelphia).
COLLEGE: East Carolina.
TRANSACTIONS/CAREER NOTES: Selected by Oakland Raiders in fifth round (153rd pick overall) of 1999 NFL draft. ... Signed by Raiders (July 24, 1999).
PLAYING EXPERIENCE: Oakland NFL, 1999. ... Games/Games started: 1999 (3/0).

COLINET, STALIN　　　　　　DE　　　　　　BROWNS

PERSONAL: Born July 19, 1974, in Bronx, N.Y. ... 6-6/288.
HIGH SCHOOL: Cardinal Hayes (Bronx, N.Y.).
COLLEGE: Boston College (degree in sociology, 1996).
TRANSACTIONS/CAREER NOTES: Selected by Minnesota Vikings in third round (78th pick overall) of 1997 NFL draft. ... Signed by Vikings (June 30, 1997). ... Traded by Vikings to Cleveland Browns for DT Jerry Ball (September 28, 1999). ... Granted free agency (February 11, 2000). ... Re-signed by Browns (April 18, 2000).
PLAYING EXPERIENCE: Minnesota NFL, 1997 and 1998; Minnesota (3)-Cleveland (11) NFL, 1999. ... Games/games started: 1997 (10/2), 1998 (11/3), 1999 (Min.-3/1; Cle.-11/9; Total: 14/10). Total: 35/15.
CHAMPIONSHIP GAME EXPERIENCE: Played in NFC championship game (1998 season).
PRO STATISTICS: 1998—Credited with one sack.

COLLINS, ANDRE　　　　　　LB

PERSONAL: Born May 4, 1968, in Riverside, N.J. ... 6-1/240. ... Full name: Andre Pierre Collins.
HIGH SCHOOL: Cinnaminson (N.J.).
COLLEGE: Penn State (degree in health planning and administration, 1991).
TRANSACTIONS/CAREER NOTES: Selected by Washington Redskins in second round (46th pick overall) of 1990 NFL draft. ... Signed by Redskins (July 22, 1990). ... Granted free agency (March 1, 1993). ... Re-signed by Redskins for 1993 season. ... Released by Redskins (April 11, 1995). ... Signed by Cincinnati Bengals (May 7, 1995). ... Granted free agency (February 16, 1996). ... Re-signed by Bengals (August 22, 1996). ... Granted free agency (February 14, 1997). ... Re-signed by Bengals (July 2, 1997). ... Granted unconditional free agency (February 13, 1998). ... Signed by Chicago Bears (May 27, 1998). ... Released by Bears (August 18, 1999). ... Signed by Detroit Lions (August 31, 1999). ... Released by Lions (December 4, 1999).
CHAMPIONSHIP GAME EXPERIENCE: Played in NFC championship game (1991 season). ... Member of Super Bowl championship team (1991 season).
HONORS: Named inside linebacker on THE SPORTING NEWS college All-America second team (1989).
PRO STATISTICS: 1991—Fumbled once. 1992—Recovered one fumble for 40 yards. 1994—Returned one kickoff for no yards and recovered one fumble for 16 yards. 1995—Returned one kickoff for minus three yards. 1997—Recovered one fumble. 1999—Recovered one fumble.

				INTERCEPTIONS			SACKS
Year　Team	G	GS	No.	Yds.	Avg.	TD	No.
1990—Washington NFL	16	16	0	0	0.0	0	6.0
1991—Washington NFL	16	16	2	33	16.5	∞1	3.0
1992—Washington NFL	14	14	1	59	59.0	0	2.0
1993—Washington NFL	13	13	1	5	5.0	0	6.0
1994—Washington NFL	16	16	4	150	37.5	2	1.5
1995—Cincinnati NFL	16	6	2	3	1.5	0	4.0
1996—Cincinnati NFL	14	0	0	0	0.0	0	0.0
1997—Cincinnati NFL	16	0	0	0	0.0	0	3.0
1998—Chicago NFL	16	2	3	29	9.7	0	0.0
1999—Detroit NFL	7	0	0	0	0.0	0	0.0
Pro totals (10 years)	144	83	13	279	21.5	3	25.5

COLLINS, BOBBY　　　　　　TE　　　　　　BILLS

PERSONAL: Born August 20, 1976, in York, Ala. ... 6-4/249. ... Full name: Bobby Eugene Collins.
HIGH SCHOOL: Sumter County (York, Ala.).

JUNIOR COLLEGE: East Mississippi Junior College.
COLLEGE: North Alabama.
TRANSACTIONS/CAREER NOTES: Selected by Buffalo Bills in fourth round (122nd pick overall) of 1999 NFL draft. ... Signed by Bills (July 12, 1999).
PRO STATISTICS: 1999—Returned one kickoff for six yards.
SINGLE GAME HIGHS (regular season): Receptions—2 (January 2, 2000, vs. Indianapolis); yards—45 (November 28, 1999, vs. New England); and touchdown receptions—1 (January 2, 2000, vs. Indianapolis).

| | | | RECEIVING | | |
Year Team	G	GS	No.	Yds.	Avg.	TD
1999—Buffalo NFL	14	4	9	124	13.8	2

COLLINS, CALVIN G/C FALCONS

PERSONAL: Born January 5, 1974, in Beaumont, Texas. ... 6-2/310. ... Full name: Calvin Lewis Collins.
HIGH SCHOOL: West Brook (Beaumont, Texas).
COLLEGE: Texas A&M.
TRANSACTIONS/CAREER NOTES: Selected by Atlanta Falcons in sixth round (180th pick overall) of 1997 NFL draft. ... Signed by Falcons (June 22, 1997). ... Granted free agency (February 11, 2000).
PLAYING EXPERIENCE: Atlanta NFL, 1997-1999. ... Games/Games started: 1997 (15/13), 1998 (16/16), 1999 (14/8). Total: 45/37.
CHAMPIONSHIP GAME EXPERIENCE: Played in NFC championship game (1998 season). ... Played in Super Bowl XXXIII (1998 season).
PRO STATISTICS: 1998—Recovered one fumble.

COLLINS, CECIL RB

PERSONAL: Born November 19, 1976, in Fort Knox, Ky. ... 5-10/209. ... Full name: Cecil J.P. Collins.
HIGH SCHOOL: Leesville (La.).
COLLEGE: Louisiana State, then McNeese State.
TRANSACTIONS/CAREER NOTES: Selected after junior season by Miami Dolphins in fifth round (134th pick overall) of 1999 NFL draft. ... Signed by Dolphins (July 27, 1999). ... Suspended by Dolphins for personal reasons (December 16, 1999-remainder of season). ... Released by Dolphins (February 8, 2000).
SINGLE GAME HIGHS (regular season): Attempts—26 (October 24, 1999, vs. Philadelphia); yards—97 (October 24, 1999, vs. Philadelphia); and rushing touchdowns—1 (October 31, 1999, vs. Oakland).

| | | | RUSHING | | | | RECEIVING | | | | TOTALS | | | |
Year Team	G	GS	Att.	Yds.	Avg.	TD	No.	Yds.	Avg.	TD	TD	2pt.	Pts.	Fum.
1999—Miami NFL	8	6	131	414	3.2	2	6	32	5.3	0	2	0	12	2

COLLINS, KERRY QB GIANTS

PERSONAL: Born December 30, 1972, in Lebanon, Pa. ... 6-5/250. ... Full name: Kerry Michael Collins.
HIGH SCHOOL: Wilson (West Lawn, Pa.).
COLLEGE: Penn State.
TRANSACTIONS/CAREER NOTES: Selected by Carolina Panthers in first round (fifth pick overall) of 1995 NFL draft. ... Signed by Panthers (July 17, 1995). ... Granted free agency (February 13, 1998). ... Re-signed by Panthers (July 24, 1998). ... Claimed on waivers by New Orleans Saints (October 14, 1998). ... Granted unconditional free agency (February 12, 1999). ... Signed by New York Giants (February 19, 1999).
CHAMPIONSHIP GAME EXPERIENCE: Played in NFC championship game (1996 season).
HONORS: Maxwell Award winner (1994). ... Davey O'Brien Award winner (1994). ... Named quarterback on THE SPORTING NEWS college All-America first team (1994). ... Played in Pro Bowl (1996 season).
PRO STATISTICS: 1995—Fumbled 13 times and recovered four fumbles for minus 15 yards. 1996—Fumbled six times and recovered one fumble. 1997—Fumbled eight times and recovered two fumbles for minus 14 yards. 1998—Caught one pass for minus 11 yards, fumbled 13 times and recovered two fumbles for minus nine yards. 1999—Fumbled 11 times and recovered two fumbles for minus 27 yards.
SINGLE GAME HIGHS (regular season): Attempts—53 (September 27, 1998, vs. Green Bay); completions—31 (December 26, 1999, vs. Minnesota); passing yards—341 (December 5, 1999, vs. New York Jets); and touchdown passes—3 (December 5, 1999, vs. New York Jets).
STATISTICAL PLATEAUS: 300-yard passing games: 1995 (2), 1996 (1), 1997 (1), 1998 (2), 1999 (2). Total: 8.
MISCELLANEOUS: Selected by Detroit Tigers organization in 26th round of free-agent draft (June 4, 1990); did not sign. ... Selected by Toronto Blue Jays organization in 58th round of free-agent draft (June 4, 1994); did not sign. ... Regular-season record as starting NFL quarterback: 26-30 (.464). ... Postseason record as starting NFL quarterback: 1-1 (.500).

| | | | PASSING | | | | | | | | RUSHING | | | | TOTALS | | |
Year Team	G	GS	Att.	Cmp.	Pct.	Yds.	TD	Int.	Avg.	Rat.	Att.	Yds.	Avg.	TD	TD	2pt.	Pts.
1995—Carolina NFL	15	13	433	214	49.4	2717	14	19	6.27	61.9	42	74	1.8	3	3	0	18
1996—Carolina NFL	13	12	364	204	56.0	2454	14	9	6.74	79.4	32	38	1.2	0	0	1	2
1997—Carolina NFL	13	13	381	200	52.5	2124	11	*21	5.57	55.7	26	65	2.5	1	1	0	6
1998—Carolina NFL	4	4	162	76	46.9	1011	8	5	6.24	70.8	7	40	5.7	0	0	1	2
—New Orleans NFL	7	7	191	94	49.2	1202	4	10	6.29	54.5	23	113	4.9	1	1	0	6
1999—N.Y. Giants NFL	10	7	331	190	57.4	2318	8	11	7.00	73.3	19	36	1.9	2	2	†1	14
Pro totals (5 years)	62	56	1862	978	52.5	11826	59	75	6.35	66.1	149	366	2.5	7	7	3	48

COLLINS, MO OT RAIDERS

PERSONAL: Born September 22, 1976, in Charlotte. ... 6-4/325. ... Full name: Damon Jamal Collins.
HIGH SCHOOL: West Charlotte.
COLLEGE: Florida.
TRANSACTIONS/CAREER NOTES: Selected after junior season by Oakland Raiders in first round (23rd pick overall) of 1998 NFL draft. ... Signed by Raiders (July 15, 1998).
PLAYING EXPERIENCE: Oakland NFL, 1998 and 1999. ... Games/Games started: 1998 (16/11), 1999 (13/12). Total: 29/23.

COLLINS, RYAN   TE   RAVENS

PERSONAL: Born November 1, 1975, in Minneapolis. ... 6-6/259.
HIGH SCHOOL: Robbinsdale Cooper (Minneapolis).
COLLEGE: St. Thomas (Minneapolis).
TRANSACTIONS/CAREER NOTES: Signed as non-drafted free agent by Minnesota Vikings (May 4, 1998). ... Released by Vikings (August 30, 1998). ... Re-signed by Vikings to practice squad (August 31, 1998). ... Granted free agency following 1998 season. ... Signed by Cleveland Browns (February 22, 1999). ... Inactive for three games with Browns (1999). ... Released by Browns (September 27, 1999). ... Signed by Baltimore Ravens to practice squad (October 12, 1999). ... Activated (December 3, 1999). ... On injured reserve with ankle injury (December 30, 1999-remainder of season).
PLAYING EXPERIENCE: Baltimore NFL, 1999. ... Games/Games started: 1999 (4/3).
PRO STATISTICS: 1999—Caught four passes for 62 yards.
SINGLE GAME HIGHS (regular season): Receptions—3 (December 26, 1999, vs. Cincinnati); yards—41 (December 26, 1999, vs. Cincinnati); and touchdown receptions—0.

COLLINS, TODD   LB   RAMS

PERSONAL: Born May 27, 1970, in New Market, Tenn. ... 6-2/248. ... Full name: Todd Franklin Collins.
HIGH SCHOOL: Jefferson County (Dandridge, Tenn.).
COLLEGE: Georgia (did not play football), then Tennessee (did not play football), then Carson-Newman (Tenn.).
TRANSACTIONS/CAREER NOTES: Selected after junior season by New England Patriots in third round (64th pick overall) of 1992 NFL draft. ... Signed by Patriots (July 23, 1992). ... On injured reserve with neck injury (October 16-November 13, 1992); on practice squad (November 11-13, 1992). ... On injured reserve with knee injury (November 15, 1994-remainder of season). ... Granted free agency (February 17, 1995). ... Re-signed by Patriots (April 20, 1995). ... On reserved/retired list (July 21, 1995-April 16, 1996). ... Granted unconditional free agency (February 14, 1997). ... Re-signed by Patriots (April 4, 1997). ... Granted unconditional free agency (February 12, 1999). ... Signed by St. Louis Rams (March 11, 1999).
PLAYING EXPERIENCE: New England NFL, 1992-1994 and 1996-1998; St. Louis NFL, 1999. ... Games/Games started: 1992 (10/0), 1993 (16/12), 1994 (7/7), 1996 (16/9), 1997 (15/15), 1998 (12/10), 1999 (16/13). Total: 92/66.
CHAMPIONSHIP GAME EXPERIENCE: Played in AFC championship game (1996 season). ... Played in Super Bowl XXXI (1996 season). ... Played in NFC championship game (1999 season). ... Member of Super Bowl championship team (1999 season).
PRO STATISTICS: 1992—Recovered two fumbles. 1993—Credited with one sack, intercepted one pass for eight yards and recovered one fumble for two yards. 1996—Intercepted one pass for seven yards. 1997—Credited with $1^1/_2$ sacks.

COLLINS, TODD   QB   CHIEFS

PERSONAL: Born November 5, 1971, in Walpole, Mass. ... 6-4/228.
HIGH SCHOOL: Walpole (Mass.).
COLLEGE: Michigan.
TRANSACTIONS/CAREER NOTES: Selected by Buffalo Bills in second round (45th pick overall) of 1995 NFL draft. ... Signed by Bills (July 10, 1995). ... Claimed on waivers by Kansas City Chiefs (August 25, 1998). ... Active for three games (1998); did not play. ... Active for all 16 games (1999); did not play.
PRO STATISTICS: 1996—Fumbled three times. 1997—Fumbled 10 times for minus 30 yards.
SINGLE GAME HIGHS (regular season): Attempts—44 (October 6, 1996, vs. Indianapolis); completions—25 (November 23, 1997, vs. Tennessee); yards—309 (October 6, 1996, vs. Indianapolis); and touchdown passes—3 (September 7, 1997, vs. New York Jets).
STATISTICAL PLATEAUS: 300-yard passing games: 1996 (1).
MISCELLANEOUS: Regular-season record as starting NFL quarterback: 7-10 (.412).

				PASSING							RUSHING				TOTALS		
Year Team	G	GS	Att.	Cmp.	Pct.	Yds.	TD	Int.	Avg.	Rat.	Att.	Yds.	Avg.	TD	TD	2pt.	Pts.
1995—Buffalo NFL	7	1	29	14	48.3	112	0	1	3.86	44.0	9	23	2.6	0	0	0	0
1996—Buffalo NFL	7	3	99	55	55.6	739	4	5	7.46	71.9	21	43	2.0	0	0	0	0
1997—Buffalo NFL	14	13	391	215	55.0	2367	12	13	6.05	69.5	30	77	2.6	0	0	0	0
1998—Kansas City NFL						Did not play.											
1999—Kansas City NFL						Did not play.											
Pro totals (3 years)	28	17	519	284	54.7	3218	16	19	6.20	68.5	60	143	2.4	0	0	0	0

COLLONS, FERRIC   DE

PERSONAL: Born December 4, 1969, in Scott Air Force Base (Belleville, Ill.). ... 6-6/285. ... Full name: Ferric Jason Collons.
HIGH SCHOOL: Jesuit (Carmichael, Calif.).
COLLEGE: California.
TRANSACTIONS/CAREER NOTES: Signed as non-drafted free agent by Los Angeles Raiders (April 1992). ... Released by Raiders (August 31, 1992). ... Re-signed by Raiders to practice squad (September 2, 1992). ... Inactive for all 16 games (1993). ... Released by Raiders (August 23, 1994). ... Inactive for two games (1994). ... Released by Jaguars (May 1, 1995). ... Signed by Green Bay Packers (May 22, 1995). ... Traded by Packers to New England Patriots for past considerations (August 27, 1995). ... Granted free agency (February 14, 1997). ... Tendered offer sheet by Philadelphia Eagles (April 14, 1997). ... Offer matched by Patriots (April 18, 1997). ... On injured reserve with shoulder injury (October 30, 1997-remainder of season). ... Released by Patriots (February 11, 1999). ... Signed by Oakland Raiders (June 17, 1999). ... Released by Raiders (September 4, 1999). ... Signed by Patriots (September 9, 1999). ... Granted unconditional free agency (February 11, 2000).
CHAMPIONSHIP GAME EXPERIENCE: Played in AFC championship game (1996 season). ... Played in Super Bowl XXXI (1996 season).
PRO STATISTICS: 1997—Recovered one fumble for five yards.

Year Team	G	GS	SACKS
1992—Los Angeles Raiders NFL			Did not play.
1993—Los Angeles Raiders NFL			Did not play.

Year—Team	G		
1994—Jacksonville NFL	Did not play.		
1995—New England NFL	16	4	4.0
1996—New England NFL	15	5	0.5
1997—New England NFL	6	5	1.0
1998—New England NFL	14	13	0.0
1999—New England NFL	14	0	2.0
Pro totals (5 years)	65	27	7.5

COLMAN, DOUG — LB

PERSONAL: Born June 4, 1973, in Somers Point, N.J. ... 6-2/250.
HIGH SCHOOL: Ocean City (N.J.).
COLLEGE: Nebraska.
TRANSACTIONS/CAREER NOTES: Selected by New York Giants in sixth round (171st pick overall) of 1996 NFL draft. ... Signed by Giants (June 18, 1996). ... Granted free agency (February 12, 1999). ... Re-signed by Giants (June 8, 1999). ... Released by Giants (September 5, 1999). ... Signed by Tennessee Titans (September 9, 1999). ... Granted unconditional free agency (February 11, 2000).
PLAYING EXPERIENCE: New York Giants NFL, 1996-1998; Tennessee NFL, 1999. ... Games/Games started: 1996 (13/0), 1997 (14/0), 1998 (16/0), 1999 (16/1). Total: 59/1.
CHAMPIONSHIP GAME EXPERIENCE: Played in AFC championship game (1999 season). ... Played in Super Bowl XXXIV (1999 season).

COLVIN, ROSEVELT — LB — BEARS

PERSONAL: Born September 5, 1977, in Indianapolis. ... 6-3/260.
HIGH SCHOOL: Broad Ripple (Indianapolis).
COLLEGE: Purdue.
TRANSACTIONS/CAREER NOTES: Selected by Chicago Bears in fourth round (111th pick overall) of 1999 NFL draft. ... Signed by Bears (July 21, 1999).
PRO STATISTICS: 1999—Recovered one fumble.

Year Team	G	GS	SACKS
1999—Chicago NFL	11	0	2.0

COMELLA, GREG — FB — GIANTS

PERSONAL: Born July 29, 1975, in Wellesley, Mass. ... 6-1/248. ... Name pronounced ka-MELL-uh.
HIGH SCHOOL: Xaverian Brothers (Westwood, Mass.).
COLLEGE: Stanford.
TRANSACTIONS/CAREER NOTES: Signed as non-drafted free agent by New York Giants (April 24, 1998).
PLAYING EXPERIENCE: New York Giants NFL, 1998 and 1999. ... Games/Games started: 1998 (16/0), 1999 (16/3). Total: 32/3.
PRO STATISTICS: 1998—Rushed once for six yards, caught one pass for three yards, returned one kickoff for 12 yards and recovered one fumble. 1999—Rushed once for no yards, caught eight passes for 39 yards and returned two kickoffs for 31 yards.
SINGLE GAME HIGHS (regular season): Attempts—1 (December 12, 1999, vs. Buffalo); yards—6 (September 21, 1998, vs. Dallas); and rushing touchdowns—0.

COMPTON, MIKE — C — LIONS

PERSONAL: Born September 18, 1970, in Richlands, Va. ... 6-6/298. ... Full name: Michael Eugene Compton.
HIGH SCHOOL: Richlands (Va.).
COLLEGE: West Virginia.
TRANSACTIONS/CAREER NOTES: Selected by Detroit Lions in third round (68th pick overall) of 1993 NFL draft. ... Signed by Lions (June 4, 1993).
PLAYING EXPERIENCE: Detroit NFL, 1993-1999. ... Games/Games started: 1993 (8/0), 1994 (2/0), 1995 (16/8), 1996 (15/15), 1997 (16/16), 1998 (16/16), 1999 (15/15). Total: 88/70.
HONORS: Named center on THE SPORTING NEWS college All-America first team (1992).
PRO STATISTICS: 1996—Fumbled once. 1999—Recovered two fumbles for eight yards.

CONATY, BILLY — OL — BILLS

PERSONAL: Born March 8, 1973, in Baltimore. ... 6-2/300. ... Full name: William B. Conaty. ... Name pronounced CON-uh-tee.
HIGH SCHOOL: Milford (Conn.) Academy, then Camden Catholic (Cherry Hill, N.J.).
COLLEGE: Virginia Tech.
TRANSACTIONS/CAREER NOTES: Signed as non-drafted free agent by Buffalo Bills (April 25, 1997). ... Released by Bills (August 24, 1997). ... Re-signed by Bills to practice squad (August 26, 1997). ... Activated (September 6, 1997). ... Released by Bills (September 22, 1997). ... Re-signed by Bills to practice squad (September 24, 1997).
PLAYING EXPERIENCE: Buffalo NFL, 1997-1999. ... Games/Games started: 1997 (1/0), 1998 (15/1), 1999 (7/1). Totals: 23/2.
HONORS: Named center on THE SPORTING NEWS college All-America first team (1996).

CONNELL, ALBERT — WR — REDSKINS

PERSONAL: Born May 13, 1974, in Fort Lauderdale, Fla. ... 6-0/179. ... Full name: Albert Gene Anthony Connell.
HIGH SCHOOL: Piper (Fort Lauderdale, Fla.).
JUNIOR COLLEGE: Trinity Valley Community College (Texas).

C

COLLEGE: Texas A&M.
TRANSACTIONS/CAREER NOTES: Selected by Washington Redskins in fourth round (115th pick overall) of 1997 NFL draft. ... Signed by Redskins (May 28, 1997). ... Granted free agency (February 11, 2000). ... Re-signed by Redskins (April 14, 2000).
PRO STATISTICS: 1997—Rushed once for three yards. 1999—Rushed once for eight yards and recovered one fumble.
SINGLE GAME HIGHS (regular season): Receptions—8 (October 17, 1999, vs. Arizona); yards—137 (September 12, 1999, vs. Dallas); and touchdown receptions—2 (October 3, 1999, vs. Carolina).
STATISTICAL PLATEAUS: 100-yard receiving games: 1998 (1), 1999 (4). Total: 5.

				RECEIVING				TOTALS		
Year Team	G	GS	No.	Yds.	Avg.	TD	TD	2pt.	Pts.	Fum.
1997—Washington NFL	5	1	9	138	15.3	2	2	0	12	0
1998—Washington NFL	14	5	28	451	16.1	2	2	0	12	0
1999—Washington NFL	15	14	62	1132	18.3	7	7	0	42	1
Pro totals (3 years)	34	20	99	1721	17.4	11	11	0	66	1

CONRAD, CHRIS   OT   STEELERS

PERSONAL: Born May 27, 1975, in Fullerton, Calif. ... 6-6/310. ... Full name: Christopher Lee Conrad.
HIGH SCHOOL: Brea (Calif.) Olinda.
COLLEGE: Fresno State.
TRANSACTIONS/CAREER NOTES: Selected by Pittsburgh Steelers in third round (66th pick overall) of 1998 NFL draft. ... Signed by Steelers (July 9, 1998).
PLAYING EXPERIENCE: Pittsburgh NFL, 1998 and 1999. ... Games/Games started: 1998 (6/1), 1999 (11/3). Total: 17/4.

C

CONWAY, BRETT   K   REDSKINS

PERSONAL: Born March 8, 1975, in Atlanta. ... 6-2/192. ... Full name: Brett Alan Conway.
HIGH SCHOOL: Parkview (Lilburn, Ga.).
COLLEGE: Penn State.
TRANSACTIONS/CAREER NOTES: Selected by Green Bay Packers in third round (90th pick overall) of 1997 NFL draft. ... Signed by Packers (July 8, 1997). ... On injured reserve with thigh injury (September 3, 1997-entire season). ... Traded by Packers to New York Jets for an undisclosed draft pick (August 21, 1998). ... Released by Jets (August 30, 1998). ... Re-signed by Jets to practice squad (September 1, 1998). ... Released by Jets (September 23, 1998). ... Signed by Washington Redskins (November 12, 1998). ... Granted free agency (February 11, 2000).
PRO STATISTICS: 1999—Attempted one pass without a completion and recovered one fumble.

				KICKING					
Year Team	G	XPM	XPA	FGM	FGA	Lg.	50+	Pts.	
1997—Green Bay NFL				Did not play.					
1998—Washington NFL	6	0	0	0	0		0-0	0	
1999—Washington NFL	16	49	50	22	∞32	51	3-9	115	
Pro totals (2 years)	22	49	50	22	32	51	3-9	115	

CONWAY, CURTIS   WR   CHARGERS

PERSONAL: Born January 13, 1971, in Los Angeles. ... 6-1/196. ... Full name: Curtis LaMont Conway.
HIGH SCHOOL: Hawthorne (Calif.).
JUNIOR COLLEGE: El Camino College (Calif.).
COLLEGE: Southern California.
TRANSACTIONS/CAREER NOTES: Selected after junior season by Chicago Bears in first round (seventh pick overall) of 1993 NFL draft. ... Signed by Bears (May 24, 1993). ... Granted free agency (February 16, 1996). ... Re-signed by Bears (March 4, 1996). ... On injured reserve with shoulder injury (December 22, 1999-remainder of season). ... Granted unconditional free agency (February 11, 2000). ... Signed by San Diego Chargers (February 22, 2000).
HONORS: Named kick returner on THE SPORTING NEWS college All-America second team (1992).
PRO STATISTICS: 1993—Fumbled once. 1994—Completed only pass attempt for 23 yards and a touchdown, fumbled twice and recovered one fumble. 1994—Returned eight punts for 63 yards. 1995—Attempted one pass without a completion. 1996—Completed only pass attempt for 33 yards and a touchdown. 1997—Attempted one pass without a completion. 1998—Attempted one pass without a completion and recovered one fumble.
SINGLE GAME HIGHS (regular season): Receptions—9 (September 12, 1999, vs. Kansas City); yards—148 (September 12, 1994, vs. Philadelphia); and touchdown receptions—3 (October 15, 1995, vs. Jacksonville).
STATISTICAL PLATEAUS: 100-yard receiving games: 1994 (1), 1995 (3), 1996 (4), 1997 (3), 1999 (1). Total: 12.

			RUSHING				RECEIVING				KICKOFF RETURNS				TOTALS			
Year Team	G	GS	Att.	Yds.	Avg.	TD	No.	Yds.	Avg.	TD	No.	Yds.	Avg.	TD	TD	2pt.	Pts.	Fum.
1993—Chicago NFL	16	7	5	44	8.8	0	19	231	12.2	2	21	450	21.4	0	2	0	12	1
1994—Chicago NFL	13	12	6	31	5.2	0	39	546	14.0	2	10	228	22.8	0	2	1	14	2
1995—Chicago NFL	16	16	5	77	15.4	0	62	1037	16.7	12	0	0	0.0	0	12	0	72	0
1996—Chicago NFL	16	16	8	50	6.3	0	81	1049	13.0	7	0	0	0.0	0	7	0	42	1
1997—Chicago NFL	7	7	3	17	5.7	0	30	476	15.9	1	0	0	0.0	0	1	0	6	0
1998—Chicago NFL	15	15	5	48	9.6	0	54	733	13.6	3	0	0	0.0	0	3	0	18	1
1999—Chicago NFL	9	8	1	-2	-2.0	0	44	426	9.7	4	0	0	0.0	0	4	0	24	2
Pro totals (7 years)	92	81	33	265	8.0	0	329	4498	13.7	31	31	678	21.9	0	31	1	188	7

CONWELL, ERNIE   TE   RAMS

PERSONAL: Born August 17, 1972, in Renton, Wash. ... 6-1/265. ... Full name: Ernest Harold Conwell.
HIGH SCHOOL: Kentwood (Kent, Wash.).

COLLEGE: Washington (degree in sociology, 1995).
TRANSACTIONS/CAREER NOTES: Selected by St. Louis Rams in second round (59th pick overall) of 1996 NFL draft. ... Signed by Rams (June 25, 1996). ... On injured reserve with knee injury (October 28, 1998-remainder of season). ... On physically unable to perform list with knee injury (August 30-November 9, 1999). ... Granted unconditional free agency (February 11, 2000). ... Re-signed by Rams (February 11, 2000).
CHAMPIONSHIP GAME EXPERIENCE: Played in NFC championship game (1999 season). ... Member of Super Bowl championship team (1999 season).
PRO STATISTICS: 1996—Recovered one fumble. 1997—Recovered one fumble.
SINGLE GAME HIGHS (regular season): Receptions—5 (September 13, 1998, vs. Minnesota); yards—75 (November 23, 1997, vs. Carolina); and touchdown receptions—1 (December 20, 1997, vs. Carolina).

| | | | RECEIVING | | | | TOTALS | | |
Year Team	G	GS	No.	Yds.	Avg.	TD	TD	2pt.	Pts.	Fum.
1996—St. Louis NFL	10	8	15	164	10.9	0	0	0	0	0
1997—St. Louis NFL	16	16	38	404	10.6	4	4	0	24	0
1998—St. Louis NFL	7	7	15	105	7.0	0	0	0	0	0
1999—St. Louis NFL	3	0	1	11	11.0	0	0	0	0	0
Pro totals (4 years)	36	31	69	684	9.9	4	4	0	24	0

COOK, ANTHONY   DE   REDSKINS

PERSONAL: Born May 30, 1972, in Bennettsville, S.C. ... 6-3/295. ... Full name: Anthony Andrew Cook.
HIGH SCHOOL: Marlboro County (Bennettsville, S.C.).
COLLEGE: South Carolina State.
TRANSACTIONS/CAREER NOTES: Selected by Houston Oilers in second round (35th pick overall) of 1995 NFL draft. ... Signed by Oilers (July 20, 1995). ... Oilers franchise moved to Tennessee for 1997 season. ... On injured reserve with chest injury (December 12, 1998-remainder of season). ... Granted unconditional free agency (February 12, 1999). ... Signed by Washington Redskins (March 29, 1999).
PRO STATISTICS: 1997—Recovered two fumbles. 1999—Recovered one fumble.

Year Team	G	GS	SACKS
1995—Houston NFL	11	5	4.5
1996—Houston NFL	12	11	7.5
1997—Tennessee NFL	16	16	0.0
1998—Tennessee NFL	13	3	2.0
1999—Washington NFL	16	7	3.0
Pro totals (5 years)	68	42	17.0

COOK, RASHARD   S   EAGLES

PERSONAL: Born April 18, 1977, in San Diego. ... 5-11/197.
HIGH SCHOOL: Samuel F.B. Morse (San Diego).
COLLEGE: Southern California.
TRANSACTIONS/CAREER NOTES: Selected by Chicago Bears in sixth round (184th pick overall) of 1999 NFL draft. ... Signed by Bears (June 25, 1999). ... Claimed on waivers by Philadelphia Eagles (September 7, 1999).
PLAYING EXPERIENCE: Philadelphia NFL, 1999. ... Games/Games started: 1999 (13/0).
PRO STATISTICS: 1999—Intercepted one pass for 29 yards and credited with one sack.

COOPER, ANDRE   WR   BRONCOS

PERSONAL: Born June 21, 1975, in Camden, S.C. ... 6-2/210. ... Full name: Andre Damon Cooper.
HIGH SCHOOL: Fletcher (Jacksonville).
COLLEGE: Florida State.
TRANSACTIONS/CAREER NOTES: Signed as non-drafted free agent by Seattle Seahawks (April 25, 1997). ... Released by Seahawks (August 17, 1997). ... Signed by Denver Broncos (January 2, 1998). ... Released by Broncos (August 25, 1998). ... Re-signed by Broncos to practice squad (August 31, 1998).
PLAYING EXPERIENCE: Denver NFL, 1999. ... Games/Games started: 1999 (10/1).
PRO STATISTICS: 1999—Caught nine passes for 98 yards.
SINGLE GAME HIGHS (regular season): Receptions—4 (October 31, 1999, vs. Minnesota); yards—38 (October 31, 1999, vs. Minnesota); and touchdown receptions—0.

COPELAND, JOHN   DE   BENGALS

PERSONAL: Born September 20, 1970, in Lanett, Ala. ... 6-3/280.
HIGH SCHOOL: Valley (Ala.).
JUNIOR COLLEGE: Hinds Community College (Miss.).
COLLEGE: Alabama.
TRANSACTIONS/CAREER NOTES: Selected by Cincinnati Bengals in first round (fifth pick overall) of 1993 NFL draft. ... Signed by Bengals (August 13, 1993). ... Granted unconditional free agency (February 13, 1998). ... Re-signed by Bengals (February 20, 1998). ... On physically unable to perform list with heel injury (August 25-November 17, 1998).
HONORS: Named defensive lineman on THE SPORTING NEWS college All-America first team (1992).
PRO STATISTICS: 1997—Recovered two fumbles for 25 yards and one touchdown. 1998—Intercepted one pass for three yards. 1999—Intercepted two passes for 16 yards.

C

Year Team	G	GS	SACKS
1993—Cincinnati NFL	14	14	3.0
1994—Cincinnati NFL	12	12	1.0
1995—Cincinnati NFL	16	16	9.0
1996—Cincinnati NFL	13	13	3.0
1997—Cincinnati NFL	15	15	3.0
1998—Cincinnati NFL	5	0	0.0
1999—Cincinnati NFL	16	16	4.0
Pro totals (7 years)	91	86	23.0

CORTEZ, JOSE   K   CHARGERS

PERSONAL: Born May 27, 1975, in San Vicente, El Salvador. ... 5-11/205. ... Full name: Jose Antonio Cortez.
HIGH SCHOOL: Van Nuys (Calif.).
JUNIOR COLLEGE: Los Angeles Valley College.
COLLEGE: Oregon State.
TRANSACTIONS/CAREER NOTES: Signed as non-drafted free agent by Cleveland Browns (April 23, 1999). ... Released by Browns (June 3, 1999). ... Signed by San Diego Chargers (June 14, 1999). ... Released by Chargers (August 30, 1999). ... Signed by New York Giants to practice squad (December 14, 1999). ... Activated (December 17, 1999). ... Released by Giants (December 21, 1999). ... Signed by San Diego Chargers (January 18, 2000).
PLAYING EXPERIENCE: New York Giants NFL, 1999. ... Games/Games started: 1999 (1/0).

C

CORYATT, QUENTIN   LB

PERSONAL: Born August 1, 1970, in St. Croix, Virgin Islands. ... 6-3/250. ... Full name: Quentin John Coryatt.
HIGH SCHOOL: Robert E. Lee (Baytown, Texas).
COLLEGE: Texas A&M.
TRANSACTIONS/CAREER NOTES: Selected by Indianapolis Colts in first round (second pick overall) of 1992 NFL draft. ... Signed by Colts (April 24, 1992). ... On injured reserve with displaced wrist bone (October 27, 1992-remainder of season). ... Designated by Colts as transition player (February 25, 1993). ... Tendered offer sheet by Jacksonville Jaguars (February 22, 1996). ... Offer matched by Colts (February 28, 1996). ... On injured reserve with pectoral injury (December 11, 1996-remainder of season). ... Released by Colts (August 31, 1998). ... Signed by Dallas Cowboys (April 17, 1999). ... Released by Cowboys (September 22, 1999). ... Re-signed by Cowboys (December 7, 1999). ... Granted unconditional free agency (February 11, 2000).
CHAMPIONSHIP GAME EXPERIENCE: Played in AFC championship game (1995 season).
PRO STATISTICS: 1992—Recovered one fumble. 1994—Recovered one fumble for 78 yards and a touchdown. 1995—Intercepted one pass for six yards and recovered three fumbles. 1996—Recovered two fumbles for seven yards. 1997—Intercepted two passes for three yards.

Year Team	G	GS	SACKS
1992—Indianapolis NFL	7	7	2.0
1993—Indianapolis NFL	16	16	1.0
1994—Indianapolis NFL	16	16	1.0
1995—Indianapolis NFL	16	16	2.5
1996—Indianapolis NFL	8	7	0.0
1997—Indianapolis NFL	15	15	2.0
1998—		Did not play.	
1999—Dallas NFL	4	1	0.0
Pro totals (7 years)	82	78	8.5

COSTELLO, BRAD   P   BENGALS

PERSONAL: Born December 12, 1974, in Burlington, N.J. ... 6-1/230. ... Full name: Bradford L. Costello.
HIGH SCHOOL: Fairfield (Conn.) Prep, then Holy Cross (Delran, N.J.).
COLLEGE: Boston University (school of hospitality administration, 1998).
TRANSACTIONS/CAREER NOTES: Signed as non-drafted free agent by Cincinnati Bengals (April 23, 1998). ... Released by Bengals (August 25, 1998). ... Re-signed by Bengals to practice squad (November 11, 1998). ... Activated (December 7, 1998). ... Released by Bengals (September 1, 1999). ... Re-signed by Bengals (November 23, 1999).
PRO STATISTICS: 1998—Rushed once for no yards.

Year Team	G	PUNTING No.	Yds.	Avg.	Net avg.	In. 20	Blk.
1998—Cincinnati NFL	3	10	495	49.5	32.7	0	1
1999—Cincinnati NFL	5	22	744	33.8	28.7	1	0
Pro totals (2 years)	8	32	1239	38.7	30.0	1	1

COTA, CHAD   DB   COLTS

PERSONAL: Born August 8, 1971, in Ashland, Ore. ... 6-1/195. ... Full name: Chad Garrett Cota.
HIGH SCHOOL: Ashland (Ore.).
COLLEGE: Oregon (degree in sociology).
TRANSACTIONS/CAREER NOTES: Selected by Carolina Panthers in seventh round (209th pick overall) of 1995 NFL draft. ... Signed by Panthers (July 14, 1995). ... Granted free agency (February 13, 1998). ... Tendered offer sheet by New Orleans Saints (March 11, 1998). ... Panthers declined to match offer (March 19, 1998). ... Granted unconditional free agency (February 12, 1999). ... Signed by Indianapolis Colts (February 23, 1999).
CHAMPIONSHIP GAME EXPERIENCE: Played in NFC championship game (1996 season).
PRO STATISTICS: 1995—Recovered one fumble. 1996—Credited with one sack, fumbled once and recovered one fumble. 1997—Credited with one sack and recovered one fumble. 1998—Credited with two sacks and recovered one fumble. 1999—Recovered one fumble for 25 yards and a touchdown.

Year Team	G	GS	No.	Yds.	Avg.	TD
			INTERCEPTIONS			
1995—Carolina NFL	16	0	0	0	0.0	0
1996—Carolina NFL	16	2	5	63	12.6	0
1997—Carolina NFL	16	16	2	28	14.0	0
1998—New Orleans NFL	16	16	4	16	4.0	0
1999—Indianapolis NFL	15	15	0	0	0.0	0
Pro totals (5 years)	79	49	11	107	9.7	0

COUCH, TIM — QB — BROWNS

PERSONAL: Born July 31, 1977, in Hyden, Ky. ... 6-4/227. ... Full name: Timothy Scott Couch.
HIGH SCHOOL: Leslie County (Hyden, Ky.).
COLLEGE: Kentucky.
TRANSACTIONS/CAREER NOTES: Selected after junior season by Cleveland Browns in first round (first pick overall) of 1999 NFL draft. ... Signed by Browns (April 17, 1999).
HONORS: Named quarterback on The Sporting News college All-America third team (1998).
PRO STATISTICS: 1999—Fumbled 14 times and recovered four fumbles for minus 11 yards.
SINGLE GAME HIGHS (regular season): Attempts—46 (November 21, 1999, vs. Carolina); completions—29 (November 21, 1999, vs. Carolina); passing yards—262 (November 28, 1999, vs. Tennessee); and touchdown passes—3 (October 31, 1999, vs. New Orleans).
MISCELLANEOUS: Regular-season record as starting NFL quarterback: 2-12 (.143).

			PASSING							RUSHING				TOTALS		
Year Team	G	GS	Att.	Cmp.	Pct.	Yds.	TD	Int.	Avg.	Rat.	Att.	Yds.	Avg.	TD	TD	2pt.	Pts.
1999—Cleveland NFL	15	14	399	223	55.9	2447	15	13	6.13	73.2	40	267	6.7	1	1	†1	8

COUSIN, TERRY — CB — BEARS

PERSONAL: Born April 11, 1975, in Miami. ... 5-9/182.
HIGH SCHOOL: Miami Beach Senior.
COLLEGE: South Carolina.
TRANSACTIONS/CAREER NOTES: Signed as non-drafted free agent by Chicago Bears (April 25, 1997). ... Released by Bears (August 24, 1997). ... Re-signed by Bears to practice squad (August 26, 1997). ... Activated (October 25, 1997). ... Released by Bears (October 28, 1997). ... Re-signed by Bears to practice squad (October 30, 1997). ... Activated (November 15, 1997). ... Granted free agency (February 11, 2000). ... Re-signed by Bears (April 18, 2000).
PRO STATISTICS: 1998—Recovered two fumbles. 1999—Recovered one fumble.

			INTERCEPTIONS			
Year Team	G	GS	No.	Yds.	Avg.	TD
1997—Chicago NFL	6	0	0	0	0.0	0
1998—Chicago NFL	16	12	1	0	0.0	0
1999—Chicago NFL	16	9	2	1	0.5	0
Pro totals (3 years)	38	21	3	1	0.3	0

COVINGTON, SCOTT — QB — BENGALS

PERSONAL: Born January 17, 1976, in Laguna Niguel, Calif. ... 6-2/217.
HIGH SCHOOL: Dana Hills (Dana Point, Calif.).
COLLEGE: Miami (Fla.).
TRANSACTIONS/CAREER NOTES: Selected by Cincinnati Bengals in seventh round (245th pick overall) of 1999 NFL draft. ... Signed by Bengals (June 14, 1999).
SINGLE GAME HIGHS (regular season): Attempts—3 (November 7, 1999, vs. Seattle); completions—2 (November 7, 1999, vs. Seattle); passing yards—15 (November 7, 1999, vs. Seattle); and touchdown passes—0.

			PASSING							RUSHING				TOTALS		
Year Team	G	GS	Att.	Cmp.	Pct.	Yds.	TD	Int.	Avg.	Rat.	Att.	Yds.	Avg.	TD	TD	2pt.	Pts.
1999—Cincinnati NFL	3	0	5	4	80.0	23	0	0	4.60	85.8	2	-4	-2.0	0	0	0	0

COWART, SAM — LB — BILLS

PERSONAL: Born February 26, 1975, in Jacksonville. ... 6-2/245.
HIGH SCHOOL: Mandarin (Jacksonville).
COLLEGE: Florida State.
TRANSACTIONS/CAREER NOTES: Selected by Buffalo Bills in second round (39th pick overall) of 1998 NFL draft. ... Signed by Bills (July 20, 1998).
PLAYING EXPERIENCE: Buffalo NFL, 1998 and 1999. ... Games/Games started: 1998 (16/11), 1999 (16/16). Total: 32/27.
HONORS: Named outside linebacker on The Sporting News college All-America first team (1997).
PRO STATISTICS: 1998—Intercepted two passes for 23 yards. 1999—Recovered one fumble and credited with one sack.

COX, BRYAN — LB — JETS

PERSONAL: Born February 17, 1968, in St. Louis. ... 6-4/250. ... Full name: Bryan Keith Cox.
HIGH SCHOOL: East St. Louis (Ill.) Senior.
COLLEGE: Western Illinois (bachelor of science degree in mass communications).

TRANSACTIONS/CAREER NOTES: Selected by Miami Dolphins in fifth round (113th pick overall) of 1991 NFL draft. ... Signed by Dolphins (July 11, 1991). ... On injured reserve with sprained ankle (October 5-November 2, 1991). ... Granted unconditional free agency (February 16, 1996). ... Signed by Chicago Bears (February 20, 1996). ... On injured reserve with thumb injury (November 5, 1996-remainder of season). ... Released by Bears (June 2, 1998). ... Signed by New York Jets (August 1, 1998). ... On injured reserve with abdominal injury (December 10, 1999-remainder of season).

CHAMPIONSHIP GAME EXPERIENCE: Played in AFC championship game (1992 and 1998 seasons).

HONORS: Played in Pro Bowl (1992, 1994 and 1995 seasons).

PRO STATISTICS: 1992—Recovered one fumble. 1993—Recovered four fumbles for one yard. 1995—Recovered one fumble. 1996—Recovered three fumbles, including one in end zone for a touchdown. 1997—Recovered one fumble. 1998—Credited with a safety. 1999—Recovered one fumble.

				INTERCEPTIONS				SACKS
Year	Team	G	GS	No.	Yds.	Avg.	TD	No.
1991—Miami NFL		13	13	0	0	0.0	0	2.0
1992—Miami NFL		16	16	1	0	0.0	0	14.0
1993—Miami NFL		16	16	1	26	26.0	0	5.0
1994—Miami NFL		16	16	0	0	0.0	0	3.0
1995—Miami NFL		16	16	1	12	12.0	0	7.5
1996—Chicago NFL		9	9	0	0	0.0	0	3.0
1997—Chicago NFL		16	15	0	0	0.0	0	5.0
1998—New York Jets NFL		16	10	0	0	0.0	0	6.0
1999—New York Jets NFL		12	11	1	27	27.0	1	0.0
Pro totals (9 years)		130	122	4	65	16.3	1	45.5

C

CRAFT, JASON   CB   JAGUARS

PERSONAL: Born February 13, 1976, in Denver. ... 5-10/178. ... Full name: Jason Donell Andre Craft.

HIGH SCHOOL: Denver East.

JUNIOR COLLEGE: Denver Community College.

COLLEGE: Colorado State.

TRANSACTIONS/CAREER NOTES: Selected by Jacksonville Jaguars in fifth round (160th pick overall) of 1999 NFL draft. ... Signed by Jaguars (May 18, 1999).

PLAYING EXPERIENCE: Jacksonville NFL, 1999. ... Games/Games started: 1999 (16/0).

CHAMPIONSHIP GAME EXPERIENCE: Played in AFC championship game (1999 season).

PRO STATISTICS: 1999—Recovered one fumble for 23 yards and a touchdown.

CRAVER, AARON   FB   SAINTS

PERSONAL: Born December 18, 1968, in Los Angeles. ... 6-0/232. ... Full name: Aaron LeRenze Craver.

HIGH SCHOOL: Compton (Calif.).

JUNIOR COLLEGE: El Camino College (Calif.).

COLLEGE: Fresno State.

TRANSACTIONS/CAREER NOTES: Selected by Miami Dolphins in third round (60th pick overall) of 1991 NFL draft. ... Signed by Dolphins (July 23, 1991). ... On injured reserve with pulled hamstring (October 21-December 12, 1992). ... On practice squad (December 12-January 9, 1993). ... On injured reserve with knee injury (August 23, 1993-entire season). ... Granted free agency (February 17, 1994). ... Re-signed by Dolphins (May 31, 1994). ... Released by Dolphins (August 28, 1994). ... Re-signed by Dolphins (September 26, 1994). ... Released by Dolphins (October 4, 1994). ... Re-signed by Dolphins (November 9, 1994). ... Granted unconditional free agency (February 17, 1995). ... Signed by Denver Broncos (March 9, 1995). ... Granted unconditional free agency (February 14, 1997). ... Signed by San Diego Chargers (April 24, 1997). ... Granted unconditional free agency (February 13, 1998). ... Signed by New Orleans Saints (April 16, 1998). ... Granted unconditional free agency (February 12, 1999). ... Re-signed by Saints (February 24, 1999).

CHAMPIONSHIP GAME EXPERIENCE: Played in AFC championship game (1992 season).

PRO STATISTICS: 1991—Recovered two fumbles. 1994—Recovered one fumble. 1995—Recovered one fumble. 1996—Attempted one pass without a completion. 1997—Recovered one fumble. 1998—Attempted one pass without a completion and recovered one fumble. 1999—Recovered one fumble.

SINGLE GAME HIGHS (regular season): Attempts—20 (December 24, 1995, vs. Oakland); yards—108 (December 24, 1995, vs. Oakland); and rushing touchdowns—1 (December 27, 1998, vs. Buffalo).

STATISTICAL PLATEAUS: 100-yard rushing games: 1995 (1).

				RUSHING				RECEIVING				KICKOFF RETURNS				TOTALS			
Year	Team	G	GS	Att.	Yds.	Avg.	TD	No.	Yds.	Avg.	TD	No.	Yds.	Avg.	TD	TD	2pt.	Pts.	Fum.
1991—Miami NFL		14	0	20	58	2.9	1	8	67	8.4	0	32	615	19.2	0	1	0	6	2
1992—Miami NFL		6	0	3	9	3.0	0	0	0	0.0	0	8	174	21.8	0	0	0	0	0
1993—Miami NFL										Did not play.									
1994—Miami NFL		8	0	6	43	7.2	0	24	237	9.9	0	0	0	0.0	0	0	1	2	1
1995—Denver NFL		16	10	73	333	4.6	5	43	369	8.6	1	7	50	7.1	0	6	0	36	1
1996—Denver NFL		15	15	59	232	3.9	2	39	297	7.6	1	0	0	0.0	0	3	0	18	1
1997—San Diego NFL		15	5	20	71	3.6	0	4	26	6.5	0	3	68	22.7	0	0	0	0	0
1998—New Orleans NFL		16	10	45	180	4.0	2	33	214	6.5	2	7	212	30.3	1	5	0	30	2
1999—New Orleans NFL		13	10	17	40	2.4	0	19	154	8.1	0	1	3	3.0	0	0	0	0	1
Pro totals (8 years)		103	50	243	966	4.0	10	170	1364	8.0	4	58	1122	19.3	1	15	1	92	8

CRAWFORD, KEITH   WR

PERSONAL: Born November 21, 1970, in Palestine, Texas. ... 6-2/195. ... Full name: Keith L. Crawford.

HIGH SCHOOL: Westwood (Palestine, Texas).

COLLEGE: Howard Payne University (Texas).

TRANSACTIONS/CAREER NOTES: Signed as non-drafted free agent by New York Giants (May 1, 1993). ... Released by Giants (October 7, 1993). ... Re-signed by Giants to practice squad (October 8, 1993). ... Activated (October 20, 1993). ... Released by Giants (August 22, 1994).

... Signed by Green Bay Packers (October 28, 1994). ... Inactive for four games (1994). ... Released by Packers (November 22, 1994). ... Re-signed by Packers (December 27, 1994). ... Claimed on waivers by St. Louis Rams (August 26, 1996). ... Granted free agency (February 14, 1997). ... Re-signed by Rams (May 20, 1997). ... Granted unconditional free agency (February 13, 1998). ... Signed by Atlanta Falcons (March 16, 1998). ... Released by Falcons (August 29, 1998). ... Signed by Kansas City Chiefs (November 3, 1998). ... Released by Chiefs (August 31, 1999). ... Signed by Packers (November 9, 1999). ... Released by Packers (December 6, 1999).
PLAYING EXPERIENCE: New York Giants NFL, 1993; Green Bay NFL, 1995 and 1999; St. Louis NFL, 1996 and 1997; Kansas City NFL, 1998. ... Games/Games started: 1993 (7/0), 1995 (13/0), 1996 (16/0), 1997 (15/2), 1998 (8/0), 1999 (3/0). Total: 62/2.
CHAMPIONSHIP GAME EXPERIENCE: Played in NFC championship game (1995 season).
PRO STATISTICS: 1993—Caught one pass for six yards. 1996—Returned four kickoffs for 47 yards. 1997—Rushed twice for 32 yards, caught 11 passes for 232 yards and recovered one fumble. 1999—Caught one pass for 14 yards.
SINGLE GAME HIGHS (regular season): Receptions—4 (October 26, 1997, vs. Kansas City); yards—86 (October 12, 1997, vs. San Francisco); and touchdown receptions—0.

CRAWFORD, VERNON   LB

PERSONAL: Born June 25, 1974, in Texas City, Texas ... 6-4/245. ... Full name: Vernon Dean Crawford Jr.
HIGH SCHOOL: Texas City (Texas).
JUNIOR COLLEGE: San Francisco City College.
COLLEGE: Florida State.
TRANSACTIONS/CAREER NOTES: Selected by New England Patriots in fifth round (159th pick overall) of 1997 NFL draft. ... Signed by Patriots (June 19, 1997). ... Granted free agency (February 11, 2000).
PLAYING EXPERIENCE: New England NFL, 1997-1999. ... Games/games started: 1997 (16/0), 1998 (16/1), 1999 (9/0). Total: 41/1.
PRO STATISTICS: 1997—Recovered one fumble.

C

CROCKETT, HENRI   LB   FALCONS

PERSONAL: Born October 28, 1974, in Pompano Beach, Fla. ... 6-2/238. ... Full name: Henri W. Crockett. ... Brother of Zack Crockett, fullback, Oakland Raiders.
HIGH SCHOOL: Ely (Pompano Beach, Fla.).
COLLEGE: Florida State (degree in criminology, 1996).
TRANSACTIONS/CAREER NOTES: Selected by Atlanta Falcons in fourth round (100th pick overall) of 1997 NFL draft. ... Signed by Falcons (July 14, 1997). ... Granted free agency (February 11, 2000).
CHAMPIONSHIP GAME EXPERIENCE: Played in NFC championship game (1998 season). ... Played in Super Bowl XXXIII (1998 season).
PRO STATISTICS: 1997—Recovered one fumble.

Year Team	G	GS	SACKS
1997—Atlanta NFL	16	10	2.0
1998—Atlanta NFL	10	10	1.0
1999—Atlanta NFL	16	14	1.5
Pro totals (3 years)	42	34	4.5

CROCKETT, RAY   CB   BRONCOS

PERSONAL: Born January 5, 1967, in Dallas. ... 5-10/184. ... Full name: Donald Ray Crockett.
HIGH SCHOOL: Duncanville (Texas).
COLLEGE: Baylor.
TRANSACTIONS/CAREER NOTES: Selected by Detroit Lions in fourth round (86th pick overall) of 1989 NFL draft. ... Signed by Lions (July 18, 1989). ... Granted unconditional free agency (February 17, 1994). ... Signed by Denver Broncos (March 9, 1994).
CHAMPIONSHIP GAME EXPERIENCE: Played in NFC championship game (1991 season). ... Played in AFC championship game (1997 and 1998 seasons). ... Member of Super Bowl championship team (1997 and 1998 seasons).
PRO STATISTICS: 1989—Returned one kickoff for eight yards and recovered one fumble. 1990—Recovered two fumbles for 22 yards and a touchdown. 1992—Recovered one fumble for 15 yards. 1993—Recovered one fumble. 1994—Recovered two fumbles for 43 yards. 1995—Ran four yards with lateral from punt return and recovered one fumble for 50 yards and a touchdown. 1999—Recovered one fumble.

Year Team	G	GS	INTERCEPTIONS No.	Yds.	Avg.	TD	SACKS No.
1989—Detroit NFL	16	0	1	5	5.0	0	0.0
1990—Detroit NFL	16	6	3	17	5.7	0	1.0
1991—Detroit NFL	16	16	∞6	141	23.5	∞1	1.0
1992—Detroit NFL	15	15	4	50	12.5	0	1.0
1993—Detroit NFL	16	16	2	31	15.5	0	1.0
1994—Denver NFL	14	14	2	6	3.0	0	0.0
1995—Denver NFL	16	16	0	0	0.0	0	3.0
1996—Denver NFL	15	15	2	34	17.0	0	4.0
1997—Denver NFL	16	16	4	18	4.5	0	0.0
1998—Denver NFL	16	16	3	105	35.0	1	0.5
1999—Denver NFL	16	16	2	14	7.0	0	2.0
Pro totals (11 years)	172	146	29	421	14.5	2	13.5

CROCKETT, ZACK   RB   RAIDERS

PERSONAL: Born December 2, 1972, in Pompano Beach, Fla. ... 6-2/240. ... Brother of Henri Crockett, linebacker, Atlanta Falcons.
HIGH SCHOOL: Ely (Pompano Beach, Fla.).
JUNIOR COLLEGE: Hinds Community College (Miss.).
COLLEGE: Florida State.

TRANSACTIONS/CAREER NOTES: Selected by Indianapolis Colts in third round (79th pick overall) of 1995 NFL draft. ... Signed by Colts (July 21, 1995). ... On injured reserve with knee injury (October 22, 1996-remainder of season). ... Granted free agency (February 13, 1998). ... Re-signed by Colts (July 23, 1998). ... Claimed on waivers by Jacksonville Jaguars (October 21, 1998). ... Granted unconditional free agency (February 12, 1999). ... Signed by Oakland Raiders (March 16, 1999).
CHAMPIONSHIP GAME EXPERIENCE: Played in AFC championship game (1995 season).
SINGLE GAME HIGHS (regular season): Attempts—15 (December 7, 1997, vs. New York Jets); yards—81 (November 2, 1997, vs. Tampa Bay); and rushing touchdowns—1 (December 26, 1999, vs. San Diego).

			RUSHING				RECEIVING				TOTALS			
Year Team	G	GS	Att.	Yds.	Avg.	TD	No.	Yds.	Avg.	TD	TD	2pt.	Pts.	Fum.
1995—Indianapolis NFL	16	0	1	0	0.0	0	2	35	17.5	0	0	0	0	0
1996—Indianapolis NFL	5	5	31	164	5.3	0	11	96	8.7	1	1	0	6	2
1997—Indianapolis NFL	16	12	95	300	3.2	1	15	112	7.5	0	1	0	6	3
1998—Indianapolis NFL	2	1	2	5	2.5	0	1	1	1.0	0	0	0	0	1
—Jacksonville NFL	10	1	0	0	0.0	0	1	4	4.0	0	0	0	0	0
1999—Oakland NFL	13	1	45	91	2.0	4	8	56	7.0	1	5	0	30	0
Pro totals (5 years)	62	20	174	560	3.2	5	38	304	8.0	2	7	0	42	6

CROSBY, CLIFTON   CB   RAMS

PERSONAL: Born September 17, 1974, in Erie, Pa. ... 5-9/172.
HIGH SCHOOL: East (Erie, Pa.).
COLLEGE: Maryland.
TRANSACTIONS/CAREER NOTES: Signed as non-drafted free agent by St. Louis Rams (April 20, 1999). ... Released by Rams (September 5, 1999). ... Re-signed by Rams (September 6, 1999). ... Released by Rams (September 13, 1999). ... Re-signed by Rams to practice squad (September 30, 1999).
PLAYING EXPERIENCE: St. Louis NFL, 1999. ... Games/Games started: 1999 (1/0).

CROSS, HOWARD   TE   GIANTS

PERSONAL: Born August 8, 1967, in Huntsville, Ala. ... 6-5/285. ... Full name: Howard E. Cross.
HIGH SCHOOL: New Hope (Ala.).
COLLEGE: Alabama.
TRANSACTIONS/CAREER NOTES: Selected by New York Giants in sixth round (158th pick overall) of 1989 NFL draft. ... Signed by Giants (July 24, 1989). ... Granted free agency (February 1, 1991). ... Re-signed by Giants (July 24, 1991). ... Granted free agency (March 1, 1993). ... Re-signed by Giants (July 16, 1993). ... Designated by Giants as transition player (February 15, 1994).
CHAMPIONSHIP GAME EXPERIENCE: Played in NFC championship game (1990 season). ... Member of Super Bowl championship team (1990 season).
PRO STATISTICS: 1992—Recovered one fumble. 1993—Recovered one fumble. 1994—Recovered one fumble. 1997—Recovered one fumble.
SINGLE GAME HIGHS (regular season): Receptions—6 (September 13, 1992, vs. Dallas); yards—77 (September 13, 1992, vs. Dallas); and touchdown receptions—2 (September 11, 1994, vs. Arizona).

			RECEIVING				KICKOFF RETURNS				TOTALS			
Year Team	G	GS	No.	Yds.	Avg.	TD	No.	Yds.	Avg.	TD	TD	2pt.	Pts.	Fum.
1989—New York Giants NFL	16	4	6	107	17.8	1	0	0	0.0	0	1	0	6	1
1990—New York Giants NFL	16	8	8	106	13.3	0	1	10	10.0	0	0	0	0	0
1991—New York Giants NFL	16	16	20	283	14.2	2	1	11	11.0	0	2	0	12	1
1992—New York Giants NFL	16	16	27	357	13.2	2	0	0	0.0	0	2	0	12	2
1993—New York Giants NFL	16	16	21	272	13.0	5	2	15	7.5	0	5	0	30	0
1994—New York Giants NFL	16	16	31	364	11.7	4	0	0	0.0	0	4	0	24	0
1995—New York Giants NFL	15	15	18	197	10.9	0	0	0	0.0	0	0	0	0	1
1996—New York Giants NFL	16	16	22	178	8.1	1	0	0	0.0	0	1	0	6	1
1997—New York Giants NFL	16	16	21	150	7.1	2	0	0	0.0	0	2	0	12	1
1998—New York Giants NFL	16	16	13	90	6.9	0	0	0	0.0	0	0	0	0	2
1999—New York Giants NFL	16	15	9	55	6.1	0	0	0	0.0	0	0	0	0	0
Pro totals (11 years)	175	154	196	2159	11.0	17	4	36	9.0	0	17	0	102	8

CROWELL, GERMANE   WR   LIONS

PERSONAL: Born September 13, 1976, in Winston-Salem, N.C. ... 6-3/216. ... Full name: Germane L. Crowell.
HIGH SCHOOL: North Forsyth (Winston-Salem, N.C.).
COLLEGE: Virginia.
TRANSACTIONS/CAREER NOTES: Selected by Detroit Lions in second round (50th pick overall) of 1998 NFL draft. ... Signed by Lions (July 20, 1998).
PRO STATISTICS: 1999—Recovered one fumble.
SINGLE GAME HIGHS (regular season): Receptions—8 (January 2, 2000, vs. Minnesota); yards—163 (November 7, 1999, vs. St. Louis); and touchdown receptions—2 (September 12, 1999, vs. Seattle).
STATISTICAL PLATEAUS: 100-yard receiving games: 1999 (6).

			RUSHING				RECEIVING				TOTALS			
Year Team	G	GS	Att.	Yds.	Avg.	TD	No.	Yds.	Avg.	TD	TD	2pt.	Pts.	Fum.
1998—Detroit NFL	14	2	1	35	35.0	0	25	464	18.6	3	3	0	18	1
1999—Detroit NFL	16	15	5	38	7.6	0	81	1338	16.5	7	7	†1	44	1
Pro totals (2 years)	30	17	6	73	12.2	0	106	1802	17.0	10	10	1	62	2

CRUMPLER, CARLESTER   TE   VIKINGS

PERSONAL: Born September 5, 1971, in Greenville, N.C. ... 6-6/253. ... Full name: Carlester Crumpler Jr.
HIGH SCHOOL: J.H. Rose (Greenville, N.C.).
COLLEGE: East Carolina (degree in finance, 1995).
TRANSACTIONS/CAREER NOTES: Selected by Seattle Seahawks in seventh round (202nd pick overall) of 1994 NFL draft. ... Signed by Seahawks (July 6, 1994). ... Granted unconditional free agency (February 13, 1998). ... Re-signed by Seahawks (April 21, 1998). ... Granted unconditional free agency (February 12, 1999). ... Signed by Minnesota Vikings (April 12, 1999). ... Granted unconditional free agency (February 11, 2000). ... Re-signed by Vikings (February 25, 2000).
HONORS: Named tight end on The Sporting News college All-America second team (1993).
SINGLE GAME HIGHS (regular season): Receptions—6 (December 15, 1996, vs. Jacksonville); yards—59 (October 29, 1995, vs. Arizona); and touchdown receptions—1 (September 19, 1999, vs. Oakland).

Year Team	G	GS	No.	Yds.	Avg.	TD	TD	2pt.	Pts.	Fum.
1994—Seattle NFL	9	4	2	19	9.5	0	0	0	0	0
1995—Seattle NFL	16	7	23	254	11.0	1	1	0	6	1
1996—Seattle NFL	16	7	26	258	9.9	0	0	0	0	1
1997—Seattle NFL	15	12	31	361	11.6	1	1	0	6	0
1998—Seattle NFL	11	1	6	52	8.7	1	1	0	6	0
1999—Minnesota NFL	11	1	2	35	17.5	1	1	0	6	0
Pro totals (6 years)	78	32	90	979	10.9	4	4	0	24	2

(RECEIVING columns: No., Yds., Avg., TD; TOTALS columns: TD, 2pt., Pts., Fum.)

CRUTCHFIELD, BUDDY   CB   JETS   C

PERSONAL: Born March 7, 1976, in Raleigh, N.C. ... 6-0/196.
HIGH SCHOOL: Athens (Raleigh, N.C.).
COLLEGE: North Carolina Central.
TRANSACTIONS/CAREER NOTES: Signed as non-drafted free agent by Washington Redskins (April 24, 1998). ... Released by Redskins (August 30, 1999). ... Signed by New York Jets to practice squad (November 10, 1999). ... Activated (November 16, 1999).
PLAYING EXPERIENCE: Washington NFL, 1998; New York Jets NFL, 1999. ... Games/Games started: 1998 (2/0), 1999 (4/0). Total: 6/0.

CULPEPPER, BRAD   DT   BUCCANEERS

PERSONAL: Born May 8, 1969, in Tallahassee, Fla. ... 6-1/270. ... Full name: John Broward Culpepper.
HIGH SCHOOL: Leon (Tallahassee, Fla.).
COLLEGE: Florida (degree in history, 1991).
TRANSACTIONS/CAREER NOTES: Selected by Minnesota Vikings in 10th round (264th pick overall) of 1992 NFL draft. ... Signed by Vikings (July 20, 1992). ... On injured reserve with toe injury (November 23, 1992-remainder of season). ... Claimed on waivers by Tampa Bay Buccaneers (August 30, 1994).
CHAMPIONSHIP GAME EXPERIENCE: Played in NFC championship game (1999 season).
HONORS: Named defensive lineman on The Sporting News college All-America first team (1991).
PRO STATISTICS: 1994—Returned two kickoffs for 30 yards and recovered one fumble. 1995—Recovered one fumble for 12 yards. 1998—Recovered one fumble. 1999—Credited with a safety.

Year Team	G	GS	SACKS
1992—Minnesota NFL	11	2	0.0
1993—Minnesota NFL	15	0	0.0
1994—Tampa Bay NFL	16	15	4.0
1995—Tampa Bay NFL	16	4	4.0
1996—Tampa Bay NFL	13	13	1.5
1997—Tampa Bay NFL	16	16	8.5
1998—Tampa Bay NFL	16	16	9.0
1999—Tampa Bay NFL	16	16	6.0
Pro totals (8 years)	119	82	33.0

CULPEPPER, DAUNTE   QB   VIKINGS

PERSONAL: Born January 28, 1977, in Ocala, Fla. ... 6-4/250.
HIGH SCHOOL: Vanguard (Ocala, Fla.).
COLLEGE: Central Florida.
TRANSACTIONS/CAREER NOTES: Selected by Minnesota Vikings in first round (11th pick overall) of 1999 NFL draft. ... Signed by Vikings (July 30, 1999).
PRO STATISTICS: 1999—Fumbled once and recovered one fumble for minus two yards.
MISCELLANEOUS: Selected by New York Yankees organization in 26th round of free-agent baseball draft (June 1, 1995); did not sign.

Year Team	G	GS	Att.	Cmp.	Pct.	Yds.	TD	Int.	Avg.	Rat.	Att.	Yds.	Avg.	TD	TD	2pt.	Pts.
1999—Minnesota NFL	1	0	0	0	0.0	0	0	0	0.0	...	3	6	2.0	0	0	0	0

(PASSING columns: Att., Cmp., Pct., Yds., TD, Int., Avg., Rat.; RUSHING columns: Att., Yds., Avg., TD; TOTALS columns: TD, 2pt., Pts.)

CUMMINGS, JOE   LB

PERSONAL: Born June 8, 1974, in Missoula, Mont. ... 6-2/242. ... Full name: Joe Edward Cummings. ... Son of Ed Cummings, linebacker with New York Jets (1964) and Denver Broncos (1965).
HIGH SCHOOL: Stevensville (Mont.).
COLLEGE: Wyoming.

TRANSACTIONS/CAREER NOTES: Sighed as non-drafted free agent by Philadelphia Eagles (April 26, 1996). ... Released by Eagles (August 20, 1996). ... Signed by San Diego Chargers (October 5, 1996). ... Released by Chargers (October 9, 1996). ... Re-signed by Chargers to practice squad (October 11, 1996). ... Activated (October 25, 1996). ... Released by Chargers (November 12, 1996). ... Re-signed by Chargers to practice squad (November 20, 1996). ... Activated (November 20, 1996). ... Released by Chargers (June 2, 1997). ... Signed by Green Bay Packers (June 3, 1997). ... Released by Packers (August 24, 1997). ... Signed by Buffalo Bills (February 2, 1998). ... Assigned by Bills to Barcelona Dragons in 1998 NFL Europe enhancement allocation program (February 18, 1998). ... Released by Bills (August 30, 1998). ... Re-signed by Bills to practice squad (August 31, 1998). ... Activated (September 30, 1998). ... Granted free agency (February 11, 2000).
PLAYING EXPERIENCE: San Diego NFL, 1996; Barcelona Dragons NFLE, 1998; Buffalo NFL, 1998 and 1999. ... Games/Games started: 1996 (3/0), NFLE 1998 (games played unavailable), NFL 1998 (9/2), 1999 (16/2). Total NFL: 28/4.
PRO STATISTICS: 1998—Returned one kickoff for 21 yards. 1999—Credited with one sack.

CUNNINGHAM, RANDALL   QB   COWBOYS

PERSONAL: Born March 27, 1963, in Santa Barbara, Calif. ... 6-4/213. ... Son of Sam Cunningham, running back with New England Patriots (1973-79 and 1981).
HIGH SCHOOL: Santa Barbara (Calif.).
COLLEGE: UNLV.
TRANSACTIONS/CAREER NOTES: Selected by Arizona Outlaws in 1985 USFL territorial draft. ... Selected by Philadelphia Eagles in second round (37th pick overall) of 1985 NFL draft. ... Signed by Eagles (July 22, 1985). ... On injured reserve with knee injury (September 3, 1991-remainder of season). ... Granted unconditional free agency (February 16, 1996). ... On retired list (August 30, 1996-April 15, 1997). ... Signed by Minnesota Vikings (April 15, 1997). ... Granted unconditional free agency (February 13, 1998). ... Re-signed by Vikings (March 24, 1998). ... Released by Vikings (June 2, 2000). ... Signed by Dallas Cowboys (June 8, 2000).
CHAMPIONSHIP GAME EXPERIENCE: Played in NFC championship game (1998 season).
HONORS: Named punter on THE SPORTING NEWS college All-America first team (1984). ... Played in Pro Bowl (1988-1990 and 1998 seasons). ... Named Outstanding Player of Pro Bowl (1988 season).
RECORDS: Holds NFL single-season record for most times sacked—72 (1986). ... Shares NFL single-game records for most own fumbles recovered—4 (November 30, 1986, OT, at Los Angeles Raiders); and most own and opponents' fumbles recovered—4 (November 30, 1986, OT, at Los Angeles Raiders).
PRO STATISTICS: 1985—Fumbled three times. 1986—Punted twice for 54 yards, fumbled seven times and recovered four fumbles. 1987—Caught one pass for minus three yards, led league with 12 fumbles and recovered six fumbles for minus seven yards. 1988—Punted three times for 167 yards, led league with 12 fumbles and recovered six fumbles. 1989—Punted six times for 319 yards, led the NFC with 17 fumbles and recovered four fumbles for minus six yards. 1990—Fumbled nine times and recovered three fumbles for minus four yards. 1992—Led league with 13 fumbles and recovered three fumbles. 1993—Fumbled three times. 1994—Punted once for 80 yards, fumbled 10 times and recovered two fumbles for minus 15 yards. 1995—Fumbled three times and recovered one fumble for minus five yards. 1997—Fumbled four times and recovered two fumbles. 1998—Caught one pass for minus three yards and fumbled twice. 1999—Fumbled twice for minus one yard.
SINGLE GAME HIGHS (regular season): Attempts—62 (October 2, 1989, vs. Chicago); completions—34 (September 17, 1989, vs. Washington); passing yards—447 (September 17, 1989, vs. Washington); and touchdown passes—5 (September 17, 1989, vs. Washington).
STATISTICAL PLATEAUS: 300-yard passing games: 1987 (1), 1988 (2), 1989 (3), 1992 (1), 1993 (1), 1994 (4), 1998 (4), 1999 (2). Total: 18. ... 100-yard rushing games: 1986 (1), 1990 (1), 1992 (1). Total: 3.
MISCELLANEOUS: Regular-season record as starting NFL quarterback: 79-50-1 (.612). ... Postseason record as starting NFL quarterback: 3-6 (.333).

					PASSING						RUSHING				TOTALS		
Year Team	G	GS	Att.	Cmp.	Pct.	Yds.	TD	Int.	Avg.	Rat.	Att.	Yds.	Avg.	TD	TD	2pt.	Pts.
1985—Philadelphia NFL	6	4	81	34	42.0	548	1	8	6.77	29.8	29	205	7.1	0	0	0	0
1986—Philadelphia NFL	15	5	209	111	53.1	1391	8	7	6.66	72.9	66	540	8.2	5	5	0	30
1987—Philadelphia NFL	12	12	406	223	54.9	2786	23	12	6.86	83.0	76	505	6.6	3	3	0	18
1988—Philadelphia NFL	16	16	‡560	301	53.8	3808	24	16	6.80	77.6	93	624	6.7	6	6	0	36
1989—Philadelphia NFL	16	16	532	290	54.5	3400	21	15	6.39	75.5	104	621	*6.0	4	4	0	24
1990—Philadelphia NFL	16	16	465	271	58.3	3466	‡30	13	7.45	91.6	118	942	*8.0	5	5	0	30
1991—Philadelphia NFL	1	1	4	1	25.0	19	0	0	4.75	46.9	0	0	0.0	0	0	0	0
1992—Philadelphia NFL	15	15	384	233	60.7	2775	19	11	7.23	87.3	87	549	6.3	5	5	0	30
1993—Philadelphia NFL	4	4	110	76	69.1	850	5	5	7.73	88.1	18	110	6.1	1	1	0	6
1994—Philadelphia NFL	14	14	490	265	54.1	3229	16	13	6.59	74.4	65	288	4.4	3	3	0	18
1995—Philadelphia NFL	7	4	121	69	57.0	605	3	5	5.00	61.5	21	98	4.7	0	0	0	0
1996—									Did not play.								
1997—Minnesota NFL	6	3	88	44	50.0	501	6	4	5.69	71.3	19	127	6.7	0	0	0	0
1998—Minnesota NFL	15	14	425	259	60.9	3704	34	10	8.72	*106.0	32	132	4.1	1	1	1	8
1999—Minnesota NFL	6	6	200	124	62.0	1475	8	9	7.38	79.1	10	58	5.8	0	0	0	0
Pro totals (14 years)	149	130	4075	2301	56.5	28557	198	128	7.01	81.4	738	4799	6.5	33	33	1	200

CUNNINGHAM, RICHIE   K   PANTHERS

PERSONAL: Born August 18, 1970, in Terrebonne, La. ... 5-10/167. ... Full name: Richard Anthony Cunningham.
HIGH SCHOOL: Terrebonne (La.).
COLLEGE: Southwestern Louisiana (degree in marketing).
TRANSACTIONS/CAREER NOTES: Signed as non-drafted free agent by Dallas Cowboys (May 2, 1994). ... Released by Cowboys (August 17, 1994). ... Signed by Green Bay Packers (April 22, 1996). ... Released by Packers (August 19, 1996). ... Signed by Cowboys (April 15, 1997). ... Released by Cowboys (December 7, 1999). ... Signed by Carolina Panthers (December 14, 1999).
HONORS: Named kicker on THE SPORTING NEWS NFL All-Pro team (1997).

		KICKING						
Year Team	G	XPM	XPA	FGM	FGA	Lg.	50+	Pts.
1997—Dallas NFL	16	24	24	*34	∞37	53	1-1	‡126
1998—Dallas NFL	16	40	40	29	35	54	1-3	127
1999—Dallas NFL	12	31	31	12	22	47	0-1	67
—Carolina NFL	3	13	14	3	3	43	0-0	22
Pro totals (3 years)	47	108	109	78	97	54	2-5	342

CURRY, ERIC   DE   JAGUARS

PERSONAL: Born February 3, 1970, in Thomasville, Ga. ... 6-6/277. ... Full name: Eric Felece Curry. ... Cousin of William Andrews, running back with Atlanta Falcons (1979-83 and 1986); cousin of Lomas Brown, offensive tackle, New York Giants; and cousin of Guy McIntyre, guard with San Francisco 49ers (1984-93), Green Bay Packers (1994) and Philadelphia Eagles (1995 and 1996).
HIGH SCHOOL: Thomasville (Ga.).
COLLEGE: Alabama (degree in criminal justice, 1992).
TRANSACTIONS/CAREER NOTES: Selected by Tampa Bay Buccaneers in first round (sixth pick overall) of 1993 NFL draft. ... Signed by Buccaneers (August 16, 1993). ... Designated by Buccaneers as transition player (February 15, 1994). ... Released by Buccaneers (August 23, 1997). ... Re-signed by Buccaneers (August 25, 1997). ... Granted unconditional free agency (February 13, 1998). ... Signed by Green Bay Packers (April 2, 1998). ... Released by Packers (August 30, 1998). ... Signed by Jacksonville Jaguars (September 9, 1998). ... Granted unconditional free agency (February 12, 1999). ... Re-signed by Jaguars (April 8, 1999). ... On injured reserve with knee injury (October 13, 1999-remainder of season). ... Granted unconditional free agency (February 11, 2000). ... Re-signed by Jaguars (February 22, 2000).
HONORS: Named defensive lineman on THE SPORTING NEWS college All-America first team (1992).
PRO STATISTICS: 1993—Recovered one fumble. 1995—Recovered one fumble.

Year Team	G	GS	SACKS
1993—Tampa Bay NFL	10	10	5.0
1994—Tampa Bay NFL	15	14	3.0
1995—Tampa Bay NFL	16	16	2.0
1996—Tampa Bay NFL	12	3	2.0
1997—Tampa Bay NFL	6	1	0.0
1998—Jacksonville NFL	11	0	0.0
1999—Jacksonville NFL	5	0	0.5
Pro totals (7 years)	**75**	**44**	**12.5**

CURRY, SCOTT   OT   PACKERS

PERSONAL: Born December 25, 1975, in Conrad, Mont. ... 6-5/300. ... Full name: Scott Richard Curry.
HIGH SCHOOL: Valier (Mont.).
COLLEGE: Montana (degree in business administration).
TRANSACTIONS/CAREER NOTES: Selected by Green Bay Packers in sixth round (203rd pick overall) of 1999 NFL draft. ... Signed by Packers (July 21, 1999).
PLAYING EXPERIENCE: Green Bay NFL, 1999. ... Games/Games started: 1999 (5/0).

CURTIS, CANUTE   LB   BENGALS

PERSONAL: Born August 4, 1974, in Amityville, N.Y. ... 6-2/256. ... Name pronounced kuh-NOOT.
HIGH SCHOOL: Farmingdale (N.Y.).
COLLEGE: West Virginia.
TRANSACTIONS/CAREER NOTES: Selected by Cincinnati Bengals in sixth round (176th pick overall) of 1997 NFL draft. ... Signed by Bengals (July 11, 1997). ... Released by Bengals (August 24, 1997). ... Re-signed by Bengals to practice squad (August 26, 1997). ... Activated (October 21, 1997). ... Released by Bengals (August 30, 1998). ... Re-signed by Bengals to practice squad (August 31, 1998). ... Activated (November 10, 1998). ... Granted free agency (February 11, 2000). ... Re-signed by Bengals (March 1, 2000).
PLAYING EXPERIENCE: Cincinnati NFL, 1997-1999. ... Games/games started: 1997 (3/0), 1998 (5/0), 1999 (15/0). Total: 23/0.
HONORS: Named outside linebacker on THE SPORTING NEWS college All-America first team (1996).
PRO STATISTICS: 1999—Credited with one sack.

CUSHING, MATT   TE   STEELERS

PERSONAL: Born July 2, 1975, in Chicago ... 6-3/258. ... Full name: Matt Jay Cushing.
HIGH SCHOOL: Mount Carmel (Chicago).
COLLEGE: Illinois.
TRANSACTIONS/CAREER NOTES: Signed as non-drafted free agent by Pittsburgh Steelers (April 24, 1998). ... Released by Steelers (August 24, 1998). ... Re-signed by Steelers (February 22, 1999). ... Assigned by Steelers to Amsterdam Admirals in 1999 NFL Europe enhancement allocation program (February 22, 1999). ... Released by Steelers (September 5, 1999). ... Re-signed by Steelers (October 28, 1999).
SINGLE GAME HIGHS (regular season): Receptions—2 (January 2, 2000, vs. Tennessee); yards—29 (January 2, 2000, vs. Tennessee); and touchdown receptions—0.

				RECEIVING				TOTALS		
Year Team	G	GS	No.	Yds.	Avg.	TD	TD	2pt.	Pts.	Fum.
1999—Amsterdam NFLE	...	...	6	62	10.3	0	0	0	0	0
—Pittsburgh NFL	7	1	2	29	14.5	0	0	0	0	0
NFL Europe totals (1 year)	...	...	6	62	10.3	0	0	0	0	0
NFL totals (1 year)	7	1	2	29	14.5	0	0	0	0	0
Pro totals (2 years)	...	...	8	91	11.4	0	0	0	0	0

DAILEY, CASEY   LB   JETS

PERSONAL: Born June 11, 1975, in La Verne, Calif. ... 6-3/249.
HIGH SCHOOL: Damien (La Verne, Calif.).
COLLEGE: Northwestern.
TRANSACTIONS/CAREER NOTES: Selected by New York Jets in fifth round (134th pick overall) of 1998 NFL draft. ... Signed by Jets (July 8, 1998). ... On injured reserve with foot injury (July 31, 1998-entire season). ... Released by Jets (September 5, 1999). ... Re-signed by Jets to practice squad (September 6, 1999). ... Activated (October 6, 1999).
PLAYING EXPERIENCE: New York Jets NFL, 1999. ... Games/Games started: 1999 (6/0).

C
D

DALMAN, CHRIS   C   49ERS

PERSONAL: Born March 15, 1970, in Salinas, Calif. ... 6-3/297. ... Full name: Christopher William Dalman.
HIGH SCHOOL: Palma (Salinas, Calif.).
COLLEGE: Stanford (degree in political science, 1992).
TRANSACTIONS/CAREER NOTES: Selected by San Francisco 49ers in sixth round (166th pick overall) of 1993 NFL draft. ... Signed by 49ers (June 24, 1993). ... Granted unconditional free agency (February 14, 1997). ... Re-signed by 49ers (April 25, 1997).
PLAYING EXPERIENCE: San Francisco NFL, 1993-1999. ... Games/Games started: 1993 (15/0), 1994 (16/4), 1995 (15/1), 1996 (16/16), 1997 (13/13), 1998 (15/15), 1999 (15/15). Total: 105/64.
CHAMPIONSHIP GAME EXPERIENCE: Played in NFC championship game (1993, 1994 and 1997 seasons). ... Member of Super Bowl championship team (1994 season).
PRO STATISTICS: 1993—Recovered one fumble. 1994—Fumbled once. 1995—Caught one pass for minus one yard, returned three kickoffs for 29 yards and recovered one fumble. 1997—Recovered one fumble.

DALTON, ANTICO   LB   VIKINGS

PERSONAL: Born December 31, 1975, in Eden, N.C. ... 6-1/241.
HIGH SCHOOL: J.M. Morehead (Eden, N.C.).
COLLEGE: Hampton University.
TRANSACTIONS/CAREER NOTES: Selected by Minnesota Vikings in sixth round (199th pick overall) of 1999 NFL draft. ... Signed by Vikings (June 8, 1999). ... Released by Vikings (October 12, 1999). ... Re-signed by Vikings to practice squad (October 13, 1999).
PLAYING EXPERIENCE: Minnesota NFL, 1999. ... Games/Games started: 1999 (2/0).

DALTON, LIONAL   DT   RAVENS

PERSONAL: Born February 21, 1975, in Detroit. ... 6-1/320.
HIGH SCHOOL: Cooley (Detroit).
COLLEGE: Eastern Michigan.
TRANSACTIONS/CAREER NOTES: Signed as non-drafted free agent by Baltimore Ravens (April 23, 1998).
PLAYING EXPERIENCE: Baltimore NFL, 1998 and 1999. ... Games/Games started: 1998 (2/1), 1999 (16/2). Total: 18/3.
PRO STATISTICS: 1999—Credited with one sack.

D

DALUISO, BRAD   K   GIANTS

PERSONAL: Born December 31, 1967, in San Diego. ... 6-1/180. ... Full name: Bradley William Daluiso.
HIGH SCHOOL: Valhalla (El Cajon, Calif.).
JUNIOR COLLEGE: Grossmont College (Calif.).
COLLEGE: San Diego State, then UCLA.
TRANSACTIONS/CAREER NOTES: Signed as non-drafted free agent by Green Bay Packers (May 2, 1991). ... Traded by Packers to Atlanta Falcons for an undisclosed pick in 1992 draft (August 26, 1991). ... Claimed on waivers by Buffalo Bills (September 10, 1991). ... Granted unconditional free agency (February 1, 1992). ... Signed by Dallas Cowboys (February 18, 1992). ... Claimed on waivers by Denver Broncos (September 1, 1992). ... Released by Broncos (August 23, 1993). ... Signed by New York Giants (September 1, 1993). ... Granted free agency (February 17, 1994). ... Re-signed by Giants (June 21, 1994). ... Granted unconditional free agency (February 17, 1995). ... Re-signed by Giants (February 22, 1995). ... Granted unconditional free agency (February 13, 1998). ... Re-signed by Giants (February 13, 1998). ... On injured reserve with knee injury (October 20, 1999-remainder of season).
CHAMPIONSHIP GAME EXPERIENCE: Played in AFC championship game (1991 season). ... Played in Super Bowl XXVI (1991 season).
PRO STATISTICS: 1992—Punted 10 times for 467 yards.

		KICKING						
Year Team	G	XPM	XPA	FGM	FGA	Lg.	50+	Pts.
1991—Atlanta NFL	2	2	2	2	3	23	0-0	8
—Buffalo NFL	14	0	0	0	0		0-0	0
1992—Denver NFL	16	0	0	0	1	0	0-1	0
1993—New York Giants NFL	15	0	0	1	3	54	1-3	3
1994—New York Giants NFL	16	5	5	11	11	52	1-1	38
1995—New York Giants NFL	16	28	28	20	28	51	2-2	88
1996—New York Giants NFL	16	22	22	24	27	46	0-0	94
1997—New York Giants NFL	16	27	29	22	32	52	1-4	93
1998—New York Giants NFL	16	32	32	21	27	51	1-1	95
1999—New York Giants NFL	6	9	9	7	9	36	0-0	30
Pro totals (9 years)	**133**	**125**	**127**	**108**	**141**	**54**	**6-12**	**449**

DANIELS, PHILLIP   DE   BEARS

PERSONAL: Born March 4, 1973, in Donaldsonville, Ga. ... 6-5/284. ... Full name: Phillip Bernard Daniels.
HIGH SCHOOL: Seminole County (Donaldsonville, Ga.).
COLLEGE: Georgia.
TRANSACTIONS/CAREER NOTES: Selected by Seattle Seahawks in fourth round (99th pick overall) of 1996 NFL draft. ... Signed by Seahawks (July 17, 1996). ... Granted free agency (February 12, 1999). ... Re-signed by Seahawks (April 6, 1999). ... Granted unconditional free agency (February 11, 2000). ... Signed by Chicago Bears (February 12, 2000).
PRO STATISTICS: 1996—Recovered one fumble. 1997—Returned one kickoff for minus two yards and fumbled once. 1998—Recovered two fumbles.

Year Team	G	GS	SACKS
1996—Seattle NFL	15	0	2.0
1997—Seattle NFL	13	10	4.0
1998—Seattle NFL	16	15	6.5
1999—Seattle NFL	16	16	9.0
Pro totals (4 years)	60	41	21.5

DARIUS, DONOVIN   S   JAGUARS

PERSONAL: Born August 12, 1975, in Camden, N.J. ... 6-1/212. ... Full name: Donovin Lee Darius.
HIGH SCHOOL: Woodrow Wilson (Camden, N.J.).
COLLEGE: Syracuse (degree in exercise science, 1997).
TRANSACTIONS/CAREER NOTES: Selected by Jacksonville Jaguars in first round (25th pick overall) of 1998 NFL draft. ... Signed by Jaguars (July 23, 1998).
PLAYING EXPERIENCE: Jacksonville NFL, 1998 and 1999. ... Games/Games started: 1998 (14/14), 1999 (16/16). Total: 30/30.
CHAMPIONSHIP GAME EXPERIENCE: Played in AFC championship game (1999 season).
HONORS: Named free safety on THE SPORTING NEWS college All-America first team (1997).
PRO STATISTICS: 1998—Recovered one fumble for 83 yards and a touchdown. 1999—Intercepted four passes for 37 yards.

DARLING, JAMES   LB   EAGLES

PERSONAL: Born December 29, 1974, in Denver. ... 6-0/250. ... Full name: James Jackson Darling.
HIGH SCHOOL: Kettle Falls (Wash.).
COLLEGE: Washington State.
TRANSACTIONS/CAREER NOTES: Selected by Philadelphia Eagles in second round (57th pick overall) of 1997 NFL draft. ... Signed by Eagles (July 16, 1997). ... Granted free agency (February 11, 2000). ... Re-signed by Eagles (April 10, 2000).
PLAYING EXPERIENCE: Philadelphia NFL, 1997-1999. ... Games/Games started: 1997 (16/6), 1998 (12/8), 1999 (15/10). Total: 43/24.
HONORS: Named inside linebacker on THE SPORTING NEWS college All-America second team (1996).
PRO STATISTICS: 1998—Credited with two sacks. 1999—Intercepted one pass for 33 yards.

DAVIDDS-GARRIDO, NORBERTO   OT   CARDINALS   D

PERSONAL: Born June 11, 1972, in La Puente, Calif. ... 6-5/315. ... Full name: Norberto Davidds-Garrido Jr. ... Formerly known as Norberto Garrido.
HIGH SCHOOL: Workman (City of Industry, Calif.).
JUNIOR COLLEGE: Mt. San Antonio College (Calif.).
COLLEGE: Southern California.
TRANSACTIONS/CAREER NOTES: Selected by Carolina Panthers in fourth round (106th pick overall) of 1996 NFL draft. ... Signed by Panthers (June 17, 1996). ... On injured reserve with ankle injury (December 15, 1997-remainder of season). ... Granted free agency (February 12, 1999). ... Re-signed by Panthers (July 27, 1999). ... Granted unconditional free agency (February 11, 2000). ... Signed by Arizona Cardinals (April 28, 2000).
PLAYING EXPERIENCE: Carolina NFL, 1996-1999. ... Games/Games started: 1996 (12/8), 1997 (15/15), 1998 (16/16), 1999 (16/0). Total: 59/39.
CHAMPIONSHIP GAME EXPERIENCE: Played in NFC championship game (1996 season).
PRO STATISTICS: 1998—Recovered one fumble.

DAVIS, ANTHONY   LB

PERSONAL: Born March 7, 1969, in Kennewick, Wash. ... 6-0/235. ... Full name: Anthony D. Davis.
HIGH SCHOOL: Pasco (Wash.).
JUNIOR COLLEGE: Spokane Falls Community College (Wash.).
COLLEGE: Utah.
TRANSACTIONS/CAREER NOTES: Selected by Houston Oilers in 11th round (301st pick overall) of 1992 NFL draft. ... Signed by Oilers for 1992 season. ... Released by Oilers (August 24, 1992). ... Re-signed by Oilers to practice squad (September 2, 1992). ... Released by Oilers (October 6, 1992). ... Signed by Seattle Seahawks to practice squad (December 9, 1992). ... Released by Seahawks (August 30, 1993). ... Re-signed by Seahawks to practice squad (September 1, 1993). ... Activated (October 11, 1993). ... Released by Seahawks (August 22, 1994). ... Signed by Kansas City Chiefs (November 24, 1994). ... Granted unconditional free agency (February 12, 1999). ... Signed by Green Bay Packers (July 29, 1999). ... On injured reserve with hamstring injury (January 1, 2000-remainder of season). ... Granted unconditional free agency (February 11, 2000).
PRO STATISTICS: 1997—Recovered one fumble for two yards.

Year Team	G	GS	INTERCEPTIONS No.	Yds.	Avg.	TD	SACKS No.
1993—Seattle NFL	10	0	0	0	0.0	0	0.0
1994—Kansas City NFL	5	0	0	0	0.0	0	0.0
1995—Kansas City NFL	16	2	1	11	11.0	0	2.0
1996—Kansas City NFL	16	15	2	37	18.5	0	2.5
1997—Kansas City NFL	15	15	0	0	0.0	0	3.5
1998—Kansas City NFL	16	16	2	27	13.5	0	4.5
1999—Green Bay NFL	14	1	0	0	0.0	0	0.0
Pro totals (7 years)	92	49	5	75	15.0	0	12.5

DAVIS, BILLY   WR   RAVENS

PERSONAL: Born July 6, 1972, in El Paso, Texas. ... 6-1/205. ... Full name: William Augusta Davis III.
HIGH SCHOOL: Irvin (El Paso, Texas).
COLLEGE: Pittsburgh.
TRANSACTIONS/CAREER NOTES: Signed as non-drafted free agent by Dallas Cowboys (April 27, 1995). ... Granted free agency (February 13, 1998). ... Re-signed by Cowboys (February 27, 1998). ... Released by Cowboys (June 1, 1999). ... Signed by Baltimore Ravens (June 18, 1999). ... Granted unconditional free agency (February 11, 2000). ... Re-signed by Ravens (April 28, 2000).
CHAMPIONSHIP GAME EXPERIENCE: Played in NFC championship game (1995 season). ... Member of Super Bowl championship team (1995 season).
PRO STATISTICS: 1998—Rushed four times for 15 yards, returned one kickoff for 10 yards and recovered one fumble. 1999—Recovered one fumble.
SINGLE GAME HIGHS (regular season): Receptions—4 (December 27, 1998, vs. Washington); yards—87 (September 27, 1998, vs. Oakland); and touchdown receptions—1 (November 22, 1998, vs. Seattle).

			RECEIVING				TOTALS			
Year Team	G	GS	No.	Yds.	Avg.	TD	TD	2pt.	Pts.	Fum.
1995—Dallas NFL	16	0	0	0	0.0	0	0	0	0	0
1996—Dallas NFL	13	0	0	0	0.0	0	0	0	0	0
1997—Dallas NFL	16	0	3	33	11.0	0	0	0	0	0
1998—Dallas NFL	16	11	39	691	17.7	3	3	0	18	1
1999—Baltimore NFL	16	0	6	121	20.2	0	0	0	0	0
Pro totals (5 years)	77	11	48	845	17.6	3	3	0	18	1

DAVIS, DON   LB

PERSONAL: Born December 17, 1972, in Olathe, Kan. ... 6-1/240.
HIGH SCHOOL: Olathe (Kan.) South.
COLLEGE: Kansas.
TRANSACTIONS/CAREER NOTES: Signed as non-drafted free agent by New York Jets (April 28, 1995). ... Released by Jets (August 27, 1995). ... Signed by Kansas City Chiefs (January 9, 1996). ... Released by Chiefs (August 20, 1996). ... Signed by New Orleans Saints to practice squad (August 27, 1996). ... Activated (October 4, 1996). ... On injured reserve with wrist injury (November 19, 1997-remainder of season). ... Claimed on waivers by Tampa Bay Buccaneers (November 25, 1998). ... Granted free agency (February 12, 1999). ... Re-signed by Buccaneers (May 21, 1999). ... Released by Buccaneers (October 9, 1999). ... Re-signed by Buccaneers (October 19, 1999). ... Granted unconditional free agency (February 11, 2000).
PLAYING EXPERIENCE: New Orleans NFL, 1996 and 1997; New Orleans (4)-Tampa Bay (5) NFL, 1998; Tampa Bay NFL, 1999. ... Games/Games started: 1996 (11/0), 1997 (11/0), 1998 (N.O.-4/0; T.B.-5/0; Total: 9/0), 1999 (14/0). Total: 45/0.
CHAMPIONSHIP GAME EXPERIENCE: Played in NFC championship game (1999 season).
PRO STATISTICS: 1996—Recovered one fumble.

DAVIS, ERIC   CB   PANTHERS

PERSONAL: Born January 26, 1968, in Anniston, Ala. ... 5-11/185. ... Full name: Eric Wayne Davis.
HIGH SCHOOL: Anniston (Ala.).
COLLEGE: Jacksonville (Ala.) State.
TRANSACTIONS/CAREER NOTES: Selected by San Francisco 49ers in second round (53rd pick overall) of 1990 NFL draft. ... Signed by 49ers (July 28, 1990). ... On injured reserve with shoulder injury (September 11, 1991-remainder of season). ... Granted free agency (March 1, 1993). ... Re-signed by 49ers (July 20, 1993). ... Granted unconditional free agency (February 16, 1996). ... Signed by Carolina Panthers (February 21, 1996).
CHAMPIONSHIP GAME EXPERIENCE: Played in NFC championship game (1990, 1992-1994 and 1996 seasons). ... Member of Super Bowl championship team (1994 season).
HONORS: Played in Pro Bowl (1995 and 1996 seasons).
POST SEASON RECORDS: Shares NFL postseason career record for most consecutive games with one or more interception—3.
PRO STATISTICS: 1990—Returned five punts for 38 yards and recovered one fumble for 34 yards. 1992—Recovered two fumbles. 1993—Recovered one fumble for 47 yards and a touchdown. 1994—Recovered two fumbles. 1995—Credited with one sack. 1997—Recovered one fumble for two yards. 1998—Credited with one sack and recovered one fumble. 1999—Fumbled once and recovered one fumble.
MISCELLANEOUS: Holds Carolina Panthers all-time record for most interceptions (20).

			INTERCEPTIONS			
Year Team	G	GS	No.	Yds.	Avg.	TD
1990—San Francisco NFL	16	0	1	13	13.0	0
1991—San Francisco NFL	2	2	0	0	0.0	0
1992—San Francisco NFL	16	16	3	52	17.3	0
1993—San Francisco NFL	16	16	4	45	11.3	1
1994—San Francisco NFL	16	16	1	8	8.0	0
1995—San Francisco NFL	15	15	3	84	28.0	1
1996—Carolina NFL	16	16	5	57	11.4	0
1997—Carolina NFL	14	14	5	25	5.0	0
1998—Carolina NFL	16	16	5	81	16.2	2
1999—Carolina NFL	16	16	5	49	9.8	0
Pro totals (10 years)	143	127	32	414	12.9	4

DAVIS, JOHN   TE

PERSONAL: Born May 14, 1973, in Jasper, Texas. ... 6-4/262.
HIGH SCHOOL: Jasper (Texas).
JUNIOR COLLEGE: Cisco (Texas) Junior College.

COLLEGE: Emporia (Kan.) State.
TRANSACTIONS/CAREER NOTES: Selected by Dallas Cowboys in fifth round of 1994 supplemental draft. ... Signed by Cowboys for 1994 season. ... Released by Cowboys (August 28, 1994). ... Re-signed by Cowboys to practice squad (August 30, 1994). ... On injured reserve with ankle injury (prior to 1995 season-October 31, 1995). ... Released by Cowboys (October 31, 1995). ... Signed by New Orleans Saints (June 3, 1996). ... Released by Saints (August 12, 1996). ... Signed by Tampa Bay Buccaneers (January 20, 1997). ... Granted free agency (February 12, 1999). ... Re-signed by Buccaneers (April 18, 1999). ... Granted unconditional free agency (February 11, 2000).
CHAMPIONSHIP GAME EXPERIENCE: Played in NFC championship game (1999 season).
SINGLE GAME HIGHS (regular season): Receptions—1 (November 21, 1999, vs. Atlanta); yards—16 (December 21, 1997, vs. Chicago); and touchdown receptions—1 (November 7, 1999, vs. New Orleans).

			RECEIVING				TOTALS			
Year Team	G	GS	No.	Yds.	Avg.	TD	TD	2pt.	Pts.	Fum.
1997—Tampa Bay NFL	8	2	3	35	11.7	0	0	0	0	0
1998—Tampa Bay NFL	16	0	2	12	6.0	1	1	0	6	0
1999—Tampa Bay NFL	16	0	2	7	3.5	1	1	0	6	0
Pro totals (3 years)	40	2	7	54	7.7	2	2	0	12	0

DAVIS, NATHAN　　　　　DT　　　　　BRONCOS

PERSONAL: Born February 6, 1974, in Hartford, Conn. ... 6-5/312. ... Full name: Nathan Michael Davis. ... Cousin of Barry Larkin, shortstop, Cincinnati Reds.
HIGH SCHOOL: Richmond (Ind.).
COLLEGE: Indiana.
TRANSACTIONS/CAREER NOTES: Selected by Atlanta Falcons in second round (32nd pick overall) of 1997 NFL draft. ... Signed by Falcons (July 14, 1997). ... Released by Falcons (July 28, 1998). ... Signed by Dallas Cowboys (October 5, 1998). ... Inactive for 11 games (1998). ... Released by Cowboys (November 9, 1999). ... Signed by Denver Broncos (February 22, 2000).
PLAYING EXPERIENCE: Atlanta NFL, 1997; Dallas NFL, 1999. ... Games/games started: 1997 (2/0), 1999 (4/0). Total: 6/0.

DAVIS, PERNELL　　　　　DT　　　　　EAGLES

PERSONAL: Born May 19, 1976, in Birmingham, Ala. ... 6-2/320.
HIGH SCHOOL: West End (Birmingham, Ala.).
COLLEGE: Alabama-Birmingham.
TRANSACTIONS/CAREER NOTES: Selected by Philadelphia Eagles in seventh round (251st pick overall) of 1999 NFL draft. ... Signed by Eagles (July 22, 1999). ... Assigned by Eagles to Frankfurt Galaxy in 2000 NFL Europe enhancement allocation program (February 18, 2000).
PLAYING EXPERIENCE: Philadelphia NFL, 1999. ... Games/Games started: 1999 (2/0).

DAVIS, REGGIE　　　　　TE　　　　　CHARGERS

PERSONAL: Born September 3, 1976, in Long Beach, Calif. ... 6-3/233. ... Full name: Reginald DeSean Davis.
HIGH SCHOOL: Brethren Christian (Huntington Beach, Calif.).
COLLEGE: Washington.
TRANSACTIONS/CAREER NOTES: Signed as non-drafted free agent by San Diego Chargers (May 12, 1999).
PRO STATISTICS: 1999—Recovered one fumble.
SINGLE GAME HIGHS (regular season): Receptions—6 (November 21, 1999, vs. Chicago); yards—46 (September 26, 1999, vs. Indianapolis); and touchdown receptions—1 (November 21, 1999, vs. Chicago).

			RECEIVING				TOTALS			
Year Team	G	GS	No.	Yds.	Avg.	TD	TD	2pt.	Pts.	Fum.
1999—San Diego NFL	16	3	12	137	11.4	1	1	0	6	0

DAVIS, ROB　　　　　C　　　　　PACKERS

PERSONAL: Born December 10, 1968, in Washington, D.C. ... 6-3/285. ... Full name: Robert Emmett Davis.
HIGH SCHOOL: Eleanor Roosevelt (Greenbelt, Md.).
COLLEGE: Shippensburg, Pa. (degree in criminal justice/law enforcement).
TRANSACTIONS/CAREER NOTES: Signed as non-drafted free agent by New York Jets (April 27, 1993). ... Released by Jets (August 24, 1993). ... Re-signed by Jets (April 29, 1994). ... Released by Jets (August 22, 1994). ... Signed by Baltimore Stallions of CFL (April 1995). ... Signed by Kansas City Chiefs (April 22, 1996). ... Released by Chiefs (August 20, 1996). ... Signed by Chicago Bears (August 28, 1996). ... Released by Bears (August 27, 1997). ... Signed by Green Bay Packers (November 4, 1997). ... On physically unable to perform list with back injury (July 18-August 10, 1999).
PLAYING EXPERIENCE: Baltimore CFL, 1995; Chicago NFL, 1996; Green Bay NFL, 1997-1999. ... Games/Games started: 1995 (18/games started unavailable), 1996 (16/0), 1997 (7/0), 1998 (16/0), 1999 (16/0). Total CFL: 18/-. Total NFL: 55/0. Total Pro: 73/-.
CHAMPIONSHIP GAME EXPERIENCE: Played in NFC championship game (1997 season). ... Played in Super Bowl XXXII (1997 season).

DAVIS, RUSSELL　　　　　DE　　　　　BEARS

PERSONAL: Born March 28, 1975, in Fayetteville, N.C. ... 6-4/295. ... Full name: Russell Morgan Davis.
HIGH SCHOOL: E.E. Smith (Fayetteville, N.C.).
COLLEGE: North Carolina.
TRANSACTIONS/CAREER NOTES: Selected by Chicago Bears in second round (48th pick overall) of 1999 NFL draft. ... Signed by Bears (July 22, 1999).

D

Year Team	G	GS	SACKS
1999—Chicago NFL	11	8	2.0

DAVIS, STEPHEN   RB   REDSKINS

PERSONAL: Born March 1, 1974, in Spartanburg, S.C. ... 6-0/234.
HIGH SCHOOL: Spartanburg (S.C.).
COLLEGE: Auburn (degree in vocational education, 1995).
TRANSACTIONS/CAREER NOTES: Selected by Washington Redskins in fourth round (102nd pick overall) of 1996 NFL draft. ... Signed by Redskins (July 16, 1996). ... Granted free agency (February 12, 1999). ... Re-signed by Redskins (May 12, 1999). ... Designated by Redskins as franchise player (February 11, 2000).
HONORS: Played in Pro Bowl (1999 season).
PRO STATISTICS: 1997—Returned three kickoffs for 62 yards and recovered one fumble. 1999—Recovered two fumbles.
SINGLE GAME HIGHS (regular season): Attempts—37 (December 12, 1999, vs. Arizona); yards—189 (December 12, 1999, vs. Arizona); and rushing touchdowns—3 (September 26, 1999, vs. New York Jets).
STATISTICAL PLATEAUS: 100-yard rushing games: 1999 (6). ... 100-yard receiving games: 1998 (1).

			RUSHING				RECEIVING				TOTALS			
Year Team	G	GS	Att.	Yds.	Avg.	TD	No.	Yds.	Avg.	TD	TD	2pt.	Pts.	Fum.
1996—Washington NFL	12	0	23	139	6.0	2	0	0	0.0	0	2	0	12	0
1997—Washington NFL	14	6	141	567	4.0	3	18	134	7.4	0	3	0	18	1
1998—Washington NFL	16	12	34	109	3.2	0	21	263	12.5	2	2	0	12	0
1999—Washington NFL	14	14	290	‡1405	4.8	*17	23	111	4.8	0	†17	†1	104	4
Pro totals (4 years)	56	32	488	2220	4.5	22	62	508	8.2	2	24	1	146	5

DAVIS, TERRELL   RB   BRONCOS

D

PERSONAL: Born October 28, 1972, in San Diego. ... 5-11/210.
HIGH SCHOOL: Abraham Lincoln Prep (San Diego).
COLLEGE: Long Beach State, then Georgia.
TRANSACTIONS/CAREER NOTES: Selected by Denver Broncos in sixth round (196th pick overall) of 1995 NFL draft. ... Signed by Broncos (June 30, 1995). ... On injured reserve with knee injury (October 6, 1999-remainder of season).
CHAMPIONSHIP GAME EXPERIENCE: Played in AFC championship game (1997 and 1998 seasons). ... Member of Super Bowl championship team (1997 and 1998 seasons).
HONORS: Named running back on THE SPORTING NEWS NFL All-Pro team (1996-1998). ... Played in Pro Bowl (1996 and 1997 seasons). ... Named Most Valuable Player of Super Bowl XXXII (1997 season). ... Named to play in Pro Bowl (1998 season); replaced by Curtis Martin due to injury. ... Named NFL Player of the Year by THE SPORTING NEWS (1998).
POST SEASON RECORDS: Holds Super Bowl single-game record for most rushing touchdowns—3 (January 25, 1998, vs. Green Bay). ... Shares Super Bowl single-game records for most points—18; and most touchdowns—3 (January 25, 1998, vs. Green Bay). ... Holds NFL postseason career record for highest average gain—5.41. ... Holds NFL postseason record for most consecutive games with 100 or more yards rushing—7 (1997-present). ... Shares NFL postseason career record for most games with 100 or more yards rushing—7.
PRO STATISTICS: 1995—Recovered one fumble. 1996—Recovered two fumbles. 1997—Recovered two fumbles for minus seven yards. 1998—Recovered one fumble. 1999—Recovered one fumble.
SINGLE GAME HIGHS (regular season): Attempts—42 (October 26, 1997, vs. Buffalo); yards—215 (September 21, 1997, vs. Cincinnati); and rushing touchdowns—3 (December 6, 1998, vs. Kansas City).
STATISTICAL PLATEAUS: 100-yard rushing games: 1995 (3), 1996 (6), 1997 (10), 1998 (11). Total: 30.
MISCELLANEOUS: Holds Denver Broncos all-time records for most yards rushing (6,624), most touchdowns (63) and most rushing touchdowns (58).

			RUSHING				RECEIVING				TOTALS			
Year Team	G	GS	Att.	Yds.	Avg.	TD	No.	Yds.	Avg.	TD	TD	2pt.	Pts.	Fum.
1995—Denver NFL	14	14	237	1117	§4.7	7	49	367	7.5	1	8	0	48	5
1996—Denver NFL	16	16	§345	§1538	4.5	13	36	310	8.6	2	15	0	90	5
1997—Denver NFL	15	15	369	§1750	4.7	†15	42	287	6.8	0	15	3	†96	4
1998—Denver NFL	16	16	§392	*2008	*5.1	*21	25	217	8.7	2	*23	0	138	2
1999—Denver NFL	4	4	67	211	3.1	2	3	26	8.7	0	2	0	12	1
Pro totals (5 years)	65	65	1410	6624	4.7	58	155	1207	7.8	5	63	3	384	17

DAVIS, TRAVIS   S

PERSONAL: Born January 10, 1973, in Harbor City, Calif. ... 6-0/209. ... Full name: Travis Horace Davis.
HIGH SCHOOL: Banning (Wilmington, Calif.).
COLLEGE: Notre Dame (degree in psychology, 1997).
TRANSACTIONS/CAREER NOTES: Selected by New Orleans Saints in seventh round (242nd pick overall) of 1995 NFL draft. ... Signed by Saints (July 14, 1995). ... Released by Saints (September 5, 1995). ... Re-signed by Saints to practice squad (September 6, 1995). ... Signed by Jacksonville Jaguars off Saints practice squad (October 17, 1995). ... Granted free agency (February 13, 1998). ... Re-signed by Jaguars (June 12, 1998). ... Granted unconditional free agency (February 12, 1999). ... Signed by Pittsburgh Steelers (April 5, 1999). ... Released by Steelers (May 30, 2000).
CHAMPIONSHIP GAME EXPERIENCE: Played in AFC championship game (1996 season).
PRO STATISTICS: 1995—Recovered one fumble. 1996—Recovered two fumbles. 1997—Credited with two sacks, returned one kickoff for nine yards and recovered three fumbles for 10 yards. 1998—Credited with 1/2 sack and recovered one fumble. 1999—Recovered one fumble for 102 yards and a touchdown.

			INTERCEPTIONS			
Year Team	G	GS	No.	Yds.	Avg.	TD
1995—Jacksonville NFL	9	5	0	0	0.0	0
1996—Jacksonville NFL	16	7	2	0	0.0	0
1997—Jacksonville NFL	16	16	1	23	23.0	0
1998—Jacksonville NFL	16	5	2	34	17.0	0

1999—Pittsburgh NFL	16	16	1	1	1.0	0
Pro totals (5 years)	73	49	6	58	9.7	0

DAVIS, TROY   RB

PERSONAL: Born September 14, 1975, in Miami. ... 5-7/191.
HIGH SCHOOL: Miami Southridge.
COLLEGE: Iowa State.
TRANSACTIONS/CAREER NOTES: Selected after junior season by New Orleans Saints in third round (62nd pick overall) of 1997 NFL draft. ... Signed by Saints (June 13, 1997). ... Released by Saints (February 10, 2000).
HONORS: Named running back on THE SPORTING NEWS college All-America first team (1995 and 1996).
SINGLE GAME HIGHS (regular season): Attempts—18 (October 25, 1998, vs. Tampa Bay); yards—48 (October 25, 1998, vs. Tampa Bay); and rushing touchdowns—1 (December 27, 1998, vs. Buffalo).

			RUSHING				RECEIVING				KICKOFF RETURNS				TOTALS		
Year Team	G	GS	Att.	Yds.	Avg.	TD	No.	Yds.	Avg.	TD	No.	Yds.	Avg.	TD	TD 2pt.	Pts.	Fum.
1997—New Orleans NFL	16	7	75	271	3.6	0	13	85	6.5	0	9	173	19.2	0	0 0	0	3
1998—New Orleans NFL	14	2	55	143	2.6	1	16	99	6.2	0	2	21	10.5	0	1 0	6	1
1999—New Orleans NFL	16	2	20	32	1.6	0	7	53	7.6	0	20	424	21.2	0	0 0	0	1
Pro totals (3 years)	46	11	150	446	3.0	1	36	237	6.6	0	31	618	19.9	0	1 0	6	5

DAVIS, TYRONE   TE   PACKERS

PERSONAL: Born June 30, 1972, in Halifax, Va. ... 6-4/255.
HIGH SCHOOL: Halifax County (South Boston, Va.), then Fork Union (Va.) Military Academy.
COLLEGE: Virginia.
TRANSACTIONS/CAREER NOTES: Selected by New York Jets in fourth round (107th pick overall) of 1995 NFL draft. ... Signed by Jets (June 14, 1995). ... Released by Jets (September 13, 1995). ... Re-signed by Jets to practice squad (September 15, 1995). ... Activated (December 11, 1995). ... Granted free agency (February 14, 1997). ... Re-signed by Jets for 1997 season. ... Traded by Jets to Green Bay Packers for past considerations (August 25, 1997). ... Released by Packers (September 24, 1997). ... Re-signed by Packers (September 29, 1997).
CHAMPIONSHIP GAME EXPERIENCE: Played in NFC championship game (1997 season). ... Played in Super Bowl XXXII (1997 season).
PRO STATISTICS: 1997—Recovered one fumble in end zone for a touchdown.
SINGLE GAME HIGHS (regular season): Receptions—3 (November 29, 1999, vs. San Francisco); yards—83 (November 15, 1998, vs. New York Giants); and touchdown receptions—2 (November 22, 1998, vs. Minnesota).

			RECEIVING				TOTALS		
Year Team	G	GS	No.	Yds.	Avg.	TD	TD	2pt.	Pts.	Fum.
1995—New York Jets NFL	4	0	1	9	9.0	0	0	0	0	0
1996—New York Jets NFL	2	0	1	6	6.0	0	0	0	0	0
1997—Green Bay NFL	13	0	2	28	14.0	1	2	0	12	0
1998—Green Bay NFL	13	1	18	250	13.9	7	7	0	42	1
1999—Green Bay NFL	16	13	20	204	10.2	2	2	0	12	0
Pro totals (5 years)	48	14	42	497	11.8	10	11	0	66	1

DAVIS, WENDELL   CB

PERSONAL: Born June 27, 1973, in Wichita, Kan. ... 5-10/201.
HIGH SCHOOL: North (Wichita, Kan.).
JUNIOR COLLEGE: Coffeyville (Kan.) Community College.
COLLEGE: Oklahoma.
TRANSACTIONS/CAREER NOTES: Selected by Dallas Cowboys in sixth round (207th pick overall) of 1996 NFL draft. ... Signed by Cowboys (July 15, 1996). ... Released by Cowboys (August 27, 1996). ... Re-signed by Cowboys to practice squad (August 28, 1996). ... Activated (September 6, 1996). ... On injured reserve with knee injury (July 19, 1998-entire season). ... Released by Cowboys (February 12, 1999). ... Signed by Washington Redskins (August 9, 1999). ... Released by Redskins (September 4, 1999). ... Signed by Cowboys (November 16, 1999). ... Granted unconditional free agency (February 11, 2000).
PLAYING EXPERIENCE: Dallas NFL, 1996, 1997 and 1999. ... Games/Games started: 1996 (13/0), 1997 (15/0), 1999 (6/0). Total: 34/0.
PRO STATISTICS: 1997—Recovered two fumbles.

DAVIS, ZOLA   WR   BROWNS

PERSONAL: Born January 16, 1975, in Charleston, S.C. ... 6-0/185. ... Full name: Zola Nakia Davis.
HIGH SCHOOL: Burke (Charleston, S.C.).
COLLEGE: South Carolina.
TRANSACTIONS/CAREER NOTES: Signed as non-drafted free agent by Green Bay Packers (April 23, 1999). ... Claimed on waivers by Cleveland Browns (August 31, 1999). ... Released by Browns (September 5, 1999). ... Re-signed by Browns to practice squad (September 6, 1999). ... Activated (November 16, 1999).
PLAYING EXPERIENCE: Cleveland NFL, 1999. ... Games/Games started: 1999 (6/1).
PRO STATISTICS: 1999—Caught two passes for 38 yards.
SINGLE GAME HIGHS (regular season): Receptions—1 (December 26, 1999, vs. Indianapolis); yards—25 (December 19, 1999, vs. Jacksonville); and touchdown receptions—0.

DAWKINS, BRIAN   S   EAGLES

PERSONAL: Born October 13, 1973, in Jacksonville. ... 5-11/200.
HIGH SCHOOL: Raines (Jacksonville).

D

COLLEGE: Clemson (degree in education, 1995).
TRANSACTIONS/CAREER NOTES: Selected by Philadelphia Eagles in second round (61st pick overall) of 1996 NFL draft. ... Signed by Eagles (July 17, 1996).
HONORS: Named defensive back on THE SPORTING NEWS college All-America second team (1995). ... Played in Pro Bowl (1999 season).
PRO STATISTICS: 1996—Recovered two fumbles for 23 yards. 1998—Recovered one fumble. 1999—Recovered two fumbles.

| | | | INTERCEPTIONS | | | | SACKS |
Year Team	G	GS	No.	Yds.	Avg.	TD	No.
1996—Philadelphia NFL	14	13	3	41	13.7	0	1.0
1997—Philadelphia NFL	15	15	3	76	25.3	1	0.0
1998—Philadelphia NFL	14	14	2	39	19.5	0	1.0
1999—Philadelphia NFL	16	16	4	127	31.8	1	1.5
Pro totals (4 years)	59	58	12	283	23.6	2	3.5

DAWKINS, SEAN · WR

PERSONAL: Born February 3, 1971, in Red Bank, N.J. ... 6-4/218. ... Full name: Sean Russell Dawkins.
HIGH SCHOOL: Homestead (Cupertino, Calif.).
COLLEGE: California.
TRANSACTIONS/CAREER NOTES: Selected after junior season by Indianapolis Colts in first round (16th pick overall) of 1993 NFL draft. ... Signed by Colts (August 4, 1993). ... Granted unconditional free agency (February 13, 1998). ... Signed by New Orleans Saints (May 1, 1998). ... Granted unconditional free agency (February 12, 1999). ... Signed by Seattle Seahawks (April 15, 1999). ... Released by Seahawks (June 8, 2000).
CHAMPIONSHIP GAME EXPERIENCE: Played in AFC championship game (1995 season).
HONORS: Named wide receiver on THE SPORTING NEWS college All-America first team (1992).
SINGLE GAME HIGHS (regular season): Receptions—8 (November 22, 1998, vs. San Francisco); yards—148 (November 22, 1998, vs. San Francisco); and touchdown receptions—2 (September 12, 1999, vs. Detroit).
STATISTICAL PLATEAUS: 100-yard receiving games: 1993 (1), 1994 (1), 1995 (2), 1997 (1), 1998 (3), 1999 (2). Total: 10.

D

| | | | RECEIVING | | | | TOTALS | | | |
Year Team	G	GS	No.	Yds.	Avg.	TD	TD	2pt.	Pts.	Fum.
1993—Indianapolis NFL	16	7	26	430	16.5	1	1	0	6	0
1994—Indianapolis NFL	16	16	51	742	14.5	5	5	0	30	1
1995—Indianapolis NFL	16	13	52	784	15.1	3	3	0	18	1
1996—Indianapolis NFL	15	14	54	751	13.9	1	1	0	6	1
1997—Indianapolis NFL	14	12	68	804	11.8	2	2	0	12	0
1998—New Orleans NFL	15	15	53	823	15.5	1	1	0	6	2
1999—Seattle NFL	16	13	58	992	17.1	7	7	0	42	1
Pro totals (7 years)	108	90	362	5326	14.7	20	20	0	120	6

DAWSEY, LAWRENCE · WR

PERSONAL: Born November 16, 1967, in Dothan, Ala. ... 6-0/192. ... Full name: Lawrence L. Dawsey.
HIGH SCHOOL: Northview (Dothan, Ala.).
COLLEGE: Florida State.
TRANSACTIONS/CAREER NOTES: Selected by Tampa Bay Buccaneers in third round (66th pick overall) of 1991 NFL draft. ... Signed by Buccaneers (July 17, 1991). ... On injured reserve with knee injury (October 5, 1993-remainder of season). ... On physically unable to perform list with knee injury (August 28-October 21, 1994). ... Released by Buccaneers (May 13, 1996). ... Signed by New York Giants (June 12, 1996). ... Granted unconditional free agency (February 14, 1997). ... Signed by Miami Dolphins (March 24, 1997). ... Released by Dolphins (August 24, 1997). ... Signed by New Orleans Saints (May 4, 1999). ... Granted unconditional free agency (February 11, 2000).
HONORS: Named wide receiver on THE SPORTING NEWS college All-America second team (1990).
PRO STATISTICS: 1991—Rushed once for nine yards and a touchdown. 1992—Recovered one fumble. 1996—Recovered one fumble. 1999—Returned one kickoff for 20 yards.
SINGLE GAME HIGHS (regular season): Receptions—9 (September 26, 1993, vs. Chicago); yards—116 (December 18, 1994, vs. Washington); and touchdown receptions—1 (September 12, 1999, vs. San Francisco).
STATISTICAL PLATEAUS: 100-yard receiving games: 1991 (1), 1992 (1), 1993 (1), 1994 (1). Total: 4.

| | | | RECEIVING | | | | TOTALS | | | |
Year Team	G	GS	No.	Yds.	Avg.	TD	TD	2pt.	Pts.	Fum.
1991—Tampa Bay NFL	16	10	55	818	14.9	3	4	0	24	0
1992—Tampa Bay NFL	15	12	60	776	12.9	1	1	0	6	1
1993—Tampa Bay NFL	4	4	15	203	13.5	0	0	0	0	0
1994—Tampa Bay NFL	10	5	46	673	14.6	1	1	0	6	0
1995—Tampa Bay NFL	12	10	30	372	12.4	0	0	0	0	0
1996—New York Giants NFL	16	4	18	233	12.9	0	0	0	0	0
1997—						Did not play.				
1998—						Did not play.				
1999—New Orleans NFL	10	0	16	196	12.3	1	1	0	6	0
Pro totals (7 years)	83	45	240	3271	13.6	6	7	0	42	1

DAWSON, DERMONTTI · C · STEELERS

PERSONAL: Born June 17, 1965, in Lexington, Ky. ... 6-2/292. ... Full name: Dermontti Farra Dawson. ... Cousin of Marc Logan, running back with four NFL teams (1987-97); and cousin of George Adams, running back with New York Giants (1985-89) and New England Patriots (1990-91).
HIGH SCHOOL: Bryan Station (Lexington, Ky.).
COLLEGE: Kentucky (degree in kinesiology and health promotions, 1988).
TRANSACTIONS/CAREER NOTES: Selected by Pittsburgh Steelers in second round (44th pick overall) of 1988 NFL draft. ... Signed by Steelers (August 1, 1988). ... On injured reserve with knee injury (September 26-November 26, 1988). ... Designated by Steelers as transition player (February 25, 1993). ... On injured reserve with hamstring injury (December 14, 1999-remainder of season).

PLAYING EXPERIENCE: Pittsburgh NFL, 1988-1999. ... Games: 1988 (8/5), 1989 (16/16), 1990 (16/16), 1991 (16/16), 1992 (16/16), 1993 (16/16), 1994 (16/16), 1995 (16/16), 1996 (16/16), 1997 (16/16), 1998 (16/16), 1999 (7/7). Total: 175/172.
CHAMPIONSHIP GAME EXPERIENCE: Played in AFC championship game (1994, 1995 and 1997 seasons). ... Played in Super Bowl XXX (1995 season).
HONORS: Played in Pro Bowl (1992-1998 seasons). ... Named center on THE SPORTING NEWS NFL All-Pro team (1994-1998).
PRO STATISTICS: 1991—Fumbled twice and recovered one fumble for two yards. 1993—Fumbled once. 1998—Fumbled once for minus 25 yards.

DAWSON, PHIL　　　　　　K　　　　　　BROWNS

PERSONAL: Born January 23, 1975, in West Palm Beach, Fla. ... 5-11/190.
HIGH SCHOOL: Lake Highlands (Dallas).
COLLEGE: Texas.
TRANSACTIONS/CAREER NOTES: Signed as non-drafted free agent by Oakland Raiders (April 24, 1998). ... Claimed on waivers by New England Patriots (August 21, 1998). ... Released by Patriots (August 30, 1998). ... Re-signed by Patriots to practice squad (August 31, 1998). ... Granted free agency after 1998 season. ... Signed by Cleveland Browns (March 25, 1999).
PRO STATISTICS: 1999—Rushed once for four yards and a touchdown.

				KICKING				
Year　Team	G	XPM	XPA	FGM	FGA	Lg.	50+	Pts.
1999—Cleveland NFL	15	23	24	8	12	49	0-0	53

DEARTH, JAMES　　　　　　TE

PERSONAL: Born January 22, 1976, in Scurry, Texas. ... 6-3/269.
HIGH SCHOOL: Scurry (Texas)-Rosser.
COLLEGE: Tulsa, then Tarleton State (Texas).
TRANSACTIONS/CAREER NOTES: Selected by Cleveland Browns in sixth round (191st pick overall) of 1999 NFL draft. ... Signed by Browns (July 22, 1999). ... Released by Browns (September 3, 1999). ... Re-signed by Browns to practice squad (November 23, 1999). ... Activated (December 14, 1999). ... Assigned by Browns to Scottish Claymores in 2000 NFL Europe enhancement allocation program (February 18, 2000). ... Released by Browns (April 27, 2000).
PLAYING EXPERIENCE: Cleveland NFL, 1999. ... Games/Games started: 1999 (2/0).

D

DEESE, DERRICK　　　　　　OT　　　　　　49ERS

PERSONAL: Born May 17, 1970, in Culver City, Calif. ... 6-3/289.
HIGH SCHOOL: Culver City (Calif.).
JUNIOR COLLEGE: El Camino Junior College (Calif.).
COLLEGE: Southern California.
TRANSACTIONS/CAREER NOTES: Signed as non-drafted free agent by San Francisco 49ers (May 8, 1992). ... On injured reserve with elbow injury (August 4, 1992-entire season). ... Inactive for six games (1993). ... On injured reserve with broken wrist (October 23, 1993-remainder of season). ... Granted free agency (February 17, 1995). ... Tendered offer sheet by St. Louis Rams (April 20, 1995). ... Offer matched by 49ers (April 21, 1995). ... Granted unconditional free agency (February 16, 1996). ... Re-signed by 49ers (June 4, 1996). ... Granted unconditional free agency (February 14, 1997). ... Re-signed by 49ers (April 22, 1997).
PLAYING EXPERIENCE: San Francisco NFL, 1994-1999. ... Games/Games started: 1994 (16/15), 1995 (2/2), 1996 (16/0), 1997 (16/13), 1998 (16/16), 1999 (16/16). Total: 82/62.
CHAMPIONSHIP GAME EXPERIENCE: Played in NFC championship game (1994 and 1997 seasons). ... Member of Super Bowl championship team (1994 season).
PRO STATISTICS: 1996—Returned two kickoffs for 20 yards. 1997—Recovered one fumble. 1998—Recovered one fumble. 1999—Recovered four fumbles.

DEL GRECO, AL　　　　　　K　　　　　　TITANS

PERSONAL: Born March 2, 1962, in Providence, R.I. ... 5-10/202. ... Full name: Albert Louis Del Greco Jr.
HIGH SCHOOL: Coral Gables (Fla.).
COLLEGE: Auburn (degree in business transportation).
TRANSACTIONS/CAREER NOTES: Signed as non-drafted free agent by Miami Dolphins (May 17, 1984). ... Released by Dolphins (August 27, 1984). ... Signed by Green Bay Packers (October 17, 1984). ... Released by Packers (November 25, 1987). ... Signed by St. Louis Cardinals (December 8, 1987). ... Cardinals franchise moved to Phoenix (March 15, 1988). ... Granted unconditional free agency (February 1-April 1, 1991). ... Re-signed by Cardinals (July 1, 1991). ... Released by Cardinals (August 19, 1991). ... Signed by Houston Oilers (November 5, 1991). ... Granted unconditional free agency (February 1-April 1, 1992). ... Re-signed by Oilers for 1992 season. ... Granted unconditional free agency (February 17, 1995). ... Re-signed by Oilers (June 2, 1995). ... Oilers franchise moved to Tennessee for 1997 season. ... Oilers franchise renamed Tennessee Titans for 1999 season (December 26, 1998).
CHAMPIONSHIP GAME EXPERIENCE: Played in AFC championship game (1999 season). ... Played in Super Bowl XXXIV (1999 season).
PRO STATISTICS: 1988—Rushed once for eight yards. 1990—Recovered one fumble. 1995—Punted once for 15 yards. 1997—Punted once for 32 yards.

				KICKING				
Year　Team	G	XPM	XPA	FGM	FGA	Lg.	50+	Pts.
1984—Green Bay NFL	9	34	34	9	12	45	0-1	61
1985—Green Bay NFL	16	38	40	19	26	46	0-1	95
1986—Green Bay NFL	16	29	29	17	27	50	2-4	80
1987—Green Bay NFL	5	11	11	5	10	47	0-0	26
——St. Louis NFL	3	8	9	4	5	37	0-0	20
1988—Phoenix NFL	16	42	44	12	21	51	1-2	78
1989—Phoenix NFL	16	28	29	18	26	50	1-2	82

1990—Phoenix NFL	16	31	31	17	27	50	2-6	82
1991—Houston NFL	7	16	16	10	13	52	1-1	46
1992—Houston NFL	16	41	41	21	27	†54	1-1	104
1993—Houston NFL	16	39	40	29	34	52	4-7	126
1994—Houston NFL	16	18	18	16	20	50	1-3	66
1995—Houston NFL	16	33	33	27	31	53	3-5	114
1996—Houston NFL	16	35	35	32	38	*56	1-3	131
1997—Tennessee NFL	16	32	32	27	35	52	2-2	113
1998—Tennessee NFL	16	28	28	*36	39	48	0-0	136
1999—Tennessee NFL	16	43	43	21	25	50	1-1	106
Pro totals (16 years)	**232**	**506**	**513**	**320**	**416**	**56**	**20-39**	**1466**

DELHOMME, JAKE — QB — SAINTS

PERSONAL: Born January 10, 1975, in Lafayette, La. ... 6-2/205.
HIGH SCHOOL: Teurlings (La.).
COLLEGE: Southwestern Louisiana.
TRANSACTIONS/CAREER NOTES: Signed as non-drafted free agent by New Orleans Saints (June 10, 1997). ... Released by Saints (August 18, 1997). ... Re-signed by Saints to practice saqud (November 19, 1997). ... Assigned by Saints to Amsterdam Admirals in 1998 NFL Europe enhancement allocation program (February 18, 1998). ... Inactive for five games (1998). ... Released by Saints (October 14, 1998). ... Re-signed by Saints to practice squad (October 15, 1998). ... Assigned by Saints to Frankfurt Galaxy in 1999 NFL Europe enhancement allocation program (February 22, 1999). ... Released by Saints (September 5, 1999). ... Re-signed by Saints (November 23, 1999).
PRO STATISTICS: 1999—Fumbled once.
SINGLE GAME HIGHS (regular season): Attempts—49 (January 2, 2000, vs. Carolina); completions—26 (January 2, 2000, vs. Carolina); passing yards—278 (December 24, 1999, vs. Dallas); and touchdown passes—2 (December 24, 1999, vs. Dallas).
MISCELLANEOUS: Regular-season record as starting NFL quarterback: 1-1 (.500).

				PASSING						RUSHING				TOTALS		
Year Team	G	GS	Att.	Cmp.	Pct.	Yds.	TD	Int.	Avg.	Rat.	Att.	Yds.	Avg.	TD	TD	2pt.	Pts.
1998—Amsterdam NFLE	...	...	47	15	31.9	247	0	4	5.26	15.1	2	20	10.0	0	0	0	0
1999—Frankfurt NFLE	...	...	202	136	67.3	1410	12	5	6.98	96.8	21	126	6.0	0	0	0	0
—New Orleans NFL	2	2	76	42	55.3	521	3	5	6.86	62.4	11	72	6.5	2	2	0	12
NFL Europe totals (2 years)	...	...	249	151	60.6	1657	12	9	6.65	81.4	23	146	6.3	0	0	0	0
NFL totals (1 year)	2	2	76	42	55.3	521	3	5	6.86	62.4	11	72	6.5	2	2	0	12
Pro totals (3 years)	...	...	325	193	59.4	2178	15	14	6.70	76.9	34	218	6.4	2	2	0	12

DELLENBACH, JEFF — C/G

PERSONAL: Born February 14, 1963, in Wausau, Wis. ... 6-6/300. ... Full name: Jeffrey Alan Dellenbach. ... Name pronounced del-en-BOK.
HIGH SCHOOL: East (Wausau, Wis.).
COLLEGE: Wisconsin.
TRANSACTIONS/CAREER NOTES: Selected by Jacksonville Bulls in 1985 USFL territorial draft. ... Selected by Miami Dolphins in fourth round (111th pick overall) of 1985 NFL draft. ... Signed by Dolphins (July 15, 1985). ... Granted free agency (February 1, 1990). ... Re-signed by Dolphins (August 30, 1990). ... Granted roster exemption (August 30-September 8, 1990). ... Granted free agency (February 1, 1992). ... Re-signed by Dolphins (May 4, 1992). ... Granted unconditional free agency (February 17, 1995). ... Signed by New England Patriots (March 6, 1995). ... Released by Patriots (September 10, 1996). ... Signed by Green Bay Packers (December 3, 1996). ... Granted unconditional free agency (February 14, 1997). ... Re-signed by Packers (July 25, 1997). ... Granted unconditional free agency (February 13, 1998). ... Re-signed by Packers (July 18, 1998). ... Granted unconditional free agency (February 12, 1999). ... Signed by Philadelphia Eagles (September 8, 1999). ... Granted unconditional free agency (February 11, 2000).
PLAYING EXPERIENCE: Miami NFL, 1985-1994; New England NFL, 1995; New England (2)-Green Bay (3) NFL, 1996; Green Bay NFL, 1997 and 1998; Philadelphia NFL, 1999. ... Games/Games started: 1985 (11/1), 1986 (13/6), 1987 (11/6), 1988 (16/16), 1989 (16/16), 1990 (15/0), 1991 (15/2), 1992 (16/8), 1993 (16/16), 1994 (16/16), 1995 (15/5), 1996 (N.E.-2/0; G.B.-3/0; Total: 5/0), 1997 (13/5), 1998 (16/3), 1999 (16/15). Total: 210/115.
CHAMPIONSHIP GAME EXPERIENCE: Played in AFC championship game (1985 and 1992 seasons). ... Played in NFC championship game (1996 season). ... Member of Super Bowl championship team (1996 season). ... Member of Packers for NFC championship game (1997 season); did not play. ... Member of Packers for Super Bowl XXXII (1997 season); did not play.
PRO STATISTICS: 1987—Fumbled once for minus 13 yards. 1988—Fumbled once for minus nine yards. 1991—Returned one kickoff for no yards. 1992—Recovered one fumble. 1993—Fumbled once and recovered one fumble for minus six yards. 1994—Fumbled once. 1998—Recovered two fumbles.

DeLONG, GREG — TE — RAVENS

PERSONAL: Born April 3, 1973, in Orefield, Pa. ... 6-4/255. ... Full name: Gregory A. DeLong.
HIGH SCHOOL: Parkland Senior (Orefield, Pa.).
COLLEGE: North Carolina.
TRANSACTIONS/CAREER NOTES: Signed as non-drafted free agent by Cleveland Browns (May 2, 1995). ... Released by Browns (August 21, 1995). ... Signed by Minnesota Vikings to practice squad (August 28, 1995). ... Activated (November 15, 1995). ... Granted free agency (February 13, 1998). ... Re-signed by Vikings (April 23, 1998). ... Granted unconditional free agency (February 12, 1999). ... Signed by Baltimore Ravens (February 26, 1999).
CHAMPIONSHIP GAME EXPERIENCE: Played in NFC championship game (1998 season).
PRO STATISTICS: 1996—Returned one kickoff for three yards and recovered one fumble. 1999—Returned one kickoff for 11 yards.
SINGLE GAME HIGHS (regular season): Receptions—4 (November 21, 1999, vs. Cincinnati); yards—28 (September 20, 1998, vs. Detroit); and touchdown receptions—1 (November 21, 1999, vs. Cincinnati).

			RECEIVING				TOTALS			
Year Team	G	GS	No.	Yds.	Avg.	TD	TD	2pt.	Pts.	Fum.
1995—Minnesota NFL	2	2	6	38	6.3	0	0	0	0	0
1996—Minnesota NFL	16	8	8	34	4.3	0	0	0	0	0

1997—Minnesota NFL	16	3	8	75	9.4	0	0	0	0	1
1998—Minnesota NFL	15	5	8	58	7.3	0	0	0	0	0
1999—Baltimore NFL	16	7	13	52	4.0	1	1	0	6	0
Pro totals (5 years)	65	25	43	257	6.0	1	1	0	6	1

DeMARCO, BRIAN   G   BENGALS

PERSONAL: Born April 9, 1972, in Berea, Ohio. ... 6-7/323. ... Full name: Brian Thomas DeMarco.
HIGH SCHOOL: Admiral King (Lorain, Ohio).
COLLEGE: Michigan State.
TRANSACTIONS/CAREER NOTES: Selected by Jacksonville Jaguars in second round (40th pick overall) of 1995 NFL draft. ... Signed by Jaguars (June 1, 1995). ... Granted unconditional free agency (February 12, 1999). ... Signed by Cincinnati Bengals (April 2, 1999). ... On injured reserve with elbow injury (December 16, 1999-remainder of season).
PLAYING EXPERIENCE: Jacksonville NFL, 1995-1998; Cincinnati NFL, 1999. ... Games/Games started: 1995 (16/16), 1996 (10/9), 1997 (14/5), 1998 (16/9), 1999 (7/7). Total: 63/46.
CHAMPIONSHIP GAME EXPERIENCE: Played in AFC championship game (1996 season).

DENSON, AUTRY   RB   DOLPHINS

PERSONAL: Born December 8, 1976, in Davie, Fla. ... 5-10/193. ... Full name: Autry Lamont Denson.
HIGH SCHOOL: Nova (Fort Lauderdale, Fla.).
COLLEGE: Notre Dame.
TRANSACTIONS/CAREER NOTES: Selected by Tampa Bay Buccaneers in seventh round (233rd pick overall) of 1999 NFL draft. ... Signed by Buccaneers (July 29, 1999). ... Released by Buccaneers (September 5, 1999). ... Re-signed by Buccaneers to practice squad (September 6, 1999). ... Signed by Miami Dolphins off Buccaneers practice squad (October 20, 1999).
SINGLE GAME HIGHS (regular season): Attempts—21 (January 2, 2000, vs. Washington); yards—80 (January 2, 2000, vs. Washington); and rushing touchdowns—0.

			RUSHING				RECEIVING				TOTALS			
Year Team	G	GS	Att.	Yds.	Avg.	TD	No.	Yds.	Avg.	TD	TD	2pt.	Pts.	Fum.
1999—Miami NFL	6	1	28	98	3.5	0	4	28	7.0	0	0	0	0	0

DENSON, DAMON   G   RAVENS

PERSONAL: Born February 8, 1975, in Pittsburgh. ... 6-4/310. ... Full name: Damon Michael Denson.
HIGH SCHOOL: Baldwin (Pittsburgh).
COLLEGE: Michigan.
TRANSACTIONS/CAREER NOTES: Selected by New England Patriots in fourth round (97th pick overall) of 1997 NFL draft. ... Signed by Patriots (July 16, 1997). ... Released by Patriots (September 5, 1999). ... Re-signed by Patriots (September 15, 1999). ... Released by Patriots (September 29, 1999). ... Signed by Baltimore Ravens (February 11, 2000).
PLAYING EXPERIENCE: New England NFL, 1997-1999. ... Games/Games started: 1997 (2/0), 1998 (11/4), 1999 (2/0). Total: 15/4.

DENTON, TIM   DB   REDSKINS

PERSONAL: Born February 2, 1973, in Galveston, Texas ... 5-11/182.
HIGH SCHOOL: Ball (Galveston, Texas).
JUNIOR COLLEGE: Blinn College (Texas).
COLLEGE: Oklahoma, then Sam Houston State.
TRANSACTIONS/CAREER NOTES: Signed as non-drafted free agent by Atlanta Falcons (April 22, 1996). ... Released by Falcons (August 31, 1996). ... Re-signed by Falcons (February 10, 1997). ... Released by Falcons (August 18, 1997). ... Re-signed by Falcons to practice squad (August 26, 1997). ... Granted free agency after 1997 season. ... Signed by Washington Redskins (February 18, 1998). ... Assigned by Redskins to Rhein Fire in 1998 NFL Europe enhancement allocation program (February 18, 1998).
PLAYING EXPERIENCE: Rhein Fire NFLE, 1998; Washington NFL, 1998 and 1999. ... Games/Games started: NFLE 1998 (games played unavailable), NFL 1998 (16/0), 1999 (16/0). Total NFL: 32/0.
PRO STATISTICS: NFLE: 1998—Intercepted two passes for no yards.

DERCHER, DAN   OT   49ERS

PERSONAL: Born June 26, 1976, in Kansas City, Kan. ... 6-5/293. ... Full name: Daniel Lawrence Dercher.
HIGH SCHOOL: Bishop Miege (Mission, Kan.).
COLLEGE: Kansas.
TRANSACTIONS/CAREER NOTES: Signed as non-drafted free agent by San Francisco 49ers (April 23, 1999).
PLAYING EXPERIENCE: San Francisco NFL, 1999. ... Games/Games started: 1999 (9/0).

DETMER, KOY   QB   EAGLES

PERSONAL: Born July 5, 1973, in San Antonio. ... 6-1/195. ... Brother of Ty Detmer, quarterback, Cleveland Browns.
HIGH SCHOOL: Mission (Texas).
COLLEGE: Colorado (degree in communications, 1996).
TRANSACTIONS/CAREER NOTES: Selected by Philadelphia Eagles in seventh round (207th pick overall) of 1997 NFL draft. ... Signed by Eagles (June 4, 1997). ... On injured reserve with knee injury (August 22, 1997-entire season). ... Granted free agency (February 11, 2000). ... Re-signed by Eagles (April 17, 2000).

PRO STATISTICS: 1998—Fumbled once.
SINGLE GAME HIGHS (regular season): Attempts—43 (December 20, 1998, vs. Dallas); completions—24 (December 20, 1998, vs. Dallas); yards—231 (December 20, 1998, vs. Dallas); and touchdown passes—3 (December 19, 1999, vs. New England).
MISCELLANEOUS: Regular-season record as starting NFL quarterback: 2-4 (.333).

			PASSING								RUSHING				TOTALS		
Year Team	G	GS	Att.	Cmp.	Pct.	Yds.	TD	Int.	Avg.	Rat.	Att.	Yds.	Avg.	TD	TD	2pt.	Pts.
1997—Philadelphia NFL							Did not play.										
1998—Philadelphia NFL	8	5	181	97	53.6	1011	5	5	5.59	67.7	7	20	2.9	0	0	0	0
1999—Philadelphia NFL	1	1	29	10	34.5	181	3	2	6.24	62.6	2	-2	-1.0	0	0	0	0
Pro totals (2 years)	9	6	210	107	51.0	1192	8	7	5.68	67.0	9	18	2.0	0	0	0	0

DETMER, TY   QB   BROWNS

PERSONAL: Born October 30, 1967, in San Marcos, Texas. ... 6-0/194. ... Full name: Ty Hubert Detmer. ... Brother of Koy Detmer, quarterback, Philadelphia Eagles.
HIGH SCHOOL: Southwest (San Antonio).
COLLEGE: Brigham Young (degree in recreation administration, 1991).
TRANSACTIONS/CAREER NOTES: Selected by Green Bay Packers in ninth round (230th pick overall) of 1992 NFL draft. ... Signed by Packers (July 22, 1992). ... Active for two games (1992); did not play. ... Active for five games (1994); did not play. ... On injured reserve with thumb injury (November 8, 1995-remainder of season). ... Granted unconditional free agency (February 16, 1996). ... Signed by Philadelphia Eagles (March 1, 1996). ... Granted unconditional free agency (February 13, 1998). ... Signed by San Francisco 49ers (March 12, 1998). ... Traded by 49ers with fourth-round pick (LB Wali Rainer) in 1999 draft to Cleveland Browns for fourth- (traded to Indianapolis) and fifth-round (traded to Miami) picks in 1999 draft (February 23, 1999).
HONORS: Heisman Trophy winner (1990). ... Maxwell Award winner (1990). ... Davey O'Brien Award winner (1990 and 1991). ... Named quarterback on THE SPORTING NEWS college All-America first team (1990 and 1991).
PRO STATISTICS: 1995—Fumbled once and recovered one fumble. 1996—Fumbled seven times and recovered one fumble. 1997—Fumbled six times and recovered one fumble for minus two yards. 1998—Fumbled once.
SINGLE GAME HIGHS (regular season): Attempts—45 (September 28, 1997, vs. Minnesota); completions—28 (September 28, 1997, vs. Minnesota); yards—342 (October 27, 1996, vs. Carolina); and touchdown passes—4 (October 20, 1996, vs. Miami).
STATISTICAL PLATEAUS: 300-yard passing games: 1996 (3).
MISCELLANEOUS: Regular-season record as starting NFL quarterback: 10-11 (.476). ... Postseason record as starting NFL quarterback: 0-1.

			PASSING								RUSHING				TOTALS		
Year Team	G	GS	Att.	Cmp.	Pct.	Yds.	TD	Int.	Avg.	Rat.	Att.	Yds.	Avg.	TD	TD	2pt.	Pts.
1992—Green Bay NFL							Did not play.										
1993—Green Bay NFL	3	0	5	3	60.0	26	0	0	5.20	73.8	1	-2	-2.0	0	0	0	0
1994—Green Bay NFL							Did not play.										
1995—Green Bay NFL	4	0	16	8	50.0	81	1	1	5.06	59.6	3	3	1.0	0	0	0	0
1996—Philadelphia NFL	13	11	401	238	59.4	2911	15	13	7.26	80.8	31	59	1.9	1	1	0	6
1997—Philadelphia NFL	8	7	244	134	54.9	1567	7	6	6.42	73.9	14	46	3.3	1	1	0	6
1998—San Francisco NFL	16	1	38	24	63.2	312	4	3	8.21	91.1	8	7	0.9	0	0	0	0
1999—Cleveland NFL	5	2	91	47	51.6	548	4	2	6.02	75.7	6	38	6.3	1	1	0	6
Pro totals (6 years)	49	21	795	454	57.1	5445	31	25	6.85	78.1	63	151	2.4	3	3	0	18

DEVINE, KEVIN   DB

PERSONAL: Born December 11, 1974, in Jackson, Miss. ... 5-9/179. ... Full name: Kevin L. Devine.
HIGH SCHOOL: West Nogales (West Covina, Calif.).
COLLEGE: California.
TRANSACTIONS/CAREER NOTES: Signed as non-drafted free agent by Jacksonville Jaguars (April 21, 1997). ... Assigned by Jaguars to Amsterdam Admirals in 1998 NFL Europe enhancement allocation program (February 18, 1998). ... Selected by Cleveland Browns from Jaguars in NFL expansion draft (February 9, 1999). ... Claimed on waivers by Minnesota Vikings (September 6, 1999). ... Released by Vikings (September 21, 1999).
PLAYING EXPERIENCE: Jacksonville NFL, 1997 and 1998; Amsterdam NFLE 1998; Minnesota NFL, 1999. ... Games/Games started: 1997 (12/0), NFLE 1998 (games played unavailable), NFL 1998 (5/0), 1999 (2/0). Total NFL: 19/0.
PRO STATISTICS: 1998—Intercepted one pass for no yards.

DEVLIN, MIKE   C   CARDINALS

PERSONAL: Born November 16, 1969, in Blacksburg, Va. ... 6-2/325. ... Full name: Michael R. Devlin. ... Cousin of Joe Devlin, offensive tackle/guard with Buffalo Bills (1976-82 and 1984-89).
HIGH SCHOOL: Cherokee (Marlton, N.J.).
COLLEGE: Iowa.
TRANSACTIONS/CAREER NOTES: Selected by Buffalo Bills in fifth round (136th pick overall) of 1993 NFL draft. ... Signed by Bills (July 12, 1993). ... Granted unconditional free agency (February 16, 1996). ... Signed by Arizona Cardinals (March 8, 1996). ... Granted unconditional free agency (February 14, 1997). ... Re-signed by Cardinals (February 25, 1997). ... Granted unconditional free agency (February 12, 1999). ... Re-signed by Cardinals (April 12, 1999). ... Granted unconditional free agency (February 11, 2000). ... Re-signed by Cardinals (April 10, 2000).
PLAYING EXPERIENCE: Buffalo NFL, 1993-1995; Arizona NFL, 1996-1999. ... Games/Games started: 1993 (12/0), 1994 (16/0), 1995 (16/0), 1996 (11/11), 1997 (15/13), 1998 (15/3), 1999 (16/0). Total: 101/27.
CHAMPIONSHIP GAME EXPERIENCE: Played in AFC championship game (1993 season). ... Played in Super Bowl XXVIII (1993 season).
PRO STATISTICS: 1997—Recovered one fumble. 1998—Recovered one fumble.

DeVRIES, JARED   DE   LIONS

PERSONAL: Born June 11, 1976, in Aplington, Iowa. ... 6-4/280.
HIGH SCHOOL: Aplington-Parkersburg (Aplington, Iowa).
COLLEGE: Iowa.
TRANSACTIONS/CAREER NOTES: Selected by Detroit Lions in third round (70th pick overall) of 1999 NFL draft. ... Signed by Lions (July 28, 1999).
PLAYING EXPERIENCE: Detroit NFL, 1999. ... Games/Games started: 1999 (2/0).
HONORS: Named defensive tackle on THE SPORTING NEWS college All-America third team (1997). ... Named defensive tackle on THE SPORTING NEWS college All-America first team (1998).

DEXTER, JAMES   OL   PANTHERS

PERSONAL: Born March 3, 1973, in Fort Ord, Calif. ... 6-7/320.
HIGH SCHOOL: West Springfield (Va.).
COLLEGE: South Carolina (degree in criminal justice, 1996).
TRANSACTIONS/CAREER NOTES: Selected by Arizona Cardinals in fifth round (137th pick overall) of 1996 NFL draft. ... Signed by Cardinals (July 21, 1996). ... Granted free agency (February 12, 1999). ... Re-signed by Cardinals (May 21, 1999). ... Granted unconditional free agency (February 11, 2000). ... Signed by Carolina Panthers (April 25, 2000).
PLAYING EXPERIENCE: Arizona NFL, 1996-1999. ... Games/Games started: 1996 (6/1), 1997 (10/9), 1998 (16/16), 1999 (9/5). Total: 41/31.
PRO STATISTICS: 1998—Recovered two fumbles.

DIAZ, JORGE   G   COWBOYS

PERSONAL: Born November 15, 1973, in New York. ... 6-4/315. ... Full name: Jorge Armando Diaz. ... Name pronounced George.
HIGH SCHOOL: Katy (Texas).
JUNIOR COLLEGE: Kilgore (Texas) College.
COLLEGE: Texas A&M-Kingsville.
TRANSACTIONS/CAREER NOTES: Signed as a non-drafted free agent by Tampa Bay Buccaneers (April 23, 1996). ... Released by Buccaneers (March 17, 2000). ... Signed by Dallas Cowboys (March 31, 2000).
PLAYING EXPERIENCE: Tampa Bay NFL, 1996-1999. ... Games/Games started: 1996 (11/6), 1997 (16/16), 1998 (12/12), 1999 (13/11). Total: 52/45.
CHAMPIONSHIP GAME EXPERIENCE: Played in NFC championship game (1999 season).
PRO STATISTICS: 1997—Recovered one fumble. 1999—Recovered one fumble.

DIAZ-INFANTE, DAVID   G   BRONCOS

PERSONAL: Born March 31, 1964, in San Jose, Calif. ... 6-3/296. ... Full name: Gustavo David Mienez Diaz-Infante. ... Name pronounced DEE-oz in-FON-tay.
HIGH SCHOOL: Bellarmine Prep (San Jose, Calif.).
COLLEGE: San Jose State.
TRANSACTIONS/CAREER NOTES: Signed as non-drafted free agent by San Diego Chargers prior to 1987 season. ... Released by Chargers prior to 1987 season. ... Re-signed by Chargers as replacement player for 1987 season. ... Released by Chargers (October 1987). ... Signed by Los Angeles Rams for 1988 season. ... Released by Rams prior to 1988 season. ... Re-signed by Rams for 1989 season. ... Released by Rams prior to 1989 season. ... Selected by Franfurt Galaxy in third round (fourth offensive lineman) of 1991 WLAF positional draft. ... Signed by Galaxy (January 11, 1991). ... Signed by San Francisco 49ers (May 25, 1993). ... Released by 49ers (August 22, 1993). ... Signed by Sacramento Gold Miners of CFL (September 1993). ... Signed by Denver Broncos (March 30, 1995). ... Released by Broncos (August 27, 1995). ... Re-signed by Broncos to practice squad (August 28, 1995). ... Released by Broncos (September 5, 1999). ... Signed by Philadelphia Eagles (September 14, 1999). ... Granted unconditional free agency (February 11, 2000). .. Signed by Broncos (May 25, 2000).
PLAYING EXPERIENCE: San Diego NFL, 1987; Frankfurt WL, 1991 and 1992; Sacramento CFL, 1993 and 1994; Denver NFL, 1996-1998; Philadelphia NFL, 1999. ... Games/Games started: 1987 (3/0; replacement games), 1991, 1992 and 1994 games played unavailable, 1993 (8/-), 1996 (9/2), 1997 (16/7), 1998 (10/0), 1999 (15/0). Total NFL: 53/9; including 3/0 as replacement player.
CHAMPIONSHIP GAME EXPERIENCE: Played in AFC championship game (1997 and 1998 seasons). ... Member of Super Bowl championship team (1997 and 1998 seasons).

DILFER, TRENT   QB   RAVENS

PERSONAL: Born March 13, 1972, in Santa Cruz, Calif. ... 6-4/229. ... Full name: Trent Farris Dilfer.
HIGH SCHOOL: Aptos (Calif.).
COLLEGE: Fresno State.
TRANSACTIONS/CAREER NOTES: Selected after junior season by Tampa Bay Buccaneers in first round (sixth pick overall) of 1994 NFL draft. ... Signed by Buccaneers (August 3, 1994). ... Granted unconditional free agency (February 11, 2000). ... Signed by Baltimore Ravens (March 8, 2000).
CHAMPIONSHIP GAME EXPERIENCE: Member of Buccaneers for NFC championship game (1999 season); inactive.
HONORS: Played in Pro Bowl (1997 season).
PRO STATISTICS: 1994—Fumbled twice. 1995—Fumbled 13 times and recovered one fumble for minus nine yards. 1996—Fumbled 10 times and recovered four fumbles for minus four yards. 1997—Fumbled nine times and recovered three fumbles for minus 22 yards. 1998—Fumbled nine times and recovered two fumbles for minus five yards. 1999—Fumbled six times for minus four yards.
SINGLE GAME HIGHS (regular season): Attempts—48 (November 26, 1995, vs. Green Bay); completions—30 (November 17, 1996, vs. San Diego); yards—327 (November 17, 1996, vs. San Diego); and touchdown passes—4 (September 21, 1997, vs. Miami).
STATISTICAL PLATEAUS: 300-yard passing games: 1995 (1), 1996 (1), 1999 (1). Total: 3.
MISCELLANEOUS: Regular-season record as starting NFL quarterback: 38-38 (.500). ... Postseason record as starting NFL quarterback: 1-1 (.500).

			PASSING							RUSHING				TOTALS		
Year Team	G	GS	Att.	Cmp.	Pct.	Yds.	TD	Int.	Avg.	Rat.	Att.	Yds.	Avg.	TD	TD	2pt.	Pts.
1994—Tampa Bay NFL	5	2	82	38	46.3	433	1	6	5.28	36.3	2	27	13.5	0	0	0	0
1995—Tampa Bay NFL	16	16	415	224	54.0	2774	4	18	6.68	60.1	23	115	5.0	2	2	0	12
1996—Tampa Bay NFL	16	16	482	267	55.4	2859	12	19	5.93	64.8	32	124	3.9	0	0	0	0
1997—Tampa Bay NFL	16	16	386	217	56.2	2555	21	11	6.62	82.8	33	99	3.0	1	1	0	6
1998—Tampa Bay NFL	16	16	429	225	52.4	2729	21	15	6.36	74.0	40	141	3.5	2	2	0	12
1999—Tampa Bay NFL	10	10	244	146	59.8	1619	11	11	6.64	75.8	35	144	4.1	0	0	0	0
Pro totals (6 years)	79	76	2038	1117	54.8	12969	70	80	6.36	69.4	165	650	3.9	5	5	0	30

DILGER, KEN — TE — COLTS

PERSONAL: Born February 2, 1971, in Mariah Hill, Ind. ... 6-5/255. ... Full name: Kenneth Ray Dilger. ... Name pronounced DIL-gur.
HIGH SCHOOL: Heritage Hills (Lincoln City, Ind.).
COLLEGE: Illinois (degree in marketing).
TRANSACTIONS/CAREER NOTES: Selected by Indianapolis Colts in second round (48th pick overall) of 1995 NFL draft. ... Signed by Colts (July 15, 1995).
CHAMPIONSHIP GAME EXPERIENCE: Played in AFC championship game (1995 season).
PRO STATISTICS: 1998—Returned one kickoff for 14 yards. 1999—Recovered one fumble.
SINGLE GAME HIGHS (regular season): Receptions—7 (September 8, 1996, vs. New York Jets); yards—156 (September 8, 1996, vs. New York Jets); and touchdown receptions—3 (December 14, 1997, vs. Miami).
STATISTICAL PLATEAUS: 100-yard receiving games: 1995 (1), 1996 (1), 1997 (1). Total: 3.

			RECEIVING				TOTALS			
Year Team	G	GS	No.	Yds.	Avg.	TD	TD	2pt.	Pts.	Fum.
1995—Indianapolis NFL	16	13	42	635	15.1	4	4	0	24	0
1996—Indianapolis NFL	16	16	42	503	12.0	4	4	0	24	1
1997—Indianapolis NFL	14	14	27	380	14.1	3	3	0	18	0
1998—Indianapolis NFL	16	16	31	303	9.8	1	1	1	8	0
1999—Indianapolis NFL	15	15	40	479	12.0	2	2	0	12	1
Pro totals (5 years)	77	74	182	2300	12.6	14	14	1	86	2

DILLON, COREY — RB — BENGALS

PERSONAL: Born October 24, 1975, in Seattle. ... 6-1/225.
HIGH SCHOOL: Franklin (Seattle).
JUNIOR COLLEGE: Garden City (Kan.) Community College, then Dixie College (Utah).
COLLEGE: Washington.
TRANSACTIONS/CAREER NOTES: Selected after junior season by Cincinnati Bengals in second round (43rd pick overall) of 1997 NFL draft. ... Signed by Bengals (July 21, 1997). ... Granted free agency (February 11, 2000).
HONORS: Named running back on THE SPORTING NEWS college All-America second team (1996). ... Played in Pro Bowl (1999 season).
PRO STATISTICS: 1997—Recovered one fumble for four yards. 1999—Recovered one fumble.
SINGLE GAME HIGHS (regular season): Attempts—39 (December 4, 1997, vs. Tennessee); yards—246 (December 4, 1997, vs. Tennessee); and rushing touchdowns—4 (December 4, 1997, vs. Tennessee).
STATISTICAL PLATEAUS: 100-yard rushing games: 1997 (4), 1998 (4), 1999 (5). Total: 13.
MISCELLANEOUS: Selected by San Diego Padres organization in 34th round of free agent draft (June 3, 1993); did not sign.

			RUSHING				RECEIVING				KICKOFF RETURNS				TOTALS		
Year Team	G	GS	Att.	Yds.	Avg.	TD	No.	Yds.	Avg.	TD	No.	Yds.	Avg.	TD	TD	2pt.	Pts. Fum.
1997—Cincinnati NFL............	16	6	233	1129	4.8	10	27	259	9.6	0	6	182	30.3	0	10	0	60 1
1998—Cincinnati NFL............	15	15	262	1130	4.3	4	28	178	6.4	1	0	0	0.0	0	5	0	30 2
1999—Cincinnati NFL............	15	15	263	1200	4.6	5	31	290	9.4	1	1	4	4.0	0	6	0	36 3
Pro totals (3 years)	46	36	758	3459	4.6	19	86	727	8.5	2	7	186	26.6	0	21	0	126 6

DIMRY, CHARLES — CB

PERSONAL: Born January 31, 1966, in San Diego. ... 6-0/176. ... Full name: Charles Louis Dimry III.
HIGH SCHOOL: Oceanside (Calif.).
COLLEGE: UNLV.
TRANSACTIONS/CAREER NOTES: Selected by Atlanta Falcons in fifth round (110th pick overall) of 1988 NFL draft. ... Signed by Falcons (July 16, 1988). ... Granted unconditional free agency (February 1, 1991). ... Signed by Denver Broncos (March 28, 1991). ... Granted unconditional free agency (February 17, 1994). ... Signed by Tampa Bay Buccaneers (May 23, 1994). ... Released by Buccaneers (July 20, 1997). ... Signed by Philadelphia Eagles (July 29, 1997). ... Granted unconditional free agency (February 13, 1998). ... Signed by San Diego Chargers (June 10, 1998). ... Announced retirement (February 11, 2000).
CHAMPIONSHIP GAME EXPERIENCE: Played in AFC championship game (1991 season).
PRO STATISTICS: 1989—Credited with one sack. 1991—Recovered one fumble. 1992—Returned one punt for four yards. 1994—Recovered one fumble. 1995—Recovered two fumbles. 1996—Recovered one fumble. 1997—Fumbled once and recovered two fumbles for 34 yards.

			INTERCEPTIONS			
Year Team	G	GS	No.	Yds.	Avg.	TD
1988—Atlanta NFL	16	1	0	0	0.0	0
1989—Atlanta NFL	16	4	2	72	36.0	0
1990—Atlanta NFL	16	12	3	16	5.3	0
1991—Denver NFL	16	1	3	35	11.7	1
1992—Denver NFL	16	6	1	2	2.0	0
1993—Denver NFL	12	11	1	0	0.0	0
1994—Tampa Bay NFL	16	16	1	0	0.0	0
1995—Tampa Bay NFL	16	16	1	0	0.0	0

1996—Tampa Bay NFL	16	7	2	1	0.5	0
1997—Philadelphia NFL	15	9	2	25	12.5	0
1998—San Diego NFL	16	15	3	38	12.7	0
1999—San Diego NFL	12	7	2	1	0.5	0
Pro totals (12 years)	183	105	21	190	9.0	1

DiNAPOLI, GENNARO   G   RAIDERS

PERSONAL: Born May 25, 1975, in Manhassat, N.Y. ... 6-3/300. ... Full name: Gennaro L. DiNapoli. ... Name pronounced den-ah-POLE-ee.
HIGH SCHOOL: Cazenovia (N.Y.), then Milford (Conn.) Academy.
COLLEGE: Virginia Tech.
TRANSACTIONS/CAREER NOTES: Selected by Oakland Raiders in fourth round (109th pick overall) of 1998 NFL draft. ... Signed by Raiders (July 24, 1998). ... Active for four games (1998); did not play.
PLAYING EXPERIENCE: Oakland NFL, 1999. ... Games/Games started: 1999 (11/9).

DINGLE, ANTONIO   DT   PANTHERS

PERSONAL: Born October 7, 1976, in Fayetteville, N.C. ... 6-2/315. ... Full name: Antonio Demetric Dingle.
HIGH SCHOOL: South View (Hope Mills, N.C.).
COLLEGE: Virginia.
TRANSACTIONS/CAREER NOTES: Selected by Pittsburgh Steelers in seventh round (214th pick overall) of 1999 NFL draft. ... Signed by Steelers (June 29, 1999). ... Claimed on waivers by Green Bay Packers (August 31, 1999). ... Claimed on waivers by Carolina Panthers (December 7, 1999). ... Assigned by Panthers to Scottish Claymores in 2000 NFL Europe enhancement allocation program (February 18, 2000).
PLAYING EXPERIENCE: Green Bay (6)-Carolina (3) NFL, 1999. ... Games/Games started: 1999 (G.B.-6/0; Car.-3/0; Total: 9/0).

DISHMAN, CHRIS   G   CARDINALS

PERSONAL: Born February 27, 1974, in Cozad, Neb. ... 6-3/338.
HIGH SCHOOL: Cozad (Neb.).
COLLEGE: Nebraska.
TRANSACTIONS/CAREER NOTES: Selected by Arizona Cardinals in fourth round (106th pick overall) of 1997 NFL draft. ... Signed by Cardinals (July 9, 1997). ... Granted free agency (February 11, 2000). ... Re-signed by Cardinals (April 28, 2000)
PLAYING EXPERIENCE: Arizona NFL, 1997-1999. ... Games/Games started: 1997 (8/0), 1998 (12/11), 1999 (13/10). Total: 33/21.
PRO STATISTICS: 1998—Recovered one fumble. 1999—Returned one kickoff for nine yards.

D

DISHMAN, CRIS   CB   CHIEFS

PERSONAL: Born August 13, 1965, in Louisville, Ky. ... 6-0/196. ... Full name: Cris Edward Dishman.
HIGH SCHOOL: DeSales (Louisville, Ky.).
COLLEGE: Purdue.
TRANSACTIONS/CAREER NOTES: Selected by Houston Oilers in fifth round (125th pick overall) of 1988 NFL draft. ... Signed by Oilers (July 15, 1988). ... Granted free agency (February 1, 1991). ... Re-signed by Oilers (August 18, 1991). ... Granted free agency (February 1, 1992). ... Re-signed by Oilers (September 10, 1992). ... Designated by Oilers as transition player (February 15, 1994). ... Free agency status changed by Oilers from transitional to franchise player (February 15, 1996). ... Granted unconditional free agency (February 14, 1997). ... Signed by Washington Redskins (April 5, 1997). ... Released by Redskins (April 19, 1999). ... Signed by Kansas City Chiefs (May 13, 1999).
HONORS: Played in Pro Bowl (1991 and 1997 seasons).
PRO STATISTICS: 1988—Returned blocked punt 10 yards for a touchdown and recovered one fumble. 1989—Returned blocked punt seven yards for a touchdown and recovered one fumble. 1991—Recovered three fumbles for 19 yards and one touchdown. 1993—Recovered two fumbles for 69 yards and one touchdown. 1994—Returned one punt for no yards and recovered one fumble for 29 yards. 1995—Recovered two fumbles for 15 yards. 1996—Recovered two fumbles. 1997—Credited with $1\frac{1}{2}$ sacks and recovered one fumble. 1999—Recovered three fumbles for 40 yards and one touchdown.

			INTERCEPTIONS				TOTALS			
Year Team	G	GS	No.	Yds.	Avg.	TD	TD	2pt.	Pts.	Fum.
1988—Houston NFL	15	2	0	0	0.0	0	1	0	6	0
1989—Houston NFL	16	0	4	31	7.8	0	1	0	6	0
1990—Houston NFL	16	14	4	50	12.5	0	0	0	0	0
1991—Houston NFL	15	15	6	61	10.2	0	1	0	6	0
1992—Houston NFL	15	15	3	34	11.3	0	0	0	0	0
1993—Houston NFL	16	16	6	74	12.3	0	1	0	6	0
1994—Houston NFL	16	16	4	74	18.5	1	1	0	6	0
1995—Houston NFL	15	15	3	17	5.7	0	0	0	0	0
1996—Houston NFL	16	16	1	7	7.0	0	0	0	0	0
1997—Washington NFL	16	15	4	47	11.8	1	1	0	6	0
1998—Washington NFL	16	16	2	60	30.0	0	0	0	0	0
1999—Kansas City NFL	16	16	5	95	19.0	1	2	0	12	0
Pro totals (12 years)	188	156	42	550	13.1	3	8	0	48	0

DIXON, ANDRE   CB   LIONS

PERSONAL: Born December 4, 1975, in Philadelphia. ... 6-1/200. ... Full name: Andre Lee Dixon.
HIGH SCHOOL: Chestnut Hill Academy (Philadelphia).
COLLEGE: Northeastern.

TRANSACTIONS/CAREER NOTES: Signed as non-drafted free agent by Green Bay Packers (April 23, 1999). ... Released by Packers (August 5, 1999). ... Signed by Detroit Lions to practice squad (October 6, 1999). ... Activated (November 24, 1999). ... Released by Lions (November 29, 1999). ... Re-signed by Lions to practice squad (December 1, 1999). ... Activated (December 18, 1999). ... On injured reserve with hamstring injury (January 4, 2000-remainder of playoffs).
PLAYING EXPERIENCE: Detroit NFL, 1999. ... Games/Games started: 1999 (4/0).

DIXON, DAVID — G — VIKINGS

PERSONAL: Born January 5, 1969, in Papakura, New Zealand. ... 6-5/346. ... Full name: David Tukatahi Dixon.
HIGH SCHOOL: Pukekohe (New Zealand).
JUNIOR COLLEGE: Ricks College (Idaho).
COLLEGE: Arizona State.
TRANSACTIONS/CAREER NOTES: Selected by New England Patriots in ninth-round (232nd pick overall) of 1992 draft. ... Signed by Patriots for 1992 season. ... Released by Patriots (August 1992). ... Signed by Minnesota Vikings to practice squad (October 20, 1992). ... Released by Vikings (August 23, 1993). ... Signed by Dallas Cowboys to practice squad (September 8, 1993). ... Granted free agency after 1993 season. ... Signed by Vikings (July 12, 1994). ... Granted free agency (February 14, 1997). ... Re-signed by Vikings (May 1, 1997). ... Granted unconditional free agency (February 13, 1998). ... Re-signed by Vikings (February 17, 1998). ... On physically unable to perform list with knee injury (August 1-10, 1999).
PLAYING EXPERIENCE: Minnesota NFL, 1994-1999. ... Games/Games started: 1994 (1/0), 1995 (15/6), 1996 (13/6), 1997 (13/13), 1998 (16/16), 1999 (16/16). Total: 74/57.
CHAMPIONSHIP GAME EXPERIENCE: Played in NFC championship game (1998 season).
PRO STATISTICS: 1998—Recovered one fumble.

DIXON, GERALD — LB — CHARGERS

PERSONAL: Born June 20, 1969, in Charlotte. ... 6-3/250. ... Full name: Gerald Scott Dixon.
HIGH SCHOOL: Rock Hill (S.C.).
JUNIOR COLLEGE: Garden City (Kan.) Community College.
COLLEGE: South Carolina.
TRANSACTIONS/CAREER NOTES: Selected by Cleveland Browns in third round (78th pick overall) of 1992 NFL draft. ... Signed by Browns (July 15, 1992). ... On injured reserve with ankle injury (September 2, 1992-entire season). ... Granted free agency (February 17, 1995). ... Re-signed by Browns for 1995 season. ... Granted unconditional free agency (February 16, 1996). ... Signed by Cincinnati Bengals (March 14, 1996). ... Granted unconditional free agency (February 13, 1998). ... Signed by San Diego Chargers (March 24, 1998). ... Granted unconditional free agency (February 11, 2000). ... Re-signed by Chargers (March 15, 2000).
PRO STATISTICS: 1995—Intercepted two passes for 48 yards and one touchdown, returned one kickoff for 10 yards and recovered one fumble. 1999—Recovered one fumble for 27 yards and a touchdown.

Year Team	G	GS	SACKS
1992—Cleveland NFL	Did not play.		
1993—Cleveland NFL	11	0	0.0
1994—Cleveland NFL	16	0	1.0
1995—Cleveland NFL	16	9	0.0
1996—Cincinnati NFL	16	1	0.0
1997—Cincinnati NFL	15	12	8.5
1998—San Diego NFL	16	6	2.5
1999—San Diego NFL	14	1	4.0
Pro totals (7 years)	104	29	16.0

DIXON, MARK — G — DOLPHINS

PERSONAL: Born November 6, 1970, in Charlottesville, N.C. ... 6-4/300. ... Full name: Mark Keller Dixon.
HIGH SCHOOL: Ragsdale (Jamestown, N.C.).
COLLEGE: Virginia.
TRANSACTIONS/CAREER NOTES: Signed as non-drafted free agent by Philadelphia Eagles (April 1994). ... Released by Eagles (August 1994). ... Played with Frankfurt Galaxy of World League (1995). ... Signed by Atlanta Falcons (July 18, 1995). ... Released by Falcons (August 21, 1995). ... Signed by Baltimore Stallions of CFL (August 30, 1995). ... Signed by Miami Dolphins (January 22, 1998). ... On injured reserve with neck injury (November 24, 1998-remainder of season).
PLAYING EXPERIENCE: Frankfurt W.L., 1995; Baltimore Stallions CFL, 1995; Montreal Alouettes CFL, 1996 and 1997; Miami NFL, 1998 and 1999. ... Games/Games started: W.L. 1995 (games played unavailable), CFL 1995 (9/5), 1996 (18/18), 1997 (7/7), 1998 (11/10), 1999 (13/13). Total CFL: 33/30. Total NFL 24/23. Total Pro: 57/53.
CHAMPIONSHIP GAME EXPERIENCE: Member of CFL championship team (1995).
PRO STATISTICS: 1998—Recovered two fumbles.

DOERING, CHRIS — WR — BRONCOS

PERSONAL: Born May 19, 1973, in Gainesville, Fla. ... 6-4/195. ... Full name: Christopher Paul Doering. ... Name pronounced DOOR-ing.
HIGH SCHOOL: P.K. Yonge (Gainesville, Fla.).
COLLEGE: Florida.
TRANSACTIONS/CAREER NOTES: Selected by Jacksonville Jaguars in sixth round (185th pick overall) of 1996 NFL draft. ... Signed by Jaguars (June 5, 1996). ... Claimed on waivers by New York Jets (August 20, 1996). ... Released by Jets (August 25, 1996). ... Signed by Indianapolis Colts to practice squad (August 27, 1996). ... Activated (December 5, 1997). ... Re-signed by Colts (August 24, 1997). ... Re-signed by Colts to practice squad (August 25, 1997). ... Activated (December 5, 1997). ... Claimed on waivers by Cincinnati Bengals (February 25, 1998). ... Released by Bengals (September 2, 1998). ... Signed by Denver Broncos (February 3, 1999).
PLAYING EXPERIENCE: Indianapolis NFL, 1996 and 1997; Denver NFL, 1999. ... Games/Games started: 1996 (1/0), 1997 (2/0), 1999 (3/0). Total: 6/0.
PRO STATISTICS: 1996—Caught one pass for 10 yards. 1997—Caught two passes for 12 yards. 1999—Caught three passes for 22 yards.

SINGLE GAME HIGHS (regular season): Receptions—3 (September 13, 1999, vs. Miami); yards—22 (September 13, 1999, vs. Miami); and touchdown receptions—0.

DOGINS, KEVIN — C/G — BUCCANEERS

PERSONAL: Born December 7, 1972, in Eagle Lake, Texas. ... 6-1/301. ... Full name: Kevin Ray Dogins.
HIGH SCHOOL: Rice (Texas).
COLLEGE: Texas A&M-Kingsville.
TRANSACTIONS/CAREER NOTES: Signed as non-drafted free agent by Dallas Cowboys (April 25, 1996). ... Released by Cowboys (August 19, 1996). ... Signed by Tampa Bay Buccaneers to practice squad (August 27, 1996). ... Activated (December 17, 1996). ... Inactive for all 16 games (1997). ... Granted free agency (February 11, 2000).
PLAYING EXPERIENCE: Tampa Bay NFL, 1996, 1998 and 1999. ... Games/Games started: 1996 (1/0), 1998 (6/4), 1999 (11/5). Total: 18/9.
CHAMPIONSHIP GAME EXPERIENCE: Played in NFC championship game (1999 season).

DOLEMAN, CHRIS — DE

PERSONAL: Born October 16, 1961, in Indianapolis. ... 6-5/289. ... Full name: Christopher John Doleman.
HIGH SCHOOL: William Penn (York, Pa.).
COLLEGE: Pittsburgh.
TRANSACTIONS/CAREER NOTES: Selected by Baltimore Stars in 1985 USFL territorial draft. ... Selected by Minnesota Vikings in first round (fourth pick overall) of 1985 NFL draft. ... Signed by Vikings (August 8, 1985). ... Granted free agency (February 1, 1991). ... Re-signed by Vikings (July 25, 1991). ... Traded by Vikings with second-round pick (WR Bert Emanuel) in 1994 draft to Atlanta Falcons for second-round pick (RB/WR/KR David Palmer) in 1994 draft and first-round pick (DE Derrick Alexander) in 1995 draft (April 24, 1994). ... Granted unconditional free agency (February 16, 1996). ... Signed by San Francisco 49ers (March 14, 1996). ... Announced retirement (January 9, 1999). ... Released by 49ers (June 18, 1999). ... Signed by Minnesota Vikings (September 21, 1999). ... Granted unconditional free agency (February 11, 2000).
CHAMPIONSHIP GAME EXPERIENCE: Played in NFC championship game (1987 and 1997 seasons).
HONORS: Played in Pro Bowl (1987-1990, 1992, 1993, 1995 and 1997 seasons). ... Named defensive end on THE SPORTING NEWS NFL All-Pro team (1989 and 1992).
PRO STATISTICS: 1985—Recovered three fumbles. 1989—Recovered five fumbles for seven yards. 1990—Credited with a safety. 1991—Recovered two fumbles for seven yards. 1992—Credited with a safety and recovered three fumbles. 1993—Recovered one fumble. 1995—Recovered two fumbles. 1996—Recovered three fumbles for 13 yards and one touchdown. 1997—Recovered one fumble. 1998—Recovered two fumbles. 1999—Recovered two fumbles for seven yards.

Year Team	G	GS	INTERCEPTIONS				SACKS
			No.	Yds.	Avg.	TD	No.
1985—Minnesota NFL	16	13	1	5	5.0	0	0.5
1986—Minnesota NFL	16	9	1	59	59.0	1	3.0
1987—Minnesota NFL	12	12	0	0	0.0	0	11.0
1988—Minnesota NFL	16	16	0	0	0.0	0	8.0
1989—Minnesota NFL	16	16	0	0	0.0	0	21.0
1990—Minnesota NFL	16	16	1	30	30.0	0	11.0
1991—Minnesota NFL	16	16	0	0	0.0	0	7.0
1992—Minnesota NFL	16	16	1	27	27.0	1	14.5
1993—Minnesota NFL	16	16	1	-3	-3.0	0	12.5
1994—Atlanta NFL	14	7	1	2	2.0	0	7.0
1995—Atlanta NFL	16	16	0	0	0.0	0	9.0
1996—San Francisco NFL	16	16	2	1	0.5	0	11.0
1997—San Francisco NFL	16	16	0	0	0.0	0	12.0
1998—San Francisco NFL	16	16	0	0	0.0	0	15.0
1999—Minnesota NFL	14	12	0	0	0.0	0	8.0
Pro totals (15 years)	232	213	8	121	15.1	2	150.5

DONNALLEY, KEVIN — G

PERSONAL: Born June 10, 1968, in St. Louis. ... 6-5/310. ... Full name: Kevin Thomas Donnalley. ... Brother of Rick Donnalley, center with Pittsburgh Steelers (1982 and 1983), Washington Redskins (1984 and 1985) and Kansas City Chiefs (1986 and 1987).
HIGH SCHOOL: Athens Drive Senior (Raleigh, N.C.).
COLLEGE: Davidson, then North Carolina (degree in economics).
TRANSACTIONS/CAREER NOTES: Selected by Houston Oilers in third round (79th pick overall) of 1991 NFL draft. ... Signed by Oilers (July 10, 1991). ... Granted free agency (February 17, 1994). ... Tendered offer sheet by Los Angeles Rams (March 17, 1994). ... Offer matched by Oilers (March 23, 1994). ... Oilers franchise moved to Tennessee for 1997 season. ... Granted unconditional free agency (February 13, 1998). ... Signed by Miami Dolphins (February 17, 1998). ... Released by Dolphins (June 2, 2000).
PLAYING EXPERIENCE: Houston NFL, 1991-1996; Tennessee NFL, 1997; Miami NFL, 1998 and 1999. ... Games/Games started: 1991 (16/0), 1992 (16/2), 1993 (16/6), 1994 (13/11), 1995 (16/16), 1996 (16/16), 1997 (16/16), 1998 (14/14), 1999 (16/9). Total: 139/90.
PRO STATISTICS: 1995—Recovered one fumble. 1998—Recovered one fumble.

DORSETT, ANTHONY — S — RAIDERS

PERSONAL: Born September 14, 1973, in Aliquippa, Pa. ... 5-11/200. ... Full name: Anthony Drew Dorsett Jr. ... Son of Tony Dorsett, Hall of Fame running back with Dallas Cowboys (1977-87) and Denver Broncos (1988).
HIGH SCHOOL: Richland (Dallas), then J.J. Pearce (Dallas).
COLLEGE: Pittsburgh.
TRANSACTIONS/CAREER NOTES: Selected by Houston Oilers in sixth round (177th pick overall) of 1996 NFL draft. ... Signed by Oilers (June 21, 1996). ... Assigned by Oilers to Barcelona Dragons in 1997 World League enhancement allocation program (February 19, 1997). ... Oilers franchise moved to Tennessee for 1997 season. ... Oilers franchise renamed Tennessee Titans for 1999 season (December 26, 1998). ...

Granted free agency (February 12, 1999). ... Re-signed by Titans (June 15, 1999). ... Granted unconditional free agency (February 11, 2000). ... Signed by Oakland Raiders (March 21, 2000).
PLAYING EXPERIENCE: Houston NFL, 1996; Barcelona W.L., 1997; Tennessee NFL, 1997-1999. ... Games/Games started: 1996 (8/0), W.L. 1997 (games played unavailable), 1997 (16/0), 1998 (16/0), 1999 (16/1). Total: 56/1.
CHAMPIONSHIP GAME EXPERIENCE: Played in AFC championship game (1999 season). ... Played in Super Bowl XXXIV (1999 season).
PRO STATISTICS: 1999—Intercepted one pass for 43 yards.

DOTSON, EARL — OT — PACKERS

PERSONAL: Born December 17, 1970, in Beaumont, Texas. ... 6-4/310. ... Full name: Earl Christopher Dotson.
HIGH SCHOOL: Westbrook (Texas).
JUNIOR COLLEGE: Tyler (Texas) Junior College.
COLLEGE: Texas A&I.
TRANSACTIONS/CAREER NOTES: Selected by Green Bay Packers in third round (81st pick overall) of 1993 NFL draft. ... Signed by Packers (June 14, 1993).
PLAYING EXPERIENCE: Green Bay NFL, 1993-1999. ... Games/Games started: 1993 (13/0), 1994 (4/0), 1995 (16/16), 1996 (15/15), 1997 (13/13), 1998 (16/16), 1999 (15/15). Total: 92/75.
CHAMPIONSHIP GAME EXPERIENCE: Played in NFC championship game (1995-97 seasons). ... Member of Super Bowl championship team (1996 season). ... Played in Super Bowl XXXII (1997 season).
PRO STATISTICS: 1996—Recovered one fumble. 1997—Recovered one fumble.

DOTSON, SANTANA — DT — PACKERS

PERSONAL: Born December 19, 1969, in New Orleans. ... 6-5/290. ... Full name: Santana N. Dotson. ... Son of Alphonse Dotson, defensive tackle with Kansas City Chiefs (1965), Miami Dolphins (1966) and Oakland Raiders (1968-70).
HIGH SCHOOL: Jack Yates (Houston).
COLLEGE: Baylor.
TRANSACTIONS/CAREER NOTES: Selected by Tampa Bay Buccaneers in fifth round (132nd pick overall) of 1992 NFL draft. ... Signed by Buccaneers (July 7, 1992). ... Granted free agency (February 17, 1995). ... Re-signed by Buccaneers (June 14, 1995). ... Granted unconditional free agency (February 16, 1996). ... Signed by Green Bay Packers (March 7, 1996). ... Granted unconditional free agency (February 12, 1999). ... Re-signed by Packers (February 19, 1999).
CHAMPIONSHIP GAME EXPERIENCE: Played in NFC championship game (1996 and 1997 seasons). ... Member of Super Bowl championship team (1996 season). ... Played in Super Bowl XXXII (1997 season).
HONORS: Named defensive lineman on THE SPORTING NEWS college All-America first team (1991). ... Named NFL Rookie of the Year by THE SPORTING NEWS (1992).
PRO STATISTICS: 1992—Recovered two fumbles for 42 yards and one touchdown. 1995—Recovered two fumbles. 1996—Recovered one fumble for eight yards. 1998—Recovered one fumble.

Year Team	G	GS	SACKS
1992—Tampa Bay NFL	16	16	10.0
1993—Tampa Bay NFL	16	13	5.0
1994—Tampa Bay NFL	16	9	3.0
1995—Tampa Bay NFL	16	8	5.0
1996—Green Bay NFL	16	15	5.5
1997—Green Bay NFL	16	16	5.5
1998—Green Bay NFL	16	16	3.0
1999—Green Bay NFL	12	12	2.5
Pro totals (8 years)	**124**	**105**	**39.5**

DOUGLAS, DAMEANE — WR — EAGLES

PERSONAL: Born March 15, 1976, in Hanford, Calif. ... 6-0/195.
HIGH SCHOOL: Hanford (Calif.).
COLLEGE: California.
TRANSACTIONS/CAREER NOTES: Selected by Oakland Raiders in fourth round (102nd pick overall) of 1999 NFL draft. ... Signed by Raiders for 1999 season. ... Claimed on waivers by Philadelphia Eagles (September 7, 1999).
SINGLE GAME HIGHS (regular season): Receptions—3 (December 5, 1999, vs. Arizona); yards—47 (December 5, 1999, vs. Arizona); and touchdown receptions—1 (December 5, 1999, vs. Arizona).

Year Team	G	GS	RECEIVING No.	Yds.	Avg.	TD	TOTALS TD	2pt.	Pts.	Fum.
1999—Philadelphia NFL	14	0	8	79	9.9	1	1	0	6	0

DOUGLAS, HUGH — LB/DE — EAGLES

PERSONAL: Born August 23, 1971, in Mansfield, Ohio. ... 6-2/280.
HIGH SCHOOL: Mansfield (Ohio).
COLLEGE: Central State (Ohio).
TRANSACTIONS/CAREER NOTES: Selected after junior season by New York Jets in first round (16th pick overall) of 1995 NFL draft. ... Signed by Jets (June 8, 1995). ... Traded by Jets to Philadelphia Eagles for second- (traded to Pittsburgh) and fifth-round (LB Casey Dailey) picks in 1998 draft (March 13, 1998). ... On injured reserve with bicep injury (October 20, 1999-remainder of season).
PRO STATISTICS: 1995—Recovered two fumbles. 1996—Recovered three fumbles for 64 yards and one touchdown.

Year Team	G	GS	SACKS
1995—New York Jets NFL	15	3	10.0
1996—New York Jets NFL	10	10	8.0
1997—New York Jets NFL	15	15	4.0
1998—Philadelphia NFL	15	13	12.5
1999—Philadelphia NFL	4	2	2.0
Pro totals (5 years)	59	43	36.5

DRAFT, CHRIS   LB   FALCONS

PERSONAL: Born February 26, 1976, in Anaheim. ... 5-11/230.
HIGH SCHOOL: Valencia (Placentia, Calif.).
COLLEGE: Stanford.
TRANSACTIONS/CAREER NOTES: Selected by Chicago Bears in sixth round (157th pick overall) of 1998 NFL draft. ... Signed by Bears (June 16, 1998). ... Released by Bears (August 30, 1998). ... Re-signed by Bears to practice squad (August 31, 1998). ... Activated (December 2, 1998). ... Released by Bears (August 30, 1999). ... Signed by San Francisco 49ers to practice squad (September 29, 1999). ... Activated (November 19, 1999). ... Claimed on waivers by Atlanta Falcons (February 14, 2000).
PLAYING EXPERIENCE: Chicago NFL, 1998; San Francisco NFL, 1999. ... Games/Games started: 1998 (1/0), 1999 (7/0). Total: 8/0.

DRAKE, JERRY   DE   CARDINALS

PERSONAL: Born July 9, 1969, in Kingston, N.Y. ... 6-5/312.
HIGH SCHOOL: Kingston (N.Y.).
JUNIOR COLLEGE: Ulster Community College (N.Y.).
COLLEGE: Hastings (Neb.) College.
TRANSACTIONS/CAREER NOTES: Signed as non-drafted free agent by Arizona Cardinals (May 2, 1995). ... Released by Cardinals (August 21, 1995). ... Re-signed by Cardinals to practice squad (August 30, 1995). ... Activated (November 24, 1995). ... Assigned by Cardinals to London Monarchs in 1996 World League enhancement allocation program (February 19, 1996). ... On injured reserve with neck injury (August 19, 1997-entire season). ... On injured reserve with back injury (October 2, 1998-remainder of season). ... Granted unconditional free agency (February 11, 2000). ... Re-signed by Cardinals (May 24, 2000).
PLAYING EXPERIENCE: Arizona NFL, 1995, 1996, 1998 and 1999; London W.L., 1996. ... Games/Games started: 1995 (2/0), W.L. 1996 (10/10); NFL 1996 (11/0); 1998 (1/1), 1999 (16/16). Total: W.L.: 10/10. Total NFL: 30/17. Total Pro: 40/27.
PRO STATISTICS: W.L.: 1996—Credited with eight sacks. NFL: 1999—Intercepted one pass for no yards, credited with one sack and recovered one fumble.

DRAKEFORD, TYRONNE   CB

PERSONAL: Born June 21, 1971, in Camden, S.C. ... 5-11/185. ... Full name: Tyronne James Drakeford.
HIGH SCHOOL: North Central (Kershaw, S.C.).
COLLEGE: Virginia Tech (degree in finance).
TRANSACTIONS/CAREER NOTES: Selected by San Francisco 49ers in second round (62nd pick overall) of 1994 NFL draft. ... Signed by 49ers (July 20, 1994). ... Granted free agency (February 14, 1997). ... Re-signed by 49ers (April 8, 1997). ... Granted unconditional free agency (February 13, 1998). ... Signed by New Orleans Saints (February 19, 1998). ... Released by Saints (May 11, 2000).
CHAMPIONSHIP GAME EXPERIENCE: Played in NFC championship game (1994 and 1997 seasons). ... Member of Super Bowl championship team (1994 season).
PRO STATISTICS: 1995—Credited with one sack, fumbled once and recovered one fumble for 12 yards. 1996—Credited with two sacks and recovered one fumble for eight yards. 1997—Returned one kickoff for 24 yards. 1999—Recovered one fumble for 20 yards.

				INTERCEPTIONS		
Year Team	G	GS	No.	Yds.	Avg.	TD
1994—San Francisco NFL	13	0	1	6	6.0	0
1995—San Francisco NFL	16	2	5	54	10.8	0
1996—San Francisco NFL	16	16	1	11	11.0	0
1997—San Francisco NFL	16	2	5	15	3.0	0
1998—New Orleans NFL	16	15	4	76	19.0	1
1999—New Orleans NFL	10	5	0	0	0.0	0
Pro totals (6 years)	87	40	16	162	10.1	1

DRAYTON, TROY   TE

PERSONAL: Born June 29, 1970, in Harrisburg, Pa. ... 6-3/270. ... Full name: Troy Anthony Drayton. ... Cousin of Kevin Mitchell, linebacker, New Orleans Saints.
HIGH SCHOOL: Steelton Highspire (Steelton, Pa.).
COLLEGE: Penn State.
TRANSACTIONS/CAREER NOTES: Selected by Los Angeles Rams in second round (39th pick overall) of 1993 NFL draft. ... Signed by Rams (July 20, 1993). ... Rams franchise moved to St. Louis (April 12, 1995). ... Granted free agency (February 16, 1996). ... Re-signed by Rams (April 17, 1996). ... Traded by Rams to Miami Dolphins for OT Bill Milner (October 1, 1996). ... Released by Dolphins (February 10, 2000).
PRO STATISTICS: 1993—Rushed once for seven yards and returned one kickoff for minus 15 yards. 1994—Rushed once for four yards. 1996—Recovered one fumble.
SINGLE GAME HIGHS (regular season): Receptions—8 (November 19, 1995, vs. Atlanta); yards—106 (September 24, 1995, vs. Chicago); and touchdown receptions—2 (October 12, 1998, vs. Jacksonville).
STATISTICAL PLATEAUS: 100-yard receiving games: 1995 (1).

			RECEIVING				TOTALS			
Year Team	G	GS	No.	Yds.	Avg.	TD	TD	2pt.	Pts.	Fum.
1993—Los Angeles Rams NFL	16	2	27	319	11.8	4	4	0	24	1

1994—Los Angeles Rams NFL	16	16	32	276	8.6	6	6	0	36	0
1995—St. Louis NFL	16	16	47	458	9.7	4	4	0	24	2
1996—St. Louis NFL	3	3	2	11	5.5	0	0	0	0	0
—Miami NFL	10	10	26	320	12.3	0	0	1	2	0
1997—Miami NFL	16	15	39	558	14.3	4	4	0	24	0
1998—Miami NFL	15	15	30	334	11.1	3	3	0	18	0
1999—Miami NFL	14	13	32	299	9.3	1	1	0	6	0
Pro totals (7 years)	106	90	235	2575	11.0	22	22	1	134	3

DRIVER, DONALD   WR   PACKERS

PERSONAL: Born February 2, 1975, in Houston. ... 6-0/175. ... Full name: Donald Jerome Driver.
HIGH SCHOOL: Milby (Houston).
COLLEGE: Alcorn State (degree in accounting).
TRANSACTIONS/CAREER NOTES: Selected by Green Bay Packers in seventh round (213th pick overall) of 1999 NFL draft. ... Signed by Packers (June 2, 1999).
PLAYING EXPERIENCE: Green Bay NFL, 1999. ... Games/Games started: 1999 (6/0).
PRO STATISTICS: 1999—Caught three passes for 31 yards and one touchdown.
SINGLE GAME HIGHS (regular season): Receptions—3 (December 12, 1999, vs. Carolina); yards—31 (December 12, 1999, vs. Carolina); and touchdown receptions—1 (December 12, 1999, vs. Carolina).

DRONETT, SHANE   DE   FALCONS

PERSONAL: Born January 12, 1971, in Orange, Texas. ... 6-6/300.
HIGH SCHOOL: Bridge City (Texas).
COLLEGE: Texas.
TRANSACTIONS/CAREER NOTES: Selected after junior season by Denver Broncos in second round (54th pick overall) of 1992 NFL draft. ... Signed by Broncos (July 15, 1992). ... Granted free agency (February 17, 1995). ... Re-signed by Broncos (May 12, 1995). ... Granted unconditional free agency (February 16, 1996). ... Signed by Atlanta Falcons (April 9, 1996). ... Released by Falcons (October 7, 1996). ... Signed by Detroit Lions (October 9, 1996). ... Granted unconditional free agency (February 14, 1997). ... Signed by Lions for 1997 season. ... Released by Lions (August 24, 1997). ... Signed by Falcons (August 27, 1997). ... Granted unconditional free agency (February 13, 1998). ... Re-signed by Falcons (February 20, 1998).
CHAMPIONSHIP GAME EXPERIENCE: Played in NFC championship game (1998 season). ... Played in Super Bowl XXXIII (1998 season).
PRO STATISTICS: 1992—Recovered two fumbles for minus five yards. 1993—Intercepted two passes for 13 yards. 1998—Recovered one fumble. 1999—Recovered one fumble for 15 yards.

Year Team	G	GS	SACKS
1992—Denver NFL	16	2	6.5
1993—Denver NFL	16	16	7.0
1994—Denver NFL	16	15	6.0
1995—Denver NFL	13	2	2.0
1996—Atlanta NFL	5	0	0.0
—Detroit NFL	7	0	0.0
1997—Atlanta NFL	16	1	3.0
1998—Atlanta NFL	16	16	6.5
1999—Atlanta NFL	16	16	6.5
Pro totals (8 years)	121	68	37.5

DRUCKENMILLER, JIM   QB   DOLPHINS

PERSONAL: Born September 19, 1972, in Northhampton, Pa. ... 6-5/234. ... Full name: James David Druckenmiller Jr.
HIGH SCHOOL: Northhampton (Pa.), then Fork Union (Va.) Military Academy.
COLLEGE: Virginia Tech.
TRANSACTIONS/CAREER NOTES: Selected by San Francisco 49ers in first round (26th pick overall) of 1997 NFL draft. ... Signed by 49ers (July 31, 1997). ... Traded by 49ers to Miami Dolphins for seventh-round pick (TE Brian Jennings) in 2000 draft and seventh-round pick in 2001 draft (September 6, 1999).
CHAMPIONSHIP GAME EXPERIENCE: Member of 49ers for NFC championship game (1997 season); inactive.
SINGLE GAME HIGHS (regular season): Attempts—28 (September 7, 1997, vs. St. Louis); completions—10 (September 7, 1997, vs. St. Louis); yards—102 (September 7, 1997, vs. St. Louis); and touchdown passes—1 (September 7, 1997, vs. St. Louis).
MISCELLANEOUS: Regular-season record as starting NFL quarterback: 1-0.

			PASSING								RUSHING				TOTALS		
Year Team	G	GS	Att.	Cmp.	Pct.	Yds.	TD	Int.	Avg.	Rat.	Att.	Yds.	Avg.	TD	TD	2pt.	Pts.
1997—San Francisco NFL	4	1	52	21	40.4	239	1	4	4.60	29.2	10	-6	-0.6	0	0	0	0
1998—San Francisco NFL	2	0	0	0	0.0	0	0	0	0.00	...	3	-4	-1.3	0	0	0	0
1999—Miami NFL								Did not play.									
Pro totals (2 years)	6	1	52	21	40.4	239	1	4	4.60	29.2	13	-10	-0.8	0	0	0	0

DUDLEY, RICKEY   TE   RAIDERS

PERSONAL: Born July 15, 1972, in Henderson, Texas. ... 6-6/255.
HIGH SCHOOL: Henderson (Texas).
COLLEGE: Ohio State.
TRANSACTIONS/CAREER NOTES: Selected by Oakland Raiders in first round (ninth pick overall) of 1996 NFL draft. ... Signed by Raiders (July 12, 1996).
PRO STATISTICS: 1998—Rushed once for minus two yards.

SINGLE GAME HIGHS (regular season): Receptions—6 (November 8, 1998, vs. Baltimore); yards—116 (November 9, 1997, vs. New Orleans); and touchdown receptions—2 (November 28, 1999, vs. Kansas City).
STATISTICAL PLATEAUS: 100-yard receiving games: 1997 (2), 1998 (1). Total: 3.
MISCELLANEOUS: Member of Ohio State basketball team (1991-92 through 1993-94).

				RECEIVING				TOTALS		
Year Team	G	GS	No.	Yds.	Avg.	TD	TD	2pt.	Pts.	Fum.
1996—Oakland NFL	16	15	34	386	11.4	4	4	0	24	1
1997—Oakland NFL	16	16	48	787	16.4	7	7	0	42	0
1998—Oakland NFL	16	15	36	549	15.3	5	5	1	32	1
1999—Oakland NFL	16	16	39	555	14.2	9	9	0	54	0
Pro totals (4 years)	64	62	157	2277	14.5	25	25	1	152	2

DUFF, BILL — DL — BROWNS

PERSONAL: Born February 24, 1974, in Willingboro, N.J. ... 6-3/285. ... Full name: William Brian Duff.
HIGH SCHOOL: Delran (N.J.).
COLLEGE: Tennessee.
TRANSACTIONS/CAREER NOTES: Signed as non-drafted free agent by San Francisco 49ers (April 24, 1998). ... Released by 49ers (August 25, 1998). ... Signed by Cleveland Browns (February 11, 1999). ... Released by Browns (September 4, 1999). ... Re-signed by Browns to practice squad (September 6, 1999). ... Activated (September 7, 1999). ... Released by Browns (September 14, 1999). ... Re-signed by Browns (October 6, 1999). ... Released by Browns (October 25, 1999). ... Re-signed by Browns (November 9, 1999). ... Assigned by Browns to Berlin Thunder in 2000 NFL Europe enhancement allocation program (February 18, 2000).
PLAYING EXPERIENCE: Cleveland NFL, 1999. ... Games/Games started: 1999 (5/0).

DUFFY, ROGER — G/C — STEELERS

PERSONAL: Born July 16, 1967, in Pittsburgh. ... 6-3/299. ... Full name: Roger Thomas Duffy.
HIGH SCHOOL: Canton (Ohio) Central Catholic.
COLLEGE: Penn State (degree in communications, 1990).
TRANSACTIONS/CAREER NOTES: Selected by New York Jets in eighth round (196th pick overall) of 1990 NFL draft. ... Signed by Jets (July 18, 1990). ... Granted free agency (February 1, 1992). ... Re-signed by Jets (May 15, 1992). ... Granted unconditional free agency (February 17, 1994). ... Re-signed by Jets (March 2, 1994). ... Granted unconditional free agency (February 16, 1996). ... Re-signed by Jets (April 1, 1996). ... Granted unconditional free agency (February 13, 1998). ... Signed by Pittsburgh Steelers (March 13, 1998).
PLAYING EXPERIENCE: New York Jets NFL, 1990-1997; Pittsburgh NFL, 1998 and 1999. ... Games/Games started: 1990 (16/2), 1991 (12/0), 1992 (16/6), 1993 (16/1), 1994 (16/14), 1995 (16/16), 1996 (16/16), 1997 (15/15), 1998 (15/4), 1999 (16/11). Total: 154/85.
PRO STATISTICS: 1991—Returned one kickoff for eight yards. 1992—Returned one kickoff for seven yards and recovered one fumble. 1993—Recovered one fumble. 1995—Recovered two fumbles. 1996—Recovered one fumble. 1997—Fumbled twice and recovered one fumble for minus 22 yards.

DUMAS, MIKE — S — CHARGERS

PERSONAL: Born March 18, 1969, in Grand Rapids, Mich. ... 6-0/202. ... Full name: Michael Dion Dumas.
HIGH SCHOOL: Lowell (Mich.).
COLLEGE: Indiana.
TRANSACTIONS/CAREER NOTES: Selected by Houston Oilers in second round (28th pick overall) of 1991 NFL draft. ... Signed by Oilers (August 12, 1991). ... On injured reserve with Achilles' tendon injury (August 23, 1993-entire season). ... Granted free agency (February 17, 1994). ... Re-signed by Oilers (June 1994). ... Released by Oilers (July 14, 1994). ... Signed by Buffalo Bills (July 25, 1994). ... Granted unconditional free agency (February 17, 1995). ... Signed by Jacksonville Jaguars (April 24, 1995). ... Released by Jaguars (April 24, 1996). ... Signed by San Diego Chargers (March 4, 1997). ... Granted unconditional free agency (February 13, 1998). ... Re-signed by Chargers (February 20, 1998). ... On injured reserve with knee injury (September 26, 1998-remainder of season). ... Granted unconditional free agency (February 11, 2000). ... Re-signed by Chargers (April 20, 2000).
HONORS: Named defensive back on THE SPORTING NEWS college All-America second team (1990).
PRO STATISTICS: 1991—Recovered three fumbles for 19 yards and one touchdown. 1992—Recovered one fumble. 1994—Recovered two fumbles for 40 yards. 1995—Recovered two fumbles. 1997—Credited with one sack and recovered one fumble. 1998—Credited with one sack. 1999—Credited with two sacks.

				INTERCEPTIONS		
Year Team	G	GS	No.	Yds.	Avg.	TD
1991—Houston NFL	13	0	1	19	19.0	0
1992—Houston NFL	16	1	1	0	0.0	0
1993—Houston NFL			Did not play.			
1994—Buffalo NFL	14	0	0	0	0.0	0
1995—Jacksonville NFL	14	8	1	0	0.0	0
1996—			Did not play.			
1997—San Diego NFL	16	15	1	0	0.0	0
1998—San Diego NFL	3	3	0	0	0.0	0
1999—San Diego NFL	14	14	2	92	46.0	0
Pro totals (7 years)	90	41	6	111	18.5	0

DUNCAN, JAMIE — LB — BUCCANEERS

PERSONAL: Born July 20, 1975, in Wilmington, Del. ... 6-0/242.
HIGH SCHOOL: Christiana (Newark, Del.).
COLLEGE: Vanderbilt (degree in human and organizational development, 1998).
TRANSACTIONS/CAREER NOTES: Selected by Tampa Bay Buccaneers in third round (84th pick overall) of 1998 NFL draft. ... Signed by Buccaneers (July 10, 1998).

PLAYING EXPERIENCE: Tampa Bay NFL, 1998 and 1999. ... Games/Games started: 1998 (14/6), 1999 (16/0). Total: 30/6.
CHAMPIONSHIP GAME EXPERIENCE: Played in NFC championship game (1999 season).
HONORS: Named inside linebacker on THE SPORTING NEWS college All-America second team (1997).

DUNN, DAMON   WR   BROWNS

PERSONAL: Born March 15, 1976, in Fort Worth, Texas ... 5-9/182. ... Full name: Damon Jerrel Dunn.
HIGH SCHOOL: Sam Houston (Arlington, Texas).
COLLEGE: Stanford.
TRANSACTIONS/CAREER NOTES: Signed as non-drafted free agent by Jacksonville Jaguars (April 23, 1998). ... Released by Jaguars (August 25, 1998). ... Re-signed by Jaguars to practice squad (August 31, 1998). ... Released by Jaguars (August 29, 1999). ... Signed by Cleveland Browns to practice squad (November 16, 1999). ... Activated (December 14, 1999). ... Assigned by Browns to Berlin Thunder in 2000 NFL Europe enhancement allocation program (February 18, 2000).
PLAYING EXPERIENCE: Cleveland NFL, 1999. ... Games/Games started: 1999 (1/0).

DUNN, DAVID   WR   RAIDERS

PERSONAL: Born June 10, 1972, in San Diego. ... 6-3/210.
HIGH SCHOOL: Samuel F.B. Morse (San Diego).
JUNIOR COLLEGE: Bakersfield (Calif.) College.
COLLEGE: Fresno State.
TRANSACTIONS/CAREER NOTES: Selected by Cincinnati Bengals in fifth round (139th pick overall) of 1995 NFL draft. ... Signed by Bengals (July 31, 1995). ... Granted free agency (February 13, 1998). ... Re-signed by Bengals (April 23, 1998). ... Released by Bengals (September 9, 1998). ... Signed by Pittsburgh Steelers (October 14, 1998). ... Released by Steelers (August 30, 1999). ... Signed by Cleveland Browns (September 28, 1999). ... Released by Browns (November 9, 1999). ... Signed by Oakland Raiders (February 29, 2000).
HONORS: Named kick returner on THE SPORTING NEWS college All-America second team (1994).
PRO STATISTICS: 1995—Rushed once for minus 13 yards. 1997—Recovered one fumble. 1999—Recovered one fumble.
SINGLE GAME HIGHS (regular season): Receptions—7 (December 15, 1996, vs. Houston); yards—95 (December 15, 1996, vs. Houston); and touchdown receptions—1 (December 14, 1997, vs. Dallas).

				RECEIVING				PUNT RETURNS				KICKOFF RETURNS				TOTALS		
Year Team	G	GS	No.	Yds.	Avg.	TD	No.	Yds.	Avg.	TD	No.	Yds.	Avg.	TD	TD	2pt.	Pts.	Fum.
1995—Cincinnati NFL............	16	0	17	209	12.3	1	0	0	0.0	0	50	1092	21.8	0	1	0	6	2
1996—Cincinnati NFL............	16	0	32	509	15.9	1	7	54	7.7	0	35	782	22.3	▲1	3	0	18	1
1997—Cincinnati NFL............	14	5	27	414	15.3	2	0	0	0.0	0	19	487	25.6	0	2	0	12	1
1998—Cincinnati NFL............	1	0	0	0	0.0	0	0	0	0.0	0	0	0	0.0	0	0	0	0	0
—Pittsburgh NFL............	10	0	9	87	9.7	0	0	0	0.0	0	21	525	25.0	0	0	0	0	1
1999—Cleveland NFL	6	0	1	4	4.0	0	4	25	6.3	0	9	180	20.0	0	0	0	0	3
Pro totals (5 years)	63	5	86	1223	14.2	4	11	79	7.2	0	134	3066	22.9	1	6	0	36	8

DUNN, WARRICK   RB   BUCCANEERS

PERSONAL: Born January 5, 1975, in Baton Rouge, La. ... 5-8/180. ... Full name: Warrick De'Mon Dunn.
HIGH SCHOOL: Catholic (Baton Rouge, La.).
COLLEGE: Florida State (degree in information studies, 1997).
TRANSACTIONS/CAREER NOTES: Selected by Tampa Bay Buccaneers in first round (12th pick overall) of 1997 NFL draft. ... Signed by Buccaneers (July 24, 1997).
CHAMPIONSHIP GAME EXPERIENCE: Played in NFC championship game (1999 season).
HONORS: Named NFL Rookie of the Year by THE SPORTING NEWS (1997). ... Played in Pro Bowl (1997 season).
PRO STATISTICS: 1997—Returned five punts for 48 yards and recovered four fumbles. 1998—Recovered one fumble. 1999—Recovered one fumble.
SINGLE GAME HIGHS (regular season): Attempts—24 (September 19, 1999, vs. Philadelphia); yards—130 (September 7, 1997, vs. Detroit); and rushing touchdowns—1 (November 1, 1998, vs. Minnesota).
STATISTICAL PLATEAUS: 100-yard rushing games: 1997 (5), 1998 (2). Total: 7. ... 100-yard receiving games: 1997 (1), 1999 (1). Total: 2.

			RUSHING				RECEIVING				KICKOFF RETURNS				TOTALS		
Year Team	G	GS	Att.	Yds.	Avg.	TD	No.	Yds.	Avg.	TD	No.	Yds.	Avg.	TD	TD	2pt.	Pts.	Fum.
1997—Tampa Bay NFL..........	16	10	224	978	4.4	4	39	462	11.8	3	6	129	21.5	0	7	0	42	4
1998—Tampa Bay NFL..........	16	14	245	1026	4.2	2	44	344	7.8	0	1	25	25.0	0	2	0	12	1
1999—Tampa Bay NFL..........	15	15	195	616	3.2	0	64	589	9.2	2	8	156	19.5	0	2	0	12	3
Pro totals (3 years)	47	39	664	2620	3.9	6	147	1395	9.5	5	15	310	20.7	0	11	0	66	8

DWIGHT, TIM   WR/KR   FALCONS

PERSONAL: Born July 13, 1975, in Iowa City, Iowa. ... 5-8/180.
HIGH SCHOOL: Iowa City (Iowa) High.
COLLEGE: Iowa.
TRANSACTIONS/CAREER NOTES: Selected by Atlanta Falcons in fourth round (114th pick overall) of 1998 NFL draft. ... Signed by Falcons (June 25, 1998).
CHAMPIONSHIP GAME EXPERIENCE: Played in NFC championship game (1998 season). ... Played in Super Bowl XXXIII (1998 season).
HONORS: Named kick returner on THE SPORTING NEWS college All-America second team (1996). ... Named kick returner on THE SPORTING NEWS college All-America first team (1997).
POST SEASON RECORDS: Holds Super Bowl career record for highest kickoff return average (minimum four returns)—42.0. ... Shares Super Bowl single-game record for most touchdowns by kickoff return—1 (January 31, 1999, vs. Denver).
PRO STATISTICS: 1998—Attempted two passes with one completion for 22 yards and fumbled three times. 1999—Fumbled twice.

SINGLE GAME HIGHS (regular season): Receptions—7 (January 3, 2000, vs. San Francisco); yards—162 (January 3, 2000, vs. San Francisco); and touchdown receptions—2 (January 3, 2000, vs. San Francisco).
STATISTICAL PLATEAUS: 100-yard receiving games: 1999 (2).

			RUSHING				RECEIVING				PUNT RETURNS				KICKOFF RETURNS				TOTALS	
Year Team	G	GS	Att.	Yds.	Avg.	TD	No.	Yds.	Avg.	TD	No.	Yds.	Avg.	TD	No.	Yds.	Avg.	TD	TD	2pt. Pts.
1998—Atlanta NFL........	12	0	8	19	2.4	0	4	94	23.5	1	31	263	8.5	0	36	973	27.0	1	2	0 12
1999—Atlanta NFL........	12	8	5	28	5.6	1	32	669	*20.9	7	20	220	11.0	∞1	44	944	21.5	0	9	0 54
Pro totals (2 years)	24	8	13	47	3.6	1	36	763	21.2	8	51	483	9.5	1	80	1917	24.0	1	11	0 66

DYSON, KEVIN — WR — TITANS

PERSONAL: Born June 23, 1975, in Logan, Utah ... 6-1/201.
HIGH SCHOOL: Clearfield (Utah).
COLLEGE: Utah.
TRANSACTIONS/CAREER NOTES: Selected by Tennessee Oilers in first round (16th pick overall) of 1998 NFL draft. ... Signed by Oilers (July 24, 1998). ... Oilers franchise renamed Tennessee Titans for 1999 season (December 26, 1998).
CHAMPIONSHIP GAME EXPERIENCE: Played in AFC championship game (1999 season). ... Played in Super Bowl XXXIV (1999 season).
PRO STATISTICS: 1998—Rushed once for four yards. 1999—Rushed once for three yards.
SINGLE GAME HIGHS (regular season): Receptions—9 (September 12, 1999, vs. Cincinnati); yards—162 (September 12, 1999, vs. Cincinnati); and touchdown receptions—2 (September 12, 1999, vs. Cincinnati).
STATISTICAL PLATEAUS: 100-yard receiving games: 1999 (1).

			RECEIVING				TOTALS			
Year Team	G	GS	No.	Yds.	Avg.	TD	TD	2pt.	Pts.	Fum.
1998—Tennessee NFL	13	9	21	263	12.5	2	2	0	12	0
1999—Tennessee NFL	16	16	54	658	12.2	4	4	0	24	0
Pro totals (2 years)	29	25	75	921	12.3	6	6	0	36	0

EARLY, QUINN — WR

PERSONAL: Born April 13, 1965, in West Hempstead, N.Y. ... 6-0/190. ... Full name: Quinn Remar Early.
HIGH SCHOOL: Great Neck (N.Y.).
COLLEGE: Iowa (degree in art, 1988).
TRANSACTIONS/CAREER NOTES: Selected by San Diego Chargers in third round (60th pick overall) of 1988 NFL draft. ... Signed by Chargers (July 11, 1988). ... On injured reserve with knee injury (October 21-December 13, 1989). ... On developmental squad (December 14-15, 1989). ... Activated (December 16, 1989). ... Granted unconditional free agency (February 1, 1991). ... Signed by New Orleans Saints (April 1, 1991). ... Granted unconditional free agency (February 16, 1996). ... Signed by Buffalo Bills (March 8, 1996). ... Released by Bills (February 10, 1999). ... Signed by New York Jets (August 18, 1999). ... Granted unconditional free agency (February 11, 2000).
PRO STATISTICS: 1991—Returned nine kickoffs for 168 yards.
SINGLE GAME HIGHS (regular season): Receptions—9 (November 19, 1995, vs. Minnesota); yards—150 (November 19, 1995, vs. Minnesota); and touchdown receptions—2 (November 23, 1997, vs. Tennessee).
STATISTICAL PLATEAUS: 100-yard receiving games: 1991 (1), 1994 (1), 1995 (2), 1996 (2), 1997 (2). Total: 8.

			RUSHING				RECEIVING				TOTALS			
Year Team	G	GS	Att.	Yds.	Avg.	TD	No.	Yds.	Avg.	TD	TD	2pt.	Pts.	Fum.
1988—San Diego NFL	16	10	7	63	9.0	0	29	375	12.9	4	4	0	24	1
1989—San Diego NFL	6	3	1	19	19.0	0	11	126	11.5	0	0	0	0	0
1990—San Diego NFL	14	4	0	0	0.0	0	15	238	15.9	1	1	0	6	0
1991—New Orleans NFL.............................	15	12	3	13	4.3	0	32	541	16.9	2	2	0	12	2
1992—New Orleans NFL.............................	16	16	3	-1	-0.3	0	30	566	18.9	5	5	0	30	0
1993—New Orleans NFL.............................	16	15	2	32	16.0	0	45	670	14.9	6	6	0	36	1
1994—New Orleans NFL.............................	16	13	2	10	5.0	0	82	894	10.9	4	4	0	24	0
1995—New Orleans NFL.............................	16	15	2	-3	-1.5	0	81	1087	13.4	8	8	0	48	1
1996—Buffalo NFL	16	13	3	39	13.0	0	50	798	16.0	4	4	1	26	0
1997—Buffalo NFL	16	16	0	0	0.0	0	60	853	14.2	5	5	0	30	0
1998—Buffalo NFL	16	2	0	0	0.0	0	19	217	11.4	1	1	0	6	0
1999—New York Jets NFL	16	3	0	0	0.0	0	6	83	13.8	0	0	0	0	0
Pro totals (12 years)	179	122	23	172	7.5	0	460	6448	14.0	40	40	1	242	5

EATON, CHAD — DT — PATRIOTS

PERSONAL: Born April 6, 1972, in Exeter, N.H. ... 6-5/300. ... Full name: Chad Everett Eaton.
HIGH SCHOOL: Rogers (Puyallup, Wash.).
COLLEGE: Washington State.
TRANSACTIONS/CAREER NOTES: Selected by Arizona Cardinals in seventh round (241st pick overall) of 1995 NFL draft. ... Signed by Cardinals (July 24, 1995). ... Released by Cardinals (August 14, 1995). ... Signed by New York Jets (August 15, 1995). ... Released by Jets (August 27, 1995). ... Signed by Cleveland Browns to practice squad (September 28, 1995). ... Activated (December 15, 1995); did not play. ... Browns franchise moved to Baltimore and renamed Ravens for 1996 season (March 11, 1996). ... Released by Ravens (August 19, 1996). ... Signed by New England Patriots to practice squad (August 27, 1996). ... Activated (November 28, 1996).
CHAMPIONSHIP GAME EXPERIENCE: Played in AFC championship game (1996 season). ... Played in Super Bowl XXXI (1996 season).
HONORS: Named defensive lineman on THE SPORTING NEWS college All-America second team (1994).
PRO STATISTICS: 1998—Returned one kickoff for 13 yards and recovered one fumble for two yards. 1999—Recovered three fumbles for 53 yards and one touchdown.

Year Team	G	GS	SACKS
1995—Cleveland NFL		Did not play.	
1996—New England NFL	4	0	1.0
1997—New England NFL	16	1	1.0
1998—New England NFL	15	14	6.0
1999—New England NFL	16	16	3.0
Pro totals (4 years)	51	31	11.0

EDWARDS, ANTONIO　　　DE

PERSONAL: Born March 10, 1970, in Moultrie, Ga. ... 6-3/271.
HIGH SCHOOL: Colquitt County (Moultrie, Ga.).
COLLEGE: Valdosta (Ga.) State.
TRANSACTIONS/CAREER NOTES: Selected by Seattle Seahawks in eighth round (204th pick overall) of 1993 NFL draft. ... Signed by Seahawks (July 14, 1993). ... Released by Seahawks (August 5, 1997). ... Re-signed by Seahawks (September 23, 1997). ... Released by Seahawks (October 20, 1997). ... Signed by New York Giants (December 2, 1997). ... Granted unconditional free agency (February 13, 1998). ... Signed by Atlanta Falcons (June 19, 1998). ... Granted unconditional free agency (February 12, 1999). ... Signed by Carolina Panthers (March 3, 1999). ... Released by Panthers (February 24, 2000).
CHAMPIONSHIP GAME EXPERIENCE: Played in NFC championship game (1998 season). ... Played in Super Bowl XXXIII (1998 season).
PRO STATISTICS: 1993—Credited with a safety. 1995—Recovered one fumble for 83 yards and a touchdown. 1998—Recovered one fumble for two yards and a touchdown.

Year Team	G	GS	SACKS
1993—Seattle NFL	9	0	3.0
1994—Seattle NFL	15	14	2.5
1995—Seattle NFL	13	8	5.5
1996—Seattle NFL	12	3	2.0
1997—Seattle NFL	1	0	0.0
—New York Giants NFL	3	0	0.0
1998—Atlanta NFL	15	0	1.0
1999—Carolina NFL	14	7	2.0
Pro totals (7 years)	82	32	16.0

EDWARDS, ANTUAN　　　CB　　　PACKERS

PERSONAL: Born May 26, 1977, in Starkville, Miss. ... 6-1/205. ... Full name: Antuan Minye' Edwards. ... Name pronounced AN-twan.
HIGH SCHOOL: Starkville (Miss.).
COLLEGE: Clemson.
TRANSACTIONS/CAREER NOTES: Selected by Green Bay Packers in first round (25th pick overall) of 1999 NFL draft. ... Signed by Packers (June 7, 1999).

Year Team	G	GS	INTERCEPTIONS				PUNT RETURNS				TOTALS			
			No.	Yds.	Avg.	TD	No.	Yds.	Avg.	TD	TD	2pt.	Pts.	Fum.
1999—Green Bay NFL	16	1	4	26	6.5	1	10	90	9.0	0	1	0	6	1

EDWARDS, DONNIE　　　LB　　　CHIEFS

PERSONAL: Born April 6, 1973, in San Diego ... 6-2/235. ... Full name: Donnie Lewis Edwards Jr.
HIGH SCHOOL: Chula Vista (San Diego).
COLLEGE: UCLA (degree in political science).
TRANSACTIONS/CAREER NOTES: Selected by Kansas City Chiefs in fourth round (98th pick overall) of 1996 NFL draft. ... Signed by Chiefs (July 24, 1996).
PRO STATISTICS: 1997—Recovered one fumble. 1998—Recovered one fumble. 1999—Recovered two fumbles for 79 yards and one touchdown.

Year Team	G	GS	INTERCEPTIONS				SACKS
			No.	Yds.	Avg.	TD	No.
1996—Kansas City NFL	15	1	1	22	22.0	0	0.0
1997—Kansas City NFL	16	16	2	15	7.5	0	2.5
1998—Kansas City NFL	15	15	0	0	0.0	0	6.0
1999—Kansas City NFL	16	16	5	50	10.0	1	3.0
Pro totals (4 years)	62	48	8	87	10.9	1	11.5

EDWARDS, MARC　　　FB　　　BROWNS

PERSONAL: Born November 17, 1974, in Cincinnati. ... 6-0/229. ... Full name: Marc Alexander Edwards.
HIGH SCHOOL: Norwood (Cincinnati).
COLLEGE: Notre Dame (degree in business management, 1996).
TRANSACTIONS/CAREER NOTES: Selected by San Francisco 49ers in second round (55th pick overall) of 1997 NFL draft. ... Signed by 49ers (July 23, 1997). ... On physically unable to perform list with back injury (July 17-August 10, 1998). ... Traded by 49ers to Cleveland Browns for fourth-round pick (DB Pierson Prioleau) in 1999 draft (April 18, 1999).
CHAMPIONSHIP GAME EXPERIENCE: Played in NFC championship game (1997 season).
PRO STATISTICS: 1997—Returned one kickoff for 30 yards.
SINGLE GAME HIGHS (regular season): Attempts—3 (December 27, 1998, vs. St. Louis); yards—41 (September 27, 1998, vs. Atlanta); and rushing touchdowns—1 (September 27, 1998, vs. Atlanta).

Year Team	G	GS	RUSHING				RECEIVING				TOTALS			
			Att.	Yds.	Avg.	TD	No.	Yds.	Avg.	TD	TD	2pt.	Pts.	Fum.
1997—San Francisco NFL	15	1	5	17	3.4	0	6	48	8.0	0	0	0	0	0
1998—San Francisco NFL	16	11	22	94	4.3	1	22	218	9.9	2	3	0	18	0
1999—Cleveland NFL	16	14	6	35	5.8	0	27	212	7.9	2	2	0	12	1
Pro totals (3 years)	47	26	33	146	4.4	1	55	478	8.7	4	5	0	30	1

EDWARDS, ROBERT   RB   PATRIOTS

PERSONAL: Born October 2, 1974, in Tennille, Ga. ... 5-11/218. ... Full name: Robert Lee Edwards III.
HIGH SCHOOL: Washington County (Sandersville, Ga.).
COLLEGE: Georgia.
TRANSACTIONS/CAREER NOTES: Selected by New England Patriots in first round (18th pick overall) of 1998 NFL draft. ... Signed by Patriots (July 17, 1998). ... On non-football injury list with knee injury (August 31, 1999-entire season).
PRO STATISTICS: 1998—Recovered two fumbles.
SINGLE GAME HIGHS (regular season): Attempts—28 (December 6, 1998, vs. Pittsburgh); yards—196 (December 13, 1998, vs. St. Louis); and rushing touchdowns—1 (December 20, 1998, vs. San Francisco).
STATISTICAL PLATEAUS: 100-yard rushing games: 1998 (4).

Year Team	G	GS	RUSHING				RECEIVING				TOTALS			
			Att.	Yds.	Avg.	TD	No.	Yds.	Avg.	TD	TD	2pt.	Pts.	Fum.
1998—New England NFL	16	15	291	1115	3.8	9	35	331	9.5	3	12	0	72	5
1999—New England NFL							Did not play.							
Pro totals (1 years)	16	15	291	1115	3.8	9	35	331	9.5	3	12	0	72	5

EDWARDS, TROY   WR   STEELERS

PERSONAL: Born April 7, 1977, in Shreveport, La. ... 5-9/192.
HIGH SCHOOL: Huntington (Shreveport, La.).
COLLEGE: Louisiana Tech.
TRANSACTIONS/CAREER NOTES: Selected by Pittsburgh Steelers in first round (13th pick overall) of 1999 NFL draft. ... Signed by Steelers (July 28, 1999).
HONORS: Fred Biletnikoff Award winner (1998). ... Named wide receiver on THE SPORTING NEWS college All-America second team (1998).
PRO STATISTICS: 1999—Recovered three fumbles.
SINGLE GAME HIGHS (regular season): Receptions—7 (November 28, 1999, vs. Cincinnati); yards—86 (November 28, 1999, vs. Cincinnati); and touchdown receptions—1 (December 18, 1999, vs. Kansas City).

Year Team	G	GS	RECEIVING				PUNT RETURNS				KICKOFF RETURNS				TOTALS			
			No.	Yds.	Avg.	TD	No.	Yds.	Avg.	TD	No.	Yds.	Avg.	TD	TD	2pt.	Pts.	Fum.
1999—Pittsburgh NFL	16	6	61	714	11.7	5	25	234	9.4	0	13	234	18.0	0	5	0	30	4

EKUBAN, EBENEZER   DE   COWBOYS

PERSONAL: Born May 29, 1976, in Ghana, Africa. ... 6-3/265. ... Full name: Ebenezer Ekuban Jr. ... Name pronounced ECK-you-bon.
HIGH SCHOOL: Bladensburg (Md.).
COLLEGE: North Carolina.
TRANSACTIONS/CAREER NOTES: Selected by Dallas Cowboys in first round (20th pick overall) of 1999 NFL draft. ... Signed by Cowboys (July 27, 1999).

Year Team	G	GS	SACKS
1999—Dallas NFL	16	2	2.5

ELAM, JASON   K   BRONCOS

PERSONAL: Born March 8, 1970, in Fort Walton Beach, Fla. ... 5-11/200. ... Name pronounced EE-lum.
HIGH SCHOOL: Brookwood (Snellville, Ga.).
COLLEGE: Hawaii.
TRANSACTIONS/CAREER NOTES: Selected by Denver Broncos in third round (70th pick overall) of 1993 NFL draft. ... Signed by Broncos (July 12, 1993).
CHAMPIONSHIP GAME EXPERIENCE: Played in AFC championship game (1997 and 1998 seasons). ... Member of Super Bowl championship team (1997 and 1998 seasons).
HONORS: Named kicker on THE SPORTING NEWS college All-America second team (1989 and 1991). ... Played in Pro Bowl (1995 and 1998 seasons).
RECORDS: Holds NFL career record for highest PAT percentage—99.65. ... Shares NFL career record for longest field goal—63 (October 25, 1998, vs. Jacksonville).
PRO STATISTICS: 1995—Punted once for 17 yards.

Year Team	G	KICKING						
		XPM	XPA	FGM	FGA	Lg.	50+	Pts.
1993—Denver NFL	16	§41	§42	26	35	54	4-6	119
1994—Denver NFL	16	29	29	30	37	†54	1-3	119
1995—Denver NFL	16	39	39	31	38	§56	5-7	132
1996—Denver NFL	16	§46	§46	21	28	51	1-3	109
1997—Denver NFL	15	§46	§46	26	36	53	3-5	124
1998—Denver NFL	16	§58	§58	23	27	*63	3-4	§127
1999—Denver NFL	16	29	29	29	36	*55	5-8	116
Pro totals (7 years)	111	288	289	186	237	63	22-36	846

E

ELIAS, KEITH RB

PERSONAL: Born February 3, 1972, in Lacey Township, N.J. ... 5-9/203.
HIGH SCHOOL: Lacey Township (Lanoka Harbor, N.J.).
COLLEGE: Princeton.
TRANSACTIONS/CAREER NOTES: Signed as non-drafted free agent by New York Giants (April 29, 1994). ... On injured reserve with knee injury (December 19, 1996-remainder of season). ... Granted unconditional free agency (February 14, 1997). ... Signed by Indianapolis Colts (January 12, 1998). ... Granted unconditional free agency (February 11, 2000).
SINGLE GAME HIGHS (regular season): Attempts—12 (November 21, 1999, vs. Philadelphia); yards—34 (November 21, 1999, vs. Philadelphia); and rushing touchdowns—0.

			RUSHING				RECEIVING				KICKOFF RETURNS				TOTALS			
Year Team	G	GS	Att.	Yds.	Avg.	TD	No.	Yds.	Avg.	TD	No.	Yds.	Avg.	TD	TD	2pt.	Pts.	Fum.
1994—New York Giants NFL..	2	0	2	4	2.0	0	0	0	0.0	0	0	0	0.0	0	0	0	0	0
1995—New York Giants NFL..	15	0	10	44	4.4	0	9	69	7.7	0	0	0	0.0	0	0	0	0	0
1996—New York Giants NFL..	9	0	9	24	2.7	0	8	51	6.4	0	0	0	0.0	0	0	0	0	0
1997—									Did not play.									
1998—Indianapolis NFL.........	13	0	8	24	3.0	0	1	11	11.0	0	14	317	22.6	0	0	0	0	0
1999—Indianapolis NFL.........	14	0	13	28	2.2	0	4	16	4.0	0	5	82	16.4	0	0	0	0	0
Pro totals (5 years)...............	53	0	42	124	3.0	0	22	147	6.7	0	19	399	21.0	0	0	0	0	0

ELLIOTT, JUMBO OT

PERSONAL: Born April 1, 1965, in Lake Ronkonkoma, N.Y. ... 6-7/308. ... Full name: John Elliott.
HIGH SCHOOL: Sachem (Lake Ronkonkoma, N.Y.).
COLLEGE: Michigan.
TRANSACTIONS/CAREER NOTES: Selected by New York Giants in second round (36th pick overall) of 1988 NFL draft. ... Signed by Giants (July 18, 1988). ... Granted free agency (February 1, 1991). ... Re-signed by Giants (August 22, 1991). ... Designated by Giants as franchise player (February 25, 1993). ... On injured reserve with back injury (January 7, 1994-remainder of playoffs). ... Granted unconditional free agency (February 16, 1996). ... Signed by New York Jets (February 24, 1996). ... On injured reserve with ankle injury (December 1, 1997-remainder of season). ... Announced retirement (March 6, 2000).
PLAYING EXPERIENCE: New York Giants NFL, 1988-1995; New York Jets NFL, 1996-1999. ... Games/Games started: 1988 (16/5), 1989 (13/11), 1990 (8/8), 1991 (16/16), 1992 (16/16), 1993 (11/11), 1994 (16/15), 1995 (16/16), 1996 (14/14), 1997 (13/13), 1998 (16/16), 1999 (16/15). Total: 171/156.
CHAMPIONSHIP GAME EXPERIENCE: Played in NFC championship game (1990 season). ... Member of Super Bowl championship team (1990 season). ... Played in AFC championship game (1998 season).
HONORS: Played in Pro Bowl (1993 season).
PRO STATISTICS: 1988—Recovered one fumble.

ELLIS, ED OT PATRIOTS

PERSONAL: Born October 13, 1975, in Hamden, Conn. ... 6-7/330. ... Full name: Edward Key Ellis.
HIGH SCHOOL: Hamden (Conn.).
COLLEGE: Buffalo.
TRANSACTIONS/CAREER NOTES: Selected by New England Patriots in fourth round (125th pick overall) of 1997 NFL draft. ... Signed by Patriots (June 19, 1997). ... Granted free agency (February 11, 2000). ... Assigned by Patriots to Barcelona Dragons in 2000 NFL Europe enhancement allocation program (February 18, 2000). ... Re-signed by Patriots (March 13, 2000).
PLAYING EXPERIENCE: New England NFL, 1997-1999. ... Games/Games started: 1997 (1/0), 1998 (7/0), 1999 (1/1). Total: 9/1.

ELLIS, GREG DE COWBOYS

PERSONAL: Born August 14, 1975, in Wendell. N.C. ... 6-6/286. ... Full name: Gregory Lemont Ellis.
HIGH SCHOOL: East Wake (Wendell, N.C.).
COLLEGE: North Carolina.
TRANSACTIONS/CAREER NOTES: Selected by Dallas Cowboys in first round (eighth pick overall) of 1998 NFL draft. ... Signed by Cowboys (July 13, 1998). ... On injured reserve with leg injury (December 16, 1999-remainder of season).
HONORS: Named defensive end on THE SPORTING NEWS college All-America second team (1996 and 1997).
PRO STATISTICS: 1998—Recovered one fumble for two yards. 1999—Intercepted one pass for 87 yards and a touchdown and recovered one fumble for 98 yards and a touchdown.

Year Team	G	GS	SACKS
1998—Dallas NFL...	16	16	3.0
1999—Dallas NFL...	13	13	7.5
Pro totals (2 years)..	29	29	10.5

ELLISON, JERRY RB BUCCANEERS

PERSONAL: Born December 20, 1971, in Augusta, Ga. ... 5-10/204. ... Full name: Jerry Ernest Ellison.
HIGH SCHOOL: Glenn Hills (Augusta, Ga.).
COLLEGE: Tennessee-Chattanooga.
TRANSACTIONS/CAREER NOTES: Signed as non-drafted free agent by Tampa Bay Buccaneers (May 5, 1994). ... Released by Buccaneers (August 23, 1994). ... Re-signed by Buccaneers to practice squad (September 7, 1994). ... Released by Buccaneers (September 12, 1994). ... Re-signed by Buccaneers to practice squad (September 27, 1994). ... Granted free agency (February 13, 1998). ... Re-signed by Buccaneers (June 11, 1998). ... Granted unconditional free agency (February 12, 1999). ... Signed by New England Patriots (September 29, 1999). ... Granted unconditional free agency (February 11, 2000). ... Signed by Buccaneers (February 22, 2000).

E

PRO STATISTICS: 1995—Recovered one fumble. 1996—Recovered one fumble. 1997—Recovered one fumble. 1998—Recovered two fumbles.

SINGLE GAME HIGHS (regular season): Attempts—8 (September 8, 1996, vs. Detroit); yards—91 (December 23, 1995, vs. Detroit); and rushing touchdowns—2 (November 12, 1995, vs. Detroit).

			RUSHING				RECEIVING				KICKOFF RETURNS				TOTALS		
Year Team	G	GS	Att.	Yds.	Avg.	TD	No.	Yds.	Avg.	TD	No.	Yds.	Avg.	TD	TD	2pt.	Pts. Fum.
1994—Tampa Bay NFL								Did not play.									
1995—Tampa Bay NFL	16	3	26	218	8.4	5	7	44	6.3	0	15	261	17.4	0	5	0	30	0
1996—Tampa Bay NFL	16	2	35	106	3.0	0	18	208	11.6	0	0	0	0.0	0	0	0	0	2
1997—Tampa Bay NFL	16	0	2	10	5.0	0	1	8	8.0	0	2	61	30.5	0	0	0	0	0
1998—Tampa Bay NFL	16	0	9	24	2.7	0	0	0	0.0	0	1	19	19.0	0	0	0	0	0
1999—New England NFL	12	0	2	10	5.0	0	4	50	12.5	0	1	13	13.0	0	0	0	0	0
Pro totals (5 years)	76	5	74	368	5.0	5	30	310	10.3	0	19	354	18.6	0	5	0	30	2

ELLISS, LUTHER   DT   LIONS

PERSONAL: Born March 22, 1973, in Mancos, Colo. ... 6-5/305.
HIGH SCHOOL: Mancos (Colo.).
COLLEGE: Utah.
TRANSACTIONS/CAREER NOTES: Selected by Detroit Lions in first round (20th pick overall) of 1995 NFL draft. ... Signed by Lions (July 19, 1995).
HONORS: Named defensive lineman on THE SPORTING NEWS college All-America first team (1994). ... Played in Pro Bowl (1999 season).
PRO STATISTICS: 1997—Recovered two fumbles. 1998—Recovered one fumble. 1999—Recovered two fumbles for 11 yards and one touchdown.

Year Team	G	GS	SACKS
1995—Detroit NFL	16	16	0.0
1996—Detroit NFL	14	14	6.5
1997—Detroit NFL	16	16	8.5
1998—Detroit NFL	16	16	3.0
1999—Detroit NFL	15	14	3.5
Pro totals (5 years)	77	76	21.5

ELLSWORTH, PERCY   S   BROWNS

PERSONAL: Born October 19, 1974, in Drewryville, Va. ... 6-2/225.
HIGH SCHOOL: Southampton (Courtland, Va.).
COLLEGE: Virginia.
TRANSACTIONS/CAREER NOTES: Signed as non-drafted free agent by New York Giants (April 27, 1996). ... Granted free agency (February 12, 1999). ... Re-signed by Giants (July 19, 1999). ... Granted unconditional free agency (February 11, 2000). ... Signed by Cleveland Browns (February 18, 2000).
PRO STATISTICS: 1996—Recovered one fumble. 1997—Recovered two fumbles for 24 yards. 1999—Recovered one fumble for 15 yards.

			INTERCEPTIONS			
Year Team	G	GS	No.	Yds.	Avg.	TD
1996—New York Giants NFL	14	4	3	62	20.7	0
1997—New York Giants NFL	16	1	4	40	10.0	0
1998—New York Giants NFL	16	9	5	92	18.4	2
1999—New York Giants NFL	14	14	6	80	13.3	0
Pro totals (4 years)	60	28	18	274	15.2	2

ELOMS, JOEY   CB   SEAHAWKS

PERSONAL: Born April 4, 1976, in Fort Wayne, Ind. ... 5-10/183. ... Name pronounced ELL-ums.
HIGH SCHOOL: Concordia Lutheran (Fort Wayne, Ind.).
COLLEGE: Indiana.
TRANSACTIONS/CAREER NOTES: Signed as non-drafted free agent by Seattle Seahawks (April 28, 1998). ... Released by Seahawks (August 30, 1998). ... Re-signed by Seahawks to practice squad (August 31, 1998). ... Released by Seahawks (September 9, 1998). ... Re-signed by Seahawks to practice squad (September 22, 1998). ... Activated (November 28, 1998). ... Assigned by Seahawks to Scottish Claymores in 1999 NFL Europe enhancement allocation program (February 22, 1999). ... Released by Seahawks (September 5, 1999). ... Signed by Pittsburgh Steelers to practice squad (November 17, 1999). ... Signed by Seahawks off Steelers practice squad (December 7, 1999).
PLAYING EXPERIENCE: Seattle NFL, 1998 and 1999; Scottish NFLE, 1999. ... Games/Games started: 1998 (1/0), NFLE 1999 (games played unavailable); NFL 1999 (4/0). Total NFL: 5/0.
PRO STATISTICS: NFLE: 1999—Intercepted three passes for 98 yards and one touchdown and returned five punts for 23 yards.

EMANUEL, BERT   WR   DOLPHINS

PERSONAL: Born October 28, 1970, in Kansas City, Mo. ... 5-10/175. ... Full name: Bert Tyrone Emanuel.
HIGH SCHOOL: Langham Creek (Houston).
COLLEGE: UCLA, then Rice (degree in business, 1993).
TRANSACTIONS/CAREER NOTES: Selected by Atlanta Falcons in second round (45th pick overall) of 1994 NFL draft. ... Signed by Falcons (July 11, 1994). ... Granted free agency (February 14, 1997). ... Re-signed by Falcons (July 16, 1997). ... Designated by Falcons as transition player (February 13, 1998). ... Tendered offer sheet by Tampa Bay Buccaneers (April 10, 1998). ... Falcons declined to match offer (April 14, 1998). ... Released by Buccaneers (April 12, 2000). ... Signed by Miami Dolphins (May 2, 2000).
CHAMPIONSHIP GAME EXPERIENCE: Played in NFC championship game (1999 season).
PRO STATISTICS: 1994—Rushed twice for four yards and had only pass attempt intercepted. 1995—Rushed once for no yards. 1997—Recovered two fumbles. 1998—Rushed once for 11 yards.

SINGLE GAME HIGHS (regular season): Receptions—9 (December 15, 1996, vs. St. Louis); yards—173 (December 15, 1996, vs. St. Louis); and touchdown receptions—2 (November 2, 1997, vs. St. Louis).
STATISTICAL PLATEAUS: 100-yard receiving games: 1994 (1), 1995 (4), 1996 (3), 1997 (1), 1998 (1). Total: 10.
MISCELLANEOUS: Selected by Toronto Blue Jays organization in 75th round of free-agent baseball draft (June 5, 1989); did not sign. ... Selected by Pittsburgh Pirates organization in 49th round of free-agent baseball draft (June 1, 1992); did not sign.

| | | | | RECEIVING | | | TOTALS | | | |
Year Team	G	GS	No.	Yds.	Avg.	TD	TD	2pt.	Pts.	Fum.
1994—Atlanta NFL	16	16	46	649	14.1	4	4	0	24	0
1995—Atlanta NFL	16	16	74	1039	14.0	5	5	0	30	2
1996—Atlanta NFL	14	13	75	921	12.3	6	6	0	36	0
1997—Atlanta NFL	16	16	65	991	15.2	9	9	0	54	2
1998—Tampa Bay NFL	11	11	41	636	15.5	2	2	0	12	0
1999—Tampa Bay NFL	11	10	22	238	10.8	1	1	0	6	0
Pro totals (6 years)	84	82	323	4474	13.9	27	27	0	162	4

EMMONS, CARLOS   LB   EAGLES

PERSONAL: Born September 3, 1973, in Greenwood, Miss. ... 6-5/250. ... Name pronounced EM-mins.
HIGH SCHOOL: Greenwood (Miss.).
COLLEGE: Arkansas State (degree in business management, 1995).
TRANSACTIONS/CAREER NOTES: Selected by Pittsburgh Steelers in seventh round (242nd pick overall) of 1996 NFL draft. ... Signed by Steelers (July 16, 1996). ... Granted free agency (February 12, 1999). ... Re-signed by Steelers (April 23, 1999). ... Granted unconditional free agency (February 11, 2000). ... Signed by Philadelphia Eagles (March 23, 2000).
CHAMPIONSHIP GAME EXPERIENCE: Played in AFC championship game (1997 season).
PRO STATISTICS: 1996—Recovered one fumble. 1998—Intercepted one pass for two yards and recovered one fumble. 1999—Intercepted one pass for 22 yards and recovered three fumbles for two yards.

Year Team	G	GS	SACKS
1996—Pittsburgh NFL	15	0	2.5
1997—Pittsburgh NFL	5	0	0.0
1998—Pittsburgh NFL	15	13	3.5
1999—Pittsburgh NFL	16	16	6.0
Pro totals (4 years)	51	29	12.0

ENGEL, GREG   C

PERSONAL: Born January 18, 1971, in Davenport, Iowa. ... 6-3/285. ... Full name: Gregory Allen Engel.
HIGH SCHOOL: Bloomington (Ill.).
COLLEGE: Illinois.
TRANSACTIONS/CAREER NOTES: Signed as non-drafted free agent by San Diego Chargers (April 28, 1994). ... Inactive for all 16 games (1994). ... Granted free agency (February 14, 1997). ... Signed by Chargers prior to 1997 season. ... Granted unconditional free agency (February 13, 1998). ... Re-signed by Chargers (February 13, 1998). ... Released by Chargers (July 23, 1998). ... Signed by Oakland Raiders (July 1998). ... Released by Raiders (August 25, 1998). ... Signed by Detroit Lions (August 10, 1999). ... Released by Lions (October 8, 1999).
PLAYING EXPERIENCE: San Diego NFL, 1995-1997; Detroit NFL, 1999. ... Games/Games started: 1995 (10/0), 1996 (12/9), 1997 (9/0), 1999 (1/0). Total: 32/9.
PRO STATISTICS: 1995—Ran one yard with lateral from kickoff return.

ENGLER, DEREK   C   GIANTS

PERSONAL: Born July 11, 1974, in St. Paul, Minn. ... 6-5/300.
HIGH SCHOOL: Cretin-Derham Hall (St. Paul, Minn.).
COLLEGE: Wisconsin.
TRANSACTIONS/CAREER NOTES: Signed as non-drafted free agent by New York Giants (April 28, 1997). ... Granted free agency (February 11, 2000). ... Re-signed by Giants (April 10, 2000).
PLAYING EXPERIENCE: New York Giants NFL, 1997-1999. ... Games/Games started: 1997 (5/5), 1998 (11/0), 1999 (10/4). Total: 26/9.
PRO STATISTICS: 1997—Fumbled once for minus two yards.

ENGRAM, BOBBY   WR   BEARS

PERSONAL: Born January 7, 1973, in Camden, S.C. ... 5-10/192. ... Full name: Simon Engram III.
HIGH SCHOOL: Camden (S.C.).
COLLEGE: Penn State.
TRANSACTIONS/CAREER NOTES: Selected by Chicago Bears in second round (52nd pick overall) of 1996 NFL draft. ... Signed by Bears (July 17, 1996). ... Granted free agency (February 12, 1999). ... Re-signed by Bears (April 16, 1999). ... Granted unconditional free agency (February 11, 2000). ... Re-signed by Bears (April 26, 2000).
HONORS: Named wide receiver on THE SPORTING NEWS college All-America second team (1994 and 1995).
PRO STATISTICS: 1997—Recovered one fumble. 1998—Rushed once for three yards. 1999—Rushed twice for 11 yards and recovered two fumbles.
SINGLE GAME HIGHS (regular season): Receptions—13 (December 26, 1999, vs. St. Louis); yards—143 (December 26, 1999, vs. St. Louis); and touchdown receptions—2 (December 26, 1999, vs. St. Louis).
STATISTICAL PLATEAUS: 100-yard receiving games: 1998 (3), 1999 (2). Total: 5.

| | | | RECEIVING | | | | PUNT RETURNS | | | | KICKOFF RETURNS | | | | TOTALS | | |
Year Team	G	GS	No.	Yds.	Avg.	TD	No.	Yds.	Avg.	TD	No.	Yds.	Avg.	TD	TD	2pt.	Pts.	Fum.
1996—Chicago NFL	16	2	33	389	11.8	6	31	282	9.1	0	25	580	23.2	0	6	0	36	2
1997—Chicago NFL	11	11	45	399	8.9	2	1	4	4.0	0	2	27	13.5	0	2	1	14	1

E

1998—Chicago NFL................	16	16	64	987	15.4	5	0	0	0.0	0	0	0	0.0	0	5	0	30	1
1999—Chicago NFL................	16	14	88	947	10.8	4	0	0	0.0	0	0	0	0.0	0	4	0	24	2
Pro totals (4 years)...............	59	43	230	2722	11.8	17	32	286	8.9	0	27	607	22.5	0	17	1	104	6

ENIS, CURTIS　　　　　　RB　　　　　　BEARS

PERSONAL: Born June 15, 1976, in Union City, Ohio. ... 6-0/240. ... Full name: Curtis D. Enis.
HIGH SCHOOL: Mississinawa Valley (Union City, Ohio), then Kiski Prep (Saltsburg, Pa.).
COLLEGE: Penn State.
TRANSACTIONS/CAREER NOTES: Selected after junior season by Chicago Bears in first round (fifth pick overall) of 1998 NFL draft. ... Signed by Bears (August 18, 1998). ... On injured reserve with knee injury (November 11, 1998-remainder of season). ... On injured reserve with shoulder and elbow injuries (December 31, 1999-remainder of season).
HONORS: Named running back on THE SPORTING NEWS college All-America second team (1997).
PRO STATISTICS: 1999—Recovered two fumbles.
SINGLE GAME HIGHS (regular season): Attempts—27 (October 10, 1999, vs. Minnesota); yards—94 (September 19, 1999, vs. Seattle); and rushing touchdowns—1 (December 5, 1999, vs. Green Bay).

			RUSHING				RECEIVING				TOTALS			
Year Team	G	GS	Att.	Yds.	Avg.	TD	No.	Yds.	Avg.	TD	TD	2pt.	Pts.	Fum.
1998—Chicago NFL	9	1	133	497	3.7	0	6	20	3.3	0	0	0	0	1
1999—Chicago NFL	15	12	287	916	3.2	3	45	340	7.6	2	5	0	30	4
Pro totals (2 years)..	24	13	420	1413	3.4	3	51	360	7.1	2	5	0	30	5

EVANS, CHUCK　　　　　　FB　　　　　　RAVENS

PERSONAL: Born April 16, 1967, in Augusta, Ga. ... 6-1/245. ... Full name: Charles Evans Jr.
HIGH SCHOOL: Glenn Hills (Augusta, Ga.).
COLLEGE: Clark Atlanta University.
TRANSACTIONS/CAREER NOTES: Selected by Minnesota Vikings in 11th round (295th pick overall) of 1992 NFL draft. ... Signed by Vikings (June 10, 1992). ... Released by Vikings (August 31, 1992). ... Re-signed by Vikings (February 10, 1993). ... On injured reserve with wrist injury (October 11, 1993-remainder of season). ... Granted free agency (February 16, 1996). ... Re-signed by Vikings (May 9, 1996). ... Granted unconditional free agency (February 14, 1997). ... Re-signed by Vikings (April 11, 1997). ... Granted unconditional free agency (February 12, 1999). ... Signed by Baltimore Ravens (February 17, 1999).
CHAMPIONSHIP GAME EXPERIENCE: Played in NFC championship game (1998 season).
PRO STATISTICS: 1993—Returned one kickoff for 11 yards. 1994—Returned one kickoff for four yards. 1997—Recovered one fumble. 1999—Recovered one fumble.
SINGLE GAME HIGHS (regular season): Attempts—10 (December 9, 1995, vs. Cleveland); yards—50 (November 9, 1997, vs. Chicago); and rushing touchdowns—1 (December 20, 1998, vs. Jacksonville).

			RUSHING				RECEIVING				TOTALS			
Year Team	G	GS	Att.	Yds.	Avg.	TD	No.	Yds.	Avg.	TD	TD	2pt.	Pts.	Fum.
1993—Minnesota NFL	3	0	14	32	2.3	0	4	39	9.8	0	0	0	0	0
1994—Minnesota NFL	14	0	6	20	3.3	0	1	2	2.0	0	0	0	0	0
1995—Minnesota NFL	16	7	19	59	3.1	1	18	119	6.6	1	2	0	12	0
1996—Minnesota NFL	16	6	13	29	2.2	0	22	135	6.1	0	0	0	0	0
1997—Minnesota NFL	16	13	43	157	3.7	2	21	152	7.2	0	2	1	14	0
1998—Minnesota NFL	16	8	23	67	2.9	1	12	84	7.0	0	1	0	6	0
1999—Baltimore NFL	16	10	38	134	3.5	0	32	235	7.3	1	1	†1	8	0
Pro totals (7 years)..	97	44	156	498	3.2	4	110	766	7.0	2	6	2	40	0

EVANS, DOUG　　　　　　CB　　　　　　PANTHERS

PERSONAL: Born May 13, 1970, in Shreveport, La. ... 6-1/190. ... Full name: Douglas Edwards Evans. ... Brother of Bobby Evans, safety with Winnipeg Blue Bombers of the CFL (1990-94).
HIGH SCHOOL: Haynesville (La.).
COLLEGE: Louisiana Tech (degree in finance).
TRANSACTIONS/CAREER NOTES: Selected by Green Bay Packers in sixth round (141st pick overall) of 1993 NFL draft. ... Signed by Packers (July 9, 1993). ... Granted unconditional free agency (February 13, 1998). ... Signed by Carolina Panthers (February 18, 1998). ... On injured reserve with broken collarbone (November 10, 1998-remainder of season).
CHAMPIONSHIP GAME EXPERIENCE: Played in NFC championship game (1995-1997 seasons). ... Member of Super Bowl championship team (1996 season). ... Played in Super Bowl XXXII (1997 season).
PRO STATISTICS: 1993—Recovered two fumbles. 1994—Recovered one fumble for three yards. 1995—Returned one punt for no yards and fumbled once. 1996—Fumbled once and recovered one fumble for two yards.

			INTERCEPTIONS				SACKS
Year Team	G	GS	No.	Yds.	Avg.	TD	No.
1993—Green Bay NFL	16	0	1	0	0.0	0	0.0
1994—Green Bay NFL	16	15	1	0	0.0	0	1.0
1995—Green Bay NFL	16	16	2	24	12.0	0	1.0
1996—Green Bay NFL	16	16	5	102	20.4	1	3.0
1997—Green Bay NFL	15	15	3	33	11.0	0	1.0
1998—Carolina NFL	9	7	2	18	9.0	0	0.0
1999—Carolina NFL	16	16	2	1	0.5	0	0.0
Pro totals (7 years)..	104	85	16	178	11.1	1	6.0

E

EVANS, JOSH   DT/DE   TITANS

PERSONAL: Born September 6, 1972, in Langdale, Ala. ... 6-2/288. ... Full name: Mijoshki Antwon Evans.
HIGH SCHOOL: Lanett (Ala.).
COLLEGE: Alabama-Birmingham.
TRANSACTIONS/CAREER NOTES: Signed as non-drafted free agent by Dallas Cowboys (April 27, 1995). ... Released by Cowboys (August 22, 1995). ... Signed by Houston Oilers to practice squad (September 1, 1995). ... Activated (November 10, 1995). ... On injured reserve with knee injury (November 29, 1996-remainder of season). ... Oilers franchise moved to Tennessee for 1997 season. ... Granted free agency (February 13, 1998). ... Re-signed by Oilers (July 25, 1998). ... Oilers franchise renamed Tennessee Titans for 1999 season (December 26, 1998). ... On suspended list for violating league substance abuse policy (September 6-October 4, 1999). ... On suspended list for violating league substance abuse policy (March 1, 2000-present).
CHAMPIONSHIP GAME EXPERIENCE: Played in AFC championship game (1999 season). ... Played in Super Bowl XXXIV (1999 season).
PRO STATISTICS: 1997—Recovered one fumble. 1999—Recovered two fumbles.

Year Team	G	GS	SACKS
1995—Houston NFL	7	0	0.0
1996—Houston NFL	8	0	0.0
1997—Tennessee NFL	15	0	2.0
1998—Tennessee NFL	14	11	3.5
1999—Tennessee NFL	11	10	3.5
Pro totals (5 years)	55	21	9.0

EVANS, LEOMONT   S

PERSONAL: Born July 12, 1974, in Abbeville, S.C. ... 6-1/202.
HIGH SCHOOL: Abbeville (S.C.).
COLLEGE: Clemson.
TRANSACTIONS/CAREER NOTES: Selected by Washington Redskins in fifth round (138th pick overall) of 1996 NFL draft. ... Signed by Redskins (June 4, 1996). ... Granted free agency (February 12, 1999). ... Re-signed by Redskins (February 25, 1999). ... Granted unconditional free agency (February 11, 2000).
PLAYING EXPERIENCE: Washington NFL, 1996-1999. ... Games/Games started: 1996 (12/0), 1997 (16/0), 1998 (16/13), 1999 (15/15). Total: 59/28.
PRO STATISTICS: 1997—Recovered one fumble. 1998—Intercepted three passes for 77 yards and credited with one sack. 1999—Recovered one fumble.

EVERITT, STEVE   C

PERSONAL: Born August 21, 1970, in Miami. ... 6-5/310. ... Full name: Steven Michael Everitt.
HIGH SCHOOL: Southridge (Miami).
COLLEGE: Michigan (degree in fine arts, 1993).
TRANSACTIONS/CAREER NOTES: Selected by Cleveland Browns in first round (14th pick overall) of 1993 NFL draft. ... Signed by Browns (July 15, 1993). ... Designated by Browns as transition player (February 15, 1994). ... Browns franchise moved to Baltimore and renamed Ravens for 1996 season (March 11, 1996). ... Free agency status changed by Ravens from transitional to unconditional (February 14, 1997). ... Signed by Philadelphia Eagles (March 6, 1997). ... Released by Eagles (April 25, 2000).
PLAYING EXPERIENCE: Cleveland NFL, 1993-1995; Baltimore NFL, 1996; Philadelphia NFL, 1997-1999. ... Games/Games started: 1993 (16/16), 1994 (15/15), 1995 (15/14), 1996 (8/7), 1997 (16/16), 1998 (13/13), 1999 (16/16). Total: 99/97.
HONORS: Named center on The Sporting News college All-America second team (1992).
PRO STATISTICS: 1993—Recovered two fumbles. 1995—Recovered one fumble. 1997—Recovered one fumble. 1999—Recovered one fumble.

FABINI, JASON   OT   JETS

PERSONAL: Born August 25, 1974, in Fort Wayne, Ind. ... 6-7/312.
HIGH SCHOOL: Bishop Dwenger (Fort Wayne, Ind.).
COLLEGE: Cincinnati.
TRANSACTIONS/CAREER NOTES: Selected by New York Jets in fourth round (111th pick overall) of 1998 NFL draft. ... Signed by Jets (July 13, 1998). ... On injured reserve with knee injury (November 16, 1999-remainder of season).
PLAYING EXPERIENCE: New York Jets NFL, 1998 and 1999. ... Games/Games started: 1998 (16/16), 1999 (9/9). Total: 25/25.
CHAMPIONSHIP GAME EXPERIENCE: Played in AFC championship game (1998 season).

FAIR, TERRY   CB   LIONS

PERSONAL: Born July 20, 1976, in Phoenix. ... 5-9/183. ... Full name: Terrance Delon Fair.
HIGH SCHOOL: South Mountain (Phoenix).
COLLEGE: Tennessee.
TRANSACTIONS/CAREER NOTES: Selected by Detroit Lions in first round (20th pick overall) of 1998 NFL draft. ... Signed by Lions (July 20, 1998). ... On non-football injury list with hand injury (December 14, 1999-remainder of season).
HONORS: Named kick returner on The Sporting News NFL All-Pro team (1998).
PRO STATISTICS: 1998—Credited with one sack and recovered one fumble. 1999—Recovered one fumble for 35 yards and a touchdown.

			INTERCEPTIONS			PUNT RETURNS				KICKOFF RETURNS				TOTALS			
Year Team	G	GS	No.	Yds.	Avg.	TD	No.	Yds.	Avg.	TD	No.	Yds.	Avg.	TD	TD	2pt.	Pts. Fum.
1998—Detroit NFL	14	10	0	0	0.0	0	30	189	6.3	0	51	1428	*28.0	†2	2	0	12 5
1999—Detroit NFL	11	11	3	49	16.3	1	11	97	8.8	0	34	752	22.1	0	2	0	12 2
Pro totals (2 years)	25	21	3	49	16.3	1	41	286	7.0	0	85	2180	25.6	2	4	0	24 7

FANECA, ALAN G STEELERS

PERSONAL: Born December 7, 1976, in New Orleans. ... 6-4/315. ... Full name: Alan Joseph Faneca Jr.
HIGH SCHOOL: John Curtis Christian (New Orleans), then Lamar (Houston).
COLLEGE: Louisiana State.
TRANSACTIONS/CAREER NOTES: Selected after junior season by Pittsburgh Steelers in first round (26th pick overall) of 1998 NFL draft. ... Signed by Steelers (July 29, 1998).
PLAYING EXPERIENCE: Pittsburgh NFL, 1998 and 1999. ... Games/Games started: 1998 (16/12), 1999 (15/14). Total: 31/26.
HONORS: Named guard on THE SPORTING NEWS college All-America first team (1997).

FANN, CHAD TE VIKINGS

PERSONAL: Born June 7, 1970, in Jacksonville. ... 6-3/250. ... Full name: Chad Fitzgerald Fann.
HIGH SCHOOL: Jean Ribault (Jacksonville).
COLLEGE: Mississippi, then Florida A&M.
TRANSACTIONS/CAREER NOTES: Signed as non-drafted free agent by Phoenix Cardinals (April 28, 1993). ... Released by Cardinals (August 23, 1993). ... Re-signed by Cardinals to practice squad (October 24, 1993). ... Activated (November 4, 1993). ... Cardinals franchise renamed Arizona Cardinals for 1994 season. ... Granted free agency (February 16, 1996). ... Signed by San Francisco 49ers (June 11, 1996). ... Released by 49ers (August 21, 1996). ... Re-signed by 49ers (January 29, 1997). ... Granted unconditional free agency (February 13, 1998). ... Re-signed by 49ers (June 1, 1998). ... Granted unconditional free agency (February 12, 1999). ... Re-signed by 49ers (March 2, 1999). ... Released by 49ers (February 7, 2000). ... Signed by Minnesota Vikings (March 31, 2000).
CHAMPIONSHIP GAME EXPERIENCE: Played in NFC championship game (1997 season).
PRO STATISTICS: 1997—Returned one kickoff for no yards. 1999—Recovered one fumble.
SINGLE GAME HIGHS (regular season): Receptions—6 (November 27, 1994, vs. Chicago); yards—50 (December 21, 1997, vs. Seattle); and touchdown receptions—0.

				RECEIVING				TOTALS			
Year Team	G	GS	No.	Yds.	Avg.	TD	TD	2pt.	Pts.	Fum.
1993—Phoenix NFL	1	0	0	0	0.0	0	0	0	0	0
1994—Arizona NFL	16	9	12	96	8.0	0	0	0	0	1
1995—Arizona NFL	16	3	5	41	8.2	0	0	0	0	1
1996—					Did not play.					
1997—San Francisco NFL	11	0	5	78	15.6	0	0	0	0	0
1998—San Francisco NFL	12	0	0	0	0.0	0	0	0	0	0
1999—San Francisco NFL	16	3	2	8	4.0	0	0	0	0	1
Pro totals (6 years)	72	15	24	223	9.3	0	0	0	0	3

FARMER, ROBERT RB JETS

PERSONAL: Born March 4, 1974, in Lincoln, Neb. ... 5-11/217.
HIGH SCHOOL: Bolingbrook (Ill.).
COLLEGE: Notre Dame.
TRANSACTIONS/CAREER NOTES: Signed as non-drafted free agent by New York Jets (April 25, 1997). ... Released by Jets (August 24, 1997). ... Re-signed by Jets to practice squad (August 26, 1997). ... Activated (December 23, 1997); did not play. ... Released by Jets (August 30, 1998). ... Re-signed by Jets to practice squad (August 31, 1998). ... Released by Jets (September 5, 1999). ... Re-signed by Jets (September 14, 1999).
PLAYING EXPERIENCE: New York Jets NFL, 1999. ... Games/Games started: 1999 (13/0).
PRO STATISTICS: 1999—Returned four kickoffs for 84 yards, fumbled once and recovered one fumble.

FARR, D'MARCO DT RAMS

PERSONAL: Born June 9, 1971, in San Pablo, Calif. ... 6-1/280. ... Full name: D'Marco Marcellus Farr. ... Cousin of Mel Farr Sr., running back with Detroit Lions (1967-73); cousin of Mel Farr Jr., running back with Los Angeles Rams (1989) and Sacramento Surge of World League (1991); and cousin of Mike Farr, wide receiver with Detroit Lions (1990-92).
HIGH SCHOOL: John F. Kennedy (Richmond, Calif.).
COLLEGE: Washington (degree in society and justice, 1993).
TRANSACTIONS/CAREER NOTES: Signed as non-drafted free agent by Los Angeles Rams (May 4, 1994). ... On injured reserve with dislocated left elbow (December 7, 1994-remainder of season). ... Rams franchise moved to St. Louis (April 12, 1995).
CHAMPIONSHIP GAME EXPERIENCE: Played in NFC championship game (1999 season). ... Member of Super Bowl championship team (1999 season).
PRO STATISTICS: 1994—Returned one kickoff for 16 yards. 1995—Intercepted one pass for five yards. 1996—Intercepted one pass for five yards. 1997—Intercepted one pass for 22 yards and recovered two fumbles. 1998—Recovered one fumble for 18 yards.

Year Team	G	GS	SACKS
1994—Los Angeles Rams NFL	10	3	1.0
1995—St. Louis NFL	16	16	11.5
1996—St. Louis NFL	16	16	4.5
1997—St. Louis NFL	16	16	3.0
1998—St. Louis NFL	16	16	7.0
1999—St. Louis NFL	16	16	8.5
Pro totals (6 years)	90	83	35.5

FARRIOR, JAMES LB JETS

PERSONAL: Born January 6, 1975, in Ettrick, Va. ... 6-2/244. ... Full name: James Alfred Farrior.
HIGH SCHOOL: Matoaca (Ettrick, Va.).

F

COLLEGE: Virginia.

TRANSACTIONS/CAREER NOTES: Selected by New York Jets in first round (eighth pick overall) of 1997 NFL draft. ... Signed by Jets (July 20, 1997).

CHAMPIONSHIP GAME EXPERIENCE: Played in AFC championship game (1998 season).

PRO STATISTICS: 1998—Recovered one fumble.

Year Team	G	GS	SACKS
1997—New York Jets NFL	16	15	1.5
1998—New York Jets NFL	12	2	0.0
1999—New York Jets NFL	16	4	2.0
Pro totals (3 years)	44	21	3.5

FAULK, KEVIN · RB · PATRIOTS

PERSONAL: Born June 15, 1976, in Lafayette, La. ... 5-8/197. ... Full name: Kevin Tony Faulk.

HIGH SCHOOL: Carencro (Lafayette, La.).

COLLEGE: Louisiana State (degree in kinesiology).

TRANSACTIONS/CAREER NOTES: Selected by New England Patriots in second round (46th pick overall) of 1999 NFL draft. ... Signed by Patriots (July 28, 1999). ... On injured reserve with broken ankle (December 15, 1999-remainder of season).

HONORS: Named kick returner on THE SPORTING NEWS college All-America second team (1998).

PRO STATISTICS: 1999—Fumbled three times for minus nine yards.

SINGLE GAME HIGHS (regular season): Attempts—17 (October 31, 1999, vs. Arizona); yards—61 (November 21, 1999, vs. Miami); and rushing touchdowns—1 (October 24, 1999, vs. Denver).

			RUSHING				RECEIVING				PUNT RETURNS				KICKOFF RETURNS				TOTALS		
Year Team	G	GS	Att.	Yds.	Avg.	TD	No.	Yds.	Avg.	TD	No.	Yds.	Avg.	TD	No.	Yds.	Avg.	TD	TD	2pt.	Pts.
1999—New England NFL	11	2	67	227	3.4	1	12	98	8.2	1	10	90	9.0	0	39	943	24.2	0	2	0	12

FAULK, MARSHALL · RB · RAMS

PERSONAL: Born February 26, 1973, in New Orleans. ... 5-10/211. ... Full name: Marshall William Faulk.

HIGH SCHOOL: G. W. Carver (New Orleans).

COLLEGE: San Diego State.

TRANSACTIONS/CAREER NOTES: Selected after junior season by Indianapolis Colts in first round (second pick overall) of 1994 NFL draft. ... Signed by Colts (July 24, 1994). ... Traded by Colts to St. Louis Rams for second- (LB Mike Peterson) and fifth-round (DE Brad Scioli) picks in 1999 draft (April 15, 1999).

CHAMPIONSHIP GAME EXPERIENCE: Member of Colts for AFC championship game (1995 season); inactive due to injury. ... Played in NFC championship game (1999 season). ... Member of Super Bowl championship team (1999 season).

HONORS: Named running back on THE SPORTING NEWS college All-America first team (1991-1993). ... Named NFL Rookie of the Year by THE SPORTING NEWS (1994). ... Played in Pro Bowl (1994, 1995, 1998 and 1999 seasons). ... Named Outstanding Player of Pro Bowl (1994 season). ... Named running back on THE SPORTING NEWS NFL All-Pro team (1999).

PRO STATISTICS: 1994—Recovered one fumble. 1995—Recovered one fumble. 1997—Recovered one fumble. 1998—Recovered two fumbles for 13 yards. 1999—Attempted one pass without a completion.

SINGLE GAME HIGHS (regular season): Attempts—29 (December 12, 1999, vs. New Orleans); yards—192 (November 29, 1998, vs. Baltimore); and rushing touchdowns—3 (October 1, 1995, vs. St. Louis).

STATISTICAL PLATEAUS: 100-yard rushing games: 1994 (4), 1995 (1), 1996 (1), 1997 (4), 1998 (4), 1999 (7). Total: 21. ... 100-yard receiving games: 1994 (1), 1998 (3), 1999 (1). Total: 5.

			RUSHING				RECEIVING				TOTALS			
Year Team	G	GS	Att.	Yds.	Avg.	TD	No.	Yds.	Avg.	TD	TD	2pt.	Pts.	Fum.
1994—Indianapolis NFL	16	16	314	1282	4.1	11	52	522	10.0	1	▲12	0	72	5
1995—Indianapolis NFL	16	16	289	1078	3.7	11	56	475	8.5	3	14	0	84	8
1996—Indianapolis NFL	13	13	198	587	3.0	7	56	428	7.6	0	7	0	42	2
1997—Indianapolis NFL	16	16	264	1054	4.0	7	47	471	10.0	1	8	0	48	5
1998—Indianapolis NFL	16	15	324	1319	4.1	6	86	908	10.6	4	10	0	60	3
1999—St. Louis NFL	16	16	253	1381	*5.5	7	87	1048	12.0	5	12	†1	74	2
Pro totals (6 years)	93	92	1642	6701	4.1	49	384	3852	10.0	14	63	1	380	25

F

FAURIA, CHRISTIAN · TE · SEAHAWKS

PERSONAL: Born September 22, 1971, in Harbor City, Calif. ... 6-4/245. ... Name pronounced FOUR-ee-ah.

HIGH SCHOOL: Crespi Carmelite (Encino, Calif.).

COLLEGE: Colorado (degree in communications, 1995).

TRANSACTIONS/CAREER NOTES: Selected by Seattle Seahawks in second round (39th pick overall) of 1995 NFL draft. ... Signed by Seahawks (July 17, 1995). ... Re-signed by Seahawks (April 20, 1998). ... Granted unconditional free agency (February 12, 1999). ... Re-signed by Seahawks (March 5, 1999).

PRO STATISTICS: 1996—Returned one kickoff for eight yards. 1998—Returned one kickoff for no yards and recovered one fumble. 1999—Returned two kickoffs for 15 yards.

SINGLE GAME HIGHS (regular season): Receptions—6 (December 26, 1999, vs. Kansas City); yards—84 (December 26, 1999, vs. Kansas City); and touchdown receptions—1 (November 15, 1998, vs.Oakland).

			RECEIVING				TOTALS			
Year Team	G	GS	No.	Yds.	Avg.	TD	TD	2pt.	Pts.	Fum.
1995—Seattle NFL	14	9	17	181	10.6	1	1	0	6	0
1996—Seattle NFL	10	9	18	214	11.9	1	1	0	6	0
1997—Seattle NFL	16	3	10	110	11.0	0	0	0	0	0
1998—Seattle NFL	16	15	37	377	10.2	2	2	0	12	1
1999—Seattle NFL	16	16	35	376	10.7	0	0	0	0	1
Pro totals (5 years)	72	52	117	1258	10.8	4	4	0	24	2

FAVORS, GREG · LB · TITANS

PERSONAL: Born September 30, 1974, in Atlanta. ... 6-1/244. ... Full name: Gregory Bernard Favors.
HIGH SCHOOL: Southside (Atlanta).
COLLEGE: Mississippi State (degree in correction, 1997).
TRANSACTIONS/CAREER NOTES: Selected by Kansas City Chiefs in fourth round (120th pick overall) of 1998 NFL draft. ... Signed by Chiefs (July 17, 1998). ... Claimed on waivers by Tennessee Titans (September 8, 1999).
CHAMPIONSHIP GAME EXPERIENCE: Played in AFC championship game (1999 season). ... Played in Super Bowl XXXIV (1999 season).
PRO STATISTICS: 1998—Recovered one fumble for 41 yards. 1999—Recovered one fumble.

Year Team	G	GS	SACKS
1998—Kansas City NFL	16	4	2.0
1999—Tennessee NFL	15	0	0.0
Pro totals (2 years)	31	4	2.0

FAVRE, BRETT · QB · PACKERS

PERSONAL: Born October 10, 1969, in Gulfport, Miss. ... 6-2/220. ... Full name: Brett Lorenzo Favre. ... Name pronounced FARVE.
HIGH SCHOOL: Hancock North Central (Kiln, Miss.).
COLLEGE: Southern Mississippi.
TRANSACTIONS/CAREER NOTES: Selected by Atlanta Falcons in second round (33rd pick overall) of 1991 NFL draft. ... Signed by Falcons (July 18, 1991). ... Traded by Falcons to Green Bay Packers for first-round pick (OT Bob Whitfield) in 1992 draft (February 11, 1992). ... Granted free agency (February 17, 1994). ... Re-signed by Packers (July 14, 1994).
CHAMPIONSHIP GAME EXPERIENCE: Played in NFC championship game (1995-1997 seasons). ... Member of Super Bowl championship team (1996 season). ... Played in Super Bowl XXXII (1997 season).
HONORS: Played in Pro Bowl (1992, 1993, 1995 and 1996 seasons). ... Named NFL Player of the Year by THE SPORTING NEWS (1995 and 1996). ... Named quarterback on THE SPORTING NEWS NFL All-Pro team (1995-97). ... Named to play in Pro Bowl (1997 season); replaced by Chris Chandler due to injury.
RECORDS: Shares NFL record for longest pass completion (to Robert Brooks)—99 yards, touchdown (September 11, 1995, at Chicago).
POST SEASON RECORDS: Holds Super Bowl record for longest pass completion (to Antonio Freeman)—81 yards (January 26, 1997, vs. New England).
PRO STATISTICS: 1992—Caught one pass for minus seven yards, fumbled 12 times and recovered three fumbles for minus 12 yards. 1993—Fumbled 12 times and recovered two fumbles for minus one yard. 1994—Fumbled seven times and recovered one fumble for minus two yards. 1995—Fumbled eight times. 1996—Fumbled 11 times and recovered five fumbles for minus 10 yards. 1997—Fumbled seven times and recovered one fumble for minus 10 yards. 1998—Fumbled eight times and recovered three fumbles for minus one yard. 1999—Fumbled nine times and recovered one fumble for minus two yards.
SINGLE GAME HIGHS (regular season): Attempts—61 (October 14, 1996, vs. San Francisco); completions—36 (December 5, 1993, vs. Chicago); yards—402 (December 5, 1993, vs. Chicago); and touchdown passes—5 (September 27, 1998, vs. Carolina).
STATISTICAL PLATEAUS: 300-yard passing games: 1993 (1), 1994 (4), 1995 (7), 1996 (2), 1997 (2), 1998 (4), 1999 (6). Total: 26.
MISCELLANEOUS: Regular-season record as starting NFL quarterback: 82-43 (.656). ... Postseason record as starting NFL quarterback: 9-5 (.643). ... Holds Green Bay Packers all-time records for most yards passing (30,894) and most touchdown passes (235).

			PASSING							RUSHING				TOTALS		
Year Team	G	GS	Att.	Cmp.	Pct.	Yds.	TD	Int.	Avg.	Rat.	Att.	Yds.	Avg.	TD	TD	2pt.	Pts.
1991—Atlanta NFL	2	0	5	0	0.0	0	0	2	0.0	0.0	0	0	0.0	0	0	0	0
1992—Green Bay NFL	15	13	471	∞302	64.1	3227	18	13	6.85	85.3	47	198	4.2	1	1	0	6
1993—Green Bay NFL	16	16	‡522	‡318	60.9	3303	19	*24	6.33	72.2	58	216	3.7	1	1	0	6
1994—Green Bay NFL	16	16	582	363	62.4	3882	33	14	6.67	90.7	42	202	4.8	2	2	0	12
1995—Green Bay NFL	16	16	570	359	63.0	*4413	*38	13	‡7.74	‡99.5	39	181	4.6	3	3	0	18
1996—Green Bay NFL	16	16	‡543	‡325	59.9	‡3899	*39	13	7.18	95.8	49	136	2.8	2	2	0	12
1997—Green Bay NFL	16	16	513	‡304	59.3	‡3867	*35	16	7.54	92.6	58	187	3.2	1	1	0	6
1998—Green Bay NFL	16	16	‡551	*347	*63.0	*4212	31	‡23	7.64	87.8	40	133	3.3	1	1	0	6
1999—Green Bay NFL	16	16	*595	341	57.3	4091	22	23	6.88	74.7	28	142	5.1	0	0	0	0
Pro totals (9 years)	129	125	4352	2659	61.1	30894	235	141	7.10	87.1	361	1395	3.9	11	11	0	66

FAZANDE, JERMAINE · RB · CHARGERS

PERSONAL: Born January 14, 1975, in Marrero, La. ... 6-2/255. ... Full name: Jermaine Keith Fazande. ... Name pronounced FUH-zand.
HIGH SCHOOL: John Ehret (Marrero, La.).
COLLEGE: Oklahoma.
TRANSACTIONS/CAREER NOTES: Selected by San Diego Chargers in second round (60th pick overall) of 1999 NFL draft. ... Signed by Chargers (July 23, 1999).
SINGLE GAME HIGHS (regular season): Attempts—30 (January 2, 2000, vs. Denver); yards—183 (January 2, 2000, vs. Denver); and rushing touchdowns—1 (January 2, 2000, vs. Denver).
STATISTICAL PLATEAUS: 100-yard rushing games: 1999 (1).

			RUSHING				TOTALS			
Year Team	G	GS	Att.	Yds.	Avg.	TD	TD	2pt.	Pts.	Fum.
1999—San Diego NFL	7	3	91	365	4.0	2	2	0	12	2

FEAGLES, JEFF · P · SEAHAWKS

PERSONAL: Born August 7, 1966, in Anaheim ... 6-1/207. ... Full name: Jeffrey Allan Feagles.
HIGH SCHOOL: Gerard Catholic (Phoenix).
JUNIOR COLLEGE: Scottsdale (Ariz.) Community College.
COLLEGE: Miami, Fla. (degree in business administration, 1988).

F

TRANSACTIONS/CAREER NOTES: Signed as non-drafted free agent by New England Patriots (May 1, 1988). ... Claimed on waivers by Philadelphia Eagles (June 5, 1990). ... Granted unconditional free agency (February 1-April 1, 1992). ... Re-signed by Eagles for 1992 season. ... Granted unconditional free agency (February 17, 1994). ... Signed by Phoenix Cardinals (March 2, 1994). ... Cardinals franchise renamed Arizona Cardinals for 1994 season. ... Granted unconditional free agency (February 13, 1998). ... Signed by Seattle Seahawks (March 4, 1998).
HONORS: Played in Pro Bowl (1995 season).
PRO STATISTICS: 1988—Rushed once for no yards and recovered one fumble. 1989—Attempted two passes without a completion, fumbled once and recovered one fumble. 1990—Rushed twice for three yards and attempted one pass without a completion. 1991—Rushed three times for minus one yard, fumbled once and recovered one fumble. 1993—Rushed twice for six yards and recovered one fumble. 1994—Rushed twice for eight yards. 1995—Rushed twice for four yards and fumbled once for minus 22 yards. 1996—Rushed once for no yards and fumbled once for minus seven yards. 1997—Fumbled once and recovered one fumble. 1999—Rushed twice for no yards.

			PUNTING					
Year Team	G	No.	Yds.	Avg.	Net avg.	In. 20	Blk.	
1988—New England NFL	16	▲91	3482	38.3	34.1	24	0	
1989—New England NFL	16	63	2392	38.0	31.3	13	1	
1990—Philadelphia NFL	16	72	3026	42.0	35.5	20	2	
1991—Philadelphia NFL	16	*87	3640	41.8	34.0	*29	1	
1992—Philadelphia NFL	16	‡82	‡3459	42.2	36.8	‡26	0	
1993—Philadelphia NFL	16	83	3323	40.0	35.2	*31	0	
1994—Arizona NFL	16	*98	‡3997	40.8	36.0	‡33	0	
1995—Arizona NFL	16	72	3150	43.8	‡38.2	20	0	
1996—Arizona NFL	16	76	3328	43.8	36.3	23	1	
1997—Arizona NFL	16	91	4028	44.3	36.8	24	1	
1998—Seattle NFL	16	81	3568	44.0	36.5	27	0	
1999—Seattle NFL	16	84	3425	40.8	35.2	34	0	
Pro totals (12 years)	192	980	40818	41.7	35.5	304	6	

FERGUSON, JASON　　　　DT　　　　JETS

PERSONAL: Born November 28, 1974, in Nettleton, Miss. ... 6-3/305. ... Full name: Jason O. Ferguson. ... Cousin of Terance Mathis, wide receiver, Atlanta Falcons.
HIGH SCHOOL: Nettleton (Miss.).
JUNIOR COLLEGE: Itawamba Junior College (Miss.).
COLLEGE: Georgia.
TRANSACTIONS/CAREER NOTES: Selected by New York Jets in seventh round (229th pick overall) of 1997 NFL draft. ... Signed by Jets (April 30, 1997). ... On suspended list for violating league substance abuse policy (November 24-December 22, 1999). ... Granted free agency (February 11, 2000). ... Re-signed by Jets (May 24, 2000).
CHAMPIONSHIP GAME EXPERIENCE: Played in AFC championship game (1998 season).
PRO STATISTICS: 1997—Returned one kickoff for one yard.

Year Team	G	GS	SACKS
1997—New York Jets NFL	13	1	3.5
1998—New York Jets NFL	16	16	4.0
1999—New York Jets NFL	9	9	1.0
Pro totals (3 years)	38	26	8.5

FIALA, JOHN　　　　LB　　　　STEELERS

PERSONAL: Born November 25, 1973, in Fullerton, Calif. ... 6-2/235. ... Full name: John Charles Fiala. ... Name pronounced FEE-ah-lah.
HIGH SCHOOL: Lake Washington (Kirkland, Wash.).
COLLEGE: Washington.
TRANSACTIONS/CAREER NOTES: Selected by Miami Dolphins in sixth round (166th pick overall) of 1997 NFL draft. ... Signed by Dolphins (June 17, 1997). ... Released by Dolphins (July 31, 1997). ... Signed by Pittsburgh Steelers to practice squad (August 26, 1997).
PLAYING EXPERIENCE: Pittsburgh NFL, 1998 and 1999. ... Games/Games started: 1998 (16/0), 1999 (16/0). Total: 32/0.

FIEDLER, JAY　　　　QB　　　　DOLPHINS

PERSONAL: Born December 29, 1971, in Oceanside, N.Y. ... 6-2/220. ... Full name: Jay Brian Fiedler.
HIGH SCHOOL: Oceanside (N.Y.).
COLLEGE: Dartmouth (degree in engineering sciences).
TRANSACTIONS/CAREER NOTES: Signed as non-drafted free agent by Philadelphia Eagles (April 29, 1994). ... Inactive for all 16 games (1994). ... Claimed on waivers by Cincinnati Bengals (July 31, 1996). ... Released by Bengals (August 25, 1996). ... Played for Amsterdam Admirals of World League (1997). ... Signed by Minnesota Vikings (April 3, 1998). ... Released by Vikings (August 30, 1998). ... Re-signed by Vikings (September 15, 1998). ... Granted free agency (February 12, 1999). ... Signed by Jacksonville Jaguars (April 16, 1999). ... Granted unconditional free agency (February 11, 2000). ... Signed by Miami Dolphins (February 17, 2000).
CHAMPIONSHIP GAME EXPERIENCE: Member of Vikings for NFC championship game (1998 season); inactive. ... Member of Jaguars for AFC championship game (1999 season); did not play.
PRO STATISTICS: 1999—Fumbled once.
SINGLE GAME HIGHS (regular season): Attempts—39 (January 2, 2000, vs. Cincinnati); completions—28 (January 2, 2000, vs.Cincinnati); yards—317 (January 2, 2000, vs.Cincinnati); and touchdown passes—1 (January 2, 2000, vs. Cincinnati).
STATISTICAL PLATEAUS: 300-yard passing games: 1999 (1).
MISCELLANEOUS: Regular-season record as starting NFL quarterback: 1-0 (1.000).

			PASSING								RUSHING				TOTALS		
Year Team	G	GS	Att.	Cmp.	Pct.	Yds.	TD	Int.	Avg.	Rat.	Att.	Yds.	Avg.	TD	TD	2pt.	Pts.
1994—Philadelphia NFL							Did not play.										
1995—Philadelphia NFL							Did not play.										
1996—							Did not play.										
1997—Amsterdam W.L.	...	...	109	46	42.2	678	2	8	6.22	38.7	16	93	5.8	0	0	0	0

1998—Minnesota NFL............	5	0	7	3	42.9	41	0	1	5.86	22.6	4	-6	-1.5	0	0	0	0
1999—Jacksonville NFL........	7	1	94	61	64.9	656	2	2	6.98	83.5	13	26	2.0	0	0	0	0
W.L. totals (1 year).............	...	...	109	46	42.2	678	2	8	6.22	38.7	16	93	5.8	0	0	0	0
NFL totals (3 years).............	13	1	101	64	63.4	697	2	3	6.90	77.9	17	20	1.2	0	0	0	0
Pro totals (4 years).............	...	...	210	110	52.4	1375	4	11	6.55	57.5	33	113	3.4	0	0	0	0

FIELDS, MARK — LB — SAINTS

PERSONAL: Born November 9, 1972, in Los Angeles. ... 6-2/244. ... Full name: Mark Lee Fields.
HIGH SCHOOL: Washington (Cerritos, Calif.).
JUNIOR COLLEGE: Los Angeles Southwest Community College.
COLLEGE: Washington State.
TRANSACTIONS/CAREER NOTES: Selected by New Orleans Saints in first round (13th pick overall) of 1995 NFL draft. ... Signed by Saints (July 20, 1995).
PRO STATISTICS: 1996—Recovered one fumble for 20 yards. 1997—Recovered two fumbles for 28 yards and one touchdown. 1998—Recovered one fumble for 36 yards and a touchdown. 1999—Intercepted two passes for no yards and recovered one fumble.

Year Team	G	GS	SACKS
1995—New Orleans NFL........................	16	3	1.0
1996—New Orleans NFL........................	16	15	2.0
1997—New Orleans NFL........................	16	15	8.0
1998—New Orleans NFL........................	15	15	6.0
1999—New Orleans NFL........................	14	14	4.0
Pro totals (5 years)............................	77	62	21.0

FIELDS, SCOTT — LB — LIONS

PERSONAL: Born April 22, 1973, in Ontario, Calif. ... 6-2/220.
HIGH SCHOOL: Bishop Amat (La Puente, Calif.).
COLLEGE: Southern California.
TRANSACTIONS/CAREER NOTES: Signed as non-drafted free agent by Atlanta Falcons (April 22, 1996). ... Released by Falcons (June 12, 1997). ... Selected by England Monarchs in 1998 NFL Europe draft (February 18, 1998). ... Signed by Tampa Bay Buccaneers (July 21, 1998). ... Released by Buccaneers (August 25, 1998). ... Signed by Seattle Seahawks (July 9, 1999). ... Released by Seahawks (September 5, 1999). ... Re-signed by Seahawks to practice squad (September 6, 1999). ... Activated (September 17, 1999). ... Released by Seahawks (September 28, 1999). ... Re-signed by Seahawks to practice squad (September 30, 1999). ... Released by Seahawks (October 19, 1999). ... Signed by Detroit Lions to practice squad (December 22, 1999).
PLAYING EXPERIENCE: Atlanta NFL, 1996; Seattle NFL, 1999. ... Games/Games started: 1996 (6/0), 1999 (2/0). Total: 8/0.

FINA, JOHN — OT — BILLS

PERSONAL: Born March 11, 1969, in Rochester, Minn. ... 6-4/300. ... Full name: John Joseph Fina. ... Name pronounced FEE-nuh.
HIGH SCHOOL: Salpointe Catholic (Tucson, Ariz.).
COLLEGE: Arizona.
TRANSACTIONS/CAREER NOTES: Selected by Buffalo Bills in first round (27th pick overall) of 1992 NFL draft. ... Signed by Bills (July 21, 1992). ... Designated by Bills as franchise player (February 16, 1996).
PLAYING EXPERIENCE: Buffalo NFL, 1992-1999. ... Games/Games started: 1992 (16/0), 1993 (16/16), 1994 (12/12), 1995 (16/16), 1996 (15/15), 1997 (16/16), 1998 (14/14), 1999 (16/16). Total: 121/105.
CHAMPIONSHIP GAME EXPERIENCE: Played in AFC championship game (1992 and 1993 seasons). ... Played in Super Bowl XXVII (1992 season) and Super Bowl XXVIII (1993 season).
PRO STATISTICS: 1992—Caught one pass for one yard and a touchdown. 1993—Rushed once for minus two yards. 1996—Recovered two fumbles for minus one yard. 1997—Recovered one fumble.

F

FINNERAN, BRIAN — WR — FALCONS

PERSONAL: Born January 31, 1976, in Mission Viejo, Calif. ... 6-5/208.
HIGH SCHOOL: Santa Margarita (Mission Viejo, Calif.).
COLLEGE: Villanova.
TRANSACTIONS/CAREER NOTES: Signed as non-drafted free agent by Seattle Seahawks (April 21, 1998). ... Released by Seahawks (August 24, 1998). ... Selected by Barcelona Dragons in 1999 NFL Europe draft (February 18, 1999). ... Signed by Philadelphia Eagles (July 6, 1999). ... Released by Eagles (October 12, 1999). ... Signed by Atlanta Falcons to practice squad (December 13, 1999).
HONORS: Won Walter Payton Award (1997).
PRO STATISTICS: NFLE: 1999—Returned one kickoff for no yards.
SINGLE GAME HIGHS (regular season): Receptions—1 (September 26, 1999, vs. Buffalo); yards—11 (September 26, 1999, vs. Buffalo); and touchdown receptions—0.

Year Team	G	GS	RECEIVING				TOTALS			
			No.	Yds.	Avg.	TD	TD	2pt.	Pts.	Fum.
1999—Barcelona NFLE..................................	...	...	54	844	15.6	8	8	1	50	0
—Philadelphia NFL..................................	3	0	2	21	10.5	0	0	0	0	0
NFL Europe totals (1 year)........................	...	...	54	844	15.6	8	8	1	50	0
NFL totals (1 year)..................................	3	0	2	21	10.5	0	0	0	0	0
Pro totals (1years)	...	...	56	865	15.4	8	8	1	50	0

FIORE, DAVE — OT — 49ERS

PERSONAL: Born August 10, 1974, in Hackensack, N.J. ... 6-4/290. ... Full name: David Fiore. ... Name pronounced fee-OR-ee.

HIGH SCHOOL: Waldwick (N.J.).
COLLEGE: Hofstra.
TRANSACTIONS/CAREER NOTES: Signed as non-drafted free agent by San Francisco 49ers (April 23, 1996). ... Claimed on waivers by New York Jets (October 14, 1996). ... Active for nine games (1996); did not play. ... Released by Jets (July 31, 1997). ... Signed by 49ers (August 1, 1997). ... On injured reserve with knee injury (August 19, 1997-entire season).
PLAYING EXPERIENCE: San Francisco NFL, 1998 and 1999. ... Games/Games started: 1998 (9/3), 1999 (16/16). Total: 25/19.

FISHER, CHARLES   CB   BENGALS

PERSONAL: Born February 2, 1976, in Aliquippa, Pa. ... 6-0/185.
HIGH SCHOOL: Aliquippa (Pa.).
COLLEGE: West Virginia.
TRANSACTIONS/CAREER NOTES: Selected by Cincinnati Bengals in second round (33rd pick overall) of 1999 NFL draft. ... Signed by Bengals (August 1, 1999). ... On injured reserve with knee injury (September 13, 1999-remainder of season).
PLAYING EXPERIENCE: Cincinnati NFL, 1999. ... Games/Games started: 1999 (1/1).

FISK, JASON   DT   TITANS

PERSONAL: Born September 4, 1972, in Davis, Calif. ... 6-3/295.
HIGH SCHOOL: Davis (Calif.).
COLLEGE: Stanford.
TRANSACTIONS/CAREER NOTES: Selected by Minnesota Vikings in seventh round (243rd pick overall) of 1995 NFL draft. ... Signed by Vikings (July 24, 1995). ... Granted unconditional free agency (February 12, 1999). ... Signed by Tennessee Titans (March 3, 1999).
CHAMPIONSHIP GAME EXPERIENCE: Played in NFC championship game (1998 season). ... Played in AFC championship game (1999 season). ... Played in Super Bowl XXXIV (1999 season).
PRO STATISTICS: 1996—Intercepted one pass for no yards and recovered one fumble. 1997—Intercepted one pass for one yard and recovered one fumble. 1998—Recovered one fumble. 1999—Intercepted one pass for 17 yards.

Year Team	G	GS	SACKS
1995—Minnesota NFL	8	0	0.0
1996—Minnesota NFL	16	6	1.0
1997—Minnesota NFL	16	10	3.0
1998—Minnesota NFL	16	0	1.5
1999—Tennessee NFL	16	16	4.0
Pro totals (5 years)	72	32	9.5

FLANAGAN, MIKE   C   PACKERS

PERSONAL: Born November 10, 1973, in Washington, D.C. ... 6-5/295. ... Full name: Michael Christopher Flanagan.
HIGH SCHOOL: Rio Americano (Sacramento).
COLLEGE: UCLA.
TRANSACTIONS/CAREER NOTES: Selected by Green Bay Packers in third round (90th pick overall) of 1996 NFL draft. ... Signed by Packers (July 17, 1996). ... On injured reserve with ankle injury (August 19, 1996-entire season). ... Traded by Packers to Carolina Panthers for an undisclosed draft pick (August 31, 1998); trade later voided because Flanagan failed physical (September 1, 1998). ... Granted free agency (February 12, 1999). ... Re-signed by Packers (March 25, 1999).
PLAYING EXPERIENCE: Green Bay NFL, 1998 and 1999. ... Games/Games started: 1998 (2/0), 1999 (15/0). Total: 17/0.

FLANIGAN, JIM   DT   BEARS

F

PERSONAL: Born August 27, 1971, in Green Bay. ... 6-2/288. ... Full name: James Michael Flanigan. ... Son of Jim Flanigan, linebacker with Green Bay Packers (1967-70) and New Orleans Saints (1971).
HIGH SCHOOL: Southern Door (Brussels, Wis.).
COLLEGE: Notre Dame.
TRANSACTIONS/CAREER NOTES: Selected by Chicago Bears in third round (74th pick overall) of 1994 NFL draft. ... Signed by Bears (July 14, 1994). ... Granted free agency (February 14, 1997). ... Re-signed by Bears (June 1, 1997). ... Granted unconditional free agency (February 13, 1998). ... Re-signed by Bears (February 13, 1998).
PRO STATISTICS: 1994—Returned two kickoffs for 26 yards. 1995—Rushed once for no yards, caught two passes for six yards and two touchdowns and recovered one fumble. 1996—Caught one pass for one yard and a touchdown. 1997—Recovered three fumbles for three yards and credited with one two-point conversion. 1998—Recovered one fumble. 1999—Intercepted one pass for six yards and recovered one fumble.

Year Team	G	GS	SACKS
1994—Chicago NFL	14	0	0.0
1995—Chicago NFL	16	12	11.0
1996—Chicago NFL	14	14	5.0
1997—Chicago NFL	16	16	6.0
1998—Chicago NFL	16	16	8.5
1999—Chicago NFL	16	16	6.0
Pro totals (6 years)	92	74	36.5

FLETCHER, LONDON   LB   RAMS

PERSONAL: Born May 19, 1975, in Cleveland. ... 5-10/241. ... Full name: London Levi Fletcher.
HIGH SCHOOL: Villa Angela-St. Joseph (Cleveland).

COLLEGE: John Carroll (degree in sociology).
TRANSACTIONS/CAREER NOTES: Signed as non-drafted free agent by St. Louis Rams (April 28, 1998).
PLAYING EXPERIENCE: St. Louis NFL, 1998 and 1999. ... Games/started: 1998 (16/1), 1999 (16/16). Total: 32/17.
CHAMPIONSHIP GAME EXPERIENCE: Played in NFC championship game (1999 season). ... Member of Super Bowl championship team (1999 season).
PRO STATISTICS: 1998—Returned five kickoffs for 72 yards and fumbled once. 1999—Returned two kickoffs for 13 yards, credited with three sacks and credited with a safety.

FLETCHER, TERRELL RB CHARGERS

PERSONAL: Born September 14, 1973, in St. Louis. ... 5-8/196. ... Full name: Terrell Antoine Fletcher.
HIGH SCHOOL: Hazelwood East (St. Louis).
COLLEGE: Wisconsin (degree in English, 1994).
TRANSACTIONS/CAREER NOTES: Selected by San Diego Chargers in second round (51st pick overall) of 1995 NFL draft. ... Signed by Chargers (July 12, 1995). ... On injured reserve with knee injury (December 17, 1997-remainder of season). ... Granted free agency (February 13, 1998). ... Re-signed by Chargers (June 1998).
PRO STATISTICS: 1995—Returned three punts for 12 yards and recovered two fumbles. 1996—Recovered one fumble. 1998—Completed only pass attempt for 23 yards and a touchdown and recovered two fumbles for 21 yards. 1999—Recovered one fumble.
SINGLE GAME HIGHS (regular season): Attempts—34 (December 6, 1998, vs. Washington); yards—127 (December 27, 1998, vs. Arizona); and rushing touchdowns—2 (November 22, 1998, vs. Kansas City).
STATISTICAL PLATEAUS: 100-yard rushing games: 1998 (2).

			RUSHING				RECEIVING				KICKOFF RETURNS				TOTALS			
Year Team	G	GS	Att.	Yds.	Avg.	TD	No.	Yds.	Avg.	TD	No.	Yds.	Avg.	TD	TD	2pt.	Pts.	Fum.
1995—San Diego NFL............	16	0	26	140	5.4	1	3	26	8.7	0	4	65	16.3	0	1	0	6	2
1996—San Diego NFL............	16	0	77	282	3.7	0	61	476	7.8	2	0	0	0.0	0	2	0	12	1
1997—San Diego NFL............	13	1	51	161	3.2	0	39	292	7.5	0	0	0	0.0	0	0	0	0	4
1998—San Diego NFL............	12	5	153	543	3.5	5	30	188	6.3	0	3	71	23.7	0	5	0	30	1
1999—San Diego NFL............	15	2	48	126	2.6	0	45	360	8.0	0	7	112	16.0	0	0	0	0	1
Pro totals (5 years)................	72	8	355	1252	3.5	6	178	1342	7.5	2	14	248	17.7	0	8	0	48	9

FLOWERS, LEE S STEELERS

PERSONAL: Born January 14, 1973, in Columbia, S.C. ... 6-0/211. ... Full name: Lethon Flowers III.
HIGH SCHOOL: Spring Valley (Columbia, S.C.).
COLLEGE: Georgia Tech.
TRANSACTIONS/CAREER NOTES: Selected by Pittsburgh Steelers in fifth round (151st pick overall) of 1995 NFL draft. ... Signed by Steelers (July 18, 1995). ... Granted free agency (February 13, 1998). ... Re-signed by Steelers (June 9, 1998). ... Granted unconditional free agency (February 12, 1999). ... Re-signed by Steelers (February 16, 1999).
PLAYING EXPERIENCE: Pittsburgh NFL, 1995-1999. ... Games/Games started: 1995 (10/0), 1996 (16/0), 1997 (10/0), 1998 (16/16), 1999 (15/15). Total: 67/31.
CHAMPIONSHIP GAME EXPERIENCE: Played in AFC championship game (1995 and 1997 seasons). ... Played in Super Bowl XXX (1995 season).
PRO STATISTICS: 1997—Recovered one fumble. 1998—Intercepted one pass for two yards, credited with one sack and recovered two fumbles. 1999—Credited with five sacks.

FLOYD, CHRIS FB PATRIOTS

PERSONAL: Born June 23, 1975, in Detroit. ... 6-2/235. ... Full name: Christopher Michael Floyd.
HIGH SCHOOL: Cooley (Detroit).
COLLEGE: Michigan (degree in sports management and communications).
TRANSACTIONS/CAREER NOTES: Selected by New England Patriots in third round (81st pick overall) of 1998 NFL draft. ... Signed by Patriots (July 15, 1998).
SINGLE GAME HIGHS (regular season): Attempts—3 (October 3, 1999, vs. Cleveland); yards—14 (December 20, 1998, vs. San Francisco); and rushing touchdowns—0.

			RUSHING				RECEIVING				TOTALS			
Year Team	G	GS	Att.	Yds.	Avg.	TD	No.	Yds.	Avg.	TD	TD	2pt.	Pts.	Fum.
1998—New England NFL	16	2	6	22	3.7	0	1	6	6.0	0	0	0	0	0
1999—New England NFL	13	0	6	12	2.0	0	2	16	8.0	0	0	0	0	0
Pro totals (2 years)..	29	2	12	34	2.8	0	3	22	7.3	0	0	0	0	0

FLOYD, WILLIAM FB PANTHERS

PERSONAL: Born February 17, 1972, in St. Petersburg, Fla. ... 6-1/242. ... Full name: William Ali Floyd.
HIGH SCHOOL: Lakewood Senior (St. Petersburg, Fla.).
COLLEGE: Florida State.
TRANSACTIONS/CAREER NOTES: Selected after junior season by San Francisco 49ers in first round (28th pick overall) of 1994 NFL draft. ... Signed by 49ers (July 28, 1994). ... On injured reserve with knee injury (October 31, 1995-remainder of season). ... On physically unable to perform list with knee injury (August 20-October 12, 1996). ... Granted unconditional free agency (February 13, 1998). ... Signed by Carolina Panthers (March 6, 1998).
CHAMPIONSHIP GAME EXPERIENCE: Played in NFC championship game (1994 and 1997 seasons). ... Member of Super Bowl championship team (1994 season).
POST SEASON RECORDS: Holds postseason single-game record for most touchdowns by rookie—3 (January 7, 1995, vs Chicago).
PRO STATISTICS: 1996—Recovered one fumble. 1998—Had only pass attempt intercepted. 1999—Recovered one fumble.

F

SINGLE GAME HIGHS (regular season): Attempts—12 (October 1, 1995, vs. New York Giants); yards—61 (December 4, 1994, vs. Atlanta); and rushing touchdowns—2 (November 21, 1999, vs. Cleveland).

				RUSHING				RECEIVING				TOTALS		
Year Team	G	GS	Att.	Yds.	Avg.	TD	No.	Yds.	Avg.	TD	TD	2pt.	Pts.	Fum.
1994—San Francisco NFL	16	11	87	305	3.5	6	19	145	7.6	0	6	0	36	0
1995—San Francisco NFL	8	8	64	237	3.7	2	47	348	7.4	1	3	0	18	1
1996—San Francisco NFL	9	8	47	186	4.0	2	26	197	7.6	1	3	0	18	4
1997—San Francisco NFL	15	15	78	231	3.0	3	37	321	8.7	1	4	0	24	2
1998—Carolina NFL	16	13	28	71	2.5	3	24	123	5.1	1	4	0	24	1
1999—Carolina NFL	16	16	35	78	2.2	3	21	179	8.5	0	3	0	18	1
Pro totals (6 years)	80	71	339	1108	3.3	19	174	1313	7.5	4	23	0	138	9

FLUTIE, DOUG   QB   BILLS

PERSONAL: Born October 23, 1962, in Manchester, Md. ... 5-10/178. ... Full name: Douglas Richard Flutie. ... Brother of Darren Flutie, wide receiver with San Diego Chargers (1998), B.C. Lions of CFL (1991-95), Edmonton Eskimos of CFL (1996 and 1997) and Hamilton Tiger-Cats of CFL (1998).

HIGH SCHOOL: Natick (Mass.).

COLLEGE: Boston College (degrees in computer science and speech communications, 1984.).

TRANSACTIONS/CAREER NOTES: Selected by New Jersey Generals in 1985 USFL territorial draft. ... Signed by Generals (February 4, 1985). ... Granted roster exemption (February 4-14, 1985). ... Activated (February 15, 1985). ... On developmental squad for three games with Generals (1985). ... Selected by Los Angeles Rams in 11th round (285th pick overall) of 1985 NFL draft. ... On developmental squad (June 10, 1995-remainder of season). ... Rights traded by Rams with fourth-round pick in 1987 draft to Chicago Bears for third- and sixth-round picks in 1987 draft (October 14, 1986). ... Signed by Bears (October 21, 1986). ... Granted roster exemption (October 21-November 3, 1986). ... Activated (November 4, 1986). ... Crossed picket line during players strike (October 13, 1987). ... Traded by Bears to New England Patriots for eighth-round pick in 1988 draft (October 13, 1987). ... Released by Patriots after 1989 season. ... Signed by B.C. Lions of CFL (June 1990). ... Granted free agency (February 1992). ... Signed by Calgary Stampeders of CFL (March 1992). ... Rights assigned to Toronto Argonauts of CFL (March 15, 1996). ... Signed by Buffalo Bills (January 16, 1998).

CHAMPIONSHIP GAME EXPERIENCE: Member of CFL championship team (1992, 1996 and 1997). ... Named Most Valuable Player of Grey Cup, CFL championship game (1992, 1996 and 1997). ... Played in Grey Cup (1993 and 1995).

HONORS: Heisman Trophy winner (1984). ... Named College Football Player of the Year by THE SPORTING NEWS (1984). ... Named quarterback on THE SPORTING NEWS college All-America first team (1984). ... Most Outstanding Player of CFL (1991-1994, 1996 and 1997). ... Played in Pro Bowl (1998 season).

PRO STATISTICS: USFL: 1985—Recovered two fumbles. NFL: 1986—Recovered two fumbles and fumbled three times for minus four yards. 1987—Recovered one fumble. 1988—Fumbled three times. 1989—Fumbled once. CFL: 1990—Fumbled six times. 1991—Fumbled seven times. 1992—Fumbled five times. 1993—Caught one pass for 11 yards and fumbled five times. 1994—Fumbled eight times. 1995—Fumbled twice. 1996—Fumbled once. 1997—Fumbled three times. NFL: 1998—Fumbled three times and recovered four fumbles for minus 13 yards. 1999—Fumbled six times and recovered one fumble for minus five yards.

SINGLE GAME HIGHS (regular season): Attempts—50 (October 24, 1999, vs. Seattle); completions—24 (October 24, 1999, vs. Seattle); yards—339 (November 29, 1998, vs. New England); and touchdown passes—4 (October 30, 1988, vs. Chicago).

STATISTICAL PLATEAUS: 300-yard passing games: 1998 (2), 1999 (1). Total: 3.

MISCELLANEOUS: Regular-season record as starting NFL quarterback: 26-13 (.667). ... Postseason record as starting NFL quarterback: 0-2.

			PASSING								RUSHING				TOTALS		
Year Team	G	GS	Att.	Cmp.	Pct.	Yds.	TD	Int.	Avg.	Rat.	Att.	Yds.	Avg.	TD	TD	2pt.	Pts.
1985—New Jersey USFL	15	...	281	134	47.7	2109	13	14	7.51	67.8	65	465	7.2	6	6	0	36
1986—Chicago NFL	4	1	46	23	50.0	361	3	2	7.85	80.1	9	36	4.0	1	1	0	6
1987—Chicago NFL							Did not play.										
—New England NFL	1	1	25	15	60.0	199	1	0	7.96	98.6	6	43	7.2	0	0	0	0
1988—New England NFL	11	9	179	92	51.4	1150	8	10	6.42	63.3	38	179	4.7	1	1	0	6
1989—New England NFL	5	3	91	36	39.6	493	2	4	5.42	46.6	16	87	5.4	0	0	0	0
1990—British Columbia CFL	16	...	392	207	52.8	2960	16	19	7.55	71.0	79	662	8.4	3	3	0	18
1991—British Columbia CFL	18	...	730	466	63.8	6619	38	24	9.07	96.7	120	610	5.1	14	14	1	86
1992—Calgary CFL	18	...	688	396	57.6	5945	32	30	8.64	83.4	96	669	7.0	11	11	0	66
1993—Calgary CFL	18	...	703	416	59.2	6092	44	17	8.67	98.3	74	373	5.0	11	11	0	66
1994—Calgary CFL	18	...	659	403	61.2	5726	48	19	8.69	101.5	96	760	7.9	8	8	0	48
1995—Calgary CFL	12	...	332	223	67.2	2788	16	5	8.40	102.8	46	288	6.3	5	5	0	30
1996—Toronto CFL	18	...	677	434	64.1	5720	29	17	8.45	94.5	101	756	7.5	9	9	0	54
1997—Toronto CFL	18	18	673	430	63.9	5505	47	24	8.18	97.8	92	542	5.9	9	9	0	54
1998—Buffalo NFL	13	10	354	202	57.1	2711	20	11	7.66	87.4	48	248	5.2	1	1	0	6
1999—Buffalo NFL	15	15	478	264	55.2	3171	19	16	6.63	75.1	88	476	5.4	1	1	0	6
USFL totals (1 year)	15	...	281	134	47.7	2109	13	14	7.51	67.8	65	465	7.2	6	6	0	36
CFL totals (8 years)	136	...	4854	2975	61.3	41355	270	155	8.52	93.9	704	4660	6.6	70	70	1	422
NFL totals (6 years)	49	39	1173	632	53.9	8085	53	43	6.89	75.5	205	1069	5.2	4	4	0	24
Pro totals (15 years)	200	...	6308	3741	59.3	51549	336	212	8.17	89.3	974	6194	6.4	80	80	1	482

FLYNN, MIKE   OL   RAVENS

PERSONAL: Born June 15, 1974, in Doylestown, Pa. ... 6-3/295. ... Full name: Michael Patrick Flynn.

HIGH SCHOOL: Cathedral (Springfield, Mass.).

COLLEGE: Maine.

TRANSACTIONS/CAREER NOTES: Signed as non-drafted free agent by Baltimore Ravens (April 25, 1997). ... Released by Ravens (August 24, 1997). ... Signed by Tampa Bay Buccaneers to practice squad (August 27, 1997). ... Released by Buccaneers (September 2, 1997). ... Signed by Jacksonville Jaguars to practice squad (November 4, 1997). ... Signed by Ravens off Jaguars practice squad (December 3, 1997). ... Inactive for three games (1997).

PLAYING EXPERIENCE: Baltimore NFL, 1998 and 1999. ... Games/Games started: 1998 (2/0), 1999 (12/0). Total: 14/0.

F

FOLAU, SPENCER OT RAVENS

PERSONAL: Born April 5, 1973, in Nuk 'Alofa, Tonga, Samoan Islands. ... 6-5/300. ... Full name: Spencer Sione Folau. ... Name pronounced fah-LOWE.
HIGH SCHOOL: Sequoia (Redwood City, Calif.).
COLLEGE: Idaho.
TRANSACTIONS/CAREER NOTES: Signed as non-drafted free agent by Baltimore Ravens (April 26, 1996). ... Released by Ravens (August 25, 1996). ... Re-signed by Ravens to practice squad (October 29, 1996). ... Assigned by Ravens to Rhein Fire in 1997 World League enhancement allocation program (February 1997). ... Released by Ravens (October 28, 1998). ... Re-signed by Ravens (November 3, 1998). ... Granted free agency (February 11, 2000). ... Tendered offer sheet by New England Patriots (April 10, 2000). ... Offer matched by Ravens (April 12, 2000).
PLAYING EXPERIENCE: Rhein W.L., 1997; Baltimore NFL, 1997-1999. ... Games/Games started: W.L. 1997 (games played unavailable), NFL 1997 (10/0), 1998 (3/3), 1999 (5/1). Total NFL: 18/4.

FOLEY, GLENN QB SEAHAWKS

PERSONAL: Born October 10, 1970, in Cherry Hill, N.J. ... 6-2/220. ... Full name: Glenn Edward Foley.
HIGH SCHOOL: Cherry Hill (N.J.) East.
COLLEGE: Boston College (degree in sociology).
TRANSACTIONS/CAREER NOTES: Selected by New York Jets in seventh round (208th pick overall) of 1994 NFL draft. ... Signed by Jets (June 21, 1994). ... On injured reserve with shoulder injury (November 8, 1995-remainder of season). ... On physically unable to perform list with knee injury (July 18-21, 1997). ... Traded by Jets to Seattle Seahawks for seventh-round pick (OT Ryan Young) in 1999 draft (March 19, 1999).
CHAMPIONSHIP GAME EXPERIENCE: Member of Jets for AFC championship game (1998 season); inactive.
PRO STATISTICS: 1995—Caught one pass for minus nine yards. 1996—Fumbled once for minus four yards. 1997—Fumbled once. 1998—Fumbled once. 1999—Fumbled once.
SINGLE GAME HIGHS (regular season): Attempts—58 (September 6, 1998, vs. San Francisco); completions—30 (September 6, 1998, vs. San Francisco); yards—415 (September 6, 1998, vs. San Francisco); and touchdown passes—3 (September 6, 1998, vs. San Francisco).
STATISTICAL PLATEAUS: 300-yard passing games: 1997 (1), 1998 (1). Total: 2.
MISCELLANEOUS: Regular-season record as starting NFL quarterback: 2-7 (.222).

				PASSING							RUSHING				TOTALS		
Year Team	G	GS	Att.	Cmp.	Pct.	Yds.	TD	Int.	Avg.	Rat.	Att.	Yds.	Avg.	TD	TD	2pt.	Pts.
1994—New York Jets NFL......	1	0	8	5	62.5	45	0	1	5.63	38.0	0	0	0.0	0	0	0	0
1995—New York Jets NFL......	1	0	29	16	55.2	128	0	1	4.41	52.1	1	9	9.0	0	0	0	0
1996—New York Jets NFL......	5	3	110	54	49.1	559	3	7	5.08	46.7	7	40	5.7	0	0	0	0
1997—New York Jets NFL......	6	2	97	56	57.7	705	3	1	7.27	86.5	3	-5	-1.7	0	0	0	0
1998—New York Jets NFL......	5	3	108	58	53.7	749	4	6	6.94	64.9	5	-11	-2.2	0	0	0	0
1999—Seattle NFL................	3	1	30	18	60.0	283	2	0	9.43	113.6	3	-1	-0.3	0	0	0	0
Pro totals (6 years)...............	21	9	382	207	54.2	2469	12	16	6.46	67.2	19	32	1.7	0	0	0	0

FOLEY, STEVE LB BENGALS

PERSONAL: Born September 9, 1975, in Little Rock, Ark. ... 6-3/260.
HIGH SCHOOL: Hall (Little Rock, Ark.).
COLLEGE: Northeast Louisiana.
TRANSACTIONS/CAREER NOTES: Selected by Cincinnati Bengals in third round (75th pick overall) of 1998 NFL draft. ... Signed by Bengals (July 19, 1998).
PRO STATISTICS: 1999—Recovered two fumbles.

Year Team	G	GS	SACKS
1998—Cincinnati NFL	10	1	2.0
1999—Cincinnati NFL	16	16	3.5
Pro totals (2 years)..	26	17	5.5

FOLSTON, JAMES LB CARDINALS

PERSONAL: Born August 14, 1971, in Cocoa, Fla. ... 6-3/240. ... Full name: James Edward Folston.
HIGH SCHOOL: Cocoa (Fla.).
COLLEGE: Northeast Louisiana.
TRANSACTIONS/CAREER NOTES: Selected by Los Angeles Raiders in second round (52nd pick overall) of 1994 NFL draft. ... Signed by Raiders (July 13, 1994). ... Raiders franchise moved to Oakland (July 21, 1995). ... Granted free agency (February 14, 1997). ... Re-signed by Raiders for 1997 season. ... Released by Raiders (September 4, 1999). ... Signed by Arizona Cardinals (November 17, 1999).
PLAYING EXPERIENCE: Los Angeles Raiders NFL, 1994; Oakland NFL, 1995-1998; Arizona NFL, 1999. ... Games/Games started: 1994 (7/0), 1995 (15/0), 1996 (12/0), 1997 (16/7), 1998 (16/5), 1999 (6/0). Total: 72/12.
PRO STATISTICS: 1997—Recovered one fumble. 1998—Caught one pass for minus one yard and credited with one sack.

FONTENOT, AL DE CHARGERS

PERSONAL: Born September 17, 1970, in Houston. ... 6-4/287. ... Full name: Albert Paul Fontenot.
HIGH SCHOOL: Jack Yates (Houston).
JUNIOR COLLEGE: Navarro College (Texas).
COLLEGE: Baylor (degree in communications).
TRANSACTIONS/CAREER NOTES: Selected by Chicago Bears in fourth round (112th pick overall) of 1993 NFL draft. ... Signed by Bears (July 16, 1993). ... Granted free agency (February 16, 1996). ... Re-signed by Bears (April 18, 1996). ... Granted unconditional free agency (February 14, 1997). ... Signed by Indianapolis Colts (April 3, 1997). ... On injured reserve with calf injury (November 25, 1998-remainder of season).

F

... Released by Colts (April 28, 1999). ... Signed by San Diego Chargers (May 12, 1999). ... Granted unconditional free agency (February 11, 2000). ... Re-signed by Chargers (March 10, 2000).

PRO STATISTICS: 1993—Returned one kickoff for eight yards. 1995—Credited with one safety and recovered one fumble. 1997—Recovered three fumbles for 35 yards and one touchdown. 1998—Recovered one fumble. 1999—Recovered one fumble.

Year Team	G	GS	SACKS
1993—Chicago NFL	16	0	1.0
1994—Chicago NFL	16	8	4.0
1995—Chicago NFL	13	5	2.5
1996—Chicago NFL	16	15	4.5
1997—Indianapolis NFL	16	16	4.5
1998—Indianapolis NFL	7	5	1.0
1999—San Diego NFL	15	15	5.0
Pro totals (7 years)	**99**	**64**	**22.5**

FONTENOT, JERRY   C   SAINTS

PERSONAL: Born November 21, 1966, in Lafayette, La. ... 6-3/300. ... Full name: Jerry Paul Fontenot.
HIGH SCHOOL: Lafayette (La.).
COLLEGE: Texas A&M.
TRANSACTIONS/CAREER NOTES: Selected by Chicago Bears in third round (65th pick overall) of 1989 NFL draft. ... Signed by Bears (July 27, 1989). ... Granted free agency (March 1, 1993). ... Re-signed by Bears (June 16, 1993). ... Granted free agency (February 16, 1996). ... Re-signed by Bears (July 10, 1996). ... Granted unconditional free agency (February 14, 1997). ... Signed by New Orleans Saints (May 28, 1997). ... On injured reserve with knee injury (October 14, 1998-remainder of season). ... Granted unconditional free agency (February 12, 1999). ... Re-signed by Saints (February 15, 1999).
PLAYING EXPERIENCE: Chicago NFL, 1989-1996; New Orleans NFL, 1997-1999. ... Games/Games started: 1989 (16/0), 1990 (16/2), 1991 (16/7), 1992 (16/16), 1993 (16/16), 1994 (16/16), 1995 (16/16), 1996 (16/16), 1997 (16/16), 1998 (4/4), 1999 (16/16). Total: 164/125.
PRO STATISTICS: 1989—Recovered one fumble. 1990—Fumbled once. 1992—Fumbled once for minus two yards. 1993—Recovered one fumble. 1997—Fumbled three times. 1999—Recovered one fumble.

FORBES, MARLON   DB

PERSONAL: Born December 25, 1971, in Long Island, N.Y. ... 6-1/215.
HIGH SCHOOL: Central Islip (N.Y.).
COLLEGE: Penn State.
TRANSACTIONS/CAREER NOTES: Signed as non-drafted free agent by Chicago Bears (April 1, 1995). ... Released by Bears (August 27, 1995). ... Re-signed by Bears to practice squad (December 1, 1995). ... Released by Bears (August 27, 1996). ... Re-signed by Bears to practice squad (September 4, 1996). ... Activated (September 9, 1996). ... Selected by Cleveland Browns from Bears in NFL expansion draft (February 9, 1999). ... Granted free agency (February 12, 1999). ... Signed by Browns (June 16, 1999). ... Granted unconditional free agency (February 11, 2000).
PLAYING EXPERIENCE: Chicago NFL, 1996-1998; Cleveland NFL, 1999. ... Games/Games started: 1996 (15/0), 1997 (16/1), 1998 (16/2), 1999 (16/1). Total: 63/4.
PRO STATISTICS: 1996—Recovered one fumble.

FORD, HENRY   DT   TITANS

PERSONAL: Born October 30, 1971, in Fort Worth, Texas. ... 6-3/295.
HIGH SCHOOL: Trimble Technical (Fort Worth, Texas).
COLLEGE: Arkansas.
TRANSACTIONS/CAREER NOTES: Selected by Houston Oilers in first round (26th pick overall) of 1994 NFL draft. ... Signed by Oilers (June 16, 1994). ... Oilers franchise moved to Tennessee for 1997 season. ... Granted unconditional free agency (February 13, 1998). ... Re-signed by Oilers (March 2, 1998). ... Oilers franchise renamed Tennessee Titans for 1999 season (December 26, 1998).
CHAMPIONSHIP GAME EXPERIENCE: Played in AFC championship game (1999 season). ... Played in Super Bowl XXXIV (1999 season).
PRO STATISTICS: 1997—Recovered two fumbles for 13 yards. 1998—Recovered one fumble. 1999—Recovered two fumbles.

Year Team	G	GS	SACKS
1994—Houston NFL	11	0	0.0
1995—Houston NFL	16	16	4.5
1996—Houston NFL	15	14	1.0
1997—Tennessee NFL	16	16	5.0
1998—Tennessee NFL	13	5	1.5
1999—Tennessee NFL	12	9	5.5
Pro totals (6 years)	**83**	**60**	**17.5**

FOREMAN, JAY   LB   BILLS

PERSONAL: Born December 16, 1976, in Eden Prairie, Minn. ... 6-1/240. ... Full name: Jamal A. Foreman. ... Son of Chuck Foreman, running back with Minnesota Vikings (1973-79) and New England Patriots (1980).
HIGH SCHOOL: Eden Prairie (Minn.).
COLLEGE: Nebraska (degree in business administration).
TRANSACTIONS/CAREER NOTES: Selected by Buffalo Bills in fifth round (156th pick overall) of 1999 NFL draft. ... Signed by Bills (July 27, 1999).
PLAYING EXPERIENCE: Buffalo NFL, 1999. ... Games/Games started: 1999 (7/0).

F

FORTIN, ROMAN   C/G   CHARGERS

PERSONAL: Born February 26, 1967, in Columbus, Ohio. ... 6-5/297. ... Full name: Roman Brian Fortin.
HIGH SCHOOL: Ventura (Calif.).
COLLEGE: Oregon, then San Diego State.
TRANSACTIONS/CAREER NOTES: Selected by Detroit Lions in eighth round (203rd pick overall) of 1990 NFL draft. ... On injured reserve (September 5, 1990-entire season). ... Granted unconditional free agency (February 1, 1992). ... Signed by Atlanta Falcons (March 31, 1992). ... Granted unconditional free agency (February 17, 1994). ... Re-signed by Falcons (February 24, 1994). ... Granted unconditional free agency (February 16, 1996). ... Re-signed by Falcons (February 20, 1996). ... Released by Falcons (February 11, 1998). ... Signed by San Diego Chargers (March 17, 1998). ... Granted unconditional free agency (February 11, 2000). ... Re-signed by Chargers (February 17, 2000).
PLAYING EXPERIENCE: Detroit NFL, 1991; Atlanta NFL, 1992-1997; San Diego NFL, 1998 and 1999. ... Games/Games started: 1991 (16/2), 1992 (16/1), 1993 (16/1), 1994 (16/16), 1995 (16/16), 1996 (16/16), 1997 (3/3), 1998 (16/16), 1999 (16/16). Total: 131/87.
CHAMPIONSHIP GAME EXPERIENCE: Played in NFC championship game (1991 season).
PRO STATISTICS: 1991—Caught one pass for four yards. 1992—Returned one kickoff for five yards and recovered one fumble. 1995—Fumbled twice for minus six yards. 1996—Recovered two fumbles. 1999—Recovered two fumbles.

FRANCIS, JAMES   LB

PERSONAL: Born August 4, 1968, in Houston. ... 6-5/257. ... Brother of Ron Francis, cornerback with Dallas Cowboys (1987-90).
HIGH SCHOOL: La Marque (Texas).
COLLEGE: Baylor.
TRANSACTIONS/CAREER NOTES: Selected by Cincinnati Bengals in first round (12th pick overall) of 1990 NFL draft. ... Signed by Bengals (July 19, 1990). ... On injured reserve with knee injury (December 26, 1992-remainder of season). ... Designated by Bengals as transition player (February 25, 1993). ... On injured reserve with broken leg (November 22, 1995-remainder of season). ... Released by Bengals (September 5, 1999). ... Signed by Washington Redskins (October 26, 1999). ... Granted free agency (February 11, 2000).
HONORS: Named special-teams player on THE SPORTING NEWS college All-America first team (1989).
PRO STATISTICS: 1990—Credited with a safety. 1991—Recovered one fumble. 1992—Recovered two fumbles for three yards. 1993—Recovered one fumble. 1996—Recovered three fumbles. 1997—Recovered one fumble.

			INTERCEPTIONS				SACKS
Year Team	G	GS	No.	Yds.	Avg.	TD	No.
1990—Cincinnati NFL	16	16	1	17	17.0	▲1	8.0
1991—Cincinnati NFL	16	16	1	0	0.0	0	3.0
1992—Cincinnati NFL	14	13	3	108	36.0	1	6.0
1993—Cincinnati NFL	14	12	2	12	6.0	0	2.0
1994—Cincinnati NFL	16	16	0	0	0.0	0	4.5
1995—Cincinnati NFL	11	11	0	0	0.0	0	3.0
1996—Cincinnati NFL	16	15	3	61	20.3	1	3.0
1997—Cincinnati NFL	16	16	1	7	7.0	0	3.5
1998—Cincinnati NFL	14	14	0	0	0.0	0	0.0
1999—Washington NFL	10	1	0	0	0.0	0	0.5
Pro totals (10 years)	143	130	11	205	18.6	3	33.5

FRANKLIN, P.J.   WR   SAINTS

PERSONAL: Born September 28, 1977, in Independence, La. ... 5-10/180. ... Full name: David L. Franklin Jr.
HIGH SCHOOL: Amite (La.).
COLLEGE: Tulane.
TRANSACTIONS/CAREER NOTES: Signed as non-drafted free agent by New Orleans Saints (April 23, 1999). ... Released by Saints (September 5, 1999). ... Re-signed by Saints to practice squad (September 6, 1999). ... Activated (December 16, 1999).
PLAYING EXPERIENCE: New Orleans NFL, 1999. ... Games/Games started: 1999 (3/0).
PRO STATISTICS: 1999—Rushed once for no yards and caught two passes for 13 yards.
SINGLE GAME HIGHS (regular season): Receptions—1 (January 2, 2000, vs. Carolina); yards—8 (January 2, 2000, vs. Carolina); and touchdown receptions—0.

FREDERICK, MIKE   DE

PERSONAL: Born August 6, 1972, in Abington, Pa. ... 6-5/280. ... Full name: Thomas Michael Frederick.
HIGH SCHOOL: Neshaminy (Langhorne, Pa.).
COLLEGE: Virginia (degree in management).
TRANSACTIONS/CAREER NOTES: Selected by Cleveland Browns in third round (94th pick overall) of 1995 NFL draft. ... Signed by Browns (July 14, 1995). ... Browns franchise moved to Baltimore and renamed Ravens for 1996 season (March 11, 1996). ... Granted free agency (February 13, 1998). ... Re-signed by Ravens (June 10, 1998). ... Granted unconditional free agency (February 12, 1999). ... Signed by New York Jets (February 17, 1999). ... Released by Jets (August 30, 1999). ... Signed by Tennessee Titans (September 5, 1999). ... Granted unconditional free agency (February 11, 2000).
PLAYING EXPERIENCE: Cleveland NFL, 1995; Baltimore NFL, 1996-1998; Tennessee NFL, 1999. ... Games/Games started: 1995 (16/0), 1996 (16/11), 1997 (16/1), 1998 (10/0), 1999 (13/0). Total: 71/12.
CHAMPIONSHIP GAME EXPERIENCE: Member of Titans for AFC championship game (1999 season); inactive. ... Member of Titans for Super Bowl XXXIV (1999 season); inactive.
PRO STATISTICS: 1995—Credited with one sack and returned two kickoffs for 16 yards. 1996—Lost one yard with lateral from kickoff return. 1997—Recovered one fumble. 1999—Credited with $1/2$ sack.

FREDRICKSON, ROB   LB   CARDINALS

PERSONAL: Born May 13, 1971, in Saint Joseph, Mich. ... 6-4/235. ... Full name: Robert J. Fredrickson.

F

HIGH SCHOOL: Saint Joseph (Mich.) Senior.

COLLEGE: Michigan State.

TRANSACTIONS/CAREER NOTES: Selected by Los Angeles Raiders in first round (22nd pick overall) of 1994 NFL draft. ... Signed by Raiders (July 19, 1994). ... Raiders franchise moved to Oakland (July 21, 1995). ... On injured reserve with shoulder injury (November 20, 1996-remainder of season). ... Traded by Raiders to Detroit Lions for fourth-round pick (traded to Washington) in 1998 draft (March 25, 1998). ... Granted unconditional free agency (February 12, 1999). ... Signed by Arizona Cardinals (March 26, 1999).

PRO STATISTICS: 1995—Recovered four fumbles for 35 yards and one touchdown. 1999—Recovered one fumble.

				INTERCEPTIONS			SACKS
Year Team	G	GS	No.	Yds.	Avg.	TD	No.
1994—Los Angeles Raiders NFL	16	12	0	0	0.0	0	3.0
1995—Oakland NFL	16	15	1	14	14.0	0	0.0
1996—Oakland NFL	10	10	0	0	0.0	0	0.0
1997—Oakland NFL	16	13	0	0	0.0	0	2.0
1998—Detroit NFL	16	16	1	0	0.0	0	2.5
1999—Arizona NFL	16	16	2	57	28.5	1	2.0
Pro totals (6 years)	90	82	4	71	17.8	1	9.5

FREEMAN, ANTONIO — WR — PACKERS

PERSONAL: Born May 27, 1972, in Baltimore. ... 6-1/198. ... Full name: Antonio Michael Freeman.

HIGH SCHOOL: Polytechnic (Baltimore).

COLLEGE: Virginia Tech.

TRANSACTIONS/CAREER NOTES: Selected by Green Bay Packers in third round (90th pick overall) of 1995 NFL draft. ... Signed by Packers (June 22, 1995). ... Granted free agency (February 13, 1998). ... Re-signed by Packers (June 16, 1998). ... Designated by Packers as franchise player (February 12, 1999).

CHAMPIONSHIP GAME EXPERIENCE: Played in NFC championship game (1995-1997 seasons). ... Member of Super Bowl championship team (1996 season). ... Played in Super Bowl XXXII (1997 season).

HONORS: Named wide receiver on THE SPORTING NEWS NFL All-Pro team (1998). ... Played in Pro Bowl (1998 season).

POST SEASON RECORDS: Holds Super Bowl record for longest pass reception (from Brett Favre)—81 yards (January 26, 1997, vs. New England). ... Shares NFL postseason record for most touchdowns by punt return—1(December 31, 1995, vs. Atlanta).

PRO STATISTICS: 1995—Recovered four fumbles. 1996—Recovered one fumble for 14 yards. 1997—Rushed once for 14 yards. 1998—Rushed three times for five yards. 1999—Rushed once for minus two yards and recovered one fumble.

SINGLE GAME HIGHS (regular season): Receptions—10 (December 14, 1997, vs. Carolina); yards—193 (November 1, 1998, vs. San Francisco); and touchdown receptions—3 (December 20, 1998, vs. Tennessee).

STATISTICAL PLATEAUS: 100-yard receiving games: 1996 (4), 1997 (3), 1998 (6), 1999 (3). Total: 16.

			RECEIVING				PUNT RETURNS				KICKOFF RETURNS				TOTALS			
Year Team	G	GS	No.	Yds.	Avg.	TD	No.	Yds.	Avg.	TD	No.	Yds.	Avg.	TD	TD	2pt.	Pts.	Fum.
1995—Green Bay NFL	11	0	8	106	13.3	1	37	292	7.9	0	24	556	23.2	0	1	0	6	7
1996—Green Bay NFL	12	12	56	933	16.7	9	0	0	0.0	0	1	16	16.0	0	9	0	54	3
1997—Green Bay NFL	16	16	81	1243	15.3	12	0	0	0.0	0	0	0	0.0	0	12	0	72	1
1998—Green Bay NFL	15	15	84	*1424	17.0	14	0	0	0.0	0	0	0	0.0	0	14	1	86	0
1999—Green Bay NFL	16	16	74	1074	14.5	6	0	0	0.0	0	0	0	0.0	0	6	0	36	1
Pro totals (5 years)	70	59	303	4780	15.8	42	37	292	7.9	0	25	572	22.9	0	42	1	254	12

FREROTTE, GUS — QB — BRONCOS

PERSONAL: Born August 3, 1971, in Kittanning, Pa. ... 6-3/230. ... Full name: Gustave Joseph Frerotte. ... Brother of Mitch Frerotte, guard with Buffalo Bills (1987 and 1990-92).

HIGH SCHOOL: Ford City (Pa.) Junior-Senior.

COLLEGE: Tulsa.

TRANSACTIONS/CAREER NOTES: Selected by Washington Redskins in seventh round (197th pick overall) of 1994 NFL draft. ... Signed by Redskins (July 19, 1994). ... Granted free agency (February 14, 1997). ... Re-signed by Redskins (July 18, 1997). ... On injured reserve with hip injury (December 2, 1997-remainder of season). ... Released by Redskins (February 11, 1999). ... Signed by Detroit Lions (March 3, 1999). ... Granted unconditional free agency (February 11, 2000). ... Signed by Denver Broncos (March 3, 2000).

HONORS: Played in Pro Bowl (1996 season).

PRO STATISTICS: 1994—Fumbled four times and recovered two fumbles for minus four yards. 1995—Fumbled seven times and recovered four fumbles for minus 16 yards. 1996—Fumbled 12 times and recovered one fumble for minus 12 yards. 1997—Fumbled eight times and recovered two fumbles for minus 16 yards. 1999—Fumbled three times and recovered one fumble.

SINGLE GAME HIGHS (regular season): Attempts—45 (November 30, 1997, vs. St. Louis); completions—29 (November 25, 1999, vs. Chicago); yards—375 (November 14, 1999, vs. Arizona); and touchdown passes—3 (September 28, 1997, vs. Jacksonville).

STATISTICAL PLATEAUS: 300-yard passing games: 1995 (1), 1996 (1), 1999 (2). Total: 4.

MISCELLANEOUS: Regular-season record as starting NFL quarterback: 21-30-1 (.413). ... Postseason record as starting NFL quarterback: 0-1.

			PASSING								RUSHING				TOTALS		
Year Team	G	GS	Att.	Cmp.	Pct.	Yds.	TD	Int.	Avg.	Rat.	Att.	Yds.	Avg.	TD	TD	2pt.	Pts.
1994—Washington NFL	4	4	100	46	46.0	600	5	5	6.00	61.3	4	1	0.3	0	0	0	0
1995—Washington NFL	16	11	396	199	50.3	2751	13	13	6.95	70.2	22	16	0.7	1	1	0	6
1996—Washington NFL	16	16	470	270	57.4	3453	12	11	7.35	79.3	28	16	0.6	0	0	0	0
1997—Washington NFL	13	13	402	204	50.7	2682	17	12	6.67	73.8	24	65	2.7	2	2	0	12
1998—Washington NFL	3	2	54	25	46.3	283	1	3	5.24	45.5	3	20	6.7	0	0	0	0
1999—Detroit NFL	9	6	288	175	60.8	2117	9	7	7.35	83.6	15	33	2.2	0	0	0	0
Pro totals (6 years)	61	52	1710	919	53.7	11886	57	51	6.95	74.5	96	151	1.6	3	3	0	18

FRICKE, BEN — G/C — COWBOYS

PERSONAL: Born November 3, 1975, in Austin, Texas. ... 6-0/295.

HIGH SCHOOL: L.C. Anderson (Austin, Texas).

F

COLLEGE: Houston.

TRANSACTIONS/CAREER NOTES: Selected by New York Giants in seventh round (213th pick overall) of 1998 NFL draft. ... Signed by Giants (July 20, 1998). ... Released by Giants (August 22, 1998). ... Selected by Amsterdam Admirals in 1999 NFL Europe draft (February 23, 1999). ... Signed by Dallas Cowboys (August 3, 1999). ... Released by Cowboys (September 22, 1999). ... Re-signed by Cowboys (October 5, 1999). ... Released by Cowboys (October 27, 1999). ... Re-signed by Cowboys to practice squad (October 28, 1999). ... Activated (November 19, 1999). ... Assigned by Cowboys to Admirals in 2000 NFL Europe enhancement allocation program (February 18, 2000).

PLAYING EXPERIENCE: Amsterdam Admirals NFLE, 1999; Dallas NFL, 1999. ... Games/Games started: NFLE 1999 (games played unavailable), NFL 1999 (3/0).

HONORS: Named center on THE SPORTING NEWS college All-America second team (1997).

FRIESZ, JOHN　　　　　　QB　　　　　　PATRIOTS

PERSONAL: Born May 19, 1967, in Missoula, Mont. ... 6-4/223. ... Full name: John Melvin Friesz. ... Name pronounced FREEZE.

HIGH SCHOOL: Coeur D'Alene (Idaho).

COLLEGE: Idaho.

TRANSACTIONS/CAREER NOTES: Selected by San Diego Chargers in sixth round (138th pick overall) of 1990 NFL draft. ... Signed by Chargers (July 20, 1990). ... On injured reserve with elbow injury (September 4-October 3, 1990). ... On practice squad (October 3-December 28, 1990). ... Granted free agency (February 1, 1992). ... Re-signed by Chargers (July 27, 1992). ... On injured reserve with knee injury (August 25, 1992-entire season). ... Granted unconditional free agency (February 17, 1994). ... Signed by Washington Redskins (April 18, 1994). ... Granted unconditional free agency (February 17, 1995). ... Signed by Seattle Seahawks (March 17, 1995). ... Released by Seahawks (February 10, 1999). ... Signed by New England Patriots (April 22, 1999).

HONORS: Walter Payton Award winner (1989).

PRO STATISTICS: 1991—Fumbled 10 times and recovered two fumbles for minus 21 yards. 1993—Fumbled twice and recovered one fumble for minus three yards. 1994—Fumbled twice and recovered one fumble. 1995—Fumbled twice and recovered one fumble for minus three yards. 1996—Fumbled seven times and recovered two fumbles for minus six yards. 1997—Fumbled once and recovered one fumble for minus two yards.

SINGLE GAME HIGHS (regular season): Attempts—54 (October 20, 1991, vs. Cleveland); completions—33 (October 20, 1991, vs. Cleveland); yards—381 (September 18, 1994, vs. New York Giants); and touchdown passes—4 (September 11, 1994, vs. New Orleans).

STATISTICAL PLATEAUS: 300-yard passing games: 1991 (2), 1994 (1), 1996 (1). Total: 4.

MISCELLANEOUS: Regular-season record as starting NFL quarterback: 13-25 (.342).

| | | | PASSING | | | | | | | | RUSHING | | | | TOTALS | | |
Year　Team	G	GS	Att.	Cmp.	Pct.	Yds.	TD	Int.	Avg.	Rat.	Att.	Yds.	Avg.	TD	TD	2pt.	Pts.
1990—San Diego NFL...........	1	1	22	11	50.0	98	1	1	4.45	58.5	1	3	3.0	0	0	0	0
1991—San Diego NFL...........	16	16	487	262	53.8	2896	12	15	5.95	67.1	10	18	1.8	0	0	0	0
1992—San Diego NFL...........							Did not play.										
1993—San Diego NFL...........	12	6	238	128	53.8	1402	6	4	5.89	72.8	10	3	0.3	0	0	0	0
1994—Washington NFL.........	16	4	180	105	58.3	1266	10	9	7.03	77.7	1	1	1.0	0	0	0	0
1995—Seattle NFL.................	6	3	120	64	53.3	795	6	3	6.63	80.4	11	0	0.0	0	0	0	0
1996—Seattle NFL.................	8	6	211	120	56.9	1629	8	4	7.72	86.4	12	1	0.1	0	0	0	0
1997—Seattle NFL.................	2	1	36	15	41.7	138	0	3	3.83	18.1	1	0	0.0	0	0	0	0
1998—Seattle NFL.................	6	1	49	29	59.2	409	2	2	8.35	82.8	5	5	1.0	0	0	0	0
1999—New England NFL.......	1	0	0	0	0.0	0	0	0	0.0	...	2	-2	-1.0	0	0	0	0
Pro totals (9 years)...............	68	38	1343	734	54.7	8633	45	41	6.43	72.9	53	29	0.5	0	0	0	0

FROST, SCOTT　　　　　　S　　　　　　JETS

PERSONAL: Born January 4, 1975, in Wood River, Neb. ... 6-3/219.

HIGH SCHOOL: Wood River (Neb.).

COLLEGE: Stanford, then Nebraska (degree in finance, 1997).

TRANSACTIONS/CAREER NOTES: Selected by New York Jets in third round (67th pick overall) of 1998 NFL draft. ... Signed by Jets (July 21, 1998).

PLAYING EXPERIENCE: New York Jets NFL, 1998 and 1999. ... Games/Games started: 1998 (13/0), 1999 (14/0). Total: 27/0.

CHAMPIONSHIP GAME EXPERIENCE: Played in AFC championship game (1998 season).

PRO STATISTICS: 1998—Returned one punt for no yards and fumbled once.

F

FRYAR, IRVING　　　　　　WR　　　　　　REDSKINS

PERSONAL: Born September 28, 1962, in Mount Holly, N.J. ... 6-0/198. ... Full name: Irving Dale Fryar.

HIGH SCHOOL: Rancocas Valley (Mount Holly, N.J.).

COLLEGE: Nebraska (degree in bible study).

TRANSACTIONS/CAREER NOTES: Selected by Chicago Blitz in first round (third pick overall) of 1984 USFL draft. ... Signed by New England Patriots (April 11, 1984). ... Selected officially by Patriots in first round (first pick overall) of 1984 NFL draft. ... Traded by Patriots to Miami Dolphins for second-round pick (OL Todd Rucci) in 1993 draft and third-round pick (C Joe Burch) in 1994 draft (April 1, 1993). ... Granted unconditional free agency (February 16, 1996). ... Signed by Philadelphia Eagles (March 19, 1996). ... Announced retirement (December 23, 1998). ... Signed by Washington Redskins (August 19, 1999).

CHAMPIONSHIP GAME EXPERIENCE: Played in Super Bowl XX (1985 season).

HONORS: Named wide receiver on THE SPORTING NEWS college All-America first team (1983). ... Played in Pro Bowl (1985, 1993, 1994, 1996 and 1997 seasons).

PRO STATISTICS: 1984—Fumbled four times and recovered one fumble. 1985—Fumbled four times. 1986—Fumbled four times and recovered one fumble. 1987—Fumbled twice. 1988—Fumbled twice. 1989—Fumbled twice. 1990—Fumbled once and recovered one fumble. 1991—Attempted one pass without a completion and fumbled twice. 1994—Ran two yards with lateral from reception for a touchdown and recovered one fumble for seven yards. 1997—Fumbled once.

SINGLE GAME HIGHS (regular season): Receptions—10 (October 12, 1997, vs. Jacksonville); yards—211 (September 4, 1994, vs. New England); and touchdown receptions—4 (October 20, 1996, vs. Miami).

STATISTICAL PLATEAUS: 100-yard receiving games: 1985 (1), 1986 (2), 1987 (1), 1988 (1), 1989 (1), 1990 (1), 1991 (3), 1992 (2), 1993 (2), 1994 (6), 1995 (2), 1996 (4), 1997 (6). Total: 32.

Year	Team	G	GS	RUSHING				RECEIVING				PUNT RETURNS				KICKOFF RETURNS				TOTALS		
				Att.	Yds.	Avg.	TD	No.	Yds.	Avg.	TD	No.	Yds.	Avg.	TD	No.	Yds.	Avg.	TD	TD	2pt	Pts.
1984—New England NFL		14	2	2	-11	-5.5	0	11	164	14.9	1	36	347	9.6	0	5	95	19.0	0	1	0	6
1985—New England NFL		16	14	7	27	3.9	1	39	670	17.2	7	37	520*14.1	†2		3	39	13.0	0	10	0	60
1986—New England NFL		14	13	4	80	20.0	0	43	737	17.1	6	35	366	10.5	▲1	10	192	19.2	0	7	0	42
1987—New England NFL		12	12	9	52	5.8	0	31	467	15.1	5	18	174	9.7	0	6	119	19.8	0	5	0	30
1988—New England NFL		15	14	6	12	2.0	0	33	490	14.8	5	38	398	10.5	0	1	3	3.0	0	5	0	30
1989—New England NFL		11	5	2	15	7.5	0	29	537	18.5	3	12	107	8.9	0	1	47	47.0	0	3	0	18
1990—New England NFL		16	15	0	0	0.0	0	54	856	15.9	4	28	133	4.8	0	0	0	0.0	0	4	0	24
1991—New England NFL		16	15	2	11	5.5	0	68	1014	14.9	3	2	10	5.0	0	0	0	0.0	0	3	0	18
1992—New England NFL		15	14	1	6	6.0	0	55	791	14.4	4	0	0	0.0	0	0	0	0.0	0	4	0	24
1993—Miami NFL		16	16	3	-4	-1.3	0	64	1010	15.8	5	0	0	0.0	0	1	10	10.0	0	5	0	30
1994—Miami NFL		16	16	0	0	0.0	0	73	1270	17.4	7	0	0	0.0	0	0	0	0.0	0	7	2	46
1995—Miami NFL		16	16	0	0	0.0	0	62	910	14.7	8	0	0	0.0	0	0	0	0.0	0	8	0	48
1996—Philadelphia NFL		16	16	1	-4	-4.0	0	88	1195	13.6	‡11	0	0	0.0	0	0	0	0.0	0	11	0	66
1997—Philadelphia NFL		16	16	0	0	0.0	0	86	1316	15.3	6	0	0	0.0	0	0	0	0.0	0	6	0	36
1998—Philadelphia NFL		16	16	3	46	15.3	0	48	556	11.6	2	0	0	0.0	0	0	0	0.0	0	2	0	12
1999—Washington NFL		16	1	0	0	0.0	0	26	254	9.8	2	0	0	0.0	0	0	0	0.0	0	2	0	12
Pro totals (16 years)		241	201	40	230	5.8	1	810	12237	15.1	79	206	2055	10.0	3	27	505	18.7	0	83	2	502

FUAMATU-MA'AFALA, CHRIS   RB   STEELERS

PERSONAL: Born March 4, 1977, in Honolulu. ... 5-11/252. ... Name pronounced fu-ah-MAH-tu ma-ah-FAH-la.
HIGH SCHOOL: St. Louis (Honolulu).
COLLEGE: Utah.
TRANSACTIONS/CAREER NOTES: Selected after junior season by Pittsburgh Steelers in sixth round (178th pick overall) of 1998 NFL draft. ... Signed by Steelers (July 10, 1998).
PRO STATISTICS: 1999—Returned one kickoff for nine yards.
SINGLE GAME HIGHS (regular season): Attempts—2 (October 18, 1998, vs. Baltimore); yards—10 (September 27, 1998, vs. Seattle); and rushing touchdowns—1 (November 9, 1998, vs. Green Bay).

Year Team	G	GS	RUSHING				RECEIVING				TOTALS			
			Att.	Yds.	Avg.	TD	No.	Yds.	Avg.	TD	TD	2pt.	Pts.	Fum.
1998—Pittsburgh NFL	12	0	7	30	4.3	2	9	84	9.3	1	3	0	18	0
1999—Pittsburgh NFL	10	0	1	4	4.0	0	0	0	0.0	0	0	0	0	0
Pro totals (2 years)	22	0	8	34	4.3	2	9	84	9.3	1	3	0	18	0

FULLER, COREY   DB   BROWNS

PERSONAL: Born May 1, 1971, in Tallahassee, Fla. ... 5-10/217.
HIGH SCHOOL: James S. Rickards (Tallahassee, Fla.).
COLLEGE: Florida State (degree in criminology and child development, 1994).
TRANSACTIONS/CAREER NOTES: Selected by Minnesota Vikings in second round (55th pick overall) of 1995 NFL draft. ... Signed by Vikings (July 24, 1995). ... Granted unconditional free agency (February 12, 1999). ... Signed by Cleveland Browns (February 18, 1999).
CHAMPIONSHIP GAME EXPERIENCE: Played in NFC championship game (1998 season).
PRO STATISTICS: 1995—Credited with 1/2 sack and recovered one fumble for 12 yards and a touchdown. 1998—Credited with one sack. 1999—Recovered two fumbles.

Year Team	G	GS	INTERCEPTIONS			
			No.	Yds.	Avg.	TD
1995—Minnesota NFL	16	11	1	0	0.0	0
1996—Minnesota NFL	16	14	3	3	1.0	0
1997—Minnesota NFL	16	16	2	24	12.0	0
1998—Minnesota NFL	16	16	4	36	9.0	0
1999—Cleveland NFL	16	16	0	0	0.0	0
Pro totals (5 years)	80	73	10	63	6.3	0

FULLER, RANDY   CB

PERSONAL: Born June 2, 1970, in Griffin, Ga. ... 5-10/184. ... Full name: Randy Lamar Fuller.
HIGH SCHOOL: William H. Spencer (Columbus, Ga.).
COLLEGE: Tennessee State.
TRANSACTIONS/CAREER NOTES: Selected by Denver Broncos in fourth round (123rd pick overall) of 1994 NFL draft. ... Signed by Broncos (July 22, 1994). ... Released by Broncos (August 22, 1995). ... Signed by Pittsburgh Steelers (September 12, 1995). ... Granted free agency (February 14, 1997). ... Re-signed by Steelers for 1997 season. ... Granted unconditional free agency (February 13, 1998). ... Signed by Atlanta Falcons (March 19, 1998). ... Released by Falcons (September 5, 1999). ... Signed by Seattle Seahawks (December 8, 1999). ... Granted unconditional free agency (February 11, 2000).
PLAYING EXPERIENCE: Denver NFL, 1994; Pittsburgh NFL, 1995-1997; Atlanta NFL, 1998; Seattle NFL, 1999. ... Games/Games started: 1994 (10/1), 1995 (13/0), 1996 (14/1), 1997 (12/3), 1998 (13/0), 1999 (2/0). Total: 64/5.
CHAMPIONSHIP GAME EXPERIENCE: Played in AFC championship game (1995 and 1997 seasons). ... Played in Super Bowl XXX (1995 season) and Super Bowl XXXIII (1998 season). ... Played in NFC championship game (1998 season).
PRO STATISTICS: 1996—Intercepted one pass for no yards. 1997—Credited with one sack. 1998—Credited with two sacks and recovered two fumbles.

GADSDEN, ORONDE   WR   DOLPHINS

PERSONAL: Born August 20, 1971, in Charleston, S.C. ... 6-2/215. ... Full name: Oronde Benjamin Gadsden. ... Name pronounced o-RON-day.

F
G

HIGH SCHOOL: Burke (Charleston, S.C.).

COLLEGE: Winston-Salem (degree in marketing).

TRANSACTIONS/CAREER NOTES: Signed by Dallas Cowboys as non-drafted free agent (August 1995). ... Released by Cowboys (August 22, 1995). ... Re-signed by Cowboys to practice squad (August 30, 1995). ... Activated (January 8, 1996). ... On injured reserve with left ankle sprain (January 11, 1996-remainder of playoffs). ... Released by Cowboys (August 27, 1996). ... Signed by Pittsburgh Steelers (February 4, 1997). ... Released by Steelers (August 19, 1997). ... Signed by Cowboys (August 21, 1997). ... Released by Cowboys (August 24, 1997). ... Played with Portland Forest Dragons of Arena League (1998). ... Signed by Miami Dolphins (August 3, 1998).

SINGLE GAME HIGHS (regular season): Receptions—9 (January 2, 2000, vs. Washington); yards—153 (December 27, 1998, vs. Atlanta); and touchdown receptions—2 (November 21, 1999, vs. New England).

STATISTICAL PLATEAUS: 100-yard receiving games: 1998 (1), 1999 (3). Total: 4.

				RECEIVING				TOTALS		
Year Team	G	GS	No.	Yds.	Avg.	TD	TD	2pt.	Pts.	Fum.
1995—Dallas NFL						Did not play.				
1996—						Did not play.				
1997—						Did not play.				
1998—Miami NFL	16	12	48	713	14.9	7	7	0	42	2
1999—Miami NFL	16	7	48	803	16.7	6	6	0	36	0
Pro totals (2 years)	32	19	96	1516	15.8	13	13	0	78	2

GALLOWAY, JOEY   WR   COWBOYS

PERSONAL: Born November 20, 1971, in Bellaire, Ohio. ... 5-11/188.

HIGH SCHOOL: Bellaire (Ohio).

COLLEGE: Ohio State (degree in business/marketing, 1994).

TRANSACTIONS/CAREER NOTES: Selected by Seattle Seahawks in first round (eighth pick overall) of 1995 NFL draft. ... Signed by Seahawks (July 20, 1995). ... On did not report list (September 4-November 9, 1999). ... Designated by Seahawks as franchise player (February 11, 2000). ... Traded by Seahawks to Dallas Cowboys for first-round pick (RB Shaun Alexander) in 2000 draft and first round pick in 2001 draft (February 12, 2000).

PRO STATISTICS: 1995—Returned two kickoffs for 30 yards. 1997—Recovered one fumble.

SINGLE GAME HIGHS (regular season): Receptions—8 (November 2, 1997, vs. Denver); yards—142 (September 6, 1998, vs. Philadelphia); and touchdown receptions—3 (October 26, 1997, vs. Oakland).

STATISTICAL PLATEAUS: 100-yard receiving games: 1995 (3), 1996 (2), 1997 (3), 1998 (4). Total: 12.

			RUSHING				RECEIVING				PUNT RETURNS				TOTALS		
Year Team	G	GS	Att.	Yds.	Avg.	TD	No.	Yds.	Avg.	TD	No.	Yds.	Avg.	TD	TD	2pt.	Pts. Fum.
1995—Seattle NFL	16	16	11	154	14.0	1	67	1039	15.5	7	36	360	10.0	†1	9	0	54 1
1996—Seattle NFL	16	16	15	127	8.5	0	57	987	17.3	7	15	158	10.5	▲1	8	0	48 2
1997—Seattle NFL	15	15	9	72	8.0	0	72	1049	14.6 ▲12		0	0	0.0	0	12	0	72 1
1998—Seattle NFL	16	16	9	26	2.9	0	65	1047	16.1 ▲10		25	251	10.0	†2	12	0	72 1
1999—Seattle NFL	8	4	1	-1	-1.0	0	22	335	15.2	1	3	54	18.0	0	1	0	6 0
Pro totals (5 years)	71	67	45	378	8.4	1	283	4457	15.7	37	79	823	10.4	4	42	0	252 5

GALYON, SCOTT   LB   DOLPHINS

PERSONAL: Born March 23, 1974, in Seymour, Tenn. ... 6-2/245. ... Name pronounced GAL-yun.

HIGH SCHOOL: Seymour (Tenn.).

COLLEGE: Tennessee.

TRANSACTIONS/CAREER NOTES: Selected by New York Giants in sixth round (182nd pick overall) of 1996 NFL draft. ... Signed by Giants (July 17, 1996). ... On injured reserve with knee injury (December 8, 1998-remainder of season). ... Granted free agency (February 12, 1999). ... Re-signed by Giants (May 3, 1999). ... Granted unconditional free agency (February 11, 2000). ... Signed by Miami Dolphins (February 25, 2000).

PLAYING EXPERIENCE: New York Giants NFL, 1996-1999. ... Games/Games started: 1996 (16/0), 1997 (16/0), 1998 (10/1), 1999 (16/0). Total: 58/1.

PRO STATISTICS: 1997—Credited with three sacks. 1998—Credited with one sack and recovered one fumble. 1999—Credited with one sack.

GAMMON, KENDALL   TE   CHIEFS

PERSONAL: Born October 23, 1968, in Wichita, Kan. ... 6-4/260. ... Full name: Kendall Robert Gammon.

HIGH SCHOOL: Rose Hill (Kan.).

COLLEGE: Pittsburg (Kan.) State (degree in physical education).

TRANSACTIONS/CAREER NOTES: Selected by Pittsburgh Steelers in 11th round (291st pick overall) of 1992 NFL draft. ... Signed by Steelers (July 14, 1992). ... Released by Steelers (August 30, 1993). ... Re-signed by Steelers (August 31, 1993). ... Granted unconditional free agency (February 17, 1995). ... Re-signed by Steelers (May 8, 1995). ... Released by Steelers (August 26, 1996). ... Signed by New Orleans Saints (August 28, 1996). ... Granted unconditional free agency (February 11, 2000). ... Signed by Kansas City Chiefs (February 23, 2000).

PLAYING EXPERIENCE: Pittsburgh NFL, 1992-1995; New Orleans NFL, 1996-1999. ... Games/Games started: 1992 (16/0), 1993 (16/0), 1994 (16/0), 1995 (16/0), 1996 (16/0), 1997 (16/0), 1998 (16/0), 1999 (16/0). Total: 128/0.

CHAMPIONSHIP GAME EXPERIENCE: Played in AFC championship game (1994 and 1995 seasons). ... Played in Super Bowl XXX (1995 season).

PRO STATISTICS: 1999—Returned one kickoff for nine yards.

G

GANDY, WAYNE   OT   STEELERS

PERSONAL: Born February 10, 1971, in Haines City, Fla. ... 6-5/310. ... Full name: Wayne Lamar Gandy.

HIGH SCHOOL: Haines City (Fla.).

COLLEGE: Auburn.

TRANSACTIONS/CAREER NOTES: Selected by Los Angeles Rams in first round (15th pick overall) of 1994 NFL draft. ... Signed by Rams (July 23, 1994). ... Rams franchise moved to St. Louis (April 12, 1995). ... Granted unconditional free agency (February 12, 1999). ... Signed by Pittsburgh Steelers (April 6, 1999).

PLAYING EXPERIENCE: Los Angeles Rams NFL, 1994; St. Louis NFL, 1995-1998; Pittsburgh NFL, 1999. ... Games/Games started: 1994 (16/9), 1995 (16/16), 1996 (16/16), 1997 (16/16), 1998 (16/16), 1999 (16/16). Total: 96/89.

HONORS: Named offensive lineman on THE SPORTING NEWS college All-America first team (1993).

GANNON, RICH   QB   RAIDERS

PERSONAL: Born December 20, 1965, in Philadelphia. ... 6-3/210. ... Full name: Richard Joseph Gannon.
HIGH SCHOOL: St. Joseph's Prep (Philadelphia).
COLLEGE: Delaware (degree in criminal justice, 1987).
TRANSACTIONS/CAREER NOTES: Selected by New England Patriots in fourth round (98th pick overall) of 1987 NFL draft. ... Rights traded by Patriots to Minnesota Vikings for fourth- (WR Sammy Martin) and 11th-round (traded) picks in 1988 draft (May 6, 1987). ... Signed by Vikings (July 30, 1987). ... Active for 13 games (1989); did not play. ... Granted free agency (February 1, 1990). ... Re-signed by Vikings (July 30, 1990). ... Granted free agency (February 1, 1991). ... Re-signed by Vikings (July 25, 1991). ... Granted free agency (February 1, 1992). ... Re-signed by Vikings (August 8, 1992). ... Traded by Vikings to Washington Redskins for conditional draft pick (August 20, 1993). ... Granted unconditional free agency (February 17, 1994). ... Signed by Kansas City Chiefs (March 29, 1995). ... Released by Chiefs (February 15, 1996). ... Re-signed by Chiefs (April 3, 1996). ... Granted unconditional free agency (February 12, 1999). ... Signed by Oakland Raiders (February 16, 1999).
CHAMPIONSHIP GAME EXPERIENCE: Member of Vikings for NFC championship game (1987 season); did not play.
HONORS: Played in Pro Bowl (1999 season).
PRO STATISTICS: 1990—Recovered six fumbles for minus three yards. 1991—Caught one pass for no yards. 1993—Recovered one fumble. 1996—Fumbled once. 1997—Fumbled five times. 1998—Fumbled nine times and recovered four fumbles for minus 15 yards. 1999—Caught one pass for minus three yards, fumbled eight times and recovered one fumble for minus five yards.
SINGLE GAME HIGHS (regular season): Attempts—63 (October 20, 1991, vs. New England); completions—35 (October 20, 1991, vs. New England); yards—352 (October 24, 1999, vs. New York Jets); and touchdown passes—4 (November 14, 1999, vs. San Diego).
STATISTICAL PLATEAUS: 300-yard passing games: 1991 (1), 1992 (1), 1997 (1), 1998 (1), 1999 (2). Total: 6.
MISCELLANEOUS: Regular-season record as starting NFL quarterback: 39-35 (.527).

			PASSING								RUSHING				TOTALS		
Year Team	G	GS	Att.	Cmp.	Pct.	Yds.	TD	Int.	Avg.	Rat.	Att.	Yds.	Avg.	TD	TD	2pt.	Pts.
1987—Minnesota NFL	4	0	6	2	33.3	18	0	1	3.00	2.8	0	0	0.0	0	0	0	0
1988—Minnesota NFL	3	0	15	7	46.7	90	0	0	6.00	66.0	4	29	7.3	0	0	0	0
1989—Minnesota NFL						Did not play.											
1990—Minnesota NFL	14	12	349	182	52.1	2278	16	16	6.53	68.9	52	268	5.2	1	1	0	6
1991—Minnesota NFL	15	11	354	211	59.6	2166	12	6	6.12	81.5	43	236	5.5	2	2	0	12
1992—Minnesota NFL	12	12	279	159	57.0	1905	12	13	6.83	72.9	45	187	4.2	0	0	0	0
1993—Washington NFL	8	4	125	74	59.2	704	3	7	5.63	59.6	21	88	4.2	1	1	0	6
1994—						Did not play.											
1995—Kansas City NFL	2	0	11	7	63.6	57	0	0	5.18	76.7	8	25	3.1	1	0	0	0
1996—Kansas City NFL	4	3	90	54	60.0	491	6	1	5.46	92.4	12	81	6.8	0	0	0	0
1997—Kansas City NFL	9	6	175	98	56.0	1144	7	4	6.54	79.8	33	109	3.3	2	2	0	12
1998—Kansas City NFL	12	10	354	206	58.2	2305	10	6	6.51	80.1	44	168	3.8	3	3	0	18
1999—Oakland NFL	16	16	515	304	59.0	3840	24	14	7.46	86.5	46	298	6.5	2	2	0	12
Pro totals (11 years)	99	74	2273	1304	57.4	14998	90	68	6.60	78.1	308	1489	4.8	12	11	0	66

GARCIA, FRANK   C   PANTHERS

PERSONAL: Born January 28, 1972, in Phoenix. ... 6-2/302. ... Full name: Frank Christopher Garcia.
HIGH SCHOOL: Maryvale (Phoenix).
COLLEGE: Washington.
TRANSACTIONS/CAREER NOTES: Selected by Carolina Panthers in fourth round (132nd pick overall) of 1995 NFL draft. ... Signed by Panthers (July 14, 1995). ... Granted free agency (February 13, 1998). ... Re-signed by Panthers (March 16, 1998).
PLAYING EXPERIENCE: Carolina NFL, 1995-1999. ... Games/Games started: 1995 (15/14), 1996 (14/8), 1997 (16/16), 1998 (14/14), 1999 (16/16). Total: 75/68.
CHAMPIONSHIP GAME EXPERIENCE: Played in NFC championship game (1996 season).
PRO STATISTICS: 1995—Fumbled once and recovered one fumble for 10 yards. 1996—Recovered two fumbles. 1997—Returned one kickoff for 11 yards. 1998—Recovered two fumbles for two yards. 1999—Recovered two fumbles.

GARCIA, JEFF   QB   49ERS

PERSONAL: Born February 24, 1970, in Gilroy, Calif. ... 6-1/195.
HIGH SCHOOL: Gilroy (Calif.).
JUNIOR COLLEGE: Gavilan College (Calif.).
COLLEGE: San Jose State.
TRANSACTIONS/CAREER NOTES: Signed by Calgary Stampeders of CFL (1994). ... Granted free agency (February 16, 1997). ... Re-signed by Stampeders (April 30, 1997). ... Signed as non-drafted free agent by San Francisco 49ers (February 16, 1999).
CHAMPIONSHIP GAME EXPERIENCE: Played in Grey Cup (1995). ... Member of CFL Championship team (1998). ... Named Most Valuable Player of Grey Cup, CFL championship game (1998).
PRO STATISTICS: 1999—Fumbled five times and recovered one fumble for minus one yard.
SINGLE GAME HIGHS (regular season): Attempts—49 (December 5, 1999, vs. Cincinnati); completions—33 (December 5, 1999, vs. Cincinnati); passing yards—437 (December 5, 1999, vs. Cincinnati); and touchdown passes—3 (December 5, 1999, vs. Cincinnati).
STATISTICAL PLATEAUS: 300-yard passing games: 1999 (3).
MISCELLANEOUS: Regular-season record as starting NFL quarterback: 2-8 (.200).

G

						PASSING						RUSHING				TOTALS	
Year Team	G	GS	Att.	Cmp.	Pct.	Yds.	TD	Int.	Avg.	Rat.	Att.	Yds.	Avg.	TD	TD	2pt.	Pts.
1994—Calgary CFL	7	...	3	2	66.7	10	0	0	3.33	71.5	2	3	1.5	0	0	0	0
1995—Calgary CFL	18	...	364	230	63.2	3358	25	7	9.23	108.1	61	396	6.5	5	5	0	30
1996—Calgary CFL	18	...	537	315	58.7	4225	25	16	7.87	86.9	92	657	7.1	6	6	0	36
1997—Calgary CFL	17	...	566	354	62.5	4573	33	14	8.08	97.0	135	727	5.4	7	7	...	42
1998—Calgary CFL	18	...	554	348	62.8	4276	28	15	7.72	92.2	94	575	6.1	6	6	0	36
1999—San Francisco NFL	13	10	375	225	60.0	2544	11	11	6.78	77.9	45	231	5.1	2	2	0	12
CFL totals (4 years)	61	...	1458	895	61.4	11869	78	38	8.14	94.1	249	1631	6.6	17	17	0	102
NFL totals (1 year)	13	10	375	225	60.0	2544	11	11	6.78	77.9	45	231	5.1	2	2	0	12
Pro totals (5 years)	74	...	1833	1120	61.1	14413	89	49	7.86	90.8	294	1862	6.3	19	19	0	114

GARDENER, DARYL   DT   DOLPHINS

PERSONAL: Born February 25, 1973, in Baltimore. ... 6-6/315. ... Full name: Daryl Ronald Gardener.
HIGH SCHOOL: Lawton (Okla.).
COLLEGE: Baylor.
TRANSACTIONS/CAREER NOTES: Selected by Miami Dolphins in first round (20th pick overall) of 1996 NFL draft. ... Signed by Dolphins (June 6, 1996).
PRO STATISTICS: 1996—Recovered one fumble. 1997—Recovered one fumble. 1998—Intercepted one pass for minus one yard. 1999—Recovered one fumble for 33 yards.

Year Team	G	GS	SACKS
1996—Miami NFL	16	12	1.0
1997—Miami NFL	16	16	1.5
1998—Miami NFL	16	16	1.0
1999—Miami NFL	16	15	5.0
Pro totals (4 years)	64	59	8.5

GARDNER, BARRY   LB   EAGLES

PERSONAL: Born December 13, 1976, in Harvey, Ill. ... 6-0/248. ... Full name: Barry Allan Gardner.
HIGH SCHOOL: Thornton (Harvey, Ill.).
COLLEGE: Northwestern.
TRANSACTIONS/CAREER NOTES: Selected by Philadelphia Eagles in second round (35th pick overall) of 1999 NFL draft. ... Signed by Eagles (July 25, 1999).
PLAYING EXPERIENCE: Philadelphia NFL, 1999. ... Games/Games started: 1999 (16/5).
PRO STATISTICS: 1999—Recovered one fumble for 20 yards.

GARDNER, DERRICK   CB   FALCONS

PERSONAL: Born March 10, 1977, in Oakland. ... 6-0/185.
HIGH SCHOOL: Skyline (Oakland).
COLLEGE: California.
TRANSACTIONS/CAREER NOTES: Signed as non-drafted free agent by Atlanta Falcons (April 20, 1999). ... Released by Falcons (September 5, 1999). ... Re-signed by Falcons to practice squad (September 7, 1999). ... Activated (October 20, 1999). ... Released by Falcons (November 17, 1999). ... Re-signed by Falcons (November 30, 1999). ... Assigned by Falcons to Rhein Fire in 2000 NFL Europe enhancement allocation program (February 18, 2000).
PLAYING EXPERIENCE: Atlanta NFL, 1999. ... Games/Games started: 1999 (7/0).

GARDOCKI, CHRIS   P   BROWNS

PERSONAL: Born February 7, 1970, in Stone Mountain, Ga. ... 6-1/200. ... Full name: Christopher Allen Gardocki.
HIGH SCHOOL: Redan (Stone Mountain, Ga.).
COLLEGE: Clemson.
TRANSACTIONS/CAREER NOTES: Selected after junior season by Chicago Bears in third round (78th pick overall) of 1991 NFL draft. ... Signed by Bears (June 24, 1991). ... On injured reserve with groin injury (August 27-November 27, 1991). ... Granted unconditional free agency (February 17, 1995). ... Signed by Indianapolis Colts (February 24, 1995). ... Granted unconditional free agency (February 12, 1999). ... Signed by Cleveland Browns (February 16, 1999).
CHAMPIONSHIP GAME EXPERIENCE: Played in AFC championship game (1995 season).
HONORS: Named kicker on The Sporting News college All-America second team (1990). ... Named punter on The Sporting News NFL All-Pro team (1996). ... Played in Pro Bowl (1996 season).
PRO STATISTICS: 1992—Attempted three passes with one completion for 43 yards and recovered one fumble. 1993—Attempted two passes without a completion, fumbled once and recovered one fumble. 1995—Attempted one pass without a completion.

			PUNTING				
Year Team	G	No.	Yds.	Avg.	Net avg.	In. 20	Blk.
1991—Chicago NFL	4	0	0	0.0	.0	0	0
1992—Chicago NFL	16	79	3393	42.9	36.2	19	0
1993—Chicago NFL	16	80	3080	38.5	36.6	28	0
1994—Chicago NFL	16	76	2871	37.8	32.3	23	0
1995—Indianapolis NFL	16	63	2681	42.6	33.3	16	0
1996—Indianapolis NFL	16	68	3105	45.7	§39.0	23	0
1997—Indianapolis NFL	16	67	3034	45.3	36.2	18	0
1998—Indianapolis NFL	16	79	3583	45.4	37.1	23	0
1999—Cleveland NFL	16	§106	*4645	43.8	34.6	20	0
Pro totals (9 years)	132	618	26392	42.7	35.6	170	0

GARNER, CHARLIE   RB   49ERS

PERSONAL: Born February 13, 1972, in Falls Church, Va. ... 5-9/187.
HIGH SCHOOL: Jeb Stuart (Falls Church, Va.).
JUNIOR COLLEGE: Scottsdale (Ariz.) Community College.
COLLEGE: Tennessee.
TRANSACTIONS/CAREER NOTES: Selected by Philadelphia Eagles in second round (42nd pick overall) of 1994 NFL draft. ... Signed by Eagles (July 18, 1994). ... Granted free agency (February 14, 1997). ... Re-signed by Eagles (June 16, 1997). ... Granted unconditional free agency (February 13, 1998). ... Re-signed by Eagles (February 23, 1998). ... On injured reserve with rib injury (December 10, 1998-remainder of season). ... Released by Eagles (April 20, 1999). ... Signed by San Francisco 49ers (July 19, 1999).
SINGLE GAME HIGHS (regular season): Attempts—28 (October 9, 1994, vs. Washington); yards—166 (November 7, 1999, vs. Pittsburgh); and rushing touchdowns—3 (October 8, 1995, vs. Washington).
STATISTICAL PLATEAUS: 100-yard rushing games: 1994 (2), 1995 (1), 1997 (1), 1998 (1), 1999 (3). Total: 8.

Year Team	G	GS	RUSHING Att.	Yds.	Avg.	TD	RECEIVING No.	Yds.	Avg.	TD	KICKOFF RETURNS No.	Yds.	Avg.	TD	TOTALS TD	2pt.	Pts.	Fum.
1994—Philadelphia NFL	10	8	109	399	3.7	3	8	74	9.3	0	0	0	0.0	0	3	0	18	3
1995—Philadelphia NFL	15	2	108	588	*5.4	6	10	61	6.1	0	29	590	20.3	0	6	0	36	2
1996—Philadelphia NFL	15	1	66	346	5.2	1	14	92	6.6	0	6	117	19.5	0	1	0	6	1
1997—Philadelphia NFL	16	2	116	547	4.7	3	24	225	9.4	0	0	0	0.0	0	3	0	18	1
1998—Philadelphia NFL	10	3	96	381	4.0	4	19	110	5.8	0	0	0	0.0	0	4	0	24	1
1999—San Francisco NFL	16	15	241	1229	5.1	4	56	535	9.6	2	0	0	0.0	0	6	0	36	4
Pro totals (6 years)	82	31	736	3490	4.7	21	131	1097	8.4	2	35	707	20.2	0	23	0	138	12

GARNES, SAM   S   GIANTS

PERSONAL: Born July 12, 1974, in Bronx, N.Y. ... 6-3/225. ... Full name: Sam Aaron Garnes.
HIGH SCHOOL: DeWitt Clinton (Bronx, N.Y.).
COLLEGE: Cincinnati.
TRANSACTIONS/CAREER NOTES: Selected by New York Giants in fifth round (136th pick overall) of 1997 NFL draft. Signed by Giants for 1997 season. ... Granted free agency (February 11, 2000). ... Re-signed by Giants (February 12, 2000).
PRO STATISTICS: 1999—Credited with one sack.

Year Team	G	GS	INTERCEPTIONS No.	Yds.	Avg.	TD
1997—New York Giants NFL	16	15	1	95	95.0	1
1998—New York Giants NFL	11	11	1	13	13.0	0
1999—New York Giants NFL	16	16	2	7	3.5	0
Pro totals (3 years)	43	42	4	115	28.8	1

GARRETT, JASON   QB   GIANTS

PERSONAL: Born March 28, 1966, in Abington, Pa. ... 6-2/200. ... Full name: Jason Calvin Garrett. ... Son of Jim Garrett, scout, Dallas Cowboys; brother of John Garrett, wide receiver with Cincinnati Bengals (1989) and San Antonio Riders of World League (1991); and brother of Judd Garrett, running back with London of World League (1991-92).
HIGH SCHOOL: University (Chargin Falls, Ohio).
COLLEGE: Princeton (degree in history).
TRANSACTIONS/CAREER NOTES: Signed as non-drafted free agent by New Orleans Saints (1989). ... Released by Saints (August 30, 1989). ... Re-signed by Saints to developmental squad (September 6, 1989). ... Released by Saints (December 29, 1989). ... Re-signed by Saints for 1990 season. ... Released by Saints (September 3, 1990). ... Signed by WLAF (January 3, 1991). ... Selected by San Antonio Riders in first round (seventh quarterback) of 1991 WLAF positional draft. ... Signed by Ottawa Rough Riders of CFL (1991). ... Released by San Antonio Riders (March 3, 1992). ... Signed by Dallas Cowboys (March 23, 1992). ... Released by Cowboys (August 31, 1992). ... Re-signed by Cowboys to practice squad (September 1, 1992). ... Granted unconditional free agency (February 16, 1996). ... Re-signed by Cowboys (April 3, 1996). ... Granted unconditional free agency (February 14, 1997). ... Re-signed by Cowboys (April 8, 1997). ... Granted unconditional free agency (February 11, 2000). ... Signed by New York Giants (February 22, 2000).
CHAMPIONSHIP GAME EXPERIENCE: Member of Cowboys for NFC championship game (1993-1995 seasons); inactive. ... Member of Super Bowl championship team (1993 and 1995 seasons).
PRO STATISTICS: W.L.: 1991—Fumbled twice. CFL: 1991—Fumbled once. NFL: 1993—Fumbled once. 1994—Recovered one fumble. 1998—Fumbled four times for minus 17 yards.
SINGLE GAME HIGHS (regular season): Attempts—33 (September 27, 1998, vs. Oakland); completions—18 (September 27, 1998, vs. Oakland); yards—311 (November 24, 1994, vs. Green Bay); and touchdown passes—2 (November 14, 1999, vs. Green Bay).
STATISTICAL PLATEAUS: 300-yard passing games: 1994 (1).
MISCELLANEOUS: Regular-season record as starting NFL quarterback: 6-3 (.667).

Year Team	G	GS	PASSING Att.	Cmp.	Pct.	Yds.	TD	Int.	Avg.	Rat.	RUSHING Att.	Yds.	Avg.	TD	TOTALS TD	2pt.	Pts.
1991—San Antonio W.L.	5	3	113	66	58.4	609	3	3	5.39	71.0	7	7	1.0	0	0	0	0
—Ottawa CFL	13	0	3	2	66.7	28	0	0	9.33	96.5	0	0	0.0	0	0	0	0
1992—Dallas NFL..................						Did not play.											
1993—Dallas NFL..................	5	1	19	9	47.4	61	0	0	3.21	54.9	8	-8	-1.0	0	0	0	0
1994—Dallas NFL..................	2	1	31	16	51.6	315	2	1	10.16	95.5	3	-2	-0.7	0	0	0	0
1995—Dallas NFL..................	1	0	5	4	80.0	46	1	0	9.20	144.6	1	-1	-1.0	0	0	0	0
1996—Dallas NFL..................	1	0	3	3	100.0	44	0	0	14.67	118.8	0	0	0.0	0	0	0	0
1997—Dallas NFL..................	1	0	14	10	71.4	56	0	0	4.00	78.3	0	0	0.0	0	0	0	0
1998—Dallas NFL..................	8	5	158	91	57.6	1206	5	3	7.63	84.5	11	14	1.3	0	0	0	0
1999—Dallas NFL..................	9	2	64	32	50.0	314	3	1	4.91	73.3	6	12	2.0	0	0	0	0
W.L. totals (1 year)...............	5	3	113	66	58.4	609	3	3	5.39	71.0	7	7	1.0	0	0	0	0
CFL totals (1 year)	13	0	3	2	66.7	28	0	0	9.33	96.5	0	0	0.0	0	0	0	0
NFL totals (7 years)	27	9	294	165	56.1	2042	11	5	6.95	83.2	29	15	0.5	0	0	0	0
Pro totals (9 years)	45	12	410	233	56.8	2679	14	8	6.53	79.9	36	22	0.6	0	0	0	0

G

GARY, OLANDIS   RB   BRONCOS

PERSONAL: Born May 18, 1975, in Washington, D.C. ... 5-11/218. ... Full name: Olandis C. Gary.
HIGH SCHOOL: Riverdale Baptist (Upper Marlboro, Md.).
COLLEGE: Marshall, then Georgia.
TRANSACTIONS/CAREER NOTES: Selected by Denver Broncos in fourth round (127th pick overall) of 1999 NFL draft. ... Signed by Broncos (July 20, 1999).
PRO STATISTICS: 1999—Recovered one fumble.
SINGLE GAME HIGHS (regular season): Attempts—37 (October 17, 1999, vs. Green Bay); yards—185 (December 25, 1999, vs. Detroit); and rushing touchdowns—2 (November 7, 1999, vs. San Diego).
STATISTICAL PLATEAUS: 100-yard rushing games: 1999 (4).

			RUSHING				RECEIVING				TOTALS			
Year Team	G	GS	Att.	Yds.	Avg.	TD	No.	Yds.	Avg.	TD	TD	2pt.	Pts.	Fum.
1999—Denver NFL	12	12	276	1159	4.2	7	21	159	7.6	0	7	†1	44	2

GASH, SAM   FB

PERSONAL: Born March 7, 1969, in Hendersonville, N.C. ... 6-0/235. ... Full name: Samuel Lee Gash Jr. ... Cousin of Thane Gash, safety with Cleveland Browns (1988-90) and San Francisco 49ers (1992).
HIGH SCHOOL: Hendersonville (N.C.).
COLLEGE: Penn State (degree in liberal arts).
TRANSACTIONS/CAREER NOTES: Selected by New England Patriots in eighth round (205th pick overall) of 1992 NFL draft. ... Signed by Patriots (June 10, 1992). ... Granted free agency (February 17, 1995). ... Re-signed by Patriots (May 5, 1995). ... On injured reserve with knee injury (December 10, 1996-remainder of season). ... Granted unconditional free agency (February 13, 1998). ... Signed by Buffalo Bills (March 5, 1998). ... Released by Bills (April 14, 2000).
HONORS: Played in Pro Bowl (1998 and 1999 seasons).
PRO STATISTICS: 1992—Recovered two fumbles. 1994—Returned one kickoff for nine yards and recovered one fumble. 1998—Returned three kickoffs for 41 yards. 1999—Returned one kickoff for 13 yards and recovered one fumble.
SINGLE GAME HIGHS (regular season): Attempts—15 (December 18, 1994, vs. Buffalo); yards—56 (December 18, 1994, vs. Buffalo); and rushing touchdowns—1 (September 19, 1993, vs. Seattle).

			RUSHING				RECEIVING				TOTALS			
Year Team	G	GS	Att.	Yds.	Avg.	TD	No.	Yds.	Avg.	TD	TD	2pt.	Pts.	Fum.
1992—New England NFL	15	0	5	7	1.4	1	0	0	0.0	0	1	0	6	1
1993—New England NFL	15	4	48	149	3.1	1	14	93	6.6	0	1	0	6	1
1994—New England NFL	13	6	30	86	2.9	0	9	61	6.8	0	0	0	0	1
1995—New England NFL	15	12	8	24	3.0	0	26	242	9.3	1	1	0	6	0
1996—New England NFL	14	9	8	15	1.9	0	33	276	8.4	2	2	1	14	0
1997—New England NFL	16	5	6	10	1.7	0	22	154	7.0	3	3	0	18	0
1998—Buffalo NFL	16	13	11	32	2.9	0	19	165	8.7	3	3	0	18	0
1999—Buffalo NFL	15	11	0	0	0.0	0	20	163	8.2	2	2	0	12	0
Pro totals (8 years)	119	60	116	323	2.8	2	143	1154	8.1	11	13	1	80	3

GEORGE, EDDIE   RB   TITANS

PERSONAL: Born September 24, 1973, in Philadelphia. ... 6-3/240. ... Full name: Edward Nathan George.
HIGH SCHOOL: Abington (Philadelphia), then Fork Union (Va.) Military Academy.
COLLEGE: Ohio State.
TRANSACTIONS/CAREER NOTES: Selected by Houston Oilers in first round (14th pick overall) of 1996 NFL draft. ... Signed by Oilers (July 20, 1996). ... Oilers franchise moved to Tennessee for 1997 season. ... Oilers franchise renamed Tennessee Titans for 1999 season (December 26, 1998).
CHAMPIONSHIP GAME EXPERIENCE: Played in AFC championship game (1999 season). ... Played in Super Bowl XXXIV (1999 season).
HONORS: Heisman Trophy winner (1995). ... Maxwell Award winner (1995). ... Doak Walker Award winner (1995). ... Named running back on THE SPORTING NEWS college All-America first team (1995). ... Named NFL Rookie of the Year by THE SPORTING NEWS (1996). ... Played in Pro Bowl (1997-1999 seasons).
PRO STATISTICS: 1996—Recovered one fumble. 1998—Recovered five fumbles. 1999—Recovered one fumble.
SINGLE GAME HIGHS (regular season): Attempts—35 (August 31, 1997, vs. Oakland); yards—216 (August 31, 1997, vs. Oakland); and rushing touchdowns—2 (December 9, 1999, vs. Oakland).
STATISTICAL PLATEAUS: 100-yard rushing games: 1996 (4), 1997 (8), 1998 (6), 1999 (5). Total: 23.

			RUSHING				RECEIVING				TOTALS			
Year Team	G	GS	Att.	Yds.	Avg.	TD	No.	Yds.	Avg.	TD	TD	2pt.	Pts.	Fum.
1996—Houston NFL	16	16	335	1368	4.1	8	23	182	7.9	0	8	0	48	3
1997—Tennessee NFL	16	16	357	1399	3.9	6	7	44	6.3	1	7	1	44	4
1998—Tennessee NFL	16	16	348	1294	3.7	5	37	310	8.4	1	6	1	38	7
1999—Tennessee NFL	16	16	320	1304	4.1	9	47	458	9.7	4	13	0	78	5
Pro totals (4 years)	64	64	1360	5365	3.9	28	114	994	8.7	6	34	2	208	19

GEORGE, JEFF   QB   REDSKINS

PERSONAL: Born December 8, 1967, in Indianapolis. ... 6-4/215. ... Full name: Jeffrey Scott George.
HIGH SCHOOL: Warren Central (Indianapolis).
COLLEGE: Purdue, then Illinois (degree in speech communications, 1991).
TRANSACTIONS/CAREER NOTES: Signed after junior season by Indianapolis Colts (April 20, 1990). ... Selected officially by Colts in first round (first pick overall) of 1990 NFL draft. ... On reserve/did not report list (July 23-August 20, 1993). ... Traded by Colts to Atlanta Falcons for first- (LB Trev Alberts) and third-round (OT Jason Mathews) picks in 1994 draft and a first-round pick (WR Marvin Harrison) in 1996 draft (March

G

24, 1994). ... Designated by Falcons as transition player (February 16, 1996). ... Released by Falcons (October 22, 1996). ... Signed by Oakland Raiders (February 15, 1997). ... Granted unconditional free agency (February 12, 1999). ... Signed by Minnesota Vikings (April 6, 1999). ... Granted unconditional free agency (February 11, 2000). ... Signed by Washington Redskins (April 19, 2000).

PRO STATISTICS: 1990—Fumbled four times and recovered two fumbles. 1991—Fumbled eight times and recovered two fumbles for minus four yards. 1992—Fumbled six times and recovered one fumble for minus two yards. 1993—Fumbled four times. 1994—Led league with 12 fumbles and recovered six fumbles for minus 12 yards. 1995—Fumbled six times and recovered two fumbles for minus 15 yards. 1996—Fumbled three times and recovered two fumbles for minus 24 yards. 1997—Fumbled seven times and recovered three fumbles for minus 14 yards. 1998—Fumbled seven times and recovered one fumble for minus six yards. 1999—Fumbled eight times and recovered two fumbles.

SINGLE GAME HIGHS (regular season): Attempts—59 (November 7, 1993, vs. Washington); completions—37 (November 7, 1993, vs. Washington); yards—386 (September 17, 1995, vs. New Orleans); and touchdown passes—4 (November 28, 1999, vs. San Diego).

STATISTICAL PLATEAUS: 300-yard passing games: 1991 (2), 1992 (3), 1993 (2), 1994 (2), 1995 (3), 1997 (2), 1998 (1), 1999 (2). Total: 17.

MISCELLANEOUS: Regular-season record as starting NFL quarterback: 45-72 (.385). ... Postseason record as starting NFL quarterback: 1-2 (.333).

					PASSING						RUSHING			TOTALS		
Year	Team	G	GS	Att.	Cmp.	Pct.	Yds.	TD	Int.	Avg.	Rat.	Att.	Yds.	Avg.	TD	TD	2pt.	Pts.
1990—Indianapolis NFL		13	12	334	181	54.2	2152	16	13	6.44	73.8	11	2	0.2	1	1	0	6
1991—Indianapolis NFL		16	16	485	292	60.2	2910	10	12	6.00	73.8	16	36	2.3	0	0	0	0
1992—Indianapolis NFL		10	10	306	167	54.6	1963	7	15	6.42	61.5	14	26	1.9	1	1	0	6
1993—Indianapolis NFL		13	11	407	234	57.5	2526	8	6	6.21	76.3	13	39	3.0	0	0	0	0
1994—Atlanta NFL		16	16	524	322	61.5	3734	23	18	7.13	83.3	30	66	2.2	0	0	0	0
1995—Atlanta NFL		16	16	557	336	60.3	4143	24	11	7.44	89.5	27	17	0.6	0	0	0	0
1996—Atlanta NFL		3	3	99	56	56.6	698	3	3	7.05	76.1	5	10	2.0	0	0	0	0
1997—Oakland NFL		16	16	521	290	55.7	*3917	§29	9	7.52	91.2	17	44	2.6	0	0	0	0
1998—Oakland NFL		8	7	169	93	55.0	1186	4	5	7.02	72.7	8	2	0.3	0	0	0	0
1999—Minnesota NFL		12	10	329	191	58.1	2816	23	12	8.56	94.2	16	41	2.6	0	0	0	0
Pro totals (10 years)		123	117	3731	2162	57.9	26045	147	104	6.98	81.0	157	283	1.8	2	2	0	12

GEORGE, RON   LB   CHIEFS

PERSONAL: Born March 20, 1970, in Heidelberg, West Germany. ... 6-2/247. ... Full name: Ronald L. George.
HIGH SCHOOL: Heidelberg (West Germany) American.
COLLEGE: Air Force, then Stanford (degree in economics, 1992).
TRANSACTIONS/CAREER NOTES: Selected by Atlanta Falcons in fifth round (121st pick overall) of 1993 NFL draft. ... Signed by Falcons (June 4, 1993). ... Granted free agency (February 16, 1996). ... Re-signed by Falcons (June 12, 1996). ... Granted unconditional free agency (February 14, 1997). ... Signed by Minnesota Vikings (June 9, 1997). ... Released by Vikings (February 11, 1998). ... Signed by Kansas City Chiefs (April 9, 1998).
PLAYING EXPERIENCE: Atlanta NFL, 1993-1996; Minnesota NFL, 1997; Kansas City NFL, 1998 and 1999. ... Games/Games started: 1993 (12/4), 1994 (16/9), 1995 (16/0), 1996 (16/15), 1997 (16/0), 1998 (16/0), 1999 (16/0). Total: 108/28.
HONORS: Named linebacker on THE SPORTING NEWS college All-America second team (1992).
PRO STATISTICS: 1993—Credited with one sack. 1994—Recovered one fumble. 1995—Returned three kickoffs for 45 yards. 1996—Credited with two sacks and recovered three fumbles for 14 yards. 1997—Returned one kickoff for 10 yards. 1998—Recovered one fumble.

GEORGE, SPENCER   RB   TITANS

PERSONAL: Born October 28, 1973, in Beaumont, Texas. ... 5-9/200. ... Full name: Spencer James George.
HIGH SCHOOL: Hamshire-Fannett (Hamshire, Texas).
COLLEGE: Rice (degree in Managerial studies/economics).
TRANSACTIONS/CAREER NOTES: Signed as non-drafted free agent by Tennessee Oilers (May 5, 1997). ... Released by Oilers (August 25, 1997). ... Re-signed by Oilers to practice squad (August 26, 1997). ... Activated (November 18, 1997). ... Released by Oilers (August 30, 1998). ... Resigned by Oilers to practice squad (September 29, 1998). ... Activated (November 4, 1998). ... Released by Oilers (December 16, 1998). ... Re-signed by Oilers to practice squad (December 16, 1998). ... Oilers franchise renamed Tennessee Titans for 1999 season (December 26, 1998).
PLAYING EXPERIENCE: Tennessee NFL, 1997-1999. ... Games/Games started: 1997 (5/0), 1998 (5/0), 1999 (8/0). Total: 18/0.
CHAMPIONSHIP GAME EXPERIENCE: Member of Titans for AFC championship game (1999 season); inactive. ... Member of Titans for Super Bowl XXXIV (1999 season); inactive.
PRO STATISTICS: 1999—Returned one punt for 18 yards and returned four kickoffs for 63 yards.

GEORGE, TONY   S   PATRIOTS

PERSONAL: Born August 10, 1975, in Cincinnati. ... 5-11/200. ... Full name: Houston Antonio George Jr.
HIGH SCHOOL: Winton Woods (Cincinnati).
COLLEGE: Florida.
TRANSACTIONS/CAREER NOTES: Selected by New England Patriots in third round (91st pick overall) of 1999 NFL draft. ... Signed by Patriots (July 28, 1999).
PLAYING EXPERIENCE: New England NFL, 1999. ... Games/Games started: 1999 (16/1).

G

GERMAINE, JOE   QB   RAMS

PERSONAL: Born August 11, 1975, in Denver. ... 6-0/203. ... Full name: Joe Berton Germaine.
HIGH SCHOOL: Mountain View (Mesa, Ariz.).
JUNIOR COLLEGE: Scottsdale (Ariz.) Community College.
COLLEGE: Ohio State.
TRANSACTIONS/CAREER NOTES: Selected by St. Louis Rams in fourth round (101st pick overall) of 1999 NFL draft. ... Signed by Rams (July 19, 1999).

CHAMPIONSHIP GAME EXPERIENCE: Member of Rams for NFC championship game (1999 season); inactive. ... Member of Super Bowl championship team (1999 season); inactive

PRO STATISTICS: 1999—Fumbled once.

SINGLE GAME HIGHS (regular season): Attempts—12 (January 2, 2000, vs. Philadelphia); completions—9 (January 2, 2000, vs. Philadelphia); passing yards—136 (January 2, 2000, vs. Philadelphia); and touchdown passes—1 (January 2, 1999, vs. Philadelphia).

MISCELLANEOUS: Selected by Colorado Rockies organization in 25th round of free-agent baseball draft (June 2, 1994); did not sign.

					PASSING							RUSHING				TOTALS	
Year Team	G	GS	Att.	Cmp.	Pct.	Yds.	TD	Int.	Avg.	Rat.	Att.	Yds.	Avg.	TD	TD	2pt.	Pts.
1999—St. Louis NFL	3	0	16	9	56.3	136	1	2	8.50	65.6	3	0	0.0	0	0	0	0

GERMAN, JAMMI — WR — FALCONS

PERSONAL: Born July 4, 1974, in Fort Myers, Fla. ... 6-1/192. ... Full name: Jammi Darnell German.

HIGH SCHOOL: Fort Myers (Fla.).

COLLEGE: Miami (Fla.).

TRANSACTIONS/CAREER NOTES: Selected by Atlanta Falcons in third round (74th pick overall) of 1998 NFL draft. ... Signed by Falcons (July 8, 1998). ... On injured reserve with knee injury (November 10, 1998-remainder of season). ... Released by Falcons (September 5, 1999). ... Re-signed by Falcons to practice squad (September 7, 1999). ... Activated (September 14, 1999).

PLAYING EXPERIENCE: Atlanta NFL, 1998 and 1999. ... Games/Games started: 1998 (6/0), 1999 (14/0). Total: 20/0.

PRO STATISTICS: 1999—Caught 12 passes for 219 yards and three touchdowns and returned one kickoff for one yard.

SINGLE GAME HIGHS (regular season): Receptions—3 (December 19, 1999, vs. Seattle); yards—62 (October 10, 1999, vs. New Orleans); and touchdown receptions—2 (December 19, 1999, vs. Tennessee).

GIBSON, DAMON — WR

PERSONAL: Born February 25, 1975, in Houston ... 5-9/184.

HIGH SCHOOL: Forest Brook (Houston).

COLLEGE: Iowa.

TRANSACTIONS/CAREER NOTES: Signed as non-drafted free agent by Cincinnati Bengals (April 20, 1998). ... Selected by Cleveland Browns from Bengals in 1999 NFL expansion draft (February 9, 1999). ... Released by Browns (September 28, 1999). ... Selected by Scottish Claymores in 2000 NFL Europe draft (February 22, 2000).

PRO STATISTICS: 1998—Rushed once for nine yards and recovered one fumble.

SINGLE GAME HIGHS (regular season): Receptions—3 (November 1, 1998, vs. Denver); yards—76 (October 18, 1998, vs. Tennessee); and touchdown receptions—1 (November 8, 1998, vs. Jacksonville).

			RECEIVING				PUNT RETURNS				KICKOFF RETURNS				TOTALS			
Year Team	G	GS	No.	Yds.	Avg.	TD	No.	Yds.	Avg.	TD	No.	Yds.	Avg.	TD	TD	2pt.	Pts.	Fum.
1998—Cincinnati NFL	16	0	19	258	13.6	3	27	218	8.1	1	17	372	21.9	0	4	0	24	3
1999—Cleveland NFL	2	0	0	0	0.0	0	2	9	4.5	0	0	0	0.0	0	0	0	0	0
Pro totals (2 years)	18	0	19	258	13.6	3	29	227	7.8	1	17	372	21.9	0	4	0	24	3

GIBSON, OLIVER — DT — BENGALS

PERSONAL: Born March 15, 1972, in Chicago. ... 6-2/290. ... Full name: Oliver Donnovan Gibson. ... Cousin of Godfrey Myles, linebacker with Dallas Cowboys (1991-96).

HIGH SCHOOL: Romeoville (Ill.).

COLLEGE: Notre Dame (degree in economics, 1994).

TRANSACTIONS/CAREER NOTES: Selected by Pittsburgh Steelers in fourth round (120th pick overall) of 1995 NFL draft. ... Signed by Steelers (July 18, 1995). ... Granted free agency (February 13, 1998). ... Re-signed by Steelers (June 9, 1998). ... Granted unconditional free agency (February 12, 1999). ... Signed by Cincinnati Bengals (March 9, 1999).

CHAMPIONSHIP GAME EXPERIENCE: Member of Steelers for AFC championship game (1995 season); inactive. ... Played in AFC championship game (1997 season).

HONORS: Earned first-team All-Independent honors from THE SPORTING NEWS (1994).

PRO STATISTICS: 1995—Returned one kickoff for 10 yards. 1997—Recovered one fumble. 1998—Returned one kickoff for nine yards. 1999—Recovered one fumble.

Year Team	G	GS	SACKS
1995—Pittsburgh NFL	12	0	0.0
1996—Pittsburgh NFL	16	0	2.5
1997—Pittsburgh NFL	16	0	1.0
1998—Pittsburgh NFL	16	0	2.0
1999—Cincinnati NFL	16	16	4.5
Pro totals (5 years)	76	16	10.0

G

GILBERT, SEAN — DT — PANTHERS

PERSONAL: Born April 10, 1970, in Aliquippa, Pa. ... 6-5/318.

HIGH SCHOOL: Aliquippa (Pa.).

COLLEGE: Pittsburgh.

TRANSACTIONS/CAREER NOTES: Selected after junior season by Los Angeles Rams in first round (third pick overall) of 1992 NFL draft. ... Signed by Rams (July 28, 1992). ... Designated by Rams as transition player (February 25, 1993). ... Rams franchise moved to St. Louis (April 12, 1995). ... Traded by Rams to Washington Redskins for first-round pick (RB Lawrence Phillips) in 1996 draft (April 8, 1996). ... Designated by Redskins as franchise player (February 12, 1997). ... Sat out 1997 season due to contract dispute. ... Designated by Redskins as franchise player (February 11, 1998). ... Tendered offer sheet by Carolina Panthers (March 24, 1998). ... Redskins declined to match offer (April 21, 1998).

HONORS: Played in Pro Bowl (1993 season).

PRO STATISTICS: 1992—Recovered one fumble. 1994—Credited with one safety. 1995—Recovered one fumble. 1999—Intercepted one pass for four yards.

Year Team	G	GS	SACKS
1992—Los Angeles Rams NFL	16	16	5.0
1993—Los Angeles Rams NFL	16	16	10.5
1994—Los Angeles Rams NFL	14	14	3.0
1995—St. Louis NFL	14	14	5.5
1996—Washington NFL	16	16	3.0
1997—Washington NFL	Did not play.		
1998—Carolina NFL	16	16	6.0
1999—Carolina NFL	16	16	2.5
Pro totals (7 years)	108	108	35.5

GILDON, JASON   LB   STEELERS

PERSONAL: Born July 31, 1972, in Altus, Okla. ... 6-3/255. ... Full name: Jason Larue Gildon. ... Related to Wendall Gaines, guard with Arizona Cardinals (1995).
HIGH SCHOOL: Altus (Okla.).
COLLEGE: Oklahoma State.
TRANSACTIONS/CAREER NOTES: Selected by Pittsburgh Steelers in third round (88th pick overall) of 1994 NFL draft. ... Signed by Steelers (July 15, 1994). ... Granted free agency (February 14, 1997). ... Re-signed by Steelers (July 21, 1997). ... Granted unconditional free agency (February 13, 1998). ... Re-signed by Steelers (April 7, 1998).
CHAMPIONSHIP GAME EXPERIENCE: Played in AFC championship game (1994, 1995 and 1997 seasons). ... Played in Super Bowl XXX (1995 season).
PRO STATISTICS: 1995—Recovered one fumble. 1997—Recovered two fumbles for 32 yards and one touchdown. 1998—Recovered one fumble.

Year Team	G	GS	SACKS
1994—Pittsburgh NFL	16	1	2.0
1995—Pittsburgh NFL	16	0	3.0
1996—Pittsburgh NFL	14	13	7.0
1997—Pittsburgh NFL	16	16	5.0
1998—Pittsburgh NFL	16	16	11.0
1999—Pittsburgh NFL	16	16	8.5
Pro totals (6 years)	94	62	36.5

GISLER, MIKE   C/G   JETS

PERSONAL: Born August 26, 1969, in Runge, Texas. ... 6-4/300. ... Full name: Michael Gisler. ... Name pronounced GHEE-sler.
HIGH SCHOOL: Runge (Texas).
COLLEGE: Houston.
TRANSACTIONS/CAREER NOTES: Selected by New Orleans Saints in 11th round (303rd pick overall) of 1992 NFL draft. ... Signed by Saints (July 15, 1992). ... Released by Saints (August 31, 1992). ... Re-signed by Saints to practice squad (September 2, 1992). ... Released by Saints (September 7, 1992). ... Signed by Houston Oilers to practice squad (September 9, 1992). ... Granted free agency after 1992 season. ... Signed by New England Patriots (March 3, 1993). ... Granted free agency (February 16, 1996). ... Re-signed by Patriots (May 20, 1996). ... Released by Patriots (August 25, 1996). ... Re-signed by Patriots (September 10, 1996). ... Granted unconditional free agency (February 14, 1997). ... Re-signed by Patriots (April 22, 1997). ... Granted unconditional free agency (February 13, 1998). ... Signed by New York Jets (February 18, 1998).
PLAYING EXPERIENCE: New England NFL, 1993-1997; New York Jets NFL, 1998 and 1999. ... Games/Games started: 1993 (12/0), 1994 (15/5), 1995 (16/0), 1996 (14/0), 1997 (16/2), 1998 (16/0), 1999 (16/0). Total: 105/7.
CHAMPIONSHIP GAME EXPERIENCE: Played in AFC championship game (1996 and 1998 seasons). ... Played in Super Bowl XXXI (1996 season).
PRO STATISTICS: 1995—Returned two kickoffs for 19 yards and fumbled once. 1996—Returned one kickoff for nine yards.

GIVENS, REGGIE   LB   REDSKINS

PERSONAL: Born October 3, 1971, in Emporia, Va. ... 6-0/234. ... Full name: Reginald Alonzo Givens.
HIGH SCHOOL: Sussex (Va.) Central.
COLLEGE: Penn State.
TRANSACTIONS/CAREER NOTES: Selected by Dallas Cowboys in eighth round (213rd pick overall) of 1993 NFL draft. ... Signed by Cowboys (July 15, 1993). ... Released by Cowboys (August 30, 1993). ... Signed by Chicago Bears (April 20, 1994). ... Released by Bears (August 18, 1994). ... Signed by Winnipeg Blue Bombers of CFL (October 1994). ... Released by Blue Bombers (July 11, 1995). ... Signed by Baltimore Stallions of CFL (August 9, 1995). ... Transferred to Saskatchewan Roughriders of CFL (May 16, 1996). ... Released by Roughriders (June 3, 1996). ... Signed by Toronto Argonauts of CFL (June 6, 1996). ... Granted free agency (February 16, 1998). ... Signed by San Francisco 49ers (March 12, 1998). ... Granted free agency (February 11, 2000). ... Signed by Washington Redskins (April 13, 2000).
PLAYING EXPERIENCE: Winnipeg CFL, 1994; Winnipeg (1)-Baltimore (4) CFL, 1995; Toronto CFL, 1996 and 1997; San Francisco NFL, 1998 and 1999. ... Games/Games started: 1994 (4/games started unavailable), 1995 (Win.-1/-; Bal.-4/-; Total: 5/-), 1996 (18/-), 1997 (18/-), 1998 (16/0), 1999 (16/0). Total CFL: 45/-. Total NFL: 32/0. Total Pro: 77/-.
PRO STATISTICS: CFL: 1994—Intercepted one pass for no yards and credited with two sacks. 1996—Rushed once for one yard, intercepted one pass for no yards, credited with eight sacks, fumbled once and recovered four fumbles. 1997—Intercepted one pass for six yards, credited with six sacks and recovered two fumbles for 182 yards and two touchdowns. 1999—Returned one punt for no yards and fumbled once.

GLENN, AARON   CB/KR   JETS

PERSONAL: Born July 16, 1972, in Humble, Texas. ... 5-9/185. ... Full name: Aaron DeVon Glenn.
HIGH SCHOOL: Nimitz (Irving, Texas).

G

JUNIOR COLLEGE: Navarro College (Texas).
COLLEGE: Texas A&M.
TRANSACTIONS/CAREER NOTES: Selected by New York Jets in first round (12th pick overall) of 1994 NFL draft. ... Signed by Jets (July 21, 1994).
CHAMPIONSHIP GAME EXPERIENCE: Played in AFC championship game (1998 season).
HONORS: Named defensive back on THE SPORTING NEWS college All-America first team (1993). ... Played in Pro Bowl (1997 season). ... Named to play in Pro Bowl (1998 season); replaced by Charles Woodson due to injury.
PRO STATISTICS: 1994—Recovered one fumble. 1995—Recovered one fumble. 1998—Recovered one fumble and returned a missed field goal attempt 104 yards for a touchdown. 1999—Recovered one fumble.

				INTERCEPTIONS				KICKOFF RETURNS				TOTALS		
Year Team	G	GS	No.	Yds.	Avg.	TD	No.	Yds.	Avg.	TD	TD	2pt.	Pts.	Fum.
1994—New York Jets NFL	15	15	0	0	0.0	0	27	582	21.6	0	0	0	0	2
1995—New York Jets NFL	16	16	1	17	17.0	0	1	12	12.0	0	0	0	0	0
1996—New York Jets NFL	16	16	4	113	28.3	†2	1	6	6.0	0	2	0	12	0
1997—New York Jets NFL	16	16	1	5	5.0	0	28	741	§26.5	▲1	1	0	6	1
1998—New York Jets NFL	13	13	6	23	3.8	0	24	585	24.4	0	1	0	6	1
1999—New York Jets NFL	16	16	3	20	6.7	0	27	601	22.3	0	0	0	0	0
Pro totals (6 years)................................	92	92	15	178	11.9	2	108	2527	23.4	1	4	0	24	4

GLENN, TARIK   OT   COLTS

PERSONAL: Born May 25, 1976, in Cleveland. ... 6-5/335.
HIGH SCHOOL: Bishop O'Dowd (Oakland).
COLLEGE: California.
TRANSACTIONS/CAREER NOTES: Selected by Indianapolis Colts in first round (19th pick overall) of 1997 NFL draft. ... Signed by Colts (August 11, 1997).
PLAYING EXPERIENCE: Indianapolis NFL, 1997-1999. ... Games/Games started: 1997 (16/16), 1998 (16/16), 1999 (16/16). Total: 48/48.
HONORS: Named offensive tackle on THE SPORTING NEWS college All-America second team (1996).
PRO STATISTICS: 1997—Caught one pass for three yards and recovered one fumble.

GLENN, TERRY   WR   PATRIOTS

PERSONAL: Born July 23, 1974, in Columbus, Ohio. ... 5-11/185.
HIGH SCHOOL: Brookhaven (Columbus, Ohio).
COLLEGE: Ohio State.
TRANSACTIONS/CAREER NOTES: Selected after junior season by New England Patriots in first round (seventh pick overall) of 1996 NFL draft. ... Signed by Patriots (July 12, 1996). ... On injured reserve with fractured ankle (December 18, 1998-remainder of season).
CHAMPIONSHIP GAME EXPERIENCE: Played in AFC championship game (1996 season). ... Played in Super Bowl XXXI (1996 season).
HONORS: Fred Biletnikoff Award winner (1995). ... Named wide receiver on THE SPORTING NEWS college All-America first team (1995).
RECORDS: Holds NFL single-season record for most receptions by a rookie—90 (1996).
PRO STATISTICS: 1999—Recovered one fumble.
SINGLE GAME HIGHS (regular season): Receptions—13 (October 3, 1999, vs. Cleveland); yards—214 (October 3, 1999, vs. Cleveland); and touchdown receptions—1 (November 28, 1999, vs. Buffalo).
STATISTICAL PLATEAUS: 100-yard receiving games: 1996 (2), 1997 (1), 1998 (4), 1999 (4). Total: 11.

				RUSHING				RECEIVING				TOTALS		
Year Team	G	GS	Att.	Yds.	Avg.	TD	No.	Yds.	Avg.	TD	TD	2pt.	Pts.	Fum.
1996—New England NFL	15	15	5	42	8.4	0	90	1132	12.6	6	6	0	36	1
1997—New England NFL	9	9	0	0	0.0	0	27	431	16.0	2	2	0	12	1
1998—New England NFL	10	9	2	-1	-0.5	0	50	792	15.8	3	3	0	18	0
1999—New England NFL	14	13	0	0	0.0	0	69	1147	16.6	4	4	0	24	2
Pro totals (4 years)................................	48	46	7	41	5.9	0	236	3502	14.8	15	15	0	90	4

GLOVER, ANDREW   TE   SAINTS

PERSONAL: Born August 12, 1967, in New Orleans. ... 6-6/252. ... Full name: Andrew Lee Glover.
HIGH SCHOOL: East Ascension (Gonzales, La.).
COLLEGE: Grambling State (degree in criminal justice, 1990).
TRANSACTIONS/CAREER NOTES: Selected by Los Angeles Raiders in 10th round (274th pick overall) of 1991 NFL draft. ... Signed by Raiders (1991). ... On injured reserve with knee injury (December 27, 1993-remainder of season). ... Raiders franchise moved to Oakland (July 21, 1995). ... Granted unconditional free agency (February 16, 1996). ... Re-signed by Raiders (May 24, 1996). ... Granted unconditional free agency (February 14, 1997). ... Signed by Minnesota Vikings (July 28, 1997). ... Granted unconditional free agency (February 13, 1998). ... Re-signed by Vikings (February 18, 1998). ... Released by Vikings (February 10, 2000). ... Signed by New Orleans Saints (February 18, 2000).
CHAMPIONSHIP GAME EXPERIENCE: Played in NFC championship game (1998 season).
PRO STATISTICS: 1992—Recovered one fumble.
SINGLE GAME HIGHS (regular season): Receptions—9 (November 8, 1998, vs. New Orleans); yards—93 (November 8, 1998, vs. New Orleans); and touchdown receptions—2 (December 20, 1998, vs. Jacksonville).

				RECEIVING				TOTALS		
Year Team	G	GS	No.	Yds.	Avg.	TD	TD	2pt.	Pts.	Fum.
1991—Los Angeles Raiders NFL	16	1	5	45	9.0	3	3	0	18	0
1992—Los Angeles Raiders NFL	16	2	15	178	11.9	1	1	0	6	1
1993—Los Angeles Raiders NFL	15	0	4	55	13.8	1	1	0	6	0
1994—Los Angeles Raiders NFL	16	16	33	371	11.2	2	2	0	12	0
1995—Oakland NFL...	16	7	26	220	8.5	3	3	0	18	0
1996—Oakland NFL...	14	4	9	101	11.2	1	1	0	6	0
1997—Minnesota NFL..	13	11	32	378	11.8	3	3	0	18	0

G

1998—Minnesota NFL	16	12	35	522	14.9	5	5	0	30	0
1999—Minnesota NFL	16	13	28	327	11.7	1	1	0	6	0
Pro totals (9 years)	138	66	187	2197	11.7	20	20	0	120	1

GLOVER, KEVIN   C

PERSONAL: Born June 17, 1963, in Washington, D.C. ... 6-2/282. ... Full name: Kevin Bernard Glover.
HIGH SCHOOL: Largo (Md.).
COLLEGE: Maryland.
TRANSACTIONS/CAREER NOTES: Selected by Tampa Bay Bandits in 1985 USFL territorial draft. ... Selected by Detroit Lions in second round (34th pick overall) of 1985 NFL draft. ... Signed by Lions (July 23, 1985). ... On injured reserve with knee injury (December 7, 1985-remainder of season). ... On injured reserve with knee injury (September 29-December 20, 1986). ... Granted free agency (February 1, 1992). ... Re-signed by Lions (August 25, 1992). ... On injured reserve with ankle injury (October 27, 1992-remainder of season). ... Designated by Lions as franchise player (February 16, 1996). ... Granted unconditional free agency (February 13, 1998). ... Signed by Seattle Seahawks (February 21, 1998). ... On injured reserve with back injury (November 29, 1998-remainder of season). ... On injured reserve with chest injury (October 27, 1999-remainder of season). ... Released by Seahawks (February 9, 2000).
PLAYING EXPERIENCE: Detroit NFL, 1985-1997; Seattle NFL, 1998 and 1999. ... Games/Games started: 1985 (10/0), 1986 (4/1), 1987 (12/9), 1988 (16/16), 1989 (16/16), 1990 (16/16), 1991 (16/16), 1992 (7/7), 1993 (16/16), 1994 (16/16), 1995 (16/16), 1996 (16/16), 1997 (16/16), 1998 (8/8), 1999 (6/6). Total: 191/175.
CHAMPIONSHIP GAME EXPERIENCE: Played in NFC championship game (1991 season).
HONORS: Named center on THE SPORTING NEWS college All-America first team (1984). ... Played in Pro Bowl (1995-1997 seasons).
PRO STATISTICS: 1987—Returned one kickoff for 19 yards. 1988—Recovered two fumbles. 1990—Recovered one fumble. 1992—Recovered one fumble. 1995—Fumbled twice and recovered one fumble for minus 14 yards. 1996—Recovered two fumbles. 1997—Recovered one fumble.

GLOVER, La'ROI   DT   SAINTS

PERSONAL: Born July 4, 1974, in San Diego. ... 6-2/285. ... Full name: La'Roi Damon Glover. ... Name pronounced la-ROY.
HIGH SCHOOL: Point Loma (San Diego).
COLLEGE: San Diego State.
TRANSACTIONS/CAREER NOTES: Selected by Oakland Raiders in fifth round (166th pick overall) of 1996 NFL draft. ... Signed by Raiders (July 12, 1996). ... Assigned by Raiders to Barcelona Dragons in 1997 World League enhancement allocation program (February 19, 1997). ... Claimed on waivers by New Orleans Saints (August 25, 1997).
PRO STATISTICS: 1997—Recovered one fumble. 1998—Intercepted one pass for no yards. 1999—Recovered one fumble for two yards.

Year Team	G	GS	SACKS
1996—Oakland NFL	2	0	0.0
1997—Barcelona W.L.	10	10	6.5
—New Orleans NFL	15	2	6.5
1998—New Orleans NFL	16	15	10.0
1999—New Orleans NFL	16	16	8.5
W.L. totals (1 year)	10	10	6.5
NFL totals (4 years)	49	33	25.0
Pro totals (5 years)	59	43	31.5

GLOVER, PHIL   LB   TITANS

PERSONAL: Born December 17, 1975, in San Fernando Calif. ... 5-11/241. ... Full name: Phil Dwyain Glover.
HIGH SCHOOL: Clark (Las Vegas, Nev.).
COLLEGE: Washington State, then Utah.
TRANSACTIONS/CAREER NOTES: Selected by Tennessee Titans in seventh round (222nd pick overall) of 1999 NFL draft. ... Signed by Titans (July 26, 1999). ... Assigned by Titans to Scottish Claymores in 2000 NFL Europe enhancement allocation program (February 18, 2000).
PLAYING EXPERIENCE: Tennessee NFL, 1999. ... Games/Games started: 1999 (1/0).
CHAMPIONSHIP GAME EXPERIENCE: Member of Titans for AFC championship game (1999 season); inactive. ... Member of Titans for Super Bowl XXXIV (1999 season); inactive.

GODFREY, RANDALL   LB   TITANS

PERSONAL: Born April 6, 1973, in Valdosta, Ga. ... 6-2/245. ... Full name: Randall Euralentris Godfrey.
HIGH SCHOOL: Lowndes County (Valdosta, Ga.).
COLLEGE: Georgia.
TRANSACTIONS/CAREER NOTES: Selected by Dallas Cowboys in second round (49th pick overall) of 1996 NFL draft. ... Signed by Cowboys (July 17, 1996). ... Granted free agency (February 12, 1999). ... Re-signed by Cowboys (June 25, 1999). ... Granted unconditional free agency (February 11, 2000). ... Signed by Tennessee Titans (February 16, 2000).
PLAYING EXPERIENCE: Dallas NFL, 1996-1999. ... Games/Games started: 1996 (16/6), 1997 (16/16), 1998 (16/16), 1999 (16/16). Total: 64/54.
PRO STATISTICS: 1997—Credited with one sack and recovered one fumble. 1998—Intercepted one pass for no yards, credited with three sacks and recovered one fumble. 1999—Intercepted one pass for 10 yards and credited with one sack.

GOFF, MIKE   G   BENGALS

PERSONAL: Born January 6, 1976, in Spring Valley, Ill. ... 6-5/316. ... Full name: Michael J. Goff.
HIGH SCHOOL: Lasalle-Peru (Peru, Ill.).
COLLEGE: Iowa.

G

TRANSACTIONS/CAREER NOTES: Selected by Cincinnati Bengals in third round (78th pick overall) of 1998 NFL draft. ... Signed by Bengals (July 20, 1998).
PLAYING EXPERIENCE: Cincinnati NFL, 1998 and 1999. ... Games/Games started: 1998 (10/5), 1999 (12/1). Total: 22/6.
PRO STATISTICS: 1999—Recovered one fumble.

GOGAN, KEVIN G CHARGERS

PERSONAL: Born November 2, 1964, in Pacifica, Calif. ... 6-7/330. ... Full name: Kevin Patrick Gogan.
HIGH SCHOOL: Sacred Heart (San Francisco).
COLLEGE: Washington (degree in sociology, 1987).
TRANSACTIONS/CAREER NOTES: Selected by Dallas Cowboys in eighth round (206th pick overall) of 1987 NFL draft. ... Signed by Cowboys (July 18, 1987). ... On non-football injury list with substance abuse problem (August 5-31, 1988). ... Granted roster exemption (August 31-September 5, 1988). ... Granted unconditional free agency (February 17, 1994). ... Signed by Los Angeles Raiders (April 18, 1994). ... Raiders franchise moved to Oakland (July 21, 1995). ... Granted unconditional free agency (February 14, 1997). ... Signed by San Francisco 49ers (February 25, 1997). ... On physically unable to perform list with hamstring injury (July 21-28, 1998). ... Traded by 49ers to Miami Dolphins for fifth-round pick (RB Terry Jackson) in 1999 draft (March 1, 1999). ... Released by Dolphins (February 25, 2000). ... Signed by San Diego Chargers (June 6, 2000).
PLAYING EXPERIENCE: Dallas NFL, 1987-1993; Los Angeles Raiders NFL, 1994; Oakland NFL, 1995 and 1996; San Francisco NFL, 1997 and 1998; Miami NFL, 1999. ... Games/Games started: 1987 (11/10), 1988 (15/15), 1989 (13/13), 1990 (16/4), 1991 (16/16), 1992 (16/1), 1993 (16/16), 1994 (16/16), 1995 (16/16), 1996 (16/16), 1997 (16/16), 1998 (16/16), 1999 (16/10). Total: 199/165.
CHAMPIONSHIP GAME EXPERIENCE: Played in NFC championship game (1992, 1993 and 1997 seasons). ... Member of Super Bowl championship team (1992 and 1993 seasons).
HONORS: Played in Pro Bowl (1994, 1997 and 1998 seasons).
PRO STATISTICS: 1987—Recovered one fumble. 1990—Recovered one fumble. 1996—Recovered one fumble. 1999—Recovered one fumble.

GONZALEZ, PETE QB COLTS

PERSONAL: Born July 4, 1974, in Miami. ... 6-1/217.
HIGH SCHOOL: Miami-Coral Park Senior.
COLLEGE: Pittsburgh.
TRANSACTIONS/CAREER NOTES: Signed as non-drafted free agent by Pittsburgh Steelers (April 24, 1998). ... Inactive for all 16 games (1998). ... Granted unconditional free agency (February 12, 2000). ... Signed by Indianapolis Colts (February 29, 2000).
PLAYING EXPERIENCE: Pittsburgh NFL, 1999. ... Games/Games started: 1999 (1/0).
PRO STATISTICS: 1999—Completed only pass attempt for eight yards and rushed twice for minus three yards.
SINGLE GAME HIGHS (regular season): Attempts—1 (September 12, 1999, vs. Cleveland); completions—1 (September 12, 1999, vs. Cleveland); passing yards—8 (September 12, 1999, vs. Cleveland); and touchdown passes—0.

GONZALEZ, TONY TE CHIEFS

PERSONAL: Born February 27, 1976, in Torrance, Calif. ... 6-4/251. ... Full name: Anthony Gonzalez.
HIGH SCHOOL: Huntington Beach (Calif.).
COLLEGE: California.
TRANSACTIONS/CAREER NOTES: Selected by Kansas City Chiefs in first round (13th pick overall) of 1997 NFL draft. ... Signed by Chiefs (July 29, 1997).
HONORS: Named tight end on THE SPORTING NEWS college All-America first team (1996). ... Named tight end on THE SPORTING NEWS NFL All-Pro team (1999). ... Played in Pro Bowl (1999 season).
PRO STATISTICS: 1999—Recovered one fumble.
SINGLE GAME HIGHS (regular season): Receptions—9 (December 26, 1999, vs. Seattle); yards—93 (December 18, 1999, vs. Pittsburgh); and touchdown receptions—2 (December 18, 1999, vs. Pittsburgh).

			RECEIVING				TOTALS			
Year Team	G	GS	No.	Yds.	Avg.	TD	TD	2pt.	Pts.	Fum.
1997—Kansas City NFL	16	0	33	368	11.2	2	2	1	14	0
1998—Kansas City NFL	16	16	59	621	10.5	2	2	0	12	3
1999—Kansas City NFL	15	15	76	849	11.2	11	11	0	66	2
Pro totals (3 years)	47	31	168	1838	10.9	15	15	1	92	5

GOOCH, JEFF LB BUCCANEERS

PERSONAL: Born October 31, 1974, in Nashville. ... 5-11/225. ... Full name: Jeffery Lance Gooch.
HIGH SCHOOL: Overton (Nashville).
COLLEGE: Austin Peay State.
TRANSACTIONS/CAREER NOTES: Signed as non-drafted free agent by Tampa Bay Buccaneers (April 23, 1996). ... On injured reserve with knee injury (December 17, 1996-remainder of season). ... Granted free agency (February 12, 1999). ... Re-signed by Buccaneers (April 13, 1999).
PLAYING EXPERIENCE: Tampa Bay NFL, 1996-1999. ... Games/Games started: 1996 (15/0), 1997 (14/5), 1998 (16/16), 1999 (15/0). Total: 60/21.
CHAMPIONSHIP GAME EXPERIENCE: Played in NFC championship game (1999 season).
PRO STATISTICS: 1996—Recovered one fumble. 1998—Credited with one sack and recovered one fumble.

G

GOODWIN, HUNTER TE DOLPHINS

PERSONAL: Born October 10, 1972, in Bellville, Texas. ... 6-5/270. ... Full name: Robert Hunter Goodwin.
HIGH SCHOOL: Bellville (Texas).

COLLEGE: Texas A&M-Kingsville, then Texas A&M.
TRANSACTIONS/CAREER NOTES: Selected by Minnesota Vikings in fourth round (97th pick overall) of 1996 NFL draft. ... Signed by Vikings (July 20, 1996). ... Granted free agency (February 12, 1999). ... Tendered offer sheet by Miami Dolphins (April 8, 1999). ... Vikings declined to match offer (April 9, 1999).
CHAMPIONSHIP GAME EXPERIENCE: Played in NFC championship game (1998 season).
PRO STATISTICS: 1998—Recovered one fumble.
SINGLE GAME HIGHS (regular season): Receptions—3 (December 27, 1999, vs. New York Jets); yards—24 (December 1, 1996, vs. Arizona); and touchdown receptions—0.

				RECEIVING			TOTALS			
Year Team	G	GS	No.	Yds.	Avg.	TD	TD	2pt.	Pts.	Fum.
1996—Minnesota NFL	9	6	1	24	24.0	0	0	0	0	0
1997—Minnesota NFL	16	5	7	61	8.7	0	0	0	0	0
1998—Minnesota NFL	15	0	3	16	5.3	0	0	0	0	0
1999—Miami NFL	15	5	8	55	6.9	0	0	0	0	1
Pro totals (4 years)	55	16	19	156	8.2	0	0	0	0	1

GORDON, DARRIEN — CB — RAIDERS

PERSONAL: Born November 14, 1970, in Shawnee, Okla. ... 5-11/190. ... Full name: Darrien Jamal Gordon.
HIGH SCHOOL: Shawnee (Okla.).
COLLEGE: Stanford.
TRANSACTIONS/CAREER NOTES: Selected by San Diego Chargers in first round (22nd pick overall) of 1993 NFL draft. ... Signed by Chargers (July 16, 1993). ... Inactive for all 16 games due to shoulder injury (1995 season). ... Granted unconditional free agency (February 14, 1997). ... Signed by Denver Broncos (April 30, 1997). ... Granted unconditional free agency (February 12, 1999). ... Signed by Oakland Raiders (June 9, 1999). ... Released by Raiders (February 10, 2000). ... Re-signed by Raiders (February 28, 2000).
CHAMPIONSHIP GAME EXPERIENCE: Played in AFC championship game (1994, 1997 and 1998 seasons). ... Played in Super Bowl XXIX (1994 season). ... Member of Super Bowl championship team (1997 and 1998 seasons).
HONORS: Named punt returner on THE SPORTING NEWS NFL All-Pro team (1997).
RECORDS: Shares NFL single-game records for most touchdowns by punt return—2; and most touchdowns by combined kick return—2 (November 9, 1997, vs. Carolina).
POST SEASON RECORDS: Holds Super Bowl career and single-game records for most interception return yards—108 (January 31, 1999, vs. Atlanta).
PRO STATISTICS: 1993—Recovered two fumbles for minus two yards. 1994—Recovered three fumbles for 15 yards. 1996—Credited with two sacks. 1997—Credited with two sacks and recovered four fumbles. 1998—Recovered one fumble. 1999—Credited with one sack and recovered two fumbles for 40 yards.

			INTERCEPTIONS				PUNT RETURNS				TOTALS			
Year Team	G	GS	No.	Yds.	Avg.	TD	No.	Yds.	Avg.	TD	TD	2pt.	Pts.	Fum.
1993—San Diego NFL	16	7	1	3	3.0	0	31	395	12.7	0	0	0	0	4
1994—San Diego NFL	16	16	4	32	8.0	0	36	475	§13.2	†2	2	0	12	2
1995—San Diego NFL									Did not play.					
1996—San Diego NFL	16	6	2	55	27.5	0	36	537	§14.9	▲1	1	0	6	3
1997—Denver NFL	16	16	4	64	16.0	1	40	543	13.6	†3	4	0	24	3
1998—Denver NFL	16	16	4	125	31.3	1	34	379	11.1	0	1	0	6	1
1999—Oakland NFL	16	2	3	44	14.7	0	42	397	9.5	0	0	0	0	3
Pro totals (6 years)	96	63	18	323	17.9	2	219	2726	12.4	6	8	0	48	16

GORDON, DWAYNE — LB — JETS

PERSONAL: Born November 2, 1969, in White Plains, N.Y. ... 6-1/245. ... Full name: Dwayne K. Gordon.
HIGH SCHOOL: Arlington North (LaGrangeville, N.Y.).
COLLEGE: New Hampshire.
TRANSACTIONS/CAREER NOTES: Selected by Miami Dolphins in eighth round (218th pick overall) of 1993 NFL draft. ... Signed by Dolphins for 1993 season. ... Released by Dolphins (July 12, 1993). ... Signed by Atlanta Falcons (July 19, 1993). ... Released by Falcons (August 27, 1995). ... Signed by San Diego Chargers (August 28, 1995). ... Granted free agency (February 16, 1996). ... Re-signed by Chargers (June 14, 1996). ... Granted unconditional free agency (February 17, 1997). ... Signed by New York Jets (June 4, 1997). ... Granted unconditional free agency (February 12, 1999). ... Re-signed by Jets (March 10, 1999).
PLAYING EXPERIENCE: Atlanta NFL, 1993 and 1994; San Diego NFL, 1995 and 1996; New York Jets NFL, 1997-1999. ... Games/Games started: 1993 (5/0), 1994 (16/0), 1995 (16/3), 1996 (13/0), 1997 (16/8), 1998 (16/4), 1999 (16/4). Total: 98/19.
CHAMPIONSHIP GAME EXPERIENCE: Played in AFC championship game (1998 season).
PRO STATISTICS: 1993—Fumbled once. 1995—Credited with one sack and recovered one fumble. 1997—Credited with one sack. 1998—Intercepted one pass for 31 yards and a touchdown. 1999—Credited with one sack.

GORDON, LENNOX — RB — BILLS

PERSONAL: Born April 9, 1978, in Higley, Ariz. ... 6-0/201. ... Full name: Lennox Constantine Gordon.
HIGH SCHOOL: Red Mountain (Mesa, Ariz.).
COLLEGE: New Mexico.
TRANSACTIONS/CAREER NOTES: Signed as non-drafted free agent by Buffalo Bills (April 19, 1999).
PLAYING EXPERIENCE: Buffalo NFL, 1999. ... Games/Games started: 1999 (8/0).
PRO STATISTICS: 1999—Rushed 11 times for 38 yards and returned one kickoff for 11 yards.
SINGLE GAME HIGHS (regular season): Attempts—5 (November 14, 1999, vs. Miami); yards—18 (November 28, 1999, vs. New England); and rushing touchdowns—0.

G

GOUVEIA, KURT — LB

PERSONAL: Born September 14, 1964, in Honolulu. ... 6-1/240. ... Full name: Kurt Keola Gouveia. ... Name pronounced goo-VAY-uh.
HIGH SCHOOL: Waianae (Hawaii).
COLLEGE: Brigham Young.
TRANSACTIONS/CAREER NOTES: Selected by Washington Redskins in eighth round (213th pick overall) of 1986 NFL draft. ... Signed by Redskins (July 18, 1986). ... On injured reserve with knee injury (August 25, 1986-entire season). ... Granted unconditional free agency (March 1, 1993). ... Re-signed by Redskins for 1993 season. ... Granted free agency (February 17, 1995). ... Signed by Philadelphia Eagles (April 23, 1995). ... Granted unconditional free agency (February 16, 1996). ... Signed by San Diego Chargers (February 27, 1996). ... On injured reserve with neck injury (October 22, 1997-remainder of season). ... Granted unconditional free agency (February 12, 1999). ... Signed by Redskins (October 11, 1999). ... Granted unconditional free agency (February 11, 2000).
CHAMPIONSHIP GAME EXPERIENCE: Played in NFC championship game (1987 and 1991 seasons). ... Member of Super Bowl championship team (1987 and 1991 seasons).
POST SEASON RECORDS: Shares NFL postseason career record for most consecutive games with one or more interception—3.
PRO STATISTICS: 1990—Recovered one fumble for 39 yards and a touchdown. 1995—Recovered one fumble.

Year Team	G	GS	INTERCEPTIONS No.	Yds.	Avg.	TD	SACKS No.	KICKOFF RETURNS No.	Yds.	Avg.	TD	TOTALS TD	2pt.	Pts.	Fum.
1986—Washington NFL							Did not play.								
1987—Washington NFL	11	1	0	0	0.0	0	0.0	0	0	0.0	0	0	0	0	0
1988—Washington NFL	16	0	0	0	0.0	0	0.0	0	0	0.0	0	0	0	0	0
1989—Washington NFL	15	1	1	1	1.0	0	0.0	1	0	0.0	0	0	0	0	0
1990—Washington NFL	16	7	0	0	0.0	0	1.0	2	23	11.5	0	1	0	6	0
1991—Washington NFL	14	1	1	22	22.0	0	0.0	3	12	4.0	0	0	0	0	0
1992—Washington NFL	16	14	3	43	14.3	0	1.0	1	7	7.0	0	0	0	0	0
1993—Washington NFL	16	16	1	59	59.0	1	1.5	0	0	0.0	0	1	0	6	0
1994—Washington NFL	14	1	1	7	7.0	0	0.0	0	0	0.0	0	0	0	0	0
1995—Philadelphia NFL	16	16	1	20	20.0	0	0.0	0	0	0.0	0	0	0	0	0
1996—San Diego NFL	16	16	3	41	13.7	0	1.0	0	0	0.0	0	0	0	0	0
1997—San Diego NFL	7	6	1	0	0.0	0	0.0	0	0	0.0	0	0	0	0	0
1998—San Diego NFL	15	12	0	0	0.0	0	0.5	0	0	0.0	0	0	0	0	0
1999—Washington NFL	12	0	0	0	0.0	0	0.0	0	0	0.0	0	0	0	0	0
Pro totals (13 years)	184	91	12	193	16.1	1	5.0	7	42	6.0	0	2	0	12	0

GOWIN, TOBY — P — SAINTS

PERSONAL: Born March 30, 1975, in Jacksonville, Texas. ... 5-10/167. ... Name pronounced GO-in.
HIGH SCHOOL: Jacksonville (Texas).
COLLEGE: North Texas (degree in kinesiology).
TRANSACTIONS/CAREER NOTES: Signed as non-drafted free agent by Dallas Cowboys (April 24, 1997). ... Granted free agency (February 11, 2000). ... Tendered offer sheet by New Orleans Saints (April 6, 2000). ... Cowboys declined to match offer (April 6, 2000).
PRO STATISTICS: 1997—Missed only field-goal attempt.

Year Team	G	PUNTING No.	Yds.	Avg.	Net avg.	In. 20	Blk.
1997—Dallas NFL	16	86	3592	41.8	35.4	26	0
1998—Dallas NFL	16	77	3342	43.4	36.6	31	∞1
1999—Dallas NFL	16	81	3500	43.2	35.1	24	0
Pro totals (3 years)	48	244	10434	42.8	35.7	81	1

GOWINS, BRIAN — K

PERSONAL: Born June 3, 1976, in Birmingham, Ala. ... 5-9/174.
HIGH SCHOOL: Shades Valley (Birmingham, Ala.).
COLLEGE: Northwestern.
TRANSACTIONS/CAREER NOTES: Signed as non-drafted free agent by Detroit Lions (April 23, 1999). ... Released by Lions (August 18, 1999). ... Signed by Chicago Bears (August 26, 1999). ... Released by Bears (August 31, 1999). ... Re-signed by Bears to practice squad (September 6, 1999). ... Activated (September 11, 1999). ... Released by Bears (September 13, 1999). ... Re-signed by Bears to practice squad (September 13, 1999). ... Activated (September 18, 1999). ... Released by Bears (September 20, 1999). ... Re-signed by Bears to practice squad (September 21, 1999). ... Released by Bears (September 28, 1999).

Year Team	G	KICKING XPM	XPA	FGM	FGA	Lg.	50+	Pts.
1999—Chicago NFL	2	3	3	4	6	43	0-1	15

GRAGG, SCOTT — OT

PERSONAL: Born February 28, 1972, in Silverton, Ore. ... 6-8/325.
HIGH SCHOOL: Silverton (Ore.) Union.
COLLEGE: Montana.
TRANSACTIONS/CAREER NOTES: Selected by New York Giants in second round (54th pick overall) of 1995 NFL draft. ... Signed by Giants (July 23, 1995). ... Granted free agency (February 13, 1998). ... Re-signed by Giants (September 4, 1998). ... Released by Giants (March 28, 2000).
PLAYING EXPERIENCE: New York Giants NFL, 1995-1999. ... Games/Games started: 1995 (13/0), 1996 (16/16), 1997 (16/16), 1998 (16/16), 1999 (16/16). Total: 77/64.
PRO STATISTICS: 1997—Recovered one fumble. 1998—Recovered one fumble. 1999—Recovered one fumble.

G

GRAHAM, AARON   C/G   CHIEFS

PERSONAL: Born May 22, 1973, in Las Vegas, N.M. ... 6-4/301.
HIGH SCHOOL: Denton (Texas).
COLLEGE: Nebraska.
TRANSACTIONS/CAREER NOTES: Selected by Arizona Cardinals in fourth round (112th pick overall) of 1996 NFL draft. ... Signed by Cardinals for 1996 season. ... Granted free agency (February 12, 1999). ... Re-signed by Cardinals (May 21, 1999). ... Granted unconditional free agency (February 11, 2000). ... Signed by Kansas City Chiefs (April 13, 2000)
PLAYING EXPERIENCE: Arizona NFL, 1996-1999. ... Games/Games started: 1996 (16/7), 1997 (16/4), 1998 (14/13), 1999 (16/16). Total: 62/40.
PRO STATISTICS: 1997—Recovered one fumble. 1999—Fumbled once and recovered one fumble.

GRAHAM, DeMINGO   G/OT   CHARGERS

PERSONAL: Born September 10, 1973, in Newark, N.J. ... 6-3/310.
HIGH SCHOOL: Newark (N.J.) Central.
COLLEGE: Hofstra.
TRANSACTIONS/CAREER NOTES: Signed as non-drafted free agent by San Diego Chargers (April 20, 1998). ... Inactive for all 16 games (1998).
PLAYING EXPERIENCE: San Diego NFL, 1999. ... Games/Games started: 1999 (16/10).

GRAHAM, JAY   RB   RAVENS

PERSONAL: Born July 14, 1975, in Concord, N.C. ... 5-11/215. ... Full name: Herman Jason Graham.
HIGH SCHOOL: Concord (N.C.).
COLLEGE: Tennessee.
TRANSACTIONS/CAREER NOTES: Selected by Baltimore Ravens in third round (64th pick overall) of 1997 NFL draft. ... Signed by Ravens (June 19, 1997). ... On injured reserve with knee injury (December 10, 1998-remainder of season). ... Granted free agency (February 11, 2000).
PRO STATISTICS: 1997—Returned six kickoffs for 115 yards and recovered one fumble. 1998—Returned three kickoffs for 52 yards.
SINGLE GAME HIGHS (regular season): Attempts—35 (November 16, 1997, vs. Philadelphia); yards—154 (November 16, 1997, vs. Philadelphia); and rushing touchdowns—1 (September 14, 1997, vs. New York Giants).
STATISTICAL PLATEAUS: 100-yard rushing games: 1997 (1).

			RUSHING				RECEIVING				TOTALS			
Year Team	G	GS	Att.	Yds.	Avg.	TD	No.	Yds.	Avg.	TD	TD	2pt.	Pts.	Fum.
1997—Baltimore NFL	13	3	81	299	3.7	2	12	51	4.3	0	2	0	12	2
1998—Baltimore NFL	5	2	35	109	3.1	0	5	41	8.2	0	0	0	0	0
1999—Baltimore NFL	4	0	0	0	0.0	0	0	0	0.0	0	0	0	0	0
Pro totals (3 years)	22	5	116	408	3.5	2	17	92	5.4	0	2	0	12	2

GRAHAM, JEFF   WR   CHARGERS

PERSONAL: Born February 14, 1969, in Dayton, Ohio. ... 6-2/206. ... Full name: Jeff Todd Graham.
HIGH SCHOOL: Archbishop Hoban (Akron, Ohio).
COLLEGE: Ohio State.
TRANSACTIONS/CAREER NOTES: Selected by Pittsburgh Steelers in second round (46th pick overall) of 1991 NFL draft. ... Signed by Steelers (August 3, 1991). ... Traded by Steelers to Chicago Bears for fifth-round pick (DB Lethon Flowers) in 1995 draft (April 29, 1994). ... Granted unconditional free agency (February 16, 1996). ... Signed by New York Jets (March 14, 1996). ... Traded by Jets to Philadelphia Eagles for sixth-round pick (DE Eric Ogbogu) in 1998 draft (April 19, 1998). ... Released by Eagles (February 13, 1999). ... Signed by San Diego Chargers (March 19, 1999). ... Granted unconditional free agency (February 11, 2000). ... Re-signed by Chargers (February 21, 2000).
PRO STATISTICS: 1991—Returned three kickoffs for 48 yards. 1994—Recovered one fumble. 1995—Returned one kickoff for 12 yards. 1997—Recovered one fumble.
SINGLE GAME HIGHS (regular season): Receptions—9 (December 12, 1999, vs. Seattle); yards—192 (December 19, 1993, vs. Houston); and touchdown receptions—3 (November 17, 1996, vs. Indianapolis).
STATISTICAL PLATEAUS: 100-yard receiving games: 1992 (2), 1993 (2), 1994 (2), 1995 (7), 1996 (3), 1997 (1), 1999 (4). Total: 21.

			RECEIVING				PUNT RETURNS				TOTALS			
Year Team	G	GS	No.	Yds.	Avg.	TD	No.	Yds.	Avg.	TD	TD	2pt.	Pts.	Fum.
1991—Pittsburgh NFL	13	1	2	21	10.5	0	8	46	5.8	0	0	0	0	0
1992—Pittsburgh NFL	14	10	49	711	14.5	1	0	0	0.0	0	1	0	6	0
1993—Pittsburgh NFL	15	12	38	579	15.2	0	0	0	0.0	0	0	0	0	0
1994—Chicago NFL	16	15	68	944	13.9	4	15	140	9.3	1	5	1	32	1
1995—Chicago NFL	16	16	82	1301	15.9	4	23	183	8.0	0	4	0	24	3
1996—New York Jets NFL	11	9	50	788	15.8	6	0	0	0.0	0	6	0	36	0
1997—New York Jets NFL	16	16	42	542	12.9	2	0	0	0.0	0	2	0	12	0
1998—Philadelphia NFL	15	15	47	600	12.8	2	0	0	0.0	0	2	0	12	0
1999—San Diego NFL	16	11	57	968	17.0	2	0	0	0.0	0	2	0	12	0
Pro totals (9 years)	132	105	435	6454	14.8	21	46	369	8.0	1	22	1	134	4

GRAHAM, KENT   QB   STEELERS

PERSONAL: Born November 1, 1968, in Wheaton, Ill. ... 6-5/245. ... Full name: Kent Douglas Graham.
HIGH SCHOOL: Wheaton (Ill.) North.
COLLEGE: Notre Dame, then Ohio State.

G

TRANSACTIONS/CAREER NOTES: Selected by New York Giants in eighth round (211th pick overall) of 1992 NFL draft. ... Signed by Giants (July 21, 1992). ... On injured reserve with elbow injury (September 18-October 14, 1992). ... Granted free agency (February 17, 1995). ... Re-signed by Giants (July 1995). ... Released by Giants (August 30, 1995). ... Signed by Detroit Lions (September 5, 1995). ... Granted unconditional free agency (February 16, 1996). ... Signed by Arizona Cardinals (March 7, 1996). ... Granted unconditional free agency (February 13, 1998). ... Signed by New York Giants (February 17, 1998). ... Released by Giants (February 10, 2000). ... Signed by Pittsburgh Steelers (February 28, 2000).

PRO STATISTICS: 1992—Fumbled once and recovered one fumble. 1994—Fumbled twice and recovered one fumble. 1996—Fumbled five times. 1997—Fumbled five times. 1998—Caught one pass for 16 yards and fumbled twice for minus three yards. 1999—Caught one pass for minus one yard, fumbled four times and recovered two fumbles.

SINGLE GAME HIGHS (regular season): Attempts—58 (September 29, 1996, vs. St. Louis); completions—37 (September 29, 1996, vs. St. Louis); yards—366 (September 29, 1996, vs. St. Louis); and touchdown passes—4 (September 29, 1996, vs. St. Louis).

STATISTICAL PLATEAUS: 300-yard passing games: 1996 (1), 1997 (1). Total: 2.

MISCELLANEOUS: Regular-season record as starting NFL quarterback: 15-18 (.455).

					PASSING						RUSHING				TOTALS	
Year Team	G	GS	Att.	Cmp.	Pct.	Yds.	TD	Int.	Avg.	Rat.	Att.	Yds.	Avg.	TD	TD	2pt.	Pts.
1992—N.Y. Giants NFL	6	3	97	42	43.3	470	1	4	4.85	44.6	6	36	6.0	0	0	0	0
1993—N.Y. Giants NFL	9	0	22	8	36.4	79	0	0	3.59	47.3	2	-3	-1.5	0	0	0	0
1994—N.Y. Giants NFL	13	1	53	24	45.3	295	3	2	5.57	66.2	2	11	5.5	0	0	0	0
1995—Detroit NFL	2	0	0	0	0.0	0	0	0	0.0	...	0	0	0.0	0	0	0	0
1996—Arizona NFL	10	8	274	146	53.3	1624	12	7	5.93	75.1	21	87	4.1	0	0	0	0
1997—Arizona NFL	8	6	250	130	52.0	1408	4	5	5.63	65.9	13	23	1.8	2	2	0	12
1998—N.Y. Giants NFL	11	6	205	105	51.2	1219	7	5	5.95	70.8	27	138	5.1	2	2	0	12
1999—N.Y. Giants NFL	9	9	271	160	59.0	1697	9	9	6.26	74.6	35	132	3.8	1	1	0	6
Pro totals (8 years)	68	33	1172	615	52.5	6792	36	32	5.80	68.8	106	424	4.0	5	5	0	30

GRAMATICA, MARTIN   K   BUCCANEERS

PERSONAL: Born November 27, 1975, in Buenos Aires, Argentina. ... 5-8/170. ... Name pronounced mar-TEEN gruh-MAT-ee-ka.
HIGH SCHOOL: La Belle (Fla.).
COLLEGE: Kansas State.
TRANSACTIONS/CAREER NOTES: Selected by Tampa Bay Buccaneers in third round (80th pick overall) of 1999 NFL draft. ... Signed by Buccaneers (July 29, 1999).
CHAMPIONSHIP GAME EXPERIENCE: Played in NFC championship game (1999 season).
HONORS: Won Lou Groza Award (1997). ... Named kicker on THE SPORTING NEWS college All-America first team (1997). ... Named kicker on THE SPORTING NEWS college All-America second team (1998).
PRO STATISTICS: 1999—Recovered one fumble.

		KICKING						
Year Team	G	XPM	XPA	FGM	FGA	Lg.	50+	Pts.
1999—Tampa Bay NFL	16	25	25	‡27	∞32	∞53	3-4	106

GRANVILLE, BILLY   LB   BENGALS

PERSONAL: Born March 11, 1974, in Lawrenceville, N.J. ... 6-3/246.
HIGH SCHOOL: Lawrenceville (N.J.).
COLLEGE: Duke (degree in sociology, 1997).
TRANSACTIONS/CAREER NOTES: Signed as non-drafted free agent by Cincinnati Bengals (April 25, 1997). ... Granted free agency (February 11, 2000). ... Re-signed by Bengals (April 18, 2000).
PLAYING EXPERIENCE: Cincinnati NFL, 1997-1999. ... Games/Games started: 1997 (12/4), 1998 (16/0), 1999 (16/0). Total: 44/4.
PRO STATISTICS: 1998—Recovered one fumble.

GRASMANIS, PAUL   DT   EAGLES

PERSONAL: Born August 2, 1974, in Grand Rapids, Mich. ... 6-2/298. ... Full name: Paul Ryan Grasmanis.
HIGH SCHOOL: Jenison (Mich.).
COLLEGE: Notre Dame.
TRANSACTIONS/CAREER NOTES: Selected by Chicago Bears in fourth round (116th pick overall) of 1996 NFL draft. ... Signed by Bears (June 13, 1996). ... Granted free agency (February 12, 1999). ... Re-signed by Bears (April 13, 1999). ... Released by Bears (September 5, 1999). ... Signed by St. Louis Rams (September 7, 1999). ... Inactive for one game with Rams (1999). ... Released by Rams (September 13, 1999). ... Signed by Denver Broncos (November 1, 1999). ... Granted unconditional free agency (February 11, 2000). ... Signed by Philadelphia Eagles (March 3, 2000).
PLAYING EXPERIENCE: Chicago NFL, 1996-1998; Denver NFL, 1999. ... Games/Games started: 1996 (14/3), 1997 (16/0), 1998 (15/0), 1999 (5/0). Total: 50/3.
PRO STATISTICS: 1997—Credited with 1/2 sack and recovered one fumble. 1998—Credited with one sack.

G

GRAY, CARLTON   CB   CHIEFS

PERSONAL: Born June 26, 1971, in Cincinnati. ... 6-0/198. ... Full name: Carlton Patrick Gray.
HIGH SCHOOL: Forest Park (Cincinnati).
COLLEGE: UCLA.
TRANSACTIONS/CAREER NOTES: Selected by Seattle Seahawks in second round (30th pick overall) of 1993 NFL draft. ... Signed by Seahawks (July 22, 1993). ... On injured reserve with forearm injury (November 23, 1994-remainder of season). ... Granted free agency (February 16, 1996). ... Re-signed by Seahawks (February 16, 1996). ... Granted unconditional free agency (February 14, 1997). ... Signed by Indianapolis Colts (March 3, 1997). ... Released by Colts (September 3, 1998). ... Signed by New York Giants (September 9, 1998). ... Released by Giants (February 11, 1999). ... Signed by Kansas City Chiefs (February 26, 1999).

HONORS: Named defensive back on The Sporting News college All-America first team (1992).
PRO STATISTICS: 1993—Credited with one sack. 1995—Fumbled once. 1996—Ran three yards with lateral from interception return and recovered one fumble for 62 yards. 1998—Credited with one sack.

			INTERCEPTIONS			
Year Team	G	GS	No.	Yds.	Avg.	TD
1993—Seattle NFL	10	2	3	33	11.0	0
1994—Seattle NFL	11	11	2	0	0.0	0
1995—Seattle NFL	16	16	4	45	11.3	0
1996—Seattle NFL	16	16	0	3	0.0	0
1997—Indianapolis NFL	15	13	2	0	0.0	0
1998—New York Giants NFL	14	3	1	36	36.0	0
1999—Kansas City NFL	16	0	0	0	0.0	0
Pro totals (7 years)	98	61	12	117	9.8	0

GRAY, CHRIS — C/G — SEAHAWKS

PERSONAL: Born June 19, 1970, in Birmingham, Ala. ... 6-4/305. ... Full name: Christopher William Gray.
HIGH SCHOOL: Homewood (Ala.).
COLLEGE: Auburn (degree in marketing, 1992).
TRANSACTIONS/CAREER NOTES: Selected by Miami Dolphins in fifth round (132nd pick overall) of 1993 NFL draft. ... Signed by Dolphins (July 12, 1993). ... On injured reserve with ankle injury (November 15, 1995-remainder of season). ... On injured reserve with broken leg (November 19, 1996-remainder of season). ... Released by Dolphins (August 12, 1997). ... Signed by Chicago Bears (September 9, 1997). ... Granted unconditional free agency (February 13, 1998). ... Signed by Seattle Seahawks (February 20, 1998).
PLAYING EXPERIENCE: Miami NFL, 1993-1996; Chicago NFL, 1997; Seattle NFL, 1998 and 1999. ... Games/Games started: 1993 (5/0), 1994 (16/2), 1995 (10/10), 1996 (11/11), 1997 (8/2), 1998 (15/8), 1999 (16/10). Total: 81/43.
PRO STATISTICS: 1994—Recovered one fumble. 1999—Recovered one fumble.

GRAZIANI, TONY — QB — FALCONS

PERSONAL: Born December 23, 1973, in Las Vegas, Nev. ... 6-2/215. ... Full name: Anthony Robert Graziani. ... Name pronounced gra-zee-ON-ee.
HIGH SCHOOL: Downey (Calif.).
COLLEGE: Oregon.
TRANSACTIONS/CAREER NOTES: Selected by Atlanta Falcons in seventh round (204th pick overall) of 1997 NFL draft. ... Signed by Falcons for 1997 season. ... Granted free agency (February 11, 2000). ... Assigned by Falcons to Barcelona Dragons in 2000 NFL Europe enhancement allocation program (February 18, 2000). ... Re-signed by Falcons (April 14, 2000)
CHAMPIONSHIP GAME EXPERIENCE: Member of Falcons for NFC championship game (1998 season); inactive. ... Member of Falcons for Super Bowl XXXIII (1998 season); inactive.
PRO STATISTICS: 1999—Fumbled four times and recovered two fumbles for minus eight yards.
SINGLE GAME HIGHS (regular season): Attempts—22 (September 26, 1999, vs. St. Louis); completions—14 (September 26, 1999, vs. St. Louis); yards—162 (September 26, 1999, vs. St. Louis); and touchdown passes—1 (October 10, 1999, vs. New Orleans).
MISCELLANEOUS: Regular-season record as starting NFL quarterback: 2-3 (.400).

			PASSING							RUSHING				TOTALS		
Year Team	G	GS	Att.	Cmp.	Pct.	Yds.	TD	Int.	Avg.	Rat.	Att.	Yds.	Avg.	TD	TD	2pt.	Pts.
1997—Atlanta NFL	3	1	23	7	30.4	41	0	2	1.78	3.7	3	19	6.3	0	0	0	0
1998—Atlanta NFL	4	1	33	16	48.5	199	0	2	6.03	42.4	4	21	5.3	0	0	0	0
1999—Atlanta NFL	11	3	118	62	52.5	759	2	4	6.43	64.2	9	11	1.2	0	0	0	0
Pro totals (3 years)	18	5	174	85	48.9	999	2	8	5.74	51.4	16	51	3.2	0	0	0	0

GRBAC, ELVIS — QB — CHIEFS

PERSONAL: Born August 13, 1970, in Cleveland. ... 6-5/237. ... Name pronounced ger-BACK.
HIGH SCHOOL: St. Joseph (Cleveland).
COLLEGE: Michigan (degree in graphic design, 1993).
TRANSACTIONS/CAREER NOTES: Selected by San Francisco 49ers in eighth round (219th pick overall) of 1993 NFL draft. ... Signed by 49ers (July 13, 1993). ... Inactive for all 16 games (1993). ... Granted unconditional free agency (February 14, 1997). ... Signed by Kansas City Chiefs (March 17, 1997).
CHAMPIONSHIP GAME EXPERIENCE: Member of 49ers for NFC championship game (1993 season); inactive. ... Member of 49ers for NFC championship game (1994 season); did not play. ... Member of Super Bowl championship team (1994 season).
PRO STATISTICS: 1994—Fumbled five times. 1995—Fumbled twice and recovered two fumbles for minus one yard. 1997—Fumbled once. 1998—Fumbled once and recovered one fumble. 1999—Fumbled seven times and recovered one fumble.
SINGLE GAME HIGHS (regular season): Attempts—49 (November 21, 1999, vs. Seattle); completions—31 (November 20, 1995, vs. Miami); yards—382 (November 20, 1995, vs. Miami); and touchdown passes—4 (November 20, 1995, vs. Miami).
STATISTICAL PLATEAUS: 300-yard passing games: 1995 (3), 1997 (1), 1999 (1). Total: 5.
MISCELLANEOUS: Regular-season record as starting NFL quarterback: 25-16 (.610). ... Postseason record as starting NFL quarterback: 0-1.

			PASSING							RUSHING				TOTALS		
Year Team	G	GS	Att.	Cmp.	Pct.	Yds.	TD	Int.	Avg.	Rat.	Att.	Yds.	Avg.	TD	TD	2pt.	Pts.
1993—San Francisco NFL									Did not play.								
1994—San Francisco NFL	11	0	50	35	70.0	393	2	1	7.86	98.2	13	1	0.1	0	0	0	0
1995—San Francisco NFL	16	5	183	127	69.4	1469	8	5	8.03	96.6	20	3	1.7	2	2	0	12
1996—San Francisco NFL	15	4	197	122	61.9	1236	8	10	6.27	72.2	23	21	0.9	2	2	0	12
1997—Kansas City NFL	10	10	314	179	57.0	1943	11	6	6.19	79.1	30	168	5.6	1	1	0	6
1998—Kansas City NFL	8	6	188	98	52.1	1142	5	12	6.07	53.1	7	27	3.9	0	0	0	0
1999—Kansas City NFL	16	16	499	294	58.9	3389	22	15	6.79	81.7	19	10	0.5	0	0	0	0
Pro totals (6 years)	76	41	1431	855	59.7	9572	56	49	6.69	78.5	112	260	2.3	5	5	0	30

G

GREEN, AHMAN   RB   PACKERS

PERSONAL: Born February 16, 1977, in Omaha, Neb. ... 6-0/215.
HIGH SCHOOL: North (Omaha, Neb.), then Central Christian (Omaha, Neb.).
COLLEGE: Nebraska.
TRANSACTIONS/CAREER NOTES: Selected after junior season by Seattle Seahawks in third round (76th pick overall) of 1998 NFL draft. ... Signed by Seahawks (July 18, 1998). ... Traded by Seahawks with fifth-round pick (WR/KR Joey Jamison) in 2000 draft to Green Bay Packers for CB Fred Vinson and sixth-round pick (DT Tim Watson) in 2000 draft (April 14, 2000).
HONORS: Named running back on THE SPORTING NEWS college All-America second team (1997).
PRO STATISTICS: 1998—Recovered one fumble. 1999—Recovered one fumble.
SINGLE GAME HIGHS (regular season): Attempts—9 (November 7, 1999, vs. Cincinnati); yards—100 (September 6, 1998, vs. Philadelphia); and rushing touchdowns—1 (September 6, 1998, vs. Philadelphia).
STATISTICAL PLATEAUS: 100-yard rushing games: 1998 (1).

			RUSHING				RECEIVING				KICKOFF RETURNS				TOTALS		
Year Team	G	GS	Att.	Yds.	Avg.	TD	No.	Yds.	Avg.	TD	No.	Yds.	Avg.	TD	TD	2pt.	Pts. Fum.
1998—Seattle NFL	16	0	35	209	6.0	1	3	2	0.7	0	27	620	23.0	0	1	0	6 1
1999—Seattle NFL	14	0	26	120	4.6	0	0	0	0.0	0	36	818	22.7	0	0	0	0 2
Pro totals (2 years)	30	0	61	329	5.4	1	3	2	0.7	0	63	1438	22.8	0	1	0	6 3

GREEN, DARRELL   CB   REDSKINS

PERSONAL: Born February 15, 1960, in Houston. ... 5-8/184.
HIGH SCHOOL: Jesse H. Jones Senior (Houston).
COLLEGE: Texas A&I.
TRANSACTIONS/CAREER NOTES: Selected by Denver Gold in 10th round (112th pick overall) of 1983 USFL draft. ... Selected by Washington Redskins in first round (28th pick overall) of 1983 NFL draft. ... Signed by Redskins (June 10, 1983). ... On injured reserve with broken hand (December 13, 1988-remainder of season). ... On injured reserve with broken bone in wrist (October 24, 1989-remainder of season). ... Granted free agency (February 1, 1992). ... Re-signed by Redskins (August 25, 1992). ... On injured reserve with broken forearm (September 16-November 23, 1992). ... Granted unconditional free agency (February 17, 1995). ... Re-signed by Redskins (March 10, 1995). ... Granted unconditional free agency (February 14, 1997). ... Re-signed by Redskins (April 25, 1997).
CHAMPIONSHIP GAME EXPERIENCE: Played in NFC championship game (1983, 1986, 1987 and 1991 seasons). ... Played in Super Bowl XVIII (1983 season). ... Member of Super Bowl championship team (1987 and 1991 seasons).
HONORS: Played in Pro Bowl (1984, 1986, 1987, 1990, 1991, 1996 and 1997 seasons). ... Named cornerback on THE SPORTING NEWS NFL All-Pro team (1991).
POST SEASON RECORDS: Shares NFL postseason career record for most touchdowns by punt return—1 (January 10, 1988, at Chicago).
PRO STATISTICS: 1983—Recovered one fumble. 1985—Rushed once for six yards and recovered one fumble. 1986—Recovered one fumble. 1987—Recovered one fumble for 26 yards and a touchdown. 1988—Credited with one sack and recovered one fumble. 1989—Recovered one fumble. 1993—Recovered one fumble for 78 yards and a touchdown. 1996—Recovered one fumble for 15 yards. 1997—Returned one kickoff for nine yards. 1999—Recovered one fumble for four yards.
MISCELLANEOUS: Holds Washington Redskins all-time record for most interceptions (50).

			INTERCEPTIONS				PUNT RETURNS				TOTALS			
Year Team	G	GS	No.	Yds.	Avg.	TD	No.	Yds.	Avg.	TD	TD	2pt.	Pts.	Fum.
1983—Washington NFL	16	16	2	7	3.5	0	4	29	7.3	0	0	0	0	1
1984—Washington NFL	16	16	5	91	18.2	1	2	13	6.5	0	1	0	6	0
1985—Washington NFL	16	16	2	0	0.0	0	16	214	13.4	0	0	0	0	2
1986—Washington NFL	16	15	5	9	1.8	0	12	120	10.0	0	0	0	0	1
1987—Washington NFL	12	12	3	65	21.7	0	5	53	10.6	0	1	0	6	0
1988—Washington NFL	15	15	1	12	12.0	0	9	103	11.4	0	0	0	0	0
1989—Washington NFL	7	7	2	0	0.0	0	1	11	11.0	0	0	0	0	1
1990—Washington NFL	16	16	4	20	5.0	1	1	6	6.0	0	1	0	6	0
1991—Washington NFL	16	16	5	47	9.4	0	0	0	0.0	0	0	0	0	0
1992—Washington NFL	8	7	1	15	15.0	0	0	0	0.0	0	0	0	0	0
1993—Washington NFL	16	16	4	10	2.5	0	1	27	27.0	0	1	0	6	0
1994—Washington NFL	16	16	3	32	10.7	1	0	0	0.0	0	1	0	6	0
1995—Washington NFL	16	16	3	42	14.0	1	0	0	0.0	0	1	0	6	0
1996—Washington NFL	16	16	3	84	28.0	1	0	0	0.0	0	1	0	6	0
1997—Washington NFL	16	16	1	83	83.0	1	0	0	0.0	0	1	0	6	0
1998—Washington NFL	16	16	3	36	12.0	0	0	0	0.0	0	0	0	0	0
1999—Washington NFL	16	16	3	33	11.0	0	0	0	0.0	0	0	0	0	0
Pro totals (17 years)	250	248	50	586	11.7	6	51	576	11.3	0	8	0	48	6

GREEN, E.G.   WR   COLTS   G

PERSONAL: Born June 28, 1975, in Fort Walton Beach, Fla. ... 5-11/190. ... Full name: Ernie G. Green.
HIGH SCHOOL: Fort Walton Beach (Fla.).
COLLEGE: Florida State.
TRANSACTIONS/CAREER NOTES: Selected by Indianapolis Colts in third round (71st pick overall) of 1998 NFL draft. ... Signed by Colts (July 21, 1998).
SINGLE GAME HIGHS (regular season): Receptions—5 (September 19, 1999, vs. New England); yards—124 (September 12, 1999, vs. Buffalo); and touchdown receptions—1 (December 13, 1998, vs. Cincinnati).
STATISTICAL PLATEAUS: 100-yard receiving games: 1999 (1).

			RECEIVING				TOTALS			
Year Team	G	GS	No.	Yds.	Avg.	TD	TD	2pt.	Pts.	Fum.
1998—Indianapolis NFL	12	0	15	177	11.8	1	1	0	6	0
1999—Indianapolis NFL	11	4	21	287	13.7	0	0	0	0	0
Pro totals (2 years)	23	4	36	464	12.9	1	1	0	6	0

GREEN, ERIC — TE

PERSONAL: Born June 22, 1967, in Savannah, Ga. ... 6-5/285. ... Full name: Bernard Eric Green.
HIGH SCHOOL: A.E. Beach (Savannah, Ga.).
COLLEGE: Liberty University, Va. (degree in finance, 1991).
TRANSACTIONS/CAREER NOTES: Selected by Pittsburgh Steelers in first round (21st pick overall) of 1990 NFL draft. ... Signed by Steelers (September 10, 1990). ... Granted roster exemption (September 10-24, 1990). ... On injured reserve with ankle injury (November 23, 1991-remainder of season). ... On injured reserve with shoulder injury (September 9-October 5, 1992). ... On practice squad (October 5-10, 1992). ... On reserve/suspended list for substance abuse (November 9-December 21, 1992). ... Granted roster exemption (December 21-27, 1992). ... Designated by Steelers as franchise player (February 15, 1994). ... Free agency status changed by Steelers from franchise to unconditional (February 15, 1995). ... Signed by Miami Dolphins (March 10, 1995). ... Released by Dolphins (July 9, 1996). ... Signed by Baltimore Ravens (September 24, 1996). ... Granted unconditional free agency (February 14, 1997). ... Re-signed by Ravens (July 18, 1997). ... Granted unconditional free agency (February 13, 1998). ... Re-signed by Ravens (February 18, 1998). ... Granted unconditional free agency (February 12, 1999). ... Signed by New York Jets (February 17, 1999). ... On injured reserve with neck injury (December 15, 1999-remainder of season). ... Released by Jets (February 2, 2000).
CHAMPIONSHIP GAME EXPERIENCE: Played in AFC championship game (1994 season).
HONORS: Played in Pro Bowl (1993 and 1994 seasons).
PRO STATISTICS: 1990—Returned one kickoff for 16 yards and recovered one fumble.
SINGLE GAME HIGHS (regular season): Receptions—9 (November 2, 1997, vs. New York Jets); yards—158 (September 22, 1991, vs. Philadelphia); and touchdown receptions—3 (October 14, 1990, vs. Denver).
STATISTICAL PLATEAUS: 100-yard receiving games: 1990 (1), 1991 (1), 1993 (2). Total: 4.

				RECEIVING				TOTALS		
Year Team	G	GS	No.	Yds.	Avg.	TD	TD	2pt.	Pts.	Fum.
1990—Pittsburgh NFL	13	7	34	387	11.4	7	7	0	42	1
1991—Pittsburgh NFL	11	11	41	582	14.2	6	6	0	36	2
1992—Pittsburgh NFL	7	5	14	152	10.9	2	2	0	12	0
1993—Pittsburgh NFL	16	16	63	942	15.0	5	5	0	30	3
1994—Pittsburgh NFL	15	14	46	618	13.4	4	4	0	24	2
1995—Miami NFL	14	14	43	499	11.6	3	3	1	20	0
1996—Baltimore NFL	6	3	15	150	10.0	1	1	0	6	0
1997—Baltimore NFL	16	15	65	601	9.2	5	5	0	30	1
1998—Baltimore NFL	12	12	34	422	12.4	1	1	0	6	4
1999—New York Jets NFL	10	7	7	37	5.3	2	2	0	12	0
Pro totals (10 years)	120	104	362	4390	12.1	36	36	1	218	13

GREEN, JACQUEZ — WR — BUCCANEERS

PERSONAL: Born January 15, 1976, in Fort Valley, Ga. ... 5-9/168. ... Full name: D'Tanyian Jacquez Green.
HIGH SCHOOL: Peach County (Fort Valley, Ga.).
COLLEGE: Florida.
TRANSACTIONS/CAREER NOTES: Selected after junior season by Tampa Bay Buccaneers in second round (34th pick overall) of 1998 NFL draft. ... Signed by Buccaneers (July 19, 1998).
CHAMPIONSHIP GAME EXPERIENCE: Played in NFC championship game (1999 season).
HONORS: Named wide receiver on THE SPORTING NEWS college All-America second team (1997).
PRO STATISTICS: 1998—Fumbled five times and recovered two fumbles. 1999—Fumbled once.
SINGLE GAME HIGHS (regular season): Receptions—10 (January 2, 2000, vs. Chicago); yards—164 (November 14, 1999, vs. Kansas City); and touchdown receptions—1 (December 6, 1999, vs. Minnesota).
STATISTICAL PLATEAUS: 100-yard receiving games: 1999 (2).

			RUSHING				RECEIVING				PUNT RETURNS				KICKOFF RETURNS				TOTALS		
Year Team	G	GS	Att.	Yds.	Avg.	TD	No.	Yds.	Avg.	TD	No.	Yds.	Avg.	TD	No.	Yds.	Avg.	TD	TD	2pt.	Pts.
1998—Tampa Bay NFL	12	1	3	12	4.0	0	14	251	17.9	2	30	453	15.1	1	10	229	22.9	0	3	0	18
1999—Tampa Bay NFL	16	10	3	8	2.7	0	56	791	14.1	3	23	204	8.9	0	10	185	18.5	0	3	0	18
Pro totals (2 years)	28	11	6	20	3.3	0	70	1042	14.9	5	53	657	12.4	1	20	414	20.7	0	6	0	36

GREEN, LAMONT — LB — PANTHERS

PERSONAL: Born July 10, 1976, in Miami. ... 6-3/230.
HIGH SCHOOL: Southridge (Miami).
COLLEGE: Florida State.
TRANSACTIONS/CAREER NOTES: Signed as non-drafted free agent by Atlanta Falcons (April 19, 1999). ... Released by Falcons (August 30, 1999). ... Re-signed by Falcons to practice squad (September 7, 1999). ... Activated (October 13, 1999). ... Released by Falcons (October 19, 1999). ... Re-signed by Falcons to practice squad (October 21, 1999). ... Released by Falcons (November 2, 1999). ... Signed by Carolina Panthers to practice squad (December 29, 1999).
PLAYING EXPERIENCE: Atlanta NFL, 1999. ... Games/Games started: 1999 (1/0).
HONORS: Named outside linebacker on THE SPORTING NEWS college All-America second team (1998).

GREEN, TRENT — QB — RAMS

PERSONAL: Born July 9, 1970, in Cedar Rapids, Iowa. ... 6-3/215. ... Full name: Trent Jason Green.
HIGH SCHOOL: Vianney (St. Louis).
COLLEGE: Indiana.
TRANSACTIONS/CAREER NOTES: Selected by San Diego Chargers in eighth round (222nd pick overall) of 1993 NFL draft. ... Signed by Chargers (July 15, 1993). ... Inactive for all 16 games (1993). ... Released by Chargers (August 22, 1994). ... Signed by Washington Redskins (April 5, 1995). ... Inactive for all 16 games (1995). ... Inactive for all 16 games (1996). ... Granted free agency (February 14, 1997). ... Re-

G

signed by Redskins (June 6, 1997). ... Granted unconditional free agency (February 12, 1999). ... Signed by St. Louis Rams (February 16, 1999). ... On injured reserve with knee injury (August 30, 1999-entire season).
PRO STATISTICS: 1998—Caught two passes for minus eight yards, led NFL with 14 fumbles and recovered four fumbles.
SINGLE GAME HIGHS (regular season): Attempts—54 (September 20, 1998, vs. Seattle); completions—30 (November 22, 1998, vs. Arizona); yards—383 (September 20, 1998, vs. Seattle); and touchdown passes—4 (November 22, 1998, vs. Arizona).
STATISTICAL PLATEAUS: 300-yard passing games: 1998 (2).
MISCELLANEOUS: Regular-season record as starting NFL quarterback: 6-8 (.429).

				PASSING							RUSHING				TOTALS		
Year Team	G	GS	Att.	Cmp.	Pct.	Yds.	TD	Int.	Avg.	Rat.	Att.	Yds.	Avg.	TD	TD	2pt.	Pts.
1993—San Diego NFL............						Did not play.											
1994—						Did not play.											
1995—Washington NFL						Did not play.											
1996—Washington NFL						Did not play.											
1997—Washington NFL	1	0	1	0	0.0	0	0	0	0.0	39.6	0	0	0.0	0	0	0	0
1998—Washington NFL	15	14	509	278	54.6	3441	23	11	6.76	81.8	42	117	2.8	2	2	0	12
1999—St. Louis NFL						Did not play.											
Pro totals (2 years)...............	16	14	510	278	54.5	3441	23	11	6.75	81.7	42	117	2.8	2	2	0	12

GREEN, VICTOR   S   JETS

PERSONAL: Born December 8, 1969, in Americus, Ga. ... 5-11/210. ... Full name: Victor Bernard Green. ... Cousin of Tommy Sims, defensive back with Indianapolis Colts (1986).
HIGH SCHOOL: Americus (Ga.).
JUNIOR COLLEGE: Copiah-Lincoln Junior College (Miss.).
COLLEGE: Akron (degree in criminal justice, 1993).
TRANSACTIONS/CAREER NOTES: Signed as non-drafted free agent by New York Jets (April 29, 1993). ... Released by Jets (August 30, 1993). ... Re-signed by Jets to practice squad (September 1, 1993). ... Activated (September 28, 1993).
CHAMPIONSHIP GAME EXPERIENCE: Played in AFC championship game (1998 season).
PRO STATISTICS: 1994—Recovered one fumble. 1995—Recovered one fumble. 1996—Recovered three fumbles. 1998—Recovered one fumble. 1999—Recovered two fumbles for nine yards.

			INTERCEPTIONS				SACKS
Year Team	G	GS	No.	Yds.	Avg.	TD	No.
1993—New York Jets NFL......................................	11	0	0	0	0.0	0	0.0
1994—New York Jets NFL......................................	16	0	0	0	0.0	0	1.0
1995—New York Jets NFL......................................	16	12	1	2	2.0	0	2.0
1996—New York Jets NFL......................................	16	16	2	27	13.5	0	2.0
1997—New York Jets NFL......................................	16	16	3	89	29.7	0	1.0
1998—New York Jets NFL......................................	16	16	4	99	24.8	0	1.0
1999—New York Jets NFL......................................	16	16	5	92	18.4	0	0.0
Pro totals (7 years)...	107	76	15	309	20.6	0	7.0

GREEN, YATIL   WR   DOLPHINS

PERSONAL: Born November 25, 1973, in Gainesville, Fla. ... 6-2/205. ... Full name: Yatil Devon Green. ... Name pronounced yuh-TEEL.
HIGH SCHOOL: Columbia (Lake City, Fla.).
COLLEGE: Miami (Fla.).
TRANSACTIONS/CAREER NOTES: Selected by Miami Dolphins in first round (15th pick overall) of 1997 NFL draft. ... Signed by Dolphins (June 13, 1997). ... On injured reserve with knee injury (August 18, 1997-entire season). ... On injured reserve with knee injury (August 24, 1998-entire season).
SINGLE GAME HIGHS (regular season): Receptions—5 (December 5, 1999, vs. Indianapolis); yards—73 (December 12, 1999, vs. New York Jets); and touchdown receptions—0.

			RECEIVING				TOTALS			
Year Team	G	GS	No.	Yds.	Avg.	TD	TD	2pt.	Pts.	Fum.
1997—Miami NFL...					Did not play.					
1998—Miami NFL...					Did not play.					
1999—Miami NFL...	8	1	18	234	13.0	0	0	0	0	0
Pro totals (1 years)..	8	1	18	234	13.0	0	0	0	0	0

GREENE, KEVIN   LB

G

PERSONAL: Born July 31, 1962, in New York. ... 6-3/247. ... Full name: Kevin Darwin Greene.
HIGH SCHOOL: South (Granite City, Ill.).
COLLEGE: Auburn.
TRANSACTIONS/CAREER NOTES: Selected by Birmingham Stallions in 1985 USFL territorial draft. ... Selected by Los Angeles Rams in fifth round (113th pick overall) of 1985 NFL draft. ... Signed by Rams (July 12, 1985). ... Crossed picket line during players strike (October 14, 1987). ... Granted free agency (February 1, 1990). ... Re-signed by Rams (September 1, 1990). ... Granted roster exemption (September 1-7, 1990). ... Granted unconditional free agency (March 1, 1993). ... Signed by Pittsburgh Steelers (April 3, 1993). ... Granted unconditional free agency (February 16, 1996). ... Signed by Carolina Panthers (May 3, 1996). ... On reserve/did not report list (July 21-August 25, 1997). ... Released by Panthers (August 25, 1997). ... Signed by San Francisco 49ers (August 28, 1997). ... Released by 49ers (February 9, 1998). ... Signed by Panthers (March 16, 1998). ... Announced retirement (January 27, 2000). ... Granted unconditional free agency (February 11, 2000).
CHAMPIONSHIP GAME EXPERIENCE: Played in NFC championship game (1985, 1989, 1996 and 1997 seasons). ... Played in AFC championship game (1994 and 1995 seasons). ... Played in Super Bowl XXX (1995 season).
HONORS: Named outside linebacker on The Sporting News NFL All-Pro team (1989 and 1994). ... Played in Pro Bowl (1989, 1994-1996 and 1998 seasons).
PRO STATISTICS: 1986—Recovered one fumble for 13 yards. 1987—Intercepted one pass for 25 yards. 1988—Credited with a safety and intercepted one pass for 10 yards. 1989—Recovered two fumbles. 1990—Recovered four fumbles. 1991—Credited with one safety. 1992—

Credited with one safety and recovered four fumbles for two yards. 1993—Recovered three fumbles for five yards. 1994—Recovered three fumbles. 1995—Intercepted one pass for no yards. 1996—Recovered three fumbles for 66 yards and a touchdown. 1997—Recovered two fumbles for 40 yards and one touchdown. 1998—Intercepted two passes for 18 yards and recovered one fumble for two yards. 1999—Recovered three fumbles for eight yards.

MISCELLANEOUS: Holds Carolina Panthers all-time record for most sacks (41.5).

Year Team	G	GS	SACKS
1985—Los Angeles Rams NFL	15	0	0.0
1986—Los Angeles Rams NFL	16	0	7.0
1987—Los Angeles Rams NFL	9	0	6.5
1988—Los Angeles Rams NFL	16	14	16.5
1989—Los Angeles Rams NFL	16	16	16.5
1990—Los Angeles Rams NFL	15	15	13.0
1991—Los Angeles Rams NFL	16	16	3.0
1992—Los Angeles Rams NFL	16	16	10.0
1993—Pittsburgh NFL	16	16	12.5
1994—Pittsburgh NFL	16	16	*14.0
1995—Pittsburgh NFL	16	16	9.0
1996—Carolina NFL	16	16	*14.5
1997—San Francisco NFL	14	4	10.5
1998—Carolina NFL	15	15	15.0
1999—Carolina NFL	16	16	12.0
Pro totals (15 years)	228	176	160.0

GREENE, SCOTT — RB

PERSONAL: Born June 1, 1972, in Honeoye, N.Y. ... 5-11/230. ... Full name: Scott Clayton Greene.
HIGH SCHOOL: Canandaigua (N.Y.) Academy.
COLLEGE: Michigan State.
TRANSACTIONS/CAREER NOTES: Selected by Carolina Panthers in sixth round (193rd pick overall) of 1996 NFL draft. ... Signed by Panthers (July 17, 1996). ... Released by Panthers (August 21, 1996). ... Re-signed by Panthers to practice squad (August 27, 1996). ... Activated (October 29, 1996). ... Released by Panthers (August 26, 1998). ... Signed by Indianapolis Colts (October 20, 1998). ... Granted free agency (February 12, 1999). ... Re-signed by Colts (June 2, 1999). ... Released by Colts (October 13, 1999). ... Re-signed by Colts (October 28, 1999). ... Granted unconditional free agency (February 11, 2000).
CHAMPIONSHIP GAME EXPERIENCE: Played in NFC championship game (1996 season).
PRO STATISTICS: 1996—Returned two kickoffs for 10 yards. 1997—Returned three kickoffs for 18 yards. 1999—Returned one kickoff for 14 yards.
SINGLE GAME HIGHS (regular season): Attempts—7 (November 30, 1997, vs. New Orleans); yards—30 (November 30, 1997, vs. New Orleans); and rushing touchdowns—1 (November 2, 1997, vs. Oakland).

			RUSHING				RECEIVING				TOTALS			
Year Team	G	GS	Att.	Yds.	Avg.	TD	No.	Yds.	Avg.	TD	TD	2pt.	Pts.	Fum.
1996—Carolina NFL	8	0	0	0	0.0	0	2	7	3.5	1	1	0	6	0
1997—Carolina NFL	16	14	45	157	3.5	1	40	277	6.9	1	2	0	12	1
1998—Indianapolis NFL	5	0	0	0	0.0	0	1	2	2.0	0	0	0	0	0
1999—Indianapolis NFL	5	0	0	0	0.0	0	1	4	4.0	0	0	0	0	0
Pro totals (4 years)	34	14	45	157	3.5	1	44	290	6.6	2	3	0	18	1

GREER, DONOVAN — DB — BILLS

PERSONAL: Born September 11, 1974, in Houston. ... 5-9/178.
HIGH SCHOOL: Elsik (Alief, Texas).
COLLEGE: Texas A&M.
TRANSACTIONS/CAREER NOTES: Signed as non-drafted free agent by New Orleans Saints (April 25, 1997). ... Released by Saints (August 24, 1997). ... Signed by Atlanta Falcons (August 26, 1997). ... Released by Falcons (September 3, 1997). ... Signed by Saints to practice squad (September 4, 1997). ... Activated (November 15, 1997). ... Released by Saints (August 24, 1998). ... Signed by Buffalo Bills to practice squad (September 9, 1998). ... Activated (September 30, 1998). ... Granted free agency (February 11, 2000). ... Re-signed by Bills (April 14, 2000).
PLAYING EXPERIENCE: Atlanta (1)-New Orleans (6) NFL, 1997; Buffalo NFL, 1998 and 1999. ... Games/Games started: 1997 (Atl.-1/0; N.O.-6/1; Total: 7/1), 1998 (11/2), 1999 (16/0). Total: 34/3.
PRO STATISTICS: 1998—Recovered one fumble for 18 yards. 1999—Intercepted one pass for no yards.

GREGG, KELLY — DT — EAGLES

G

PERSONAL: Born November 1, 1976, in Edmond, Okla. ... 6-0/285.
HIGH SCHOOL: Edmond (Okla.).
COLLEGE: Oklahoma.
TRANSACTIONS/CAREER NOTES: Selected by Cincinnati Bengals in sixth round (173rd pick overall) of 1999 NFL draft. ... Signed by Bengals (June 23, 1999). ... Released by Bengals (September 6, 1999). ... Re-signed by Bengals to practice squad (September 7, 1999). ... Signed by Philadelphia Eagles off Bengals practice squad (December 7, 1999).
PLAYING EXPERIENCE: Philadelphia NFL, 1999. ... Games/Games started: 1999 (3/0).

GREISEN, CHRIS — QB — CARDINALS

PERSONAL: Born July 2, 1976, in Sturgeon Bay, Wis. ... 6-3/225.
HIGH SCHOOL: Sturgeon Bay (Wis.).
COLLEGE: Northwest Missouri State (degree in physical education).

RANSACTIONS/CAREER NOTES: Selected by Arizona Cardinals in seventh round (239th pick overall) of 1999 NFL draft. ... Signed by ardinals (June 18, 1999).
LAYING EXPERIENCE: Arizona NFL, 1999. ... Games/Games started: 1999 (2/0).
RO STATISTICS: 1999—Attempted six passes with one completion for four yards.
INGLE GAME HIGHS (regular season): Attempts—6 (October 31, 1999, vs. New England); completions—1 (October 31, 1999, vs. New ngland); passing yards—4 (October 31, 1999, vs. New England); and touchdown passes—0.

GRIESE, BRIAN QB BRONCOS

ERSONAL: Born March 18, 1975, in Miami. ... 6-3/215. ... Full name: Brian David Griese. ... Son of Bob Griese, Hall of Fame quarterback with Miami Dolphins (1967-80). ... Name pronounced GREE-see.
IIGH SCHOOL: Columbus (Miami).
:OLLEGE: Michigan.
RANSACTIONS/CAREER NOTES: Selected by Denver Broncos in third round (91st pick overall) of 1998 NFL draft. ... Signed by Broncos (July 2, 1998).
HAMPIONSHIP GAME EXPERIENCE: Member of Broncos for AFC championship game (1998 season); inactive. ... Member of Super Bowl hampionship team (1998 season); inactive.
RO STATISTICS: 1998—Fumbled once for minus one yard. 1999—Led league with 16 fumbles and recovered nine fumbles for minus 46 ards.
INGLE GAME HIGHS (regular season): Attempts—46 (January 2, 2000, vs. San Diego); completions—25 (October 24, 1999, vs. New ngland); yards—363 (October 17, 1999, vs. Green Bay); and touchdown passes—3 (September 13, 1999, vs. Miami).
TATISTICAL PLATEAUS: 300-yard passing games: 1999 (2).
MISCELLANEOUS: Regular-season record as starting NFL quarterback: 4-9 (.308).

			PASSING								RUSHING				TOTALS		
ear Team	G	GS	Att.	Cmp.	Pct.	Yds.	TD	Int.	Avg.	Rat.	Att.	Yds.	Avg.	TD	TD	2pt.	Pts.
998—Denver NFL	1	0	3	1	33.3	2	0	1	0.67	2.8	4	-4	-1.0	0	0	0	0
999—Denver NFL	14	13	452	261	57.7	3032	14	14	6.71	75.6	46	138	3.0	2	2	0	12
ro totals (2 years)	15	13	455	262	57.6	3034	14	15	6.67	74.4	50	134	2.7	2	2	0	12

GRIFFIN, DAMON WR BENGALS

ERSONAL: Born June 14, 1976, in Los Angeles. ... 5-9/186. ... Full name: Damon Gilbert Griffin.
IIGH SCHOOL: Monrovia (Los Angeles).
:OLLEGE: Oregon.
RANSACTIONS/CAREER NOTES: Signed as non-drafted free agent by San Francisco 49ers (April 23, 1999). ... Claimed on waivers by 'incinnati Bengals (September 6, 1999).
RO STATISTICS: 1999—Recovered two fumbles.
INGLE GAME HIGHS (regular season): Receptions—4 (October 17, 1999, vs. Pittsburgh); yards—46 (October 17, 1999, vs. Pittsburgh); nd touchdown receptions—0.

			RECEIVING				PUNT RETURNS				KICKOFF RETURNS				TOTALS			
ear Team	G	GS	No.	Yds.	Avg.	TD	No.	Yds.	Avg.	TD	No.	Yds.	Avg.	TD	TD	2pt.	Pts.	Fum.
999—Cincinnati NFL	13	0	12	112	9.3	0	23	195	8.5	0	15	296	19.7	0	0	0	0	5

GRIFFITH, HOWARD FB BRONCOS

ERSONAL: Born November 17, 1967, in Chicago. ... 6-0/230. ... Full name: Howard Thomas Griffith.
IIGH SCHOOL: Percy L. Julian (Chicago).
:OLLEGE: Illinois.
RANSACTIONS/CAREER NOTES: Selected by Indianapolis Colts in ninth round (237th pick overall) of 1991 NFL draft. ... Signed by Colts July 12, 1991). ... Released by Colts (August 26, 1991). ... Signed by Buffalo Bills to practice squad (September 4, 1991). ... Released by ills (August 31, 1992). ... Re-signed by Bills to practice squad (September 2, 1992). ... Released by Bills (October 21, 1992). ... Signed by an Diego Chargers to practice squad (October 23, 1992). ... Released by Chargers (October 28, 1992). ... Re-signed by Chargers to practice quad (October 30, 1992). ... Released by Chargers (December 9, 1992). ... Re-signed by Chargers to practice squad (December 14, 1992). . Released by Chargers (August 30, 1993). ... Signed by Los Angeles Rams (September 2, 1993). ... Selected by Carolina Panthers from tams in NFL expansion draft (February 15, 1995). ... Granted free agency (February 16, 1996). ... Re-signed by Panthers (July 20, 1996). ... ranted unconditional free agency (February 14, 1997). ... Signed by Denver Broncos (February 18, 1997).
HAMPIONSHIP GAME EXPERIENCE: Played in NFC championship game (1996 season). ... Played in AFC championship game (1997 and 998 seasons). ... Member of Super Bowl championship team (1997 and 1998 seasons).
RO STATISTICS: 1995—Recovered one fumble. 1996—Recovered one fumble. 1997—Recovered one fumble. 1999—Recovered one fumble.
INGLE GAME HIGHS (regular season): Attempts—25 (November 19, 1995, vs. Arizona); yards—88 (November 19, 1995, vs. Arizona); and ushing touchdowns—1 (November 22, 1999, vs. Oakland).

			RUSHING				RECEIVING				KICKOFF RETURNS				TOTALS			
ear Team	G	GS	Att.	Yds.	Avg.	TD	No.	Yds.	Avg.	TD	No.	Yds.	Avg.	TD	TD	2pt.	Pts.	Fum.
991—Buffalo NFL							Did not play.											
992—San Diego NFL							Did not play.											
993—LA Rams NFL	15	0	0	0	0.0	0	0	0	0.0	0	8	169	21.1	0	0	0	0	0
994—LA Rams NFL	16	10	9	30	3.3	0	16	113	7.1	1	2	35	17.5	0	1	0	6	0
995—Carolina NFL	15	7	65	197	3.0	1	11	63	5.7	1	0	0	0.0	0	2	0	12	1
996—Carolina NFL	16	14	12	7	0.6	1	27	223	8.3	1	0	0	0.0	0	2	0	12	1
997—Denver NFL	15	13	9	34	3.8	0	11	55	5.0	0	0	0	0.0	0	0	0	0	0
998—Denver NFL	14	13	4	13	3.3	0	15	97	6.5	3	0	0	0.0	0	3	0	18	0
999—Denver NFL	16	16	17	66	3.9	1	26	192	7.4	1	0	0	0.0	0	2	0	12	0
ro totals (7 years)	107	73	116	347	3.0	3	106	743	7.0	7	10	204	20.4	0	10	0	60	2

G

GRIFFITH, RICH   TE   JAGUARS

PERSONAL: Born July 31, 1969, in Tucson, Ariz. ... 6-5/260. ... Full name: Richard Pope Griffith.
HIGH SCHOOL: Catalina (Tucson, Ariz.).
COLLEGE: Arizona (degree in communications, 1993).
TRANSACTIONS/CAREER NOTES: Selected by New England Patriots in fifth round (138th pick overall) of 1993 NFL draft. ... Signed by Patriots (July 16, 1993). ... Released by Patriots (August 20, 1994). ... Signed by Jacksonville Jaguars (January 6, 1995). ... Granted free agency (February 14, 1997). ... Re-signed by Jaguars (April 15, 1997). ... Granted unconditional free agency (February 13, 1998). ... Re-signed by Jaguars (February 16, 1998). ... On injured reserve with knee injury (October 28, 1998-remainder of season). ... Granted unconditional free agency (February 11, 2000). ... Re-signed by Jaguars (March 21, 2000).
PLAYING EXPERIENCE: New England NFL, 1993; Jacksonville NFL, 1995-1999. ... Games/Games started: 1993 (3/0), 1995 (16/15), 1996 (16/2), 1997 (16/1), 1998 (7/0), 1999 (16/0). Total: 74/18.
CHAMPIONSHIP GAME EXPERIENCE: Played in AFC championship game (1996 and 1999 seasons).
PRO STATISTICS: 1995—Caught 16 passes for 243 yards and returned one kickoff for nine yards. 1996—Caught five passes for 53 yards, returned two kickoffs for 24 yards and recovered one fumble.
SINGLE GAME HIGHS (regular season): Receptions—4 (December 10, 1995, vs. Indianapolis); yards—54 (December 10, 1995, vs. Indianapolis); and touchdown receptions—0.

GRIFFITH, ROBERT   S   VIKINGS

PERSONAL: Born November 30, 1970, in Landham, Md. ... 5-11/198. ... Full name: Robert Otis Griffith.
HIGH SCHOOL: Mount Miguel (Spring Valley, Calif.).
COLLEGE: San Diego State.
TRANSACTIONS/CAREER NOTES: Signed by Sacramento Gold Miners of CFL to practice squad (August 8, 1993). ... Granted free agency after 1993 season. ... Signed as non-drafted free agent by Minnesota Vikings (April 21, 1994). ... Granted free agency (February 14, 1997). ... Re-signed by Vikings (May 7, 1997).
CHAMPIONSHIP GAME EXPERIENCE: Played in NFC championship game (1998 season).
HONORS: Named safety on THE SPORTING NEWS NFL All-Pro team (1998).
PRO STATISTICS: 1996—Fumbled once.

			INTERCEPTIONS				SACKS
Year Team	G	GS	No.	Yds.	Avg.	TD	No.
1994—Minnesota NFL	15	0	0	0	0.0	0	0.0
1995—Minnesota NFL	16	0	0	0	0.0	0	0.5
1996—Minnesota NFL	14	14	4	67	16.8	0	2.0
1997—Minnesota NFL	16	16	2	26	13.0	0	0.0
1998—Minnesota NFL	16	16	5	25	5.0	0	0.0
1999—Minnesota NFL	16	16	3	0	0.0	0	4.0
Pro totals (6 years)	93	62	14	118	8.4	0	6.5

GROCE, CLIF   FB   BENGALS

PERSONAL: Born July 30, 1972, in College Station, Texas. ... 5-11/245. ... Full name: Clifton Allen Groce. ... Name pronounced gross.
HIGH SCHOOL: A&M Consolidated (College Station, Texas).
COLLEGE: Texas A&M.
TRANSACTIONS/CAREER NOTES: Signed as non-drafted free agent by Indianapolis Colts (April 27, 1995). ... Released by Colts (August 22, 1995). ... Re-signed by Colts to practice squad (August 28, 1995). ... Activated (December 7, 1995). ... Released by Colts (August 28, 1998). ... Signed by New England Patriots (December 16, 1998). ... Claimed on waivers by Cincinnati Bengals (December 24, 1998). ... Inactive for two games (1998). ... Released by Bengals (August 30, 1999). ... Re-signed by Bengals (September 2, 1999).
CHAMPIONSHIP GAME EXPERIENCE: Played in AFC championship game (1995 season).
PRO STATISTICS: 1996—Returned one kickoff for 18 yards and recovered one fumble. 1997—Returned one kickoff for 15 yards.
SINGLE GAME HIGHS (regular season): Attempts—11 (October 13, 1996, vs. Baltimore); yards—55 (October 13, 196, vs. Baltimore); and rushing touchdowns—1 (December 12, 1999, vs. Cleveland).

			RUSHING				RECEIVING				TOTALS			
Year Team	G	GS	Att.	Yds.	Avg.	TD	No.	Yds.	Avg.	TD	TD	2pt.	Pts.	Fum.
1995—Indianapolis NFL	1	0	0	0	0.0	0	0	0	0.0	0	0	0	0	0
1996—Indianapolis NFL	15	8	46	184	4.0	0	13	106	8.2	0	0	0	0	2
1997—Indianapolis NFL	7	0	10	66	6.6	0	0	0	0.0	0	0	0	0	0
1998—Cincinnati NFL							Did not play.							
1999—Cincinnati NFL	16	15	8	22	2.8	1	25	154	6.2	0	1	0	6	0
Pro totals (4 years)	39	23	64	272	4.3	1	38	260	6.8	0	1	0	6	2

G

GRUBER, PAUL   OT

PERSONAL: Born February 24, 1965, in Madison, Wis. ... 6-5/292. ... Full name: Paul Blake Gruber.
HIGH SCHOOL: Sauk Prairie (Prairie du Sac, Wis.).
COLLEGE: Wisconsin (degree in communication arts, 1988).
TRANSACTIONS/CAREER NOTES: Selected by Tampa Bay Buccaneers in first round (fourth pick overall) of 1988 NFL draft. ... Signed by Buccaneers (August 7, 1988). ... Designated by Buccaneers as franchise player (February 25, 1993). ... Re-signed by Buccaneers (October 20, 1993). ... Granted roster exemption (October 20-23, 1993). ... On injured reserve with broken leg (January 5, 2000-remainder of playoffs). ... Granted unconditional free agency (February 11, 2000).
PLAYING EXPERIENCE: Tampa Bay NFL, 1988-1999. ... Games/Games started: 1988 (16/16), 1989 (16/16), 1990 (16/16), 1991 (16/16), 1992 (16/16), 1993 (10/10), 1994 (16/16), 1995 (16/16), 1996 (13/13), 1997 (16/16), 1998 (16/16), 1999 (16/16). Total: 183/183.
HONORS: Named offensive tackle on THE SPORTING NEWS college All-America first team (1987).

PRO STATISTICS: 1988—Recovered two fumbles. 1990—Recovered one fumble. 1991—Recovered one fumble. 1992—Recovered one fumble. 1994—Recovered one fumble. 1995—Recovered two fumbles. 1997—Recovered one fumble.

GRUNHARD, TIM   C   CHIEFS

PERSONAL: Born May 17, 1968, in Chicago. ... 6-2/311. ... Full name: Timothy Gerard Grunhard.
HIGH SCHOOL: St. Laurence (Burbank, Ill.).
COLLEGE: Notre Dame (degree in political science).
TRANSACTIONS/CAREER NOTES: Selected by Kansas City Chiefs in second round (40th pick overall) of 1990 NFL draft. ... Signed by Chiefs (July 22, 1990).
PLAYING EXPERIENCE: Kansas City NFL, 1990-1999. ... Games/Games started: 1990 (14/9), 1991 (16/16), 1992 (12/12), 1993 (16/16), 1994 (16/16), 1995 (16/16), 1996 (16/16), 1997 (16/16), 1998 (16/16), 1999 (16/16). Total: 154/149.
CHAMPIONSHIP GAME EXPERIENCE: Played in AFC championship game (1993 season).
PRO STATISTICS: 1991—Recovered one fumble. 1992—Recovered two fumbles. 1993—Fumbled once. 1995—Recovered one fumble. 1996—Recovered one fumble. 1997—Recovered one fumble. 1999—Recovered one fumble.

GRUTTADAURIA, MIKE   C   CARDINALS

PERSONAL: Born December 6, 1972, in Fort Lauderdale, Fla. ... 6-3/297. ... Full name: Michael Jason Gruttadauria. ... Name pronounced GRU-da-DOOR-ri-ah.
HIGH SCHOOL: Tarpon Springs (Fla.).
COLLEGE: Central Florida.
TRANSACTIONS/CAREER NOTES: Signed as non-drafted free agent by Dallas Cowboys (April 26, 1995). ... Released by Cowboys (August 22, 1995). ... Signed by St. Louis Rams (February 9, 1996). ... Granted free agency (February 12, 1999). ... Re-signed by Rams (June 8, 1999). ... Granted unconditional free agency (February 11, 2000). ... Signed by Arizona Cardinals (February 19, 2000).
PLAYING EXPERIENCE: St. Louis NFL, 1996-1999. ... Games/Games started: 1996 (9/3), 1997 (14/14), 1998 (12/3), 1999 (16/16). Total: 51/36.
CHAMPIONSHIP GAME EXPERIENCE: Played in NFC championship game (1999 season). ... Member of Super Bowl championship team (1999 season).
PRO STATISTICS: 1997—Caught one pass for no yards.

GUTIERREZ, BROCK   C   BENGALS

PERSONAL: Born September 25, 1973, in Charlotte, Mich. ... 6-3/304.
HIGH SCHOOL: Charlotte (Mich.).
COLLEGE: Central Michigan.
TRANSACTIONS/CAREER NOTES: Signed as non-drafted free agent by Cincinnati Bengals (April 23, 1996). ... Active for two games (1996). ... Released by Bengals (August 30, 1998). ... Re-signed by Bengals (November 4, 1998). ... Released by Bengals (November 17, 1998). ... Signed by Jacksonville Jaguars to practice squad (November 30, 1998). ... Signed by Bengals off Jaguars practice squad (December 15, 1998). ... Granted free agency (February 11, 2000). ... Re-signed by Bengals (March 17, 2000).
PLAYING EXPERIENCE: Cincinnati NFL, 1997-1999. ... Games/Games started: 1997 (5/0), 1998 (1/0), 1999 (16/0). Total: 22/0

HABIB, BRIAN   G

PERSONAL: Born December 2, 1964, in Ellensburg, Wash. ... 6-7/299. ... Full name: Brian Richard Habib. ... Name pronounced ha-BEEB.
HIGH SCHOOL: Ellensburg (Wash.).
COLLEGE: Washington.
TRANSACTIONS/CAREER NOTES: Selected by Minnesota Vikings in 10th round (264th pick overall) of 1988 NFL draft. ... Signed by Vikings (July 19, 1988). ... On injured reserve with shoulder injury (September 3-December 24, 1988). ... Granted free agency (February 1, 1991). ... Re-signed by Vikings (July 18, 1991). ... Granted free agency (February 1, 1992). ... Re-signed by Vikings (July 24, 1992). ... Granted unconditional free agency (March 1, 1993). ... Signed by Denver Broncos (March 8, 1993). ... Granted unconditional free agency (February 13, 1998). ... Signed by Seattle Seahawks (March 6, 1998). ... Released by Seahawks (February 8, 2000).
PLAYING EXPERIENCE: Minnesota NFL, 1989-1992; Denver NFL, 1993-1997; Seattle NFL, 1998 and 1999. ... Games/Games started: 1989 (16/0), 1990 (16/0), 1991 (16/8), 1992 (16/15), 1993 (16/16), 1994 (16/16), 1995 (16/16), 1996 (16/16), 1997 (14/14), 1998 (16/16), 1999 (16/16). Total: 174/133.
CHAMPIONSHIP GAME EXPERIENCE: Played in AFC championship game (1997 season). ... Member of Super Bowl championship team (1997 season).
PRO STATISTICS: 1994—Recovered one fumble. 1998—Recovered two fumbles.

HAKIM, Az-ZAHIR   WR   RAMS

PERSONAL: Born June 3, 1977, in Los Angeles. ... 5-10/178. ... Full name: Az-Zahir Ali Hakim. ... Name pronounced oz-za-HERE ha-KEEM.
HIGH SCHOOL: Fairfax (Los Angeles).
COLLEGE: San Diego State.
TRANSACTIONS/CAREER NOTES: Selected by St. Louis Rams in fourth round (96th pick overall) of 1998 NFL draft. ... Signed by Rams (July 13, 1998).
CHAMPIONSHIP GAME EXPERIENCE: Played in NFC championship game (1999 season). ... Member of Super Bowl championship team (1999 season).
PRO STATISTICS: 1998—Fumbled once. 1999—Fumbled six times and recovered three fumbles.
SINGLE GAME HIGHS (regular season): Receptions—5 (October 31, 1999, vs. Tennessee); yards—122 (December 5, 1999, vs. Carolina); and touchdown receptions—3 (October 3, 1999, vs. Cincinnati).
STATISTICAL PLATEAUS: 100-yard receiving games: 1999 (1).

G
H

Year Team	G	GS	RUSHING				RECEIVING				PUNT RETURNS				KICKOFF RETURNS				TOTALS		
			Att.	Yds.	Avg.	TD	No.	Yds.	Avg.	TD	No.	Yds.	Avg.	TD	No.	Yds.	Avg.	TD	TD	2pt.	Pts.
1998—St. Louis NFL	9	4	2	30	15.0	1	20	247	12.4	0	0	0	0.0	0	0	0	0.0	0	2	0	12
1999—St. Louis NFL	15	0	4	44	11.0	0	36	677	18.8	8	∞44	461	10.5	∞1	2	35	17.5	0	9	0	54
Pro totals (2 years)	24	4	6	74	12.3	1	56	924	16.5	9	44	461	10.5	1	2	35	17.5	0	11	0	66

HALAPIN, MIKE   OT   SAINTS

PERSONAL: Born July 1, 1973, in New Kinsington, Pa. ... 6-5/310. ... Full name: Michael R. Halapin.
HIGH SCHOOL: Kiski (Saltsburg, Penn.).
COLLEGE: Pittsburgh.
TRANSACTIONS/CAREER NOTES: Signed as non-drafted free agent by Houston Oilers (April 23, 1996). ... Oilers franchise moved to Tennessee for 1997 season. ... On injured reserve with shoulder injury (November 21, 1997-remainder of season). ... Released by Oilers (August 30, 1998). ... Signed by New Orleans Saints (January 27, 1999). ... Assigned by Saints to Rhein Fire in 1999 NFL Europe enhancement allocation program (February 22, 1999). ... Granted free agency (February 11, 2000). ... Re-signed by Saints (March 3, 2000).
PLAYING EXPERIENCE: Houston NFL, 1996; Tennessee NFL, 1997; Rhein Fire NFLE, 1999; New Orleans NFL, 1999. ... Games/Games started: 1996 (9/0), 1997 (3/1), NFLE 1999 (games played unavailable), NFL 1999 (9/3). Total NFL: 21/4.

HALE, RYAN   DT   GIANTS

PERSONAL: Born July 10, 1975, in Rogers, Ark ... 6-4/295.
HIGH SCHOOL: Rogers (Ark.).
COLLEGE: Arkansas.
TRANSACTIONS/CAREER NOTES: Selected by New York Giants in seventh round (225th pick overall) of 1999 NFL draft. ... Signed by Giants (July 29, 1999).
PLAYING EXPERIENCE: New York Giants NFL, 1999. ... Games/Games started: 1999 (8/0).

HALEY, CHARLES   DE

PERSONAL: Born January 6, 1964, in Gladys, Va. ... 6-5/260. ... Full name: Charles Lewis Haley.
HIGH SCHOOL: William Campbell (Naruna, Va.).
COLLEGE: James Madison.
TRANSACTIONS/CAREER NOTES: Selected by San Francisco 49ers in fourth round (96th pick overall) of 1986 NFL draft. ... Signed by 49ers (May 27, 1986). ... On reserve/did not report list (July 24-August 23, 1989). ... Granted free agency (February 1, 1990). ... Re-signed by 49ers (August 23, 1990). ... Traded by 49ers to Dallas Cowboys for second-round pick (traded to Los Angeles Raiders) in 1993 draft (August 27, 1992). ... Granted unconditional free agency (March 1, 1993). ... Re-signed by Cowboys (March 16, 1993). ... Announced retirement (July 15, 1997). ... Signed by 49ers (January 3, 1999). ... Granted unconditional free agency (February 12, 1999). ... Re-signed by 49ers (July 21, 1999). ... Announced retirement (February 7, 2000).
CHAMPIONSHIP GAME EXPERIENCE: Played in NFC championship game (1988-1990 and 1992-1995 seasons). ... Member of Super Bowl championship team (1988, 1989, 1992, 1993 and 1995 seasons).
HONORS: Played in Pro Bowl (1988, 1990, 1991, 1994 and 1995 seasons). ... Named defensive end on THE SPORTING NEWS NFL All-Pro team (1994).
POST SEASON RECORDS: Holds Super Bowl career records for most games played on winning team—5; and most sacks—4.5.
PRO STATISTICS: 1986—Intercepted one pass for eight yards, fumbled once and recovered two fumbles for three yards. 1988—Credited with one safety and recovered two fumbles. 1989—Recovered one fumble for three yards and a touchdown. 1990—Recovered one fumble. 1991—Recovered one fumble for three yards. 1993—Recovered one fumble. 1994—Intercepted one pass for one yard.

Year Team	G	GS	SACKS
1986—San Francisco NFL	16	1	12.0
1987—San Francisco NFL	12	2	6.5
1988—San Francisco NFL	16	14	11.5
1989—San Francisco NFL	16	16	10.5
1990—San Francisco NFL	16	16	‡16.0
1991—San Francisco NFL	14	14	7.0
1992—Dallas NFL	15	13	6.0
1993—Dallas NFL	14	11	4.0
1994—Dallas NFL	16	16	12.5
1995—Dallas NFL	13	11	10.5
1996—Dallas NFL	5	5	1.0
1997—	Out of pro football.		
1998—	Out of pro football.		
1999—San Francisco NFL	16	1	3.0
Pro totals (12 years)	169	120	100.5

HALL, CORY   S   BENGALS

PERSONAL: Born December 5, 1976, in Bakersfield, Calif. ... 6-0/205.
HIGH SCHOOL: South (Bakersfield, Calif.).
COLLEGE: Fresno State.
TRANSACTIONS/CAREER NOTES: Selected by Cincinnati Bengals in third round (65th pick overall) of 1999 NFL draft. ... Signed by Bengals (May 7, 1999).
PLAYING EXPERIENCE: Cincinnati NFL, 1999. ... Games/Games started: 1999 (16/12).
PRO STATISTICS: 1999—Intercepted one pass for no yards and recovered one fumble.

H

HALL, JOHN   K   JETS

PERSONAL: Born March 17, 1974, in Port Charlotte, Fla. ... 6-3/228.
HIGH SCHOOL: Port Charlotte (Fla.).
COLLEGE: Wisconsin.
TRANSACTIONS/CAREER NOTES: Signed as non-drafted free agent by New York Jets (April 25, 1997). ... Granted free agency (February 11, 2000). ... Re-signed by Jets (April 13, 2000).
CHAMPIONSHIP GAME EXPERIENCE: Played in AFC championship game (1998 season).
PRO STATISTICS: 1997—Punted three times for 144 yards. 1999—Punted once for 34 yards.

| | | KICKING | | | | | | |
Year Team	G	XPM	XPA	FGM	FGA	Lg.	50+	Pts.
1997—New York Jets NFL	16	36	36	28	†41	†55	4-6	120
1998—New York Jets NFL	16	45	46	25	35	54	1-3	120
1999—New York Jets NFL	16	27	29	27	33	48	0-0	108
Pro totals (3 years)	48	108	111	80	109	55	5-9	348

HALL, LAMONT   TE   PACKERS

PERSONAL: Born November 16, 1974, in York, S.C. ... 6-4/260. ... Full name: James Lamont Hall.
HIGH SCHOOL: Clover (S.C.).
COLLEGE: Clemson (degree in history).
TRANSACTIONS/CAREER NOTES: Signed as non-drafted free agent by Tampa Bay Buccaneers (April 24, 1998). ... Released by Buccaneers (August 25, 1998). ... Re-signed by Buccaneers to practice squad (October 21, 1998). ... Granted free agency following 1998 season. ... Selected by Rhein Fire in 1999 NFL Europe draft (February 18, 1999). ... Signed by Green Bay Packers (July 7, 1999).
PRO STATISTICS: NFLE: 1999—Returned one kickoff for 15 yards.
SINGLE GAME HIGHS (regular season): Receptions—1 (December 20, 1999, vs. Minnesota); yards—13 (November 1, 1999, vs. Seattle); and touchdown receptions—0.

| | | | RECEIVING | | | | | TOTALS | | |
Year Team	G	GS	No.	Yds.	Avg.	TD	TD	2pt.	Pts.	Fum.
1998—Tampa Bay NFL						Did not play.				
1999—Rhein NFLE	...	...	5	60	12.0	0	0	0	0	0
—Green Bay NFL	14	0	3	33	11.0	0	0	0	0	0
NFL Europe totals (1 year)	...	...	5	60	12.0	0	0	0	0	0
NFL totals (1 year)	14	0	3	33	11.0	0	0	0	0	0
Pro totals (1 years)	...	...	8	93	11.6	0	0	0	0	0

HALL, LEMANSKI   LB   VIKINGS

PERSONAL: Born November 24, 1970, in Valley, Ala. ... 6-0/235. ... Full name: Lemanski S. Hall.
HIGH SCHOOL: Valley (Ala.).
COLLEGE: Alabama.
TRANSACTIONS/CAREER NOTES: Selected by Houston Oilers in seventh round (220th pick overall) of 1994 NFL draft. ... Signed by Oilers (June 20, 1994). ... Released by Oilers (August 28, 1994). ... Re-signed by Oilers to practice squad (August 30, 1994). ... Activated (December 23, 1994); did not play. ... Assigned by Oilers to Frankfurt Galaxy in 1995 World League enhancement allocation program (February 20, 1995). ... Assigned by Oilers to Amsterdam Admirals in 1996 World League enhancement allocation program (February 19, 1996). ... Oilers franchise moved to Tennessee for 1997 season. ... Granted free agency (February 13, 1998). ... Re-signed by Oilers (May 28, 1998). ... Traded by Oilers to Chicago Bears for seventh pick (RB Mike Green) in 2000 draft (September 1, 1998). ... Released by Bears (September 5, 1999). ... Signed by Dallas Cowboys (October 27, 1999). ... Granted unconditional free agency (February 11, 2000). ... Signed by Minnesota Vikings (February 24, 2000).
PLAYING EXPERIENCE: Frankfurt W.L., 1995; Houston NFL, 1995 and 1996; Amsterdam W.L., 1996; Tennessee NFL, 1997; Chicago NFL, 1998; Dallas NFL, 1999. ... Games/Games started: W.L.1995 (games played unavailable), NFL 1995 (12/0), W.L. 1996(-), NFL 1996 (3/0), 1997 (16/2), 1998 (15/0), 1999 (10/0). Total: 56/2.
PRO STATISTICS: 1997—Credited with two sacks. 1998—Recovered one fumble for five yards.

HALL, TRAVIS   DT   FALCONS

PERSONAL: Born August 3, 1972, in Kenai, Alaska. ... 6-5/297.
HIGH SCHOOL: West Jordan (Utah).
COLLEGE: Brigham Young.
TRANSACTIONS/CAREER NOTES: Selected by Atlanta Falcons in sixth round (181st pick overall) of 1995 NFL draft. ... Signed by Falcons (June 30, 1995).
CHAMPIONSHIP GAME EXPERIENCE: Played in NFC championship game (1998 season). ... Played in Super Bowl XXXIII (1998 season).
PRO STATISTICS: 1996—Recovered one fumble. 1997—Recovered one fumble. 1998—Recovered four fumbles. 1999—Recovered one fumble.

Year Team	G	GS	SACKS
1995—Atlanta NFL	1	0	0.0
1996—Atlanta NFL	14	13	6.0
1997—Atlanta NFL	16	16	10.5
1998—Atlanta NFL	14	13	4.5
1999—Atlanta NFL	16	15	4.5
Pro totals (5 years)	61	57	25.5

H

HALLEN, BOB   C/G   FALCONS

PERSONAL: Born March 9, 1975, in Mentor, Ohio. ... 6-4/292. ... Full name: Robert Joseph Hallen.
HIGH SCHOOL: Kent.
COLLEGE: Mentor (Ohio).
TRANSACTIONS/CAREER NOTES: Selected by Atlanta Falcons in second round (53rd pick overall) of 1998 NFL draft. ... Signed by Falcons (June 3, 1998).
PLAYING EXPERIENCE: Atlanta NFL, 1998 and 1999. ... Games/Games started: 1998 (12/0), 1999 (16/14). Total: 28/14.
CHAMPIONSHIP GAME EXPERIENCE: Played in NFC championship game (1998 season). ... Played in Super Bowl XXXIII (1998 season).

HALLOCK, TY   LB   BEARS

PERSONAL: Born April 30, 1971, in Grand Rapids, Mich. ... 6-2/254. ... Full name: Ty Edward Hallock.
HIGH SCHOOL: Greenville (Mich.).
COLLEGE: Michigan State (degree in employee relations, 1997).
TRANSACTIONS/CAREER NOTES: Selected by Detroit Lions in seventh round (174th pick overall) of 1993 NFL draft. ... Signed by Lions (July 15, 1993). ... Released by Lions (August 30, 1993). ... Re-signed by Lions to practice squad (August 31, 1993). ... Activated (September 3, 1993). ... Traded by Lions to Jacksonville Jaguars for CB Corey Raymond (May 30, 1995). ... On reserve/retired list (July 10, 1995-February 12, 1996). ... Granted free agency (February 14, 1997). ... Re-signed by Jaguars (June 9, 1997). ... Granted unconditional free agency (February 13, 1998). ... Signed by Chicago Bears (February 16, 1998).
CHAMPIONSHIP GAME EXPERIENCE: Played in AFC championship game (1996 season).
PRO STATISTICS: 1993—Returned one kickoff for 11 yards. 1997—Returned one kickoff for six yards. 1998—Recovered one fumble. 1999—Returned two kickoffs for 10 yards and recovered one fumble.
SINGLE GAME HIGHS (regular season): Attempts—3 (December 6, 1998, vs. Minnesota); yards—17 (December 6, 1998, vs. Minnesota); and rushing touchdowns—1 (October 25, 1998, vs. Tennessee).
MISCELLANEOUS: Played fullback and tight end (1993-99).

			RUSHING				RECEIVING				TOTALS		
Year Team	G	GS	Att.	Yds.	Avg.	TD	No.	Yds.	Avg.	TD	TD	2pt.	Pts.	Fum.
1993—Detroit NFL	16	4	0	0	0.0	0	8	88	11.0	2	2	0	12	0
1994—Detroit NFL	15	10	0	0	0.0	0	7	75	10.7	0	0	0	0	0
1995—Jacksonville NFL							Did not play.							
1996—Jacksonville NFL	7	0	0	0	0.0	0	1	5	5.0	0	0	0	0	0
1997—Jacksonville NFL	15	8	4	21	5.3	0	18	131	7.3	1	1	0	6	0
1998—Chicago NFL	16	12	13	41	3.2	1	25	166	6.6	0	1	0	6	3
1999—Chicago NFL	15	4	0	0	0.0	0	6	22	3.7	0	0	0	0	0
Pro totals (6 years)	84	38	17	62	3.6	1	65	487	7.5	3	4	0	24	3

HAMBRICK, DARREN   LB   COWBOYS

PERSONAL: Born August 30, 1975, in Lacoochee, Fla. ... 6-2/227. ... Nephew of Mudcat Grant, pitcher for seven major league teams (1958-71).
HIGH SCHOOL: Pasco (Dade City, Fla.).
COLLEGE: Florida, then South Carolina.
TRANSACTIONS/CAREER NOTES: Selected by Dallas Cowboys in fifth round (130th pick overall) of 1998 NFL draft. ... Signed by Cowboys (July 14, 1998).
PLAYING EXPERIENCE: Dallas NFL, 1998 and 1999. ... Games/Games started: 1998 (14/0), 1999 (16/12). Total: 30/12.
PRO STATISTICS: 1999—Intercepted two passes for 44 yards, credited with 2$\frac{1}{2}$ sacks and credited with a safety.

HAMILTON, BOBBY   DE/DT

PERSONAL: Born January 7, 1971, in Denver. ... 6-5/280.
HIGH SCHOOL: East Marion (Columbia, Miss.).
COLLEGE: Southern Mississippi.
TRANSACTIONS/CAREER NOTES: Signed as non-drafted free agent by Seattle Seahawks (April 19, 1994). ... On injured reserve with knee injury (August 17, 1994-entire season). ... Assigned by Seahawks to Amsterdam Admirals in 1995 World League enhancement allocation draft. ... Released by Seahawks (August 15, 1995). ... Signed by New York Jets (June 1996). ... Released by Jets (August 24, 1996). ... Re-signed by Jets to practice squad (August 26, 1996). ... Activated (September 4, 1996). ... Granted unconditional free agency (February 11, 2000).
CHAMPIONSHIP GAME EXPERIENCE: Played in AFC championship game (1998 season).
PRO STATISTICS: 1996—Recovered one fumble for seven yards. 1997—Returned one kickoff for no yards.

Year Team	G	GS	SACKS
1994—Seattle NFL		Did not play.	
1995—Amsterdam W.L.	10	9	5.0
1996—Amsterdam W.L.	11	9	5.0
—New York Jets NFL	15	11	4.5
1997—New York Jets NFL	16	0	1.0
1998—New York Jets NFL	16	1	0.0
1999—New York Jets NFL	7	0	0.0
W.L. totals (2 years)	21	18	10.0
NFL totals (3 years)	54	12	5.5
Pro totals (5 years)	75	30	15.5

H

HAMILTON, CONRAD   CB   GIANTS

PERSONAL: Born November 5, 1974, in Alamogordo, N.M. ... 5-10/195.
HIGH SCHOOL: Alamogordo (N.M.).

JUNIOR COLLEGE: New Mexico Military Institute.
COLLEGE: Eastern New Mexico.
TRANSACTIONS/CAREER NOTES: Selected by New York Giants in seventh round (214th pick overall) of 1996 NFL draft. ... Signed by Giants (July 18, 1996). ... Granted free agency (February 12, 1999). ... Re-signed by Giants (May 13, 1999). ... Granted unconditional free agency (February 11, 2000). ... Re-signed by Giants (February 22, 2000).
PRO STATISTICS: 1998—Credited with one sack and recovered one fumble.

Year Team	G	GS	INTERCEPTIONS				KICKOFF RETURNS				TOTALS			
			No.	Yds.	Avg.	TD	No.	Yds.	Avg.	TD	TD	2pt.	Pts.	Fum.
1996—New York Giants NFL	15	1	1	29	29.0	0	19	382	20.1	0	0	0	0	0
1997—New York Giants NFL	14	0	1	18	18.0	0	0	0	0.0	0	0	0	0	0
1998—New York Giants NFL	16	15	1	17	17.0	0	0	0	0.0	0	0	0	0	0
1999—New York Giants NFL	3	2	0	0	0.0	0	0	0	0.0	0	0	0	0	0
Pro totals (4 years)	48	18	3	64	21.3	0	19	382	20.1	0	0	0	0	0

HAMILTON, KEITH   DT   GIANTS

PERSONAL: Born May 25, 1971, in Paterson, N.J. ... 6-6/295. ... Full name: Keith Lamarr Hamilton.
HIGH SCHOOL: Heritage (Lynchburg, Va.).
COLLEGE: Pittsburgh.
TRANSACTIONS/CAREER NOTES: Selected after junior season by New York Giants in fourth round (99th pick overall) of 1992 NFL draft. ... Signed by Giants (July 21, 1992).
PRO STATISTICS: 1992—Recovered one fumble for four yards. 1993—Credited with a safety and recovered one fumble for 10 yards. 1994—Recovered three fumbles. 1995—Fumbled once and recovered three fumbles for 87 yards. 1997—Recovered three fumbles. 1998—Recovered one fumble. 1999—Recovered two fumbles.

Year Team	G	GS	SACKS
1992—New York Giants NFL	16	0	3.5
1993—New York Giants NFL	16	16	11.5
1994—New York Giants NFL	15	15	6.5
1995—New York Giants NFL	14	14	2.0
1996—New York Giants NFL	14	14	3.0
1997—New York Giants NFL	16	16	8.0
1998—New York Giants NFL	16	16	7.0
1999—New York Giants NFL	16	16	4.0
Pro totals (8 years)	123	107	45.5

HAMILTON, MALCOLM   LB

PERSONAL: Born December 31, 1972, in Dallas. ... 6-1/235.
HIGH SCHOOL: Permian (Odessa, Texas).
COLLEGE: Baylor.
TRANSACTIONS/CAREER NOTES: Signed as non-drafted free agent by Washington Redskins (April 29, 1997). ... Released by Redskins (August 19, 1997). ... Re-signed by Redskins to practice squad (September 2, 1997). ... Released by Redskins (August 29, 1998). ... Signed by Atlanta Falcons to practice squad (September 23, 1998). ... Released by Falcons (November 25, 1998). ... Signed by Redskins (November 25, 1998). ... On injured reserve with shoulder injury (December 15, 1998-remainder of season). ... On injured reserve with back injury (October 11, 1999-remainder of season). ... Granted free agency (February 11, 2000).
PLAYING EXPERIENCE: Washington NFL, 1998 and 1999. ... Games/Games started: 1998 (2/0), 1999 (4/0). Total: 6/0.

HAMILTON, MICHAEL   LB   CHARGERS

PERSONAL: Born December 3, 1973, in Greenville, S.C. ... 6-2/245. ... Full name: Michael Antonio Hamilton.
HIGH SCHOOL: Southside (Greenville, S.C.).
COLLEGE: North Carolina A&T.
TRANSACTIONS/CAREER NOTES: Selected by San Diego Chargers in third round (74th pick overall) of 1997 NFL draft. ... Signed by Chargers (June 11, 1997). ... Released by Chargers (September 2, 1997). ... Re-signed by Chargers to practice squad (September 3, 1997). ... Activated (November 4, 1997). ... Granted free agency (February 11, 2000).
PLAYING EXPERIENCE: San Diego NFL, 1997-1999. ... Games/ Games started: 1997 (6/0), 1998 (13/0), 1999 (14/2). Total: 33/2.
PRO STATISTICS: 1998—Recovered one fumble.

HAMILTON, RUFFIN   LB

PERSONAL: Born March 2, 1971, in Detroit. ... 6-1/235. ... Full name: Ruffin Hamilton III.
HIGH SCHOOL: Northeast (Zachary, La.).
COLLEGE: Tulane.
TRANSACTIONS/CAREER NOTES: Selected by Green Bay Packers in sixth round (175th pick overall) of 1994 NFL draft. ... Signed by Packers (July 19, 1994). ... Released by Packers (October 6, 1994). ... Re-signed by Packers to practice squad (October 7, 1994). ... Activated (December 6, 1994). ... Released by Packers (August 27, 1995). ... Signed by Atlanta Falcons (January 30, 1996). ... Released by Falcons (August 25, 1996). ... Re-signed by Falcons (February 13, 1997). ... On injured reserve with hamstring injury (January 1, 2000-remainder of season). ... Granted unconditional free agency (February 11, 2000).
PLAYING EXPERIENCE: Green Bay NFL, 1994; Atlanta NFL, 1997-1999. ... Games/Games started: 1994 (5/0), 1997 (13/0), 1998 (16/0), 1999 (11/1). Total: 45/1.
CHAMPIONSHIP GAME EXPERIENCE: Played in NFC championship game (1998 season). ... Played in Super Bowl XXXIII (1998 season).

H

HAMITER, UHURU DE SAINTS

PERSONAL: Born March 14, 1973, in Kingstree, S.C. ... 6-4/280.
HIGH SCHOOL: Mastbaum Area Vo-Tech (Philadelphia).
COLLEGE: Delaware State.
TRANSACTIONS/CAREER NOTES: Selected by England Monarchs in 1998 NFL Europe draft (February 18, 1998). ... Signed as non-drafted free agent by Philadelphia Eagles (June 19, 1998). ... Claimed on waivers by New Orleans Saints (August 31, 1998). ... Active for one game (1998); did not play. ... Released by Saints (September 28, 1999). ... Re-signed by Saints to practice squad (September 30, 1999). ... Activated (November 19, 1999).
PLAYING EXPERIENCE: England NFLE, 1998; New Orleans NFL, 1999. ... Games/Games started: 1998 (10/games started unavailable), 1999 (5/0). Total NFLE: (10/-). Total NFL: (5/0). Total Pro: (15/-).
PRO STATISTICS: 1998—Credited with seven sacks.

HAND, NORMAN DT SAINTS

PERSONAL: Born September 4, 1972, in Queens, N.Y. ... 6-3/310. ... Full name: Norman L. Hand.
HIGH SCHOOL: Walterboro (S.C.).
JUNIOR COLLEGE: Itawamba Community College (Miss.).
COLLEGE: Mississippi.
TRANSACTIONS/CAREER NOTES: Selected by Miami Dolphins in fifth round (158th pick overall) of 1995 NFL draft. ... Signed by Dolphins (May 17, 1995). ... Inactive for all 16 games (1995). ... Claimed on waivers by San Diego Chargers (August 25, 1997). ... Granted free agency (February 13, 1998). ... Re-signed by Chargers (July 14, 1998). ... Designated by Chargers as franchise player (February 11, 2000). ... Free agency status changed from franchise to unconditional (February 16, 2000). ... Signed by New Orleans Saints (February 23, 2000).
PRO STATISTICS: 1998—Intercepted two passes for 47 yards.

Year Team	G	GS	SACKS
1995—Miami NFL	Did not play.		
1996—Miami NFL	9	0	0.5
1997—San Diego NFL	15	1	1.0
1998—San Diego NFL	16	16	6.0
1999—San Diego NFL	14	14	4.0
Pro totals (4 years)	54	31	11.5

HANKS, MERTON S

PERSONAL: Born March 12, 1968, in Dallas. ... 6-2/181. ... Full name: Merton Edward Hanks.
HIGH SCHOOL: Lake Highlands (Dallas).
COLLEGE: Iowa (degree in liberal arts, 1990).
TRANSACTIONS/CAREER NOTES: Selected by San Francisco 49ers in fifth round (122nd pick overall) of 1991 NFL draft. ... Signed by 49ers (July 10, 1991). ... Released by 49ers (September 7, 1999). ... Signed by Seattle Seahawks (September 14, 1999). ... Granted unconditional free agency (February 11, 2000).
CHAMPIONSHIP GAME EXPERIENCE: Played in NFC championship game (1992-1994 and 1997 seasons). ... Member of Super Bowl championship team (1994 season).
HONORS: Named free safety on THE SPORTING NEWS NFL All-Pro team (1994 and 1995). ... Played in Pro Bowl (1994, 1995 and 1997 seasons).
PRO STATISTICS: 1991—Recovered two fumbles. 1992—Returned one punt for 48 yards. 1993—Recovered one fumble. 1994—Credited with 1/2 sack, fumbled once and recovered two fumbles. 1995—Returned one punt for no yards and recovered two fumbles for 69 yards and one touchdown. 1997—Recovered two fumbles for 38 yards and one touchdown. 1998—Credited with 1/2 sack and recovered one fumble. 1999—Credited with two sacks.

Year Team	G	GS	INTERCEPTIONS				TOTALS			
			No.	Yds.	Avg.	TD	TD	2pt.	Pts.	Fum.
1991—San Francisco NFL	13	8	0	0	0.0	0	0	0	0	0
1992—San Francisco NFL	16	5	2	5	2.5	0	0	0	0	0
1993—San Francisco NFL	16	14	3	104	34.7	1	1	0	6	0
1994—San Francisco NFL	16	16	7	93	13.3	0	0	0	0	1
1995—San Francisco NFL	16	16	5	31	6.2	0	1	0	6	0
1996—San Francisco NFL	16	16	4	7	1.8	0	0	0	0	0
1997—San Francisco NFL	16	16	6	103	17.2	1	2	0	12	0
1998—San Francisco NFL	16	16	4	37	9.3	0	0	0	0	0
1999—Seattle NFL	12	1	2	30	15.0	1	1	0	6	0
Pro totals (9 years)	137	108	33	410	12.4	3	5	0	30	1

HANSEN, BRIAN P

PERSONAL: Born October 26, 1960, in Hawarden, Iowa. ... 6-4/215. ... Full name: Brian Dean Hansen.
HIGH SCHOOL: West Sioux Community (Hawarden, Iowa).
COLLEGE: Sioux Falls (S.D.) College.
TRANSACTIONS/CAREER NOTES: Selected by New Orleans Saints in ninth round (237th pick overall) of 1984 NFL draft. ... Signed by Saints for 1984 season. ... Released by Saints (September 5, 1989). ... Signed by New England Patriots (May 3, 1990). ... Granted unconditional free agency (February 1, 1991). ... Signed by Cleveland Browns (April 1, 1991). ... Granted unconditional free agency (February 1-April 1, 1992). ... Re-signed by Browns for 1992 season. ... Granted unconditional free agency (February 17, 1994). ... Signed by New York Jets (April 19, 1994). ... Released by Jets (August 25, 1997). ... Re-signed by Jets (August 27, 1997). ... Traded by Jets to Green Bay Packers for undisclosed terms (August 17, 1998). ... Released by Packers (August 21, 1998). ... Signed by Jets (September 13, 1998). ... Released by Jets (November 3, 1998). ... Signed by Washington Redskins (October 22, 1999). ... Released by Redskins (November 9, 1999).
HONORS: Played in Pro Bowl (1984 season).
PRO STATISTICS: 1984—Rushed twice for minus 27 yards. 1985—Completed only pass attempt for eight yards. 1986—Rushed once for no yards, fumbled once and recovered one fumble. 1987—Rushed twice for minus six yards. 1988—Rushed once for 10 yards. 1990—Rushed

H

once for no yards, fumbled once and recovered two fumbles for minus 18 yards. 1991—Completed only pass attempt for 11 yards and a touchdown, rushed twice for minus three yards and recovered one fumble. 1992—Fumbled once and recovered one fumble. 1996—Rushed once for one yard. 1997—Completed only pass attempt for 26 yards.

Year Team	G	No.	Yds.	Avg.	Net avg.	In. 20	Blk.
					PUNTING		
1984—New Orleans NFL	16	69	3020	‡43.8	33.2	9	1
1985—New Orleans NFL	16	89	3763	42.3	36.5	14	0
1986—New Orleans NFL	16	81	3456	42.7	36.6	17	1
1987—New Orleans NFL	12	52	2104	40.5	35.6	19	0
1988—New Orleans NFL	16	72	2913	40.5	34.2	19	1
1989—					Did not play.		
1990—New England NFL	16	*90	*3752	41.7	33.6	18	2
1991—Cleveland NFL	16	80	3397	42.5	36.1	20	0
1992—Cleveland NFL	16	74	3083	41.7	36.1	28	1
1993—Cleveland NFL	16	82	3632	44.3	35.6	15	2
1994—New York Jets NFL	16	84	3534	42.1	36.1	25	0
1995—New York Jets NFL	16	*99	*4090	41.3	31.8	23	1
1996—New York Jets NFL	16	74	3293	44.5	36.5	13	0
1997—New York Jets NFL	15	71	3068	43.2	35.3	20	1
1998—New York Jets NFL	7	31	1233	39.8	32.7	6	0
1999—Washington NFL	2	9	362	40.2	24.7	1	0
Pro totals (15 years)	212	1057	44700	42.3	35.0	247	10

HANSEN, PHIL   DE   BILLS

PERSONAL: Born May 20, 1968, in Ellendale, N.D. ... 6-5/278. ... Full name: Phillip Allen Hansen.
HIGH SCHOOL: Oakes (N.D.).
COLLEGE: North Dakota State (degree in agricultural economics).
TRANSACTIONS/CAREER NOTES: Selected by Buffalo Bills in second round (54th pick overall) of 1991 NFL draft. ... Signed by Bills (July 10, 1991). ... Granted free agency (February 17, 1994). ... Re-signed by Bills (April 29, 1994).
CHAMPIONSHIP GAME EXPERIENCE: Played in AFC championship game (1991-1993 seasons). ... Played in Super Bowl XXVI (1991 season), Super Bowl XXVII (1992 season) and Super Bowl XXVIII (1993 season).
PRO STATISTICS: 1991—Recovered one fumble. 1995—Recovered one fumble. 1996—Recovered two fumbles. 1997—Credited with a safety. 1998—Recovered three fumbles for 13 yards and one touchdown. 1999—Recovered two fumbles for 24 yards.

Year Team	G	GS	SACKS
1991—Buffalo NFL	14	10	2.0
1992—Buffalo NFL	16	16	8.0
1993—Buffalo NFL	11	9	3.5
1994—Buffalo NFL	16	16	5.5
1995—Buffalo NFL	16	16	10.0
1996—Buffalo NFL	16	16	8.0
1997—Buffalo NFL	16	16	6.0
1998—Buffalo NFL	15	15	7.5
1999—Buffalo NFL	14	14	6.0
Pro totals (9 years)	134	128	56.5

HANSON, CHRIS   P   DOLPHINS

PERSONAL: Born October 25, 1976, in Riverdale, Ga. ... 6-1/214.
HIGH SCHOOL: East Coweta (Ga.).
COLLEGE: Marshall.
TRANSACTIONS/CAREER NOTES: Signed as non-drafted free agent by Cleveland Browns (April 23, 1999). ... Claimed on waivers by Green Bay Packers (September 1, 1999). ... Released by Packers (September 14, 1999). ... Re-signed by Packers to practice squad (September 16, 1999). ... Released by Packers (October 12, 1999). ... Signed by Miami Dolphins (February 8, 2000).

Year Team	G	No.	Yds.	Avg.	Net avg.	In. 20	Blk.
					PUNTING		
1999—Green Bay NFL	1	4	157	39.3	38.5	0	0

HANSON, JASON   K   LIONS

PERSONAL: Born June 17, 1970, in Spokane, Wash. ... 5-11/182. ... Full name: Jason Douglas Hanson.
HIGH SCHOOL: Mead (Spokane, Wash.).
COLLEGE: Washington State (degree in pre-med).
TRANSACTIONS/CAREER NOTES: Selected by Detroit Lions in second round (56th pick overall) of 1992 NFL draft. ... Signed by Lions (July 23, 1992). ... Designated by Lions as transition player (February 15, 1994).
HONORS: Named kicker on THE SPORTING NEWS college All-America first team (1989). ... Named kicker on THE SPORTING NEWS NFL All-Pro team (1993). ... Played in Pro Bowl (1997 and 1999 season).
PRO STATISTICS: 1995—Punted once for 34 yards. 1996—Punted once for 24 yards. 1998—Punted three times for 94 yards.

Year Team	G	XPM	XPA	FGM	FGA	Lg.	50+	Pts.
				KICKING				
1992—Detroit NFL	16	30	30	21	26	52	2-5	93
1993—Detroit NFL	16	28	28	‡34	‡43	53	3-7	‡130
1994—Detroit NFL	16	39	40	18	27	49	0-5	93
1995—Detroit NFL	16	*48	†48	28	34	56	1-1	132
1996—Detroit NFL	16	36	36	12	17	51	1-3	72
1997—Detroit NFL	16	39	40	26	29	†55	3-5	117

H

1998—Detroit NFL	16	27	29	29	33	51	1-3	114
1999—Detroit NFL	16	28	29	26	∞32	52	4-8	106
Pro totals (8 years)	128	275	280	194	241	56	15-37	857

HANSPARD, BYRON   RB   FALCONS

PERSONAL: Born January 23, 1976, in Dallas. ... 5-10/200. ... Cousin of Essex Johnson, running back with Cincinnati Bengals (1968-75).
HIGH SCHOOL: DeSoto (Texas).
COLLEGE: Texas Tech.
TRANSACTIONS/CAREER NOTES: Selected by Atlanta Falcons in second round (41st pick overall) of 1997 NFL draft. ... Signed by Falcons (July 14, 1997). ... On injured reserve with knee injury (August 30, 1998-entire season). ... Granted free agency (February 11, 2000).
HONORS: Doak Walker Award winner (1996). ... Named running back on THE SPORTING NEWS college All-America first team (1996).
PRO STATISTICS: 1997—Recovered two fumbles.
SINGLE GAME HIGHS (regular season): Attempts—26 (December 26, 1999, vs. Arizona); yards—102 (December 26, 1999, vs. Arizona); and rushing touchdowns—1 (December 26, 1999, vs. Arizona).
STATISTICAL PLATEAUS: 100-yard rushing games: 1999 (1).

			RUSHING				RECEIVING				KICKOFF RETURNS				TOTALS			
Year Team	G	GS	Att.	Yds.	Avg.	TD	No.	Yds.	Avg.	TD	No.	Yds.	Avg.	TD	TD	2pt.	Pts.	Fum.
1997—Atlanta NFL	16	0	53	335	6.3	0	6	53	8.8	1	40	987	24.7	*2	3	0	18	3
1998—Atlanta NFL								Did not play.										
1999—Atlanta NFL	12	4	136	383	2.8	1	10	93	9.3	0	0	0	0.0	0	1	0	6	1
Pro totals (2 years)	28	4	189	718	3.8	1	16	146	9.1	1	40	987	24.7	2	4	0	24	4

HAPE, PATRICK   TE   BUCCANEERS

PERSONAL: Born June 6, 1974, in Killen, Ala. ... 6-4/262. ... Full name: Patrick Stephen Hape.
HIGH SCHOOL: Brooks (Killen, Ala.).
COLLEGE: Alabama.
TRANSACTIONS/CAREER NOTES: Selected by Tampa Bay Buccaneers in fifth round (137th pick overall) of 1997 NFL draft. ... Signed by Buccaneers (July 20, 1997). ... Granted free agency (February 11, 2000).
CHAMPIONSHIP GAME EXPERIENCE: Played in NFC championship game (1999 season).
PRO STATISTICS: 1997—Rushed once for one yard.
SINGLE GAME HIGHS (regular season): Receptions—2 (October 31, 1999, vs. Detroit); yards—13 (October 5, 1997, vs. Green Bay); and touchdown receptions—1 (November 28, 1999, vs. Seattle).

			RECEIVING				TOTALS			
Year Team	G	GS	No.	Yds.	Avg.	TD	TD	2pt.	Pts.	Fum.
1997—Tampa Bay NFL	14	3	4	22	5.5	1	1	0	6	1
1998—Tampa Bay NFL	16	2	4	27	6.8	0	0	1	2	1
1999—Tampa Bay NFL	15	1	5	12	2.4	1	1	0	6	0
Pro totals (3 years)	45	6	13	61	4.7	2	2	1	14	2

HARBAUGH, JIM   QB   CHARGERS

PERSONAL: Born December 23, 1963, in Toledo, Ohio. ... 6-3/215. ... Full name: James Joseph Harbaugh. ... Son of Jack Harbaugh, head coach, Western Kentucky University; and cousin of Mike Gottfried, ESPN college football analyst; and former head coach, Murray State University, University of Cincinnati, University of Kansas and University of Pittsburgh.
HIGH SCHOOL: Pioneer (Ann Arbor, Mich.), then Palo Alto (Calif.).
COLLEGE: Michigan (degree in communications, 1987).
TRANSACTIONS/CAREER NOTES: Selected by Chicago Bears in first round (26th pick overall) of 1987 NFL draft. ... Signed by Bears (August 3, 1987). ... On injured reserve with separated shoulder (December 19, 1990-remainder of season). ... Granted free agency (February 1, 1991). ... Re-signed by Bears (July 22, 1991). ... Granted unconditional free agency (March 1, 1993). ... Re-signed by Bears (March 19, 1993). ... Released by Bears (March 16, 1994). ... Signed by Indianapolis Colts (April 7, 1994). ... Designated by Colts as franchise player (February 16, 1996). ... Traded by Colts with fourth-round pick (traded to Tampa Bay) in 1998 draft to Baltimore Ravens for third- (WR E.G. Green) and fourth-round (traded back to Baltimore) picks in 1998 draft (February 14, 1998). ... Traded by Ravens to San Diego Chargers for fifth-round pick (G Richard Mercier) in 2000 draft (March 15, 1999).
CHAMPIONSHIP GAME EXPERIENCE: Member of Bears for NFC championship game (1988 season); did not play. ... Played in AFC championship game (1995 season).
HONORS: Played in Pro Bowl (1995 season).
PRO STATISTICS: 1988—Fumbled once. 1989—Fumbled twice. 1990—Fumbled eight times and recovered three fumbles for minus four yards. 1991—Fumbled six times. 1992—Fumbled six times and recovered three fumbles. 1993—Caught one pass for one yard, led league with 15 fumbles and recovered four fumbles for minus one yard. 1994—Fumbled once. 1995—Caught one pass for minus nine yards, fumbled four times and recovered one fumble for minus 20 yards. 1996—Fumbled eight times and recovered four fumbles for minus three yards. 1997—Fumbled four times and recovered one fumble. 1998—Fumbled seven times and recovered three fumbles for minus seven yards. 1999—Fumbled 12 times and recovered four fumbles for minus 20 yards.
SINGLE GAME HIGHS (regular season): Attempts—47 (November 28, 1991, vs. Detroit); completions—30 (September 7, 1997, vs. New England); yards—404 (November 28, 1999, vs. Minnesota); and touchdown passes—4 (December 14, 1997, vs. Miami).
STATISTICAL PLATEAUS: 300-yard passing games: 1991 (1), 1992 (1), 1995 (1), 1997 (1), 1999 (2). Total: 6.
MISCELLANEOUS: Regular-season record as starting NFL quarterback: 66-69 (.489). ... Postseason record as starting NFL quarterback: 2-3 (.400).

			PASSING								RUSHING				TOTALS		
Year Team	G	GS	Att.	Cmp.	Pct.	Yds.	TD	Int.	Avg.	Rat.	Att.	Yds.	Avg.	TD	TD	2pt.	Pts.
1987—Chicago NFL	6	0	11	8	72.7	62	0	0	5.64	86.2	4	15	3.8	0	0	0	0
1988—Chicago NFL	10	2	97	47	48.5	514	0	2	5.30	55.9	19	110	5.8	1	1	0	6
1989—Chicago NFL	12	5	178	111	62.4	1204	5	9	6.76	70.5	45	276	6.1	3	3	0	18
1990—Chicago NFL	14	14	312	180	57.7	2178	10	6	6.98	81.9	51	321	6.3	4	4	0	24

H

Year—Team																	
1991—Chicago NFL	16	16	478	275	57.5	3121	15	16	6.53	73.7	70	338	4.8	2	2	0	12
1992—Chicago NFL	16	13	358	202	56.4	2486	13	12	6.94	76.2	47	272	5.8	1	1	0	6
1993—Chicago NFL	15	15	325	200	61.5	2002	7	11	6.16	72.1	60	277	4.6	4	4	0	24
1994—Indianapolis NFL	12	9	202	125	61.9	1440	9	6	7.13	85.8	39	223	5.7	0	0	0	0
1995—Indianapolis NFL	15	12	314	200	63.7	2575	17	5	*8.20	*100.7	52	235	4.5	2	2	0	12
1996—Indianapolis NFL	14	14	405	232	57.3	2630	13	11	6.49	76.3	48	192	4.0	1	1	0	6
1997—Indianapolis NFL	12	11	309	189	§61.2	2060	10	4	6.67	86.2	36	206	5.7	0	0	0	0
1998—Baltimore NFL	14	12	293	164	56.0	1839	12	11	6.28	72.9	40	172	4.3	0	0	0	0
1999—San Diego NFL	14	12	434	249	57.4	2761	10	14	6.36	70.6	34	126	3.7	0	0	0	0
Pro totals (13 years)	170	135	3716	2182	58.7	24872	121	107	6.69	77.8	545	2763	5.1	18	18	0	108

HARDEN, CEDRIC   DE   CHARGERS

PERSONAL: Born October 19, 1974, in Atlanta. ... 6-6/260. ... Full name: Cedric Bernard Harden.
HIGH SCHOOL: D.M. Therrell (Atlanta).
COLLEGE: Florida A&M.
TRANSACTIONS/CAREER NOTES: Selected by San Diego Chargers in fifth round (126th pick overall) of 1998 NFL draft. ... Signed by Chargers (July 10, 1998). ... On injured reserve with shoulder injury (August 30, 1998-entire season). ... Assigned by Chargers to Amsterdam Admirals in 2000 NFL Europe enhancement allocation program (February 18, 2000).
PLAYING EXPERIENCE: San Diego NFL, 1999. ... Games/Games started: 1999 (5/0).
PRO STATISTICS: 1999—Credited with 1/2 sack.

HARDY, KEVIN   LB   JAGUARS

PERSONAL: Born July 24, 1973, in Evansville, Ind. ... 6-4/247. ... Full name: Kevin Lamont Hardy.
HIGH SCHOOL: Harrison (Evansville, Ind.).
COLLEGE: Illinois (degree in marketing, 1995).
TRANSACTIONS/CAREER NOTES: Selected by Jacksonville Jaguars in first round (second pick overall) of 1996 NFL draft. ... Signed by Jaguars (July 17, 1996).
CHAMPIONSHIP GAME EXPERIENCE: Played in AFC championship game (1996 and 1999 seasons).
HONORS: Butkus Award winner (1995). ... Named linebacker on THE SPORTING NEWS college All-America first team (1995). ... Named linebacker on THE SPORTING NEWS NFL All-Pro team (1999). ... Played in Pro Bowl (1999 season).
PRO STATISTICS: 1996—Recovered one fumble for 13 yards. 1998—Recovered one fumble. 1999—Recovered one fumble.

			INTERCEPTIONS				SACKS
Year Team	G	GS	No.	Yds.	Avg.	TD	No.
1996—Jacksonville NFL	16	15	2	19	9.5	0	5.5
1997—Jacksonville NFL	13	11	0	0	0.0	0	2.5
1998—Jacksonville NFL	16	16	2	40	20.0	0	1.5
1999—Jacksonville NFL	16	16	0	0	0.0	0	10.5
Pro totals (4 years)	61	58	4	59	14.8	0	20.0

HARDY, TERRY   TE   CARDINALS

PERSONAL: Born May 31, 1976, in Montgomery, Ala. ... 6-4/271.
HIGH SCHOOL: Carver (Montgomery, Ala.).
COLLEGE: Southern Mississippi (degree in coaching and sports information, 1997).
TRANSACTIONS/CAREER NOTES: Selected by Arizona Cardinals in fifth round (125th pick overall) of 1998 NFL draft. ... Signed by Cardinals (June 15, 1998).
SINGLE GAME HIGHS (regular season): Receptions—5 (October 3, 1999, vs. Dallas); yards—49 (September 12, 1999, vs. Philadelphia); and touchdown receptions—0.

			RECEIVING				TOTALS			
Year Team	G	GS	No.	Yds.	Avg.	TD	TD	2pt.	Pts.	Fum.
1998—Arizona NFL	9	0	0	0	0.0	0	0	0	0	0
1999—Arizona NFL	16	16	30	222	7.4	0	0	0	0	1
Pro totals (2 years)	25	16	30	222	7.4	0	0	0	0	1

HARPER, ALVIN   WR

PERSONAL: Born July 6, 1968, in Frostproof, Fla. ... 6-4/218. ... Full name: Alvin Craig Harper.
HIGH SCHOOL: Frostproof (Fla.).
COLLEGE: Tennessee (degree in criminal justice).
TRANSACTIONS/CAREER NOTES: Selected by Dallas Cowboys in first round (12th pick overall) of 1991 NFL draft. ... Signed by Cowboys (April 22, 1991). ... Granted free agency (February 17, 1994). ... Re-signed by Cowboys (June 1, 1994). ... Granted unconditional free agency (February 17, 1995). ... Signed by Tampa Bay Buccaneers (March 8, 1995). ... Released by Buccaneers (June 10, 1997). ... Signed by Washington Redskins (June 11, 1997). ... Claimed on waivers by New Orleans Saints (December 2, 1997). ... Released by Saints (July 24, 1998). ... Signed by Cowboys (October 14, 1999). ... Released by Cowboys (December 7, 1999).
CHAMPIONSHIP GAME EXPERIENCE: Played in NFC championship game (1992-1994 seasons). ... Member of Super Bowl championship team (1992 and 1993 seasons).
POST SEASON RECORDS: Holds NFL postseason career records for highest average gain (minimum 20 receptions)—27.3; and longest reception (from Troy Aikman)—94 yards (January 8, 1995, vs. Green Bay).
PRO STATISTICS: 1992—Rushed once for 15 yards and intercepted one pass for one yard. 1993—Completed only pass attempt for 46 yards.
SINGLE GAME HIGHS (regular season): Receptions—6 (November 26, 1995, vs. Green Bay); yards—140 (September 6, 1993, vs. Washington); and touchdown receptions—2 (November 7, 1993, vs. New York Giants).
STATISTICAL PLATEAUS: 100-yard receiving games: 1991 (1), 1993 (2), 1994 (3), 1995 (1). Total: 7.

H

Year Team	G	GS	RECEIVING				TOTALS			
			No.	Yds.	Avg.	TD	TD	2pt.	Pts.	Fum.
1991—Dallas NFL	15	5	20	326	16.3	1	1	0	6	0
1992—Dallas NFL	16	13	35	562	16.1	4	4	0	24	1
1993—Dallas NFL	16	15	36	777	‡21.6	5	5	0	30	1
1994—Dallas NFL	16	14	33	821	*24.9	8	8	0	48	2
1995—Tampa Bay NFL	13	13	46	633	13.8	2	2	0	12	0
1996—Tampa Bay NFL	12	7	19	289	15.2	1	1	0	6	1
1997—Washington NFL	12	0	2	65	32.5	0	0	0	0	0
1998—					Did not play.					
1999—Dallas NFL	2	0	0	0	0.0	0	0	0	0	0
Pro totals (8 years)	102	67	191	3473	18.2	21	21	0	126	5

HARPER, DWAYNE CB

PERSONAL: Born March 29, 1966, in Orangeburg, S.C. ... 5-11/175. ... Full name: Dwayne Anthony Harper.
HIGH SCHOOL: Orangeburg-Wilkinson (Orangeburg, S.C.).
COLLEGE: South Carolina State (degree in marketing, 1987).
TRANSACTIONS/CAREER NOTES: Selected by Seattle Seahawks in 11th round (299th pick overall) of 1988 NFL draft. ... Signed by Seahawks (July 16, 1988). ... Granted free agency (February 1, 1992). ... Re-signed by Seahawks (August 10, 1992). ... Granted unconditional free agency (February 17, 1994). ... Signed by San Diego Chargers (March 3, 1994). ... Granted unconditional free agency (February 14, 1997). ... Re-signed by Chargers (February 16, 1997). ... On injured reserve with hamstring injury (December 17, 1997-remainder of season). ... On injured reserve with neck injury (October 21, 1998-remainder of season). ... Released by Chargers (September 6, 1999). ... Signed by Detroit Lions (December 14, 1999). ... Granted unconditional free agency (February 11, 2000).
CHAMPIONSHIP GAME EXPERIENCE: Played in AFC championship game (1994 season). ... Played in Super Bowl XXIX (1994 season).
PRO STATISTICS: 1988—Credited with a sack and recovered one fumble. 1989—Recovered one fumble. 1991—Returned one punt for five yards. 1992—Fumbled once and recovered two fumbles for 52 yards and one touchdown. 1993—Recovered one fumble. 1995—Recovered one fumble for one yard. 1997—Recovered one fumble.

Year Team	G	GS	INTERCEPTIONS			
			No.	Yds.	Avg.	TD
1988—Seattle NFL	16	1	0	0	0.0	0
1989—Seattle NFL	16	13	2	15	7.5	0
1990—Seattle NFL	16	16	3	69	23.0	0
1991—Seattle NFL	16	16	4	84	21.0	0
1992—Seattle NFL	16	16	3	74	24.7	0
1993—Seattle NFL	14	14	1	0	0.0	0
1994—San Diego NFL	16	16	3	28	9.3	0
1995—San Diego NFL	16	16	4	12	3.0	0
1996—San Diego NFL	6	6	1	0	0.0	0
1997—San Diego NFL	12	12	2	43	21.5	0
1998—San Diego NFL	1	1	1	12	12.0	0
1999—Detroit NFL	3	1	0	0	0.0	0
Pro totals (12 years)	148	128	24	337	14.0	0

HARRIS, AL CB EAGLES

PERSONAL: Born December 7, 1974, in Pompano Beach, Fla. ... 6-1/185. ... Full name: Alshinard Harris.
HIGH SCHOOL: Ely (Pompano Beach, Fla.).
JUNIOR COLLEGE: Trinity Valley Community College (Texas).
COLLEGE: Texas A&M-Kingsville.
TRANSACTIONS/CAREER NOTES: Selected by Tampa Bay Buccaneers in sixth round (169th pick overall) of 1997 NFL draft. ... Signed by Buccaneers (July 1, 1997). ... Released by Buccaneers (August 24, 1997). ... Re-signed by Buccaneers to practice squad (August 26, 1997). ... Claimed on waivers by Philadelphia Eagles (August 31, 1998).
PLAYING EXPERIENCE: Philadelphia NFL, 1998 and 1999. ... Games/Games started: 1998 (16/7), 1999 (16/6). Total: 32/13.
PRO STATISTICS: 1998—Returned one punt for minus two yards and fumbled once. 1999—Intercepted four passes for 151 yards and one touchdown and fumbled once.

HARRIS, ANTHONY LB PACKERS

PERSONAL: Born January 25, 1973, in Fort Pierce, Fla. ... 6-1/240. ... Full name: Anthony Jerrod Harris.
HIGH SCHOOL: Westwood Christian (Miami).
COLLEGE: Auburn.
TRANSACTIONS/CAREER NOTES: Signed as non-drafted free agent by Miami Dolphins (April 21, 1996). ... Granted free agency (February 12, 1999). ... Re-signed by Dolphins (April 8, 1999). ... Released by Dolphins (February 18, 2000). ... Signed by Green Bay Packers (April 6, 2000).
PLAYING EXPERIENCE: Miami NFL, 1996-1999. ... Games/Games started: 1996 (7/3), 1997 (16/16), 1998 (5/0), 1999 (4/0). Total: 32/19.
PRO STATISTICS: 1996—Recovered one fumble. 1997—Returned one kickoff for no yards and credited with one sack.

HARRIS, BERNARDO LB PACKERS

PERSONAL: Born October 15, 1971, in Chapel Hill, N.C. ... 6-2/250. ... Full name: Bernardo Jamaine Harris.
HIGH SCHOOL: Chapel Hill (N.C.).
COLLEGE: North Carolina.
TRANSACTIONS/CAREER NOTES: Signed as non-drafted free agent by Kansas City Chiefs (June 2, 1994). ... Released by Chiefs (August 2, 1994). ... Signed by Green Bay Packers (January 20, 1995).

H

PLAYING EXPERIENCE: Green Bay NFL, 1995-1999. ... Games/Games started: 1995 (11/0), 1996 (16/0), 1997 (16/16), 1998 (16/16), 1999 (16/15). Total: 75/47.
CHAMPIONSHIP GAME EXPERIENCE: Played in NFC championship game (1995-1997 seasons). ... Member of Super Bowl championship team (1996 season). ... Played in Super Bowl XXXII (1997 season).
PRO STATISTICS: 1997—Intercepted one pass for no yards and credited with one sack. 1998—Credited with two sacks. 1999—Recovered one fumble.

HARRIS, COREY — CB — SAINTS

PERSONAL: Born November 28, 1976, in Warner Robins, Ga. ... 5-10/191.
HIGH SCHOOL: Northside (Warner Robins, Ga.).
COLLEGE: The Citadel, then North Alabama.
TRANSACTIONS/CAREER NOTES: Signed as non-drafted free agent by New Orleans Saints (May 20, 1999). ... Released by Saints (September 5, 1999). ... Re-signed by Saints to practice squad (September 6, 1999). ... Released by Saints (September 28, 1999). ... Re-signed by Saints to practice squad (October 27, 1999). ... Activated (December 17, 1999).
PLAYING EXPERIENCE: New Orleans NFL, 1999. ... Games/Games started: 1999 (3/0).

HARRIS, COREY — S — RAVENS

PERSONAL: Born October 25, 1969, in Indianapolis. ... 5-11/200. ... Full name: Corey Lamont Harris.
HIGH SCHOOL: Ben Davis (Indianapolis).
COLLEGE: Vanderbilt (degree in human resources).
TRANSACTIONS/CAREER NOTES: Selected by Houston Oilers in third round (77th pick overall) of 1992 NFL draft. ... Signed by Oilers (August 5, 1992). ... Claimed on waivers by Green Bay Packers (October 14, 1992). ... Granted free agency (February 17, 1995). ... Tendered offer sheet by Seattle Seahawks (March 3, 1995). ... Packers declined to match offer (March 10, 1995). ... Granted unconditional free agency (February 14, 1997). ... Signed by Miami Dolphins (March 17, 1997). ... Released by Dolphins (August 3, 1998). ... Signed by Baltimore Ravens (August 17, 1998). ... Granted unconditional free agency (February 12, 1999). ... Re-signed by Ravens (May 17, 1999). ... Granted unconditional free agency (February 11, 2000). ... Re-signed by Ravens (March 21, 2000).
PRO STATISTICS: 1992—Rushed twice for 10 yards and returned six punts for 17 yards. 1993—Caught two passes for 11 yards. 1994—Recovered one fumble. 1995—Recovered one fumble for 57 yards and a touchdown. 1996—Credited with one sack and recovered three fumbles for 28 yards. 1998—Credited with one sack and recovered one fumble. 1999—Credited with one sack.
MISCELLANEOUS: Played wide receiver (1992 and 1993).

| | | | INTERCEPTIONS | | | | KICKOFF RETURNS | | | | TOTALS | | | |
Year Team	G	GS	No.	Yds.	Avg.	TD	No.	Yds.	Avg.	TD	TD	2pt.	Pts.	Fum.
1992—Houston NFL	5	0	0	0	0.0	0	0	0	0.0	0	0	0	0	0
—Green Bay NFL	10	0	0	0	0.0	0	33	691	20.9	0	0	0	0	0
1993—Green Bay NFL	11	0	0	0	0.0	0	16	482	30.1	0	0	0	0	0
1994—Green Bay NFL	16	2	0	0	0.0	0	29	618	21.3	0	0	0	0	1
1995—Seattle NFL	16	16	3	-5	-1.7	0	19	397	20.9	0	1	0	6	0
1996—Seattle NFL	16	16	1	25	25.0	0	7	166	23.7	0	0	0	0	0
1997—Miami NFL	16	7	0	0	0.0	0	11	224	20.4	0	0	0	0	0
1998—Baltimore NFL	16	6	0	0	0.0	0	35	965	§27.6	▲1	1	0	6	2
1999—Baltimore NFL	16	0	1	24	24.0	1	38	843	22.2	0	1	0	6	0
Pro totals (8 years)	122	47	5	44	8.8	1	188	4386	23.3	1	3	0	18	3

HARRIS, DERRICK — FB — CHARGERS

PERSONAL: Born September 18, 1972, in Angleton, Texas ... 6-0/252. ... Full name: Sidney Derrick Harris.
HIGH SCHOOL: Angleton (Texas), then Willowridge (Sugar Land, Texas).
COLLEGE: Miami, Fla. (degree in business management, 1995).
TRANSACTIONS/CAREER NOTES: Selected by St. Louis Rams in sixth round (175th pick overall) of 1996 NFL draft. ... Signed by Rams (July 9, 1996). ... Active for one game (1997); did not play. ... Granted free agency (February 12, 1999). ... Re-signed by Rams (June 14, 1999). ... Released by Rams (September 13, 1999). ... Signed by San Diego Chargers (January 18, 2000).
PRO STATISTICS: 1996—Recovered one fumble. 1998—Recovered two fumbles.
SINGLE GAME HIGHS (regular season): Attempts—5 (October 11, 1998, vs. New York Jets); yards—15 (September 20, 1998, vs. Buffalo); and rushing touchdowns—0.

| | | | RUSHING | | | | RECEIVING | | | | TOTALS | | | |
Year Team	G	GS	Att.	Yds.	Avg.	TD	No.	Yds.	Avg.	TD	TD	2pt.	Pts.	Fum.
1996—St. Louis NFL	11	6	3	5	1.7	0	4	17	4.3	0	0	0	0	0
1997—St. Louis NFL							Did not play.							
1998—St. Louis NFL	16	14	14	38	2.7	0	12	57	4.8	2	2	0	12	1
1999—St. Louis NFL	1	0	0	0	0.0	0	0	0	0.0	0	0	0	0	0
Pro totals (3 years)	28	20	17	43	2.5	0	16	74	4.6	2	2	0	12	1

HARRIS, JACKIE — TE — COWBOYS

PERSONAL: Born January 4, 1968, in Pine Bluff, Ark. ... 6-4/250. ... Full name: Jackie Bernard Harris. ... Secound cousin of Chris Akins, safety, Dallas Cowboys.
HIGH SCHOOL: Dollarway (Pine Bluff, Ark.).
COLLEGE: Northeast Louisiana.
TRANSACTIONS/CAREER NOTES: Selected by Green Bay Packers in fourth round (102nd pick overall) of 1990 NFL draft. ... Signed by Packers (July 22, 1990). ... Granted free agency (February 1, 1992). ... Re-signed by Packers (August 14, 1992). ... Designated by Packers as transition player (February 25, 1993). ... Tendered offer sheet by Tampa Bay Buccaneers (June 15, 1994). ... Packers declined to match offer (June 22, 1994). ... On injured reserve with shoulder injury (November 22, 1994-remainder of season). ... On injured reserve with hernia (January 2, 1998-remainder of 1997 playoffs). ... Granted unconditional free agency (February 13, 1998). ... Signed by Tennessee Oilers (March 11,

H

1998). ... Oilers franchise renamed Tennessee Titans for 1999 season (December 26, 1998). ... Granted unconditional free agency (February 11, 2000). ... Signed by Dallas Cowboys (March 17, 2000).

CHAMPIONSHIP GAME EXPERIENCE: Played in AFC championship game (1999 season). ... Played in Super Bowl XXXIV (1999 season).

PRO STATISTICS: 1991—Rushed once for one yard and recovered one fumble. 1998—Returned one kickoff for three yards.

SINGLE GAME HIGHS (regular season): Receptions—10 (November 26, 1995, vs. Green Bay); yards—128 (October 10, 1993, vs. Denver); and touchdown receptions—1 (December 26, 1999, vs. Jacksonville).

STATISTICAL PLATEAUS: 100-yard receiving games: 1993 (1), 1995 (2). Total: 3.

				RECEIVING				TOTALS			
Year Team	G	GS	No.	Yds.	Avg.	TD	TD	2pt.	Pts.	Fum.
1990—Green Bay NFL	16	3	12	157	13.1	0	0	0	0	0
1991—Green Bay NFL	16	6	24	264	11.0	3	3	0	18	1
1992—Green Bay NFL	16	11	55	595	10.8	2	2	0	12	1
1993—Green Bay NFL	12	12	42	604	14.4	4	4	0	24	0
1994—Tampa Bay NFL	9	9	26	337	13.0	3	3	1	20	0
1995—Tampa Bay NFL	16	16	62	751	12.1	1	1	0	6	2
1996—Tampa Bay NFL	13	12	30	349	11.6	1	1	1	8	1
1997—Tampa Bay NFL	12	11	19	197	10.4	1	1	0	6	0
1998—Tennessee NFL	16	16	43	412	9.6	2	2	0	12	0
1999—Tennessee NFL	12	1	26	297	11.4	1	1	†1	8	0
Pro totals (10 years)	138	97	339	3963	11.7	18	18	3	114	5

HARRIS, JAMES   DE

PERSONAL: Born May 13, 1968, in East St. Louis, Ill. ... 6-6/280. ... Full name: James Edward Harris.

HIGH SCHOOL: East St. Louis (Ill.) Senior, then East St. Louis (Ill.) Lincoln.

COLLEGE: Temple.

TRANSACTIONS/CAREER NOTES: Signed as non-drafted free agent by Seattle Seahawks (April 30, 1992). ... Released by Seahawks (August 24, 1992). ... Signed by Minnesota Vikings to practice squad (September 8, 1992). ... On injured reserve with ankle injury (October 29, 1992-remainder of season). ... On physically unable to perform list with foot injury (July 24-September 10, 1995). ... Granted unconditional free agency (February 16, 1996). ... Signed by St. Louis Rams (April 23, 1996). ... Granted unconditional free agency (February 14, 1997). ... Re-signed by Rams (Februaty 24, 1997). ... Released by Rams (August 17, 1997). ... Signed by Oakland Raiders (March 11, 1998). ... Granted unconditional free agency (February 11, 2000).

PRO STATISTICS: 1994—Intercepted one pass for 21 yards, fumbled twice and recovered three fumbles for 18 yards and one touchdown, . 1995—Recovered one fumble. 1996—Recovered one fumble for 22 yards. 1998—Recovered one fumble for one yard.

Year Team	G	GS	SACKS
1992—Minnesota NFL		Did not play.	
1993—Minnesota NFL	6	0	0.0
1994—Minnesota NFL	16	16	3.0
1995—Minnesota NFL	12	3	1.0
1996—St. Louis NFL	16	0	2.0
1998—Oakland NFL	16	16	1.0
1999—Oakland NFL	16	16	2.5
Pro totals (6 years)	82	51	9.5

HARRIS, JOHNNIE   S   RAIDERS

PERSONAL: Born August 21, 1972, in Chicago. ... 6-2/210.

HIGH SCHOOL: Martin Luther King (Chicago).

JUNIOR COLLEGE: San Bernardino (Calif.) Valley.

COLLEGE: Mississippi State.

TRANSACTIONS/CAREER NOTES: Signed by San Antonio Texans of CFL (October 17, 1995). ... Selected by Edmonton Eskimos in 1996 U.S. Team Dispersal draft. ... Released by Eskimos (June 5, 1996). ... Played with Tampa Bay Storm of Arena League (1996-98). ... Signed by Toronto Argonauts of CFL (October 12, 1996). ... Released by Argonauts (May 15, 1997). ... Re-signed by Argonauts (June 2, 1997). ... Signed as non-drafted free agent by Oakland Raiders (February 28, 1999). ... Released by Raiders (September 5, 1999). ... Re-signed by Raiders to practice squad (September 7, 1999). ... Activated (December 1999).

PLAYING EXPERIENCE: Toronto Argonauts CFL, 1996 and 1997; Oakland NFL, 1999. ... Games/Games started: 1996 (4/games started unavailable), 1997 (18/-), 1999 (4/0). Total CFL: 22/-. Total NFL: 4/0. Total Pro: 26/-.

CHAMPIONSHIP GAME EXPERIENCE: Member of CFL championship team (1996).

PRO STATISTICS: CFL: 1996—Returned one kickoff for seven yards. 1997—Intercepted five passes for 72 yards.

HARRIS, MARK   WR

PERSONAL: Born April 28, 1970, in Clovis, N.M ... 6-4/201. ... Full name: Mark Edward Harris.

HIGH SCHOOL: Box Elder (Brigham City, Utah).

JUNIOR COLLEGE: Ricks College (Idaho).

COLLEGE: Southern Utah, then Stanford (degree in psychology, 1995).

TRANSACTIONS/CAREER NOTES: Signed as non-drafted free agent by Dallas Cowboys (April, 25, 1996). ... Released by Cowboys (July 30, 1996). ... Signed by San Francisco 49ers (August 8, 1996). ... Released by 49ers (August 21, 1996). ... Re-signed by 49ers to practice squad (August 26, 1996). ... Activated (October 6, 1996). ... Released by 49ers (October 21, 1996). ... Re-signed by 49ers to practice squad (October 23, 1996). ... Granted free agency (February 11, 2000).

CHAMPIONSHIP GAME EXPERIENCE: Member of 49ers for NFC championship game (1997 season); inactive.

PRO STATISTICS: 1999—Returned four punts for eight yards and returned two kickoffs for 26 yards.

SINGLE GAME HIGHS (regular season): Receptions—2 (October 12, 1997, vs. St. Louis); yards—42 (November 15, 1998, vs. Atlanta); and touchdown receptions—0.

H

Year Team				RECEIVING					TOTALS		
	G	GS	No.	Yds.	Avg.	TD	TD	2pt.	Pts.	Fum.
1996—San Francisco NFL	1	0	0	0	0.0	0	0	0	0	0
1997—San Francisco NFL	10	0	5	53	10.6	0	0	0	0	0
1998—San Francisco NFL	10	0	2	67	33.5	0	0	0	0	0
1999—San Francisco NFL	16	2	6	66	11.0	0	0	0	0	1
Pro totals (4 years)	37	2	13	186	14.3	0	0	0	0	1

HARRIS, RAYMONT   RB   PATRIOTS

PERSONAL: Born December 23, 1970, in Lorain, Ohio. ... 6-0/230. ... Full name: Raymont LeShawn Harris.

HIGH SCHOOL: Lorain (Ohio) Admiral King.

COLLEGE: Ohio State.

TRANSACTIONS/CAREER NOTES: Selected by Chicago Bears in fourth round (114th pick overall) of 1994 NFL draft. ... Signed by Bears (June 21, 1994). ... On injured reserve with broken collarbone (November 29, 1995-remainder of season). ... Granted free agency (February 14, 1997). ... On injured reserve with ankle injury (December 9, 1997-remainder of season). ... Designated by Bears as transition player (February 12, 1998). ... Free agency status changed from transitional to unconditional (April 20, 1998). ... Signed by Green Bay Packers (July 20, 1998). ... Released by Packers (December 8, 1998). ... Signed by New England Patriots (February 14, 2000).

PRO STATISTICS: 1994—Returned one kickoff for 18 yards and recovered three fumbles.

SINGLE GAME HIGHS (regular season): Attempts—33 (November 23, 1997, vs. Tampa Bay); yards—122 (September 1, 1997, vs. Green Bay); and rushing touchdowns—2 (September 1, 1997, vs. Green Bay).

STATISTICAL PLATEAUS: 100-yard rushing games: 1996 (3), 1997 (5). Total: 8. ... 100-yard receiving games: 1996 (1).

Year Team			RUSHING				RECEIVING				TOTALS			
	G	GS	Att.	Yds.	Avg.	TD	No.	Yds.	Avg.	TD	TD	2pt.	Pts.	Fum.
1994—Chicago NFL	16	11	123	464	3.8	1	39	236	6.1	0	1	0	6	1
1995—Chicago NFL	2	1	0	0	0.0	0	1	4	4.0	0	0	0	0	0
1996—Chicago NFL	12	10	194	748	3.9	4	32	296	9.3	1	5	0	30	3
1997—Chicago NFL	13	13	275	1033	3.8	10	28	115	4.1	0	10	0	60	1
1998—Green Bay NFL	8	3	79	228	2.9	1	10	68	6.8	0	1	0	6	3
1999—							Did not play.							
Pro totals (5 years)	51	38	671	2473	3.7	16	110	719	6.5	1	17	0	102	8

HARRIS, ROBERT   DT

PERSONAL: Born June 13, 1969, in Riviera Beach, Fla. ... 6-4/300. ... Full name: Robert Lee Harris.

HIGH SCHOOL: Sun Coast (Riviera Beach, Fla.).

COLLEGE: Southern.

TRANSACTIONS/CAREER NOTES: Selected by Minnesota Vikings in second round (39th pick overall) of 1992 NFL draft. ... Signed by Vikings (July 20, 1992). ... On injured reserve with knee injury (September 30-November 12, 1992). ... Granted free agency (February 17, 1995). ... Tendered offer sheet by New York Giants (March 13, 1995). ... Vikings declined to match offer (March 20, 1995). ... On injured reserve with leg injury (November 11, 1999-remainder of season). ... Released by Giants (March 2, 2000).

PRO STATISTICS: 1995—Recovered two fumbles for five yards. 1997—Recovered two fumbles.

Year Team	G	GS	SACKS
1992—Minnesota NFL	7	0	0.0
1993—Minnesota NFL	16	0	1.0
1994—Minnesota NFL	11	1	2.0
1995—New York Giants NFL	15	15	5.0
1996—New York Giants NFL	16	16	4.5
1997—New York Giants NFL	16	16	10.0
1998—New York Giants NFL	10	10	3.5
1999—New York Giants NFL	6	6	1.0
Pro totals (8 years)	97	64	27.0

HARRIS, RONNIE   WR   FALCONS

PERSONAL: Born June 4, 1970, in Granada Hills, Calif. ... 5-11/180. ... Full name: Ronnie James Harris.

HIGH SCHOOL: Valley Christian (San Jose, Calif.).

COLLEGE: Oregon (degree in business and management, 1992).

TRANSACTIONS/CAREER NOTES: Signed as non-drafted free agent by New England Patriots (April 30, 1993). ... Released by Patriots (August 23, 1993). ... Re-signed by Patriots to practice squad (August 31, 1993). ... Activated (December 3, 1993). ... Re-signed by Patriots (August 20, 1994). ... Re-signed by Patriots to practice squad (August 30, 1994). ... Activated (October 15, 1994). ... Released by Patriots (October 19, 1994). ... Re-signed by Patriots to practice squad (October 19, 1994). ... Released by Patriots (November 23, 1994). ... Signed by Seattle Seahawks to practice squad (November 29, 1994). ... Activated (December 11, 1994). ... Granted free agency (February 13, 1998). ... Re-signed by Seahawks (February 27, 1998). ... Released by Seahawks (November 2, 1998). ... Signed by Atlanta Falcons (November 11, 1998). ... Granted unconditional free agency (February 12, 1999). ... Re-signed by Falcons (March 8, 1999).

CHAMPIONSHIP GAME EXPERIENCE: Played in NFC championship game (1998 season). ... Played in Super Bowl XXXIII (1998 season).

RECORDS: Shares NFL single-game record for most combined kick returns—13 (December 5, 1993, at Pittsburgh).

PRO STATISTICS: 1993—Recovered one fumble. 1997—Recovered two fumbles. 1998—Recovered one fumble.

SINGLE GAME HIGHS (regular season): Receptions—3 (December 19, 1999, vs. Tennessee); yards—63 (September 12, 1999, vs. Minnesota); and touchdown receptions—0.

Year Team			RECEIVING				PUNT RETURNS				KICKOFF RETURNS				TOTALS			
	G	GS	No.	Yds.	Avg.	TD	No.	Yds.	Avg.	TD	No.	Yds.	Avg.	TD	TD	2pt.	Pts.	Fum.
1993—New England NFL	5	0	0	0	0.0	0	23	201	8.7	0	6	90	15.0	0	0	0	0	2
1994—New England NFL	1	0	1	11	11.0	0	3	26	8.7	0	0	0	0.0	0	0	0	0	1
—Seattle NFL	1	0	0	0	0.0	0	0	0	0.0	0	0	0	0.0	0	0	0	0	0
1995—Seattle NFL	13	0	0	0	0.0	0	3	23	7.7	0	1	29	29.0	0	0	0	0	0

H

1996—Seattle NFL	15	0	2	26	13.0	0	19	194	10.2	0	12	240	20.0	0	0	0	0	0
1997—Seattle NFL	13	0	4	81	20.3	0	21	144	6.9	0	14	318	22.7	0	0	0	0	4
1998—Seattle NFL	2	0	0	0	0.0	0	1	-5	-5.0	0	0	0	0.0	0	0	0	0	1
—Atlanta NFL	6	0	1	14	14.0	0	1	-1	-1.0	0	1	16	16.0	0	0	0	0	1
1999—Atlanta NFL	13	0	10	164	16.4	0	0	0	0.0	0	1	5	5.0	0	0	0	0	1
Pro totals (7 years)	69	0	18	296	16.4	0	71	582	8.2	0	35	698	19.9	0	0	0	0	10

HARRIS, SEAN — LB — BEARS

PERSONAL: Born February 25, 1972, in Tucson, Ariz. ... 6-3/252. ... Full name: Sean Eugene Harris.
HIGH SCHOOL: Tucson (Ariz.) High Magnet School.
COLLEGE: Arizona.
TRANSACTIONS/CAREER NOTES: Selected by Chicago Bears in third round (83rd pick overall) of 1995 NFL draft. ... Signed by Bears (July 18, 1995). ... Granted free agency (February 13, 1998). ... Re-signed by Bears (May 12, 1998). ... Granted unconditional free agency (February 12, 1999). ... Re-signed by Bears (March 11, 1999).
PLAYING EXPERIENCE: Chicago NFL, 1995-1999. ... Games/Games started: 1995 (11/0), 1996 (15/0), 1997 (11/1), 1998 (16/14), 1999 (14/10). Total: 67/25.
PRO STATISTICS: 1998—Intercepted one pass for no yards and credited with one sack. 1999—Intercepted one pass for no yards and recovered two fumbles, including one in end zone for a touchdown.

HARRIS, WALT — CB — BEARS

PERSONAL: Born August 10, 1974, in La Grange, Ga. ... 5-11/195. ... Full name: Walter Lee Harris.
HIGH SCHOOL: La Grange (Ga.).
COLLEGE: Mississippi State.
TRANSACTIONS/CAREER NOTES: Selected by Chicago Bears in first round (13th pick overall) of 1996 NFL draft. ... Signed by Bears (July 11, 1996). ... On injured reserve with knee injury (December 22, 1998-remainder of season).
PRO STATISTICS: 1996—Recovered two fumbles for eight yards. 1997—Fumbled once and recovered one fumble. 1998—Recovered one fumble. 1999—Credited with one sack and recovered one fumble.

			INTERCEPTIONS			
Year Team	G	GS	No.	Yds.	Avg.	TD
1996—Chicago NFL	15	13	2	0	0.0	0
1997—Chicago NFL	16	16	5	30	6.0	0
1998—Chicago NFL	14	14	4	41	10.3	1
1999—Chicago NFL	15	15	1	-1	-1.0	0
Pro totals (4 years)	60	58	12	70	5.8	1

HARRISON, MARTIN — DE

PERSONAL: Born September 20, 1967, in Livermore, Calif. ... 6-5/285. ... Full name: Martin Allen Harrison.
HIGH SCHOOL: Newport (Bellevue, Wash.).
COLLEGE: Washington (degree in sociology, 1990).
TRANSACTIONS/CAREER NOTES: Selected by San Francisco 49ers in 10th round (276th pick overall) of 1990 NFL draft. ... Signed by 49ers (July 18, 1990). ... On injured reserve with shoulder injury (September 18-December 13, 1990). ... Released by 49ers (December 13, 1990). ... Re-signed by 49ers (1991). ... Released by 49ers (August 26, 1991). ... Re-signed by 49ers to practice squad (August 28, 1991). ... Granted free agency after 1991 season. ... Re-signed by 49ers (March 25, 1992). ... Released by 49ers (August 31, 1992). ... Re-signed by 49ers (September 1, 1992). ... Granted unconditional free agency (February 17, 1994). ... Re-signed by 49ers (June 1, 1994). ... Released by 49ers (August 27, 1994). ... Signed by Minnesota Vikings (September 12, 1994). ... Granted unconditional free agency (February 17, 1995). ... Re-signed by Vikings (March 27, 1995). ... Granted unconditional free agency (February 16, 1996). ... Re-signed by Vikings (March 20, 1996). ... Granted unconditional free agency (February 14, 1997). ... Signed by Seattle Seahawks (June 9, 1997). ... Granted unconditional free agency (February 13, 1998). ... Signed by Denver Broncos (May 28, 1998). ... Released by Broncos (August 19, 1998). ... Signed by Chicago Bears (August 21, 1998). ... Released by Bears (August 30, 1998). ... Signed by Vikings (March 11, 1999). ... Released by Vikings (September 1, 1999). ... Re-signed by Vikings (September 6, 1999). ... Released by Vikings (November 4, 1999).
CHAMPIONSHIP GAME EXPERIENCE: Played in NFC championship game (1992 season). ... Member of 49ers for NFC championship game (1993 season); inactive.
PRO STATISTICS: 1995—Intercepted one pass for 15 yards. 1997—Recovered one fumble.

Year Team	G	GS	SACKS
1990—San Francisco NFL	2	0	0.0
1991—San Francisco NFL	Did not play.		
1992—San Francisco NFL	16	1	3.5
1993—San Francisco NFL	11	1	6.0
1994—Minnesota NFL	13	0	0.0
1995—Minnesota NFL	11	0	4.5
1996—Minnesota NFL	16	8	7.0
1997—Seattle NFL	8	0	0.0
1998—	Did not play.		
1999—Minnesota NFL	4	0	0.0
Pro totals (8 years)	81	10	21.0

HARRISON, MARVIN — WR — COLTS

H

PERSONAL: Born August 25, 1972, in Philadelphia. ... 6-0/181. ... Full name: Marvin Daniel Harrison.
HIGH SCHOOL: Roman Catholic (Philadelphia).
COLLEGE: Syracuse.

TRANSACTIONS/CAREER NOTES: Selected by Indianapolis Colts in first round (19th pick overall) of 1996 NFL draft. ... Signed by Colts (July 8, 1996). ... On injured reserve with shoulder injury (December 2, 1998-remainder of season).

HONORS: Named kick returner on THE SPORTING NEWS All-America first team (1995). ... Named wide receiver on THE SPORTING NEWS NFL All-Pro team (1999). ... Played in Pro Bowl (1999 season).

PRO STATISTICS: 1996—Rushed three times for 15 yards. 1997—Recovered one fumble for five yards. 1999—Rushed once for four yards and recovered one fumble.

SINGLE GAME HIGHS (regular season): Receptions—14 (December 26, 1999, vs. Cleveland); yards—196 (September 26, 1999, vs. San Diego); and touchdown receptions—3 (September 19, 1999, vs. New England).

STATISTICAL PLATEAUS: 100-yard receiving games: 1996 (2), 1998 (2), 1999 (9). Total: 13.

				RECEIVING				PUNT RETURNS				TOTALS		
Year Team	G	GS	No.	Yds.	Avg.	TD	No.	Yds.	Avg.	TD	TD	2pt.	Pts.	Fum.
1996—Indianapolis NFL	16	15	64	836	13.1	8	18	177	9.8	0	8	0	48	1
1997—Indianapolis NFL	16	15	73	866	11.9	6	0	0	0.0	0	6	2	40	2
1998—Indianapolis NFL	12	12	59	776	13.2	7	0	0	0.0	0	7	1	44	0
1999—Indianapolis NFL	16	16	115	*1663	14.5	§12	0	0	0.0	0	12	†1	74	2
Pro totals (4 years)	60	58	311	4141	13.3	33	18	177	9.8	0	33	4	206	5

HARRISON, NOLAN   DE

PERSONAL: Born January 25, 1969, in Chicago. ... 6-5/291. ... Full name: Nolan Harrison III.

HIGH SCHOOL: Homewood-Flossmoor (Flossmoor, Ill.).

COLLEGE: Indiana (degree in criminal justice, 1991).

TRANSACTIONS/CAREER NOTES: Selected by Los Angeles Raiders in sixth round (146th pick overall) of 1991 NFL draft. ... Signed by Raiders (1991). ... Raiders franchise moved to Oakland (July 21, 1995). ... Granted unconditional free agency (February 16, 1996). ... Signed by Pittsburgh Steelers (May 20, 1997). ... On injured reserve with chest injury (December 15, 1999-remainder of season). ... Granted unconditional free agency (February 11, 2000).

CHAMPIONSHIP GAME EXPERIENCE: Played in AFC championship game (1997 season).

PRO STATISTICS: 1992—Credited with a safety. 1993—Recovered one fumble for five yards. 1994—Recovered two fumbles. 1999—Recovered one fumble.

Year Team	G	GS	SACKS
1991—Los Angeles Raiders NFL	14	3	1.0
1992—Los Angeles Raiders NFL	14	14	2.5
1993—Los Angeles Raiders NFL	16	14	3.0
1994—Los Angeles Raiders NFL	16	16	5.0
1995—Oakland NFL	7	6	0.0
1996—Oakland NFL	15	2	2.0
1997—Pittsburgh NFL	16	16	4.0
1998—Pittsburgh NFL	9	7	3.5
1999—Pittsburgh NFL	5	3	0.0
Pro totals (9 years)	112	81	21.0

HARRISON, RODNEY   S   CHARGERS

PERSONAL: Born December 15, 1972, in Markham, Ill. ... 6-1/207. ... Full name: Rodney Scott Harrison.

HIGH SCHOOL: Marian Catholic (Chicago Heights, Ill.).

COLLEGE: Western Illinois.

TRANSACTIONS/CAREER NOTES: Selected after junior season by San Diego Chargers in fifth round (145th pick overall) of 1994 NFL draft. ... Signed by Chargers (June 29, 1994).

CHAMPIONSHIP GAME EXPERIENCE: Played in AFC championship game (1994 season). ... Played in Super Bowl XXIX (1994 season).

HONORS: Named safety on THE SPORTING NEWS NFL All-Pro team (1998). ... Played in Pro Bowl (1998 season).

PRO STATISTICS: 1994—Recovered one fumble. 1996—Returned one kickoff for 10 yards, fumbled once and recovered two fumbles for four yards. 1997—Returned one punt for no yards, returned one kickoff for 40 yards and a touchdown and recovered three fumbles, including one in the end zone for a touchdown.

			INTERCEPTIONS				SACKS
Year Team	G	GS	No.	Yds.	Avg.	TD	No.
1994—San Diego NFL	15	0	0	0	0.0	0	0.0
1995—San Diego NFL	11	0	5	22	4.4	0	0.0
1996—San Diego NFL	16	16	5	56	11.2	0	1.0
1997—San Diego NFL	16	16	2	75	37.5	1	4.0
1998—San Diego NFL	16	16	3	42	14.0	0	4.0
1999—San Diego NFL	6	6	1	0	0.0	0	1.0
Pro totals (6 years)	80	54	16	195	12.2	1	10.0

HARTINGS, JEFF   G   LIONS

PERSONAL: Born September 7, 1972, in St. Henry, Ohio. ... 6-3/295. ... Full name: Jeffrey Allen Hartings.

HIGH SCHOOL: St. Henry (Ohio).

COLLEGE: Penn State.

TRANSACTIONS/CAREER NOTES: Selected by Detroit Lions in first round (23rd pick overall) of 1996 NFL draft. ... Signed by Lions (September 27, 1996).

PLAYING EXPERIENCE: Detroit NFL, 1996-1999. ... Games/Games started: 1996 (11/10), 1997 (16/16), 1998 (13/13), 1999 (16/16). Total: 56/55.

HONORS: Named offensive lineman on THE SPORTING NEWS college All-America second team (1994). ... Named offensive lineman on THE SPORTING NEWS college All-America first team (1995).

PRO STATISTICS: 1996—Recovered one fumble. 1999—Recovered two fumbles for one yard.

H

HARVEY, RICHARD   LB

PERSONAL: Born September 11, 1966, in Pascagoula, Miss. ... 6-1/235. ... Full name: Richard Clemont Harvey. ... Son of Richard Harvey Sr., defensive back with Philadelphia Eagles (1970) and New Orleans Saints (1971).
HIGH SCHOOL: Pascagoula (Miss.).
COLLEGE: Tulane.
TRANSACTIONS/CAREER NOTES: Selected by Buffalo Bills in 11th round (305th pick overall) of 1989 NFL draft. ... Signed by Bills for 1989 season. ... On injured reserve with shoulder injury (September 4, 1989-entire season). ... Granted unconditional free agency (February 1, 1990). ... Signed by New England Patriots (March 23, 1990). ... Released by Patriots (September 2, 1991). ... Signed by Bills (February 3, 1992). ... Selected by Ohio Glory in first round of 1992 World League supplemental draft. ... Granted unconditional free agency (February 17, 1994). ... Signed by Denver Broncos (May 9, 1994). ... Granted unconditional free agency (February 17, 1995). ... Signed by New Orleans Saints (April 3, 1995). ... Granted unconditional free agency (February 14, 1997). ... Re-signed by Saints (May 1, 1997). ... On injured reserve with foot injury (December 20, 1997-remainder of season). ... Granted unconditional free agency (February 13, 1998). ... Re-signed by Saints (March 2, 1998). ... Released by Saints (August 24, 1998). ... Signed by Oakland Raiders (August 26, 1998). ... Released by Raiders (February 10, 2000).
CHAMPIONSHIP GAME EXPERIENCE: Member of Bills for AFC championship game (1992 season); inactive. ... Member of Bills for Super Bowl XXVII (1992 season); inactive. ... Played in AFC championship game (1993 season). ... Played in Super Bowl XXVIII (1993 season).
PRO STATISTICS: 1992—Recovered one fumble. 1994—Recovered one fumble. 1997—Intercepted one pass for seven yards and recovered one fumble. 1998—Intercepted one pass for two yards.

Year Team	G	GS	SACKS
1989—Buffalo NFL	Did not play.		
1990—New England NFL	16	9	0.0
1991—New England NFL	1	0	0.0
1992—Buffalo NFL	12	0	0.0
1993—Buffalo NFL	15	0	0.0
1994—Denver NFL	16	1	0.0
1995—New Orleans NFL	16	14	2.0
1996—New Orleans NFL	14	7	2.0
1997—New Orleans NFL	14	13	3.0
1998—Oakland NFL	16	16	4.0
1999—Oakland NFL	15	15	2.0
Pro totals (10 years)	135	75	13.0

HASSELBACH, HARALD   DE   BRONCOS

PERSONAL: Born September 22, 1967, in Amsterdam, Holland. ... 6-6/285. ... Name pronounced HASS-el-back.
HIGH SCHOOL: South Delta (Delta, B.C.).
COLLEGE: Washington.
TRANSACTIONS/CAREER NOTES: Selected by Calgary Stampeders in fifth round (34th pick overall) of 1989 CFL draft. ... Granted free agency after 1993 season. ... Signed as non-drafted free agent by Denver Broncos (April 11, 1994).
CHAMPIONSHIP GAME EXPERIENCE: Played in Grey Cup (1992). ... Played in AFC championship game (1997 and 1998 seasons). ... Member of Super Bowl championship team (1997 and 1998 seasons).
PRO STATISTICS: CFL: 1992—Recovered two fumbles. 1993—Recovered four fumbles for 16 yards, intercepted one pass for no yards and fumbled once. NFL: 1995—Recovered four fumbles.

Year Team	G	GS	SACKS
1990—Calgary CFL	3	...	0.0
1991—Calgary CFL	11	...	3.0
1992—Calgary CFL	18	...	4.0
1993—Calgary CFL	18	...	7.0
1994—Denver NFL	16	9	2.0
1995—Denver NFL	16	10	4.0
1996—Denver NFL	16	1	2.0
1997—Denver NFL	16	3	1.5
1998—Denver NFL	16	3	3.0
1999—Denver NFL	16	2	2.5
CFL totals (4 years)	50	...	14.0
NFL totals (6 years)	96	28	15.0
Pro totals (10 years)	146	...	29.0

HASSELBECK, MATT   QB   PACKERS

PERSONAL: Born September 25, 1975, in Boulder, Colo. ... 6-4/220. ... Full name: Matthew Michael Hasselbeck. ... Son of Don Hasselbeck, tight end with New England Patriots (1977-85).
HIGH SCHOOL: Westwood (Mass.).
COLLEGE: Boston College (degree in marketing and finance, 1997).
TRANSACTIONS/CAREER NOTES: Selected by Green Bay Packers in sixth round (187th pick overall) of 1998 NFL draft. ... Signed by Packers (July 17, 1998). ... Released by Packers (September 3, 1998). ... Re-signed by Packers to practice squad (September 5, 1998).
PRO STATISTICS: 1999—Fumbled once and recovered one fumble for minus 16 yards.
SINGLE GAME HIGHS (regular season): Attempts—6 (November 1, 1999, vs. Seattle); completions—2 (November 1, 1999, vs. Seattle); passing yards—32 (November 1, 1999, vs. Seattle); and touchdown passes—1 (December 20, 1999, vs. Minnesota).

			PASSING							RUSHING				TOTALS		
Year Team	G	GS	Att.	Cmp.	Pct.	Yds.	TD	Int.	Avg.	Rat.	Att.	Yds.	Avg.	TD	TD	2pt.	Pts.
1999—Green Bay NFL	16	0	10	3	30.0	41	1	0	4.10	77.5	6	15	2.5	0	0	0	0

H

HASTINGS, ANDRE   WR

PERSONAL: Born November 7, 1970, in Atlanta. ... 6-1/190. ... Full name: Andre Orlando Hastings.
HIGH SCHOOL: Morrow (Ga.).
COLLEGE: Georgia.
TRANSACTIONS/CAREER NOTES: Selected after junior season by Pittsburgh Steelers in third round (76th pick overall) of 1993 NFL draft. ... Signed by Steelers (July 18, 1993). ... Granted free agency (February 16, 1996). ... Re-signed by Steelers (August 9, 1996). ... Granted unconditional free agency (February 14, 1997). ... Signed by New Orleans Saints (May 28, 1997). ... Released by Saints (February 10, 1998). ... Re-signed by Saints (March 6, 1998). ... Released by Saints (April 24, 2000).
CHAMPIONSHIP GAME EXPERIENCE: Played in AFC championship game (1994 and 1995 seasons). ... Played in Super Bowl XXX (1995 season).
PRO STATISTICS: 1996—Recovered one fumble. 1998—Recovered one fumble.
SINGLE GAME HIGHS (regular season): Receptions—10 (September 18, 1995, vs. Miami); yards—122 (December 6, 1998, vs. Dallas); and touchdown receptions—2 (December 1, 1996, vs. Baltimore).
STATISTICAL PLATEAUS: 100-yard receiving games: 1997 (1), 1998 (1), 1999 (1). Total: 3.

			RUSHING				RECEIVING				PUNT RETURNS				KICKOFF RETURNS				TOTALS		
Year Team	G	GS	Att.	Yds.	Avg.	TD	No.	Yds.	Avg.	TD	No.	Yds.	Avg.	TD	No.	Yds.	Avg.	TD	TD	2pt.	Pts.
1993—Pittsburgh NFL....	6	0	0	0	0.0	0	3	44	14.7	0	0	0	0.0	0	12	177	14.8	0	0	0	0
1994—Pittsburgh NFL....	16	8	0	0	0.0	0	20	281	14.1	2	2	15	7.5	0	0	0	0.0	0	2	0	12
1995—Pittsburgh NFL....	16	0	1	14	14.0	0	48	502	10.5	1	48	474	9.9	†1	0	0	0.0	0	2	0	12
1996—Pittsburgh NFL....	16	10	4	71	17.8	0	72	739	10.3	6	37	242	6.5	0	1	42	42.0	0	6	0	36
1997—New Orleans NFL	16	16	4	35	8.8	0	48	722	15.0	5	1	-2	-2.0	0	0	0	0.0	0	5	1	32
1998—New Orleans NFL	16	12	3	32	10.7	0	35	455	13.0	3	22	307	14.0	0	1	16	16.0	0	3	0	18
1999—New Orleans NFL	15	5	1	4	4.0	0	40	564	14.1	1	0	0	0.0	0	0	0	0.0	0	1	0	6
Pro totals (7 years)........	101	51	13	156	12.0	0	266	3307	12.4	18	110	1036	9.4	1	14	235	16.8	0	19	1	116

HASTY, JAMES   CB   CHIEFS

PERSONAL: Born May 23, 1965, in Seattle. ... 6-0/213. ... Full name: James Edward Hasty.
HIGH SCHOOL: Franklin (Seattle).
COLLEGE: Central Washington, then Washington State (degree in communications, 1988).
TRANSACTIONS/CAREER NOTES: Selected by New York Jets in third round (74th pick overall) of 1988 NFL draft. ... Signed by Jets (July 12, 1988). ... Designated by Jets as transition player (February 25, 1993). ... Tendered offer sheet by Cincinnati Bengals (April 29, 1993). ... Offer matched by Jets (May 4, 1993). ... Granted unconditional free agency (February 17, 1995). ... Signed by Kansas City Chiefs (March 29, 1995). ... On reserve/did not report list (July 20-August 3, 1997). ... Granted unconditional free agency (February 13, 1998). ... Re-signed by Chiefs (February 17, 1998).
HONORS: Played in Pro Bowl (1997 and 1999 seasons).
PRO STATISTICS: 1988—Recovered three fumbles for 35 yards. 1989—Fumbled once and recovered two fumbles for two yards. 1990—Returned one punt for no yards, fumbled once and recovered three fumbles. 1991—Recovered four fumbles for seven yards. 1992—Recovered two fumbles. 1993—Recovered two fumbles for 28 yards. 1994—Recovered two fumbles. 1995—Recovered one fumble for 20 yards. 1996—Recovered one fumble for 80 yards and a touchdown. 1997—Recovered one fumble. 1998—Recovered one fumble.

			INTERCEPTIONS				SACKS
Year Team	G	GS	No.	Yds.	Avg.	TD	No.
1988—New York Jets NFL................	15	15	5	20	4.0	0	1.0
1989—New York Jets NFL................	16	16	5	62	12.4	1	0.0
1990—New York Jets NFL................	16	16	2	0	0.0	0	0.0
1991—New York Jets NFL................	16	16	3	39	13.0	0	0.0
1992—New York Jets NFL................	16	16	2	18	9.0	0	0.0
1993—New York Jets NFL................	16	16	2	22	11.0	0	0.0
1994—New York Jets NFL................	16	16	5	90	18.0	0	3.0
1995—Kansas City NFL....................	16	16	3	89	29.7	▲1	0.0
1996—Kansas City NFL....................	15	14	0	0	0.0	0	1.0
1997—Kansas City NFL....................	16	15	3	22	7.3	0	2.0
1998—Kansas City NFL....................	16	14	4	42	10.5	0	1.0
1999—Kansas City NFL....................	15	15	†7	98	14.0	†2	1.0
Pro totals (12 years)......................	189	185	41	502	12.2	4	9.0

HATCHETTE, MATTHEW   WR   VIKINGS

PERSONAL: Born May 1, 1974, in Cleveland. ... 6-2/201. ... Full name: Matthew Isaac Hatchette.
HIGH SCHOOL: Jefferson (Delphos, Ohio).
COLLEGE: Mercyhurst College (Pa.), then Langston University (Okla.).
TRANSACTIONS/CAREER NOTES: Selected by Minnesota Vikings in seventh round (235th pick overall) of 1997 NFL draft. ... Signed by Vikings (June 20, 1997). ... Granted free agency (February 11, 2000). ... Re-signed by Vikings (April 11, 2000).
CHAMPIONSHIP GAME EXPERIENCE: Played in NFC championship game (1998 season).
SINGLE GAME HIGHS (regular season): Receptions—6 (December 13, 1998, vs. Baltimore); yards—95 (December 13, 1998, vs. Baltimore); and touchdown receptions—1 (December 12, 1999, vs. Kansas City).

			RECEIVING				TOTALS			
Year Team	G	GS	No.	Yds.	Avg.	TD	TD	2pt.	Pts.	Fum.
1997—Minnesota NFL	16	0	3	54	18.0	0	0	0	0	0
1998—Minnesota NFL	5	0	15	216	14.4	0	0	0	0	0
1999—Minnesota NFL	13	0	9	180	20.0	2	2	0	12	0
Pro totals (3 years)	34	0	27	450	16.7	2	2	0	12	0

H

HAUCK, TIM   S

PERSONAL: Born December 20, 1966, in Butte, Mont. ... 5-10/187. ... Full name: Timothy Christian Hauck. ... Name pronounced HOWK.
HIGH SCHOOL: Sweet Grass County (Big Timber, Mont.).
COLLEGE: Pacific (Ore.), then Montana.
TRANSACTIONS/CAREER NOTES: Signed as non-drafted free agent by New England Patriots (May 1, 1990). ... Released by Patriots (August 26, 1990). ... Re-signed by Patriots to practice squad (October 1, 1990). ... Activated (October 27, 1990). ... Granted unconditional free agency (February 1, 1991). ... Signed by Green Bay Packers (April 1, 1991). ... Granted unconditional free agency (February 1-April 1, 1992). ... Re-signed by Packers for 1992 season. ... Granted free agency (March 1, 1993). ... Re-signed by Packers (July 13, 1993). ... Granted unconditional free agency (February 17, 1994). ... Re-signed by Packers (July 20, 1994). ... Granted unconditional free agency (February 17, 1995). ... Signed by Denver Broncos (March 6, 1995). ... Granted unconditional free agency (February 14, 1997). ... Signed by Seattle Seahawks (June 2, 1997). ... Granted unconditional free agency (February 13, 1998). ... Signed by Indianapolis Colts (July 26, 1998). ... Granted unconditional free agency (February 12, 1999). ... Signed by Philadelphia Eagles (April 20, 1999). ... Granted unconditional free agency (February 11, 2000).
PLAYING EXPERIENCE: New England NFL, 1990; Green Bay NFL, 1991-1994; Denver NFL, 1995 and 1996; Seattle NFL, 1997; Indianapolis NFL, 1998; Philadelphia NFL, 1999. ... Games/Games started: 1990 (10/0), 1991 (16/0), 1992 (16/0), 1993 (13/0), 1994 (13/3), 1995 (16/0), 1996 (16/0), 1997 (16/0), 1998 (16/7), 1999 (16/15). Total: 148/25.
PRO STATISTICS: 1991—Recovered one fumble. 1992—Returned one punt for two yards. 1993—Recovered one fumble. 1997—Recovered one fumble for eight yards. 1999—Intercepted one pass for two yards and recovered one fumble.

HAWKINS, ARTRELL   CB   BENGALS

PERSONAL: Born November 24, 1975, in Johnstown, Pa. ... 5-10/190. ... Cousin of Carlton Haselrig, guard with Pittsburgh Steelers (1990-93) and New York Jets (1995).
HIGH SCHOOL: Bishop McCort (Johnstown, Pa.).
COLLEGE: Cincinnati.
TRANSACTIONS/CAREER NOTES: Selected by Cincinnati Bengals in second round (43rd pick overall) of 1998 NFL draft. ... Signed by Bengals (May 14, 1998).
PRO STATISTICS: 1998—Credited with one sack and recovered one fumble for 25 yards. 1999—Recovered one fumble.

			INTERCEPTIONS			
Year Team	G	GS	No.	Yds.	Avg.	TD
1998—Cincinnati NFL	16	16	3	21	7.0	0
1999—Cincinnati NFL	14	13	0	0	0.0	0
Pro totals (2 years)	30	29	3	21	7.0	0

HAWKINS, COURTNEY   WR

PERSONAL: Born December 12, 1969, in Flint, Mich. ... 5-9/190. ... Full name: Courtney Tyrone Hawkins Jr. ... Cousin of Roy Marble, guard/forward with Atlanta Hawks (1989-90) and Denver Nuggets (1993-94).
HIGH SCHOOL: Beecher (Flint, Mich.).
COLLEGE: Michigan State.
TRANSACTIONS/CAREER NOTES: Selected by Tampa Bay Buccaneers in second round (44th pick overall) of 1992 NFL draft. ... Signed by Buccaneers (July 16, 1992). ... On injured reserve with knee injury (December 16, 1994-remainder of season). ... Granted free agency (February 17, 1995). ... Re-signed by Buccaneers (July 21, 1995). ... Granted unconditional free agency (February 16, 1996). ... Re-signed by Buccaneers (April 27, 1996). ... Granted free agency (February 14, 1997). ... Signed by Pittsburgh Steelers (June 2, 1997). ... Granted unconditional free agency (February 11, 2000).
CHAMPIONSHIP GAME EXPERIENCE: Played in AFC championship game (1997 season).
PRO STATISTICS: 1992—Returned nine kickoffs for 118 yards and recovered one fumble. 1995—Rushed four times for five yards. 1996—Rushed once for minus 13 yards. 1998—Rushed 10 times for 41 yards and recovered one fumble.
SINGLE GAME HIGHS (regular season): Receptions—14 (November 1, 1998, vs. Tennessee); yards—147 (November 1, 1998, vs. Tennessee); and touchdown receptions—2 (November 20, 1994, vs. Seattle).
STATISTICAL PLATEAUS: 100-yard receiving games: 1992 (1), 1993 (2), 1996 (1), 1998 (1). Total: 5.

			RECEIVING				PUNT RETURNS				TOTALS			
Year Team	G	GS	No.	Yds.	Avg.	TD	No.	Yds.	Avg.	TD	TD	2pt.	Pts.	Fum.
1992—Tampa Bay NFL	16	5	20	336	16.8	2	13	53	4.1	0	2	0	12	2
1993—Tampa Bay NFL	16	12	62	933	15.0	5	15	166	11.1	0	5	0	30	2
1994—Tampa Bay NFL	13	12	37	438	11.8	5	5	28	5.6	0	5	0	30	0
1995—Tampa Bay NFL	16	3	41	493	12.0	0	0	0	0.0	0	0	0	0	1
1996—Tampa Bay NFL	16	16	46	544	11.8	1	1	-1	-1.0	0	1	0	6	1
1997—Pittsburgh NFL	15	3	45	555	12.3	3	4	68	17.0	0	3	0	18	1
1998—Pittsburgh NFL	15	14	66	751	11.4	1	15	175	11.7	0	1	0	6	1
1999—Pittsburgh NFL	11	11	30	285	9.5	0	11	49	4.5	0	0	0	0	0
Pro totals (8 years)	118	76	347	4335	12.5	17	64	538	8.4	0	17	0	102	8

HAWTHORNE, DUANE   CB   COWBOYS

PERSONAL: Born August 26, 1976, in St. Louis. ... 5-10/175. ... Name pronounced DUH-wann.
HIGH SCHOOL: Ladue (Mo.).
COLLEGE: Northern Illinois.
TRANSACTIONS/CAREER NOTES: Signed as non-drafted free agent by Dallas Cowboys (April 23, 1999). ... Assigned by Cowboys to Scottish Claymores in 2000 NFL Europe enhancement allocation program (February 18, 2000).

			INTERCEPTIONS			
Year Team	G	GS	No.	Yds.	Avg.	TD
1999—Dallas NFL	13	0	3	-2	-0.7	0

H

HAYES, CHRIS   S   JETS

PERSONAL: Born May 7, 1972, in San Bernardino, Calif. ... 6-0/206.
HIGH SCHOOL: San Gorgonio (San Bernardino, Calif.).
COLLEGE: Washington State.
TRANSACTIONS/CAREER NOTES: Selected by New York Jets in seventh round (210th pick overall) of 1996 NFL draft. ... Signed by Jets (June 26, 1996). ... Released by Jets (August 19, 1996). ... Signed by Washington Redskins to practice squad (September 11, 1996). ... Released by Redskins (October 2, 1996). ... Signed by Green Bay Packers to practice squad (October 4, 1996). ... Activated (December 9, 1996). ... Traded by Packers to Jets for CB Carl Greenwood (June 5, 1997). ... Granted free agency (February 11, 2000). ... Re-signed by Jets (May 8, 2000).
PLAYING EXPERIENCE: Green Bay NFL, 1996; New York Jets NFL, 1997-1999. ... Games/Games started: 1996 (2/0), 1997 (16/0), 1998 (15/0), 1999 (15/0). Total: 48/0.
CHAMPIONSHIP GAME EXPERIENCE: Played in NFC championship game (1996 season). ... Member of Super Bowl championship team (1996 season). ... Played in AFC championship game (1998 season).

HAYES, DONALD   WR   PANTHERS

PERSONAL: Born July 13, 1975, in Madison, Wis. ... 6-4/208. ... Full name: Donald Ross Hayes Jr.
HIGH SCHOOL: Madison (Wis.) East.
COLLEGE: Wisconsin.
TRANSACTIONS/CAREER NOTES: Selected by Carolina Panthers in fourth round (106th pick overall) of 1998 NFL draft. ... Signed by Panthers (July 8, 1998).
SINGLE GAME HIGHS (regular season): Receptions—5 (November 28, 1999, vs. Atlanta); yards—133 (November 28, 1999, vs. Atlanta); and touchdown receptions—1 (December 5, 1999, vs. St. Louis).
STATISTICAL PLATEAUS: 100-yard receiving games: 1999 (1).

				RECEIVING		
Year Team	G	GS	No.	Yds.	Avg.	TD
1998—Carolina NFL	8	0	3	62	20.7	0
1999—Carolina NFL	13	1	11	270	24.5	2
Pro totals (2 years)	21	1	14	332	23.7	2

HEARST, GARRISON   RB   49ERS

PERSONAL: Born January 4, 1971, in Lincolnton, Ga. ... 5-11/215. ... Full name: Gerald Garrison Hearst.
HIGH SCHOOL: Lincoln County (Lincolnton, Ga.).
COLLEGE: Georgia.
TRANSACTIONS/CAREER NOTES: Selected after junior season by Phoenix Cardinals in first round (third pick overall) of 1993 NFL draft. ... Signed by Cardinals (August 28, 1993). ... On injured reserve with knee injury (November 4, 1993-remainder of season). ... Cardinals franchise renamed Arizona Cardinals for 1994 season. ... On physically unable to perform list with knee injury (August 23-October 13, 1994). ... Granted free agency (February 16, 1996). ... Re-signed by Cardinals (May 23, 1996). ... Claimed on waivers by Cincinnati Bengals (August 21, 1996). ... Granted unconditional free agency (February 14, 1997). ... Signed by San Francisco 49ers (March 7, 1997). ... On physically unable to perform list with leg injury (July 30, 1999-entire season).
CHAMPIONSHIP GAME EXPERIENCE: Played in NFC championship game (1997 season).
HONORS: Doak Walker Award winner (1992). ... Named running back on THE SPORTING NEWS college All-America first team (1992). ... Named to play in Pro Bowl (1998 season); replaced by Emmitt Smith due to injury.
PRO STATISTICS: 1993—Had only pass attempt intercepted. 1994—Completed only pass attempt for 10 yards and a touchdown. 1995—Attempted two passes with one completion for 16 yards and recovered two fumbles. 1996—Recovered one fumble. 1997—Recovered two fumbles. 1998—Recovered one fumble.
SINGLE GAME HIGHS (regular season): Attempts—28 (September 29, 1997, vs. Carolina); yards—198 (December 14, 1998, vs. Detroit); and rushing touchdowns—2 (September 6, 1998, vs. New York Jets).
STATISTICAL PLATEAUS: 100-yard rushing games: 1995 (3), 1997 (3), 1998 (6). Total: 12. ... 100-yard receiving games: 1998 (2).

			RUSHING				RECEIVING				TOTALS			
Year Team	G	GS	Att.	Yds.	Avg.	TD	No.	Yds.	Avg.	TD	TD	2pt.	Pts.	Fum.
1993—Phoenix NFL	6	5	76	264	3.5	1	6	18	3.0	0	1	0	6	2
1994—Arizona NFL	8	0	37	169	4.6	1	6	49	8.2	0	1	0	6	0
1995—Arizona NFL	16	15	284	1070	3.8	1	29	243	8.4	1	2	0	12	12
1996—Cincinnati NFL	16	12	225	847	3.8	0	12	131	10.9	1	1	1	8	1
1997—San Francisco NFL	13	13	234	1019	4.4	4	21	194	9.2	2	6	0	36	2
1998—San Francisco NFL	16	16	310	1570	‡5.1	7	39	535	13.7	2	9	1	56	4
1999—San Francisco NFL					Did not play.									
Pro totals (6 years)	75	61	1166	4939	4.2	14	113	1170	10.4	6	20	2	124	21

HEATH, RODNEY   CB   BENGALS

PERSONAL: Born October 29, 1974, in Cincinnati. ... 5-10/170. ... Full name: Rodney Larece Heath.
HIGH SCHOOL: Western Hills (Cincinnati).
COLLEGE: Minnesota (degree in sports studies).
TRANSACTIONS/CAREER NOTES: Signed as non-drafted free agent by Cincinnati Bengals (January 27, 1999).
PRO STATISTICS: 1999—Recovered two fumbles for minus four yards.

			INTERCEPTIONS				TOTALS			
Year Team	G	GS	No.	Yds.	Avg.	TD	TD	2pt.	Pts.	Fum.
1999—Cincinnati NFL	16	9	3	72	24.0	1	1	0	6	0

H

HECK, ANDY   OT   REDSKINS

PERSONAL: Born January 1, 1967, in Fargo, N.D. ... 6-6/298. ... Full name: Andrew Robert Heck.
HIGH SCHOOL: W.T. Woodson (Fairfax, Va.).
COLLEGE: Notre Dame (degree in American studies, 1989).
TRANSACTIONS/CAREER NOTES: Selected by Seattle Seahawks in first round (15th pick overall) of 1989 NFL draft. ... Signed by Seahawks (July 31, 1989). ... On injured reserve with ankle injury (October 21-November 20, 1992); on practice squad (November 18-20, 1992). ... Designated by Seahawks as transition player (February 25, 1993). ... Tendered offer sheet by Chicago Bears (February 21, 1994). ... Seahawks declined to match offer (March 1, 1994). ... Released by Bears (June 2, 1999). ... Signed by Washington Redskins (June 17, 1999). ... Granted unconditional free agency (February 11, 2000). ... Re-signed by Redskins (March 20, 2000).
PLAYING EXPERIENCE: Seattle NFL, 1989-1993; Chicago NFL, 1994-1998; Washington NFL, 1999. ... Games/Games started: 1989 (16/9), 1990 (16/16), 1991 (16/16), 1992 (13/13), 1993 (16/16), 1994 (14/14), 1995 (16/16), 1996 (16/16), 1997 (16/16), 1998 (14/14), 1999 (16/16). Total: 169/162.
HONORS: Named offensive tackle on THE SPORTING NEWS college All-America first team (1988).
PRO STATISTICS: 1989—Recovered one fumble. 1990—Recovered one fumble. 1993—Recovered two fumbles.

HEGAMIN, GEORGE   OT   BUCCANEERS

PERSONAL: Born February 14, 1973, in Camden, N.J. ... 6-7/331. ... Full name: George Russell Hegamin. ... Name pronounced HEG-a-min.
HIGH SCHOOL: Camden (N.J.).
COLLEGE: North Carolina State.
TRANSACTIONS/CAREER NOTES: Selected after junior season by Dallas Cowboys in third round (102nd pick overall) of 1994 NFL draft. ... Signed by Cowboys (July 15, 1994). ... Active for four games (1995); did not play. ... Assigned by Cowboys to Frankfurt Galaxy in 1996 World League enhancement allocation program (February 19, 1996). ... Granted unconditional free agency (February 13, 1998). ... Signed by Philadelphia Eagles (February 19, 1998). ... Released by Eagles (September 4, 1999). ... Signed by Tampa Bay Buccaneers (November 10, 1999).
PLAYING EXPERIENCE: Dallas NFL, 1994, 1996 and 1997; Frankfurt W.L., 1996, Philadelphia NFL, 1998; Tampa Bay NFL, 1999. ... Games/Games started: 1994 (2/0), W.L. 1996 (games played unavailable), NFL 1996 (16/1), 1997 (13/9), 1998 (16/6), 1999 (1/0). Total: 48/16.
CHAMPIONSHIP GAME EXPERIENCE: Member of Cowboys for NFC championship game (1994 season); inactive. ... Member of Cowboys for NFC championship game (1995 season); did not play. ... Member of Super Bowl championship team (1995 season). ... Played in NFC championship game (1999 season).
PRO STATISTICS: 1997—Recovered one fumble.

HEIDEN, STEVE   TE   CHARGERS

PERSONAL: Born September 21, 1976, in Rushford, Minn. ... 6-5/270. ... Full name: Steve Allen Heiden. ... Name pronounced HIGH-den.
HIGH SCHOOL: Rushford-Peterson (Rushford, Minn.).
COLLEGE: South Dakota State.
TRANSACTIONS/CAREER NOTES: Selected by San Diego Chargers in third round (69th pick overall) of 1999 NFL draft. ... Signed by Chargers (July 22, 1999).
PLAYING EXPERIENCE: San Diego NFL, 1999. ... Games/Games started: 1999 (11/0).

HEIMBURGER, CRAIG   G   PACKERS

PERSONAL: Born February 3, 1977, in Belleville, Ill. ... 6-2/318. ... Full name: Craig Andre Heimburger. ... Name pronounced HIME-burger.
HIGH SCHOOL: Belleville (Ill.) East.
COLLEGE: Missouri.
TRANSACTIONS/CAREER NOTES: Selected by Green Bay Packers in fifth round (163rd pick overall) of 1999 NFL draft. ... Signed by Packers (July 13, 1999). ... Released by Packers (September 5, 1999). ... Re-signed by Packers to practice squad (September 7, 1999). ... Activated (November 23, 1999). ... Assigned by Packers to Rhein Fire in 2000 NFL Europe enhancement allocation program (February 18, 2000).
PLAYING EXPERIENCE: Green Bay NFL, 1999. ... Games/Games started: 1999 (2/0).

HELLESTRAE, DALE   G/C

PERSONAL: Born July 11, 1962, in Phoenix. ... 6-5/291. ... Full name: Dale Robert Hellestrae. ... Name pronounced HELL-uh-stray.
HIGH SCHOOL: Saguaro (Scottsdale, Ariz.).
COLLEGE: Southern Methodist (degree in business administration).
TRANSACTIONS/CAREER NOTES: Selected by Houston Gamblers in 1985 USFL territorial draft. ... Selected by Buffalo Bills in fourth round (112th pick overall) of 1985 NFL draft. ... Signed by Bills (July 19, 1985). ... On injured reserve with broken thumb (October 4, 1985-remainder of season). ... On injured reserve with broken wrist (September 17-November 15, 1986). ... On injured reserve with hip injury (September 1, 1987-entire season). ... Granted unconditional free agency (February 1, 1989). ... Signed by Los Angeles Raiders (February 24, 1989). ... On injured reserve with broken leg (August 29, 1989-entire season). ... Traded by Raiders to Dallas Cowboys for seventh-round pick (traded to Chicago) in 1991 draft (August 20, 1990). ... Granted unconditional free agency (February 1-April 1, 1991). ... Re-signed by Cowboys for 1991 season. ... Granted unconditional free agency (February 1-April 1, 1992). ... Re-signed by Cowboys for 1992 season. ... Released by Cowboys (August 31, 1992). ... Re-signed by Cowboys (September 2, 1992). ... Granted unconditional free agency (March 1, 1993). ... Re-signed by Cowboys (June 2, 1993). ... Released by Cowboys (August 30, 1993). ... Re-signed by Cowboys (August 31, 1993). ... Granted unconditional free agency (February 17, 1994). ... Re-signed by Cowboys (July 14, 1994). ... Granted unconditional free agency (February 16, 1996). ... Re-signed by Cowboys (April 9, 1996). ... Granted unconditional free agency (February 13, 1998). ... Re-signed by Cowboys (April 7, 1998). ... Granted unconditional free agency (February 12, 1999). ... Re-signed by Cowboys (June 23, 1999). ... Granted unconditional free agency (February 11, 2000).
PLAYING EXPERIENCE: Buffalo NFL, 1985, 1986 and 1988; Dallas NFL, 1990-1999. ... Games/Games started: 1985 (4/0), 1986 (8/0), 1988 (16/2), 1990 (16/0), 1991 (16/0), 1992 (16/0), 1993 (16/0), 1994 (16/0), 1995 (16/0), 1996 (16/0), 1997 (16/0), 1998 (16/0), 1999 (16/0). Total: 188/2.

H

CHAMPIONSHIP GAME EXPERIENCE: Played in AFC championship game (1988 season). ... Played in NFC championship game (1992-1995 seasons). ... Member of Super Bowl championship team (1992, 1993 and 1995 seasons).
PRO STATISTICS: 1986—Fumbled once for minus 14 yards.

HEMSLEY, NATE — LB

PERSONAL: Born May 15, 1974, in Willingboro, N.J. ... 6-0/228. ... Full name: Nathaniel Richard Hemsley.
HIGH SCHOOL: Delran (N.J.).
COLLEGE: Syracuse.
TRANSACTIONS/CAREER NOTES: Signed as non-drafted free agent by Tennessee Oilers (April 23, 1997). ... Released by Oilers (August 13, 1997). ... Signed by Dallas Cowboys to practice squad (September 3, 1997). ... Activated (December 10, 1997). ... On injured reserve with ankle injury (October 5, 1998-remainder of season). ... Released by Cowboys (October 27, 1999).
PLAYING EXPERIENCE: Dallas NFL, 1997-1999. ... Games/Games started: 1997 (2/0), 1998 (3/0), 1999 (6/0). Total: 11/0.

HENDERSON, WILLIAM — FB — PACKERS

PERSONAL: Born February 19, 1971, in Richmond, Va. ... 6-1/250. ... Full name: William Terrelle Henderson.
HIGH SCHOOL: Thomas Dale (Chester, Va.).
COLLEGE: North Carolina.
TRANSACTIONS/CAREER NOTES: Selected by Green Bay Packers in third round (66th pick overall) of 1995 NFL draft. ... Signed by Packers (July 17, 1995). ... Granted free agency (February 13, 1998). ... Re-signed by Packers (June 15, 1998). ... Granted unconditional free agency (February 12, 1999). ... Re-signed by Packers (April 6, 1999).
CHAMPIONSHIP GAME EXPERIENCE: Played in NFC championship game (1995-1997 seasons). ... Member of Super Bowl championship team (1996 season). ... Played in Super Bowl XXXII (1997 season).
PRO STATISTICS: 1996—Returned two kickoffs for 38 yards. 1997—Recovered two fumbles. 1999—Returned two kickoffs for 23 yards.
SINGLE GAME HIGHS (regular season): Attempts—6 (September 7, 1997, vs. Philadelphia); yards—40 (September 9, 1996, vs. Philadelphia); and rushing touchdowns—1 (December 12, 1999, vs. Carolina).

| | | | RUSHING | | | | RECEIVING | | | | TOTALS | | |
Year Team	G	GS	Att.	Yds.	Avg.	TD	No.	Yds.	Avg.	TD	TD	2pt.	Pts.	Fum.
1995—Green Bay NFL	15	2	7	35	5.0	0	3	21	7.0	0	0	0	0	0
1996—Green Bay NFL	16	11	39	130	3.3	0	27	203	7.5	1	1	0	6	1
1997—Green Bay NFL	16	14	31	113	3.6	0	41	367	9.0	1	1	0	6	1
1998—Green Bay NFL	16	10	23	70	3.0	2	37	241	6.5	1	3	0	18	1
1999—Green Bay NFL	16	13	7	29	4.1	2	30	203	6.8	1	3	0	18	1
Pro totals (5 years)	79	50	107	377	3.5	4	138	1035	7.5	4	8	0	48	4

HENNINGS, CHAD — DT — COWBOYS

PERSONAL: Born October 20, 1965, in Elberton, Iowa. ... 6-6/291. ... Full name: Chad William Hennings.
HIGH SCHOOL: Benton Community (Van Horne, Iowa).
COLLEGE: Air Force (degree in management).
TRANSACTIONS/CAREER NOTES: Selected by Dallas Cowboys in 11th round (290th pick overall) of 1988 NFL draft. ... Signed by Cowboys (November 22, 1988). ... Served in military (1988-1992). ... Granted unconditional free agency (February 17, 1994). ... Re-signed by Cowboys for 1994 season.
CHAMPIONSHIP GAME EXPERIENCE: Played in NFC championship game (1992, 1994 and 1995 seasons). ... Member of Cowboys for NFC championship game (1993 season); inactive. ... Member of Super Bowl championship team (1992, 1993 and 1995 seasons).
HONORS: Outland Trophy winner (1987). ... Named defensive lineman on The Sporting News college All-America first team (1987).
PRO STATISTICS: 1993—Returned one kickoff for seven yards. 1994—Recovered one fumble. 1995—Recovered one fumble. 1996—Recovered one fumble. 1997—Recovered one fumble for four yards and a touchdown. 1998—Recovered one fumble.

Year Team	G	GS	SACKS
1992—Dallas NFL	8	0	0.0
1993—Dallas NFL	13	0	0.0
1994—Dallas NFL	16	0	7.0
1995—Dallas NFL	16	7	5.5
1996—Dallas NFL	15	15	4.5
1997—Dallas NFL	11	10	4.5
1998—Dallas NFL	16	16	1.0
1999—Dallas NFL	16	16	5.0
Pro totals (8 years)	111	64	27.5

HENRY, KEVIN — DE — STEELERS

PERSONAL: Born October 23, 1968, in Mound Bayou, Miss. ... 6-4/285. ... Full name: Kevin Lerell Henry. ... Name pronounced KEE-vin.
HIGH SCHOOL: John F. Kennedy (Mound Bayou, Miss.).
COLLEGE: Mississippi State.
TRANSACTIONS/CAREER NOTES: Selected by Pittsburgh Steelers in fourth round (108th pick overall) of 1993 NFL draft. ... Signed by Steelers (July 9, 1993). ... Granted free agency (February 16, 1996). ... Re-signed by Steelers (August 2, 1996). ... Granted unconditional free agency (February 14, 1997). ... Re-signed by Steelers (April 3, 1997).
CHAMPIONSHIP GAME EXPERIENCE: Played in AFC championship game (1994, 1995 and 1997 seasons). ... Played in Super Bowl XXX (1995 season).
PRO STATISTICS: 1993—Intercepted one pass for 10 yards. 1994—Recovered one fumble. 1996—Recovered one fumble for four yards. 1997—Intercepted one pass for 36 yards and recovered two fumbles.

H

Year Team	G	GS	SACKS
1993—Pittsburgh NFL	12	1	1.0
1994—Pittsburgh NFL	16	5	0.0
1995—Pittsburgh NFL	13	5	2.0
1996—Pittsburgh NFL	12	10	1.5
1997—Pittsburgh NFL	16	16	4.5
1998—Pittsburgh NFL	16	16	4.0
1999—Pittsburgh NFL	16	13	1.0
Pro totals (7 years)	101	66	14.0

HENTRICH, CRAIG   P   TITANS

PERSONAL: Born May 18, 1971, in Alton, Ill. ... 6-3/205. ... Full name: Craig Anthony Hentrich. ... Name pronounced HEN-trick.
HIGH SCHOOL: Marquette (Ottawa, Ill.).
COLLEGE: Notre Dame.
TRANSACTIONS/CAREER NOTES: Selected by New York Jets in eighth round (200th pick overall) of 1993 NFL draft. ... Signed by Jets (July 14, 1993). ... Released by Jets (August 24, 1993). ... Signed by Green Bay Packers to practice squad (September 7, 1993). ... Activated (January 14, 1994); did not play. ... Granted unconditional free agency (February 13, 1998). ... Signed by Tennessee Oilers (February 19, 1998). ... Oilers franchise renamed Tennessee Titans for 1999 season (December 26, 1998).
CHAMPIONSHIP GAME EXPERIENCE: Played in NFC championship game (1995-1997 seasons). ... Member of Super Bowl championship team (1996 season). ... Played in Super Bowl XXXII (1997 season) and Super Bowl XXXIV (1999 season). ... Played in AFC championship game (1999 season).
HONORS: Named punter on THE SPORTING NEWS NFL All-Pro team (1998). ... Played in Pro Bowl (1998 season).
PRO STATISTICS: 1996—Attempted one pass without a completion and recovered one fumble. 1998—Rushed once for minus one yard and completed only pass attempt for 13 yards. 1999—Rushed twice for one yard and recovered two fumbles.

				PUNTING						KICKING					
Year Team	G	No.	Yds.	Avg.	Net avg.	In. 20	Blk.	XPM	XPA	FGM	FGA	Lg.	50+	Pts.
1993—Green Bay NFL					Did not play.									
1994—Green Bay NFL	16	81	3351	41.4	35.5	24	0	0	0	0	0	0	0-0	0
1995—Green Bay NFL	16	65	2740	42.2	34.6	26	2	5	5	3	5	49	0-0	14
1996—Green Bay NFL	16	68	2886	42.4	36.2	28	0	0	0	0	0	0	0-0	0
1997—Green Bay NFL	16	75	3378	45.0	36.0	26	0	0	0	0	0	0	0-0	0
1998—Tennessee NFL	16	69	3258	*47.2	*39.2	18	0	0	0	0	1	0	0-0	0
1999—Tennessee NFL	16	90	3824	42.5	38.1	35	0	0	0	0	0	0	0-0	0
Pro totals (6 years)	96	448	19437	43.4	36.7	157	2	5	5	3	6	49	0-0	14

HERRING, KIM   S   RAVENS

PERSONAL: Born September 10, 1975, in Cleveland. ... 6-0/200. ... Full name: Kimani Masai Herring.
HIGH SCHOOL: Solon (Ohio).
COLLEGE: Penn State.
TRANSACTIONS/CAREER NOTES: Selected by Baltimore Ravens in second round (58th pick overall) of 1997 NFL draft. ... Signed by Ravens (July 18, 1997). ... On injured reserve with shoulder injury (December 2, 1998-remainder of season). ... Granted free agency (February 11, 2000). ... Re-signed by Ravens (April 18, 2000)
PLAYING EXPERIENCE: Baltimore NFL, 1997-1999. ... Games/Games started: 1997 (15/4), 1998 (7/7), 1999 (16/16). Total: 38/27.
HONORS: Named free safety on THE SPORTING NEWS college All-America first team (1996).
PRO STATISTICS: 1997—Credited with one sack and recovered one fumble. 1999—Recovered two fumbles.

HETHERINGTON, CHRIS   FB   PANTHERS

PERSONAL: Born November 27, 1972, in North Branford, Conn. ... 6-3/249. ... Full name: Christopher Raymond Hetherington.
HIGH SCHOOL: Avon (Conn.) Old Farms.
COLLEGE: Yale (degree in psychology).
TRANSACTIONS/CAREER NOTES: Signed as non-drafted free agent by Cincinnati Bengals (April 23, 1996). ... Released by Bengals (August 21, 1996). ... Re-signed by Bengals to practice squad (August 26, 1996). ... Signed by Indianapolis Colts off Bengals practice squad (October 22, 1996). ... Released by Colts (August 24, 1998). ... Re-signed by Colts (August 31, 1998). ... Released by Colts (February 12, 1999). ... Signed by Carolina Panthers (March 5, 1999). ... Granted unconditional free agency (February 11, 2000). ... Re-signed by Panthers (February 23, 2000).
PRO STATISTICS: 1999—Rushed twice for seven yards and recovered one fumble.
SINGLE GAME HIGHS (regular season): Attempts—2 (November 7, 1999, vs. Philadelphia); yards—7 (November 7, 1999, vs. Philadelphia); and rushing touchdowns—0.

			KICKOFF RETURNS				TOTALS			
Year Team	G	GS	No.	Yds.	Avg.	TD	TD	2pt.	Pts.	Fum.
1996—Indianapolis NFL	6	0	1	16	16.0	0	0	0	0	0
1997—Indianapolis NFL	16	0	2	23	11.5	0	0	0	0	0
1998—Indianapolis NFL	14	1	5	71	14.2	0	0	0	0	1
1999—Carolina NFL	14	0	1	16	16.0	0	0	0	0	0
Pro totals (4 years)	50	1	9	126	14.0	0	0	0	0	1

H   HEWITT, CHRIS   S

PERSONAL: Born July 22, 1974, in Kingston, Jamaica. ... 6-0/210. ... Full name: Christopher Horace Hewitt.
HIGH SCHOOL: Dwight Morrow (Englewood, N.J.).
COLLEGE: Cincinnati.

TRANSACTIONS/CAREER NOTES: Signed as non-drafted free agent by New Orleans Saints (April 25, 1997). ... Released by Saints (August 18, 1997). ... Re-signed by Saints to practice squad (August 25, 1997). ... Activated (October 1, 1997). ... On injured reserve with knee injury (December 17, 1999-remainder of season). ... Granted free agency (February 11, 2000).
PLAYING EXPERIENCE: New Orleans NFL, 1997-1999. ... Games/Games started: 1997 (11/2), 1998 (16/2), 1999 (12/0). Total: 39/4.
PRO STATISTICS: 1997—Recovered one fumble. 1998—Credited with two sacks. 1999—Credited with one sack.

HICKS, ERIC   DE   CHIEFS

PERSONAL: Born June 17, 1976, in Erie, Pa. ... 6-6/278. ... Full name: Eric David Hicks.
HIGH SCHOOL: Mercyhurst (Erie, Pa.).
COLLEGE: Maryland.
TRANSACTIONS/CAREER NOTES: Signed as non-drafted free agent by Kansas City Chiefs (April 25, 1998).
PLAYING EXPERIENCE: Kansas City NFL, 1998 and 1999. ... Games/Games started: 1998 (3/0), 1999 (16/16). Total: 19/16.
PRO STATISTICS: 1998—Recovered one fumble. 1999—Credited with four sacks and recovered two fumbles for 44 yards and one touchdown.

HICKS, ROBERT   OT   BILLS

PERSONAL: Born November 17, 1974, in Atlanta ... 6-7/338. ... Full name: Robert Otis Hicks Jr.
HIGH SCHOOL: Douglass (Atlanta).
COLLEGE: Mississippi State.
TRANSACTIONS/CAREER NOTES: Selected by Buffalo Bills in third round (68th pick overall) of 1998 NFL draft. ... Signed by Bills (July 20, 1998).
PLAYING EXPERIENCE: Buffalo NFL, 1998 and 1999. ... Games/Games started: 1998 (9/2), 1999 (14/14). Total: 23/16.
PRO STATISTICS: 1999—Rushed once for minus two yards and caught one pass for minus six yards.

HICKS, SKIP   RB   REDSKINS

PERSONAL: Born October 13, 1974, in Corsicana, Texas. ... 6-0/230. ... Full name: Brian LaVell Hicks.
HIGH SCHOOL: Burkburnett (Texas).
COLLEGE: UCLA.
TRANSACTIONS/CAREER NOTES: Selected by Washington Redskins in third round (69th pick overall) of 1998 NFL draft. ... Signed by Redskins (July 7, 1998).
HONORS: Named running back on THE SPORTING NEWS college All-America first team (1997).
SINGLE GAME HIGHS (regular season): Attempts—26 (November 15, 1998, vs. Philadelphia); yards—94 (November 15, 1998, vs. Philadelphia); and rushing touchdowns—3 (November 15, 1998, vs. Philadelphia).

				RUSHING				RECEIVING				TOTALS		
Year Team	G	GS	Att.	Yds.	Avg.	TD	No.	Yds.	Avg.	TD	TD	2pt.	Pts.	Fum.
1998—Washington NFL	9	5	122	433	3.5	8	4	23	5.8	0	8	0	48	0
1999—Washington NFL	10	2	78	257	3.3	3	8	72	9.0	0	3	0	18	1
Pro totals (2 years)	19	7	200	690	3.5	11	12	95	7.9	0	11	0	66	1

HILL, ERIC   LB   CHARGERS

PERSONAL: Born November 14, 1966, in Galveston, Texas. ... 6-2/265.
HIGH SCHOOL: Ball (Galveston, Texas).
COLLEGE: Louisiana State.
TRANSACTIONS/CAREER NOTES: Selected by Phoenix Cardinals in first round (10th pick overall) of 1989 NFL draft. ... Signed by Cardinals (August 18, 1989). ... Granted free agency (March 1, 1993). ... Re-signed by Cardinals (September 4, 1993). ... Activated (September 26, 1993). ... Designated by Cardinals as transition player (February 15, 1994). ... Cardinals franchise renamed Arizona Cardinals for 1994 season. ... Granted unconditional free agency (February 13, 1998). ... Signed by St. Louis Rams (February 26, 1998). ... Released by Rams (March 11, 1999). ... Signed by San Diego Chargers (March 26, 1999).
PRO STATISTICS: 1989—Recovered one fumble. 1991—Recovered one fumble for 85 yards and a touchdown. 1992—Fumbled once and recovered one fumble for minus two yards. 1993—Recovered one fumble. 1998—Intercepted one pass for no yards.

Year Team	G	GS	SACKS
1989—Phoenix NFL	15	14	1.0
1990—Phoenix NFL	16	16	1.5
1991—Phoenix NFL	16	15	1.0
1992—Phoenix NFL	16	16	0.0
1993—Phoenix NFL	13	12	1.0
1994—Arizona NFL	16	15	1.5
1995—Arizona NFL	14	14	2.0
1996—Arizona NFL	16	16	0.0
1997—Arizona NFL	11	10	0.0
1998—St. Louis NFL	15	13	1.0
1999—San Diego NFL	12	10	0.0
Pro totals (11 years)	160	151	9.0

HILL, GREG   RB

PERSONAL: Born February 23, 1972, in Dallas. ... 5-11/212. ... Full name: Gregory Lamonte' Hill.
HIGH SCHOOL: David W. Carter (Dallas).
COLLEGE: Texas A&M.

H

TRANSACTIONS/CAREER NOTES: Selected after junior season by Kansas City Chiefs in first round (25th pick overall) of 1994 NFL draft. ... Signed by Chiefs (August 2, 1994). ... Granted unconditional free agency (February 13, 1998). ... Signed by St. Louis Rams (August 4, 1998). ... On injured reserve with broken leg (September 29, 1998-remainder of season). ... Traded by Rams to Detroit Lions for fifth- (traded to Chicago) and seventh-round (G Andrew Kline) picks in 2000 draft (August 31, 1999). ... Released by Lions (February 4, 2000).
HONORS: Named running back on THE SPORTING NEWS college All-America second team (1992).
SINGLE GAME HIGHS (regular season): Attempts—21 (September 13, 1998, vs. Minnesota); yards—158 (September 20, 1998, vs. Buffalo); and rushing touchdowns—2 (September 20, 1998, vs. Buffalo).
STATISTICAL PLATEAUS: 100-yard rushing games: 1995 (2), 1996 (2), 1998 (1), 1999 (1). Total: 6.

| | | | RUSHING | | | | RECEIVING | | | | TOTALS | | | |
Year Team	G	GS	Att.	Yds.	Avg.	TD	No.	Yds.	Avg.	TD	TD	2pt.	Pts.	Fum.
1994—Kansas City NFL	16	1	141	574	4.1	1	16	92	5.8	0	1	0	6	1
1995—Kansas City NFL	16	1	155	667	4.3	1	7	45	6.4	0	1	0	6	2
1996—Kansas City NFL	15	1	135	645	4.8	4	3	60	20.0	1	5	0	30	1
1997—Kansas City NFL	16	16	157	550	3.5	0	12	126	10.5	0	0	0	0	1
1998—St. Louis NFL	2	2	40	240	6.0	4	1	6	6.0	0	4	0	24	0
1999—Detroit NFL	14	8	144	542	3.8	2	13	77	5.9	0	2	0	12	1
Pro totals (6 years)	79	29	772	3218	4.2	12	52	406	7.8	1	13	0	78	6

HILL, MADRE   RB   BROWNS

PERSONAL: Born January 2, 1976, in Malvern, Ark. ... 5-11/199.
HIGH SCHOOL: Malvern (Ark.).
COLLEGE: Arkansas.
TRANSACTIONS/CAREER NOTES: Selected by Cleveland Browns in seventh round (207th pick overall) of 1999 NFL draft. ... Signed by Browns (July 22, 1999). ... Released by Browns (September 5, 1999). ... Re-signed by Browns to practice squad (September 6, 1999). ... Activated (November 23, 1999).

| | | | KICKOFF RETURNS | | | | TOTALS | | | |
Year Team	G	GS	No.	Yds.	Avg.	TD	TD	2pt.	Pts.	Fum.
1999—Cleveland NFL	5	0	8	137	17.1	0	0	0	0	0

HILL, RAY   CB   DOLPHINS

PERSONAL: Born August 7, 1975, in Detroit. ... 6-0/195. ... Full name: Raymond Millous Hill.
HIGH SCHOOL: Chadsey (Detroit).
COLLEGE: Michigan State.
TRANSACTIONS/CAREER NOTES: Signed as non-drafted free agent by Buffalo Bills (April 23, 1998). ... Released by Bills (August 30, 1998). ... Re-signed by Bills to practice squad (August 31, 1998). ... Activated (September 9, 1998). ... Claimed on waivers by Miami Dolphins (November 19, 1998).
PLAYING EXPERIENCE: Buffalo (4)-Miami (2) NFL, 1998; Miami NFL, 1999. ... Games/Games started: 1998 (Buf.-4/0; Mia.-2/0; Total: 6/0), 1999 (16/0). Total: 22/0.
PRO STATISTICS: 1999—Recovered one fumble for one yard.

HILLIARD, IKE   WR   GIANTS

PERSONAL: Born April 5, 1976, in Patterson, La. ... 5-11/198. ... Full name: Isaac Jason Hilliard. ... Nephew of Dalton Hilliard, running back with New Orleans Saints (1986-93).
HIGH SCHOOL: Patterson (La.).
COLLEGE: Florida.
TRANSACTIONS/CAREER NOTES: Selected by New York Giants in first round (seventh pick overall) of 1997 NFL draft. ... Signed by Giants (July 19, 1997). ... On injured reserve with neck injury (September 30, 1997-remainder of season).
PRO STATISTICS: 1998—Rushed once for four yards. 1999—Rushed three times for 16 yards.
SINGLE GAME HIGHS (regular season): Receptions—8 (September 19, 1999, vs. New York Giants); yards—141 (November 30, 1998, vs. San Francisco); and touchdown receptions—1 (December 19, 1999, vs. St. Louis).
STATISTICAL PLATEAUS: 100-yard receiving games: 1998 (1), 1999 (3). Total: 4.

| | | | RECEIVING | | | | TOTALS | | | |
Year Team	G	GS	No.	Yds.	Avg.	TD	TD	2pt.	Pts.	Fum.
1997—New York Giants NFL	2	2	2	42	21.0	0	0	0	0	0
1998—New York Giants NFL	16	16	51	715	14.0	2	2	0	12	0
1999—New York Giants NFL	16	16	72	996	13.8	3	3	0	18	0
Pro totals (3 years)	34	34	125	1753	14.0	5	5	0	30	2

HITCHCOCK, JIMMY   CB   PANTHERS

PERSONAL: Born November 9, 1970, in Concord, N.C. ... 5-10/187. ... Full name: Jimmy Davis Hitchcock Jr.
HIGH SCHOOL: Concord (N.C.).
COLLEGE: North Carolina.
TRANSACTIONS/CAREER NOTES: Selected by New England Patriots in third round (88th pick overall) of 1995 NFL draft. ... Signed by Patriots (July 19, 1995). ... Granted free agency (February 13, 1998). ... Re-signed by Patriots (April 18, 1998). ... Traded by Patriots to Minnesota Vikings for third-round pick (S Tony George) in 1999 draft (April 18, 1998). ... Granted unconditional free agency (February 11, 2000). ... Signed by Carolina Panthers (February 24, 2000).
CHAMPIONSHIP GAME EXPERIENCE: Member of Patriots for AFC championship game (1996 season); inactive. ... Member of Patriots for Super Bowl XXXI (1996 season); inactive. ... Played in NFC championship game (1998 season).
PRO STATISTICS: 1998—Recovered one fumble for one yard. 1999—Credited with two sacks.

H

Year	Team	G	GS	INTERCEPTIONS No.	Yds.	Avg.	TD
1995—New England NFL		8	0	0	0	0.0	0
1996—New England NFL		13	5	2	14	7.0	0
1997—New England NFL		15	15	2	104	52.0	1
1998—Minnesota NFL		16	16	7	*242	‡34.6	*3
1999—Minnesota NFL		16	16	2	0	0.0	0
Pro totals (5 years)		68	52	13	360	27.7	4

HOARD, LEROY   RB

PERSONAL: Born May 15, 1968, in New Orleans. ... 5-11/224.

HIGH SCHOOL: St. Augustine (New Orleans).

COLLEGE: Michigan.

TRANSACTIONS/CAREER NOTES: Selected after junior season by Cleveland Browns in second round (45th pick overall) of 1990 NFL draft. ... Signed by Browns (July 29, 1990). ... Granted free agency (March 1, 1993). ... Re-signed by Browns for 1993 season.. ... On physically unable to perform list with rib injury (July 22-24, 1995). ... On injured reserve with rib injury (December 16, 1995-remainder of season). ... Browns franchise moved to Baltimore and renamed Ravens for 1996 season (March 11, 1996). ... Released by Ravens (September 24, 1996). ... Signed by Carolina Panthers (October 1, 1996). ... Released by Panthers (October 22, 1996). ... Signed by Minnesota Vikings (November 5, 1996). ... Granted unconditional free agency (February 14, 1997). ... Re-signed by Vikings (April 3, 1997). ... Granted unconditional free agency (February 11, 2000).

CHAMPIONSHIP GAME EXPERIENCE: Played in NFC championship game (1998 season).

HONORS: Played in Pro Bowl (1994 season).

PRO STATISTICS: 1991—Recovered one fumble for four yards. 1992—Recovered one fumble. 1993—Attempted one pass without a completion. 1998—Recovered one fumble.

SINGLE GAME HIGHS (regular season): Attempts—26 (December 13, 1998, vs. Baltimore); yards—123 (November 6, 1994, vs. New England); and rushing touchdowns—2 (December 26, 1999, vs. New York Giants).

STATISTICAL PLATEAUS: 100-yard rushing games: 1994 (2), 1996 (2), 1999 (1). Total: 5. ... 100-yard receiving games: 1991 (1).

Year	Team	G	GS	RUSHING Att.	Yds.	Avg.	TD	RECEIVING No.	Yds.	Avg.	TD	KICKOFF RETURNS No.	Yds.	Avg.	TD	TOTALS TD	2pt.	Pts.	Fum.
1990—Cleveland NFL		14	5	58	149	2.6	3	10	73	7.3	0	2	18	9.0	0	3	0	18	6
1991—Cleveland NFL		16	9	37	154	4.2	2	48	567	11.8	9	0	0	0.0	0	11	0	66	1
1992—Cleveland NFL		16	9	54	236	4.4	0	26	310	11.9	1	2	34	17.0	0	1	0	6	3
1993—Cleveland NFL		16	7	56	227	4.1	0	35	351	10.0	0	13	286	22.0	0	0	0	0	4
1994—Cleveland NFL		16	12	209	890	4.3	5	45	445	9.9	4	2	30	15.0	0	9	0	54	8
1995—Cleveland NFL		12	12	136	547	4.0	0	13	103	7.9	0	1	13	13.0	0	0	0	0	5
1996—Baltimore NFL		2	1	15	61	4.1	0	1	4	4.0	0	0	0	0.0	0	0	0	0	0
—Carolina NFL		3	0	5	11	2.2	0	0	0	0.0	0	1	19	19.0	0	0	0	0	0
—Minnesota NFL		6	6	105	420	4.0	3	10	129	12.9	0	0	0	0.0	0	3	0	18	3
1997—Minnesota NFL		12	1	80	235	2.9	4	11	84	7.6	0	0	0	0.0	0	4	0	24	0
1998—Minnesota NFL		16	1	115	479	4.2	0	22	198	9.0	1	0	0	0.0	0	10	0	60	1
1999—Minnesota NFL		15	3	138	555	4.0	10	17	166	9.8	0	0	0	0.0	0	10	0	60	4
Pro totals (10 years)		144	66	1008	3964	3.9	36	238	2430	10.2	15	21	400	19.0	0	51	0	306	35

HOBERT, BILLY JOE   QB

PERSONAL: Born January 8, 1971, in Puyallup, Wash. ... 6-3/230.

HIGH SCHOOL: Puyallup (Wash.).

COLLEGE: Washington.

TRANSACTIONS/CAREER NOTES: Selected after junior season by Los Angeles Raiders in third round (58th pick overall) of 1993 NFL draft. ... Raiders franchise moved to Oakland (July 21, 1995). ... Traded by Raiders to Buffalo Bills for undisclosed draft pick (February 17, 1997). ... Released by Bills (October 15, 1997). ... Signed by New Orleans Saints (November 19, 1997). ... On injured reserve with Achilles' tendon injury (September 9, 1998-remainder of season). ... Granted unconditional free agency (February 11, 2000).

PRO STATISTICS: 1996—Punted nine times for 371 yards (41.2 avg./35.1 net avg.) and fumbled six times. 1997—Fumbled three times and recovered one fumble for minus five yards. 1999—Fumbled twice and recovered one fumble for minus eight yards.

SINGLE GAME HIGHS (regular season): Attempts—42 (December 7, 1997, vs. St. Louis); completions—23 (November 28, 1999, vs. St. Louis); yards—259 (December 7, 1997, vs. St. Louis); and touchdown passes—3 (September 19, 1999, vs. San Francisco).

MISCELLANEOUS: Regular-season record as starting quarterback: 4-13 (.235).

Year	Team	G	GS	PASSING Att.	Cmp.	Pct.	Yds.	TD	Int.	Avg.	Rat.	RUSHING Att.	Yds.	Avg.	TD	TOTALS TD	2pt.	Pts.
1993—L.A. Raiders NFL							Did not play.											
1994—L.A. Raiders NFL							Did not play.											
1995—Oakland NFL		4	2	80	44	55.0	540	6	4	6.75	80.2	3	5	1.7	0	0	0	0
1996—Oakland NFL		8	3	104	57	54.8	667	4	5	6.41	67.3	2	13	6.5	0	0	0	0
1997—Buffalo NFL		2	0	30	17	56.7	133	0	2	4.43	40.0	2	7	3.5	0	0	0	0
—New Orleans NFL		5	4	131	61	46.6	891	6	8	6.80	59.0	12	36	3.0	0	0	0	0
1998—New Orleans NFL		1	1	23	11	47.8	170	1	0	7.39	87.2	2	13	6.5	0	0	0	0
1999—New Orleans NFL		9	7	159	85	53.5	970	6	6	6.10	68.9	12	47	3.9	1	1	0	6
Pro totals (5 years)		29	17	527	275	52.2	3371	23	25	6.40	67.0	33	121	3.7	1	1	0	6

RECORD AS BASEBALL PLAYER

TRANSACTIONS/CAREER NOTES: Threw right, batted left. ... Selected by Chicago White Sox organization in 16th round of free-agent baseball draft (June 3, 1993).

Year	Team (League)	Pos.	G	BATTING AB	R	H	2B	3B	HR	RBI	Avg.	BB	SO	SB	FIELDING PO	A	E	Avg.
1988—GC White Sox (GCL)		OF	15	39	3	10	2	0	0	4	.256	6	5	1	13	1	0	1.000

H

HOBGOOD-CHITTICK, NATE   DT   RAMS

PERSONAL: Born November 30, 1974, in New Haven, Conn. ... 6-3/290. ... Full name: Nate Broe Hobgood-Chittick.
HIGH SCHOOL: William Allen (Allentown, Pa.).
COLLEGE: North Carolina.
TRANSACTIONS/CAREER NOTES: Signed as non drafted free agent by New York Giants (April 24, 1998). ... Inactive for four games with Giants (1998). ... Released by Giants (September 30, 1998). ... Re-signed by Giants to practice squad (October 2, 1998). ... Signed by Indianapolis Colts off Giants practice squad (November 25, 1998). ... Inactive for five games with Colts (1998). ... Released by Colts (September 7, 1999). ... Signed by St. Louis Rams (September 13, 1999).
PLAYING EXPERIENCE: St. Louis NFL, 1999. ... Games/Games started: 1999 (10/1).
CHAMPIONSHIP GAME EXPERIENCE: Played in NFC championship game (1999 season). ... Member of Super Bowl championship team (1999 season).
PRO STATISTICS: 1999—Credited with $1/2$ sack.

HODGINS, JAMES   RB   RAMS

PERSONAL: Born April 30, 1977, in San Jose, Calif. ... 5-11/230.
HIGH SCHOOL: Oak Grove (San Jose, Calif.).
COLLEGE: San Jose State.
TRANSACTIONS/CAREER NOTES: Signed as non-drafted free agent by St. Louis Rams (April 20, 1999).
CHAMPIONSHIP GAME EXPERIENCE: Played in NFC championship game (1999 season). ... Member of Super Bowl championship team (1999 season).
PRO STATISTICS: 1999—Returned two kickoffs for four yards.
SINGLE GAME HIGHS (regular season): Attempts—3 (November 28, 1999, vs. New Orleans); yards—3 (November 28, 1999, vs. New Orleans); and rushing touchdowns—1 (November 28, 1999, vs. New Orleans).

			RUSHING				RECEIVING				TOTALS			
Year Team	G	GS	Att.	Yds.	Avg.	TD	No.	Yds.	Avg.	TD	TD	2pt.	Pts.	Fum.
1999—St. Louis NFL.........................	15	0	7	10	1.4	1	6	35	5.8	0	1	0	6	0

HOLCOMB, KELLY   QB   COLTS

PERSONAL: Born July 9, 1973, in Fayetteville, Tenn. ... 6-2/212. ... Full name: Bryan Kelly Holcomb.
HIGH SCHOOL: Lincoln County (Fayetteville, Tenn.).
COLLEGE: Middle Tennessee State.
TRANSACTIONS/CAREER NOTES: Signed as non-drafted free agent by Tampa Bay Buccaneers (May 1, 1995). ... Released by Buccaneers (August 22, 1995). ... Re-signed by Buccaneers to practice squad (August 29, 1995). ... Released by Buccaneers (September 19, 1995). ... Re-signed by Buccaneers to practice squad (October 4, 1995). ... Released by Buccaneers (October 17, 1995). ... Re-signed by Buccaneers to practice squad (December 19, 1995). ... Played for Barcelona Dragons of World League (1996). ... Released by Buccaneers (August 19, 1996). ... Signed by Indianapolis Colts to practice squad (November 27, 1996). ... Active (December 12, 1996). ... Active for all 16 games (1998); did not play. ... Granted free agency (February 11, 2000). ... Re-signed by Colts (February 26, 2000).
PRO STATISTICS: W.L.: 1995—Caught one pass for minus eight yards. 1997—Fumbled four times and recovered one fumble for minus eight yards.
SINGLE GAME HIGHS (regular season): Attempts—32 (November 9, 1997, vs. Cincinnati); completions—19 (November 9, 1997, vs. Cincinnati); yards—236 (November 9, 1997, vs. Cincinnati); touchdown passes—1 (November 9, 1997, vs. Cincinnati).
MISCELLANEOUS: Regular-season record as starting NFL quarterback: 0-1.

			PASSING								RUSHING				TOTALS		
Year Team	G	GS	Att.	Cmp.	Pct.	Yds.	TD	Int.	Avg.	Rat.	Att.	Yds.	Avg.	TD	TD	2pt.	Pts.
1995—Tampa Bay NFL..........								Did not play.									
1996—Barcelona W.L............	10	10	319	191	59.9	2382	14	16	7.47	76.8	38	111	2.9	2	2	0	12
—Indianapolis NFL........								Did not play.									
1997—Indianapolis NFL........	5	1	73	45	61.6	454	1	8	6.22	44.3	5	5	1.0	0	0	0	0
1998—Indianapolis NFL........								Did not play.									
1999—Indianapolis NFL........								Did not play.									
W.L. totals (1 year)..............	10	10	319	191	59.9	2382	14	16	7.47	76.8	38	111	2.9	2	2	0	12
NFL totals (2 years).............	5	1	73	45	61.6	454	1	8	6.22	44.3	5	5	1.0	0	0	0	0
Pro totals (3 years)..............	15	11	392	236	60.2	2836	15	24	7.23	69.6	43	116	2.7	2	2	0	12

HOLCOMBE, ROBERT   RB   RAMS

PERSONAL: Born December 11, 1975, in Houston. ... 5-11/220. ... Full name: Robert Wayne Holcombe.
HIGH SCHOOL: Jeff Davis Senior (Houston), then Mesa (Ariz.).
COLLEGE: Illinois.
TRANSACTIONS/CAREER NOTES: Selected by St. Louis Rams in second round (37th pick overall) of 1998 NFL draft. ... Signed by Rams (July 2, 1998).
CHAMPIONSHIP GAME EXPERIENCE: Played in NFC championship game (1999 season). ... Member of Super Bowl championship team (1999 season).
SINGLE GAME HIGHS (regular season): Attempts—21 (September 27, 1998, vs. Arizona); yards—84 (September 27, 1998, vs. Arizona); and rushing touchdowns—2 (September 27, 1998, vs. Arizona).

H

			RUSHING				RECEIVING				TOTALS			
Year Team	G	GS	Att.	Yds.	Avg.	TD	No.	Yds.	Avg.	TD	TD	2pt.	Pts.	Fum.
1998—St. Louis NFL.........................	13	7	98	230	2.3	2	6	34	5.7	0	2	0	12	0
1999—St. Louis NFL.........................	15	7	78	294	3.8	4	14	163	11.6	1	5	0	30	4
Pro totals (2 years)..................	28	14	176	524	3.0	6	20	197	9.9	1	7	0	42	4

HOLDMAN, WARRICK — LB — BEARS

PERSONAL: Born November 22, 1975, in Alief, Texas. ... 6-1/238. ... Full name: Warrick Donte Holdman.
HIGH SCHOOL: Elsik (Alief, Texas).
COLLEGE: Texas A&M.
TRANSACTIONS/CAREER NOTES: Selected by Chicago Bears in fourth round (106th pick overall) of 1999 NFL draft. ... Signed by Bears (July 25, 1999).
PRO STATISTICS: 1999—Recovered one fumble for 33 yards.

Year Team	G	GS	SACKS
1999—Chicago NFL	16	5	2.0

HOLECEK, JOHN — LB — BILLS

PERSONAL: Born May 7, 1972, in Steger, Ill. ... 6-2/242. ... Full name: John Francis Holecek. ... Name pronounced HOLL-uh-sek.
HIGH SCHOOL: Marian Catholic (Chicago Heights, Ill.).
COLLEGE: Illinois.
TRANSACTIONS/CAREER NOTES: Selected by Buffalo Bills in fifth round (144th pick overall) of 1995 NFL draft. ... Signed by Bills (June 12, 1995). ... On physically unable to perform list with hamstring injury (August 22-November 21, 1995). ... On injured reserve with knee injury (August 16, 1996-entire season). ... Granted free agency (February 13, 1998). ... Re-signed by Bills (April 27, 1998).
PLAYING EXPERIENCE: Buffalo NFL, 1995 and 1997-1999. ... Games/Games started: 1995 (1/0), 1997 (14/8), 1998 (13/13), 1999 (14/14). Total: 42/35.
PRO STATISTICS: 1997—Credited with 1½ sacks. 1999—Intercepted one pass for 35 yards and credited with one sack.

HOLLAND, DARIUS — DT — BROWNS

PERSONAL: Born November 10, 1973, in Petersburg, Va. ... 6-5/320. ... Full name: Darius Jerome Holland.
HIGH SCHOOL: Mayfield (Las Cruces, N.M.).
COLLEGE: Colorado.
TRANSACTIONS/CAREER NOTES: Selected by Green Bay Packers in third round (65th pick overall) of 1995 NFL draft. ... Signed by Packers (July 18, 1995). ... Granted free agency (February 13, 1998). ... Re-signed by Packers (April 10, 1998). ... Traded by Packers to Kansas City Chiefs for DE Vaughn Booker (May 13, 1998). ... Released by Chiefs (October 13, 1998). ... Signed by Detroit Lions (October 19, 1998). ... Granted unconditional free agency (February 12, 1999). ... Signed by Cleveland Browns (April 23, 1999). ... Granted unconditional free agency (February 11, 2000). ... Re-signed by Browns (February 11, 2000).
PLAYING EXPERIENCE: Green Bay NFL, 1995-1997; Kansas City (6)-Detroit (10) NFL, 1998; Cleveland NFL, 1999. ... Games/Games started: 1995 (14/4), 1996 (16/0), 1997 (12/1), 1998 (K.C.-6/0; Det.-10/4; Total: 16/4), 1999 (15/11). Total: 73/20.
CHAMPIONSHIP GAME EXPERIENCE: Played in NFC championship game (1995-1997 seasons). ... Member of Super Bowl championship team (1996 season). ... Played in Super Bowl XXXII (1997 season).
PRO STATISTICS: 1995—Credited with 1½ sacks. 1999—Credited with two sacks and recovered one fumble for 14 yards.

HOLLIDAY, VONNIE — DE — PACKERS

PERSONAL: Born December 11, 1975, in Camden, S.C. ... 6-5/300. ... Full name: Dimetry Giovonni Holliday. ... Cousin of Corey Holliday, wide receiver with Pittsburgh Steelers (1995-97).
HIGH SCHOOL: Camden (S.C.).
COLLEGE: North Carolina.
TRANSACTIONS/CAREER NOTES: Selected by Green Bay Packers in first round (19th pick overall) of 1998 NFL draft. ... Signed by Packers (June 15, 1998).
PRO STATISTICS: 1998—Recovered two fumbles. 1999—Recovered one fumble.

Year Team	G	GS	SACKS
1998—Green Bay NFL	12	12	8.0
1999—Green Bay NFL	16	16	6.0
Pro totals (2 years)	28	28	14.0

HOLLIER, DWIGHT — LB

PERSONAL: Born April 21, 1969, in Hampton, Va. ... 6-2/242. ... Full name: Dwight Leon Hollier Jr. ... Name pronounced HALL-yer.
HIGH SCHOOL: Kecoughtan (Hampton, Va.).
COLLEGE: North Carolina (degree in speech communications and psychology).
TRANSACTIONS/CAREER NOTES: Selected by Miami Dolphins in fourth round (97th pick overall) of 1992 NFL draft. ... Signed by Dolphins (July 10, 1992). ... Granted free agency (February 17, 1995). ... Re-signed by Dolphins (May 9, 1995). ... Granted unconditional free agency (February 14, 1997). ... Re-signed by Dolphins (April 17, 1997). ... Granted unconditional free agency (February 11, 2000).
PLAYING EXPERIENCE: Miami NFL, 1992-1999. ... Games/Games started: 1992 (16/5), 1993 (16/10), 1994 (11/7), 1995 (16/14), 1996 (16/15), 1997 (16/3), 1998 (16/0), 1999 (15/0). Total: 122/54.
CHAMPIONSHIP GAME EXPERIENCE: Played in AFC championship game (1992 season).
PRO STATISTICS: 1992—Credited with one sack and recovered three fumbles. 1993—Recovered one fumble. 1994—Intercepted one pass for 36 yards. 1995—Recovered one fumble. 1996—Intercepted one pass for 11 yards and credited with one sack. 1997—Returned one kickoff for no yards. 1998—Recovered one fumble. 1999—Recovered one fumble.

HOLLIS, MIKE — K — JAGUARS

PERSONAL: Born May 22, 1972, in Kellogg, Idaho. ... 5-7/178. ... Full name: Michael Shane Hollis.
HIGH SCHOOL: Central Valley (Veradale, Wash.).

H

COLLEGE: Idaho (degree in sports science, 1996).
TRANSACTIONS/CAREER NOTES: Signed as non-drafted free agent by San Diego Chargers (May 6, 1994). ... Released by Chargers (August 22, 1994). ... Signed by Jacksonville Jaguars (June 5, 1995).
CHAMPIONSHIP GAME EXPERIENCE: Played in AFC championship game (1996 and 1999 seasons).
HONORS: Played in Pro Bowl (1997 season).

				KICKING				
Year Team	G	XPM	XPA	FGM	FGA	Lg.	50+	Pts.
1995—Jacksonville NFL	16	27	28	20	27	53	2-3	87
1996—Jacksonville NFL	16	27	27	30	36	53	2-3	117
1997—Jacksonville NFL	16	41	41	31	36	52	2-2	*134
1998—Jacksonville NFL	16	45	45	21	26	47	0-1	108
1999—Jacksonville NFL	16	37	37	31	38	50	1-1	130
Pro totals (5 years)	80	177	178	133	163	53	7-10	576

HOLMBERG, ROB   LB

PERSONAL: Born May 6, 1971, in McKeesport, Pa. ... 6-3/230. ... Full name: Robert Anthony Holmberg.
HIGH SCHOOL: Mt. Pleasant (Pa.).
COLLEGE: Navy, then Penn State.
TRANSACTIONS/CAREER NOTES: Selected by Los Angeles Raiders in seventh round (217th pick overall) of 1994 NFL draft. ... Signed by Raiders for 1994 season. ... Raiders franchise moved to Oakland (July 21, 1995). ... Released by Raiders (August 30, 1998). ... Signed by Indianapolis Colts (September 9, 1998). ... Released by Colts (September 29, 1998). ... Signed by New York Jets (October 27, 1998). ... Released by Jets (September 5, 1999). ... Signed by Minnesota Vikings (September 6, 1999). ... Released by Vikings (March 31, 2000).
PLAYING EXPERIENCE: Los Angeles Raiders NFL, 1994; Oakland NFL, 1995-1997; Indianapolis (3)-New York Jets (9) NFL, 1998; Minnesota NFL, 1999. ... Games/Games started: 1994 (16/0), 1995 (16/0), 1996 (13/1), 1997 (16/0), 1998 (Ind.-3/0; NYJ-9/0; Total: 12/0), 1999 (16/0). Total: 89/1.
CHAMPIONSHIP GAME EXPERIENCE: Played in AFC championship game (1998 season).
PRO STATISTICS: 1995—Credited with one sack and recovered one fumble. 1996—Credited with one sack. 1997—Returned one kickoff for 15 yards and recovered one fumble.

HOLMES, DARICK   RB

PERSONAL: Born July 1, 1971, in Pasadena, Calif. ... 6-0/226.
HIGH SCHOOL: John Muir (Pasadena, Calif.).
JUNIOR COLLEGE: Sacramento City College.
COLLEGE: Portland State.
TRANSACTIONS/CAREER NOTES: Selected by Buffalo Bills in seventh round (244th pick overall) of 1995 NFL draft. ... Signed by Bills (June 19, 1995). ... Granted free agency (February 13, 1998). ... Re-signed by Bills (April 24, 1998). ... Traded by Bills to Green Bay Packers for fourth-round pick (TE Bobby Collins) in 1999 draft (September 29, 1998). ... Granted unconditional free agency (February 12, 1999). ... Signed by Indianapolis Colts (April 12, 1999). ... On injured reserve with leg injury (October 28, 1999-remainder of season). ... Released by Colts (February 8, 2000).
PRO STATISTICS: 1995—Recovered two fumbles. 1996—Recovered one fumble. 1997—Recovered one fumble. 1998—Recovered one fumble.
SINGLE GAME HIGHS (regular season): Attempts—30 (December 1, 1996 vs. Indianapolis); yards—163 (November 29, 1998, vs. Philadelphia); and rushing touchdowns—3 (November 3, 1996, vs. Washington).
STATISTICAL PLATEAUS: 100-yard rushing games: 1996 (1), 1998 (2). Total: 3.

			RUSHING				RECEIVING				KICKOFF RETURNS				TOTALS			
Year Team	G	GS	Att.	Yds.	Avg.	TD	No.	Yds.	Avg.	TD	No.	Yds.	Avg.	TD	TD	2pt.	Pts.	Fum.
1995—Buffalo NFL	16	2	172	698	4.1	4	24	214	8.9	0	39	799	20.5	0	4	0	24	4
1996—Buffalo NFL	16	1	189	571	3.0	4	16	102	6.4	1	0	0	0.0	0	5	1	32	2
1997—Buffalo NFL	13	0	22	106	4.8	2	13	106	8.2	0	23	430	18.7	0	2	0	12	1
1998—Buffalo NFL	3	0	2	8	4.0	0	1	9	9.0	0	1	20	20.0	0	0	0	0	0
—Green Bay NFL	11	4	93	386	4.2	1	19	179	9.4	0	0	0	0.0	0	1	0	6	1
1999—Indianapolis NFL	1	0	0	0	0.0	0	0	0	0.0	0	0	0	0.0	0	0	0	0	0
Pro totals (5 years)	60	7	478	1769	3.7	11	73	610	8.4	1	63	1249	19.8	0	12	1	74	8

HOLMES, EARL   LB   STEELERS

PERSONAL: Born April 28, 1973, in Tallahassee, Fla. ... 6-2/250. ... Full name: Earl L. Holmes.
HIGH SCHOOL: Florida A&M University (Tallahassee, Fla.).
COLLEGE: Florida A&M.
TRANSACTIONS/CAREER NOTES: Selected by Pittsburgh Steelers in fourth round (126th pick overall) of 1996 NFL draft. ... Signed by Steelers (July 16, 1996).
CHAMPIONSHIP GAME EXPERIENCE: Played in AFC championship game (1997 season).
PRO STATISTICS: 1997—Recovered one fumble. 1998—Intercepted one pass for 36 yards. 1999—Recovered one fumble.

Year Team	G	GS	SACKS
1996—Pittsburgh NFL	3	1	1.0
1997—Pittsburgh NFL	16	16	4.0
1998—Pittsburgh NFL	14	14	1.5
1999—Pittsburgh NFL	16	16	0.0
Pro totals (4 years)	49	47	6.5

H

HOLMES, JARET   K   BEARS

PERSONAL: Born March 3, 1976, in Clinton, Miss. ... 6-0/203. ... Full name: Jaret D. Holmes.
HIGH SCHOOL: Clinton (Miss.).
JUNIOR COLLEGE: Hinds Community College (Miss.).
COLLEGE: Auburn.
TRANSACTIONS/CAREER NOTES: Signed as non-drafted free agent by Philadelphia Eagles (April 21, 1998). ... Released by Eagles (August 17, 1998). ... Signed by Buffalo Bills (April 23, 1999). ... Released by Bills (August 30, 1999). ... Signed by Chicago Bears to practice squad (November 18, 1999). ... Released by Bears (November 23, 1999). ... Signed by New York Giants to practice squad (December 2, 1999). ... Signed by Bears off Giants practice squad (December 13, 1999).

				KICKING				
Year Team	G	XPM	XPA	FGM	FGA	Lg.	50+	Pts.
1999—Chicago NFL	3	0	0	2	2	39	0-0	6

HOLMES, KENNY   DE   TITANS

PERSONAL: Born October 24, 1973, in Vero Beach, Fla. ... 6-4/270. ... Full name: Kenneth Holmes.
HIGH SCHOOL: Vero Beach (Fla.).
COLLEGE: Miami, Fla. (degree in criminal justice).
TRANSACTIONS/CAREER NOTES: Selected by Houston Oilers in first round (18th pick overall) of 1997 NFL draft. ... Oilers franchise moved to Tennessee for 1997 season. ... Signed by Oilers (July 18, 1997). ... Oilers franchise renamed Tennessee Titans for 1999 season (December 26, 1998).
CHAMPIONSHIP GAME EXPERIENCE: Played in AFC championship game (1999 season). ... Played in Super Bowl XXXIV (1999 season).
PRO STATISTICS: 1997—Recovered one fumble. 1999—Intercepted two passes for 17 yards.

Year Team	G	GS	SACKS
1997—Tennessee NFL	16	5	7.0
1998—Tennessee NFL	14	11	2.5
1999—Tennessee NFL	14	7	4.0
Pro totals (3 years)	44	23	13.5

HOLMES, LESTER   G   CARDINALS

PERSONAL: Born September 27, 1969, in Tylertown, Miss. ... 6-5/330.
HIGH SCHOOL: Tylertown (Miss.).
COLLEGE: Jackson State.
TRANSACTIONS/CAREER NOTES: Selected by Philadelphia Eagles in first round (19th pick overall) of 1993 NFL draft. ... Signed by Eagles (August 2, 1993). ... On injured reserve with knee injury (November 28, 1995-remainder of season). ... Granted free agency (February 16, 1996). ... Re-signed by Eagles (July 17, 1996). ... Granted unconditional free agency (February 14, 1997). ... Signed by Oakland Raiders (May 17, 1997). ... Released by Raiders (February 12, 1998). ... Signed by Arizona Cardinals (February 26, 1998).
PLAYING EXPERIENCE: Philadelphia NFL, 1993-1996; Oakland NFL, 1997; Arizona NFL, 1998 and 1999. ... Games/Games started: 1993 (12/6), 1994 (16/16), 1995 (2/2), 1996 (16/14), 1997 (15/15), 1998 (16/16), 1999 (13/13). Total: 90/82.
PRO STATISTICS: 1993—Recovered one fumble. 1994—Recovered three fumbles. 1999—Recovered one fumble.

HOLMES, PRIEST   RB   RAVENS

PERSONAL: Born October 7, 1973, in Fort Smith, Ark. ... 5-9/205. ... Full name: Priest Anthony Holmes.
HIGH SCHOOL: Marshall (Texas).
COLLEGE: Texas.
TRANSACTIONS/CAREER NOTES: Signed as non-drafted free agent by Baltimore Ravens (April 25, 1997). ... Granted free agency (February 11, 2000).
PRO STATISTICS: 1997—Returned one kickoff for 14 yards. 1998—Had only pass attempt intercepted, returned two kickoffs for 30 yards and recovered one fumble for one yard. 1999—Recovered one fumble.
SINGLE GAME HIGHS (regular season): Attempts—36 (November 22, 1998, vs. Cincinnati); yards—227 (November 22, 1998, vs. Cincinnati); and rushing touchdowns—2 (November 29, 1998, vs. Indianapolis).
STATISTICAL PLATEAUS: 100-yard rushing games: 1998 (4), 1999 (2). Total: 6.
MISCELLANEOUS: Holds Baltimore Ravens all-time record for most yards rushing (1,514). ... Shares Baltimore Ravens all-time record for most rushing touchdowns (8).

			RUSHING				RECEIVING				TOTALS			
Year Team	G	GS	Att.	Yds.	Avg.	TD	No.	Yds.	Avg.	TD	TD	2pt.	Pts.	Fum.
1997—Baltimore NFL	7	0	0	0	0.0	0	0	0	0.0	0	0	0	0	0
1998—Baltimore NFL	16	13	233	1008	4.3	7	43	260	6.0	0	7	0	42	3
1999—Baltimore NFL	9	4	89	506	5.7	1	13	104	8.0	1	2	0	12	0
Pro totals (3 years)	32	17	322	1514	4.7	8	56	364	6.5	1	9	0	54	3

HOLSEY, BERNARD   DL   COLTS

PERSONAL: Born December 10, 1973, in Cave Spring, Ga. ... 6-2/285.
HIGH SCHOOL: Coosa (Rome, Ga.).
COLLEGE: Duke.
TRANSACTIONS/CAREER NOTES: Signed as non-drafted free agent by New York Giants (April 26, 1996). ... Granted free agency (February 12, 1999). ... Re-signed by Giants (June 2, 1999). ... Granted unconditional free agency (February 11, 2000). ... Signed by Indianapolis Colts (March 15, 2000).

H

PLAYING EXPERIENCE: New York Giants NFL, 1996-1999. ... Games/Games started: 1996 (16/0), 1997 (16/4), 1998 (16/0), 1999 (16/0). Total: 64/4.
PRO STATISTICS: 1997—Credited with 3½ sacks. 1999—Recovered one fumble.

HOLT, TORRY   WR   RAMS

PERSONAL: Born June 5, 1976, in Greensboro, N.C. ... 6-0/190. ... Full name: Torry Jabar Holt.
HIGH SCHOOL: Eastern Guilford (Gibsonville, N.C.).
COLLEGE: North Carolina State.
TRANSACTIONS/CAREER NOTES: Selected by St. Louis Rams in first round (sixth pick overall) of 1999 NFL draft. ... Signed by Rams (June 5, 1999).
CHAMPIONSHIP GAME EXPERIENCE: Played in NFC championship game (1999 season). ... Member of Super Bowl championship team (1999 season).
HONORS: Named wide receiver on THE SPORTING NEWS college All-America first team (1998).
PRO STATISTICS: 1999—Recovered one fumble.
SINGLE GAME HIGHS (regular season): Receptions—6 (December 12, 1999, vs. New Orleans); yards—122 (January 2, 2000, vs. Philadelphia); and touchdown receptions—2 (January 2, 2000, vs. Philadelphia).
STATISTICAL PLATEAUS: 100-yard receiving games: 1999 (2).

			RUSHING				RECEIVING				PUNT RETURNS				TOTALS			
Year Team	G	GS	Att.	Yds.	Avg.	TD	No.	Yds.	Avg.	TD	No.	Yds.	Avg.	TD	TD	2pt.	Pts.	Fum.
1999—St. Louis NFL	16	15	3	25	8.3	0	52	788	15.2	6	3	15	5.0	0	6	0	36	4

HOPKINS, BRAD   OT   TITANS

PERSONAL: Born September 5, 1970, in Columbia, S.C. ... 6-3/305. ... Full name: Bradley D. Hopkins.
HIGH SCHOOL: Moline (Ill.).
COLLEGE: Illinois (degree in speech communications, 1993).
TRANSACTIONS/CAREER NOTES: Selected by Houston Oilers in first round (13th pick overall) of 1993 NFL draft. ... Signed by Oilers (August 10, 1993). ... Granted unconditional free agency (February 14, 1997). ... Re-signed by Oilers (March 10, 1997). ... Oilers franchise moved to Tennessee for 1997 season. ... Oilers franchise renamed Tennessee Titans for 1999 season (December 26, 1998).
PLAYING EXPERIENCE: Houston NFL, 1993-1996; Tennessee NFL, 1997-1999. ... Games/Games started: 1993 (16/11), 1994 (16/15), 1995 (16/16), 1996 (16/16), 1997 (16/16), 1998 (13/13), 1999 (16/16). Total: 109/103.
CHAMPIONSHIP GAME EXPERIENCE: Played in AFC championship game (1999 season). ... Played in Super Bowl XXXIV (1999 season).
PRO STATISTICS: 1994—Recovered one fumble. 1995—Recovered three fumbles. 1996—Recovered one fumble. 1997—Recovered one fumble.

HOPSON, TYRONE   G   49ERS

PERSONAL: Born May 28, 1976, in Hopkinsville, Ky. ... 6-2/305. ... Full name: Tyrone Hopson Jr.
HIGH SCHOOL: Davies County (Owensboro, Ky.).
COLLEGE: Eastern Kentucky.
TRANSACTIONS/CAREER NOTES: Selected by San Francisco 49ers in fifth round (161st pick overall) of 1999 NFL draft. ... Signed by 49ers (July 26, 1999). ... On injured reserve with shoulder injury (October 20, 1999-remainder of season).
PLAYING EXPERIENCE: San Francisco NFL, 1999. ... Games/Games started: 1999 (1/0).

HORAN, MIKE   P

PERSONAL: Born February 1, 1959, in Orange, Calif. ... 5-11/192. ... Full name: Michael William Horan.
HIGH SCHOOL: Sunny Hills (Fullerton, Calif.).
JUNIOR COLLEGE: Fullerton (Calif.) College.
COLLEGE: Long Beach State (degree in mechanical engineering).
TRANSACTIONS/CAREER NOTES: Selected by Atlanta Falcons in ninth round (235th pick overall) of 1982 NFL draft. ... Signed by Falcons for 1982 season. ... Released by Falcons (September 4, 1982). ... Signed by Green Bay Packers (March 15, 1983). ... Released by Packers after failing physical (May 6, 1983). ... Signed by Buffalo Bills (May 25, 1983). ... Released by Bills (August 22, 1983). ... Signed by Philadelphia Eagles (May 7, 1984). ... Released by Eagles (August 28, 1986). ... Signed by Minnesota Vikings (October 31, 1986). ... Active for one game with Vikings (1986); did not play. ... Released by Vikings (November 3, 1986). ... Signed by Denver Broncos (November 25, 1986). ... Granted unconditional free agency (February 1-April 1, 1991). ... Re-signed by Broncos for 1991 season. ... Granted unconditional free agency (February 1-April 1, 1992). ... Re-signed by Broncos for 1992 season. ... On injured reserve with knee injury (October 22, 1992-remainder of season). ... Released by Broncos (August 30, 1993). ... Signed by New York Giants (November 9, 1993). ... Granted unconditional free agency (February 16, 1996). ... Re-signed by Giants (May 6, 1996). ... Released by Giants (February 14, 1997). ... Signed by St. Louis Rams (October 12, 1997). ... Granted unconditional free agency (February 13, 1998). ... Signed by Chicago Bears (September 23, 1998). ... Granted unconditional free agency (February 12, 1999). ... Signed by Rams (November 10, 1998). ... Granted unconditional free agency (February 11, 2000).
CHAMPIONSHIP GAME EXPERIENCE: Played in AFC championship game (1986, 1987, 1989 and 1991 seasons). ... Played in Super Bowl XXI (1986 season), Super Bowl XXII (1987 season) and Super Bowl XXIV (1989 season). ... Played in NFC championship game (1999 season). ... Member of Super Bowl championship team (1999 season).
HONORS: Named punter on THE SPORTING NEWS NFL All-Pro team (1988). ... Played in Pro Bowl (1988 season).
POST SEASON RECORDS: Shares NFL postseason career record for longest punt—76 yards (January 12, 1991, at Buffalo).
PRO STATISTICS: 1985—Rushed once for 12 yards. 1986—Rushed once for no yards, fumbled once and recovered one fumble for minus 12 yards. 1991—Rushed twice for nine yards and recovered one fumble. 1995—Rushed once for no yards, fumbled once and recovered one fumble for minus 18 yards. 1997—Rushed once for minus three yards. 1998—Attempted two passes with one completion for 18 yards and a touchdown.

		PUNTING					
Year Team	G	No.	Yds.	Avg.	Net avg.	In. 20	Blk.
1984—Philadelphia NFL	16	‡92	‡3880	42.2	35.6	21	0

H

1985—Philadelphia NFL	16	‡91	‡3777	41.5	34.2	20	0
1986—Denver NFL	4	13	571	43.9	34.5	8	0
1987—Denver NFL	12	44	1807	41.1	33.1	11	*2
1988—Denver NFL	16	65	2861	44.0	*37.8	19	0
1989—Denver NFL	16	77	3111	40.4	34.2	24	0
1990—Denver NFL	15	58	2575	*44.4	*38.9	14	1
1991—Denver NFL	16	72	3012	41.8	36.7	24	1
1992—Denver NFL	7	37	1681	45.4	40.2	7	1
1993—New York Giants NFL	8	44	1882	42.8	*39.9	13	0
1994—New York Giants NFL	16	85	3521	41.4	35.2	25	*2
1995—New York Giants NFL	16	72	3063	42.5	36.2	15	0
1996—New York Giants NFL	16	*102	*4289	42.0	35.8	*32	0
1997—St. Louis NFL	10	53	2272	42.9	36.3	10	0
1998—Chicago NFL	13	64	2643	41.3	35.4	12	0
1999—St. Louis NFL	8	26	1048	40.3	35.3	7	0
Pro totals (16 years)	205	995	41993	42.2	36.1	262	7

HORN, JOE   WR   SAINTS

PERSONAL: Born January 16, 1972, in New Haven, Conn. ... 6-1/206. ... Full name: Joseph Horn.
HIGH SCHOOL: Douglas Bird (Fayetteville, N.C.).
JUNIOR COLLEGE: Itawamba Junior College (Miss.).
COLLEGE: None.
TRANSACTIONS/CAREER NOTES: Signed by Memphis Mad Dogs of CFL (March 25, 1995). ... Selected by Kansas City Chiefs in fifth round (135th pick overall) of 1996 NFL draft. ... Signed by Chiefs (June 25, 1996). ... Granted free agency (February 12, 1999). ... Re-signed by Chiefs (June 16, 1999). ... Granted unconditional free agency (February 11, 2000). ... Signed by New Orleans Saints (February 13, 2000).
PRO STATISTICS: 1996—Rushed once for eight yards. 1998—Rushed once for no yards, returned one punt for six yards and recovered three fumbles for minus eight yards. 1999—Rushed twice for 15 yards, returned one punt for 18 yards and recovered one fumble.
SINGLE GAME HIGHS (regular season): Receptions—4 (January 2, 2000, vs. Oakland); yards—92 (December 26, 1999, vs. Seattle); and touchdown receptions—1 (January 2, 2000, vs. Oakland).

			RECEIVING				KICKOFF RETURNS				TOTALS			
Year Team	G	GS	No.	Yds.	Avg.	TD	No.	Yds.	Avg.	TD	TD	2pt.	Pts.	Fum.
1995—Memphis CFL	17	17	71	1415	19.9	5	2	17	8.5	0	5	0	30	0
1996—Kansas City NFL	9	0	2	30	15.0	0	0	0	0.0	0	0	0	0	0
1997—Kansas City NFL	8	0	2	65	32.5	0	0	0	0.0	0	0	0	0	0
1998—Kansas City NFL	16	1	14	198	14.1	1	11	233	21.2	0	1	0	6	2
1999—Kansas City NFL	16	1	35	586	16.7	6	9	165	18.3	0	6	0	36	0
CFL totals (1 year)	17	17	71	1415	19.9	5	2	17	8.5	0	5	0	30	0
NFL totals (4 years)	49	2	53	879	16.6	7	20	398	19.9	0	7	0	42	2
Pro totals (5 years)	66	19	124	2294	18.5	12	22	415	18.9	0	12	0	72	2

HORNE, TONY   WR   RAMS

PERSONAL: Born March 21, 1976, in Montgomery County, N.C. ... 5-9/173. ... Full name: Tony Tremaine Horne.
HIGH SCHOOL: Richmond City (Rockingham, N.C.).
COLLEGE: Clemson.
TRANSACTIONS/CAREER NOTES: Signed as non-drafted free agent by St. Louis Rams (April 20, 1998). ... On suspended list for violating league substance abuse policy (October 20-November 16, 1999).
CHAMPIONSHIP GAME EXPERIENCE: Played in NFC championship game (1999 season). ... Member of Super Bowl championship team (1999 season).
HONORS: Named kick returner on THE SPORTING NEWS NFL All-Pro team (1999).
RECORDS: Holds NFL rookie-season record for most kickoff returns—56 (1998).

			PUNT RETURNS				KICKOFF RETURNS				TOTALS			
Year Team	G	GS	No.	Yds.	Avg.	TD	No.	Yds.	Avg.	TD	TD	2pt.	Pts.	Fum.
1998—St. Louis NFL	16	0	1	0	0.0	0	56	1306	23.3	1	1	0	6	1
1999—St. Louis NFL	12	0	5	22	4.4	0	30	892	*29.7	†2	2	0	12	0
Pro totals (2 years)	28	0	6	22	3.7	0	86	2198	25.6	3	3	0	18	1

HOWARD, CHRIS   RB   JAGUARS

PERSONAL: Born May 5, 1975, in Kenner, La. ... 5-10/226. ...Full name: Christopher L. Howard.
HIGH SCHOOL: John Curtis (River Ridge, La.).
COLLEGE: Michigan.
TRANSACTIONS/CAREER NOTES: Selected by Denver Broncos in fifth round (153rd pick overall) of 1998 NFL draft. ... Signed by Broncos (July 22, 1998). ... Released by Broncos (August 30, 1998). ... Re-signed by Broncos to practice squad (September 8, 1998). ... Released by Broncos (September 22, 1998). ... Signed by Jacksonville Jaguars (September 22, 1998).
CHAMPIONSHIP GAME EXPERIENCE: Played in AFC championship game (1999 season).
SINGLE GAME HIGHS (regular season): Attempts—7 (October 18, 1998, vs. Buffalo); yards—29 (December 19, 1999, vs. Cleveland); and rushing touchdowns—0.

			RUSHING				RECEIVING				TOTALS			
Year Team	G	GS	Att.	Yds.	Avg.	TD	No.	Yds.	Avg.	TD	TD	2pt.	Pts.	Fum.
1998—Jacksonville NFL	8	0	7	16	2.3	0	1	3	3.0	0	0	0	0	0
1999—Jacksonville NFL	12	0	13	55	4.2	0	1	8	8.0	0	0	0	0	0
Pro totals (2 years)	20	0	20	71	3.6	0	2	11	5.5	0	0	0	0	0

H

HOWARD, DESMOND   WR

PERSONAL: Born May 15, 1970, in Cleveland. ... 5-10/185. ... Full name: Desmond Kevin Howard.
HIGH SCHOOL: St. Joseph (Cleveland) Academy.
COLLEGE: Michigan (degree in communication studies).
TRANSACTIONS/CAREER NOTES: Selected by Washington Redskins in first round (fourth pick overall) of 1992 NFL draft. ... Signed by Redskins (August 25, 1992). ... On injured reserve with separated shoulder (December 29, 1992-remainder of 1992 playoffs). ... Selected by Jacksonville Jaguars from Redskins in NFL expansion draft (February 15, 1995). ... Granted unconditional free agency (February 16, 1996). ... Signed by Green Bay Packers (July 11, 1996). ... Granted unconditional free agency (February 14, 1997). ... Signed by Oakland Raiders (March 4, 1997). ... Released by Raiders (June 9, 1999). ... Signed by Packers (June 29, 1999). ... Released by Packers (November 30, 1999). ... Signed by Detroit Lions (December 4, 1999). ... Granted unconditional free agency (February 11, 2000).
CHAMPIONSHIP GAME EXPERIENCE: Played in NFC championship game (1996 season). ... Member of Super Bowl championship team (1996 season).
HONORS: Heisman Trophy winner (1991). ... Named College Football Player of the Year by The Sporting News (1991). ... Maxwell Award winner (1991). ... Named wide receiver on The Sporting News college All-America first team (1991). ... Named punt returner on The Sporting News NFL All-Pro team (1996). ... Named Most Valuable Player of Super Bowl XXXI (1996 season).
RECORDS: Holds NFL single-season record for most yards by punt return—875 (1996).
POST SEASON RECORDS: Holds Super Bowl and NFL postseason record for longest kickoff return—99 yards (January 26, 1997, vs. New England). ... Holds Super Bowl single-game record for most yards by punt return—90 (January 26, 1997, vs. New England). ... Shares Super Bowl career and single-game records for most punt returns—6. ... Shares Super Bowl single-game records for most combined yards—244; most combined yards by kick returns—244; most touchdowns by kickoff return—1 (January 26, 1997, vs. New England). ... Shares NFL postseason single-game record for most combined yards —244; most combined kick return yards—244; and most touchdowns by kickoff return—1 (January 26, 1997, vs. New England).
PRO STATISTICS: 1992—Fumbled once. 1996—Fumbled twice and recovered one fumble. 1997—Fumbled twice and recovered two fumbles. 1998—Fumbled four times.
SINGLE GAME HIGHS (regular season): Receptions—7 (November 20, 1994, vs. Dallas); yards—130 (December 4, 1994, vs. Tampa Bay); and touchdown receptions—1 (October 1, 1995, vs. Houston).
STATISTICAL PLATEAUS: 100-yard receiving games: 1994 (2).

Year Team	G	GS	RUSHING				RECEIVING				PUNT RETURNS				KICKOFF RETURNS				TOTALS		
			Att.	Yds.	Avg.	TD	No.	Yds.	Avg.	TD	No.	Yds.	Avg.	TD	No.	Yds.	Avg.	TD	TD	2pt.	Pts.
1992—Washington NFL .	16	1	3	14	4.7	0	3	20	6.7	0	6	84	14.0	1	22	462	21.0	0	1	0	6
1993—Washington NFL .	16	5	2	17	8.5	0	23	286	12.4	0	4	25	6.3	0	21	405	19.3	0	0	0	0
1994—Washington NFL .	16	15	1	4	4.0	0	40	727	18.2	0	0	0	0.0	0	0	0	0.0	0	5	1	32
1995—Jacksonville NFL .	13	7	1	8	8.0	0	26	276	10.6	1	24	246	10.3	0	10	178	17.8	0	1	0	6
1996—Green Bay NFL....	16	0	0	0	0.0	0	13	95	7.3	0	*58	*875	*15.1	*3	22	460	20.9	0	3	0	18
1997—Oakland NFL........	15	0	0	0	0.0	0	4	30	7.5	0	27	210	7.8	0	*61	§1318	21.6	0	0	0	0
1998—Oakland NFL........	15	1	0	0	0.0	0	2	16	8.0	0	§45	541	12.0	†2	§49	1040	21.2	0	2	0	12
1999—Green Bay NFL....	8	0	0	0	0.0	0	0	0	0.0	0	12	93	7.8	0	19	364	19.2	0	0	0	0
—Detroit NFL..........	5	0	0	0	0.0	0	0	0	0.0	0	6	115	19.2	∞1	15	298	19.9	0	1	0	6
Pro totals (8 years)........	120	29	7	43	6.1	0	111	1450	13.1	6	182	2189	12.0	7	219	4525	20.7	0	13	1	80

HOWARD, TY   CB   BENGALS

PERSONAL: Born November 30, 1973, in Columbus, Ohio. ... 5-10/185.
HIGH SCHOOL: Briggs (Columbus, Ohio).
COLLEGE: Ohio State.
TRANSACTIONS/CAREER NOTES: Selected by Arizona Cardinals in third round (84th pick overall) of 1997 NFL draft. ... Signed by Cardinals (June 10, 1997). ... Claimed on waivers by Cincinnati Bengals (September 6, 1999). ... Granted free agency (February 11, 2000). ... Re-signed by Bengals (April 11, 2000).
PLAYING EXPERIENCE: Arizona NFL, 1997 and 1998; Cincinnati NFL, 1999. ... Games/Games started: 1997 (15/2), 1998 (9/0), 1999 (12/3). Total: 36/5.
PRO STATISTICS: 1997—Credited with one sack.

HOYING, BOBBY   QB   RAIDERS

PERSONAL: Born September 20, 1972, in St. Henry, Ohio. ... 6-3/220. ... Full name: Robert Carl Hoying.
HIGH SCHOOL: St. Henry (Ohio).
COLLEGE: Ohio State (degree in production and operations management).
TRANSACTIONS/CAREER NOTES: Selected by Philadelphia Eagles in third round (85th pick overall) of 1996 NFL draft. ... Signed by Eagles (July 15, 1996). ... Granted free agency (February 12, 1999). ... Re-signed by Eagles (April 15, 1999). ... Traded by Eagles to Oakland Raiders for sixth-round pick (DE John Frank) in 2000 draft (August 24, 1999).
PRO STATISTICS: 1997—Fumbled seven times and recovered one fumble. 1998—Fumbled six times and recovered two fumbles for minus two yards.
SINGLE GAME HIGHS (regular season): Attempts—42 (November 30, 1997, vs. Cincinnati); completions—26 (November 30, 1997, vs. Cincinnati); yards—313 (November 30, 1997, vs. Cincinnati); and touchdown passes—4 (November 30, 1997, vs. Cincinnati).
STATISTICAL PLATEAUS: 300-yard passing games: 1997 (1).
MISCELLANEOUS: Regular-season record as starting NFL quarterback: 3-9-1 (.269).

Year Team	G	GS	PASSING								RUSHING				TOTALS		
			Att.	Cmp.	Pct.	Yds.	TD	Int.	Avg.	Rat.	Att.	Yds.	Avg.	TD	TD	2pt.	Pts.
1996—Philadelphia NFL	1	0	0	0	0.0	0	0	0	0.0	...	0	0	0.0	0	0	0	0
1997—Philadelphia NFL	7	6	225	128	56.9	1573	11	6	6.99	83.8	16	78	4.9	0	0	0	0
1998—Philadelphia NFL	8	7	224	114	50.9	961	0	9	4.29	45.6	22	84	3.8	0	0	0	0
1999—Oakland NFL........	2	0	5	2	40.0	10	0	0	2.00	47.9	2	-3	-1.5	0	0	0	0
Pro totals (4 years)...............	18	13	454	244	53.7	2544	11	15	5.60	64.5	40	159	4.0	0	0	0	0

H

HUARD, DAMON   QB   DOLPHINS

PERSONAL: Born July 9, 1973, in Yakima, Wash. ... 6-3/215.
HIGH SCHOOL: Puyallup (Wash.).
COLLEGE: Washington.
TRANSACTIONS/CAREER NOTES: Signed as non-drafted free agent by Cincinnati Bengals (April 23, 1996). ... Released by Bengals (August 19, 1996). ... Signed by Miami Dolphins (April 24, 1997). ... Released by Dolphins (August 24, 1997). ... Re-signed by Dolphins to practice squad (August 26, 1997). ... Activated (September 6, 1997); did not play. ... Assigned by Dolphins to Frankfurt Galaxy in 1998 NFL Europe enhancement allocation progarm (February 18, 1998).
PRO STATISTICS: 1999—Caught one pass for no yards, fumbled three times and recovered one fumble for minus five yards.
SINGLE GAME HIGHS (regular season): Attempts—42 (October 17, 1999, vs. New England); completions—24 (October 17, 1999, vs. New England); yards—240 (October 17, 1999, vs. New England); and touchdown passes—2 (November 21, 1999, vs. New England).
MISCELLANEOUS: Regular-season record as starting NFL quarterback: 4-1 (.800).

				PASSING							RUSHING				TOTALS	
Year Team	G	GS	Att.	Cmp.	Pct.	Yds.	TD	Int.	Avg.	Rat.	Att.	Yds.	Avg.	TD	TD	2pt.	Pts.
1997—Miami NFL							Did not play.										
1998—Frankfurt NFLE	10	10	290	159	54.8	1857	12	7	6.40	78.2	28	65	2.3	1	1	0	6
—Miami NFL	2	0	9	6	66.7	85	0	1	9.44	57.4	0	0	0.0	0	0	0	0
1999—Miami NFL	16	5	216	125	57.9	1288	8	4	5.96	79.8	28	124	4.4	0	0	0	0
NFL Europe totals (1 year)	10	10	290	159	54.8	1857	12	7	6.40	78.2	28	65	2.3	1	1	0	6
NFL totals (1 year)	18	5	225	131	58.2	1373	8	5	6.10	78.6	28	124	4.4	0	0	0	0
Pro totals (2 years)	28	15	515	290	56.3	3230	20	12	6.27	78.4	56	189	3.4	1	1	0	6

HUDSON, CHRIS   S

PERSONAL: Born October 6, 1971, in Houston. ... 5-10/199. ... Full name: Christopher Reshard Hudson.
HIGH SCHOOL: E.E. Worthing (Houston).
COLLEGE: Colorado (degree in business, 1995).
TRANSACTIONS/CAREER NOTES: Selected by Jacksonville Jaguars in third round (71st pick overall) of 1995 NFL draft. ... Signed by Jaguars (June 1, 1995). ... On injured reserve with groin injury (September 28, 1995-remainder of season). ... Granted free agency (February 13, 1998). ... Re-signed by Jaguars (June 10, 1998). ... Granted unconditional free agency (February 12, 1999). ... Signed by Chicago Bears (April 22, 1999). ... Granted unconditional free agency (February 11, 2000).
CHAMPIONSHIP GAME EXPERIENCE: Played in AFC championship game (1996 season).
HONORS: Jim Thorpe Award winner (1994).
PRO STATISTICS: 1996—Recovered two fumbles. 1997—Returned blocked field goal attempt 58 yards for a touchdown and recovered two fumbles for 32 yards and one touchdown. 1998—Recovered one fumble. 1999—Credited with one sack.

			INTERCEPTIONS				PUNT RETURNS				TOTALS			
Year Team	G	GS	No.	Yds.	Avg.	TD	No.	Yds.	Avg.	TD	TD	2pt.	Pts.	Fum.
1995—Jacksonville NFL	1	0	0	0	0.0	0	0	0	0.0	0	0	0	0	0
1996—Jacksonville NFL	16	16	2	25	12.5	0	32	348	10.9	0	0	0	0	3
1997—Jacksonville NFL	16	16	3	26	8.7	0	0	0	0.0	0	2	0	12	1
1998—Jacksonville NFL	13	13	3	10	3.3	0	0	0	0.0	0	0	0	0	0
1999—Chicago NFL	16	16	3	28	9.3	0	0	0	0.0	0	0	0	0	0
Pro totals (5 years)	62	61	11	89	8.1	0	32	348	10.9	0	2	0	12	4

HUDSON, JOHN   C/G

PERSONAL: Born January 29, 1968, in Memphis, Tenn. ... 6-2/270. ... Full name: John Lewis Hudson.
HIGH SCHOOL: Henry County (Paris, Tenn.).
COLLEGE: Auburn.
TRANSACTIONS/CAREER NOTES: Selected by Philadelphia Eagles in 11th round (294th pick overall) of 1990 NFL draft. ... Signed by Eagles (July 31, 1990). ... On physically unable to perform list with knee laceration (August 2, 1990-entire season). ... Granted unconditional free agency (February 1-April 1, 1992). ... Re-signed by Eagles (July 23, 1992). ... On injured reserve with broken hand (September 28, 1992-remainder of season). ... Granted free agency (March 1, 1993). ... Re-signed by Eagles (May 12, 1993). ... Granted unconditional free agency (February 17, 1994). ... Re-signed by Eagles (April 7, 1994). ... Granted unconditional free agency (February 16, 1996). ... Signed by New York Jets (February 26, 1996). ... Granted unconditional free agency (February 1, 2000).
PLAYING EXPERIENCE: Philadelphia NFL, 1991-1995; New York Jets NFL, 1996-1999. ... Games/Games started: 1991 (16/0), 1992 (3/0), 1993 (16/0), 1994 (16/0), 1995 (16/0), 1996 (16/0), 1997 (16/0), 1998 (16/0), 1999 (16/0). Total: 131/0.
CHAMPIONSHIP GAME EXPERIENCE: Played in AFC championship game (1998 season).
PRO STATISTICS: 1991—Fumbled once. 1993—Fumbled once.

HUNDON, JAMES   WR   BENGALS

PERSONAL: Born April 9, 1971, in Daly City, Calif. ... 6-1/173.
HIGH SCHOOL: Jefferson (Daly City, Calif.).
JUNIOR COLLEGE: San Francisco Community College.
COLLEGE: Portland State.
TRANSACTIONS/CAREER NOTES: Signed as non-drafted free agent by Cincinnati Bengals (April 23, 1996). ... Released by Bengals (August 27, 1996). ... Re-signed by Bengals to practice squad (November 19, 1996). ... Activated (November 22, 1996). ... Granted free agency (February 11, 2000). ... Re-signed by Bengals (April 3, 2000).
PRO STATISTICS: 1996—Returned one punt for minus seven yards.
SINGLE GAME HIGHS (regular season): Receptions—5 (November 30, 1997, vs. Philadelphia); yards—118 (November 30, 1997, vs. Philadelphia); and touchdown receptions—2 (November 30, 1997, vs. Philadelphia).
STATISTICAL PLATEAUS: 100-yard receiving games: 1997 (1).

H

Year Team	G	GS	RECEIVING No.	Yds.	Avg.	TD	KICKOFF RETURNS No.	Yds.	Avg.	TD	TOTALS TD	2pt.	Pts.	Fum.
1996—Cincinnati NFL	5	0	1	14	14.0	1	10	237	23.7	0	1	0	6	1
1997—Cincinnati NFL	16	0	16	285	17.8	2	10	169	16.9	0	2	0	12	1
1998—Cincinnati NFL	9	3	10	112	11.2	1	0	0	0.0	0	1	0	6	0
1999—Cincinnati NFL	6	0	1	5	5.0	0	0	0	0.0	0	0	0	0	0
Pro totals (4 years)	36	3	28	416	14.9	4	20	406	20.3	0	4	0	24	2

HUNT, CLETIDUS — DE — PACKERS

PERSONAL: Born January 2, 1976, in Memphis, Tenn. ... 6-4/295. ... Full name: Cletidus Marquell Hunt.
HIGH SCHOOL: Whitehaven (Memphis, Tenn.).
JUNIOR COLLEGE: Northwest Mississippi Community College.
COLLEGE: Kentucky State.
TRANSACTIONS/CAREER NOTES: Selected by Green Bay Packers in third round (94th pick overall) of NFL draft. ... Signed by Packers (July 26, 1999).
PLAYING EXPERIENCE: Green Bay NFL, 1999. ... Games/Games started: 1999 (11/1).
PRO STATISTICS: 1999—Credited with $1/2$ sack and recovered one fumble.

HUNTLEY, RICHARD — RB — STEELERS

PERSONAL: Born September 18, 1972, in Monroe, N.C. ... 5-11/225. ... Full name: Richard Earl Huntley.
HIGH SCHOOL: Monroe (N.C.).
COLLEGE: Winston-Salem (N.C.) State.
TRANSACTIONS/CAREER NOTES: Selected by Atlanta Falcons in fourth round (117th pick overall) of 1996 NFL draft. ... Signed by Falcons for 1996 season. ... Released by Falcons (August 18, 1997). ... Signed by Pittsburgh Steelers (February 13, 1998). ... Granted free agency (February 11, 2000). ... Re-signed by Steelers (March 14, 2000).
SINGLE GAME HIGHS (regular season): Attempts—21 (October 18, 1998, vs. Baltimore); yards—85 (October 11, 1998, vs. Cincinnati); and rushing touchdowns—1 (January 2, 2000, vs. Tennessee).

Year Team	G	GS	RUSHING Att.	Yds.	Avg.	TD	RECEIVING No.	Yds.	Avg.	TD	KICKOFF RETURNS No.	Yds.	Avg.	TD	TOTALS TD	2pt.	Pts.	Fum.
1996—Atlanta NFL	1	0	2	8	4.0	0	1	14	14.0	0	0	0	0.0	0	0	0	0	0
1997—									Did not play.									
1998—Pittsburgh NFL	16	1	55	242	4.4	1	3	18	6.0	0	6	119	19.8	0	1	0	6	5
1999—Pittsburgh NFL	16	2	93	567	6.1	5	27	253	9.4	3	15	336	22.4	0	8	0	48	3
Pro totals (3 years)	33	3	150	817	5.4	6	31	285	9.2	3	21	455	21.7	0	9	0	54	8

HUSTED, MICHAEL — K — RAIDERS

PERSONAL: Born June 16, 1970, in El Paso, Texas. ... 6-0/195. ... Full name: Michael James Husted.
HIGH SCHOOL: Hampton (Va.).
COLLEGE: Virginia (degree in sociology, 1992).
TRANSACTIONS/CAREER NOTES: Signed as non-drafted free agent by Tampa Bay Buccaneers (May 3, 1993). ... Granted free agency (February 16, 1996). ... Tendered offer sheet by San Francisco 49ers (February 21, 1996). ... Offer matched by Buccaneers (February 28, 1996). ... Released by Buccaneers (February 11, 1999). ... Signed by Oakland Raiders (February 24, 1999).
PRO STATISTICS: 1994—Punted twice for 53 yards. 1998—Rushed once for 20 yards.

Year Team	G	KICKING XPM	XPA	FGM	FGA	Lg.	50+	Pts.
1993—Tampa Bay NFL	16	27	27	16	22	‡57	3-5	75
1994—Tampa Bay NFL	16	20	20	23	35	53	1-5	89
1995—Tampa Bay NFL	16	25	25	19	26	53	3-3	82
1996—Tampa Bay NFL	16	18	19	25	32	50	1-3	93
1997—Tampa Bay NFL	16	32	35	13	17	54	1-3	71
1998—Tampa Bay NFL	16	29	30	21	28	52	1-1	92
1999—Oakland NFL	13	30	30	20	31	49	0-3	90
Pro totals (7 years)	109	181	186	137	191	57	10-23	592

HUTSON, TONY — G/OT — COWBOYS

PERSONAL: Born March 13, 1974, in Houston ... 6-3/317.
HIGH SCHOOL: MacArthur (Houston).
JUNIOR COLLEGE: Kilgore (Texas) College.
COLLEGE: Northeastern Oklahoma State.
TRANSACTIONS/CAREER NOTES: Signed as non-drafted free agent by Dallas Cowboys (April 23, 1996). ... Released by Cowboys (August 25, 1996). ... Re-signed by Cowboys to practice squad (August 27, 1996). ... Activated (January 5, 1997). ... Released by Cowboys (August 24, 1997). ... Re-signed by Cowboys to practice squad (August 26, 1997). ... Activated (November 4, 1997). ... On injured reserve with knee injury (October 5, 1999-remainder of season). ... Granted free agency (February 11, 2000). ... Re-signed by Cowboys (March 14, 2000).
PLAYING EXPERIENCE: Dallas NFL, 1997-1999. ... Games/Games started: 1997 (5/1), 1998 (9/1), 1999 (2/2). Total: 16/4.

H

HUTTON, TOM — P — PACKERS

PERSONAL: Born July 8, 1972, in Memphis, Tenn. ... 6-1/193. ... Full name: William Thomas Hutton.
HIGH SCHOOL: Memphis University High.

COLLEGE: Tennessee (degree in public relations, 1994).
TRANSACTIONS/CAREER NOTES: Signed as non-drafted free agent by Philadelphia Eagles (April 26, 1995). ... Granted unconditional free agency (February 12, 1999). ... Signed by Miami Dolphins (September 27, 1999). ... Granted unconditional free agency (February 11, 2000). ... Signed by Green Bay Packers (May 16, 2000).
PRO STATISTICS: 1995—Fumbled once for minus 19 yards. 1996—Recovered one fumble. 1997—Rushed once for no yards, fumbled once and recovered one fumble for minus one yard.

				PUNTING			
Year Team	G	No.	Yds.	Avg.	Net avg.	In. 20	Blk.
1995—Philadelphia NFL	16	85	3682	43.3	3.3	20	1
1996—Philadelphia NFL	16	73	3107	42.6	35.1	17	1
1997—Philadelphia NFL	16	87	3660	42.1	34.6	19	1
1998—Philadelphia NFL	16	*104	4339	41.7	34.9	21	0
1999—Miami NFL	14	73	2978	40.8	35.1	22	0
Pro totals (5 years)	78	422	17766	42.1	28.5	99	3

HYDER, GAYLON　　　　DT　　　　RAMS

PERSONAL: Born October 18, 1974, in Longview, Texas. ... 6-5/290.
HIGH SCHOOL: Longview (Texas).
COLLEGE: Texas Christian.
TRANSACTIONS/CAREER NOTES: Signed as non-drafted free agent by St. Louis Rams (July 30, 1999). ... On injured reserve with back injury (November 19, 1999-remainder of season).
PLAYING EXPERIENCE: St. Louis NFL, 1999. ... Games/Games started: 1999 (4/0).

INGRAM, STEPHEN　　　　G/OT　　　　JAGUARS

PERSONAL: Born May 8, 1971, in Cheverly, Md. ... 6-4/315.
HIGH SCHOOL: DuVal (Greenbelt, Md.).
COLLEGE: Maryland (degree in criminal justice, 1994).
TRANSACTIONS/CAREER NOTES: Selected by Tampa Bay Buccaneers in seventh round (215th pick overall) of 1995 NFL draft. ... Signed by Buccaneers (May 3, 1995). ... Released by Buccaneers (August 22, 1996). ... Re-signed by Buccaneers (November 13, 1996). ... On injured reserve with leg injury (August 17, 1997-entire season). ... Granted free agency (February 13, 1998). ... Re-signed by Buccaneers for 1998 season. ... Released by Buccaneers (August 30, 1998). ... Re-signed by Buccaneers to practice squad (December 3, 1998). ... Granted free agency following 1998 season. ... Signed by Jacksonville Jaguars (January 15, 1999). ... Granted unconditional free agency (February 11, 2000). ... Re-signed by Jaguars (February 22, 2000).
PLAYING EXPERIENCE: Tampa Bay NFL, 1995; Jacksonville NFL, 1999. ... Games/Games played: 1995 (2/0), 1999 (6/0). Total: 8/0.
CHAMPIONSHIP GAME EXPERIENCE: Played in AFC championship game (1999 season).

IRVIN, KEN　　　　CB　　　　BILLS

PERSONAL: Born July 11, 1972, in Rome, Ga. ... 5-10/186. ... Full name: Kenneth Irvin.
HIGH SCHOOL: Pepperell (Lindale, Ga.).
COLLEGE: Memphis (degree in criminal justice, 1998).
TRANSACTIONS/CAREER NOTES: Selected by Buffalo Bills in fourth round (109th pick overall) of 1995 NFL draft. ... Signed by Bills (July 10, 1995). ... Granted free agency (February 13, 1998). ... Re-signed by Bills (April 17, 1998). ... Granted unconditional free agency (February 12, 1999). ... Re-signed by Bills (March 17, 1999). ... On injured reserve with foot injury (December 23, 1999-remainder of season).
PLAYING EXPERIENCE: Buffalo NFL, 1995-1999. ... Games/Games started: 1995 (16/3), 1996 (16/1), 1997 (16/0), 1998 (16/16), 1999 (14/14). Total: 78/34.
PRO STATISTICS: 1995—Returned one kickoff for 12 yards. 1996—Credited with two sacks and recovered one fumble. 1997—Intercepted two passes for 28 yards. 1998—Intercepted one pass for 43 yards. 1999—Intercepted one pass for one yard.

IRVIN, MICHAEL　　　　WR

PERSONAL: Born March 5, 1966, in Fort Lauderdale, Fla. ... 6-2/207. ... Full name: Michael Jerome Irvin. ... Cousin of Sedrick Irvin, running back, Detroit Lions.
HIGH SCHOOL: St. Thomas Aquinas (Fort Lauderdale, Fla.).
COLLEGE: Miami, Fla. (degree in business management, 1988).
TRANSACTIONS/CAREER NOTES: Selected by Dallas Cowboys in first round (11th pick overall) of 1988 NFL draft. ... Signed by Cowboys (July 9, 1988). ... On injured reserve with knee injury (October 17, 1989-remainder of season). ... On injured reserve with knee injury (September 4-October 7, 1990). ... Granted free agency (February 1, 1992). ... Re-signed by Cowboys (September 3, 1992). ... Designated by Cowboys as transition player (February 25, 1993). ... On suspended list for violating league substance abuse policy (August 26-October 1, 1996). ... On injured reserve with neck injury (December 4, 1999-remainder of season). ... Granted unconditional free agency (February 11, 2000).
CHAMPIONSHIP GAME EXPERIENCE: Played in NFC championship game (1992-1995 seasons). ... Member of Super Bowl championship team (1992, 1993 and 1995 seasons).
HONORS: Named wide receiver on THE SPORTING NEWS college All-America second team (1986). ... Named wide receiver on THE SPORTING NEWS NFL All-Pro team (1991). ... Played in Pro Bowl (1991-1995 seasons). ... Named Outstanding Player of Pro Bowl (1991 season).
RECORDS: Holds NFL single-season record for most games with 100 or more yards receiving—11 (1995). ... Shares NFL record for most consecutive games with 100 or more yards receiving—7 (1995).
PRO STATISTICS: 1988—Rushed once for two yards. 1989—Rushed once for six yards and recovered one fumble. 1991—Recovered one fumble. 1992—Rushed once for minus nine yards and recovered one fumble. 1993—Rushed twice for six yards. 1998—Rushed once for one yard.
SINGLE GAME HIGHS (regular season): Receptions—12 (October 27, 1996, vs. Miami); yards—210 (September 20, 1992, vs. Arizona); and touchdown receptions—3 (September 20, 1992, vs. Arizona).

H
I

STATISTICAL PLATEAUS: 100-yard receiving games: 1988 (1), 1989 (1), 1991 (7), 1992 (6), 1993 (5), 1994 (5), 1995 (11), 1996 (3), 1997 (4), 1998 (3), 1999 (1). Total: 47.
MISCELLANEOUS: Holds Dallas Cowboys all-time records for most receptions (750) and most yards receiving (11,904).

				RECEIVING				TOTALS		
Year Team	G	GS	No.	Yds.	Avg.	TD	TD	2pt.	Pts.	Fum.
1988—Dallas NFL	14	10	32	654	‡20.4	5	5	0	30	0
1989—Dallas NFL	6	6	26	378	14.5	2	2	0	12	0
1990—Dallas NFL	12	7	20	413	20.7	5	5	0	30	0
1991—Dallas NFL	16	16	‡93	*1523	16.4	8	8	0	48	3
1992—Dallas NFL	16	14	78	1396	17.9	7	7	0	42	1
1993—Dallas NFL	16	16	88	1330	15.1	7	7	0	42	0
1994—Dallas NFL	16	16	79	1241	15.7	6	6	0	36	0
1995—Dallas NFL	16	16	111	1603	14.4	10	10	0	60	1
1996—Dallas NFL	11	11	64	962	15.0	2	2	1	14	1
1997—Dallas NFL	16	16	75	1180	15.7	9	9	0	54	0
1998—Dallas NFL	16	15	74	1057	14.3	1	1	0	6	1
1999—Dallas NFL	4	4	10	167	16.7	3	3	0	18	0
Pro totals (12 years)	159	147	750	11904	15.9	65	65	1	392	7

IRVIN, SEDRICK — RB — LIONS

PERSONAL: Born March 30, 1978, in Miami. ... 5-11/226. ... Cousin of Michael Irvin, wide receiver with Dallas Cowboys (1988-99).
HIGH SCHOOL: Miami Southridge, then Miami High.
COLLEGE: Michigan State.
TRANSACTIONS/CAREER NOTES: Selected after junior season by Detroit Lions in fourth round (103rd pick overall) of 1999 NFL draft. ... Signed by Lions (July 25, 1999).
PRO STATISTICS: 1999—Fumbled twice.
SINGLE GAME HIGHS (regular season): Attempts—8 (November 21, 1999, vs. Green Bay); yards—62 (November 21, 1999, vs. Green Bay); and rushing touchdowns—1 (November 21, 1999, vs. Green Bay).

			RUSHING				RECEIVING				PUNT RETURNS				KICKOFF RETURNS				TOTALS	
Year Team	G	GS	Att.	Yds.	Avg.	TD	No.	Yds.	Avg.	TD	No.	Yds.	Avg.	TD	No.	Yds.	Avg.	TD	TD	2pt. Pts.
1999—Detroit NFL	14	0	36	133	3.7	4	25	233	9.3	0	2	15	7.5	0	3	21	7.0	0	4	0 24

IRWIN, HEATH — G — DOLPHINS

PERSONAL: Born June 27, 1973, in Boulder, Colo. ... 6-4/300. ... Nephew of Hale Irwin, professional golfer.
HIGH SCHOOL: Boulder (Colo.).
COLLEGE: Colorado.
TRANSACTIONS/CAREER NOTES: Selected by New England Patriots in fourth round (101st pick overall) of 1996 NFL draft. ... Signed by Patriots (July 17, 1996). ... Inactive for all 16 games (1996). ... Granted free agency (February 12, 1999). ... Re-signed by Patriots (June 24, 1999). ... Granted unconditional free agency (February 11, 2000). ... Signed by Miami Dolphins (February 25, 2000).
PLAYING EXPERIENCE: New England NFL, 1997-1999. ... Games/Games started: 1997 (15/1), 1998 (13/3), 1999 (15/13). Total: 43/17.
CHAMPIONSHIP GAME EXPERIENCE: Member of Patriots for AFC championship game (1996 season); inactive. ... Member of Patriots for Super Bowl XXXI (1996 season); inactive.

ISMAIL, QADRY — WR — RAVENS

PERSONAL: Born November 8, 1970, in Newark, N.J. ... 6-0/200. ... Full name: Qadry Rahmadan Ismail. ... Brother of Rocket Ismail, wide receiver, Dallas Cowboys. ... Name pronounced KAH-dree ISS-my-el.
HIGH SCHOOL: Elmer L. Meyers (Wilkes-Barre, Pa.).
COLLEGE: Syracuse (degree in communications).
TRANSACTIONS/CAREER NOTES: Selected by Minnesota Vikings in second round (52nd pick overall) of 1993 NFL draft. ... Signed by Vikings (July 20, 1993). ... Granted unconditional free agency (February 14, 1997). ... Signed by Green Bay Packers (June 2, 1997). ... Traded by Packers to Miami Dolphins for first-round pick in (DT Vonnie Holliday) in 1998 draft (August 24, 1997). ... Granted unconditional free agency (February 13, 1998). ... Signed by New Orleans Saints (February 27, 1998). ... Released by Saints (February 10, 1999). ... Signed by Baltimore Ravens (April 27, 1999). ... Granted unconditional free agency (February 11, 2000). ... Re-signed by Ravens (April 28, 2000).
HONORS: Named kick returner on THE SPORTING NEWS college All-America second team (1991).
PRO STATISTICS: 1993—Rushed three times for 14 yards. 1994—Recovered one fumble. 1995—Rushed once for seven yards. 1996—Recovered one fumble. 1999—Rushed once for four yards.
SINGLE GAME HIGHS (regular season): Receptions—7 (December 19, 1999, vs. New Orleans); yards—258 (December 12, 1999, vs. Pittsburgh); and touchdown receptions—3 (December 12, 1999, vs. Pittsburgh).
STATISTICAL PLATEAUS: 100-yard receiving games: 1994 (2), 1995 (1), 1999 (3). Total: 6.

				RECEIVING				KICKOFF RETURNS				TOTALS		
Year Team	G	GS	No.	Yds.	Avg.	TD	No.	Yds.	Avg.	TD	TD	2pt.	Pts.	Fum.
1993—Minnesota NFL	15	3	19	212	11.2	1	‡42	902	21.5	0	1	0	6	1
1994—Minnesota NFL	16	3	45	696	15.5	5	35	807	23.1	0	5	0	30	2
1995—Minnesota NFL	16	2	32	597	18.7	3	42	1037	24.7	0	3	0	18	3
1996—Minnesota NFL	16	2	22	351	16.0	3	28	527	18.8	0	3	0	18	2
1997—Miami NFL	3	0	0	0	0.0	0	8	166	20.8	0	0	0	0	0
1998—New Orleans NFL	10	1	0	0	0.0	0	28	590	21.1	0	0	0	0	2
1999—Baltimore NFL	16	16	68	1105	16.3	6	4	55	13.8	0	6	0	36	2
Pro totals (7 years)	92	27	186	2961	15.9	18	187	4084	21.8	0	18	0	108	12

ISMAIL, ROCKET   WR/KR   COWBOYS

PERSONAL: Born November 18, 1969, in Elizabeth, N.J. ... 5-11/190. ... Full name: Raghib Ramadian Ismail. ... Brother of Qadry Ismail, wide receiver, Baltimore Ravens. ... Name pronounced rah-GIBB ISS-my-ell.
HIGH SCHOOL: Elmer L. Meyers (Wilkes-Barre, Pa.).
COLLEGE: Notre Dame (degree in sociology, 1994).
TRANSACTIONS/CAREER NOTES: Signed after junior season by Toronto Argonauts of CFL (April 21, 1991). ... Selected by Los Angeles Raiders in fourth round (100th pick overall) of 1991 NFL draft. ... Granted free agency from Argonauts (February 15, 1993). ... Signed by Raiders (August 30, 1993). ... Raiders franchise moved to Oakland (July 21, 1995). ... Granted free agency (February 16, 1996). ... Re-signed by Raiders (August 25, 1996). ... Traded by Raiders to Carolina Panthers for fifth-round pick (traded to Miami) in 1997 draft (August 25, 1996). ... Granted unconditional free agency (February 14, 1997). ... Re-signed by Panthers (February 26, 1997). ... Granted unconditional free agency (February 13, 1998). ... Re-signed by Panthers (June 2, 1998). ... Granted unconditional free agency (February 12, 1999). ... Signed by Dallas Cowboys (April 15, 1999).
CHAMPIONSHIP GAME EXPERIENCE: Played in Grey Cup, CFL championship game (1991). ... Played in NFC championship game (1996 season).
HONORS: Named kick returner on THE SPORTING NEWS college All-America first team (1989). ... Named College Football Player of the Year by THE SPORTING NEWS (1990). ... Named wide receiver on THE SPORTING NEWS college All-America first team (1990).
PRO STATISTICS: CFL: 1991—Returned two unsuccessful field-goals for 90 yards, attempted one pass without a completion, fumbled eight times and recovered two fumbles. 1992—Fumbled seven times and recovered two fumbles. NFL: 1993—Recovered one fumble. 1995—Fumbled four times and recovered one fumble. 1998—Fumbled twice and recovered one fumble. 1999—Fumbled once.
SINGLE GAME HIGHS (regular season): Receptions—8 (December 5, 1999, vs. New England); yards—149 (September 12, 1999, vs. Washington); and touchdown receptions—2 (October 11, 1998, vs. Dallas).
STATISTICAL PLATEAUS: 100-yard receiving games: 1995 (1), 1996 (1), 1997 (1), 1998 (3), 1999 (3). Total: 9.

			RUSHING				RECEIVING				PUNT RETURNS				KICKOFF RETURNS				TOTALS		
Year Team	G	GS	Att.	Yds.	Avg.	TD	No.	Yds.	Avg.	TD	No.	Yds.	Avg.	TD	No.	Yds.	Avg.	TD	TD	2pt.	Pts.
1991—Toronto CFL	17	17	36	271	7.5	3	64	1300	20.3	9	48	602	12.5	1	31	786	25.4	0	13	0	78
1992—Toronto CFL	16	16	34	154	4.5	3	36	651	18.1	4	59	614	10.4	1	43	*1139	26.5	0	8	0	48
1993—LA Raiders NFL	13	0	4	-5	-1.3	0	26	353	13.6	1	0	0	0.0	0	25	605	§24.2	0	1	0	6
1994—LA Raiders NFL	16	0	4	31	7.8	0	34	513	15.1	5	0	0	0.0	0	43	923	21.5	0	5	0	30
1995—Oakland NFL	16	16	6	29	4.8	0	28	491	17.5	3	0	0	0.0	0	36	706	19.6	0	3	0	18
1996—Carolina NFL	13	5	8	80	10.0	1	12	214	17.8	0	0	0	0.0	0	5	100	20.0	0	1	0	6
1997—Carolina NFL	13	2	4	32	8.0	0	36	419	11.6	2	0	0	0.0	0	0	0	0.0	0	2	0	12
1998—Carolina NFL	16	15	3	42	14.0	0	69	1024	14.8	8	0	0	0.0	0	0	0	0.0	0	8	0	48
1999—Dallas NFL	16	14	13	110	8.5	1	80	1097	13.7	6	0	0	0.0	0	0	0	0.0	0	7	0	42
CFL totals (2 years)	33	33	70	425	6.1	6	100	1951	19.5	13	107	1216	11.4	2	74	1925	26.0	0	21	0	126
NFL totals (7 years)	103	52	42	319	7.6	2	285	4111	14.4	25	0	0	0.0	0	109	2334	21.4	0	27	0	162
Pro totals (9 years)	136	85	112	744	6.6	8	385	6062	15.7	38	107	1216	11.4	2	183	4259	23.3	0	48	0	288

ISRAEL, STEVE   CB   SAINTS

PERSONAL: Born March 16, 1969, in Lawnside, N.J. ... 5-11/197. ... Full name: Steven Douglas Israel.
HIGH SCHOOL: Haddon Heights (N.J.).
COLLEGE: Pittsburgh (degree in economics).
TRANSACTIONS/CAREER NOTES: Selected by Los Angeles Rams in second round (30th pick overall) of 1992 NFL draft. ... Signed by Rams (August 23, 1992). ... Granted roster exemption (August 25-September 4, 1992). ... Claimed on waivers by Green Bay Packers (August 7, 1995). ... Released by Packers (August 25, 1995). ... Signed by San Francisco 49ers (October 3, 1995). ... Granted unconditional free agency (February 16, 1996). ... Re-signed by 49ers (March 1, 1996). ... Granted unconditional free agency (February 14, 1997). ... Signed by New England Patriots (March 24, 1997). ... Granted unconditional free agency (February 11, 2000). ... Signed by New Orleans Saints (April 21, 2000).
PLAYING EXPERIENCE: Los Angeles Rams NFL, 1992-1994; San Francisco, NFL, 1995 and 1996; New England NFL, 1997-1999. ... Games/Games started: 1992 (16/1), 1993 (16/12), 1994 (10/2), 1995 (8/0), 1996 (14/2), 1997 (5/0), 1998 (11/7), 1999 (13/13). Total: 93/37.
PRO STATISTICS: 1992—Returned one kickoff for minus three yards and recovered one fumble. 1993—Returned five kickoffs for 92 yards. 1996—Intercepted one pass for three yards and recovered one fumble. 1997—Credited with one sack. 1998—Intercepted three passes for 13 yards and credited with two sacks. 1999—Intercepted one pass for no yards, credited with one sack and recovered two fumbles.

IZZO, LARRY   LB   DOLPHINS

PERSONAL: Born September 26, 1974, in Fort Belvoir, Va. ... 5-10/228. ... Full name: Lawrence Alexander Izzo.
HIGH SCHOOL: McCullough (Houston).
COLLEGE: Rice.
TRANSACTIONS/CAREER NOTES: Signed as non-drafted free agent by Miami Dolphins (April 25, 1996). ... On injured reserve with foot injury (August 18, 1997-entire season). ... Granted free agency (February 12, 1999). ... Re-signed by Dolphins (March 31, 1999).
PLAYING EXPERIENCE: Miami NFL, 1996, 1998 and 1999. ... Games/Games started: 1996 (16/0), 1998 (13/0), 1999 (16/0). Total: 45/0.
PRO STATISTICS: 1996—Rushed once for 26 yards. 1999—Recovered one fumble.

JACKE, CHRIS   K

PERSONAL: Born March 12, 1966, in Richmond, Va. ... 6-0/205. ... Full name: Christopher Lee Jacke.
HIGH SCHOOL: J.J. Pearce (Richardson, Texas).
COLLEGE: Texas-El Paso (degree in business, 1989).
TRANSACTIONS/CAREER NOTES: Selected by Green Bay Packers in sixth round (142nd pick overall) of 1989 NFL draft. ... Signed by Packers (July 28, 1989). ... Granted free agency (February 1, 1991). ... Re-signed by Packers (August 26, 1991). ... Granted unconditional free agency (February 14, 1997). ... Signed by Pittsburgh Steelers (July 9, 1997). ... Released by Steelers (October 14, 1997). ... Signed by Washington Redskins (December 16, 1997). ... Released by Redskins (February 3, 1998). ... Signed by Arizona Cardinals (December 1, 1998). ... Granted

unconditional free agency (February 12, 1999). ... Re-signed by Cardinals (April 9, 1999). ... Granted unconditional free agency (February 11, 2000).
CHAMPIONSHIP GAME EXPERIENCE: Played in NFC championship game (1995 of 1996 seasons). ... Member of Super Bowl championship team (1996 season).

					KICKING			
Year Team	G	XPM	XPA	FGM	FGA	Lg.	50+	Pts.
1989—Green Bay NFL	16	42	42	22	28	52	1-3	108
1990—Green Bay NFL	16	28	29	23	30	53	2-4	97
1991—Green Bay NFL	16	31	31	18	24	53	1-1	85
1992—Green Bay NFL	16	30	30	22	29	53	2-3	96
1993—Green Bay NFL	16	35	35	31	37	54	6-7	128
1994—Green Bay NFL	16	41	43	19	26	50	1-3	98
1995—Green Bay NFL	14	43	43	17	23	51	3-4	94
1996—Green Bay NFL	16	*51	*53	21	27	53	1-1	114
1997—Washington NFL	1	5	5	0	0	0	0-0	5
1998—Arizona NFL	4	6	6	10	14	52	1-2	36
1999—Arizona NFL	16	26	26	19	27	49	0-3	83
Pro totals (11 years)	147	338	343	202	265	54	18-31	944

JACKSON, BRAD — LB — RAVENS

PERSONAL: Born January 11, 1975, in Canton, Ohio. ... 6-0/230. ... Full name: Bradley Michael Jackson.
HIGH SCHOOL: Firestone (Akron, Ohio).
COLLEGE: Cincinnati.
TRANSACTIONS/CAREER NOTES: Selected by Miami Dolphins in third round (79th pick overall) of 1998 NFL draft. ... Signed by Dolphins (July 21, 1998). ... Released by Dolphins (August 25, 1998). ... Signed by Tennessee Oilers to practice squad (September 1, 1998). ... Released by Oilers (September 29, 1998). ... Signed by Baltimore Ravens to practice squad (September 30, 1998). ... Activated (December 17, 1998); did not play.
PLAYING EXPERIENCE: Baltimore NFL, 1999. ... Games/Games started: 1999 (13/0).
HONORS: Named outside linebacker on The Sporting News college All-America third team (1997).
PRO STATISTICS: 1999—Recovered one fumble.

JACKSON, CALVIN — S — DOLPHINS

PERSONAL: Born October 28, 1972, in Miami. ... 5-9/195. ... Full name: Calvin Bernard Jackson.
HIGH SCHOOL: Dillard (Fort Lauderdale, Fla.).
COLLEGE: Auburn.
TRANSACTIONS/CAREER NOTES: Signed as non-drafted free agent by Miami Dolphins (July 21, 1994). ... Released by Dolphins (August 22, 1994). ... Re-signed by Dolphins to practice squad (August 29, 1994). ... Activated (September 17, 1994). ... Released by Dolphins (October 26, 1994). ... Re-signed by Dolphins to practice squad (October 27, 1994). ... On practice squad injured reserve with knee injury (December 24, 1994-remainder of season). ... Released by Dolphins (August 27, 1995). ... Re-signed by Dolphins to practice squad (August 30, 1995). ... Activated (September 9, 1995). ... Granted unconditional free agency (February 11, 2000). ... Re-signed by Dolphins (March 22, 2000).
PRO STATISTICS: 1996—Fumbled once. 1997—Recovered one fumble.

			INTERCEPTIONS				SACKS
Year Team	G	GS	No.	Yds.	Avg.	TD	No.
1994—Miami NFL	2	0	0	0	0.0	0	0.0
1995—Miami NFL	9	1	1	23	23.0	0	0.0
1996—Miami NFL	16	15	3	82	27.3	1	1.5
1997—Miami NFL	16	16	0	0	0.0	0	0.5
1998—Miami NFL	16	15	0	0	0.0	0	1.0
1999—Miami NFL	16	10	0	0	0.0	0	1.0
Pro totals (6 years)	75	57	4	105	26.3	1	4.0

JACKSON, DEXTER — S — BUCCANEERS

PERSONAL: Born July 28, 1977, in Quincy, Fla. ... 6-0/196. ... Full name: Dexter Lamar Jackson.
HIGH SCHOOL: James A. Shanks (Quincy, Fla.).
COLLEGE: Florida State.
TRANSACTIONS/CAREER NOTES: Selected by Tampa Bay Buccaneers in fourth round (113th pick overall) of 1999 NFL draft. ... Signed by Buccaneers (July 29, 1999).
PLAYING EXPERIENCE: Tampa Bay NFL, 1999. ... Games/Games started: 1999 (12/0).
CHAMPIONSHIP GAME EXPERIENCE: Played in NFC championship game (1999 season).

JACKSON, GRADY — DT — RAIDERS

PERSONAL: Born January 21, 1973, in Greensboro, Ala. ... 6-2/325.
HIGH SCHOOL: Greensboro (Ala.) East.
JUNIOR COLLEGE: Hinds Community College (Miss.).
COLLEGE: Knoxville (Tenn.) College.
TRANSACTIONS/CAREER NOTES: Selected by Oakland Raiders in sixth round (193rd pick overall) of 1997 NFL draft. ... Signed by Raiders for 1997 season.
PRO STATISTICS: 1998—Recovered one fumble for two yards. 1999—Recovered one fumble.

Year Team	G	GS	SACKS
1997—Oakland NFL	5	0	0.0
1998—Oakland NFL	15	1	3.0
1999—Oakland NFL	15	0	4.0
Pro totals (3 years)	35	1	7.0

JACKSON, GREG S CHARGERS

PERSONAL: Born August 20, 1966, in Hialeah, Fla. ... 6-1/217. ... Full name: Greg Allen Jackson.
HIGH SCHOOL: American (Hialeah, Fla.).
COLLEGE: Louisiana State.
TRANSACTIONS/CAREER NOTES: Selected by New York Giants in third round (78th pick overall) of 1989 NFL draft. ... Signed by Giants (July 24, 1989). ... Granted free agency (February 1, 1992). ... Re-signed by Giants (August 3, 1992). ... Granted unconditional free agency (February 17, 1994). ... Signed by Philadelphia Eagles (June 30, 1994). ... Granted unconditional free agency (February 16, 1996). ... Signed by New Orleans Saints (June 18, 1996). ... Granted unconditional free agency (February 14, 1997). ... Signed by San Diego Chargers (June 13, 1997). ... On injured reserve with leg injury (December 1, 1997-remainder of season). ... Granted unconditional free agency (February 13, 1998). ... Re-signed by Chargers (May 4, 1998). ... Released by Chargers (August 26, 1998). ... Re-signed by Chargers (August 30, 1998). ... Granted unconditional free agency (February 12, 1999). ... Re-signed by Chargers (August 9, 1999). ... Granted unconditional free agency (February 11, 2000). ... Re-signed by Chargers (April 24, 2000).
CHAMPIONSHIP GAME EXPERIENCE: Played in NFC championship game (1990 season). ... Member of Super Bowl championship team (1990 season).
PRO STATISTICS: 1989—Recovered one fumble. 1990—Credited with four sacks. 1991—Fumbled once. 1992—Recovered one fumble. 1993—Recovered three fumbles for three yards. 1995—Recovered three fumbles for 45 yards and one touchdown. 1996—Fumbled once. 1997—Returned one punt for no yards and recovered one fumble for 41 yards and a touchdown. 1998—Recovered one fumble. 1999—Recovered one fumble.

			INTERCEPTIONS			
Year Team	G	GS	No.	Yds.	Avg.	TD
1989—New York Giants NFL	16	1	0	0	0.0	0
1990—New York Giants NFL	14	14	5	8	1.6	0
1991—New York Giants NFL	13	12	1	3	3.0	0
1992—New York Giants NFL	16	16	4	71	17.8	0
1993—New York Giants NFL	16	16	4	32	8.0	0
1994—Philadelphia NFL	16	16	6	86	14.3	1
1995—Philadelphia NFL	16	16	1	18	18.0	0
1996—New Orleans NFL	16	15	3	24	8.0	0
1997—San Diego NFL	13	0	2	37	18.5	1
1998—San Diego NFL	16	13	6	50	8.3	0
1999—San Diego NFL	14	9	0	0	0.0	0
Pro totals (11 years)	166	128	32	329	10.3	2

JACKSON, JOHN OT CHARGERS

PERSONAL: Born January 4, 1965, in Camp Kwe, Okinawa, Japan. ... 6-6/297.
HIGH SCHOOL: Woodward (Cincinnati).
COLLEGE: Eastern Kentucky (degree in police administration, 1991).
TRANSACTIONS/CAREER NOTES: Selected by Pittsburgh Steelers in 10th round (252nd pick overall) of 1988 NFL draft. ... Signed by Steelers (May 17, 1988). ... Granted unconditional free agency (February 13, 1998). ... Signed by San Diego Chargers (February 18, 1998).
PLAYING EXPERIENCE: Pittsburgh NFL, 1988-1997; San Diego NFL, 1998 and 1999. ... Games/Games started: 1988 (16/0), 1989 (14/12), 1990 (16/16), 1991 (16/16), 1992 (16/13), 1993 (16/16), 1994 (16/16), 1995 (11/9), 1996 (16/16), 1997 (16/16), 1998 (16/16), 1999 (15/15). Total: 184/161.
CHAMPIONSHIP GAME EXPERIENCE: Played in AFC championship game (1994, 1995 and 1997 seasons). ... Played in Super Bowl XXX (1995 season).
PRO STATISTICS: 1988—Returned one kickoff for 10 yards. 1991—Recovered one fumble. 1993—Recovered one fumble. 1994—Recovered two fumbles. 1996—Recovered one fumble.

JACKSON, LENZIE WR JAGUARS

PERSONAL: Born June 17, 1977, in Santa Clara, Calif. ... 6-0/187. ... Full name: Lenzie Maurice Jackson.
HIGH SCHOOL: Milpitas (Calif.).
COLLEGE: Arizona State (degree in justice studies).
TRANSACTIONS/CAREER NOTES: Signed as non-drafted free agent by Jacksonville Jaguars (April 22, 1999). ... Released by Jaguars (September 5, 1999). ... Re-signed by Jaguars to practice squad (September 6, 1999). ... Activated (November 10, 1999).
PLAYING EXPERIENCE: Jacksonville NFL, 1999. ... Games/Games started: 1999 (4/0).
CHAMPIONSHIP GAME EXPERIENCE: Member of Jaguars for AFC championship game (1999 season); inactive.
PRO STATISTICS: 1999—Returned three kickoffs for 58 yards.

JACKSON, RAYMOND DB BROWNS

PERSONAL: Born February 17, 1973, in East Chicago, Ind. ... 5-10/189. ... Full name: Raymond DeWayne Jackson.
HIGH SCHOOL: Montbello (Denver).
COLLEGE: Colorado State.
TRANSACTIONS/CAREER NOTES: Selected by Buffalo Bills in fifth round (156th pick overall) of 1996 NFL draft. ... Signed by Bills (June 25, 1996). ... Selected by Cleveland Browns from Bills in NFL expansion draft (February 9, 1999). ... Granted free agency (February 12, 1999). ... Re-signed by Browns (April 14, 1999). ... Granted unconditional free agency (February 11, 2000). ... Re-signed by Browns (February 24, 2000).

PRO STATISTICS: 1997—Returned one punt for no yards and fumbled once.

Year Team	G	GS	INTERCEPTIONS			
			No.	Yds.	Avg.	TD
1996—Buffalo NFL	12	0	1	0	0.0	0
1997—Buffalo NFL	9	0	0	0	0.0	0
1998—Buffalo NFL	14	0	2	27	13.5	0
1999—Cleveland NFL	14	0	0	0	0.0	0
Pro totals (4 years)	49	0	3	27	9.0	0

JACKSON, SHELDON — TE — BILLS

PERSONAL: Born July 24, 1976, in Diamond Bar, Calif. ... 6-3/250. ... Full name: Sheldon B. Jackson Jr.
HIGH SCHOOL: Damien (La Verne, Calif.).
COLLEGE: Nebraska (degree in psychology).
TRANSACTIONS/CAREER NOTES: Selected by Buffalo Bills in seventh round (230th pick overall) of 1999 NFL draft. ... Signed by Bills (June 22, 1999).
PLAYING EXPERIENCE: Buffalo NFL, 1999. ... Games/Games started: 1999 (13/4).
PRO STATISTICS: 1999—Caught four passes for 34 yards.
SINGLE GAME HIGHS (regular season): Receptions—2 (January 2, 2000, vs. Indianapolis); yards—22 (January 2, 2000, vs. Indianapolis); and touchdown receptions—0.

JACKSON, STEVE — CB

PERSONAL: Born April 8, 1969, in Houston. ... 5-8/188. ... Full name: Steven Wayne Jackson.
HIGH SCHOOL: Klein Forest (Houston).
COLLEGE: Purdue.
TRANSACTIONS/CAREER NOTES: Selected by Houston Oilers in third round (71st pick overall) of 1991 NFL draft. ... Signed by Oilers (July 11, 1991). ... Granted free agency (February 17, 1994). ... Re-signed by Oilers (June 10, 1994). ... Granted unconditional free agency (February 14, 1997). ... Re-signed by Oilers (March 26, 1997). ... Oilers franchise moved to Tennessee for 1997 season. ... Oilers franchise renamed Tennessee Titans for 1999 season (December 26, 1998). ... Released by Titans (February 9, 2000).
CHAMPIONSHIP GAME EXPERIENCE: Played in AFC championship game (1999 season). ... Played in Super Bowl XXXIV (1999 season).
PRO STATISTICS: 1991—Returned one punt for no yards and recovered two fumbles. 1994—Returned 14 kickoffs for 285 yards. 1996—Credited with a safety and recovered one fumble. 1999—Recovered two fumbles.

Year Team	G	GS	INTERCEPTIONS				SACKS
			No.	Yds.	Avg.	TD	No.
1991—Houston NFL	15	2	0	0	0.0	0	1.0
1992—Houston NFL	16	1	3	18	6.0	0	1.0
1993—Houston NFL	16	12	5	54	10.8	▲1	0.0
1994—Houston NFL	11	0	1	0	0.0	0	1.0
1995—Houston NFL	10	1	2	0	0.0	0	1.0
1996—Houston NFL	16	1	0	0	0.0	0	2.0
1997—Tennessee NFL	12	6	0	0	0.0	0	1.0
1998—Tennessee NFL	14	4	1	0	0.0	0	1.5
1999—Tennessee NFL	8	0	1	2	2.0	0	0.5
Pro totals (9 years)	118	27	13	74	5.7	1	9.0

JACKSON, TERRY — RB — 49ERS

PERSONAL: Born January 10, 1976, in Gainesville, Fla. ... 6-0/218. ... Full name: Terrance Bernard Jackson. ... Brother of Willie Jackson Jr., wide receiver, New Orleans Saints.
HIGH SCHOOL: P.K. Yonge (Gainesville, Fla.).
COLLEGE: Florida.
TRANSACTIONS/CAREER NOTES: Selected by San Francisco 49ers in fifth round (157th pick overall) of 1999 NFL draft. ... Signed by 49ers (July 26, 1999).
SINGLE GAME HIGHS (regular season): Attempts—5 (January 3, 2000, vs. Atlanta); yards—35 (January 3, 2000, vs. Atlanta); and rushing touchdowns—0.

Year Team	G	GS	RUSHING				RECEIVING				TOTALS			
			Att.	Yds.	Avg.	TD	No.	Yds.	Avg.	TD	TD	2pt.	Pts.	Fum.
1999—San Francisco NFL	16	0	15	75	5.0	0	3	6	2.0	0	0	0	0	1

JACKSON, TYOKA — DL — BUCCANEERS

PERSONAL: Born November 22, 1971, in Washington, D.C. ... 6-2/280. ... Name pronounced tie-OH-kah.
HIGH SCHOOL: Bishop McNamara (Forestville, Md.).
COLLEGE: Penn State.
TRANSACTIONS/CAREER NOTES: Signed as non-drafted free agent by Atlanta Falcons (May 2, 1994). ... Released by Falcons (August 29, 1994). ... Re-signed by Falcons to practice squad (August 30, 1994). ... Signed by Miami Dolphins off Falcons practice squad (November 16, 1994). ... Released by Dolphins (August 27, 1995). ... Signed by Tampa Bay Buccaneers (December 27, 1995). ... Granted free agency (February 13, 1998). ... Re-signed by Buccaneers (June 22, 1998).
CHAMPIONSHIP GAME EXPERIENCE: Member of Buccaneers for NFC championship game (1999 season); inactive.
PRO STATISTICS: 1994—Recovered one fumble.

Year—Team	G	GS	SACKS
1994—Miami NFL	1	0	0.0
1995—	Did not play.		
1996—Tampa Bay NFL	13	2	0.0
1997—Tampa Bay NFL	12	0	2.5
1998—Tampa Bay NFL	16	12	3.0
1999—Tampa Bay NFL	6	0	1.0
Pro totals (5 years)	48	14	6.5

JACKSON, WAVERLY   G   COLTS

PERSONAL: Born December 19, 1972, in South Hill, Va. ... 6-2/315.
HIGH SCHOOL: Park View (Sterling, Va.).
COLLEGE: Virginia Tech.
TRANSACTIONS/CAREER NOTES: Signed as non-drafted free agent by Carolina Panthers (April 19, 1997). ... Released by Panthers (August 25, 1997). ... Re-signed by Panthers to practice squad (August 26, 1997). ... Granted free agency after 1997 season. ... Signed by Indianapolis Colts (January 12, 1998).
PLAYING EXPERIENCE: Indianapolis NFL, 1998 and 1999. ... Games/Games started: 1998 (7/2), 1999 (16/16). Total: 23/18.

JACKSON, WILLIE   WR   SAINTS

PERSONAL: Born August 16, 1971, in Gainesville, Fla. ... 6-1/212. ... Full name: Willie Bernard Jackson Jr. ... Brother of Terry Jackson, running back, San Francisco 49ers.
HIGH SCHOOL: P.K. Yonge (Gainesville, Fla.).
COLLEGE: Florida (degree in telecommunications, 1993).
TRANSACTIONS/CAREER NOTES: Selected by Dallas Cowboys in fourth round (109th pick overall) of 1994 NFL draft. ... Signed by Cowboys (July 16, 1994). ... Inactive for 16 games (1994). ... Selected by Jacksonville Jaguars from Cowboys in NFL expansion draft (February 15, 1995). ... Granted free agency (February 14, 1997). ... Re-signed by Jaguars (March 26, 1997). ... Released by Jaguars (August 30, 1998). ... Signed by Cincinnati Bengals (September 10, 1998). ... Granted unconditional free agency (February 11, 2000). ... Signed by New Orleans Saints (April 28, 2000)
CHAMPIONSHIP GAME EXPERIENCE: Member of Cowboys for NFC championship game (1994 season); inactive. ... Played in AFC championship game (1996 season).
PRO STATISTICS: 1995—Returned one punt for minus two yards and recovered one fumble. 1996—Rushed once for two yards. 1997—Rushed three times for 14 yards. 1999—Returned two punts for six yards and recovered one fumble.
SINGLE GAME HIGHS (regular season): Receptions—8 (November 17, 1996, vs. Pittsburgh); yards—113 (December 10, 1995, vs. Indianapolis); and touchdown receptions—2 (December 10, 1995, vs. Indianapolis).
STATISTICAL PLATEAUS: 100-yard receiving games: 1995 (1), 1996 (1). Total: 2.

			RECEIVING				KICKOFF RETURNS				TOTALS			
Year—Team	G	GS	No.	Yds.	Avg.	TD	No.	Yds.	Avg.	TD	TD	2pt.	Pts.	Fum.
1994—Dallas NFL							Did not play.							
1995—Jacksonville NFL	14	10	53	589	11.1	5	19	404	21.3	0	5	1	32	2
1996—Jacksonville NFL	16	2	33	486	14.7	3	7	149	21.3	0	3	1	20	0
1997—Jacksonville NFL	16	1	17	206	12.1	2	32	653	20.4	0	2	1	14	1
1998—Cincinnati NFL	8	0	7	165	23.6	0	0	0	0.0	0	0	0	0	0
1999—Cincinnati NFL	16	2	31	369	11.9	2	6	179	29.8	0	2	†1	14	1
Pro totals (5 years)	70	15	141	1815	12.9	12	64	1385	21.6	0	12	4	80	4

JACOBY, MITCH   TE   CHIEFS

PERSONAL: Born December 8, 1973, in Port Washington, Wis. ... 6-4/260. ... Full name: Mitchel Ray Jacoby.
HIGH SCHOOL: Fredonia (Wis.).
COLLEGE: Northern Illinois.
TRANSACTIONS/CAREER NOTES: Signed as non-drafted free agent by St. Louis Rams (April 29, 1997). ... Released by Rams (August 30, 1998). ... Re-signed by Rams (November 17, 1998). ... Traded by Rams to Kansas City Chiefs for sixth-round pick (traded to Denver) in 2000 draft (August 30, 1999). ... Granted free agency (February 11, 2000). ... Re-signed by Chiefs (March 28, 2000).
PLAYING EXPERIENCE: St. Louis NFL, 1997 and 1998; Kansas City NFL, 1999. ... Games/Games started: 1997 (14/2), 1998 (5/0), 1999 (5/0). Total: 24/2.
PRO STATISTICS: 1997—Caught two passes for 10 yards. 1999—Caught one pass for six yards.
SINGLE GAME HIGHS (regular season): Receptions—1 (October 31, 1999, vs. San Diego); yards—10 (September 28, 1997. vs. Oakland); and touchdown receptions—0.

JACOX, KENDYL   C/G   CHARGERS

PERSONAL: Born June 10, 1975, in Dallas. ... 6-2/330. ... Full name: Kendyl LaMarc Jacox. ... Name pronounced JAY-cox.
HIGH SCHOOL: Carter (Dallas).
COLLEGE: Kansas State.
TRANSACTIONS/CAREER NOTES: Signed as non-drafted free agent by San Diego Chargers (April 20, 1998). ... On injured reserve with knee injury (December 4, 1999-remainder of season).
PLAYING EXPERIENCE: San Diego NFL, 1998 and 1999. ... Games/Games started: 1998 (16/6), 1999 (10/5). Total: 26/11.
PRO STATISTICS: 1998—Returned one kickoff for no yards.

JACQUET, NATE   WR   DOLPHINS

PERSONAL: Born September 2, 1975, in Duarte, Calif. ... 6-0/185. ... Full name: Nathaniel Martin Jacquet.
HIGH SCHOOL: Duarte (Calif.).

JUNIOR COLLEGE: Mt. San Antonio College (Calif.).
COLLEGE: San Diego State.
TRANSACTIONS/CAREER NOTES: Selected by Indianapolis Colts in fifth round (150th pick overall) of 1997 NFL draft. ... Signed by Colts (June 26, 1997). ... Released by Colts (August 24, 1997). ... Re-signed by Colts to practice squad (August 25, 1997). ... Activated (November 4, 1997). ... Claimed on waivers by Miami Dolphins (August 26, 1998). ... Released by Dolphins (August 30, 1998). ... Re-signed by Dolphins to practice squad (August 31, 1998). ... Activated (September 9, 1998). ... Released by Dolphins (September 5, 1999). ... Re-signed by Dolphins (October 8, 1999). ... Granted free agency (February 11, 2000). ... Re-signed by Dolphins (April 28, 2000).
PRO STATISTICS: 1997—Recovered one fumble. 1999—Rushed once for four yards.
SINGLE GAME HIGHS (regular season): Receptions—5 (December 13, 1998, vs. New York Jets); yards—68 (December 13, 1998, vs. New York Jets); and touchdown receptions—0.

Year Team	G	GS	RECEIVING No.	Yds.	Avg.	TD	PUNT RETURNS No.	Yds.	Avg.	TD	KICKOFF RETURNS No.	Yds.	Avg.	TD	TOTALS TD	2pt.	Pts.	Fum.
1997—Indianapolis NFL	5	0	0	0	0.0	0	13	96	7.4	0	8	156	19.5	0	0	0	0	1
1998—Miami NFL	15	0	8	122	15.3	0	0	0	0.0	0	4	103	25.8	0	0	0	0	0
1999—Miami NFL	13	0	1	18	18.0	0	28	351	12.5	0	1	26	26.0	0	0	0	0	1
Pro totals (3 years)	33	0	9	140	15.6	0	41	447	10.9	0	13	285	21.9	0	0	0	0	2

JAEGER, JEFF — K

PERSONAL: Born November 26, 1964, in Tacoma, Wash. ... 5-11/190. ... Full name: Jeff Todd Jaeger.
HIGH SCHOOL: Meridian (Bellingham, Wash.).
COLLEGE: Washington.
TRANSACTIONS/CAREER NOTES: Selected by Cleveland Browns in third round (82nd pick overall) of 1987 NFL draft. ... Signed by Browns (July 26, 1987). ... Crossed picket line during players strike (October 14, 1987). ... On injured reserve with foot injury (August 26, 1988-entire season). ... Granted unconditional free agency (February 1, 1989). ... Signed by Los Angeles Raiders (March 20, 1989). ... Granted free agency (February 1, 1991). ... Re-signed by Raiders (July 13, 1991). ... Granted free agency (February 1, 1993). ... Re-signed by Raiders (August 30, 1993). ... Re-signed by Raiders (August 31, 1993). ... Raiders franchise moved to Oakland (July 21, 1995). ... Released by Raiders (August 25, 1996). ... Signed by Chicago Bears (September 17, 1996). ... Released by Bears (September 11, 1999). ... Re-signed by Bears (September 13, 1999). ... Released by Bears (September 18, 1999). ... Re-signed by Bears (September 20, 1999). ... On injured reserve with hip injury (October 13, 1999-remainder of season). ... Granted unconditional free agency (February 11, 2000).
CHAMPIONSHIP GAME EXPERIENCE: Played in AFC championship game (1990 season).
HONORS: Played in Pro Bowl (1991 season).
PRO STATISTICS: 1987—Attempted one pass without a completion and recovered one fumble. 1997—Punted once for 18 yards. 1998—Punted once for 27 yards.

Year Team	G	KICKING XPM	XPA	FGM	FGA	Lg.	50+	Pts.
1987—Cleveland NFL	10	33	33	14	22	48	0-1	75
1988—Cleveland NFL				Did not play.				
1989—Los Angeles Raiders NFL	16	34	34	23	34	50	1-2	103
1990—Los Angeles Raiders NFL	16	40	42	15	20	50	1-2	85
1991—Los Angeles Raiders NFL	16	29	30	29	34	53	2-4	§116
1992—Los Angeles Raiders NFL	16	28	28	15	26	†54	3-6	73
1993—Los Angeles Raiders NFL	16	27	29	*35	*44	53	4-7	*132
1994—Los Angeles Raiders NFL	16	31	31	22	28	51	2-2	97
1995—Oakland NFL	11	22	22	13	18	46	0-1	61
1996—Chicago NFL	13	23	23	19	23	49	0-0	80
1997—Chicago NFL	16	20	20	21	26	52	1-1	83
1998—Chicago NFL	16	27	28	21	26	52	1-1	90
1999—Chicago NFL	3	7	7	2	8	52	1-1	13
Pro totals (12 years)	165	321	327	229	309	54	16-28	1008

JAMES, EDGERRIN — RB — COLTS

PERSONAL: Born August 1, 1978, in Immokalee, Fla. ... 6-0/216. ... Full name: Edgerrin Tyree James. ... Name pronounced EDGE-rin.
HIGH SCHOOL: Immokalee (Fla.).
COLLEGE: Miami (Fla.).
TRANSACTIONS/CAREER NOTES: Selected after junior season by Indianapolis Colts in first round (fourth pick overall) of 1999 NFL draft. ... Signed by Colts (August 12, 1999).
HONORS: Named NFL Rookie of the Year by THE SPORTING NEWS (1999). ... Named running back on THE SPORTING NEWS NFL All-Pro team (1999). ... Played in Pro Bowl (1999 season).
PRO STATISTICS: 1999—Recovered two fumbles.
SINGLE GAME HIGHS (regular season): Attempts—32 (September 19, 1999, vs. New England); yards—152 (November 21, 1999, vs. Philadelphia); and rushing touchdowns—3 (December 26, 1999, vs. Cleveland).
STATISTICAL PLATEAUS: 100-yard rushing games: 1999 (10).

Year Team	G	GS	RUSHING Att.	Yds.	Avg.	TD	RECEIVING No.	Yds.	Avg.	TD	TOTALS TD	2pt.	Pts.	Fum.
1999—Indianapolis NFL	16	16	*369	*1553	4.2	▲13	62	586	9.5	4	†17	0	102	8

JAMES, TORY — CB — RAIDERS

PERSONAL: Born May 18, 1973, in New Orleans. ... 6-2/185. ... Full name: Tory Steven James.
HIGH SCHOOL: Archbishop Shaw (Marrero, La.).
COLLEGE: Louisiana State.
TRANSACTIONS/CAREER NOTES: Selected by Denver Broncos in second round (44th pick overall) of 1996 NFL draft. ... Signed by Broncos (July 22, 1996). ... On injured reserve with knee injury (August 18, 1997-entire season). ... Granted unconditional free agency (February 11, 2000). ... Signed by Oakland Raiders (February 28, 2000).

CHAMPIONSHIP GAME EXPERIENCE: Played in AFC championship game (1998 season). ... Member of Super Bowl championship team (1998 season).
PRO STATISTICS: 1996—Recovered one fumble for 15 yards. 1998—Recovered one fumble.

				INTERCEPTIONS		
Year Team	G	GS	No.	Yds.	Avg.	TD
1996—Denver NFL	16	2	2	15	7.5	0
1997—Denver NFL				Did not play.		
1998—Denver NFL	16	0	0	0	0.0	0
1999—Denver NFL	16	4	5	59	11.8	0
Pro totals (3 years)	48	6	7	74	10.6	0

JANSEN, JON   OT   REDSKINS

PERSONAL: Born January 28, 1976, in Clawson, Mich. ... 6-6/302. ... Full name: Jonathan Ward Jansen.
HIGH SCHOOL: Clawson (Mich.).
COLLEGE: Michigan.
TRANSACTIONS/CAREER NOTES: Selected by Washington Redskins in second round (37th pick overall) of 1999 NFL draft. ... Signed by Redskins (July 9, 1999).
PLAYING EXPERIENCE: Washington NFL, 1999. ... Games/Games started: 1999 (16/16).

JASPER, ED   DT   FALCONS

PERSONAL: Born January 18, 1973, in Tyler, Texas. ... 6-2/295. ... Full name: Edward Vidal Jasper.
HIGH SCHOOL: Troup (Texas).
COLLEGE: Texas A&M.
TRANSACTIONS/CAREER NOTES: Selected by Philadelphia Eagles in sixth round (198th pick overall) of 1997 NFL draft. ... Signed by Eagles (July 16, 1997). ... Released by Eagles (August 30, 1998). ... Re-signed by Eagles (September 17, 1998). ... Released by Eagles (October 23, 1998). ... Re-signed by Eagles (December 9, 1998). ... Released by Eagles (February 12, 1999). ... Signed by Atlanta Falcons (March 5, 1999).
PLAYING EXPERIENCE: Philadelphia NFL, 1997 and 1998; Atlanta NFL, 1999. ... Games/Games started: 1997 (9/1), 1998 (7/0), 1999 (13/0). Total: 29/1.

JEFFERS, PATRICK   WR   PANTHERS

PERSONAL: Born February 2, 1973, in Fort Campbell, Ky. ... 6-3/218. ... Full name: Patrick Christopher Jeffers.
HIGH SCHOOL: Fort Worth (Texas) Country Day.
COLLEGE: Virginia.
TRANSACTIONS/CAREER NOTES: Selected by Denver Broncos in fifth round (159th pick overall) of 1996 NFL draft. ... Signed by Broncos (July 17, 1996). ... Traded by Broncos to Dallas Cowboys for past considerations (August 30, 1998). ... Granted free agency (February 12, 1999). ... Tendered offer sheet by Carolina Panthers (April 12, 1999). ... Cowboys declined to match offer (April 15, 1999).
CHAMPIONSHIP GAME EXPERIENCE: Played in AFC championship game (1997 season). ... Member of Super Bowl championship team (1997 season).
PRO STATISTICS: 1996—Returned one kickoff for 18 yards. 1999—Rushed twice for 16 yards and recovered one fumble for three yards.
SINGLE GAME HIGHS (regular season): Receptions—8 (December 18, 1999, vs. San Francisco); yards—165 (January 2, 2000, vs. New Orleans); and touchdown receptions—2 (January 2, 2000, vs. New Orleans).
STATISTICAL PLATEAUS: 100-yard receiving games: 1999 (5).

			RECEIVING				TOTALS			
Year Team	G	GS	No.	Yds.	Avg.	TD	TD	2pt.	Pts.	Fum.
1996—Denver NFL	4	0	0	0	0.0	0	0	0	0	0
1997—Denver NFL	10	0	3	24	8.0	0	0	0	0	0
1998—Dallas NFL	8	1	18	330	18.3	2	2	0	12	0
1999—Carolina NFL	15	10	63	1082	17.2	12	12	0	72	0
Pro totals (4 years)	37	11	84	1436	17.1	14	14	0	84	0

JEFFERSON, GREG   DE   EAGLES

PERSONAL: Born August 31, 1971, in Orlando. ... 6-3/280. ... Full name: Greg Benton Jefferson.
HIGH SCHOOL: Bartow (Fla.).
COLLEGE: Central Florida.
TRANSACTIONS/CAREER NOTES: Selected by Philadelphia Eagles in third round (72nd pick overall) of 1995 NFL draft. ... Signed by Eagles (June 29, 1995). ... On injured reserve with knee injury (September 21, 1995-remainder of season). ... Granted free agency (February 13, 1998). ... Re-signed by Eagles (June 3, 1998).
PRO STATISTICS: 1997—Recovered one fumble. 1999—Recovered two fumbles for four yards.

Year Team	G	GS	SACKS
1995—Philadelphia NFL	3	0	0.0
1996—Philadelphia NFL	11	0	2.5
1997—Philadelphia NFL	12	11	3.0
1998—Philadelphia NFL	15	14	4.0
1999—Philadelphia NFL	16	16	4.0
Pro totals (5 years)	57	41	13.5

JEFFERSON, SHAWN   WR   FALCONS

PERSONAL: Born February 22, 1969, in Jacksonville. ... 5-11/180. ... Full name: Vanchi LaShawn Jefferson.
HIGH SCHOOL: Raines (Jacksonville).

COLLEGE: Central Florida.
TRANSACTIONS/CAREER NOTES: Selected by Houston Oilers in ninth round (240th pick overall) of 1991 NFL draft. ... Signed by Oilers (July 15, 1991). ... Traded by Oilers with first-round pick (DE Chris Mims) in 1992 draft to San Diego Chargers for DL Lee Williams (August 22, 1991). ... Granted free agency (March 1, 1993). ... Re-signed by Chargers (July 15, 1993). ... Granted free agency (February 17, 1994). ... Re-signed by Chargers (May 2, 1994). ... Released by Chargers (February 29, 1996). ... Signed by New England Patriots (March 14, 1996). ... Granted unconditional free agency (February 11, 2000). ... Signed by Atlanta Falcons (February 12, 2000).
CHAMPIONSHIP GAME EXPERIENCE: Played in AFC championship game (1994 and 1996 seasons). ... Played in Super Bowl XXIX (1994 season) and Super Bowl XXXI (1996 season).
PRO STATISTICS: 1998—Recovered one fumble. 1999—Recovered one fumble.
SINGLE GAME HIGHS (regular season): Receptions—7 (December 12, 1999, vs. Indianapolis); yards—131 (November 23, 1998, vs. Miami); and touchdown receptions—2 (October 31, 1999, vs. Arizona).
STATISTICAL PLATEAUS: 100-yard receiving games: 1995 (1), 1997 (1), 1998 (2), 1999 (1). Total: 5.

			RUSHING				RECEIVING				TOTALS			
Year Team	G	GS	Att.	Yds.	Avg.	TD	No.	Yds.	Avg.	TD	TD	2pt.	Pts.	Fum.
1991—San Diego NFL	16	3	1	27	27.0	0	12	125	10.4	1	1	0	6	0
1992—San Diego NFL	16	1	0	0	0.0	0	29	377	13.0	2	2	0	12	0
1993—San Diego NFL	16	4	5	53	10.6	0	30	391	13.0	2	2	0	12	0
1994—San Diego NFL	16	16	3	40	13.3	0	43	627	14.6	3	3	0	18	0
1995—San Diego NFL	16	15	2	1	0.5	0	48	621	12.9	2	2	0	12	0
1996—New England NFL	15	15	1	6	6.0	0	50	771	15.4	4	4	0	24	2
1997—New England NFL	16	14	0	0	0.0	0	54	841	15.6	2	2	0	12	2
1998—New England NFL	16	16	1	15	15.0	0	34	771	*22.7	2	2	0	12	0
1999—New England NFL	16	16	0	0	0.0	0	40	698	§17.5	6	6	0	36	0
Pro totals (9 years)	143	100	13	142	10.9	0	340	5222	15.4	24	24	0	144	4

JEFFRIES, GREG CB DOLPHINS

PERSONAL: Born October 16, 1971, in High Point, N.C. ... 5-9/195. ... Full name: Greg Lemont Jeffries.
HIGH SCHOOL: T.W. Andrews (High Point, N.C.).
COLLEGE: Virginia.
TRANSACTIONS/CAREER NOTES: Selected by Detroit Lions in sixth round (147th pick overall) of 1993 NFL draft. ... Signed by Lions (July 17, 1993). ... Granted unconditional free agency (February 14, 1997). ... Re-signed by Lions (February 19, 1997). ... Granted unconditional free agency (February 12, 1999). ... Signed by Miami Dolphins (February 19, 1999).
PLAYING EXPERIENCE: Detroit NFL, 1993-1998; Miami NFL, 1999. ... Games/Games started: 1993 (7/0), 1994 (16/1), 1995 (14/0), 1996 (16/4), 1997 (15/2), 1998 (15/3), 1999 (16/0). Total: 99/10.
PRO STATISTICS: 1993—Recovered one fumble. 1995—Credited with 1/2 sack. 1996—Intercepted one pass for no yards. 1997—Intercepted one pass for no yards and credited with one sack. 1998—Recovered one fumble.

JELLS, DIETRICH WR EAGLES

PERSONAL: Born April 11, 1972, in Brooklyn, N.Y. ... 5-10/185. ... Name pronounced DEE-trick.
HIGH SCHOOL: Tech Memorial (Erie, Pa.).
COLLEGE: Pittsburgh (degree in business).
TRANSACTIONS/CAREER NOTES: Selected by Kansas City Chiefs in sixth round (176th pick overall) of 1996 NFL draft. ... Signed by Chiefs (July 26, 1996). ... Claimed on waivers by New England Patriots (August 21, 1996). ... Traded by Patriots to Philadelphia Eagles for conditional draft pick (August 30, 1998). ... Granted free agency (February 12, 1999). ... Re-signed by Eagles (March 29, 1999). ... Released by Eagles (November 16, 1999). ... Re-signed by Eagles (November 24, 1999). ... Granted unconditional free agency (February 11, 2000). ... Re-signed by Eagles (April 5, 2000).
CHAMPIONSHIP GAME EXPERIENCE: Member of Patriots for AFC championship game (1996 season); inactive. ... Member of Patriots for Super Bowl XXXI (1996 season); inactive.
PRO STATISTICS: 1998—Rushed twice for nine yards.
SINGLE GAME HIGHS (regular season): Receptions—2 (December 12, 1999, vs. Dallas); yards—69 (October 17, 1999, vs. Chicago); and touchdown receptions—1 (December 19, 1999, vs. New England).

			RECEIVING				TOTALS			
Year Team	G	GS	No.	Yds.	Avg.	TD	TD	2pt.	Pts.	Fum.
1996—New England NFL	7	1	1	5	5.0	0	0	0	0	0
1997—New England NFL	11	0	1	9	9.0	0	0	0	0	0
1998—Philadelphia NFL	9	0	2	53	26.5	0	0	0	0	0
1999—Philadelphia NFL	14	3	10	180	18.0	2	2	0	12	0
Pro totals (4 years)	41	4	14	247	17.6	2	2	0	12	0

JENKINS, BILLY S BRONCOS

PERSONAL: Born July 8, 1974, in Albuquerque, N.M. ... 5-10/205.
HIGH SCHOOL: Albuquerque (N.M.).
COLLEGE: Howard.
TRANSACTIONS/CAREER NOTES: Signed as non-drafted free agent by St. Louis Rams (April 29, 1997). ... Granted free agency (February 11, 2000). ... Re-signed by Rams (March 3, 2000). ... Traded by Rams to Denver Broncos for fifth-round pick (DL Brian Young) in 2000 draft and conditional pick in 2001 draft (March 3, 2000).
CHAMPIONSHIP GAME EXPERIENCE: Played in NFC championship game (1999 season). ... Member of Super Bowl championship team (1999 season).

			INTERCEPTIONS				SACKS
Year Team	G	GS	No.	Yds.	Avg.	TD	No.
1997—St. Louis NFL	16	2	0	0	0.0	0	0.0
1998—St. Louis NFL	16	13	2	31	15.5	0	3.0

| 1999—St. Louis NFL | 16 | 16 | 2 | 16 | 8.0 | 0 | 1.0 |
| Pro totals (3 years) | 48 | 31 | 4 | 47 | 11.8 | 0 | 4.0 |

JENKINS, DeRON — CB — CHARGERS

PERSONAL: Born November 14, 1973, in St. Louis. ... 5-11/192. ... Full name: DeRon Charles Jenkins.
HIGH SCHOOL: Ritenour (St. Louis).
COLLEGE: Tennessee.
TRANSACTIONS/CAREER NOTES: Selected by Baltimore Ravens in second round (55th pick overall) of 1996 NFL draft. ... Signed by Ravens (July 19, 1996). ... Granted free agency (February 12, 1999). ... Re-signed by Ravens (July 28, 1999). ... Granted unconditional free agency (February 11, 2000). ... Signed by San Diego Chargers (February 21, 2000).
PLAYING EXPERIENCE: Baltimore NFL, 1996-1999. ... Games/Games started: 1996 (15/2), 1997 (16/6), 1998 (16/7), 1999 (16/15). Total: 63/30.
PRO STATISTICS: 1996—Recovered one fumble. 1997—Intercepted one pass for 15 yards and recovered one fumble. 1998—Intercepted one pass for no yards and recovered one fumble. 1999—Credited with one sack.

JENKINS, JAMES — TE — REDSKINS

PERSONAL: Born August 17, 1967, in Staten Island, N.Y. ... 6-2/249.
HIGH SCHOOL: Curtis (Staten Island, N.Y.).
COLLEGE: Rutgers.
TRANSACTIONS/CAREER NOTES: Signed as non-drafted free agent by Washington Redskins (April 25, 1991). ... Released by Redskins (August 26, 1991). ... Re-signed by Redskins to practice squad (August 27, 1991). ... Activated (November 30, 1991). ... Released by Redskins (August 31, 1992). ... Re-signed by Redskins (September 1, 1992). ... On injured reserve with back injury (September-November 28, 1992). ... On injured reserve with shoulder injury (December 28, 1993-remainder of season). ... Granted free agency (February 17, 1995). ... Re-signed by Redskins (July 19, 1995). ... Granted unconditional free agency (February 14, 1997). ... Re-signed by Redskins (July 16, 1997). ... Granted unconditional free agency (February 12, 1999). ... Re-signed by Redskins (May 11, 1999).
CHAMPIONSHIP GAME EXPERIENCE: Played in NFC championship game (1991 season). ... Member of Super Bowl championship team (1991 season).
PRO STATISTICS: 1994—Returned one kickoff for four yards. 1995—Returned one kickoff for 12 yards and recovered one fumble. 1996—Recovered one fumble. 1998—Returned one kickoff for no yards and recovered one fumble. 1999—Returned one kickoff for 10 yards.
SINGLE GAME HIGHS (regular season): Receptions—2 (October 23, 1994, vs. Indianapolis); yards—30 (November 21, 1999, vs. New York Giants); and touchdown receptions—2 (October 23, 1994, vs. Indianapolis).

| | | | | RECEIVING | | | | TOTALS | | |
Year Team	G	GS	No.	Yds.	Avg.	TD	TD	2pt.	Pts.	Fum.
1991—Washington NFL	4	0	0	0	0.0	0	0	0	0	0
1992—Washington NFL	5	1	0	0	0.0	0	0	0	0	0
1993—Washington NFL	15	5	0	0	0.0	0	0	0	0	0
1994—Washington NFL	16	3	8	32	4.0	4	4	0	24	0
1995—Washington NFL	16	5	1	2	2.0	0	0	0	0	0
1996—Washington NFL	16	5	1	7	7.0	0	0	0	0	0
1997—Washington NFL	16	4	4	43	10.8	3	3	0	18	0
1998—Washington NFL	16	4	0	0	0.0	0	0	0	0	0
1999—Washington NFL	16	4	1	30	30.0	0	0	0	0	0
Pro totals (9 years)	120	31	15	114	7.6	7	7	0	42	0

JENKINS, KERRY — G/OT — JETS

PERSONAL: Born September 6, 1973, in Tuscaloosa, Ala. ... 6-5/305.
HIGH SCHOOL: Holt (Ala.).
COLLEGE: Louisiana State, then Troy (Ala.) State.
TRANSACTIONS/CAREER NOTES: Signed as non-drafted free agent by Chicago Bears (April 25, 1997). ... Released by Bears (August 24, 1997). ... Re-signed by Bears to practice squad (August 27, 1997). ... Signed by New York Jets off Bears practice squad (December 3, 1997).
PLAYING EXPERIENCE: New York Jets NFL, 1997-1999. ... Games/Games started: 1997 (2/2), 1998 (16/0), 1999 (16/16). Total: 34/18.
CHAMPIONSHIP GAME EXPERIENCE: Played in AFC championship game (1998 season).
PRO STATISTICS: 1999—Recovered one fumble.

JENKINS, MARTAY — WR — CARDINALS

PERSONAL: Born February 28, 1975, in Waterloo, Iowa ... 5-11/193.
HIGH SCHOOL: Waterloo (Iowa) North.
JUNIOR COLLEGE: North Iowa Area Community College.
COLLEGE: Nebraska-Omaha (degree in sociology).
TRANSACTIONS/CAREER NOTES: Selected by Dallas Cowboys in sixth round (193rd pick overall) of 1999 NFL draft. ... Signed by Cowboys (July 27, 1999). ... Claimed on waivers by Arizona Cardinals (September 6, 1999).
PLAYING EXPERIENCE: Arizona NFL, 1999. ... Games/Games started: 1999 (3/0).

JERVEY, TRAVIS — RB — 49ERS

PERSONAL: Born May 5, 1972, in Columbia, S.C. ... 6-0/222. ... Full name: Travis Richard Jervey.
HIGH SCHOOL: Wando (Mount Pleasant, S.C.).
COLLEGE: The Citadel.

TRANSACTIONS/CAREER NOTES: Selected by Green Bay Packers in fifth round (170th pick overall) of 1995 NFL draft. ... Signed by Packers (May 23, 1995). ... Granted free agency (February 13, 1998). ... Re-signed by Packers (June 16, 1998). ... On injured reserve with knee and ankle injuries (November 11, 1998-remainder of season). ... Granted unconditional free agency (February 12, 1999). ... Signed by San Francisco 49ers (March 22, 1999). ... On physically unable to perform list with ankle injury (July 27-August 26, 1999). ... On suspended list for violating league substance abuse policy (October 21-November 26, 1999).

CHAMPIONSHIP GAME EXPERIENCE: Played in NFC championship game (1995-97 seasons). ... Member of Super Bowl championship team (1996 season). ... Played in Super Bowl XXXII (1997 season).

HONORS: Played in Pro Bowl (1997 season).

PRO STATISTICS: 1995—Recovered one fumble. 1996—Recovered one fumble.

SINGLE GAME HIGHS (regular season): Attempts—29 (October 25, 1998, vs. Baltimore); yards—95 (November 1, 1998, vs. San Francisco); and rushing touchdowns—1 (January 3, 2000, vs. Atlanta).

			RUSHING				RECEIVING				KICKOFF RETURNS				TOTALS		
Year Team	G	GS	Att.	Yds.	Avg.	TD	No.	Yds.	Avg.	TD	No.	Yds.	Avg.	TD	TD 2pt.	Pts.	Fum.
1995—Green Bay NFL	16	0	0	0	0.0	0	0	0	0.0	0	8	165	20.6	0	0	0	0
1996—Green Bay NFL	16	0	26	106	4.1	0	0	0	0.0	0	1	17	17.0	0	0	0	4
1997—Green Bay NFL	16	0	0	0	0.0	0	0	0	0.0	0	0	0	0.0	0	0	0	0
1998—Green Bay NFL	8	5	83	325	3.9	1	9	33	3.7	0	0	0	0.0	0	1	6	0
1999—San Francisco NFL	8	0	6	49	8.2	1	1	2	2.0	0	8	191	23.9	0	1	6	0
Pro totals (5 years)	64	5	115	480	4.2	2	10	35	3.5	0	17	373	21.9	0	2	12	4

JETT, JAMES — WR — RAIDERS

PERSONAL: Born December 28, 1970, in Charles Town, W.Va. ... 5-10/170.

HIGH SCHOOL: Jefferson (Shenandoah Junction, W.Va.).

COLLEGE: West Virginia.

TRANSACTIONS/CAREER NOTES: Signed as non-drafted free agent by Los Angeles Raiders (May 1993). ... Raiders franchise moved to Oakland (July 21, 1995).

PRO STATISTICS: 1993—Rushed once for no yards. 1994—Recovered two fumbles for 15 yards. 1997—Recovered one fumble. 1998—Rushed once for three yards and recovered one fumble for four yards.

SINGLE GAME HIGHS (regular season): Receptions—7 (October 13, 1996, vs. Detroit); yards—148 (September 21, 1997, vs. New York Jets); and touchdown receptions—2 (October 26, 1997, vs. Seattle).

STATISTICAL PLATEAUS: 100-yard receiving games: 1993 (2), 1996 (1), 1997 (1), 1998 (2). Total: 6.

			RECEIVING				TOTALS			
Year Team	G	GS	No.	Yds.	Avg.	TD	TD	2pt.	Pts.	Fum.
1993—Los Angeles Raiders NFL	16	1	33	771	*23.4	3	3	0	18	1
1994—Los Angeles Raiders NFL	16	1	15	253	16.9	0	0	0	0	0
1995—Oakland NFL	16	0	13	179	13.8	1	1	0	6	1
1996—Oakland NFL	16	16	43	601	14.0	4	4	0	24	0
1997—Oakland NFL	16	16	46	804	17.5	▲12	12	0	72	2
1998—Oakland NFL	16	16	45	882	19.6	6	6	0	36	0
1999—Oakland NFL	16	11	39	552	14.2	2	2	†1	14	0
Pro totals (7 years)	112	61	234	4042	17.3	28	28	1	170	4

JETT, JOHN — P — LIONS

PERSONAL: Born November 11, 1968, in Richmond, Va. ... 6-0/197.

HIGH SCHOOL: Northumberland (Heathsville, Va.).

COLLEGE: East Carolina.

TRANSACTIONS/CAREER NOTES: Signed as non-drafted free agent by Minnesota Vikings (June 22, 1992). ... Released by Vikings (August 25, 1992). ... Signed by Dallas Cowboys (March 10, 1993). ... Granted unconditional free agency (February 16, 1996). ... Re-signed by Cowboys (April 15, 1996). ... Granted unconditional free agency (February 14, 1997). ... Signed by Detroit Lions (March 7, 1997). ... Granted unconditional free agency (February 11, 2000). ... Re-signed by Lions (February 21, 2000).

CHAMPIONSHIP GAME EXPERIENCE: Played in NFC championship game (1993-1995 seasons). ... Member of Super Bowl championship team (1993 and 1995 seasons).

PRO STATISTICS: 1996—Rushed once for minus 23 yards. 1998—Attempted one pass without a completion. 1999—Rushed twice for minus eight yards and fumbled once.

				PUNTING			
Year Team	G	No.	Yds.	Avg.	Net avg.	In. 20	Blk.
1993—Dallas NFL	16	56	2342	41.8	37.7	22	0
1994—Dallas NFL	16	70	2935	41.9	35.3	26	0
1995—Dallas NFL	16	53	2166	40.9	34.5	17	0
1996—Dallas NFL	16	74	3150	42.6	36.7	22	0
1997—Detroit NFL	16	84	3576	42.6	35.6	24	†2
1998—Detroit NFL	14	66	2892	43.8	36.0	17	0
1999—Detroit NFL	16	86	3637	42.3	34.8	27	0
Pro totals (7 years)	110	489	20698	42.3	35.8	155	2

JOHNSON, ANTHONY — RB — PANTHERS

PERSONAL: Born October 25, 1967, in Indianapolis. ... 6-0/225. ... Full name: Anthony Scott Johnson.

HIGH SCHOOL: John Adams (South Bend, Ind.).

COLLEGE: Notre Dame.

TRANSACTIONS/CAREER NOTES: Selected by Indianapolis Colts in second round (36th pick overall) of 1990 NFL draft. ... Signed by Colts (July 27, 1990). ... On injured reserve with eye injury (November 5, 1991-remainder of season). ... Granted unconditional free agency (February 17, 1994). ... Signed by New York Jets (June 21, 1994). ... Granted unconditional free agency (February 17, 1995). ... Signed by Chicago Bears (March 21, 1995). ... Claimed on waivers by Carolina Panthers (November 7, 1995). ... Granted unconditional free agency

(February 14, 1997). ... Re-signed by Panthers (February 24, 1997). ... Granted unconditional free agency (February 11, 2000). ... Re-signed by Panthers (April 27, 2000).

CHAMPIONSHIP GAME EXPERIENCE: Played in NFC championship game (1996 season).

PRO STATISTICS: 1992—Attempted one pass without a completion and recovered four fumbles. 1993—Had only pass attempt intercepted and recovered two fumbles. 1994—Returned one punt for three yards. 1997—Recovered two fumbles. 1998—Returned two kickoffs for 12 yards and recovered one fumble. 1999—Returned one punt for three yards and returned one kickoff for nine yards.

SINGLE GAME HIGHS (regular season): Attempts—29 (October 20, 1996, vs. New Orleans); yards—134 (August 31, 1997, vs. Washington); and rushing touchdowns—1 (December 15, 1996, vs. Baltimore).

STATISTICAL PLATEAUS: 100-yard rushing games: 1996 (5), 1997 (1). Total: 6. ... 100-yard receiving games: 1991 (1), 1992 (1). Total: 2.

MISCELLANEOUS: Holds Carolina Panthers all-time record for most yards rushing (1,795).

				RUSHING				RECEIVING				TOTALS		
Year Team	G	GS	Att.	Yds.	Avg.	TD	No.	Yds.	Avg.	TD	TD	2pt.	Pts.	Fum.
1990—Indianapolis NFL	16	0	0	0	0.0	0	5	32	6.4	2	2	0	12	0
1991—Indianapolis NFL	9	6	22	94	4.3	0	42	344	8.2	0	0	0	0	2
1992—Indianapolis NFL	15	13	178	592	3.3	0	49	517	10.6	3	3	0	18	6
1993—Indianapolis NFL	13	8	95	331	3.5	1	55	443	8.1	0	1	0	6	5
1994—New York Jets NFL	15	0	5	12	2.4	0	5	31	6.2	0	0	0	0	0
1995—Chicago NFL	8	0	6	30	5.0	0	13	86	6.6	0	0	0	0	2
—Carolina NFL	7	0	24	110	4.6	1	16	121	7.6	0	1	0	6	0
1996—Carolina NFL	16	11	300	1120	3.7	6	26	192	7.4	0	6	0	36	2
1997—Carolina NFL	16	7	97	358	3.7	0	21	158	7.5	1	1	1	8	2
1998—Carolina NFL	16	2	36	135	3.8	0	27	242	9.0	1	1	0	6	3
1999—Carolina NFL	16	0	25	72	2.9	0	13	103	7.9	0	0	0	0	1
Pro totals (10 years)	147	47	788	2854	3.6	8	272	2269	8.3	7	15	1	92	23

JOHNSON, BILL　　DT

PERSONAL: Born December 9, 1968, in Chicago. ... 6-4/305. ... Full name: William Edward Johnson.

HIGH SCHOOL: Neal F. Simeon (Chicago).

COLLEGE: Michigan State.

TRANSACTIONS/CAREER NOTES: Selected by Cleveland Browns in third round (65th pick overall) of 1992 NFL draft. ... Signed by Browns (July 19, 1992). ... Granted free agency (February 17, 1995). ... Re-signed by Browns (April 13, 1995). ... Claimed on waivers by Cincinnati Bengals (August 1, 1995); released after failing physical. ... Signed by Pittsburgh Steelers (October 25, 1995). ... Granted unconditional free agency (February 14, 1997). ... Signed by St. Louis Rams (June 10, 1997). ... Granted unconditional free agency (February 13, 1998). ... Signed by Philadelphia Eagles (February 21, 1998). ... On injured reserve with knee injury (December 4, 1998-remainder of season). ... Released by Eagles (November 9, 1999).

CHAMPIONSHIP GAME EXPERIENCE: Played in AFC championship game (1995 season). ... Played in Super Bowl XXX (1995 season).

PRO STATISTICS: 1994—Recovered one fumble. 1995—Recovered one fumble. 1996—Recovered one fumble. 1997—Recovered one fumble.

Year Team	G	GS	SACKS
1992—Cleveland NFL	16	2	2.0
1993—Cleveland NFL	10	0	1.0
1994—Cleveland NFL	14	13	1.0
1995—Pittsburgh NFL	9	0	0.0
1996—Pittsburgh NFL	15	8	1.0
1997—St. Louis NFL	16	16	4.0
1998—Philadelphia NFL	13	13	2.5
1999—Philadelphia NFL	6	0	1.0
Pro totals (8 years)	99	52	12.5

JOHNSON, BRAD　　QB　　REDSKINS

PERSONAL: Born September 13, 1968, in Marietta, Ga. ... 6-5/224. ... Full name: James Bradley Johnson.

HIGH SCHOOL: Charles D. Owen (Black Mountain, N.C.).

COLLEGE: Florida State (degree in physical education, 1991).

TRANSACTIONS/CAREER NOTES: Selected by Minnesota Vikings in ninth round (227th pick overall) of 1992 NFL draft. ... Signed by Vikings (July 17, 1992). ... Active for one game (1992); did not play. ... Inactive for all 16 games (1993). ... Granted free agency (February 17, 1995). ... Assigned by Vikings to London Monarchs in 1995 World League enhancement allocation program (February 20, 1995). ... Re-signed by Vikings (March 27, 1995). ... On injured reserve with neck injury (December 5, 1997-remainder of season). ... Traded by Vikings to Washington Redskins for first- (QB Daunte Culpepper) and third-round (traded to Pittsburgh) picks in 1999 draft and second-round pick (DE Michael Boireau) in 2000 draft (February 15, 1999).

CHAMPIONSHIP GAME EXPERIENCE: Member of Vikings for NFC championship game (1998 season); did not play.

HONORS: Played in Pro Bowl (1999 season).

PRO STATISTICS: 1995—Fumbled twice. 1996—Fumbled five times and recovered three fumbles for minus eight yards. 1997—Caught one pass for three yards and a touchdown, fumbled four times and recovered three fumbles. 1998—Fumbled once. 1999—Tied for NFC lead with 12 fumbles and recovered two fumbles for minus eight yards.

SINGLE GAME HIGHS (regular season): Attempts—47 (December 26, 1999, vs. San Francisco); completions—33 (September 7, 1997, vs. Chicago); yards—471 (December 26, 1999, vs. San Francisco); and touchdown passes—4 (October 3, 1999, vs. Carolina).

STATISTICAL PLATEAUS: 300-yard passing games: 1997 (2), 1998 (1), 1999 (4). Total: 7.

MISCELLANEOUS: Regular-season record as starting NFL quarterback: 25-14 (.641). ... Postseason record as starting NFL quarterback: 1-2 (.333).

					PASSING						RUSHING				TOTALS	
Year Team	G	GS	Att.	Cmp.	Pct.	Yds.	TD	Int.	Avg.	Rat.	Att.	Yds.	Avg.	TD	TD	2pt.	Pts.
1992—Minnesota NFL						Did not play.											
1993—Minnesota NFL						Did not play.											
1994—Minnesota NFL	4	0	37	22	59.5	150	0	0	4.05	68.5	2	-2	-1.0	0	0	0	0
1995—London W.L.	...	...	328	194	59.1	2227	13	14	6.79	75.1	24	99	4.1	1	1	1	8

	G	GS	Att	Yds												
—Minnesota NFL	5	0	36	25	69.4	272	0	2	7.56	68.3	9	-9	-1.0	0	0	0	0
1996—Minnesota NFL	12	8	311	195	62.7	2258	17	10	7.26	89.4	34	90	2.6	1	1	0	6
1997—Minnesota NFL	13	13	452	275	60.8	3036	20	12	6.72	84.5	35	139	4.0	0	1	2	10
1998—Minnesota NFL	4	2	101	65	64.4	747	7	5	7.40	89.0	12	15	1.3	0	0	0	0
1999—Washington NFL	16	16	519	316	60.9	4005	24	13	7.72	90.0	26	31	1.2	2	2	0	12
W.L. totals (1 year)	...	...	328	194	59.1	2227	13	14	6.79	75.1	24	99	4.1	1	1	1	8
NFL totals (6 years)	54	39	1456	898	61.7	10468	68	42	7.19	87.0	118	264	2.2	3	4	2	28
Pro totals (7 years)	...	...	1784	1092	61.2	12695	81	56	7.12	84.8	142	363	2.6	4	5	3	36

JOHNSON, CHARLES　　　WR　　　EAGLES

PERSONAL: Born January 3, 1972, in San Bernardino, Calif. ... 6-0/200. ... Full name: Charles Everett Johnson.
HIGH SCHOOL: Cajon (San Bernardino, Calif.).
COLLEGE: Colorado (degree in marketing, 1993).
TRANSACTIONS/CAREER NOTES: Selected by Pittsburgh Steelers in first round (17th pick overall) of 1994 NFL draft. ... Signed by Steelers (July 21, 1994). ... On injured reserve with knee injury (December 23, 1995-remainder of season). ... Granted unconditional free agency (February 12, 1999). ... Signed by Philadelphia Eagles (February 16, 1999). ... On injured reserve with knee injury (December 3, 1999-remainder of season).
CHAMPIONSHIP GAME EXPERIENCE: Played in AFC championship game (1994 and 1997 seasons).
HONORS: Named wide receiver on THE SPORTING NEWS college All-America second team (1993).
RECORDS: Shares NFL single-game record for most two-point converstions—2 (November 1, 1998).
PRO STATISTICS: 1994—Fumbled twice. 1995—Recovered one fumble. 1996—Fumbled once. 1999—Credited with a safety, fumbled twice and recovered one fumble.
SINGLE GAME HIGHS (regular season): Receptions—9 (November 1, 1998, vs. Tennessee); yards—165 (December 24, 1994, vs. San Diego); and touchdown receptions—3 (November 1, 1998, vs. Tennessee).
STATISTICAL PLATEAUS: 100-yard receiving games: 1994 (1), 1996 (4), 1997 (1), 1998 (1). Total: 7.

			RUSHING				RECEIVING				PUNT RETURNS				KICKOFF RETURNS				TOTALS		
Year　Team	G	GS	Att.	Yds.	Avg.	TD	No.	Yds.	Avg.	TD	No.	Yds.	Avg.	TD	No.	Yds.	Avg.	TD	TD	2pt.	Pts.
1994—Pittsburgh NFL....	16	9	4	-1	-0.3	0	38	577	15.2	3	15	90	6.0	0	16	345	21.6	0	3	0	18
1995—Pittsburgh NFL....	14	12	1	-10	-10.0	0	38	432	11.4	0	0	0	0.0	0	2	47	23.5	0	0	0	0
1996—Pittsburgh NFL....	16	12	0	0	0.0	0	60	1008	16.8	3	0	0	0.0	0	6	111	18.5	0	3	1	20
1997—Pittsburgh NFL....	13	11	0	0	0.0	0	46	568	12.3	2	0	0	0.0	0	0	0	0.0	0	2	0	12
1998—Pittsburgh NFL....	16	16	1	4	4.0	0	65	815	12.5	7	0	0	0.0	0	0	0	0.0	0	7	†2	46
1999—Philadelphia NFL.	11	11	0	0	0.0	0	34	414	12.2	1	1	0	0.0	0	0	0	0.0	0	1	0	8
Pro totals (6 years)	86	71	6	-7	-1.2	0	281	3814	13.6	16	16	90	5.6	0	24	503	21.0	0	16	3	104

JOHNSON, DARRIUS　　　CB

PERSONAL: Born September 17, 1972, in Terrell, Texas. ... 5-9/185.
HIGH SCHOOL: Terrell (Texas).
COLLEGE: Oklahoma.
TRANSACTIONS/CAREER NOTES: Selected by Denver Broncos in fourth round (122nd pick overall) of 1996 NFL draft. ... Signed by Broncos (July 17, 1996). ... Released by Broncos (March 8, 2000). ... On suspended list for violating league substance abuse policy (March 9, 2000-present).
PLAYING EXPERIENCE: Denver NFL, 1996-1999. ... Games/Games started: 1996 (13/0), 1997 (16/0), 1998 (16/2), 1999 (16/2). Total: 61/4.
CHAMPIONSHIP GAME EXPERIENCE: Played in AFC championship game (1997 and 1998 seasons). ... Member of Super Bowl championship team (1997 and 1998 seasons).
PRO STATISTICS: 1997—Recovered one fumble for six yards and a touchdown. 1998—Intercepted two passes for 79 yards and credited with one sack. 1999—Recovered two fumbles.

JOHNSON, DUSTIN　　　FB

PERSONAL: Born August 5, 1973, in Eagar, Ariz. ... 6-2/236.
HIGH SCHOOL: Round Valley (Springerville, Ariz.).
COLLEGE: Brigham Young.
TRANSACTIONS/CAREER NOTES: Selected by New York Jets in sixth round (183rd pick overall) of 1998 NFL draft. ... Signed by Jets (July 15, 1998). ... Released by Jets (August 13, 1998). ... Signed by Seattle Seahawks (June 14, 1999). ... On injured reserve with head injury (September 24, 1999-remainder of season). ... Released by Seahawks (January 15, 2000).
PLAYING EXPERIENCE: Seattle NFL, 1999. ... Games/Games started: 1999 (1/0).

JOHNSON, ELLIS　　　DT　　　COLTS

PERSONAL: Born October 30, 1973, in Wildwood, Fla. ... 6-2/288. ... Full name: Ellis Bernard Johnson.
HIGH SCHOOL: Wildwood (Fla.).
COLLEGE: Florida.
TRANSACTIONS/CAREER NOTES: Selected by Indianapolis Colts in first round (15th pick overall) of 1995 NFL draft. ... Signed by Colts (June 7, 1995).
CHAMPIONSHIP GAME EXPERIENCE: Played in AFC championship game (1995 season).
PRO STATISTICS: 1997—Intercepted one pass for 18 yards and recovered two fumbles. 1999—Recovered one fumble.

Year　　Team	G	GS	SACKS
1995—Indianapolis NFL	16	2	4.5
1996—Indianapolis NFL	12	6	0.0

1997—Indianapolis NFL	15	15	4.5		
1998—Indianapolis NFL		16	16	8.0	
1999—Indianapolis NFL		16	16	7.5	
Pro totals (5 years)		75	55	24.5	

JOHNSON, J.J.   RB   DOLPHINS

PERSONAL: Born April 20, 1974, in Mobile, Ala. ... 6-1/230. ... Full name: James E. Johnson.
HIGH SCHOOL: Dothan (Ala.), then Davidson (Mobile, Ala.).
JUNIOR COLLEGE: East Mississippi Junior College.
COLLEGE: Mississippi State.
TRANSACTIONS/CAREER NOTES: Selected by Miami Dolphins in second round (39th pick overall) of 1999 NFL draft. ... Signed by Dolphins (July 27, 1999).
HONORS: Named running back on THE SPORTING NEWS college All-America second team (1998).
PRO STATISTICS: 1999—Returned two kickoffs for 26 yards and recovered one fumble.
SINGLE GAME HIGHS (regular season): Attempts—31 (November 21, 1999, vs. New England); yards—106 (November 21, 1999, vs. New England); and rushing touchdowns—1 (December 27, 1999, vs. New York Jets).
STATISTICAL PLATEAUS: 100-yard rushing games: 1999 (1).

			RUSHING				RECEIVING				TOTALS			
Year Team	G	GS	Att.	Yds.	Avg.	TD	No.	Yds.	Avg.	TD	TD	2pt.	Pts.	Fum.
1999—Miami NFL	13	4	164	558	3.4	4	15	100	6.7	0	4	0	24	2

JOHNSON, JASON   C   BRONCOS

PERSONAL: Born February 6, 1974, in Kansas City, Mo. ... 6-3/290. ... Full name: Jason Joseph Johnson.
HIGH SCHOOL: Oak Park (Kansas City, Mo.).
COLLEGE: Kansas State.
TRANSACTIONS/CAREER NOTES: Signed as non-drafted free agent by Indianapolis Colts (April 25, 1997). ... Released by Colts (September 13, 1997). ... Re-signed by Colts to practice squad (September 15, 1997). ... Granted free agency (February 11, 2000). ... Signed by Denver Broncos (May 19, 2000).
PLAYING EXPERIENCE: Indianapolis NFL, 1998 and 1999. ... Games/Games started: 1998 (14/0), 1999 (16/0). Total: 30/0.

JOHNSON, JOE   DE   SAINTS

PERSONAL: Born July 11, 1972, in St. Louis. ... 6-4/270. ... Full name: Joe T. Johnson.
HIGH SCHOOL: Jennings (Mo.).
COLLEGE: Louisville.
TRANSACTIONS/CAREER NOTES: Selected after junior season by New Orleans Saints in first round (13th pick overall) of 1994 NFL draft. ... Signed by Saints (June 7, 1994). ... Designated by Saints as franchise player (February 13, 1998). ... Re-signed by Saints (September 2, 1998). ... On injured reserve with knee injury (August 31, 1999-entire season).
HONORS: Played in Pro Bowl (1998 season).
PRO STATISTICS: 1994—Recovered one fumble. 1997—Recovered one fumble. 1998—Recovered one fumble for five yards and a touchdown.

Year Team	G	GS	SACKS
1994—New Orleans NFL	15	14	1.0
1995—New Orleans NFL	14	14	5.5
1996—New Orleans NFL	13	13	7.5
1997—New Orleans NFL	16	16	8.5
1998—New Orleans NFL	16	16	7.0
1999—New Orleans NFL	Did not play.		
Pro totals (5 years)	74	73	29.5

JOHNSON, KEVIN   WR   BROWNS

PERSONAL: Born July 15, 1975, in Trenton, N.J. ... 5-10/188. ... Full name: Kevin L. Johnson.
HIGH SCHOOL: Hamilton West (Trenton, N.J.).
COLLEGE: Syracuse.
TRANSACTIONS/CAREER NOTES: Selected by Cleveland Browns in second round (32nd pick overall) of 1999 NFL draft. ... Signed by Browns (July 22, 1999).
PRO STATISTICS: 1999—Attempted one pass without a completion, returned one kickoff for 25 yards and recovered one fumble.
SINGLE GAME HIGHS (regular season): Receptions—7 (December 12, 1999, vs. Cincinnati); yards—135 (December 12, 1999, vs. Cincinnati); and touchdown receptions—2 (October 31, 1999, vs. New Orleans).
STATISTICAL PLATEAUS: 100-yard receiving games: 1999 (2).

			RUSHING				RECEIVING				PUNT RETURNS				TOTALS			
Year Team	G	GS	Att.	Yds.	Avg.	TD	No.	Yds.	Avg.	TD	No.	Yds.	Avg.	TD	TD	2pt.	Pts.	Fum.
1999—Cleveland NFL	16	16	1	-6	-6.0	0	66	986	14.9	8	19	128	6.7	0	8	0	48	1

JOHNSON, KEYSHAWN   WR   BUCCANEERS

PERSONAL: Born July 22, 1972, in Los Angeles. ... 6-4/212. ... Cousin of Chris Miller, wide receiver with Green Bay Packers (1997), Detroit Lions (1997) and Chicago Bears (1998); and cousin of Ed Gray, guard with Atlanta Hawks (1997-98 and 1998-99).
HIGH SCHOOL: Dorsey (Los Angeles).
JUNIOR COLLEGE: West Los Angeles College.
COLLEGE: Southern California (degree in history).
TRANSACTIONS/CAREER NOTES: Selected by New York Jets in first round (first pick overall) of 1996 NFL draft. ... Signed by Jets (August 6, 1996). ... Traded by Jets to Tampa Bay Buccaneers for two first-round picks (LB John Abraham and TE Anthony Becht) in 2000 draft (April 12, 2000).
CHAMPIONSHIP GAME EXPERIENCE: Played in AFC championship game (1998 season).
HONORS: Named wide receiver on THE SPORTING NEWS college All-America first team (1995). ... Played in Pro Bowl (1998 and 1999 seasons). ... Named co-Oustanding Player of Pro Bowl (1998 season).
PRO STATISTICS: 1998—Rushed twice for 60 yards and one touchdown. 1999—Rushed five times for six yards and attempted one pass without a completion.
SINGLE GAME HIGHS (regular season): Receptions—11 (December 12, 1999, vs. Miami); yards—194 (September 12, 1999, vs. New England); and touchdown receptions—2 (December 12, 1999, vs. Miami).
STATISTICAL PLATEAUS: 100-yard receiving games: 1997 (1), 1998 (4), 1999 (2). Total: 7.

			RECEIVING				TOTALS			
Year Team	G	GS	No.	Yds.	Avg.	TD	TD	2pt.	Pts.	Fum.
1996—New York Jets NFL	14	11	63	844	13.4	8	8	1	50	0
1997—New York Jets NFL	16	16	70	963	13.8	5	5	0	30	0
1998—New York Jets NFL	16	16	83	1131	13.6	▲10	11	0	66	0
1999—New York Jets NFL	16	16	89	1170	13.1	8	8	0	48	0
Pro totals (4 years)	62	59	305	4108	13.5	31	32	1	194	0

JOHNSON, LEE   P   PATRIOTS

PERSONAL: Born November 27, 1961, in Dallas. ... 6-2/200.
HIGH SCHOOL: McCullough (The Woodlands, Texas).
COLLEGE: Brigham Young.
TRANSACTIONS/CAREER NOTES: Selected by Houston Gamblers in ninth round (125th pick overall) of 1985 USFL draft. ... Selected by Houston Oilers in fifth round (138th pick overall) of 1985 NFL draft. ... Signed by Oilers (June 25, 1985). ... Crossed picket line during players strike (October 14, 1987). ... Claimed on waivers by Buffalo Bills (December 2, 1987). ... Claimed on waivers by Cleveland Browns (December 10, 1987). ... Claimed on waivers by Cincinnati Bengals (September 23, 1988). ... Granted free agency (February 1, 1991). ... Re-signed by Bengals (1991). ... Granted unconditional free agency (March 1, 1993). ... Re-signed by Bengals (May 10, 1993). ... Released by Bengals (December 7, 1998). ... Signed by New England Patriots (February 18, 1999).
CHAMPIONSHIP GAME EXPERIENCE: Played in AFC championship game (1987 and 1988 seasons). ... Played in Super Bowl XXIII (1988 season).
POST SEASON RECORDS: Holds Super Bowl career record for longest punt—63 yards (January 22, 1989, vs. San Francisco).
PRO STATISTICS: 1985—Rushed once for no yards, fumbled twice and recovered one fumble for seven yards. 1987—Had 32.8-yard net punting average. 1988—Had 33.4-yard net punting average. 1989—Rushed once for minus seven yards. 1990—Attempted one pass with a completion for four yards and a touchdown. 1991—Attempted one pass with a completion for three yards, rushed once for minus two yards and fumbled once. 1993—Attempted one pass without a completion. 1994—Attempted one pass with a completion for seven yards and one touchdown. 1995—Attempted one pass with a completion for five yards, rushed once for minus 16 yards and fumbled once. 1997—Rushed once for no yards and recovered two fumbles. 1999—Rushed twice for 13 yards.

				PUNTING				KICKING						
Year Team	G	No.	Yds.	Avg.	Net avg.	In. 20	Blk.	XPM	XPA	FGM	FGA	Lg.	50+	Pts.
1985—Houston NFL	16	83	3464	41.7	35.7	22	0	0	0	0	0	0	0-0	0
1986—Houston NFL	16	88	3623	41.2	35.7	26	0	0	0	0	0	0	0-0	0
1987—Houston NFL	9	25	1008	40.3	.0	5	1	0	0	0	0	0	0-0	0
—Cleveland NFL	3	9	317	35.2	32.2	3	0	0	0	0	0	0	0-0	0
1988—Cleveland NFL	3	31	1237	39.9	.0	6	0	0	0	1	2	50	1-2	3
—Cincinnati NFL	12	14	594	42.4	.0	4	0	0	0	0	0	0	0-0	0
1989—Cincinnati NFL	16	61	2446	40.1	30.1	14	2	0	1	0	0	0	0-0	0
1990—Cincinnati NFL	16	64	2705	42.3	34.2	12	0	0	0	1	0	0	0-0	0
1991—Cincinnati NFL	16	64	2795	43.7	34.7	15	0	0	0	1	3	53	1-3	3
1992—Cincinnati NFL	16	76	3196	42.1	35.8	15	0	0	0	0	1	0	0-1	0
1993—Cincinnati NFL	16	▲90	3954	43.9	36.6	24	0	0	0	0	0	0	0-0	0
1994—Cincinnati NFL	16	79	3461	43.8	35.2	19	1	0	0	0	0	0	0-0	0
1995—Cincinnati NFL	16	68	2861	42.1	38.6	26	0	0	0	0	0	0	0-0	0
1996—Cincinnati NFL	16	80	3630	45.4	34.3	16	1	0	0	0	0	0	0-0	0
1997—Cincinnati NFL	16	81	3471	42.9	35.9	27	0	0	0	0	0	0	0-0	0
1998—Cincinnati NFL	13	69	3083	44.7	35.6	14	1	0	0	0	0	0	0-0	0
1999—New England NFL	16	90	3735	41.5	34.6	23	0	0	0	0	0	0	0-0	0
Pro totals (15 years)	232	1072	45580	42.5	32.9	271	6	0	1	2	7	53	2-6	6

JOHNSON, LEON   RB/KR   JETS

PERSONAL: Born July 13, 1974, in Morganton, N.C.. ... 6-0/218. ... Full name: William Leon Johnson.
HIGH SCHOOL: Freedom (Morganton, N.C.).
COLLEGE: North Carolina.
TRANSACTIONS/CAREER NOTES: Selected by New York Jets in fourth round (104th pick overall) of 1997 NFL draft. ... Signed by Jets (July 17, 1997). ... On injured reserve with rib injury (December 16, 1998-remainder of season). ... On injured reserve with knee injury (September 13, 1999-remainder of season). ... Granted free agency (February 11, 2000). ... Re-signed by Jets (May 8, 2000).
PRO STATISTICS: 1997—Attempted two passes without a completion and one interception, fumbled five times and recovered five fumbles. 1998—Fumbled three times and recovered three fumbles. 1999—Fumbled once.

SINGLE GAME HIGHS (regular season): Attempts—13 (October 11, 1998, vs. St. Louis); yards—56 (October 11, 1998, vs. St. Louis); and rushing touchdowns—2 (September 20, 1998, vs Indianapolis).

				RUSHING			RECEIVING				PUNT RETURNS				KICKOFF RETURNS				TOTALS		
Year	Team	G	GS	Att.	Yds.	Avg.	TD	No.	Yds.	Avg.	TD	No.	Yds.	Avg.	TD	No.	Yds.	Avg.	TD	TD	2pt.	Pts.
1997—N.Y. Jets NFL		16	1	48	158	3.3	2	16	142	8.9	0	§51	*619	12.1	1	12	319	26.6	▲1	4	0	24
1998—N.Y. Jets NFL		12	2	41	185	4.5	2	13	222	17.1	2	29	203	7.0	0	16	366	22.9	0	4	0	24
1999—N.Y. Jets NFL		1	0	1	2	2.0	0	0	0	0.0	0	1	6	6.0	0	2	31	15.5	0	0	0	0
Pro totals (3 years)		29	3	90	345	3.8	4	29	364	12.6	2	81	828	10.2	1	30	716	23.9	1	8	0	48

JOHNSON, LeSHON — RB

PERSONAL: Born January 15, 1971, in Haskell, Okla. ... 6-0/214. ... Full name: LeShon Eugene Johnson.
HIGH SCHOOL: Haskell (Okla.).
JUNIOR COLLEGE: Northeastern Oklahoma A&M Junior College.
COLLEGE: Northern Illinois (degree in studio art).
TRANSACTIONS/CAREER NOTES: Selected by Green Bay Packers in third round (84th pick overall) of 1994 NFL draft. ... Signed by Packers (July 19, 1994). ... On injured reserve with knee injury (January 3, 1995-remainder of 1994 playoffs). ... On physically unable to perform list with knee injury (August 27-October 21, 1995). ... Claimed on waivers by Arizona Cardinals (November 29, 1995). ... Granted free agency (February 14, 1997). ...Re-signed by Cardinals for 1997 season. ... Granted unconditional free agency (February 13, 1998). ... Signed by New York Giants (March 7, 1998). ... On non-football injury list with lymphoma (July 25, 1998-entire season). ... Granted unconditional free agency (February 11, 2000).
HONORS: Named running back on THE SPORTING NEWS college All-America first team (1993).
PRO STATISTICS: 1995—Recovered one fumble. 1996—Recovered two fumbles.
SINGLE GAME HIGHS (regular season): Attempts—21 (September 22, 1996, vs. New Orleans); yards—214 (September 22, 1996, vs. New Orleans); and rushing touchdowns—2 (September 22, 1996, vs. New Orleans).
STATISTICAL PLATEAUS: 100-yard rushing games: 1996 (1).

				RUSHING				RECEIVING				KICKOFF RETURNS				TOTALS			
Year	Team	G	GS	Att.	Yds.	Avg.	TD	No.	Yds.	Avg.	TD	No.	Yds.	Avg.	TD	TD	2pt.	Pts.	Fum.
1994—Green Bay NFL		12	0	26	99	3.8	0	13	168	12.9	0	0	0	0.0	0	0	0	0	0
1995—Green Bay NFL		2	0	2	-2	-1.0	0	0	0	0.0	0	0	0	0.0	0	0	0	0	0
—Arizona NFL		3	0	0	0	0.0	0	0	0	0.0	0	11	259	23.5	0	0	0	0	1
1996—Arizona NFL		15	8	141	634	4.5	3	15	176	11.7	1	10	198	19.8	0	4	0	24	5
1997—Arizona NFL		14	0	23	81	3.5	0	3	4	1.3	0	1	26	0.0	0	0	0	0	0
1998—New York Giants NFL							Did not play.												
1999—New York Giants NFL		16	4	61	143	2.3	2	12	86	7.2	1	0	0	0.0	0	3	0	18	2
Pro totals (5 years)		62	12	253	955	3.8	5	43	434	10.1	2	21	483	23.0	0	7	0	42	8

JOHNSON, LONNIE — TE

PERSONAL: Born February 14, 1971, in Miami. ... 6-3/240. ... Full name: Lonnie Demetrius Johnson.
HIGH SCHOOL: Miami Senior High.
COLLEGE: Florida State.
TRANSACTIONS/CAREER NOTES: Selected by Buffalo Bills in second round (61st pick overall) of 1994 NFL draft. ... Signed by Bills (July 15, 1994). ... Granted free agency (February 14, 1997). ... Re-signed by Bills (June 12, 1997). ... Granted unconditional free agency (February 13, 1998). ... Re-signed by Bills (March 30, 1998). ... Granted unconditional free agency (February 12, 1999). ... Signed by Kansas City Chiefs (April 12, 1999). ... Granted free agency (February 11, 2000).
PRO STATISTICS: 1995—Recovered one fumble. 1996—Recovered four fumbles. 1997—Rushed once for six yards and recovered one fumble. 1998—Returned three kickoffs for 18 yards. 1999—Returned one kickoff for 11 yards.
SINGLE GAME HIGHS (regular season): Receptions—7 (October 15, 1995, vs. Seattle); yards—90 (October 20, 1996, vs. New York Jets); and touchdown receptions—1 (December 26, 1999, vs. Seattle).

			RECEIVING				TOTALS			
Year	Team	G	GS	No.	Yds.	Avg.	TD	TD	2pt.	Pts.	Fum.
1994—Buffalo NFL	10	1	3	42	14.0	0	0	0	0	0
1995—Buffalo NFL	16	16	49	504	10.3	1	1	0	6	0
1996—Buffalo NFL	16	15	46	457	9.9	0	0	0	0	1
1997—Buffalo NFL	16	16	41	340	8.3	2	2	0	12	2
1998—Buffalo NFL	16	16	14	146	10.4	2	2	0	12	1
1999—Kansas City NFL	14	2	10	98	9.8	1	1	0	6	0
Pro totals (6 years)	88	66	163	1587	9.7	6	6	0	36	4

JOHNSON, MALCOLM — WR — STEELERS

PERSONAL: Born August 27, 1977, in Washington, D.C. ... 6-5/215. ... Full name: Malcolm Alexander Johnson.
HIGH SCHOOL: Gonzaga (Washington, D.C.).
COLLEGE: Notre Dame (degree in marketing).
TRANSACTIONS/CAREER NOTES: Selected by Pittsburgh Steelers in fifth round (195th pick overall) of 1999 NFL draft. ... Signed by Steelers (July 12, 1999).
PLAYING EXPERIENCE: Pittsburgh NFL, 1999. ... Games/Games started: 1999 (6/0).
PRO STATISTICS: 1999—Caught two passes for 23 yards.
SINGLE GAME HIGHS (regular season): Receptions—1 (January 2, 2000, vs. Tennessee); yards—18 (December 12, 1999, vs. Baltimore); and touchdown receptions—0.

J

JOHNSON, NORM — K

PERSONAL: Born May 31, 1960, in Garden Grove, Calif. ... 6-2/202. ... Full name: Norm Douglas Johnson.
HIGH SCHOOL: Pacifica (Garden Grove, Calif.).
COLLEGE: UCLA.
TRANSACTIONS/CAREER NOTES: Signed as non-drafted free agent by Seattle Seahawks (May 4, 1982). ... Crossed picket line during players strike (October 14, 1987). ... Granted free agency (February 1, 1991). ... Re-signed by Seahawks (July 19, 1991). ... Released by Seahawks (August 26, 1991). ... Signed by Atlanta Falcons (September 9, 1991). ... Granted free agency (February 1, 1992). ... Re-signed by Falcons for 1992 season. ... Released by Falcons (July 20, 1995). ... Signed by Pittsburgh Steelers (August 22, 1995). ... Released by Steelers (July 9, 1997). ... Re-signed by Steelers (August 25, 1997). ... Granted unconditional free agency (February 12, 1999). ... Signed by Philadelphia Eagles (August 17, 1999). ... Released by Eagles (April 25, 2000).
CHAMPIONSHIP GAME EXPERIENCE: Played in AFC championship game (1983, 1995 and 1997 seasons). ... Played in Super Bowl XXX (1995 season).
HONORS: Named kicker on THE SPORTING NEWS NFL All-Pro team (1984). ... Played in Pro Bowl (1984 and 1993 seasons).
RECORDS: Holds NFL career record for most consecutive PATs made—301 (1991-present).
PRO STATISTICS: 1982—Attempted one pass with one completion for 27 yards. 1991—Punted once for 21 yards. 1992—Punted once for 37 yards.

		KICKING						
Year Team	G	XPM	XPA	FGM	FGA	Lg.	50+	Pts.
1982—Seattle NFL	9	13	14	10	14	48	0-1	43
1983—Seattle NFL	16	49	50	18	25	54	1-3	103
1984—Seattle NFL	16	50	51	20	24	50	1-3	110
1985—Seattle NFL	16	40	41	14	25	51	1-3	82
1986—Seattle NFL	16	42	42	22	35	§54	5-7	108
1987—Seattle NFL	13	§40	§40	15	20	49	0-1	85
1988—Seattle NFL	16	39	39	22	28	47	0-0	105
1989—Seattle NFL	16	27	27	15	25	50	1-5	72
1990—Seattle NFL	16	33	34	23	32	51	1-3	102
1991—Atlanta NFL	14	38	39	19	23	50	1-2	95
1992—Atlanta NFL	16	39	39	18	22	†54	4-4	93
1993—Atlanta NFL	15	34	34	26	27	54	2-2	112
1994—Atlanta NFL	16	32	32	21	25	50	1-5	95
1995—Pittsburgh NFL	16	39	39	*34	*41	50	1-1	§141
1996—Pittsburgh NFL	16	37	37	23	30	49	0-1	106
1997—Pittsburgh NFL	16	40	40	22	25	52	1-2	106
1998—Pittsburgh NFL	15	21	21	26	31	49	0-2	99
1999—Philadelphia NFL	15	25	25	18	25	49	0-2	79
Pro totals (18 years)	273	638	644	366	477	54	20-47	1736

JOHNSON, OLRICK — LB — VIKINGS

PERSONAL: Born August 20, 1977, in Miami. ... 6-0/244. ... Nephew of Cecil Johnson, linebacker with Tampa Bay Buccaneers (1977-85).
HIGH SCHOOL: Northwestern (Miami).
COLLEGE: Florida A&M.
TRANSACTIONS/CAREER NOTES: Signed as non-drafted free agent by New York Jets (April 19, 1999). ... Released by Jets (September 5, 1999). ... Re-signed by Jets to practice squad (September 6, 1999). ... Activated (November 5, 1999). ... Released by Jets (November 23, 1999). ... Signed by Minnesota Vikings (November 27, 1999).
PLAYING EXPERIENCE: New York Jets (3)-Minnesota (5) NFL, 1999. ... Games/Games started: 1999 (NYJ-3/0; Min.-5/0; Total: 8/0).

JOHNSON, PATRICK — WR — RAVENS

PERSONAL: Born August 10, 1976, in Gainesville, Ga. ... 5-10/180. ... Full name: Patrick Jevon Johnson.
HIGH SCHOOL: Redlands (Calif.).
COLLEGE: Oregon.
TRANSACTIONS/CAREER NOTES: Selected by Baltimore Ravens in second round (42nd pick overall) of 1998 NFL draft. ... Signed by Ravens (June 24, 1998).
HONORS: Named kick returner on THE SPORTING NEWS college All-America second team (1997).
PRO STATISTICS: 1998—Returned one punt for six yards. 1999—Rushed once for 12 yards and recovered one fumble for 12 yards.
SINGLE GAME HIGHS (regular season): Receptions—9 (January 2, 2000, vs. New England); yards—114 (January 2, 2000, vs. New England); and touchdown receptions—1 (December 5, 1999, vs. Tennessee).
STATISTICAL PLATEAUS: 100-yard receiving games: 1999 (1).

			RECEIVING				KICKOFF RETURNS				TOTALS			
Year Team	G	GS	No.	Yds.	Avg.	TD	No.	Yds.	Avg.	TD	TD	2pt.	Pts.	Fum.
1998—Baltimore NFL	13	0	12	159	13.3	1	16	399	24.9	▲1	2	0	12	1
1999—Baltimore NFL	10	6	29	526	18.1	3	0	0	0.0	0	3	0	18	1
Pro totals (2 years)	23	6	41	685	16.7	4	16	399	24.9	1	5	0	30	2

JOHNSON, RAYLEE — DE — CHARGERS

PERSONAL: Born June 1, 1970, in Chicago, Ill. ... 6-3/272. ... Full name: Raylee Terrell Johnson.
HIGH SCHOOL: Fordyce (Ark.).
COLLEGE: Arkansas.
TRANSACTIONS/CAREER NOTES: Selected by San Diego Chargers in fourth round (95th pick overall) of 1993 NFL draft. ... Signed by Chargers (July 15, 1993). ... Granted unconditional free agency (February 14, 1997). ... Re-signed by Chargers (March 11, 1997).
CHAMPIONSHIP GAME EXPERIENCE: Played in AFC championship game (1994 season). ... Played in Super Bowl XXIX (1994 season).

PRO STATISTICS: 1999—Recovered one fumble.

Year Team	G	GS	SACKS
1993—San Diego NFL	9	0	0.0
1994—San Diego NFL	15	0	1.5
1995—San Diego NFL	16	1	3.0
1996—San Diego NFL	16	1	3.0
1997—San Diego NFL	16	0	2.5
1998—San Diego NFL	16	3	5.5
1999—San Diego NFL	16	16	10.5
Pro totals (7 years)	104	21	26.0

JOHNSON, ROB   QB   BILLS

PERSONAL: Born March 18, 1973, in Newport Beach, Calif. ... 6-4/212. ... Full name: Rob Garland Johnson. ... Brother of Bret Johnson, quarterback with Toronto Argonauts of CFL (1993); and cousin of Bart Johnson, pitcher with Chicago White Sox (1969-74, 1976 and 1977).
HIGH SCHOOL: El Toro (Calif.).
COLLEGE: Southern California.
TRANSACTIONS/CAREER NOTES: Selected by Jacksonville Jaguars in fourth round (99th pick overall) of 1995 NFL draft. ... Signed by Jaguars (June 1, 1995). ... Traded by Jaguars to Buffalo Bills for first- (RB Fred Taylor) and fourth-round (RB Tavian Banks) picks in 1998 draft (February 13, 1998).
CHAMPIONSHIP GAME EXPERIENCE: Member of Jaguars for AFC championship game (1996 season); did not play.
PRO STATISTICS: 1998—Fumbled twice and recovered one fumble for minus one yard.
SINGLE GAME HIGHS (regular season): Attempts—32 (January 2, 2000, vs. Indianapolis); completions—24 (January 2, 2000, vs. Indianapolis); yards—294 (August 31, 1997, vs. Baltimore); and touchdown passes—3 (December 27, 1998, vs. New Orleans).
MISCELLANEOUS: Selected by Minnesota Twins organization in 16th round of free-agent draft (June 4, 1991); did not sign. ... Regular-season record as starting NFL quarterback: 5-3 (.625). ... Postseason record as starting NFL quarterback: 0-1.

				PASSING							RUSHING				TOTALS		
Year Team	G	GS	Att.	Cmp.	Pct.	Yds.	TD	Int.	Avg.	Rat.	Att.	Yds.	Avg.	TD	TD	2pt.	Pts.
1995—Jacksonville NFL	1	0	7	3	42.9	24	0	1	3.43	12.5	3	17	5.7	0	0	0	0
1996—Jacksonville NFL	2	0	0	0	0.0	0	0	0	0.0	...	0	0	0.0	0	0	0	0
1997—Jacksonville NFL	5	1	28	22	78.6	344	2	2	12.29	111.9	10	34	3.4	1	1	0	6
1998—Buffalo NFL	8	6	107	67	62.6	910	8	3	8.50	102.9	24	123	5.1	1	1	0	6
1999—Buffalo NFL	2	1	34	25	73.5	298	2	0	8.76	119.5	8	61	7.6	0	0	0	0
Pro totals (5 years)	18	8	176	117	66.5	1576	12	6	8.95	103.3	45	235	5.2	2	2	0	12

JOHNSON, TED   LB   PATRIOTS

PERSONAL: Born December 4, 1972, in Alameda, Calif. ... 6-4/250. ... Full name: Ted Curtis Johnson.
HIGH SCHOOL: Carlsbad (Calif.).
COLLEGE: Colorado.
TRANSACTIONS/CAREER NOTES: Selected by New England Patriots in second round (57th pick overall) of 1995 NFL draft. ... Signed by Patriots (July 18, 1995). ... On injured reserve with bicep injury (December 11, 1998-remainder of season).
CHAMPIONSHIP GAME EXPERIENCE: Played in AFC championship game (1996 season). ... Played in Super Bowl XXXI (1996 season).
HONORS: Named linebacker on THE SPORTING NEWS college All-America second team (1994).
PRO STATISTICS: 1995—Recovered two fumbles. 1996—Intercepted one pass for no yards and recovered one fumble.

Year Team	G	GS	SACKS
1995—New England NFL	12	11	0.5
1996—New England NFL	16	16	0.0
1997—New England NFL	16	16	4.0
1998—New England NFL	13	13	2.0
1999—New England NFL	5	5	2.0
Pro totals (5 years)	62	61	8.5

JOHNSON, TRE'   G   REDSKINS

PERSONAL: Born August 30, 1971, in Manhattan, N.Y. ... 6-2/326. ... Full name: Edward Stanton Johnson III.
HIGH SCHOOL: Peekskill (N.Y.).
COLLEGE: Temple (degree in social administration, 1993).
TRANSACTIONS/CAREER NOTES: Selected by Washington Redskins in second round (31st pick overall) of 1994 NFL draft. ... Signed by Redskins (July 22, 1994). ... On injured reserve with shoulder injury (December 16, 1997-remainder of season). ... Granted unconditional free agency (February 13, 1998). ... Re-signed by Redskins (February 13, 1998). ... On injured reserve with knee injury (November 24, 1998-remainder of season).
PLAYING EXPERIENCE: Washington NFL, 1994-1999. ... Games/Games started: 1994 (14/1), 1995 (10/9), 1996 (15/15), 1997 (11/10), 1998 (10/10), 1999 (16/16). Total: 76/61.
HONORS: Played in Pro Bowl (1999 season).
PRO STATISTICS: 1994—Ran four yards with lateral from kickoff return. 1996—Recovered one fumble. 1999—Recovered three fumbles.

JOHNSTON, DARYL   FB   COWBOYS

PERSONAL: Born February 10, 1966, in Youngstown, N.Y. ... 6-2/242. ... Full name: Daryl Peter Johnston. ... Nickname: Moose.
HIGH SCHOOL: Lewiston-Porter Central (Youngstown, N.Y.).
COLLEGE: Syracuse (degree in economics, 1989).
TRANSACTIONS/CAREER NOTES: Selected by Dallas Cowboys in second round (39th pick overall) of 1989 NFL draft. ... Signed by Cowboys (July 24, 1989). ... Granted free agency (March 1, 1993). ... Re-signed by Cowboys (July 16, 1993). ... Granted unconditional free agency

(February 17, 1994). ... Re-signed by Cowboys (April 7, 1994). ... Granted unconditional free agency (February 14, 1997). ... Re-signed by Cowboys (March 19, 1997). ... On injured reserve with neck injury (September 16, 1999-remainder of season).

CHAMPIONSHIP GAME EXPERIENCE: Played in NFC championship game (1992-1995 seasons). ... Member of Super Bowl championship team (1992, 1993 and 1995 seasons).

HONORS: Played in Pro Bowl (1993 and 1994 seasons).

PRO STATISTICS: 1990—Recovered one fumble. 1992—Recovered one fumble. 1993—Recovered one fumble. 1995—Recovered one fumble. 1996—Recovered one fumble. 1999—Recovered one fumble.

SINGLE GAME HIGHS (regular season): Attempts—16 (December 24, 1989, vs. Green Bay); yards—60 (December 24, 1989, vs. Green Bay); and rushing touchdowns—1 (October 29, 1995, vs. Atlanta).

				RUSHING				RECEIVING				TOTALS		
Year Team	G	GS	Att.	Yds.	Avg.	TD	No.	Yds.	Avg.	TD	TD	2pt.	Pts.	Fum.
1989—Dallas NFL	16	10	67	212	3.2	0	16	133	8.3	3	3	0	18	3
1990—Dallas NFL	16	0	10	35	3.5	1	14	148	10.6	1	2	0	12	1
1991—Dallas NFL	16	14	17	54	3.2	0	28	244	8.7	1	1	0	6	0
1992—Dallas NFL	16	16	17	61	3.6	0	32	249	7.8	2	2	0	12	0
1993—Dallas NFL	16	16	24	74	3.1	3	50	372	7.4	1	4	0	24	1
1994—Dallas NFL	16	16	40	138	3.5	2	44	325	7.4	2	4	0	24	2
1995—Dallas NFL	16	16	25	111	4.4	2	30	248	8.3	1	3	0	18	1
1996—Dallas NFL	16	15	22	48	2.2	0	43	278	6.5	1	1	0	6	1
1997—Dallas NFL	6	6	2	3	1.5	0	18	166	9.2	1	1	0	6	1
1998—Dallas NFL	16	13	8	17	2.1	0	18	60	3.3	1	1	0	6	0
1999—Dallas NFL	1	0	0	0	0.0	0	1	4	4.0	0	0	0	0	0
Pro totals (11 years)	151	122	232	753	3.2	8	294	2227	7.6	14	22	0	132	10

JOHNSTONE, LANCE   DE   RAIDERS

PERSONAL: Born June 11, 1973, in Philadelphia. ... 6-4/250.
HIGH SCHOOL: Germantown (Philadelphia).
COLLEGE: Temple.
TRANSACTIONS/CAREER NOTES: Selected by Oakland Raiders in second round (57th pick overall) of 1996 NFL draft. ... Signed by Raiders for 1996 season.
PRO STATISTICS: 1997—Recovered one fumble for two yards. 1998—Recovered one fumble for 40 yards and a touchdown. 1999—Intercepted one pass for no yards and recovered one fumble for 13 yards and a touchdown.

Year Team	G	GS	SACKS
1996—Oakland NFL	16	10	1.0
1997—Oakland NFL	14	6	3.5
1998—Oakland NFL	16	15	11.0
1999—Oakland NFL	16	16	10.0
Pro totals (4 years)	62	47	25.5

JONES, CEDRIC   DE   GIANTS

PERSONAL: Born April 30, 1974, in Houston. ... 6-4/275.
HIGH SCHOOL: Lamar (Houston).
COLLEGE: Oklahoma.
TRANSACTIONS/CAREER NOTES: Selected by New York Giants in first round (fifth pick overall) of 1996 NFL draft. ... Signed by Giants (July 27, 1996). ... On injured reserve with leg injury (December 11, 1997-remainder of season).
HONORS: Named defensive lineman on THE SPORTING NEWS college All-America first team (1995).
PRO STATISTICS: 1998—Recovered one fumble.

Year Team	G	GS	SACKS
1996—New York Giants NFL	16	0	0.0
1997—New York Giants NFL	9	2	0.0
1998—New York Giants NFL	16	1	4.0
1999—New York Giants NFL	16	16	7.5
Pro totals (4 years)	57	19	11.5

JONES, CHARLIE   WR   CHARGERS

PERSONAL: Born December 1, 1972, in Hanford, Calif. ... 5-8/175. ... Full name: Charlie Edward Jones.
HIGH SCHOOL: Lemoore (Calif.).
COLLEGE: Fresno State.
TRANSACTIONS/CAREER NOTES: Selected by San Diego Chargers in fourth round (114th pick overall) of 1996 NFL draft. ... Signed by Chargers for 1996 season. ... Granted free agency (February 12, 1999). ... Re-signed by Chargers (April 1, 1999).
PRO STATISTICS: 1996—Returned one punt for 21 yards. 1997—Rushed four times for 42 yards. 1998—Rushed four times for 39 yards and returned two kickoffs for 25 yards. 1999—Rushed once for minus eight yards, returned nine punts for 93 yards and recovered one fumble.
SINGLE GAME HIGHS (regular season): Receptions—7 (October 27, 1996, vs. Seattle); yards—86 (November 16, 1997, vs. Oakland); and touchdown receptions—1 (November 7, 1999, vs. Denver).

			RECEIVING				TOTALS			
Year Team	G	GS	No.	Yds.	Avg.	TD	TD	2pt.	Pts.	Fum.
1996—San Diego NFL	14	4	41	524	12.8	4	4	0	24	0
1997—San Diego NFL	16	11	32	423	13.2	1	1	0	6	0
1998—San Diego NFL	16	11	46	699	15.2	3	3	0	18	1
1999—San Diego NFL	8	1	10	90	9.0	1	1	0	6	1
Pro totals (4 years)	54	27	129	1736	13.5	9	9	0	54	2

JONES, CLARENCE   OT   PANTHERS

PERSONAL: Born May 6, 1968, in Brooklyn, N.Y. ... 6-6/300. ... Full name: Clarence Thomas Jones.
HIGH SCHOOL: Central Islip (N.Y.).
COLLEGE: Maryland.
TRANSACTIONS/CAREER NOTES: Selected by New York Giants in fourth round (111th pick overall) of 1991 NFL draft. ... On injured reserve with ankle injury (October 1991). ... Activated (November 1991). ... Granted free agency (February 17, 1994). ... Released by Giants (May 6, 1994). ... Signed by Los Angeles Rams (June 1, 1994). ... Rams franchise moved to St. Louis (April 12, 1995). ... Granted unconditional free agency (February 16, 1996). ... Signed by New Orleans Saints (February 20, 1996). ... Granted unconditional free agency (February 12, 1999). ... Signed by Carolina Panthers (March 26, 1999).
PLAYING EXPERIENCE: New York Giants NFL, 1991-1993; Los Angeles Rams NFL, 1994; St. Louis NFL, 1995; New Orleans NFL, 1996-1998; Carolina NFL, 1999. ... Games/Games started: 1991 (3/0), 1992 (3/0), 1993 (4/0), 1994 (16/16), 1995 (13/0), 1996 (16/16), 1997 (15/15), 1998 (14/14), 1999 (16/16). Total: 100/77.
PRO STATISTICS: 1997—Recovered two fumbles. 1998—Recovered one fumble.

J

JONES, DAMON   TE   JAGUARS

PERSONAL: Born September 18, 1974, in Evanston, Ill. ... 6-5/266.
HIGH SCHOOL: Evanston (Ill.).
COLLEGE: Michigan, then Southern Illinois (degree in consumer economics, 1997).
TRANSACTIONS/CAREER NOTES: Selected by Jacksonville Jaguars in fifth round (147th pick overall) of 1997 NFL draft. ... Signed by Jaguars (May 30, 1997). ... Granted free agency (February 11, 2000). ... Re-signed by Jaguars (April 10, 2000).
CHAMPIONSHIP GAME EXPERIENCE: Played in AFC championship game (1999 season).
PRO STATISTICS: 1998—Returned two kickoffs for minus one yard.
SINGLE GAME HIGHS (regular season): Receptions—2 (December 26, 1999, vs. Tennessee); yards—34 (November 30, 1997, vs. Baltimore); and touchdown receptions—1 (December 19, 1999, vs. Cleveland).

			RECEIVING				TOTALS		
Year Team	G	GS	No.	Yds.	Avg.	TD	TD	2pt.	Pts.	Fum.
1997—Jacksonville NFL	11	3	5	87	17.4	2	2	0	12	0
1998—Jacksonville NFL	16	7	8	90	11.3	4	4	0	24	1
1999—Jacksonville NFL	15	8	19	221	11.6	4	4	0	24	0
Pro totals (3 years)	42	18	32	398	12.4	10	10	0	60	1

JONES, DONTA   LB   PANTHERS

PERSONAL: Born August 27, 1972, in Washington, D.C. ... 6-2/235. ... Full name: Markeysia Donta Jones. ... Name pronounced DON-tay.
HIGH SCHOOL: McDonough (Pomfret, Md.).
COLLEGE: Nebraska (degree in accounting and business administration, 1994).
TRANSACTIONS/CAREER NOTES: Selected by Pittsburgh Steelers in fourth round (125th pick overall) of 1995 NFL draft. ... Signed by Steelers (July 19, 1995). ... Granted free agency (February 13, 1998). ... Re-signed by Steelers (June 9, 1998). ... Granted unconditional free agency (February 12, 1999). ... Signed by Carolina Panthers (February 15, 1999).
PLAYING EXPERIENCE: Pittsburgh NFL, 1995-1998; Carolina NFL, 1999. ... Games/Games started: 1995 (16/0), 1996 (15/2), 1997 (16/4), 1998 (16/4), 1999 (16/0). Total: 79/10.
CHAMPIONSHIP GAME EXPERIENCE: Played in AFC championship game (1995 and 1997 seasons). ... Played in Super Bowl XXX (1995 season).
PRO STATISTICS: 1996—Credited with one sack and returned one punt for three yards. 1997—Recovered one fumble for six yards. 1998—Credited with three sacks.

JONES, ERNEST   LB

PERSONAL: Born April 1, 1971, in Utica, N.Y. ... 6-2/255. ... Full name: Ernest Lee Jones.
HIGH SCHOOL: Utica (N.Y.) Senior Academy.
COLLEGE: Oregon.
TRANSACTIONS/CAREER NOTES: Selected by Los Angeles Rams in third round (100th pick overall) of 1994 NFL draft. ... Signed by Rams (June 20, 1994). ... On injured reserve with knee injury (August 28, 1994-entire season). ... Released by Rams (August 21, 1995). ... Signed by New Orleans Saints to practice squad (August 28, 1995). ... Activated (October 21, 1995). ... Released by Saints (October 30, 1995). ... Re-signed by Saints to practice squad (November 1, 1995). ... Granted free agency (February 16, 1996) ... Signed by Denver Broncos (March 25, 1996). ... Granted free agency (February 13, 1998). ... Re-signed by Broncos (April 7, 1998). ... Claimed on waivers by Saints (October 14, 1998). ... Inactive for three games with Saints (1998). ... Claimed on waivers by Carolina Panthers (November 5, 1998). ... Granted unconditional free agency (February 12, 1999). ... Re-signed by Panthers (March 17, 1999). ... Granted unconditional free agency (February 11, 2000).
PLAYING EXPERIENCE: New Orleans NFL, 1995; Denver NFL, 1996 and 1997; Denver (1)-Carolina (7) NFL, 1998; Carolina NFL, 1999. ... Games/Games started: 1995 (1/0), 1996 (6/0), 1997 (1/0), 1998 (Den.-1/0; Car.-7/0; Total: 8/0), 1999 (13/0). Total: 29/0.
CHAMPIONSHIP GAME EXPERIENCE: Member of Broncos for AFC championship game (1997 season); inactive. ... Member of Super Bowl championship team (1997 season); inactive.
PRO STATISTICS: 1999—Credited with $2\frac{1}{2}$ sacks.

JONES, FREDDIE   TE   CHARGERS

PERSONAL: Born September 16, 1974, in Cheverly, Md. ... 6-5/270. ... Full name: Freddie Ray Jones Jr.
HIGH SCHOOL: McKinley (Landover, Md.).
COLLEGE: North Carolina.

TRANSACTIONS/CAREER NOTES: Selected by San Diego Chargers in second round (45th pick overall) of 1997 NFL draft. ... Signed by Chargers (May 21, 1997). ... On injured reserve with leg injury (December 12, 1997-remainder of season). ... Granted free agency (February 11, 2000). ... Re-signed by Chargers (May 2, 2000).
SINGLE GAME HIGHS (regular season): Receptions—7 (October 24, 1999, vs. Green Bay); yards—87 (October 24, 1999, vs. Green Bay); and touchdown receptions—1 (November 14, 1999, vs. Oakland).

			RECEIVING				TOTALS		
Year Team	G	GS	No.	Yds.	Avg.	TD	TD	2pt.	Pts.	Fum.
1997—San Diego NFL	13	8	41	505	12.3	2	2	0	12	0
1998—San Diego NFL	16	16	57	602	10.6	3	3	1	20	1
1999—San Diego NFL	16	16	56	670	12.0	2	2	0	12	0
Pro totals (3 years)	45	40	154	1777	11.5	7	7	1	44	1

JONES, GEORGE — RB

PERSONAL: Born December 31, 1973, in Greenville, S.C. ... 5-9/212. ... Full name: George Dee Jones.
HIGH SCHOOL: Eastside (Taylors, S.C.).
JUNIOR COLLEGE: Bakersfield (Calif.) College.
COLLEGE: San Diego State.
TRANSACTIONS/CAREER NOTES: Selected by Pittsburgh Steelers in fifth round (154th pick overall) of 1997 NFL draft. ... Signed by Steelers (July 15, 1997). ... Released by Steelers (August 25, 1998). ... Signed by Jacksonville Jaguars (September 22, 1998). ... Released by Jaguars (September 5, 1999). ... Signed by Cleveland Browns (September 14, 1999). ... Released by Browns (November 23, 1999).
CHAMPIONSHIP GAME EXPERIENCE: Member of Steelers for AFC championship game (1997 season); inactive.
PRO STATISTICS: 1997—Recovered one fumble. 1998—Returned one kickoff for 21 yards. 1999—Returned one kickoff for 12 yards.
SINGLE GAME HIGHS (regular season): Attempts—16 (December 21, 1997, vs. Tennessee); yards—64 (November 16, 1997, vs. Cincinnati); and rushing touchdowns—1 (November 9, 1997, vs. Baltimore).

			RUSHING				RECEIVING				TOTALS			
Year Team	G	GS	Att.	Yds.	Avg.	TD	No.	Yds.	Avg.	TD	TD	2pt.	Pts.	Fum.
1997—Pittsburgh NFL	16	1	72	235	3.3	1	16	96	6.0	1	2	0	12	3
1998—Jacksonville NFL	12	0	39	121	3.1	0	1	9	9.0	0	0	0	0	0
1999—Cleveland NFL	6	0	8	15	1.9	0	0	0	0.0	0	0	0	0	0
Pro totals (3 years)	34	1	119	371	3.1	1	17	105	6.2	1	2	0	12	3

JONES, GREG — LB — REDSKINS

PERSONAL: Born May 22, 1974, in Denver. ... 6-4/238. ... Full name: Greg Phillip Jones.
HIGH SCHOOL: John F. Kennedy (Denver).
COLLEGE: Colorado (degree in small business management, 1996).
TRANSACTIONS/CAREER NOTES: Selected by Washington Redskins in second round (51st pick overall) of 1997 NFL draft. ... Signed by Redskins (July 11, 1997).
PRO STATISTICS: 1997—Returned one kickoff for six yards. 1998—Intercepted one pass for nine yards.

Year Team	G	GS	SACKS
1997—Washington NFL	16	3	3.5
1998—Washington NFL	16	5	1.0
1999—Washington NFL	15	15	0.5
Pro totals (3 years)	47	23	5.0

JONES, HENRY — S — BILLS

PERSONAL: Born December 29, 1967, in St. Louis. ... 6-0/197.
HIGH SCHOOL: St. Louis University High.
COLLEGE: Illinois (degree in psychology, 1990).
TRANSACTIONS/CAREER NOTES: Selected by Buffalo Bills in first round (26th pick overall) of 1991 NFL draft. ... Signed by Bills (August 30, 1991). ... Activated (September 7, 1991). ... Designated by Bills as transition player (February 15, 1994). ... On injured reserve with broken leg (October 9, 1996-remainder of season).
CHAMPIONSHIP GAME EXPERIENCE: Played in AFC championship game (1991-1993 seasons). ... Played in Super Bowl XXVI (1991 season), Super Bowl XXVII (1992 season) and Super Bowl XXVIII (1993 season).
HONORS: Named strong safety on THE SPORTING NEWS NFL All-Pro team (1992). ... Played in Pro Bowl (1992 season).
RECORDS: Shares NFL single-game record for most touchdowns scored by interception—2 (September 20, 1992, vs. Indianapolis).
PRO STATISTICS: 1991—Recovered one fumble. 1992—Recovered two fumbles. 1993—Credited with a safety and recovered two fumbles. 1994—Recovered one fumble. 1995—Recovered one fumble. 1997—Returned one punt for no yards, fumbled once and recovered one fumble. 1999—Returned one kickoff for 37 yards and a touchdown.

			INTERCEPTIONS				SACKS
Year Team	G	GS	No.	Yds.	Avg.	TD	No.
1991—Buffalo NFL	15	0	0	0	0.0	0	0.0
1992—Buffalo NFL	16	16	†8	*263	32.9	▲2	0.0
1993—Buffalo NFL	16	16	2	92	46.0	▲1	2.0
1994—Buffalo NFL	16	16	2	45	22.5	0	1.0
1995—Buffalo NFL	13	13	1	10	10.0	0	0.0
1996—Buffalo NFL	5	5	0	0	0.0	0	0.0
1997—Buffalo NFL	15	15	0	0	0.0	0	2.0
1998—Buffalo NFL	16	16	3	0	0.0	0	0.0
1999—Buffalo NFL	16	16	0	0	0.0	0	0.0
Pro totals (9 years)	128	113	16	410	25.6	3	5.0

JONES, ISAAC WR COLTS

PERSONAL: Born December 7, 1975, in Wallingford, Pa. ... 6-0/190. ... Full name: Isaac Douglas Jones.
HIGH SCHOOL: Strath Haven (Wallingford, Pa.).
COLLEGE: Purdue.
TRANSACTIONS/CAREER NOTES: Signed as non-drafted free agent by Indianapolis Colts (April 20, 1999). ... On physically unable to perform list with leg injury (August 26-October 23, 1999).
PLAYING EXPERIENCE: Indianapolis NFL, 1999. ... Games/Games started: 1999 (1/1).
PRO STATISTICS: 1999—Caught one pass for eight yards.
SINGLE GAME HIGHS (regular season): Receptions—1 (November 21, 1999, vs. Philadelphia); yards—8 (November 21, 1999, vs. Philadelphia); and touchdown receptions—0.

JONES, JAMES DT LIONS

PERSONAL: Born February 6, 1969, in Davenport, Iowa. ... 6-2/295. ... Full name: James Alfie Jones. ... Nickname: J.J.
HIGH SCHOOL: Davenport (Iowa) Central.
COLLEGE: Northern Iowa (degree in science, 1992).
TRANSACTIONS/CAREER NOTES: Selected by Cleveland Browns in third round (57th pick overall) of 1991 NFL draft. ... Signed by Browns (1991). ... Granted unconditional free agency (February 17, 1995). ... Signed by Denver Broncos (February 24, 1995). ... Released by Broncos (July 17, 1996). ... Signed by Baltimore Ravens (August 21, 1996). ... Granted unconditional free agency (February 12, 1999). ... Signed by Detroit Lions (February 16, 1999).
PRO STATISTICS: 1991—Credited with a safety, intercepted one pass for 20 yards and a touchdown and recovered three fumbles for 15 yards. 1992—Recovered one fumble. 1993—Rushed twice for two yards and one touchdown. 1994—Rushed once for no yards, caught one pass for one yard and recovered two fumbles. 1995—Recovered two fumbles. 1996—Caught one pass for two yards and a touchdown. 1997—Recovered one fumble. 1998—Recovered one fumble. 1999—Recovered one fumble.

Year Team	G	GS	SACKS
1991—Cleveland NFL	16	16	1.0
1992—Cleveland NFL	16	16	4.0
1993—Cleveland NFL	16	12	5.5
1994—Cleveland NFL	16	5	3.0
1995—Denver NFL	16	16	1.0
1996—Baltimore NFL	16	11	1.0
1997—Baltimore NFL	16	16	6.0
1998—Baltimore NFL	16	16	5.5
1999—Detroit NFL	16	16	7.0
Pro totals (9 years)	144	124	34.0

JONES, JERMAINE CB BEARS

PERSONAL: Born July 25, 1976, in Morgan City, La. ... 5-8/183.
HIGH SCHOOL: Central Catholic (Morgan City, La.).
COLLEGE: Northwestern (La.) State.
TRANSACTIONS/CAREER NOTES: Selected by New York Jets in fifth round (162nd pick overall) of 1999 NFL draft. ... Signed by Jets (July 7, 1999). ... Released by Jets (September 5, 1999). ... Re-signed by Jets to practice squad (September 6, 1999). ... Released by Jets (September 14, 1999). ... Signed by Chicago Bears to practice squad (September 21, 1999). ... Activated (December 1, 1999).
PLAYING EXPERIENCE: New York Jets (1)-Chicago (1) NFL, 1999. ... Games/Games started: 1999 (NYJ-1/0; Chi.-1/0; Total: 2/0).

JONES, LENOY LB BROWNS

PERSONAL: Born September 25, 1974, in Marlin, Texas. ... 6-1/235.
HIGH SCHOOL: Groesbeck (Texas).
COLLEGE: Texas Christian.
TRANSACTIONS/CAREER NOTES: Signed as non-drafted free agent by Houston Oilers (April 23, 1996). ... Released by Oilers (August 20, 1996). ... Re-signed by Oilers to practice squad (August 26, 1996). ... Activated (October 9, 1996). ... Oilers franchise moved to Tennessee for 1997 season. ... Oilers franchise renamed Tennessee Titans for 1999 season (December 26, 1998). ... Selected by Cleveland Browns from Titans in NFL expansion draft (February 9, 1999). ... Granted free agency (February 12, 1999). ... Re-signed by Browns (May 26, 1999). ... Granted unconditional free agency (February 11, 2000). ... Re-signed by Browns (March 6, 2000).
PLAYING EXPERIENCE: Houston NFL, 1996; Tennessee NFL, 1997 and 1998; Cleveland NFL, 1999. ... Games/Games started: 1996 (11/0), 1997 (16/0), 1998 (9/0), 1999 (16/1). Total: 52/1.
PRO STATISTICS: 1996—Recovered one fumble. 1997—Credited with one sack. 1999—Intercepted one pass for three yards and fumbled once.

JONES, MARCUS DE BUCCANEERS

PERSONAL: Born August 15, 1973, in Jacksonville, N.C. ... 6-6/278. ... Full name: Marcus Edward Jones.
HIGH SCHOOL: Southwest Onslow (Jacksonville, N.C.).
COLLEGE: North Carolina.
TRANSACTIONS/CAREER NOTES: Selected by Tampa Bay Buccaneers in first round (22nd pick overall) of 1996 NFL draft. ... Signed by Buccaneers (July 21, 1996). ... On injured reserve with ankle injury (December 23, 1997-remainder of season).
PLAYING EXPERIENCE: Tampa Bay NFL, 1996-1999. ... Games/Games started: 1996 (16/3), 1997 (7/1), 1998 (15/0), 1999 (16/4). Total: 54/8.
CHAMPIONSHIP GAME EXPERIENCE: Played in NFC championship game (1999 season).

HONORS: Named defensive lineman on THE SPORTING NEWS college All-America second team (1995).
PRO STATISTICS: 1996—Credited with one sack. 1997—Recovered one fumble. 1998—Recovered one fumble. 1999—Credited with seven sacks.

JONES, MARVIN   LB   JETS

PERSONAL: Born June 28, 1972, in Miami. ... 6-2/250. ... Full name: Marvin Maurice Jones.
HIGH SCHOOL: Miami Northwestern.
COLLEGE: Florida State.
TRANSACTIONS/CAREER NOTES: Selected after junior season by New York Jets in first round (fourth pick overall) of 1993 NFL draft. ... Signed by Jets (August 5, 1993). ... On injured reserve with hip injury (November 16, 1993-remainder of season). ... On injured reserve with knee injury (July 29, 1998-entire season).
HONORS: Butkus Award winner (1992). ... Named College Football Player of the Year by THE SPORTING NEWS (1992). ... Named linebacker on THE SPORTING NEWS college All-America first team (1992).
PRO STATISTICS: 1993—Recovered one fumble. 1997—Recovered one fumble. 1999—Intercepted one pass for 15 yards and recovered one fumble.

Year Team	G	GS	SACKS
1993—New York Jets NFL	9	0	0.0
1994—New York Jets NFL	15	11	0.5
1995—New York Jets NFL	10	10	1.5
1996—New York Jets NFL	12	12	1.0
1997—New York Jets NFL	16	16	3.0
1998—New York Jets NFL	Did not play.		
1999—New York Jets NFL	16	16	1.0
Pro totals (6 years)	78	65	7.0

JONES, MIKE A.   LB   RAMS

PERSONAL: Born April 15, 1969, in Kansas City, Mo. ... 6-1/240. ... Full name: Michael Anthony Jones.
HIGH SCHOOL: Southwest (Kansas City, Mo.).
COLLEGE: Missouri.
TRANSACTIONS/CAREER NOTES: Signed as non-drafted free agent by Los Angeles Raiders (April 1991). ... Assigned by Raiders to Sacramento Surge in 1992 World League enhancement allocation program (February 20, 1992). ... Raiders franchise moved to Oakland (July 21, 1995). ... Granted unconditional free agency (February 14, 1997). ... Signed by St. Louis Rams (March 18, 1997).
CHAMPIONSHIP GAME EXPERIENCE: Played in NFC championship game (1999 season). ... Member of Super Bowl championship team (1999 season).
PRO STATISTICS: 1995—Recovered two fumbles for 52 yards and one touchdown. 1999—Fumbled once and recovered two fumbles for 42 yards and one touchdown.

Year Team	G	GS	No.	Yds.	Avg.	TD	SACKS No.
1991—Los Angeles Raiders NFL	16	0	0	0	0.0	0	0.0
1992—Sacramento W.L.	7	7	0	0	0.0	0	2.0
—Los Angeles Raiders NFL	16	0	0	0	0.0	0	0.0
1993—Los Angeles Raiders NFL	16	2	0	0	0.0	0	0.0
1994—Los Angeles Raiders NFL	16	1	0	0	0.0	0	0.0
1995—Oakland NFL	16	16	1	23	23.0	0	0.0
1996—Oakland NFL	15	15	0	0	0.0	0	1.0
1997—St. Louis NFL	16	16	1	0	0.0	0	2.0
1998—St. Louis NFL	16	16	2	13	6.5	0	3.0
1999—St. Louis NFL	16	16	4	96	24.0	†2	1.0
W.L. totals (1 year)	7	7	0	0	0.0	0	2.0
NFL totals (9 years)	153	82	8	132	16.5	2	7.0
Pro totals (9 years)	160	89	8	132	16.5	2	9.0

JONES, MIKE D.   DT/DE   TITANS

PERSONAL: Born August 25, 1969, in Columbia, S.C. ... 6-4/280. ... Full name: Michael David Jones.
HIGH SCHOOL: C.A. Johnson (Columbia, S.C.).
COLLEGE: North Carolina State.
TRANSACTIONS/CAREER NOTES: Selected by Phoenix Cardinals in second round (32nd pick overall) of 1991 NFL draft. ... Signed by Cardinals (July 15, 1991). ... Granted free agency (February 17, 1994). ... Signed by New England Patriots (June 7, 1994). ... Granted unconditional free agency (February 14, 1997). ... Re-signed by Patriots (March 10, 1997). ... Traded by Patriots to St. Louis Rams for fifth-round pick (DT Jeff Marriott) in 2000 draft (August 30, 1998). ... Granted unconditional free agency (February 12, 1999). ... Signed by Tennessee Titans (February 15, 1999).
CHAMPIONSHIP GAME EXPERIENCE: Played in Super Bowl XXXI (1996 season). ... Played in AFC championship game (1999 season).
PRO STATISTICS: 1994—Recovered one fumble. 1996—Recovered one fumble for 31 yards. 1997—Recovered one fumble. 1998—Returned one kickoff for two yards and recovered two fumbles for 43 yards. 1999—Recovered one fumble.

Year Team	G	GS	SACKS
1991—Phoenix NFL	16	1	0.0
1992—Phoenix NFL	15	15	6.0
1993—Phoenix NFL	16	2	3.0
1994—New England NFL	16	16	6.0
1995—New England NFL	13	3	3.0
1996—New England NFL	16	12	2.0
1997—New England NFL	16	7	4.0

1998—St. Louis NFL	16	15	2.5
1999—Tennessee NFL	11	3	1.0
Pro totals (9years)	135	74	27.5

JONES, ROBERT   LB   DOLPHINS

PERSONAL: Born September 27, 1969, in Blackstone, Va. ... 6-3/245. ... Full name: Robert Lee Jones.
HIGH SCHOOL: Nottoway (Va.), then Fork Union (Va.) Military Academy.
COLLEGE: East Carolina.
TRANSACTIONS/CAREER NOTES: Selected by Dallas Cowboys in first round (24th pick overall) of 1992 NFL draft. ... Signed by Cowboys (April 26, 1992). ... Granted unconditional free agency (February 16, 1996). ... Signed by St. Louis Rams (March 5, 1996). ... Released by Rams (June 2, 1998). ... Signed by Miami Dolphins (June 10, 1998). ... Granted unconditional free agency (February 12, 1999). ... Re-signed by Dolphins (February 19, 1999).
PLAYING EXPERIENCE: Dallas NFL, 1992-1995; St. Louis NFL, 1996 and 1997; Miami NFL, 1998 and 1999. ... Games/Games started: 1992 (15/13), 1993 (13/3), 1994 (16/16), 1995 (12/12), 1996 (16/13), 1997 (16/15), 1998 (16/16), 1999 (16/15). Total: 120/103.
CHAMPIONSHIP GAME EXPERIENCE: Played in NFC championship game (1992-1995 seasons). ... Member of Super Bowl championship team (1992, 1993 and 1995 seasons).
HONORS: Named linebacker on THE SPORTING NEWS college All-America second team (1990). ... Named linebacker on THE SPORTING NEWS college All-America first team (1991).
PRO STATISTICS: 1992—Credited with one sack and recovered one fumble. 1993—Returned one kickoff for 12 yards. 1994—Returned one kickoff for eight yards and recovered one fumble. 1995—Credited with one sack. 1996—Intercepted one pass for no yards. 1997—Credited with one sack. 1998—Intercepted two passes for 14 yards and one touchdown and credited with five sacks.

JONES, ROD   OT   BENGALS

PERSONAL: Born January 11, 1974, in Detroit. ... 6-4/325. ... Full name: Rodrek E. Jones.
HIGH SCHOOL: Henry Ford (Detroit).
COLLEGE: Kansas (degree in human development/family living).
TRANSACTIONS/CAREER NOTES: Selected by Cincinnati Bengals in seventh round (219th pick overall) of 1996 NFL draft. ... Signed by Bengals (July 15, 1996). ... Granted free agency (February 12, 1999). ... Re-signed by Bengals (April 15, 1999).
PLAYING EXPERIENCE: Cincinnati NFL, 1996-1999. ... Games/Games started: 1996 (6/1), 1997 (13/8), 1998 (7/2), 1999 (16/15). Total: 42/26.

JONES, TEBUCKY   CB   PATRIOTS

PERSONAL: Born October 6, 1974, in New Britain, Conn. ... 6-2/219. ... Full name: Tebucky Shermaine Jones.
HIGH SCHOOL: New Britain (Conn.).
COLLEGE: Syracuse.
TRANSACTIONS/CAREER NOTES: Selected by New England Patriots in first round (22nd pick overall) of 1998 NFL draft. ... Signed by Patriots (July 18, 1998). ... On injured reserve with knee injury (December 31, 1999-remainder of season).
PLAYING EXPERIENCE: New England NFL, 1998 and 1999. ... Games/Games started: 1998 (16/0), 1999 (11/2). Total: 27/2.
PRO STATISTICS: 1998—Recovered one fumble. 1999—Returned five kickoffs for 113 yards.

JONES, TONY   OT   BRONCOS

PERSONAL: Born May 24, 1966, in Royston, Ga. ... 6-5/291. ... Full name: Tony Edward Jones.
HIGH SCHOOL: Franklin County (Carnesville, Ga.).
COLLEGE: Western Carolina (degree in management, 1989).
TRANSACTIONS/CAREER NOTES: Signed as non-drafted free agent by Cleveland Browns (May 2, 1988). ... On injured reserve with toe injury (August 29-October 22, 1988). ... On injured reserve with toe injury (September 20-November 7, 1989). ... Granted free agency (February 1, 1992). ... Re-signed by Browns (July 29, 1992). ... Browns franchise moved to Baltimore and renamed Ravens for 1996 season (March 11, 1996). ... Traded by Ravens to Denver Broncos for second-round pick (S Kim Herring) in 1997 draft (February 14, 1997). ... On injured reserve with arm injury (December 31, 1999-remainder of season).
PLAYING EXPERIENCE: Cleveland NFL, 1988-1995; Baltimore NFL, 1996; Denver NFL, 1997-1999. ... Games/Games started: 1988 (4/0), 1989 (9/3), 1990 (16/16), 1991 (16/16), 1992 (16/16), 1993 (16/16), 1994 (16/16), 1995 (16/16), 1996 (15/15), 1997 (16/16), 1998 (16/16), 1999 (12/12). Total: 168/158.
CHAMPIONSHIP GAME EXPERIENCE: Played in AFC championship game (1989, 1997 and 1998 seasons). ... Member of Super Bowl championship team (1997 and 1998 seasons).
HONORS: Played in Pro Bowl (1998 season).
PRO STATISTICS: 1989—Recovered one fumble. 1991—Recovered one fumble. 1994—Recovered one fumble. 1995—Recovered one fumble.

JONES, WALTER   OT   SEAHAWKS

PERSONAL: Born January 19, 1974, in Aliceville, Ala. ... 6-5/300.
HIGH SCHOOL: Aliceville (Ala.).
JUNIOR COLLEGE: Holmes Junior College (Miss.).
COLLEGE: Florida State.
TRANSACTIONS/CAREER NOTES: Selected by Seattle Seahawks in first round (sixth pick overall) of 1997 NFL draft. ... Signed by Seahawks (August 6, 1997).
PLAYING EXPERIENCE: Seattle NFL, 1997-1999. ... Games/Games started: 1997 (12/12), 1998 (16/16), 1999 (16/16). Total: 44/44.
HONORS: Played in Pro Bowl (1999 season).
PRO STATISTICS: 1999—Recovered one fumble.

JORDAN, ANDREW   TE   VIKINGS

PERSONAL: Born June 21, 1972, in Charlotte. ... 6-6/272. ... Full name: Andrew Jordan Jr.
HIGH SCHOOL: West Charlotte.
COLLEGE: North Greenville College (S.C.), then Western Carolina (degree in criminal justice, 1993).
TRANSACTIONS/CAREER NOTES: Selected by Minnesota Vikings in sixth round (179th pick overall) of 1994 NFL draft. ... Signed by Vikings (June 17, 1994). ... Released by Vikings (September 23, 1997). ... Signed by Tampa Bay Buccaneers (December 9, 1997). ... Released by Buccaneers (August 25, 1998). ... Signed by Philadelphia Eagles (December 1, 1998). ... Granted unconditional free agency (February 12, 1999). ... Re-signed by Eagles (February 18, 1999). ... Released by Eagles (September 7, 1999). ... Signed by Vikings (October 13, 1999).
PRO STATISTICS: 1994—Returned one kickoff for eight yards and recovered a fumble. 1999—Returned one kickoff for no yards.
SINGLE GAME HIGHS (regular season): Receptions—5 (November 13, 1994, vs. New England); yards—57 (November 13, 1994, vs. New England); and touchdown receptions—1 (October 24, 1999, vs. San Francisco).

| | | | RECEIVING | | | | TOTALS | | | |
Year Team	G	GS	No.	Yds.	Avg.	TD	TD	2pt.	Pts.	Fum.
1994—Minnesota NFL	16	12	35	336	9.6	0	0	1	2	1
1995—Minnesota NFL	13	7	27	185	6.9	2	2	0	12	1
1996—Minnesota NFL	13	9	19	128	6.7	0	0	1	2	0
1997—Minnesota NFL	2	0	0	0	0.0	0	0	0	0	0
—Tampa Bay NFL	2	0	1	0	0.0	0	0	0	0	0
1998—Philadelphia NFL	3	0	2	9	4.5	0	0	0	0	0
1999—Minnesota NFL	11	1	5	40	8.0	1	1	0	6	0
Pro totals (6 years)	60	29	89	698	7.8	3	3	2	22	2

JORDAN, CHARLES   WR

PERSONAL: Born October 9, 1969, in Los Angeles. ... 5-11/185. ... Full name: Charles Alexander Jordan.
HIGH SCHOOL: Morningside (Inglewood, Calif.).
JUNIOR COLLEGE: Long Beach (Calif.) City College.
COLLEGE: None.
TRANSACTIONS/CAREER NOTES: Signed as non-drafted free agent by Los Angeles Raiders (May 4, 1993). ... Inactive for six games (1993). ... On injured reserve with abdominal injury (October 27, 1993-remainder of season). ... Traded by Raiders to Green Bay Packers for fifth-round pick (traded to Washington in 1995 draft (August 28, 1994). ... Granted free agency (February 16, 1996). ... Tendered offer sheet by Miami Dolphins (March 7, 1996). ... Packers declined to match offer (March 13, 1996). ... On injured reserve with groin injury (October 8, 1998-remainder of season). ... Granted unconditional free agency (February 12, 1999). ... Signed by Seattle Seahawks (June 4, 1999). ... Released by Seahawks (November 26, 1999). ... Re-signed by Seahawks (November 30, 1999). ... Claimed on waivers by Packers (December 9, 1999). ... Granted unconditional free agency (February 11, 2000).
CHAMPIONSHIP GAME EXPERIENCE: Member of Packers for NFC championship game (1995 season); inactive.
PRO STATISTICS: 1994—Rushed once for five yards. 1995—Recovered one fumble. 1997—Rushed three times for 12 yards and recovered one fumble. 1998—Recovered one fumble. 1999—Recovered one fumble.
SINGLE GAME HIGHS (regular season): Receptions—5 (December 7, 1997, vs. Detroit); yards—106 (November 30, 1997, vs. Oakland); and touchdown receptions—2 (November 30, 1997, vs. Oakland).
STATISTICAL PLATEAUS: 100-yard receiving games: 1997 (2).

| | | | RECEIVING | | | | PUNT RETURNS | | | | KICKOFF RETURNS | | | | TOTALS | | | |
Year Team	G	GS	No.	Yds.	Avg.	TD	No.	Yds.	Avg.	TD	No.	Yds.	Avg.	TD	TD	2pt.	Pts.	Fum.
1993—LA Raiders NFL										Did not play.								
1994—Green Bay NFL	10	0	0	0	0.0	0	1	0	0.0	0	5	115	23.0	0	0	0	0	1
1995—Green Bay NFL	6	1	7	117	16.7	2	21	213	10.1	0	21	444	21.1	0	2	0	12	1
1996—Miami NFL	6	0	7	152	21.7	0	0	0	0.0	0	4	81	20.3	0	0	0	0	0
1997—Miami NFL	14	1	27	471	17.4	3	26	273	10.5	0	1	6	6.0	0	3	0	18	2
1998—Miami NFL	3	0	2	17	8.5	0	5	47	9.4	0	0	0	0.0	0	0	0	0	2
1999—Seattle NFL	4	1	1	6	6.0	0	5	47	9.4	0	3	62	20.7	0	0	0	0	0
—Green Bay NFL	4	0	2	54	27.0	0	5	29	5.8	0	6	95	15.8	0	0	0	0	1
Pro totals (6 years)	47	3	46	817	17.8	5	63	609	9.7	0	40	803	20.1	0	5	0	30	7

JORDAN, RANDY   RB   RAIDERS

PERSONAL: Born June 6, 1970, in Henderson, N.C. ... 5-11/215. ... Full name: Randy Loment Jordan.
HIGH SCHOOL: Warren County (Warrenton, N.C.).
COLLEGE: North Carolina.
TRANSACTIONS/CAREER NOTES: Signed as non-drafted free agent by Los Angeles Raiders (May 1993). ... Released by Raiders (August 25, 1993). ... Re-signed by Raiders to practice squad (August 31, 1993). ... Activated (October 30, 1993). ... Released by Raiders (August 28, 1994). ... Signed by Jacksonville Jaguars (December 15, 1994). ... Granted free agency (February 14, 1997). ... Re-signed by Jaguars (May 5, 1997). ... Released by Jaguars (August 19, 1997). ... Re-signed by Jaguars (September 24, 1997). ... Granted unconditional free agency (February 13, 1998). ... Signed by Oakland Raiders (June 2, 1998).
CHAMPIONSHIP GAME EXPERIENCE: Played in AFC championship game (1996 season).
PRO STATISTICS: 1996—Recovered one fumble.
SINGLE GAME HIGHS (regular season): Attempts—24 (December 20, 1998, vs. San Diego); yards—82 (December 20, 1998, vs. San Diego); and rushing touchdowns—2 (September 12, 1999, vs. Green Bay).

| | | | RUSHING | | | | RECEIVING | | | | KICKOFF RETURNS | | | | TOTALS | | | |
Year Team	G	GS	Att.	Yds.	Avg.	TD	No.	Yds.	Avg.	TD	No.	Yds.	Avg.	TD	TD	2pt.	Pts.	Fum.
1993—LA Raiders NFL	10	2	12	33	2.8	0	4	42	10.5	0	0	0	0.0	0	0	0	0	2
1994—Jacksonville NFL										Did not play.								
1995—Jacksonville NFL	12	2	21	62	3.0	0	5	89	17.8	1	2	41	20.5	0	1	0	6	0
1996—Jacksonville NFL	15	0	0	0	0.0	0	0	0	0.0	0	26	553	21.3	0	0	0	0	1
1997—Jacksonville NFL	7	0	1	2	2.0	0	0	0	0.0	0	0	0	0.0	0	0	0	0	1
1998—Oakland NFL	16	0	47	159	3.4	1	3	2	0.7	0	0	0	0.0	0	1	0	6	1

	16	0	9	32	3.6	2	8	82	10.3	0	10	207	20.7	0	2	0	12	2
1999—Oakland NFL................																		
Pro totals (6 years)	76	4	90	288	3.2	3	20	215	10.8	1	38	801	21.1	0	4	0	24	6

JORDAN, RICHARD — LB — LIONS

PERSONAL: Born December 1, 1974, in Holdenville, Okla. ... 6-1/256. ... Full name: Richard Lamont Jordan.
HIGH SCHOOL: Vian (Okla.).
COLLEGE: Missouri Southern.
TRANSACTIONS/CAREER NOTES: Selected by Detroit Lions in seventh round (239th pick overall) of 1997 NFL draft. ... Signed by Lions (May 22, 1997). ... Released by Lions (August 25, 1997). ... Re-signed by Lions to practice squad (August 27, 1997). ... Activated (September 27, 1997). ... On injured reserve with knee injury (November 17, 1999-remainder of season). ... Granted free agency (February 11, 2000). ... Re-signed by Lions (April 5, 2000).
PLAYING EXPERIENCE: Detroit NFL, 1997-1999. ... Games/Games started: 1997 (10/0), 1998 (16/3), 1999 (9/0). Total: 35/3.
PRO STATISTICS: 1998—Intercepted one pass for four yards.

JOSEPH, KERRY — S — SEAHAWKS

PERSONAL: Born October 4, 1973, in New Iberia, La. ... 6-2/205.
HIGH SCHOOL: New Iberia (La.).
COLLEGE: McNeese State.
TRANSACTIONS/CAREER NOTES: Signed as non-drafted free agent by Cincinnati Bengals (April 22, 1996). ... Inactive for all 16 games (1996). ... Released by Bengals (May 6, 1997). ... Signed by Washington Redskins (May 16, 1997). ... Released by Redskins (August 25, 1997). ... Selected by Rhein Fire in 1998 NFL Europe draft (February 18, 1998). ... Signed by Seattle Seahawks (June 29, 1998). ... Granted free agency (February 11, 2000). ... Re-signed by Seahawks (April 19, 2000).
PRO STATISTICS: 1999—Recovered one fumble.

			INTERCEPTIONS				PUNT RETURNS				KICKOFF RETURNS				TOTALS			
Year Team	G	GS	No.	Yds.	Avg.	TD	No.	Yds.	Avg.	TD	No.	Yds.	Avg.	TD	TD	2pt.	Pts.	Fum.
1996—Cincinnati NFL............								Did not play.										
1997—								Did not play.										
1998—Rhein NFLE..............	...	...	4	25	6.3	0	4	43	10.8	0	0	0	0.0	0	0	0	0	0
—Seattle NFL	16	0	0	0	0.0	0	15	182	12.1	0	2	49	24.5	0	0	0	0	1
1999—Seattle NFL	16	4	3	82	27.3	0	0	0	0.0	0	6	132	22.0	0	0	0	0	0
NFL Europe totals (1 year)	...	...	4	25	6.3	0	4	43	10.8	0	0	0	0.0	0	0	0	0	0
NFL totals (1 year)	32	4	3	82	27.3	0	15	182	12.1	0	8	181	22.6	0	0	0	0	1
Pro totals (2 years)	...	...	7	107	15.3	0	19	225	11.8	0	8	181	22.6	0	0	0	0	1

JOYCE, MATT — OL — CARDINALS

PERSONAL: Born March 30, 1972, in La Crosse, Wis. ... 6-7/305.
HIGH SCHOOL: New York Military Academy (Cornwall Hudson, N.Y.).
COLLEGE: Richmond (degree in health science, 1994).
TRANSACTIONS/CAREER NOTES: Signed as non-drafted free agent by Dallas Cowboys (May 2, 1994). ... Claimed on waivers by Cincinnati Bengals (August 28, 1994); released after failing physical. ... Signed by Cowboys to practice squad (September 5, 1994). ... Granted free agency after 1994 season. ... Signed by Seattle Seahawks (March 1, 1995). ... Released by Seahawks (August 25, 1996). ... Signed by Arizona Cardinals (December 3, 1996). ... Assigned by Cardinals to Scottish Claymores in 1997 World League enhancement allocation program (February 19, 1997). ... Granted free agency (February 12, 1999). ... Re-signed by Cardinals (April 1, 1999). ... Granted unconditional free agency (February 11, 2000). ... Re-signed by Cardinals (February 21, 2000).
PLAYING EXPERIENCE: Seattle NFL, 1995; Scottish Claymores W.L., 1997; Arizona NFL, 1996-1999. ... Games/Games started: 1995 (16/13), 1996 (2/0), W.L. 1997 (games played unavailable), NFL 1997 (9/6), 1998 (11/0), 1999 (15/15). Total NFL: 53/34.
PRO STATISTICS: 1995—Recovered one fumble. 1999—Recovered one fumble.

JUNKIN, TREY — TE — CARDINALS

PERSONAL: Born January 23, 1961, in Conway, Ark. ... 6-2/245. ... Full name: Abner Kirk Junkin. ... Brother of Mike Junkin, linebacker with Cleveland Browns (1987 and 1988) and Kansas City Chiefs (1989).
HIGH SCHOOL: North Little Rock (Ark.).
COLLEGE: Louisiana Tech.
TRANSACTIONS/CAREER NOTES: Selected by Buffalo Bills in fourth round (93rd pick overall) of 1983 NFL draft. ... Signed by Bills for 1983 season. ... Released by Bills (September 12, 1984). ... Signed by Washington Redskins (September 25, 1984). ... Rights relinquished by Redskins (February 1, 1985). ... Signed by Los Angeles Raiders (March 10, 1985). ... On injured reserve with knee injury (September 24, 1986-remainder of season). ... Released by Raiders (September 3, 1990). ... Signed by Seattle Seahawks (October 3, 1990). ... Granted unconditional free agency (February 1-April 1, 1991). ... Re-signed by Seahawks (July 9, 1991). ... Granted unconditional free agency (February 1-April 1, 1992). ... Re-signed by Seahawks for 1992 season. ... Granted unconditional free agency (March 1, 1993). ... Re-signed by Seahawks (March 11, 1993). ... Released by Seahawks (August 30, 1993). ... Re-signed by Seahawks (August 31, 1993). ... Granted unconditional free agency (February 17, 1994). ... Re-signed by Seahawks (May 31, 1994). ... Granted unconditional free agency (February 17, 1995). ... Re-signed by Seahawks (March 20, 1995). ... Granted unconditional free agency (February 16, 1996). ... Signed by Oakland Raiders (June 10, 1996). ... Claimed on waivers by Arizona Cardinals (October 14, 1996).
PRO STATISTICS: 1983—Recovered one fumble. 1984—Recovered one fumble. 1989—Returned one kickoff for no yards.
SINGLE GAME HIGHS (regular season): Receptions—2 (November 22, 1992, vs. Kansas City); yards—38 (September 21, 1986, vs. New York Giants); and touchdown receptions—1 (September 25, 1994, vs. Pittsburgh).

			RECEIVING				TOTALS			
Year Team	G	GS	No.	Yds.	Avg.	TD	TD	2pt.	Pts.	Fum.
1983—Buffalo NFL	16	0	0	0	0.0	0	0	0	0	0
1984—Buffalo NFL..	2	0	0	0	0.0	0	0	0	0	0
—Washington NFL...	12	0	0	0	0.0	0	0	0	0	0

Year—Team	G	GS	No.	Yds.	Avg.	TD	TD	2pt.	Pts.	Fum.
1985—Los Angeles Raiders NFL	16	0	2	8	4.0	1	1	0	6	0
1986—Los Angeles Raiders NFL	3	0	2	38	19.0	0	0	0	0	0
1987—Los Angeles Raiders NFL	12	1	2	15	7.5	0	0	0	0	0
1988—Los Angeles Raiders NFL	16	1	4	25	6.3	2	2	0	12	0
1989—Los Angeles Raiders NFL	16	0	3	32	10.7	2	2	0	12	0
1990—Seattle NFL	12	0	0	0	0.0	0	0	0	0	0
1991—Seattle NFL	16	0	0	0	0.0	0	0	0	0	0
1992—Seattle NFL	16	1	3	25	8.3	1	1	0	6	0
1993—Seattle NFL	16	1	0	0	0.0	0	0	0	0	0
1994—Seattle NFL	16	0	1	1	1.0	1	1	0	6	0
1995—Seattle NFL	16	0	0	0	0.0	0	0	0	0	0
1996—Oakland NFL	6	0	0	0	0.0	0	0	0	0	0
—Arizona NFL	10	0	0	0	0.0	0	0	0	0	0
1997—Arizona NFL	16	0	0	0	0.0	0	0	0	0	0
1998—Arizona NFL	16	0	0	0	0.0	0	0	0	0	0
1999—Arizona NFL	16	0	0	0	0.0	0	0	0	0	0
Pro totals (17 years)	249	4	17	144	8.5	7	7	0	42	0

JUREVICIUS, JOE WR GIANTS

PERSONAL: Born December 23, 1974, in Cleveland. ... 6-5/230. ... Full name: Joe Michael Jurevicius. ... Name pronounced jur-uh-VISH-us.
HIGH SCHOOL: Lake Catholic (Mentor, Ohio).
COLLEGE: Penn State.
TRANSACTIONS/CAREER NOTES: Selected by New York Giants in second round (55th pick overall) of 1998 NFL draft. ... Signed by Giants (July 28, 1998).
SINGLE GAME HIGHS (regular season): Receptions—3 (January 2, 2000, vs. Dallas); yards—86 (January 2, 2000, vs. Dallas); and touchdown receptions—1 (October 24, 1999, vs. New Orleans).

Year Team	G	GS	RECEIVING				TOTALS			
			No.	Yds.	Avg.	TD	TD	2pt.	Pts.	Fum.
1998—New York Giants NFL	14	1	9	146	16.2	0	0	0	0	0
1999—New York Giants NFL	16	1	18	318	17.7	1	1	0	6	1
Pro totals (2 years)	30	2	27	464	17.2	1	1	0	6	1

JURKOVIC, JOHN DT

PERSONAL: Born August 18, 1967, in Friedrischafen, West Germany. ... 6-2/301. ... Full name: Ivan Jurkovic. ... Name pronounced YUR-kuh-vitch.
HIGH SCHOOL: Thornton Fractional North (Calumet City, Ill.).
COLLEGE: Eastern Illinois (degree in business).
TRANSACTIONS/CAREER NOTES: Signed as non-drafted free agent by Miami Dolphins (April 27, 1990). ... Released by Dolphins (August 28, 1990). ... Re-signed by Dolphins to practice squad (October 3, 1990). ... Granted free agency after 1990 season. ... Signed by Green Bay Packers (March 8, 1991). ... Released by Packers (August 26, 1991). ... Re-signed by Packers to practice squad (August 28, 1991). ... Activated (November 22, 1991). ... Granted unconditional free agency (February 1-April 1, 1992). ... Re-signed by Packers (April 2, 1992). ... Granted unconditional free agency (February 16, 1996). ... Signed by Jacksonville Jaguars (April 13, 1996). ... On injured reserve with leg injury (September 23, 1997-remainder of season). ... Granted unconditional free agency (February 12, 1999). ... Signed by Cleveland Browns (March 25, 1999). ... On injured reserve with hamstring injury (November 23, 1999-remainder of season). ... Released by Browns (March 9, 2000).
CHAMPIONSHIP GAME EXPERIENCE: Played in NFC championship game (1995 season). ... Played in AFC championship game (1996 season).
PRO STATISTICS: 1992—Returned three kickoffs for 39 yards. 1993—Returned two kickoffs for 22 yards. 1994—Returned four kickoffs for 57 yards. 1995—Returned one kickoff for 17 yards. 1996—Recovered two fumbles.

Year Team	G	GS	SACKS
1990—Miami NFL	Did not play.		
1991—Green Bay NFL	5	0	0.0
1992—Green Bay NFL	16	12	2.0
1993—Green Bay NFL	16	12	5.5
1994—Green Bay NFL	16	15	0.0
1995—Green Bay NFL	16	14	0.0
1996—Jacksonville NFL	16	14	1.0
1997—Jacksonville NFL	3	3	0.0
1998—Jacksonville NFL	16	16	0.5
1999—Cleveland NFL	10	9	0.0
Pro totals (9 years)	114	95	9.0

JUSTIN, PAUL QB COWBOYS

PERSONAL: Born May 19, 1968, in Schaumburg, Ill. ... 6-4/211. ... Full name: Paul Donald Justin.
HIGH SCHOOL: Schaumburg (Ill.).
COLLEGE: Arizona State.
TRANSACTIONS/CAREER NOTES: Selected by Chicago Bears in seventh round (190th pick overall) of 1991 NFL draft. ... Signed by Bears for 1991 season. ... Released by Bears (August 27, 1991). ... Re-signed by Bears to practice squad (August 28, 1991). ... Released by Bears (August 31, 1992). ... Signed by Indianapolis Colts (April 11, 1994). ... Released by Colts (August 25, 1994). ... Re-signed by Colts to practice squad (August 29, 1994). ... Assigned by Colts to Frankfurt Galaxy in 1995 World League enhancement allocation program (February 20, 1995). ... On injured reserve with knee injury (December 5, 1997-remainder of season). ... Granted free agency (February 13, 1998). ... Re-signed by Colts (March 26, 1998). ... Traded by Colts to Cincinnati Bengals for fifth-round pick (LB Antony Jordon) in 1998 draft (March 26, 1998). ... Released by Bengals (April 20, 1999). ... Signed by Oakland Raiders (July 1999). ... Traded by Raiders to St. Louis Rams for seventh-round pick (traded to Indianapolis) in 2000 draft (August 29, 1999). ... Granted unconditional free agency (February 11, 2000). ... Signed by Dallas Cowboys (April 7, 2000).

CHAMPIONSHIP GAME EXPERIENCE: Member of Colts for AFC championship game (1995 season); inactive. ... Member of Rams for NFC championship game (1999 season); did not play. ... Member of Super Bowl championship team (1999 season); did not play.
PRO STATISTICS: 1995—Fumbled once and recovered one fumble for minus one yard. 1996—Fumbled once and recovered one fumble. 1997—Fumbled once.
SINGLE GAME HIGHS (regular season): Attempts—40 (December 1, 1996, vs. Buffalo); completions—24 (November 16, 1997, vs. Green Bay); yards—340 (November 16, 1997, vs. Green Bay); and touchdown passes—2 (October 26, 1997, vs. San Diego).
STATISTICAL PLATEAUS: 300-yard passing games: 1997 (1).
MISCELLANEOUS: Regular-season record as starting NFL quarterback: 3-7 (.300).

					PASSING						RUSHING				TOTALS	
Year Team	G	GS	Att.	Cmp.	Pct.	Yds.	TD	Int.	Avg.	Rat.	Att.	Yds.	Avg.	TD	TD	2pt.	Pts.
1991—Chicago NFL...............							Did not play.										
1992—							Did not play.										
1993—							Did not play.										
1994—Indianapolis NFL							Did not play.										
1995—Frankfurt W.L............	...	...	279	172	61.6	2394	17	12	8.58	91.6	14	50	3.6	0	0	0	0
—Indianapolis NFL	3	1	36	20	55.6	212	0	2	5.89	49.8	3	1	0.3	0	0	0	0
1996—Indianapolis NFL	8	2	127	74	58.3	839	2	0	6.61	83.4	2	7	3.5	0	0	0	0
1997—Indianapolis NFL	8	4	140	83	59.3	1046	5	5	7.47	79.6	6	2	0.3	0	0	0	0
1998—Cincinnati NFL.............	5	3	63	34	54.0	426	1	3	6.76	60.7	1	2	2.0	0	0	1	2
1999—St. Louis NFL..............	10	0	14	9	64.3	91	0	0	6.50	82.7	5	-1	-0.2	0	0	0	0
W.L. totals (1 year)............	...	...	279	172	61.6	2394	17	12	8.58	91.6	14	50	3.6	0	0	0	0
NFL totals (4 years)	34	10	380	220	57.9	2614	8	10	6.88	75.0	17	11	0.6	0	0	1	2
Pro totals (5 years)	...	...	659	392	59.5	5008	25	22	7.60	82.1	31	61	2.0	0	0	1	2

KALU, NDUKWE   DE   REDSKINS

PERSONAL: Born August 3, 1975, in Baltimore. ... 6-3/246. ... Full name: Ndukwe Dike Kalu. ... Name pronounced EN-doo-kway ka-LOO.
HIGH SCHOOL: John Marshall (San Antonio).
COLLEGE: Rice.
TRANSACTIONS/CAREER NOTES: Selected by Philadelphia Eagles in fifth round (152nd pick overall) of 1997 NFL draft. ... Signed by Eagles (July 15, 1997). ... Released by Eagles (August 25, 1998). ... Signed by Washington Redskins (August 30, 1998). ... Granted free agency (February 11, 2000). ... Re-signed by Redskins (May 18, 2000).

Year Team	G	GS	SACKS
1997—Philadelphia NFL..	3	0	0.0
1998—Washington NFL...	13	1	3.0
1999—Washington NFL...	12	0	3.5
Pro totals (3 years)...	28	1	6.5

KANELL, DANNY   QB   FALCONS

PERSONAL: Born November 21, 1973, in Fort Lauderdale, Fla. ... 6-3/218. ... Son of Dan Kanell, team physician, Miami Dolphins and spring training physician, New York Yankees. ... Name pronounced KA-nell.
HIGH SCHOOL: Westminster Academy (Fort Lauderdale, Fla.).
COLLEGE: Florida State.
TRANSACTIONS/CAREER NOTES: Selected by New York Giants in fourth round (130th pick overall) of 1996 NFL draft. ... Signed by Giants (July 18, 1996). ... Released by Giants (February 19, 1999). ... Signed by Atlanta Falcons (March 19, 1999). ... On injured reserve with knee injury (December 22, 1999-remainder of season).
PRO STATISTICS: 1996—Fumbled twice for minus one yard. 1997—Fumbled six times for minus 10 yards. 1998—Fumbled six times and recovered one fumble.
SINGLE GAME HIGHS (regular season): Attempts—45 (September 21, 1998, vs. Dallas); completions—25 (September 21, 1998, vs. Dallas); yards—259 (October 18, 1998, vs. Arizona); and touchdown passes—3 (October 18, 1998, vs. Arizona).\
MISCELLANEOUS: Selected by Milwaukee Brewers organization in 19th round of free-agent baseball draft (June 1, 1992); did not sign. ... Selected by New York Yankees organization in 25th round of free-agent baseball draft (June 1, 1995); did not sign. ... Regular-season record as starting NFL quarterback: 10-10-1 (.500). ... Postseason record as starting NFL quarterback: 0-1.

					PASSING						RUSHING				TOTALS	
Year Team	G	GS	Att.	Cmp.	Pct.	Yds.	TD	Int.	Avg.	Rat.	Att.	Yds.	Avg.	TD	TD	2pt.	Pts.
1996—N.Y. Giants NFL..........	4	0	60	23	38.3	227	1	1	3.78	48.4	7	6	0.9	0	0	0	0
1997—N.Y. Giants NFL..........	16	10	294	156	53.1	1740	11	9	5.92	70.7	15	2	0.1	0	0	0	0
1998—N.Y. Giants NFL..........	10	10	299	160	53.5	1603	11	10	5.36	67.3	15	36	2.4	0	0	0	0
1999—Atlanta NFL	3	1	84	42	50.0	593	4	4	7.06	69.2	0	0	0.0	0	0	0	0
Pro totals (4 years)	33	21	737	381	51.7	4163	27	24	5.65	67.3	37	44	1.2	0	0	0	0

KASAY, JOHN   K   PANTHERS

PERSONAL: Born October 27, 1969, in Athens, Ga. ... 5-10/198. ... Full name: John David Kasay. ... Name pronounced CASEY.
HIGH SCHOOL: Clarke Central (Athens, Ga.).
COLLEGE: Georgia (degree in journalism, 1994).
TRANSACTIONS/CAREER NOTES: Selected by Seattle Seahawks in fourth round (98th pick overall) of 1991 NFL draft. ... Signed by Seahawks (July 19, 1991). ... Granted free agency (February 17, 1994). ... Re-signed by Seahawks (July 19, 1994). ... Granted unconditional free agency (February 17, 1995). ... Signed by Carolina Panthers (February 20, 1995). ... On injured reserve with knee injury (December 14, 1999-remainder of season).
CHAMPIONSHIP GAME EXPERIENCE: Played in NFC championship game (1996 season).
HONORS: Played in Pro Bowl (1996 season).
PRO STATISTICS: 1993—Recovered one fumble. 1995—Punted once for 32 yards. 1996—Punted once for 30 yards.

Year Team	G	XPM	XPA	FGM	FGA	Lg.	50+	Pts.
1991—Seattle NFL	16	27	28	25	31	54	2-3	102
1992—Seattle NFL	16	14	14	14	22	43	0-0	56
1993—Seattle NFL	16	29	29	23	28	55	3-5	98
1994—Seattle NFL	16	25	26	20	24	50	1-2	85
1995—Carolina NFL	16	27	28	26	33	52	1-1	105
1996—Carolina NFL	16	34	35	*37	*45	53	3-7	*145
1997—Carolina NFL	16	25	25	22	26	54	3-6	91
1998—Carolina NFL	16	35	37	19	26	56	4-7	92
1999—Carolina NFL	13	33	33	22	25	52	2-4	99
Pro totals (9 years)	141	249	255	208	260	56	19-35	873

KATZENMOYER, ANDY   LB   PATRIOTS

PERSONAL: Born December 2, 1977, in Westerville, Ohio. ... 6-3/255. ... Full name: Andrew Warren Katzenmoyer.
HIGH SCHOOL: Westerville (Ohio) North.
COLLEGE: Ohio State.
TRANSACTIONS/CAREER NOTES: Selected after junior season by New England Patriots in first round (28th pick overall) of 1999 NFL draft. ... Signed by Patriots (July 30, 1999).
HONORS: Butkus Award winner (1997). ... Named inside linebacker on THE SPORTING NEWS college All-America third team (1997).

			INTERCEPTIONS				SACKS
Year Team	G	GS	No.	Yds.	Avg.	TD	No.
1999—New England NFL	16	11	1	57	57.0		3.5

KAUFMAN, NAPOLEON   RB/KR   RAIDERS

PERSONAL: Born June 7, 1973, in Kansas City, Mo. ... 5-9/185.
HIGH SCHOOL: Lompoc (Calif.).
COLLEGE: Washington.
TRANSACTIONS/CAREER NOTES: Selected by Los Angeles Raiders in first round (18th pick overall) of 1995 NFL draft. ... Signed by Raiders (May 24, 1995). ... Raiders franchise moved to Oakland (July 21, 1995).
HONORS: Named running back on THE SPORTING NEWS college All-America second team (1994).
PRO STATISTICS: 1997—Attempted one pass without a completion and recovered one fumble. 1998—Recovered one fumble. 1999—Recovered two fumbles.
SINGLE GAME HIGHS (regular season): Attempts—31 (October 25, 1998, vs. Cincinnati); yards—227 (October 19, 1997, vs. Denver); and rushing touchdowns—2 (December 19, 1999, vs. Tampa Bay).
STATISTICAL PLATEAUS: 100-yard rushing games: 1996 (3), 1997 (6), 1998 (4), 1999 (1). Total: 14. ... 100-yard receiving games: 1997 (1).

			RUSHING				RECEIVING				KICKOFF RETURNS				TOTALS			
Year Team	G	GS	Att.	Yds.	Avg.	TD	No.	Yds.	Avg.	TD	No.	Yds.	Avg.	TD	TD	2pt.	Pts.	Fum.
1995—Oakland NFL	16	1	108	490	4.5	1	9	62	6.9	0	22	572	26.0	1	2	0	12	0
1996—Oakland NFL	16	9	150	874	*5.8	1	22	143	6.5	1	25	548	21.9	0	2	0	12	3
1997—Oakland NFL	16	16	272	1294	4.8	6	40	403	10.1	2	0	0	0.0	0	8	0	48	7
1998—Oakland NFL	13	13	217	921	4.2	2	25	191	7.6	0	0	0	0.0	0	2	0	12	2
1999—Oakland NFL	16	5	138	714	§5.2	2	18	181	10.1	1	42	831	19.8	0	3	0	18	3
Pro totals (5 years)	77	44	885	4293	4.9	12	114	980	8.6	4	89	1951	21.9	1	17	0	102	15

KEARSE, JEVON   DE   TITANS

PERSONAL: Born September 3, 1976, in Fort Myers, Fla. ... 6-4/265. ... Name pronounced juh-VAUGHN CURSE.
HIGH SCHOOL: North Fort Myers (Fla.).
COLLEGE: Florida.
TRANSACTIONS/CAREER NOTES: Selected after junior season by Tennessee Titans in first round (16th pick overall) of 1999 NFL draft. ... Signed by Titans (July 27, 1999).
CHAMPIONSHIP GAME EXPERIENCE: Played in AFC championship game (1999 season). ... Played in Super Bowl XXXIV (1999 season).
HONORS: Named outside linebacker on THE SPORTING NEWS college All-America second team (1998). ... Named defensive end on THE SPORTING NEWS NFL All-Pro team (1999). ... Played in Pro Bowl (1999 season).
RECORDS: Holds NFL rookie-season record for most sacks—14.5 (1999).
PRO STATISTICS: 1999—Recovered one fumble for 14 yards and a touchdown.

Year Team	G	GS	SACKS
1999—Tennessee NFL	16	16	§14.5

KELLY, BRIAN   CB   BUCCANEERS

PERSONAL: Born January 14, 1976, in Las Vegas, Nev. ... 5-11/193.
HIGH SCHOOL: Overland (Aurora, Colo.).
COLLEGE: Southern California.
TRANSACTIONS/CAREER NOTES: Selected by Tampa Bay Buccaneers in second round (45th pick overall) of 1998 NFL draft. ... Signed by Buccaneers (July 19, 1998).
PLAYING EXPERIENCE: Tampa Bay NFL, 1998 and 1999. ... Games/Games started: 1998 (16/3), 1999 (16/3). Total: 32/6.
CHAMPIONSHIP GAME EXPERIENCE: Played in NFC championship game (1999 season).
PRO STATISTICS: 1998—Intercepted one pass for four yards, fumbled once and recovered one fumble for 15 yards. 1999—Intercepted one pass for 26 yards.

KELLY, JEFF   LB   FALCONS

PERSONAL: Born December 13, 1975, in La Grange, Texas. ... 5-11/245.
HIGH SCHOOL: La Grange (Texas).
JUNIOR COLLEGE: Garden City (Kan.) Community College.
COLLEGE: Stephen F. Austin State, then Kansas State.
TRANSACTIONS/CAREER NOTES: Selected by Atlanta Falcons in sixth round (198th pick overall) of 1999 NFL draft. ... Signed by Falcons (June 28, 1999).
PLAYING EXPERIENCE: Atlanta NFL, 1999. ... Games/Games started: 1999 (16/1).
HONORS: Named inside linebacker on THE SPORTING NEWS college All-America second team (1998).
PRO STATISTICS: 1999—Recovered one fumble.

KELLY, REGGIE   TE   FALCONS

PERSONAL: Born February 22, 1977, in Aberdeen, Miss. ... 6-3/255. ... Full name: Reginald Kuta Kelly.
HIGH SCHOOL: Aberdeen (Miss.).
COLLEGE: Mississippi State.
TRANSACTIONS/CAREER NOTES: Selected by Atlanta Falcons in second round (42nd pick overall) of 1999 NFL draft. ... Signed by Falcons (June 25, 1999).
PLAYING EXPERIENCE: Atlanta NFL, 1999. ... Games/Games started: 1999 (16/2).
PRO STATISTICS: 1999—Caught eight passes for 146 yards.
SINGLE GAME HIGHS (regular season): Receptions—3 (October 17, 1999, vs. St. Louis); yards—70 (October 17, 1999, vs. St. Louis); and touchdown receptions—0.

KELLY, ROB   S   SAINTS

PERSONAL: Born June 21, 1974, in Newark, Ohio. ... 6-0/199. ... Full name: Robert James Kelly.
HIGH SCHOOL: Newark Catholic (Ohio).
COLLEGE: Ohio State.
TRANSACTIONS/CAREER NOTES: Selected by New Orleans Saints in second round (33rd pick overall) of 1997 NFL draft. ... Signed by Saints (July 17, 1997). ... Granted free agency (February 11, 2000). ... Re-signed by Saints (April 24, 2000).
PRO STATISTICS: 1999—Recovered one fumble.

| | | | | INTERCEPTIONS | | |
Year Team	G	GS	No.	Yds.	Avg.	TD
1997—New Orleans NFL	16	2	1	15	15.0	0
1998—New Orleans NFL	16	3	2	104	52.0	1
1999—New Orleans NFL	16	7	1	6	6.0	0
Pro totals (3 years)	48	12	4	125	31.3	1

KELSAY, CHAD   LB   STEELERS

PERSONAL: Born April 9, 1977, in Auburn, Neb. ... 6-2/252.
HIGH SCHOOL: Auburn (Neb.).
COLLEGE: Nebraska.
TRANSACTIONS/CAREER NOTES: Selected by Pittsburgh Steelers in seventh round (219th pick overall) of 1999 NFL draft. ... Signed by Steelers (July 8, 1999).
PLAYING EXPERIENCE: Pittsburgh NFL, 1999. ... Games/Games started: 1999 (6/0).

KENDALL, PETE   G   SEAHAWKS

PERSONAL: Born July 9, 1973, in Quincy, Mass. ... 6-5/292. ... Full name: Peter Marcus Kendall.
HIGH SCHOOL: Archbishop Williams (Braintree, Mass.).
COLLEGE: Boston College (degree in marketing, 1995).
TRANSACTIONS/CAREER NOTES: Selected by Seattle Seahawks in first round (21st pick overall) of 1996 NFL draft. ... Signed by Seahawks (July 21, 1996).
PLAYING EXPERIENCE: Seattle NFL, 1996-1999. ... Games/Games started: 1996 (12/11), 1997 (16/16), 1998 (16/16), 1999 (16/16). Total: 60/59.

KENELEY, MATT   DT   SEAHAWKS

PERSONAL: Born December 1, 1973, in Santa Ana, Calif. ... 6-5/284. ... Full name: Matthew Edward Keneley.
HIGH SCHOOL: Mission Viejo (Calif.).
COLLEGE: Southern California.
TRANSACTIONS/CAREER NOTES: Selected by New York Giants in seventh round (208th pick overall) of 1997 NFL draft. ... Signed by Giants for 1997 season. ... Released by Giants (August 24, 1997). ... Signed by New York Jets (December 23, 1997). ... Released by Jets (June 5, 1998). ... Played for San Jose Sabercats of Arena League (1998). ... Signed by Detroit Lions (August 17, 1998). ... Released by Lions (August 25, 1998). ... Signed by San Francisco 49ers (April 22, 1999). ... Released by 49ers (September 5, 1999). ... Re-signed by 49ers to practice squad (September 7, 1999). ... Activated (November 12, 1999). ... Claimed on waivers by Green Bay Packers (February 11, 2000). ... Released by Packers (April 17, 2000). ... Signed by Seattle Seahawks (April 28, 2000).
PLAYING EXPERIENCE: San Francisco NFL, 1999. ... Games/Games started: 1999 (7/0).

K

KENNEDY, CORTEZ   DT   SEAHAWKS

PERSONAL: Born August 23, 1968, in Osceola, Ark. ... 6-3/306.
HIGH SCHOOL: Rivercrest (Wilson, Ark.).
JUNIOR COLLEGE: Northwest Mississippi Community College.
COLLEGE: Miami, Fla. (degree in criminal justice).
TRANSACTIONS/CAREER NOTES: Selected by Seattle Seahawks in first round (third pick overall) of 1990 NFL draft. ... Signed by Seahawks (September 3, 1990). ... Granted roster exemption (September 3-9, 1990). ... On injured reserve with ankle injury (December 10, 1997-remainder of season).
HONORS: Named defensive tackle on THE SPORTING NEWS college All-America first team (1989). ... Played in Pro Bowl (1991-1996, 1998 and 1999 seasons). ... Named defensive tackle on THE SPORTING NEWS NFL All-Pro team (1992 and 1993).
PRO STATISTICS: 1990—Recovered one fumble. 1991—Recovered one fumble. 1992—Fumbled once and recovered one fumble for 19 yards. 1993—Recovered one fumble. 1994—Recovered one fumble. 1998—Recovered one fumble for 39 yards and a touchdown. 1999—Intercepted two passes for 12 yards.

Year Team	G	GS	SACKS
1990—Seattle NFL	16	2	1.0
1991—Seattle NFL	16	16	6.5
1992—Seattle NFL	16	16	14.0
1993—Seattle NFL	16	16	6.5
1994—Seattle NFL	16	16	4.0
1995—Seattle NFL	16	16	6.5
1996—Seattle NFL	16	16	8.0
1997—Seattle NFL	8	8	2.0
1998—Seattle NFL	15	15	2.0
1999—Seattle NFL	16	16	6.5
Pro totals (10 years)	151	137	57.0

KENNEDY, LINCOLN   OT   RAIDERS

PERSONAL: Born February 12, 1971, in York, Pa. ... 6-6/335. ... Full name: Tamerlane Lincoln Kennedy.
HIGH SCHOOL: Samuel F.B. Morse (San Diego).
COLLEGE: Washington (degree in speech and drama, 1993).
TRANSACTIONS/CAREER NOTES: Selected by Atlanta Falcons in first round (ninth pick overall) of 1993 NFL draft. ... Signed by Falcons (August 2, 1993). ... Granted free agency (February 16, 1996). ... Re-signed by Falcons (May 13, 1996). ... Traded by Falcons to Oakland Raiders for fifth-round pick (traded to Washington) in 1997 draft (May 13, 1996).
PLAYING EXPERIENCE: Atlanta NFL, 1993-1995; Oakland NFL, 1996-1999. ... Games/Games started: 1993 (16/16), 1994 (16/2), 1995 (16/4), 1996 (16/16), 1997 (16/16), 1998 (16/16), 1999 (15/15). Total: 111/85.
HONORS: Named offensive tackle on THE SPORTING NEWS college All-America first team (1992).
PRO STATISTICS: 1993—Recovered one fumble. 1994—Recovered one fumble. 1996—Recovered one fumble. 1998—Recovered one fumble for 27 yards.

KENNISON, EDDIE   WR   BEARS

PERSONAL: Born January 20, 1973, in Lake Charles, La. ... 6-0/195. ... Full name: Eddie Joseph Kennison III.
HIGH SCHOOL: Washington-Marion (Lake Charles, La.).
COLLEGE: Louisiana State.
TRANSACTIONS/CAREER NOTES: Selected after junior season by St. Louis Rams in first round (18th pick overall) of 1996 NFL draft. ... Signed by Rams (July 27, 1996). ... Traded by Rams to New Orleans Saints for second-round pick (DB Dre' Bly) in 1999 draft (February 18, 1999). ... Traded by Saints to Chicago Bears for fifth-round pick (traded to Indianapolis) in 2000 draft (February 21, 2000).
PRO STATISTICS: 1996—Fumbled five times. 1997—Fumbled twice. 1998—Fumbled four times and recovered one fumble. 1999—Fumbled six times and recovered four fumbles.
SINGLE GAME HIGHS (regular season): Receptions—8 (December 8, 1996, vs. Chicago); yards—226 (December 15, 1996, vs. Atlanta); and touchdown receptions—3 (December 15, 1996, vs. Atlanta).
STATISTICAL PLATEAUS: 100-yard receiving games: 1996 (2), 1999 (1). Total: 3.

			RUSHING			RECEIVING			PUNT RETURNS			KICKOFF RETURNS			TOTALS		
Year Team	G	GS	Att.	Yds.	Avg.	TD	No.	Yds.	Avg.	TD	No.	Yds.	Avg.	TD	No.	Yds.	Avg.	TD	TD	2pt.	Pts.
1996—St. Louis NFL	15	14	0	0	0.0	0	54	924	17.1	9	29	423	14.6	2	23	454	19.7	0	11	0	66
1997—St. Louis NFL	14	9	3	13	4.3	0	25	404	16.2	0	34	247	7.3	0	1	14	14.0	0	0	0	0
1998—St. Louis NFL	16	13	2	9	4.5	0	17	234	13.8	1	40	415	10.4	1	0	0	0.0	0	2	0	12
1999—New Orleans NFL	16	16	3	20	6.7	0	61	835	13.7	4	35	258	7.4	0	0	0	0.0	0	4	†1	26
Pro totals (4 years)	61	52	8	42	5.3	0	157	2397	15.3	14	138	1343	9.7	3	24	468	19.5	0	17	1	104

KENT, JOEY   WR   TITANS

PERSONAL: Born April 23, 1974, in Huntsville, Ala. ... 6-1/191. ... Full name: Joseph Edward Kent III.
HIGH SCHOOL: J.O. Johnson (Huntsville, Ala.).
COLLEGE: Tennessee (degree in marketing).
TRANSACTIONS/CAREER NOTES: Selected by Houston Oilers in second round (46th pick overall) of 1997 NFL draft. ... Oilers franchise moved to Tennessee for 1997 season. ... Signed by Oilers (July 17, 1997). ... Oilers franchise renamed Tennessee Titans for 1999 season (December 26, 1998). ... Granted free agency (February 11, 2000).
CHAMPIONSHIP GAME EXPERIENCE: Member of Titans for AFC championship game (1999 season); inactive. ... Played in Super Bowl XXXIV (1999 season).
HONORS: Named wide receiver on THE SPORTING NEWS college All-America second team (1996).
PRO STATISTICS: 1999—Returned two kickoffs for 24 yards.

SINGLE GAME HIGHS (regular season): Receptions—2 (November 28, 1999, vs. Cleveland); yards—26 (October 11, 1998, vs. Baltimore); and touchdown receptions—1 (December 4, 1997, vs. Cincinnati).

				RECEIVING				TOTALS		
Year Team	G	GS	No.	Yds.	Avg.	TD	TD	2pt.	Pts.	Fum.
1997—Tennessee NFL	12	0	6	55	9.2	1	1	0	6	0
1998—Tennessee NFL	10	0	4	62	15.5	0	0	0	0	0
1999—Tennessee NFL	8	0	3	42	14.0	0	0	0	0	0
Pro totals (3 years)	30	0	13	159	12.2	1	1	0	6	0

KERNEY, PATRICK   DE   FALCONS

PERSONAL: Born December 30, 1976, in Trenton, N.J. ... 6-5/272. ... Full name: Patrick Manning Kerney.
HIGH SCHOOL: Taft Prep (Watertown, Conn.)
COLLEGE: Virginia.
TRANSACTIONS/CAREER NOTES: Selected by Atlanta Falcons in first round (30th pick overall) of 1999 NFL draft. ... Signed by Falcons (June 25, 1999).
HONORS: Named defensive end on THE SPORTING NEWS college All-America second team (1998).

Year Team	G	GS	SACKS
1999—Atlanta NFL	16	2	2.5

KIGHT, DANNY   K   COLTS

K

PERSONAL: Born August 18, 1971, in Atlanta. ... 6-0/214.
HIGH SCHOOL: Druid Hills (Ga.).
COLLEGE: Augusta (Ga.) State.
TRANSACTIONS/CAREER NOTES: Signed as non-drafted free agent by San Diego Chargers (April 23, 1996). ... Released by Chargers (August 14, 1996). ... Signed by Dallas Cowboys (April 15, 1997). ... Released by Cowboys (August 12, 1997). ... Signed by Washington Redskins (February 11, 1998). ... On non-football injury list with leg injury (July 20-September 22, 1998). ... Released by Redskins (September 22, 1998). ... Signed by Tampa Bay Buccaneers (April 7, 1999). ... Claimed on waivers by Cleveland Browns (April 20, 1999). ... Released by Browns (August 25, 1999). ... Signed by Indianapolis Colts (October 13, 1999).
PLAYING EXPERIENCE: Indianapolis NFL, 1999. ... Games/Games started: 1999 (12/0).

KILLENS, TERRY   LB   TITANS

PERSONAL: Born March 24, 1974, in Cincinnati. ... 6-1/235. ... Full name: Terry Deleon Killens.
HIGH SCHOOL: Purcell (Cincinnati).
COLLEGE: Penn State.
TRANSACTIONS/CAREER NOTES: Selected by Houston Oilers in third round (74th pick overall) of 1996 NFL draft. ... Signed by Oilers (July 20, 1996). ... Oilers franchise moved to Tennessee for 1997 season. ... Oilers franchise renamed Tennessee Titans for 1999 season (December 26, 1998). ... Granted free agency (February 12, 1999). ... Re-signed by Titans (June 2, 1999). ... Granted unconditional free agency (February 11, 2000). ... Re-signed by Titans (May 26, 2000).
PLAYING EXPERIENCE: Houston NFL, 1996; Tennessee NFL, 1997-1999. ... Games/Games started: 1996 (14/0), 1997 (16/0), 1998 (16/1), 1999 (16/1). Total: 62/2.
CHAMPIONSHIP GAME EXPERIENCE: Played in AFC championship game (1999 season). ... Played in Super Bowl XXXIV (1999 season).
PRO STATISTICS: 1999—Recovered one fumble.

KINCHEN, BRIAN   TE   PANTHERS

PERSONAL: Born August 6, 1965, in Baton Rouge, La. ... 6-2/240. ... Full name: Brian Douglas Kinchen. ... Brother of Todd Kinchen, wide receiver/kick returner with four NFL teams (1992-98).
HIGH SCHOOL: University (Baton Rouge, La.).
COLLEGE: Louisiana State.
TRANSACTIONS/CAREER NOTES: Selected by Miami Dolphins in 12th round (320th pick overall) of 1988 NFL draft. ... Signed by Dolphins (June 6, 1988). ... On injured reserve with hamstring injury (October 4, 1990-remainder of season). ... Granted unconditional free agency (February 1, 1991). ... Signed by Green Bay Packers (April 1, 1991). ... Released by Packers (August 26, 1991). ... Signed by Cleveland Browns (September 13, 1991). ... Granted unconditional free agency (February 1-April 1, 1992). ... Re-signed by Browns for 1992 season. ... Granted unconditional free agency (February 17, 1994). ... Re-signed by Browns (March 4, 1994). ... Granted unconditional free agency (February 16, 1996). ... Browns franchise moved to Baltimore and renamed Ravens for 1996 season (March 11, 1996). ... Re-signed by Ravens (April 3, 1996). ... Granted unconditional free agency (February 12, 1999). ... Signed by Carolina Panthers (March 8, 1999).
PRO STATISTICS: 1995—Recovered one fumble. 1999—Recovered one fumble.
SINGLE GAME HIGHS (regular season): Receptions—9 (November 24, 1996, vs. Jacksonville); yards—87 (December 15, 1996, vs. Carolina); and touchdown receptions—1 (December 12, 1999, vs. Green Bay).

			RECEIVING				KICKOFF RETURNS				TOTALS			
Year Team	G	GS	No.	Yds.	Avg.	TD	No.	Yds.	Avg.	TD	TD	2pt.	Pts.	Fum.
1988—Miami NFL	16	0	1	3	3.0	0	0	0	0.0	0	0	0	0	0
1989—Miami NFL	16	0	1	12	12.0	0	2	26	13.0	0	0	0	0	2
1990—Miami NFL	4	0	0	0	0.0	0	1	16	16.0	0	0	0	0	0
1991—Cleveland NFL	14	0	0	0	0.0	0	0	0	0.0	0	0	0	0	1
1992—Cleveland NFL	16	0	0	0	0.0	0	0	0	0.0	0	0	0	0	0
1993—Cleveland NFL	16	15	29	347	12.0	2	1	0	0.0	0	2	0	12	1
1994—Cleveland NFL	16	11	24	232	9.7	1	3	38	12.7	0	1	0	6	1
1995—Cleveland NFL	13	12	20	216	10.8	0	0	0	0.0	0	0	0	0	1
1996—Baltimore NFL	16	16	55	581	10.6	1	1	19	19.0	0	1	0	6	1
1997—Baltimore NFL	16	6	11	95	8.6	1	0	0	0.0	0	1	0	6	0

1998—Baltimore NFL	16	5	13	110	8.5	0	2	33	16.5	0	0	0	0	0
1999—Carolina NFL	16	0	5	45	9.0	2	3	29	9.7	0	2	0	12	0
Pro totals (12 years)	175	65	159	1641	10.3	7	13	161	12.4	0	7	0	42	7

KING, LAMAR — DE — SEAHAWKS

PERSONAL: Born August 10, 1975, in Boston. ... 6-3/294.
HIGH SCHOOL: Chesapeake (Md.).
JUNIOR COLLEGE: Montgomery College (Md.).
COLLEGE: Saginaw Valley State (Mich.).
TRANSACTIONS/CAREER NOTES: Selected by Seattle Seahawks in first round (22nd pick overall) of 1999 NFL draft. ... Signed by Seahawks (August 12, 1999).

Year Team	G	GS	SACKS
1999—Seattle NFL	14	0	2.0

KING, SHAUN — QB — BUCCANEERS

PERSONAL: Born May 29, 1977, in St. Petersburg, Fla. ... 6-0/225. ... Full name: Shaun Earl King.
HIGH SCHOOL: Gibbs (St. Petersburg, Fla.).
COLLEGE: Tulane.
TRANSACTIONS/CAREER NOTES: Selected by Tampa Bay Buccaneers in second round (50th pick overall) of 1999 NFL draft. ... Signed by Buccaneers (August 1, 1999).
CHAMPIONSHIP GAME EXPERIENCE: Played in NFC championship game (1999 season).
PRO STATISTICS: 1999—Fumbled four times and recovered one fumble.
SINGLE GAME HIGHS (regular season): Attempts—37 (December 12, 1999, vs. Detroit); completions—23 (December 12, 1999, vs. Detroit); passing yards—297 (December 12, 1999, vs. Detroit); and touchdown passes—2 (December 12, 1999, vs. Detroit).
MISCELLANEOUS: Regular-season record as starting NFL quarterback: 4-1 (.800). ... Postseason record as starting NFL quarterback: 1-1 (.500).

			PASSING								RUSHING				TOTALS		
Year Team	G	GS	Att.	Cmp.	Pct.	Yds.	TD	Int.	Avg.	Rat.	Att.	Yds.	Avg.	TD	TD	2pt.	Pts.
1999—Tampa Bay NFL	6	5	146	89	61.0	875	7	4	5.99	82.4	18	38	2.1	0	0	0	0

KING, SHAWN — DE — COLTS

PERSONAL: Born June 24, 1972, in West Monroe, La. ... 6-3/278.
HIGH SCHOOL: West Monroe (La.).
COLLEGE: Louisiana State, then Northeast Louisiana.
TRANSACTIONS/CAREER NOTES: Selected by Carolina Panthers in second round (36th pick overall) of 1995 NFL draft. ... Signed by Panthers (July 15, 1995). ... On reserve/suspended list for violating league substance abuse policy (August 24-October 17, 1997). ... On injured reserve with knee injury (December 15, 1997-remainder of season). ... On injured reserve with arm injury (August 24, 1998-entire season). ... Granted unconditional free agency (February 12, 1999). ... Signed by Indianapolis Colts (February 15, 1999). ... On suspended list for violating league substance abuse policy (December 20, 1999-present).
PRO STATISTICS: 1996—Intercepted one pass for one yard and recovered one fumble for 12 yards and a touchdown.

Year Team	G	GS	SACKS
1995—Carolina NFL	13	0	2.0
1996—Carolina NFL	16	0	3.0
1997—Carolina NFL	9	2	2.0
1998—Carolina NFL		Did not play.	
1999—Indianapolis NFL	9	8	1.5
Pro totals (4 years)	47	10	8.5

KIRBY, TERRY — RB — BROWNS

PERSONAL: Born January 20, 1970, in Hampton, Va. ... 6-1/213. ... Full name: Terry Gayle Kirby. ... Brother of Wayne Kirby, outfielder, Baltimore Orioles organizations; and cousin of Chris Slade, linebacker, New England Patriots.
HIGH SCHOOL: Tabb (Va.).
COLLEGE: Virginia (degree in psychology).
TRANSACTIONS/CAREER NOTES: Selected by Miami Dolphins in third round (78th pick overall) of 1993 NFL draft. ... Signed by Dolphins (July 19, 1993). ... On injured reserve with knee injury (September 26, 1994-remainder of season). ... Granted free agency (February 16, 1996). ... Traded by Dolphins to San Francisco 49ers for fourth-round pick (traded to Oakland) in 1997 draft (August 19, 1996). ... Released by 49ers (March 3, 1998). ... Re-signed by 49ers (September 23, 1998). ... Granted unconditional free agency (February 12, 1999). ... Signed by Cleveland Browns (March 9, 1999).
CHAMPIONSHIP GAME EXPERIENCE: Played in NFC championship game (1997 season).
PRO STATISTICS: 1993—Recovered four fumbles. 1995—Completed only pass attempt for 31 yards and a touchdown. 1996—Attempted two passes with one completion for 24 yards and a touchdown and returned one punt for three yards. 1997—Recovered two fumbles. 1998—Completed only pass attempt for 28 yards and a touchdown. 1999—Completed only pass attempt for two yards and recovered two fumbles.
SINGLE GAME HIGHS (regular season): Attempts—22 (October 17, 1999, vs. Jacksonville); yards—105 (December 2, 1996, vs. Atlanta); and rushing touchdowns—2 (December 26, 1999, vs. Indianapolis).
STATISTICAL PLATEAUS: 100-yard rushing games: 1994 (1), 1996 (1). Total: 2. ... 100-yard receiving games: 1993 (2).

			RUSHING				RECEIVING				KICKOFF RETURNS				TOTALS			
Year Team	G	GS	Att.	Yds.	Avg.	TD	No.	Yds.	Avg.	TD	No.	Yds.	Avg.	TD	TD	2pt.	Pts.	Fum.
1993—Miami NFL	16	8	119	390	3.3	3	75	874	11.7	3	4	85	21.3	0	6	0	36	5
1994—Miami NFL	4	4	60	233	3.9	2	14	154	11.0	0	0	0	0.0	0	2	1	14	2
1995—Miami NFL	16	4	108	414	3.8	4	66	618	9.4	3	0	0	0.0	0	7	0	42	2

1996—San Francisco NFL	14	10	134	559	4.2	3	52	439	8.4	1	1	22	22.0	0	4	0	24	1
1997—San Francisco NFL	16	3	125	418	3.3	6	23	279	12.1	1	3	124	41.3	1	8	2	52	3
1998—San Francisco NFL	9	0	48	258	5.4	3	16	134	8.4	0	17	340	20.0	0	3	0	18	0
1999—Cleveland NFL	16	10	130	452	3.5	6	58	528	9.1	3	11	230	20.9	0	9	0	54	4
Pro totals (7 years)	91	39	724	2724	3.8	27	304	3026	10.0	11	36	801	22.3	1	39	3	240	17

KIRK, RANDY　　　　　　LB

PERSONAL: Born December 27, 1964, in San Jose, Calif. ... 6-2/242. ... Full name: Randall Scott Kirk.
HIGH SCHOOL: Bellarmine College Prep (San Jose, Calif.).
JUNIOR COLLEGE: De Anza College (Calif.).
COLLEGE: San Diego State.
TRANSACTIONS/CAREER NOTES: Signed as non-drafted free agent by New York Giants (May 10, 1987). ... Released by Giants (August 31, 1987). ... Signed as replacement player by San Diego Chargers (September 24, 1987). ... Granted unconditional free agency (February 1, 1989). ... Signed by Phoenix Cardinals (March 31, 1989). ... On injured reserve with broken ankle (October 16, 1989-remainder of season). ... On injured reserve with foot injury (August 27-September 18, 1990). ... Released by Cardinals (September 18, 1990). ... Signed by Washington Redskins (November 7, 1990). ... Released by Redskins (November 13, 1990). ... Signed by Cleveland Browns (July 27, 1991). ... On injured reserve with back injury (September 13-November 19, 1991). ... Claimed on waivers by Chargers (November 19, 1991). ... Granted unconditional free agency (February 1, 1992). ... Signed by Cincinnati Bengals (March 3, 1992). ... Granted unconditional free agency (February 17, 1994). ... Signed by Cardinals (March 7, 1994). ... Cardinals franchise renamed Arizona Cardinals for 1994 season. ... Granted unconditional free agency (February 16, 1996). ... Signed by San Francisco 49ers (March 26, 1996). ... Released by 49ers (February 10, 1999). ... Re-signed by 49ers (December 15, 1999). ... Granted unconditional free agency (February 11, 2000).
PLAYING EXPERIENCE: San Diego NFL, 1987 and 1988; Phoenix NFL, 1989; Washington NFL, 1990; Cleveland (2)-San Diego (5) NFL, 1991; Cincinnati NFL, 1992 and 1993; Arizona NFL, 1994 and 1995; San Francisco NFL, 1996-1999. ... Games/Games started: 1987 (13/1), 1988 (16/0), 1989 (6/0), 1990 (1/0), 1991 (Cle.-2/0; S.D.-5/0; Total: 7/0), 1992 (15/0), 1993 (16/0), 1994 (16/0), 1995 (16/0), 1996 (16/0), 1997 (16/0), 1998 (16/0), 1999 (3/0). Total: 157/1.
CHAMPIONSHIP GAME EXPERIENCE: Played in NFC championship game (1997 season).
PRO STATISTICS: 1987—Credited with one sack. 1988—Recovered one fumble. 1992—Recovered two fumbles for seven yards. 1998—Fumbled once for minus 18 yards.

KIRKLAND, LEVON　　　　　　LB　　　　　　STEELERS

PERSONAL: Born February 17, 1969, in Lamar, S.C. ... 6-1/270. ... Full name: Lorenzo Levon Kirkland. ... Name pronounced luh-VON.
HIGH SCHOOL: Lamar (S.C.).
COLLEGE: Clemson.
TRANSACTIONS/CAREER NOTES: Selected by Pittsburgh Steelers in second round (38th pick overall) of 1992 NFL draft. ... Signed by Steelers (July 25, 1992).
CHAMPIONSHIP GAME EXPERIENCE: Played in AFC championship game (1994, 1995 and 1997 seasons). ... Played in Super Bowl XXX (1995 season).
HONORS: Named linebacker on THE SPORTING NEWS college All-America first team (1991). ... Played in Pro Bowl (1996 and 1997 seasons). ... Named inside linebacker on THE SPORTING NEWS NFL All-Pro team (1997).
PRO STATISTICS: 1993—Recovered two fumbles for 24 yards and one touchdown. 1995—Recovered two fumbles. 1997—Recovered one fumble. 1999—Recovered two fumbles.

			INTERCEPTIONS				SACKS
Year　Team	G	GS	No.	Yds.	Avg.	TD	No.
1992—Pittsburgh NFL	16	0	0	0	0.0	0	0.0
1993—Pittsburgh NFL	16	13	0	0	0.0	0	1.0
1994—Pittsburgh NFL	16	15	2	0	0.0	0	3.0
1995—Pittsburgh NFL	16	16	0	0	0.0	0	1.0
1996—Pittsburgh NFL	16	16	4	12	3.0	0	4.0
1997—Pittsburgh NFL	16	16	2	14	7.0	0	5.0
1998—Pittsburgh NFL	16	16	1	1	1.0	0	2.5
1999—Pittsburgh NFL	16	16	1	23	23.0	0	2.0
Pro totals (8 years)	128	108	10	50	5.0	0	18.5

KIRSCHKE, TRAVIS　　　　　　DE　　　　　　LIONS

PERSONAL: Born September 6, 1974, in Fullerton, Calif. ... 6-3/287.
HIGH SCHOOL: Esperanza (Anaheim, Calif.).
COLLEGE: UCLA.
TRANSACTIONS/CAREER NOTES: Signed as non-drafted free agent by Detroit Lions (April 24, 1997). ... Inactive for three games (1998). ... On injured reserve with abdominal injury (September 24, 1998-remainder of season). ... Granted free agency (February 11, 2000). ... Re-signed by Lions (April 25, 2000).
PLAYING EXPERIENCE: Detroit NFL, 1997 and 1999. ... Games/Games started: 1997 (3/0), 1999 (15/7). Total: 18/7.
PRO STATISTICS: 1999—Credited with two sacks and recovered one fumble.

KITNA, JON　　　　　　QB　　　　　　SEAHAWKS

PERSONAL: Born September 21, 1972, in Tacoma, Wash. ... 6-2/217.
HIGH SCHOOL: Lincoln (Tacoma, Wash.).
COLLEGE: Central Washington (degree in math education, 1995).
TRANSACTIONS/CAREER NOTES: Signed as non-drafted free agent by Seattle Seahawks (April 25, 1996) ... Released by Seahawks (August 19, 1996) ... Re-signed by Seahawks to practice squad (August 20, 1996). ... Assigned by Seahawks to Barcelona Dragons in 1997 World League enhancement allocation program (April 7, 1997). ... Granted free agency (February 11, 2000). ... Re-signed by Seahawks (March 15, 2000).

K

PRO STATISTICS: 1997—Fumbled once and recovered one fumble for minus two yards. 1998—Fumbled six times and recovered four fumbles for minus 10 yards. 1999—Fumbled 14 times and recovered six fumbles for minus nine yards.

SINGLE GAME HIGHS (regular season): Attempts—45 (January 2, 2000, vs. New York Jets); completions—25 (December 12, 1999, vs. San Diego); yards—298 (November 29, 1998, vs. Tennessee); and touchdown passes—3 (November 7, 1999, vs. Cincinnati).

MISCELLANEOUS: Regular-season record as starting NFL quarterback: 12-9 (.571). ... Postseason record as starting NFL quarterback: 0-1.

					PASSING						RUSHING				TOTALS		
Year Team	G	GS	Att.	Cmp.	Pct.	Yds.	TD	Int.	Avg.	Rat.	Att.	Yds.	Avg.	TD	TD	2pt.	Pts.
1997—Barcelona W.L.	10	...	317	171	53.9	2448	22	15	7.72	82.6	50	334	6.7	3	3	0	18
—Seattle NFL	3	1	45	31	68.9	371	1	2	8.24	82.7	10	9	0.9	1	1	0	6
1998—Seattle NFL	6	5	172	98	57.0	1177	7	8	6.84	72.3	20	67	3.4	1	1	0	6
1999—Seattle NFL	15	15	495	270	54.5	3346	23	16	6.76	77.7	35	56	1.6	0	0	0	0
W.L. totals (1 year)	10	...	317	171	53.9	2448	22	15	7.72	82.6	50	334	6.7	3	3	0	18
NFL totals (3 years)	24	21	712	399	56.0	4894	31	26	6.87	76.7	65	132	2.0	2	2	0	12
Pro totals (4 years)	34	...	1029	570	55.4	7342	53	41	7.14	78.5	115	466	4.1	5	5	0	30

KLEINSASSER, JIM FB VIKINGS

PERSONAL: Born January 31, 1977, in Carrington, N.D. ... 6-3/272.
HIGH SCHOOL: Carrington (N.D.).
COLLEGE: North Dakota.
TRANSACTIONS/CAREER NOTES: Selected by Minnesota Vikings in second round (44th pick overall) of 1999 NFL draft. ... Signed by Vikings (August 1, 1999).
PLAYING EXPERIENCE: Minnesota NFL, 1999. ... Games/Games started: 1999 (13/7).
PRO STATISTICS: 1999—Caught six passes for 13 yards, returned one kickoff for no yards and fumbled twice.

K

KNIGHT, SAMMY S SAINTS

PERSONAL: Born September 10, 1975, in Fontana, Calif. ... 6-0/205.
HIGH SCHOOL: Rubidoux (Riverside, Calif.).
COLLEGE: Southern California.
TRANSACTIONS/CAREER NOTES: Signed as non-drafted free agent by New Orleans Saints (April 25, 1997).
PRO STATISTICS: 1997—Recovered one fumble. 1998—Recovered two fumbles for three yards. 1999—Recovered one fumble.

			INTERCEPTIONS			
Year Team	G	GS	No.	Yds.	Avg.	TD
1997—New Orleans NFL	16	12	5	75	15.0	0
1998—New Orleans NFL	14	13	6	171	28.5	2
1999—New Orleans NFL	16	16	1	0	0.0	0
Pro totals (3 years)	46	41	12	246	20.5	2

KNIGHT, TOM CB CARDINALS

PERSONAL: Born December 29, 1974, in Marlton, N.J. ... 6-0/197. ... Full name: Thomas Lorenzo Knight.
HIGH SCHOOL: Cherokee (Marlton, N.J.).
COLLEGE: Iowa.
TRANSACTIONS/CAREER NOTES: Selected by Arizona Cardinals in first round (ninth pick overall) of 1997 NFL draft. ... Signed by Cardinals (July 16, 1997).
PLAYING EXPERIENCE: Arizona NFL, 1997-1999. ... Games/Games Started: 1997 (15/14), 1998 (8/5), 1999 (16/11). Total: 39/30.
PRO STATISTICS: 1998—Credited with one sack. 1999—Intercepted two passes for 16 yards and returned three punts for 38 yards.

KONRAD, ROB FB DOLPHINS

PERSONAL: Born November 12, 1976, in Rochester, N.Y. ... 6-3/255. ... Full name: Robert L. Konrad.
HIGH SCHOOL: St. John's (Andover, Mass.).
COLLEGE: Syracuse.
TRANSACTIONS/CAREER NOTES: Selected by Miami Dolphins in second round (43rd pick overall) of 1999 NFL draft. ... Signed by Dolphins (July 27, 1999).
PRO STATISTICS: 1999—Recovered one fumble.
SINGLE GAME HIGHS (regular season): Attempts—3 (September 19, 1999, vs. Arizona); yards—7 (September 13, 1999, vs. Denver); and rushing touchdowns—0.

			RUSHING				RECEIVING				TOTALS			
Year Team	G	GS	Att.	Yds.	Avg.	TD	No.	Yds.	Avg.	TD	TD	2pt.	Pts.	Fum.
1999—Miami NFL	15	9	9	16	1.8	0	34	251	7.4	1	1	0	6	3

KOONCE, GEORGE LB

PERSONAL: Born October 15, 1968, in New Bern, N.C. ... 6-1/245. ... Full name: George Earl Koonce Jr.
HIGH SCHOOL: West Craven (Vanceboro, N.C.).
COLLEGE: Chowan College (N.C.), then East Carolina.
TRANSACTIONS/CAREER NOTES: Signed as non-drafted free agent by Atlanta Falcons (April 30, 1991). ... Released by Falcons (August 26, 1991). ... Selected by Ohio Glory in 13th round (143rd pick overall) of 1992 World League draft. ... Signed by Green Bay Packers (June 2, 1992). ... On injured reserve with shoulder injury (January 3, 1994-entire 1993 playoffs). ... Granted free agency (February 17, 1995). ... Re-signed by Packers (June 2, 1995). ... On injured reserve with knee injury (January 10, 1997-remainder of 1996 playoffs). ...

On physically unable to perform list with knee injury (August 19-November 18, 1997). ... Granted unconditional free agency (February 12, 1999). ... Re-signed by Packers (February 18, 1999). ... Released by Packers (June 5, 2000).
CHAMPIONSHIP GAME EXPERIENCE: Played in NFC championship game (1995 and 1997 seasons). ... Member of Packers for NFC championship game (1996); inactive. ... Member of Super Bowl championship team (1996 season); inactive. ... Played in Super Bowl XXXII (1997 season).
PRO STATISTICS: W.L.: 1992—Recovered two fumbles for 35 yards. NFL: 1992—Recovered one fumble. 1993—Recovered one fumble. 1994—Recovered two fumbles. 1996—Recovered one fumble. 1998—Recovered one fumble for four yards.

				INTERCEPTIONS			SACKS
Year Team	G	GS	No.	Yds.	Avg.	TD	No.
1992—Ohio W.L.	10	9	0	0	0.0	0	2.5
—Green Bay NFL	16	10	0	0	0.0	0	1.5
1993—Green Bay NFL	15	15	0	0	0.0	0	3.0
1994—Green Bay NFL	16	16	0	0	0.0	0	1.0
1995—Green Bay NFL	16	16	1	12	12.0	0	1.0
1996—Green Bay NFL	16	16	3	84	28.0	1	0.0
1997—Green Bay NFL	4	0	0	0	0.0	0	0.0
1998—Green Bay NFL	14	14	0	0	0.0	0	1.0
1999—Green Bay NFL	15	15	0	0	0.0	0	0.0
W.L. totals (1 year)	10	9	0	0	0.0	0	2.5
NFL totals (8 years)	112	102	4	96	24.0	1	7.5
Pro totals (9 years)	122	111	4	96	24.0	1	10.0

KOPP, JEFF　　　　　LB　　　　　SEAHAWKS

K

PERSONAL: Born July 8, 1971, in Danville, Calif. ... 6-4/244. ... Full name: Jeffery Blair Kopp.
HIGH SCHOOL: San Ramon (Danville, Calif.).
COLLEGE: Southern California (degree in communications, 1994).
TRANSACTIONS/CAREER NOTES: Selected by Miami Dolphins in sixth round (194th pick overall) of 1995 NFL draft. ... Signed by Dolphins for 1995 season. ... Released by Dolphins (August 25, 1996). ... Signed by Jacksonville Jaguars (September 24, 1996). ... Released by Jaguars (October 21, 1998). ... Signed by Baltimore Ravens (October 28, 1998). ... Granted unconditional free agency (February 12, 1999). ... Re-signed by Ravens (April 22, 1999). ... Released by Ravens (September 4, 1999). ... Re-signed by Ravens (September 26, 1999). ... Inactive for two games with Ravens (1999). ... Released by Ravens (October 6, 1999). ... Signed by New England Patriots (October 27, 1999). ... Granted unconditional free agency (February 11, 2000). ... Signed by Seattle Seahawks (April 28, 2000)
PLAYING EXPERIENCE: Miami NFL, 1995; Jacksonville NFL, 1996 and 1997; Jacksonville (6)-Baltimore (7) NFL, 1998; New England NFL, 1999. ... Games/Games started: 1995 (16/0), 1996 (12/0), 1997 (16/3), 1998 (Jax.-6/0; Bal.-7/0; Total: 13/0), 1999 (6/0). Total: 63/3.
CHAMPIONSHIP GAME EXPERIENCE: Played in AFC championship game (1996 season).
PRO STATISTICS: 1997—Intercepted one pass for nine yards and credited with one sack.

KOWALKOWSKI, SCOTT　　　　　LB　　　　　LIONS

PERSONAL: Born August 23, 1968, in Farmington Hills, Mich. ... 6-2/220. ... Full name: Scott Thomas Kowalkowski. ... Son of Bob Kowalkowski, guard with Detroit Lions (1966-76) and Green Bay Packers (1977).
HIGH SCHOOL: St. Mary's Prep (Orchard Lake, Mich.).
COLLEGE: Notre Dame (degree in American studies).
TRANSACTIONS/CAREER NOTES: Selected by Philadelphia Eagles in eighth round (217th pick overall) of 1991 NFL draft. ... Signed by Eagles (July 10, 1991). ... On injured reserve with ankle injury (August 30-November 23, 1993). ... Released by Eagles (November 23, 1993). ... Signed by Detroit Lions (February 4, 1994). ... Granted unconditional free agency (February 17, 1995). ... Re-signed by Lions (March 24, 1995). ... Granted unconditional free agency (February 16, 1996). ... Re-signed by Lions (February 29,1996). ... Granted unconditional free agency (February 14, 1997). ... Re-signed by Lions (March 18, 1997). ... Granted unconditional free agency (February 11, 2000). ... Re-signed by Lions (April 26, 2000).
PLAYING EXPERIENCE: Philadelphia NFL, 1991 and 1992; Detroit NFL, 1994-1999. ... Games/Games started: 1991 (16/0), 1992 (16/0), 1994 (16/0), 1995 (16/0), 1996 (16/1), 1997 (16/0), 1998 (15/0), 1999 (16/3). Total: 127/4.
PRO STATISTICS: 1991—Recovered one fumble. 1996—Recovered one fumble. 1998—Recovered one fumble. 1999—Intercepted one pass for 29 yards and credited with one sack.

KOZLOWSKI, BRIAN　　　　　TE　　　　　FALCONS

PERSONAL: Born October 4, 1970, in Rochester, N.Y. ... 6-3/250. ... Full name: Brian Scott Kozlowski.
HIGH SCHOOL: Webster (N.Y.).
COLLEGE: Connecticut.
TRANSACTIONS/CAREER NOTES: Signed as non-drafted free agent by New York Giants (May 1, 1993). ... Released by Giants (August 16, 1993). ... Re-signed by Giants to practice squad (December 8, 1993). ... Granted unconditional free agency (February 14, 1997). ... Signed by Atlanta Falcons (March 21, 1997). ... Granted unconditional free agency (February 13, 1998). ... Re-signed by Falcons (March 4, 1998).
CHAMPIONSHIP GAME EXPERIENCE: Played in NFC championship game (1998 season). ... Played in Super Bowl XXXIII (1998 season).
PRO STATISTICS: 1995—Recovered one fumble.
SINGLE GAME HIGHS (regular season): Receptions—3 (November 28, 1999, vs. Carolina); yards—49 (November 7, 1999, vs. Jacksonville); and touchdown receptions—1 (November 28, 1999, vs. Carolina).

			RECEIVING				KICKOFF RETURNS				TOTALS			
Year Team	G	GS	No.	Yds.	Avg.	TD	No.	Yds.	Avg.	TD	TD	2pt.	Pts.	Fum.
1993—New York Giants NFL							Did not play.							
1994—New York Giants NFL	16	2	1	5	5.0	0	2	21	10.5	0	0	0	0	0
1995—New York Giants NFL	16	0	2	17	8.5	0	5	75	15.0	0	0	0	0	1
1996—New York Giants NFL	5	0	1	4	4.0	1	1	16	16.0	0	1	0	6	0
1997—Atlanta NFL	16	5	7	99	14.1	1	2	49	24.5	0	1	0	6	0
1998—Atlanta NFL	16	4	10	103	10.3	1	1	12	12.0	0	1	0	6	0

| 1999—Atlanta NFL | 16 | 3 | 11 | 122 | 11.1 | 2 | 2 | 19 | 9.5 | 0 | 2 | 0 | 12 | 1 |
| Pro totals (6 years) | 85 | 14 | 32 | 350 | 10.9 | 5 | 13 | 192 | 14.8 | 0 | 5 | 0 | 30 | 2 |

KRAMER, ERIK — QB

PERSONAL: Born November 6, 1964, in Encino, Calif. ... 6-1/204. ... Full name: William Erik Kramer.
HIGH SCHOOL: Burroughs (Ridgecrest, Calif.).
JUNIOR COLLEGE: Los Angeles Pierce Junior College.
COLLEGE: North Carolina State.
TRANSACTIONS/CAREER NOTES: Signed as non-drafted free agent by New Orleans Saints (May 6, 1987). ... Released by Saints (August 31, 1987). ... Signed as replacement player by Atlanta Falcons (September 24, 1987). ... Released by Falcons (September 1, 1988). ... Signed by Calgary Stampeders of CFL (September 28, 1988). ... Released by Stampeders (July 4, 1989). ... Signed by Detroit Lions (March 21, 1990). ... On injured reserve with shoulder injury (September 4-December 28, 1990). ... Released by Lions (December 28, 1990). ... Re-signed by Lions (March 6, 1991). ... Granted free agency (March 1, 1993). ... Tendered offer sheet by Dallas Cowboys (April 1993). ... Offer matched by Lions (April 23, 1993). ... Granted unconditional free agency (February 17, 1994). ... Signed by Chicago Bears (February 21, 1994). ... On injured reserve with neck injury (October 14, 1996-remainder of season). ... Granted unconditional free agency (February 14, 1997). ... Re-signed by Bears (March 11, 1997). ... Granted unconditional free agency (February 13, 1998). ... Re-signed by Bears (February 20, 1998). ... On injured reserve with shoulder and knee injuries (December 2, 1998-remainder of season). ... Released by Bears (July 20, 1999). ... Signed by San Diego Chargers (July 22, 1999). ... On injured reserve with neck injury (November 23, 1999-remainder of season). ... Released by Chargers (February 10, 2000).
CHAMPIONSHIP GAME EXPERIENCE: Played in NFC championship game (1991 season).
PRO STATISTICS: CFL: 1988—Fumbled seven times. NFL: 1991—Fumbled eight times and recovered four fumbles for minus five yards. 1992—Fumbled four times and recovered one fumble for minus one yard. 1993—Fumbled once. 1994—Fumbled three times and recovered two fumbles for minus five yards. 1995—Fumbled six times and recovered two fumbles for minus 13 yards. 1996—Fumbled once and recovered one fumble for minus one yard. 1997—Fumbled 11 times and recovered three fumbles for minus 14 yards. 1998—Fumbled three times. 1999—Fumbled three times and recovered one fumble for minus seven yards.
SINGLE GAME HIGHS (regular season): Attempts—60 (November 16, 1997, vs. New York Jets); completions—32 (November 16, 1997, vs. New York Jets); yards—372 (September 27, 1998, vs. Minnesota); and touchdown passes—4 (September 27, 1998, vs. Minnesofa).
STATISTICAL PLATEAUS: 300-yard passing games: 1987 (1), 1992 (1), 1994 (1), 1995 (3), 1997 (2), 1998 (1). Total: 9.
MISCELLANEOUS: Regular-season record as starting NFL quarterback: 31-36 (.463). ... Postseason record as starting NFL quarterback: 1-2 (.333).

			PASSING								RUSHING				TOTALS		
Year Team	G	GS	Att.	Cmp.	Pct.	Yds.	TD	Int.	Avg.	Rat.	Att.	Yds.	Avg.	TD	TD	2pt.	Pts.
1987—Atlanta NFL	3	2	92	45	48.9	559	4	5	6.08	60.0	2	10	5.0	0	0	0	0
1988—Calgary CFL	6	0	153	62	40.5	964	5	13	6.30	37.6	12	17	1.4	1	1	0	6
1989—								Did not play.									
1990—Detroit NFL								Did not play.									
1991—Detroit NFL	13	8	265	136	51.3	1635	11	8	6.17	71.8	35	26	0.7	1	1	0	6
1992—Detroit NFL	7	3	106	58	54.7	771	4	8	7.27	59.1	12	34	2.8	0	0	0	0
1993—Detroit NFL	5	4	138	87	63.0	1002	8	3	7.26	95.1	10	5	0.5	0	0	0	0
1994—Chicago NFL	6	5	158	99	62.7	1129	8	8	7.15	79.9	6	-2	-0.3	0	0	0	0
1995—Chicago NFL	16	16	522	315	60.3	3838	29	10	7.35	93.5	35	39	1.1	1	1	0	6
1996—Chicago NFL	4	4	150	73	48.7	781	3	6	5.21	54.3	8	4	0.5	0	0	0	0
1997—Chicago NFL	15	13	477	275	57.7	3011	14	14	6.31	74.0	27	83	3.1	2	2	0	12
1998—Chicago NFL	8	8	250	151	60.4	1823	9	7	7.29	83.1	13	17	1.3	1	1	0	6
1999—San Diego NFL	6	4	141	78	55.3	788	2	10	5.59	46.6	5	1	0.2	0	0	0	0
CFL totals (1 year)	6	0	153	62	40.5	964	5	13	6.30	37.6	12	17	1.4	1	1	0	6
NFL totals (10 years)	83	67	2299	1317	57.3	15337	92	79	6.67	76.6	153	217	1.4	5	5	0	30
Pro totals (11 years)	89	67	2452	1379	56.2	16301	97	92	6.65	74.2	165	234	1.4	6	6	0	36

KREUTZ, OLIN — C — BEARS

PERSONAL: Born June 9, 1977, in Honolulu. ... 6-2/295.
HIGH SCHOOL: St. Louis (Honolulu).
COLLEGE: Washington.
TRANSACTIONS/CAREER NOTES: Selected after junior season by Chicago Bears in third round (64th pick overall) of 1998 NFL draft. ... Signed by Bears (July 20, 1998).
PLAYING EXPERIENCE: Chicago NFL, 1998 and 1999. ... Games/Games started: 1998 (9/0), 1999 (16/16). Total: 25/16.
HONORS: Named center on THE SPORTING NEWS college All-America first team (1997).
PRO STATISTICS: 1999—Fumbled once and recovered two fumbles for minus 17 yards.

KRIEWALDT, CLINT — LB — LIONS

PERSONAL: Born March 16, 1976, in Shiocton, Wis. ... 6-1/236.
HIGH SCHOOL: Shiocton (Wis.).
COLLEGE: Wisconsin-Stevens Point.
TRANSACTIONS/CAREER NOTES: Selected by Detroit Lions in sixth round (177th pick overall) of 1999 NFL draft. ... Signed by Lions (July 22, 1999).
PLAYING EXPERIENCE: Detroit NFL, 1999. ... Games/Games started: 1999 (12/0).
PRO STATISTICS: 1999—Intercepted one pass for two yards.

KUBERSKI, BOB — DT — BRONCOS

PERSONAL: Born April 5, 1971, in Chester, Pa. ... 6-4/300. ... Full name: Robert Kenneth Kuberski Jr. ... Name pronounced KA-bear-ski.
HIGH SCHOOL: Ridley (Folsom, Pa.).

K

COLLEGE: Navy (degree in political science).
TRANSACTIONS/CAREER NOTES: Selected by Green Bay Packers in seventh round (183rd pick overall) of 1993 NFL draft. ... Signed by Packers (June 7, 1993). ... On reserve/military list (August 23, 1993-April 19, 1995). ... Granted unconditional free agency (February 12, 1999). ... Signed by Atlanta Falcons (March 2, 1999). ... Released by Falcons (August 30, 1999). ... Signed by New England Patriots (September 5, 1999). ... Granted unconditional free agency (February 11, 2000). ... Signed by Denver Broncos (April 17, 2000).
PLAYING EXPERIENCE: Green Bay NFL, 1995-1998; New England NFL, 1999. ... Games/Games started: 1995 (9/0), 1996 (1/0), 1997 (11/3), 1998 (16/0), 1999 (5/0). Total: 42/3.
CHAMPIONSHIP GAME EXPERIENCE: Played in NFC championship game (1995 and 1997 seasons). ... Member of Packers for NFC championship game (1996 season); inactive. ... Member of Super Bowl championship team (1996 season); inactive. ... Played in Super Bowl XXXII (1997 season).
PRO STATISTICS: 1995—Credited with two sacks.

KUEHL, RYAN — DT — BROWNS

PERSONAL: Born January 18, 1972, in Washington, D.C. ... 6-5/290. ... Full name: Ryan Philip Kuehl.
HIGH SCHOOL: Walt Whitman (Bethesda, Md.).
COLLEGE: Virginia (degree in marketing, 1994).
TRANSACTIONS/CAREER NOTES: Signed as non-drafted free agent by San Francisco 49ers (April 26, 1995). ... Released by 49ers (August 19, 1995). ... Signed by Washington Redskins to practice squad (August 26, 1995). ... Signed by Washington Redskins (February 16, 1996). ... Released by Redskins (August 25, 1996). ... Re-signed by Redskins to practice squad (August 26, 1996). ... Activated (October 19, 1996). ... Released by Redskins (November 6, 1996). ... Re-signed by Redskins to practice squad (November 7, 1996). ... Activated (November 11, 1996). ... Released by Redskins (August 23, 1997). ... Re-signed by Redskins (September 9, 1997). ... Released by Redskins (August 30, 1998). ... Signed by Cleveland Browns (February 11, 1999).
PLAYING EXPERIENCE: Washington NFL, 1996 and 1997; Cleveland NFL, 1999. ... Games/Games started: 1996 (2/0), 1997 (12/5), 1999 (16/0). Total: 30/5.

K
L

LaBOUNTY, MATT — DE — SEAHAWKS

PERSONAL: Born January 3, 1969, in San Francisco. ... 6-4/275. ... Full name: Matthew James LaBounty.
HIGH SCHOOL: San Marin (Novato, Calif.).
COLLEGE: Oregon.
TRANSACTIONS/CAREER NOTES: Selected by San Francisco 49ers in 12th round (327th pick overall) of 1992 NFL draft. ... Signed by 49ers (July 13, 1992). ... Released by 49ers (August 31, 1992). ... Re-signed by 49ers to practice squad (September 1, 1992). ... Released by 49ers (October 17, 1993). ... Re-signed by 49ers to practice squad (October 20, 1993). ... Activated (December 2, 1993). ... Claimed on waivers by Green Bay Packers (December 8, 1993). ... On injured reserve with back injury (August 23, 1994-entire season). ... Traded by Packers to Seattle Seahawks for S Eugene Robinson (June 27, 1996). ... Granted unconditional free agency (February 13, 1998). ... Re-signed by Seahawks (February 11, 1998).
CHAMPIONSHIP GAME EXPERIENCE: Played in NFC championship game (1995 season).
PRO STATISTICS: 1998—Fumbled once and recovered one fumble for 13 yards.

Year Team	G	GS	SACKS
1992—San Francisco NFL	Did not play.		
1993—San Francisco NFL	6	0	0.0
1994—Green Bay NFL	Did not play.		
1995—Green Bay NFL	14	2	3.0
1996—Seattle NFL	3	0	0.0
1997—Seattle NFL	15	6	3.0
1998—Seattle NFL	16	1	6.0
1999—Seattle NFL	16	1	2.0
Pro totals (6 years)	70	10	14.0

LACINA, CORBIN — G — VIKINGS

PERSONAL: Born November 2, 1970, in Mankato, Minn. ... 6-4/302.
HIGH SCHOOL: Cretin-Derham Hall (St. Paul, Minn.).
COLLEGE: Augustana (S.D.).
TRANSACTIONS/CAREER NOTES: Selected by Buffalo Bills in sixth round (167th pick overall) of 1993 NFL draft. ... Signed by Bills (July 12, 1993). ... Released by Bills (August 30, 1993). ... Re-signed by Bills to practice squad (September 1, 1993). ... Activated (December 30, 1993); did not play. ... On injured reserve with foot injury (December 22, 1994-remainder of season). ... On injured reserve with groin injury (November 30, 1996-remainder of season). ... Granted free agency (February 14, 1997). ... Re-signed by Bills (June 12, 1997). ... Granted unconditional free agency (February 13, 1998). ... Signed by Carolina Panthers (February 26, 1998). ... Released by Panthers (June 16, 1999). ... Signed by Minnesota Vikings (June 18, 1999).
PLAYING EXPERIENCE: Buffalo NFL, 1994-1997; Carolina NFL, 1998; Minnesota NFL, 1999. ... Games/Games started: 1994 (11/10), 1995 (16/3), 1996 (12/2), 1997 (16/13), 1998 (10/10), 1999 (14/0). Total: 79/38.
CHAMPIONSHIP GAME EXPERIENCE: Member of Bills for AFC championship game (1993 season); inactive. ... Member of Bills for Super Bowl XXVIII (1993 season); inactive.
PRO STATISTICS: 1997—Recovered one fumble. 1998—Recovered one fumble.

LaFLEUR, DAVID — TE — COWBOYS

PERSONAL: Born January 29, 1974, in Lake Charles, La. ... 6-7/272. ... Full name: David Alan LaFleur.
HIGH SCHOOL: Westlake (La.).
COLLEGE: Louisiana State.
TRANSACTIONS/CAREER NOTES: Selected by Dallas Cowboys in first round (22nd pick overall) of 1997 NFL draft. ... Signed by Cowboys (July 17, 1997).
PRO STATISTICS: 1998—Returned one kickoff for 12 yards. 1999—Recovered one fumble.

SINGLE GAME HIGHS (regular season): Receptions—4 (December 24, 1999, vs. New Orleans); yards—44 (December 12, 1999, vs. Philadelphia); and touchdown receptions—2 (September 12, 1999, vs. Washington).

Year Team	G	GS	RECEIVING				TOTALS			
			No.	Yds.	Avg.	TD	TD	2pt.	Pts.	Fum.
1997—Dallas NFL	16	5	18	122	6.8	2	2	0	12	1
1998—Dallas NFL	13	13	20	176	8.8	2	2	0	12	1
1999—Dallas NFL	16	16	35	322	9.2	7	7	0	42	0
Pro totals (3 years)	45	34	73	620	8.5	11	11	0	66	2

LAKE, CARNELL — S — JAGUARS

PERSONAL: Born July 15, 1967, in Salt Lake City. ... 6-1/207. ... Full name: Carnell Augustino Lake.
HIGH SCHOOL: Culver City (Calif.).
COLLEGE: UCLA (degree in political science, 1993).
TRANSACTIONS/CAREER NOTES: Selected by Pittsburgh Steelers in second round (34th pick overall) of 1989 NFL draft. ... Signed by Steelers (July 23, 1989). ... Granted free agency (February 1, 1992). ... Re-signed by Steelers (August 21, 1992). ... Granted roster exemption (August 21-28, 1992). ... Designated by Steelers as franchise player (February 15, 1995). ... Granted unconditional free agency (February 12, 1999). ... Signed by Jacksonville Jaguars (February 13, 1999).
CHAMPIONSHIP GAME EXPERIENCE: Played in AFC championship game (1994, 1995, 1997 and 1999 seasons). ... Played in Super Bowl XXX (1995 season).
HONORS: Named linebacker on THE SPORTING NEWS college All-America second team (1987). ... Played in Pro Bowl (1994-1997 and 1999 seasons). ... Named strong safety on THE SPORTING NEWS NFL All-Pro team (1997).
POST SEASON RECORDS: Shares NFL postseason single-game record for most safeties—1 (January 7, 1995, vs. Cleveland).
PRO STATISTICS: 1989—Recovered six fumbles for two yards. 1990—Recovered one fumble. 1992—Recovered one fumble for 12 yards. 1993—Recovered two fumbles. 1994—Recovered one fumble. 1995—Recovered one fumble. 1996—Recovered two fumbles for 85 yards and one touchdown. 1997—Recovered one fumble for 38 yards and a touchdown. 1998—Recovered one fumble for minus two yards.

Year Team	G	GS	INTERCEPTIONS				SACKS
			No.	Yds.	Avg.	TD	No.
1989—Pittsburgh NFL	15	15	1	0	0.0	0	1.0
1990—Pittsburgh NFL	16	16	1	0	0.0	0	1.0
1991—Pittsburgh NFL	16	16	0	0	0.0	0	1.0
1992—Pittsburgh NFL	16	16	0	0	0.0	0	2.0
1993—Pittsburgh NFL	14	14	4	31	7.8	0	5.0
1994—Pittsburgh NFL	16	16	1	2	2.0	0	1.0
1995—Pittsburgh NFL	16	16	1	32	32.0	▲1	1.5
1996—Pittsburgh NFL	13	13	1	47	47.0	1	2.0
1997—Pittsburgh NFL	16	16	3	16	5.3	0	6.0
1998—Pittsburgh NFL	16	16	4	33	8.3	1	1.0
1999—Jacksonville NFL	16	16	0	0	0.0	0	3.5
Pro totals (11 years)	170	170	16	161	10.1	3	25.0

LANDETA, SEAN — P — EAGLES

PERSONAL: Born January 6, 1962, in Baltimore. ... 6-0/215. ... Full name: Sean Edward Landeta.
HIGH SCHOOL: Loch Raven (Baltimore).
COLLEGE: Towson State.
TRANSACTIONS/CAREER NOTES: Selected by Philadelphia Stars in 14th round (161st pick overall) of 1983 USFL draft. ... Signed by Stars (January 24, 1983). ... Stars franchise moved to Baltimore (November 1, 1984). ... Granted free agency (August 1, 1985). ... Signed by New York Giants (August 5, 1985). ... On injured reserve with back injury (September 7, 1988-remainder of season). ... Granted free agency (February 1, 1990). ... Re-signed by Giants (July 23, 1990). ... On injured reserve with knee injury (November 25, 1992-remainder of season). ... Granted unconditional free agency (March 1, 1993). ... Re-signed by Giants (March 18, 1993). ... Released by Giants (November 9, 1993). ... Signed by Los Angeles Rams (November 12, 1993). ... Granted unconditional free agency (February 17, 1994). ... Re-signed by Rams (May 10, 1994). ... Granted unconditional free agency (February 17, 1995). ... Rams franchise moved to St. Louis (April 12, 1995). ... Re-signed by Rams (May 8, 1995). ... Released by Rams (March 18, 1997). ... Signed by Tampa Bay Buccaneers (October 9, 1997). ... Granted unconditional free agency (February 13, 1998). ... Signed by Green Packers (February 26, 1998). ... Granted unconditional free agency (February 12, 1999). ... Signed by Philadelphia Eagles (February 26, 1999).
CHAMPIONSHIP GAME EXPERIENCE: Played in USFL championship game (1983-1985 seasons). ... Played in NFC championship game (1986 and 1990 seasons). ... Member of Super Bowl championship team (1986 and 1990 seasons).
HONORS: Named punter on THE SPORTING NEWS USFL All-Star team (1983 and 1984). ... Named punter on THE SPORTING NEWS NFL All-Pro team (1986, 1989 and 1990). ... Played in Pro Bowl (1986 and 1990 seasons).
PRO STATISTICS: USFL: 1983—Rushed once for minus five yards, fumbled once and recovered one fumble. 1984—Recovered one fumble. NFL: 1985—Attempted one pass without a completion. 1996—Rushed twice for no yards, fumbled once and recovered one fumble for minus 11 yards. 1999—Fumbled once and recovered one fumble.

Year Team	G	PUNTING					
		No.	Yds.	Avg.	Net avg.	In. 20	Blk.
1983—Philadelphia USFL	18	86	3601	41.9	36.5	31	0
1984—Philadelphia USFL	18	53	2171	41.0	*38.1	18	0
1985—Baltimore USFL	18	65	2718	41.8	33.2	18	0
—New York Giants NFL	16	81	3472	42.9	36.3	20	0
1986—New York Giants NFL	16	79	3539	‡44.8	‡37.1	24	0
1987—New York Giants NFL	12	65	2773	42.7	31.0	13	1
1988—New York Giants NFL	1	6	222	37.0	35.7	1	0
1989—New York Giants NFL	16	70	3019	43.1	*37.7	19	0
1990—New York Giants NFL	16	75	3306	‡44.1	37.2	†24	0
1991—New York Giants NFL	15	64	2768	43.3	35.2	16	0
1992—New York Giants NFL	11	53	2317	43.7	31.5	13	*2
1993—New York Giants NFL	8	33	1390	42.1	35.0	11	1
—Los Angeles Rams NFL	8	42	1825	43.5	32.8	7	0

1994—Los Angeles Rams NFL	16	78	3494	*44.8	34.2	23	0
1995—St. Louis NFL	16	83	3679	‡44.3	36.7	23	0
1996—St. Louis NFL	16	78	3491	44.8	36.1	23	0
1997—Tampa Bay NFL	10	54	2274	42.1	34.1	15	1
1998—Green Bay NFL	16	65	2788	42.9	37.1	30	0
1999—Philadelphia NFL	16	*107	‡4524	42.3	35.1	21	1
USFL totals (3 years)	54	204	8490	41.6	35.9	67	0
NFL totals (15 years)	209	1033	44881	43.4	35.4	283	6
Pro totals (18 years)	263	1237	53371	43.1	35.4	350	6

LANDOLT, KEVIN — DT — JAGUARS

PERSONAL: Born October 25, 1975, in Mount Holly, N.J. ... 6-4/298. ... Full name: Kevin Joseph Landolt.
HIGH SCHOOL: Holy Cross (Florence, N.J.).
COLLEGE: West Virginia.
TRANSACTIONS/CAREER NOTES: Selected by Jacksonville Jaguars in fourth round (121st pick overall) of 1999 NFL draft. ... Signed by Jaguars (May 18, 1999).
PLAYING EXPERIENCE: Jacksonville NFL, 1999. ... Games/Games started: 1999 (1/0).
CHAMPIONSHIP GAME EXPERIENCE: Member of Jaguars for AFC championship game (1999 season); inactive.

LANE, FRED — RB — COLTS

PERSONAL: Born September 6, 1975, in Nashville. ... 5-10/205. ... Full name: Freddie Brown Lane Jr.
HIGH SCHOOL: Franklin (Tenn.).
COLLEGE: Lane College (Tenn.).
TRANSACTIONS/CAREER NOTES: Signed as non-drafted free agent by Carolina Panthers (April 19, 1997). ... Traded by Panthers to Indianapolis Colts for LB Spencer Reid (April 20, 2000).
PRO STATISTICS: 1997—Recovered two fumbles. 1999—Returned three kickoffs for 58 yards.
SINGLE GAME HIGHS (regular season): Attempts—35 (November 1, 1998, vs. New Orleans); yards—147 (November 2, 1997, vs. Oakland); and rushing touchdowns—3 (November 2, 1997, vs. Oakland).
STATISTICAL PLATEAUS: 100-yard rushing games: 1997 (4), 1998 (2). Total: 6.
MISCELLANEOUS: Holds Carolina Panthers all-time record for most rushing touchdowns (13).

			RUSHING				RECEIVING				TOTALS			
Year Team	G	GS	Att.	Yds.	Avg.	TD	No.	Yds.	Avg.	TD	TD	2pt.	Pts.	Fum.
1997—Carolina NFL	13	7	182	809	4.4	7	8	27	3.4	0	7	0	42	4
1998—Carolina NFL	14	11	205	717	3.5	5	12	85	7.1	0	5	0	30	4
1999—Carolina NFL	15	5	115	475	4.1	1	23	163	7.1	0	1	0	6	1
Pro totals (3 years)	42	23	502	2001	4.0	13	43	275	6.4	0	13	0	78	9

LANE, MAX — G/OT — PATRIOTS

PERSONAL: Born February 22, 1971, in Norborne, Mo. ... 6-6/320. ... Full name: Max Aaron Lane.
HIGH SCHOOL: Norborne (Mo.), then Naval Academy Preparatory (Newport, R.I.).
COLLEGE: Navy.
TRANSACTIONS/CAREER NOTES: Selected by New England Patriots in sixth round (168th pick overall) of 1994 NFL draft. ... Signed by Patriots (June 1, 1994). ... Granted free agency (February 14, 1997). ... Re-signed by Patriots (June 20, 1997).
PLAYING EXPERIENCE: New England NFL, 1994-1999. ... Games/Games started: 1994 (14/0), 1995 (16/16), 1996 (16/16), 1997 (16/16), 1998 (16/11), 1999 (16/6). Total: 94/65.
CHAMPIONSHIP GAME EXPERIENCE: Played in AFC championship game (1996 season). ... Played in Super Bowl XXXI (1996 season).
PRO STATISTICS: 1995—Recovered one fumble. 1996—Recovered three fumbles. 1997—Recovered one fumble.

LANG, KENARD — DE — REDSKINS

PERSONAL: Born January 31, 1975, in Orlando. ... 6-4/277. ... Full name: Kenard Dushun Lang.
HIGH SCHOOL: Maynard Evans (Orlando).
COLLEGE: Miami (Fla.).
TRANSACTIONS/CAREER NOTES: Selected by Washington Redskins in first round (17th pick overall) of 1997 NFL draft. ... Signed by Redskins (July 28, 1997).
PRO STATISTICS: 1997—Recovered two fumbles. 1999—Recovered one fumble.

Year Team	G	GS	SACKS
1997—Washington NFL	12	11	1.5
1998—Washington NFL	16	16	7.0
1999—Washington NFL	16	9	6.0
Pro totals (3 years)	44	36	14.5

LANGFORD, JEVON — DE — BENGALS

PERSONAL: Born February 16, 1974, in Washington, D.C. ... 6-3/290.
HIGH SCHOOL: Bishop Carroll (Washington, D.C.).
COLLEGE: Oklahoma State.
TRANSACTIONS/CAREER NOTES: Selected after junior season by Cincinnati Bengals in fourth round (108th pick overall) of 1996 NFL draft. ... Signed by Bengals (August 5, 1996). ... Granted free agency (February 12, 1999). ... Re-signed by Bengals (May 25, 1999). ... Granted unconditional free agency (February 11, 2000). ... Re-signed by Bengals (May 5, 2000).

PRO STATISTICS: 1996—Recovered one fumble.

Year Team	G	GS	SACKS
1996—Cincinnati NFL	12	3	2.0
1997—Cincinnati NFL	15	0	1.0
1998—Cincinnati NFL	14	1	0.5
1999—Cincinnati NFL	12	7	0.0
Pro totals (4 years)	53	11	3.5

LANGHAM, ANTONIO　　　CB　　　PATRIOTS

PERSONAL: Born July 31, 1972, in Town Creek, Ala. ... 6-0/184. ... Full name: Collie Antonio Langham.
HIGH SCHOOL: Hazelwood (Town Creek, Ala.).
COLLEGE: Alabama.
TRANSACTIONS/CAREER NOTES: Selected by Cleveland Browns in first round (ninth pick overall) of 1994 NFL draft. ... Signed by Browns (August 4, 1994). ... Browns franchise moved to Baltimore and renamed Ravens for 1996 season (March 11, 1996). ... Granted unconditional free agency (February 13, 1998). ... Signed by San Francisco 49ers (March 9, 1998). ... Selected by Browns from 49ers in NFL expansion draft (February 9, 1999). ... Released by Browns (February 9, 2000). ... Signed by New England Patriots (April 25, 2000).
HONORS: Jim Thorpe Award winner (1993). ... Named defensive back on THE SPORTING NEWS college All-America first team (1993).
PRO STATISTICS: 1994—Fumbled once. 1997—Credited with one sack.

Year Team	G	GS	INTERCEPTIONS No.	Yds.	Avg.	TD
1994—Cleveland NFL	16	16	2	2	1.0	0
1995—Cleveland NFL	16	16	2	29	14.5	0
1996—Baltimore NFL	15	14	5	59	11.8	0
1997—Baltimore NFL	16	15	3	40	13.3	1
1998—San Francisco NFL	11	6	1	0	0.0	0
1999—Cleveland NFL	13	2	0	0	0.0	0
Pro totals (6 years)	87	69	13	130	10.0	1

LASSITER, KWAMIE　　　S　　　CARDINALS

PERSONAL: Born December 3, 1969, in Hampton, Va. ... 6-0/197.
HIGH SCHOOL: Menchville (Newport News, Va.).
JUNIOR COLLEGE: Butler County Community College (Kan.).
COLLEGE: Kansas.
TRANSACTIONS/CAREER NOTES: Signed as non-drafted free agent by Arizona Cardinals (April 28, 1995). ... On injured reserve with ankle injury (October 5, 1995-remainder of season). ... Granted free agency (February 13, 1998). ... Re-signed by Cardinals (May 21, 1998). ... Granted unconditional free agency (February 12, 1999). ... Re-signed by Cardinals (March 9, 1999).
PRO STATISTICS: 1995—Rushed once for one yard. 1997—Credited with three sacks. 1998—Recovered one fumble. 1999—Returned one kickoff for 13 yards and recovered two fumbles.

Year Team	G	GS	INTERCEPTIONS No.	Yds.	Avg.	TD
1995—Arizona NFL	5	0	0	0	0.0	0
1996—Arizona NFL	14	0	1	20	20.0	0
1997—Arizona NFL	16	1	1	10	10.0	0
1998—Arizona NFL	16	6	‡8	80	10.0	0
1999—Arizona NFL	16	16	2	110	55.0	1
Pro totals (5 years)	67	23	12	220	18.3	1

LAW, TY　　　CB　　　PATRIOTS

PERSONAL: Born February 10, 1974, in Aliquippa, Pa. ... 5-11/200. ... Full name: Tajuan Law.
HIGH SCHOOL: Aliquippa (Pa.).
COLLEGE: Michigan.
TRANSACTIONS/CAREER NOTES: Selected after junior season by New England Patriots in first round (23rd pick overall) of 1995 NFL draft. ... Signed by Patriots (July 20, 1995). ... On injured reserve with hand injury (December 29, 1999-remainder of season).
CHAMPIONSHIP GAME EXPERIENCE: Played in AFC championship game (1996 season). ... Played in Super Bowl XXXI (1996 season).
HONORS: Named cornerback on THE SPORTING NEWS NFL All-Pro team (1998). ... Played in Pro Bowl (1998 season). ... Named co-Oustanding Player of Pro Bowl (1998 season).
PRO STATISTICS: 1995—Credited with one sack. 1997—Credited with $1/2$ sack, fumbled once and recovered one fumble. 1998—Recovered one fumble for 17 yards. 1999—Credited with $1/2$ sack, fumbled once and recovered one fumble.

Year Team	G	GS	INTERCEPTIONS No.	Yds.	Avg.	TD
1995—New England NFL	14	7	3	47	15.7	0
1996—New England NFL	13	12	3	45	15.0	1
1997—New England NFL	16	16	3	70	23.3	0
1998—New England NFL	16	16	*9	133	14.8	1
1999—New England NFL	13	13	2	20	10.0	1
Pro totals (5 years)	72	64	20	315	15.8	3

LAYMAN, JASON　　　G

PERSONAL: Born July 29, 1973, in Sevierville, Tenn. ... 6-5/310. ... Full name: Jason Todd Layman.
HIGH SCHOOL: Sevier County (Sevierville, Tenn.).

COLLEGE: Tennessee.

TRANSACTIONS/CAREER NOTES: Selected by Houston Oilers in second round (48th pick overall) of 1996 NFL draft. ... Signed by Oilers (July 20, 1996). ... Oilers franchise moved to Tennessee for 1997 season. ... Oilers franchise renamed Tennessee Titans for 1999 season (December 26, 1998). ... Granted unconditional free agency (February 11, 2000).
PLAYING EXPERIENCE: Houston NFL, 1996; Tennessee NFL, 1997-1999. ... Games/Games started: 1996 (16/0), 1997 (13/0), 1998 (16/15), 1999 (15/1). Total: 60/16.
CHAMPIONSHIP GAME EXPERIENCE: Played in AFC championship game (1999 season). ... Played in Super Bowl XXXIV (1999 season).
PRO STATISTICS: 1997—Returned one kickoff for five yards. 1998—Recovered one fumble.

LEAF, RYAN   QB   CHARGERS

PERSONAL: Born May 15, 1976, in Great Falls, Mont. ... 6-5/235. ... Full name: Ryan David Leaf.
HIGH SCHOOL: Russell (Great Falls, Mont.).
COLLEGE: Washington State.
TRANSACTIONS/CAREER NOTES: Selected after junior season by San Diego Chargers in first round (second pick overall) of 1998 NFL draft. ... Signed by Chargers (July 28, 1998). ... Inactive for 15 games (1999). ... On injured reserve with shoulder injury (December 30, 1999-remainder of season).
HONORS: Named quarterback on THE SPORTING NEWS college All-America first team (1997).
PRO STATISTICS: 1998—Fumbled eight times and recovered two fumbles for minus 18 yards.
SINGLE GAME HIGHS (regular season): Attempts—52 (October 25, 1998, vs. Seattle); completions—25 (October 25, 1998, vs. Seattle); yards—281 (October 25, 1998, vs. Seattle); and touchdown passes—1 (October 25, 1998, vs. Seattle).
MISCELLANEOUS: Regular-season record as starting NFL quarterback: 3-6 (.333).

Year Team	G	GS	Att.	Cmp.	Pct.	Yds.	TD	Int.	Avg.	Rat.	Att.	Yds.	Avg.	TD	TD	2pt.	Pts.
						PASSING						**RUSHING**				**TOTALS**	
1998—San Diego NFL	10	9	245	111	45.3	1289	2	15	5.26	39.0	27	80	3.0	0	0	0	0
1999—San Diego NFL								Did not play.									
Pro totals (1 years)	10	9	245	111	45.3	1289	2	15	5.26	39.0	27	80	3.0	0	0	0	0

LEE, AMP   RB

PERSONAL: Born October 1, 1971, in Chipley, Fla. ... 5-11/200. ... Full name: Anthonia Wayne Lee.
HIGH SCHOOL: Chipley (Fla.).
COLLEGE: Florida State.
TRANSACTIONS/CAREER NOTES: Selected after junior season by San Francisco 49ers in second round (45th pick overall) of 1992 NFL draft. ... Signed by 49ers (July 18, 1992). ... Released by 49ers (May 4, 1994). ... Signed by Minnesota Vikings (May 24, 1994). ... On physically unable to perform list (July 13-20, 1994). ... Granted unconditional free agency (February 14, 1997). ... Signed by St. Louis Rams (August 4, 1997). ... Granted unconditional free agency (February 13, 1998). ... Re-signed by Rams (February 24, 1998). ... Released by Rams (March 1, 2000).
CHAMPIONSHIP GAME EXPERIENCE: Played in NFC championship game (1992, 1993 and 1999 seasons). ... Member of Super Bowl championship team (1999 season).
PRO STATISTICS: 1992—Fumbled once and recovered three fumbles. 1993—Fumbled once. 1994—Fumbled once and recovered one fumble. 1995—Fumbled three times and recovered two fumbles. 1996—Fumbled twice and recovered one fumble. 1998—Fumbled three times. 1999—Recovered one fumble.
SINGLE GAME HIGHS (regular season): Attempts—23 (December 13, 1992, vs. Minnesota); yards—134 (December 13, 1992, vs. Minnesota); and rushing touchdowns—2 (October 11, 1998, vs. New York Jets).
STATISTICAL PLATEAUS: 100-yard rushing games: 1992 (1). ... 100-yard receiving games: 1997 (3).

Year Team	G	GS	Att.	Yds.	Avg.	TD	No.	Yds.	Avg.	TD	No.	Yds.	Avg.	TD	No.	Yds.	Avg.	TD	TD	2pt.	Pts.
			RUSHING				**RECEIVING**				**PUNT RETURNS**				**KICKOFF RETURNS**				**TOTALS**		
1992—San Fran. NFL	16	3	91	362	4.0	2	20	102	5.1	2	0	0	0.0	0	14	276	19.7	0	4	0	24
1993—San Fran. NFL	15	3	72	230	3.2	1	16	115	7.2	2	0	0	0.0	0	10	160	16.0	0	3	0	18
1994—Minnesota NFL	13	0	29	104	3.6	0	45	368	8.2	2	0	0	0.0	0	3	42	14.0	0	2	0	12
1995—Minnesota NFL	16	3	69	371	5.4	2	71	558	7.9	1	5	50	10.0	0	5	100	20.0	0	3	0	18
1996—Minnesota NFL	16	3	51	161	3.2	0	54	422	7.8	2	10	84	8.4	0	5	85	17.0	0	2	0	12
1997—St. Louis NFL	16	1	28	104	3.7	0	61	825	13.5	3	0	0	0.0	0	4	71	17.8	0	3	0	18
1998—St. Louis NFL	14	1	44	175	4.0	2	64	667	10.4	2	0	0	0.0	0	0	0	0.0	0	4	1	26
1999—St. Louis NFL	7	0	3	3	1.0	0	3	22	7.3	1	0	0	0.0	0	0	0	0.0	0	1	0	6
Pro totals (8 years)	113	14	387	1510	3.9	7	334	3079	9.2	15	15	134	8.9	0	41	734	17.9	0	22	1	134

LEE, DEL   CB   JETS

PERSONAL: Born January 19, 1976, in New Orleans. ... 5-10/187. ... Full name: Delphrine Lee.
HIGH SCHOOL: Karr (New Orleans).
COLLEGE: McNeese State.
TRANSACTIONS/CAREER NOTES: Signed as non-drafted free agent by New York Jets (April 19, 1999). ... Released by Jets (August 30, 1999). ... Re-signed by Jets to practice squad (October 13, 1999). ... Released by Jets (November 10, 1999). ... Re-signed by Jets to practice squad (November 16, 1999). ... Activated (December 10, 1999).
PLAYING EXPERIENCE: New York Jets NFL, 1999. ... Games/Games started: 1999 (4/0).

LEE, SHAWN   DT   RAIDERS

PERSONAL: Born October 24, 1966, in Brooklyn, N.Y. ... 6-2/300. ... Full name: Shawn Swaboda Lee.
HIGH SCHOOL: Erasmus Hall (Brooklyn, N.Y.).
JUNIOR COLLEGE: Westchester Community College (Valhalla, N.Y.).
COLLEGE: North Alabama.

TRANSACTIONS/CAREER NOTES: Selected by Tampa Bay Buccaneers in sixth round (163rd pick overall) of 1988 NFL draft. ... Signed by Buccaneers (July 10, 1988). ... Granted unconditional free agency (February 1-April 1, 1990). ... Re-signed by Buccaneers (July 20, 1990). ... Claimed on waivers by Atlanta Falcons (August 29, 1990). ... Traded by Falcons to Miami Dolphins for conditional pick in 1991 draft (September 3, 1990). ... On injured reserve with ankle injury (September 29-October 27, 1990). ... Granted free agency (February 1, 1991). ... Re-signed by Dolphins (August 21, 1991). ... On injured reserve with knee injury (September 17, 1991-remainder of season). ... Granted free agency (February 1, 1992). ... Re-signed by Dolphins (July 22, 1992). ... Released by Dolphins (August 31, 1992). ... Signed by San Diego Chargers (October 28, 1992). ... Granted unconditional free agency (March 1, 1993). ... Re-signed by Chargers (April 23, 1993). ... Traded by Chargers to Chicago Bears for fifth-round pick (DE Adrian Dingle) in 1999 draft (June 8, 1998). ... Granted unconditional free agency (February 12, 1999). ... Signed by Oakland Raiders (April 13, 2000).

CHAMPIONSHIP GAME EXPERIENCE: Member of Chargers for AFC championship game (1994 season); inactive. ... Played in Super Bowl XXIX (1994 season).

PRO STATISTICS: 1991—Intercepted one pass for 14 yards. 1992—Recovered one fumble. 1993—Recovered one fumble. 1994—Recovered one fumble. 1995—Recovered one fumble. 1996—Intercepted one pass for minus one yard. 1998—Recovered one fumble for 15 yards and a touchdown.

Year Team	G	GS	SACKS
1988—Tampa Bay NFL	15	0	2.0
1989—Tampa Bay NFL	15	3	1.0
1990—Miami NFL	13	10	1.5
1991—Miami NFL	3	2	0.0
1992—San Diego NFL	9	1	0.5
1993—San Diego NFL	16	15	3.0
1994—San Diego NFL	16	15	6.5
1995—San Diego NFL	16	15	8.0
1996—San Diego NFL	15	7	1.0
1997—San Diego NFL	16	15	3.0
1998—Chicago NFL	15	14	2.0
1999	Did not play.		
Pro totals (11 years)	148	97	28.5

LEEUWENBURG, JAY   C/G

PERSONAL: Born June 18, 1969, in St. Louis. ... 6-3/290. ... Full name: Jay Robert Leeuwenburg. ... Son of Richard Leeuwenburg, tackle with Chicago Bears (1965). ... Name pronounced LEW-in-berg.
HIGH SCHOOL: Kirkwood (Mo.).
COLLEGE: Colorado (degree in English).
TRANSACTIONS/CAREER NOTES: Selected by Kansas City Chiefs in ninth round (244th pick overall) of 1992 NFL draft. ... Signed by Chiefs (July 20, 1992). ... Claimed on waivers by Chicago Bears (September 2, 1992). ... Granted free agency (February 17, 1995). ... Re-signed by Bears (April 12, 1995). ... Granted unconditional free agency (February 16, 1996). ... Signed by Indianapolis Colts (February 21, 1996). ... Released by Colts (August 31, 1999). ... Signed by Cincinnati Bengals (September 3, 1999). ... Granted unconditional free agency (February 11, 2000).
PLAYING EXPERIENCE: Chicago NFL, 1992-1995; Indianapolis NFL, 1996-1998; Cincinnati NFL, 1999. ... Games/Games started: 1992 (12/0), 1993 (16/16), 1994 (16/16), 1995 (16/16), 1996 (15/7), 1997 (16/16), 1998 (16/16), 1999 (14/9). Total: 121/96.
HONORS: Named center on THE SPORTING NEWS college All-America first team (1991).
PRO STATISTICS: 1992—Returned one kickoff for 12 yards. 1995—Recovered one fumble. 1997—Fumbled once for minus 20 yards. 1998—Recovered one fumble. 1999—Fumbled once.

LEPSIS, MATT   OT   BRONCOS

PERSONAL: Born January 13, 1974, in Conroe, Texas ... 6-4/290. ... Full name: Matthew Lepsis.
HIGH SCHOOL: Frisco (Texas).
COLLEGE: Colorado.
TRANSACTIONS/CAREER NOTES: Signed as non-drafted free agent by Denver Broncos (April 22, 1997). ... On non-football injury list with knee injury (July 16, 1997-entire season). ... Assigned by Broncos to Barcelona Dragons in 1998 NFL Europe enhancement allocation program (February 18, 1998).
PLAYING EXPERIENCE: Barcelona Dragons NFLE, 1998; Denver NFL, 1998 and 1999. ... Games/Games started: NFLE 1998 (games played unavailable), NFL 1998 (16/0), 1999 (16/16). Total NFL: 32/16.
CHAMPIONSHIP GAME EXPERIENCE: Played in AFC championship game (1998 season). ... Member of Super Bowl championship team (1998 season).

LEROY, EMARLOS   DT   JAGUARS

PERSONAL: Born July 31, 1975, in Albany, Ga. ... 6-1/310. ... Full name: Emarlos S. Leroy. ... Name pronounced LEE-roy.
HIGH SCHOOL: Monroe (Albany, Ga.).
JUNIOR COLLEGE: Northwest Mississippi Community College.
COLLEGE: Georgia (degree in child and family development).
TRANSACTIONS/CAREER NOTES: Selected by Jacksonville Jaguars in sixth round (182nd pick overall) of 1999 NFL draft. ... Signed by Jaguars (May 26, 1999).
PLAYING EXPERIENCE: Jacksonville NFL, 1999. ... Games/Games started: 1999 (13/0).
CHAMPIONSHIP GAME EXPERIENCE: Played in AFC championship game (1999 season).

LESHINSKI, RON   FB

PERSONAL: Born March 6, 1974, in Sandusky, Ohio. ... 6-2/248. ... Name pronounced luh-SHIN-skee.
HIGH SCHOOL: Vermilion (Ohio).
COLLEGE: Army.

TRANSACTIONS/CAREER NOTES: Signed as non-drafted free agent by New Orleans Saints (April 25, 1997). ... On military reserve list (July 24, 1998-February 22, 1999). ... Assigned by Saints to Frankfurt Galaxy in 1999 NFL Europe enhancement allocation program (February 22, 1999). ... Claimed on waivers by Philadelphia Eagles (September 7, 1999). ... Released by Eagles (September 14, 1999).
PLAYING EXPERIENCE: Frankfurt NFLE, 1999; Philadelphia NFL, 1999. ... Games/Games started: NFLE 1999 (10/10); NFL 1999 (1/0). ... Total Pro. (11/10).
PRO STATISTICS: NFLE: 1999—Caught 10 passes for 112 yards and one touchdown and returned one kickoff for no yards.

LESTER, TIM   FB

PERSONAL: Born June 15, 1968, in Miami. ... 5-10/238. ... Full name: Timothy Lee Lester. ... Brother of Fred Lester, fullback with New York Jets (1994), Tampa Bay Buccaneers (1995-96) and Atlanta Falcons (1997).
HIGH SCHOOL: Miami Southridge.
COLLEGE: Eastern Kentucky.
TRANSACTIONS/CAREER NOTES: Selected by Los Angeles Rams in 10th round (255th pick overall) of 1992 NFL draft. ... Signed by Rams (July 13, 1992). ... Released by Rams (September 4, 1992). ... Re-signed by Rams to practice squad (September 7, 1992). ... Activated (October 7, 1992). ... Released by Rams (August 29, 1995). ... Signed by Pittsburgh Steelers (October 3, 1995). ... On physically unable to perform list with rotator cuff and knee injuries (August 25-October 17, 1998). ... Granted unconditional free agency (February 12, 1999). ... Signed by Jacksonville Jaguars (August 15, 1999). ... Released by Jaguars (September 5, 1999). ... Signed by Dallas Cowboys (September 16, 1999). ... Released by Cowboys (October 27, 1999).
CHAMPIONSHIP GAME EXPERIENCE: Played in AFC championship game (1995 and 1997 seasons). ... Played in Super Bowl XXX (1995 season).
PRO STATISTICS: 1994—Returned one kickoff for eight yards and recovered one fumble.
SINGLE GAME HIGHS (regular season): Attempts—5 (December 11, 1994, vs. Tampa Bay); yards—28 (October 14, 1993, vs. Atlanta); and rushing touchdowns—1 (November 25, 1996, vs. Miami).

			RUSHING				RECEIVING				TOTALS		
Year Team	G	GS	Att.	Yds.	Avg.	TD	No.	Yds.	Avg.	TD	TD	2pt.	Pts.	Fum.
1992—Los Angeles Rams NFL	11	0	0	0	0.0	0	0	0	0.0	0	0	0	0	0
1993—Los Angeles Rams NFL	16	14	11	74	6.7	0	18	154	8.6	0	0	0	0	0
1994—Los Angeles Rams NFL	14	4	7	14	2.0	0	1	1	1.0	0	0	0	0	1
1995—Pittsburgh NFL	6	1	5	9	1.8	1	0	0	0.0	0	1	0	6	0
1996—Pittsburgh NFL	16	13	8	20	2.5	1	7	70	10.0	0	1	0	6	1
1997—Pittsburgh NFL	16	13	2	9	4.5	0	10	51	5.1	0	0	0	0	0
1998—Pittsburgh NFL	9	7	0	0	0.0	0	9	46	5.1	0	0	0	0	0
1999—Dallas NFL	5	1	0	0	0.0	0	2	9	4.5	0	0	0	0	0
Pro totals (8 years)	93	53	33	126	3.8	2	47	331	7.0	0	2	0	12	2

LETT, LEON   DT   COWBOYS

PERSONAL: Born October 12, 1968, in Mobile, Ala. ... 6-6/290. ... Full name: Leon Lett Jr. ... Nickname: The Big Cat.
HIGH SCHOOL: Fairhope (Ala.).
JUNIOR COLLEGE: Hinds Community College (Miss.).
COLLEGE: Emporia (Kan.) State.
TRANSACTIONS/CAREER NOTES: Selected by Dallas Cowboys in seventh round (173rd pick overall) of 1991 NFL draft. ... Signed by Cowboys (July 14, 1991). ... On injured reserve with back injury (August 27-November 21, 1991). ... On suspended list for violating league substance abuse policy (November 3-24, 1995). ... On suspended list for violating league substance abuse policy (December 3, 1996-December 1, 1997). ... On suspended list for violating league substance abuse policy (June 4-November 9, 1999).
CHAMPIONSHIP GAME EXPERIENCE: Played in NFC championship game (1992-1995 seasons). ... Member of Super Bowl championship team (1992, 1993 and 1995 seasons).
HONORS: Played in Pro Bowl (1994 and 1998 seasons).
POST SEASON RECORDS: Holds Super Bowl career record for most yards by fumble recovery—64. ... Holds Super Bowl single-game record for most yards by fumble recovery—64 (January 31, 1993).
PRO STATISTICS: 1992—Recovered one fumble. 1993—Fumbled once. 1995—Recovered two fumbles. 1996—Recovered two fumbles. 1999—Recovered two fumbles.

Year Team	G	GS	SACKS
1991—Dallas NFL	5	0	0.0
1992—Dallas NFL	16	0	3.5
1993—Dallas NFL	11	6	0.0
1994—Dallas NFL	16	16	4.0
1995—Dallas NFL	12	12	4.0
1996—Dallas NFL	13	13	3.5
1997—Dallas NFL	3	3	0.5
1998—Dallas NFL	16	15	4.0
1999—Dallas NFL	8	1	1.5
Pro totals (9 years)	100	66	20.0

LEVENS, DORSEY   RB   PACKERS

PERSONAL: Born May 21, 1970, in Syracuse, N.Y. ... 6-1/228. ... Full name: Herbert Dorsey Levens.
HIGH SCHOOL: Nottingham (Syracuse, N.Y.).
COLLEGE: Notre Dame, then Georgia Tech (degree in business management).
TRANSACTIONS/CAREER NOTES: Selected by Green Bay Packers in fifth round (149th pick overall) of 1994 NFL draft. ... Signed by Packers (June 9, 1994). ... Granted free agency (February 14, 1997). ... Re-signed by Packers (June 20, 1997). ... Designated by Packers as franchise player (February 13, 1998). ... Re-signed by Packers (August 30, 1998).
CHAMPIONSHIP GAME EXPERIENCE: Played in NFC championship game (1995-97 seasons). ... Member of Super Bowl championship team (1996 season). ... Played in Super Bowl XXXII (1997 season).
HONORS: Played in Pro Bowl (1997 season).

PRO STATISTICS: 1996—Recovered one fumble. 1997—Recovered one fumble for minus seven yards.
SINGLE GAME HIGHS (regular season): Attempts—33 (November 23, 1997, vs. Dallas); yards—190 (November 23, 1997, vs. Dallas); and rushing touchdowns—4 (January 2, 2000, vs. Arizona).
STATISTICAL PLATEAUS: 100-yard rushing games: 1997 (6), 1998 (1), 1999 (3). Total: 10.

Year Team	G	GS	RUSHING				RECEIVING				KICKOFF RETURNS				TOTALS			
			Att.	Yds.	Avg.	TD	No.	Yds.	Avg.	TD	No.	Yds.	Avg.	TD	TD	2pt.	Pts.	Fum.
1994—Green Bay NFL	14	0	5	15	3.0	0	1	9	9.0	0	2	31	15.5	0	0	0	0	0
1995—Green Bay NFL	15	12	36	120	3.3	3	48	434	9.0	4	0	0	0.0	0	7	0	42	0
1996—Green Bay NFL	16	1	121	566	4.7	5	31	226	7.3	5	5	84	16.8	0	10	0	60	2
1997—Green Bay NFL	16	16	329	1435	4.4	7	53	370	7.0	5	0	0	0.0	0	12	1	74	5
1998—Green Bay NFL	7	4	115	378	3.3	1	27	162	6.0	0	0	0	0.0	0	1	0	6	0
1999—Green Bay NFL	14	14	279	1034	3.7	9	71	573	8.1	1	0	0	0.0	0	10	0	60	5
Pro totals (6 years)	82	47	885	3548	4.0	25	231	1774	7.7	15	7	115	16.4	0	40	1	242	12

LEVINGSTON, BASHIR　　CB　　GIANTS

PERSONAL: Born October 2, 1976, in Inglewood, Calif. ... 5-9/180. ... Name pronounced buh-SHEER.
HIGH SCHOOL: Seaside (Calif.).
JUNIOR COLLEGE: Monterey (Calif.) Peninsula College.
COLLEGE: Utah State, then Eastern Washington.
TRANSACTIONS/CAREER NOTES: Signed as non-drafted free agent by New York Giants (April 23, 1999). ... Assigned by Giants to Amsterdam Admirals in 2000 NFL Europe enhancement allocation program (February 18, 2000).
PRO STATISTICS: 1999—Intercepted one pass for 34 yards.

Year Team	G	GS	KICKOFF RETURNS				TOTALS			
			No.	Yds.	Avg.	TD	TD	2pt.	Pts.	Fum.
1999—New York Giants NFL	12	0	22	532	24.2	0	0	0	0	1

LEWIS, CHAD　　TE　　EAGLES

PERSONAL: Born October 5, 1971, in Fort Dix, N.J. ... 6-6/252. ... Full name: Chad Wayne Lewis.
HIGH SCHOOL: Orem (Utah).
COLLEGE: Brigham Young (degrees in communications and Chinese).
TRANSACTIONS/CAREER NOTES: Signed as non-drafted free agent by Philadelphia Eagles (April 23, 1997). ... Released by Eagles (September 15, 1998). ... Signed by St. Louis Rams (December 9, 1998). ... Inactive for three games with Rams (1998). ... Claimed on waivers by Eagles (November 16, 1999). ... Granted free agency (February 11, 2000). ... Re-signed by Eagles (March 17, 2000).
PRO STATISTICS: 1997—Returned one kickoff for 11 yards.
SINGLE GAME HIGHS (regular season): Receptions—3 (August 31, 1997, vs. New York Giants); yards—34 (August 31, 1997, vs. New York Giants); and touchdown receptions—1 (January 2, 2000, vs. St. Louis).

Year Team	G	GS	RECEIVING				TOTALS			
			No.	Yds.	Avg.	TD	TD	2pt.	Pts.	Fum.
1997—Philadelphia NFL	16	3	12	94	7.8	4	4	0	24	0
1998—Philadelphia NFL	2	0	0	0	0.0	0	0	0	0	0
1999—St. Louis NFL	6	0	1	12	12.0	0	0	0	0	0
—Philadelphia NFL	6	4	7	76	10.9	3	3	0	18	0
Pro totals (3 years)	30	7	20	182	9.1	7	7	0	42	0

LEWIS, DARRYLL　　CB　　CHARGERS

PERSONAL: Born December 16, 1968, in West Covina, Calif. ... 5-9/188. ... Full name: Darryll Lamont Lewis.
HIGH SCHOOL: Nogales (La Puente, Calif.).
COLLEGE: Arizona.
TRANSACTIONS/CAREER NOTES: Selected by Houston Oilers in second round (38th pick overall) of 1991 NFL draft. ... Signed by Oilers (July 19, 1991). ... On injured reserve with knee injury (October 25, 1993-remainder of season). ... Granted free agency (February 17, 1994). ... Re-signed by Oilers (July 17, 1994). ... Granted unconditional free agency (February 17, 1995). ... Re-signed by Oilers (March 9, 1995). ... Oilers franchise moved to Tennessee for 1997 season. ... Oilers franchise renamed Tennessee Titans for 1999 season (December 26, 1998). ... Released by Titans (September 5, 1999). ... Signed by San Diego Chargers (September 6, 1999). ... Granted unconditional free agency (February 11, 2000). ... Re-signed by Chargers (March 6, 2000).
HONORS: Jim Thorpe Award winner (1990). ... Named defensive back on THE SPORTING NEWS college All-America first team (1990). ... Played in Pro Bowl (1995 season).
PRO STATISTICS: 1991—Recovered one fumble. 1992—Returned eight kickoffs for 171 yards and recovered one fumble. 1997—Recovered three fumbles for 68 yards and fumbled once. 1999—Recovered blocked punt in end zone for a touchdown and recovered two fumbles for 42 yards and one touchdown.

Year Team	G	GS	INTERCEPTIONS				SACKS
			No.	Yds.	Avg.	TD	No.
1991—Houston NFL	16	1	1	33	33.0	1	1.0
1992—Houston NFL	13	0	0	0	0.0	0	1.0
1993—Houston NFL	4	4	1	47	47.0	▲1	0.0
1994—Houston NFL	16	15	5	57	11.4	0	0.0
1995—Houston NFL	16	15	6	§145	24.2	▲1	1.0
1996—Houston NFL	16	16	5	103	20.6	0	0.0
1997—Tennessee NFL	16	14	5	115	23.0	1	0.0
1998—Tennessee NFL	16	15	4	40	10.0	0	1.0
1999—San Diego NFL	13	8	4	9	2.3	0	0.0
Pro totals (9 years)	126	88	31	549	17.7	5	4.0

LEWIS, JEFF — QB — PANTHERS

PERSONAL: Born April 17, 1973, in Columbus, Ohio. ... 6-2/211. ... Full name: Jeffery Scott Lewis.
HIGH SCHOOL: Horizon (Scottsdale, Ariz.).
COLLEGE: Northern Arizona.
TRANSACTIONS/CAREER NOTES: Selected by Denver Broncos in fourth round (100th pick overall) of 1996 NFL draft. ... Signed by Broncos (July 19, 1996). ... On physically unable to perform list with knee injury (July 24-August 24, 1998). ... On non-football injury list with knee injury (August 25, 1998-entire season). ... Traded by Broncos to Carolina Panthers for third-round pick (CB Chris Watson) in 1999 draft and fourth-round pick (OT Cooper Carlisle) in 2000 draft (March 1, 1999).
CHAMPIONSHIP GAME EXPERIENCE: Member of Broncos for AFC championship game (1997 season); inactive. ... Member of Super Bowl championship team (1997 season); inactive.
SINGLE GAME HIGHS (regular season): Attempts—14 (December 22, 1996, vs. San Diego); completions—8 (December 22, 1996, vs. San Diego); yards—53 (December 22, 1996, vs. San Diego); and touchdown passes—0.

| | | | PASSING | | | | | | | RUSHING | | | | TOTALS | | |
Year Team	G	GS	Att.	Cmp.	Pct.	Yds.	TD	Int.	Avg.	Rat.	Att.	Yds.	Avg.	TD	TD	2pt.	Pts.
1996—Denver NFL	2	0	17	9	52.9	58	0	1	3.41	35.9	4	39	9.8	0	0	0	0
1997—Denver NFL	3	0	2	1	50.0	21	0	0	10.50	87.5	5	2	0.4	0	0	0	0
1998—Denver NFL									Did not play.								
1999—Carolina NFL	2	0	3	2	66.7	11	0	0	3.67	72.9	4	1	0.3	0	0	0	0
Pro totals (3 years)	7	0	22	12	54.5	90	0	1	4.09	45.6	13	42	3.2	0	0	0	0

LEWIS, JERMAINE — WR/PR — RAVENS

PERSONAL: Born October 16, 1974, in Lanham, Md. ... 5-7/175. ... Full name: Jermaine Edward Lewis.
HIGH SCHOOL: Eleanor Roosevelt (Greenbelt, Md.).
COLLEGE: Maryland.
TRANSACTIONS/CAREER NOTES: Selected by Baltimore Ravens in fifth round (153rd pick overall) of 1996 NFL draft. ... Signed by Ravens (July 18, 1996).
HONORS: Named punt returner on THE SPORTING NEWS NFL All-Pro team (1998). ... Played in Pro Bowl (1998 season).
RECORDS: Shares NFL single-game records for most touchdowns by punt returns—2; and most touchdowns by combined kick return—2 (December 7, 1997, vs. Seattle).
PRO STATISTICS: 1996—Fumbled four times and recovered one fumble. 1997—Fumbled three times and recovered two fumbles. 1998—Fumbled three times and recovered three fumbles. 1999—Fumbled once and recovered one fumble.
SINGLE GAME HIGHS (regular season): Receptions—8 (September 21, 1997, vs. Tennessee); yards—124 (September 21, 1997, vs. Tennessee); and touchdown receptions—2 (December 5, 1999, vs. Tennessee).
STATISTICAL PLATEAUS: 100-yard receiving games: 1997 (2), 1998 (2). Total: 4.

| | | | RUSHING | | | | RECEIVING | | | | PUNT RETURNS | | | | KICKOFF RETURNS | | | | TOTALS | | |
Year Team	G	GS	Att.	Yds.	Avg.	TD	No.	Yds.	Avg.	TD	No.	Yds.	Avg.	TD	No.	Yds.	Avg.	TD	TD	2pt.	Pts.
1996—Baltimore NFL	16	1	6	-3	-3.0	0	5	78	15.6	1	36	339	9.4	0	41	883	21.5	0	1	0	6
1997—Baltimore NFL	14	7	3	35	11.7	0	42	648	15.4	6	28	437*15.6		2	41	905	22.1	0	8	0	48
1998—Baltimore NFL	13	13	5	20	4.0	0	41	784	19.1	6	32	405	12.7	†2	6	145	24.2	0	8	0	48
1999—Baltimore NFL	15	6	5	11	2.2	0	25	281	11.2	2	*57	452	7.9	0	8	158	19.8	0	2	0	12
Pro totals (4 years)	58	27	14	63	4.5	0	113	1791	15.8	15	153	1633	10.7	4	96	2091	21.8	0	19	0	114

LEWIS, MO — LB — JETS

PERSONAL: Born October 21, 1969, in Atlanta. ... 6-3/258. ... Full name: Morris C. Lewis.
HIGH SCHOOL: J.C. Murphy (Atlanta).
COLLEGE: Georgia.
TRANSACTIONS/CAREER NOTES: Selected by New York Jets in third round (62nd pick overall) of 1991 NFL draft. ... Signed by Jets (July 18, 1991). ... Designated by Jets as franchise player (February 11, 2000).
CHAMPIONSHIP GAME EXPERIENCE: Played in AFC championship game (1998 season).
HONORS: Played in Pro Bowl (1998 and 1999 seasons).
PRO STATISTICS: 1991—Recovered one fumble. 1992—Recovered four fumbles for 22 yards. 1994—Recovered one fumble for 11 yards. 1997—Recovered one fumble for 26 yards. 1998—Fumbled once and recovered one fumble. 1999—Recovered one fumble.

| | | | INTERCEPTIONS | | | | SACKS |
Year Team	G	GS	No.	Yds.	Avg.	TD	No.
1991—New York Jets NFL	16	16	0	0	0.0	0	2.0
1992—New York Jets NFL	16	16	1	1	1.0	0	2.0
1993—New York Jets NFL	16	16	2	4	2.0	0	4.0
1994—New York Jets NFL	16	16	4	106	26.5	2	6.0
1995—New York Jets NFL	16	16	2	22	11.0	▲1	5.0
1996—New York Jets NFL	9	9	0	0	0.0	0	0.5
1997—New York Jets NFL	16	16	1	43	43.0	1	8.0
1998—New York Jets NFL	16	16	1	11	11.0	0	7.0
1999—New York Jets NFL	16	16	0	0	0.0	0	5.5
Pro totals (9 years)	137	137	11	187	17.0	4	40.0

LEWIS, RAY — LB — RAVENS

PERSONAL: Born May 15, 1975, in Bartow, Fla. ... 6-1/245. ... Full name: Ray Anthony Lewis.
HIGH SCHOOL: Kathleen (Lakeland, Fla.).
COLLEGE: Miami (Fla.).

TRANSACTIONS/CAREER NOTES: Selected after junior season by Baltimore Ravens in first round (26th pick overall) of 1996 NFL draft. ... Signed by Ravens (July 15, 1996).

HONORS: Named linebacker on THE SPORTING NEWS college All-America second team (1995). ... Played in Pro Bowl (1997 and 1998 seasons). ... Named linebacker on THE SPORTING NEWS NFL All-Pro team (1998 and 1999). ... Named to play in Pro Bowl (1999 season); replaced by Junior Seau due to personal reasons.

PRO STATISTICS: 1997—Recovered one fumble. 1999—Credited with a safety and fumbled once.

				INTERCEPTIONS			SACKS
Year Team	G	GS	No.	Yds.	Avg.	TD	No.
1996—Baltimore NFL	14	13	1	0	0.0	0	2.5
1997—Baltimore NFL	16	16	1	18	18.0	0	4.0
1998—Baltimore NFL	14	14	2	25	12.5	0	3.0
1999—Baltimore NFL	16	16	3	97	32.3	0	3.5
Pro totals (4 years)	60	59	7	140	20.0	0	13.0

LINCOLN, JEREMY — CB — BRONCOS

PERSONAL: Born April 7, 1969, in Toledo, Ohio. ... 5-10/182. ... Full name: Jeremy Arlo Lincoln.
HIGH SCHOOL: DeVilbiss (Toledo, Ohio).
COLLEGE: Tennessee.
TRANSACTIONS/CAREER NOTES: Selected by Chicago Bears in third round (80th pick overall) of 1992 NFL draft. ... Signed by Bears (July 23, 1992). ... On injured reserve with knee injury (September 1, 1992-entire season). ... Granted free agency (February 17, 1995). ... Re-signed by Bears (July 17, 1995). ... Released by Bears (August 20, 1996). ... Signed by St. Louis Rams (September 5, 1996). ... Released by Rams (February 24, 1997). ... Signed by Seattle Seahawks (June 4, 1997). ... Granted unconditional free agency (February 13, 1998). ... Signed by New York Giants (June 15, 1998). ... Granted unconditional free agency (February 12, 1999). ... Re-signed by Giants (June 14, 1999). ... Granted unconditional free agency (February 11, 2000). ... Signed by Denver Broncos (February 16, 2000).
PRO STATISTICS: 1995—Credited with one sack. 1996—Recovered one fumble. 1997—Recovered one fumble.

				INTERCEPTIONS		
Year Team	G	GS	No.	Yds.	Avg.	TD
1992—Chicago NFL				Did not play.		
1993—Chicago NFL	16	7	3	109	‡36.3	1
1994—Chicago NFL	15	14	1	5	5.0	0
1995—Chicago NFL	16	14	1	32	32.0	0
1996—St. Louis NFL	13	1	1	3	3.0	0
1997—Seattle NFL	13	3	0	0	0.0	0
1998—New York Giants NFL	16	1	1	0	0.0	0
1999—New York Giants NFL	15	7	1	0	0.0	0
Pro totals (7 years)	104	47	8	149	18.6	1

LINDSAY, EVERETT — OL — BROWNS

PERSONAL: Born September 18, 1970, in Burlington, Iowa. ... 6-4/302. ... Full name: Everett Eric Lindsay.
HIGH SCHOOL: Millbrook (Raleigh, N.C.).
COLLEGE: Mississippi (degree in general business, 1992).
TRANSACTIONS/CAREER NOTES: Selected by Minnesota Vikings in fifth round (133rd pick overall) of 1993 NFL draft. ... Signed by Vikings (July 14, 1993). ... On injured reserve with shoulder injury (December 22, 1993-remainder of season). ... On injured reserve with shoulder injury (August 23, 1994-entire season). ... On physically unable to perform list with knee injury (July 22-August 20, 1996). ... On non-football injury list with knee injury (August 20, 1996-entire season). ... Assigned by Vikings to Barcelona Dragons in 1997 World League enhancement allocation program (February 19, 1997). ... Granted unconditional free agency (February 13, 1998). ... Re-signed by Vikings (February 17, 1998). ... Traded by Vikings to Baltimore Ravens for sixth-round pick (DE Talance Sawyer) in 1999 draft (April 17, 1999). ... Granted free agency (February 11, 2000). ... Signed by Cleveland Browns (February 15, 2000).
PLAYING EXPERIENCE: Minnesota NFL, 1993, 1995, 1997 and 1998; Baltimore NFL, 1999. ... Games/Games started: 1993 (12/12), 1995 (16/0), 1997 (16/3), 1998 (16/3), 1999 (16/16). Total: 76/34.
CHAMPIONSHIP GAME EXPERIENCE: Played in NFC championship game (1998 season).
HONORS: Named offensive tackle on THE SPORTING NEWS college All-America second team (1992).

LINDSEY, STEVE — K — JAGUARS

PERSONAL: Born November 25, 1974 in Hattiesburg, Miss, ... 6-1/176. ... Full name: Steve Kendall Lindsey.
HIGH SCHOOL: North Forrest (Hattiesburg, Miss.).
COLLEGE: Mississippi.
TRANSACTIONS/CAREER NOTES: Signed as non-drafted free agent by San Francisco 49ers (April 24, 1998). ... Released by 49ers (July 15, 1998). ... Signed by Jacksonville Jaguars (January 6, 1999).
PLAYING EXPERIENCE: Jacksonville NFL, 1999. ... Games/Games started: 1999 (16/0).
CHAMPIONSHIP GAME EXPERIENCE: Played in AFC championship game (1999 season).

LINTON, JONATHAN — FB — BILLS

PERSONAL: Born November 7, 1974, in Allentown, Pa ... 6-0/238. ... Full name: Jonathan C. Linton.
HIGH SCHOOL: Catasauqua (Pa).
COLLEGE: North Carolina.
TRANSACTIONS/CAREER NOTES: Selected by Buffalo Bills in fifth round (131st pick overall) of 1998 NFL draft. ... Signed by Bills (June 8, 1998).

PRO STATISTICS: 1998—Recovered one fumble. 1999—Recovered one fumble.
SINGLE GAME HIGHS (regular season): Attempts—24 (November 7, 1999, vs. Washington); yards—96 (November 7, 1999, vs. Washington); rushing touchdowns—1 (January 2, 2000, vs. Indianapolis).

				RUSHING				RECEIVING				TOTALS		
Year Team	G	GS	Att.	Yds.	Avg.	TD	No.	Yds.	Avg.	TD	TD	2pt.	Pts.	Fum.
1998—Buffalo NFL	14	0	45	195	4.3	1	1	10	10.0	0	1	0	6	0
1999—Buffalo NFL	16	2	205	695	3.4	5	29	228	7.9	1	6	†1	38	4
Pro totals (2 years)	30	2	250	890	3.6	6	30	238	7.9	1	7	1	44	4

LITTLE, EARL — DB — BROWNS

PERSONAL: Born March 10, 1973, in Miami. ... 6-0/191. ... Full name: Earl Jerome Little.
HIGH SCHOOL: North Miami.
COLLEGE: Michigan, then Miami (Fla.).
TRANSACTIONS/CAREER NOTES: Signed as non-drafted free agent by Miami Dolphins (April 24, 1997). ... Released by Dolphins (August 24, 1997). ... Re-signed by Dolphins to practice squad (August 26, 1997). ... Released by Dolphins (August 29, 1997). ... Signed by New Orleans Saints to practice squad (October 1, 1997). ... Claimed on waivers by Cleveland Browns (October 25, 1999).
PLAYING EXPERIENCE: New Orleans NFL, 1998; New Orleans (1)-Cleveland (9) NFL, 1999. ... Games/Games started: 1998 (16/0), 1999 (N.O.-1/0; Cle.-9/0; Total: 10/0). Total: 26/0.
PRO STATISTICS: 1998—Returned four kickoffs for 64 yards. 1999—Intercepted one pass for no yards, returned two kickoffs for 34 yards and fumbled once.

LITTLE, LEONARD — LB — RAMS

PERSONAL: Born October 19, 1974, in Asheville, N.C. ... 6-3/237. ... Full name: Leonard Antonio Little.
HIGH SCHOOL: Asheville (N.C.).
JUNIOR COLLEGE: Coffeyville (Kan.) Community College.
COLLEGE: Tennessee (degree in psychology, 1997).
TRANSACTIONS/CAREER NOTES: Selected by St. Louis Rams in third round (65th pick overall) of 1998 NFL draft. ... Signed by Rams (July 2, 1998). ... On non-football injury list for personal reasons (November 17, 1998-November 16, 1999). ... On suspended list for violating league substance abuse policy (July 16-November 9, 1999).
PLAYING EXPERIENCE: St. Louis NFL, 1998 and 1999. ... Games/Games started: 1998 (6/0), 1999 (6/0). Total: 12/0.
CHAMPIONSHIP GAME EXPERIENCE: Played in NFC championship game (1999 season). ... Member of Super Bowl championship team (1999 season).
PRO STATISTICS: 1998—Credited with 1/2 sack.

LOCKETT, KEVIN — WR — CHIEFS

PERSONAL: Born September 8, 1974, in Tulsa, Okla. ... 6-0/187.
HIGH SCHOOL: Washington (Okla.).
COLLEGE: Kansas State (degree in accounting).
TRANSACTIONS/CAREER NOTES: Selected by Kansas City Chiefs in second round (47th pick overall) of 1997 NFL draft. ... Signed by Chiefs (July 25, 1997). ... Granted free agency (February 11, 2000). ... Re-signed by Chiefs (May 3, 2000)
PRO STATISTICS: 1998—Recovered two fumbles.
SINGLE GAME HIGHS (regular season): Receptions—4 (October 10, 1999, vs. New England); yards—74 (September 27, 1998, vs. Philadelphia); and touchdown receptions—1 (January 2, 2000, vs. Oakland).

			RECEIVING				PUNT RETURNS				TOTALS		
Year Team	G	GS	No.	Yds.	Avg.	TD	No.	Yds.	Avg.	TD	TD	2pt.	Pts.	Fum.
1997—Kansas City NFL	9	0	1	35	35.0	0	0	0	0.0	0	0	0	0	0
1998—Kansas City NFL	13	3	19	281	14.8	0	7	36	5.1	0	0	0	0	2
1999—Kansas City NFL	16	1	34	426	12.5	2	1	10	10.0	0	2	0	12	0
Pro totals (3 years)	38	4	54	742	13.7	2	8	46	5.8	0	2	0	12	2

LODISH, MIKE — DT — BRONCOS

PERSONAL: Born August 11, 1967, in Detroit. ... 6-3/270. ... Full name: Michael Timothy Lodish.
HIGH SCHOOL: Brother Rice (Birmingham, Mich.).
COLLEGE: UCLA (degree in history and business administration, 1990).
TRANSACTIONS/CAREER NOTES: Selected by Buffalo Bills in 10th round (265th pick overall) of 1990 NFL draft. ... Signed by Bills (July 26, 1990). ... Granted free agency (February 1, 1992). ... Re-signed by Bills (July 23, 1992). ... Granted unconditional free agency (February 17, 1995). ... Signed by Denver Broncos (April 4, 1995). ... Granted unconditional free agency (February 14, 1997). ... Re-signed by Broncos (August 6, 1997). ... Granted unconditional free agency (February 11, 2000). ... Re-signed by Broncos (March 23, 2000).
CHAMPIONSHIP GAME EXPERIENCE: Played in AFC championship game (1990-1993, 1997 and 1998 seasons). ... Played in Super Bowl XXV (1990 season), Super Bowl XXVI (1991 season), Super Bowl XXVII (1992 season) and Super Bowl XXVIII (1993 season). ... Member of Super Bowl championship team (1997 and 1998 seasons).
POST SEASON RECORDS: Holds Super Bowl career record for most games—6.
PRO STATISTICS: 1992—Recovered one fumble for 18 yards and a touchdown. 1993—Recovered one fumble. 1994—Recovered one fumble in end zone for a touchdown. 1997—Recovered one fumble.

Year Team	G	GS	SACKS
1990—Buffalo NFL	12	0	2.0
1991—Buffalo NFL	16	6	1.5
1992—Buffalo NFL	16	0	0.0
1993—Buffalo NFL	15	1	0.5
1994—Buffalo NFL	15	5	0.0
1995—Denver NFL	16	0	0.0
1996—Denver NFL	16	16	1.5
1997—Denver NFL	16	0	1.0
1998—Denver NFL	15	1	2.0
1999—Denver NFL	13	2	0.0
Pro totals (10 years)	**150**	**31**	**8.5**

LOFTON, STEVE   CB

PERSONAL: Born November 26, 1968, in Jacksonville, Texas. ... 5-9/177. ... Full name: Steven Lynn Lofton.
HIGH SCHOOL: Alto (Texas).
COLLEGE: Texas A&M.
TRANSACTIONS/CAREER NOTES: Signed as non-drafted free agent by WLAF (January 31, 1991). ... Selected by Montreal Machine in third round (34th defensive back) of 1991 WLAF positional draft. ... Signed by Phoenix Cardinals (July 9, 1991). ... On injured reserve with hamstring injury (October 12-December 2, 1992). ... On practice squad (December 2, 1992-remainder of season). ... Cardinals franchise renamed Arizona Cardinals for 1994 season. ... Claimed on waivers by Cincinnati Bengals (August 4, 1994). ... Released by Bengals (August 7, 1994). ... Signed by Carolina Panthers (April 11, 1995). ... Granted unconditional free agency (February 14, 1997). ... Signed by New England Patriots (September 30, 1997). ... On injured reserve with hamstring injury (December 9, 1997-remainder of season). ... Claimed on waivers by Panthers (October 23, 1998). ... Granted unconditional free agency (February 12, 1999). ... Re-signed by Panthers (March 30, 1999). ... Released by Panthers (February 9, 2000).
CHAMPIONSHIP GAME EXPERIENCE: Member of Panthers for NFC championship game (1996 season); did not play.
PRO STATISTICS: W.L.: 1991—Recovered one fumble. NFL: 1993—Returned one kickoff for 18 yards.

Year Team	G	GS	No.	INTERCEPTIONS Yds.	Avg.	TD
1991—Montreal W.L.	10	8	2	16	8.0	0
—Phoenix NFL	11	1	0	0	0.0	0
1992—Phoenix NFL	4	0	0	0	0.0	0
1993—Phoenix NFL	13	0	0	0	0.0	0
1994—				Did not play.		
1995—Carolina NFL	9	2	0	0	0.0	0
1996—Carolina NFL	11	3	1	42	42.0	0
1997—New England NFL	4	0	0	0	0.0	0
1998—New England NFL	6	0	0	0	0.0	0
—Carolina NFL	10	7	0	0	0.0	0
1999—Carolina NFL	5	0	0	0	0.0	0
W.L. totals (1 year)	**10**	**8**	**2**	**16**	**8.0**	**0**
NFL totals (8 years)	**73**	**13**	**1**	**42**	**42.0**	**0**
Pro totals (9 years)	**83**	**21**	**3**	**58**	**19.3**	**0**

LOGAN, ERNIE   DT/DE   JETS

PERSONAL: Born May 18, 1968, in Fort Bragg, N.C. ... 6-3/290. ... Full name: Ernest Edward Logan.
HIGH SCHOOL: Pine Forest (Fayetteville, N.C.).
COLLEGE: East Carolina.
TRANSACTIONS/CAREER NOTES: Selected by Atlanta Falcons in ninth round (226th pick overall) of 1991 NFL draft. ... Released by Falcons (August 19, 1991). ... Signed by Cleveland Browns (August 21, 1991). ... Released by Browns (September 8, 1993). ... Signed by Falcons (October 7, 1993). ... Granted free agency (February 17, 1994). ... Re-signed by Falcons (April 28, 1994). ... Released by Falcons (August 22, 1994). ... Signed by Jacksonville Jaguars (December 15, 1994). ... Granted unconditional free agency (February 14, 1997). ... Signed by New York Jets (March 20, 1997). ... On injured reserve with leg injury (December 15, 1997-remainder of season). ... Released by Jets (September 11, 1999). ... Re-signed by Jets (September 13, 1999).
CHAMPIONSHIP GAME EXPERIENCE: Member of Jaguars for AFC championship game (1996 season); inactive. ... Played in AFC championship game (1998 season).
PRO STATISTICS: 1991—Recovered one fumble.

Year Team	G	GS	SACKS
1991—Cleveland NFL	15	5	0.5
1992—Cleveland NFL	16	0	1.0
1993—Atlanta NFL	8	1	1.0
1994—		Did not play.	
1995—Jacksonville NFL	15	1	3.0
1996—Jacksonville NFL	4	0	0.0
1997—New York Jets NFL	15	14	0.0
1998—New York Jets NFL	16	12	2.5
1999—New York Jets NFL	14	7	3.0
Pro totals (8 years)	**103**	**40**	**11.0**

LOGAN, JAMES   LB   SEAHAWKS

PERSONAL: Born December 6, 1972, in Opp, Ala. ... 6-2/225.
HIGH SCHOOL: Opp (Ala.).
JUNIOR COLLEGE: Jones County Junior College (Miss.).
COLLEGE: Memphis State.

TRANSACTIONS/CAREER NOTES: Signed as non-drafted free agent by Houston Oilers (May 3, 1995). ... Released by Oilers (August 27, 1995). ... Re-signed by Oilers to practice squad (August 30, 1995). ... Activated (September 15, 1995). ... Claimed on waivers by Cincinnati Bengals (October 18, 1995). ... Claimed on waivers by Seattle Seahawks (October 31, 1995). ... Assigned by Seahawks to Scottish Claymores in 1997 World League enhancement allocation program (February 19, 1997). ... On injured reserve with fractured leg (September 30, 1998-remainder of season). ... Granted unconditional free agency (February 12, 1999). ... Re-signed by Seahawks (March 23, 1999).
PLAYING EXPERIENCE: Houston (3)-Cincinnati (1)-Seattle (6) NFL, 1995; Seattle NFL, 1996-1999; Scottish W.L., 1997. ... Games/Games started: 1995 (Hou.-3/0; Cin.-1/0; Sea.-6/0; Total: 10/0), 1996 (6/0), W.L. 1997 (games played unavailable), NFL 1997 (14/1), 1998 (4/1), 1999 (16/2). Total NFL: 50/4.
PRO STATISTICS: W.L.: 1997—Intercepted one pass for no yards, NFL: 1997—Recovered one fumble. 1998—Credited with one sack.

LOGAN, MIKE — S — JAGUARS

PERSONAL: Born September 15, 1974, in Pittsburgh. ... 6-0/211. ... Full name: Michael V. Logan.
HIGH SCHOOL: McKeesport (Pa.).
COLLEGE: West Virginia.
TRANSACTIONS/CAREER NOTES: Selected by Jacksonville Jaguars in second round (50th pick overall) of 1997 NFL draft. ... Signed by Jaguars (May 23, 1997). ... On injured reserve with ankle injury (September 20, 1999-remainder of season). ... Granted free agency (February 11, 2000). ... Re-signed by Jaguars (March 21, 2000).
PRO STATISTICS: 1998—Recovered one fumble for two yards.

| | | | PUNT RETURNS | | | | KICKOFF RETURNS | | | | TOTALS | | | |
Year Team	G	GS	No.	Yds.	Avg.	TD	No.	Yds.	Avg.	TD	TD	2pt.	Pts.	Fum.
1997—Jacksonville NFL	11	0	0	0	0.0	0	10	236	23.6	0	0	0	0	0
1998—Jacksonville NFL	15	0	2	26	13.0	0	18	414	23.0	0	0	0	0	1
1999—Jacksonville NFL	2	0	1	7	7.0	0	1	25	25.0	0	0	0	0	0
Pro totals (3 years)	28	0	3	33	11.0	0	29	675	23.3	0	0	0	0	1

LONG, KEVIN — C — TITANS

PERSONAL: Born May 2, 1975, in Summerville, S.C. ... 6-5/295. ... Full name: Kevin Dale Long.
HIGH SCHOOL: Summerville (S.C.).
COLLEGE: Florida State.
TRANSACTIONS/CAREER NOTES: Selected by Tennessee Oilers in seventh round (229th pick overall) of 1998 NFL draft. ... Signed by Oilers (July 2, 1998). ... Oilers franchise renamed Tennessee Titans for 1999 season (December 26, 1998).
PLAYING EXPERIENCE: Tennessee NFL, 1998 and 1999. ... Games/Games started: 1998 (16/2), 1999 (16/12). Total: 32/14.
CHAMPIONSHIP GAME EXPERIENCE: Played in AFC championship game (1999 season). ... Played in Super Bowl XXXIV (1999 season).
PRO STATISTICS: 1999—Fumbled once for minus 10 yards.

L

LONGWELL, RYAN — K — PACKERS

PERSONAL: Born August 16, 1974, in Seattle. ... 6-0/197. ... Full name: Ryan Walker Longwell.
HIGH SCHOOL: Bend (Ore.).
COLLEGE: California (degree in English).
TRANSACTIONS/CAREER NOTES: Signed as non-drafted free agent by San Francisco 49ers (April 28, 1997). ... Claimed on waivers by Green Bay Packers (July 10, 1997).
CHAMPIONSHIP GAME EXPERIENCE: Played in NFC championship game (1997 season). ... Played in Super Bowl XXXII (1997 season).
PRO STATISTICS: 1999—Punted once for 19 yards.

| | | KICKING | | | | | | |
Year Team	G	XPM	XPA	FGM	FGA	Lg.	50+	Pts.
1997—Green Bay NFL	16	*48	*48	24	30	50	1-1	120
1998—Green Bay NFL	16	41	43	29	33	45	0-1	128
1999—Green Bay NFL	16	38	38	25	30	50	1-2	113
Pro totals (3 years)	48	127	129	78	93	50	2-4	361

LOUD, KAMIL — WR — FALCONS

PERSONAL: Born June 25, 1976, in Richmond, Calif. ... 6-0/190. ... Full name: Kamil Kassam Loud.
HIGH SCHOOL: El Cerrito (Calif.).
COLLEGE: Cal Poly-San Luis Obispo.
TRANSACTIONS/CAREER NOTES: Selected by Buffalo Bills in seventh round (238th pick overall) of 1998 NFL draft. ... Signed by Bills (June 8, 1998). ... Claimed on waivers by Atlanta Falcons (April 20, 2000).
PLAYING EXPERIENCE: Buffalo NFL, 1998 and 1999. ... Games/Games started: 1998 (5/0), 1999 (7/0). Total: 12/0.
PRO STATISTICS: 1998—Recovered one fumble. 1999—Caught six passes for 66 yards and returned two kickoffs for 26 yards.
SINGLE GAME HIGHS (regular season): Receptions—5 (October 24, 1999, vs. Seattle); yards—55 (October 24, 1999, vs. Seattle); and touchdown receptions—0.

LOVILLE, DEREK — RB — RAMS

PERSONAL: Born July 4, 1968, in San Francisco. ... 5-10/210. ... Full name: Derek Kevin Loville. ... Name pronounced lu-VIL.
HIGH SCHOOL: Riordan (San Francisco).
COLLEGE: Oregon (degree in American studies).
TRANSACTIONS/CAREER NOTES: Signed as non-drafted free agent by Seattle Seahawks (May 9, 1990). ... Granted unconditional free agency (February 1-April 1, 1991). ... Re-signed by Seahawks for 1991 season. ... Granted unconditional free agency (February 1, 1992). ... Signed

by Los Angeles Rams (March 27, 1992). ... Released by Rams (August 31, 1992). ... Signed by San Francisco 49ers (March 22, 1993). ... On injured reserve with knee injury (August 30-November 10, 1993). ... Released by 49ers (November 10, 1993). ... Re-signed by 49ers (June 1, 1994). ... Granted unconditional free agency (February 17, 1995). ... Re-signed by 49ers (March 1, 1995). ... Released by 49ers (February 3, 1997). ... Signed by Denver Broncos (May 2, 1997). ... Granted unconditional free agency (February 13, 1998). ... Re-signed by Broncos (June 1, 1998). ... Traded by Broncos to St. Louis Rams for undisclosed draft pick (April 4, 2000).
CHAMPIONSHIP GAME EXPERIENCE: Played in NFC championship game (1994 season). ... Member of Super Bowl championship team (1994, 1997 and 1998 seasons). ... Played in AFC championship game (1997 and 1998 seasons).
PRO STATISTICS: 1991—Returned three punts for 16 yards and recovered one fumble.
SINGLE GAME HIGHS (regular season): Attempts—24 (December 3, 1995, vs. Buffalo); yards—88 (December 3, 1995, vs. Buffalo); and rushing touchdowns—1 (October 31, 1999, vs. Minnesota).

Year Team	G	GS	RUSHING				RECEIVING				KICKOFF RETURNS				TOTALS			
			Att	Yds	Avg	TD	No.	Yds	Avg	TD	No.	Yds	Avg	TD	TD	2pt	Pts.	Fum.
1990—Seattle NFL	11	1	7	12	1.7	0	0	0	0.0	0	18	359	19.9	0	0	0	0	1
1991—Seattle NFL	16	0	22	69	3.1	0	0	0	0.0	0	18	412	22.9	0	0	0	0	0
1992—									Did not play.									
1993—San Francisco NFL									Did not play.									
1994—San Francisco NFL	14	0	31	99	3.2	0	2	26	13.0	0	2	34	17.0	0	0	0	0	0
1995—San Francisco NFL	16	16	218	723	3.3	10	87	662	7.6	3	0	0	0.0	0	13	1	80	1
1996—San Francisco NFL	12	6	70	229	3.3	2	16	138	8.6	2	10	229	22.9	0	4	0	24	0
1997—Denver NFL	16	0	25	124	5.0	1	2	10	5.0	0	5	136	27.2	0	1	0	6	1
1998—Denver NFL	16	0	53	161	3.0	2	2	29	14.5	0	6	105	17.5	0	2	0	12	0
1999—Denver NFL	10	0	40	203	5.1	1	11	50	4.5	0	2	22	11.0	0	1	0	6	1
Pro totals (8 years)	111	23	466	1620	3.5	16	120	915	7.6	5	61	1297	21.3	0	21	1	128	4

LUCAS, JUSTIN — DB — CARDINALS

PERSONAL: Born July 15, 1976, in Victoria, Texas. ... 5-10/187.
HIGH SCHOOL: Stroman (Victoria, Texas).
COLLEGE: Texas A&M, then Abilene Christian (degree in industrial technology).
TRANSACTIONS/CAREER NOTES: Signed as non-drafted free agent by Arizona Cardinals (April 23, 1999). ... Released by Cardinals (September 5, 1999). ... Re-signed by Cardinals to practice squad (September 7, 1999). ... Activated (October 17, 1999). ... Released by Cardinals (October 19, 1999). ... Re-signed by Cardinals to practice squad (October 20, 1999). ... Activated (December 31, 1999).
PLAYING EXPERIENCE: Arizona NFL, 1999. ... Games/Games started: 1999 (2/0).

LUCAS, RAY — QB — JETS

PERSONAL: Born August 6, 1972, in Harrison, N.J. ... 6-3/214.
HIGH SCHOOL: Harrison (N.J.).
COLLEGE: Rutgers.
TRANSACTIONS/CAREER NOTES: Signed as non-drafted free agent by New England Patriots (May 1, 1996). ... Released by Patriots (August 25, 1996). ... Re-signed by Patriots to practice squad (August 27, 1996). ... Activated (December 12, 1996). ... Claimed on waivers by New York Jets (August 19, 1997). ... Released by Jets (August 24, 1997). ... Re-signed by Jets to practice squad (August 26, 1997). ... Activated (November 22, 1997).
CHAMPIONSHIP GAME EXPERIENCE: Played in AFC championship game (1996 season). ... Played in Super Bowl XXXI (1996 season). ... Member of Jets for AFC championship game (1998 season); did not play.
PRO STATISTICS: 1999—Fumbled eight times and recovered four fumbles for minus 28 yards.
SINGLE GAME HIGHS (regular season): Attempts—48 (December 5, 1999, vs. New York Giants); completions—31 (December 5, 1999, vs. New York Giants); yards—284 (December 5, 1999, vs. New York Giants); and touchdown passes—4 (December 5, 1999, vs. New York Giants).
MISCELLANEOUS: Regular-season record as starting NFL quarterback: 6-3 (.667).

Year Team	G	GS	PASSING								RUSHING				TOTALS		
			Att	Cmp.	Pct.	Yds	TD	Int.	Avg.	Rat.	Att.	Yds	Avg.	TD	TD	2pt.	Pts.
1996—New England NFL	2	0	0	0	0	0	0	0	0.0	...	0	0	0.0	0	0	0	0
1997—New York Jets NFL	5	0	4	3	75.0	28	0	1	7.00	54.2	6	55	9.2	0	0	0	0
1998—New York Jets NFL	15	0	3	1	33.3	27	0	0	9.00	67.4	5	23	4.6	0	0	0	0
1999—New York Jets NFL	9	9	272	161	59.2	1678	14	6	6.17	85.1	41	144	3.5	1	1	0	6
Pro totals (4 years)	31	9	279	165	59.1	1733	14	7	6.21	83.5	52	222	4.3	1	1	0	6

LUCKY, MIKE — TE — COWBOYS

PERSONAL: Born November 23, 1975, in Antioch, Calif. ... 6-6/273. ... Full name: Michael Thomas Lucky.
HIGH SCHOOL: Antioch (Calif.).
COLLEGE: Arizona (degree in political science).
TRANSACTIONS/CAREER NOTES: Selected by Dallas Cowboys in seventh round (229th pick overall) of 1999 NFL draft. ... Signed by Cowboys (July 22, 1999).
PLAYING EXPERIENCE: Dallas NFL, 1999. ... Games/Games started: 1999 (14/4).
PRO STATISTICS: 1999—Caught five passes for 25 yards.
SINGLE GAME HIGHS (regular season): Receptions—2 (November 25, 1999, vs. Miami); yards—15 (November 25, 1999, vs. Miami); and touchdown receptions—0.

LYGHT, TODD — CB — RAMS

PERSONAL: Born February 9, 1969, in Kwajalein, Marshall Islands. ... 6-0/190. ... Full name: Todd William Lyght.
HIGH SCHOOL: Luke M. Powers Catholic (Flint, Mich.).

COLLEGE: Notre Dame.

TRANSACTIONS/CAREER NOTES: Selected by Los Angeles Rams in first round (fifth pick overall) of 1991 NFL draft. ... Signed by Rams (August 16, 1991). ... On injured reserve with shoulder injury (September 22-October 22, 1992). ... On injured reserve with knee injury (November 23, 1993-remainder of season). ... Designated by Rams as transition player (February 15, 1994). ... Rams franchise moved to St. Louis (April 12, 1995). ... Tendered offer sheet by Jacksonville Jaguars (April 12, 1996). ... Offer matched by Rams (April 15, 1996). ... Designated by Rams as transition player (February 11, 2000).

CHAMPIONSHIP GAME EXPERIENCE: Played in NFC championship game (1999 season). ... Member of Super Bowl championship team (1999 season).

HONORS: Named defensive back on THE SPORTING NEWS college All-America first team (1989). ... Named defensive back on THE SPORTING NEWS college All-America second team (1990). ... Played in Pro Bowl (1999 season).

PRO STATISTICS: 1991—Fumbled once and recovered one fumble. 1993—Recovered one fumble for 13 yards. 1994—Returned one punt for 29 yards and recovered one fumble for 74 yards and a touchdown. 1995—Ran 16 yards with lateral from punt return. 1996—Fumbled once. 1997—Recovered two fumbles.

			INTERCEPTIONS				SACKS
Year Team	G	GS	No.	Yds.	Avg.	TD	No.
1991—Los Angeles Rams NFL	12	8	1	0	0.0	0	0.0
1992—Los Angeles Rams NFL	12	12	3	80	26.7	0	0.0
1993—Los Angeles Rams NFL	9	9	2	0	0.0	0	0.0
1994—Los Angeles Rams NFL	16	16	1	14	14.0	0	0.0
1995—St. Louis NFL	16	16	4	34	8.5	1	0.0
1996—St. Louis NFL	16	16	5	43	8.6	1	0.0
1997—St. Louis NFL	16	16	4	25	6.3	0	1.0
1998—St. Louis NFL	16	16	3	30	10.0	0	1.5
1999—St. Louis NFL	16	16	6	112	18.7	1	2.5
Pro totals (9 years)	129	125	29	338	11.7	3	5.0

LYLE, KEITH   S   RAMS

PERSONAL: Born April 17, 1972, in Washington, D.C. ... 6-2/210. ... Full name: Keith Allen Lyle. ... Son of Garry Lyle, free safety/running back with Chicago Bears (1968-74).

HIGH SCHOOL: Mendon (N.Y.), then George C. Marshall (Falls Church, Va.).

COLLEGE: Virginia (degree in psychology, 1993).

TRANSACTIONS/CAREER NOTES: Selected by Los Angeles Rams in third round (71st pick overall) of 1994 NFL draft. ... Signed by Rams (July 8, 1994). ... Rams franchise moved to St. Louis (April 12, 1995). ... Granted free agency (February 14, 1997). ... Re-signed by Rams (April 15, 1997).

CHAMPIONSHIP GAME EXPERIENCE: Played in NFC championship game (1999 season). ... Member of Super Bowl championship team (1999 season).

PRO STATISTICS: 1995—Rushed once for four yards. 1996—Rushed three times for 39 yards and fumbled once.

			INTERCEPTIONS				SACKS
Year Team	G	GS	No.	Yds.	Avg.	TD	No.
1994—Los Angeles Rams NFL	16	0	2	1	0.5	0	0.0
1995—St. Louis NFL	16	16	3	42	14.0	0	0.0
1996—St. Louis NFL	16	16	†9	‡152	16.9	0	0.0
1997—St. Louis NFL	16	16	8	102	12.8	0	2.0
1998—St. Louis NFL	16	16	3	20	6.7	0	1.0
1999—St. Louis NFL	9	9	2	10	5.0	0	1.0
Pro totals (6 years)	89	73	27	327	12.1	0	4.0

LYLE, RICK   DE/DT   JETS

PERSONAL: Born February 26, 1971, in Monroe, La. ... 6-5/290. ... Full name: Rick James Earl Lyle.

HIGH SCHOOL: Hickman Mills (Kansas City, Mo.).

COLLEGE: Missouri (degree in parks, recreation and tourism).

TRANSACTIONS/CAREER NOTES: Signed as non-drafted free agent by Cleveland Browns (May 2, 1994). ... On injured reserve with back injury (September 2, 1995-entire season). ... Browns franchise moved to Baltimore and renamed Ravens for 1996 season (March 11, 1996). ... Granted unconditional free agency (February 14, 1997). ... Signed by New York Jets (March 24, 1997).

PLAYING EXPERIENCE: Cleveland NFL, 1994; Baltimore NFL, 1996; New York Jets NFL, 1997-1999. ... Games/Games started: 1994 (3/0), 1996 (11/3), 1997 (16/16), 1998 (16/16), 1999 (16/16). Total: 62/51.

CHAMPIONSHIP GAME EXPERIENCE: Played in AFC championship game (1998 season).

PRO STATISTICS: 1997—Credited with three sacks and recovered one fumble for two yards. 1998—Credited with 1$\frac{1}{2}$ sacks. 1999—Credited with one sack.

LYNCH, BEN   C   49ERS

PERSONAL: Born November 18, 1972, in Santa Rosa, Calif. ... 6-4/295. ... Full name: Benjamin John Lynch.

HIGH SCHOOL: Analy (Sebastopol, Calif.).

COLLEGE: California.

TRANSACTIONS/CAREER NOTES: Selected by Kansas City Chiefs in seventh round (211th pick overall) of 1996 NFL draft. ... Signed by Chiefs (July 24, 1996). ... Released by Chiefs (August 20, 1996). ... Signed by Minnesota Vikings (February 10, 1997). ... Released by Vikings (August 18, 1997). ... Re-signed by Vikings to practice squad (December 11, 1997). ... Activated (December 30, 1997); did not play. ... Granted free agency (February 13, 1998). ... Selected by Frankfurt Galaxy in 1998 NFL Europe draft (February 18, 1998). ... Signed by Chicago Bears (July 1, 1998). ... On injured reserve with ankle injury (August 5-12, 1998). ... Released by Bears (August 12, 1998). ... Signed by San Francisco 49ers (May 4, 1999).

PLAYING EXPERIENCE: Frankfurt NFLE, 1998; San Francisco NFL, 1999. ... Games/Games started: 1998 (games played unavailable), 1999 (16/1).

PRO STATISTICS: 1999—Returned one kickoff for four yards.

LYNCH, JOHN — S — BUCCANEERS

PERSONAL: Born September 25, 1971, in Hinsdale, Ill. ... 6-2/220. ... Full name: John Terrence Lynch. ... Son of John Lynch, linebacker with Pittsburgh Steelers (1969); brother-in-law of John Allred, tight end, Chicago Bears; and brother of Ryan Lynch, pitcher in Baltimore Orioles organization.
HIGH SCHOOL: Torrey Pines (Encinitas, Calif.).
COLLEGE: Stanford.
TRANSACTIONS/CAREER NOTES: Selected by Tampa Bay Buccaneers in third round (82nd pick overall) of 1993 NFL draft. ... Signed by Buccaneers (June 1, 1993). ... On injured reserve with knee injury (December 12, 1995-remainder of season). ... Granted free agency (February 16, 1996). ... Re-signed by Buccaneers (July 13, 1996).
CHAMPIONSHIP GAME EXPERIENCE: Played in NFC championship game (1999 season).
HONORS: Played in Pro Bowl (1997 and 1999 seasons). ... Named safety on THE SPORTING NEWS NFL All-Pro team (1999).
PRO STATISTICS: 1996—Rushed once for 40 yards, credited with one sack, fumbled once and recovered one fumble. 1997—Recovered two fumbles. 1998—Credited with two sacks and recovered one fumble. 1999—Credited with $1/2$ sack.

			INTERCEPTIONS			
Year Team	G	GS	No.	Yds.	Avg.	TD
1993—Tampa Bay NFL	15	4	0	0	0.0	0
1994—Tampa Bay NFL	16	0	0	0	0.0	0
1995—Tampa Bay NFL	9	6	3	3	1.0	0
1996—Tampa Bay NFL	16	14	3	26	8.7	0
1997—Tampa Bay NFL	16	16	2	28	14.0	0
1998—Tampa Bay NFL	15	15	2	29	14.5	0
1999—Tampa Bay NFL	16	16	2	32	16.0	0
Pro totals (7 years)	103	71	12	118	9.8	0

RECORD AS BASEBALL PLAYER

TRANSACTIONS/CAREER NOTES: Threw right, batted right. ... Selected by Florida Marlins organization in second round (66th pick overall) of free-agent draft (June 1, 1992).

PITCHING TOTALS

Year Team (League)	W	L	Pct.	ERA	G	GS	CG	ShO	Sv.	IP	H	R	ER	BB	SO
1992—Erie (N.Y.-Penn.)	0	3	.000	2.15	7	7	0	0	0	29 $1/3$	24	15	7	17	16
1993—Kane County (Midwest)	1	0	1.000	3.00	2	2	0	0	0	9	4	4	3	12	3
Totals (2 years)	1	3	.250	2.35	9	9	0	0	0	38 $1/3$	28	19	10	29	10

LYNN, ANTHONY — FB — BRONCOS

PERSONAL: Born December 21, 1968, in McKinney, Texas. ... 6-3/230. ... Full name: Anthony Ray Lynn.
HIGH SCHOOL: Celina (Texas).
COLLEGE: Texas Tech.
TRANSACTIONS/CAREER NOTES: Signed as non-drafted free agent by New York Giants (May 5, 1992). ... Released by Giants (August 31, 1992). ... Signed by Denver Broncos (April 21, 1993). ... Released by Broncos (August 23, 1994). ... Signed by San Francisco 49ers (March 28, 1995). ... Granted unconditional free agency (February 14, 1997). ... Signed by Broncos (March 4, 1997).
PLAYING EXPERIENCE: Denver NFL, 1993 and 1997-1999; San Francisco NFL, 1995 and 1996. ... Games/Games started: 1993 (13/0), 1995 (6/0), 1996 (16/1), 1997 (16/0), 1998 (16/0), 1999 (16/0). Total: 83/1.
CHAMPIONSHIP GAME EXPERIENCE: Played in AFC championship game (1997 and 1998 seasons). ... Member of Super Bowl championship team (1997 and 1998 seasons).
PRO STATISTICS: 1995—Rushed twice for 11 yards. 1996—Rushed 24 times for 164 yards and caught two passes for 14 yards. 1997—Caught one pass for 21 yards. 1999—Rushed twice for two yards and recovered one fumble.
SINGLE GAME HIGHS (regular season): Attempts—7 (October 6, 1996, vs. St. Louis); yards—67 (September 29, 1996, vs. Atlanta); and rushing touchdowns—0.

LYON, BILLY — DT — PACKERS

PERSONAL: Born December 10, 1973, in Ashland, Ky. ... 6-5/300. ... Full name: William Morton Lyon.
HIGH SCHOOL: Lloyd (Erlanger, Ky.).
COLLEGE: Marshall (degree in occupational safety).
TRANSACTIONS/CAREER NOTES: Signed as non-drafted free agent by Kansas City Chiefs (April 28, 1997). ... Released by Chiefs (August 15, 1997). ... Signed by Green Bay Packers to practice squad (November 20, 1997)
PLAYING EXPERIENCE: Green Bay NFL, 1998 and 1999. ... Games/Games started: 1998 (4/0), 1999 (16/4). Total: 20/4.
PRO STATISTICS: 1998—Credited with one sack. 1999—Intercepted one pass for no yards and credited with two sacks.

LYONS, MITCH — TE

PERSONAL: Born May 13, 1970, in Grand Rapids, Mich. ... 6-5/268. ... Full name: Mitchell Warren Lyons.
HIGH SCHOOL: Forest Hills Northern (Grand Rapids, Mich.).
COLLEGE: Michigan State.
TRANSACTIONS/CAREER NOTES: Selected by Atlanta Falcons in sixth round (151st pick overall) of 1993 NFL draft. ... Signed by Falcons (May 26, 1993). ... Granted free agency (February 16, 1996). ... Re-signed by Falcons (June 12, 1996). ... Granted unconditional free agency (February 14, 1997). ... Signed by Pittsburgh Steelers (April 21, 1997). ... On injured reserve with knee injury (November 11, 1997-remainder of season). ... Released by Steelers (September 26, 1998). ... Re-signed by Steelers (September 28, 1998). ... On injured reserve with knee injury (December 31, 1999-remainder of season). ... Granted unconditional free agency (February 11, 2000).
PRO STATISTICS: 1998—Rushed twice for minus four yards. 1999—Returned three kickoffs for 42 yards.

SINGLE GAME HIGHS (regular season): Receptions—4 (October 23, 1994, vs. Los Angeles Raiders); yards—34 (November 26, 1995, vs. Arizona); and touchdown receptions—1 (December 8, 1996, vs. New Orleans).

				RECEIVING				TOTALS		
Year Team	G	GS	No.	Yds.	Avg.	TD	TD	2pt.	Pts.	Fum.
1993—Atlanta NFL	16	8	8	63	7.9	0	0	0	0	0
1994—Atlanta NFL	7	2	7	54	7.7	0	0	0	0	0
1995—Atlanta NFL	13	5	5	83	16.6	0	0	0	0	0
1996—Atlanta NFL	14	4	4	16	4.0	1	1	0	6	0
1997—Pittsburgh NFL	10	3	4	29	7.3	0	0	0	0	0
1998—Pittsburgh NFL	15	0	3	19	6.3	0	0	0	0	0
1999—Pittsburgh NFL	14	2	8	81	10.1	0	0	0	0	0
Pro totals (7 years)	89	24	39	345	8.8	1	1	0	6	0

MACHADO, J.P. G JETS

PERSONAL: Born January 6, 1976, in Monmouth, Ill. ... 6-4/300.
HIGH SCHOOL: Monmouth (Ill.).
COLLEGE: Illinois.
TRANSACTIONS/CAREER NOTES: Selected by New York Jets in sixth round (197th pick overall) of 1999 NFL draft. ... Signed by Jets (July 27, 1999).
PLAYING EXPERIENCE: New York Jets NFL, 1999. ... Games/Games started: 1999 (5/0).
PRO STATISTICS: 1999—Recovered one fumble.

MACK, STACEY FB JAGUARS

PERSONAL: Born June 26, 1975, in Orlando, Fla. ... 6-1/237. ... Full name: Stacey Lamar Mack.
HIGH SCHOOL: Boone (Orlando, Fla.).
JUNIOR COLLEGE: Southwest Mississippi College.
COLLEGE: Temple.
TRANSACTIONS/CAREER NOTES: Signed as non-drafted free agent by Jacksonville Jaguars (April 22, 1999).
PLAYING EXPERIENCE: Jacksonville NFL, 1999. ... Games/Games started: 1999 (12/0).
CHAMPIONSHIP GAME EXPERIENCE: Member of Jaguars for AFC championship game (1999 season); inactive.
PRO STATISTICS: 1999—Rushed seven times for 40 yards and returned six kickoffs for 112 yards.
SINGLE GAME HIGHS (regular season): Attempts—6 (November 21, 1999, vs. New Orleans); yards—27 (November 21, 1999, vs. New Orleans); and rushing touchdowns—0.

MACK, TREMAIN S/KR BENGALS

PERSONAL: Born November 21, 1974, in Tyler, Texas. ... 6-0/193. ... Nephew of Phillip Epps, wide receiver with Green Bay Packers (1982-88) and New York Jets (1989).
HIGH SCHOOL: Chapel Hill (Tyler, Texas).
COLLEGE: Miami (Fla.).
TRANSACTIONS/CAREER NOTES: Selected by Cincinnati Bengals in fourth round (111th pick overall) of 1997 NFL draft. ... Signed by Bengals (June 5, 1997). ... On non-football injury list with illness (November 5-December 1, 1997). ... On exempt/left squad list (December 3, 1998-remainder of season). ... On suspended list for violating league substance abuse policy (September 5-October 3, 1999).
HONORS: Played in Pro Bowl (1999 season).
PRO STATISTICS: 1997—Intercepted one pass for 29 yards. 1998—Recovered one fumble. 1999—Recovered one fumble.

				KICKOFF RETURNS				TOTALS		
Year Team	G	GS	No.	Yds.	Avg.	TD	TD	2pt.	Pts.	Fum.
1997—Cincinnati NFL	4	4	0	0	0.0	0	0	0	0	0
1998—Cincinnati NFL	12	0	45	1165	25.9	▲1	1	0	6	2
1999—Cincinnati NFL	12	0	51	1382	§27.1	▲1	1	0	6	3
Pro totals (3 years)	28	4	96	2547	26.5	2	2	0	12	5

MADDOX, MARK LB CARDINALS

PERSONAL: Born March 23, 1968, in Milwaukee. ... 6-1/238. ... Full name: Mark Anthony Maddox.
HIGH SCHOOL: James Madison Memorial (Madison, Wis.).
COLLEGE: Northern Michigan.
TRANSACTIONS/CAREER NOTES: Selected by Buffalo Bills in ninth round (249th pick overall) of 1991 NFL draft. ... Signed by Bills (June 18, 1991). ... On injured reserve with knee injury (August 27, 1991-entire season). ... On injured reserve with knee injury (October 10, 1995-remainder of season). ... Granted unconditional free agency (February 16, 1996). ... Re-signed by Bills (March 4, 1996). ... Released by Bills (June 2, 1997). ... Re-signed by Bills (July 2, 1997). ... Released by Bills (August 12, 1997). ... Re-signed by Bills (October 28, 1997). ... Granted unconditional free agency (February 13, 1998). ... Signed by Arizona Cardinals (March 19, 1998). ... Granted unconditional free agency (February 12, 1999). ... Re-signed by Cardinals (April 2, 1999). ... Granted unconditional free agency (February 11, 2000). ... Re-signed by Cardinals (March 28, 2000).
PLAYING EXPERIENCE: Buffalo NFL, 1992-1997; Arizona NFL, 1998 and 1999. ... Games/Games started: 1992 (15/1), 1993 (11/8), 1994 (15/14), 1995 (4/4), 1996 (14/14), 1997 (8/1), 1998 (14/3), 1999 (16/2). Total: 97/47.
CHAMPIONSHIP GAME EXPERIENCE: Played in AFC championship game (1992 and 1993 season). ... Played in Super Bowl XXVII (1992 season) and Super Bowl XXVIII (1993 season).
PRO STATISTICS: 1993—Recovered two fumbles. 1994—Intercepted one pass for 11 yards and recovered one fumble. 1997—Intercepted one pass for 25 yards. 1998—Credited with one sack and recovered one fumble.

MADISON, SAM   CB   DOLPHINS

PERSONAL: Born April 23, 1974, in Thomasville, Ga. ... 5-11/185. ... Full name: Samuel A. Madison Jr.
HIGH SCHOOL: Florida A&M High (Monticello, Fla.).
COLLEGE: Louisville.
TRANSACTIONS/CAREER NOTES: Selected by Miami Dolphins in second round (44th pick overall) of 1997 NFL draft. ... Signed by Dolphins (June 16, 1997).
HONORS: Named cornerback on THE SPORTING NEWS NFL All-Pro team (1999). ... Played in Pro Bowl (1999 season).
PRO STATISTICS: 1998—Credited with one sack. 1999—Credited with a safety.

			INTERCEPTIONS				TOTALS			
Year Team	G	GS	No.	Yds.	Avg.	TD	TD	2pt.	Pts.	Fum.
1997—Miami NFL	14	3	1	21	21.0	0	0	0	0	0
1998—Miami NFL	16	16	8	114	14.3	0	0	0	0	0
1999—Miami NFL	16	16	†7	164	23.4	1	1	0	8	0
Pro totals (3 years)	46	35	16	299	18.7	1	1	0	8	0

MAKOVICKA, JOEL   FB   CARDINALS

PERSONAL: Born October 6, 1975, in Brainard, Neb. ... 5-11/246. ... Name pronounced mack-oh-VIK-uh.
HIGH SCHOOL: East Butler (Brainard, Neb.).
COLLEGE: Nebraska.
TRANSACTIONS/CAREER NOTES: Selected by Arizona Cardinals in fourth round (116th pick overall) of 1999 NFL draft. ... Signed by Cardinals (June 18, 1999).
PRO STATISTICS: 1999—Returned one kickoff for 10 yards and recovered one fumble.
SINGLE GAME HIGHS (regular season): Attempts—2 (October 31, 1999, vs. New England); yards—7 (December 26, 1999, vs. Atlanta); and rushing touchdowns—0.

			RUSHING				RECEIVING				TOTALS			
Year Team	G	GS	Att.	Yds.	Avg.	TD	No.	Yds.	Avg.	TD	TD	2pt.	Pts.	Fum.
1999—Arizona NFL	16	10	8	7	0.9	0	10	70	7.0	1	1	0	6	1

MALAMALA, SIUPELI   OT

PERSONAL: Born January 15, 1969, in Tofoa, Tonga. ... 6-5/305. ... Cousin of Viliami Maumau, defensive tackle, Carolina Panthers. ... Name pronounced soo-PAY-lee.
HIGH SCHOOL: Kalahoe (Kailua, Hawaii).
COLLEGE: Washington.
TRANSACTIONS/CAREER NOTES: Selected by New York Jets in third round (68th pick overall) of 1992 NFL draft. ... Signed by Jets (July 14, 1992). ... On injured reserve with shoulder injury (August 31-September 29, 1992). ... On practice squad (September 29-October 9, 1992). ... Granted free agency (February 17, 1995). ... Re-signed by Jets (March 29, 1995). ... On injured reserve with knee injury (October 31, 1995-remainder of season). ... On physically unable to perform list with knee injury (July 21-October 18, 1996). ... Released by Jets (September 20, 1997). ... Re-signed by Jets (September 21, 1997). ... Released by Jets (September 21, 1998). ... Signed by Oakland Raiders (February 18, 1999). ... Released by Raiders (September 4, 1999). ... Re-signed by Raiders (October 14, 1999). ... Released by Raiders (October 27, 1999). ... Signed by New York Jets (November 24, 1999). ... Granted unconditional free agency (February 11, 2000).
PLAYING EXPERIENCE: New York Jets NFL, 1992-1997 and 1999. ... Games/Games started: 1992 (9/5), 1993 (15/15), 1994 (12/10), 1995 (6/4), 1996 (4/1), 1997 (10/5), 1999 (6/1). Total: 62/41.
PRO STATISTICS: 1993—Recovered one fumble.

MAMULA, MIKE   LB/DE   EAGLES

PERSONAL: Born August 14, 1973, in Lackawanna, N.Y. ... 6-4/252. ... Full name: Michael David Mamula. ... Name pronounced muh-MOO-la.
HIGH SCHOOL: Lackawanna (N.Y.) Secondary.
COLLEGE: Boston College (degree in sociology, 1994).
TRANSACTIONS/CAREER NOTES: Selected after junior season by Philadelphia Eagles in first round (seventh pick overall) of 1995 NFL draft. ... Signed by Eagles (July 19, 1995). ... On injured reserve with knee injury (August 18, 1998-entire season). ... Granted unconditional free agency (February 12, 1999). ... Re-signed by Eagles (February 12, 1999).
PRO STATISTICS: 1995—Recovered one fumble for 25 yards. 1996—Recovered three fumbles for four yards and a touchdown. 1999—Intercepted one pass for 41 yards and a touchdown and recovered two fumbles.

Year Team	G	GS	SACKS
1995—Philadelphia NFL	14	13	5.5
1996—Philadelphia NFL	16	16	8.0
1997—Philadelphia NFL	16	16	4.0
1998—Philadelphia NFL		Did not play.	
1999—Philadelphia NFL	16	13	8.5
Pro totals (4 years)	62	58	26.0

MANGUM, KRIS   TE   PANTHERS

PERSONAL: Born August 15, 1973, in Magee, Miss. ... 6-4/249. ... Full name: Kris Thomas Mangum. ... Son of John Mangum, defensive tackle with Boston Patriots (1966 and 1967) of AFL; and brother of John Mangum, cornerback with Chicago Bears (1990-98).
HIGH SCHOOL: Magee (Miss.).
COLLEGE: Mississippi.

M

TRANSACTIONS/CAREER NOTES: Selected by Carolina Panthers in seventh round (228th pick overall) of 1997 NFL draft. ... Signed by Panthers (May 20, 1997). ... Released by Panthers (September 2, 1997). ... Re-signed by Panthers to practice squad (September 4, 1997). ... Activated (December 5, 1997).
PRO STATISTICS: 1999—Returned two kickoffs for 20 yards.
SINGLE GAME HIGHS (regular season): Receptions—4 (December 20, 1997, vs. St. Louis); yards—56 (December 20, 1997, vs. St. Louis); and touchdown receptions—0.

				RECEIVING			TOTALS			
Year Team	G	GS	No.	Yds.	Avg.	TD	TD	2pt.	Pts.	Fum.
1997—Carolina NFL..	2	1	4	56	14.0	0	0	0	0	0
1998—Carolina NFL..	6	0	1	5	5.0	0	0	0	0	0
1999—Carolina NFL..	11	0	1	6	6.0	0	0	0	0	0
Pro totals (3 years)	19	1	6	67	11.2	0	0	0	0	0

MANNELLY, PATRICK　　　　OT　　　　BEARS

PERSONAL: Born April 18, 1975, in Atlanta. ... 6-5/285. ... Full name: James Patrick Mannelly.
HIGH SCHOOL: Marist (Atlanta).
COLLEGE: Duke.
TRANSACTIONS/CAREER NOTES: Selected by Chicago Bears in sixth round (189th pick overall) of 1998 NFL draft. ... Signed by Bears (June 11, 1998).
PLAYING EXPERIENCE: Chicago NFL, 1998 and 1999. ... Games/Games started: 1998 (16/0), 1999 (16/0). Total: 32/0.

MANNING, PEYTON　　　　QB　　　　COLTS

PERSONAL: Born March 24, 1976, in New Orleans. ... 6-5/230. ... Full name: Peyton Williams Manning. ... Son of Archie Manning, quarterback with New Orleans Saints (1971-82), Houston Oilers (1982-83) and Minnesota Vikings (1983-84).
HIGH SCHOOL: Isidore Newman (New Orleans).
COLLEGE: Tennessee (degree in speech communication).
TRANSACTIONS/CAREER NOTES: Selected by Indianapolis Colts in first round (first pick overall) of 1998 NFL draft. ... Signed by Colts (July 28, 1998).
HONORS: Davey O'Brien Award winner (1997). ... Named College Player of the Year by THE SPORTING NEWS (1997). ... Named quarterback on THE SPORTING NEWS college All-America second team (1997). ... Played in Pro Bowl (1999 season).
RECORDS: Holds NFL rookie-season records for most passes attempted—575 (1998); most passes completed—326 (1998); and most yards passing—3,739.
PRO STATISTICS: 1998—Fumbled three times. 1999—Fumbled six times and recovered two fumbles for minus five yards.
SINGLE GAME HIGHS (regular season): Attempts—54 (September 26, 1999, vs. San Diego); completions—30 (November 1, 1998, vs. New England); yards—404 (September 26, 1999, vs. San Diego); and touchdown passes—3 (November 21, 1999, vs. Philadelphia).
STATISTICAL PLATEAUS: 300-yard passing games: 1998 (4), 1999 (2). Total: 6.
MISCELLANEOUS: Regular-season record as starting NFL quarterback: 16-16 (.500). ... Postseason record as starting NFL quarterback: 0-1.

			PASSING							RUSHING				TOTALS		
Year Team	G	GS	Att.	Cmp.	Pct.	Yds.	TD	Int.	Avg.	Rat.	Att.	Yds.	Avg.	TD	TD	2pt.	Pts.
1998—Indianapolis NFL	16	16	*575	§326	56.7	§3739	26	*28	6.50	71.2	15	62	4.1	0	0	0	0
1999—Indianapolis NFL	16	16	533	§331	§62.1	§4135	§26	15	§7.76	§90.7	35	73	2.1	2	2	0	12
Pro totals (2 years)	32	32	1108	657	59.3	7874	52	43	7.11	80.6	50	135	2.7	2	2	0	12

MANUSKY, GREG　　　　LB

PERSONAL: Born August 12, 1966, in Wilkes-Barre, Pa. ... 6-1/234. ... Full name: Gregory Manusky. ... Name pronounced MAN-eh-ski.
HIGH SCHOOL: Dallas (Pa.).
COLLEGE: Colgate (degrees in education and geology, 1988).
TRANSACTIONS/CAREER NOTES: Signed as non-drafted free agent by Washington Redskins (May 3, 1988). ... On injured reserve with thigh injury (August 29-November 4, 1988). ... Granted unconditional free agency (February 1, 1991). ... Signed by Minnesota Vikings (March 27, 1991). ... On injured reserve with kidney injury (November 24-December 23, 1992). ... Granted unconditional free agency (March 1, 1993). ... Re-signed by Vikings for 1993 season. ... Released by Vikings (August 30, 1993). ... Re-signed by Vikings (August 31, 1993). ... Released by Vikings (August 22, 1994). ... Signed by Kansas City Chiefs (August 31, 1994). ... Granted unconditional free agency (February 16, 1996). ... Re-signed by Chiefs (April 9, 1996). ... Granted unconditional free agency (February 13, 1998). ... Re-signed by Chiefs (April 24, 1998). ... Released by Chiefs (February 9, 2000).
PLAYING EXPERIENCE: Washington NFL, 1988-1990; Minnesota NFL, 1991-1993; Kansas City NFL, 1994-1999. ... Games/Games started: 1988 (7/0), 1989 (16/7), 1990 (16/8), 1991 (16/0), 1992 (11/0), 1993 (16/0), 1994 (16/2), 1995 (16/1), 1996 (16/1), 1997 (16/1), 1998 (16/1), 1999 (16/0). Total: 178/21.
PRO STATISTICS: 1989—Recovered one fumble. 1994—Recovered two fumbles. 1996—Returned two kickoffs for 32 yards, fumbled once and recovered three fumbles. 1997—Returned one kickoff for 16 yards and recovered one fumble. 1998—Returned three kickoffs for 20 yards and recovered two fumbles for seven yards. 1999—Returned two kickoffs for six yards and recovered one fumble.

MARE, OLINDO　　　　K　　　　DOLPHINS

PERSONAL: Born June 6, 1973, in Hollywood, Fla. ... 5-10/190. ... Full name: Olindo Franco Mare. ... Name pronounced o-LEND-o MAR-ray.
HIGH SCHOOL: Cooper City (Fla.).
JUNIOR COLLEGE: Valencia Community College (Fla.).
COLLEGE: Syracuse.
TRANSACTIONS/CAREER NOTES: Signed as non-drafted free agent by New York Giants (May 2, 1996). ... Released by Giants (August 25, 1996). ... Re-signed by Giants to practice squad (August 27, 1996). ... Granted free agency after 1996 season. ... Signed by Miami Dolphins (February 27, 1997). ... Granted free agency (February 11, 2000).
HONORS: Named kicker on THE SPORTING NEWS NFL All-Pro team (1999). ... Played in Pro Bowl (1999 season).

RECORDS: Holds NFL single-season record for most field goals made—39 (1999).

Year Team	G	No.	Yds.	PUNTING Avg.Net avg.		In. 20	Blk.	KICKING XPM	XPA	FGM	FGA	Lg.	50+	Pts.
1996—New York Giants NFL								Did not play.						
1997—Miami NFL	16	5	235	47.0	46.2	2	0	33	33	28	36	50	1-3	117
1998—Miami NFL	16	3	115	38.3	31.7	1	0	33	34	22	27	48	0-2	99
1999—Miami NFL	16	1	36	36.0	30.0	0	0	27	27	*39	*46	54	3-5	144
Pro totals (3 years)	48	9	386	42.9	39.6	3	0	93	94	89	109	54	4-10	360

MARINO, DAN   QB

PERSONAL: Born September 15, 1961, in Pittsburgh. ... 6-4/228. ... Full name: Daniel Constantine Marino Jr. ... Brother-in-law of Bill Maas, nose tackle with Kansas City Chiefs (1984-92) and Green Bay Packers (1993); and current NFL broadcaster, Fox Sports.

HIGH SCHOOL: Central Catholic (Pittsburgh).

COLLEGE: Pittsburgh (degree in communications).

TRANSACTIONS/CAREER NOTES: Selected by Los Angeles Express in first round (first pick overall) of 1983 USFL draft. ... Selected by Miami Dolphins in first round (27th pick overall) of 1983 NFL draft. ... Signed by Dolphins (July 9, 1983). ... Left Dolphins camp voluntarily (July 25-August 31, 1985). ... Granted roster exemption (September 1-5, 1985). ... On injured reserve with Achilles' tendon injury (October 13, 1993-remainder of season). ... Granted unconditional free agency (February 11, 2000). ... Announced retirement (March 13, 2000).

CHAMPIONSHIP GAME EXPERIENCE: Played in AFC championship game (1984, 1985 and 1992 seasons). ... Played in Super Bowl XIX (1984 season).

HONORS: Named quarterback on THE SPORTING NEWS college All-America first team (1981). ... Named NFL Rookie of the Year by THE SPORTING NEWS (1983). ... Named to play in Pro Bowl (1983 season); replaced by Bill Kenney due to injury. ... Named NFL Player of the Year by THE SPORTING NEWS (1984). ... Named quarterback on THE SPORTING NEWS NFL All-Pro team (1984-1986). ... Played in Pro Bowl (1984 and 1992 seasons). ... Named to play in Pro Bowl (1985 season); replaced by Ken O'Brien due to injury. ... Named to play in Pro Bowl (1986 season); replaced by Boomer Esiason due to injury. ... Named to play in Pro Bowl (1987 season); replaced by Jim Kelly due to injury. ... Named to play in Pro Bowl (1991 season); replaced by John Elway due to injury. Elway replaced by Ken O'Brien due to injury. ... Named to play in Pro Bowl (1994 season); replaced by Jeff Hostetler due to injury. ... Named to play in Pro Bowl (1995 season); replaced by Steve Bono due to injury.

RECORDS: Holds NFL career records for most touchdown passes—420; most yards passing—61,361; most passes attempted—8,358; most passes completed—4,967; most games with 400 or more yards passing—12; and most games with four or more touchdown passes—21. ... Holds NFL records for most seasons with 4,000 or more yards passing—6; most seasons with 3,000 or more yards passing—13; most consecutive seasons with 3,000 or more yards passing—9 (1984-1992); most games with 300 or more yards passing—63; most consecutive games with four or more touchdown passes—4 (November 26-December 17, 1984); most seasons leading league in pass attempts—5; and most seasons leading league in pass completions—6. ... Holds NFL single-season records for most yards passing—5,084 (1984); most touchdown passes—48 (1984); most games with 400 or more yards passing—4 (1984); most games with four or more touchdown passes—6 (1984); and most consecutive games with four or more touchdown passes—4 (1984). ... Holds NFL rookie-season records for highest pass completion percentage—58.45 (1983); and highest passer rating—96.0 (1983). ... Shares NFL records for most seasons leading league in yards passing—5; most consecutive seasons leading league in pass completions—3 (1984-1986); and most consecutive games with 400 or more yards passing—2 (December 2 and 9, 1984). ... Shares NFL single-season record for most games with 300 or more yards passing—9 (1984).

POST SEASON RECORDS: Holds NFL postseason career record for most consecutive games with one or more touchdown passes—13. ... Shares NFL postseason single-game record for pass attempts—64 (December 30, 1995, vs. Buffalo).

PRO STATISTICS: 1983—Fumbled five times and recovered two fumbles. 1984—Fumbled six times and recovered two fumbles for minus three yards. 1985—Fumbled nine times and recovered two fumbles for minus four yards. 1986—Fumbled eight times and recovered four fumbles for minus 12 yards. 1987—Fumbled five times and recovered four fumbles for minus 25 yards. 1988—Fumbled 10 times and recovered eight fumbles for minus 31 yards. 1989—Fumbled seven times. 1990—Fumbled three times and recovered two fumbles. 1991—Fumbled six times and recovered three fumbles for minus eight yards. 1992—Fumbled five times and recovered two fumbles for minus 12 yards. 1993—Fumbled four times and recovered two fumbles for minus 13 yards. 1994—Fumbled nine times and recovered three fumbles for minus four yards. 1995—Caught one pass for minus six yards, fumbled seven times and recovered three fumbles for minus 14 yards. 1996—Fumbled four times and recovered one fumble for minus three yards. 1997—Fumbled eight times and recovered three fumbles for minus 17 yards. 1998—Fumbled nine times and recovered two fumbles for minus nine yards. 1999—Fumbled five times.

SINGLE GAME HIGHS (regular season): Attempts—60 (November 23, 1997, vs. New England); completions—39 (November 16, 1986, vs. Buffalo); yards—521 (October 23, 1988, vs. New York Jets); and touchdown passes—6 (September 21, 1986, vs. New York Jets).

STATISTICAL PLATEAUS: 300-yard passing games: 1983 (1), 1984 (9), 1985 (6), 1986 (6), 1987 (4), 1988 (6), 1989 (5), 1990 (1), 1991 (3), 1992 (4), 1994 (5), 1995 (3), 1997 (4), 1998 (4), 1999 (3). Total: 63.

MISCELLANEOUS: Selected by Kansas City Royals organization in fourth round of free-agent baseball draft (June 5, 1979); did not sign. ... Regular-season record as starting NFL quarterback: 147-93 (.613). ... Postseason record as starting NFL quarterback: 8-10 (.444). ... Holds Miami Dolphins all-time records for most yards passing (61,361) and most touchdown passes (420).

Year Team	G	GS	Att.	PASSING Cmp.	Pct.	Yds.	TD	Int.	Avg.	Rat.	RUSHING Att.	Yds.	Avg.	TD	TOTALS TD	2pt.	Pts.
1983—Miami NFL	11	9	296	173	58.4	2210	20	6	7.47	§96.0	28	45	1.6	2	2	0	12
1984—Miami NFL	16	16	*564	*362	§64.2	*5084	*48	17	*9.01	*108.9	28	-7	-0.3	0	0	0	0
1985—Miami NFL	16	16	567	*336	59.3	*4137	*30	21	7.30	84.1	26	-24	-0.9	0	0	0	0
1986—Miami NFL	16	16	*623	*378	60.7	*4746	*44	23	7.62	§92.5	12	-3	-0.3	0	0	0	0
1987—Miami NFL	12	12	§444	§263	59.2	3245	§26	13	7.31	89.2	12	-5	-0.4	1	1	0	6
1988—Miami NFL	16	16	*606	*354	58.4	*4434	▲28	§23	7.32	80.8	20	-17	-0.9	0	0	0	0
1989—Miami NFL	16	16	§550	§308	56.0	§3997	24	†22	7.27	76.9	14	-7	-0.5	2	2	0	12
1990—Miami NFL	16	16	531	306	57.6	3563	21	11	6.71	82.6	16	29	1.8	0	0	0	0
1991—Miami NFL	16	16	549	318	57.9	3970	25	13	7.23	85.8	27	32	1.2	1	1	0	6
1992—Miami NFL	16	16	*554	*330	59.6	*4116	§24	16	7.43	85.1	20	66	3.3	0	0	0	0
1993—Miami NFL	5	5	150	91	60.7	1218	8	3	8.12	95.9	9	-4	-0.4	1	1	0	6
1994—Miami NFL	16	16	615	385	62.6	4453	§30	17	7.24	§89.2	22	-6	-0.3	1	1	0	6
1995—Miami NFL	14	14	482	309	§64.1	3668	24	15	7.61	90.8	11	14	1.3	0	0	0	0
1996—Miami NFL	13	13	373	221	59.2	2795	17	9	7.49	87.8	11	-3	-0.3	0	0	0	0
1997—Miami NFL	16	16	*548	*319	58.2	3780	16	11	6.90	80.7	18	-14	-0.8	0	0	0	0
1998—Miami NFL	16	16	537	310	57.7	3497	23	15	6.51	80.0	21	-3	-0.1	1	1	0	6
1999—Miami NFL	11	11	369	204	55.3	2448	12	17	6.63	67.4	6	-6	-1.0	0	0	0	0
Pro totals (17 years)	242	240	8358	4967	59.4	61361	420	252	7.34	86.4	301	87	0.3	9	9	0	54

M

MARION, BROCK   S   DOLPHINS

PERSONAL: Born June 11, 1970, in Bakersfield, Calif. ... 5-11/205. ... Full name: Brock Elliot Marion. ... Son of Jerry Marion, wide receiver with Pittsburgh Steelers (1967); and nephew of Brent McClanahan, running back with Minnesota Vikings (1973-79).
HIGH SCHOOL: West (Bakersfield, Calif.).
COLLEGE: Nevada.
TRANSACTIONS/CAREER NOTES: Selected by Dallas Cowboys in seventh round (196th overall) of 1993 NFL draft. ... Signed by Cowboys (July 14, 1993). ... Granted free agency (February 16, 1996). ... Re-signed by Cowboys (May 2, 1996). ... Granted unconditional free agency (February 14, 1997). ... Re-signed by Cowboys (April 7, 1997). ... Granted unconditional free agency (February 13, 1998). ... Signed by Miami Dolphins (March 3, 1998).
CHAMPIONSHIP GAME EXPERIENCE: Played in NFC championship game (1993-1995 seasons). ... Member of Super Bowl championship team (1993 and 1995 seasons).
PRO STATISTICS: 1993—Recovered one fumble. 1994—Credited with one sack and returned two kickoffs for 39 yards. 1996—Fumbled once and recovered one fumble for 45 yards. 1997—Recovered one fumble for 13 yards. 1998—Recovered one fumble for two yards. 1999—Credited with one sack and recovered one fumble.

			INTERCEPTIONS				KICKOFF RETURNS				TOTALS		
Year Team	G	GS	No.	Yds.	Avg.	TD	No.	Yds.	Avg.	TD	TD	2pt.	Pts.	Fum.
1993—Dallas NFL	15	0	1	2	2.0	0	0	0	0.0	0	0	0	0	0
1994—Dallas NFL	14	1	1	11	11.0	0	2	39	19.5	0	0	0	0	0
1995—Dallas NFL	16	16	6	40	6.7	1	1	16	16.0	0	1	0	6	0
1996—Dallas NFL	10	10	0	0	0.0	0	3	68	22.7	0	0	0	0	1
1997—Dallas NFL	16	16	0	0	0.0	0	10	311	31.1	0	0	0	0	0
1998—Miami NFL	16	16	0	0	0.0	0	6	109	18.2	0	0	0	0	0
1999—Miami NFL	16	16	2	30	15.0	0	*62	*1524	24.6	0	0	0	0	2
Pro totals (7 years)	103	75	10	83	8.3	1	84	2067	24.6	0	1	0	6	3

MARSHALL, WHIT   LB   FALCONS

PERSONAL: Born January 6, 1973, in Atlanta. ... 6-2/242. ... Full name: Thomas Whitfield Marshall.
HIGH SCHOOL: The Lovett School (Atlanta).
COLLEGE: Georgia.
TRANSACTIONS/CAREER NOTES: Selected by Philadelphia Eagles in fifth round (147th pick overall) of 1996 NFL draft. ... Signed by Eagles (July 15, 1996). ... Released by Eagles (August 25, 1996). ... Re-signed by Eagles to practice squad (August 28, 1996). ... Activated (November 19, 1996). ... Released by Eagles (August 19, 1997). ... Signed by Indianapolis Colts (March 3, 1998). ... On injured reserve with hamstring injury (August 24-September 7, 1998). ... Released by Colts (September 7, 1998). ... Selected by Frankfurt Galaxy in 1999 NFL Europe draft (February 23, 1999). ... Signed by Atlanta Falcons (July 7, 1999).
PLAYING EXPERIENCE: Philadelphia NFL, 1996; Frankfurt NFLE, 1999; Atlanta NFL, 1999. ... Games/Games started: 1996 (1/0), NFLE 1999 (games played unavailable); NFL 1999 (15/0). Total NFL: 16/0.
PRO STATISTICS: NFLE: 1999—Credited with three sacks. NFL: 1999—Returned one kickoff for minus two yards.

MARTIN, CECIL   FB   EAGLES

PERSONAL: Born July 8, 1975, in Chicago. ... 6-0/235.
HIGH SCHOOL: Evanston (Ill.).
COLLEGE: Wisconsin.
TRANSACTIONS/CAREER NOTES: Selected by Philadelphia Eagles in sixth round (172nd pick overall) of 1999 NFL draft. ... Signed by Eagles (July 25, 1999).
SINGLE GAME HIGHS (regular season): Attempts—1 (December 5, 1999, vs. Arizona); yards—2 (December 5, 1999, vs. Arizona); and rushing touchdowns—0.

			RUSHING				RECEIVING				TOTALS		
Year Team	G	GS	Att.	Yds.	Avg.	TD	No.	Yds.	Avg.	TD	TD	2pt.	Pts.	Fum.
1999—Philadelphia NFL	12	5	3	3	1.0	0	11	22	2.0	0	0	0	0	0

MARTIN, CURTIS   RB   JETS

PERSONAL: Born May 1, 1973, in Pittsburgh. ... 5-11/210.
HIGH SCHOOL: Taylor-Allderdice (Pittsburgh).
COLLEGE: Pittsburgh.
TRANSACTIONS/CAREER NOTES: Selected after junior season by New England Patriots in third round (74th pick overall) of 1995 NFL draft. ... Signed by Patriots (July 18, 1995). ... Granted free agency (February 13, 1998). ... Tendered offer sheet by New York Jets (March 20, 1998). ... Patriots declined to match offer (March 25, 1998).
CHAMPIONSHIP GAME EXPERIENCE: Played in AFC championship game (1996 and 1998 seasons). ... Played in Super Bowl XXXI (1996 season).
HONORS: Named NFL Rookie of the Year by THE SPORTING NEWS (1995). ... Played in Pro Bowl (1995, 1996 and 1998 seasons).
PRO STATISTICS: 1995—Recovered three fumbles. 1996—Recovered one fumble. 1998—Recovered one fumble. 1999—Recovered two fumbles.
SINGLE GAME HIGHS (regular season): Attempts—40 (September 14, 1997, vs. New York Jets); yards—199 (September 14, 1997, vs. New York Jets); and rushing touchdowns—3 (November 3, 1996, vs. Miami).
STATISTICAL PLATEAUS: 100-yard rushing games: 1995 (9), 1996 (2), 1997 (3), 1998 (8), 1999 (6). Total: 28.

			RUSHING				RECEIVING				TOTALS		
Year Team	G	GS	Att.	Yds.	Avg.	TD	No.	Yds.	Avg.	TD	TD	2pt.	Pts.	Fum.
1995—New England NFL	16	15	§368	§1487	4.0	14	30	261	8.7	1	15	1	92	5
1996—New England NFL	16	15	316	1152	3.6	§14	46	333	7.2	3	§17	1	104	4
1997—New England NFL	13	13	274	1160	4.2	4	41	296	7.2	1	5	0	30	3

1998—New York Jets NFL	15	15	369	1287	3.5	8	43	365	8.5	1	9	0	54	5
1999—New York Jets NFL	16	16	367	1464	4.0	5	45	259	5.8	0	5	0	30	2
Pro totals (5 years)	76	74	1694	6550	3.9	45	205	1514	7.4	6	51	2	310	19

MARTIN, JAMIE   QB   JAGUARS

PERSONAL: Born February 8, 1970, in Orange, Calif. ... 6-2/206. ... Full name: Jamie Blane Martin.
HIGH SCHOOL: Arroyo Grande (Calif.).
COLLEGE: Weber State.
TRANSACTIONS/CAREER NOTES: Signed as non-drafted free agent by Los Angeles Rams (May 3, 1993). ... Released by Rams (August 24, 1993). ... Re-signed by Rams to practice squad (August 31, 1993). ... Activated (November 23, 1993). ... Inactive for five games (1993). ... Released by Rams (August 27, 1994). ... Re-signed by Rams (October 4, 1994). ... Released by Rams (October 12, 1994). ... Re-signed by Rams (November 15, 1994). ... Active for one game (1994); did not play. ... Assigned by Rams to Amsterdam Admirals of World Football League (1995). ... Rams franchise moved to St. Louis (April 12, 1995). ... On physically unable to perform list with broken collarbone (June 3, 1995-entire season). ... Released by Rams (August 17, 1997). ... Signed by Washington Redskins (December 2, 1997). ... Granted free agency (February 13, 1998). ... Signed by Jacksonville Jaguars (March 6, 1998). ... On injured reserve with knee injury (December 15, 1998-remainder of season). ... Granted unconditional free agency (February 12, 1999). ... Signed by Cleveland Browns (August 25, 1999). ... Granted unconditional free agency (February 11, 2000). ... Signed by Jaguars (February 22, 2000).
HONORS: Walter Payton Award winner (1991).
PRO STATISTICS: 1996—Fumbled twice and recovered one fumble for minus two yards.
SINGLE GAME HIGHS (regular season): Attempts—23 (December 6, 1998, vs. Detroit); completions—15 (December 6, 1998, vs. Detroit); yards—228 (December 6, 1998, vs. Detroit); and touchdown passes—2 (December 6, 1998, vs. Detroit).
MISCELLANEOUS: Regular-season record as starting NFL quarterback: 0-1.

			PASSING								RUSHING				TOTALS		
Year Team	G	GS	Att.	Cmp.	Pct.	Yds.	TD	Int.	Avg.	Rat.	Att.	Yds.	Avg.	TD	TD	2pt.	Pts.
1993—L.A. Rams NFL							Did not play.										
1994—L.A. Rams NFL							Did not play.										
1995—Amsterdam W.L.	9	9	219	126	57.5	1433	11	6	6.54	82.6	0	0	0.0	0	0	0	0
—St. Louis NFL							Did not play.										
1996—St. Louis NFL	6	0	34	23	67.6	241	3	2	7.09	92.9	7	14	2.0	0	0	0	0
1997—Washington NFL							Did not play.										
1998—Jacksonville NFL	4	1	45	27	60.0	355	2	0	7.89	99.8	5	8	1.6	0	0	0	0
1999—Cleveland NFL							Did not play.										
W.L. totals (1 year)	9	9	219	126	57.5	1433	11	6	6.54	82.6	0	0	0.0	0	0	0	0
NFL totals (2 years)	10	1	79	50	63.3	596	5	2	7.54	96.8	12	22	1.8	0	0	0	0
Pro totals (3 years)	19	10	298	176	59.1	2029	16	8	6.81	86.4	12	22	1.8	0	0	0	0

MARTIN, MANNY   S

PERSONAL: Born July 31, 1969, in Miami. ... 5-11/184. ... Full name: Emanuel C. Martin.
HIGH SCHOOL: Miami Central.
COLLEGE: Alabama State.
TRANSACTIONS/CAREER NOTES: Signed as non-drafted free agent by Houston Oilers (May 17, 1993). ... Released by Oilers (August 19, 1993). ... Re-signed by Oilers to practice squad (September 29, 1993). ... Activated (October 6, 1993). ... Released by Oilers (October 25, 1993). ... Re-signed by Oilers to practice squad (October 27, 1993). ... Released by Oilers (August 28, 1994). ... Signed by Ottawa Rough Riders of CFL for 1994 season. ... Granted free agency (February 16, 1996). ... Signed by Buffalo Bills (April 4, 1996). ... Granted free agency (February 12, 1999). ... Re-signed by Bills (April 26, 1999). ... Granted unconditional free agency (February 11, 2000).
PRO STATISTICS: CFL: 1995: Returned one punt for 33 yards and a touchdown, credited with one sack and recovered one fumble.

			INTERCEPTIONS			
Year Team	G	GS	No.	Yds.	Avg.	TD
1993—Houston NFL	1	0	0	0	0.0	0
1994—Ottawa CFL	3	3	0	0	0.0	0
1995—Ottawa CFL	17	17	2	12	6.0	0
1996—Buffalo NFL	16	1	2	35	17.5	0
1997—Buffalo NFL	16	2	1	12	12.0	0
1998—Buffalo NFL	14	4	1	23	23.0	0
1999—Buffalo NFL	7	0	1	0	0.0	0
CFL totals (2 years)	20	20	2	12	6.0	0
NFL totals (5 years)	54	7	5	70	14.0	0
Pro totals (7 years)	74	27	7	82	11.7	0

MARTIN, STEVE   DT   CHIEFS

PERSONAL: Born May 31, 1974, in St. Paul, Minn. ... 6-4/303. ... Full name: Steven Albert Martin.
HIGH SCHOOL: Jefferson City (Mo.).
COLLEGE: Missouri.
TRANSACTIONS/CAREER NOTES: Selected by Indianapolis Colts in fifth round (151st pick overall) of 1996 NFL draft. ... Signed by Colts (July 5, 1996). ... Claimed on waivers by Philadelphia Eagles (October 23, 1998). ... Granted free agency (February 12, 1999). ... Re-signed by Eagles (April 9, 1999). ... Granted unconditional free agency (February 11, 2000). ... Signed by Kansas City Chiefs (February 24, 2000).
PRO STATISTICS: 1996—Recovered one fumble. 1999—Recovered one fumble.

Year Team	G	GS	SACKS
1996—Indianapolis NFL	14	5	1.0
1997—Indianapolis NFL	12	0	0.0
1998—Indianapolis NFL	4	0	0.0
—Philadelphia NFL	9	3	1.0
1999—Philadelphia NFL	16	15	2.0
Pro totals (4 years)	55	23	4.0

M

MARTIN, TONY   WR   DOLPHINS

PERSONAL: Born September 5, 1965, in Miami. ... 6-1/175. ... Full name: Tony Derrick Martin.

HIGH SCHOOL: Miami Northwestern.

COLLEGE: Bishop (Texas), then Mesa State College (Colo.).

TRANSACTIONS/CAREER NOTES: Selected by New York Jets in fifth round (126th pick overall) of 1989 NFL draft. ... Signed by New York Jets for 1989 season. ... Released by Jets (September 4, 1989). ... Signed by Miami Dolphins to developmental squad (September 5, 1989). ... Activated (December 23, 1989); did not play. ... Granted free agency (February 1, 1992). ... Re-signed by Dolphins (March 10, 1992). ... Traded by Dolphins to San Diego Chargers for fourth-round pick (traded to Arizona) in 1994 draft (March 24, 1994). ... Designated by Chargers as franchise player (February 13, 1997). ... Re-signed by Chargers (May 1, 1997). ... Traded by Chargers to Atlanta Falcons for second-round pick (RB Jermaine Fazande) in 1999 draft (June 3, 1998). ... Released by Falcons (February 26, 1999). ... Signed by Dolphins (April 9, 1999).

CHAMPIONSHIP GAME EXPERIENCE: Played in AFC championship game (1992 and 1994 seasons). ... Played in Super Bowl XXIX (1994 season) and Super Bowl XXXIII (1998 season). ... Played in NFC championship game (1998 season).

HONORS: Played in Pro Bowl (1996 season).

RECORDS: Shares NFL record for longest pass reception (from Stan Humphries)—99 yards, touchdown (September 18, 1994, at Seattle).

PRO STATISTICS: 1990—Recovered two fumbles. 1992—Attempted one pass without a completion and recovered one fumble. 1994—Attempted one pass without a completion and returned eight kickoffs for 167 yards. 1995—Attempted one pass without a completion. 1998—Attempted one pass without a completion.

SINGLE GAME HIGHS (regular season): Receptions—13 (September 10, 1995, vs. Seattle); yards—172 (December 11, 1994, vs. San Francisco); and touchdown receptions—3 (September 28, 1997, vs. Baltimore).

STATISTICAL PLATEAUS: 100-yard receiving games: 1991 (2), 1993 (1), 1994 (2), 1995 (4), 1996 (4), 1997 (2), 1998 (5), 1999 (5). Total: 25.

			RUSHING				RECEIVING				PUNT RETURNS				TOTALS			
Year Team	G	GS	Att.	Yds.	Avg.	TD	No.	Yds.	Avg.	TD	No.	Yds.	Avg.	TD	TD	2pt.	Pts.	Fum.
1990—Miami NFL	16	5	1	8	8.0	0	29	388	13.4	2	26	140	5.4	0	2	0	12	4
1991—Miami NFL	16	0	0	0	0.0	0	27	434	16.1	2	1	10	10.0	0	2	0	12	2
1992—Miami NFL	16	3	1	-2	-2.0	0	33	553	16.8	2	1	0	0.0	0	2	0	12	2
1993—Miami NFL	12	0	1	6	6.0	0	20	347	17.4	3	0	0	0.0	0	3	0	18	1
1994—San Diego NFL	16	1	2	-9	-4.5	0	50	885	17.7	7	0	0	0.0	0	7	0	42	2
1995—San Diego NFL	16	16	0	0	0.0	0	90	1224	13.6	6	0	0	0.0	0	6	0	36	3
1996—San Diego NFL	16	16	0	0	0.0	0	85	1171	13.8	†14	0	0	0.0	0	14	0	84	0
1997—San Diego NFL	16	16	0	0	0.0	0	63	904	14.3	6	0	0	0.0	0	6	0	36	0
1998—Atlanta NFL	16	16	0	0	0.0	0	66	1181	17.9	6	0	0	0.0	0	6	0	36	0
1999—Miami NFL	16	13	1	-6	-6.0	0	67	1037	15.5	5	0	0	0.0	0	5	0	30	0
Pro totals (10 years)	156	86	6	-3	-0.5	0	530	8124	15.3	53	28	150	5.4	0	53	0	318	14

MARTIN, WAYNE   DT   SAINTS

PERSONAL: Born October 26, 1965, in Forrest City, Ark. ... 6-5/275. ... Full name: Gerald Wayne Martin.

HIGH SCHOOL: Cross Country (Cherry Valley, Ark.).

COLLEGE: Arkansas (degree in criminal justice, 1990).

TRANSACTIONS/CAREER NOTES: Selected by New Orleans Saints in first round (19th pick overall) of 1989 NFL draft. ... Signed by Saints (August 10, 1989). ... On injured reserve with knee injury (December 19, 1990-remainder of season). ... Granted free agency (March 1, 1993). ... Tendered offer sheet by Washington Redskins (April 8, 1993). ... Offer matched by Saints (April 14, 1993).

HONORS: Named defensive lineman on THE SPORTING NEWS college All-America first team (1988). ... Played in Pro Bowl (1994 season).

PRO STATISTICS: 1989—Recovered two fumbles. 1991—Recovered one fumble. 1992—Recovered two fumbles. 1993—Recovered two fumbles for seven yards. 1995—Intercepted one pass for 12 yards and recovered one fumble. 1996—Recovered one fumble. 1997—Recovered one fumble. 1998—Credited with a safety and recovered one fumble. 1999—Recovered two fumbles.

Year Team	G	GS	SACKS
1989—New Orleans NFL	16	0	2.5
1990—New Orleans NFL	11	11	4.0
1991—New Orleans NFL	16	16	3.5
1992—New Orleans NFL	16	16	15.5
1993—New Orleans NFL	16	16	5.0
1994—New Orleans NFL	16	16	10.0
1995—New Orleans NFL	16	16	∞13.0
1996—New Orleans NFL	16	16	11.0
1997—New Orleans NFL	16	16	10.5
1998—New Orleans NFL	16	16	3.0
1999—New Orleans NFL	16	16	4.5
Pro totals (11 years)	171	155	82.5

MARTS, LONNIE   LB   JAGUARS

PERSONAL: Born November 10, 1968, in New Orleans. ... 6-2/246. ... Full name: Lonnie Marts Jr.

HIGH SCHOOL: St. Augustine (New Orleans).

COLLEGE: Tulane (degree in sociology).

TRANSACTIONS/CAREER NOTES: Signed as non-drafted free agent by Kansas City Chiefs (May 1, 1990). ... On injured reserve with ankle injury (September 8, 1990-entire season). ... Granted unconditional free agency (February 17, 1994). ... Signed by Tampa Bay Buccaneers (March 21, 1994). ... Granted unconditional free agency (February 14, 1997). ... Signed by Houston Oilers (April 3, 1997). ... Oilers franchise moved to Tennessee for 1997 season. ... Oilers franchise renamed Tennessee Titans for 1999 season (December 26, 1998). ... Released by Titans (July 28, 1999). ... Signed by Jacksonville Jaguars (July 30, 1999). ... Granted unconditional free agency (February 11, 2000). ... Re-signed by Jaguars (February 11, 2000).

CHAMPIONSHIP GAME EXPERIENCE: Played in AFC championship game (1993 and 1999 seasons).

PRO STATISTICS: 1991—Recovered one fumble. 1992—Recovered one fumble for two yards. 1993—Returned one kickoff for no yards and recovered one fumble. 1994—Recovered two fumbles. 1995—Recovered one fumble. 1996—Recovered two fumbles. 1997—Recovered one fumble. 1999—Recovered two fumbles for three yards.

Year Team	G	GS	INTERCEPTIONS No.	Yds.	Avg.	TD	SACKS No.
1990—Kansas City NFL			Did not play.				
1991—Kansas City NFL	16	2	0	0	0.0	0	1.0
1992—Kansas City NFL	15	3	1	36	36.0	1	0.0
1993—Kansas City NFL	16	15	1	20	20.0	0	2.0
1994—Tampa Bay NFL	16	14	0	0	0.0	0	0.0
1995—Tampa Bay NFL	15	13	1	8	8.0	0	0.0
1996—Tampa Bay NFL	16	13	0	0	0.0	0	7.0
1997—Tennessee NFL	14	14	0	0	0.0	0	1.0
1998—Tennessee NFL	16	15	1	27	27.0	1	4.0
1999—Jacksonville NFL	16	16	1	10	10.0	0	2.0
Pro totals (9 years)	140	105	5	101	20.2	2	17.0

MARYLAND, RUSSELL   DT   PACKERS

PERSONAL: Born March 22, 1969, in Chicago. ... 6-1/300.
HIGH SCHOOL: Whitney-Young (Chicago).
COLLEGE: Miami, Fla. (degree in psychology, 1990).
TRANSACTIONS/CAREER NOTES: Selected by Dallas Cowboys in first round (first pick overall) of 1991 NFL draft. ... Signed by Cowboys (April 22, 1991). ... Granted unconditional free agency (February 16, 1996). ... Signed by Oakland Raiders (February 22, 1996). ... Released by Raiders (April 1, 2000). ... Signed by Green Bay Packers (April 20, 2000).
CHAMPIONSHIP GAME EXPERIENCE: Played in NFC championship game (1992-1995 seasons). ... Member of Super Bowl championship team (1992, 1993 and 1995 seasons).
HONORS: Named defensive tackle on THE SPORTING NEWS college All-America second team (1989). ... Outland Trophy winner (1990). ... Named defensive lineman on THE SPORTING NEWS college All-America first team (1990). ... Played in Pro Bowl (1993 season).
PRO STATISTICS: 1992—Recovered two fumbles for 26 yards and a touchdown. 1993—Recovered two fumbles. 1994—Recovered one fumble. 1999—Intercepted one pass for two yards and recovered one fumble.

Year Team	G	GS	SACKS
1991—Dallas NFL	16	7	4.5
1992—Dallas NFL	14	13	2.5
1993—Dallas NFL	16	12	2.5
1994—Dallas NFL	16	16	3.0
1995—Dallas NFL	13	13	2.0
1996—Oakland NFL	16	16	2.0
1997—Oakland NFL	16	16	4.5
1998—Oakland NFL	15	15	2.0
1999—Oakland NFL	16	16	1.5
Pro totals (9 years)	138	124	24.5

M

MASLOWSKI, MIKE   LB   CHIEFS

PERSONAL: Born July 11, 1974, in Thorp, Wis. ... 6-1/246. ... Full name: Michael John Maslowski.
HIGH SCHOOL: Thorp (Wis.).
COLLEGE: Wisconsin-La Crosse.
TRANSACTIONS/CAREER NOTES: Signed as non-drafted free agent by San Diego Chargers (April 21, 1997). ... Released by Chargers (August 1997). ... Played for San Jose Sabercats of Arena League (1998). ... Signed by Kansas City Chiefs (January 12, 1999). ... Assigned by Chiefs to Barcelona Dragons in 1999 NFL Europe enhancement allocation program (February 22, 1999).
PLAYING EXPERIENCE: Barcelona NFLE, 1999; Kansas City NFL, 1999. ... Games/Games started: NFLE 1999 (games played unavailable); NFL 1999 (15/0).
PRO STATISTICS: NFLE: 1999—Intercepted four passes for 56 yards and one touchdown and credited with two sacks.

MASON, DERRICK   WR   TITANS

PERSONAL: Born January 17, 1974, in Detroit. ... 5-10/188. ... Full name: Derrick James Mason.
HIGH SCHOOL: Mumford (Detroit).
COLLEGE: Michigan State.
TRANSACTIONS/CAREER NOTES: Selected by Houston Oilers in fourth round (98th pick overall) of 1997 NFL draft. ... Oilers franchise moved to Tennessee for 1997 season. ... Signed by Oilers (July 19, 1997). ... Oilers franchise renamed Tennessee Titans for 1999 season (December 26, 1998). ... Granted free agency (February 11, 2000).
CHAMPIONSHIP GAME EXPERIENCE: Played in AFC championship game (1999 season). ... Played in Super Bowl XXXIV (1999 season).
PRO STATISTICS: 1997—Rushed once for minus seven yards. 1998—Recovered one fumble.
SINGLE GAME HIGHS (regular season): Receptions—4 (December 20, 1998, vs. Green Bay); yards—75 (December 26, 1998, vs. Minnesota); and touchdown receptions—2 (December 20, 1998, vs. Green Bay).

Year Team	G	GS	RECEIVING No.	Yds.	Avg.	TD	PUNT RETURNS No.	Yds.	Avg.	TD	KICKOFF RETURNS No.	Yds.	Avg.	TD	TOTALS TD	2pt.	Pts.	Fum.
1997—Tennessee NFL	16	2	14	186	13.3	0	13	95	7.3	0	26	551	21.2	0	0	0	0	0
1998—Tennessee NFL	16	0	25	333	13.3	3	31	228	7.4	0	8	154	19.3	0	3	0	18	1
1999—Tennessee NFL	13	0	8	89	11.1	0	26	225	8.7	1	41	805	19.6	0	1	0	6	0
Pro totals (3 years)	45	2	47	608	12.9	3	70	548	7.8	1	75	1510	20.1	0	4	0	24	6

MASON, EDDIE   LB   REDSKINS

PERSONAL: Born January 9, 1972, in Siler City, N.C. ... 6-0/236. ... Full name: Eddie Lee Mason.
HIGH SCHOOL: Jordan-Matthews (Siler City, N.C.).
COLLEGE: North Carolina.
TRANSACTIONS/CAREER NOTES: Selected by New York Jets in sixth round (178th pick overall) of 1995 NFL draft. ... Signed by Jets (June 14, 1995). ... On injured reserve with knee injury (August 20, 1996-entire season). ... Granted unconditional free agency (February 14, 1997). ... Signed by Tampa Bay Buccaneers (April 21, 1997). ... Released by Buccaneers (August 17, 1997). ... Signed by Carolina Panthers (March 4, 1998). ... Released by Panthers (August 24, 1998). ... Signed by Jacksonville Jaguars (December 2, 1998). ... Released by Jaguars (September 5, 1999). ... Signed by Washington Redskins (September 21, 1999). ... Granted free agency (February 11, 2000). ... Re-signed by Redskins (March 23, 2000).
PLAYING EXPERIENCE: New York Jets NFL, 1995; Jacksonville NFL, 1998; Washington NFL, 1999. ... Games/Games started: 1995 (15/0), 1998 (4/0), 1999 (14/0). Total: 33/0.

MATHEWS, JASON   OT   TITANS

PERSONAL: Born February 9, 1971, in Orange, Texas. ... 6-5/304. ... Full name: Samuel Jason Mathews.
HIGH SCHOOL: Bridge City (Texas).
COLLEGE: Brigham Young, then Texas A&M.
TRANSACTIONS/CAREER NOTES: Selected by Indianapolis Colts in third round (67th pick overall) of 1994 NFL draft. ... Signed by Colts (July 23, 1994). ... Granted free agency (February 14, 1997). ... Re-signed by Colts (April 30, 1997). ... Granted unconditional free agency (February 13, 1998). ... Signed by Tampa Bay Buccaneers (May 7, 1998). ... Released by Buccaneers (August 30, 1998). ... Signed by Tennessee Oilers (September 1, 1998). ... Oilers franchise renamed Tennessee Titans for 1999 season (December 26, 1998).
PLAYING EXPERIENCE: Indianapolis NFL, 1994-1997; Tennessee NFL, 1998 and 1999. ... Games/Games started: 1994 (10/0), 1995 (16/16), 1996 (16/15), 1997 (16/0), 1998 (3/0), 1999 (16/0). Total: 66/31.
CHAMPIONSHIP GAME EXPERIENCE: Played in AFC championship game (1995 and 1999 seasons). ... Member of Titans for Super Bowl XXXIV (1999 season); did not play.
PRO STATISTICS: 1996—Recovered one fumble.

MATHIS, KEVIN   CB   SAINTS

PERSONAL: Born April 9, 1974, in Gainesville, Texas ... 5-9/181.
HIGH SCHOOL: Gainesville (Texas).
COLLEGE: East Texas State.
TRANSACTIONS/CAREER NOTES: Signed as non-drafted free agent by Dallas Cowboys (April 24, 1997). ... Granted free agency (February 11, 2000). ... Re-signed by Cowboys (April 26, 2000). ... Traded by Cowboys to New Orleans Saints for LB Chris Bordano (April 26, 2000).
PRO STATISTICS: 1997—Recovered two fumbles. 1998—Recovered four fumbles for six yards. 1999—Recovered one fumble.

			PUNT RETURNS				KICKOFF RETURNS				TOTALS			
Year Team	G	GS	No.	Yds.	Avg.	TD	No.	Yds.	Avg.	TD	TD	2pt.	Pts.	Fum.
1997—Dallas NFL	16	3	11	91	8.3	0	0	0	0.0	0	0	0	0	2
1998—Dallas NFL	13	4	2	3	1.5	0	25	621	24.8	0	0	0	0	2
1999—Dallas NFL	8	4	0	0	0.0	0	18	408	22.7	0	0	0	0	1
Pro totals (3 years)	37	11	13	94	7.2	0	43	1029	23.9	0	0	0	0	5

M

MATHIS, TERANCE   WR   FALCONS

PERSONAL: Born June 7, 1967, in Detroit. ... 5-10/185. ... Cousin of Jason Ferguson, defensive tackle, New York Jets.
HIGH SCHOOL: Redan (Stone Mountain, Ga.).
COLLEGE: New Mexico.
TRANSACTIONS/CAREER NOTES: Selected by New York Jets in sixth round (140th pick overall) of 1990 NFL draft. ... Signed by Jets (July 12, 1990). ... Granted unconditional free agency (February 17, 1994). ... Signed by Atlanta Falcons (May 3, 1994). ... Granted unconditional free agency (February 16, 1996). ... Re-signed by Falcons (April 30, 1996).
CHAMPIONSHIP GAME EXPERIENCE: Played in NFC championship game (1998 season). ... Played in Super Bowl XXXIII (1998 season).
HONORS: Named wide receiver on The Sporting News college All-America first team (1989). ... Played in Pro Bowl (1994 season).
RECORDS: Holds NFL career record for most two-point conversions—6.
PRO STATISTICS: 1990—Fumbled once. 1991—Fumbled four times and recovered one fumble. 1992—Fumbled twice and recovered one fumble. 1993—Fumbled five times and recovered one fumble. 1994—Recovered one fumble. 1995—Fumbled once. 1996—Recovered one fumble. 1998—Recovered two fumbles.
SINGLE GAME HIGHS (regular season): Receptions—13 (September 18, 1994, vs. Kansas City); yards—198 (December 13, 1998, vs. New Orleans); and touchdown receptions—3 (November 19, 1995, vs. St. Louis).
STATISTICAL PLATEAUS: 100-yard receiving games: 1992 (1), 1994 (5), 1995 (2), 1996 (2), 1997 (1), 1998 (3), 1999 (1). Total: 15.
MISCELLANEOUS: Holds Atlanta Falcons all-time records for most receptions (465).

			RUSHING				RECEIVING				PUNT RETURNS				KICKOFF RETURNS				TOTALS		
Year Team	G	GS	Att.	Yds.	Avg.	TD	No.	Yds.	Avg.	TD	No.	Yds.	Avg.	TD	No.	Yds.	Avg.	TD	TD	2pt.	Pts.
1990—N.Y. Jets NFL	16	1	2	9	4.5	0	19	245	12.9	0	11	165	15.0	†1	43	787	18.3	0	1	0	6
1991—N.Y. Jets NFL	16	0	1	19	19.0	0	28	329	11.8	1	23	157	6.8	0	29	599	20.7	0	1	0	6
1992—N.Y. Jets NFL	16	1	3	25	8.3	1	22	316	14.4	3	2	24	12.0	0	28	492	17.6	0	4	0	24
1993—N.Y. Jets NFL	16	3	2	20	10.0	0	24	352	14.7	0	14	99	7.1	0	7	102	14.6	0	1	0	6
1994—Atlanta NFL	16	16	0	0	0.0	0	111	1342	12.1	11	0	0	0.0	0	0	0	0.0	0	11	∞2	70
1995—Atlanta NFL	14	12	0	0	0.0	0	78	1039	13.3	9	0	0	0.0	0	0	0	0.0	0	9	*3	60
1996—Atlanta NFL	16	16	0	0	0.0	0	69	771	11.2	7	3	19	6.3	0	0	0	0.0	0	7	1	44
1997—Atlanta NFL	16	16	3	35	11.7	0	62	802	12.9	6	0	0	0.0	0	0	0	0.0	0	6	0	36
1998—Atlanta NFL	16	16	1	-6	-6.0	0	64	1136	17.8	11	1	0	0.0	0	0	0	0.0	0	11	0	66
1999—Atlanta NFL	16	16	1	0	0.0	0	81	1016	12.5	6	0	0	0.0	0	0	0	0.0	0	6	0	36
Pro totals (10 years)	158	97	13	102	7.8	2	558	7348	13.2	54	54	464	8.6	1	107	1980	18.5	0	57	6	354

MATTHEWS, BRUCE   G/C   TITANS

PERSONAL: Born August 8, 1961, in Raleigh, N.C. ... 6-5/305. ... Full name: Bruce Rankin Matthews. ... Son of Clay Matthews Sr., defensive end/tackle with San Francisco 49ers (1950 and 1953-55); and brother of Clay Matthews Jr., linebacker with Cleveland Browns (1978-93) and Atlanta Falcons (1994-96).
HIGH SCHOOL: Arcadia (Calif.).
COLLEGE: Southern California (degree in industrial engineering, 1983).
TRANSACTIONS/CAREER NOTES: Selected by Los Angeles Express in 1983 USFL territorial draft. ... Selected by Houston Oilers in first round (ninth pick overall) of 1983 NFL draft. ... Signed by Oilers (July 24, 1983). ... Granted free agency (February 1, 1987). ... On reserve/unsigned list (August 31-November 3, 1987). ... Re-signed by Oilers (November 4, 1987). ... Granted roster exemption (November 4-7, 1987). ... Granted unconditional free agency (February 17, 1995). ... Re-signed by Oilers (August 8, 1995). ... Oilers franchise moved to Tennessee for 1997 season. ... Oilers franchise renamed Tennessee Titans for 1999 season (December 26, 1998). ... Granted unconditional free agency (February 12, 1999). ... Re-signed by Titans (May 13, 1999).
PLAYING EXPERIENCE: Houston NFL, 1983-1996; Tennessee NFL, 1997-1999. ... Games/Games started: 1983 (16/15), 1984 (16/16), 1985 (16/16), 1986 (16/16), 1987 (8/5), 1988 (16/16), 1989 (16/16), 1990 (16/16), 1991 (16/16), 1992 (16/16), 1993 (16/16), 1994 (16/16), 1995 (16/16), 1996 (16/16), 1997 (16/16), 1998 (16/16), 1999 (16/16). Total: 264/260.
CHAMPIONSHIP GAME EXPERIENCE: Played in AFC championship game (1999 season). ... Played in Super Bowl XXXIV (1999 season).
HONORS: Named guard on THE SPORTING NEWS college All-America first team (1982). ... Named guard on THE SPORTING NEWS NFL All-Pro team (1988-1990, 1992 and 1998). ... Played in Pro Bowl (1988-1994, 1996, 1997 and 1999 seasons). ... Named center on THE SPORTING NEWS NFL All-Pro team (1993). ... Named to play in Pro Bowl (1995 season); replaced by Will Shields due to injury. ... Named to play in Pro Bowl (1998 season); replaced by Mark Schlereth due to injury.
PRO STATISTICS: 1985—Recovered three fumbles. 1986—Recovered one fumble for seven yards. 1989—Fumbled twice and recovered one fumble for minus 29 yards. 1990—Recovered one fumble. 1991—Fumbled once and recovered one fumble for minus three yards. 1994—Fumbled twice. 1997—Recovered two fumbles. 1998—Recovered one fumble.

MATTHEWS, SHANE   QB

PERSONAL: Born June 1, 1970, in Pascagoula, Miss. ... 6-3/196. ... Full name: Michael Shane Matthews.
HIGH SCHOOL: Pascagoula (Miss.).
COLLEGE: Florida.
TRANSACTIONS/CAREER NOTES: Signed as non-drafted free agent by Chicago Bears (April 29, 1993). ... Released by Bears (August 30, 1993). ... Re-signed by Bears to practice squad (September 1, 1993). ... Activated (October 8, 1993); did not play. ... Active for two games (1994); did not play. ... Released by Bears (September 15, 1995). ... Re-signed by Bears (February 12, 1996). ... Released by Bears (June 7, 1996). ... Re-signed by Bears (October 9, 1996). ... Granted unconditional free agency (February 14, 1997). ... Assigned by Bears to Rhein Fire in 1997 World League enhancement allocation program (February 19, 1997). ... Signed by Carolina Panthers (August 25, 1997). ... Released by Panthers (September 17, 1997). ... Re-signed by Panthers (October 16, 1997). ... Active for two games (1997); did not play. ... Granted unconditional free agency (February 13, 1998). ... Re-signed by Panthers (March 19, 1998). ... Active for 12 games (1998); did not play. ... Granted unconditional free agency (February 12, 1999). ... Signed by Bears (April 3, 1999). ... Granted unconditional free agency (February 11, 2000).
PRO STATISTICS: 1999—Fumbled seven times and recovered two fumbles for minus 14 yards.
SINGLE GAME HIGHS (regular season): Attempts—42 (September 19, 1999, vs. Seattle); completions—25 (October 3, 1999, vs. New Orleans); yards—266 (December 26, 1999, vs. St. Louis); and touchdown passes—2 (December 26, 1999, vs. St. Louis).
MISCELLANEOUS: Regular-season record as starting NFL quarterback: 3-4 (.429).

| | | | | | | PASSING | | | | | | RUSHING | | | | TOTALS | |
Year Team	G	GS	Att.	Cmp.	Pct.	Yds.	TD	Int.	Avg.	Rat.	Att.	Yds.	Avg.	TD	TD	2pt.	Pts.
1993—Chicago NFL						Did not play.											
1994—Chicago NFL						Did not play.											
1995—						Did not play.											
1996—Chicago NFL	2	0	17	13	76.5	158	1	0	9.29	124.1	1	2	2.0	1	0	0	0
1997—Carolina NFL						Did not play.											
1998—Carolina NFL						Did not play.											
1999—Chicago NFL	8	7	275	167	60.7	1645	10	6	5.98	80.6	14	31	2.2	0	0	0	0
Pro totals (2 years)	10	7	292	180	61.6	1803	11	6	6.17	83.2	15	33	2.2	1	0	0	0

MAUMAU, VILIAMI   DT   PANTHERS

PERSONAL: Born April 3, 1975, in Fo'ui, Tonga. ... 6-2/302. ... Full name: Viliami Akau`ola Maumau. ... Cousin of Chris Maumalanga, defensive tackle with New York Giants (1994) and Arizona Cardinals (1995-96); and cousin of Siupeli Malamala, guard/tackle, New York Jets. ... Name pronounced vil-lee-AH-mee MOW-MOW.
HIGH SCHOOL: St. Louis (Honolulu).
COLLEGE: Colorado.
TRANSACTIONS/CAREER NOTES: Selected by Carolina Panthers in seventh round (196th pick overall) of 1998 NFL draft. ... Signed by Panthers (July 15, 1998). ... Released by Panthers (August 30, 1998). ... Re-signed by Panthers to practice squad (September 1, 1998). ... Released by Panthers (October 13, 1998). ... Signed by Denver Broncos to practice squad (November 4, 1998). ... Released by Broncos (January 8, 1999). ... Re-signed by Broncos to practice squad (January 13, 1999). ... Released by Broncos (September 5, 1999). ... Re-signed by Broncos to practice squad (September 7, 1999). ... Released by Broncos (September 14, 1999). ... Re-signed by Broncos to practice squad (September 22, 1999). ... Released by Broncos (September 28, 1999). ... Re-signed by Broncos to practice squad (November 2, 1999). ... Signed by Panthers off Broncos practice squad (December 7, 1999).
PLAYING EXPERIENCE: Carolina NFL, 1999. ... Games/Games started: 1999 (1/0).

MAWAE, KEVIN   C   JETS

PERSONAL: Born January 23, 1971, in Savannah, Ga. ... 6-4/305. ... Full name: Kevin James Mawae. ... Name pronounced ma-WHY.
HIGH SCHOOL: Leesville (La.).
COLLEGE: Louisiana State (degree in general studies).

TRANSACTIONS/CAREER NOTES: Selected by Seattle Seahawks in second round (36th pick overall) of 1994 NFL draft. ... Signed by Seahawks (July 21, 1994). ... Granted free agency (February 14, 1997). ... Re-signed by Seahawks (May 5, 1997). ... Granted unconditional free agency (February 13, 1998). ... Signed by New York Jets (February 19, 1998).
PLAYING EXPERIENCE: Seattle NFL, 1994-1997; New York Jets NFL, 1998 and 1999. ... Games/Games started: 1994 (14/11), 1995 (16/16), 1996 (16/16), 1997 (16/16), 1998 (16/16), 1999 (16/16). Total: 94/91.
CHAMPIONSHIP GAME EXPERIENCE: Played in AFC championship game (1998 season).
HONORS: Named center on THE SPORTING NEWS NFL All-Pro team (1999). ... Played in Pro Bowl (1999 season).
PRO STATISTICS: 1994—Recovered one fumble. 1996—Recovered two fumbles. 1997—Recovered two fumbles.

MAY, DEEMS   TE   SEAHAWKS

PERSONAL: Born March 6, 1969, in Lexington, N.C. ... 6-4/263. ... Full name: Bert Deems May Jr.
HIGH SCHOOL: Lexington (N.C.) Senior.
COLLEGE: North Carolina (degree in political science, 1991).
TRANSACTIONS/CAREER NOTES: Selected by San Diego Chargers in seventh round (174th pick overall) of 1992 NFL draft. ... Signed by Chargers (July 16, 1992). ... On injured reserve with foot injury (November 2, 1994-remainder of season). ... Granted free agency (February 17, 1995). ... Re-signed by Chargers (May 19, 1995). ... On physically unable to perform list with foot injury (July 18-October 10, 1995). ... Granted unconditional free agency (February 14, 1997). ... Signed by Seattle Seahawks (May 7, 1997).
PRO STATISTICS: 1996—Recovered one fumble. 1997—Returned one kickoff for eight yards.
SINGLE GAME HIGHS (regular season): Receptions—4 (November 24, 1996, vs. Kansas City); yards—44 (November 17, 1996, vs. Tampa Bay); and touchdown receptions—1 (December 27, 1998, vs. Denver).

| | | | RECEIVING | | | | TOTALS | | | |
Year Team	G	GS	No.	Yds.	Avg.	TD	TD	2pt.	Pts.	Fum.
1992—San Diego NFL	16	6	0	0	0.0	0	0	0	0	0
1993—San Diego NFL	15	1	0	0	0.0	0	0	0	0	0
1994—San Diego NFL	5	2	2	22	11.0	0	0	0	0	0
1995—San Diego NFL	5	0	0	0	0.0	0	0	0	0	0
1996—San Diego NFL	16	12	19	188	9.9	0	0	0	0	0
1997—Seattle NFL	16	0	2	21	10.5	0	0	0	0	0
1998—Seattle NFL	16	1	3	7	2.3	1	1	0	6	0
1999—Seattle NFL	15	0	0	0	0.0	0	0	0	0	1
Pro totals (8 years)	104	22	26	238	9.2	1	1	0	6	1

MAYBERRY, JERMANE   G/OT   EAGLES

PERSONAL: Born August 29, 1973, in Floresville, Texas. ... 6-4/325. ... Full name: Jermane Timothy Mayberry.
HIGH SCHOOL: Floresville (Texas).
JUNIOR COLLEGE: Navarro College (Texas).
COLLEGE: Texas A&M-Kingsville.
TRANSACTIONS/CAREER NOTES: Selected by Philadelphia Eagles in first round (25th pick overall) of 1996 NFL draft. ... Signed by Eagles (June 13, 1996).
PLAYING EXPERIENCE: Philadelphia NFL, 1996-1999. ... Games/Games started: 1996 (3/1), 1997 (16/16), 1998 (15/10), 1999 (13/5). Total: 47/32.
PRO STATISTICS: 1997—Recovered one fumble.

M

MAYBERRY, TONY   C

PERSONAL: Born December 8, 1967, in Wurzburg, West Germany. ... 6-4/282. ... Full name: Eino Anthony Mayberry.
HIGH SCHOOL: Hayfield (Alexandria, Va.).
COLLEGE: Wake Forest (degree in sociology, 1989).
TRANSACTIONS/CAREER NOTES: Selected by Tampa Bay Buccaneers in fourth round (108th pick overall) of 1990 NFL draft. ... Signed by Buccaneers (July 19, 1990). ... Granted free agency (March 1, 1993). ... Tendered offer sheet by New England Patriots (March 11, 1993). ... Offer matched by Buccaneers (March 18, 1993). ... Granted unconditional free agency (February 16, 1996). ... Re-signed by Buccaneers (February 27, 1996). ... Granted unconditional free agency (February 11, 2000).
PLAYING EXPERIENCE: Tampa Bay NFL, 1990-1999. ... Games/Games started: 1990 (16/1), 1991 (16/16), 1992 (16/16), 1993 (16/16), 1994 (16/16), 1995 (16/16), 1996 (16/16), 1997 (16/16), 1998 (16/16), 1999 (16/16). Total: 160/145.
CHAMPIONSHIP GAME EXPERIENCE: Played in NFC championship game (1999 season).
HONORS: Played in Pro Bowl (1997-1999 seasons).
PRO STATISTICS: 1991—Fumbled three times for minus 17 yards. 1993—Fumbled once and recovered one fumble for minus six yards. 1994—Recovered one fumble. 1996—Recovered one fumble. 1999—Fumbled once for minus 15 yards.

MAYES, ALONZO   TE   BEARS

PERSONAL: Born June 4, 1975, in Oklahoma City. ... 6-4/268.
HIGH SCHOOL: Douglass (Oklahoma City).
JUNIOR COLLEGE: Rose State College (Okla.); did not play football.
COLLEGE: Oklahoma State.
TRANSACTIONS/CAREER NOTES: Selected by Chicago Bears in fourth round (94th pick overall) of 1998 NFL draft. ... Signed by Bears (August 2, 1998).
HONORS: Named tight end on THE SPORTING NEWS college All-America first team (1997).
SINGLE GAME HIGHS (regular season): Receptions—4 (October 18, 1998, vs. Dallas); yards—57 (October 18, 1998, vs. Dallas); and touchdown receptions—1 (November 25, 1999, vs. Detroit).

Year Team	G	GS	RECEIVING				TOTALS			
			No.	Yds.	Avg.	TD	TD	2pt.	Pts.	Fum.
1998—Chicago NFL	16	16	21	217	10.3	0	0	0	0	2
1999—Chicago NFL	16	9	8	82	10.3	1	1	0	6	0
Pro totals (2 years)	32	25	29	299	10.3	1	1	0	6	2

MAYES, DERRICK　　　WR　　　SEAHAWKS

PERSONAL: Born January 28, 1974, in Indianapolis. ... 6-0/205. ... Full name: Derrick Binet Mayes.
HIGH SCHOOL: North Central (Indianapolis).
COLLEGE: Notre Dame (degree in communications).
TRANSACTIONS/CAREER NOTES: Selected by Green Bay Packers in second round (56th pick overall) of 1996 NFL draft. ... Signed by Packers (July 17, 1996). ... Granted free agency (February 12, 1999). ... Re-signed by Packers (June 21, 1999). ... Traded by Packers to Seattle Seahawks for seventh-round pick (DT Ron Moore) in 2000 draft (August 30, 1999). ... Granted unconditional free agency (February 11, 2000). ... Re-signed by Seahawks (February 25, 2000).
CHAMPIONSHIP GAME EXPERIENCE: Member of Packers for NFC championship game (1996 season); inactive. ... Member of Super Bowl championship team (1996 season); inactive. ... Played in NFC championship game (1997 season). ... Played in Super Bowl XXXII (1997 season).
PRO STATISTICS: 1997—Returned 14 punts for 141 yards. 1998—Returned one punt for nine yards.
SINGLE GAME HIGHS (regular season): Receptions—7 (September 19, 1999, vs. Chicago); yards—137 (September 19, 1999, vs. Chicago); and touchdown receptions—3 (September 27, 1998, vs. Carolina).
STATISTICAL PLATEAUS: 100-yard receiving games: 1997 (1), 1999 (2). Total: 3.

Year Team	G	GS	RECEIVING				TOTALS			
			No.	Yds.	Avg.	TD	TD	2pt.	Pts.	Fum.
1996—Green Bay NFL	7	0	6	46	7.7	2	2	0	12	0
1997—Green Bay NFL	12	3	18	290	16.1	0	0	0	0	0
1998—Green Bay NFL	10	6	30	394	13.1	3	3	0	18	1
1999—Seattle NFL	16	15	62	829	13.4	10	10	0	60	1
Pro totals (4 years)	45	24	116	1559	13.4	15	15	0	90	2

MAYNARD, BRAD　　　P　　　GIANTS

PERSONAL: Born February 9, 1974, in Tipton, Ind. ... 6-1/190. ... Full name: Bradley Alan Maynard.
HIGH SCHOOL: Sheridan (Ind.).
COLLEGE: Ball State.
TRANSACTIONS/CAREER NOTES: Selected by New York Giants in third round (95th pick overall) of 1997 NFL draft. ... Signed by Giants (July 19, 1997). ... Granted free agency (February 11, 2000).
HONORS: Named punter on THE SPORTING NEWS college All-America second team (1996).
PRO STATISTICS: 1998—Rushed once for minus five yards and attempted one pass without a completion.

Year Team	G	PUNTING					
		No.	Yds.	Avg.	Net avg.	In. 20	Blk.
1997—New York Giants NFL	16	*111	*4531	40.8	34.6	*33	1
1998—New York Giants NFL	16	101	*4566	45.2	37.8	∞33	0
1999—New York Giants NFL	16	89	3651	41.0	35.1	‡31	0
Pro totals (3 years)	48	301	12748	42.4	35.8	97	1

MAYS, KIVUUSAMA　　　LB　　　PACKERS

PERSONAL: Born January 7, 1975, in Anniston, Ala. ... 6-3/248. ... Name pronounced KAAH-vaah-you-SUH-muh.
HIGH SCHOOL: Cole (San Antonio), then Anniston (Ala.).
COLLEGE: North Carolina.
TRANSACTIONS/CAREER NOTES: Selected by Minnesota Vikings in fourth round (110th pick overall) of 1998 NFL draft. ... Signed by Vikings (June 26, 1998). ... Claimed on waivers by Green Bay Packers (December 8, 1999).
PLAYING EXPERIENCE: Minnesota NFL, 1998; Minnesota (11)-Green Bay (3) NFL, 1999. ... Games/Games started: 1998 (16/0), 1999 (Min.-11/0; G.B.-3/0; Total: 14/0). Total: 30/0.
CHAMPIONSHIP GAME EXPERIENCE: Member of Vikings for NFC championship game (1998 season); inactive.
PRO STATISTICS: 1998—Recovered one fumble.

McAFEE, FRED　　　RB

PERSONAL: Born June 20, 1968, in Philadelphia, Miss. ... 5-10/198. ... Full name: Fred Lee McAfee.
HIGH SCHOOL: Philadelphia (Miss.).
COLLEGE: Mississippi College (degree in mass communications, 1990).
TRANSACTIONS/CAREER NOTES: Selected by New Orleans Saints in sixth round (154th pick overall) of 1991 NFL draft. ... Signed by Saints (July 14, 1991). ... Released by Saints (August 26, 1991). ... Re-signed by Saints to practice squad (August 28, 1991). ... Activated (October 18, 1991). ... On injured reserve with shoulder injury (December 15, 1992-remainder of season). ... Granted free agency (February 17, 1994). ... Signed by Arizona Cardinals (August 2, 1994). ... Released by Cardinals (October 31, 1994). ... Signed by Pittsburgh Steelers (November 9, 1994). ... Granted unconditional free agency (February 16, 1996). ... Re-signed by Steelers (April 12, 1996). ... Granted unconditional free agency (February 12, 1999). ... Signed by Kansas City Chiefs (July 30, 1999). ... Released by Chiefs (August 31, 1999). ... Signed by Tampa Bay Buccaneers (December 28, 1999). ... Granted unconditional free agency (February 11, 2000).
CHAMPIONSHIP GAME EXPERIENCE: Played in AFC championship game (1994, 1995 and 1997 seasons). ... Played in Super Bowl XXX (1995 season). ... Played in NFC championship game (1999 season).
PRO STATISTICS: 1995—Recovered one fumble. 1998—Recovered a blocked punt in end zone for a touchdown.

SINGLE GAME HIGHS (regular season): Attempts—28 (November 24, 1991, vs. Atlanta); yards—138 (November 24, 1991, vs. Atlanta); and rushing touchdowns—1 (September 10, 1995, vs. Houston).
STATISTICAL PLATEAUS: 100-yard rushing games: 1991 (1).

			RUSHING				RECEIVING				KICKOFF RETURNS				TOTALS			
Year Team	G	GS	Att.	Yds.	Avg.	TD	No.	Yds.	Avg.	TD	No.	Yds.	Avg.	TD	TD	2pt.	Pts.	Fum.
1991—New Orleans NFL	9	0	109	494	4.5	2	1	8	8.0	0	1	14	14.0	0	2	0	12	2
1992—New Orleans NFL	14	1	39	114	2.9	1	1	16	16.0	0	19	393	20.7	0	1	0	6	0
1993—New Orleans NFL	15	4	51	160	3.1	1	1	3	3.0	0	28	580	20.7	0	1	0	6	3
1994—Arizona NFL	7	0	2	-5	-2.5	0	1	4	4.0	0	7	113	16.1	0	1	0	6	1
—Pittsburgh NFL	6	0	16	56	3.5	1	0	0	0.0	0	0	0	0.0	0	1	0	6	0
1995—Pittsburgh NFL............	16	1	39	156	4.0	1	15	88	5.9	0	5	56	11.2	0	1	0	6	0
1996—Pittsburgh NFL............	14	0	7	17	2.4	0	5	21	4.2	0	0	0	0.0	0	0	0	0	0
1997—Pittsburgh NFL............	14	0	13	41	3.2	0	2	44	22.0	0	0	0	0.0	0	0	0	0	1
1998—Pittsburgh NFL............	14	0	18	111	6.2	0	9	27	3.0	0	1	10	10.0	0	1	0	6	0
1999—Tampa Bay NFL..........	1	0	0	0	0.0	0	0	0	0.0	0	0	0	0.0	0	0	0	0	0
Pro totals (9 years)...............	110	6	294	1144	3.9	7	35	211	6.0	0	61	1166	19.1	0	8	0	48	7

McALISTER, CHRIS   CB   RAVENS

PERSONAL: Born June 14, 1977, in Pasedena, Calif. ... 6-1/206. ... Full name: Christopher James McAlister. ... Son of James McAlister, running back with Philadelphia Eagles (1975 and 1976) and New England Patriots (1978).
HIGH SCHOOL: Pasadena (Calif.).
JUNIOR COLLEGE: Mt. San Antonio College (Calif.).
COLLEGE: Arizona.
TRANSACTIONS/CAREER NOTES: Selected by Baltimore Ravens in first round (10th pick overall) of 1999 NFL draft. ... Signed by Ravens (July 23, 1999).
HONORS: Named cornerback on THE SPORTING NEWS college All-America third team (1997). ... Named cornerback on THE SPORTING NEWS college All-America first team (1998).
PRO STATISTICS: 1999—Returned one kickoff for 12 yards.

			INTERCEPTIONS			
Year Team	G	GS	No.	Yds.	Avg.	TD
1999—Baltimore NFL	16	12	5	28	5.6	0

McBRIDE, TOD   S   PACKERS

PERSONAL: Born January 26, 1976, in Los Angeles. ... 6-1/208. ... Full name: Tod Anthony McBride.
HIGH SCHOOL: Walnut (Calif.).
COLLEGE: UCLA.
TRANSACTIONS/CAREER NOTES: Signed as non-drafted free agent by Seattle Seahawks (April 23, 1999). ... Claimed on waivers by Green Bay Packers (June 23, 1999).
PLAYING EXPERIENCE: Green Bay NFL, 1999. ... Games/Games started: 1999 (15/0).
PRO STATISTICS: 1999—Recovered two fumbles.

McBURROWS, GERALD   S   FALCONS

PERSONAL: Born October 7, 1973, in Detroit. ... 5-11/210. ... Full name: Gerald Lance McBurrows.
HIGH SCHOOL: Martin Luther King (Detroit).
COLLEGE: Kansas.
TRANSACTIONS/CAREER NOTES: Selected by St. Louis Rams in seventh round (214th pick overall) of 1995 NFL draft. ... Signed by Rams (June 16, 1995). ... On injured reserve with knee injury (October 29, 1997-remainder of season). ... Granted free agency (February 13, 1998). ... Re-signed by Rams (April 24, 1998). ... On injured reserve with knee injury (November 17, 1998-remainder of season). ... Granted unconditional free agency (February 12, 1999). ... Signed by Atlanta Falcons (March 2, 1999).
PLAYING EXPERIENCE: St. Louis NFL, 1995-1998; Atlanta NFL, 1999. ... Games/Games started: 1995 (14/3), 1996 (16/7), 1997 (8/3), 1998 (10/0), 1999 (16/4). Total: 64/17.
PRO STATISTICS: 1995—Credited with one sack. 1996—Intercepted one pass for three yards. 1998—Recovered one fumble. 1999—Intercepted two passes for 64 yards, credited with one sack and recovered one fumble.

McCAFFREY, ED   WR   BRONCOS

PERSONAL: Born August 17, 1968, in Waynesboro, Pa. ... 6-5/215. ... Full name: Edward McCaffrey.
HIGH SCHOOL: Allentown (Pa.) Central Catholic.
COLLEGE: Stanford.
TRANSACTIONS/CAREER NOTES: Selected by New York Giants in third round (83rd pick overall) of 1991 NFL draft. ... Signed by Giants (July 23, 1991). ... Granted free agency (February 17, 1994). ... Signed by San Francisco 49ers (July 24, 1994). ... Granted unconditional free agency (February 17, 1995). ... Signed by Denver Broncos (March 7, 1995).
CHAMPIONSHIP GAME EXPERIENCE: Played in NFC championship game (1994 season). ... Member of Super Bowl championship team (1994, 1997 and 1998 seasons). ... Played in AFC championship game (1997 and 1998 seasons).
HONORS: Named wide receiver on THE SPORTING NEWS college All-America second team (1990). ... Played in Pro Bowl (1998 season).
PRO STATISTICS: 1995—Rushed once for minus one yard. 1997—Recovered two fumbles.
SINGLE GAME HIGHS (regular season): Receptions—9 (November 8, 1998, vs. San Diego); yards—133 (November 8, 1998, vs. San Diego); and touchdown receptions—3 (September 13, 1999, vs. Miami).
STATISTICAL PLATEAUS: 100-yard receiving games: 1992 (1), 1997 (1), 1998 (4), 1999 (4). Total: 10.

Year Team	G	GS	RECEIVING				TOTALS			
			No.	Yds.	Avg.	TD	TD	2pt.	Pts.	Fum.
1991—New York Giants NFL	16	0	16	146	9.1	0	0	0	0	0
1992—New York Giants NFL	16	3	49	610	12.4	5	5	0	30	2
1993—New York Giants NFL	16	1	27	335	12.4	2	2	0	12	0
1994—San Francisco NFL	16	0	11	131	11.9	2	2	0	12	0
1995—Denver NFL	16	5	39	477	12.2	2	2	1	14	1
1996—Denver NFL	15	15	48	553	11.5	7	7	0	42	0
1997—Denver NFL	15	15	45	590	13.1	8	8	0	48	0
1998—Denver NFL	15	15	64	1053	16.5	▲10	10	1	62	1
1999—Denver NFL	15	15	71	1018	14.3	7	7	0	42	0
Pro totals (9 years)	140	69	370	4913	13.3	43	43	2	262	4

McCARDELL, KEENAN   WR   JAGUARS

PERSONAL: Born January 6, 1970, in Houston. ... 6-1/185. ... Full name: Keenan Wayne McCardell. ... Name pronounced mc-CAR-dell.
HIGH SCHOOL: Waltrip (Houston).
COLLEGE: UNLV (degree in business management, 1991).
TRANSACTIONS/CAREER NOTES: Selected by Washington Redskins in 12th round (326th pick overall) of 1991 NFL draft. ... Signed by Redskins for 1991 season. ... On injured reserve with knee injury (August 20, 1991-entire season). ... Granted unconditional free agency (February 1, 1992). ... Signed by Cleveland Browns (March 24, 1992). ... Released by Browns (September 1, 1992). ... Re-signed by Browns to practice squad (September 3, 1992). ... Activated (October 6, 1992). ... Released by Browns (October 13, 1992). ... Re-signed by Browns to practice squad (October 14, 1992). ... Activated (November 14, 1992). ... Released by Browns (November 19, 1992). ... Re-signed by Browns to practice squad (November 20, 1992). ... Activated (December 26, 1992). ... Released by Browns (September 22, 1993). ... Signed by Chicago Bears to practice squad (November 2, 1993). ... Signed by Browns off Bears practice squad (November 24, 1993). ... Granted free agency (February 17, 1994). ... Re-signed by Browns (March 4, 1994). ... Granted unconditional free agency (February 16, 1996). ... Signed by Jacksonville Jaguars (March 2, 1996).
CHAMPIONSHIP GAME EXPERIENCE: Played in AFC championship game (1996 and 1999 seasons).
HONORS: Played in Pro Bowl (1996 season).
PRO STATISTICS: 1995—Returned 13 punts for 93 yards and returned nine kickoffs for 161 yards. 1996—Returned one punt for two yards and recovered three fumbles. 1998—Returned one kickoff for 15 yards. 1999—Returned six punts for 41 yards, returned two kickoffs for 19 yards and recovered one fumble.
SINGLE GAME HIGHS (regular season): Receptions—16 (October 20, 1996, vs. St. Louis); yards—232 (October 20, 1996, vs. St. Louis); and touchdown receptions—2 (November 29, 1998, vs. Cincinnati).
STATISTICAL PLATEAUS: 100-yard receiving games: 1995 (1), 1996 (3), 1997 (4), 1998 (2), 1999 (3). Total: 13.

Year Team	G	GS	RECEIVING				TOTALS			
			No.	Yds.	Avg.	TD	TD	2pt.	Pts.	Fum.
1991—Washington NFL					Did not play.					
1992—Cleveland NFL	2	0	1	8	8.0	0	0	0	0	0
1993—Cleveland NFL	6	3	13	234	18.0	4	4	0	24	0
1994—Cleveland NFL	13	3	10	182	18.2	0	0	0	0	0
1995—Cleveland NFL	16	5	56	709	12.7	4	4	0	24	0
1996—Jacksonville NFL	16	15	85	1129	13.3	3	3	2	22	1
1997—Jacksonville NFL	16	16	85	1164	13.7	5	5	0	30	0
1998—Jacksonville NFL	15	15	64	892	13.9	6	6	1	38	0
1999—Jacksonville NFL	16	15	78	891	11.4	5	5	†1	32	1
Pro totals (8 years)	100	72	392	5209	13.3	27	27	4	170	2

McCLEON, DEXTER   CB   RAMS

PERSONAL: Born October 9, 1973, in Meridian, Miss. ... 5-10/195. ... Full name: Dexter Keith McCleon.
HIGH SCHOOL: Meridian (Miss.).
COLLEGE: Clemson (degree in management, 1996).
TRANSACTIONS/CAREER NOTES: Selected by St. Louis Rams in second round (40th pick overall) of 1997 NFL draft. ... Signed by Rams (July 3, 1997). ... Granted free agency (February 11, 2000).
CHAMPIONSHIP GAME EXPERIENCE: Played in NFC championship game (1999 season). ... Member of Super Bowl championship team (1999 season).
PRO STATISTICS: 1997—Credited with one sack. 1999—Credited with 1½ sacks.
MISCELLANEOUS: Selected by Minnesota Twins organization in 13th round of free-agent baseball draft (June 3, 1993); did not sign.

Year Team	G	GS	INTERCEPTIONS			
			No.	Yds.	Avg.	TD
1997—St. Louis NFL	16	1	1	0	0.0	0
1998—St. Louis NFL	15	6	2	29	14.5	0
1999—St. Louis NFL	15	15	4	17	4.3	0
Pro totals (3 years)	46	22	7	46	6.6	0

McCLESKEY, J.J.   CB   CARDINALS

PERSONAL: Born April 10, 1970, in Knoxville, Tenn. ... 5-8/180. ... Full name: Tommy Joe McCleskey.
HIGH SCHOOL: Karns Comprehensive (Knoxville, Tenn.).
COLLEGE: Tennessee (degree in political science, 1993).
TRANSACTIONS/CAREER NOTES: Signed as non-drafted free agent by New Orleans Saints (May 7, 1993). ... Released by Saints (August 24, 1993). ... Re-signed by Saints to practice squad (August 31, 1993). ... Activated (December 23, 1993). ... Released by Saints (August 23, 1994). ... Re-signed by Saints (September 20, 1994). ... On injured reserve with hamstring injury (October 16-18, 1996). ... Claimed on waivers by Arizona Cardinals (October 18, 1996). ... Granted free agency (February 14, 1997). ... Re-signed by Cardinals for 1997 season. ... Granted unconditional free agency (February 13, 1998). ... Re-signed by Cardinals (February 23, 1998).

M

PRO STATISTICS: 1994—Recovered one fumble. 1995—Returned one kickoff for no yards and recovered one fumble. 1997—Credited with one sack. 1999—Returned one punt for no yards.

				INTERCEPTIONS				TOTALS		
Year Team	G	GS	No.	Yds.	Avg.	TD	TD	2pt.	Pts.	Fum.
1994—New Orleans NFL	13	0	0	0	0.0	0	0	0	0	0
1995—New Orleans NFL	14	1	1	0	0.0	0	0	0	0	0
1996—New Orleans NFL	5	0	0	0	0.0	0	0	0	0	0
—Arizona NFL	5	0	0	0	0.0	0	0	0	0	0
1997—Arizona NFL	13	0	1	15	15.0	0	0	0	0	0
1998—Arizona NFL	12	0	1	1	1.0	0	0	0	0	0
1999—Arizona NFL	16	1	1	2	2.0	0	0	0	0	0
Pro totals (6 years)	78	2	4	18	4.5	0	0	0	0	0

McCOLLUM, ANDY　　　　G　　　　RAMS

PERSONAL: Born June 2, 1970, in Akron, Ohio. ... 6-4/295. ... Full name: Andrew Jon McCollum.
HIGH SCHOOL: Revere (Richfield, Ohio).
COLLEGE: Toledo.
TRANSACTIONS/CAREER NOTES: Played with Milwaukee Mustangs of Arena League (1994). ... Signed as non-drafted free agent by Cleveland Browns (June 1994). ... Released by Browns (August 28, 1994). ... Re-signed by Browns to practice squad (August 30, 1994). ... Signed by New Orleans Saints off Browns practice squad (November 15, 1994). ... Inactive for five games (1994). ... Assigned by Saints to Barcelona Dragons in 1995 World League enhancement allocation program (February 20, 1995). ... Granted unconditional free agency (February 12, 1999). ... Signed by St. Louis Rams (April 13, 1999). ... Granted unconditional free agency (February 11, 2000). ... Re-signed by Rams (February 22, 2000).
PLAYING EXPERIENCE: Barcelona W.L., 1995; New Orleans NFL, 1995-1998; St. Louis NFL, 1999. ... Games/Games started: W.L. 1995 (games played unavailable), NFL 1995 (11/9), 1996 (16/16), 1997 (16/16), 1998 (16/5), 1999 (16/2). Total NFL: 75/48.
CHAMPIONSHIP GAME EXPERIENCE: Played in NFC championship game (1999 season). ... Member of Super Bowl championship team (1999 season).
PRO STATISTICS: 1996—Recovered one fumble. 1998—Recovered one fumble. 1999—Returned one kickoff for three yards.

McCOMBS, TONY　　　　LB　　　　BROWNS

PERSONAL: Born August 24, 1974, in Hopkinsville, Ky. ... 6-2/256. ... Full name: Antonias Orlando McCombs.
HIGH SCHOOL: Christian County (Hopkinsville, Ky.).
COLLEGE: Eastern Kentucky.
TRANSACTIONS/CAREER NOTES: Selected by Arizona Cardinals in sixth round (188th pick overall) of 1997 NFL draft. ... Signed by Cardinals (June 2, 1997). ... Released by Cardinals (September 4, 1999). ... Signed by Cleveland Browns (January 10, 2000).
PLAYING EXPERIENCE: Arizona NFL, 1997 and 1998. ... Games/Games started: 1997 (12/0), 1998 (14/13). Total: 26/13.
PRO STATISTICS: 1998—Intercepted one pass for 14 yards and recovered one fumble.

McCORMACK, HURVIN　　　　DT

PERSONAL: Born April 6, 1972, in Brooklyn, N.Y. ... 6-5/275.
HIGH SCHOOL: New Dorp (Staten Island, N.Y.).
COLLEGE: Indiana.
TRANSACTIONS/CAREER NOTES: Signed as non-drafted free agent by Dallas Cowboys (April 28, 1994). ... Granted unconditional free agency (February 14, 1997). ... Re-signed by Cowboys (July 1997). ... Granted unconditional free agency (February 13, 1998). ... Re-signed by Cowboys (March 9, 1998). ... Selected by Cleveland Browns from Cowboys in NFL expansion draft (February 9, 1999). ... Granted unconditional free agency (February 11, 2000).
CHAMPIONSHIP GAME EXPERIENCE: Member of Cowboys for NFC championship game (1994 season); did not play. ... Played in NFC championship game (1995 season). ... Member of Super Bowl championship team (1995 season).
PRO STATISTICS: 1998—Recovered one fumble.

Year Team	G	GS	SACKS
1994—Dallas NFL	4	0	0.0
1995—Dallas NFL	14	2	2.0
1996—Dallas NFL	16	4	2.5
1997—Dallas NFL	13	0	0.5
1998—Dallas NFL	16	1	5.0
1999—Cleveland NFL	13	4	2.0
Pro totals (6 years)	76	11	12.0

McCOY, TONY　　　　DT

PERSONAL: Born June 10, 1969, in Orlando. ... 6-1/285. ... Full name: Anthony Bernard McCoy.
HIGH SCHOOL: Maynard Evans (Orlando).
COLLEGE: Florida.
TRANSACTIONS/CAREER NOTES: Selected by Indianapolis Colts in fourth round (105th pick overall) of 1992 NFL draft. ... Signed by Colts (July 17, 1992). ... Granted free agency (February 17, 1995). ... Re-signed by Colts (June 7, 1995). ... Released by Colts (June 2, 2000).
CHAMPIONSHIP GAME EXPERIENCE: Played in AFC championship game (1995 season).
PRO STATISTICS: 1992—Recovered one fumble. 1994—Recovered one fumble. 1996—Recovered one fumble.

Year—Team	G	GS	SACKS
1992—Indianapolis NFL	16	3	1.0
1993—Indianapolis NFL	6	0	0.0
1994—Indianapolis NFL	15	15	6.0
1995—Indianapolis NFL	16	16	2.5
1996—Indianapolis NFL	15	15	5.0
1997—Indianapolis NFL	16	11	2.5
1998—Indianapolis NFL	14	13	6.0
1999—Indianapolis NFL	10	0	0.0
Pro totals (8 years)	108	73	23.0

McCRARY, FRED   FB   CHARGERS

PERSONAL: Born September 19, 1972, in Naples, Fla. ... 6-0/235. ... Full name: Freddy Demetrius McCrary.
HIGH SCHOOL: Naples (Fla.).
COLLEGE: Mississippi State.
TRANSACTIONS/CAREER NOTES: Selected by Philadelphia Eagles in sixth round (208th pick overall) of 1995 NFL draft. ... Signed by Eagles (June 27, 1995). ... Released by Eagles (August 25, 1996). ... Signed by New Orleans Saints (March 5, 1997). ... Released by Saints (August 24, 1998). ... Signed by San Diego Chargers (March 26, 1999). ... Granted free agency (February 11, 2000). ... Re-signed by Chargers (May 22, 2000).
PRO STATISTICS: 1995—Returned one kickoff for one yard. 1997—Returned two kickoffs for 26 yards. 1999—Returned one kickoff for four yards.
SINGLE GAME HIGHS (regular season): Attempts—5 (November 23, 1997, vs. Atlanta); yards—13 (November 23, 1997, vs. Atlanta); and rushing touchdowns—1 (September 10, 1995, vs. Arizona).

			RUSHING				RECEIVING				TOTALS			
Year—Team	G	GS	Att.	Yds.	Avg.	TD	No.	Yds.	Avg.	TD	TD	2pt.	Pts.	Fum.
1995—Philadelphia NFL	13	5	3	1	0.3	1	9	60	6.7	0	1	0	6	0
1996—						Did not play.								
1997—New Orleans NFL	7	0	8	15	1.9	0	4	17	4.3	0	0	0	0	0
1999—San Diego NFL	16	14	0	0	0.0	0	37	201	5.4	1	1	0	6	0
Pro totals (3 years)	36	19	11	16	1.5	1	50	278	5.6	1	2	0	12	0

McCRARY, MICHAEL   DE   RAVENS

PERSONAL: Born July 7, 1970, in Vienna, Va. ... 6-4/260. ... Full name: Michael Curtis McCrary.
HIGH SCHOOL: George C. Marshall (Falls Church, Va.).
COLLEGE: Wake Forest.
TRANSACTIONS/CAREER NOTES: Selected by Seattle Seahawks in seventh round (170th pick overall) of 1993 NFL draft. ... Signed by Seahawks (July 13, 1993). ... Granted free agency (February 16, 1996). ... Re-signed by Seahawks (June 6, 1996). ... Granted unconditional free agency (February 14, 1997). ... Signed by Baltimore Ravens (April 7, 1997).
HONORS: Named defensive end on THE SPORTING NEWS NFL All-Pro team (1998). ... Played in Pro Bowl (1998 and 1999 seasons).
PRO STATISTICS: 1996—Recovered one fumble. 1997—Recovered two fumbles. 1999—Recovered one fumble.
MISCELLANEOUS: Holds Baltimore Ravens all-time record for most sacks (35.0).

Year—Team	G	GS	SACKS
1993—Seattle NFL	15	0	4.0
1994—Seattle NFL	16	0	1.5
1995—Seattle NFL	11	0	1.0
1996—Seattle NFL	16	13	▲13.5
1997—Baltimore NFL	15	15	9.0
1998—Baltimore NFL	16	16	14.5
1999—Baltimore NFL	16	16	11.5
Pro totals (7 years)	105	60	55.0

McCULLOUGH, ANDY   WR   CARDINALS

PERSONAL: Born November 11, 1975, in Dayton, Ohio. ... 6-3/210. ... Full name: Antwone McCullough.
HIGH SCHOOL: Meadowdale (Dayton, Ohio).
COLLEGE: Tennessee.
TRANSACTIONS/CAREER NOTES: Selected by New Orleans Saints in seventh round (204th pick overall) of 1998 NFL draft. ... Signed by Saints (May 20, 1998). ... Released by Saints (August 30, 1998). ... Signed by Miami Dolphins to practice squad (September 1, 1998). ... Released by Dolphins (September 15, 1998). ... Signed by Detroit Lions to practice squad (September 23, 1998). ... Released by Lions (October 7, 1998). ... Signed by Arizona Cardinals to practice squad (November 19, 1998). ... Assigned by Cardinals to Frankfurt Galaxy in 1999 NFL Europe enhancement allocation program (February 22, 1999).
PRO STATISTICS: NFLE: 1998—Returned two punts for 46 yards and returned eight kickoffs for 158 yards.
SINGLE GAME HIGHS (regular season): Receptions—2 (September 27, 1999, vs. San Francisco); yards—43 (September 27, 1999, vs. San Francisco); and touchdown receptions—0.

			RECEIVING				TOTALS			
Year—Team	G	GS	No.	Yds.	Avg.	TD	TD	2pt.	Pts.	Fum.
1999—Frankfurt NFLE	...	...	48	883	18.4	10	10	1	62	0
—Arizona NFL	2	0	3	45	15.0	0	0	0	0	0
NFL Europe totals (1 year)	...	...	48	883	18.4	10	10	1	62	0
NFL totals (1 year)	2	0	3	45	15.0	0	0	0	0	0
Pro totals (2 years)	...	...	51	928	18.2	10	10	1	62	0

McCULLOUGH, GEORGE   CB   TITANS

PERSONAL: Born February 18, 1975, in Galveston, Texas. ... 5-10/187. ... Full name: George Wayne McCullough Jr.
HIGH SCHOOL: Ball (Galveston, Texas).
COLLEGE: Baylor.
TRANSACTIONS/CAREER NOTES: Selected by Houston Oilers in fifth round (143rd pick overall) of 1997 NFL draft. ... Oilers franchise moved to Tennessee for 1997 season. ... Signed by Oilers (July 19, 1997). ... Released by Oilers (August 25, 1997). ... Re-signed by Oilers to practice squad (August 26, 1997). ... Activated (December 5, 1997). ... Assigned by Oilers to Barcelona Dragons in 1998 NFL Europe enhancement allocation program (February 18, 1998). ... Oilers franchise renamed Tennessee Titans for 1999 season (December 26, 1998).
PLAYING EXPERIENCE: Tennessee NFL, 1997-1999; Barcelona Dragons NFLE, 1998. ... Games/Games started: 1997 (2/0), NFLE 1998 (games played unavailable), NFL 1998 (6/0), 1999 (5/0). Total NFL: 13/0.
CHAMPIONSHIP GAME EXPERIENCE: Member of Titans for AFC championship game (1999 season); inactive. ... Played in Super Bowl XXXIV (1999 season).
PRO STATISTICS: NFLE: 1998—Intercepted three passes for 89 yards and one touchdown and credited with two sacks.

McCUTCHEON, DAYLON   CB   BROWNS

PERSONAL: Born December 9, 1976, in Walnut, Calif. ... 5-8/180. ... Son of Lawrence McCutcheon, Director of Scouting, St. Louis Rams, and former running back with four NFL teams (1972-81). ... Name pronounced mc-CUTCH-in.
HIGH SCHOOL: Bishop Amat (La Puente, Calif.).
COLLEGE: Southern California.
TRANSACTIONS/CAREER NOTES: Selected by Cleveland Browns in third round (62nd pick overall) of 1999 NFL draft. ... Signed by Browns (July 22, 1999).
PLAYING EXPERIENCE: Cleveland NFL, 1999. ... Games/Games started: 1999 (16/15).
HONORS: Named cornerback on THE SPORTING NEWS college All-America second team (1998).
PRO STATISTICS: 1999—Intercepted one pass for 12 yards and credited with one sack.

McDANIEL, ED   LB   VIKINGS

PERSONAL: Born February 23, 1969, in Battesburg, S.C. ... 5-11/229.
HIGH SCHOOL: Battesburg (S.C.)-Leesville.
COLLEGE: Clemson (degree in human resource and development, 1991).
TRANSACTIONS/CAREER NOTES: Selected by Minnesota Vikings in fifth round (125th pick overall) of 1992 NFL draft. ... Signed by Vikings (July 20, 1992). ... Released by Vikings (August 31, 1992). ... Re-signed by Vikings to practice squad (September 1, 1992). ... Activated (November 5, 1992). ... On injured reserve with knee injury (August 25, 1996-entire season). ... Granted unconditional free agency (February 12, 1999). ... Re-signed by Vikings (February 18, 1999). ... On physically unable to perform list with knee injury (August 1-10, 1999).
CHAMPIONSHIP GAME EXPERIENCE: Played in NFC championship game (1998 season).
HONORS: Named to play in Pro Bowl (1998 season); replaced by Hardy Nickerson due to injury.
PRO STATISTICS: 1995—Recovered one fumble. 1998—Recovered two fumbles for five yards. 1999—Recovered two fumbles.

			INTERCEPTIONS				SACKS
Year Team	G	GS	No.	Yds.	Avg.	TD	No.
1992—Minnesota NFL	8	0	0	0	0.0	0	0.0
1993—Minnesota NFL	7	1	0	0	0.0	0	0.0
1994—Minnesota NFL	16	16	1	0	0.0	0	1.5
1995—Minnesota NFL	16	16	1	3	3.0	0	4.5
1996—Minnesota NFL				Did not play.			
1997—Minnesota NFL	16	16	1	18	18.0	0	1.5
1998—Minnesota NFL	16	16	0	0	0.0	0	7.0
1999—Minnesota NFL	16	16	0	0	0.0	0	2.0
Pro totals (7 years)	95	81	3	21	7.0	0	16.5

McDANIEL, EMMANUEL   CB   GIANTS

PERSONAL: Born July 27, 1972, in Griffin, Ga. ... 5-9/180.
HIGH SCHOOL: Jonesboro (Ga.).
COLLEGE: East Carolina.
TRANSACTIONS/CAREER NOTES: Selected by Carolina Panthers in fourth round (111th pick overall) of 1996 NFL draft. ... Signed by Panthers (July 20, 1996). ... Released by Panthers (August 26, 1997). ... Signed by Indianapolis Colts (November 27, 1997). ... Released by Colts (August 24, 1998). ... Re-signed by Colts (September 3, 1998). ... Inactive for one game with Colts (1998). ... Released by Colts (September 9, 1998). ... Signed by Miami Dolphins (October 8, 1998). ... Inactive for one game with Dolphins (1998). ... Released by Dolphins (October 14, 1998). ... Re-signed by Dolphins to practice squad (October 15, 1998). ... Activated (January 7, 1999). ... Claimed on waivers by New York Giants (September 1, 1999). ... Released by Giants (September 5, 1999). ... Re-signed by Giants to practice squad (September 6, 1999). ... Activated (November 15, 1999).
PLAYING EXPERIENCE: Carolina NFL, 1996; Indianapolis NFL, 1997; New York Giants NFL, 1999. ... Games/Games started: 1996 (2/0), 1997 (3/0), 1999 (7/2). Total: 12/2.
CHAMPIONSHIP GAME EXPERIENCE: Member of Panthers for NFC championship game (1996 season); inactive.

McDANIEL, JEREMY   WR   BILLS

PERSONAL: Born May 2, 1976, in New Bern, N.C. ... 6-0/197. ... Full name: Jeremy Dwayne McDaniel.
HIGH SCHOOL: New Bern (N.C.).
JUNIOR COLLEGE: Fort Scott (Kan.) Community College.
COLLEGE: Arizona.

M

TRANSACTIONS/CAREER NOTES: Signed as non-drafted free agent by Buffalo Bills (April 23, 1999). ... Released by Bills (September 4, 1999). ... Re-signed by Bills to practice squad (September 7, 1999). ... Activated (December 23, 1999).
PLAYING EXPERIENCE: Buffalo NFL, 1999. ... Games/Games started: 1999 (1/0).

McDANIEL, RANDALL   G   BUCCANEERS

PERSONAL: Born December 19, 1964, in Phoenix. ... 6-3/287. ... Full name: Randall Cornell McDaniel.
HIGH SCHOOL: Agua Fria Union (Avondale, Ariz.).
COLLEGE: Arizona State (degree in physical education, 1988).
TRANSACTIONS/CAREER NOTES: Selected by Minnesota Vikings in first round (19th pick overall) of 1988 NFL draft. ... Signed by Vikings (July 22, 1988). ... Granted free agency (February 1, 1991). ... Re-signed by Vikings (July 22, 1991). ... Designated by Vikings as transition player (February 25, 1993). ... Free agency status changed by Vikings from transitional to unconditional (February 17, 1994). ... Re-signed by Vikings (April 21, 1994). ... Designated by Vikings as franchise player (February 13, 1997). ... Re-signed by Vikings (February 21, 1997). ... Released by Vikings (February 10, 2000). ... Signed by Tampa Bay Buccaneers (March 1, 2000).
PLAYING EXPERIENCE: Minnesota NFL, 1988-1999. ... Games/Games started: 1988 (16/15), 1989 (14/13), 1990 (16/16), 1991 (16/16), 1992 (16/16), 1993 (16/16), 1994 (16/16), 1995 (16/16), 1996 (16/16), 1997 (16/16), 1998 (16/16), 1999 (16/16). Total: 190/188.
CHAMPIONSHIP GAME EXPERIENCE: Played in NFC championship game (1998 season).
HONORS: Named guard on THE SPORTING NEWS college All-America second team (1987). ... Played in Pro Bowl (1989-1999 seasons). ... Named guard on THE SPORTING NEWS NFL All-Pro team (1991-1994 and 1996-1998).
PRO STATISTICS: 1991—Recovered one fumble. 1994—Recovered one fumble. 1996—Rushed twice for one yard.

McDANIELS, PELLOM   DE   FALCONS

PERSONAL: Born February 21, 1968, in San Jose, Calif. ... 6-3/280. ... Full name: Pellom McDaniels III.
HIGH SCHOOL: Silver Creek (San Jose, Calif.).
COLLEGE: Oregon State (degree in communications and political science).
TRANSACTIONS/CAREER NOTES: Selected by Birmingham Fire in fifth round of 1991 World League draft. ... Signed as non-drafted free agent by Philadelphia Eagles (June 19, 1991). ... Released by Eagles (August 12, 1991). ... Signed by Kansas City Chiefs (June 5, 1992). ... Released by Chiefs (August 31, 1992). ... Re-signed by Chiefs to practice squad (September 2, 1992). ... Released by Chiefs (September 16, 1992). ... Re-signed by Chiefs for 1993 season. ... On injured reserve with shoulder injury (December 20, 1994-remainder of season). ... On injured reserve with ankle injury (December 17, 1998-remainder of season). ... Granted unconditional free agency (February 12, 1999). ... Signed by Atlanta Falcons (April 18, 1999).
CHAMPIONSHIP GAME EXPERIENCE: Played in AFC championship game (1993 season).
PRO STATISTICS: 1994—Recovered one fumble. 1995—Returned one kickoff for no yards. 1997—Recovered one fumble.

Year Team	G	GS	SACKS
1991—Birmingham W.L.	10	6	3.0
1992—Birmingham W.L.	10	10	3.5
1993—Kansas City NFL	10	0	0.0
1994—Kansas City NFL	12	3	2.0
1995—Kansas City NFL	16	2	2.0
1996—Kansas City NFL	9	1	0.0
1997—Kansas City NFL	16	6	3.5
1998—Kansas City NFL	11	2	0.0
1999—Atlanta NFL	16	0	0.0
W.L. totals (2 years)	20	16	6.5
NFL totals (7 years)	90	14	7.5
Pro totals (9 years)	110	30	14.0

McDONALD, DARNELL   WR   BUCCANEERS

PERSONAL: Born May 26, 1976, in Fairfax, Va. ... 6-3/199. ... Full name: Darnell Ali McDonald.
HIGH SCHOOL: Hayfield (Alexandria, Va.).
JUNIOR COLLEGE: Garden City (Kan.) Community College.
COLLEGE: Kansas State.
TRANSACTIONS/CAREER NOTES: Selected by Tampa Bay Buccaneers in seventh round (240th pick overall) of 1999 NFL draft. ... Signed by Buccaneers (July 29, 1999).
CHAMPIONSHIP GAME EXPERIENCE: Played in NFC championship game (1999 season).
SINGLE GAME HIGHS (regular season): Receptions—3 (November 7, 1999, vs. New Orleans); yards—47 (November 7, 1999, vs. New Orleans); and touchdown receptions—1 (November 7, 1999, vs. New Orleans).

Year Team	G	GS	RECEIVING No.	Yds.	Avg.	TD
1999—Tampa Bay NFL	8	0	9	96	10.7	1

McDONALD, RAMOS   CB   49ERS

PERSONAL: Born April 30, 1976, in Dallas. ... 5-11/194.
HIGH SCHOOL: Liberty Eylau (Texarkana, Texas).
JUNIOR COLLEGE: Navarro College (Texas).
COLLEGE: New Mexico.
TRANSACTIONS/CAREER NOTES: Selected by Minnesota Vikings in third round (80th pick overall) of 1998 NFL draft. ... Signed by Vikings (July 25, 1998). ... Claimed on waivers by San Francisco 49ers (October 26, 1999).
PLAYING EXPERIENCE: Minnesota NFL, 1998; Minnesota (5)-San Francisco (9) NFL, 1999. ... Games/Games started: 1998 (15/0), 1999 (Min.-5/5; S.F.-9/7; Total: 14/12). Total: 29/12.
CHAMPIONSHIP GAME EXPERIENCE: Played in NFC championship game (1998 season).
PRO STATISTICS: 1999—Intercepted one pass for four yards.

McDONALD, RICARDO   LB   BRONCOS

PERSONAL: Born November 8, 1969, in Kingston, Jamaica. ... 6-2/248. ... Full name: Ricardo Milton McDonald. ... Twin brother of Devon McDonald, linebacker with Indianapolis Colts (1993-95) and Arizona Cardinals (1996).
HIGH SCHOOL: Eastside (Paterson, N.J.).
COLLEGE: Pittsburgh.
TRANSACTIONS/CAREER NOTES: Selected by Cincinnati Bengals in fourth round (88th pick overall) of 1992 NFL draft. ... Signed by Bengals (July 24, 1992). ... On injured reserve with knee injury (December 24, 1993-remainder of season). ... Granted free agency (February 17, 1995). ... Re-signed by Bengals (March 6, 1995). ... Granted unconditional free agency (February 16, 1996). ... Re-signed by Bengals (March 8, 1996). ... Granted unconditional free agency (February 13, 1998). ... Signed by Chicago Bears (May 12, 1998). ... On injured reserve with hamstring injury (December 22, 1998-remainder of season). ... Granted unconditional free agency (February 11, 2000). ... Signed by Denver Broncos (May 23, 2000).
PRO STATISTICS: 1992—Intercepted one pass for no yards and recovered one fumble for four yards. 1995—Recovered one fumble.

Year Team	G	GS	SACKS
1992—Cincinnati NFL	16	13	0.0
1993—Cincinnati NFL	14	12	1.0
1994—Cincinnati NFL	13	13	1.0
1995—Cincinnati NFL	16	15	5.0
1996—Cincinnati NFL	16	15	5.0
1997—Cincinnati NFL	13	12	1.0
1998—Chicago NFL	15	14	1.0
1999—Chicago NFL	16	16	0.5
Pro totals (8 years)	119	110	14.5

McDONALD, TIM   S

PERSONAL: Born January 6, 1965, in Fresno, Calif. ... 6-2/219. ... Full name: Timothy McDonald.
HIGH SCHOOL: Edison (Fresno, Calif.).
COLLEGE: Southern California.
TRANSACTIONS/CAREER NOTES: Selected by St. Louis Cardinals in second round (34th pick overall) of 1987 NFL draft. ... Signed by Cardinals (August 2, 1987). ... On injured reserve with broken ankle (September 1-December 12, 1987). ... Cardinals franchise moved to Phoenix (March 15, 1988). ... Granted free agency (February 1, 1990). ... Re-signed by Cardinals (August 21, 1990). ... On injured reserve with broken leg and ankle (December 3, 1991-remainder of season). ... Designated by Cardinals as franchise player (February 25, 1993). ... Signed by San Francisco 49ers (April 7, 1993); Cardinals received first-round pick (OT Ernest Dye) in 1993 draft as compensation. ... Released by 49ers (February 9, 2000).
CHAMPIONSHIP GAME EXPERIENCE: Played in NFC championship game (1993, 1994 and 1997 seasons). ... Member of Super Bowl championship team (1994 season).
HONORS: Named defensive back on THE SPORTING NEWS college All-America second team (1984). ... Named defensive back on THE SPORTING NEWS college All-America first team (1985). ... Played in Pro Bowl (1989 and 1992-1995 seasons). ... Named to play in Pro Bowl (1991 season); replaced by Shaun Gayle due to injury.
PRO STATISTICS: 1988—Recovered one fumble for nine yards. 1989—Recovered one fumble for one yard. 1990—Recovered one fumble. 1991—Recovered one fumble. 1992—Recovered three fumbles for two yards. 1993—Recovered one fumble for 15 yards. 1994—Recovered one fumble for 49 yards and a touchdown. 1996—Recovered one fumble. 1997—Recovered three fumbles. 1998—Recovered two fumbles. 1999—Recovered one fumble.

Year Team	G	GS	INTERCEPTIONS No.	Yds.	Avg.	TD	SACKS No.
1987—St. Louis NFL	3	0	0	0	0.0	0	0.0
1988—Phoenix NFL	16	15	2	11	5.5	0	2.0
1989—Phoenix NFL	16	16	7	‡170	24.3	∞1	0.0
1990—Phoenix NFL	16	16	4	63	15.8	0	0.0
1991—Phoenix NFL	13	13	5	36	7.2	0	0.0
1992—Phoenix NFL	16	16	2	35	17.5	0	0.5
1993—San Francisco NFL	16	16	3	23	7.7	0	0.0
1994—San Francisco NFL	16	16	2	79	39.5	1	0.0
1995—San Francisco NFL	16	16	4	135	33.8	†2	0.0
1996—San Francisco NFL	16	16	2	14	7.0	0	1.0
1997—San Francisco NFL	15	15	3	34	11.3	0	0.0
1998—San Francisco NFL	16	16	4	22	5.5	0	4.0
1999—San Francisco NFL	16	16	2	18	9.0	0	2.0
Pro totals (13 years)	191	187	40	640	16.0	4	9.5

McDUFFIE, O.J.   WR   DOLPHINS

PERSONAL: Born December 2, 1969, in Marion, Ohio. ... 5-10/194. ... Full name: Otis James McDuffie.
HIGH SCHOOL: Hawken (Gates Mills, Ohio).
COLLEGE: Penn State (degree in labor and industrial relations).
TRANSACTIONS/CAREER NOTES: Selected by Miami Dolphins in first round (25th pick overall) of 1993 NFL draft. ... Signed by Dolphins (July 18, 1993).
HONORS: Named wide receiver on THE SPORTING NEWS college All-America second team (1992).
POST SEASON RECORDS: Shares NFL postseason career and single-game records for most two-point conversions—1 (December 30, 1995, vs. Buffalo). ... (December 30, 1995, vs. Buffalo).
PRO STATISTICS: 1993—Fumbled four times and recovered one fumble. 1994—Fumbled three times. 1995—Fumbled four times and recovered two fumbles. 1996—Fumbled six times and recovered three fumbles. 1997—Recovered two fumbles for three yards. 1999—Fumbled twice.
SINGLE GAME HIGHS (regular season): Receptions—11 (December 13, 1998, vs. New York Jets); yards—137 (October 27, 1997, vs. Chicago); and touchdown receptions—3 (November 29, 1998, vs. New Orleans).
STATISTICAL PLATEAUS: 100-yard receiving games: 1994 (1), 1996 (2), 1997 (3), 1998 (3). Total: 9.

M

Year Team	G	GS	RUSHING				RECEIVING				PUNT RETURNS				KICKOFF RETURNS				TOTALS		
			Att.	Yds.	Avg.	TD	No.	Yds.	Avg.	TD	No.	Yds.	Avg.	TD	No.	Yds.	Avg.	TD	TD	2pt.	Pts.
1993—Miami NFL	16	0	1	-4	-4.0	0	19	197	10.4	0	28	317	11.3	†2	32	755	23.6	0	2	0	12
1994—Miami NFL	15	3	5	32	6.4	0	37	488	13.2	3	32	228	7.1	0	36	767	21.3	0	3	0	18
1995—Miami NFL	16	16	3	6	2.0	0	62	819	13.2	8	24	163	6.8	0	23	564	24.5	0	8	1	50
1996—Miami NFL	16	16	2	7	3.5	0	74	918	12.4	8	22	212	9.6	0	0	0	0.0	0	8	0	48
1997—Miami NFL	16	16	0	0	0.0	0	76	943	12.4	1	2	4	2.0	0	0	0	0.0	0	1	0	6
1998—Miami NFL	16	16	3	11	3.7	0	*90	1050	11.7	7	12	141	11.8	0	0	0	0.0	0	7	0	42
1999—Miami NFL	12	10	0	0	0.0	0	43	516	12.0	2	7	62	8.9	0	1	17	17.0	0	2	0	12
Pro totals (7 years)........	107	77	14	52	3.7	0	401	4931	12.3	29	127	1127	8.9	2	92	2103	22.9	0	31	1	188

McELMURRY, BLAINE　　　　　S　　　　　JAGUARS

PERSONAL: Born October 23, 1973, in Helena, Mont. ... 6-0/192. ... Full name: Blaine Richard McElmurry.
HIGH SCHOOL: Troy (Mont.).
COLLEGE: Montana (degree in microbiology).
TRANSACTIONS/CAREER NOTES: Signed as non-drafted free agent by Tennessee Oilers (May 2, 1997). ... Claimed on waivers by Philadelphia Eagles (August 24, 1997). ... Released by Eagles (August 29, 1997). ... Signed by Green Bay Packers to practice squad (September 3, 1997). ... Activated (November 25, 1997). ... Released by Packers (August 21, 1998). ... Signed by Tennessee Oilers to practice squad (November 4, 1998). ... Signed by Jacksonville Jaguars off Oilers practice squad (December 16, 1998).
PLAYING EXPERIENCE: Green Bay NFL, 1997, Jacksonville NFL, 1998 and 1999. ... Games/Games started: 1997 (1/0), 1998 (2/0), 1999 (16/0). Total: 19/0.
CHAMPIONSHIP GAME EXPERIENCE: Member of Packers for NFC championship team (1997 season); inactive. ... Member of Packers for Super Bowl XXXII (1997 season); inactive. ... Played in AFC championship game (1999 season).
PRO STATISTICS: 1999—Intercepted one pass for 26 yards.

McFARLAND, ANTHONY　　　　　DT　　　　　BUCCANEERS

PERSONAL: Born December 18, 1977, in Winnsboro, La. ... 6-0/300. ... Full name: Anthony Darelle McFarland.
HIGH SCHOOL: Winnsboro (La.).
COLLEGE: Louisiana State.
TRANSACTIONS/CAREER NOTES: Selected by Tampa Bay Buccaneers in first round (15th pick overall) of 1999 NFL draft. ... Signed by Buccaneers (August 3, 1999).
PLAYING EXPERIENCE: Tampa Bay NFL, 1999. ... Games/Games started: 1999 (14/0).
CHAMPIONSHIP GAME EXPERIENCE: Played in NFC championship game (1999 season).
HONORS: Named defensive tackle on THE SPORTING NEWS college All-America second team (1998).
PRO STATISTICS: 1999—Credited with one sack.

McGARITY, WANE　　　　　WR　　　　　COWBOYS

PERSONAL: Born September 30, 1976, in San Antonio. ... 5-8/197. ... Full name: Wane Keith McGarity.
HIGH SCHOOL: Clark (San Antonio).
COLLEGE: Texas.
TRANSACTIONS/CAREER NOTES: Selected by Dallas Cowboys in fourth round (118th pick overall) of 1999 NFL draft. ... Signed by Cowboys (July 26, 1999). ... On injured reserve with finger injury (December 10, 1999-remainder of season).
SINGLE GAME HIGHS (regular season): Receptions—3 (December 5, 1999, vs. New England); yards—36 (October 18, 1999, vs. New York Giants); and touchdown receptions—0.

Year Team	G	GS	RECEIVING				PUNT RETURNS				TOTALS			
			No.	Yds.	Avg.	TD	No.	Yds.	Avg.	TD	TD	2pt.	Pts.	Fum.
1999—Dallas NFL	5	1	7	70	10.0	0	3	16	5.3	0	0	0	0	0

McGARRAHAN, SCOTT　　　　　S　　　　　PACKERS

PERSONAL: Born February 12, 1974, in Arlington, Texas. ... 6-1/198. ... Full name: John Scott McGarrahan. ... Name pronounced ma-GAIR-a-han.
HIGH SCHOOL: Lamar (Arlington, Texas).
COLLEGE: New Mexico.
TRANSACTIONS/CAREER NOTES: Selected by Green Bay Packers in sixth round (156th pick overall) of 1998 NFL draft. ... Signed by Packers (July 17, 1998). ... On injured reserve with hamstring injury (December 29, 1999-remainder of season).
PLAYING EXPERIENCE: Green Bay NFL, 1998 and 1999. ... Games/Games started: 1998 (15/0), 1999 (13/0). Total: 28/0.
PRO STATISTICS: 1999—Recovered one fumble.

McGEE, TONY　　　　　TE　　　　　BENGALS

PERSONAL: Born April 21, 1971, in Terre Haute, Ind. ... 6-3/250.
HIGH SCHOOL: Terre Haute (Ind.) South.
COLLEGE: Michigan (degree in communications).
TRANSACTIONS/CAREER NOTES: Selected by Cincinnati Bengals in second round (37th pick overall) of 1993 NFL draft. ... Signed by Bengals (July 20, 1993). ... Granted free agency (February 16, 1996). ... Re-signed by Bengals for 1996 season.
PRO STATISTICS: 1994—Returned one kickoff for four yards.
SINGLE GAME HIGHS (regular season): Receptions—8 (December 22, 1996, vs. Indianapolis); yards—118 (September 3, 1995, vs. Indianapolis); and touchdown receptions—2 (November 9, 1997, vs. Indianapolis).
STATISTICAL PLATEAUS: 100-yard receiving games: 1993 (1), 1995 (1). Total: 2.

Year Team	G	GS	RECEIVING				TOTALS			
			No.	Yds.	Avg.	TD	TD	2pt.	Pts.	Fum.
1993—Cincinnati NFL	15	15	44	525	11.9	0	0	0	0	1
1994—Cincinnati NFL	16	16	40	492	12.3	1	1	0	6	0
1995—Cincinnati NFL	16	16	55	754	13.7	4	4	0	24	2
1996—Cincinnati NFL	16	16	38	446	11.7	4	4	0	24	0
1997—Cincinnati NFL	16	16	34	414	12.2	6	6	1	38	0
1998—Cincinnati NFL	16	16	22	363	16.5	1	1	0	6	0
1999—Cincinnati NFL	16	16	26	344	13.2	2	2	0	12	0
Pro totals (7 years)	111	111	259	3338	12.9	18	18	1	110	3

McGINEST, WILLIE   DE   PATRIOTS

PERSONAL: Born December 11, 1971, in Long Beach, Calif. ... 6-5/265. ... Full name: William Lee McGinest Jr.
HIGH SCHOOL: Polytechnic (Pasadena, Calif.).
COLLEGE: Southern California.
TRANSACTIONS/CAREER NOTES: Selected by New England Patriots in first round (fourth pick overall) of 1994 NFL draft. ... Signed by Patriots (May 17, 1994). ... Granted unconditional free agency (February 13, 1998). ... Re-signed by Patriots (February 12, 1998).
CHAMPIONSHIP GAME EXPERIENCE: Played in AFC championship game (1996 season). ... Played in Super Bowl XXXI (1996 season).
PRO STATISTICS: 1994—Recovered two fumbles. 1996—Intercepted one pass for 46 yards and a touchdown and recovered two fumbles, including one in end zone for a touchdown. 1997—Recovered three fumbles. 1999—Recovered two fumbles for two yards and one touchdown.

Year Team	G	GS	SACKS
1994—New England NFL	16	7	4.5
1995—New England NFL	16	16	11.0
1996—New England NFL	16	16	9.5
1997—New England NFL	11	11	2.0
1998—New England NFL	9	8	3.5
1999—New England NFL	16	16	9.0
Pro totals (6 years)	84	74	39.5

McGLOCKTON, CHESTER   DT   CHIEFS

PERSONAL: Born September 16, 1969, in Whiteville, N.C. ... 6-4/328.
HIGH SCHOOL: Whiteville (N.C.).
COLLEGE: Clemson.
TRANSACTIONS/CAREER NOTES: Selected after junior season by Los Angeles Raiders in first round (16th pick overall) of 1992 NFL draft. ... Signed by Raiders for 1992 season. ... On injured reserve (January 11, 1994-remainder of 1993 playoffs). ... Raiders franchise moved to Oakland (July 21, 1995). ... Designated by Raiders as franchise player (February 12, 1998). ... Tendered offer sheet by Kansas City Chiefs (April 10, 1998). ... Raiders declined to match offer (April 17, 1998).
HONORS: Named defensive tackle on THE SPORTING NEWS NFL All-Pro team (1994). ... Played in Pro Bowl (1994-1997 seasons).
PRO STATISTICS: 1993—Intercepted one pass for 19 yards. 1994—Recovered one fumble. 1995—Recovered two fumbles. 1997—Recovered one fumble. 1998—Recovered one fumble. 1999—Intercepted one pass for 30 yards, fumbled once and recovered one fumble for minus two yards.

Year Team	G	GS	SACKS
1992—Los Angeles Raiders NFL	10	0	3.0
1993—Los Angeles Raiders NFL	16	16	7.0
1994—Los Angeles Raiders NFL	16	16	9.5
1995—Oakland NFL	16	16	7.5
1996—Oakland NFL	16	16	8.0
1997—Oakland NFL	16	16	4.5
1998—Kansas City NFL	10	9	1.0
1999—Kansas City NFL	16	16	1.5
Pro totals (8 years)	116	105	42.0

M

McGRIFF, TRAVIS   WR   BRONCOS

PERSONAL: Born June 24, 1976, in Gainesville, Fla. ... 5-8/185. ... Full name: William Travis McGriff.
HIGH SCHOOL: P.K. Yonge (Gainesville, Fla.).
COLLEGE: Florida.
TRANSACTIONS/CAREER NOTES: Selected by Denver Broncos in third round (93rd pick overall) of 1999 NFL draft. ... Signed by Broncos (July 22, 1999).
PRO STATISTICS: 1999—Recovered one fumble.
SINGLE GAME HIGHS (regular season): Receptions—1 (January 2, 2000, vs. San Diego); yards—15 (October 31, 1999, vs. Minnesota); and touchdown receptions—0.

Year Team	G	GS	RECEIVING				PUNT RETURNS				TOTALS			
			No.	Yds.	Avg.	TD	No.	Yds.	Avg.	TD	TD	2pt.	Pts.	Fum.
1999—Denver NFL	14	0	3	37	12.3	0	7	50	7.1	0	0	0	0	1

McIVER, EVERETT   G

PERSONAL: Born August 5, 1970, in Cumberland, N.C. ... 6-5/330. ... Full name: Everett Allen McIver.
HIGH SCHOOL: 71st Senior (Fayetteville, N.C.).
COLLEGE: Elizabeth City (N.C.) State.

TRANSACTIONS/CAREER NOTES: Signed as non-drafted free agent by San Diego Chargers (April 27, 1993). ... Claimed on waivers by Dallas Cowboys (July 27, 1993). ... Released by Cowboys (August 30, 1993). ... Re-signed by Cowboys to practice squad (August 31, 1993). ... Released by Cowboys (December 7, 1993). ... Signed by New York Jets to practice squad (December 10, 1993). ... Activated (January 2, 1994). ... Assigned by Jets to London Monarchs in 1996 World League enhancement allocation program (February 19, 1996). ... Released by Jets (August 7, 1996). ... Signed by Miami Dolphins (August 13, 1996). ... Released by Dolphins (September 2, 1996). ... Re-signed by Dolphins (October 7, 1996). ... Granted unconditional free agency (February 13, 1998). ... Signed by Cowboys (February 23, 1998). ... On injured reserve with knee injury (November 24, 1998-remainder of season). ... Granted unconditional free agency (February 11, 2000).
PLAYING EXPERIENCE: New York Jets NFL, 1994 and 1995; London W.L., 1996; Miami NFL, 1996 and 1997; Dallas NFL, 1998 and 1999. ... Games/Games started: 1994 (4/0), 1995 (14/4), W.L. 1996 (games played unavailable), NFL 1996 (7/5), 1997 (14/14), 1998 (6/6), 1999 (14/14). Total NFL: 59/43.
PRO STATISTICS: 1999—Recovered one fumble.

McKENZIE, KEITH   DE   BROWNS

PERSONAL: Born October 17, 1973, in Detroit. ... 6-3/266. ... Full name: Keith Derrick McKenzie.
HIGH SCHOOL: Highland Park (Mich.).
COLLEGE: Ball State (degree in history).
TRANSACTIONS/CAREER NOTES: Selected by Green Bay Packers in seventh round (252nd pick overall) of 1996 NFL draft. ... Signed by Packers (July 15, 1996). ... Granted free agency (February 12, 1999). ... Re-signed by Packers (June 1, 1999). ... Granted unconditional free agency (February 11, 2000). ... Signed by Cleveland Browns (February 24, 2000).
CHAMPIONSHIP GAME EXPERIENCE: Member of Super Bowl championship team (1996 season). ... Played in NFC championship game (1996 and 1997 seasons). ... Played in Super Bowl XXXII (1997 season).
PRO STATISTICS: 1998—Intercepted one pass for 33 yards and a touchdown, returned one kickoff for 17 yards and recovered three fumbles for 88 yards and one touchdown. 1999—Recovered four fumbles for 63 yards and two touchdowns.

Year Team	G	GS	SACKS
1996—Green Bay NFL	10	0	1.0
1997—Green Bay NFL	16	0	1.5
1998—Green Bay NFL	16	0	8.0
1999—Green Bay NFL	16	2	8.0
Pro totals (4 years)	58	2	18.5

McKENZIE, KEVIN   WR   DOLPHINS

PERSONAL: Born September 20, 1975, in Los Angeles, Calif. ... 5-9/187. ... Full name: Kevin Eugene McKenzie.
HIGH SCHOOL: Wilson (Long Beach, Calif.).
JUNIOR COLLEGE: Long Beach City College.
COLLEGE: Washington State.
TRANSACTIONS/CAREER NOTES: Signed as non-drafted free agent by San Francisco 49ers (April 24, 1998). ... Released by 49ers (September 1, 1998). ... Re-signed by 49ers to practice squad (September 2, 1998). ... Signed by Philadelphia Eagles off 49ers practice squad (December 1, 1998). ... Inactive for four games (1998). ... Claimed on waivers by Miami Dolphins (August 31, 1999). ... Released by Dolphins (September 5, 1999). ... Re-signed by Dolphins to practice squad (September 7, 1999). ... Activated (December 29, 1999).
PLAYING EXPERIENCE: Miami NFL, 1999. ... Games/Games started: 1999 (1/0).
PRO STATISTICS: 1999—Caught two passes for 18 yards and fumbled once.
SINGLE GAME HIGHS (regular season): Receptions—2 (January 2, 2000, vs. Washington); yards—18 (January 2, 2000, vs. Washington); and touchdown receptions—0.

McKENZIE, MIKE   CB   PACKERS

PERSONAL: Born April 26, 1976, in Miami. ... 6-0/190. ... Full name: Michael Terrance McKenzie.
HIGH SCHOOL: Norland (Miami).
COLLEGE: Memphis.
TRANSACTIONS/CAREER NOTES: Selected after junior season by Green Bay Packers in third round (87th pick overall) of 1999 NFL draft. ... Signed by Packers (July 8, 1999).

Year Team	G	GS	INTERCEPTIONS No.	Yds.	Avg.	TD
1999—Green Bay NFL	16	16	6	4	0.7	0

McKENZIE, RALEIGH   G   PACKERS

PERSONAL: Born February 8, 1963, in Knoxville, Tenn. ... 6-2/290. ... Twin brother of Reggie McKenzie, linebacker with Los Angeles Raiders (1985-88), Montreal Machine of World League (1990) and San Francisco 49ers (1992).
HIGH SCHOOL: Austin-East (Knoxville, Tenn.).
COLLEGE: Tennessee.
TRANSACTIONS/CAREER NOTES: Selected by Washington Redskins in 11th round (290th pick overall) of 1985 NFL draft. ... Signed by Redskins (June 20, 1985). ... Granted free agency (February 1, 1992). ... Re-signed by Redskins for 1992 season. ... Granted unconditional free agency (February 17, 1995). ... Signed by Philadelphia Eagles (March 28, 1995). ... Granted unconditional free agency (February 14, 1997). ... Signed by San Diego Chargers (February 20, 1997). ... Granted unconditional free agency (February 12, 1999). Signed by Green Bay Packers (February 25, 1999).
PLAYING EXPERIENCE: Washington NFL, 1985-1994; Philadelphia NFL, 1995 and 1996; San Diego NFL, 1997 and 1998; Green Bay NFL, 1999. ... Games/Games started: 1985 (6/0), 1986 (15/5), 1987 (12/12), 1988 (16/14), 1989 (15/8), 1990 (16/12), 1991 (16/14), 1992 (16/16), 1993 (16/16), 1994 (16/16), 1995 (16/16), 1996 (16/16), 1997 (16/16), 1998 (16/16), 1999 (16/7). Total: 224/184.
CHAMPIONSHIP GAME EXPERIENCE: Played in NFC championship game (1986, 1987 and 1991 seasons). ... Member of Super Bowl championship team (1987 and 1991 seasons).
PRO STATISTICS: 1994—Recovered one fumble. 1995—Recovered one fumble. 1997—Recovered one fumble. 1999—Returned one kickoff for 13 yards.

M

McKINLEY, DENNIS   FB   CARDINALS

PERSONAL: Born November 3, 1976, in Kosciusko, Miss. ... 6-2/245. ... Full name: Dennis L. McKinley.
HIGH SCHOOL: Weir (Miss.) Attendance Center.
COLLEGE: Mississippi State (degree in educational psychology).
TRANSACTIONS/CAREER NOTES: Selected by Arizona Cardinals in sixth round (206th pick overall) of 1999 NFL draft. ... Signed by Cardinals for 1999 season.
PLAYING EXPERIENCE: Arizona NFL, 1999. ... Games/Games started: 1999 (16/0).
PRO STATISTICS: 1999—Caught one pass for four yards and recovered two fumbles.

McKINNEY, STEVE   G   COLTS

PERSONAL: Born October 15, 1975, in Houston. ... 6-4/302. ... Full name: Stephen Michael McKinney.
HIGH SCHOOL: Clear Lake (Houston).
COLLEGE: Texas A&M.
TRANSACTIONS/CAREER NOTES: Selected by Indianapolis Colts in fourth round (93rd pick overall) of 1998 NFL draft. ... Signed by Colts (July 23, 1998).
PLAYING EXPERIENCE: Indianapolis NFL, 1998 and 1999. ... Games/Games started: 1998 (16/16), 1999 (15/14). Total: 31/30.

McKINNON, RONALD   LB   CARDINALS

PERSONAL: Born September 20, 1973, in Fort Rucker Army Base, Ala. ... 6-0/240.
HIGH SCHOOL: Elba (Ala.).
COLLEGE: North Alabama.
TRANSACTIONS/CAREER NOTES: Signed as non-drafted free agent by Arizona Cardinals (April 23, 1996). ... Granted free agency (February 12, 1999). ... Re-signed by Cardinals (June 14, 1999). ... Granted unconditional free agency (February 11, 2000). ... Re-signed by Cardinals (February 24, 2000).
HONORS: Harlon Hill Trophy winner (1995).
PRO STATISTICS: 1996—Rushed once for minus four yards. 1997—Rushed once for three yards. 1998—Fumbled once and recovered two fumbles. 1999—Recovered one fumble.

			INTERCEPTIONS				SACKS
Year Team	G	GS	No.	Yds.	Avg.	TD	No.
1996—Arizona NFL	16	0	0	0	0.0	0	0.0
1997—Arizona NFL	16	16	3	40	13.3	0	1.0
1998—Arizona NFL	13	13	5	25	5.0	0	2.0
1999—Arizona NFL	16	16	1	0	0.0	0	1.0
Pro totals (4 years)	61	45	9	65	7.2	0	4.0

McKNIGHT, JAMES   WR   COWBOYS

PERSONAL: Born June 17, 1972, in Orlando. ... 6-1/198.
HIGH SCHOOL: Apopka (Fla.).
COLLEGE: Liberty (Va.).
TRANSACTIONS/CAREER NOTES: Signed as non-drafted free agent by Seattle Seahawks (April 29, 1994). ... Released by Seahawks (August 28, 1994). ... Re-signed by Seahawks to practice squad (August 29, 1994). ... Activated (November 19, 1994). ... Granted unconditional free agency (February 13, 1998). ... Re-signed by Seahawks (February 17, 1998). ... Traded by Seahawks to Dallas Cowboys for third-round pick (WR Darrell Jackson) in 2000 draft (June 24, 1999). ... On injured reserve with knee injury (August 27, 1999-entire season).
PRO STATISTICS: 1995—Returned one kickoff for four yards and recovered one fumble. 1996—Returned three kickoffs for 86 yards and recovered one fumble. 1997—Returned one kickoff for 14 yards.
SINGLE GAME HIGHS (regular season): Receptions—5 (November 29, 1998, vs. Tennessee); yards—113 (November 29, 1998, vs. Tennessee); and touchdown receptions—1 (November 29, 1998, vs. Tennessee).
STATISTICAL PLATEAUS: 100-yard receiving games: 1997 (1), 1998 (1). Total: 2.

			RECEIVING				TOTALS			
Year Team	G	GS	No.	Yds.	Avg.	TD	TD	2pt.	Pts.	Fum.
1994—Seattle NFL	2	0	1	25	25.0	1	1	0	6	0
1995—Seattle NFL	16	0	6	91	15.2	0	0	0	0	1
1996—Seattle NFL	16	0	1	73	73.0	0	0	0	0	0
1997—Seattle NFL	12	5	34	637	*18.7	6	6	0	36	1
1998—Seattle NFL	14	2	21	346	16.5	2	2	0	12	0
1999—Dallas NFL					Did not play.					
Pro totals (5 years)	60	7	63	1172	18.6	9	9	0	54	2

McLAUGHLIN, JOHN   DE   BUCCANEERS

PERSONAL: Born November 13, 1975, in Cleveland. ... 6-4/247. ... Full name: John Raymond McLaughlin.
HIGH SCHOOL: Hart (Newall, Calif.).
COLLEGE: Notre Dame, then California.
TRANSACTIONS/CAREER NOTES: Selected by Tampa Bay Buccaneers in fifth round (150th pick overall) of 1999 NFL draft. ... Signed by Buccaneers (July 26, 1999).
PLAYING EXPERIENCE: Tampa Bay NFL, 1999. ... Games/Games started: 1999 (12/0).
CHAMPIONSHIP GAME EXPERIENCE: Played in NFC championship game (1999 season).

McLEOD, KEVIN   FB   BUCCANEERS

PERSONAL: Born October 17, 1974, in Montego Bay, Jamaica ... 6-0/252. ... Full name: Kevin Aston McLeod.
HIGH SCHOOL: Clarkston (Ga.).
COLLEGE: Auburn.
TRANSACTIONS/CAREER NOTES: Selected by Jacksonville Jaguars in sixth round (182nd pick overall) of 1998 NFL draft. ... Signed by Jaguars (May 19, 1998). ... Released by Jaguars (August 25, 1998). ... Signed by Tampa Bay Buccaneers to practice squad (October 27, 1998). ... Released by Buccaneers (September 5, 1999). ... Re-signed by Buccaneers to practice squad (September 6, 1999). ... Activated (October 9, 1999).
PLAYING EXPERIENCE: Tampa Bay NFL, 1999. ... Games/Games started: 1999 (7/0).
CHAMPIONSHIP GAME EXPERIENCE: Played in NFC championship game (1999 season).
PRO STATISTICS: 1999—Caught two passes for five yards and one touchdown.

McMANUS, TOM   LB

PERSONAL: Born July 30, 1970, in Buffalo Grove, Ill. ... 6-2/255. ... Full name: Thomas Edward McManus.
HIGH SCHOOL: Wheeling (Ill.).
COLLEGE: Boston College (degree in marketing, 1992).
TRANSACTIONS/CAREER NOTES: Signed as non-drafted free agent by New Orleans Saints (May 7, 1993). ... Released by Saints (August 24, 1993). ... Signed by Jacksonville Jaguars (February 1, 1995). ... On injured reserve with knee injury (July 30, 1997-entire season). ... Granted free agency (February 13, 1998). ... Re-signed by Jaguars (June 3, 1998). ... Granted unconditional free agency (February 12, 1999). ... Re-signed by Jaguars (March 19, 1999). ... On injured reserve with foot injury (September 28, 1999-remainder of season). ... Granted unconditional free agency (February 11, 2000).
PLAYING EXPERIENCE: Jacksonville NFL, 1995, 1996, 1998 and 1999. ... Games/Games started: 1995 (14/2), 1996 (16/11), 1998 (16/4), 1999 (2/2). Total: 48/19.
CHAMPIONSHIP GAME EXPERIENCE: Played in AFC championship game (1996 season).

McMILLIAN, MARK   CB

PERSONAL: Born April 29, 1970, in Los Angeles. ... 5-7/148. ... Nephew of Gary Davis, running back with Miami Dolphins (1976-79) and Tampa Bay Buccaneers (1980 and 1981). ... Name pronounced mik-MILL-en.
HIGH SCHOOL: John F. Kennedy (Granada Hills, Calif.).
JUNIOR COLLEGE: Glendale (Calif.) College.
COLLEGE: Alabama.
TRANSACTIONS/CAREER NOTES: Selected by Philadelphia Eagles in 10th round (272nd pick overall) of 1992 NFL draft. ... Signed by Eagles (July 20, 1992). ... Granted unconditional free agency (February 16, 1996). ... Signed by New Orleans Saints (February 29, 1996). ... Released by Saints (May 15, 1997). ... Signed by Kansas City Chiefs (June 16, 1997). ... Released by Chiefs (February 26, 1999). ... Signed by San Francisco 49ers (June 8, 1999). ... Released by 49ers (October 19, 1999). ... Signed by Washington Redskins (October 26, 1999). ... Granted unconditional free agency (February 11, 2000).
PRO STATISTICS: 1993—Fumbled once and recovered one fumble. 1994—Recovered one fumble. 1995—Recovered two fumbles for minus one yard. 1996—Recovered one fumble for minus six yards. 1999—Credited with $1\frac{1}{2}$ sacks, fumbled once and recovered one fumble for 41 yards and a touchdown.

| | | | INTERCEPTIONS | | | |
Year Team	G	GS	No.	Yds.	Avg.	TD
1992—Philadelphia NFL	16	3	1	0	0.0	0
1993—Philadelphia NFL	16	12	2	25	12.5	0
1994—Philadelphia NFL	16	16	2	2	1.0	0
1995—Philadelphia NFL	16	16	3	27	9.0	0
1996—New Orleans NFL	16	16	2	4	2.0	0
1997—Kansas City NFL	16	2	▲8	*274	*34.3	†3
1998—Kansas City NFL	16	10	3	48	16.0	0
1999—San Francisco NFL	6	6	1	0	0.0	0
—Washington NFL	9	0	1	24	24.0	0
Pro totals (8 years)	127	81	23	404	17.6	3

McNABB, DONOVAN   QB   EAGLES

PERSONAL: Born November 25, 1976, in Chicago. ... 6-2/226. ... Full name: Donovan Jamal McNabb.
HIGH SCHOOL: Mount Carmel (Ill.).
COLLEGE: Syracuse (degree in speech communications).
TRANSACTIONS/CAREER NOTES: Selected by Philadelphia Eagles in first round (second pick overall) of 1999 NFL draft. ... Signed by Eagles (July 30, 1999).
PRO STATISTICS: 1999—Fumbled eight times for minus three yards.
SINGLE GAME HIGHS (regular season): Attempts—36 (November 21, 1999, vs. Indianapolis); completions—19 (December 5, 1999, vs. Arizona); passing yards—179 (January 2, 2000, vs. St. Louis); and touchdown passes—3 (January 2, 2000, vs. St. Louis).
MISCELLANEOUS: Regular-season record as starting NFL quarterback: 2-4 (.333).

| | | | PASSING | | | | | | | RUSHING | | | | TOTALS | | |
Year Team	G	GS	Att.	Cmp.	Pct.	Yds.	TD	Int.	Avg.	Rat.	Att.	Yds.	Avg.	TD	TD	2pt.	Pts.
1999—Philadelphia NFL	12	6	216	106	49.1	948	8	7	4.39	60.1	47	313	6.7	0	0	†1	2

McNAIR, STEVE — QB — TITANS

PERSONAL: Born February 14, 1973, in Mount Olive, Miss. ... 6-2/225. ... Full name: Steve LaTreal McNair. ... Brother of Fred McNair, quarterback with Florida Bobcats of Arena League.
HIGH SCHOOL: Mount Olive (Miss.).
COLLEGE: Alcorn State.
TRANSACTIONS/CAREER NOTES: Selected by Houston Oilers in first round (third pick overall) of 1995 NFL draft. ... Signed by Oilers (July 25, 1995). ... Oilers franchise moved to Tennessee for 1997 season. ... Oilers franchise renamed Tennessee Titans for 1999 season (December 26, 1998).
CHAMPIONSHIP GAME EXPERIENCE: Played in AFC championship game (1999 season). ... Played in Super Bowl XXXIV (1999 season).
HONORS: Walter Payton Award winner (1994).
PRO STATISTICS: 1995—Fumbled three times and recovered two fumbles for minus two yards. 1996—Fumbled seven times and recovered four fumbles. 1997—Led NFL with 16 fumbles and recovered seven fumbles for minus two yards. 1998—Fumbled five times and recovered three fumbles for minus seven yards. 1999—Fumbled three times and recovered one fumble.
SINGLE GAME HIGHS (regular season): Attempts—49 (December 20, 1998, vs. Green Bay); completions—29 (December 20, 1998, vs. Green Bay); yards—341 (September 12, 1999, vs. Cincinnati); and touchdown passes—5 (December 26, 1999, vs. Jacksonville).
STATISTICAL PLATEAUS: 300-yard passing games: 1996 (1), 1999 (1). Total: 2.
MISCELLANEOUS: Regular-season record as starting NFL quarterback: 29-20 (.592). ... Postseason record as starting NFL quarterback: 3-1 (.750).

					PASSING						RUSHING			TOTALS		
Year Team	G	GS	Att.	Cmp.	Pct.	Yds.	TD	Int.	Avg.	Rat.	Att.	Yds.	Avg.	TD	TD	2pt.	Pts.
1995—Houston NFL	6	2	80	41	51.3	569	3	1	7.11	81.7	11	38	3.5	0	0	0	0
1996—Houston NFL	9	4	143	88	61.5	1197	6	4	8.37	90.6	31	169	5.5	2	2	0	12
1997—Tennessee NFL	16	16	415	216	52.0	2665	14	13	6.42	70.4	101	674	*6.7	8	8	0	48
1998—Tennessee NFL	16	16	492	289	58.7	3228	15	10	6.56	80.1	77	559	7.3	4	4	0	24
1999—Tennessee NFL	11	11	331	187	56.5	2179	12	8	6.58	78.6	72	337	4.7	8	8	0	48
Pro totals (5 years)	58	49	1461	821	56.2	9838	50	36	6.73	78.1	292	1777	6.1	22	22	0	132

McNEIL, RYAN — CB — COWBOYS

PERSONAL: Born October 4, 1970, in Fort Pierce, Fla. ... 6-2/192. ... Full name: Ryan Darrell McNeil.
HIGH SCHOOL: Westwood Christian (Miami).
COLLEGE: Miami, Fla. (degree in psychology, 1992).
TRANSACTIONS/CAREER NOTES: Selected by Detroit Lions in second round (33rd pick overall) of 1993 NFL draft. ... Signed by Lions (August 25, 1993). ... Granted unconditional free agency (February 14, 1997). ... Signed by St. Louis Rams (July 7, 1997). ... Designated by Rams as franchise player (February 13, 1998). ... Re-signed by Rams (August 31, 1998). ... Granted unconditional free agency (February 12, 1999). ... Signed by Cleveland Browns (August 1, 1999). ... Granted unconditional free agency (February 11, 2000). ... Signed by Dallas Cowboys (March 2, 2000).
HONORS: Named defensive back on THE SPORTING NEWS college All-America second team (1992).
PRO STATISTICS: 1995—Recovered two fumbles. 1996—Recovered two fumbles. 1997—Fumbled once and recovered one fumble. 1998—Recovered one fumble. 1999—Credited with one sack and recovered four fumbles.

			INTERCEPTIONS			
Year Team	G	GS	No.	Yds.	Avg.	TD
1993—Detroit NFL	16	2	2	19	9.5	0
1994—Detroit NFL	14	13	1	14	14.0	0
1995—Detroit NFL	16	16	2	26	13.0	0
1996—Detroit NFL	16	16	5	14	2.8	0
1997—St. Louis NFL	16	16	*9	127	14.1	1
1998—St. Louis NFL	16	12	1	37	37.0	1
1999—Cleveland NFL	16	14	0	0	0.0	0
Pro totals (7 years)	110	89	20	237	11.9	2

M

McNOWN, CADE — QB — BEARS

PERSONAL: Born January 12, 1977, in Portland, Ore. ... 6-1/213. ... Full name: Cade B. McNown.
HIGH SCHOOL: San Benito (Hollister, Calif.), then West Linn (Ore.).
COLLEGE: UCLA.
TRANSACTIONS/CAREER NOTES: Selected by Chicago Bears in first round (12th pick overall) of 1999 NFL draft. ... Signed by Bears (August 2, 1999).
HONORS: Named quarterback on THE SPORTING NEWS college All-America third team (1997). ... Named quarterback on THE SPORTING NEWS college All-America second team (1998).
PRO STATISTICS: 1999—Fumbled six times and recovered two fumbles for minus two yards.
SINGLE GAME HIGHS (regular season): Attempts—42 (January 2, 2000, vs. Tampa Bay); completions—27 (December 19, 1999, vs. Detroit); passing yards—301 (December 19, 1999, vs. Detroit); and touchdown passes—4 (December 19, 1999, vs. Detroit).
STATISTICAL PLATEAUS: 300-yard passing games: 1999 (1).
MISCELLANEOUS: Regular-season record as starting NFL quarterback: 2-4 (.333).

					PASSING						RUSHING			TOTALS		
Year Team	G	GS	Att.	Cmp.	Pct.	Yds.	TD	Int.	Avg.	Rat.	Att.	Yds.	Avg.	TD	TD	2pt.	Pts.
1999—Chicago NFL	15	6	235	127	54.0	1465	8	10	6.23	66.7	32	160	5.0	0	0	†1	2

McQUARTERS, R.W. — CB/KR — BEARS

PERSONAL: Born December 21, 1976, in Tulsa, Okla. ... 5-9/198. ... Full name: Robert William McQuarters II.
HIGH SCHOOL: Washington (Okla.).

COLLEGE: Oklahoma State.
TRANSACTIONS/CAREER NOTES: Selected after junior season by San Francisco 49ers in first round (28th pick overall) of 1998 NFL draft. ... Signed by 49ers (July 28, 1998). ... On injured reserve with shoulder injury (November 30, 1999-remainder of season). ... Traded by 49ers to Chicago Bears for conditional pick in 2001 draft (June 5, 2000).
PRO STATISTICS: 1998—Recovered two fumbles. 1999—Intercepted one pass for 25 yards.

			PUNT RETURNS				KICKOFF RETURNS				TOTALS			
Year Team	G	GS	No.	Yds.	Avg.	TD	No.	Yds.	Avg.	TD	TD	2pt.	Pts.	Fum.
1998—San Francisco NFL	16	7	*47	406	8.6	1	17	339	19.9	0	1	0	6	4
1999—San Francisco NFL	11	4	18	90	5.0	0	26	568	21.8	0	0	0	0	1
Pro totals (2 years)	27	11	65	496	7.6	1	43	907	21.1	0	1	0	6	5

McTYER, TIM — DB — BROWNS

PERSONAL: Born December 14, 1975, in Los Angeles ... 5-11/181. ... Full name: Timothy Thomas McTyer.
HIGH SCHOOL: Washington (Los Angeles).
JUNIOR COLLEGE: Los Angeles Southwest Community College.
COLLEGE: Brigham Young.
TRANSACTIONS/CAREER NOTES: Signed as non-drafted free agent by Indianapolis Colts (April 25, 1997). ... Released by Colts (August 18, 1997). ... Signed by Philadelphia Eagles to practice squad (August 27, 1997). ... Released by Eagles (September 2, 1997). ... Re-signed by Eagles to practice squad (September 18, 1997). ... Activated (October 17, 1997). ... Selected by Cleveland Browns from Eagles in NFL expansion draft (February 9, 1999). ... On injured reserve with arm injury (October 1, 1999-remainder of season). ... Granted free agency (February 11, 2000). ... Re-signed by Browns (April 27, 2000).
PLAYING EXPERIENCE: Philadelphia NFL, 1997 and 1998; Cleveland NFL, 1999. ... Games/Games started: 1997 (10/0), 1998 (16/1), 1999 (2/2). Total: 28/3.
PRO STATISTICS: 1998—Intercepted one pass for 18 yards, credited with 1/2 sack and recovered one fumble.

McWILLIAMS, JOHNNY — TE

PERSONAL: Born December 14, 1972, in Ontario, Calif. ... 6-4/271.
HIGH SCHOOL: Pomona (Calif.).
COLLEGE: Southern California.
TRANSACTIONS/CAREER NOTES: Selected by Arizona Cardinals in third round (64th pick overall) of 1996 NFL draft. ... Signed by Cardinals (August 28, 1996). ... On reserve/did not report list (August 25-September 9, 1996). ... Granted free agency (February 12, 1999). ... Re-signed by Cardinals (June 17, 1999). ... Granted unconditional free agency (February 11, 2000).
PRO STATISTICS: 1999—Recovered one fumble.
SINGLE GAME HIGHS (regular season): Receptions—5 (November 10, 1996, vs. Washington); yards—54 (November 10, 1996, vs. Washington); and touchdown receptions—1 (November 28, 1999, vs. New York Giants).

			RECEIVING				TOTALS			
Year Team	G	GS	No.	Yds.	Avg.	TD	TD	2pt.	Pts.	Fum.
1996—Arizona NFL	12	0	7	80	11.4	1	1	0	6	0
1997—Arizona NFL	16	7	7	75	10.7	0	0	0	0	0
1998—Arizona NFL	16	15	26	284	10.9	4	4	0	24	0
1999—Arizona NFL	15	4	11	71	6.5	1	1	0	6	1
Pro totals (4 years)	59	26	51	510	10.0	6	6	0	36	1

MEADOWS, ADAM — OT — COLTS

PERSONAL: Born January 25, 1974, in Powder Springs, Ga. ... 6-5/295. ... Full name: Adam Jonathon Meadows.
HIGH SCHOOL: McEachern (Powder Springs, Ga.).
COLLEGE: Georgia.
TRANSACTIONS/CAREER NOTES: Selected by Indianapolis Colts in second round (48th pick overall) of 1997 NFL draft. ... Signed by Colts (July 8, 1997). ... Granted free agency (February 11, 2000). ... Re-signed by Colts (March 1, 2000).
PLAYING EXPERIENCE: Indianapolis NFL, 1997-1999. ... Games/Games started: 1997 (16/16), 1998 (14/14), 1999 (16/16). Total: 46/46.

MEANS, NATRONE — RB — PANTHERS

PERSONAL: Born April 26, 1972, in Harrisburg, N.C. ... 5-10/245. ... Full name: Natrone Jermaine Means. ... Name pronounced NAY-tron.
HIGH SCHOOL: Central Cabarrus (Concord, N.C.).
COLLEGE: North Carolina.
TRANSACTIONS/CAREER NOTES: Selected after junior season by San Diego Chargers in second round (41st pick overall) of 1993 NFL draft. ... Signed by Chargers (July 18, 1993). ... Claimed on waivers by Jacksonville Jaguars (March 11, 1996). ... Granted unconditional free agency (February 13, 1998). ... Signed by Chargers (March 4, 1998). ... On injured reserve with foot injury (November 16, 1998-remainder of season). ... Released by Chargers (March 6, 2000). ... Signed by Carolina Panthers (April 17, 2000).
CHAMPIONSHIP GAME EXPERIENCE: Played in AFC championship game (1994 and 1996 seasons). ... Played in Super Bowl XXIX (1994 season).
HONORS: Played in Pro Bowl (1994 season).
PRO STATISTICS: 1993—Attempted one pass without a completion, returned two kickoffs for 22 yards and recovered one fumble. 1994—Attempted one pass without a completion. 1996—Recovered one fumble. 1998—Recovered one fumble.
SINGLE GAME HIGHS (regular season): Attempts—37 (October 11, 1998, vs. Oakland); yards—165 (September 20, 1998, vs. Kansas City); and rushing touchdowns—3 (October 16, 1994, vs. New Orleans).
STATISTICAL PLATEAUS: 100-yard rushing games: 1993 (2), 1994 (6), 1995 (3), 1996 (1), 1998 (4). Total: 16.

			RUSHING				RECEIVING				TOTALS			
Year Team	G	GS	Att.	Yds.	Avg.	TD	No.	Yds.	Avg.	TD	TD	2pt.	Pts.	Fum.
1993—San Diego NFL	16	0	160	645	4.0	8	10	59	5.9	0	8	0	48	1

Year—Team	G	GS	Att	Yds	Avg	TD	No	Yds	Avg	TD	TD	2pt	Pts	Fum
1994—San Diego NFL	16	16	§343	1350	3.9	§12	39	235	6.0	0	▲12	0	72	5
1995—San Diego NFL	10	9	186	730	3.9	5	7	46	6.6	0	5	0	30	2
1996—Jacksonville NFL	14	4	152	507	3.3	2	7	45	6.4	1	3	0	18	3
1997—Jacksonville NFL	14	11	244	823	3.4	9	15	104	6.9	0	9	0	54	5
1998—Jacksonville NFL	10	10	212	883	4.2	5	16	91	5.7	0	5	0	30	2
1999—San Diego NFL	7	5	112	277	2.5	4	9	51	5.7	1	5	0	30	0
Pro totals (7 years)	87	55	1409	5215	3.7	45	103	631	6.1	2	47	0	282	18

METCALF, ERIC — WR

PERSONAL: Born January 23, 1968, in Seattle. ... 5-10/188. ... Full name: Eric Quinn Metcalf. ... Son of Terry Metcalf, running back with St. Louis Cardinals (1973-77), Toronto Argonauts of CFL (1978-80) and Washington Redskins (1981); and cousin of Ray Hall, defensive tackle with Jacksonville Jaguars (1995).

HIGH SCHOOL: Bishop Denis J. O'Connell (Arlington, Va.).

COLLEGE: Texas (degree in liberal arts, 1990).

TRANSACTIONS/CAREER NOTES: Selected by Cleveland Browns in first round (13th pick overall) of 1989 NFL draft. ... Signed by Browns (August 20, 1989). ... Granted free agency (February 1, 1991). ... Re-signed by Browns for 1991 season. ... On injured reserve with shoulder injury (November 2, 1991-remainder of season). ... Granted free agency (February 1, 1992). ... Re-signed by Browns (August 30, 1992). ... Granted roster exemption (August 30-September 5, 1992). ... Traded by Browns with first-round pick (DB Devin Bush) in 1995 draft to Atlanta Falcons for first-round pick (traded to San Francisco) in 1995 draft (March 25, 1995). ... Granted unconditional free agency (February 14, 1997). ... Signed by San Diego Chargers (May 8, 1997). ... Traded by Chargers with first- (DE Andre Wadsworth) and second-round (CB Corey Chavous) picks in 1998 draft, first-round pick (WR David Boston) in 1999 draft and LB Patrick Sapp to Arizona Cardinals for first-round pick (QB Ryan Leaf) in 1998 draft (March 12, 1998). ... Granted unconditional free agency (February 12, 1999). ... Signed by Baltimore Ravens (July 2, 1999). ... Released by Ravens (September 5, 1999). ... Signed by Carolina Panthers (September 7, 1999). ... Granted unconditional free agency (February 11, 2000).

CHAMPIONSHIP GAME EXPERIENCE: Played in AFC championship game (1989 season).

HONORS: Named all-purpose player on The Sporting News college All-America second team (1987). ... Named punt returner on The Sporting News NFL All-Pro team (1993 and 1994). ... Played in Pro Bowl (1993, 1994 and 1997 seasons).

RECORDS: Holds NFL career record for most touchdowns by combined kick return—11. ... Holds NFL career record for most touchdowns by punt return—9. ... Shares NFL single-game records for most touchdowns by punt return—2; and most touchdowns by combined kick return—2 (October 24, 1993, vs. Pittsburgh and November 2, 1997, vs. Cincinnati).

POST SEASON RECORDS: Shares NFL postseason career record for most touchdowns by kickoff return—1 (January 6, 1990, vs. Buffalo).

PRO STATISTICS: 1989—Attempted two passes with one completion for 32 yards and a touchdown and fumbled five times. 1990—Fumbled eight times and recovered one fumble. 1991—Fumbled once. 1992—Attempted one pass without a completion, fumbled six times and recovered two fumbles. 1993—Fumbled five times. 1994—Attempted one pass without a completion and fumbled six times. 1995—Attempted one pass without a completion, fumbled four times and recovered two fumbles. 1996—Fumbled three times. 1997—Fumbled four times and recovered two fumbles. 1998—Fumbled five times and recovered two fumbles. 1999—Fumbled twice.

SINGLE GAME HIGHS (regular season): Receptions—11 (September 17, 1995, vs. New Orleans); yards—177 (September 20, 1992, vs. Los Angeles Raiders); and touchdown receptions—3 (September 20, 1992, vs. Los Angeles Raiders).

STATISTICAL PLATEAUS: 100-yard receiving games: 1992 (1), 1993 (1), 1995 (2), 1996 (1), 1997 (1). Total: 6.

			RUSHING				RECEIVING				PUNT RETURNS				KICKOFF RETURNS				TOTALS		
Year Team	G	GS	Att	Yds	Avg	TD	No	Yds	Avg	TD	No	Yds	Avg	TD	No	Yds	Avg	TD	TD	2pt	Pts
1989—Cleveland NFL	16	11	187	633	3.4	6	54	397	7.4	4	0	0	0.0	0	31	718	23.2	0	10	0	60
1990—Cleveland NFL	16	9	80	248	3.1	1	57	452	7.9	1	0	0	0.0	0	*52	*1052	20.2	*2	4	0	24
1991—Cleveland NFL	8	3	30	107	3.6	0	29	294	10.1	0	12	100	8.3	0	23	351	15.3	0	0	0	0
1992—Cleveland NFL	16	5	73	301	4.1	1	47	614	13.1	5	*44	§429	9.8	1	9	157	17.4	0	7	0	42
1993—Cleveland NFL	16	9	129	611	4.7	1	63	539	8.6	2	36	464	§12.9	†2	15	318	21.2	0	5	0	30
1994—Cleveland NFL	16	8	93	329	3.5	2	47	436	9.3	3	35	348	9.9	†2	9	210	23.3	0	7	0	42
1995—Atlanta NFL	16	14	28	133	4.8	1	104	1189	11.4	8	39	383	9.8	†1	12	278	23.2	0	10	0	60
1996—Atlanta NFL	16	11	3	8	2.7	0	54	599	11.1	6	27	296	11.0	0	49	1034	21.1	0	6	0	36
1997—San Diego NFL	16	1	3	-5	-1.7	0	40	576	14.4	2	45	489	10.9	†3	16	355	22.2	0	5	0	30
1998—Arizona NFL	16	3	0	0	0.0	0	31	324	10.5	0	43	295	6.9	0	57	1218	21.4	0	0	0	0
1999—Carolina NFL	16	1	2	20	10.0	0	11	133	12.1	0	34	238	7.0	0	4	56	14.0	0	0	0	0
Pro totals (11 years)	168	75	628	2385	3.8	12	537	5553	10.3	31	315	3042	9.7	9	277	5747	20.7	2	54	0	324

MICKELL, DARREN — DE — CHARGERS

PERSONAL: Born August 3, 1970, in Miami. ... 6-5/285.

HIGH SCHOOL: Miami Senior.

COLLEGE: Florida.

TRANSACTIONS/CAREER NOTES: Selected by Kansas City Chiefs in second round of 1992 NFL supplemental draft (second of two supplemental drafts in 1992). ... Signed by Chiefs (September 16, 1992). ... Granted roster exemption (September 16-29, 1992). ... On injured reserve with knee injury (September 30-November 11, 1992). ... On practice squad (November 11-December 26, 1992). ... Granted unconditional free agency (February 16, 1996). ... Signed by New Orleans Saints (March 14, 1996). ... On reserve did not report list (July 14-August 12, 1996). ... On physically unable to perform list (August 12-19, 1996). ... On suspended list for violating league substance abuse policy (October 4-November 10, 1996). ... Announced retirement (February 23, 1998). ... Activated from roster exempt list (September 28, 1999). ... Released by Saints (November 10, 1999). ... Signed by San Diego Chargers (February 28, 2000).

CHAMPIONSHIP GAME EXPERIENCE: Played in AFC championship game (1993 season).

PRO STATISTICS: 1993—Recovered one fumble. 1994—Recovered one fumble. 1995—Recovered one fumble. 1997—Recovered one fumble for 11 yards.

Year Team	G	GS	SACKS
1992—Kansas City NFL	1	0	0.0
1993—Kansas City NFL	16	1	1.0
1994—Kansas City NFL	16	13	7.0
1995—Kansas City NFL	12	6	5.5
1996—New Orleans NFL	12	12	3.0
1997—New Orleans NFL	14	13	3.5
1998—	Did not play.		

		1	0	0.0	
1999—New Orleans NFL		1	0	0.0	
Pro totals (7 years)		72	45	20.0	

MICKENS, RAY   CB/KR   JETS

PERSONAL: Born January 4, 1973, in Frankfurt, West Germany. ... 5-8/184.
HIGH SCHOOL: Andress (El Paso, Texas).
COLLEGE: Texas A&M.
TRANSACTIONS/CAREER NOTES: Selected by New York Jets in third round (62nd pick overall) of 1996 NFL draft. ... Signed by Jets (July 13, 1996). ... Granted free agency (February 12, 1999). ... Re-signed by Jets (April 9, 1999).
CHAMPIONSHIP GAME EXPERIENCE: Played in AFC championship game (1998 season).
HONORS: Named defensive back on THE SPORTING NEWS college All-America second team (1995).
PRO STATISTICS: 1997—Credited with one sack and returned blocked field-goal attempt 72 yards for a touchdown. 1998—Recovered one fumble. 1999—Credited with two sacks.

			INTERCEPTIONS			
Year Team	G	GS	No.	Yds.	Avg.	TD
1996—New York Jets NFL	15	10	0	0	0.0	0
1997—New York Jets NFL	16	0	4	2	0.5	0
1998—New York Jets NFL	16	3	3	10	3.3	0
1999—New York Jets NFL	15	5	2	2	1.0	0
Pro totals (4 years)	62	18	9	14	1.6	0

MICKENS, TERRY   WR   RAIDERS

PERSONAL: Born February 21, 1971, in Tallahassee, Fla. ... 6-1/200. ... Full name: Terry KaJuan Mickens.
HIGH SCHOOL: Leon (Tallahassee, Fla.).
COLLEGE: Florida A&M.
TRANSACTIONS/CAREER NOTES: Selected by Green Bay Packers in fifth round (146th pick overall) of 1994 NFL draft. ... Signed by Packers (July 7, 1994). ... Granted unconditional free agency (February 13, 1998). ... Signed by Oakland Raiders (April 25, 1998). ... Granted unconditional free agency (February 12, 1999). ... Re-signed by Raiders (April 23, 1999). ... Granted unconditional free agency (February 11, 2000). ... Re-signed by Raiders (March 27, 2000).
CHAMPIONSHIP GAME EXPERIENCE: Played in NFC championship game (1995-1997 seasons). ... Member of Super Bowl championship team (1996 season). ... Played in Super Bowl XXXII (1997 season).
PRO STATISTICS: 1995—Returned one kickoff for no yards. 1997—Returned one kickoff for no yards. 1998—Recovered two fumbles for three yards.
SINGLE GAME HIGHS (regular season): Receptions—7 (November 3, 1996, vs. Detroit); yards—86 (November 22, 1998, vs. Denver); and touchdown receptions—2 (November 3, 1996, vs. Detroit).

			RECEIVING				TOTALS			
Year Team	G	GS	No.	Yds.	Avg.	TD	TD	2pt.	Pts.	Fum.
1994—Green Bay NFL	12	0	4	31	7.8	0	0	0	0	0
1995—Green Bay NFL	16	0	3	50	16.7	0	0	0	0	0
1996—Green Bay NFL	8	5	18	161	8.9	2	2	0	12	1
1997—Green Bay NFL	11	0	1	2	2.0	1	1	0	6	0
1998—Oakland NFL	16	2	24	346	14.4	1	1	0	6	0
1999—Oakland NFL	16	3	20	261	13.1	0	0	0	0	1
Pro totals (6 years)	79	10	70	851	12.2	4	4	0	24	2

MIDDLETON, FRANK   G   BUCCANEERS

PERSONAL: Born October 25, 1974, in Beaumont, Texas. ... 6-3/334. ... Full name: Frank Middleton Jr.
HIGH SCHOOL: West Brook (Beaumont, Texas).
JUNIOR COLLEGE: Fort Scott (Kan.) Community College.
COLLEGE: Arizona.
TRANSACTIONS/CAREER NOTES: Selected by Tampa Bay Buccaneers in third round (63rd pick overall) of 1997 NFL draft. ... Signed by Buccaneers (July 20, 1997). ... Granted free agency (February 11, 2000). ... Re-signed by Buccanners (May 2, 2000).
PLAYING EXPERIENCE: Tampa Bay NFL, 1997-1999. ... Games/Games started: 1997 (15/2), 1998 (16/16), 1999 (16/16). Total: 47/34.
CHAMPIONSHIP GAME EXPERIENCE: Played in NFC championship game (1999 season).

MILBURN, GLYN   RB/KR   BEARS

PERSONAL: Born February 19, 1971, in Santa Monica, Calif. ... 5-8/174. ... Full name: Glyn Curt Milburn. ... Cousin of Rod Milburn, gold medalist in 110-meter high hurdles in 1972 Summer Olympics.
HIGH SCHOOL: Santa Monica (Calif.).
COLLEGE: Oklahoma, then Stanford (degree in public policy).
TRANSACTIONS/CAREER NOTES: Selected by Denver Broncos in second round (43rd pick overall) of 1993 NFL draft. ... Signed by Broncos (July 15, 1993). ... Traded by Broncos to Detroit Lions for second- (traded to Baltimore) and seventh-round (P Brian Gragert) picks in 1996 NFL draft (April 12, 1996). ... Traded by Lions to Green Bay Packers for seventh-round pick (traded to Miami) in 1999 draft (April 21, 1998). ... Traded by Packers to Chicago Bears for seventh-round pick (WR Donald Driver) in 1999 draft (August 30, 1998).
HONORS: Named kick returner on THE SPORTING NEWS NFL All-Pro team (1995). ... Played in Pro Bowl (1995 and 1999 seasons). ... Named punt returner on THE SPORTING NEWS NFL All-Pro team (1999).
RECORDS: Holds NFL single-season record for most combined kick returns—102. ... Holds NFL single-game record for most combined net yards gained—404 (December 10, 1995).

M

PRO STATISTICS: 1993—Fumbled nine times and recovered one fumble. 1994—Fumbled four times and recovered one fumble. 1995—Fumbled twice. 1997—Fumbled three times and recovered two fumbles. 1998—Fumbled once. 1999—Fumbled four times and recovered two fumbles.

SINGLE GAME HIGHS (regular season): Attempts—18 (December 10, 1995, vs. Seattle); yards—131 (December 10, 1995, vs. Seattle); and rushing touchdowns—1 (November 7, 1999, vs. Green Bay). Receptions—9 (September 18, 1994 vs. Los Angeles Raiders); yards—85 (September 18, 1994 vs. Los Angeles Raiders); and touchdown receptions—1 (November 6, 1994 vs. Los Angeles Rams).

STATISTICAL PLATEAUS: 100-yard rushing games: 1995 (1).

				RUSHING				RECEIVING				PUNT RETURNS				KICKOFF RETURNS				TOTALS	
Year Team	G	GS	Att.	Yds.	Avg.	TD	No.	Yds.	Avg.	TD	No.	Yds.	Avg.	TD	No.	Yds.	Avg.	TD	TD	2pt.	Pts.
1993—Denver NFL	16	2	52	231	4.4	0	38	300	7.9	3	40	425	10.6	0	12	188	15.7	0	3	0	18
1994—Denver NFL	16	3	58	201	3.5	1	77	549	7.1	3	41	379	9.2	0	37	793	21.4	0	4	0	24
1995—Denver NFL	16	1	49	266	5.4	0	22	191	8.7	0	31	354	11.4	0	47	1269	27.0	0	0	0	0
1996—Detroit NFL	16	0	0	0	0.0	0	0	0	0.0	0	34	284	8.4	0	64	1627	25.4	0	0	0	0
1997—Detroit NFL	16	1	0	0	0.0	0	5	77	15.4	0	47	433	9.2	0	55	1315	23.9	0	0	0	0
1998—Chicago NFL	16	0	4	8	2.0	0	4	37	9.3	0	25	291	11.6	0	*62	*1550	25.0	†2	3	0	18
1999—Chicago NFL	16	1	16	102	6.4	1	20	151	7.6	0	30	346	11.5	0	‡61	‡1426	23.4	0	1	0	6
Pro totals (7 years)	112	8	179	808	4.5	2	166	1305	7.9	6	248	2512	10.1	1	338	8168	24.2	2	11	0	66

MILI, ITULA — TE — SEAHAWKS

PERSONAL: Born April 20, 1973, in Kahuku, Hawaii. ... 6-4/265. ... Name pronounced EE-too-la MEE-lee.
HIGH SCHOOL: Kahuku (Hawaii).
COLLEGE: Brigham Young.
TRANSACTIONS/CAREER NOTES: Selected by Seattle Seahawks in sixth round (174th pick overall) of 1997 NFL draft. ... Signed by Seahawks (June 11, 1997). ... On physically unable to perform list with knee injury (August 18, 1997-entire season). ... On injured reserve with knee injury (December 25, 1998-remainder of season).
SINGLE GAME HIGHS (regular season): Receptions—1 (December 19, 1999, vs. Denver); yards—20 (November 22, 1998, vs. Dallas); and touchdown receptions—1 (October 17, 1999, vs. San Diego).

			RECEIVING				TOTALS			
Year Team	G	GS	No.	Yds.	Avg.	TD	TD	2pt.	Pts.	Fum.
1997—Seattle NFL						Did not play.				
1998—Seattle NFL	7	0	1	20	20.0	0	0	0	0	0
1999—Seattle NFL	16	1	5	28	5.6	1	1	0	6	1
Pro totals (2 years)	23	1	6	48	8.0	1	1	0	6	1

MILLER, ARNOLD — DE — BROWNS

PERSONAL: Born January 3, 1975, in New Orleans. ... 6-3/239.
HIGH SCHOOL: George Washington Carver (New Orleans).
COLLEGE: Louisiana State.
TRANSACTIONS/CAREER NOTES: Signed as non-drafted free agent by Cleveland Browns (April 23, 1999).
PLAYING EXPERIENCE: Cleveland NFL, 1999. ... Games/Games started: 1999 (9/0).
PRO STATISTICS: 1999—Credited with one sack.

MILLER, BILLY — WR/TE — BRONCOS

PERSONAL: Born April 24, 1977, in Los Angeles. ... 6-3/215. ... Full name: Billy RoShawn Miller.
HIGH SCHOOL: Westlake (Westlake Village, Calif.).
COLLEGE: Southern California.
TRANSACTIONS/CAREER NOTES: Selected by Denver Broncos in seventh round (218th pick overall) of 1999 NFL draft. ... Signed by Broncos (July 20, 1999). ... Released by Broncos (September 5, 1999). ... Re-signed by Broncos to practice squad (September 6, 1999). ... Activated (October 19, 1999).
PLAYING EXPERIENCE: Denver NFL, 1999. ... Games/Games started: 1999 (10/0).
PRO STATISTICS: 1999—Caught five passes for 59 yards and returned four kickoffs for 79 yards.
SINGLE GAME HIGHS (regular season): Receptions—2 (November 7, 1999, vs. San Diego); yards—36 (November 7, 1999, vs. San Diego); and touchdown receptions—0.

MILLER, BUBBA — C/G — EAGLES

PERSONAL: Born January 24, 1973, in Nashville. ... 6-1/305. ... Full name: Stephen DeJuan Miller.
HIGH SCHOOL: Brentwood Academy (Franklin, Tenn.).
COLLEGE: Tennessee.
TRANSACTIONS/CAREER NOTES: Signed as non-drafted free agent by Philadelphia Eagles (April 26, 1996). ... Inactive for all 16 games (1996). ... Granted free agency (February 12, 1999). ... Re-signed by Eagles (April 22, 1999). ... Granted unconditional free agency (February 11, 2000). ... Re-signed by Eagles (March 1, 2000).
PLAYING EXPERIENCE: Philadelphia NFL, 1997-1999. ... Games/Games started: 1997 (13/3), 1998 (15/4), 1999 (14/0). Total: 42/7.
PRO STATISTICS: 1998—Caught one pass for 11 yards.

MILLER, CHRIS — QB

PERSONAL: Born August 9, 1965, in Pomona, Calif. ... 6-2/212. ... Full name: Christopher James Miller.
HIGH SCHOOL: Sheldon (Eugene, Ore.).
COLLEGE: Oregon.

TRANSACTIONS/CAREER NOTES: Selected by Atlanta Falcons in first round (13th pick overall) of 1987 NFL draft. ... Signed by Falcons (October 30, 1987). ... Granted roster exemption (October 30-November 9, 1987). ... On injured reserve with broken collarbone (December 4, 1990-remainder of season). ... On injured reserve with knee injury (November 1, 1992-remainder of season). ... On injured reserve with knee injury (October 7, 1993-remainder of season). ... Granted unconditional free agency (February 17, 1994). ... Signed by Los Angeles Rams (March 7, 1994). ... Rams franchise moved to St. Louis (April 12, 1995). ... On injured reserve with concussion (December 14, 1995-remainder of season). ... Released by Rams (March 11, 1996). ... Out of pro football (1996-1998 seasons). ... Signed by Denver Broncos (April 27, 1999). ... Announced retirement (January 3, 2000).

HONORS: Played in Pro Bowl (1991 season).

PRO STATISTICS: 1988—Fumbled twice and recovered one fumble. 1989—Successful on 25-yard field-goal attempt, fumbled 13 times and recovered five fumbles for minus three yards. 1990—Fumbled 11 times and recovered four fumbles for minus nine yards. 1991—Fumbled five times. 1992—Fumbled six times and recovered one fumble for minus one yard. 1993—Fumbled twice. 1994—Fumbled seven times and recovered three fumbles for minus five yards. 1995—Fumbled four times and recovered two fumbles for minus six yards. 1999—Fumbled twice for minus six yards.

SINGLE GAME HIGHS (regular season): Attempts—66 (December 24, 1989, vs. Detroit); completions—37 (December 24, 1989, vs. Detroit); passing yards—366 (October 7, 1990, vs. New Orleans); and touchdown passes—4 (September 27, 1992, vs. Chicago).

STATISTICAL PLATEAUS: 300-yard passing games: 1989 (3), 1990 (2), 1991 (2), 1992 (1), 1994 (1), 1995 (2). Total: 11.

MISCELLANEOUS: Regular-season record as starting NFL quarterback: 34-58 (.370).

						PASSING					RUSHING				TOTALS		
Year Team	G	GS	Att.	Cmp.	Pct.	Yds.	TD	Int.	Avg.	Rat.	Att.	Yds.	Avg.	TD	TD	2pt.	Pts.
1987—Atlanta NFL	3	2	92	39	42.4	552	1	9	6.00	26.4	4	21	5.3	0	0	0	0
1988—Atlanta NFL	13	13	351	184	52.4	2133	11	12	6.08	67.3	31	138	4.5	1	1	0	6
1989—Atlanta NFL	15	15	526	280	53.2	3459	16	10	6.58	76.1	10	20	2.0	0	0	0	3
1990—Atlanta NFL	12	12	388	222	57.2	2735	17	14	7.05	78.7	26	99	3.8	1	1	0	6
1991—Atlanta NFL	15	14	413	220	53.3	3103	26	18	7.51	80.6	32	229	7.2	0	0	0	0
1992—Atlanta NFL	8	8	253	152	60.1	1739	15	6	6.87	90.7	23	89	3.9	0	0	0	0
1993—Atlanta NFL	3	2	66	32	48.5	345	1	3	5.23	50.4	2	11	5.5	0	0	0	0
1994—L.A. Rams NFL	13	10	317	173	54.6	2104	16	14	6.64	73.6	20	100	5.0	0	0	0	0
1995—St. Louis NFL	13	13	405	232	57.3	2623	18	15	6.48	76.2	22	67	3.0	0	0	0	0
1996—						Did not play.											
1997—						Did not play.											
1998—						Did not play.											
1999—Denver NFL	3	3	81	46	56.8	527	2	1	6.51	79.6	8	40	5.0	0	0	0	0
Pro totals (10 years)	98	92	2892	1580	54.6	19320	123	102	6.68	74.9	178	814	4.6	2	2	0	15

MILLER, COREY   LB

PERSONAL: Born October 25, 1968, in Pageland, S.C. ... 6-2/252.

HIGH SCHOOL: Central (Pageland, S.C.).

COLLEGE: South Carolina.

TRANSACTIONS/CAREER NOTES: Selected by New York Giants in sixth round (167th pick overall) of 1991 NFL draft. ... Signed by Giants (July 15, 1991). ... Granted free agency (February 17, 1994). ... Re-signed by Giants (July 22, 1994). ... Granted unconditional free agency (February 17, 1995). ... Re-signed by Giants (March 9, 1995). ... On injured reserve with neck injury (August 25, 1998-entire season). ... Released by Giants (February 8, 1999). ... Signed by Minnesota Vikings (March 30, 1999). ... Released by Vikings (September 1, 1999). ... Re-signed by Vikings (September 21, 1999). ... Released by Vikings (November 9, 1999). ... Re-signed by Vikings (January 5, 2000). ... Granted unconditional free agency (February 11, 2000).

PRO STATISTICS: 1991—Recovered one fumble. 1993—Recovered two fumbles and fumbled once. 1994—Recovered one fumble.

			INTERCEPTIONS				SACKS
Year Team	G	GS	No.	Yds.	Avg.	TD	No.
1991—New York Giants NFL	16	1	0	0	0.0	0	2.5
1992—New York Giants NFL	16	7	2	10	5.0	0	2.0
1993—New York Giants NFL	16	14	2	18	9.0	0	6.5
1994—New York Giants NFL	15	13	2	6	3.0	0	0.0
1995—New York Giants NFL	14	9	0	0	0.0	0	0.0
1996—New York Giants NFL	14	13	0	0	0.0	0	2.0
1997—New York Giants NFL	14	13	0	0	0.0	0	1.0
1998—New York Giants NFL			Did not play.				
1999—Minnesota NFL	5	2	1	0	0.0	0	0.0
Pro totals (8 years)	110	72	7	34	4.9	0	14.0

MILLER, FRED   OT   TITANS

PERSONAL: Born February 6, 1973, in Houston. ... 6-7/315. ... Full name: Fred Miller Jr.

HIGH SCHOOL: Aldine Eisenhower (Houston).

COLLEGE: Baylor (degree in sociology, 1995).

TRANSACTIONS/CAREER NOTES: Selected by St. Louis Rams in fifth round (141st pick overall) of 1996 NFL draft. ... Signed by Rams (July 15, 1996). ... Granted free agency (February 12, 1999). ... Re-signed by Rams (May 24, 1999). ... Granted unconditional free agency (February 11, 2000). ... Signed by Tennessee Titans (February 16, 2000).

PLAYING EXPERIENCE: St. Louis NFL, 1996-1999. ... Games/Games started: 1996 (14/0), 1997 (15/7), 1998 (15/15), 1999 (16/16). Total: 60/38.

CHAMPIONSHIP GAME EXPERIENCE: Played in NFC championship game (1999 season). ... Member of Super Bowl championship team (1999 season).

MILLER, JAMIR   LB   BROWNS

PERSONAL: Born November 19, 1973, in Philadelphia. ... 6-5/266. ... Full name: Jamir Malik Miller. ... Cousin of Mark Gunn, defensive lineman with New York Jets (1991-94 and 1996) and Philadelphia Eagles (1995 and 1996). ... Name pronounced JA-meer.

HIGH SCHOOL: El Cerrito (Calif.).

M

COLLEGE: UCLA.

TRANSACTIONS/CAREER NOTES: Selected after junior season by Arizona Cardinals in first round (10th pick overall) of 1994 NFL draft. ... Signed by Cardinals (August 12, 1994). ... On suspended list for violating league substance abuse policy (September 4-October 3, 1995). ... Granted unconditional free agency (February 12, 1999). ... Signed by Cleveland Browns (May 13, 1999).

HONORS: Named linebacker on THE SPORTING NEWS college All-America first team (1993).

PRO STATISTICS: 1995—Fumbled once and recovered two fumbles for 26 yards. 1996—Recovered one fumble for 26 yards and a touchdown. 1998—Recovered two fumbles.

Year Team	G	GS	SACKS
1994—Arizona NFL	16	0	3.0
1995—Arizona NFL	11	8	1.0
1996—Arizona NFL	16	16	1.0
1997—Arizona NFL	16	16	5.5
1998—Arizona NFL	16	16	3.0
1999—Cleveland NFL	15	15	4.5
Pro totals (6 years)	90	71	18.0

MILLER, JIM   QB   BEARS

PERSONAL: Born February 9, 1971, in Grosse Pointe, Mich. ... 6-2/218. ... Full name: James Donald Miller.

HIGH SCHOOL: Kettering (Detroit).

COLLEGE: Michigan State (degree in financial administration).

TRANSACTIONS/CAREER NOTES: Selected by Pittsburgh Steelers in sixth round (178th pick overall) of 1994 NFL draft. ... Signed by Steelers (May 12, 1994). ... Inactive for all 16 games (1994). ... Assigned by Steelers to Frankfurt Galaxy in 1995 World League enhancement allocation program (February 20, 1995). ... Released by Steelers (August 23, 1997). ... Signed by Jacksonville Jaguars (September 2, 1997). ... Released by Jaguars (September 23, 1997). ... Signed by Atlanta Falcons (October 27, 1997). ... Granted unconditional free agency (February 13, 1998). ... Signed by Detroit Lions (March 2, 1998). ... Released by Lions (August 24, 1998). ... Signed by Dallas Cowboys (September 8, 1998). ... Released by Cowboys (October 1998). ... Signed by Chicago Bears (December 1, 1998). ... Active for four games (1998); did not play. ... On suspended list for violating league substance abuse policy (December 1, 1999-remainder of season). ... Granted unconditional free agency (February 11, 2000). ... Re-signed by Bears (February 17, 2000).

CHAMPIONSHIP GAME EXPERIENCE: Member of Steelers for AFC championship game (1994 and 1995 seasons); inactive. ... Member of Steelers for Super Bowl XXX (1995 season); inactive.

PRO STATISTICS: 1995—Fumbled once. 1996—Fumbled once for minus four yards. 1999—Fumbled four times and recovered three fumbles for minus 19 yards.

SINGLE GAME HIGHS (regular season): Attempts—48 (November 14, 1999, vs. Minnesota); completions—34 (November 14, 1999, vs. Minnesota); yards—422 (November 14, 1999, vs. Minnesota); and touchdown passes—3 (November 14, 1999, vs. Minnesota).

STATISTICAL PLATEAUS: 300-yard passing games: 1999 (2).

MISCELLANEOUS: Regular-season record as starting NFL quarterback: 1-3 (.250).

			PASSING							RUSHING				TOTALS		
Year Team	G	GS	Att.	Cmp.	Pct.	Yds.	TD	Int.	Avg.	Rat.	Att.	Yds.	Avg.	TD	TD	2pt.	Pts.
1994—Pittsburgh NFL							Did not play.										
1995—Frankfurt W.L.	...	...	43	23	53.5	236	1	1	5.49	67.6	3	-2	-0.7	0	0	0	0
—Pittsburgh NFL	4	0	56	32	57.1	397	2	5	7.09	53.9	1	2	2.0	0	0	0	0
1996—Pittsburgh NFL	2	1	25	13	52.0	123	0	0	4.92	65.9	2	-4	-2.0	0	0	0	0
1997—Atlanta NFL							Did not play.										
—Jacksonville NFL							Did not play.										
1998—Chicago NFL							Did not play.										
1999—Chicago NFL	5	3	174	110	63.2	1242	7	6	7.14	83.5	3	9	3.0	0	0	0	0
W.L. totals (1 year)	...	...	43	23	53.5	236	1	1	5.49	67.6	3	-2	-0.7	0	0	0	0
NFL totals (2 years)	11	4	255	155	60.8	1762	9	11	6.91	75.3	6	7	1.2	0	0	0	0
Pro totals (3 years)	...	...	298	178	59.7	1998	10	12	6.70	74.2	9	5	0.6	0	0	0	0

MILLER, JOSH   P   STEELERS

PERSONAL: Born July 14, 1970, in Rockway, N.Y. ... 6-3/219.

HIGH SCHOOL: East Brunswick (N.J.).

JUNIOR COLLEGE: Scottsdale (Ariz.) Community College.

COLLEGE: Arizona (degree in communications, 1993).

TRANSACTIONS/CAREER NOTES: Signed as non-drafted free agent by Green Bay Packers (April 1993). ... Released by Packers before 1993 season. ... Signed by Baltimore Stallions of CFL (June 1994). ... Signed by Seattle Seahawks (May 29, 1996). ... Released by Seahawks (August 13, 1996). ... Signed by Pittsburgh Steelers (August 15, 1996).

CHAMPIONSHIP GAME EXPERIENCE: Played in Grey Cup, CFL championship game (1994). ... Played in AFC championship game (1997 season).

HONORS: Named punter on THE SPORTING NEWS college All-America first team (1992).

PRO STATISTICS: CFL: 1994—Fumbled once. NFL: 1997—Rushed once for minus seven yards. 1999—Rushed twice for minus nine yards and fumbled once for minus 11 yards.

				PUNTING			
Year Team	G	No.	Yds.	Avg.	Net avg.	In. 20	Blk.
1994—Baltimore CFL	18	117	5024	42.9	36.9	0	0
1995—Baltimore CFL	18	118	5629	47.7	42.2	0	0
1996—Pittsburgh NFL	12	55	2256	41.0	33.6	18	0
1997—Pittsburgh NFL	16	64	2729	42.6	35.0	17	0
1998—Pittsburgh NFL	16	81	3530	43.6	36.8	*34	0
1999—Pittsburgh NFL	16	84	3795	45.2	38.1	27	0
CFL totals (2 years)	36	235	10653	45.3	39.6	0	0
NFL totals (4 years)	60	284	12310	43.3	36.2	96	0
Pro totals (6 years)	96	519	22963	44.2	37.7	96	0

M

MILLOY, LAWYER   S   PATRIOTS

PERSONAL: Born November 14, 1973, in St. Louis. ... 6-0/208.
HIGH SCHOOL: Lincoln (Tacoma, Wash.).
COLLEGE: Washington.
TRANSACTIONS/CAREER NOTES: Selected after junior season by New England Patriots in second round (36th pick overall) of 1996 NFL draft. ... Signed by Patriots (June 5, 1996).
CHAMPIONSHIP GAME EXPERIENCE: Played in AFC championship game (1996 season). ... Played in Super Bowl XXXI (1996 season).
HONORS: Named defensive back on THE SPORTING NEWS college All-America first team (1995). ... Played in Pro Bowl (1998 and 1999 seasons). ... Named safety on THE SPORTING NEWS NFL All-Pro team (1999).
PRO STATISTICS: 1996—Recovered one fumble. 1997—Recovered two fumbles. 1998—Recovered one fumble. 1999—Recovered two fumbles.

			INTERCEPTIONS				SACKS
Year Team	G	GS	No.	Yds.	Avg.	TD	No.
1996—New England NFL	16	10	2	14	7.0	0	1.0
1997—New England NFL	16	16	3	15	5.0	0	0.0
1998—New England NFL	16	16	6	54	9.0	1	1.0
1999—New England NFL	16	16	4	17	4.3	0	2.0
Pro totals (4 years)	64	58	15	100	6.7	1	4.0

MILLS, ERNIE   WR

PERSONAL: Born October 28, 1968, in Dunnellon, Fla. ... 5-11/196. ... Full name: Ernest Lee Mills III.
HIGH SCHOOL: Dunnellon (Fla.) Senior.
COLLEGE: Florida (degree in sports administration/exercise and sports science).
TRANSACTIONS/CAREER NOTES: Selected by Pittsburgh Steelers in third round (73rd pick overall) of 1991 NFL draft. ... Signed by Steelers (August 13, 1991). ... Granted free agency (February 17, 1994). ... Re-signed by Steelers (June 1, 1994). ... On physically unable to perform list with knee injury (August 24-October 25, 1996). ... Granted unconditional free agency (February 14, 1997). ... Signed by Carolina Panthers (March 5, 1997). ... Released by Panthers (February 9, 1998). ... Signed by Dallas Cowboys (February 27, 1998). ... On injured reserve with abdominal injury (December 2, 1998-remainder of season). ... Granted unconditional free agency (February 12, 1999). ... Re-signed by Cowboys (May 11, 1999). ... Released by Cowboys (April 4, 2000).
CHAMPIONSHIP GAME EXPERIENCE: Played in AFC championship game (1994 and 1995 seasons). ... Played in Super Bowl XXX (1995 season).
PRO STATISTICS: 1991—Recovered punt return in end zone for a touchdown, returned one punt for no yards and recovered one fumble. 1995—Recovered one fumble. 1996—Recovered one fumble for five yards.
SINGLE GAME HIGHS (regular season): Receptions—6 (October 18, 1999, vs. New York Giants); yards—110 (October 11, 1998, vs. Carolina); and touchdown receptions—2 (December 10, 1995, vs. Oakland).
STATISTICAL PLATEAUS: 100-yard receiving games: 1998 (1).

			RUSHING				RECEIVING				KICKOFF RETURNS				TOTALS			
Year Team	G	GS	Att.	Yds.	Avg.	TD	No.	Yds.	Avg.	TD	No.	Yds.	Avg.	TD	TD	2pt.	Pts.	Fum.
1991—Pittsburgh NFL	16	2	0	0	0.0	0	3	79	26.3	1	11	284	25.8	0	2	0	12	0
1992—Pittsburgh NFL	16	5	1	20	20.0	0	30	383	12.8	3	1	11	11.0	0	3	0	18	2
1993—Pittsburgh NFL	14	5	3	12	4.0	0	29	386	13.3	1	0	0	0.0	0	1	0	6	0
1994—Pittsburgh NFL	15	6	3	18	6.0	0	19	384	20.2	1	2	6	3.0	0	1	0	6	1
1995—Pittsburgh NFL	16	4	5	39	7.8	0	39	679	17.4	8	54	1306	24.2	0	8	0	48	2
1996—Pittsburgh NFL	9	3	2	24	12.0	0	7	92	13.1	1	8	146	18.3	0	1	0	6	0
1997—Carolina NFL	10	5	0	0	0.0	0	11	127	11.5	1	4	65	16.3	0	1	0	6	0
1998—Dallas NFL	11	1	3	9	3.0	0	28	479	17.1	4	0	0	0.0	0	4	0	24	0
1999—Dallas NFL	11	7	1	-1	-1.0	0	30	325	10.8	0	0	0	0.0	0	0	0	0	0
Pro totals (9 years)	118	38	18	121	6.7	0	196	2934	15.0	20	80	1818	22.7	0	21	0	126	5

MILLS, JOHN HENRY   TE

PERSONAL: Born October 31, 1969, in Jacksonville. ... 6-0/235. ... Full name: John Henry Mills.
HIGH SCHOOL: Godby (Tallahassee, Fla.).
COLLEGE: Wake Forest (degree in speech communications, 1993).
TRANSACTIONS/CAREER NOTES: Selected by Houston Oilers in fifth round (131st pick overall) of 1993 NFL draft. ... Signed by Oilers (July 16, 1993). ... Released by Oilers (August 30, 1993). ... Re-signed by Oilers (August 31, 1993). ... Granted free agency (February 16, 1996). ... Re-signed by Oilers (July 20, 1996). ... Granted unconditional free agency (February 14, 1997). ... Signed by Oakland Raiders (June 6, 1997). ... Granted unconditional free agency (February 13, 1998). ... Re-signed by Raiders (February 23, 1998). ... On injured reserve with hamstring injury (November 4-11, 1998). ... Released by Raiders (November 11, 1998). ... Signed by Cleveland Browns (December 17, 1998). ... Released by Browns (May 4, 1999). ... Signed by Minnesota Vikings (May 11, 1999). ... On injured reserve with triceps injury (January 5, 2000-remainder of playoffs). ... Granted unconditional free agency (February 11, 2000).
HONORS: Played in Pro Bowl (1996 season).
PRO STATISTICS: 1994—Caught one pass for four yards. 1996—Recovered two fumbles. 1999—Caught three passes for 30 yards.

			KICKOFF RETURNS				TOTALS			
Year Team	G	GS	No.	Yds.	Avg.	TD	TD	2pt.	Pts.	Fum.
1993—Houston NFL	16	0	11	230	20.9	0	0	0	0	0
1994—Houston NFL	16	1	15	282	18.8	0	0	0	0	1
1995—Houston NFL	16	0	0	0	0.0	0	0	0	0	0
1996—Houston NFL	16	0	0	0	0.0	0	0	0	0	0
1997—Oakland NFL	16	0	0	0	0.0	0	0	0	0	0
1998—Oakland NFL	5	0	0	0	0.0	0	0	0	0	0
1999—Minnesota NFL	15	0	0	0	0.0	0	0	0	0	0
Pro totals (7 years)	100	1	26	512	19.7	0	0	0	0	1

MILNE, BRIAN   FB

PERSONAL: Born January 7, 1973, in Waterford, Pa., ... 6-3/254. ... Full name: Brian Fitzsimons Milne.
HIGH SCHOOL: Fort Le Boeuf (Waterford, Pa.).
COLLEGE: Penn State (degree in labor and industrial relations).
TRANSACTIONS/CAREER NOTES: Selected by Indianapolis Colts in fourth round (115th pick overall) of 1996 NFL draft. ... Signed by Colts (July 5, 1996). ... Claimed on waivers by Cincinnati Bengals (August 21, 1996). ... Granted free agency (February 12, 1999). ... Re-signed by Bengals (May 20, 1999). ... Released by Bengals (September 29, 1999). ... Signed by Seattle Seahawks (October 27, 1999). ... Granted unconditional free agency (February 11, 2000).
PRO STATISTICS: 1998—Recovered one fumble.
SINGLE GAME HIGHS (regular season): Attempts—3 (September 12, 1999, vs. Tennessee); yards—30 (September 12, 1999, vs. Tennessee); and rushing touchdowns—1 (November 29, 1998, vs. Jacksonville).
MISCELLANEOUS: Won NCAA discus championship (1993).

			RUSHING				RECEIVING				TOTALS		
Year Team	G	GS	Att.	Yds.	Avg.	TD	No.	Yds.	Avg.	TD	TD	2pt.	Pts.	Fum.
1996—Cincinnati NFL	6	5	8	22	2.8	1	3	29	9.7	0	1	0	6	0
1997—Cincinnati NFL	16	16	13	32	2.5	2	23	138	6.0	0	2	0	12	0
1998—Cincinnati NFL	14	14	10	41	4.1	1	26	124	4.8	0	1	0	6	0
1999—Cincinnati NFL	1	1	3	30	10.0	0	0	0	0.0	0	0	†1	2	0
—Seattle NFL	10	0	0	0	0.0	0	0	0	0.0	0	0	0	0	0
Pro totals (4 years)	47	36	34	125	3.7	4	52	291	5.6	0	4	1	26	0

MILSTEAD, ROD   G

PERSONAL: Born November 10, 1969, in Washington, D.C. ... 6-2/290. ... Full name: Roderick Leon Milstead Jr.
HIGH SCHOOL: Lackey (Indian Head, Md.).
COLLEGE: Delaware State (degree in sociology and criminal justice).
TRANSACTIONS/CAREER NOTES: Selected by Dallas Cowboys in fifth round (121st pick overall) of 1992 NFL draft. ... Signed by Cowboys for 1992 season. ... Traded by Cowboys to Cleveland Browns for eighth-round pick (traded to Los Angeles Rams) in 1993 draft (August 24, 1992). ... On injured reserve with back injury (September 3, 1992-entire season). ... Released by Browns (August 30, 1993). ... Re-signed by Browns (October 6, 1993). ... Released by Browns (November 27, 1993). ... Re-signed by Browns (November 30, 1993). ... Inactive for 11 games (1993). ... Released by Browns (August 28, 1994). ... Signed by San Francisco 49ers (September 14, 1994). ... Granted unconditional free agency (February 14, 1997). ... Re-signed by 49ers (May 1, 1997). ... Released by 49ers (August 24, 1997). ... Re-signed by 49ers (October 22, 1997). ... Granted unconditional free agency (February 13, 1998). ... Signed by Washington Redskins (March 3, 1998). ... Granted unconditional free agency (February 12, 1999). ... Re-signed by Redskins (March 16, 1999). ... Released by Redskins (October 22, 1999). ... Re-signed by Redskins (November 9, 1999). ... Granted unconditional free agency (February 11, 2000).
PLAYING EXPERIENCE: San Francisco NFL, 1994-1997; Washington NFL, 1998 and 1999. ... Games/Games started: 1994 (5/0), 1995 (16/12), 1996 (11/0), 1997 (4/0), 1998 (14/11), 1999 (6/0). Total: 56/23.
CHAMPIONSHIP GAME EXPERIENCE: Member of 49ers for NFC championship game (1994 and 1997 seasons); inactive. ... Member of Super Bowl championship team (1994 season).
PRO STATISTICS: 1999—Returned one kickoff for no yards.

MIMS, CHRIS   DE   BEARS

PERSONAL: Born September 29, 1970, in Los Angeles. ... 6-5/300. ... Full name: Christopher Eddie Mims.
HIGH SCHOOL: Dorsey (Los Angeles).
JUNIOR COLLEGE: Los Angeles Pierce Junior College, then Los Angeles Southwest Community College.
COLLEGE: Tennessee.
TRANSACTIONS/CAREER NOTES: Selected by San Diego Chargers in first round (23rd pick overall) of 1992 NFL draft. ... Signed by Chargers (June 5, 1992). ... Released by Chargers (April 14, 1997). ... Signed by Washington Redskins (June 10, 1997). ... Granted unconditional free agency (February 13, 1998). ... Signed by Oakland Raiders (April 25, 1998). ... Released by Raiders (June 4, 1998). ... Signed by Chargers (June 10, 1998). ... Released by Chargers (October 9, 1999). ... Re-signed by Chargers (October 16, 1999). ... Released by Chargers (December 3, 1999). ... Signed by Chicago Bears (February 15, 2000).
CHAMPIONSHIP GAME EXPERIENCE: Played in AFC championship game (1994 season). ... Played in Super Bowl XXIX (1994 season).
PRO STATISTICS: 1992—Credited with one safety and recovered one fumble. 1993—Recovered two fumbles. 1994—Recovered two fumbles. 1995—Recovered one fumble. 1996—Recovered two fumbles.

Year Team	G	GS	SACKS
1992—San Diego NFL	16	4	10.0
1993—San Diego NFL	16	7	7.0
1994—San Diego NFL	16	16	11.0
1995—San Diego NFL	15	15	2.0
1996—San Diego NFL	15	15	6.0
1997—Washington NFL	11	7	4.0
1998—San Diego NFL	6	0	2.0
1999—San Diego NFL	9	0	0.0
Pro totals (8 years)	104	64	42.0

MINCY, CHARLES   S   RAIDERS

PERSONAL: Born December 16, 1969, in Los Angeles. ... 6-0/200. ... Full name: Charles Anthony Mincy.
HIGH SCHOOL: Dorsey (Los Angeles).
JUNIOR COLLEGE: Pasadena (Calif.) City College.
COLLEGE: Washington.
TRANSACTIONS/CAREER NOTES: Selected by Kansas City Chiefs in fifth round (133rd pick overall) of 1991 NFL draft. ... Signed by Chiefs (July 17, 1991). ... On injured reserve with ankle/toe injury (August 30-December 25, 1991). ... Did not play during regular season (1991);

played in two playoff games. ... Granted free agency (February 17, 1994). ... Re-signed by Chiefs (June 17, 1994). ... Granted unconditional free agency (February 17, 1995). ... Signed by Minnesota Vikings (March 6, 1995). ... Released by Vikings (February 9, 1996). ... Signed by Tampa Bay Buccaneers (October 2, 1996). ... Granted unconditional free agency (February 13, 1998). ... Re-signed by Buccaneers (March 30, 1998). ... Released by Buccaneers (February 11, 1999). ... Signed by Oakland Raiders (April 28, 1999).

CHAMPIONSHIP GAME EXPERIENCE: Played in AFC championship game (1993 season).

PRO STATISTICS: 1992—Recovered one fumble for 30 yards and a touchdown. 1993—Recovered two fumbles. 1995—Recovered two fumbles for 10 yards. 1997—Recovered one fumble. 1999—Returned one kickoff for no yards and recovered one fumble.

			INTERCEPTIONS				PUNT RETURNS				TOTALS			
Year Team	G	GS	No.	Yds.	Avg.	TD	No.	Yds.	Avg.	TD	TD	2pt.	Pts.	Fum.
1991—Kansas City NFL							Did not play.							
1992—Kansas City NFL	16	16	4	128	32.0	▲2	1	4	4.0	0	3	0	18	0
1993—Kansas City NFL	16	4	5	44	8.8	0	2	9	4.5	0	0	0	0	0
1994—Kansas City NFL	16	7	3	49	16.3	0	0	0	0.0	0	0	0	0	0
1995—Minnesota NFL	16	9	3	37	12.3	0	4	22	5.5	0	0	0	0	0
1996—Tampa Bay NFL	2	0	1	26	26.0	0	0	0	0.0	0	0	0	0	0
1997—Tampa Bay NFL	16	9	1	14	14.0	0	0	0	0.0	0	0	0	0	0
1998—Tampa Bay NFL	16	16	4	58	14.5	1	0	0	0.0	0	1	0	6	0
1999—Oakland NFL	16	6	2	23	11.5	0	0	0	0.0	0	0	0	0	0
Pro totals (8 years)	114	67	23	379	16.5	3	7	35	5.0	0	4	0	24	0

MINTER, BARRY   LB   BEARS

PERSONAL: Born January 28, 1970, in Mount Pleasant, Texas. ... 6-2/245. ... Full name: Barry Antoine Minter.

HIGH SCHOOL: Mount Pleasant (Texas).

COLLEGE: Tulsa.

TRANSACTIONS/CAREER NOTES: Selected by Dallas Cowboys in sixth round (168th pick overall) of 1993 NFL draft. ... Signed by Cowboys (July 14, 1993). ... Traded by Cowboys with LB Vinson Smith and sixth-round pick (DE Carl Reeves) in 1995 draft to Chicago Bears for TE Kelly Blackwell, S Markus Paul and LB John Roper (August 17, 1993). ... Granted free agency (February 16, 1996). ... Re-signed by Bears (February 26, 1996). ... Granted unconditional free agency (February 13, 1998). ... Re-signed by Bears (February 20, 1998).

PRO STATISTICS: 1994—Recovered one fumble. 1997—Recovered three fumbles. 1998—Recovered one fumble for 11 yards. 1999— Recovered one fumble.

			INTERCEPTIONS				SACKS
Year Team	G	GS	No.	Yds.	Avg.	TD	No.
1993—Chicago NFL	2	0	0	0	0.0	0	0.0
1994—Chicago NFL	13	1	0	0	0.0	0	0.0
1995—Chicago NFL	16	3	1	2	2.0	1	0.0
1996—Chicago NFL	16	7	1	5	5.0	0	1.5
1997—Chicago NFL	16	16	0	0	0.0	0	6.0
1998—Chicago NFL	16	16	1	17	17.0	0	1.0
1999—Chicago NFL	16	16	2	66	33.0	1	3.0
Pro totals (7 years)	95	59	5	90	18.0	2	11.5

M

MINTER, MIKE   S   PANTHERS

PERSONAL: Born January 15, 1974, in Cleveland. ... 5-10/188. ... Full name: Michael Christopher Minter.

HIGH SCHOOL: Lawton (Okla.).

COLLEGE: Nebraska (degree in engineering, 1996).

TRANSACTIONS/CAREER NOTES: Selected by Carolina Panthers in second round (56th pick overall) of 1997 NFL draft. ... Signed by Panthers (June 12, 1997).

PRO STATISTICS: 1997—Recovered two fumbles. 1999—Recovered two fumbles for 30 yards.

			INTERCEPTIONS				SACKS
Year Team	G	GS	No.	Yds.	Avg.	TD	No.
1997—Carolina NFL	16	11	0	0	0.0	0	3.5
1998—Carolina NFL	6	4	1	7	7.0	0	0.0
1999—Carolina NFL	16	16	3	69	23.0	0	1.0
Pro totals (3 years)	38	31	4	76	19.0	0	4.5

MIRANDA, PAUL   DB   COLTS

PERSONAL: Born May 2, 1976, in Thomasville, Ga. ... 5-10/184. ... Full name: Paul Nathaniel Miranda.

HIGH SCHOOL: Thomas County Central (Thomasville, Ga.).

JUNIOR COLLEGE: Holmes Junior College (Miss.).

COLLEGE: Central Florida (degree in health services administration).

TRANSACTIONS/CAREER NOTES: Selected by Indianapolis Colts in fourth round (96th pick overall) of 1999 NFL draft. ... Signed by Colts (July 22, 1999).

PLAYING EXPERIENCE: Indianapolis NFL, 1999. ... Games/Games started: 1999 (5/0).

MIRER, RICK   QB

PERSONAL: Born March 19, 1970, in Goshen, Ind. ... 6-3/212. ... Full name: Rick F. Mirer.

HIGH SCHOOL: Goshen (Ind.).

COLLEGE: Notre Dame.

TRANSACTIONS/CAREER NOTES: Selected by Seattle Seahawks in first round (second pick overall) of 1993 NFL draft. ... Signed by Seahawks (August 2, 1993). ... On injured reserve with thumb injury (December 20, 1994-remainder of season). ... Traded by Seahawks with fourth-round pick (RB Darnell Autry) in 1997 draft to Chicago Bears for first-round pick (traded to Atlanta) in 1997 draft (February 18, 1997). ... Released by Bears (August 30, 1998). ... Signed by Green Bay Packers (September 2, 1998). ... Active for four games (1998); did not play. ... Traded by Packers to New York Jets for fourth-round pick (traded to San Francisco) in 2000 draft (August 20, 1999). ... Released by Jets (February 2, 2000).

PRO STATISTICS: 1993—Fumbled 13 times and recovered five fumbles for minus 14 yards. 1994—Fumbled twice and recovered one fumble for minus seven yards. 1995—Fumbled five times and recovered one fumble for minus one yard. 1996—Fumbled four times. 1997—Fumbled four times and recovered one fumble for minus four yards. 1999—Fumbled three times and recovered two fumbles for minus one yard.

SINGLE GAME HIGHS (regular season): Attempts—43 (October 24, 1993, vs. New England); completions—25 (October 3, 1993, vs. San Diego); yards—287 (December 5, 1993, vs. Kansas City); and touchdown passes—3 (September 11, 1994, vs. Los Angeles Raiders).

MISCELLANEOUS: Regular-season record as starting NFL quarterback: 22-38 (.367).

					PASSING						RUSHING				TOTALS		
Year Team	G	GS	Att.	Cmp.	Pct.	Yds.	TD	Int.	Avg.	Rat.	Att.	Yds.	Avg.	TD	TD	2pt.	Pts.
1993—Seattle NFL	16	16	486	274	56.4	2833	12	17	5.83	67.0	68	343	5.0	3	3	0	18
1994—Seattle NFL	13	13	381	195	51.2	2151	11	7	5.65	70.2	34	153	4.5	0	0	0	0
1995—Seattle NFL	15	13	391	209	53.5	2564	13	§20	6.56	63.7	43	193	4.5	1	1	0	6
1996—Seattle NFL	11	9	265	136	51.3	1546	5	12	5.83	56.6	33	191	5.8	2	2	0	12
1997—Chicago NFL	7	3	103	53	51.5	420	0	6	4.08	37.7	20	78	3.9	1	1	1	8
1998—Green Bay NFL							Did not play.										
1999—New York Jets NFL	8	6	176	95	54.0	1062	5	9	6.03	60.4	21	89	4.2	1	1	0	6
Pro totals (6 years)	70	60	1802	962	53.4	10576	46	71	5.87	63.1	219	1047	4.8	8	8	1	50

MITCHELL, BASIL　　　　RB　　　　PACKERS

PERSONAL: Born September 7, 1975, in Pittsburg, Texas. ... 5-10/200. ... Full name: Basil Mucktar Mitchell.
HIGH SCHOOL: Mount Pleasant (Texas).
COLLEGE: Texas Christian (degree in psychology).
TRANSACTIONS/CAREER NOTES: Signed as non-drafted free agent by Green Bay Packers (April 26, 1999).
PRO STATISTICS: 1999—Returned two punts for no yards and recovered two fumbles.
SINGLE GAME HIGHS (regular season): Attempts—12 (December 12, 1999, vs. Carolina); yards—49 (December 12, 1999, vs. Carolina); and rushing touchdowns—0.

			RUSHING				RECEIVING				KICKOFF RETURNS				TOTALS			
Year Team	G	GS	Att.	Yds.	Avg.	TD	No.	Yds.	Avg.	TD	No.	Yds.	Avg.	TD	TD	2pt.	Pts.	Fum.
1999—Green Bay NFL	16	2	29	117	4.0	0	6	48	8.0	0	21	464	22.1	1	1	0	6	2

MITCHELL, BRANDON　　　　DE　　　　PATRIOTS

PERSONAL: Born June 19, 1975, in Abbeville, La. ... 6-3/289. ... Full name: Brandon Pete Mitchell.
HIGH SCHOOL: Abbeville (La.).
COLLEGE: Texas A&M.
TRANSACTIONS/CAREER NOTES: Selected by New England Patriots in second round (59th pick overall) of 1997 NFL draft. ... Signed by Patriots (June 6, 1997). ... On injured reserve with ankle injury (October 30, 1998-remainder of season). ... Granted free agency (February 11, 2000).
PLAYING EXPERIENCE: New England NFL, 1997-1999. ... Games/Games started: 1997 (11/0), 1998 (7/1), 1999 (16/16). Total: 34/17.
PRO STATISTICS: 1998—Credited with two sacks. 1999—Credited with three sacks and recovered one fumble.

MITCHELL, BRIAN　　　　RB/KR

PERSONAL: Born August 18, 1968, in Fort Polk, La. ... 5-10/221. ... Full name: Brian Keith Mitchell.
HIGH SCHOOL: Plaquemine (La.).
COLLEGE: Southwestern Louisiana.
TRANSACTIONS/CAREER NOTES: Selected by Washington Redskins in fifth round (130th pick overall) of 1990 NFL draft. ... Signed by Redskins (July 22, 1990). ... Granted free agency (February 1, 1992). ... Re-signed by Redskins for 1992 season. ... Granted unconditional free agency (February 17, 1994). ... Re-signed by Redskins (May 24, 1994). ... Granted free agency (February 17, 1995). ... Re-signed by Redskins (March 27, 1995). ... Granted unconditional free agency (February 13, 1998). ... Re-signed by Redskins (February 12, 1998). ... Released by Redskins (June 1, 2000).
CHAMPIONSHIP GAME EXPERIENCE: Played in NFC championship game (1991 season). ... Member of Super Bowl championship team (1991 season).
HONORS: Named punt returner on THE SPORTING NEWS NFL All-Pro team (1995). ... Played in Pro Bowl (1995 season).
RECORDS: Holds NFL career record for most combined kick returns—738; and most yards by combined kick returns—13,062. ... Holds NFL single-season record for most yards by combined kick return—1,930 (1994). ... Shares NFL career record for most kickoff returns—421.
PRO STATISTICS: 1990—Attempted six passes with three completions for 40 yards and fumbled twice. 1991—Fumbled eight times and recovered one fumble. 1992—Attempted one pass without a completion, fumbled four times and recovered two fumbles. 1993—Attempted two passes with one completion for 50 yards and an interception, fumbled three times and recovered one fumble. 1994—Had only pass attempt intercepted and fumbled four times. 1995—Fumbled twice and recovered one fumble. 1996—Attempted one pass without a completion, fumbled once and recovered two fumbles. 1997—Fumbled three times. 1998—Attempted two passes with one completion for no yards and fumbled three times. 1999—Fumbled twice and recovered two fumbles for five yards.
SINGLE GAME HIGHS (regular season): Attempts—21 (September 6, 1993, vs. Dallas); yards—116 (September 6, 1993, vs. Dallas); and rushing touchdowns—2 (September 6, 1993, vs. Dallas).
STATISTICAL PLATEAUS: 100-yard rushing games: 1993 (1).

			RUSHING				RECEIVING				PUNT RETURNS				KICKOFF RETURNS				TOTALS		
Year Team	G	GS	Att.	Yds.	Avg.	TD	No.	Yds.	Avg.	TD	No.	Yds.	Avg.	TD	No.	Yds.	Avg.	TD	TD	2pt.	Pts.
1990—Washington NFL	15	0	15	81	5.4	1	2	5	2.5	0	12	107	8.9	0	18	365	20.3	0	1	0	6
1991—Washington NFL	16	0	3	14	4.7	0	0	0	0.0	0	45	*600	13.3	*2	29	583	20.1	0	2	0	12
1992—Washington NFL	16	0	6	70	11.7	0	3	30	10.0	0	29	271	9.3	1	23	492	21.4	0	1	0	6
1993—Washington NFL	16	4	63	246	3.9	3	20	157	7.9	0	29	193	6.7	0	33	678	20.5	0	3	0	18

Year—Team	G	GS																			
1994—Washington NFL .	16	7	78	311	4.0	0	26	236	9.1	1	32	‡452	*14.1	†2	58	1478	25.5	0	3	1	20
1995—Washington NFL .	16	1	46	301	6.5	1	38	324	8.5	1	25	315	12.6	†1	55	1408	‡25.6	0	3	0	18
1996—Washington NFL .	16	2	39	193	4.9	0	32	286	8.9	0	23	258	11.2	0	56	1258	22.5	0	0	0	0
1997—Washington NFL .	16	1	23	107	4.7	1	36	438	12.2	1	38	442	11.6	∞1	47	1094	23.3	1	4	0	24
1998—Washington NFL .	16	0	39	208	5.3	2	44	306	7.0	0	44	‡506	11.5	0	59	1337	22.7	1	3	0	18
1999—Washington NFL .	16	0	40	220	5.5	1	31	305	9.8	0	40	332	8.3	0	43	893	20.8	0	1	0	6
Pro totals (10 years)	159	15	352	1751	5.0	9	232	2087	9.0	3	317	3476	11.0	7	421	9586	22.8	2	21	1	128

MITCHELL, DONALD   CB   TITANS

PERSONAL: Born December 14, 1976, in Beaumont, Texas. ... 5-9/185. ... Full name: Donald Roosevelt Mitchell.
HIGH SCHOOL: Central (Beaumont, Texas).
COLLEGE: Southern Methodist.
TRANSACTIONS/CAREER NOTES: Selected by Tennessee Titans in fourth round (117th pick overall) of 1999 NFL draft. ... Signed by Titans (July 27, 1999).
PLAYING EXPERIENCE: Tennessee NFL, 1999. ... Games/Games started: 1999 (16/0).
CHAMPIONSHIP GAME EXPERIENCE: Played in AFC championship game (1999 season). ... Played in Super Bowl XXXIV (1999 season).
PRO STATISTICS: 1999—Intercepted one pass for 42 yards and a touchdown and recovered one fumble.

MITCHELL, JEFF   C   RAVENS

PERSONAL: Born January 29, 1974, in Dallas ... 6-4/300. ... Full name: Jeffrey Clay Mitchell.
HIGH SCHOOL: Countryside (Clearwater, Fla.).
COLLEGE: Florida.
TRANSACTIONS/CAREER NOTES: Selected by Baltimore Ravens in fifth round (134th pick overall) of 1997 NFL draft. ... Signed by Ravens (July 10, 1997). ... On injured reserve with knee injury (August 18, 1997-entire season). ... Granted free agency (February 11, 2000). ... Re-signed by Ravens (April 17, 2000)
PLAYING EXPERIENCE: Baltimore NFL, 1998 and 1999. ... Games/Games started: 1998 (11/10), 1999 (16/16). Total: 27/26.
PRO STATISTICS: 1998—Fumbled once for minus 11 yards. 1999—Fumbled twice for minus 36 yards.

MITCHELL, KEITH   LB   SAINTS

PERSONAL: Born July 24, 1974, in Garland, Texas ... 6-2/245. ... Full name: Clarence Marquis Mitchell.
HIGH SCHOOL: Lakeview (Garland, Texas).
COLLEGE: Texas A&M.
TRANSACTIONS/CAREER NOTES: Signed as non-drafted free agent by New Orleans Saints (April 25, 1997).
HONORS: Named outside linebacker on THE SPORTING NEWS college All-America second team (1996).
PRO STATISTICS: 1998—Recovered three fumbles for 63 yards and one touchdown. 1999—Intercepted three passes for 22 yards and recovered one fumble.

Year Team	G	GS	SACKS
1997—New Orleans NFL	16	2	4.0
1998—New Orleans NFL	16	15	2.5
1999—New Orleans NFL	16	16	3.5
Pro totals (3 years)	48	33	10.0

MITCHELL, KEVIN   LB   REDSKINS

PERSONAL: Born January 1, 1971, in Harrisburg, Pa. ... 6-1/254. ... Full name: Kevin Danyelle Mitchell. ... Cousin of Troy Drayton, tight end, Miami Dolphins.
HIGH SCHOOL: Harrisburg (Pa.).
COLLEGE: Syracuse (degree in sociology).
TRANSACTIONS/CAREER NOTES: Selected by San Francisco 49ers in second round (53rd pick overall) of 1994 NFL draft. ... Signed by 49ers (July 20, 1994). ... Granted free agency (February 14, 1997). ... Re-signed by 49ers (April 24, 1997). ... Granted free agency (February 13, 1998). ... Signed by New Orleans Saints (February 19, 1998). ... Granted unconditional free agency (February 11, 2000). ... Signed by Washington Redskins (February 29, 2000).
PLAYING EXPERIENCE: San Francisco NFL, 1994-1997; New Orleans NFL, 1998 and 1999. ... Games/Games started: 1994 (16/0), 1995 (15/0), 1996 (12/3), 1997 (16/0), 1998 (8/8), 1999 (16/1). Total: 83/12.
CHAMPIONSHIP GAME EXPERIENCE: Played in NFC championship game (1994 and 1997 seasons). ... Member of Super Bowl championship team (1994 season).
HONORS: Named defensive lineman on THE SPORTING NEWS college All-America second team (1992 and 1993).
PRO STATISTICS: 1996—Credited with one sack and recovered one fumble. 1998—Credited with 2½ sacks.

MITCHELL, PETE   TE   GIANTS

PERSONAL: Born October 9, 1971, in Royal Oak, Mich. ... 6-2/248. ... Full name: Peter Clark Mitchell.
HIGH SCHOOL: Brother Rice (Bloomfield Hills, Mich.).
COLLEGE: Boston College (degree in communications, 1994).
TRANSACTIONS/CAREER NOTES: Selected by Miami Dolphins in fourth round (122nd pick overall) of 1995 NFL draft. ... Signed by Dolphins (July 14, 1995). ... Traded by Dolphins to Jacksonville Jaguars for WR Mike Williams (August 27, 1995). ... Granted free agency (February 13, 1998). ... Re-signed by Jaguars (April 13, 1998). ... Designated by Jaguars as transition player (February 12, 1999). ... Free agency status changed from transition to unconditional (February 18, 1999). ... Signed by New York Giants (March 23, 1999).
CHAMPIONSHIP GAME EXPERIENCE: Played in AFC championship game (1996 season).
HONORS: Named tight end on THE SPORTING NEWS college All-America first team (1993 and 1994).

PRO STATISTICS: 1997—Returned two kickoffs for 17 yards and recovered one fumble. 1998—Returned two kickoffs for 27 yards and recovered one fumble.

SINGLE GAME HIGHS (regular season): Receptions—10 (November 19, 1995, vs. Tampa Bay); yards—161 (November 19, 1995, vs. Tampa Bay); and touchdown receptions—1 (December 26, 1999, vs. Minnesota).

STATISTICAL PLATEAUS: 100-yard receiving games: 1995 (1).

			RECEIVING				TOTALS			
Year Team	G	GS	No.	Yds.	Avg.	TD	TD	2pt.	Pts.	Fum.
1995—Jacksonville NFL	16	4	41	527	12.9	2	2	0	12	0
1996—Jacksonville NFL	16	7	52	575	11.1	1	1	0	6	1
1997—Jacksonville NFL	16	12	35	380	10.9	4	4	0	24	0
1998—Jacksonville NFL	16	16	38	363	9.6	2	2	0	12	0
1999—New York Giants NFL	15	6	58	520	9.0	3	3	0	18	1
Pro totals (5 years)	79	45	224	2365	10.6	12	12	0	72	2

MITCHELL, SCOTT QB BENGALS

PERSONAL: Born January 2, 1968, in Salt Lake City. ... 6-6/240. ... Full name: William Scott Mitchell.

HIGH SCHOOL: Springville (Utah).

COLLEGE: Utah.

TRANSACTIONS/CAREER NOTES: Selected after junior season by Miami Dolphins in fourth round (93rd pick overall) of 1990 NFL draft. ... Signed by Dolphins (July 20, 1990). ... Inactive for 16 games (1990). ... Granted free agency (February 1, 1992). ... Assigned by Dolphins to Orlando Thunder in 1992 World League enhancement allocation program (February 20, 1992). ... Re-signed by Dolphins (February 21, 1992). ... Granted unconditional free agency (February 17, 1994). ... Signed by Detroit Lions (March 6, 1994). ... On injured reserve with wrist injury (November 8, 1994-remainder of season). ... Traded by Lions to Baltimore Ravens for third-round pick (traded to Miami) in 1999 draft and fifth-round pick (traded to St. Louis) in 2000 draft (March 16, 1999). ... Granted unconditional free agency (February 11, 2000). ... Signed by Cincinnati Bengals (March 9, 2000).

CHAMPIONSHIP GAME EXPERIENCE: Played in AFC championship game (1992 season).

PRO STATISTICS: W.L.: 1992—Fumbled six times and recovered two fumbles for minus 19 yards. NFL: 1993—Fumbled once and recovered one fumble for minus four yards. 1994—Fumbled eight times and recovered two fumbles for minus five yards. 1995—Fumbled eight times and recovered one fumble. 1996—Fumbled nine times and recovered five fumbles for minus three yards. 1997—Tied for NFC lead with 15 fumbles and recovered four fumbles for minus 15 yards. 1998—Fumbled once for minus nine yards. 1999—Fumbled once.

SINGLE GAME HIGHS (regular season): Attempts—50 (September 7, 1997, vs. Tampa Bay); completions—31 (October 13, 1996, vs. Oakland); yards—410 (November 23, 1995, vs. Minnesota); and touchdown passes—4 (September 22, 1996, vs. Chicago).

STATISTICAL PLATEAUS: 300-yard passing games: 1993 (1), 1995 (5), 1996 (2), 1997 (1). Total: 9.

MISCELLANEOUS: Regular-season record as starting NFL quarterback: 30-36 (.455). ... Postseason record as starting NFL quarterback: 0-2.

			PASSING							RUSHING				TOTALS		
Year Team	G	GS	Att.	Cmp.	Pct.	Yds.	TD	Int.	Avg.	Rat.	Att.	Yds.	Avg.	TD	TD	2pt.	Pts.
1990—Miami NFL							Did not play.										
1991—Miami NFL	2	0	0	0	0.0	0	0	0	0.0	...	0	0	0.0	0	0	0	0
1992—Orlando W.L.	10	10	*361	*201	55.7	2213	12	7	6.13	77.0	21	45	2.1	1	1	0	6
—Miami NFL	16	0	8	2	25.0	32	0	1	4.00	4.2	8	10	1.3	0	0	0	0
1993—Miami NFL	13	7	233	133	57.1	1773	12	8	7.61	84.2	21	89	4.2	0	0	0	0
1994—Detroit NFL	9	9	246	119	48.4	1456	10	11	5.92	62.0	15	24	1.6	1	1	0	6
1995—Detroit NFL	16	16	583	346	59.3	4338	32	12	7.44	92.3	36	104	2.9	4	4	0	24
1996—Detroit NFL	14	14	437	253	57.9	2917	17	17	6.68	74.9	37	83	2.2	4	4	0	24
1997—Detroit NFL	16	16	509	293	57.6	3484	19	14	6.84	79.6	37	83	2.2	1	1	0	6
1998—Detroit NFL	2	2	75	38	50.7	452	1	3	6.03	57.2	7	30	4.3	0	0	0	0
1999—Baltimore NFL	2	2	56	24	42.9	236	1	4	4.21	31.5	1	1	1.0	0	0	0	0
W.L. totals (1 year)	10	10	361	201	55.7	2213	12	7	6.13	77.0	21	45	2.1	1	1	0	6
NFL totals (9 years)	90	66	2147	1208	56.3	14688	92	70	6.84	78.2	162	424	2.6	10	10	0	60
Pro totals (10 years)	100	76	2508	1409	56.2	16901	104	77	6.74	78.0	183	469	2.6	11	11	0	66

MIXON, KENNY DE DOLPHINS

PERSONAL: Born May 31, 1975, in Sun Valley, Calif. ... 6-4/282. ... Full name: Kenneth Jermaine Mixon.

HIGH SCHOOL: Pineville (La.).

COLLEGE: Louisiana State.

TRANSACTIONS/CAREER NOTES: Selected by Miami Dolphins in second round (49th pick overall) of 1998 NFL draft. ... Signed by Dolphins (July 21, 1998).

PLAYING EXPERIENCE: Miami NFL, 1998 and 1999. ... Games/Games started: 1998 (16/16), 1999 (11/2). Total: 27/18.

PRO STATISTICS: 1998—Credited with two sacks.

MOBLEY, JOHN LB BRONCOS

PERSONAL: Born October 10, 1973, in Chester, Pa. ... 6-1/236. ... Full name: John Ulysses Mobley.

HIGH SCHOOL: Chichester (Marcus Hook, Pa.).

COLLEGE: Kutztown (Pa.) University.

TRANSACTIONS/CAREER NOTES: Selected by Denver Broncos in first round (15th pick overall) of 1996 NFL draft. ... Signed by Broncos (July 23, 1996). ... On injured reserve with knee injury (September 22, 1999-remainder of season).

CHAMPIONSHIP GAME EXPERIENCE: Played in AFC championship game (1997 and 1998 seasons). ... Member of Super Bowl championship team (1997 and 1998 seasons).

HONORS: Named outside linebacker on THE SPORTING NEWS NFL All-Pro team (1997).

PRO STATISTICS: 1997—Recovered one fumble. 1998—Recovered one fumble.

M

| Year Team | G | GS | INTERCEPTIONS | | | | SACKS |
			No.	Yds.	Avg.	TD	No.
1996—Denver NFL	16	16	1	8	8.0	0	1.5
1997—Denver NFL	16	16	1	13	13.0	1	4.0
1998—Denver NFL	16	15	1	-2	-2.0	0	1.0
1999—Denver NFL	2	2	0	0	0.0	0	0.0
Pro totals (4 years)	50	49	3	19	6.3	1	6.5

MOBLEY, SINGOR — S

PERSONAL: Born October 12, 1972, in Tacoma, Wash. ... 5-11/195. ... Full name: Singor A. Mobley. ... Name pronounced sin-GORE.
HIGH SCHOOL: Curtis Senior (University Place, Wash.).
COLLEGE: Washington State.
TRANSACTIONS/CAREER NOTES: Signed by Edmonton Eskimos CFL (April 1995). ... Signed as non-drafted free-agent by Dallas Cowboys (February 12, 1997). ... Granted free agency (February 11, 2000). ... Signed by Eskimos CFL (May 23, 2000).
PLAYING EXPERIENCE: Edmonton CFL, 1995 and 1996; Dallas NFL, 1997-1999. ... Games/Games started: 1995 (17/games started unavailable), 1996 (16/games started unavailable); 1997 (12/0), 1998 (16/0), 1999 (16/0). Total CFL: 33/-. Total NFL: 44/0. Total Pro: 77/-.
PRO STATISTICS: CFL: 1995—Intercepted one pass for four yards, credited with one sack and recovered three fumbles for 129 yards and one touchdown. 1996—Credited with five sacks and recovered one fumble. NFL: 1998—Recovered one fumble.

MOHR, CHRIS — P — BILLS

PERSONAL: Born May 11, 1966, in Atlanta. ... 6-5/215. ... Full name: Christopher Garrett Mohr.
HIGH SCHOOL: Briarwood Academy (Warrenton, Ga.).
COLLEGE: Alabama (degree in criminal justice).
TRANSACTIONS/CAREER NOTES: Selected by Tampa Bay Buccaneers in sixth round (146th pick overall) of 1989 NFL draft. ... Signed by Buccaneers (July 15, 1989). ... Released by Buccaneers (September 2, 1990). ... Signed by WLAF (January 31, 1991). ... Selected by Montreal Machine in first round (eighth punter) of 1991 WLAF positional draft. ... Signed by Buffalo Bills (June 6, 1991). ... Granted unconditional free agency (February 17, 1994). ... Re-signed by Bills (March 3, 1994). ... Granted unconditional free agency (February 14, 1997). ... Re-signed by Bills (March 4, 1997).
CHAMPIONSHIP GAME EXPERIENCE: Played in AFC championship game (1991-1993 seasons). ... Played in Super Bowl XXVI (1991 season), Super Bowl XXVII (1992 season) and Super Bowl XXVIII (1993 season).
HONORS: Named punter on All-World League team (1991).
PRO STATISTICS: NFL: 1989—Converted one extra point. 1991—Completed only pass attempt for minus nine yards. 1992—Rushed once for 11 yards and recovered one fumble. 1993—Fumbled once and recovered one fumble. 1994—Rushed once for minus nine yards. 1997—Rushed once for no yards, attempted one pass with a completion for 29 yards, fumbled once and recovered one fumble for minus 10 yards. 1999—Rushed once for no yards. W.L.: 1991—Had only pass attempt intercepted and rushed three times for minus four yards.

| Year Team | G | PUNTING | | | | | |
		No.	Yds.	Avg.	Net avg.	In. 20	Blk.
1989—Tampa Bay NFL	16	∞84	3311	39.4	32.1	10	2
1990—				Did not play.			
1991—Montreal W.L.	10	57	2436	*42.7	34.0	13	2
—Buffalo NFL	16	54	2085	38.6	36.1	12	0
1992—Buffalo NFL	15	60	2531	42.2	36.7	12	0
1993—Buffalo NFL	16	74	2991	40.4	36.0	19	0
1994—Buffalo NFL	16	67	2799	41.8	36.0	13	0
1995—Buffalo NFL	16	86	3473	40.4	36.2	23	0
1996—Buffalo NFL	16	§101	§4194	41.5	36.5	§27	0
1997—Buffalo NFL	16	90	3764	41.8	36.0	24	1
1998—Buffalo NFL	16	69	2882	41.8	33.2	18	0
1999—Buffalo NFL	16	73	2840	38.9	33.9	20	0
W.L. totals (1 year)	10	57	2436	42.7	34.0	13	2
NFL totals (10 years)	159	758	30870	40.7	35.3	178	3
Pro totals (11 years)	169	815	33306	40.9	35.2	191	5

MOHRING, MICHAEL — DT/DE — CHARGERS

PERSONAL: Born March 22, 1974, in Glen Cove, N.Y. ... 6-5/295. ... Full name: Michael Joseph Mohring. ... Cousin of John Mohring, line-backer with Detroit Lions (1980) and Cleveland Browns (1980). ... Name pronounced MORE-ing.
HIGH SCHOOL: West Chester (Pa.) East.
COLLEGE: Pittsburgh.
TRANSACTIONS/CAREER NOTES: Signed as non-drafted free agent by Miami Dolphins (April 24, 1997). ... Released by Dolphins (August 18, 1997). ... Signed by San Diego Chargers to practice squad (August 25, 1997). ... Activated (December 12, 1997).
PLAYING EXPERIENCE: San Diego NFL, 1997-1999. ... Games/Games started: 1997 (2/0), 1998 (10/0), 1999 (16/1). Total: 28/1.
PRO STATISTICS: 1998—Credited with one sack. 1999—Credited with two sacks.

MOLDEN, ALEX — CB — SAINTS

PERSONAL: Born August 4, 1973, in Detroit. ... 5-10/190. ... Full name: Alex M. Molden.
HIGH SCHOOL: Sierra (Colorado Springs, Colo.).
COLLEGE: Oregon.
TRANSACTIONS/CAREER NOTES: Selected by New Orleans Saints in first round (11th pick overall) of 1996 NFL draft. ... Signed by Saints (July 21, 1996).
HONORS: Named defensive back on THE SPORTING NEWS college All-America second team (1995).
PRO STATISTICS: 1997—Recovered two fumbles.

M

Year Team	G	GS	INTERCEPTIONS No.	Yds.	Avg.	TD	SACKS No.
1996—New Orleans NFL	14	2	2	2	1.0	0	2.0
1997—New Orleans NFL	16	15	0	0	0.0	0	4.0
1998—New Orleans NFL	16	15	2	35	17.5	0	0.0
1999—New Orleans NFL	13	0	1	2	2.0	0	0.0
Pro totals (4 years)	59	32	5	39	7.8	0	6.0

MONROE, ROD   TE   FALCONS

PERSONAL: Born July 30, 1975, in Hearne, Texas. ... 6-4/245. ... Full name: Rodrick Monroe.
HIGH SCHOOL: Heane (Texas).
JUNIOR COLLEGE: McLennan Community College (Texas); did not play.
COLLEGE: Cincinnati.
TRANSACTIONS/CAREER NOTES: Selected by Dallas Cowboys in seventh round (237th pick overall) of 1998 NFL draft. ... Signed by Cowboys (July 13, 1998). ... Released by Cowboys (August 24, 1998). ... Signed by Atlanta Falcons to practice squad (September 1, 1998). ... Activated (December 15, 1998); did not play.
PLAYING EXPERIENCE: Atlanta NFL, 1999. ... Games/Games started: 1999 (2/0).
CHAMPIONSHIP GAME EXPERIENCE: Member of Falcons for NFC championship game (1998 season); inactive. ... Member of Falcons for Super Bowl XXXIII (1998 season); inactive.
SINGLE GAME HIGHS (regular season): Receptions—1 (December 12, 1999, vs. San Francisco); yards—8 (December 12, 1999, vs. San Francisco); and touchdown receptions—0.

MONTGOMERY, JOE   RB   GIANTS

PERSONAL: Born June 8, 1976, in Robbins, Ill. ... 5-10/230.
HIGH SCHOOL: Richards (Oak Lawn, Ill.).
COLLEGE: Ohio State.
TRANSACTIONS/CAREER NOTES: Selected by New York Giants in second round (49th pick overall) of 1999 NFL draft. ... Signed by Giants (July 29, 1999).
SINGLE GAME HIGHS (regular season): Attempts—38 (December 5, 1999, vs. New York Jets); yards—111 (December 5, 1999, vs. New York Jets); and rushing touchdowns—1 (January 2, 2000, vs. Dallas).
STATISTICAL PLATEAUS: 100-yard rushing games: 1999 (1).

Year Team	G	GS	RUSHING Att.	Yds.	Avg.	TD	TOTALS TD	2pt.	Pts.	Fum.
1999—New York Giants NFL	7	5	115	348	3.0	3	3	†1	20	2

MONTGOMERY, MONTY   CB   49ERS

PERSONAL: Born December 8, 1973, in Dallas. ... 5-11/197. ... Full name: Delmonico Montgomery.
HIGH SCHOOL: Gladewater (Texas).
COLLEGE: Houston.
TRANSACTIONS/CAREER NOTES: Selected by Indianapolis Colts in fourth round (117th pick overall) of 1997 NFL draft. ... Signed by Colts (July 7, 1997). ... Released by Colts (September 15, 1999). ... Re-signed by Colts (September 17, 1999). ... Released by Colts (September 29, 1999). ... Signed by San Francisco 49ers (October 4, 1999). ... On injured reserve with broken arm (December 8, 1999-remainder of season).
PRO STATISTICS: 1998—Intercepted one pass for 22 yards and recovered two fumbles for 14 yards.

Year Team	G	GS	SACKS
1997—Indianapolis NFL	16	3	1.0
1998—Indianapolis NFL	16	5	2.0
1999—Indianapolis NFL	3	0	0.0
—San Francisco NFL	4	2	0.0
Pro totals (3 years)	39	10	3.0

MONTY, PETE   LB   GIANTS

PERSONAL: Born July 3, 1974, in Fort Collins, Colo. ... 6-2/250. ... Full name: Peter Monty.
HIGH SCHOOL: Fort Collins (Colo.).
COLLEGE: Wisconsin.
TRANSACTIONS/CAREER NOTES: Selected by New York Giants in fourth round (103rd pick overall) of 1997 NFL draft. ... Signed by Giants (July 19, 1997). ... On injured reserve with knee injury (September 30, 1997-remainder of season). ... Granted free agency (February 11, 2000). ... Re-signed by Giants (April 13, 2000).
PLAYING EXPERIENCE: New York Giants NFL, 1997-1999. ... Games/Games started: 1997 (3/0), 1998 (11/0), 1999 (16/3). Total: 30/3.

MOON, WARREN   QB   CHIEFS

PERSONAL: Born November 18, 1956, in Los Angeles. ... 6-3/218. ... Full name: Harold Warren Moon.
HIGH SCHOOL: Hamilton (Los Angeles).
JUNIOR COLLEGE: West Los Angeles Junior College.
COLLEGE: Washington.
TRANSACTIONS/CAREER NOTES: Signed by Edmonton Eskimos of CFL (March 1978). ... USFL rights traded by Memphis Showboats to Los Angeles Express for future draft pick (August 30, 1983). ... Granted free agency (March 1, 1984). ... Signed by Houston Oilers (March 1, 1984). ... On injured reserve with fractured scapula (September 5-October 15, 1988). ... Traded by Oilers to Minnesota Vikings for third-round pick (WR Malcolm Seabron) in 1994 draft and third-round pick (RB Rodney Thomas) in 1995 draft (April 14, 1994). ... Released by Vikings

M

(February 21, 1997). ... Signed by Seattle Seahawks (March 7, 1997). ... Released by Seahawks (February 11, 1999). ... Signed by Kansas City Chiefs (April 27, 1999).

CHAMPIONSHIP GAME EXPERIENCE: Played in Grey Cup, CFL championship game (1978-1982 seasons).

HONORS: Played in Pro Bowl (1988-1995 and 1997 seasons). ... Named quarterback on THE SPORTING NEWS NFL All-Pro team (1990). ... Named Outstanding Player of Pro Bowl (1997 season).

RECORDS: Holds NFL career records for most fumbles—160; most own and opponents' fumbles recovered—55; and most own fumbles recovered—55. ... Holds NFL single-season record for most passes completed—404 (1991). ... Shares NFL single-season record for most games with 300 or more yards passing—9 (1990). ... Shares NFL single-game record for most times sacked—12 (September 29, 1985, vs. Dallas).

POST SEASON RECORDS: Holds NFL postseason career records for most fumbles—16; and most own fumbles recovered—8. ... Holds NFL postseason single-game records for most passes completed—36 (January 3, 1993, OT, at Buffalo); and most fumbles—5 (January 16, 1994, vs. Kansas City).

PRO STATISTICS: CFL: 1978—Fumbled once. 1979—Fumbled once. 1981—Fumbled once. 1982—Fumbled once and recovered one fumble. 1983—Fumbled seven times. NFL: 1984—Led league with 17 fumbles and recovered seven fumbles for minus one yard. 1985—Fumbled 12 times and recovered five fumbles for minus eight yards. 1986—Fumbled 11 times and recovered three fumbles for minus four yards. 1987—Fumbled eight times and recovered six fumbles for minus seven yards. 1988—Fumbled eight times and recovered four fumbles for minus 12 yards. 1989—Fumbled 11 times and recovered six fumbles for minus 13 yards. 1990—Led league with 18 fumbles and recovered four fumbles. 1991—Fumbled 11 times and recovered four fumbles for minus four yards. 1992—Fumbled seven times. 1993—Fumbled 13 times and recovered five fumbles for minus seven yards. 1994—Fumbled nine times and recovered two fumbles for minus five yards. 1995—Fumbled 13 times and recovered five fumbles for minus 12 yards. 1996—Fumbled seven times and recovered two fumbles. 1997—Fumbled seven times and recovered one fumble for minus two yards. 1998—Fumbled eight times and recovered one fumble for minus 12 yards.

SINGLE GAME HIGHS (regular season): Attempts—57 (November 6, 1994, vs. New Orleans); completions—41 (November 10, 1991, vs. Dallas); yards—527 (December 16, 1990, vs. Kansas City); and touchdown passes—5 (October 26, 1997, vs. Oakland).

STATISTICAL PLATEAUS: 300-yard passing games: 1984 (4), 1985 (3), 1986 (3), 1987 (2), 1989 (4), 1990 (9), 1991 (6), 1992 (4), 1993 (3), 1994 (6), 1995 (4), 1997 (1). Total: 49.

MISCELLANEOUS: Regular-season record as starting NFL quarterback: 102-100 (.505). ... Postseason record as starting NFL quarterback: 3-7 (.300). ... Active NFL leader for career passing yards (49,117) and touchdown passes (290). ... Holds Oilers franchise all-time records for most yards passing (33,685) and most touchdown passes (196).

			PASSING								RUSHING				TOTALS		
Year Team	G	GS	Att.	Cmp.	Pct.	Yds.	TD	Int.	Avg.	Rat.	Att.	Yds.	Avg.	TD	TD	2pt.	Pts.
1978—Edmonton CFL	16	...	173	89	51.4	1112	5	7	6.43	64.5	30	114	3.8	1	1	0	6
1979—Edmonton CFL	16	...	274	149	54.4	2382	20	12	8.69	89.7	56	150	2.7	2	2	0	12
1980—Edmonton CFL	16	...	331	181	54.7	3127	25	11	9.45	98.3	55	352	6.4	3	3	0	18
1981—Edmonton CFL	15	9	378	237	62.7	3959	27	12	10.47	108.6	50	298	6.0	3	3	0	18
1982—Edmonton CFL	16	16	562	333	59.3	5000	36	16	8.90	98.0	54	259	4.8	4	4	0	24
1983—Edmonton CFL	16	16	664	380	57.2	5648	31	19	8.51	88.9	85	527	6.2	3	3	0	18
1984—Houston NFL	16	16	450	259	57.6	3338	12	14	7.42	76.9	58	211	3.6	1	1	0	6
1985—Houston NFL	14	14	377	200	53.1	2709	15	19	7.19	68.5	39	130	3.3	0	0	0	0
1986—Houston NFL	15	15	488	256	52.5	3489	13	*26	7.15	62.3	42	157	3.7	2	2	0	12
1987—Houston NFL	12	12	368	184	50.0	2806	21	18	7.63	74.2	34	112	3.3	3	3	0	18
1988—Houston NFL	11	11	294	160	54.4	2327	17	8	7.91	88.4	33	88	2.7	5	5	0	30
1989—Houston NFL	16	16	464	280	60.3	3631	23	14	7.83	88.9	70	268	3.8	4	4	0	24
1990—Houston NFL	15	15	*584	*362	62.0	*4689	*33	13	8.03	96.8	55	215	3.9	2	2	0	12
1991—Houston NFL	16	16	*655	*404	61.7	*4690	23	*21	7.16	81.7	33	68	2.1	2	2	0	12
1992—Houston NFL	11	10	346	224	64.7	2521	18	12	7.29	§89.3	27	147	5.4	1	1	0	6
1993—Houston NFL	15	14	520	303	58.3	3485	21	§21	6.70	75.2	48	145	3.0	1	1	0	6
1994—Minnesota NFL	15	15	‡601	‡371	61.7	‡4264	18	‡19	7.09	79.9	27	55	2.0	0	0	0	0
1995—Minnesota NFL	16	16	‡606	*377	62.2	4228	33	14	6.98	91.5	33	82	2.5	0	0	0	0
1996—Minnesota NFL	8	8	247	134	54.3	1610	7	9	6.52	68.7	9	6	0.7	0	0	0	0
1997—Seattle NFL	15	14	528	313	59.3	3678	25	16	6.97	83.7	17	40	2.4	1	1	0	6
1998—Seattle NFL	10	10	258	145	56.2	1632	11	8	6.33	76.6	16	10	0.6	0	0	0	0
1999—Kansas City NFL	1	0	3	1	33.3	20	0	0	6.67	57.6	0	0	0.0	0	0	0	0
CFL totals (6 years)	95	...	2382	1369	57.5	21228	144	77	8.91	93.8	330	1700	5.2	16	16	0	96
NFL totals (16 years)	206	202	6789	3973	58.5	49117	290	232	7.23	81.0	541	1734	3.2	22	22	0	132
Pro totals (22 years)	301	...	9171	5342	58.2	70345	434	309	7.67	84.3	871	3434	3.9	38	38	0	228

M

MOORE, DAMON   S   EAGLES

PERSONAL: Born September 15, 1976, in Fostoria, Ohio. ... 5-11/215.
HIGH SCHOOL: Fostoria (Ohio).
COLLEGE: Ohio State.
TRANSACTIONS/CAREER NOTES: Selected by Philadelphia Eagles in fourth round (128th pick overall) of 1999 NFL draft. ... Signed by Eagles (July 28, 1999).
PLAYING EXPERIENCE: Philadelphia NFL, 1999. ... Games/Games started: 1999 (16/1).
HONORS: Named strong safety on THE SPORTING NEWS college All-America first team (1998).
PRO STATISTICS: 1999—Intercepted one pass for 28 yards and recovered one fumble.

MOORE, DAVE   TE   BUCCANEERS

PERSONAL: Born November 11, 1969, in Morristown, N.J. ... 6-2/258. ... Full name: David Edward Moore.
HIGH SCHOOL: Roxbury (Succasunna, N.J.).
COLLEGE: Pittsburgh (degree in justice administration, 1991).
TRANSACTIONS/CAREER NOTES: Selected by Miami Dolphins in seventh round (191st pick overall) of 1992 NFL draft. ... Signed by Dolphins (July 15, 1992). ... Released by Dolphins (August 31, 1992). ... Re-signed by Dolphins to practice squad (September 1, 1992). ... Released by Dolphins (September 16, 1992). ... Re-signed by Dolphins to practice squad (October 21, 1992). ... Activated (October 24, 1992). ... Released by Dolphins (October 28, 1992). ... Re-signed by Dolphins to practice squad (October 28, 1992). ... Released by Dolphins (November 18, 1992). ... Signed by Tampa Bay Buccaneers to practice squad (November 24, 1992). ... Activated (December 4, 1992). ... Granted free agency (February 16, 1996). ... Re-signed by Buccaneers (May 31, 1996). ... Granted unconditional free agency (February 14, 1997). ... Re-

signed by Buccaneers (February 18, 1997). ... Granted unconditional free agency (February 11, 2000). ... Re-signed by Buccaneers (March 20, 2000).

CHAMPIONSHIP GAME EXPERIENCE: Played in NFC championship game (1999 season).

PRO STATISTICS: 1993—Attempted one pass without a completion and recovered one fumble. 1995—Rushed once for four yards.

SINGLE GAME HIGHS (regular season): Receptions—6 (November 2, 1997, vs. Indianapolis); yards—62 (November 3, 1996, vs. Chicago); and touchdown receptions—1 (January 2, 2000, vs. Chicago).

				RECEIVING			TOTALS			
Year Team	G	GS	No.	Yds.	Avg.	TD	TD	2pt.	Pts.	Fum.
1992—Miami NFL	1	0	0	0	0.0	0	0	0	0	0
—Tampa Bay NFL	4	2	1	10	10.0	0	0	0	0	0
1993—Tampa Bay NFL	15	1	4	47	11.8	1	1	0	6	0
1994—Tampa Bay NFL	15	5	4	57	14.3	0	0	0	0	0
1995—Tampa Bay NFL	16	9	13	102	7.8	0	0	0	0	0
1996—Tampa Bay NFL	16	8	27	237	8.8	3	3	0	18	0
1997—Tampa Bay NFL	16	7	19	217	11.4	4	4	0	24	0
1998—Tampa Bay NFL	16	16	24	255	10.6	4	4	0	24	1
1999—Tampa Bay NFL	16	16	23	276	12.0	5	5	0	30	0
Pro totals (8 years)	115	64	115	1201	10.4	17	17	0	102	1

MOORE, HERMAN   WR   LIONS

PERSONAL: Born October 20, 1969, in Danville, Va. ... 6-4/224. ... Full name: Herman Joseph Moore.

HIGH SCHOOL: George Washington (Danville, Va.).

COLLEGE: Virginia (degree in rhetoric and communication studies, 1991).

TRANSACTIONS/CAREER NOTES: Selected after junior season by Detroit Lions in first round (10th pick overall) of 1991 NFL draft. ... Signed by Lions (July 19, 1991). ... On injured reserve with quadricep injury (September 11-October 9, 1992). ... On practice squad (October 9-14, 1992). ... Designated by Lions as transition player (February 25, 1993).

CHAMPIONSHIP GAME EXPERIENCE: Played in NFC championship game (1991 season).

HONORS: Named wide receiver on THE SPORTING NEWS college All-America first team (1990). ... Played in Pro Bowl (1994-1997 seasons). ... Named wide receiver on THE SPORTING NEWS NFL All-Pro team (1995-1997).

RECORDS: Holds NFL single-season record for most pass receptions—123 (1995).

POST SEASON RECORDS: Shares NFL postseason career and single-game records for most two-point conversions—1 (December 30, 1995, vs. Philadelphia).

SINGLE GAME HIGHS (regular season): Receptions—14 (December 4, 1995, vs. Chicago); yards—183 (December 4, 1995, vs. Chicago); and touchdown receptions—3 (October 29, 1995, vs. Green Bay).

STATISTICAL PLATEAUS: 100-yard receiving games: 1992 (3), 1993 (3), 1994 (3), 1995 (10), 1996 (5), 1997 (6), 1998 (4). Total: 34.

MISCELLANEOUS: Holds Detroit Lions all-time records for most yards receiving (8,664), most receptions (626), and most touchdown receptions (59).

				RECEIVING			TOTALS			
Year Team	G	GS	No.	Yds.	Avg.	TD	TD	2pt.	Pts.	Fum.
1991—Detroit NFL	13	1	11	135	12.3	0	0	0	0	0
1992—Detroit NFL	12	11	51	966	‡18.9	4	4	0	24	0
1993—Detroit NFL	15	15	61	935	15.3	6	6	0	36	2
1994—Detroit NFL	16	16	72	1173	16.3	11	11	0	66	1
1995—Detroit NFL	16	16	*123	1686	13.7	14	14	0	84	2
1996—Detroit NFL	16	16	106	1296	12.2	9	9	1	56	0
1997—Detroit NFL	16	16	†104	1293	12.4	8	8	1	50	0
1998—Detroit NFL	15	15	82	983	12.0	5	5	0	30	0
1999—Detroit NFL	8	4	16	197	12.3	2	2	0	12	0
Pro totals (9 years)	127	110	626	8664	13.8	59	59	2	358	5

M

MOORE, JASON   S   BRONCOS

PERSONAL: Born January 15, 1976, in San Bernardino, Calif. ... 5-10/191. ... Full name: Jason Dwayne Moore.

HIGH SCHOOL: Pacific (San Bernardino, Calif.).

COLLEGE: San Diego State.

TRANSACTIONS/CAREER NOTES: Signed as non-drafted free agent by Cincinnati Bengals (April 19, 1998). ... Released by Bengals (August 24, 1998). ... Signed by Denver Broncos (March 12, 1999). ... Released by Broncos (August 31, 1999). ... Re-signed by Broncos to practice squad (September 14, 1999). ... Activated (November 18, 1999).

PLAYING EXPERIENCE: Denver NFL, 1999. ... Games/Games started: 1999 (6/0).

MOORE, LARRY   C   COLTS

PERSONAL: Born June 1, 1975, in San Diego. ... 6-2/212.

HIGH SCHOOL: Monte Vista (Spring Valley, Calif.).

JUNIOR COLLEGE: Grossmont College (Calif.).

COLLEGE: Brigham Young.

TRANSACTIONS/CAREER NOTES: Signed as non-drafted free agent by Seattle Seahawks (April 25, 1997). ... Released by Seahawks (August 17, 1997). ... Signed by Washington Redskins to practice squad (August 26, 1997). ... Released by Redskins (September 3, 1997). ... Signed by Indianapolis Colts (January 29, 1998).

PLAYING EXPERIENCE: Indianapolis NFL, 1998 and 1999. ... Games/Games started: 1998 (6/5), 1999 (16/16). Total: 22/21.

PRO STATISTICS: 1999—Fumbled twice for minus 25 yards.

MOORE, MARTY   LB   BROWNS

PERSONAL: Born March 19, 1971, in Phoenix. ... 6-1/245. ... Full name: Martin Neff Moore.
HIGH SCHOOL: Highlands (Fort Thomas, Ky.).
COLLEGE: Kentucky.
TRANSACTIONS/CAREER NOTES: Selected by New England Patriots in seventh round (222nd pick overall) of 1994 NFL draft. ... Signed by Patriots (June 1, 1994). ... Granted free agency (February 14, 1997). ... Re-signed by Patriots (June 6, 1997). ... Granted unconditional free agency (February 13, 1998). ... Re-signed by Patriots (April 3, 1998). ... Granted unconditional free agency (February 11, 2000). ... Signed by Cleveland Browns (March 2, 2000).
PLAYING EXPERIENCE: New England NFL, 1994-1999. ... Games/Games started: 1994 (16/4), 1995 (16/3), 1996 (16/0), 1997 (16/0), 1998 (14/2), 1999 (15/2). Total: 93/11.
CHAMPIONSHIP GAME EXPERIENCE: Played in AFC championship game (1996 season). ... Played in Super Bowl XXXI (1996 season).
PRO STATISTICS: 1997—Intercepted two passes for seven yards. 1998—Recovered one fumble.

MOORE, ROB   WR   CARDINALS

PERSONAL: Born September 27, 1968, in New York. ... 6-3/202. ... Full name: Robert S. Moore.
HIGH SCHOOL: Hempstead (N.Y.).
COLLEGE: Syracuse (degree in sociology, 1990).
TRANSACTIONS/CAREER NOTES: Selected by New York Jets in first round of 1990 NFL supplemental draft. ... Signed by Jets (July 22, 1990). ... Designated by Jets as transition player (February 25, 1993). ... Free agency status changed by Jets from transitional to restricted (February 17, 1994). ... Re-signed by Jets (July 12, 1994). ... Designated by Jets as franchise player (February 15, 1995). ... Traded by Jets to Arizona Cardinals for RB Ronald Moore and first- (DE Hugh Douglas) and fourth-round (OT Melvin Hayes) picks in 1995 draft (April 21, 1995). ... Designated by Cardinals as franchise player (February 12, 1999).
HONORS: Named wide receiver on THE SPORTING NEWS college All-America first team (1989). ... Played in Pro Bowl (1994 and 1997 seasons).
PRO STATISTICS: 1990—Rushed twice for minus four yards. 1992—Rushed once for 21 yards. 1993—Rushed once for minus six yards. 1994—Rushed once for minus three yards and recovered one fumble. 1995—Attempted two passes with one completion for 33 yards and an interception.
SINGLE GAME HIGHS (regular season): Receptions—9 (December 20, 1998, vs. New Orleans); yards—188 (November 30, 1997, vs. Pittsburgh); and touchdown receptions—3 (December 7, 1997, vs. Washington).
STATISTICAL PLATEAUS: 100-yard receiving games: 1990 (1), 1993 (2), 1994 (2), 1995 (3), 1996 (3), 1997 (8), 1998 (2), 1999 (2). Total: 23.

			RECEIVING				TOTALS			
Year Team	G	GS	No.	Yds.	Avg.	TD	TD	2pt.	Pts.	Fum.
1990—New York Jets NFL	15	14	44	692	15.7	6	6	0	36	1
1991—New York Jets NFL	16	16	70	987	14.1	5	5	0	30	2
1992—New York Jets NFL	16	15	50	726	14.5	4	4	0	24	0
1993—New York Jets NFL	13	13	64	843	13.2	1	1	0	6	2
1994—New York Jets NFL	16	16	78	1010	12.9	6	6	2	40	0
1995—Arizona NFL	15	15	63	907	14.4	5	5	1	32	0
1996—Arizona NFL	16	16	58	1016	17.5	4	4	1	26	0
1997—Arizona NFL	16	16	97	*1584	16.3	8	8	1	50	0
1998—Arizona NFL	16	16	67	982	14.7	5	5	0	30	0
1999—Arizona NFL	14	10	37	621	16.8	5	5	0	30	0
Pro totals (10 years)	153	147	628	9368	14.9	49	49	5	304	5

MOORE, STEVON   S

PERSONAL: Born February 9, 1967, in Wiggins, Miss. ... 5-11/210. ... Full name: Stevon Nathaniel Moore. ... Name pronounced stee-VON.
HIGH SCHOOL: Stone County (Wiggins, Miss.).
COLLEGE: Mississippi.
TRANSACTIONS/CAREER NOTES: Selected by New York Jets in seventh round (181st pick overall) of 1989 NFL draft. ... Signed by Jets (July 22, 1989). ... On injured reserve with knee injury (August 28, 1989-entire season). ... Granted unconditional free agency (February 1, 1990). ... Signed by Miami Dolphins (March 30, 1990). ... On physically unable to perform list with knee injury (July 21-August 27, 1990). ... On physically unable to perform list with knee injury (August 28-October 18, 1990). ... On injured reserve with hamstring injury (November 8-December 8, 1990). ... On injured reserve with knee injury (August 27, 1991-entire season). ... Granted unconditional free agency (February 1, 1992). ... Signed by Cleveland Browns (March 25, 1992). ... On injured reserve with separated shoulder (December 15, 1992-remainder of season). ... Browns franchise moved to Baltimore and renamed Ravens for 1996 season (March 11, 1996). ... Granted unconditional free agency (February 14, 1997). ... Re-signed by Ravens (April 2, 1997). ... On injured reserve with knee injury (November 9, 1999-remainder of season). ... Released by Ravens (February 23, 2000).
PRO STATISTICS: 1990—Recovered one fumble. 1992—Recovered three fumbles for 115 yards and one touchdown. 1993—Recovered one fumble for 22 yards and a touchdown. 1994—Recovered five fumbles for three yards. 1996—Recovered one fumble.

			INTERCEPTIONS				SACKS
Year Team	G	GS	No.	Yds.	Avg.	TD	No.
1989—New York Jets NFL				Did not play.			
1990—Miami NFL	7	0	0	0	0.0	0	0.0
1991—Miami NFL				Did not play.			
1992—Cleveland NFL	14	4	0	0	0.0	0	2.0
1993—Cleveland NFL	16	16	0	0	0.0	0	0.0
1994—Cleveland NFL	16	16	0	0	0.0	0	0.0
1995—Cleveland NFL	16	16	5	55	11.0	0	1.0
1996—Baltimore NFL	16	16	1	10	10.0	0	0.0
1997—Baltimore NFL	13	12	4	56	14.0	0	0.0
1998—Baltimore NFL	16	16	0	0	0.0	0	0.0
1999—Baltimore NFL	8	0	0	0	0.0	0	0.0
Pro totals (9 years)	122	96	10	121	12.1	0	3.0

M

MORABITO, TIM   DT   PANTHERS

PERSONAL: Born October 12, 1973, in Garnerville, N.Y. ... 6-3/296. ... Full name: Timothy Robert Morabito. ... Name pronounced more-ah-BEE-toe.
HIGH SCHOOL: St. Joseph's Regional (Garnerville, N.Y.).
COLLEGE: Boston College (degree in sociology).
TRANSACTIONS/CAREER NOTES: Signed as non-drafted free agent by Cincinnati Bengals (April 23, 1996). ... Released by Bengals (September 11, 1996). ... Re-signed by Bengals to practice squad (September 12, 1996). ... Activated (November 5, 1996). ... Claimed on waivers by Carolina Panthers (August 26, 1997). ... Granted free agency (February 12, 1999). ... Re-signed by Panthers (June 4, 1999). ... Granted unconditional free agency (February 11, 2000). ... Re-signed by Panthers (March 22, 2000).
PLAYING EXPERIENCE: Cincinnati NFL, 1996; Carolina NFL, 1997-1999. ... Games/Games started: 1996 (7/1), 1997 (8/0), 1998 (8/8), 1999 (16/16). Total: 39/25.
PRO STATISTICS: 1997—Recovered one fumble.

MORAN, SEAN   DE   RAMS

PERSONAL: Born June 5, 1973, in Denver. ... 6-3/275. ... Full name: Sean Farrell Moran.
HIGH SCHOOL: Overland (Aurora, Colo.).
COLLEGE: Colorado State.
TRANSACTIONS/CAREER NOTES: Selected by Buffalo Bills in fourth round (120th pick overall) of 1996 NFL draft. ... Signed by Bills (July 9, 1996). ... Granted free agency (February 12, 1999). ... Re-signed by Bills (April 1, 1999). ... Granted unconditional free agency (February 11, 2000). ... Signed by St. Louis Rams (March 15, 2000).
PLAYING EXPERIENCE: Buffalo NFL, 1996-1999. ... Games/Games started: 1996 (16/0), 1997 (16/7), 1998 (10/2), 1999 (16/0). Total: 58/9.
PRO STATISTICS: 1997—Intercepted two passes for 12 yards, credited with 4$\frac{1}{2}$ sacks and recovered one fumble. 1999—Credited with $\frac{1}{2}$ sack.

MORENO, MOSES   QB   CHARGERS

PERSONAL: Born September 5, 1975, in Chula Vista, Calif. ... 6-1/205. ... Full name: Moses Nathaniel Moreno. ... Name pronounced mo-REH-no.
HIGH SCHOOL: Castle Park (Chula Vista, Calif.).
COLLEGE: Colorado State.
TRANSACTIONS/CAREER NOTES: Selected by Chicago Bears in seventh round (232nd pick overall) of 1998 NFL draft. ... Signed by Bears (June 20, 1998). ... On injured reserve with ankle injury (December 15, 1998-remainder of season). ... Released by Bears (August 30, 1999). ... Signed by San Diego Chargers to practice squad (September 14, 1999). ... Activated (November 20, 1999).
PRO STATISTICS: 1998—Fumbled twice for minus four yards.
SINGLE GAME HIGHS (regular season): Attempts—41 (November 29, 1998, vs. Tampa Bay); completions—18 (November 29, 1998, vs. Tampa Bay); yards—153 (November 29, 1998, vs. Tampa Bay); and touchdown passes—1 (November 29, 1998, vs. Tampa Bay).
MISCELLANEOUS: Regular-season record as starting NFL quarterback: 0-1.

			PASSING							RUSHING				TOTALS		
Year Team	G	GS	Att.	Cmp.	Pct.	Yds.	TD	Int.	Avg.	Rat.	Att.	Yds.	Avg.	TD	TD	2pt.	Pts.
1998—Chicago NFL	2	1	43	19	44.2	166	1	0	3.86	62.7	4	9	2.3	0	0	0	0
1999—San Diego NFL	1	0	7	5	71.4	78	0	0	11.14	108.0	0	0	0.0	0	0	0	0
Pro totals (2 years)	3	1	50	24	48.0	244	1	0	4.88	69.1	4	9	2.3	0	0	0	0

MOREY, SEAN   WR   PATRIOTS

PERSONAL: Born February 26, 1976, in Marshfield, Mass. ... 5-11/190. ... Full name: Sean Joseph Morey.
HIGH SCHOOL: Marshfield (Mass.).
COLLEGE: Brown.
TRANSACTIONS/CAREER NOTES: Selected by New England Patriots in seventh round (241st pick overall) of 1999 NFL draft. ... Signed by Patriots (June 10, 1999). ... Released by Patriots (September 15, 1999). ... Re-signed by Patriots to practice squad (September 16, 1999). ... Activated (December 7, 1999). ... Assigned by Patriots to Barcelona Dragons in 2000 NFL Europe enhancement allocation program (February 18, 2000).
PLAYING EXPERIENCE: New England NFL, 1999. ... Games/Games started: 1999 (2/0).

MORGAN, DON   S   VIKINGS

PERSONAL: Born September 18, 1975, in Stockton, Calif. ... 5-11/200.
HIGH SCHOOL: Manteca (Calif.).
COLLEGE: Nevada-Reno.
TRANSACTIONS/CAREER NOTES: Signed as non-drafted free agent by Minnesota Vikings (April 19, 1999). ... Released by Vikings (September 5, 1999). ... Re-signed by Vikings to practice squad (September 6, 1999). ... Activated (December 23, 1999).
PLAYING EXPERIENCE: Minnesota NFL, 1999. ... Games/Games started: 1999 (2/0).

MORRIS, BAM   RB

PERSONAL: Born January 13, 1972, in Cooper, Texas. ... 6-0/248. ... Full name: Byron Morris. ... Brother of Ron Morris, wide receiver with Chicago Bears (1987-92); and cousin of Terry Norris, former World Boxing Council junior middleweight champion.
HIGH SCHOOL: Cooper (Texas).
COLLEGE: Texas Tech.

M

TRANSACTIONS/CAREER NOTES: Selected after junior season by Pittsburgh Steelers in third round (91st pick overall) of 1994 NFL draft. ... Signed by Steelers (July 15, 1994). ... Released by Steelers (July 10, 1996). ... On suspended list for violating league substance abuse policy (September 1-22, 1996). ... Signed by Baltimore Ravens (September 24, 1996). ... On suspended list for violating league substance abuse policy (August 31-September 22, 1997). ... Granted unconditional free agency (February 13, 1998). ... Signed by Chicago Bears (August 4, 1998). ... Traded by Bears to Kansas City Chiefs for fifth-round pick (RB Jerry Azumah) in 1999 draft (October 13, 1998). ... Announced retirement (January 29, 2000).
CHAMPIONSHIP GAME EXPERIENCE: Played in AFC championship game (1994 and 1995 seasons). ... Played in Super Bowl XXX (1995 season).
HONORS: Doak Walker Award winner (1993). ... Named running back on THE SPORTING NEWS college All-America second team (1993).
PRO STATISTICS: 1994—Recovered one fumble. 1997—Recovered four fumbles. 1998—Recovered one fumble. 1999—Recovered one fumble.
SINGLE GAME HIGHS (regular season): Attempts—36 (October 26, 1997, vs. Washington); yards—176 (October 26, 1997, vs. Washington); and rushing touchdowns—3 (November 22, 1998, vs. San Diego).
STATISTICAL PLATEAUS: 100-yard rushing games: 1994 (2), 1995 (2), 1996 (3), 1997 (2), 1998 (1). Total: 10.
MISCELLANEOUS: Shares Baltimore Ravens all-time record for most rushing touchdowns (8).

Year Team	G	GS	RUSHING Att.	Yds.	Avg.	TD	RECEIVING No.	Yds.	Avg.	TD	KICKOFF RETURNS No.	Yds.	Avg.	TD	TOTALS TD	2pt.	Pts.	Fum.
1994—Pittsburgh NFL	15	6	198	836	4.2	7	22	204	9.3	0	4	114	28.5	0	7	0	42	3
1995—Pittsburgh NFL	13	4	148	559	3.8	9	8	36	4.5	0	0	0	0.0	0	9	0	54	3
1996—Baltimore NFL	11	7	172	737	4.3	4	25	242	9.7	1	1	3	3.0	0	5	0	30	0
1997—Baltimore NFL	11	8	204	774	3.8	4	29	176	6.1	0	1	23	23.0	0	4	0	24	4
1998—Chicago NFL	2	0	3	8	2.7	0	0	0	0.0	0	0	0	0.0	0	0	0	0	0
—Kansas City NFL	10	5	129	481	3.7	8	12	95	7.9	0	0	0	0.0	0	8	0	48	3
1999—Kansas City NFL	12	8	120	414	3.5	3	7	37	5.3	0	0	0	0.0	0	3	0	18	3
Pro totals (6 years)	74	38	974	3809	3.9	35	103	790	7.7	1	6	140	23.3	0	36	0	216	16

MORRIS, MIKE   C

PERSONAL: Born February 22, 1961, in Centerville, Iowa. ... 6-5/272. ... Full name: Michael Stephen Morris.
HIGH SCHOOL: Centerville (Iowa).
COLLEGE: Northeast Missouri State (degree in psychology and physical education, 1982).
TRANSACTIONS/CAREER NOTES: Signed as non-drafted free agent by Arizona Outlaws of USFL (November 1, 1984). ... Released by Outlaws (February 11, 1985). ... Signed by Denver Broncos (May 8, 1986). ... Released by Broncos (July 21, 1986). ... Signed by St. Louis Cardinals (May 20, 1987). ... Crossed picket line during players strike (October 7, 1987). ... Cardinals franchise moved to Phoenix (March 15, 1988). ... On injured reserve with knee injury (August 23, 1988-entire season). ... Granted unconditional free agency (February 1, 1989). ... Signed by Washington Redskins (March 20, 1989). ... Claimed on waivers by Kansas City Chiefs (August 30, 1989). ... Released by Chiefs (October 11, 1989). ... Signed by New England Patriots (October 13, 1989). ... Granted unconditional free agency (February 1, 1990). ... Signed by Chiefs (April 1, 1990). ... Released by Chiefs (July 28, 1990). ... Signed by Seattle Seahawks (August, 1990). ... Released by Seahawks (October 4, 1990). ... Signed by Cleveland Browns (October 16, 1990). ... Granted unconditional free agency (February 1-April 1, 1991). ... Re-signed by Browns for 1991 season. ... Released by Browns (July 22, 1991). ... Signed by Minnesota Vikings (August 10, 1991). ... Released by Vikings (August 26, 1991). ... Re-signed by Vikings (August 29, 1991). ... Granted unconditional free agency (February 1-April 1, 1992). ... Re-signed by Vikings for 1992 season. ... Granted unconditional free agency (February 17, 1994). ... Re-signed by Vikings (May 17, 1994). ... Granted unconditional free agency (February 17, 1995). ... Re-signed by Vikings (March 27, 1995). ... Granted unconditional free agency (February 12, 1999). ... Re-signed by Vikings (March 11, 1999). ... On physically unable to perform list with blurred vision (August 1-10, 1999). ... Released by Vikings (September 5, 1999). ... Re-signed by Vikings (September 9, 1999). ... Granted unconditional free agency (February 11, 2000).
PLAYING EXPERIENCE: St. Louis NFL, 1987; Kansas City (5)-New England (11) NFL, 1989; Seattle (4)-Cleveland (10) NFL, 1990; Minnesota NFL, 1991-1999. ... Games/Games started: 1987 (14/0), 1989 (K.C.-5/0; N.E.-11/0; Total: 16/0), 1990 (Sea.-4/0; Clev.-10/0; Total: 14/0), 1991 (16/0), 1992 (16/0), 1993 (16/0), 1994 (16/0), 1995 (16/0), 1996 (16/0), 1997 (16/0), 1998 (16/0), 1999 (16/0). Total: 188/0.
CHAMPIONSHIP GAME EXPERIENCE: Played in NFC championship game (1998 season).
PRO STATISTICS: 1990—Fumbled once for minus 23 yards.

MORROW, HAROLD   FB   VIKINGS

PERSONAL: Born February 24, 1973, in Maplesville, Ala. ... 5-11/224. ... Full name: Harold Morrow Jr. ... Cousin of Tommie Agee, fullback with Seattle Seahawks (1988), Kansas City Chiefs (1989) and Dallas Cowboys (1990-94).
HIGH SCHOOL: Maplesville (Ala.).
COLLEGE: Auburn.
TRANSACTIONS/CAREER NOTES: Signed as non-drafted free agent by Dallas Cowboys (April 25, 1996). ... Claimed on waivers by Minnesota Vikings (August 26, 1996). ... Granted free agency (February 12, 1999). ... Re-signed by Vikings (April 23, 1999). ... Granted unconditional free agency (February 11, 2000). ... Re-signed by Vikings (March 7, 2000).
PLAYING EXPERIENCE: Minnesota NFL, 1996-1999. ... Games/Games started: 1996 (8/0), 1997 (16/0), 1998 (11/0), 1999 (16/0). Total: 51/0.
CHAMPIONSHIP GAME EXPERIENCE: Played in NFC championship game (1998 season).
PRO STATISTICS: 1996—Returned six kickoffs for 117 yards. 1997—Returned five kickoffs for 99 yards. 1998—Rushed three times for seven yards and recovered one fumble. 1999—Rushed twice for one yard, returned one kickoff for 20 yards and recovered one fumble.
SINGLE GAME HIGHS (regular season): Attempts—3 (December 20, 1998, vs. Jacksonville); yards—7 (December 20, 1998, vs. Jacksonville); and rushing touchdowns—0.

MORTON, JOHNNIE   WR   ·LIONS

PERSONAL: Born October 7, 1971, in Inglewood, Calif. ... 6-0/190. ... Full name: Johnnie James Morton. ... Brother of Chad Morton, running back, New Orleans Saints; half brother of Michael Morton, running back with Tampa Bay Buccaneers (1982-84), Washington Redskins (1985) and Seattle Seahawks (1987).
HIGH SCHOOL: South Torrance (Calif.).
COLLEGE: Southern California (degree in communications).
TRANSACTIONS/CAREER NOTES: Selected by Detroit Lions in first round (21st pick overall) of 1994 NFL draft. ... Signed by Lions (July 18, 1994).

HONORS: Named wide receiver on THE SPORTING NEWS college All-America first team (1993).
PRO STATISTICS: 1994—Recovered one fumble. 1995—Returned seven punts for 48 yards.
SINGLE GAME HIGHS (regular season): Receptions—10 (January 2, 2000, vs. Minnesota); yards—174 (September 22, 1996, vs. Chicago); and touchdown receptions—2 (January 2, 2000, vs. Minnesota).
STATISTICAL PLATEAUS: 100-yard receiving games: 1995 (1), 1996 (2), 1997 (3), 1998 (3), 1999 (5). Total: 14.

			RUSHING				RECEIVING				KICKOFF RETURNS				TOTALS		
Year Team	G	GS	Att.	Yds.	Avg.	TD	No.	Yds.	Avg.	TD	No.	Yds.	Avg.	TD	TD	2pt.	Pts. Fum.
1994—Detroit NFL	14	0	0	0	0.0	0	3	39	13.0	1	4	143	35.8	1	2	0	12 1
1995—Detroit NFL	16	14	3	33	11.0	0	44	590	13.4	8	18	390	21.7	0	8	0	48 1
1996—Detroit NFL	16	15	9	35	3.9	0	55	714	13.0	6	0	0	0.0	0	6	0	36 1
1997—Detroit NFL	16	16	3	33	11.0	0	80	1057	13.2	6	0	0	0.0	0	6	0	36 2
1998—Detroit NFL	16	16	1	11	11.0	0	69	1028	14.9	2	0	0	0.0	0	2	0	12 0
1999—Detroit NFL	16	12	0	0	0.0	0	80	1129	14.1	5	1	22	22.0	0	5	0	30 0
Pro totals (6 years)	94	73	16	112	7.0	0	331	4557	13.8	28	23	555	24.1	1	29	0	174 5

MORTON, MIKE — LB — PACKERS

PERSONAL: Born March 28, 1972, in Kannapolis, N.C. ... 6-4/235. ... Full name: Michael Anthony Morton Jr.
HIGH SCHOOL: A.L. Brown (Kannapolis, N.C.).
COLLEGE: North Carolina.
TRANSACTIONS/CAREER NOTES: Selected by Los Angeles Raiders in fourth round (118th pick overall) of 1995 NFL draft. ... Signed by Raiders (July 21, 1995). ... Raiders franchise moved to Oakland (July 21, 1995). ... Granted unconditional free agency (February 12, 1999). ... Signed by Green Bay Packers (July 30, 1999). ... Traded by Packers to St. Louis Rams for undisclosed draft pick (July 23, 1999). ... Granted unconditional free agency (February 11, 2000). ... Signed by Packers (May 5, 2000).
PLAYING EXPERIENCE: Oakland NFL, 1995-1998; St. Louis NFL, 1999. ... Games/Games started: 1995 (12/0), 1996 (16/6), 1997 (11/11), 1998 (16/0), 1999 (16/0). Total: 71/17.
CHAMPIONSHIP GAME EXPERIENCE: Played in NFC championship game (1999 season). ... Member of Super Bowl championship team (1999 season).
PRO STATISTICS: 1995—Recovered one fumble. 1996—Intercepted two passes for 13 yards and credited with one sack. 1997—Returned one kickoff for 14 yards and recovered one fumble. 1998—Returned one kickoff for three yards and recovered two fumbles.

MOSS, RANDY — WR — VIKINGS

PERSONAL: Born February 13, 1977, in Rand, W.Va. ... 6-4/198. ... Half brother of Eric Moss, offensive lineman with Minnesota Vikings (1997-99).
HIGH SCHOOL: DuPont (Belle, W.Va.).
COLLEGE: Florida State (did not play), then Marshall.
TRANSACTIONS/CAREER NOTES: Selected after sophomore season by Minnesota Vikings in first round (21st pick overall) of 1998 NFL draft. ... Signed by Minnesota Vikings (July 26, 1998).
CHAMPIONSHIP GAME EXPERIENCE: Played in NFC championship game (1998 season).
HONORS: Fred Biletnikoff Award winner (1997). ... Named wide receiver on THE SPORTING NEWS college All-America first team (1997). ... Named NFL Rookie of the Year by THE SPORTING NEWS (1998). ... Named wide receiver on THE SPORTING NEWS NFL All-Pro team (1998). ... Played in Pro Bowl (1998 and 1999 seasons). ... Named Outstanding Player of Pro Bowl (1999).
RECORDS: Holds NFL rookie-season record for most touchdowns—17 (1998).
PRO STATISTICS: 1998—Rushed once for four yards. 1999—Rushed four times for 43 yards and completed only pass attempt for 27 yards and a touchdown.
SINGLE GAME HIGHS (regular season): Receptions—12 (November 14, 1999, vs. Chicago); yards—204 (November 14, 1999, vs. Chicago); and touchdown receptions—3 (December 6, 1998, vs. Chicago).
STATISTICAL PLATEAUS: 100-yard receiving games: 1998 (4), 1999 (7). Total: 11.

			RECEIVING				PUNT RETURNS				TOTALS		
Year Team	G	GS	No.	Yds.	Avg.	TD	No.	Yds.	Avg.	TD	TD	2pt.	Pts. Fum.
1998—Minnesota NFL	16	11	69	1313	‡19.0	*17	1	0	0.0	0	‡17	†2	106 2
1999—Minnesota NFL	16	16	80	‡1413	17.7	11	17	162	9.5	∞1	12	0	72 3
Pro totals (2 years)	32	27	149	2726	18.3	28	18	162	9.0	1	29	2	178 5

MOSS, ZEFROSS — OT

PERSONAL: Born August 17, 1966, in Holt, Ala. ... 6-6/325. ... Name pronounced ZEFF-russ.
HIGH SCHOOL: Holt (Ala.).
COLLEGE: Alabama State.
TRANSACTIONS/CAREER NOTES: Signed as non-drafted free agent by Dallas Cowboys (April 29, 1988). ... Released by Cowboys (August 24, 1988). ... Re-signed by Cowboys (December 8, 1988). ... Traded by Cowboys to Indianapolis Colts for 10th-round pick (traded to Minnesota) in 1990 draft (August 22, 1989). ... On injured reserve with ankle injury (December 20, 1991-remainder of season). ... Granted unconditional free agency (February 14, 1997). ... Signed by Detroit Lions (April 28, 1995). ... Granted unconditional free agency (February 17, 1995). ... Signed by New England Patriots (March 31, 1997). ... Released by Patriots (March 23, 2000).
PLAYING EXPERIENCE: Indianapolis NFL, 1989-1994; Detroit NFL, 1995 and 1996; New England NFL, 1997-1999. ... Games/Games started: 1989 (16/0), 1990 (16/16), 1991 (11/10), 1992 (13/13), 1993 (16/16), 1994 (11/11), 1995 (14/14), 1996 (15/15), 1997 (15/15), 1998 (14/14), 1999 (14/13). Total: 155/137.

MOULDS, ERIC — WR — BILLS

PERSONAL: Born July 17, 1973, in Lucedale, Miss. ... 6-0/204. ... Full name: Eric Shannon Moulds.
HIGH SCHOOL: George County (Lucedale, Miss.).
COLLEGE: Mississippi State.

M

TRANSACTIONS/CAREER NOTES: Selected by Buffalo Bills in first round (24th pick overall) of 1996 NFL draft. ... Signed by Bills (July 16, 1996).
HONORS: Played in Pro Bowl (1998 season).
POST SEASON RECORDS: Holds NFL postseason single-game record for most yards receiving—240 (January 2, 1999, vs. Miami).
PRO STATISTICS: 1997—Returned two punts for 20 yards and recovered one fumble.
SINGLE GAME HIGHS (regular season): Receptions—10 (September 12, 1999, vs. Indianapolis); yards—196 (December 6, 1998, vs. Cincinnati); and touchdown receptions—2 (December 6, 1998, vs. Cincinnati).
STATISTICAL PLATEAUS: 100-yard receiving games: 1998 (4), 1999 (3). Total: 7.

			RUSHING				RECEIVING				KICKOFF RETURNS				TOTALS			
Year Team	G	GS	Att.	Yds.	Avg.	TD	No.	Yds.	Avg.	TD	No.	Yds.	Avg.	TD	TD	2pt.	Pts.	Fum.
1996—Buffalo NFL	16	5	12	44	3.7	0	20	279	14.0	2	52	1205	23.2	▲1	3	0	18	1
1997—Buffalo NFL	16	8	4	59	14.8	0	29	294	10.1	0	43	921	21.4	0	0	1	2	3
1998—Buffalo NFL	16	15	0	0	0.0	0	67	§1368	20.4	9	0	0	0.0	0	9	0	54	0
1999—Buffalo NFL	14	14	1	1	1.0	0	65	994	15.3	7	0	0	0.0	0	7	0	42	1
Pro totals (4 years)	62	42	17	104	6.1	0	181	2935	16.2	18	95	2126	22.4	1	19	1	116	5

MUHAMMAD, MUHSIN — WR — PANTHERS

PERSONAL: Born May 5, 1973, in Lansing, Mich. ... 6-2/217. ... Full name: Muhsin Muhammad II. ... Name pronounced moo-SIN moo-HAH-med.
HIGH SCHOOL: Waverly (Lansing, Mich.).
COLLEGE: Michigan State.
TRANSACTIONS/CAREER NOTES: Selected by Carolina Panthers in second round (43rd pick overall) of 1996 NFL draft. ... Signed by Panthers (July 23, 1996).
CHAMPIONSHIP GAME EXPERIENCE: Played in NFC championship game (1996 season).
HONORS: Played in Pro Bowl (1999 season).
PRO STATISTICS: 1996—Rushed once for minus one yard. 1998—Recovered one fumble.
SINGLE GAME HIGHS (regular season): Receptions—11 (December 18, 1999, vs. San Francisco); yards—192 (September 13, 1998, vs. New Orleans); and touchdown receptions—3 (December 18, 1999, vs. San Francisco).
STATISTICAL PLATEAUS: 100-yard receiving games: 1998 (3), 1999 (5). Total: 8.
MISCELLANEOUS: Holds Carolina Panthers all-time record for most receiving yards (2,918).

			RECEIVING				TOTALS			
Year Team	G	GS	No.	Yds.	Avg.	TD	TD	2pt.	Pts.	Fum.
1996—Carolina NFL	9	5	25	407	16.3	1	1	0	6	0
1997—Carolina NFL	13	5	27	317	11.7	0	0	1	2	0
1998—Carolina NFL	16	16	68	941	13.8	6	6	1	38	2
1999—Carolina NFL	15	15	‡96	1253	13.1	8	8	0	48	1
Pro totals (4 years)	53	41	216	2918	13.5	15	15	2	94	3

M

MUHAMMAD, MUSTAFAH — DB — COLTS

PERSONAL: Born October 19, 1973, in Los Angeles. ... 5-10/180. ... Full name: Mustafah Jaleel Muhammad. ... Formerly known as Steve Wilson.
HIGH SCHOOL: Moreno Valley (Calif.).
JUNIOR COLLEGE: Shasta College (Calif.), then Chaffey College (Calif.).
COLLEGE: Fresno State.
TRANSACTIONS/CAREER NOTES: Signed by B.C. Lions of CFL (March 11, 1998). ... Signed as non-drafted free agent by Indianapolis Colts (February 2, 1999).
HONORS: Named CFL Most Outstanding Rookie (1998).
PRO STATISTICS: CFL: 1998—Recovered three fumbles for 60 yards and one touchdown.

			INTERCEPTIONS				PUNT RETURNS				KICKOFF RETURNS				TOTALS			
Year Team	G	GS	No.	Yds.	Avg.	TD	No.	Yds.	Avg.	TD	No.	Yds.	Avg.	TD	TD	2pt.	Pts.	Fum.
1998—British Columbia CFL	17	...	10	165	16.5	0	6	51	8.5	0	1	56	56.0	0	1	0	6	1
1999—Indianapolis NFL	11	1	0	0	0.0	0	0	0	0.0	0	2	41	20.5	0	0	0	0	0
CFL totals (1 year)	17	...	10	165	16.5	0	6	51	8.5	0	1	56	56.0	0	1	0	6	1
NFL totals (1 year)	11	1	0	0	0.0	0	0	0	0.0	0	2	41	20.5	0	0	0	0	0
Pro totals (2 years)	28	...	10	165	16.5	0	6	51	8.5	0	3	97	32.3	0	1	0	6	1

MULITALO, EDWIN — OL — RAVENS

PERSONAL: Born September 1, 1974, in Daly City, Calif. ... 6-3/340. ... Full name: Edwin Moliki Mulitalo. ... Name pronounced moo-lih-TAHL-oh.
HIGH SCHOOL: Jefferson (Daly City, Calif.).
JUNIOR COLLEGE: Ricks College (Idaho).
COLLEGE: Arizona.
TRANSACTIONS/CAREER NOTES: Selected by Baltimore Ravens in fourth round (129th pick overall) of 1999 NFL draft. ... Signed by Ravens (July 29, 1999).
PLAYING EXPERIENCE: Baltimore NFL, 1999. ... Games/Games started: 1999 (10/8).

MULLEN, RODERICK — DB

PERSONAL: Born December 5, 1972, in St. Francisville, La. ... 6-1/204. ... Full name: Roderick Louis Mullen.
HIGH SCHOOL: West Feleciana (St. Francisville, La.).

COLLEGE: Grambling State (degree in criminal justice).
TRANSACTIONS/CAREER NOTES: Selected by New York Giants in fifth round (153rd pick overall) of 1995 NFL draft. ... Signed by Giants (July 23, 1995). ... Released by Giants (August 29, 1995). ... Signed by Green Bay Packers (October 18, 1995). ... On injured reserve with shoulder injury (August 6, 1998-entire season). ... Granted unconditional free agency (February 12, 1999). ... Signed by Carolina Panthers (March 8, 1999). ... Released by Panthers (February 9, 2000).
PLAYING EXPERIENCE: Green Bay NFL, 1995-1997; Carolina NFL, 1999. ... Games/Games started: 1995 (8/0), 1996 (14/0), 1997 (16/1), 1999 (15/0). Total: 53/1.
CHAMPIONSHIP GAME EXPERIENCE: Played in NFC championship game (1995-1997 seasons). ... Member of Super Bowl championship team (1996 season). ... Played in Super Bowl XXXII (1997 season).
PRO STATISTICS: 1997—Intercepted one pass for 17 yards and recovered one fumble for one yard.

MURPHY, YO — WR — BUCCANEERS

PERSONAL: Born May 11, 1971, in Moscow, Idaho. ... 5-10/178.
COLLEGE: Idaho.
TRANSACTIONS/CAREER NOTES: Signed by B.C. Lions CFL (April 1993). ... Granted free agency (February 16, 1996). ... Re-signed by Lions (August 20, 1996). ... Released by Lions (August 26, 1996). ... Signed as non-drafted free agent by Minnesota Vikings (February 7, 1998). ... Released by Vikings (August 24, 1998). ... Signed by Tampa Bay Buccaneers (July 12, 1999). ... Claimed on waivers by Vikings (December 2, 1999). ... Released by Vikings (January 11, 1999). ... Signed by Buccaneers (February 2, 2000).
PRO STATISTICS: NFLE: 1999—Rushed once for two yards.
SINGLE GAME HIGHS (regular season): Receptions—4 (October 31, 1999, vs. Detroit); yards—28 (October 31, 1999, vs. Detroit); and touchdown receptions—0.

			RECEIVING				PUNT RETURNS				KICKOFF RETURNS				TOTALS			
Year Team	G	GS	No.	Yds.	Avg.	TD	No.	Yds.	Avg.	TD	No.	Yds.	Avg.	TD	TD	2pt.	Pts.	Fum.
1993—B.C. Lions CFL	1	...	0	0	0.0	0	0	0	0.0	0	0	0	0.0	0	0	0	0	0
1994—B.C. Lions CFL	7	...	14	127	9.1	0	0	0	0.0	0	0	0	0.0	0	0	0	0	0
1995—B.C. Lions CFL	10	...	31	510	16.5	2	7	65	9.3	0	0	0	0.0	0	2	0	12	0
1996—B.C. Lions CFL	1	...	0	0	0.0	0	0	0	0.0	0	1	20	20.0	0	0	0	0	0
1997—							Did not play.											
1998—							Did not play.											
1999—Scottish	...	...	45	752	16.7	4	7	65	9.3	0	23	600	26.1	1	5	0	30	0
—Tampa Bay NFL	7	0	4	28	7.0	0	0	0	0.0	0	14	307	21.9	0	0	0	0	0
—Minnesota NFL	1	0	0	0	0.0	0	3	14	4.7	0	4	80	20.0	0	0	0	0	1
CFL totals (4 years)	19	...	45	637	14.2	2	0	0	0.0	0	1	20	20.0	0	2	0	12	0
NFL Europe totals (1 year)	...	...	45	752	16.7	4	7	65	9.3	0	23	600	26.1	1	5	0	30	0
NFL totals (1 year)	8	0	4	28	7.0	0	3	14	4.7	0	18	387	21.5	0	0	0	0	1
Pro totals (5 years)	...	...	94	1417	15.1	6	10	79	7.9	0	42	1007	24.0	1	6	0	36	0

MURRAY, EDDIE — K

PERSONAL: Born August 29, 1956, in Halifax, Nova Scotia. ... 5-11/195. ... Full name: Edward Peter Murray. ... Cousin of Mike Rogers, center with Edmonton Oilers, New England/Hartford Whalers and New York Rangers of World Hockey Association and NHL (1974-75 through 1985-86).
HIGH SCHOOL: Spectrum (Victoria, B.C.).
COLLEGE: Tulane (degree in education, 1980).
TRANSACTIONS/CAREER NOTES: Selected by Detroit Lions in seventh round (166th pick overall) of 1980 NFL draft. ... Signed by Lions for 1980 season. ... On suspended list (September 10-November 20, 1982). ... On injured reserve with hip injury (October 12-November 20, 1990). ... Granted unconditional free agency (February 1-April 1, 1991). ... Re-signed by Lions for 1991 season. ... Granted unconditional free agency (February 1-April 1, 1992). ... Rights relinquished by Lions (April 29, 1992). ... Signed by Kansas City Chiefs (October 24, 1992). ... Released by Chiefs (October 28, 1992). ... Signed by Tampa Bay Buccaneers (November 10, 1992). ... Granted unconditional free agency (March 1, 1993). ... Re-signed by Buccaneers for 1993 season. ... Released by Buccaneers (August 23, 1993). ... Signed by Dallas Cowboys (September 14, 1993). ... Granted unconditional free agency (February 17, 1994). ... Signed by Philadelphia Eagles (March 22, 1994). ... Released by Eagles (July 23, 1995). ... Signed by Washington Redskins (August 8, 1995). ... Granted unconditional free agency (February 16, 1996). ... Re-signed by Redskins (May 15, 1996). ... Released by Redskins (August 25, 1996). ... Signed by Minnesota Vikings (September 24, 1997). ... Granted unconditional free agency (February 13, 1998). ... Signed by Detroit Lions (June 2, 1999). ... Announced retirement (June 3, 1999). ... Signed by Cowboys (December 8, 1999). ... Granted unconditional free agency (February 11, 2000).
CHAMPIONSHIP GAME EXPERIENCE: Played in NFC championship game (1991 and 1993 seasons). ... Member of Super Bowl championship team (1993 season).
HONORS: Played in Pro Bowl (1980 and 1989 seasons). ... Named Outstanding Player of Pro Bowl (1980 season).
PRO STATISTICS: 1986—Punted once for 37 yards. 1987—Punted four times for 155 yards (38.8-yard average).

		KICKING						
Year Team	G	XPM	XPA	FGM	FGA	Lg.	50+	Pts.
1980—Detroit NFL	16	35	36	*27	*42	52	1-4	‡116
1981—Detroit NFL	16	46	46	25	35	53	3-4	†121
1982—Detroit NFL	7	16	16	11	12	49	0-0	49
1983—Detroit NFL	16	38	38	25	32	54	3-4	113
1984—Detroit NFL	16	31	31	20	27	52	1-4	91
1985—Detroit NFL	16	31	33	26	31	51	2-3	109
1986—Detroit NFL	16	31	32	18	25	52	2-5	85
1987—Detroit NFL	12	21	21	20	32	53	1-2	81
1988—Detroit NFL	16	22	23	20	21	48	0-1	82
1989—Detroit NFL	16	36	36	20	21	50	1-1	96
1990—Detroit NFL	11	34	34	13	19	47	0-2	73
1991—Detroit NFL	16	40	40	19	28	50	2-4	97
1992—Kansas City NFL	1	0	0	1	1	52	1-1	3
—Tampa Bay NFL	7	13	13	4	8	47	0-0	25
1993—Dallas NFL	14	38	38	28	33	52	3-5	122
1994—Philadelphia NFL	16	33	33	21	25	42	0-0	96

M

1995—Washington NFL	16	33	33	27	36	52	1-2	114
1996—				Did not play.				
1997—Minnesota NFL	12	23	24	12	17	49	0-1	59
1998—				Did not play.				
1999—Dallas NFL	4	10	10	7	9	40	0-0	31
Pro totals (18 years)	244	531	537	344	454	54	21-43	1563

MURRELL, ADRIAN — RB — REDSKINS

PERSONAL: Born October 16, 1970, in Fayetteville, N.C. ... 5-11/210. ... Full name: Adrian Bryan Murrell.
HIGH SCHOOL: Leilehua (Wahiawa, Hawaii).
COLLEGE: West Virginia.
TRANSACTIONS/CAREER NOTES: Selected by New York Jets in fifth round (120th pick overall) of 1993 NFL draft. ... Signed by Jets (July 22, 1993). ... Granted free agency (February 16, 1996). ... Re-signed by Jets (April 21, 1996). ... Traded by Jets with seventh-round pick (DE Jomo Cousins) in 1998 draft to Arizona Cardinals for third-round pick (traded to St. Louis) in 1998 draft (April 7, 1998). ... Granted unconditional free agency (February 11, 2000). ... Signed by Washington Redskins (March 22, 2000).
PRO STATISTICS: 1993—Recovered two fumbles. 1995—Recovered two fumbles. 1996—Recovered two fumbles for minus 16 yards. 1997—Recovered two fumbles. 1998—Recovered one fumble.
SINGLE GAME HIGHS (regular season): Attempts—40 (September 28, 1997, vs. Cincinnati); yards—199 (October 27, 1996, vs. Arizona); and rushing touchdowns—2 (November 10, 1996, vs. New England).
STATISTICAL PLATEAUS: 100-yard rushing games: 1995 (1), 1996 (5), 1997 (3), 1998 (3). Total: 12.

			RUSHING				RECEIVING				KICKOFF RETURNS				TOTALS			
Year Team	G	GS	Att.	Yds.	Avg.	TD	No.	Yds.	Avg.	TD	No.	Yds.	Avg.	TD	TD	2pt.	Pts.	Fum.
1993—New York Jets NFL	16	0	34	157	4.6	1	5	12	2.4	0	23	342	14.9	0	1	0	6	4
1994—New York Jets NFL	10	1	33	160	4.8	0	7	76	10.9	0	14	268	19.1	0	0	0	0	1
1995—New York Jets NFL	15	9	192	795	4.1	1	71	465	6.5	2	1	5	5.0	0	3	0	18	2
1996—New York Jets NFL	16	16	301	1249	4.1	6	17	81	4.8	1	0	0	0.0	0	7	0	42	4
1997—New York Jets NFL	16	15	300	1086	3.6	7	27	106	3.9	0	0	0	0.0	0	7	0	42	4
1998—Arizona NFL	15	14	274	1042	3.8	8	18	169	9.4	2	0	0	0.0	0	10	0	60	6
1999—Arizona NFL	16	12	193	553	2.9	0	49	335	6.8	0	0	0	0.0	0	0	0	0	6
Pro totals (7 years)	104	67	1327	5042	3.8	23	194	1244	6.4	5	38	615	16.2	0	28	0	168	27

MYERS, GREG — S — BENGALS

PERSONAL: Born September 30, 1972, in Tampa. ... 6-1/202. ... Full name: Gregory Jay Myers.
HIGH SCHOOL: Windsor (Colo.).
COLLEGE: Colorado State.
TRANSACTIONS/CAREER NOTES: Selected by Cincinnati Bengals in fifth round (144th pick overall) of 1996 NFL draft. ... Signed by Bengals (July 2, 1996). ... Granted free agency (February 12, 1999). ... Re-signed by Bengals (May 6, 1999). ... Granted unconditional free agency (February 11, 2000). ... Re-signed by Bengals (April 3, 2000).
HONORS: Named defensive back on The Sporting News college All-America first team (1994 and 1995). ... Jim Thorpe Award winner (1995).
PRO STATISTICS: 1996—Fumbled once. 1997—Recovered two fumbles. 1998—Recovered one fumble. 1999—Recovered one fumble for 21 yards.

			INTERCEPTIONS				PUNT RETURNS				TOTALS			
Year Team	G	GS	No.	Yds.	Avg.	TD	No.	Yds.	Avg.	TD	TD	2pt.	Pts.	Fum.
1996—Cincinnati NFL	14	0	2	10	5.0	0	9	51	5.7	0	0	0	0	1
1997—Cincinnati NFL	16	14	1	25	25.0	0	26	201	7.7	0	0	0	0	3
1998—Cincinnati NFL	16	16	0	0	0.0	0	0	0	0.0	0	0	0	0	0
1999—Cincinnati NFL	12	4	1	0	0.0	0	0	0	0.0	0	0	0	0	0
Pro totals (4 years)	58	34	4	35	8.8	0	35	252	7.2	0	0	0	0	4

MYERS, MICHAEL — DL — COWBOYS

PERSONAL: Born January 20, 1976, in Vicksburg, Miss. ... 6-2/288.
HIGH SCHOOL: Vicksburg (Miss.).
JUNIOR COLLEGE: Hinds Community College (Miss.).
COLLEGE: Alabama.
TRANSACTIONS/CAREER NOTES: Selected by Dallas Cowboys in fourth round (100th pick overall) of 1998 NFL draft. ... Signed by Cowboys (July 10, 1998).
HONORS: Named defensive tackle on The Sporting News college All-America first team (1996).

Year Team	G	GS	SACKS
1998—Dallas NFL	16	1	3.0
1999—Dallas NFL	6	0	0.0
Pro totals (2 years)	22	1	3.0

MYLES, DESHONE — LB — SEAHAWKS

PERSONAL: Born October 31, 1974, in Las Vegas, Nev. ... 6-2/235. ... Name pronounced da-SHAWN.
HIGH SCHOOL: Cheyenne (North Las Vegas, Nev.).
COLLEGE: Nevada.
TRANSACTIONS/CAREER NOTES: Selected by Seattle Seahawks in fourth round (108th pick overall) of 1998 NFL draft. ... Signed by Seahawks (July 15, 1998). ... On injured reserve with knee injury (December 7, 1999-remainder of season).
PLAYING EXPERIENCE: Seattle NFL, 1998 and 1999. ... Games/Games started: 1998 (12/7), 1999 (5/0). Total: 17/7.
PRO STATISTICS: 1998—Recovered one fumble.

M

MYLES, TOBY   OT   RAIDERS

PERSONAL: Born July 23, 1975, in Jackson, Miss. ... 6-5/320. ... Full name: Tobiath Myles.
HIGH SCHOOL: Callaway (Jackson, Miss.).
COLLEGE: Mississippi State, then Jackson State.
TRANSACTIONS/CAREER NOTES: Selected by New York Giants in fifth round (147th pick overall) of 1998 NFL draft. ... Signed by Giants (July 24, 1998). ... Active for four games (1998); did not play. ... Released by Giants (March 6, 2000). ... Signed by Oakland Raiders (March 14, 2000).
PLAYING EXPERIENCE: New York Giants NFL, 1999. ... Games/Games started: 1999 (8/0).

MYSLINSKI, TOM   G   STEELERS

PERSONAL: Born December 7, 1968, in Rome, N.Y. ... 6-3/293. ... Full name: Thomas Joseph Myslinski.
HIGH SCHOOL: Free Academy (Owego, N.Y.).
COLLEGE: Tennessee (dedegree in exercise physiology).
TRANSACTIONS/CAREER NOTES: Selected by Dallas Cowboys in fourth round (109th pick overall) of 1992 NFL draft. ... Signed by Cowboys (July 15, 1992). ... Released by Cowboys (August 31, 1992). ... Re-signed by Cowboys to practice squad (September 1, 1992). ... Signed by Cleveland Browns off Cowboys practice squad (September 8, 1992). ... Inactive for three games with Browns (1992). ... Released by Browns (October 9, 1992). ... Re-signed by Browns to practice squad (October 14, 1992). ... Released by Browns (October 17, 1992). ... Signed by Washington Redskins to practice squad (October 21, 1992). ... Activated (November 11, 1992). ... Released by Redskins (November 28, 1992). ... Signed by Buffalo Bills (April 6, 1993). ... Released by Bills (August 30, 1993). ... Re-signed by Bills (August 31, 1993). ... Released by Bills (November 15, 1993). ... Signed by Chicago Bears (November 30, 1993). ... Selected by Jacksonville Jaguars from Bears in NFL expansion draft (February 15, 1995). ... Granted free agency (February 17, 1995). ... Re-signed by Jaguars (April 19, 1995). ... Granted free agency (February 16, 1996). ... Signed by Pittsburgh Steelers (April 24, 1996). ... Released by Steelers (August 24, 1996). ... Re-signed by Steelers (August 27, 1996). ... Granted unconditional free agency (February 13, 1998). ... Signed by Indianapolis Colts (February 19, 1998). ... Released by Colts (July 21, 1999). ... Signed by Cowboys (September 22, 1999). ... Granted unconditional free agency (February 11, 2000). ... Signed by Steelers (April 10, 2000).
PLAYING EXPERIENCE: Washington NFL, 1992; Buffalo (1)-Chicago (1) NFL, 1993; Chicago NFL, 1994; Jacksonville NFL, 1995; Pittsburgh NFL, 1996 and 1997; Indianapolis NFL, 1998; Dallas NFL, 1999. ... Games/Games started: 1992 (1/0), 1993 (Buf.-1/0; Chi.-1/0; Total: 2/0), 1994 (4/0), 1995 (9/9), 1996 (8/6), 1997 (16/7), 1998 (1/0), 1999 (10/2). Total: 51/24.
CHAMPIONSHIP GAME EXPERIENCE: Played in AFC championship game (1997 season).

NAEOLE, CHRIS   G   SAINTS

PERSONAL: Born December 25, 1974, in Kailua, Hawaii. ... 6-3/313. ... Full name: Chris Kealoha Naeole. ... Name pronounced NAY-oh-lee.
HIGH SCHOOL: Kahuka (Kaaava, Hawaii).
COLLEGE: Colorado.
TRANSACTIONS/CAREER NOTES: Selected by New Orleans Saints in first round (10th pick overall) of 1997 NFL draft. ... Signed by Saints (July 17, 1997). ... On injured reserve with ankle injury (October 17, 1997-remainder of season).
PLAYING EXPERIENCE: New Orleans NFL, 1997-1999. ... Games/Games started: 1997 (4/0), 1998 (16/16), 1999 (15/15). Total: 35/31.
HONORS: Named guard on THE SPORTING NEWS college All-America second team (1996).
PRO STATISTICS: 1998—Recovered one fumble.

NAILS, JAMIE   OT   BILLS

PERSONAL: Born March 3, 1975, in Baxley, Ga. ... 6-6/354. ... Full name: Jamie Marcellus Nails.
HIGH SCHOOL: Appling County (Baxley, Ga.).
COLLEGE: Florida A&M.
TRANSACTIONS/CAREER NOTES: Selected by Buffalo Bills in fourth round (120th pick overall) of 1997 NFL draft. ... Signed by Bills (July 2, 1997). ... Granted free agency (February 11, 2000). ... Re-signed by Bills (April 28, 2000)
PLAYING EXPERIENCE: Buffalo NFL, 1997-1999. ... Games/Games started: 1997 (2/0), 1998 (15/3), 1999 (16/3). Total: 33/6.

NALEN, TOM   C   BRONCOS

PERSONAL: Born May 13, 1971, in Foxboro, Mass. ... 6-2/286. ... Full name: Thomas Andrew Nalen.
HIGH SCHOOL: Foxboro (Mass.).
COLLEGE: Boston College.
TRANSACTIONS/CAREER NOTES: Selected by Denver Broncos in seventh round (218th pick overall) of 1994 NFL draft. ... Signed by Broncos (July 15, 1994). ... Released by Broncos (September 2, 1994). ... Re-signed by Broncos to practice squad (September 6, 1994). ... Activated (October 7, 1994).
PLAYING EXPERIENCE: Denver NFL, 1994-1999. ... Games/Games started: 1994 (7/1), 1995 (15/15), 1996 (16/16), 1997 (16/16), 1998 (16/16), 1999 (16/16). Total: 86/80.
CHAMPIONSHIP GAME EXPERIENCE: Played in AFC championship game (1997 and 1998 seasons). ... Member of Super Bowl championship team (1997 and 1998 seasons).
HONORS: Played in Pro Bowl (1997-1999 seasons). ... Named center on THE SPORTING NEWS NFL All-Pro team (1999).
PRO STATISTICS: 1997—Caught one pass for minus one yard.

NASH, MARCUS   WR   RAVENS

PERSONAL: Born February 1, 1976, in Tulsa, Okla. ... 6-3/195. ... Full name: Marcus DeLando Nash.
HIGH SCHOOL: Edmond (Okla.) Memorial.
COLLEGE: Tennessee.

M
N

TRANSACTIONS/CAREER NOTES: Selected by Denver Broncos in first round (30th pick overall) of 1998 NFL draft. ... Signed by Broncos (July 26, 1998). ... Traded by Broncos to Miami Dolphins for RB John Avery (September 21, 1999). ... Released by Dolphins (September 28, 1999). ... Signed by Baltimore Ravens (October 25, 1999).
PLAYING EXPERIENCE: Denver NFL, 1998; Denver (2)-Baltimore (1) NFL, 1999. ... Games/Games started: 1998 (8/0). 1999 (Den.-2/1; Balt.-1/0; Total: 3/1). Total: 11/1.
CHAMPIONSHIP GAME EXPERIENCE: Played in AFC championship game (1998 season). ... Member of Super Bowl championship team (1998 season).
PRO STATISTICS: 1998—Caught four passes for 76 yards.
SINGLE GAME HIGHS (regular season): Receptions—2 (November 16, 1998, vs. Kansas City); yards—36 (November 16, 1998, vs. Kansas City); and touchdown receptions—0.

NAVIES, HANNIBAL　　　LB　　　PANTHERS

PERSONAL: Born July 19, 1977, in Chicago. ... 6-2/240. ... Full name: Hannibal Carter Navies. ... Name pronounced NAY-vees.
HIGH SCHOOL: St. Patrick (Chicago), then Berkeley (Oakland).
COLLEGE: Colorado.
TRANSACTIONS/CAREER NOTES: Selected by Carolina Panthers in fourth round (100th pick overall) of 1999 NFL draft. ... Signed by Panthers (July 21, 1999).
PLAYING EXPERIENCE: Carolina NFL, 1999. ... Games/Games started: 1999 (9/0).

NEAL, LORENZO　　　FB　　　TITANS

PERSONAL: Born December 27, 1970, in Hanford, Calif. ... 5-11/240. ... Full name: Lorenzo LaVonne Neal.
HIGH SCHOOL: Lemoore (Calif.).
COLLEGE: Fresno State.
TRANSACTIONS/CAREER NOTES: Selected by New Orleans Saints in fourth round (89th pick overall) of 1993 NFL draft. ... Signed by Saints (July 15, 1993). ... On injured reserve with ankle injury (September 15, 1993-remainder of season). ... Granted free agency (February 16, 1996). ... Re-signed by Saints (July 1, 1996). ... Granted unconditional free agency (February 14, 1997). ... Signed by New York Jets (March 31, 1997). ... Traded by Jets to Tampa Bay Buccaneers for fifth-round pick (TE Blake Spence) in 1998 draft (March 12, 1998). ... Released by Buccaneers (February 11, 1999). ... Signed by Tennessee Titans (March 2, 1999).
CHAMPIONSHIP GAME EXPERIENCE: Played in AFC championship game (1999 season). ... Played in Super Bowl XXXIV (1999 season).
PRO STATISTICS: 1994—Returned one kickoff for 17 yards. 1995—Returned two kickoffs for 28 yards. 1996—Recovered two fumbles. 1997—Returned two kickoffs for 22 yards. 1999—Returned two kickoffs for 15 yards.
SINGLE GAME HIGHS (regular season): Attempts—14 (October 9, 1994, vs. Chicago); yards—89 (September 5, 1993, vs. Houston); and rushing touchdowns—1 (October 10, 1999, vs. Baltimore).

| | | | RUSHING | | | | RECEIVING | | | | TOTALS | | | |
Year Team	G	GS	Att.	Yds.	Avg.	TD	No.	Yds.	Avg.	TD	TD	2pt.	Pts.	Fum.
1993—New Orleans NFL	2	2	21	175	8.3	1	0	0	0.0	0	1	0	6	1
1994—New Orleans NFL	16	7	30	90	3.0	1	2	9	4.5	0	1	0	6	1
1995—New Orleans NFL	16	7	5	3	0.6	0	12	123	10.3	1	1	0	6	2
1996—New Orleans NFL	16	11	21	58	2.8	1	31	194	6.3	1	2	0	12	1
1997—New York Jets NFL	16	3	10	28	2.8	0	8	40	5.0	1	1	0	6	0
1998—Tampa Bay NFL	16	1	5	25	5.0	0	5	14	2.8	1	1	0	6	0
1999—Tennessee NFL	16	14	2	1	0.5	1	7	27	3.9	2	3	0	18	0
Pro totals (7 years)	98	45	94	380	4.0	4	65	407	6.3	6	10	0	60	5

NEDNEY, JOE　　　K　　　RAIDERS

PERSONAL: Born March 22, 1973, in San Jose, Calif. ... 6-5/220. ... Full name: Joseph Thomas Nedney. ... Name pronounced NED-nee.
HIGH SCHOOL: Santa Teresa (San Jose, Calif.).
COLLEGE: San Jose State (degree in recreation administration, 1998).
TRANSACTIONS/CAREER NOTES: Signed as non-drafted free agent by Green Bay Packers (April 1995). ... Released by Packers (August 27, 1995). ... Signed by Oakland Raiders to practice squad (August 29, 1995). ... Released by Raiders (September 6, 1995). ... Signed by Miami Dolphins to practice squad (September 21, 1995). ... Claimed on waivers by New York Jets (August 12, 1997). ... Released by Jets (August 25, 1997). ... Signed by Dolphins (October 3, 1997). ... Released by Dolphins (October 6, 1997). ... Signed by Arizona Cardinals (October 15, 1997). ... On injured reserve with knee injury (December 1, 1998-remainder of season). ... Released by Cardinals (February 12, 1999). ... Re-signed by Cardinals (March 31, 1999). ... Claimed on waivers by Baltimore Ravens (October 6, 1999). ... Inactive for four games with Ravens (1999). ... Released by Ravens (November 9, 1999). ... Signed by Raiders (December 14, 1999).

| | | KICKING | | | | | | |
Year Team	G	XPM	XPA	FGM	FGA	Lg.	50+	Pts.
1995—Miami NFL				Did not play.				
1996—Miami NFL	16	35	36	18	29	44	0-2	89
1997—Arizona NFL	10	19	19	11	17	45	0-2	52
1998—Arizona NFL	12	30	30	13	19	53	1-4	69
1999—Arizona NFL	1	0	0	0	0	0	0-0	0
—Oakland NFL	3	13	13	5	7	52	1-2	28
Pro totals (4 years)	42	97	98	47	72	53	2-10	238

NEIL, DAN　　　G　　　BRONCOS

PERSONAL: Born October 21, 1973, in Houston. ... 6-2/281. ... Full name: Daniel Neil.
HIGH SCHOOL: Cypress Creek (Houston).
COLLEGE: Texas.

TRANSACTIONS/CAREER NOTES: Selected by Denver Broncos in third round (67th pick overall) of 1997 NFL draft. ... Signed by Broncos (July 17, 1997). ... Granted free agency (February 11, 2000). ... Re-signed by Broncos (April 28, 2000)
PLAYING EXPERIENCE: Denver NFL, 1997-1999. ... Games/Games started: 1997 (3/0), 1998 (16/16), 1999 (15/15). Total: 34/31.
CHAMPIONSHIP GAME EXPERIENCE: Member of Broncos for AFC championship game (1997 season); inactive. ... Member of Super Bowl championship team (1997 season); inactive. ... Played in AFC championship game (1998 season). ... Member of Super Bowl championship team (1998 season).
HONORS: Named guard on THE SPORTING NEWS college All-America first team (1996).

NELSON, JIM — LB — PACKERS

PERSONAL: Born April 16, 1975, in Riverside, Calif. ... 6-1/238. ... Full name: James Robert Nelson.
HIGH SCHOOL: McDonough (Waldorf, Md.).
COLLEGE: Penn State (degree in criminal justice).
TRANSACTIONS/CAREER NOTES: Signed as non-drafted free agent by San Francisco 49ers (April 24, 1998). ... Claimed on waivers by Green Bay Packers (July 20, 1998). ... Released by Packers (August 25, 1998). ... Re-signed by Packers to practice squad (September 14, 1998). ... Activated (December 29, 1998).
PLAYING EXPERIENCE: Green Bay NFL, 1999. ... Games/Games started: 1999 (16/0).
PRO STATISTICS: 1999—Intercepted one pass for no yards and recovered one fumble.

NELSON, REGGIE — G — CHARGERS

PERSONAL: Born June 23, 1976, in Alexandria, La. ... 6-4/310. ... Full name: Reginald DeWayne Nelson.
HIGH SCHOOL: Alexandria (La.).
COLLEGE: McNeese State (degree in psychology).
TRANSACTIONS/CAREER NOTES: Selected by San Diego Chargers in fifth round (141st pick overall) of 1999 NFL draft. ... Signed by Chargers (July 22, 1999). ... Released by Chargers (September 4, 1999). ... Re-signed by Chargers to practice squad (September 6, 1999). ... Released by Chargers (September 20, 1999). ... Re-signed by Chargers (September 21, 1999). ... Released by Chargers (October 22, 1999). ... Re-signed by Chargers to practice squad (October 27, 1999). ... Activated (December 30, 1999).
PLAYING EXPERIENCE: San Diego NFL, 1999. ... Games/Games started: 1999 (2/0).

NESBIT, JAMAR — C — PANTHERS

PERSONAL: Born December 17, 1976, in Summerville, S.C. ... 6-4/330. ... Full name: Jamar Kendric Nesbit.
HIGH SCHOOL: Summerville (S.C.).
COLLEGE: South Carolina.
TRANSACTIONS/CAREER NOTES: Signed as non-drafted free agent by Carolina Panthers (April 18, 1999).
PLAYING EXPERIENCE: Carolina NFL, 1999. ... Games/Games started: 1999 (7/0).

NEUFELD, RYAN — FB — COWBOYS

PERSONAL: Born November 22, 1975, in Morgan Hill, Calif. ... 6-4/240. ... Full name: Ryan Matthew Neufeld.
HIGH SCHOOL: Live Oak (Morgan Hill, Calif.).
COLLEGE: UCLA.
TRANSACTIONS/CAREER NOTES: Signed as non-drafted free agent by Dallas Cowboys (April 23, 1999). ... Released by Cowboys (September 5, 1999). ... Re-signed by Cowboys to practice squad (September 6, 1999). ... Activated (October 27, 1999). ... Assigned by Cowboys to Rhein Fire in 2000 NFL Europe enhancement allocation program (February 18, 2000).
PLAYING EXPERIENCE: Dallas NFL, 1999. ... Games/Games started: 1999 (6/0).

NEUJAHR, QUENTIN — C — JAGUARS

PERSONAL: Born January 30, 1971, in Seward, Neb. ... 6-4/294. ... Full name: Quentin Troy Neujahr.
HIGH SCHOOL: Centennial (Utica, Neb.).
COLLEGE: Kansas State.
TRANSACTIONS/CAREER NOTES: Signed as non-drafted free agent by Los Angeles Raiders (May 3, 1994). ... Released by Raiders (August 23, 1994). ... Signed by Cleveland Browns to practice squad (December 27, 1994). ... Active for one game (1995); did not play. ... Browns franchise moved to Baltimore and renamed Ravens for 1996 season (March 11, 1996). ... Granted free agency (February 13, 1998). ... Tendered offer sheet by Jacksonville Jaguars (February 24, 1998). ... Ravens declined to match offer (March 3, 1998).
PLAYING EXPERIENCE: Baltimore NFL, 1996 and 1997; Jacksonville NFL, 1998 and 1999. ... Games/Games started: 1996 (5/0), 1997 (9/7), 1998 (16/16), 1999 (16/0). Total: 46/23.
CHAMPIONSHIP GAME EXPERIENCE: Played in AFC championship game (1999 season).
PRO STATISTICS: 1996—Recovered one fumble.

NEWBERRY, JEREMY — G — 49ERS

PERSONAL: Born March 23, 1976, in Antioch, Calif. ... 6-5/315. ... Full name: Jeremy David Newberry.
HIGH SCHOOL: Antioch (Calif.).
COLLEGE: California.
TRANSACTIONS/CAREER NOTES: Selected by after junior season San Francisco 49ers in second round (58th pick overall) of 1998 NFL draft. ... Signed by San Francisco 49ers (July 18, 1998). ... On physically unable to perform list with knee injury (July 17-November 7, 1998). ... Active for one game (1998); did not play.
PLAYING EXPERIENCE: San Francisco NFL, 1999. ... Games/Games started: 1999 (16/16).

NEWKIRK, ROBERT   DT   SAINTS

PERSONAL: Born March 6, 1977, in Belle Glade, Fla. ... 6-3/290.
HIGH SCHOOL: Glade Central (Belle Glade, Fla.).
COLLEGE: Michigan State.
TRANSACTIONS/CAREER NOTES: Signed as non-drafted free agent by Dallas Cowboys (April 23, 1999). ... Released by Cowboys (September 5, 1999). ... Re-signed by Cowboys to practice squad (September 6, 1999). ... Signed by New Orleans Saints off Cowboys practice squad (December 1, 1999).
PLAYING EXPERIENCE: New Orleans NFL, 1999. ... Games/Games started: 1999 (5/0).

NEWMAN, ANTHONY   DB

PERSONAL: Born November 21, 1965, in Bellingham, Wash. ... 6-0/215. ... Full name: Anthony Q. Newman.
HIGH SCHOOL: Beaverton (Ore.).
COLLEGE: Oregon.
TRANSACTIONS/CAREER NOTES: Selected by Los Angeles Rams in second round (35th pick overall) of 1988 NFL draft. ... Signed by Rams (July 11, 1988). ... On injured reserve with fractured elbow (December 21, 1989-remainder of season). ... Granted free agency (February 1, 1992). ... Re-signed by Rams (July 21, 1992). ... Rams franchise moved to St. Louis (April 12, 1995). ... Released by Rams (August 27, 1995). ... Signed by New Orleans Saints (August 28, 1995). ... Granted unconditional free agency (February 16, 1996). ... Re-signed by Saints (March 6, 1996). ... Granted unconditional free agency (February 13, 1998). ... Signed by Oakland Raiders (March 26, 1998). ... Released by Raiders (February 10, 2000).
PRO STATISTICS: 1988—Recovered one fumble. 1990—Recovered one fumble. 1991—Credited with a sack and recovered one fumble for 17 yards and a touchdown. 1992—Recovered three fumbles. 1994—Recovered one fumble. 1995—Caught one pass for 18 yards. 1996—Recovered two fumbles. 1997—Recovered one fumble. 1999—Recovered one fumble.
MISCELLANEOUS: Selected by Toronto Blue Jays organization in 26th round of free-agent baseball draft (June 4, 1984); did not sign. ... Selected by Cleveland Indians organization in secondary phase of free-agent baseball draft (January 9, 1985); did not sign. ... Selected by Texas Rangers organization in secondary phase of free-agent baseball draft (June 3, 1985); did not sign.

			INTERCEPTIONS			
Year Team	G	GS	No.	Yds.	Avg.	TD
1988—Los Angeles Rams NFL	16	0	2	27	13.5	0
1989—Los Angeles Rams NFL	15	1	0	0	0.0	0
1990—Los Angeles Rams NFL	16	6	2	0	0.0	0
1991—Los Angeles Rams NFL	16	1	1	58	58.0	0
1992—Los Angeles Rams NFL	16	16	4	33	8.3	0
1993—Los Angeles Rams NFL	16	16	0	0	0.0	0
1994—Los Angeles Rams NFL	16	14	2	46	23.0	1
1995—New Orleans NFL	13	1	0	0	0.0	0
1996—New Orleans NFL	16	16	3	40	13.3	0
1997—New Orleans NFL	12	12	3	19	6.3	0
1998—Oakland NFL	11	11	2	17	8.5	0
1999—Oakland NFL	16	13	2	16	8.0	0
Pro totals (12 years)	179	107	21	256	12.2	1

NEWMAN, KEITH   LB   BILLS

PERSONAL: Born January 19, 1977, in Tampa. ... 6-2/243. ... Full name: Keith Anthony Newman.
HIGH SCHOOL: Thomas Jefferson (Tampa).
COLLEGE: North Carolina.
TRANSACTIONS/CAREER NOTES: Selected by Buffalo Bills in fourth round (119th pick overall) of 1999 NFL draft. ... Signed by Bills (July 27, 1999).
PLAYING EXPERIENCE: Buffalo NFL, 1999. ... Games/Games started: 1999 (3/0).

N

NEWSOME, CRAIG   CB

PERSONAL: Born August 10, 1971, in San Bernardino, Calif. ... 6-0/190.
HIGH SCHOOL: Eisenhower (Rialto, Calif.).
JUNIOR COLLEGE: San Bernardino (Calif.) Valley.
COLLEGE: Arizona State.
TRANSACTIONS/CAREER NOTES: Selected by Green Bay Packers in first round (32nd pick overall) of 1995 NFL draft. ... Signed by Packers (May 23, 1995). ... On injured reserve with knee injury (September 3, 1997-remainder of season). ... Traded by Packers to San Francisco 49ers for fifth-round pick (traded back to San Francisco) in 2000 draft (September 7, 1999). ... Granted unconditional free agency (February 11, 2000).
CHAMPIONSHIP GAME EXPERIENCE: Played in NFC championship game (1995 and 1996 seasons). ... Member of Super Bowl championship team (1996 season).
PRO STATISTICS: 1996—Recovered one fumble.

			INTERCEPTIONS			
Year Team	G	GS	No.	Yds.	Avg.	TD
1995—Green Bay NFL	16	16	1	3	3.0	0
1996—Green Bay NFL	16	16	2	22	11.0	0
1997—Green Bay NFL	1	1	0	0	0.0	0
1998—Green Bay NFL	13	13	1	26	26.0	0
1999—San Francisco NFL	7	2	0	0	0.0	0
Pro totals (5 years)	53	48	4	51	12.8	0

NEWTON, NATE — G

PERSONAL: Born December 20, 1961, in Orlando. ... 6-3/318. ... Full name: Nathaniel Newton Jr. ... Brother of Tim Newton, defensive tackle with Minnesota Vikings (1985-89), Tampa Bay Buccaneers (1990-91) and Kansas City Chiefs (1993).
HIGH SCHOOL: Jones (Orlando).
COLLEGE: Florida A&M.
TRANSACTIONS/CAREER NOTES: Selected by Tampa Bay Bandits in 1983 USFL territorial draft. ... Signed as non-drafted free agent by Washington Redskins (May 5, 1983). ... Released by Redskins (August 29, 1983). ... Signed by Bandits (November 6, 1983). ... Granted free agency when USFL suspended operations (August 7, 1986). ... Signed by Dallas Cowboys (August 14, 1986). ... Granted roster exemption (August 14-21, 1986). ... Crossed picket line during players strike (October 24, 1987). ... Granted unconditional free agency (February 17, 1994). ... Re-signed by Cowboys (April 7, 1994). ... Granted unconditional free agency (February 12, 1999). ... Signed by Carolina Panthers (June 16, 1999). ... On injured reserve with triceps injury (December 14, 1999-remainder of season). ... Granted unconditional free agency (February 11, 2000). ... Announced retirement (March 8, 2000).
PLAYING EXPERIENCE: Tampa Bay USFL, 1984 and 1985; Dallas NFL, 1986-1998; Carolina NFL, 1999. ... Games/Games started: 1984 (18/18), 1985 (18/18), 1986 (11/0), 1987 (11/11), 1988 (15/15), 1989 (16/16), 1990 (16/16), 1991 (14/14), 1992 (15/15), 1993 (16/16), 1994 (16/16), 1995 (16/16), 1996 (16/16), 1997 (13/13), 1998 (16/16), 1999 (7/0). Total USFL: 36/36. Total NFL: 198/180. Total Pro: 234/216.
CHAMPIONSHIP GAME EXPERIENCE: Played in NFC championship game (1992-1995 seasons). ... Member of Super Bowl championship team (1992, 1993 and 1995 seasons).
HONORS: Played in Pro Bowl (1992-1996 and 1998 seasons). ... Named guard on THE SPORTING NEWS NFL All-Pro team (1995).
PRO STATISTICS: 1988—Caught one pass for two yards. 1990—Recovered two fumbles. 1991—Recovered one fumble. 1992—Recovered one fumble. 1997—Recovered one fumble.

NGUYEN, DAT — LB — COWBOYS

PERSONAL: Born September 25, 1975, in Fulton, Texas. ... 5-11/231. ... Name pronounced WIN.
HIGH SCHOOL: Rockport-Fulton (Rockport, Texas).
COLLEGE: Texas A&M (degree in agricultural development).
TRANSACTIONS/CAREER NOTES: Selected by Dallas Cowboys in third round (85th pick overall) of 1999 NFL draft. ... Signed by Cowboys (July 26, 1999).
PLAYING EXPERIENCE: Dallas NFL, 1999. ... Games/Games started: 1999 (16/0).
HONORS: Lombardi Award winner (1998). ... Chuck Bednarik Award winner (1998). ... Named inside linebacker on THE SPORTING NEWS college All-America first team (1998).
PRO STATISTICS: 1999—Intercepted one pass for six yards and credited with one sack.

NICKERSON, HARDY — LB — JAGUARS

PERSONAL: Born September 1, 1965, in Compton, Calif. ... 6-2/236. ... Full name: Hardy Otto Nickerson.
HIGH SCHOOL: Verbum Dei (Los Angeles).
COLLEGE: California (degree in sociology, 1986).
TRANSACTIONS/CAREER NOTES: Selected by Pittsburgh Steelers in fifth round (122nd pick overall) of 1987 NFL draft. ... Signed by Steelers (July 26, 1987). ... On injured reserve with ankle and knee injuries (November 3-December 16, 1989). ... Granted free agency (February 1, 1992). ... Re-signed by Steelers (June 15, 1992). ... Granted unconditional free agency (March 1, 1993). ... Signed by Tampa Bay Buccaneers (March 18, 1993). ... Granted unconditional free agency (February 16, 1996). ... Re-signed by Buccaneers (February 22, 1996). ... On injured reserve with heart problems (November 25, 1998-remainder of season). ... Granted unconditional free agency (February 11, 2000). ... Signed by Jacksonville Jaguars (February 22, 2000).
CHAMPIONSHIP GAME EXPERIENCE: Played in NFC championship game (1999 season).
HONORS: Named linebacker on THE SPORTING NEWS college All-America second team (1985). ... Named inside linebacker on THE SPORTING NEWS NFL All-Pro team (1993). ... Played in Pro Bowl (1993 and 1996-1999 seasons).
PRO STATISTICS: 1987—Recovered one fumble. 1988—Intercepted one pass for no yards and recovered one fumble. 1992—Recovered two fumbles for 44 yards. 1993—Intercepted one pass for six yards and recovered one fumble. 1994—Intercepted two passes for nine yards. 1995—Recovered three fumbles. 1996—Intercepted two passes for 24 yards and recovered two fumbles. 1997—Recovered two fumbles. 1998—Recovered one fumble. 1999—Intercepted two passes for 18 yards.

Year Team	G	GS	SACKS
1987—Pittsburgh NFL	12	0	0.0
1988—Pittsburgh NFL	15	10	3.5
1989—Pittsburgh NFL	10	8	1.0
1990—Pittsburgh NFL	16	14	2.0
1991—Pittsburgh NFL	16	14	1.0
1992—Pittsburgh NFL	15	15	2.0
1993—Tampa Bay NFL	16	16	1.0
1994—Tampa Bay NFL	14	14	1.0
1995—Tampa Bay NFL	16	16	1.5
1996—Tampa Bay NFL	16	16	3.0
1997—Tampa Bay NFL	16	16	1.0
1998—Tampa Bay NFL	10	10	1.0
1999—Tampa Bay NFL	16	16	0.5
Pro totals (13 years)	188	165	18.5

NOBLE, BRANDON — DT — COWBOYS

PERSONAL: Born April 10, 1974, in San Rafael, Calif. ... 6-2/285. ... Full name: Brandon Patrick Noble.
HIGH SCHOOL: First Colonial (Virginia Beach, Va.).
COLLEGE: Penn State.
TRANSACTIONS/CAREER NOTES: Signed as non-drafted free agent by San Francisco 49ers (April 29, 1997). ... Released by 49ers (August 19, 1997). ... Re-signed by 49ers to practice squad (November 12, 1997). ... Released by 49ers (November 19, 1997). ... Re-signed by 49ers

(January 13, 1998). ...Assigned by 49ers to Barcelona Dragons in 1998 NFL Europe enhancement allocation program (February 18, 1998). ... Released by 49ers (August 25, 1998). ... Re-signed by 49ers to practice squad (December 3, 1998). ... Granted free agency after 1998 season. ... Signed by Dallas Cowboys (February 2, 1999). ... Assigned by Cowboys to Barcelona Dragons in 1999 NFL Europe enhancement allocation program (February 22, 1999).

PRO STATISTICS: NFLE: 1998—Intercepted one pass for no yards, returned one kickoff for 12 yards and recovered one fumble for a touchdown. 1999—Returned one kickoff for 17 yards. NFL: 1999—Returned one kickoff for nine yards and recovered one fumble.

Year Team	G	GS	SACKS
1998—Barcelona NFLE	...	...	2.0
1999—Barcelona NFLE	...	...	5.0
—Dallas NFL	16	0	3.0
NFL Europe totals (2 years)	...	...	7.0
NFL totals (1 year)	16	0	3.0
Pro totals (3 years)	...	...	10.0

NORTHERN, GABE   LB

PERSONAL: Born June 8, 1974, in Baton Rouge, La. ... 6-2/240. ... Full name: Gabriel O'Kara Northern.
HIGH SCHOOL: Southern University Lab (Baton Rouge, La.), then Glen Oaks (Baton Rouge, La.).
COLLEGE: Louisiana State.
TRANSACTIONS/CAREER NOTES: Selected by Buffalo Bills in second round (53rd pick overall) of 1996 NFL draft. ... Signed by Bills (July 17, 1996). ... Granted unconditional free agency (February 11, 2000).
PRO STATISTICS: 1996—Returned blocked punt 18 yards for a touchdown. 1998—Intercepted one pass for 40 yards and a touchdown. 1999—Recovered one fumble for 59 yards and a touchdown.

Year Team	G	GS	SACKS
1996—Buffalo NFL	16	2	5.0
1997—Buffalo NFL	16	1	0.0
1998—Buffalo NFL	16	16	2.0
1999—Buffalo NFL	16	16	3.5
Pro totals (4 years)	64	35	10.5

NORTON, KEN   LB   49ERS

PERSONAL: Born September 29, 1966, in Lincoln, Ill. ... 6-2/254. ... Full name: Kenneth Howard Norton Jr. ... Son of Ken Norton Sr., former world heavyweight boxing champion.
HIGH SCHOOL: Westchester (Los Angeles).
COLLEGE: UCLA (degree in sociology, 1998).
TRANSACTIONS/CAREER NOTES: Selected by Dallas Cowboys in second round (41st pick overall) of 1988 NFL draft. ... Signed by Cowboys (July 13, 1988). ... On injured reserve with broken arm (August 23-December 3, 1988). ... On injured reserve with knee injury (December 24, 1990-remainder of season). ... Granted free agency (February 1, 1992). ... Re-signed by Cowboys (August 12, 1992). ... Granted unconditional free agency (February 17, 1994). ... Signed by San Francisco 49ers (April 20, 1994).
CHAMPIONSHIP GAME EXPERIENCE: Played in NFC championship game (1992-1994 and 1997 seasons). ... Member of Super Bowl championship team (1992-1994 seasons).
HONORS: Named linebacker on THE SPORTING NEWS college All-America first team (1987). ... Played in Pro Bowl (1993, 1995 and 1997 seasons).
POST SEASON RECORDS: Shares Super Bowl career record for most touchdowns by fumble recovery—1 (January 31, 1993, vs. Buffalo).
PRO STATISTICS: 1988—Recovered one fumble. 1990—Recovered two fumbles. 1992—Recovered two fumbles. 1993—Recovered one fumble for three yards. 1996—Recovered one fumble for 21 yards. 1997—Recovered two fumbles. 1998—Recovered three fumbles for 12 yards.

Year Team	G	GS	INTERCEPTIONS No.	Yds.	Avg.	TD	SACKS No.
1988—Dallas NFL	3	0	0	0	0.0	0	0.0
1989—Dallas NFL	13	13	0	0	0.0	0	2.5
1990—Dallas NFL	15	15	0	0	0.0	0	2.5
1991—Dallas NFL	16	16	0	0	0.0	0	0.0
1992—Dallas NFL	16	16	0	0	0.0	0	0.0
1993—Dallas NFL	16	16	1	25	25.0	0	2.0
1994—San Francisco NFL	16	16	1	0	0.0	0	0.0
1995—San Francisco NFL	16	16	3	102	‡34.0	†2	1.0
1996—San Francisco NFL	16	16	0	0	0.0	0	0.0
1997—San Francisco NFL	16	16	0	0	0.0	0	1.5
1998—San Francisco NFL	16	16	0	0	0.0	0	2.0
1999—San Francisco NFL	16	16	0	0	0.0	0	1.0
Pro totals (12 years)	175	172	5	127	25.4	2	12.5

NUTTEN, TOM   G   RAMS

PERSONAL: Born June 8, 1971, in Magog, Quebec. ... 6-5/300. ... Full name: Thomas Nutten. ... Name pronounced NEW-ton.
HIGH SCHOOL: Champlain Regional (Lennoxville, Quebec).
COLLEGE: Western Michigan (degree in marketing, 1994).
TRANSACTIONS/CAREER NOTES: Selected by Hamilton Tiger-Cats in first round (first pick overall) of 1995 CFL draft. ... Selected by Buffalo Bills in seventh round (221st pick overall) of 1995 NFL draft. ... Signed by Bills (June 12, 1995). ... Released by Bills (August 27, 1995). ... Re-signed by Bills to practice squad (August 29, 1995). ... Activated (October 10, 1995). ... Waived by Bills (August 26, 1996). ... Signed by Denver Broncos (January 14, 1997). ... Released by Broncos (July 16, 1997). ... Signed by Hamilton Tiger-Cats of CFL (July 28, 1997). ... Signed by St. Louis Rams (January 16, 1998). ... Assigned by Rams to Amsterdam Admirals in 1998 NFL Europe enhancement allocation pro-

gram (February 18, 1998). ... On injured reserve with neck injury (November 17, 1998-remainder of season). ... Granted free agency (February 11, 2000). ... Re-signed by Rams (February 12, 2000).
PLAYING EXPERIENCE: Buffalo NFL, 1995; Hamilton CFL, 1997; Amsterdam Admirals NFLE, 1998; St. Louis NFL, 1998 and 1999. ... Games/Games started: 1995 (1/0), 1997 (13/games started unavailable), NFLE 1998 (games played unavailable), NFL 1998 (4/2), 1999 (14/14). Total NFL: 19/16. Total CFL: 13/-.
CHAMPIONSHIP GAME EXPERIENCE: Played in NFC championship game (1999 season). ... Member of Super Bowl championship team (1999 season).
PRO STATISTICS: 1997—Recovered one fumble. 1999—Recovered one fumble.

NWKORIE, CHUKIE DE COLTS

PERSONAL: Born July 10, 1975, in Alabama. ... 6-2/286. ... Full name: Chijioke O. Nwkorie. ... Name pronounced CHEW-key wuh-CORE-e.
HIGH SCHOOL: Lafayette-Jefferson (Lafayette, Ind.).
COLLEGE: Purdue.
TRANSACTIONS/CAREER NOTES: Signed as non-drafted free agent by Indianapolis Colts (April 20, 1999).
PLAYING EXPERIENCE: Indianapolis NFL, 1999. ... Games/Games started: 1999 (1/0).

OBEN, ROMAN OT BROWNS

PERSONAL: Born October 9, 1972, in Cameroon, West Africa. ... 6-4/305. ... Name pronounced OH-bin.
HIGH SCHOOL: Gonzaga (Washington, D.C.), then Fork Union (Va.) Military Academy.
COLLEGE: Louisville (degree in economics).
TRANSACTIONS/CAREER NOTES: Selected by New York Giants in third round (66th pick overall) of 1996 NFL draft. ... Signed by Giants (July 20, 1996). ... Granted free agency (February 12, 1999). ... Re-signed by Giants (July 28, 1999). ... Granted unconditional free agency (February 11, 2000). ... Signed by Cleveland Browns (March 9, 2000).
PLAYING EXPERIENCE: New York Giants NFL, 1996-1999. ... Games/Games started: 1996 (2/0), 1997 (16/16), 1998 (16/16), 1999 (16/16). Total: 50/48.
PRO STATISTICS: 1999—Recovered two fumbles.

ODOM, JASON OT BUCCANEERS

PERSONAL: Born March 31, 1974, in Winter Haven, Fla. ... 6-5/312. ... Full name: Jason Brian Odom.
HIGH SCHOOL: Bartow (Fla.).
COLLEGE: Florida (degree in sports management, 1995).
TRANSACTIONS/CAREER NOTES: Selected by Tampa Bay Buccaneers in fourth round (96th pick overall) of 1996 NFL draft. ... Signed by Buccaneers (July 16, 1996). ... Granted free agency (February 12, 1999). ... Re-signed by Buccaneers (June 2, 1999). ... On injured reserve with back injury (November 24, 1999-remainder of season). ... Granted unconditional free agency (February 11, 2000). ... Re-signed by Buccaneers (March 1, 2000).
PLAYING EXPERIENCE: Tampa Bay NFL, 1996-1999. ... Games/Games started: 1996 (12/7), 1997 (16/16), 1998 (15/15), 1999 (3/3). Total: 46/41.
HONORS: Named offensive lineman on THE SPORTING NEWS college All-America first team (1995).
PRO STATISTICS: 1996—Recovered one fumble.

O'DONNELL, NEIL QB TITANS

PERSONAL: Born July 3, 1966, in Morristown, N.J. ... 6-3/228. ... Full name: Neil Kennedy O'Donnell.
HIGH SCHOOL: Madison-Boro (Madison, N.J.).
COLLEGE: Maryland (degree in economics, 1990).
TRANSACTIONS/CAREER NOTES: Selected by Pittsburgh Steelers in third round (70th pick overall) of 1990 NFL draft. ... Signed by Steelers (August 8, 1990). ... Active for three games (1990); did not play. ... Granted free agency (March 1, 1993). ... Tendered offer sheet by Tampa Bay Buccaneers (April 2, 1993). ... Offer matched by Steelers (April 12, 1993). ... Granted unconditional free agency (February 16, 1996). ... Signed by New York Jets (February 29, 1996). ... Released by Jets (June 24, 1998). ... Signed by Cincinnati Bengals (July 7, 1998). ... On injured reserve with hand injury (December 9, 1998-remainder of season). ... Released by Bengals (April 19, 1999). ... Signed by Tennessee Titans (July 23, 1999). ... Granted unconditional free agency (February 11, 2000). ... Re-signed by Titans (April 25, 2000).
CHAMPIONSHIP GAME EXPERIENCE: Played in AFC championship game (1994, 1995 and 1999 seasons). ... Played in Super Bowl XXX (1995 season). ... Member of Titans for Super Bowl XXXIV (1999 season); did not play.
HONORS: Played in Pro Bowl (1992 season).
RECORDS: Holds NFL career record for lowest interception percentage—2.03.
POST SEASON RECORDS: Holds NFL postseason single-game record for most passes attempted without an interception—54 (January 15, 1995, vs. San Diego).
PRO STATISTICS: 1991—Fumbled 11 times and recovered two fumbles for minus three yards. 1992—Fumbled six times and recovered four fumbles for minus 20 yards. 1993—Fumbled five times. 1994—Fumbled four times and recovered one fumble. 1995—Fumbled twice and recovered one fumble. 1996—Fumbled twice. 1997—Fumbled nine times and recovered two fumbles for minus one yard. 1998—Fumbled six times and recovered one fumble for minus two yards. 1999—Fumbled five times and recovered three fumbles for minus 14 yards.
SINGLE GAME HIGHS (regular season): Attempts—55 (December 24, 1995, vs. Green Bay); completions—34 (November 5, 1995, vs. Chicago); yards—377 (November 19, 1995, vs. Cincinnati); and touchdown passes—5 (August 31, 1997, vs. Seattle).
STATISTICAL PLATEAUS: 300-yard passing games: 1991 (1), 1993 (1), 1995 (4), 1996 (2), 1997 (1), 1998 (1), 1999 (2). Total: 12.
MISCELLANEOUS: Regular-season record as starting NFL quarterback: 53-44 (.546). ... Postseason record as starting NFL quarterback: 3-4 (.429).

N
O

Year Team	G	GS	Att.	Cmp.	Pct.	Yds.	TD	Int.	Avg.	Rat.	Att.	Yds.	Avg.	TD	TD	2pt.	Pts.
						PASSING						RUSHING				TOTALS	
1990—Pittsburgh NFL...........						Did not play.											
1991—Pittsburgh NFL...........	12	8	286	156	54.5	1963	11	7	6.86	78.8	18	82	4.6	1	1	0	6
1992—Pittsburgh NFL...........	12	12	313	185	59.1	2283	13	9	7.29	83.6	27	5	0.2	1	1	0	6
1993—Pittsburgh NFL...........	16	15	486	270	55.6	3208	14	7	6.60	79.5	26	111	4.3	0	0	0	0
1994—Pittsburgh NFL...........	14	14	370	212	57.3	2443	13	9	6.60	78.9	31	80	2.6	1	1	0	6
1995—Pittsburgh NFL...........	12	12	416	246	59.1	2970	17	7	7.14	87.7	24	45	1.9	0	0	0	0
1996—New York Jets NFL........	6	6	188	110	58.5	1147	4	7	6.10	67.8	6	30	5.0	0	0	0	0
1997—New York Jets NFL........	15	14	460	259	56.3	2796	17	7	6.08	80.3	32	36	1.1	1	1	0	6
1998—Cincinnati NFL............	13	11	343	212	§61.8	2216	15	4	6.46	90.2	13	34	2.6	0	0	0	0
1999—Tennessee NFL...........	8	5	195	116	59.5	1382	10	5	7.09	87.6	19	1	0.1	0	0	0	0
Pro totals (9 years)................	108	97	3057	1766	57.8	20408	114	62	6.68	82.0	196	424	2.2	4	4	0	24

O'DWYER, MATT — G — BENGALS

PERSONAL: Born September 1, 1972, in Lincolnshire, Ill. ... 6-5/300. ... Full name: Matthew Phillip O'Dwyer.
HIGH SCHOOL: Adlai E. Stevenson (Prairie View, Ill.).
COLLEGE: Northwestern.
TRANSACTIONS/CAREER NOTES: Selected by New York Jets in second round (33rd pick overall) of 1995 NFL draft. ... Signed by Jets (July 20, 1995). ... Granted unconditional free agency (February 12, 1999). ... Signed by Cincinnati Bengals (June 19, 1999). ... Suspended two games by NFL for involvement in bar fight (March 14, 2000).
PLAYING EXPERIENCE: New York Jets NFL, 1995-1998; Cincinnati NFL, 1999. ... Games/Games started: 1995 (12/2), 1996 (16/16), 1997 (16/16), 1998 (16/16), 1999 (16/16). Total: 76/66.
CHAMPIONSHIP GAME EXPERIENCE: Played in AFC championship game (1998 season).

OFODILE, A.J. — TE

PERSONAL: Born October 9, 1973, in Detroit. ... 6-6/260. ... Full name: Anselm Aniagboso Ofodile Jr. ... Name pronounced oh-FAH-da-lay.
HIGH SCHOOL: Cass Technical (Detroit).
COLLEGE: Missouri.
TRANSACTIONS/CAREER NOTES: Selected after junior season by Buffalo Bills in fifth round (158th pick overall) of 1994 NFL draft. ... Signed by Bills (July 15, 1994). ... On physically unable to perform list with knee injury (August 23, 1994-entire season). ... Released by Bills (August 22, 1995). ... Signed by Pittsburgh Steelers to practice squad (August 29, 1995). ... Released by Steelers (August 19, 1996). ... Signed by Baltimore Ravens (February 12, 1997). ... Assigned by Ravens to Rhein Fire in 1997 World League enhancement allocation program (February 19, 1997). ... Released by Ravens (August 30, 1998). ... Re-signed by Ravens (September 3, 1998). ... Granted free agency (February 12, 1999). ... Re-signed by Ravens (May 19, 1999). ... Granted unconditional free agency (February 11, 2000).
PLAYING EXPERIENCE: Rhein W.L., 1997; Baltimore NFL, 1997-1999. ... Games/Games started: W.L. 1997 (games played unavailable), NFL 1997 (12/0), 1998 (5/0), 1999 (7/3). Total NFL: 24/3.
PRO STATISTICS: W.L.: 1997—Caught 10 passes for 146 yards and one touchdown. NFL: 1999—Caught four passes for 25 yards.
SINGLE GAME HIGHS (regular season): Receptions—2 (October 21, 1999, vs. Kansas City); yards—13 (October 21, 1999, vs. Kansas City); and touchdown receptions—0.

OGBOGU, ERIC — DE — JETS

PERSONAL: Born July 18, 1975, in Irvington, N.Y. ... 6-4/285. ... Name pronounced oh-BOG-u.
HIGH SCHOOL: Archbishop Stepinac (White Plains, N.Y.).
COLLEGE: Maryland.
TRANSACTIONS/CAREER NOTES: Selected by New York Jets in sixth round (163rd pick overall) of 1998 NFL draft. ... Signed by Jets (July 2, 1998).
PLAYING EXPERIENCE: New York Jets NFL, 1998 and 1999. ... Games/Games started: 1998 (12/0), 1999 (14/0). Total: 26/0.
CHAMPIONSHIP GAME EXPERIENCE: Played in AFC championship game (1998 season).
PRO STATISTICS: 1999—Credited with one sack and recovered two fumbles, including one in end zone for a touchdown.

OGDEN, JEFF — WR — COWBOYS

PERSONAL: Born February 22, 1975, in Snohomish, Wash. ... 6-0/190. ... Full name: Jeffery Ogden.
HIGH SCHOOL: Snohomish (Wash.).
COLLEGE: Eastern Washington.
TRANSACTIONS/CAREER NOTES: Signed as non-drafted free agent by Dallas Cowboys (April 21, 1998). ... Assigned by Cowboys to Rhein Fire in 2000 NFL Europe enhancement allocation program (February 18, 2000).
PRO STATISTICS: 1998—Rushed once for 12 yards and returned three kickoffs for 65 yards. 1999—Returned four punts for 28 yards and returned 12 kickoffs for 252 yards.
SINGLE GAME HIGHS (regular season): Receptions—4 (November 22, 1998, vs. Seattle); yards—28 (January 2, 2000, vs. New York Giants); and touchdown receptions—0.

Year Team	G	GS	No.	Yds.	Avg.	TD	TD	2pt.	Pts.	Fum.
			RECEIVING				TOTALS			
1998—Dallas NFL........................	16	0	8	63	7.9	0	0	0	0	1
1999—Dallas NFL........................	16	0	12	144	12.0	0	0	0	0	0
Pro totals (2 years)	32	0	20	207	10.4	0	0	0	0	1

O

OGDEN, JONATHAN   OL   RAVENS

PERSONAL: Born July 31, 1974, in Washington, D.C. ... 6-8/335. ... Full name: Jonathan Phillip Ogden.
HIGH SCHOOL: St. Alban's (Washington, D.C.).
COLLEGE: UCLA.
TRANSACTIONS/CAREER NOTES: Selected by Baltimore Ravens in first round (fourth pick overall) of 1996 NFL draft. ... Signed by Ravens (July 15, 1996).
PLAYING EXPERIENCE: Baltimore NFL, 1996-1999. ... Games/Games started: 1996 (16/16), 1997 (16/16), 1998 (13/13), 1999 (16/16). Total: 61/61.
HONORS: Outland Trophy winner (1995). ... Named offensive lineman on THE SPORTING NEWS college All-America first team (1995). ... Named offensive tackle on the THE SPORTING NEWS NFL All-Pro team (1997). ... Played in Pro Bowl (1997-1999 seasons).
PRO STATISTICS: 1996—Caught one pass for one yard and a touchdown. 1999—Recovered two fumbles for two yards.

OGLE, KENDELL   LB   BROWNS

PERSONAL: Born November 25, 1975, in Hillside, N.J. ... 6-0/231.
HIGH SCHOOL: Hillside (N.J.).
COLLEGE: Maryland.
TRANSACTIONS/CAREER NOTES: Selected by Cleveland Browns in sixth round (187th pick overall) of 1999 NFL draft. ... Signed by Browns (July 22, 1999). ... Assigned by Browns to Rhein Fire in 2000 NFL Europe enhancement allocation program (February 18, 2000).
PLAYING EXPERIENCE: Cleveland NFL, 1999. ... Games/Games started: 1999 (2/0).

OKEAFOR, CHIKE   DE   49ERS

PERSONAL: Born March 27, 1976, in West Lafayette, Ind. ... 6-4/248. ... Full name: Chikeze Russell Okeafor. ... Name pronounced chee-KAY oh-KEY-fer.
HIGH SCHOOL: West Lafayette (Ind.).
COLLEGE: Purdue.
TRANSACTIONS/CAREER NOTES: Selected by San Francisco 49ers in third round (89th pick overall) of 1999 NFL draft. ... Signed by 49ers (July 27, 1999). ... On non-football injury list with back injury (July 27-September 5, 1999).
PLAYING EXPERIENCE: San Francisco NFL, 1999. ... Games/Games started: 1999 (12/0).
PRO STATISTICS: 1999—Credited with one sack.

OLDHAM, CHRIS   DB   SAINTS

PERSONAL: Born October 26, 1968, in Sacramento. ... 5-9/200. ... Full name: Christopher Martin Oldham. ... Name pronounced OLD-um.
HIGH SCHOOL: O. Perry Walker (New Orleans).
COLLEGE: Oregon (degree in communications).
TRANSACTIONS/CAREER NOTES: Selected by Detroit Lions in fourth round (105th pick overall) of 1990 NFL draft. ... Signed by Lions (July 19, 1990). ... Released by Lions (August 26, 1991). ... Signed by Buffalo Bills (September 25, 1991). ... Released by Bills (October 8, 1991). ... Signed by Phoenix Cardinals (October 15, 1991). ... Released by Cardinals (November 13, 1991). ... Signed by San Diego Chargers (February 15, 1992). ... Assigned by Chargers to San Antonio Riders in 1992 World League enhancement allocation program (February 20, 1992). ... Released by Chargers (August 25, 1992). ... Signed by Cardinals (December 22, 1992). ... Granted unconditional free agency (February 17, 1994). ... Cardinals franchise renamed Arizona Cardinals for 1994 season. ... Re-signed by Cardinals (June 7, 1994). ... Granted unconditional free agency (February 17, 1995). ... Signed by Pittsburgh Steelers (April 12, 1995). ... Granted unconditional free agency (February 11, 2000). ... Signed by New Orleans Saints (February 14, 2000).
CHAMPIONSHIP GAME EXPERIENCE: Played in AFC championship game (1995 and 1997 seasons). ... Played in Super Bowl XXX (1995 season).
PRO STATISTICS: NFL: 1990—Returned 13 kickoffs for 234 yards and fumbled twice. 1995—Recovered one fumble for 23 yards and a touchdown. 1998—Recovered five fumbles for 79 yards and one touchdown. 1999—Recovered one fumble. W.L.: 1992—Returned one kickoff for 11 yards, credited with one sack and recovered one fumble.

| | | | | INTERCEPTIONS | | | SACKS |
Year Team	G	GS	No.	Yds.	Avg.	TD	No.
1990—Detroit NFL	16	0	1	28	28.0	0	0.0
1991—Buffalo NFL	2	0	0	0	0.0	0	0.0
—Phoenix NFL	2	0	0	0	0.0	0	0.0
1992—San Antonio W.L.	9	9	3	52	17.3	*1	0.0
—Phoenix NFL	1	0	0	0	0.0	0	0.0
1993—Phoenix NFL	16	6	1	0	0.0	0	1.0
1994—Arizona NFL	11	1	0	0	0.0	0	0.0
1995—Pittsburgh NFL	15	0	1	12	12.0	0	0.0
1996—Pittsburgh NFL	16	0	0	0	0.0	0	2.0
1997—Pittsburgh NFL	16	0	2	16	8.0	0	4.0
1998—Pittsburgh NFL	16	1	1	14	14.0	0	0.5
1999—Pittsburgh NFL	15	0	1	9	9.0	0	3.0
W.L. totals (1 year)	9	9	3	52	17.3	1	0.0
NFL totals (10 years)	126	8	7	79	11.3	0	10.5
Pro totals (11 years)	135	17	10	131	13.1	1	10.5

OLIVER, WINSLOW   RB/PR   FALCONS

PERSONAL: Born March 3, 1973, in Houston. ... 5-7/200. ... Full name: Winslow Paul Oliver.
HIGH SCHOOL: Clements (Sugar Land, Texas), then Kempner (Sugar Land, Texas).
COLLEGE: New Mexico.

TRANSACTIONS/CAREER NOTES: Selected by Carolina Panthers in third round (73rd pick overall) of 1996 NFL draft. ... Signed by Panthers (July 20, 1996). ... Released by Panthers (September 7, 1999). ... Signed by Atlanta Falcons (September 22, 1999). ... Granted unconditional free agency (February 11, 2000). ... Re-signed by Falcons (March 8, 2000).
CHAMPIONSHIP GAME EXPERIENCE: Played in NFC championship game (1996 season).
PRO STATISTICS: 1996—Fumbled four times. 1997—Fumbled twice. 1998—Fumbled once. 1999—Fumbled twice.
SINGLE GAME HIGHS (regular season): Attempts—8 (November 10, 1996, vs. New York Giants); yards—37 (September 1, 1996, vs. Atlanta); and rushing touchdowns—0.

Year Team	G	GS	RUSHING				RECEIVING				PUNT RETURNS				KICKOFF RETURNS				TOTALS		
			Att.	Yds.	Avg.	TD	No.	Yds.	Avg.	TD	No.	Yds.	Avg.	TD	No.	Yds.	Avg.	TD	TD	2pt.	Pts.
1996—Carolina NFL	16	0	47	183	3.9	0	15	144	9.6	0	52	598	11.5	1	7	160	22.9	0	1	0	6
1997—Carolina NFL	6	0	1	0	0.0	0	6	47	7.8	0	14	111	7.9	0	0	0	0.0	0	0	0	0
1998—Carolina NFL	16	0	0	0	0.0	0	0	0	0.0	0	44	464	10.5	0	2	43	21.5	0	0	0	0
1999—Atlanta NFL	14	0	8	32	4.0	0	8	74	9.3	0	12	152	12.7	∞1	24	441	18.4	0	1	0	6
Pro totals (4 years)	52	0	56	215	3.8	0	29	265	9.1	0	122	1325	10.9	2	33	644	19.5	0	2	0	12

OLIVO, BROCK   FB   LIONS

PERSONAL: Born June 24, 1976, in St. Louis. ... 6-0/232. ... Name pronounced o-LEEV-o.
HIGH SCHOOL: St. Francis Borgia (Washington, Mo.).
COLLEGE: Missouri.
TRANSACTIONS/CAREER NOTES: Signed as non-drafted free agent by San Francisco 49ers (April 24, 1998). ... Released by 49ers (August 30, 1998). ... Re-signed by 49ers to practice squad (September 1, 1998). ... Signed by Detroit Lions off 49ers practice squad (September 23, 1998). ... Released by Lions (December 8, 1998). ... Re-signed by Lions to practice squad (December 9, 1998). ... On injured reserve with knee injury (December 22, 1999-remainder of season).
PRO STATISTICS: 1999—Recovered one fumble.
SINGLE GAME HIGHS (regular season): Attempts—1 (December 12, 1999, vs. Tampa Bay); yards—1 (December 12, 1999, vs. Tampa Bay); and rushing touchdowns—0.

Year Team	G	GS	RUSHING				RECEIVING				KICKOFF RETURNS				TOTALS			
			Att.	Yds.	Avg.	TD	No.	Yds.	Avg.	TD	No.	Yds.	Avg.	TD	TD	2pt.	Pts.	Fum.
1998—Detroit NFL	1	0	0	0	0.0	0	0	0	0.0	0	0	0	0.0	0	0	0	0	0
1999—Detroit NFL	14	0	1	1	1.0	0	4	24	6.0	0	11	198	18.0	0	0	0	0	0
Pro totals (2 years)	15	0	1	1	1.0	0	4	24	6.0	0	11	198	18.0	0	0	0	0	0

OLSON, BENJI   G   TITANS

PERSONAL: Born June 5, 1975, in Bremerton, Wash. ... 6-3/315. ... Full name: Benji Dempsey Olson.
HIGH SCHOOL: South Kitsap (Port Orchard, Wash.).
COLLEGE: Washington.
TRANSACTIONS/CAREER NOTES: Selected after junior season by Tennessee Oilers in fifth round (139th pick overall) of 1998 NFL draft. ... Signed by Oilers (June 29, 1998). ... Oilers franchise renamed Tennessee Titans for 1999 season (December 26, 1998).
PLAYING EXPERIENCE: Tennessee NFL, 1998 and 1999. ... Games/Games started: 1998 (13/1), 1999 (16/16). Total: 29/17.
CHAMPIONSHIP GAME EXPERIENCE: Played in AFC championship game (1999 season). ... Played in Super Bowl XXXIV (1999 season).
HONORS: Named guard on The Sporting News college All-America first team (1996).
PRO STATISTICS: 1999—Recovered one fumble.

O'NEAL, LESLIE   DE   CHIEFS

PERSONAL: Born May 7, 1964, in Little Rock, Ark. ... 6-4/281. ... Full name: Leslie Cornelius O'Neal.
HIGH SCHOOL: Hall (Little Rock, Ark.).
COLLEGE: Oklahoma State.
TRANSACTIONS/CAREER NOTES: Selected by New Jersey Generals in 1986 USFL territorial draft. ... Selected by San Diego Chargers in first round (eighth pick overall) of 1986 NFL draft. ... Signed by Chargers (August 5, 1986). ... On injured reserve with knee injury (December 4, 1986-remainder of season). ... On physically unable to perform list with knee injury (August 30, 1987-entire season). ... On physically unable to perform list with knee injury (July 23-August 21, 1988). ... On physically unable to perform list with knee injury (August 22-October 15, 1988). ... Granted free agency (February 1, 1990). ... Re-signed by Chargers (August 21, 1990). ... Granted free agency (February 1, 1992). ... Re-signed by Chargers (July 23, 1992). ... Designated by Chargers as franchise player (February 25, 1993). ... Free agency status changed by Chargers from franchise player to restricted free agent (June 15, 1993). ... Re-signed by Chargers (August 19, 1993). ... Granted unconditional free agency (February 16, 1996). ... Signed by St. Louis Rams (March 1, 1996). ... Released by Rams (February 23, 1998). ... Signed by Kansas City Chiefs (April 17, 1998).
CHAMPIONSHIP GAME EXPERIENCE: Played in AFC championship game (1994 season). ... Played in Super Bowl XXIX (1994 season).
HONORS: Named defensive lineman on The Sporting News college All-America first team (1984 and 1985). ... Played in Pro Bowl (1989, 1990 and 1992-1995 seasons).
PRO STATISTICS: 1986—Intercepted two passes for 22 yards and one touchdown and recovered two fumbles. 1989—Recovered two fumbles for 10 yards. 1990—Fumbled once and recovered two fumbles for 10 yards. 1992—Recovered one fumble. 1993—Recovered one fumble for 13 yards. 1994—Recovered one fumble. 1996—Recovered three fumbles. 1997—Intercepted one pass for five yards and recovered two fumbles for 66 yards and one touchdown. 1998—Recovered two fumbles.
MISCELLANEOUS: Active AFC leader for career sacks (132.5). ... Holds San Diego Chargers all-time record for most sacks (105.5).

Year Team	G	GS	SACKS
1986—San Diego NFL	13	13	12.5
1987—San Diego NFL	Did not play.		

O

1988—San Diego NFL	9	1	4.0
1989—San Diego NFL	16	16	12.5
1990—San Diego NFL	16	16	13.5
1991—San Diego NFL	16	16	9.0
1992—San Diego NFL	15	15	§17.0
1993—San Diego NFL	16	16	12.0
1994—San Diego NFL	16	16	12.5
1995—San Diego NFL	16	16	12.5
1996—St. Louis NFL	16	16	7.0
1997—St. Louis NFL	15	14	10.0
1998—Kansas City NFL	16	13	4.5
1999—Kansas City NFL	16	10	5.5
Pro totals (13 years)	196	178	132.5

O'NEILL, KEVIN   LB   LIONS

PERSONAL: Born April 14, 1975, in Twinsburg, Ohio. ... 6-2/249.
HIGH SCHOOL: Walsh Jesuit (Cuyahoga Falls, Ohio).
COLLEGE: Bowling Green State.
TRANSACTIONS/CAREER NOTES: Signed as non-drafted free agent by Detroit Lions (April 24, 1998). ... On physically unable to perform list with knee injury (August 30-November 17, 1999).
PLAYING EXPERIENCE: Detroit NFL, 1998 and 1999. ... Games/Games started: 1998 (11/0), 1999 (4/0). Total: 15/0.

OSBORNE, CHUCK   DT   RAIDERS

PERSONAL: Born November 2, 1973, in Los Angeles. ... 6-2/290. ... Full name: Charles Wayne Osborne.
HIGH SCHOOL: Canyon Country (Calif.).
COLLEGE: Arizona.
TRANSACTIONS/CAREER NOTES: Selected by St. Louis Rams in seventh round (222nd pick overall) of 1996 NFL draft. ... Signed by Rams (June 21, 1996). ... Released by Rams (August 19, 1997). ... Selected by Amsterdam Admirals in 1998 NFL Europe draft (February 18, 1998). ... Signed by Oakland Raiders (June 24, 1998). ... On injured reserve with knee injury (October 21, 1998-remainder of season). ... Granted free agency (February 11, 2000).
PLAYING EXPERIENCE: St. Louis NFL, 1996; Amsterdam Admirals NFLE, 1998; Oakland NFL, 1998 and 1999. ... Games/Games started: 1996 (15/1), NFLE 1998 (games played unavailable), NFL 1998 (6/0), 1999 (16/0). Total NFL: 37/1.
PRO STATISTICS: 1996—Credited with one sack. 1999—Credited with one sack. NFLE: 1998—Credited with eight sacks.

OSTROSKI, JERRY   C   BILLS

PERSONAL: Born July 12, 1970, in Collegeville, Pa. ... 6-4/326. ... Full name: Gerald Ostroski Jr.
HIGH SCHOOL: Owen J. Roberts (Pottstown, Pa.).
COLLEGE: Tulsa.
TRANSACTIONS/CAREER NOTES: Selected by Kansas City Chiefs in 10th round (271st pick overall) of 1992 NFL draft. ... Signed by Chiefs (July 21, 1992). ... Released by Chiefs (August 25, 1992). ... Signed by Atlanta Falcons (May 7, 1993). ... Released by Falcons (August 24, 1993). ... Signed by Buffalo Bills to practice squad (November 18, 1993). ... Released by Bills (August 28, 1994). ... Re-signed by Bills to practice squad (August 29, 1994). ... Activated (November 30, 1994). ... Granted free agency (February 13, 1998). ... Re-signed by Bills (April 8, 1998). ... Granted unconditional free agency (February 12, 1999). ... Re-signed by Bills (February 17, 1999).
PLAYING EXPERIENCE: Buffalo NFL, 1994-1999. ... Games/Games started: 1994 (4/3), 1995 (16/13), 1996 (16/16), 1997 (16/16), 1998 (16/16), 1999 (15/15). Total: 83/79.
PRO STATISTICS: 1997—Recovered three fumbles. 1999—Fumbled once for minus two yards.

OSTROWSKI, PHIL   G   49ERS

PERSONAL: Born September 23, 1975, in Wilkes-Barre, Pa. ... 6-4/291. ... Full name: Phillip Lucas Ostrowski. ... Name pronounced oh-STROW-ski.
HIGH SCHOOL: E.L. Meyers (Wilkes-Barre, Pa.).
COLLEGE: Penn State.
TRANSACTIONS/CAREER NOTES: Selected by San Francisco 49ers in fifth round (151st pick overall) of 1998 NFL draft. ... Signed by 49ers (July 18, 1998). ... Inactive for 16 games (1998).
PLAYING EXPERIENCE: San Francisco NFL, 1999. ... Games/Games started: 1999 (15/0).

OTTIS, BRAD   DE   CARDINALS

PERSONAL: Born August 2, 1972, in Wahoo, Neb. ... 6-5/293. ... Full name: Brad Allen Ottis. ... Name pronounced AH-tis.
HIGH SCHOOL: Bergan (Fremont, Neb.).
COLLEGE: Wayne State (Neb.).
TRANSACTIONS/CAREER NOTES: Selected by Los Angeles Rams in second round (56th pick overall) of 1994 NFL draft. ... Signed by Rams (June 23, 1994). ... Rams franchise moved to St. Louis (April 12, 1995). ... Released by Rams (August 20, 1996). ... Signed by Arizona Cardinals (October 1, 1996). ... Granted free agency (February 14, 1997). ... Re-signed by Cardinals for 1997 season. ... Granted unconditional free agency (February 13, 1998). ... Re-signed by Cardinals (February 18, 1998). ... On injured reserve with foot injury (August 30, 1998-entire season). ... Granted unconditional free agency (February 11, 2000). ... Re-signed by Cardinals (April 28, 2000).
PLAYING EXPERIENCE: Los Angeles Rams NFL, 1994; St. Louis NFL, 1995; Arizona NFL, 1996, 1997 and 1999. ... Games/Games started: 1994 (13/0), 1995 (12/0), 1996 (11/1), 1997 (16/4), 1999 (14/7). Total: 66/12.
PRO STATISTICS: 1994—Credited with one sack. 1996—Credited with one sack. 1999—Credited with one sack.

O

OWENS, DAN   DT

PERSONAL: Born March 16, 1967, in Whittier, Calif. ... 6-3/290. ... Full name: Daniel William Owens.
HIGH SCHOOL: La Habra (Calif.).
COLLEGE: Southern California.
TRANSACTIONS/CAREER NOTES: Selected by Detroit Lions in second round (35th pick overall) of 1990 NFL draft. ... Signed by Lions (July 26, 1990). ... Granted free agency (March 1, 1993). ... Re-signed by Lions (August 14, 1993). ... Granted unconditional free agency (February 17, 1995). ... Re-signed by Lions (March 13, 1995). ... Granted unconditional free agency (February 16, 1996). ... Signed by Atlanta Falcons (March 26, 1996). ... Granted unconditional free agency (February 13, 1998). ... Signed by Lions (February 18, 1998). ... On injured reserve with knee injury (November 23, 1998-remainder of season). ... On physically unable to perform list with knee injury (August 30-November 6, 1999). ... Released by Lions (February 10, 2000).
CHAMPIONSHIP GAME EXPERIENCE: Played in NFC championship game (1991 season).
PRO STATISTICS: 1991—Recovered two fumbles. 1992—Recovered one fumble. 1993—Intercepted one pass for one yard and recovered two fumbles for 17 yards. 1995—Returned one kickoff for nine yards. 1996—Recovered one fumble. 1997—Intercepted one pass for 14 yards, returned one kickoff for nine yards, fumbled once and recovered one fumble for two yards.

Year Team	G	GS	SACKS
1990—Detroit NFL	16	12	3.0
1991—Detroit NFL	16	16	5.5
1992—Detroit NFL	16	4	2.0
1993—Detroit NFL	15	11	3.0
1994—Detroit NFL	16	8	3.0
1995—Detroit NFL	16	0	0.0
1996—Atlanta NFL	16	9	5.5
1997—Atlanta NFL	15	15	8.0
1998—Detroit NFL	11	11	2.5
1999—Detroit NFL	8	0	1.0
Pro totals (10 years)	145	86	33.5

OWENS, RICH   DE   DOLPHINS

PERSONAL: Born May 22, 1972, in Philadelphia. ... 6-6/275.
HIGH SCHOOL: Lincoln (Philadelphia).
COLLEGE: Lehigh.
TRANSACTIONS/CAREER NOTES: Selected by Washington Redskins in fifth round (152nd pick overall) of 1995 NFL draft. ... Signed by Redskins (May 23, 1995). ... Granted free agency (February 13, 1998). ... Re-signed by Redskins (May 7, 1998). ... On injured reserve with knee injury (August 25, 1998-entire season). ... Granted unconditional free agency (February 12, 1999). ... Signed by Miami Dolphins (March 16, 1999).
PRO STATISTICS: 1997—Recovered one fumble. 1999—Recovered one fumble.

Year Team	G	GS	SACKS
1995—Washington NFL	10	3	3.0
1996—Washington NFL	16	16	11.0
1997—Washington NFL	16	15	2.5
1998—Washington NFL	Did not play.		
1999—Miami NFL	16	14	8.5
Pro totals (4 years)	58	48	25.0

OWENS, TERRELL   WR   49ERS

PERSONAL: Born December 7, 1973, in Alexander City, Ala. ... 6-3/217. ... Full name: Terrell Eldorado Owens. ... Name pronounced TARE-el.
HIGH SCHOOL: Benjamin Russell (Alexander City, Ala.).
COLLEGE: Tennessee-Chattanooga.
TRANSACTIONS/CAREER NOTES: Selected by San Francisco 49ers in third round (89th pick overall) of 1996 NFL draft. ... Signed by 49ers (July 18, 1996). ... On physically unable to perform list with foot injury (July 17-August 11, 1997). ... Designated by 49ers as franchise player (February 12, 1999). ... Re-signed by 49ers (June 4, 1999).
CHAMPIONSHIP GAME EXPERIENCE: Played in NFC championship game (1997 season).
PRO STATISTICS: 1996—Returned three kickoffs for 47 yards. 1997—Returned two kickoffs for 31 yards and recovered one fumble. 1998—Rushed four times for 53 yards and one touchdown and recovered one fumble for 13 yards.
SINGLE GAME HIGHS (regular season): Receptions—9 (December 5, 1999, vs. Cincinnati); yards—145 (December 5, 1999, vs. Cincinnati); and touchdown receptions—2 (September 19, 1999, vs. New Orleans).
STATISTICAL PLATEAUS: 100-yard receiving games: 1996 (1), 1998 (2), 1999 (2). Total: 5.

Year Team	G	GS	RECEIVING No.	Yds.	Avg.	TD	TOTALS TD	2pt.	Pts.	Fum.
1996—San Francisco NFL	16	10	35	520	14.9	4	4	0	24	1
1997—San Francisco NFL	16	15	60	936	15.6	8	8	0	48	1
1998—San Francisco NFL	16	8	67	1097	16.4	14	15	1	92	1
1999—San Francisco NFL	14	14	60	754	12.6	4	4	0	24	1
Pro totals (4 years)	62	47	222	3307	14.9	30	31	1	188	4

OXENDINE, KEN   RB   FALCONS

PERSONAL: Born October 4, 1975, in Richmond, Va. ... 6-0/230. ... Full name: Ken Qwarious Oxendine.
HIGH SCHOOL: Thomas Dale (Chester, Va.).
COLLEGE: Virginia Tech.
TRANSACTIONS/CAREER NOTES: Selected by Atlanta Falcons in seventh round (201st pick overall) of 1998 NFL draft. ... Signed by Falcons (May 27, 1998).

O

CHAMPIONSHIP GAME EXPERIENCE: Played in NFC championship game (1998 season).
SINGLE GAME HIGHS (regular season): Attempts—20 (October 10, 1999, vs. New Orleans); yards—85 (December 5, 1999, vs. New Orleans); and rushing touchdowns—1 (October 31, 1999, vs. Carolina).

| | | | | RUSHING | | | | RECEIVING | | | | TOTALS | | |
Year	Team	G	GS	Att.	Yds.	Avg.	TD	No.	Yds.	Avg.	TD	TD	2pt.	Pts.	Fum.
1998—Atlanta NFL		9	0	18	50	2.8	0	1	11	11.0	0	0	0	0	1
1999—Atlanta NFL		12	9	141	452	3.2	1	17	172	10.1	1	2	0	12	5
Pro totals (2 years)		21	9	159	502	3.2	1	18	183	10.2	1	2	0	12	6

PACE, ORLANDO — OT — RAMS

PERSONAL: Born November 4, 1975, in Sandusky, Ohio. ... 6-7/320. ... Full name: Orlando Lamar Pace.
HIGH SCHOOL: Sandusky (Ohio).
COLLEGE: Ohio State.
TRANSACTIONS/CAREER NOTES: Selected after junior season by St. Louis Rams in first round (first pick overall) of 1997 NFL draft. ... Signed by Rams (August 16, 1997).
PLAYING EXPERIENCE: St. Louis NFL, 1997-1999. ... Games/Games started: 1997 (13/9), 1998 (16/16), 1999 (16/16). Total: 45/41.
CHAMPIONSHIP GAME EXPERIENCE: Played in NFC championship game (1999 season). ... Member of Super Bowl championship team (1999 season).
HONORS: Lombardi Award winner (1995 and 1996). ... Named offensive tackle on The Sporting News college All-America first team (1995 and 1996). ... Outland Trophy winner (1996). ... Named offensive tackle on The Sporting News NFL All-Pro team (1999). ... Played in Pro Bowl (1999 season).
PRO STATISTICS: 1997—Recovered one fumble. 1998—Recovered one fumble.

PAGE, SOLOMON — OT — COWBOYS

PERSONAL: Born February 27, 1976, in Pittsburgh. ... 6-4/321.
HIGH SCHOOL: Brashear (Pittsburgh).
COLLEGE: West Virginia.
TRANSACTIONS/CAREER NOTES: Selected after junior season by Dallas Cowboys in second round (55th pick overall) of 1999 NFL draft. ... Signed by Cowboys (July 28, 1999).
PLAYING EXPERIENCE: Dallas NFL, 1999. ... Games/Games started: 1999 (14/6).

PALELEI, LONNIE — G — EAGLES

PERSONAL: Born October 15, 1970, in Nu'uuli, American Samoa. ... 6-3/310. ... Full name: Si'ulagi Jack Palelei.
HIGH SCHOOL: Blue Springs (Mo.).
COLLEGE: Purdue, then UNLV.
TRANSACTIONS/CAREER NOTES: Selected by Pittsburgh Steelers in fifth round (135th pick overall) of 1993 NFL draft. ... Signed by Steelers (July 9, 1993). ... Inactive for all 16 games (1994). ... On reserve/non-football injury list with knee injury (August 21-November 3, 1995). ... Claimed on waivers by Cleveland Browns (November 28, 1995). ... Browns franchise moved to Baltimore and renamed Ravens for 1996 season (March 11, 1996). ... Released by Ravens (August 25, 1996). ... Signed by New York Jets (March 3, 1997). ... Released by Jets (August 25, 1998). ... Signed by New York Giants (August 27, 1998). ... On injured reserve with heart problems (December 3, 1998-remainder of season). ... Granted unconditional free agency (February 12, 1999). ... Signed by Philadelphia Eagles (May 20, 1999).
PLAYING EXPERIENCE: Pittsburgh NFL, 1993 and 1995; New York Jets NFL, 1997; New York Giants NFL, 1998; Philadelphia NFL, 1999. ... Games/Games started: 1993 (3/0), 1995 (1/0), 1997 (15/14), 1998 (9/0), 1999 (16/12). Total: 44/26.
CHAMPIONSHIP GAME EXPERIENCE: Member of Steelers for AFC championship game (1994 season); inactive.
PRO STATISTICS: 1997—Recovered one fumble. 1998—Returned three kickoffs for 14 yards and fumbled once.

PALMER, DAVID — RB/KR — VIKINGS

PERSONAL: Born November 19, 1972, in Birmingham, Ala. ... 5-8/172. ... Full name: David L. Palmer.
HIGH SCHOOL: Jackson-Olin (Birmingham, Ala.).
COLLEGE: Alabama.
TRANSACTIONS/CAREER NOTES: Selected after junior season by Minnesota Vikings in second round (40th pick overall) of 1994 NFL draft. ... Signed by Vikings (July 19, 1994). ... Granted free agency (February 14, 1997). ... Re-signed by Vikings (May 7, 1997). ... Granted unconditional free agency (February 12, 1999). ... Re-signed by Vikings (February 22, 1999). ... On injured reserve with knee injury (November 27, 1999-remainder of season).
CHAMPIONSHIP GAME EXPERIENCE: Played in NFC championship game (1998 season).
HONORS: Named kick returner on The Sporting News college All-America first team (1993).
PRO STATISTICS: 1994—Fumbled twice. 1995—Fumbled once. 1996—Fumbled three times and recovered one fumble. 1997—Fumbled twice. 1998—Fumbled twice and recovered one fumble. 1999—Fumbled once.
SINGLE GAME HIGHS (regular season): Attempts—4 (November 16, 1997, vs. Detroit); yards—15 (September 20, 1998, vs. Detroit); and rushing touchdowns—1 (November 9, 1997, vs. Chicago).

| | | | | RUSHING | | | | RECEIVING | | | | PUNT RETURNS | | | | KICKOFF RETURNS | | | | TOTALS | | |
Year	Team	G	GS	Att.	Yds.	Avg.	TD	No.	Yds.	Avg.	TD	No.	Yds.	Avg.	TD	No.	Yds.	Avg.	TD	TD	2pt.	Pts.
1994—Minnesota NFL		13	1	1	1	1.0	0	6	90	15.0	0	30	193	6.4	0	0	0	0.0	0	0	0	0
1995—Minnesota NFL		14	0	7	15	2.1	0	12	100	8.3	0	26	342*13.2		†1	17	354	20.8	0	1	0	6
1996—Minnesota NFL		11	1	2	9	4.5	0	6	40	6.7	0	22	216	9.8	1	13	292	22.5	0	1	0	6
1997—Minnesota NFL		16	0	11	36	3.3	1	26	193	7.4	1	34	444‡13.1		0	32	711	22.2	0	2	0	12
1998—Minnesota NFL		16	0	10	52	5.2	0	18	185	10.3	0	28	289	10.3	0	50	1176	23.5	1	1	0	6
1999—Minnesota NFL		8	2	3	12	4.0	0	4	25	6.3	0	12	93	7.8	0	27	621	23.0	0	0	0	0
Pro totals (6 years)		78	4	34	125	3.7	1	72	633	8.8	1	152	1577	10.4	2	139	3154	22.7	1	5	0	30

O
P

PALMER, MITCH   LB   BUCCANEERS

PERSONAL: Born September 2, 1973, in San Diego. ... 6-4/259. ... Full name: Richard Mitchell Palmer.
HIGH SCHOOL: Poway (Calif.).
COLLEGE: Colorado State.
TRANSACTIONS/CAREER NOTES: Signed as non-drafted free agent by Carolina Panthers (April 28, 1997). ... Released by Panthers (August 17, 1997). ... Signed by Tampa Bay Buccaneers (April 28, 1998). ... On injured reserve with knee injury (October 5, 1999-remainder of season).
PLAYING EXPERIENCE: Tampa Bay NFL, 1998 and 1999. ... Games/Games started: 1998 (16/0), 1999 (4/0). Total: 20/0.

PALMER, RANDY   TE   BROWNS

PERSONAL: Born November 12, 1975, in Pleasanton, Texas. ... 6-4/235.
HIGH SCHOOL: Pleasanton (Texas).
COLLEGE: Texas A&M-Kingsville.
TRANSACTIONS/CAREER NOTES: Signed as non-drafted free agent by Oakland Raiders (April 23, 1999). ... Claimed on waivers by Cleveland Browns (September 6, 1999). ... On injured reserve with knee injury (November 16, 1999-remainder of season).
PLAYING EXPERIENCE: Cleveland NFL, 1999. ... Games/Games started: 1999 (3/0).

PANOS, JOE   G   BILLS

PERSONAL: Born January 24, 1971, in Brookfield, Wis. ... 6-2/298. ... Full name: Zois Panagiotopoulos.
HIGH SCHOOL: Brookfield (Wis.) East.
COLLEGE: Wisconsin.
TRANSACTIONS/CAREER NOTES: Selected by Philadelphia Eagles in third round (77th pick overall) of 1994 NFL draft. ... Signed by Eagles (July 11, 1994). ... On injured reserve with shoulder injury (November 12, 1995-remainder of season). ... Granted free agency (February 14, 1997). ... Re-signed by Eagles (July 19, 1997). ... Granted unconditional free agency (February 13, 1998). ... Signed by Buffalo Bills (February 20, 1998). ... Inactive for entire 1999 season due to neck injury.
PLAYING EXPERIENCE: Philadelphia NFL, 1994-1997; Buffalo NFL, 1998. ... Games/Games started: 1994 (16/2), 1995 (9/9), 1996 (16/16), 1997 (13/13), 1998 (16/16). Total: 70/56.
PRO STATISTICS: 1997—Recovered one fumble.

PARKER, De'MOND   RB   PACKERS

PERSONAL: Born December 24, 1976, in Tulsa, Okla. ... 5-10/188. ... Full name: De'Mond Keith Parker. ... Nephew of Patrick Collins, running back with Green Bay Packers (1988). ... Name pronounced de-MOND.
HIGH SCHOOL: Booker T. Washington (Tulsa, Okla.).
COLLEGE: Oklahoma.
TRANSACTIONS/CAREER NOTES: Selected after junior season by Green Bay Packers in fifth round (159th pick overall) of 1999 NFL draft. ... Signed by Packers (July 12, 1999). ... On injured reserve with knee injury (December 28, 1999-remainder of season).
PRO STATISTICS: 1999—Recovered two fumbles.
SINGLE GAME HIGHS (regular season): Attempts—19 (December 5, 1999, vs. Chicago); yards—113 (December 5, 1999, vs. Chicago); rushing touchdowns—2 (December 5, 1999, vs. Chicago).
STATISTICAL PLATEAUS: 100-yard rushing games: 1999 (1).

			RUSHING				RECEIVING				KICKOFF RETURNS				TOTALS			
Year Team	G	GS	Att.	Yds.	Avg.	TD	No.	Yds.	Avg.	TD	No.	Yds.	Avg.	TD	TD	2pt.	Pts.	Fum.
1999—Green Bay NFL	11	0	36	184	5.1	2	4	15	3.8	0	15	268	17.9	0	2	0	12	1

PARKER, GLENN   G   GIANTS

PERSONAL: Born April 22, 1966, in Westminster, Calif. ... 6-5/311. ... Full name: Glenn Andrew Parker.
HIGH SCHOOL: Edison (Huntington Beach, Calif.).
JUNIOR COLLEGE: Golden West Junior College (Calif.).
COLLEGE: Arizona.
TRANSACTIONS/CAREER NOTES: Selected by Buffalo Bills in third round (69th pick overall) of 1990 NFL draft. ... Signed by Bills (July 26, 1990). ... Granted free agency (March 1, 1993). ... Re-signed by Bills (March 11, 1993). ... Released by Bills (August 24, 1997). ... Signed by Kansas City Chiefs (August 28, 1997). ... Granted unconditional free agency (February 11, 2000). ... Signed by New York Giants (March 26, 2000).
PLAYING EXPERIENCE: Buffalo NFL, 1990-1996; Kansas City NFL, 1997-1999. ... Games/Games started: 1990 (16/3), 1991 (16/5), 1992 (13/13), 1993 (16/9), 1994 (16/16), 1995 (13/13), 1996 (14/13), 1997 (15/15), 1998 (15/15), 1999 (12/11). Total: 146/113.
CHAMPIONSHIP GAME EXPERIENCE: Played in AFC championship game (1990, 1992 and 1993 seasons). ... Member of Bills for AFC championship game (1991 season); inactive. ... Played in Super Bowl XXV (1990 season), Super Bowl XXVI (1991 season), Super Bowl XXVII (1992 season) and Super Bowl XXVIII (1993 season).
PRO STATISTICS: 1992—Recovered one fumble. 1995—Recovered one fumble. 1996—Recovered two fumbles. 1998—Recovered one fumble.

PARKER, LARRY   WR   CHIEFS

PERSONAL: Born July 14, 1976, in Bakersfield, Calif. ... 6-1/200.
HIGH SCHOOL: Bakersfield (Calif.).
COLLEGE: Southern California.

TRANSACTIONS/CAREER NOTES: Selected by Kansas City Chiefs in fourth round (108th pick overall) of 1999 NFL draft. ... Signed by Chiefs (July 29, 1999).

Year Team	G	GS	PUNT RETURNS				KICKOFF RETURNS				TOTALS			
			No.	Yds.	Avg.	TD	No.	Yds.	Avg.	TD	TD	2pt.	Pts.	Fum.
1999—Kansas City NFL	10	0	5	51	10.2	0	1	24	24.0	0	0	0	0	1

PARKER, RIDDICK   DT   SEAHAWKS

PERSONAL: Born November 20, 1972, in Emporia, Va. ... 6-3/274.
HIGH SCHOOL: Southampton (Courtland, Va.).
COLLEGE: North Carolina.
TRANSACTIONS/CAREER NOTES: Signed as non-drafted free agent by San Diego Chargers (April 28, 1995). ... Released by Chargers (August 22, 1995). ... Signed by Seattle Seahawks (July 8, 1996). ... Released by Seahawks (August 24, 1996). ... Re-signed by Seahawks to practice squad (August 26, 1996). ... Granted free agency (February 11, 2000).
PLAYING EXPERIENCE: Seattle NFL, 1997-1999. ... Games/Games started: 1997 (11/0), 1998 (8/0), 1999 (16/3). Total: 35/3.
PRO STATISTICS: 1998—Credited with one sack. 1999—Credited with two sacks.

PARKER, VAUGHN   OT   CHARGERS

PERSONAL: Born June 5, 1971, in Buffalo. ... 6-3/300. ... Full name: Vaughn Antoine Parker.
HIGH SCHOOL: Saint Joseph's Collegiate Institute (Buffalo).
COLLEGE: UCLA.
TRANSACTIONS/CAREER NOTES: Selected by San Diego Chargers in second round (63rd pick overall) of 1994 NFL draft. ... Signed by Chargers (July 12, 1994). ... Granted free agency (February 14, 1997). ... Re-signed by Chargers (June 6, 1997). ... On injured reserve with leg injury (December 12, 1998-remainder of season). ... Granted unconditional free agency (February 11, 2000). ... Re-signed by Chargers (February 11, 2000).
PLAYING EXPERIENCE: San Diego NFL, 1994-1999. ... Games/Games started: 1994 (6/0), 1995 (14/7), 1996 (16/16), 1997 (16/16), 1998 (6/6), 1999 (15/15). Total: 73/60.
CHAMPIONSHIP GAME EXPERIENCE: Played in AFC championship game (1994 season). ... Played in Super Bowl XXIX (1994 season).
PRO STATISTICS: 1994—Returned one kickoff for one yard. 1996—Recovered one fumble. 1997—Recovered two fumbles. 1999—Recovered one fumble.

PARKS, NATHAN   G/OT   RAIDERS

PERSONAL: Born October 24, 1974, in Chico, Calif. ... 6-5/305. ... Full name: Nate Jacob Parks.
HIGH SCHOOL: Durham (Calif.).
JUNIOR COLLEGE: Butte Junior College (Calif.).
COLLEGE: Stanford.
TRANSACTIONS/CAREER NOTES: Selected by Kansas City Chiefs in seventh round (214th pick overall) of 1997 NFL draft. ... Signed by Chiefs (May 1, 1997). ... Placed on reserve/left camp list (August 5, 1998). ... Assigned by Chiefs to Scottish Claymores in 1999 NFL Europe enhancement allocation program (February 22, 1999). ... Released by Chiefs (September 5, 1999). ... Signed by Oakland Raiders (October 26, 1999).
PLAYING EXPERIENCE: Kansas City NFL, 1997; Scottish NFLE, 1999; Oakland NFL, 1999. ... Games/Games started: 1997 (1/0), NFLE 1999 (games played unavailable), NFL 1999 (2/0). Total NFL: 3/0.

PARMALEE, BERNIE   RB   JETS

PERSONAL: Born September 16, 1967, in Jersey City, N.J. ... 5-11/210. ... Full name: Bernard Parmalee. ... Name pronounced PARM-uh-lee.
HIGH SCHOOL: Lincoln (Jersey City, N.J.).
COLLEGE: Ball State (degree in business administration).
TRANSACTIONS/CAREER NOTES: Signed as non-drafted free agent by Miami Dolphins (May 1, 1992). ... Released by Dolphins (August 31, 1992). ... Re-signed by Dolphins to practice squad (September 1, 1992). ... Activated (October 21, 1992). ... Deactivated for remainder of 1992 playoffs (January 16, 1993). ... Granted free agency (February 14, 1997). ... Re-signed by Dolphins (April 17, 1997). ... Granted unconditional free agency (February 13, 1998). ... Re-signed by Dolphins (March 2, 1998). ... Released by Dolphins (September 5, 1999). ... Signed by New York Jets (September 7, 1999).
PRO STATISTICS: 1994—Recovered three fumbles for 20 yards. 1998—Recovered two fumbles.
SINGLE GAME HIGHS (regular season): Attempts—30 (October 16, 1994, vs. Los Angeles Raiders); yards—150 (October 16, 1994, vs. Los Angeles Raiders); and rushing touchdowns—3 (December 25, 1994, vs. Detroit).
STATISTICAL PLATEAUS: 100-yard rushing games: 1994 (3), 1995 (3). Total: 6.

Year Team	G	GS	RUSHING				RECEIVING				KICKOFF RETURNS				TOTALS			
			Att.	Yds.	Avg.	TD	No.	Yds.	Avg.	TD	No.	Yds.	Avg.	TD	TD	2pt.	Pts.	Fum.
1992—Miami NFL	10	0	6	38	6.3	0	0	0	0.0	0	14	289	20.6	0	0	0	0	3
1993—Miami NFL	16	0	4	16	4.0	0	1	1	1.0	0	0	0	0.0	0	0	0	0	4
1994—Miami NFL	15	10	216	868	4.0	6	34	249	7.3	1	2	0	0.0	0	7	1	44	5
1995—Miami NFL	16	12	236	878	3.7	9	39	345	8.8	1	0	0	0.0	0	10	0	60	5
1996—Miami NFL	16	0	25	80	3.2	0	21	189	9.0	0	0	0	0.0	0	0	0	0	1
1997—Miami NFL	16	4	18	59	3.3	0	28	301	10.8	1	0	0	0.0	0	1	0	6	1
1998—Miami NFL	15	0	8	20	2.5	0	21	221	10.5	0	0	0	0.0	0	0	0	0	2
1999—New York Jets NFL	16	0	27	133	4.9	0	15	113	7.5	0	0	0	0.0	0	0	0	0	1
Pro totals (8 years)	120	26	540	2092	3.9	15	159	1419	8.9	3	16	289	18.1	0	18	1	110	17

P

PARRELLA, JOHN   DT   CHARGERS

PERSONAL: Born November 22, 1969, in Topeka, Kan. ... 6-3/300. ... Full name: John Lorin Parrella.
HIGH SCHOOL: Grand Island (Neb.) Central Catholic.
COLLEGE: Nebraska.
TRANSACTIONS/CAREER NOTES: Selected by Buffalo Bills in second round (55th pick overall) of 1993 NFL draft. ... Signed by Bills (July 12, 1993). ... Released by Bills (August 28, 1994). ... Signed by San Diego Chargers (September 12, 1994). ... Granted free agency (February 16, 1996). ... Re-signed by Chargers (June 14, 1996).
CHAMPIONSHIP GAME EXPERIENCE: Member of Bills for AFC championship game (1993 season); inactive. ... Member of Bills for Super Bowl XXVIII (1993 season); inactive. ... Played in AFC championship game (1994 season). ... Played in Super Bowl XXIX (1994 season).
PRO STATISTICS: 1997—Recovered one fumble. 1998—Recovered one fumble.

Year Team	G	GS	SACKS
1993—Buffalo NFL	10	0	1.0
1994—San Diego NFL	13	1	1.0
1995—San Diego NFL	16	1	2.0
1996—San Diego NFL	16	9	2.0
1997—San Diego NFL	16	16	3.5
1998—San Diego NFL	16	16	1.5
1999—San Diego NFL	16	16	5.5
Pro totals (7 years)	103	59	16.5

PARRISH, TONY   S   BEARS

PERSONAL: Born November 23, 1975, in Huntington Beach, Calif. ... 5-10/206.
HIGH SCHOOL: Marina (Huntington Beach, Calif.).
COLLEGE: Washington.
TRANSACTIONS/CAREER NOTES: Selected by Chicago Bears in second round (35th pick overall) of 1998 NFL draft. ... Signed by Bears (July 20, 1998).
PRO STATISTICS: 1998—Credited with one sack, fumbled once and recovered two fumbles for minus two yards.

Year Team	G	GS	INTERCEPTIONS No.	Yds.	Avg.	TD
1998—Chicago NFL	16	16	1	8	8.0	0
1999—Chicago NFL	16	16	1	41	41.0	0
Pro totals (2 years)	32	32	2	49	24.5	0

PARTEN, TY   DE

PERSONAL: Born October 13, 1969, in Washington, D.C. ... 6-5/290. ... Full name: Ty Daniel Parten.
HIGH SCHOOL: Horizon (Scottsdale, Ariz.).
COLLEGE: Arizona.
TRANSACTIONS/CAREER NOTES: Selected by Cincinnati Bengals in third round (63rd pick overall) of 1993 draft. ... Signed by Bengals (July 19, 1993). ... On injured reserve with left thumb injury (November 29, 1993-remainder of season). ... Released by Bengals (September 20, 1995). ... Selected by Scottish Claymores in 1996 World League draft (February 22, 1996). ... Signed by St. Louis Rams (April 2, 1997). ... Released by Rams (August 24, 1997). ... Signed by Kansas City Chiefs (December 10, 1997). ... Granted free agency (February 12, 1999). ... Re-signed by Chiefs (June 16, 1999). ... Granted unconditional free agency (February 11, 2000).
PLAYING EXPERIENCE: Cincinnati NFL, 1993-1995; Scottish NFLE, 1996; Kansas City NFL, 1997-1999. ... Games/Games started: 1993 (11/1), 1994 (14/4), 1995 (1/1), 1996 (games played unavailable), 1997 (2/0), 1998 (16/6), 1999 (16/0). Total NFL: 60/12.
PRO STATISTICS: NFLE: 1996-Credited with two sacks. NFL: 1998—Returned two kickoffs for 22 yards and recovered one fumble. 1999—Returned one kickoff for 11 yards.

PATHON, JEROME   WR   COLTS

PERSONAL: Born December 16, 1975, in Capetown, South Africa. ... 6-0/187. ... Name pronounced PAY-thin.
HIGH SCHOOL: Carson Graham Secondary School (North Vancouver).
COLLEGE: Acadia (Nova Scotia), then Washington.
TRANSACTIONS/CAREER NOTES: Selected by Indianapolis Colts in second round (32nd pick overall) of 1998 NFL draft. ... Signed by Colts (July 26, 1998).
HONORS: Named wide receiver on THE SPORTING NEWS college All-America second team (1997).
PRO STATISTICS: 1998—Rushed three times for minus two yards. 1999—Returned six kickoffs for 123 yards.
SINGLE GAME HIGHS (regular season): Receptions—7 (November 1, 1998, vs. New England); yards—66 (December 20, 1998, vs. Seattle); and touchdown receptions—1 (November 29, 1998, vs. Baltimore).

Year Team	G	GS	RECEIVING No.	Yds.	Avg.	TD	TOTALS TD	2pt.	Pts.	Fum.
1998—Indianapolis NFL	16	15	50	511	10.2	1	1	0	6	0
1999—Indianapolis NFL	10	2	14	163	11.6	0	0	0	0	0
Pro totals (2 years)	26	17	64	674	10.5	1	1	0	6	0

PATTEN, DAVID   WR/KR   BROWNS

PERSONAL: Born August 19, 1974, in Hopkins, S.C. ... 5-9/193.
HIGH SCHOOL: Lower Richland (Hopkins, S.C.).
COLLEGE: Western Carolina.

P

TRANSACTIONS/CAREER NOTES: Played for Albany Firebirds of Arena League (1996). ... Signed as non-drafted free agent by New York Giants (March 24, 1997). ... Released by Giants (August 24, 1997). ... Re-signed by Giants to practice squad (August 25, 1997). ... Activated (August 27, 1997). ... On injured reserve with knee injury (December 16, 1998-remainder of season). ... Granted free agency (February 11, 2000). ... Signed by Cleveland Browns (March 16, 2000).
PRO STATISTICS: 1997—Rushed once for two yards and recovered one fumble. 1999—Rushed once for 27 yards.
SINGLE GAME HIGHS (regular season): Receptions—3 (November 21, 1999, vs. Washington); yards—66 (October 12, 1997, vs. Arizona); and touchdown receptions—1 (October 11, 1998, vs. Atlanta).

			RECEIVING				KICKOFF RETURNS				TOTALS		
Year Team	G	GS	No.	Yds.	Avg.	TD	No.	Yds.	Avg.	TD	TD	2pt.	Pts.	Fum.
1997—New York Giants NFL	16	3	13	226	17.4	2	8	123	15.4	0	2	0	12	2
1998—New York Giants NFL	12	0	11	119	10.8	1	43	928	21.6	1	2	0	12	0
1999—New York Giants NFL	16	0	9	115	12.8	0	33	673	20.4	0	0	0	0	0
Pro totals (3 years)	44	3	33	460	13.9	3	84	1724	20.5	1	4	0	24	2

PATTON, JOE   G   CHARGERS

PERSONAL: Born January 5, 1972, in Birmingham, Ala. ... 6-4/310. ... Full name: Joseph Patton.
HIGH SCHOOL: Jones Valley (Birmingham, Ala.).
COLLEGE: Alabama A&M.
TRANSACTIONS/CAREER NOTES: Selected by Washington Redskins in third round (97th pick overall) of 1994 NFL draft. ... Signed by Redskins (July 19, 1994). ... Granted free agency (February 14, 1997). ... Re-signed by Redskins (June 2, 1997). ... Granted unconditional free agency (February 13, 1998). ... Re-signed by Redskins (February 19, 1998). ... Released by Redskins (August 30, 1999). ... Signed by Jacksonville Jaguars (January 5, 2000). ... Granted unconditional free agency (February 11, 2000). ... Signed by San Diego Chargers (March 9, 2000).
PLAYING EXPERIENCE: Washington NFL, 1994-1998. ... Games/Games started: 1994 (2/0), 1995 (16/13), 1996 (16/15), 1997 (16/16), 1998 (11/10). Total: 61/54.
CHAMPIONSHIP GAME EXPERIENCE: Member of Jaguars for AFC championship game (1999 season); inactive.
PRO STATISTICS: 1995—Recovered one fumble. 1996—Recovered one fumble. 1997—Recovered one fumble.

PATTON, MARVCUS   LB   CHIEFS

PERSONAL: Born May 1, 1967, in Los Angeles. ... 6-2/243. ... Full name: Marvcus Raymond Patton.
HIGH SCHOOL: Leuzinger (Lawndale, Calif.).
COLLEGE: UCLA (degree in political science, 1990).
TRANSACTIONS/CAREER NOTES: Selected by Buffalo Bills in eighth round (208th pick overall) of 1990 NFL draft. ... Signed by Bills (July 27, 1990). ... On injured reserve with broken leg (January 26, 1991-remainder of 1990 playoffs). ... Granted free agency (February 1, 1992). ... Re-signed by Bills (July 23, 1992). ... Granted unconditional free agency (February 17, 1995). ... Signed by Washington Redskins (February 22, 1995). ... Granted unconditional free agency (February 12, 1999). ... Signed by Kansas City Chiefs (April 27, 1999).
CHAMPIONSHIP GAME EXPERIENCE: Played in AFC championship game (1991-1993 seasons). ... Played in Super Bowl XXVI (1991 season), Super Bowl XXVII (1992 season) and Super Bowl XXVIII (1993 season).
PRO STATISTICS: 1993—Recovered three fumbles for five yards. 1994—Recovered one fumble and fumbled once. 1995—Recovered one fumble. 1997—Returned one kickoff for 10 yards and recovered one fumble. 1999—Recovered three fumbles.

			INTERCEPTIONS				SACKS
Year Team	G	GS	No.	Yds.	Avg.	TD	No.
1990—Buffalo NFL	16	0	0	0	0.0	0	0.5
1991—Buffalo NFL	16	2	0	0	0.0	0	0.0
1992—Buffalo NFL	16	4	0	0	0.0	0	2.0
1993—Buffalo NFL	16	16	2	0	0.0	0	1.0
1994—Buffalo NFL	16	16	2	8	4.0	0	0.0
1995—Washington NFL	16	16	2	7	3.5	0	2.0
1996—Washington NFL	16	16	2	26	13.0	0	2.0
1997—Washington NFL	16	16	2	5	2.5	0	4.5
1998—Washington NFL	16	16	0	0	0.0	0	3.0
1999—Kansas City NFL	16	16	1	0	0.0	0	6.5
Pro totals (10 years)	160	118	11	46	4.2	0	21.5

PAUL, TITO   CB

PERSONAL: Born December 7, 1971, in Kissimmee, Fla. ... 6-0/195. ... Cousin of Markus Paul, safety with Chicago Bears (1989-93) and Tampa Bay Buccaneers (1993).
HIGH SCHOOL: Osceola (Seminole, Fla.).
COLLEGE: Ohio State.
TRANSACTIONS/CAREER NOTES: Selected by Arizona Cardinals in fifth round (167th pick overall) of 1995 NFL draft. ... Signed by Cardinals (July 20, 1995). ... Released by Cardinals (September 1, 1997). ... Signed by Cincinnati Bengals (September 9, 1997). ... Released by Bengals (April 20, 1998). ... Signed by Denver Broncos (May 7, 1998). ... Traded by Broncos to Washington Redskins for conditional seventh-round pick (August 24, 1999). ... On injured reserve with knee injury (November 16, 1999-remainder of season). ... Traded by Redskins to Broncos for seventh-round pick (traded to Seattle) in 2000 draft and seventh-round pick in 2001 draft (January 26, 2000). ... Granted unconditional free agency (February 11, 2000).
PLAYING EXPERIENCE: Arizona NFL, 1995 and 1996; Arizona (1)-Cincinnati (14) NFL, 1997; Denver NFL, 1998; Washington NFL, 1999. ... Games/Games started: 1995 (14/4), 1996 (16/3), 1997 (Ari.-1/0; Cin.-14/5; Total: 15/5), 1998 (16/0), 1999 (6/0). Total: 67/12.
CHAMPIONSHIP GAME EXPERIENCE: Played in AFC championship game (1998 season). ... Member of Super Bowl championship team (1998 season).
PRO STATISTICS: 1994—Intercepted one pass for four yards. 1996—Recovered one fumble. 1997—Recovered one fumble. 1998—Returned one punt for no yards, fumbled once and recovered one fumble.

P

PAULK, JEFF   FB   FALCONS

PERSONAL: Born April 26, 1976, in Phoenix. ... 6-0/240. ... Full name: Jeffery Howard Paulk.
HIGH SCHOOL: Corona Del Sol (Tempe, Ariz.).
COLLEGE: Arizona State.
TRANSACTIONS/CAREER NOTES: Selected by Atlanta Falcons in third round (92nd pick overall) of 1999 NFL draft. ... Signed by Falcons (June 16, 1999).
PLAYING EXPERIENCE: Atlanta NFL, 1999. ... Games/Games started: 1999 (1/0).

PAUP, BRYCE   LB   VIKINGS

PERSONAL: Born February 29, 1968, in Jefferson, Iowa. ... 6-5/250. ... Full name: Bryce Eric Paup.
HIGH SCHOOL: Scranton (Iowa).
COLLEGE: Northern Iowa (degree in business).
TRANSACTIONS/CAREER NOTES: Selected by Green Bay Packers in sixth round (159th pick overall) of 1990 NFL draft. ... Signed by Packers (July 22, 1990). ... On injured reserve with hand injury (September 4-November 17, 1990). ... On injured reserve with calf injury (December 12, 1991-remainder of season). ... Granted free agency (February 1, 1992). ... Re-signed by Packers (August 13, 1992). ... Granted unconditional free agency (February 17, 1995). ... Signed by Buffalo Bills (March 9, 1995). ... Granted unconditional free agency (February 13, 1998). ... Signed by Jacksonville Jaguars (February 16, 1998). ... Released by Jaguars (June 2, 2000). ... Signed by Minnesota Vikings (June 6, 2000).
CHAMPIONSHIP GAME EXPERIENCE: Played in AFC championship game (1999 season).
HONORS: Played in Pro Bowl (1994-1997 seasons). ... Named linebacker on THE SPORTING NEWS NFL All-Pro team (1995).
PRO STATISTICS: 1991—Credited with a safety. 1992—Recovered two fumbles. 1994—Recovered two fumbles. 1995—Recovered one fumble. 1997—Recovered one fumble.

				INTERCEPTIONS			SACKS
Year Team	G	GS	No.	Yds.	Avg.	TD	No.
1990—Green Bay NFL	5	0	0	0	0.0	0	0.0
1991—Green Bay NFL	12	1	0	0	0.0	0	7.5
1992—Green Bay NFL	16	10	0	0	0.0	0	6.5
1993—Green Bay NFL	15	14	1	8	8.0	0	11.0
1994—Green Bay NFL	16	16	3	47	15.7	1	7.5
1995—Buffalo NFL	15	15	2	0	0.0	0	*17.5
1996—Buffalo NFL	12	11	0	0	0.0	0	6.0
1997—Buffalo NFL	16	16	0	0	0.0	0	9.5
1998—Jacksonville NFL	16	16	0	0	0.0	0	6.5
1999—Jacksonville NFL	15	14	0	0	0.0	0	1.0
Pro totals (10 years)	138	113	6	55	9.2	1	73.0

PAYNE, SETH   DT   JAGUARS

PERSONAL: Born February 12, 1975, in Clifton Springs, N.Y. ... 6-4/289. ... Full name: Seth Copeland Payne.
HIGH SCHOOL: Victor (N.Y.) Central.
COLLEGE: Cornell.
TRANSACTIONS/CAREER NOTES: Selected by Jacksonville Jaguars in fourth round (114th pick overall) of 1997 NFL draft. ... Signed by Jaguars (May 23, 1997). ... On injured reserve with shoulder injury (November 17, 1998-remainder of season).
PLAYING EXPERIENCE: Jacksonville NFL, 1997-1999. ... Games/Games started: 1997 (12/5), 1998 (6/1), 1999 (16/16). Total: 34/22.
CHAMPIONSHIP GAME EXPERIENCE: Played in AFC championship game (1999 season).
PRO STATISTICS: 1999—Credited with 1$\frac{1}{2}$ sacks.

PEDERSON, DOUG   QB   EAGLES

PERSONAL: Born January 31, 1968, in Bellingham, Wash. ... 6-3/216. ... Full name: Douglas Irvin Pederson.
HIGH SCHOOL: Ferndale (Wash.).
COLLEGE: Northeast Louisiana (degree in business management).
TRANSACTIONS/CAREER NOTES: Signed as non-drafted free agent by Miami Dolphins (April 30, 1991). ... Released by Dolphins (August 16, 1991). ... Selected by New York/New Jersey Knights in fifth round (49th pick overall) of 1992 World League draft. ... Re-signed by Dolphins (June 1, 1992). ... Released by Dolphins (August 31, 1992). ... Re-signed by Dolphins to practice squad (September 1, 1992). ... Released by Dolphins (October 7, 1992). ... Re-signed by Dolphins (March 3, 1993). ... Released by Dolphins (August 30, 1993). ... Re-signed by Dolphins to practice squad (August 31, 1993). ... Activated (October 22, 1993). ... Released by Dolphins (December 15, 1993). ... Re-signed by Dolphins (April 15, 1994). ... Inactive for all 16 games (1994). ... Selected by Carolina Panthers from Dolphins in NFL expansion draft (February 15, 1995). ... Released by Panthers (May 22, 1995). ... Signed by Dolphins (July 11, 1995). ... Released by Dolphins (August 21, 1995). ... Re-signed by Dolphins (October 10, 1995). ... Inactive for two games with Dolphins (1995). ... Released by Dolphins (October 25, 1995). ... Signed by Green Bay Packers (November 22, 1995). ... Inactive for five games with Packers (1995). ... Granted unconditional free agency (February 14, 1997). ... Re-signed by Packers (February 20, 1997). ... Granted unconditional free agency (February 12, 1999). ... Signed by Philadelphia Eagles (February 17, 1999).
CHAMPIONSHIP GAME EXPERIENCE: Member of Packers for NFC championship game (1995-97 seasons); inactive. ... Member of Super Bowl championship team (1996 season); inactive. ... Member of Packers for Super Bowl XXXII (1997 season); inactive.
PRO STATISTICS: 1993—Recovered one fumble for minus one yard. 1998—Fumbled once for minus two yards. 1999—Fumbled seven times.
SINGLE GAME HIGHS (regular season): Attempts—38 (October 17, 1999, vs. Chicago); completions—22 (October 17, 1999, vs. Chicago); yards—256 (October 31, 1999, vs. New York Giants); and touchdown passes—2 (October 17, 1999, vs. Chicago).
MISCELLANEOUS: Regular-season record as starting NFL quarterback: 2-7 (.222).

			PASSING							RUSHING				TOTALS		
Year Team	G	GS	Att.	Cmp.	Pct.	Yds.	TD	Int.	Avg.	Rat.	Att.	Yds.	Avg.	TD	TD	2pt.	Pts.
1992—NY/New Jersey W.L.	7	1	128	70	54.7	1077	8	3	8.41	93.8	15	46	3.1	0	0	0	0
1993—Miami NFL	7	0	8	4	50.0	41	0	0	5.13	65.1	2	-1	-0.5	0	0	0	0

Year	G	GS	Att	Cmp	Pct	Yds	TD	Int	Avg	Rat	Att	Yds	Avg	TD	TD	2pt	Pts
1994—Miami NFL										Did not play.							
1995—Miami NFL										Did not play.							
—Green Bay NFL										Did not play.							
1996—Green Bay NFL	1	0	0	0	0.0	0	0	0	0.0	...	0	0	0.0	0	0	0	0
1997—Green Bay NFL	1	0	0	0	0.0	0	0	0	0.0	...	3	-4	-1.3	0	0	0	0
1998—Green Bay NFL	12	0	24	14	58.3	128	2	0	5.33	100.7	8	-4	-0.5	0	0	0	0
1999—Philadelphia NFL	16	9	227	119	52.4	1276	7	9	5.62	62.9	20	33	1.7	0	0	0	0
W.L. totals (1 year)	7	1	128	70	54.7	1077	8	3	8.41	93.8	15	46	3.1	0	0	0	0
NFL totals (5 years)	37	9	259	137	52.9	1445	9	9	5.58	66.5	33	24	0.7	0	0	0	0
Pro totals (6 years)	44	10	387	207	53.5	2522	17	12	6.52	75.5	48	70	1.5	0	0	0	0

PEETE, RODNEY — QB

PERSONAL: Born March 16, 1966, in Mesa, Ariz. ... 6-0/225. ... Son of Willie Peete, former running backs coach and scout with Chicago Bears; cousin of Calvin Peete, professional golfer.

HIGH SCHOOL: Sahuaro (Tucson, Ariz.), then Shawnee Mission South (Overland Park, Kan.).

COLLEGE: Southern California (degree in communications, 1989).

TRANSACTIONS/CAREER NOTES: Selected by Detroit Lions in sixth round (141st pick overall) of 1989 NFL draft. ... Signed by Lions (July 13, 1989). ... On injured reserve with Achilles' tendon injury (October 30, 1991-remainder of season). ... Granted free agency (February 1, 1992). ... Re-signed by Lions (July 30, 1992). ... Granted unconditional free agency (February 17, 1994). ... Signed by Dallas Cowboys (May 4, 1994). ... Granted unconditional free agency (February 17, 1995). ... Signed by Philadelphia Eagles (April 22, 1995). ... Granted unconditional free agency (February 16, 1996). ... Re-signed by Eagles (March 14, 1996). ... On injured reserve with knee injury (October 3, 1996-remainder of season). ... Granted unconditional free agency (February 14, 1997). ... Re-signed by Eagles (April 1, 1997). ... Traded by Eagles to Washington Redskins for sixth-round pick (C John Romero) in 2000 draft (April 28, 1999). ... Released by Redskins (April 18, 2000).

CHAMPIONSHIP GAME EXPERIENCE: Member of Cowboys for NFC championship game (1994 season); did not play.

HONORS: Named quarterback on THE SPORTING NEWS college All-America second team (1988).

PRO STATISTICS: 1989—Fumbled nine times and recovered three fumbles. 1990—Fumbled nine times and recovered one fumble. 1991—Fumbled twice and recovered one fumble for minus one yard. 1992—Fumbled six times and recovered two fumbles for minus seven yards. 1993—Fumbled 11 times and recovered four fumbles for minus eight yards. 1994—Fumbled three times and recovered two fumbles for minus one yard. 1995—Fumbled 13 times and recovered five fumbles. 1996—Fumbled twice and recovered one fumble. 1997—Fumbled five times and recovered two fumbles for minus two yards. 1998—Fumbled once.

SINGLE GAME HIGHS (regular season): Attempts—45 (October 8, 1995, vs. Washington); completions—30 (October 8, 1995, vs. Washington); yards—323 (September 27, 1992, vs. Tampa Bay); and touchdown passes—4 (December 16, 1990, vs. Chicago).

STATISTICAL PLATEAUS: 300-yard passing games: 1990 (1), 1992 (1). Total: 2.

MISCELLANEOUS: Selected by Toronto Blue Jays organization in 30th round of free-agent baseball draft (June 4, 1984); did not sign. ... Selected by Oakland Athletics organization in 14th round of free-agent baseball draft (June 1, 1988); did not sign. ... Selected by Athletics organization in 13th round of free-agent baseball draft (June 5, 1989); did not sign. ... Regular-season record as starting NFL quarterback: 37-35 (.514). ... Postseason record as starting NFL quarterback: 1-1 (.500).

			PASSING								RUSHING				TOTALS		
Year Team	G	GS	Att	Cmp	Pct	Yds	TD	Int	Avg	Rat	Att	Yds	Avg	TD	TD	2pt	Pts
1989—Detroit NFL	8	8	195	103	52.8	1479	5	9	7.58	67.0	33	148	4.5	4	4	0	24
1990—Detroit NFL	11	11	271	142	52.4	1974	13	8	7.28	79.8	47	363	7.7	6	6	0	36
1991—Detroit NFL	8	8	194	116	59.8	1339	5	9	6.90	69.9	25	125	5.0	2	2	0	12
1992—Detroit NFL	10	10	213	123	57.7	1702	9	9	7.99	80.0	21	83	4.0	0	0	0	0
1993—Detroit NFL	10	10	252	157	62.3	1670	6	14	6.63	66.4	45	165	3.7	1	1	0	6
1994—Dallas NFL	7	1	56	33	58.9	470	4	1	8.39	102.5	9	-2	-0.2	0	0	0	0
1995—Philadelphia NFL	15	12	375	215	57.3	2326	8	14	6.20	67.3	32	147	4.6	1	1	0	6
1996—Philadelphia NFL	5	5	134	80	59.7	992	3	5	7.40	74.6	20	31	1.6	1	1	0	6
1997—Philadelphia NFL	5	3	118	68	57.6	869	4	4	7.36	78.0	8	37	4.6	0	1	0	6
1998—Philadelphia NFL	5	4	129	71	55.0	758	2	4	5.88	64.7	5	30	6.0	1	1	0	6
1999—Washington NFL	3	0	17	8	47.1	107	2	1	6.29	82.2	2	-1	-0.5	0	0	0	0
Pro totals (11 years)	87	72	1954	1116	57.1	13686	61	78	7.00	72.6	247	1126	4.6	16	16	0	96

PELFREY, DOUG — K — BENGALS

PERSONAL: Born September 25, 1970, in Fort Thomas, Ky. ... 5-11/185. ... Full name: William Douglas Pelfrey.

HIGH SCHOOL: Scott (Covington, Ky.).

COLLEGE: Kentucky (degree in biology, 1993).

TRANSACTIONS/CAREER NOTES: Selected by Cincinnati Bengals in eighth round (202nd pick overall) of 1993 NFL draft. ... Signed by Bengals (July 19, 1993). ... Granted free agency (February 16, 1996). ... Re-signed by Bengals (June 8, 1996).

PRO STATISTICS: 1995—Punted twice for 52 yards. 1996—Punted once for four yards. 1998—Attempted one pass without a completion.

		KICKING						
Year Team	G	XPM	XPA	FGM	FGA	Lg.	50+	Pts.
1993—Cincinnati NFL	15	13	16	24	31	53	2-3	85
1994—Cincinnati NFL	16	24	25	28	33	†54	2-4	108
1995—Cincinnati NFL	16	34	34	29	36	51	1-2	121
1996—Cincinnati NFL	16	41	41	23	28	49	0-0	110
1997—Cincinnati NFL	16	41	43	12	16	46	0-2	77
1998—Cincinnati NFL	16	21	21	19	27	51	2-5	78
1999—Cincinnati NFL	16	27	27	18	27	50	1-1	81
Pro totals (7 years)	111	201	207	153	198	54	8-17	660

PELSHAK, TROY — LB — RAMS

P

PERSONAL: Born March 6, 1977, in Charlotte, N.C. ... 6-2/242. ... Full name: Zenret Pelshak.

HIGH SCHOOL: Garringer (Charlotte, N.C.).

COLLEGE: North Carolina A&T.

TRANSACTIONS/CAREER NOTES: Signed as non-drafted free agent by St. Louis Rams (April 20, 1999).
PLAYING EXPERIENCE: St. Louis NFL, 1999. ... Games/Games started: 1999 (9/0).
CHAMPIONSHIP GAME EXPERIENCE: Member of Rams for NFC championship game (1999 season); inactive. ... Member of Super Bowl championship team (1999 season); inactive.

PENN, CHRIS — WR

PERSONAL: Born April 20, 1971, in Lenapah, Okla. ... 6-0/198. ... Full name: Christopher Anthony Penn.
HIGH SCHOOL: Lenapah (Okla.).
COLLEGE: Northwestern Oklahoma A&M, then Tulsa.
TRANSACTIONS/CAREER NOTES: Selected by Kansas City Chiefs in third round (96th pick overall) of 1994 NFL draft. ... Signed by Chiefs (June 2, 1994). ... Granted free agency (February 14, 1997). ... Re-signed by Chiefs (July 18, 1997). ... Traded by Chiefs to Chicago Bears for fifth-round pick (DB Robert Williams) in 1998 draft (August 24, 1997). ... Claimed on waivers by San Diego Chargers (September 8, 1999). ... Granted unconditional free agency (February 11, 2000).
PRO STATISTICS: 1997—Rushed once for minus one yard. 1999—Recovered one fumble.
SINGLE GAME HIGHS (regular season): Receptions—7 (October 10, 1999, vs. New York Jets); yards—106 (October 4, 1998, vs. Detroit); and touchdown receptions—2 (September 15, 1996, vs. Seattle).
STATISTICAL PLATEAUS: 100-yard receiving games: 1998 (1).

			RECEIVING				PUNT RETURNS				KICKOFF RETURNS				TOTALS			
Year Team	G	GS	No.	Yds.	Avg.	TD	No.	Yds.	Avg.	TD	No.	Yds.	Avg.	TD	TD	2pt.	Pts.	Fum.
1994—Kansas City NFL..........	8	0	3	24	8.0	0	0	0	0.0	0	9	194	21.6	0	0	0	0	0
1995—Kansas City NFL..........	2	0	1	12	12.0	0	4	12	3.0	0	2	26	13.0	0	0	0	0	0
1996—Kansas City NFL..........	16	16	49	628	12.8	5	14	148	10.6	0	0	0	0.0	0	5	0	30	3
1997—Chicago NFL................	14	4	47	576	12.3	3	0	0	0.0	0	0	0	0.0	0	3	0	18	1
1998—Chicago NFL................	14	1	31	448	14.5	3	0	0	0.0	0	0	0	0.0	0	3	1	20	1
1999—San Diego NFL............	16	3	17	257	15.1	1	21	148	7.0	0	0	0	0.0	0	1	0	6	3
Pro totals (6 years)................	70	24	148	1945	13.1	12	39	308	7.9	0	11	220	20.0	0	12	1	74	8

PERRY, ED — TE — DOLPHINS

PERSONAL: Born September 1, 1974, in Richmond, Va. ... 6-4/265. ... Full name: Edward Lewis Perry.
HIGH SCHOOL: Highlands Springs (Va.).
COLLEGE: James Madison.
TRANSACTIONS/CAREER NOTES: Selected by Miami Dolphins in sixth round (177th pick overall) of 1997 NFL draft. ... Signed by Dolphins (June 13, 1997). ... Granted free agency (February 11, 2000). ... Re-signed by Dolphins (April 28, 2000).
PRO STATISTICS: 1997—Returned one kickoff for seven yards and recovered one fumble.
SINGLE GAME HIGHS (regular season): Receptions—4 (September 13, 1998, vs. Buffalo); yards—59 (November 23, 1998, vs. New England); and touchdown receptions—1 (December 27, 1999, vs. New York Jets).

			RECEIVING				TOTALS			
Year Team	G	GS	No.	Yds.	Avg.	TD	TD	2pt.	Pts.	Fum.
1997—Miami NFL................	16	4	11	45	4.1	1	1	0	6	0
1998—Miami NFL................	14	5	25	255	10.2	0	0	0	0	0
1999—Miami NFL................	16	1	3	8	2.7	1	1	0	6	0
Pro totals (3 years)	46	10	39	308	7.9	2	2	0	12	0

PERRY, JASON — S — CHARGERS

PERSONAL: Born August 1, 1976, in Passaic, N.J. ... 6-0/200. ... Full name: Jason Robert Perry.
HIGH SCHOOL: Paterson (N.J.) Catholic.
COLLEGE: North Carolina State.
TRANSACTIONS/CAREER NOTES: Selected by San Diego Chargers in fourth round (104th pick overall) of 1999 NFL draft. ... Signed by Chargers (July 22, 1999).
PLAYING EXPERIENCE: San Diego NFL, 1999. ... Games/Games started: 1999 (16/5).
PRO STATISTICS: 1999—Recovered one fumble.

PERRY, MARLO — LB

PERSONAL: Born August 25, 1972, in Forest, Miss. ... 6-4/250. ... Full name: Malcolm Marlo Perry.
HIGH SCHOOL: Central (Forest, Miss.).
COLLEGE: Jackson State.
TRANSACTIONS/CAREER NOTES: Selected by Buffalo Bills in third round (81st pick overall) of 1994 NFL draft. ... Signed by Bills (July 18, 1994). ... Granted free agency (February 14, 1997). ... Re-signed by Bills (June 12, 1997). ... Granted unconditional free agency (February 13, 1998). ... Re-signed by Bills for 1998 season. ... Granted unconditional free agency (February 11, 2000).
PLAYING EXPERIENCE: Buffalo NFL, 1994-1999. ... Games/Games started: 1994 (2/0), 1995 (16/11), 1996 (13/0), 1997 (13/0), 1998 (16/1), 1999 (16/0). Total: 76/12.
PRO STATISTICS: 1996—Intercepted one pass for six yards. 1997—Intercepted one pass for four yards and recovered one fumble. 1999—Credited with 1 1/2 sacks.

P

PERRY, TODD — G — BEARS

PERSONAL: Born November 28, 1970, in Elizabethtown, Ky. ... 6-5/308. ... Full name: Todd Joseph Perry.
HIGH SCHOOL: North Hardin (Radcliff, Ky.).
COLLEGE: Kentucky.

TRANSACTIONS/CAREER NOTES: Selected by Chicago Bears in fourth round (97th pick overall) of 1993 NFL draft. ... Signed by Bears (June 16, 1993). ... On injured reserve with back injury (December 19, 1997-remainder of season). ... Granted unconditional free agency (February 11, 2000). ... Re-signed by Bears (May 4, 2000).
PLAYING EXPERIENCE: Chicago NFL, 1993-1999. ... Games/Games started: 1993 (13/3), 1994 (15/4), 1995 (15/15), 1996 (16/16), 1997 (11/11), 1998 (16/16), 1999 (16/16). Total: 102/81.
PRO STATISTICS: 1996—Recovered one fumble. 1999—Recovered one fumble.

PERRY, WILMONT　　　　　RB　　　　　SAINTS

PERSONAL: Born February 24, 1975, in Franklinton, N.C. ... 6-1/235. ... Full name: Wilmont Darnell Perry.
HIGH SCHOOL: Garner (N.C.) Senior.
COLLEGE: Barber-Scotia College, N.C. (did not play), then Livingstone (N.C.).
TRANSACTIONS/CAREER NOTES: Selected by New Orleans Saints in fifth round (132nd pick overall) of 1998 NFL draft. ... Signed by Saints (June 11, 1998).
PRO STATISTICS: 1999—Returned two kickoffs for six yards and recovered one fumble.
SINGLE GAME HIGHS (regular season): Attempts—16 (December 5, 1999, vs. Atlanta); yards—93 (December 5, 1999, vs. Atlanta); and rushing touchdowns—0.

| | | | RUSHING | | | | RECEIVING | | | | TOTALS | | |
Year　Team	G	GS	Att.	Yds.	Avg.	TD	No.	Yds.	Avg.	TD	TD	2pt.	Pts.	Fum.
1998—New Orleans NFL	6	2	30	122	4.1	0	1	2	2.0	0	0	0	0	1
1999—New Orleans NFL	7	3	48	180	3.8	0	4	26	6.5	0	0	0	0	0
Pro totals (2 years)	13	5	78	302	3.9	0	5	28	5.6	0	0	0	0	1

PETER, CHRISTIAN　　　　　DT　　　　　GIANTS

PERSONAL: Born October 5, 1972, in Locust, N.J. ... 6-3/300. ... Brother of Jason Peter, defensive end, Carolina Panthers.
HIGH SCHOOL: Middletown South (Middleton, N.J.), then Milford (Conn.) Academy.
COLLEGE: Nebraska.
TRANSACTIONS/CAREER NOTES: Selected by New England Patriots in fifth round (149th pick overall) of 1996 NFL draft. ... Patriots released rights (April 24, 1996). ... Signed by New York Giants (January 22, 1997). ... Granted free agency (February 11, 2000). ... Re-signed by Giants (April 12, 2000).
PRO STATISTICS: 1999—Recovered one fumble for 38 yards and a touchdown.

Year　Team	G	GS	SACKS
1997—New York Giants NFL	7	0	0.5
1998—New York Giants NFL	16	6	1.0
1999—New York Giants NFL	16	10	0.0
Pro totals (3 years)	39	16	1.5

PETER, JASON　　　　　DE　　　　　PANTHERS

PERSONAL: Born September 13, 1974, in Locust, N.J. ... 6-4/295. ... Full name: Jason Michael Peter. ... Brother of Christian Peter, defensive tackle, New York Giants.
HIGH SCHOOL: Middletown South (Middleton, N.J.), then Milford (Conn.) Academy.
COLLEGE: Nebraska (degree in communication studies, 1997).
TRANSACTIONS/CAREER NOTES: Selected by Carolina Panthers in first round (14th pick overall) of 1998 NFL draft. ... Signed by Panthers (August 31, 1998).
HONORS: Named defensive tackle on THE SPORTING NEWS college All-America first team (1997).
PRO STATISTICS: 1998—Recovered one fumble.

Year　Team	G	GS	SACKS
1998—Carolina NFL	14	11	1.0
1999—Carolina NFL	9	9	4.5
Pro totals (2 years)	23	20	5.5

PETERS, TYRELL　　　　　LB　　　　　RAVENS

PERSONAL: Born August 4, 1974, in Oklahoma City. ... 6-0/235.
HIGH SCHOOL: Norman (Okla.).
COLLEGE: Oklahoma.
TRANSACTIONS/CAREER NOTES: Signed as non-drafted free agent by Seattle Seahawks (April 25, 1997). ... Released by Seahawks (August 18, 1997). ... Signed by Baltimore Ravens (August 25, 1997). ... Released by Ravens (October 14, 1997). ... Re-signed by Ravens to practice squad (October 16, 1997). ... Activated (December 19, 1997). ... Granted free agency (February 11, 2000).
PLAYING EXPERIENCE: Baltimore NFL, 1997-1999. ... Games/Games started: 1997 (4/0), 1998 (10/0), 1999 (13/0). Total: 27/0.

PETERSON, ANTHONY　　　　　LB　　　　　REDSKINS

PERSONAL: Born January 23, 1972, in Cleveland. ... 6-1/232. ... Full name: Anthony Wayne Peterson.
HIGH SCHOOL: Ringgold (Monongahela, Pa.).
COLLEGE: Notre Dame.
TRANSACTIONS/CAREER NOTES: Selected by San Francisco 49ers in fifth round (153rd pick overall) of 1994 NFL draft. ... Signed by 49ers (July 20, 1994). ... On injured reserve with hamstring injury (January 18, 1995-remainder of 1994 playoffs). ... Granted unconditional free agency (February 14, 1997). ... Signed by Chicago Bears (March 7, 1997). ... Traded by Bears to 49ers for seventh-round pick (OT Chad Overhauser) in 1998 draft (April 15, 1998). ... Granted unconditional free agency (February 11, 2000). ... Signed by Washington Redskins (May 8, 2000).

P

PLAYING EXPERIENCE: San Francisco NFL, 1994-1996, 1998 and 1999; Chicago NFL, 1997. ... Games/Games started: 1994 (15/0), 1995 (15/0), 1996 (13/0), 1997 (16/0), 1998 (16/1), 1999 (12/0). Total: 87/1.
CHAMPIONSHIP GAME EXPERIENCE: Member of 49ers for NFC championship game (1994 season); inactive.
PRO STATISTICS: 1997—Recovered one fumble. 1998—Credited with one sack. 1999—Returned two kickoffs for 10 yards and fumbled once.

PETERSON, BEN — LB — BENGALS

PERSONAL: Born March 28, 1977, in Clay Center, Kan. ... 6-3/250.
HIGH SCHOOL: Clay Center (Kan.).
COLLEGE: Pittsburg (Kan.) State.
TRANSACTIONS/CAREER NOTES: Signed as non-drafted free agent by Cincinnati Bengals (April 22, 1999). ... Released by Bengals (September 5, 1999). ... Re-signed by Bengals to practice squad (September 6, 1999). ... Activated (October 15, 1999). ... Released by Bengals (November 4, 1999). ... Re-signed by Bengals to practice squad (November 5, 1999).
PLAYING EXPERIENCE: Cincinnati NFL, 1999. ... Games/Games started: 1999 (3/0).

PETERSON, MIKE — LB — COLTS

PERSONAL: Born June 17, 1976, in Gainesville, Fla. ... 6-2/235. ... Full name: Porter Michael Peterson. ... Couson of Freddie Solomon, wide receiver with Philadelphia Eagles (1995-98).
HIGH SCHOOL: Santa Fe (Alachua, Fla.).
COLLEGE: Florida.
TRANSACTIONS/CAREER NOTES: Selected by Indianapolis Colts in second round (36th pick overall) of 1999 NFL draft. ... Signed by Colts (July 28, 1999).
HONORS: Named outside linebacker on THE SPORTING NEWS college All-America first team (1998).
PRO STATISTICS: 1999—Recovered one fumble.

Year Team	G	GS	SACKS
1999—Indianapolis NFL	16	13	3.0

PETERSON, TODD — K — SEAHAWKS

PERSONAL: Born February 4, 1970, in Washington, D.C. ... 5-10/177. ... Full name: Joseph Todd Peterson.
HIGH SCHOOL: Valdosta (Ga.) State.
COLLEGE: Navy, then Georgia (degree in finance, 1992).
TRANSACTIONS/CAREER NOTES: Selected by New York Giants in seventh round (177th pick overall) of 1993 NFL draft. ... Signed by Giants (July 19, 1993). ... Released by Giants (August 24, 1993). ... Signed by New England Patriots to practice squad (November 30, 1993). ... Released by Patriots (December 6, 1993). ... Signed by Atlanta Falcons (May 3, 1994). ... Released by Falcons (August 29, 1994). ... Signed by Arizona Cardinals (October 12, 1994). ... Released by Cardinals (October 24, 1994). ... Signed by Seattle Seahawks (January 17, 1995). ... Granted free agency (February 13, 1998). ... Re-signed by Seahawks for 1998 season. ... Granted unconditional free agency (February 12, 1999). ... Re-signed by Seahawks (March 2, 1999).

Year Team	G	KICKING						
		XPM	XPA	FGM	FGA	Lg.	50+	Pts.
1993—New England NFL				Did not play.				
1994—Arizona NFL	2	4	4	2	4	35	0-0	10
1995—Seattle NFL	16	§40	§40	23	28	49	0-2	109
1996—Seattle NFL	16	27	27	28	34	54	2-3	111
1997—Seattle NFL	16	37	37	22	28	52	1-2	103
1998—Seattle NFL	16	41	41	19	24	51	3-7	98
1999—Seattle NFL	16	32	32	34	40	51	1-2	134
Pro totals (6 years)	82	181	181	128	158	54	7-16	565

PETITGOUT, LUKE — OT — GIANTS

PERSONAL: Born June 16, 1976, in Milford, Del. ... 6-6/315. ... Full name: Lucas George Petitgout. ... Name pronounced pet-ee-GOO.
HIGH SCHOOL: Sussex Central (Georgetown, Del.).
COLLEGE: Notre Dame.
TRANSACTIONS/CAREER NOTES: Selected by New York Giants in first round (19th pick overall) of 1999 NFL draft. ... Signed by Giants (July 29, 1999).
PLAYING EXPERIENCE: New York Giants NFL, 1999. ... Games/Games started: 1999 (15/8).

PHENIX, PERRY — S — TITANS

PERSONAL: Born November 14, 1974, in Dallas. ... 5-11/210.
HIGH SCHOOL: Hillcrest (Dallas).
JUNIOR COLLEGE: Trinity Valley Community College (Texas).
COLLEGE: Southern Mississippi.
TRANSACTIONS/CAREER NOTES: Signed as non-drafted free agent by Tennessee Oilers (April 20, 1998).
PLAYING EXPERIENCE: Tennessee NFL, 1998 and 1999. ... Games/Games started: 1998 (15/3), 1999 (16/1). Total: 31/4.
CHAMPIONSHIP GAME EXPERIENCE: Played in AFC championship game (1999 season). ... Played in Super Bowl XXXIV (1999 season).
PRO STATISTICS: 1998—Recovered one fumble for 18 yards.

P

PHIFER, ROMAN　　　　　　　　LB　　　　　　　　JETS

PERSONAL: Born March 5, 1968, in Plattsburgh, N.Y. ... 6-2/248. ... Full name: Roman Zubinsky Phifer.
HIGH SCHOOL: South Mecklenburg (Charlotte).
COLLEGE: UCLA.
TRANSACTIONS/CAREER NOTES: Selected by Los Angeles Rams in second round (31st pick overall) of 1991 NFL draft. ... Signed by Rams (July 19, 1991). ... On injured reserve with broken leg (November 26, 1991-remainder of season). ... Granted unconditional free agency (February 17, 1995). ... Re-signed by Rams (March 22, 1995). ... Rams franchise moved to St. Louis (April 12, 1995). ... Granted unconditional free agency (February 12, 1999). ... Signed by New York Jets (March 9, 1999).
PRO STATISTICS: 1992—Recovered two fumbles. 1993—Recovered two fumbles for 10 yards. 1995—Fumbled once. 1998—Fumbled once.

			INTERCEPTIONS				SACKS
Year　Team	G	GS	No.	Yds.	Avg.	TD	No.
1991—Los Angeles Rams NFL	12	5	0	0	0.0	0	2.0
1992—Los Angeles Rams NFL	16	14	1	3	3.0	0	0.0
1993—Los Angeles Rams NFL	16	16	0	0	0.0	0	0.0
1994—Los Angeles Rams NFL	16	15	2	7	3.5	0	1.5
1995—St. Louis NFL	16	16	3	52	17.3	0	3.0
1996—St. Louis NFL	15	15	0	0	0.0	0	1.5
1997—St. Louis NFL	16	15	0	0	0.0	0	2.0
1998—St. Louis NFL	13	13	1	41	41.0	0	6.5
1999—New York Jets NFL	16	12	2	20	10.0	0	4.5
Pro totals (9 years)	136	121	9	123	13.7	0	21.0

PHILLIPS, JOE　　　　　　　　DT

PERSONAL: Born July 15, 1963, in Portland, Ore. ... 6-5/305. ... Full name: Joseph Gordon Phillips.
HIGH SCHOOL: Columbia River (Vancouver, Wash.).
JUNIOR COLLEGE: Chemeketa Community College (Ore.).
COLLEGE: Oregon State, then Southern Methodist (degree in psychology, 1985).
TRANSACTIONS/CAREER NOTES: Selected by Minnesota Vikings in fourth round (93rd pick overall) of 1986 NFL draft. ... Signed by Vikings (July 28, 1986). ... Released by Vikings (September 7, 1987). ... Signed as replacement player by San Diego Chargers (September 24, 1987). ... Granted free agency (February 1, 1988). ... Re-signed by Chargers (August 29, 1988). ... On non-football injury list with head injuries (September 26, 1990-remainder of season). ... Granted free agency (February 1, 1992). ... Rights relinquished by Chargers (September 21, 1992). ... Signed by Kansas City Chiefs (September 30, 1992). ... Granted unconditional free agency (February 17, 1994). ... Re-signed by Chiefs (March 29, 1994). ... Released by Chiefs (February 13, 1998). ... Signed by St. Louis Rams (April 24, 1998). ... Released by Rams (February 18, 1999). ... Signed by Minnesota Vikings (August 5, 1999). ... Granted unconditional free agency (February 11, 2000).
CHAMPIONSHIP GAME EXPERIENCE: Played in AFC championship game (1993 season).
PRO STATISTICS: 1986—Recovered one fumble. 1991—Recovered one fumble. 1992—Recovered one fumble. 1994—Recovered one fumble. 1995—Intercepted one pass for two yards and recovered one fumble. 1997—Recovered one fumble and credited with a safety.

Year　Team	G	GS	SACKS
1986—Minnesota NFL	16	1	0.0
1987—San Diego NFL	13	7	5.0
1988—San Diego NFL	16	16	2.0
1989—San Diego NFL	16	15	1.0
1990—San Diego NFL	3	3	0.5
1991—San Diego NFL	16	15	1.0
1992—Kansas City NFL	12	10	2.5
1993—Kansas City NFL	16	16	1.5
1994—Kansas City NFL	16	16	3.0
1995—Kansas City NFL	16	16	4.5
1996—Kansas City NFL	16	16	2.0
1997—Kansas City NFL	15	15	0.5
1998—St. Louis NFL	13	4	0.0
1999—Minnesota NFL	16	2	1.0
Pro totals (14 years)	200	152	24.5

PHILLIPS, LAWRENCE　　　　　　　　RB

PERSONAL: Born May 12, 1975, in Little Rock, Ark. ... 6-0/223. ... Full name: Lawrence Lamond Phillips.
HIGH SCHOOL: Baldwin Park (Calif.).
COLLEGE: Nebraska.
TRANSACTIONS/CAREER NOTES: Selected after junior season by St. Louis Rams in first round (sixth pick overall) of 1996 NFL draft. ... Signed by Rams (July 30, 1996). ... Released by Rams (November 20, 1997). ... Signed by Miami Dolphins (December 2, 1997). ... Released by Dolphins (July 25, 1998). ... Selected by Barcelona Dragons in 1999 NFL Europe draft (February 23, 1999). ... Signed by San Francisco 49ers (July 26, 1999). ... Released by 49ers (November 23, 1999).
PRO STATISTICS: NFL: 1996—Recovered one fumble. 1999—Recovered two fumbles. NFLE: 1999—Completed only pass attempt for six yards and a touchdown.
SINGLE GAME HIGHS (regular season): Attempts—31 (October 27, 1996, vs. Baltimore Ravens); yards—125 (August 31, 1997, vs. New Orleans); and rushing touchdowns—3 (August 31, 1997, vs. New Orleans).
STATISTICAL PLATEAUS: 100-yard rushing games: 1996 (2), 1997 (1), 1999 (1). Total: 4.

			RUSHING				RECEIVING				KICKOFF RETURNS				TOTALS			
Year　Team	G	GS	Att.	Yds.	Avg.	TD	No.	Yds.	Avg.	TD	No.	Yds.	Avg.	TD	TD	2pt.	Pts.	Fum.
1996—St. Louis NFL	15	11	193	632	3.3	4	8	28	3.5	1	4	74	18.5	0	5	0	30	2
1997—St. Louis NFL	10	9	183	633	3.5	8	10	33	3.3	0	0	0	0.0	0	8	0	48	3
—Miami NFL	2	0	18	44	2.4	0	1	6	6.0	0	0	0	0.0	0	0	0	0	0
1998—							Did not play.											
1999—Barcelona NFLE	...	...	194	1021	5.3	14	25	247	9.9	0	0	0	0.0	0	14	0	84	0

P

	G	GS	Att.	Yds.	Avg.	TD	No.	Yds.	Avg.	TD	No.	Yds.	Avg.	TD	TD	2pt.	Pts.	Fum.
—San Francisco NFL	8	0	30	144	4.8	2	15	152	10.1	0	19	415	21.8	0	2	0	12	2
NFL Europe totals (1 year)	...	...	194	1021	5.3	14	25	247	9.9	0	0	0	0.0	0	14	0	84	0
NFL totals (3 years)	35	20	424	1453	3.4	14	34	219	6.4	1	23	489	21.3	0	15	0	90	7
Pro totals (4 years)	...	...	618	2474	4.0	28	59	466	7.9	1	23	489	21.3	0	29	0	174	7

PHILLIPS, RYAN   LB   GIANTS

PERSONAL: Born February 7, 1974, in Renton, Wash. ... 6-4/252.
HIGH SCHOOL: Auburn (Wash.).
COLLEGE: Idaho.
TRANSACTIONS/CAREER NOTES: Selected by New York Giants in third round (68th pick overall) of 1997 NFL draft. ... Signed by Giants (July 19, 1997). ... Granted free agency (February 11, 2000). ... Re-signed by Giants (April 12, 2000).
PLAYING EXPERIENCE: New York Giants NFL, 1997-1999. ... Games/Games started: 1997 (10/0), 1998 (16/3), 1999 (16/16). Total: 42/19.
PRO STATISTICS: 1997—Credited with one sack. 1999—Intercepted one pass for no yards.

PHILYAW, DINO   RB   SAINTS

PERSONAL: Born October 30, 1970, in Kenansville, N.C. ... 5-10/205. ... Full name: Delvic Dyvon Philyaw.
HIGH SCHOOL: Southern Wayne (Dudley, N.C.).
JUNIOR COLLEGE: Taft (Calif.) College.
COLLEGE: Oregon.
TRANSACTIONS/CAREER NOTES: Selected by New England Patriots in sixth round (195th pick overall) of 1995 NFL draft. ... Signed by Patriots (July 10, 1995). ... Released by Patriots (August 30, 1995). ... Re-signed by Patriots to practice squad (September 1, 1995). ... Signed by Carolina Panthers off Patriots practice squad (November 8, 1995). ... Granted unconditional free agency (February 14, 1997). ... Signed by St. Louis Rams (February 24, 1997). ... Released by Rams (August 17, 1997). ... Signed by Green Bay Packers (February 3, 1998). ... Assigned by Packers to Scotland Claymores in 1998 NFL Europe enhancement allocation program (February 18, 1998). ... Released by Packers (May 15, 1998). ... Signed by New Orleans Saints (February 23, 1999). ... Granted free agency (February 11, 2000). ... Re-signed by Saints (March 29, 2000).
CHAMPIONSHIP GAME EXPERIENCE: Member of Panthers for NFC championship game (1996 season); inactive.
PRO STATISTICS: 1995—Returned one kickoff for 23 yards. 1996—Rushed 12 times for 38 yards and one touchdown. 1999—Recovered one fumble.
SINGLE GAME HIGHS (regular season): Attempts—9 (October 13, 1996, vs. St. Louis Rams); yards—22 (October 13, 1996, vs. St. Louis Rams); and rushing touchdowns—1 (October 13, 1996, vs. St. Louis Rams).

			RUSHING				RECEIVING				KICKOFF RETURNS				TOTALS			
Year Team	G	GS	Att.	Yds.	Avg.	TD	No.	Yds.	Avg.	TD	No.	Yds.	Avg.	TD	TD	2pt.	Pts.	Fum.
1995—Carolina NFL	1	0	0	0	0.0	0	0	0	0.0	0	1	23	23.0	0	0	0	0	0
1996—Carolina NFL	9	0	12	38	3.2	1	0	0	0.0	0	0	0	0.0	0	1	0	6	0
1997—								Did not play.										
1998—Scottish NFLE	...	...	33	94	2.8	1	10	96	9.6	2	4	88	22.0	0	3	0	18	0
1999—New Orleans NFL	13	0	4	16	4.0	0	2	23	11.5	0	53	1165	22.0	0	0	0	0	1
NFL Europe totals (1 year)	...	...	33	94	2.8	1	10	96	9.6	2	4	88	22.0	0	3	0	18	0
NFL totals (3 years)	23	0	16	54	3.4	1	2	23	11.5	0	54	1188	22.0	0	1	0	6	1
Pro totals (4 years)	...	...	49	148	3.0	2	12	119	9.9	2	58	1276	22.0	0	4	0	24	1

PICKENS, CARL   WR   BENGALS

PERSONAL: Born March 23, 1970, in Murphy, N.C. ... 6-2/206. ... Full name: Carl McNally Pickens.
HIGH SCHOOL: Murphy (N.C.).
COLLEGE: Tennessee.
TRANSACTIONS/CAREER NOTES: Selected after junior season by Cincinnati Bengals in second round (31st pick overall) of 1992 NFL draft. ... Signed by Bengals (August 4, 1992). ... Granted free agency (February 17, 1995). ... Tendered offer sheet by Arizona Cardinals (March 17, 1995). ... Offer matched by Bengals (March 24, 1995). ... On injured reserve with groin injury (December 15, 1997-remainder of season). ... Designated by Bengals as franchise player (February 12, 1999).
HONORS: Named wide receiver on The Sporting News college All-America first team (1991). ... Played in Pro Bowl (1995 and 1996 seasons).
PRO STATISTICS: 1992—Recovered two fumbles. 1993—Attempted one pass without a completion. 1994—Recovered one fumble. 1995—Rushed once for six yards. 1996—Rushed twice for two yards and completed only pass attempt for 12 yards. 1998—Rushed twice for four yards. 1999—Completed only pass attempt for six yards.
SINGLE GAME HIGHS (regular season): Receptions—13 (October 11, 1998, vs. Pittsburgh); yards—204 (October 11, 1998, vs. Pittsburgh); and touchdown receptions—3 (December 1, 1996, vs. Jacksonville).
STATISTICAL PLATEAUS: 100-yard receiving games: 1993 (1), 1994 (5), 1995 (5), 1996 (2), 1997 (1), 1998 (2), 1999 (2). Total: 18.
MISCELLANEOUS: Holds Cincinnati Bengals all-time records for most receptions (530) and touchdown receptions (63).

			RECEIVING				PUNT RETURNS				TOTALS			
Year Team	G	GS	No.	Yds.	Avg.	TD	No.	Yds.	Avg.	TD	TD	2pt.	Pts.	Fum.
1992—Cincinnati NFL	16	10	26	326	12.5	1	18	229	12.7	1	2	0	12	3
1993—Cincinnati NFL	13	12	43	565	13.1	6	4	16	4.0	0	6	0	36	1
1994—Cincinnati NFL	15	15	71	1127	15.9	§11	9	62	6.9	0	11	0	66	1
1995—Cincinnati NFL	16	15	§99	1234	12.5	†17	5	-2	-0.4	0	§17	0	102	1
1996—Cincinnati NFL	16	16	§100	1180	11.8	12	1	2	2.0	0	12	1	74	0
1997—Cincinnati NFL	12	12	52	695	13.4	5	0	0	0.0	0	5	0	30	1
1998—Cincinnati NFL	16	16	82	1023	12.5	5	0	0	0.0	0	5	1	32	2
1999—Cincinnati NFL	16	14	57	737	12.9	6	0	0	0.0	0	6	0	36	1
Pro totals (8 years)	120	110	530	6887	13.0	63	37	307	8.3	1	64	2	388	10

P

PIERCE, AARON — TE

PERSONAL: Born September 8, 1969, in Seattle. ... 6-5/250.
HIGH SCHOOL: Franklin (Seattle).
COLLEGE: Washington.
TRANSACTIONS/CAREER NOTES: Selected by New York Giants in third round (69th pick overall) of 1992 NFL draft. ... Signed by Giants (July 21, 1992). ... On injured reserve with wrist injury (September 1-December 26, 1992); on practice squad (October 7-November 4, 1992). ... Granted free agency (February 17, 1995). ... Re-signed by Giants (April 5, 1995). ... Released by Giants (February 12, 1998). ... Signed by Baltimore Ravens (March 10, 1999). ... On injured reserve with Achilles' tendon injury (November 30, 1999-remainder of season). ... Released by Ravens (February 23, 2000).
PRO STATISTICS: 1995—Rushed once for six yards and recovered one fumble. 1996—Rushed once for one yard and a touchdown and recovered one fumble. 1997—Returned one kickoff for 10 yards. 1999—Returned one kickoff for seven yards.
SINGLE GAME HIGHS (regular season): Receptions—5 (October 30, 1994, vs. Detroit); yards—98 (December 5, 1993, vs. Miami); and touchdown receptions—1 (September 15, 1996, vs. Washington).

| | | | RECEIVING | | | | TOTALS | | |
Year Team	G	GS	No.	Yds.	Avg.	TD	TD	2pt.	Pts.	Fum.
1992—New York Giants NFL	1	0	0	0	0.0	0	0	0	0	0
1993—New York Giants NFL	13	6	12	212	17.7	0	0	0	0	2
1994—New York Giants NFL	16	11	20	214	10.7	4	4	0	24	0
1995—New York Giants NFL	16	11	33	310	9.4	0	0	0	0	0
1996—New York Giants NFL	10	3	11	144	13.1	1	2	0	12	0
1997—New York Giants NFL	16	4	10	47	4.7	0	0	0	0	0
1998—						Did not play.				
1999—Baltimore NFL	10	8	11	102	9.3	0	0	0	0	1
Pro totals (7 years)	82	43	97	1029	10.6	5	6	0	36	3

PIERSON, PETE — OT — BUCCANEERS

PERSONAL: Born February 4, 1971, in Portland, Ore. ... 6-5/315. ... Full name: Peter Samuel Pierson.
HIGH SCHOOL: David Douglas (Portland, Ore.).
COLLEGE: Washington (degree in political science, 1994).
TRANSACTIONS/CAREER NOTES: Selected by Tampa Bay Buccaneers in fifth round (136th pick overall) of 1994 NFL draft. ... Signed by Buccaneers (July 6, 1994). ... Released by Buccaneers (August 28, 1994). ... Re-signed by Buccaneers to practice squad (September 2, 1994). ... Activated (November 22, 1994). ... Released by Buccaneers (August 18, 1996). ... Re-signed by Buccaneers (September 10, 1996). ... Granted free agency (February 13, 1998). ... Re-signed by Buccaneers (June 11, 1998).
PLAYING EXPERIENCE: Tampa Bay NFL, 1995-1999. ... Games/Games started: 1995 (12/4), 1996 (11/2), 1997 (15/0), 1998 (16/0), 1999 (15/0). Total: 69/6.
CHAMPIONSHIP GAME EXPERIENCE: Played in NFC championship game (1999 season).
PRO STATISTICS: 1995—Recovered one fumble.

PILGRIM, EVAN — G — FALCONS

PERSONAL: Born August 14, 1972, in Pittsburgh, Calif. ... 6-4/305.
HIGH SCHOOL: Antioch (Calif.).
COLLEGE: Brigham Young.
TRANSACTIONS/CAREER NOTES: Selected by Chicago Bears in third round (87th pick overall) of 1995 NFL draft. ... Signed by Bears (July 19, 1995). ... Inactive for all 16 games (1995). ... Released by Bears (December 9, 1997). ... Signed by Tennessee Oilers (May 14, 1998). ... Released by Oilers (August 30, 1998). ... Re-signed by Oilers (September 9, 1998). ... Released by Oilers (November 4, 1998). ... Re-signed by Oilers (December 16, 1998). ... Oilers franchise renamed Tennessee Titans for 1999 season (December 26, 1998). ... Released by Titans (September 5, 1999). ... Signed by Denver Broncos (October 6, 1999). ... Inactive for two games with Broncos (1999). ... Released by Broncos (October 19, 1999). ... Signed by Atlanta Falcons (November 2, 1999).
PLAYING EXPERIENCE: Chicago NFL, 1996 and 1997; Tennessee NFL, 1998; Atlanta NFL, 1999. ... Games/Games started: 1996 (6/0), 1997 (13/6), 1998 (2/0), 1999 (3/1). Total: 24/7.
PRO STATISTICS: 1997—Recovered one fumble.

PILLER, ZACH — G — TITANS

PERSONAL: Born May 2, 1976, in St. Petersburg, Fla. ... 6-5/330. ... Full name: Zachary Paul Piller.
HIGH SCHOOL: Lincoln (Tallahassee, Fla.).
COLLEGE: Georgia Tech, then Florida.
TRANSACTIONS/CAREER NOTES: Selected by Tennessee Titans in third round (81st pick overall) of 1999 NFL draft. ... Signed by Titans (July 22, 1999).
PLAYING EXPERIENCE: Tennessee NFL, 1999. ... Games/Games started: 1999 (8/0).
CHAMPIONSHIP GAME EXPERIENCE: Member of Titans for AFC championship game (1999 season); inactive. ... Member of Titans for Super Bowl XXXIV (1999 season); inactive.

PITTMAN, KAVIKA — DE — BRONCOS

P

PERSONAL: Born October 9, 1974, in Frankfurt, West Germany. ... 6-6/273. ... Name pronounced kuh-VEE-kuh.
HIGH SCHOOL: Leesville (La.).
COLLEGE: McNeese State.
TRANSACTIONS/CAREER NOTES: Selected by Dallas Cowboys in second round (37th pick overall) of 1996 NFL draft. ... Signed by Cowboys (July 16, 1996). ... Granted unconditional free agency (February 11, 2000). ... Signed by Denver Broncos (February 22, 2000).

PRO STATISTICS: 1997—Returned one kickoff for no yards. 1998—Recovered two fumbles for seven yards. 1999—Recovered two fumbles.

Year Team	G	GS	SACKS
1996—Dallas NFL	15	0	0.0
1997—Dallas NFL	15	0	1.0
1998—Dallas NFL	15	15	6.0
1999—Dallas NFL	16	16	3.0
Pro totals (4 years)	61	31	10.0

PITTMAN, MICHAEL　　　　RB　　　　CARDINALS

PERSONAL: Born August 14, 1975, in New Orleans. ... 6-0/220.
HIGH SCHOOL: Mira Mesa (San Diego).
COLLEGE: Fresno State.
TRANSACTIONS/CAREER NOTES: Selected by Arizona Cardinals in fourth round (95th pick overall) of 1998 NFL draft. ... Signed by Cardinals (May 20, 1998).
PRO STATISTICS: 1998—Fumbled once and recovered one fumble. 1999—Completed only pass attempt for 26 yards, fumbled three times and recovered one fumble.
SINGLE GAME HIGHS (regular season): Attempts—23 (November 14, 1999, vs. Detroit); yards—133 (November 14, 1999, vs. Detroit); and rushing touchdowns—1 (November 14, 1999, vs. Detroit).
STATISTICAL PLATEAUS: 100-yard rushing games: 1999 (1).

			RUSHING				RECEIVING				PUNT RETURNS				KICKOFF RETURNS				TOTALS		
Year Team	G	GS	Att.	Yds.	Avg.	TD	No.	Yds.	Avg.	TD	No.	Yds.	Avg.	TD	No.	Yds.	Avg.	TD	TD	2pt.	Pts.
1998—Arizona NFL	15	0	29	91	3.1	0	0	0	0.0	0	0	0	0.0	0	4	84	21.0	0	0	0	0
1999—Arizona NFL	10	2	64	289	4.5	2	16	196	12.3	0	4	16	4.0	0	2	31	15.5	0	2	0	12
Pro totals (2 years)	25	2	93	380	4.1	2	16	196	12.3	0	4	16	4.0	0	6	115	19.2	0	2	0	12

PLAYER, SCOTT　　　　P　　　　CARDINALS

PERSONAL: Born December 17, 1969, in St. Augustine, Fla. ... 6-1/221.
HIGH SCHOOL: St. Augustine (Fla.).
JUNIOR COLLEGE: Florida Community College.
COLLEGE: Flagler College (Fla.), then Florida State (degree in education).
TRANSACTIONS/CAREER NOTES: Played with Birmingham Barracudas of CFL (1995). ... Granted free agency (March 7, 1996). ... Signed as non-drafted free agent by Arizona Cardinals (April 23, 1996). ... Released by Cardinals (August 19, 1996). ... Signed by New York Giants (February 14, 1997). ... Assigned by Giants to Frankfurt Galaxy in 1997 World League enhancement allocation program (February 18, 1997). ... Released by Giants (August 24, 1997). ... Signed by New York Jets to practice squad (August 26, 1997). ... Released by Jets (August 28, 1997). ... Re-signed by Cardinals (March 3, 1998).
PRO STATISTICS: CFL: 1995—Attempted two passes with one completion for 52 yards. NFL: 1999—Rushed once for minus 18 yards.

		PUNTING					
Year Team	G	No.	Yds.	Avg.	Net avg.	In. 20	Blk.
1995—Birmingham CFL	18	143	6247	43.7	36.5	0	0
1996—					Did not play.		
1997—Frankfurt W.L.	...	60	2617	43.6	34.3	17	1
1998—Arizona NFL	16	81	3378	41.7	35.9	12	∞1
1999—Arizona NFL	16	94	3948	42.0	36.7	18	0
W.L. totals (1 year)	...	60	2617	43.6	34.3	17	1
CFL totals (1 year)	18	143	6247	43.7	36.5	0	0
NFL totals (2 years)	32	175	7326	41.9	36.3	30	1
Pro totals (4 years)	...	378	16190	42.8	36.1	47	2

PLEASANT, ANTHONY　　　　DE

PERSONAL: Born January 27, 1968, in Century, Fla. ... 6-5/280. ... Full name: Anthony Devon Pleasant.
HIGH SCHOOL: Century (Fla.).
COLLEGE: Tennessee State.
TRANSACTIONS/CAREER NOTES: Selected by Cleveland Browns in third round (73rd pick overall) of 1990 NFL draft. ... Signed by Browns (July 22, 1990). ... Browns franchise moved to Baltimore and renamed Ravens for 1996 season (March 11, 1996). ... Granted unconditional free agency (February 14, 1997). ... Signed by Atlanta Falcons (June 21, 1997). ... Released by Falcons (February 11, 1998). ... Signed by New York Jets (March 12, 1998). ... Granted unconditional free agency (February 11, 2000).
CHAMPIONSHIP GAME EXPERIENCE: Played in AFC championship game (1998 season).
PRO STATISTICS: 1991—Recovered one fumble for four yards. 1993—Credited with a safety. 1996—Recovered one fumble for 36 yards.

Year Team	G	GS	SACKS
1990—Cleveland NFL	16	7	3.5
1991—Cleveland NFL	16	7	2.5
1992—Cleveland NFL	16	14	4.0
1993—Cleveland NFL	16	13	11.0
1994—Cleveland NFL	14	14	4.5
1995—Cleveland NFL	16	16	8.0
1996—Baltimore NFL	12	12	4.0
1997—Atlanta NFL	11	0	0.5
1998—New York Jets NFL	16	15	6.0
1999—New York Jets NFL	16	16	2.0
Pro totals (10 years)	149	114	46.0

P

PLUMMER, CHAD   WR   COLTS

PERSONAL: Born November 30, 1975, in Delray Beach, Fla. ... 6-3/218.
HIGH SCHOOL: Godby (Tallahassee, Fla.).
COLLEGE: Cincinnati (degree in communications).
TRANSACTIONS/CAREER NOTES: Selected by Denver Broncos in sixth round (204th pick overall) of 1999 NFL draft. ... Signed by Broncos (July 20, 1999). ... Released by Broncos (August 27, 1999). ... Signed by Indianapolis Colts to practice squad (September 7, 1999). ... Activated (November 20, 1999).
PLAYING EXPERIENCE: Indianapolis NFL, 1999. ... Games/Games started: 1999 (1/0).

PLUMMER, JAKE   QB   CARDINALS

PERSONAL: Born December 19, 1974, in Boise, Idaho. ... 6-2/199. ... Full name: Jason Steven Plummer.
HIGH SCHOOL: Capital (Boise, Idaho).
COLLEGE: Arizona State.
TRANSACTIONS/CAREER NOTES: Selected by Arizona Cardinals in second round (42nd pick overall) of 1997 NFL draft. ... Signed by Cardinals (July 14, 1997).
HONORS: Named quarterback on THE SPORTING NEWS college All-America second team (1996).
PRO STATISTICS: 1997—Caught one pass for two yards, fumbled six times and recovered one fumble for minus one yard. 1998—Fumbled 12 times and recovered three fumbles for minus two yards. 1999—Fumbled seven times and recovered five fumbles for minus four yards.
SINGLE GAME HIGHS (regular season): Attempts—57 (January 2, 2000, vs. Green Bay); completions—35 (January 2, 2000, vs. Green Bay); yards—465 (November 15, 1998, vs. Dallas); and touchdown passes—4 (December 7, 1997, vs. Washington).
STATISTICAL PLATEAUS: 300-yard passing games: 1997 (2), 1998 (2), 1999 (1). Total: 5.
MISCELLANEOUS: Regular-season record as starting NFL quarterback: 15-21 (.417). ... Postseason record as starting NFL quarterback: 1-1 (.500).

				PASSING							RUSHING				TOTALS	
Year Team	G	GS	Att.	Cmp.	Pct.	Yds.	TD	Int.	Avg.	Rat.	Att.	Yds.	Avg.	TD	TD	2pt.	Pts.
1997—Arizona NFL	10	9	296	157	53.0	2203	15	15	7.44	73.1	39	216	5.5	2	2	1	14
1998—Arizona NFL	16	16	547	324	59.2	3737	17	20	6.83	75.0	51	217	4.3	4	4	0	24
1999—Arizona NFL	12	11	381	201	52.8	2111	9	*24	5.54	50.8	39	121	3.1	2	2	0	12
Pro totals (3 years)	38	36	1224	682	55.7	8051	41	59	6.58	67.0	129	554	4.3	8	8	1	50

POLLARD, MARCUS   TE   COLTS

PERSONAL: Born February 8, 1972, in Valley, Ala. ... 6-4/252. ... Full name: Marcus LaJuan Pollard.
HIGH SCHOOL: Valley (Ala.).
JUNIOR COLLEGE: Seward County Community College, Kan. (did not play football).
COLLEGE: Bradley (did not play football).
TRANSACTIONS/CAREER NOTES: Signed as non-drafted free agent by Indianapolis Colts (January 24, 1995). ... Released by Colts (August 22, 1995). ... Re-signed by Colts to practice squad (August 28, 1995). ... Activated (October 10, 1995). ... Granted free agency (February 13, 1998). ... Tendered offer sheet by Philadelphia Eagles (March 4, 1998). ... Offer matched by Colts (March 9, 1998).
CHAMPIONSHIP GAME EXPERIENCE: Played in AFC championship game (1995 season).
PRO STATISTICS: 1996—Recovered one fumble. 1998—Returned one kickoff for four yards.
SINGLE GAME HIGHS (regular season): Receptions—6 (September 13, 1998, vs. New England); yards—65 (December 27, 1998, vs. Carolina); and touchdown receptions—2 (October 10, 1999, vs. Miami).
MISCELLANEOUS: Played basketball during college.

			RECEIVING				TOTALS			
Year Team	G	GS	No.	Yds.	Avg.	TD	TD	2pt.	Pts.	Fum.
1995—Indianapolis NFL	8	0	0	0	0	0	0	0	0	0
1996—Indianapolis NFL	16	4	6	86	14.3	1	1	0	6	0
1997—Indianapolis NFL	16	5	10	116	11.6	0	0	1	2	0
1998—Indianapolis NFL	16	11	24	309	12.9	4	4	†2	28	0
1999—Indianapolis NFL	16	12	34	374	11.0	4	4	0	24	2
Pro totals (5 years)	72	32	74	885	12.0	9	9	3	60	2

POOLE, KEITH   WR   SAINTS

PERSONAL: Born June 18, 1974, in San Jose, Calif. ... 6-0/193. ... Full name: Keith Robert Strohmaier Poole.
HIGH SCHOOL: Clovis (Calif.).
COLLEGE: Arizona State.
TRANSACTIONS/CAREER NOTES: Selected by New Orleans Saints in fourth round (116th pick overall) of 1997 NFL draft. ... Signed by Saints (June 10, 1997).
PRO STATISTICS: 1999—Rushed once for 14 yards.
SINGLE GAME HIGHS (regular season): Receptions—6 (January 2, 2000, vs. Carolina); yards—154 (October 18, 1998, vs. Atlanta); and touchdown receptions—2 (October 18, 1998, vs. Atlanta).
STATISTICAL PLATEAUS: 100-yard receiving games: 1998 (1), 1999 (1). Total: 2.

			RECEIVING				TOTALS			
Year Team	G	GS	No.	Yds.	Avg.	TD	TD	2pt.	Pts.	Fum.
1997—New Orleans NFL	3	0	4	98	24.5	2	2	0	12	0
1998—New Orleans NFL	15	4	24	509	21.2	2	2	0	12	0
1999—New Orleans NFL	15	15	42	796	19.0	6	6	0	36	0
Pro totals (3 years)	33	19	70	1403	20.0	10	10	0	60	0

P

POOLE, TYRONE   DB   COLTS

PERSONAL: Born February 3, 1972, in La Grange, Ga. ... 5-8/188.
HIGH SCHOOL: La Grange (Ga.).
COLLEGE: Fort Valley (Ga.) State.
TRANSACTIONS/CAREER NOTES: Selected by Carolina Panthers in first round (22nd pick overall) of 1995 NFL draft. ... Signed by Panthers (July 15, 1995). ... Traded by Panthers to Indianapolis Colts for second-round pick (OT Chris Terry) in 1999 draft (July 22, 1998).
CHAMPIONSHIP GAME EXPERIENCE: Played in NFC championship game (1996 season).
PRO STATISTICS: 1996—Recovered one fumble. 1997—Returned one kickoff for five yards and recovered three fumbles for 11 yards.

			INTERCEPTIONS			SACKS	PUNT RETURNS				TOTALS			
Year Team	G	GS	No.	Yds.	Avg.	TD	No.	No.	Yds.	Avg.	TD	TD 2pt.	Pts. Fum.		
1995—Carolina NFL	16	13	2	8	4.0	0	2.0	0	0	0.0	0	0	0	0	0
1996—Carolina NFL	15	15	1	35	35.0	0	0.0	3	26	8.7	0	0	0	0	0
1997—Carolina NFL	16	16	2	0	0.0	0	1.0	26	191	7.3	0	0	0	0	3
1998—Indianapolis NFL	15	15	1	0	0.0	0	0.0	12	107	8.9	0	0	0	0	0
1999—Indianapolis NFL	15	14	3	85	28.3	0	1.0	0	0	0.0	0	0	0	0	0
Pro totals (5 years)	77	73	9	128	14.2	0	4.0	41	324	7.9	0	0	0	0	3

POPE, DANIEL   P   CHIEFS

PERSONAL: Born March 28, 1975, in Alpharetta, Ga. ... 5-10/203.
HIGH SCHOOL: Milton (Alpharetta, Ga.).
COLLEGE: Alabama.
TRANSACTIONS/CAREER NOTES: Signed as non-drafted free agent by Detroit Lions (April 23, 1999). ... Released by Lions (August 26, 1999). ... Signed by Kansas City Chiefs (August 27, 1999).
PRO STATISTICS: 1999—Rushed once for no yards, fumbled once and recovered one fumble for minus 11 yards.

		PUNTING					
Year Team	G	No.	Yds.	Avg.	Net avg.	In. 20	Blk.
1999—Kansas City NFL	16	101	4218	41.8	35.1	20	†2

POPE, MARQUEZ   DB   RAIDERS

PERSONAL: Born October 29, 1970, in Nashville. ... 5-11/193. ... Full name: Marquez Phillips Pope. ... Name pronounced MAR-kez.
HIGH SCHOOL: Long Beach (Calif.) Polytechnic.
COLLEGE: Fresno State (degree in speech and mass communication, 1998).
TRANSACTIONS/CAREER NOTES: Selected by San Diego Chargers in second round (33rd pick overall) of 1992 NFL draft. ... Signed by Chargers (July 16, 1992). ... On non-football illness list with virus (September 1-28, 1992). ... On practice squad (September 28-November 7, 1992). ... Traded by Chargers to Los Angeles Rams for sixth-round pick (G Troy Sienkiewicz) in 1995 draft (April 11, 1994). ... Granted free agency (February 17, 1995). ... Tendered offer sheet by San Francisco 49ers (April 9, 1995). ... Rams declined to match offer (April 12, 1995); received second-round pick (OL Jesse James) in 1995 draft as compensation. ... Granted unconditional free agency (February 12, 1999). ... Signed by Cleveland Browns (March 8, 1999). ... Released by Browns (February 18, 2000). ... Signed by Oakland Raiders (May 22, 2000).
CHAMPIONSHIP GAME EXPERIENCE: Played in NFC championship game (1997 season).
PRO STATISTICS: 1993—Credited with $1/2$ sack. 1996—Recovered one fumble for four yards.

			INTERCEPTIONS			
Year Team	G	GS	No.	Yds.	Avg.	TD
1992—San Diego NFL	7	0	0	0	0.0	0
1993—San Diego NFL	16	1	2	14	7.0	0
1994—Los Angeles Rams NFL	16	16	3	66	22.0	0
1995—San Francisco NFL	16	16	1	-7	-7.0	0
1996—San Francisco NFL	16	16	6	98	16.3	1
1997—San Francisco NFL	5	5	1	7	7.0	0
1998—San Francisco NFL	6	3	1	0	0.0	0
1999—Cleveland NFL	16	15	2	15	7.5	0
Pro totals (8 years)	98	72	16	193	12.1	1

PORCHER, ROBERT   DE   LIONS

PERSONAL: Born July 30, 1969, in Wando, S.C. ... 6-3/282. ... Full name: Robert Porcher III. ... Name pronounced por-SHAY.
HIGH SCHOOL: Cainhoy (Huger, S.C.).
COLLEGE: Tennessee State, then South Carolina State (degree in criminal justice).
TRANSACTIONS/CAREER NOTES: Selected by Detroit Lions in first round (26th pick overall) of 1992 NFL draft. ... Signed by Lions (July 25, 1992). ... Granted unconditional free agency (February 16, 1996). ... Re-signed by Lions (March 29, 1996). ... Granted unconditional free agency (February 14, 1997). ... Re-signed by Lions (March 4, 1997). ... Designated by Lions as franchise player (February 11, 2000).
HONORS: Played in Pro Bowl (1999 season).
PRO STATISTICS: 1994—Recovered one fumble. 1996—Recovered two fumbles.

Year Team	G	GS	SACKS
1992—Detroit NFL	16	1	1.0
1993—Detroit NFL	16	4	8.5
1994—Detroit NFL	15	15	3.0
1995—Detroit NFL	16	16	5.0
1996—Detroit NFL	16	16	10.0
1997—Detroit NFL	16	15	12.5
1998—Detroit NFL	16	16	11.5
1999—Detroit NFL	15	14	15.0
Pro totals (8 years)	126	97	66.5

P

PORTER, DARYL   CB   BILLS

PERSONAL: Born January 16, 1974, in Fort Lauderdale, Fla. ... 5-9/190. ... Full name: Daryl Maurice Porter. ... Cousin of Bennie Blades, safety with Detroit Lions (1988-96) and Seattle Seahawks (1997); and cousin of Brian Blades, wide receiver with Seattle Seahawks (1988-98).
HIGH SCHOOL: St. Thomas Aquinas (Fort Lauderdale, Fla.).
COLLEGE: Boston College.
TRANSACTIONS/CAREER NOTES: Selected by Pittsburgh Steelers in sixth round (186th pick overall) of 1997 NFL draft. ... Signed by Steelers (June 6, 1997). ... Released by Steelers (August 19, 1997). ... Re-signed by Steelers to practice squad (August 26, 1997). ... Released by Steelers (October 20, 1997). ... Signed by Detroit Lions (October 21, 1997). ... Released by Lions (August 24, 1998). ... Signed by Steelers to practice squad (September 1, 1998). ... Signed by Buffalo Bills off Steelers practice squad (December 16, 1998).
PLAYING EXPERIENCE: Detroit NFL, 1997; Buffalo NFL, 1998 and 1999. ... Games/Games started: 1997 (7/0), 1998 (2/0), 1999 (16/0). Total: 25/0.
PRO STATISTICS: 1999—Returned two kickoffs for 41 yards.

PORTER, JOEY   LB   STEELERS

PERSONAL: Born March 22, 1977, in Kansas City, Mo. ... 6-2/240. ... Full name: Joey Eugene Porter.
HIGH SCHOOL: Foothills (Calif.).
COLLEGE: Colorado State.
TRANSACTIONS/CAREER NOTES: Selected by Pittsburgh Steelers in third round (73rd pick overall) of 1999 NFL draft. ... Signed by Steelers (July 30, 1999).
PLAYING EXPERIENCE: Pittsburgh NFL, 1999. ... Games/Games started: 1999 (16/0).
PRO STATISTICS: 1999—Credited with two sacks and recovered two fumbles for 50 yards and one touchdown.

PORTILLA, JOSE   OT   FALCONS

PERSONAL: Born September 11, 1972, in Houston ... 6-6/315. ... Full name: Jose Casiano Portilla.
HIGH SCHOOL: MacArthur (Houston).
JUNIOR COLLEGE: Ricks College (Idaho).
COLLEGE: Arizona.
TRANSACTIONS/CAREER NOTES: Signed as non-drafted free agent by Atlanta Falcons (April 20, 1998).
PLAYING EXPERIENCE: Atlanta NFL, 1998 and 1999. ... Games/Games started: 1998 (16/0), 1999 (4/0). Total: 20/0.
CHAMPIONSHIP GAME EXPERIENCE: Played in NFC championship game (1998 season). ... Played in Super Bowl XXXIII (1998 season).
PRO STATISTICS: 1998—Recovered one fumble.

POSEY, JEFF   DE   49ERS

PERSONAL: Born August 14, 1975, in Bassfield, Miss. ... 6-4/240.
HIGH SCHOOL: Greenville (Miss.).
JUNIOR COLLEGE: Pearl River Community College (Miss.).
COLLEGE: Southern Mississippi.
TRANSACTIONS/CAREER NOTES: Signed as non-drafted free agent by San Francisco 49ers (May 2, 1997) ... Released by 49ers (August 19, 1997). ... Re-signed by 49ers to practice squad (August 25, 1997).
PLAYING EXPERIENCE: San Francisco NFL, 1998 and 1999. ... Games/Games started: 1998 (16/0), 1999 (16/6). Total: 32/6.
PRO STATISTICS: 1998—Credited with $1/2$ sack. 1999—Credited with two sacks.

POUNDS, DARRYL   CB   BRONCOS

PERSONAL: Born July 21, 1972, in Fort Worth, Texas. ... 5-10/189.
HIGH SCHOOL: South Pike (Magnolia, Miss.).
COLLEGE: Nicholls State.
TRANSACTIONS/CAREER NOTES: Selected by Washington Redskins in third round (68th pick overall) of 1995 NFL draft. ... Signed by Redskins (May 26, 1995). ... On physically unable to perform list with back injury (August 22-October 17, 1995). ... Granted free agency (February 13, 1998). ... Re-signed by Redskins (April 9, 1998). ... Granted unconditional free agency (February 11, 2000). ... Signed by Denver Broncos (March 3, 2000).
PRO STATISTICS: 1995—Fumbled once. 1996—Recovered one fumble. 1997—Credited with two sacks and recovered three fumbles for 18 yards and one touchdown. 1998—Credited with $1/2$ sack and recovered one fumble. 1999—Returned one punt for no yards, credited with one sack, fumbled once and recovered one fumble for two yards.

| | | | INTERCEPTIONS | | | |
Year Team	G	GS	No.	Yds.	Avg.	TD
1995—Washington NFL	9	0	1	26	26.0	0
1996—Washington NFL	12	1	2	11	5.5	0
1997—Washington NFL	16	0	3	42	14.0	1
1998—Washington NFL	16	3	0	0	0.0	0
1999—Washington NFL	16	0	3	37	12.3	0
Pro totals (5 years)	69	4	9	116	12.9	1

POURDANESH, SHAR   OL   STEELERS

PERSONAL: Born July 19, 1970, in Tehran, Iran. ... 6-6/312. ... Full name: Shahriar Pourdanesh. ... Name pronounced shar-E-are poor-DON-esh.
HIGH SCHOOL: University (Irvine, Calif.).

P

COLLEGE: Nevada-Reno.

TRANSACTIONS/CAREER NOTES: Signed as non-drafted free agent by Cleveland Browns (April 1993). ... Released by Browns before 1993 season. ... Signed by Baltimore of CFL (1994). ... Signed by Washington Redskins (March 20, 1995). ... Traded by Redskins to Pittsburgh Steelers for seventh-round pick (DT Delbert Cowsette) in 2000 draft (August 13, 1999).

PLAYING EXPERIENCE: Baltimore CFL, 1994 and 1995; Washington NFL, 1996-1998; Pittsburgh NFL, 1999. ... Games/Games started: 1994 (18/18), 1995 (14/14), 1996 (16/8), 1997 (16/14), 1998 (16/15), 1999 (4/2). Total CFL: 32/32. Total NFL: 52/39. Total Pro: 84/71.

CHAMPIONSHIP GAME EXPERIENCE: Played in Grey Cup, CFL championship game (1994).

HONORS: Named tackle on CFL All-Star team (1994). ... Named CFL Most Outstanding Offensive Lineman (1994).

PRO STATISTICS: 1998—Fumbled once and recovered one fumble for minus four yards.

POWELL, MARVIN   FB   SAINTS

PERSONAL: Born June 6, 1976, in Van Nuys, Calif. ... 6-2/235. ... Son of Marvin Powell, offensive tackle with New York Jets (1977-85) and Tampa Bay Buccaneers (1986 and 1987).

HIGH SCHOOL: Birmingham (Van Nuys, Calif.).

COLLEGE: Southern California.

TRANSACTIONS/CAREER NOTES: Signed as non-drafted free agent by New Orleans Saints (April 23, 1999). ... Released by Saints (September 5, 1999). ... Re-signed by Saints to practice squad (September 6, 1999). ... Activated (October 23, 1999).

PLAYING EXPERIENCE: New Orleans NFL, 1999. ... Games/Games started: 1999 (9/0).

PRO STATISTICS: 1999—Rushed once for one yard.

SINGLE GAME HIGHS (regular season): Attempts—1 (October 24, 1999, vs. New York Giants); yards—1 (October 24, 1999, vs. New York Giants); and rushing touchdowns—0.

POWELL, RONNIE   WR/KR   BROWNS

PERSONAL: Born November 3, 1974, in Hope, Ark. ... 5-10/174.

HIGH SCHOOL: Hope (Ark.).

COLLEGE: Arkansas Tech, then Northwestern (La.) State.

TRANSACTIONS/CAREER NOTES: Signed as non-drafted free agent by Cleveland Browns (April 23, 1999). ... Assigned by Browns to Barcelona Dragons in 2000 NFL Europe enhancement allocation program (February 18, 2000).

PRO STATISTICS: 1999—Rushed once for minus 14 yards and caught one pass for 45 yards.

SINGLE GAME HIGHS (regular season): Receptions—1 (December 12, 1999, vs. Cincinnati); yards—45 (December 12, 1999, vs. Cincinnati); and touchdown receptions—0.

			KICKOFF RETURNS				TOTALS			
Year Team	G	GS	No.	Yds.	Avg.	TD	TD	2pt.	Pts.	Fum.
1999—Cleveland NFL	14	0	44	986	22.4	0	0	0	0	3

PRESTON, ROELL   WR/KR

PERSONAL: Born June 23, 1972, in Miami. ... 5-10/185. ... Name pronounced ROW-ell.

HIGH SCHOOL: Hialeah (Fla.).

JUNIOR COLLEGE: Northwest Mississippi Community College.

COLLEGE: Mississippi.

TRANSACTIONS/CAREER NOTES: Selected by Atlanta Falcons in fifth round (145th pick overall) of 1995 NFL draft. ... Signed by Falcons (July 13, 1995). ... Released by Falcons (August 24, 1997). ... Signed by Green Bay Packers (November 12, 1997). ... Released by Packers (November 18, 1997). ... Signed by Washington Redskins (December 3, 1997). ... Inactive for one game with Redskins (1997). ... Released by Redskins (December 9, 1997). ... Signed by Packers (February 26, 1998). ... Granted free agency (February 12, 1999). ... Signed by Tennessee Titans (September 15, 1999). ... Released by Titans (September 29, 1999). ... Signed by Miami Dolphins (October 18, 1999). ... Released by Dolphins (October 26, 1999). ... Signed by San Francisco 49ers (December 8, 1999). ... Granted unconditional free agency (February 11, 2000).

HONORS: Played in Pro Bowl (1998 season).

PRO STATISTICS: 1995—Fumbled once. 1997—Returned one punt for no yards. 1998—Recovered one fumble. 1999—Recovered one fumble.

SINGLE GAME HIGHS (regular season): Receptions—9 (October 13, 1996, vs. Houston); yards—79 (November 26, 1995, vs. Arizona); and touchdown receptions—1 (September 29, 1996, vs. San Francisco).

			RECEIVING				PUNT RETURNS				KICKOFF RETURNS				TOTALS			
Year Team	G	GS	No.	Yds.	Avg.	TD	No.	Yds.	Avg.	TD	No.	Yds.	Avg.	TD	TD	2pt.	Pts.	Fum.
1995—Atlanta NFL	14	0	7	129	18.4	1	0	0	0.0	0	30	627	20.9	0	1	0	6	1
1996—Atlanta NFL	15	2	21	208	9.9	1	0	0	0.0	0	32	681	21.3	0	1	0	6	0
1997—Green Bay NFL	1	0	0	0	0.0	0	1	0	0.0	0	7	211	30.1	0	0	0	0	0
1998—Green Bay NFL	16	0	2	23	11.5	0	44	398	9.0	1	57	1497	26.3	†2	3	0	18	7
1999—Tennessee NFL	2	0	0	0	0.0	0	8	59	7.4	0	5	119	23.8	0	0	0	0	0
—Miami NFL	1	0	0	0	0.0	0	1	6	6.0	0	0	0	0.0	0	0	0	0	0
—San Francisco NFL	4	0	0	0	0.0	0	3	6	2.0	0	16	292	18.3	0	0	0	0	1
Pro totals (5 years)	53	2	30	360	12.0	2	57	469	8.2	1	147	3427	23.3	2	5	0	30	9

PRICE, PEERLESS   WR   BILLS

P

PERSONAL: Born October 27, 1976, in Dayton, Ohio. ... 5-11/180. ... Full name: Peerless LeCross Price.

HIGH SCHOOL: Meadowdale (Dayton, Ohio).

COLLEGE: Tennessee.

TRANSACTIONS/CAREER NOTES: Selected by Buffalo Bills in second round (53rd pick overall) of 1999 NFL draft. ... Signed by Bills (July 30, 1999).

SINGLE GAME HIGHS (regular season): Receptions—5 (December 26, 1999, vs. New England); yards—106 (October 24, 1999, vs. Seattle); and touchdown receptions—1 (January 2, 2000, vs. Indianapolis).
STATISTICAL PLATEAUS: 100-yard receiving games: 1999 (1).

				RUSHING			RECEIVING				PUNT RETURNS				KICKOFF RETURNS				TOTALS		
Year Team	G	GS	Att.	Yds.	Avg.	TD	No.	Yds.	Avg.	TD	No.	Yds.	Avg.	TD	No.	Yds.	Avg.	TD	TD	2pt.	Pts.
1999—Buffalo NFL	16	4	1	-7	-7.0	0	31	393	12.7	3	1	16	16.0	0	1	27	27.0	0	3	0	18

PRICE, SHAWN — DE — BILLS

PERSONAL: Born March 28, 1970, in Van Nuys, Calif. ... 6-4/290. ... Full name: Shawn Sterling Price.
HIGH SCHOOL: North Tahoe (Nev.).
JUNIOR COLLEGE: Sierra College (Calif.).
COLLEGE: Pacific.
TRANSACTIONS/CAREER NOTES: Signed as non-drafted free agent by Tampa Bay Buccaneers (April 29, 1993). ... Released by Buccaneers (August 30, 1993). ... Re-signed by Buccaneers to practice squad (August 31, 1993). ... Activated (November 5, 1993). ... Selected by Carolina Panthers from Buccaneers in NFL expansion draft (February 15, 1995). ... Granted unconditional free agency (February 16, 1996). ... Signed by Buffalo Bills (April 12, 1996). ... Granted unconditional free agency (February 13, 1998). ... Re-signed by Bills (March 9, 1998).

Year Team	G	GS	SACKS
1993—Tampa Bay NFL	9	6	3.0
1994—Tampa Bay NFL	6	0	0.0
1995—Carolina NFL	16	0	1.0
1996—Buffalo NFL	15	0	0.0
1997—Buffalo NFL	10	0	0.0
1998—Buffalo NFL	14	2	5.0
1999—Buffalo NFL	15	1	2.5
Pro totals (7 years)	85	9	11.5

PRINGLEY, MIKE — DE — LIONS

PERSONAL: Born May 22, 1976, in Linden, N.J. ... 6-4/277. ... Full name: Michael Charles Pringley.
HIGH SCHOOL: Linden (N.J.).
COLLEGE: North Carolina.
TRANSACTIONS/CAREER NOTES: Selected by Detroit Lions in seventh round (215th pick overall) of 1999 NFL draft. ... Signed by Lions (July 22, 1999).
PLAYING EXPERIENCE: Detroit NFL, 1999. ... Games/Games started: 1999 (9/0).
PRO STATISTICS: 1999—Credited with $1\frac{1}{2}$ sacks.

PRIOLEAU, PIERSON — CB — 49ERS

PERSONAL: Born August 6, 1977, in Charleston, S.C. ... 5-10/191. ... Full name: Pierson Olin Prioleau. ... Name pronounced pray-LOW.
HIGH SCHOOL: Macedonia (Saint Stephens, S.C.).
COLLEGE: Virginia Tech.
TRANSACTIONS/CAREER NOTES: Selected by San Francisco 49ers in fourth round (110th pick overall) of 1999 NFL draft. ... Signed by 49ers (July 27, 1999).
PLAYING EXPERIENCE: San Francisco NFL, 1999. ... Games/Games started: 1999 (14/5).
HONORS: Named strong safety on THE SPORTING NEWS college All-America third team (1997).
PRO STATISTICS: 1999—Returned three kickoffs for 73 yards.

PRITCHARD, MIKE — WR — SEAHAWKS

PERSONAL: Born October 26, 1969, in Shaw Air Force Base, S.C. ... 5-10/193. ... Full name: Michael Robert Pritchard.
HIGH SCHOOL: Rancho (North Las Vegas, Nev.).
COLLEGE: Colorado (degree in economics, 1998).
TRANSACTIONS/CAREER NOTES: Selected by Atlanta Falcons in first round (13th pick overall) of 1991 NFL draft. ... Signed by Falcons (July 24, 1991). ... Traded by Falcons with seventh-round pick (WR Byron Chamberlain) in 1995 draft to Denver Broncos for first-round pick (traded to Minnesota) in 1995 draft (April 24, 1994). ... On injured reserve with kidney injury (November 2, 1994-remainder of season). ... Released by Broncos (June 3, 1996). ... Signed by Seattle Seahawks (June 19, 1996).
PRO STATISTICS: 1991—Returned one kickoff for 18 yards.
SINGLE GAME HIGHS (regular season): Receptions—10 (September 5, 1993, vs. Detroit); yards—119 (September 4, 1994, vs. San Diego); and touchdown receptions—2 (November 21, 1993, vs. Dallas). Total: 3.
STATISTICAL PLATEAUS: 100-yard receiving games: 1992 (1), 1994 (2). Total: 3.

			RUSHING				RECEIVING				TOTALS			
Year Team	G	GS	Att.	Yds.	Avg.	TD	No.	Yds.	Avg.	TD	TD	2pt.	Pts.	Fum.
1991—Atlanta NFL	16	11	0	0	0.0	0	50	624	12.5	2	2	0	12	2
1992—Atlanta NFL	16	15	5	37	7.4	0	77	827	10.7	5	5	0	30	3
1993—Atlanta NFL	15	14	2	4	2.0	0	74	736	9.9	7	7	0	42	1
1994—Denver NFL	3	0	0	0	0.0	0	19	271	14.3	1	1	0	6	1
1995—Denver NFL	15	13	6	17	2.8	0	33	441	13.4	3	3	0	18	1
1996—Seattle NFL	16	5	2	13	6.5	0	21	328	15.6	1	1	0	6	0
1997—Seattle NFL	16	15	1	14	14.0	0	64	843	13.2	2	2	0	12	2
1998—Seattle NFL	16	16	1	17	17.0	0	58	742	12.8	3	3	1	20	1
1999—Seattle NFL	14	5	0	0	0.0	0	26	375	14.4	2	2	0	12	0
Pro totals (9 years)	127	94	17	102	6.0	0	422	5187	12.3	26	26	1	158	11

P

PRITCHETT, KELVIN — DT — LIONS

PERSONAL: Born October 24, 1969, in Atlanta. ... 6-3/319. ... Full name: Kelvin Bratodd Pritchett.
HIGH SCHOOL: Therrell (Atlanta).
COLLEGE: Mississippi.
TRANSACTIONS/CAREER NOTES: Selected by Dallas Cowboys in first round (20th pick overall) of 1991 NFL draft. ... Rights traded by Cowboys to Detroit Lions for second- (LB Dixon Edwards), third- (G James Richards) and fourth-round (DE Tony Hill) picks in 1991 draft (April 21, 1991). ... Granted free agency (February 17, 1994). ... Re-signed by Lions (August 12, 1994). ... Granted unconditional free agency (February 17, 1995). ... Signed by Jacksonville Jaguars (March 11, 1995). ... On injured reserve with knee injury (November 4, 1997-remainder of season). ... Granted unconditional free agency (February 12, 1999). ... Signed by Lions (April 22, 1999). ... Granted unconditional free agency (February 11, 2000). ... Re-signed by Lions (May 15, 2000).
CHAMPIONSHIP GAME EXPERIENCE: Played in NFC championship game (1991 season). ... Played in AFC championship game (1996 season).
PRO STATISTICS: 1994—Recovered one fumble. 1996—Recovered two fumbles. 1997—Recovered one fumble.

Year Team	G	GS	SACKS
1991—Detroit NFL	16	0	1.5
1992—Detroit NFL	16	15	6.5
1993—Detroit NFL	16	5	4.0
1994—Detroit NFL	16	15	5.5
1995—Jacksonville NFL	16	16	1.5
1996—Jacksonville NFL	13	4	2.0
1997—Jacksonville NFL	8	5	3.0
1998—Jacksonville NFL	15	9	3.0
1999—Detroit NFL	16	2	1.0
Pro totals (9 years)	132	71	28.0

PRITCHETT, STANLEY — RB — EAGLES

PERSONAL: Born December 22, 1973, in Atlanta. ... 6-1/240. ... Full name: Stanley Jerome Pritchett.
HIGH SCHOOL: Frederick Douglass (College Park, Ga.).
COLLEGE: South Carolina.
TRANSACTIONS/CAREER NOTES: Selected by Miami Dolphins in fourth round (118th pick overall) of 1996 NFL draft. ... Signed by Dolphins (July 10, 1996). ... Granted free agency (February 12, 1999). ... Re-signed by Dolphins (April 13, 1999). ... Granted unconditional free agency (February 11, 2000). ... Signed by Philadelphia Eagles (March 9, 2000).
PRO STATISTICS: 1996—Recovered one fumble. 1998—Recovered one fumble.
SINGLE GAME HIGHS (regular season): Attempts—17 (December 12, 1999, vs. New York Jets); yards—68 (December 12, 1999, vs. New York Jets); and rushing touchdowns—1 (December 12, 1999, vs. New York Jets).

Year Team	G	GS	RUSHING Att.	Yds.	Avg.	TD	RECEIVING No.	Yds.	Avg.	TD	TOTALS TD	2pt.	Pts.	Fum.
1996—Miami NFL	16	16	7	27	3.9	0	33	354	10.7	2	2	0	12	3
1997—Miami NFL	6	5	3	7	2.3	0	5	35	7.0	0	0	0	0	0
1998—Miami NFL	16	12	6	19	3.2	0	17	97	5.7	0	1	0	6	0
1999—Miami NFL	14	7	47	158	3.4	1	43	312	7.3	4	5	0	30	0
Pro totals (4 years)	52	40	63	211	3.3	2	98	798	8.1	6	8	0	48	3

PROEHL, RICKY — WR — RAMS

PERSONAL: Born March 7, 1968, in Bronx, N.Y. ... 6-0/190. ... Full name: Richard Scott Proehl.
HIGH SCHOOL: Hillsborough (Belle Mead, N.J.).
COLLEGE: Wake Forest.
TRANSACTIONS/CAREER NOTES: Selected by Phoenix Cardinals in third round (58th pick overall) of 1990 NFL draft. ... Signed by Cardinals (July 23, 1990). ... Granted free agency (March 1, 1993). ... Tendered offer sheet by New England Patriots (April 13, 1993). ... Offer matched by Cardinals (April 19, 1993). ... Cardinals franchise renamed Arizona Cardinals for 1994 season. ... Traded by Cardinals to Seattle Seahawks for fourth-round pick (traded to New York Jets) in 1995 draft (April 3, 1995). ... Released by Seahawks (March 7, 1997). ... Signed by Chicago Bears (April 10, 1997). ... Granted unconditional free agency (February 13, 1998). ... Signed by St. Louis Rams (February 25, 1998).
CHAMPIONSHIP GAME EXPERIENCE: Played in NFC championship game (1999 season). ... Member of Super Bowl championship team (1999 season).
PRO STATISTICS: 1990—Returned one punt for two yards and returned four kickoffs for 53 yards. 1991—Returned four punts for 26 yards and recovered one fumble. 1992—Had only pass attempt intercepted and fumbled five times. 1993—Fumbled once. 1994—Fumbled twice and recovered two fumbles. 1997—Returned eight punts for 59 yards.
SINGLE GAME HIGHS (regular season): Receptions—11 (November 16, 1997, vs. New York Jets); yards—164 (November 27, 1997, vs. Detroit); and touchdown receptions—2 (December 27, 1998, vs. San Francisco).
STATISTICAL PLATEAUS: 100-yard receiving games: 1990 (2), 1991 (1), 1992 (3), 1993 (1), 1997 (3), 1998 (1). Total: 11.

Year Team	G	GS	RUSHING Att.	Yds.	Avg.	TD	RECEIVING No.	Yds.	Avg.	TD	TOTALS TD	2pt.	Pts.	Fum.
1990—Phoenix NFL	16	2	1	4	4.0	0	56	802	14.3	4	4	0	24	0
1991—Phoenix NFL	16	16	3	21	7.0	0	55	766	13.9	2	2	0	12	0
1992—Phoenix NFL	16	15	3	23	7.7	0	60	744	12.4	3	3	0	18	5
1993—Phoenix NFL	16	16	8	47	5.9	0	65	877	13.5	7	7	0	42	1
1994—Arizona NFL	16	16	0	0	0.0	0	51	651	12.8	5	5	0	30	2
1995—Seattle NFL	8	0	0	0	0.0	0	5	29	5.8	0	0	0	0	0
1996—Seattle NFL	16	7	0	0	0.0	0	23	309	13.4	2	2	0	12	0
1997—Chicago NFL	15	10	0	0	0.0	0	58	753	13.0	7	7	1	44	2
1998—St. Louis NFL	16	10	1	14	14.0	0	60	771	12.9	3	3	1	20	0
1999—St. Louis NFL	15	2	0	0	0.0	0	33	349	10.6	0	0	0	0	0
Pro totals (10 years)	150	94	16	109	6.8	0	466	6051	13.0	33	33	2	202	10

P

PRYCE, TREVOR — DT — BRONCOS

PERSONAL: Born August 3, 1975, in Brooklyn, N.Y. ... 6-5/295.
HIGH SCHOOL: Lake Howell (Casselberry, Fla.).
COLLEGE: Clemson.
TRANSACTIONS/CAREER NOTES: Selected by Denver Broncos in first round (28th pick overall) of 1997 NFL draft. ... Signed by Broncos (July 24, 1997).
CHAMPIONSHIP GAME EXPERIENCE: Played in AFC championship game (1997 and 1998 seasons). ... Member of Super Bowl championship team (1997 and 1998 seasons).
HONORS: Played in Pro Bowl (1999 season).
PRO STATISTICS: 1998—Intercepted one pass for one yard. 1999—Intercepted one pass for no yards, credited with a safety and recovered one fumble.

Year Team	G	GS	SACKS
1997—Denver NFL	8	3	2.0
1998—Denver NFL	16	15	8.5
1999—Denver NFL	15	15	13.0
Pro totals (3 years)	39	33	23.5

PUPUNU, AL — TE

PERSONAL: Born October 17, 1969, in Tonga. ... 6-2/260. ... Full name: Alfred Sione Pupunu. ... Name pronounced puh-POO-new.
HIGH SCHOOL: Salt Lake City South.
JUNIOR COLLEGE: Dixie College (Utah).
COLLEGE: Weber State.
TRANSACTIONS/CAREER NOTES: Signed as non-drafted free agent by Kansas City Chiefs (May 2, 1992). ... Claimed on waivers by San Diego Chargers (September 1, 1992). ... Granted unconditional free agency (February 16, 1996). ... Re-signed by Chargers (March 5, 1996). ... Released by Chargers (November 4, 1997). ... Signed by Chiefs (November 11, 1997). ... Released by Chiefs (November 25, 1997). ... Signed by New York Giants (December 22, 1997). ... On injured reserve with knee injury (November 17, 1998-remainder of season). ... Granted unconditional free agency (February 12, 1999). ... Signed by Chargers (April 7, 1999). ... Released by Chargers (November 20, 1999).
CHAMPIONSHIP GAME EXPERIENCE: Played in AFC championship game (1994 season). ... Played in Super Bowl XXIX (1994 season).
POST SEASON RECORDS: Shares Super Bowl and NFL postseason career and single-game records for most two-point conversions—1 (January 29, 1995, vs. San Francisco).
PRO STATISTICS: 1993—Recovered one fumble. 1995—Fumbled once. 1996—Returned one kickoff for 15 yards and recovered two fumbles. 1997—Recovered one fumble.
SINGLE GAME HIGHS (regular season): Receptions—6 (December 19, 1993, vs. Kansas City); yards—83 (September 29, 1996, vs. Kansas City); and touchdown receptions—1 (November 11, 1996, vs. Detroit).

			RECEIVING				TOTALS			
Year Team	G	GS	No.	Yds.	Avg.	TD	TD	2pt.	Pts.	Fum.
1992—San Diego NFL	15	2	0	0	0.0	0	0	0	0	0
1993—San Diego NFL	16	7	13	142	10.9	0	0	0	0	0
1994—San Diego NFL	13	10	21	214	10.2	2	2	0	12	0
1995—San Diego NFL	15	14	35	315	9.0	0	0	0	0	1
1996—San Diego NFL	9	8	24	271	11.3	1	1	0	6	1
1997—San Diego NFL	8	1	1	7	7.0	0	0	0	0	0
—Kansas City NFL	1	0	0	0	0.0	0	0	0	0	0
1998—New York Giants NFL	9	0	1	2	2.0	0	0	0	0	0
1999—San Diego NFL	8	0	4	17	4.3	0	0	0	0	0
Pro totals (8 years)	94	42	99	968	9.8	3	3	0	18	2

PURNELL, LOVETT — TE — BUCCANEERS

PERSONAL: Born April 7, 1972, in Seaford, Del. ... 6-3/245. ... Full name: Lovett S. Purnell.
HIGH SCHOOL: Seaford (Del.).
COLLEGE: West Virginia.
TRANSACTIONS/CAREER NOTES: Selected by New England Patriots in seventh round (216th pick overall) of 1996 NFL draft. ... Signed by Patriots (July 11, 1996). ... Released by Patriots (October 9, 1996). ... Re-signed by Patriots to practice squad (October 11, 1996). ... Activated (December 10, 1996). ... Granted free agency (February 12, 1999). ... Re-signed by Patriots (March 30, 1999). ... Traded by Patriots to Baltimore Ravens for sixth-round pick (DB Marcus Washington) in 1999 draft (March 31, 1999). ... Released by Ravens (September 26, 1999). ... Re-signed by Ravens (November 30, 1999). ... Released by Ravens (December 22, 1999). ... Signed by Tampa Bay Buccaneers (March 2, 2000).
CHAMPIONSHIP GAME EXPERIENCE: Member of Patriots for AFC championship game (1996 season); inactive. ... Member of Patriots for Super Bowl XXXI (1996 season); inactive.
PRO STATISTICS: 1997—Recovered one fumble.
SINGLE GAME HIGHS (regular season): Receptions—4 (December 13, 1998, vs. St. Louis); yards—37 (December 13, 1998, vs. St. Louis); and touchdown receptions—1 (December 13, 1998, vs. St. Louis).

			RECEIVING				TOTALS			
Year Team	G	GS	No.	Yds.	Avg.	TD	TD	2pt.	Pts.	Fum.
1996—New England NFL	2	0	0	0	0.0	0	0	0	0	0
1997—New England NFL	16	2	5	57	11.4	3	3	0	18	0
1998—New England NFL	16	5	12	92	7.7	2	2	0	12	0
1999—Baltimore NFL	2	0	2	10	5.0	0	0	0	0	0
Pro totals (4 years)	36	7	19	159	8.4	5	5	0	30	0

P

PURVIS, ANDRE   DT   BENGALS

PERSONAL: Born July 14, 1973, in Jacksonville, N.C. ... 6-4/310. ... Full name: Andre Lamont Purvis.
HIGH SCHOOL: White Oak (Jacksonville, N.C.), then Swansboro (N.C.).
COLLEGE: North Carolina.
TRANSACTIONS/CAREER NOTES: Selected by Cincinnati Bengals in fifth round (144th pick overall) of 1997 NFL draft. ... Signed by Bengals (June 5, 1997). ... Granted free agency (February 11, 2000). ... Re-signed by Bengals (March 15, 2000).
PLAYING EXPERIENCE: Cincinnati NFL, 1997-1999. ... Games/Games started: 1997 (7/1), 1998 (9/0), 1999 (5/0). Total: 21/1.
PRO STATISTICS: 1998—Credited with one sack.

PYNE, JIM   G   BROWNS

PERSONAL: Born November 23, 1971, in Milford, Conn. ... 6-2/297. ... Full name: James M. Pyne. ... Son of George Pyne III, tackle with Boston Patriots of AFL (1965); and grandson of George Pyne Jr., tackle with Providence Steamrollers of NFL (1931).
HIGH SCHOOL: Choate Prep (Wallingford, Conn.), then Milford (Mass.).
COLLEGE: Virginia Tech.
TRANSACTIONS/CAREER NOTES: Selected by Tampa Bay Buccaneers in seventh round (200th pick overall) of 1994 NFL draft. ... Signed by Buccaneers (July 14, 1994). ... On injured reserve with broken leg (December 17, 1996-remainder of season). ... Granted free agency (February 14, 1997). ... Re-signed by Buccaneers (April 18, 1997). ... Granted unconditional free agency (February 13, 1998). ... Signed by Detroit Lions (February 21, 1998). ... Selected by Cleveland Browns from Lions in NFL expansion draft (February 9, 1999).
PLAYING EXPERIENCE: Tampa Bay NFL, 1995-1997; Detroit NFL, 1998; Cleveland NFL, 1999. ... Games/Games started: 1995 (15/13), 1996 (12/11), 1997 (15/14), 1998 (16/16), 1999 (16/16). Total: 74/70.
HONORS: Named offensive lineman on THE SPORTING NEWS college All-America first team (1993).
PRO STATISTICS: 1995—Recovered one fumble. 1997—Fumbled once for minus five yards.

QUARLES, SHELTON   LB   BUCCANEERS

PERSONAL: Born September 11, 1971, in Nashville. ... 6-1/230. ... Full name: Shelton Eugene Quarles.
HIGH SCHOOL: Whites Creek (Tenn.).
COLLEGE: Vanderbilt (degree in human and organized development).
TRANSACTIONS/CAREER NOTES: Signed as non-drafted free agent by Miami Dolphins (April 29, 1994). ... Released by Dolphins (August 15, 1994). ... Signed by B.C. Lions of CFL (December 1, 1994). ... Granted free agency (February 16, 1997). ... Signed by Tampa Bay Buccaneers (March 21, 1997).
PLAYING EXPERIENCE: B.C. CFL, 1995 and 1996; Tampa Bay NFL, 1997-1999. ... Games/Games started: 1995 (16/games started unavailable), 1996 (16/-), 1997 (16/0), 1998 (16/0), 1999 (16/14). Total CFL: 32/-. Total NFL: 48/14. Total Pro: 80/-.
CHAMPIONSHIP GAME EXPERIENCE: Played in NFC championship game (1999 season).
PRO STATISTICS: 1995—Intercepted one pass for no yards and recovered one fumble for 14 yards. 1996—Credited with 10 sacks and intercepted one pass for 22 yards. 1997—Recovered two fumbles. 1998—Credited with one sack. 1999—Recovered one fumble.

QUINN, JONATHON   QB   JAGUARS

PERSONAL: Born February 27, 1975, in Turlock, Calif. ... 6-6/240. ... Full name: Jonathon Ryan Quinn.
HIGH SCHOOL: McGavock (Nashville).
COLLEGE: Tulane, then Middle Tennessee State (degree in business administration, 1997).
TRANSACTIONS/CAREER NOTES: Selected by Jacksonville Jaguars in third round (86th pick overall) of 1998 NFL draft. ... Signed by Jaguars (May 19, 1998). ... Active for one game (1999); did not play.
CHAMPIONSHIP GAME EXPERIENCE: Member of Jaguars for AFC championship game (1999 season); inactive.
PRO STATISTICS: 1998—Fumbled three times.
SINGLE GAME HIGHS (regular season): Attempts—27 (December 20, 1998, vs. Minnesota); completions—12 (December 20, 1998, vs. Minnesota); yards—192 (December 28, 1998, vs. Pittsburgh); and touchdown passes—1 (December 28, 1998, vs. Pittsburgh).
MISCELLANEOUS: Regular-season record as starting NFL quarterback: 1-1 (.500).

| Year Team | G | GS | PASSING | | | | | | | | RUSHING | | | | TOTALS | | |
			Att.	Cmp.	Pct.	Yds.	TD	Int.	Avg.	Rat.	Att.	Yds.	Avg.	TD	TD	2pt.	Pts.
1998—Jacksonville NFL	4	2	64	34	53.1	387	2	3	6.05	62.4	11	77	7.0	1	1	0	6
1999—Jacksonville NFL								Did not play.									
Pro totals (1 years)	4	2	64	34	53.1	387	2	3	6.05	62.4	11	77	7.0	1	1	0	6

RAFFERTY, IAN   OT   JETS

PERSONAL: Born September 2, 1976, in Summerville, S.C. ... 6-5/300.
HIGH SCHOOL: Summerville (N.C.).
COLLEGE: North Carolina State.
TRANSACTIONS/CAREER NOTES: Signed as non-drafted free agent by Tennessee Titans (April 20, 1999). ... Released by Titans (September 5, 1999). ... Re-signed by Titans to practice squad (September 8, 1999). ... Signed by New York Jets off Titans practice squad (November 16, 1999).
PLAYING EXPERIENCE: New York Jets NFL, 1999. ... Games/Games started: 1999 (5/0).

RAINER, WALI   LB   BROWNS

PERSONAL: Born April 19, 1977, in Rockingham, N.C. ... 6-2/235. ... Full name: Wali Rashid Rainer.
HIGH SCHOOL: West Charlotte (N.C.).
COLLEGE: Virginia.

P Q R

TRANSACTIONS/CAREER NOTES: Selected by Cleveland Browns in fourth round (124th pick overall) of 1999 NFL draft. ... Signed by Browns (July 22, 1999).
PLAYING EXPERIENCE: Cleveland NFL, 1999. ... Games/Games started: 1999 (16/15).
PRO STATISTICS: 1999—Credited with one sack.

RAMIREZ, TONY — OT — LIONS

PERSONAL: Born January 26, 1973, in Lincoln, Neb. ... 6-6/305.
HIGH SCHOOL: Northglenn (Denver), then Lincoln (Neb.).
COLLEGE: Northern Colorado.
TRANSACTIONS/CAREER NOTES: Selected by Detroit Lions in sixth round (168th pick overall) of 1997 NFL draft. ... Signed by Lions (July 11, 1997). ... Granted free agency (February 11, 2000). ... Re-signed by Lions (April 25, 2000).
PLAYING EXPERIENCE: Detroit NFL, 1997-1999. ... Games/Games started: 1997 (2/0), 1998 (16/7), 1999 (12/3). Total: 30/10.
PRO STATISTICS: 1999—Recovered one fumble.

RANDLE, JOHN — DT — VIKINGS

PERSONAL: Born December 12, 1967, in Hearne, Texas. ... 6-1/287. ... Brother of Ervin Randle, linebacker with Tampa Bay Buccaneers (1985-90) and Kansas City Chiefs (1991 and 1992).
HIGH SCHOOL: Hearne (Texas).
JUNIOR COLLEGE: Trinity Valley Community College (Texas).
COLLEGE: Texas A&I.
TRANSACTIONS/CAREER NOTES: Signed as non-drafted free agent by Minnesota Vikings (May 4, 1990). ... Designated by Vikings as transition player (January 15, 1994). ... Designated by Vikings as transition player (February 13, 1998). ... Tendered offer sheet by Miami Dolphins (February 16, 1998). ... Offer matched by Vikings (February 18, 1998).
CHAMPIONSHIP GAME EXPERIENCE: Played in NFC championship game (1998 season).
HONORS: Played in Pro Bowl (1993-1998 seasons). ... Named defensive tackle on THE SPORTING NEWS NFL All-Pro team (1994-1998).
PRO STATISTICS: 1992—Recovered one fumble. 1994—Recovered two fumbles. 1997—Recovered two fumbles for five yards. 1998—Recovered one fumble. 1999—Intercepted one pass for one yard and recovered three fumbles.

Year Team	G	GS	SACKS
1990—Minnesota NFL	16	0	1.0
1991—Minnesota NFL	16	8	9.5
1992—Minnesota NFL	16	14	11.5
1993—Minnesota NFL	16	16	12.5
1994—Minnesota NFL	16	16	∞13.5
1995—Minnesota NFL	16	16	10.5
1996—Minnesota NFL	16	16	11.5
1997—Minnesota NFL	16	16	*15.5
1998—Minnesota NFL	16	16	10.5
1999—Minnesota NFL	16	16	10.0
Pro totals (10 years)	160	134	106.0

RANDOLPH, THOMAS — CB

PERSONAL: Born October 5, 1970, in Norfolk, Va. ... 5-9/185. ... Full name: Thomas C. Randolph.
HIGH SCHOOL: Manhattan (Kan.).
COLLEGE: Kansas State.
TRANSACTIONS/CAREER NOTES: Selected by New York Giants in second round (47th pick overall) of 1994 NFL draft. ... Signed by Giants (July 17, 1994). ... Granted unconditional free agency (February 13, 1998). ... Signed by Cincinnati Bengals (March 4, 1998). ... Released by Bengals (September 1, 1999). ... Signed by Indianapolis Colts (September 7, 1999). ... Granted unconditional free agency (February 11, 2000).
PRO STATISTICS: 1995—Recovered one fumble. 1996—Recovered one fumble for 17 yards. 1999—Recovered one fumble.

Year Team	G	GS	INTERCEPTIONS No.	Yds.	Avg.	TD
1994—New York Giants NFL	16	10	1	0	0.0	0
1995—New York Giants NFL	16	16	2	15	7.5	0
1996—New York Giants NFL	16	2	0	0	0.0	0
1997—New York Giants NFL	16	4	1	1	1.0	0
1998—Cincinnati NFL	16	1	1	0	0.0	0
1999—Indianapolis NFL	15	0	1	0	0.0	0
Pro totals (6 years)	95	33	6	16	2.7	0

RANSOM, DERRICK — DT — CHIEFS

PERSONAL: Born September 13, 1976, in Indianapolis. ... 6-3/307. ... Full name: Derrick Wayne Ransom Jr.
HIGH SCHOOL: Lawrence Central (Indianapolis).
COLLEGE: Cincinnati (degree in finance).
TRANSACTIONS/CAREER NOTES: Selected by Kansas City Chiefs in sixth round (181st pick overall) of 1998 NFL draft. ... Signed by Chiefs (June 3, 1998).
PLAYING EXPERIENCE: Kansas City NFL, 1998 and 1999. ... Games/Games started: 1998 (7/0), 1999 (10/0). Total: 17/0.
PRO STATISTICS: 1998—Returned one kickoff for no yards. 1999—Credited with one sack.

RASBY, WALTER   TE   LIONS

PERSONAL: Born September 7, 1972, in Washington, D.C. ... 6-3/251. ... Full name: Walter Herbert Rasby.
HIGH SCHOOL: Washington (N.C.).
COLLEGE: Wake Forest.
TRANSACTIONS/CAREER NOTES: Signed as non-drafted free agent by Pittsburgh Steelers (April 29, 1994). ... Released by Steelers (August 27, 1995). ... Signed by Carolina Panthers (October 17, 1995). ... Granted free agency (February 14, 1997). ... Re-signed by Panthers (June 3, 1997). ... On injured reserve with knee injury (December 10, 1997-remainder of season). ... Granted unconditional free agency (February 13, 1998). ... Signed by Detroit Lions (April 13, 1998).
CHAMPIONSHIP GAME EXPERIENCE: Played in AFC championship game (1994 season). ... Played in NFC championship game (1996 season).
PRO STATISTICS: 1996—Recovered one fumble. 1997—Returned three kickoffs for 32 yards.
SINGLE GAME HIGHS (regular season): Receptions—5 (October 4, 1998, vs. Chicago); yards—39 (October 4, 1998, vs. Chicago); and touchdown receptions—1 (September 26, 1999, vs. Kansas City).

| | | | RECEIVING | | | | TOTALS | | |
Year Team	G	GS	No.	Yds.	Avg.	TD	TD	2pt.	Pts.	Fum.
1994—Pittsburgh NFL	2	0	0	0	0.0	0	0	0	0	0
1995—Carolina NFL	9	2	5	47	9.4	0	0	1	2	0
1996—Carolina NFL	16	1	0	0	0.0	0	0	0	0	0
1997—Carolina NFL	14	2	1	1	1.0	0	0	0	0	0
1998—Detroit NFL	16	16	15	119	7.9	1	1	0	6	0
1999—Detroit NFL	16	6	3	19	6.3	1	1	0	6	0
Pro totals (6 years)	73	27	24	186	7.8	2	2	1	14	0

RAY, MARCUS   S   RAIDERS

PERSONAL: Born August 14, 1976, in Columbus, Ohio. ... 5-11/215. ... Full name: Marcus Kenyon Ray.
HIGH SCHOOL: Eastmoor (Columbus, Ohio).
COLLEGE: Michigan.
TRANSACTIONS/CAREER NOTES: Signed as non-drafted free agent by Oakland Raiders (April 22, 1999). ... Assigned by Raiders to Scottish Claymores in 2000 NFL Europe enhancement allocation program (February 18, 2000).
PLAYING EXPERIENCE: Oakland NFL, 1999. ... Games/Games started: 1999 (8/0).
HONORS: Named strong safety on THE SPORTING NEWS college All-America second team (1997).

RAYMER, CORY   C   REDSKINS

PERSONAL: Born March 3, 1973, in Fond du Lac, Wis. ... 6-2/289.
HIGH SCHOOL: Goodrich (Fond du Lac, Wis.).
COLLEGE: Wisconsin.
TRANSACTIONS/CAREER NOTES: Selected by Washington Redskins in second round (37th pick overall) of 1995 NFL draft. ... Signed by Redskins (July 24, 1995). ... On injured reserve with back injury (November 25, 1996-remainder of season). ... Granted unconditional free agency (February 12, 1999). ... Re-signed by Redskins (March 16, 1999). ... Granted unconditional free agency (February 11, 2000). ... Re-signed by Redskins (February 26, 2000).
PLAYING EXPERIENCE: Washington NFL, 1995-1999. ... Games/Games started: 1995 (3/2), 1996 (6/5), 1997 (6/3), 1998 (16/16), 1999 (16/16). Total: 47/42.
HONORS: Named offensive lineman on THE SPORTING NEWS college All-America first team (1994).
PRO STATISTICS: 1996—Recovered one fumble. 1998—Recovered one fumble. 1999—Recovered one fumble.

REAGOR, MONTAE   DE   BRONCOS

PERSONAL: Born June 29, 1977, in Waxahachie, Texas. ... 6-2/256. ... Full name: Willie Montae Reagor. ... Name pronounced MON-tay RAY-ger.
HIGH SCHOOL: Waxahachie (Texas).
COLLEGE: Texas Tech (degree in exercise and sports sciences).
TRANSACTIONS/CAREER NOTES: Selected by Denver Broncos in second round (58th pick overall) of 1999 NFL draft. ... Signed by Broncos (July 13, 1999).
PLAYING EXPERIENCE: Denver NFL, 1999. ... Games/Games started: 1999 (9/0).
HONORS: Named defensive end on THE SPORTING NEWS college All-America second team (1997). ... Named defensive end on THE SPORTING NEWS college All-America first team (1998).

REDMON, ANTHONY   G   FALCONS

PERSONAL: Born April 9, 1971, in Brewton, Ala. ... 6-5/308. ... Full name: Kendrick Anthony Redmon.
HIGH SCHOOL: T. R. Miller (Brewton, Ala.).
COLLEGE: Auburn.
TRANSACTIONS/CAREER NOTES: Selected by Arizona Cardinals in fifth round (139th pick overall) of 1994 NFL draft. ... Signed by Cardinals (June 13, 1994). ... Granted free agency (February 14, 1997). ... Re-signed by Cardinals (June 13, 1997). ... Granted unconditional free agency (February 13, 1998). ... Signed by Miami Dolphins (July 24, 1998). ... Released by Dolphins (August 30, 1998). ... Signed by Carolina Panthers (October 14, 1998). ... Granted unconditional free agency (February 12, 1999). ... Re-signed Panthers (February 12, 1999). ... Released by Panthers (February 16, 2000). ... Signed by Atlanta Falcons (March 22, 2000).
PLAYING EXPERIENCE: Arizona NFL, 1994-1997; Carolina NFL, 1998 and 1999. ... Games/Games started: 1994 (6/5), 1995 (12/9), 1996 (16/16), 1997 (16/16), 1998 (10/4), 1999 (15/15). Total: 75/65.
PRO STATISTICS: 1996—Recovered one fumble.

REECE, TRAVIS — FB — LIONS

PERSONAL: Born April 3, 1975, in Detroit. ... 6-3/251.
HIGH SCHOOL: Denby (Detroit).
COLLEGE: Michigan State.
TRANSACTIONS/CAREER NOTES: Signed as non-drafted free agent by Detroit Lions (April 24, 1998). ... Released by Lions (August 30, 1998). ... Re-signed by Lions to practice squad (September 1, 1998). ... Activated (September 18, 1998). ... Released by Lions (October 5, 1998). ... Re-signed by Lions to practice squad (October 7, 1998). ... Activated (December 23, 1998). ... Released by Lions (September 15, 1999). ... Re-signed by Lions to practice squad (September 17, 1999). ... Activated (December 3, 1999). ... Released by Lions (December 18, 1999). ... Re-signed by Lions (December 22, 1999).
PLAYING EXPERIENCE: Detroit NFL, 1998 and 1999. ... Games/Games started: 1998 (3/0), 1999 (4/0). Total: 7/0.

REED, ANDRE — WR

R

PERSONAL: Born January 29, 1964, in Allentown, Pa. ... 6-2/190. ... Full name: Andre Darnell Reed.
HIGH SCHOOL: Louis E. Dieruff (Allentown, Pa.).
COLLEGE: Kutztown (Pa.) University.
TRANSACTIONS/CAREER NOTES: Selected by Orlando Renegades in third round (39th pick overall) of 1985 USFL draft. ... Selected by Buffalo Bills in fourth round (86th pick overall) of 1985 NFL draft. ... Signed by Bills (July 19, 1985). ... Granted unconditional free agency (February 16, 1996). ... Re-signed by Bills (May 7, 1996). ... On injured reserve with shoulder injury (December 18, 1997-remainder of season). ... Released by Bills (February 9, 2000).
CHAMPIONSHIP GAME EXPERIENCE: Played in AFC championship game (1988 and 1990-1993 seasons). ... Played in Super Bowl XXV (1990 season), Super Bowl XXVI (1991 season), Super Bowl XXVII (1992 season) and Super Bowl XXVIII (1993 season).
HONORS: Played in Pro Bowl (1988-1990, 1992 and 1994 seasons). ... Member of Pro Bowl squad (1991 season); did not play. ... Named to play in Pro Bowl (1993 season); replaced by Haywood Jeffires due to injury.
RECORDS: Shares NFL record for most seasons with 50 or more receptions—13.
POST SEASON RECORDS: Shares NFL postseason single-game record for most touchdown receptions—3 (January 3, 1993, OT, vs. Houston).
PRO STATISTICS: 1985—Returned five punts for 12 yards and recovered two fumbles. 1986—Recovered two fumbles for two yards. 1990—Recovered one fumble. 1994—Completed only pass attempt for 32 yards and recovered two fumbles. 1999—Recovered one fumble.
SINGLE GAME HIGHS (regular season): Receptions—15 (November 20, 1994, vs. Green Bay); yards—191 (November 20, 1994, vs. Green Bay); and touchdown receptions—3 (September 5, 1993, vs. New England).
STATISTICAL PLATEAUS: 100-yard receiving games: 1985 (1), 1987 (2), 1988 (3), 1989 (6), 1990 (2), 1991 (4), 1992 (2), 1993 (2), 1994 (5), 1996 (5), 1997 (2), 1998 (1). Total: 35.
MISCELLANEOUS: Active AFC leader for career receptions (941), receiving yards (13,095) and touchdown receptions (86). ... Shares active AFC lead in touchdowns (87). ... Holds Buffalo Bills all-time record for most receptions (941), most yards receiving (13,095) and most touchdown receptions (86). ... Shares Buffalo Bills all-time record for most touchdowns (87).

			RUSHING				RECEIVING				TOTALS		
Year Team	G	GS	Att.	Yds.	Avg.	TD	No.	Yds.	Avg.	TD	TD	2pt.	Pts.	Fum.
1985—Buffalo NFL	16	15	3	-1	-0.3	1	48	637	13.3	4	5	0	30	1
1986—Buffalo NFL	15	15	3	-8	-2.7	0	53	739	13.9	7	7	0	42	2
1987—Buffalo NFL	12	12	1	1	1.0	0	57	752	13.2	5	5	0	30	0
1988—Buffalo NFL	15	14	6	64	10.7	0	71	968	13.6	6	6	0	36	1
1989—Buffalo NFL	16	16	2	31	15.5	0	§88	§1312	14.9	9	9	0	54	4
1990—Buffalo NFL	16	16	3	23	7.7	0	71	945	13.3	8	8	0	48	1
1991—Buffalo NFL	16	16	12	136	11.3	0	81	1113	13.7	10	10	0	60	1
1992—Buffalo NFL	16	16	8	65	8.1	0	65	913	14.0	3	3	0	18	4
1993—Buffalo NFL	15	15	9	21	2.3	0	52	854	16.4	6	6	0	36	3
1994—Buffalo NFL	16	16	10	87	8.7	0	90	1303	14.5	8	8	0	48	3
1995—Buffalo NFL	6	6	7	48	6.9	0	24	312	13.0	3	3	0	18	2
1996—Buffalo NFL	16	16	8	22	2.8	0	66	1036	15.7	6	6	0	36	1
1997—Buffalo NFL	15	15	3	11	3.7	0	60	880	14.7	5	5	0	30	0
1998—Buffalo NFL	15	13	0	0	0.0	0	63	795	12.6	5	5	0	30	0
1999—Buffalo NFL	16	16	0	0	0.0	0	52	536	10.3	1	1	0	6	0
Pro totals (15 years)	221	217	75	500	6.7	1	941	13095	13.9	86	87	0	522	24

REED, JAKE — WR — SAINTS

PERSONAL: Born September 28, 1967, in Covington, Ga. ... 6-3/216. ... Full name: Willis Reed. ... Brother of Dale Carter, cornerback, Denver Broncos.
HIGH SCHOOL: Newton County (Covington, Ga.).
COLLEGE: Grambling State (degree in criminal justice, 1990).
TRANSACTIONS/CAREER NOTES: Selected by Minnesota Vikings in third round (68th pick overall) of 1991 NFL draft. ... Signed by Vikings (July 22, 1991). ... On injured reserve with ankle injury (November 2, 1991-remainder of season). ... Granted free agency (February 17, 1994). ... Re-signed by Vikings (May 6, 1994). ... Granted unconditional free agency (February 17, 1995). ... Re-signed by Vikings (February 28, 1995). ... Released by Vikings (February 10, 2000). ... Signed by New Orleans Saints (February 21, 2000).
CHAMPIONSHIP GAME EXPERIENCE: Member of Vikings for NFC championship game (1998 season); inactive.
PRO STATISTICS: 1992—Returned one kickoff for one yard. 1995—Recovered one fumble.
SINGLE GAME HIGHS (regular season): Receptions—12 (September 7, 1997, vs. Chicago); yards—157 (November 6, 1994, vs. New Orleans); and touchdown receptions—2 (November 1, 1998, vs. Tampa Bay).
STATISTICAL PLATEAUS: 100-yard receiving games: 1994 (3), 1995 (3), 1996 (3), 1997 (5), 1998 (1), 1999 (2). Total: 17.

			RECEIVING				TOTALS		
Year Team	G	GS	No.	Yds.	Avg.	TD	TD	2pt.	Pts.	Fum.
1991—Minnesota NFL	1	0	0	0	0.0	0	0	0	0	0
1992—Minnesota NFL	16	0	6	142	23.7	0	0	0	0	0
1993—Minnesota NFL	10	1	5	65	13.0	0	0	0	0	0

Year—Team	G	GS	No.	Yds.	Avg.	TD			TD	Pts.	Fum.
1994—Minnesota NFL	16	16	85	1175	13.8	4	4	0		24	3
1995—Minnesota NFL	16	16	72	1167	16.2	9	9	0		54	1
1996—Minnesota NFL	16	15	72	1320	18.3	7	7	0		42	0
1997—Minnesota NFL	16	16	68	1138	16.7	6	6	0		36	0
1998—Minnesota NFL	11	11	34	474	13.9	4	4	0		24	0
1999—Minnesota NFL	16	8	44	643	14.6	2	2	0		12	0
Pro totals (9 years)	118	83	386	6124	15.9	32	32	0		192	4

REED, ROBERT — WR — CHARGERS

PERSONAL: Born January 14, 1975, in Hinds County, Miss. ... 6-1/203. ... Full name: Robert E. Reed.
HIGH SCHOOL: Northwest Rankin (Miss.).
JUNIOR COLLEGE: Hinds Community College (Miss.).
COLLEGE: Mississippi, then Lambuth University (Tenn.).
TRANSACTIONS/CAREER NOTES: Signed as non-drafted free agent by San Diego Chargers (April 20, 1999). ... Released by Chargers (September 4, 1999). ... Re-signed by Chargers to practice squad (September 6, 1999). ... Activated (December 3, 1999).
PRO STATISTICS: 1999—Caught one pass for one yard.
SINGLE GAME HIGHS (regular season): Receptions—1 (December 5, 1999, vs. Cleveland); yards—1 (December 5, 1999, vs. Cleveland); and touchdown receptions—0.

			PUNT RETURNS				KICKOFF RETURNS				TOTALS		
Year Team	G	GS	No.	Yds.	Avg.	TD	No.	Yds.	Avg.	TD	TD	2pt.	Pts.	Fum.
1999—San Diego NFL	3	0	3	49	16.3	0	5	72	14.4	0	0	0	0	1

REESE, IKE — LB — EAGLES

PERSONAL: Born October 16, 1973, in Jacksonville, N.C. ... 6-2/222. ... Full name: Isaiah Reese.
HIGH SCHOOL: Woodward (Cincinnati), then Aiken (Cincinnati).
COLLEGE: Michigan State.
TRANSACTIONS/CAREER NOTES: Selected by Philadelphia Eagles in fifth round (142nd pick overall) of 1998 NFL draft. ... Signed by Eagles (July 14, 1998).
PLAYING EXPERIENCE: Philadelphia NFL, 1998 and 1999. ... Games/Games started: 1998 (16/0), 1999 (16/0). Total: 32/0.
PRO STATISTICS: 1999—Credited with three sacks.

REESE, IZELL — S — COWBOYS

PERSONAL: Born May 7, 1974, in Dothan, Ala. ... 6-2/190.
HIGH SCHOOL: Northview (Dothan, Ala.).
COLLEGE: Alabama-Birmingham.
TRANSACTIONS/CAREER NOTES: Selected by Dallas Cowboys in sixth round (188th pick overall) of 1998 NFL draft. ... Signed by Cowboys (July 15, 1998). ... On injured reserve with neck injury (November 19, 1999-remainder of season).

			INTERCEPTIONS			
Year Team	G	GS	No.	Yds.	Avg.	TD
1998—Dallas NFL	16	0	1	6	6.0	0
1999—Dallas NFL	8	4	3	28	9.3	0
Pro totals (2 years)	24	4	4	34	8.5	0

REEVES, JOHN — LB — CHARGERS

PERSONAL: Born February 23, 1975, in Bradenton, Fla. ... 6-3/236. ... Full name: John Edwin Reeves Jr.
HIGH SCHOOL: Southeast (Bradenton, Fla.).
COLLEGE: Purdue.
TRANSACTIONS/CAREER NOTES: Signed as non-drafted free agent by San Diego Chargers (April 20, 1999). ... Released by Chargers (September 4, 1999). ... Re-signed by Chargers to practice squad (September 6, 1999). ... Activated (November 23, 1999).
PLAYING EXPERIENCE: San Diego NFL, 1999. ... Games/Games started: 1999 (5/0).

REHBERG, SCOTT — OT — BENGALS

PERSONAL: Born November 17, 1973, in Kalamazoo, Mich. ... 6-8/330. ... Full name: Scott Joseph Rehberg. ... Name pronounced RAY-berg.
HIGH SCHOOL: Central (Kalamazoo, Mich.).
COLLEGE: Central Michigan.
TRANSACTIONS/CAREER NOTES: Selected by New England Patriots in seventh round (230th pick overall) of 1997 NFL draft. ... Signed by Patriots (June 19, 1997). ... Selected by Cleveland Browns from Patriots in NFL expansion draft (February 9, 1999). ... Granted free agency (February 11, 2000). ... Signed by Cincinnati Bengals (March 2, 2000).
PLAYING EXPERIENCE: New England NFL, 1997 and 1998; Cleveland NFL, 1999. ... Games/Games started: 1997 (6/0), 1998 (2/0), 1999 (15/13). Total: 23/13.
PRO STATISTICS: 1999—Recovered one fumble.

REID, SPENCER — LB — PANTHERS

PERSONAL: Born February 8, 1976, in Pago Pago, American Samoa. ... 6-1/247. ... Full name: Spencer Eldon Karene Reid.
HIGH SCHOOL: Leone (American Samoa).

COLLEGE: Brigham Young.
TRANSACTIONS/CAREER NOTES: Signed as non-drafted free agent by Carolina Panthers (April 18, 1998). ... Claimed on waivers by Indianapolis Colts (September 6, 1999). ... Traded by Colts to Panthers for RB Fred Lane (April 20, 2000).
PLAYING EXPERIENCE: Carolina NFL, 1998; Indianapolis NFL, 1999. ... Games/Games started: 1998 (16/0), 1999 (12/0). Total: 28/0.

RHETT, ERRICT   RB   BROWNS

PERSONAL: Born December 11, 1970, in Pembroke Pines, Fla. ... 5-11/211. ... Full name: Errict Undra Rhett.
HIGH SCHOOL: McArthur (Hollywood, Fla.).
COLLEGE: Florida (degree in commercial management).
TRANSACTIONS/CAREER NOTES: Selected by Tampa Bay Buccaneers in second round (34th pick overall) of 1994 NFL draft. ... Signed by Buccaneers (August 9, 1994). ... Granted free agency (February 13, 1998). ... Re-signed by Buccaneers (February 18, 1998). ... Traded by Buccaneers to Baltimore Ravens for third-round pick (traded back to Baltimore) in 1999 draft (February 18, 1998). ... Granted unconditional free agency (February 12, 1999). ... Re-signed by Ravens (April 26, 1999). ... Granted unconditional free agency (February 11, 2000). ... Signed by Cleveland Browns (February 19, 2000).
HONORS: Named running back on THE SPORTING NEWS college All-America second team (1993).
PRO STATISTICS: 1994—Recovered one fumble. 1995—Recovered one fumble. 1996—Recovered one fumble. 1997—Returned one kickoff for 16 yards.
SINGLE GAME HIGHS (regular season): Attempts—40 (December 4, 1994, vs. Washington); yards—192 (December 4, 1994, vs. Washington); and rushing touchdowns—2 (November 7, 1999, vs. Cleveland).
STATISTICAL PLATEAUS: 100-yard rushing games: 1994 (4), 1995 (4), 1999 (4). Total: 12.

			RUSHING				RECEIVING				TOTALS			
Year Team	G	GS	Att.	Yds.	Avg.	TD	No.	Yds.	Avg.	TD	TD	2pt.	Pts.	Fum.
1994—Tampa Bay NFL	16	8	284	1011	3.6	7	22	119	5.4	0	7	1	44	2
1995—Tampa Bay NFL	16	16	332	1207	3.6	11	14	110	7.9	0	11	0	66	2
1996—Tampa Bay NFL	9	7	176	539	3.1	3	4	11	2.8	1	4	0	24	3
1997—Tampa Bay NFL	11	0	31	96	3.1	3	0	0	0.0	0	3	0	18	0
1998—Baltimore NFL	13	1	44	180	4.1	0	11	65	5.9	0	0	0	0	0
1999—Baltimore NFL	16	10	236	852	3.6	5	24	169	7.0	2	7	0	42	0
Pro totals (6 years)	81	42	1103	3885	3.5	29	75	474	6.3	3	32	1	194	7

RHINEHART, COBY   CB   CARDINALS

PERSONAL: Born February 7, 1977, in Dallas. ... 5-10/186. ... Full name: Jacoby Rhinehart.
HIGH SCHOOL: Tyler Street Christian Academy (Dallas).
COLLEGE: Southern Methodist.
TRANSACTIONS/CAREER NOTES: Selected by Arizona Cardinals in sixth round (190th pick overall) of 1999 NFL draft. ... Signed by Cardinals (June 18, 1999).
PLAYING EXPERIENCE: Arizona NFL, 1999. ... Games/Games started: 1999 (16/0).

RICE, JERRY   WR   49ERS

PERSONAL: Born October 13, 1962, in Starkville, Miss. ... 6-2/196. ... Full name: Jerry Lee Rice.
HIGH SCHOOL: Crawford MS Moor (Crawford, Miss.).
COLLEGE: Mississippi Valley State.
TRANSACTIONS/CAREER NOTES: Selected by Birmingham Stallions in first round (first pick overall) of 1985 USFL draft. ... Selected by San Francisco 49ers in first round (16th pick overall) of 1985 NFL draft. ... Signed by 49ers (July 23, 1985). ... Granted free agency (February 1, 1992). ... Re-signed by 49ers (August 25, 1992). ... On injured reserve with knee injury (December 23, 1997-remainder of season).
CHAMPIONSHIP GAME EXPERIENCE: Played in NFC championship game (1988-1990 and 1992-1994 seasons). ... Member of Super Bowl championship team (1988, 1989 and 1994 seasons).
HONORS: Named wide receiver on THE SPORTING NEWS college All-America first team (1984). ... Named wide receiver on THE SPORTING NEWS NFL All-Pro team (1986-1996). ... Played in Pro Bowl (1986, 1987, 1989-1993, 1995 and 1998 seasons). ... Named NFL Player of the Year by THE SPORTING NEWS (1987 and 1990). ... Named Most Valuable Player of Super Bowl XXIII (1988 season). ... Named to play in Pro Bowl (1988 season); replaced by J.T. Smith due to injury. ... Named to play in Pro Bowl (1994 season); replaced by Herman Moore due to injury. ... Named Outstanding Player of Pro Bowl (1995 season). ... Named to play in Pro Bowl (1996 season); replaced by Irving Fryar due to injury.
RECORDS: Holds NFL career records for most touchdowns—180; most touchdown receptions—169; most receiving yards—18,442; most pass receptions—1,206; most seasons with 1,000 or more yards receiving—12; most games with 100 or more yards receiving—66; most consecutive games with one or more reception—209 (December 9, 1985-present); and most consecutive games with one or more touchdown reception—13 (December 19, 1986-December 27, 1987). ... Holds NFL single-season record for most yards receiving—1,848 (1995); and most touchdown receptions—22 (1987). ... Shares NFL record for most seasons with 50 or more receptions—13. ... Shares NFL single-game record for most touchdown receptions—5 (October 14, 1990, at Atlanta).
POST SEASON RECORDS: Holds Super Bowl career records for most points—42; most touchdowns—7; most touchdown receptions—7; most receptions—28; most combined yards—527; and most yards receiving—512. ... Holds Super Bowl single-game records for most touchdown receptions—3 (January 28, 1990, vs. Denver and January 29, 1995, vs. San Diego); and most yards receiving—215 (January 22, 1989, vs. Cincinnati). ... Shares Super Bowl single-game records for most points—18 (January 28, 1990, vs. Denver and January 29, 1995, vs. San Diego); and most receptions—11 (January 22, 1989, vs. Cincinnati). ... Holds NFL post-season career records for most touchdowns—19; most touchdown receptions—19; most receptions—124; most yards receiving—1,811; and most games with 100 or more yards receiving—7. ... Holds NFL postseason record for most consecutive games with one or more receptions—23 (1985-present). ... Shares NFL postseason career record for most consecutive games with 100 or more yards receiving—3 (1988-89). ... Shares NFL postseason single-game record for most touchdown receptions—3 (January 28, 1990, vs. Denver; January 1, 1989, vs. Minnesota; and January 29, 1995, vs. San Diego).
PRO STATISTICS: 1985—Returned one kickoff for six yards. 1986—Attempted two passes with one completion for 16 yards and recovered three fumbles. 1987—Recovered one fumble. 1988—Attempted three passes with one completion for 14 yards and one interception and recovered one fumble. 1993—Recovered one fumble. 1995—Completed only pass attempt for 41 yards and a touchdown and

recovered one fumble in end zone for a touchdown. 1996—Attempted one pass without a completion. 1999—Attempted one pass without a completion.

SINGLE GAME HIGHS (regular season): Receptions—16 (November 20, 1994, vs. Los Angeles Rams); yards—289 (December 18, 1995, vs. Minnesota); and touchdown receptions—5 (October 14, 1990, vs. Atlanta).

STATISTICAL PLATEAUS: 100-yard receiving games: 1985 (2), 1986 (6), 1987 (4), 1988 (5), 1989 (8), 1990 (7), 1991 (4), 1992 (3), 1993 (5), 1994 (5), 1995 (9), 1996 (3), 1998 (3), 1999 (2). Total: 66.

MISCELLANEOUS: Active NFL leader for career receptions (1,206), receiving yards (18,442), touchdown receptions (169) and touchdowns (180). ... Holds San Francisco 49ers all-time records for most yards receiving (18,442), most touchdowns (180), most receptions (1,206) and most touchdown receptions (169).

				RUSHING				RECEIVING				TOTALS			
Year Team	G	GS	Att.	Yds.	Avg.	TD	No.	Yds.	Avg.	TD	TD	2pt.	Pts.	Fum.
1985—San Francisco NFL	16	4	6	26	4.3	1	49	927	18.9	3	4	0	24	1
1986—San Francisco NFL	16	15	10	72	7.2	1	‡86	*1570	18.3	*15	16	0	96	2
1987—San Francisco NFL	12	12	8	51	6.4	1	65	1078	16.6	*22	*23	0	*138	2
1988—San Francisco NFL	16	16	13	107	8.2	1	64	1306	20.4	9	10	0	60	2
1989—San Francisco NFL	16	16	5	33	6.6	0	82	*1483	18.1	*17	17	0	102	0
1990—San Francisco NFL	16	16	2	0	0.0	0	*100	*1502	15.0	*13	13	0	78	1
1991—San Francisco NFL	16	16	1	2	2.0	0	80	1206	15.1	*14	14	0	84	1
1992—San Francisco NFL	16	16	9	58	6.4	1	84	1201	14.3	10	11	0	66	2
1993—San Francisco NFL	16	16	3	69	23.0	1	98	*1503	15.3	†15	*16	0	96	3
1994—San Francisco NFL	16	16	7	93	13.3	2	112	*1499	13.4	13	15	1	92	1
1995—San Francisco NFL	16	16	5	36	7.2	1	122	*1848	15.1	15	17	1	104	3
1996—San Francisco NFL	16	16	11	77	7.0	1	*108	1254	11.6	8	9	0	54	0
1997—San Francisco NFL	2	1	1	-10	-10.0	0	7	78	11.1	1	1	0	6	0
1998—San Francisco NFL	16	16	0	0	0.0	0	82	1157	14.1	9	9	†2	58	2
1999—San Francisco NFL	16	16	2	13	6.5	0	67	830	12.4	5	5	0	30	0
Pro totals (15 years)	222	208	83	627	7.6	10	1206	18442	15.3	169	180	4	1088	20

RICE, RON   S   LIONS

PERSONAL: Born November 9, 1972, in Detroit. ... 6-1/217. ... Full name: Ronald Wilson Rice.
HIGH SCHOOL: University of Detroit Jesuit.
COLLEGE: Eastern Michigan (degree in criminal justice).
TRANSACTIONS/CAREER NOTES: Signed as non-drafted free agent by Detroit Lions (April 24, 1995). ... Released by Lions (August 18, 1995). ... Re-signed by Lions to practice squad (August 29, 1995). ... Activated (November 1, 1995); did not play. ... Granted free agency (February 13, 1998). ... Re-signed by Lions (June 25, 1998).
PRO STATISTICS: 1999—Recovered one fumble.

			INTERCEPTIONS				SACKS
Year Team	G	GS	No.	Yds.	Avg.	TD	No.
1995—Detroit NFL			Did not play.				
1996—Detroit NFL	13	2	0	0	0.0	0	0.0
1997—Detroit NFL	12	8	1	18	18.0	0	1.0
1998—Detroit NFL	16	16	3	25	8.3	0	3.5
1999—Detroit NFL	16	16	5	82	16.4	0	1.0
Pro totals (4 years)	57	42	9	125	13.9	0	5.5

RICE, SIMEON   DE   CARDINALS

PERSONAL: Born February 24, 1974, in Chicago. ... 6-5/268.
HIGH SCHOOL: Mount Carmel (Chicago).
COLLEGE: Illinois (degree in speech communications, 1996).
TRANSACTIONS/CAREER NOTES: Selected by Arizona Cardinals in first round (third pick overall) of 1996 NFL draft. ... Signed by Cardinals (August 19, 1996). ... Designated by Cardinals as franchise player (February 11, 2000).
HONORS: Played in Pro Bowl (1999 season). ... Named linebacker on The Sporting News college All-America second team (1995).
PRO STATISTICS: 1996—Recovered one fumble. 1997—Intercepted one pass for no yards. 1998—Recovered four fumbles for 39 yards. 1999—Recovered one fumble.

Year Team	G	GS	SACKS
1996—Arizona NFL	16	15	12.5
1997—Arizona NFL	16	15	5.0
1998—Arizona NFL	16	16	10.0
1999—Arizona NFL	16	16	16.5
Pro totals (4 years)	64	62	44.0

RICHARDSON, DAMIEN   S   PANTHERS

PERSONAL: Born April 3, 1976, in Los Angeles. ... 6-1/210. ... Full name: Damien A. Richardson.
HIGH SCHOOL: Clovis West (Fresno, Calif.).
COLLEGE: Arizona State.
TRANSACTIONS/CAREER NOTES: Selected by Carolina Panthers in sixth round (165th pick overall) of 1998 NFL draft. ... Signed by Panthers (July 24, 1998).
PLAYING EXPERIENCE: Carolina NFL, 1998 and 1999. ... Games/Games started: 1998 (14/7), 1999 (15/0). Total: 29/7.
PRO STATISTICS: 1998—Recovered one fumble. 1999—Intercepted one pass for 27 yards and credited with one sack.

RICHARDSON, KYLE   P   RAVENS

PERSONAL: Born March 2, 1973, in Farmington, Mo. ... 6-2/210. ... Full name: Kyle Davis Richardson.
HIGH SCHOOL: Farmington (Mo.).
COLLEGE: Arkansas State.
TRANSACTIONS/CAREER NOTES: Played for Rhein Fire of World League (1996). ... Signed as non-drafted free agent by Miami Dolphins (September 3, 1997). ... Released by Dolphins (September 8, 1997). ... Re-signed by Dolphins (September 18, 1997). ... Released by Dolphins (October 7, 1997). ... Signed by Seattle Seahawks (November 12, 1997). ... Released by Seahawks (November 25, 1997). ... Signed by Baltimore Ravens (March 25, 1998).
PRO STATISTICS: 1997—Rushed once for no yards and fumbled once for minus 13 yards. 1998—Rushed once for no yards and recovered one fumble.

			PUNTING				
Year Team	G	No.	Yds.	Avg.	Net avg.	In. 20	Blk.
1996—Rhein W. L.			Statistics unavailable.				
1997—Miami NFL	3	11	480	43.6	33.1	0	0
—Seattle NFL	2	8	324	40.5	23.8	2	†2
1998—Baltimore NFL	16	90	3948	43.9	38.3	25	*2
1999—Baltimore NFL	16	103	4355	42.3	35.5	*39	1
Pro totals (3 years)	37	212	9107	43.0	36.1	66	5

RICHARDSON, TONY   FB   CHIEFS

PERSONAL: Born December 17, 1971, in Frankfurt, West Germany. ... 6-1/235. ... Full name: Antonio Richardson.
HIGH SCHOOL: Daleville (Ala.).
COLLEGE: Auburn.
TRANSACTIONS/CAREER NOTES: Signed as non-drafted free agent by Dallas Cowboys (April 28, 1994). ... Released by Cowboys (August 28, 1994). ... Re-signed by Cowboys to practice squad (August 30, 1994). ... Granted free agency after 1994 season. ... Signed by Kansas City Chiefs (February 28, 1995). ... On injured reserve with wrist injury (December 11, 1996-remainder of season). ... Granted unconditional free agency (February 11, 2000). ... Re-signed by Chiefs (February 16, 2000).
PRO STATISTICS: 1996—Recovered one fumble. 1998—Returned one kickoff for no yards and recovered one fumble.
SINGLE GAME HIGHS (regular season): Attempts—12 (December 5, 1999, vs. Denver); yards—80 (December 5, 1999, vs. Denver); and rushing touchdowns—1 (September 19, 1999, vs. Denver).

			RUSHING				RECEIVING				TOTALS			
Year Team	G	GS	Att.	Yds.	Avg.	TD	No.	Yds.	Avg.	TD	TD	2pt.	Pts.	Fum.
1995—Kansas City NFL	14	1	8	18	2.3	0	0	0	0.0	0	0	0	0	0
1996—Kansas City NFL	13	0	4	10	2.5	0	2	18	9.0	1	1	0	6	0
1997—Kansas City NFL	14	0	2	11	5.5	0	3	6	2.0	3	3	0	18	0
1998—Kansas City NFL	14	1	20	45	2.3	2	2	13	6.5	0	2	0	12	0
1999—Kansas City NFL	16	15	84	387	4.6	1	24	141	5.9	0	1	0	6	1
Pro totals (5 years)	71	17	118	471	4.0	3	31	178	5.7	4	7	0	42	1

RICHEY, WADE   K   49ERS

PERSONAL: Born May 19, 1976, in Lafayette, La. ... 6-4/200. ... Full name: Wade Edward Richey.
HIGH SCHOOL: Carencro (Lafayette, La.).
COLLEGE: Louisiana State.
TRANSACTIONS/CAREER NOTES: Signed as non-drafted free agent by Seattle Seahawks (April 21, 1998). ... Claimed on waivers by San Francisco 49ers (August 26, 1998).
PRO STATISTICS: 1999—Punted four times for 146 yards.

			KICKING					
Year Team	G	XPM	XPA	FGM	FGA	Lg.	50+	Pts.
1998—San Francisco NFL	16	49	51	18	27	46	0-0	103
1999—San Francisco NFL	16	30	31	21	23	52	1-1	93
Pro totals (2 years)	32	79	82	39	50	52	1-1	196

RICHIE, DAVID   DT

PERSONAL: Born September 26, 1973, in Orange, Calif. ... 6-4/280.
HIGH SCHOOL: Kelso (Wash.).
COLLEGE: Washington.
TRANSACTIONS/CAREER NOTES: Signed as non-drafted free agent by Denver Broncos (April 28, 1997). ... Traded by Broncos with C Steve Gordon to San Francisco 49ers for past considerations (August 25, 1998). ... Released by 49ers (November 7, 1998). ... Re-signed by 49ers to practice squad (November 17, 1998). ... Activated (December 2, 1998). ... Released by 49ers (September 21, 1999). ... Re-signed by 49ers (December 8, 1999). ... Granted free agency (February 11, 2000).
PLAYING EXPERIENCE: Denver NFL, 1997; San Francisco NFL, 1998 and 1999. ... Games/Games started: 1997 (2/0), 1998 (8/0), 1999 (1/0). Total: 11/0.
CHAMPIONSHIP GAME EXPERIENCE: Member of Broncos for AFC championship game (1997 season); inactive. ... Member of Super Bowl championship team (1997 season); inactive.
PRO STATISTICS: 1997—Credited with 1/2 sack. 1998—Returned one kickoff for 11 yards.

RICKS, MIKHAEL   WR   CHARGERS

PERSONAL: Born November 14, 1974, in Galveston, Texas. ... 6-5/237. ... Full name: Mikhael Roy Ricks. ... Name pronounced Michael.
HIGH SCHOOL: Anahuac (Texas).

R

COLLEGE: Stephen F. Austin State.
TRANSACTIONS/CAREER NOTES: Selected by San Diego Chargers in second round (59th pick overall) of 1998 NFL draft. ... Signed by Chargers (July 23, 1998).
PRO STATISTICS: 1999—Rushed twice for 11 yards and attempted one pass without a completion.
SINGLE GAME HIGHS (regular season): Receptions—6 (October 24, 1999,vs. Green Bay); yards—86 (September 19, 1999, vs. Cincinnati); and touchdown receptions—1 (December 20, 1998, vs. Oakland).

| | | | RECEIVING | | | | TOTALS | | |
Year Team	G	GS	No.	Yds.	Avg.	TD	TD	2pt.	Pts.	Fum.
1998—San Diego NFL	16	9	30	450	15.0	2	2	0	12	1
1999—San Diego NFL	16	15	40	429	10.7	0	0	†1	2	0
Pro totals (2 years)	32	24	70	879	12.6	2	2	1	14	1

R

RIEMERSMA, JAY　　　　　TE　　　　　BILLS

PERSONAL: Born May 17, 1973, in Evansville, Ind. ... 6-5/254. ... Full name: Allen Jay Riemersma. ... Name pronounced REEM-urz-muh.
HIGH SCHOOL: Zeeland (Mich.).
COLLEGE: Michigan.
TRANSACTIONS/CAREER NOTES: Selected by Buffalo Bills in seventh round (244th pick overall) of 1996 NFL draft. ... Signed by Bills (July 9, 1996). ... Released by Bills (August 25, 1996). ... Re-signed by Bills to practice squad (August 26, 1996). ... Activated (October 15, 1996); did not play. ... Granted free agency (February 12, 1999). ... Re-signed by Bills (April 26, 1999). ... Granted unconditional free agency (February 11, 2000). ... Re-signed by Bills (February 15, 2000).
PRO STATISTICS: 1998—Returned one kickoff for nine yards and recovered one fumble.
SINGLE GAME HIGHS (regular season): Receptions—6 (December 26, 1999, vs. New England); yards—86 (November 7, 1999, vs. Washington); and touchdown receptions—2 (November 1, 1998, vs. Miami).

| | | | RECEIVING | | | | TOTALS | | |
Year Team	G	GS	No.	Yds.	Avg.	TD	TD	2pt.	Pts.	Fum.
1996—Buffalo NFL					Did not play.					
1997—Buffalo NFL	16	8	26	208	8.0	2	2	1	14	1
1998—Buffalo NFL	16	3	25	288	11.5	6	6	0	36	0
1999—Buffalo NFL	14	11	37	496	13.4	4	4	0	24	0
Pro totals (3 years)	46	22	88	992	11.3	12	12	1	74	1

RILEY, VICTOR　　　　　OT　　　　　CHIEFS

PERSONAL: Born November 4, 1974, in Swansea, S.C. ... 6-5/334. ... Full name: Victor Allan Riley.
HIGH SCHOOL: Swansea (S.C.).
COLLEGE: Auburn.
TRANSACTIONS/CAREER NOTES: Selected by Kansas City Chiefs in first round (27th pick overall) of 1998 NFL draft. ... Signed by Chiefs (July 2, 1998).
PLAYING EXPERIENCE: Kansas City NFL, 1998 and 1999. ... Games/Games started: 1998 (16/15), 1999 (16/16). Total: 32/31.
PRO STATISTICS: 1998—Recovered one fumble.

RISON, ANDRE　　　　　WR　　　　　CHIEFS

PERSONAL: Born March 18, 1967, in Flint, Mich. ... 6-1/199. ... Full name: Andre Previn Rison. ... Name pronounced RYE-zun.
HIGH SCHOOL: Northwestern (Flint, Mich.).
COLLEGE: Michigan State.
TRANSACTIONS/CAREER NOTES: Selected by Indianapolis Colts in first round (22nd pick overall) of 1989 NFL draft. ... Signed by Colts (May 2, 1989). ... Traded by Colts with OT Chris Hinton, fifth-round pick (OT Reggie Redding) in 1990 draft and first-round pick (WR Mike Pritchard) in 1991 draft to Atlanta Falcons for first (QB Jeff George) and fourth-round (WR Stacey Simmons) picks in 1990 draft (April 20, 1990). ... Granted roster exemption for one game (September 1992). ... Designated by Falcons as transition player (February 25, 1993). ... On reserve/did not report list (July 23-August 20, 1993). ... Granted roster exemption (August 20-26, 1993). ... On suspended list (November 21-22, 1994). ... Free agency status changed by Falcons from transitional to unconditional (February 17, 1995). ... Signed by Cleveland Browns (March 24, 1995). ... Browns franchise moved to Baltimore and renamed Ravens for 1996 season (March 11, 1996). ... Released by Ravens (July 9, 1996). ... Signed by Jacksonville Jaguars (July 17, 1996). ... Released by Jaguars (November 18, 1996). ... Claimed on waivers by Green Bay Packers (November 19, 1996). ... Released by Packers (March 25, 1997). ... Signed by Kansas City Chiefs (June 18, 1997).
CHAMPIONSHIP GAME EXPERIENCE: Played in NFC championship game (1996 season). ... Member of Super Bowl championship team (1996 season).
HONORS: Named wide receiver on THE SPORTING NEWS NFL All-Pro team (1990). ... Played in Pro Bowl (1990-1993 and 1997 seasons). ... Named Outstanding Player of Pro Bowl (1993 season).
PRO STATISTICS: 1989—Rushed three times for 18 yards and returned two punts for 20 yards. 1990—Returned two punts for 10 yards. 1991—Rushed once for minus nine yards. 1995—Rushed twice for no yards and recovered one fumble. 1997—Rushed once for two yards. 1998—Rushed twice for 12 yards and recovered one fumble.
SINGLE GAME HIGHS (regular season): Receptions—14 (September 4, 1994, vs. Detroit); yards—193 (September 4, 1994, vs. Detroit); and touchdown receptions—3 (September 19, 1993, vs. San Francisco).
STATISTICAL PLATEAUS: 100-yard receiving games: 1989 (3), 1990 (5), 1991 (1), 1992 (2), 1993 (4), 1994 (3), 1995 (2), 1996 (1), 1997 (2). Total: 23.
MISCELLANEOUS: Holds Atlanta Falcons all-time records for most touchdowns (56) and most touchdown receptions (56).

| | | | RECEIVING | | | | KICKOFF RETURNS | | | | TOTALS | | |
Year Team	G	GS	No.	Yds.	Avg.	TD	No.	Yds.	Avg.	TD	TD	2pt.	Pts.	Fum.
1989—Indianapolis NFL	16	13	52	820	15.8	4	8	150	18.8	0	4	0	24	1
1990—Atlanta NFL	16	15	82	1208	14.7	10	0	0	0.0	0	10	0	60	2
1991—Atlanta NFL	16	15	81	976	12.0	12	0	0	0.0	0	12	0	72	1
1992—Atlanta NFL	15	13	93	1119	12.0	11	0	0	0.0	0	11	0	66	2
1993—Atlanta NFL	16	16	86	1242	14.4	†15	0	0	0.0	0	15	0	90	2

	15	14	81	1088	13.4	8	0	0	0.0	0	8	1	50	1
1994—Atlanta NFL	15	14	81	1088	13.4	8	0	0	0.0	0	8	1	50	1
1995—Cleveland NFL	16	14	47	701	14.9	3	0	0	0.0	0	3	0	18	1
1996—Jacksonville NFL	10	9	34	458	13.5	2	0	0	0.0	0	2	0	12	0
—Green Bay NFL	5	4	13	135	10.4	1	0	0	0.0	0	1	0	6	1
1997—Kansas City NFL	16	16	72	1092	15.2	7	0	0	0.0	0	7	0	42	0
1998—Kansas City NFL	14	13	40	542	13.6	5	0	0	0.0	0	5	0	30	1
1999—Kansas City NFL	15	14	21	218	10.4	0	0	0	0.0	0	0	0	0	0
Pro totals (11 years)	170	156	702	9599	13.7	78	8	150	18.8	0	78	1	470	12

RITCHIE, JON   RB   RAIDERS

PERSONAL: Born September 4, 1974, in Mechanicsburgh, Pa. ... 6-1/250.
HIGH SCHOOL: Cumberland Valley (Mechanicsburg, Pa.).
COLLEGE: Michigan, then Stanford.
TRANSACTIONS/CAREER NOTES: Selected by Oakland Raiders in third round (63rd pick overall) of 1998 NFL draft. ... Signed by Raiders (July 18, 1998).
SINGLE GAME HIGHS (regular season): Attempts—2 (September 12, 1999, vs. Green Bay); yards—14 (November 15, 1998, vs. Seattle); and rushing touchdowns—0.

			RUSHING				RECEIVING				TOTALS			
Year Team	G	GS	Att.	Yds.	Avg.	TD	No.	Yds.	Avg.	TD	TD	2pt.	Pts.	Fum.
1998—Oakland NFL	15	10	9	23	2.6	0	29	225	7.8	0	0	0	0	2
1999—Oakland NFL	16	14	5	12	2.4	0	45	408	9.1	1	1	0	6	0
Pro totals (2 years)	31	24	14	35	2.5	0	74	633	8.6	1	1	0	6	2

RIVERA, MARCO   G   PACKERS

PERSONAL: Born April 26, 1972, in Brooklyn, N.Y. ... 6-4/305. ... Full name: Marco Anthony Rivera.
HIGH SCHOOL: Elmont (N.Y.) Memorial.
COLLEGE: Penn State (degree in administration of justice).
TRANSACTIONS/CAREER NOTES: Selected by Green Bay Packers in sixth round (208th pick overall) of 1996 NFL draft. ... Signed by Packers (July 15, 1996). ... Inactive for all 16 games (1996). ... Assigned by Packers to Scottish Claymores in 1997 World League enhancement allocation program (February 19, 1997). ... Granted free agency (February 12, 1999). ... Re-signed by Packers (March 24, 1999).
PLAYING EXPERIENCE: Scottish W.L., 1997, Green Bay NFL, 1997-1999. ... Games/Games started: W.L. 1997 (10/10), NFL 1997 (14/0), 1998 (15/15), 1999 (16/16). Total W.L.:10/10. Total NFL: 45/31. Total Pro: 55/41.
CHAMPIONSHIP GAME EXPERIENCE: Member of Packers for NFC championship game (1996 season); inactive. ... Member of Super Bowl championship team (1996 season); inactive. ... Played in NFC championship game (1997 season). ... Played in Super Bowl XXXII (1997 season).
PRO STATISTICS: 1999—Recovered one fumble.

RIVERS, RON   RB

PERSONAL: Born November 13, 1971, in Elizabeth City, N.J. ... 5-8/205. ... Full name: Ronald Leroy Rivers.
HIGH SCHOOL: San Gorgonio (San Bernardino, Calif.).
COLLEGE: Fresno State.
TRANSACTIONS/CAREER NOTES: Signed as non-drafted free agent by San Diego Chargers (April 28, 1994). ... Released by Chargers (August 29, 1994). ... Signed by Detroit Lions to practice squad (September 21, 1994). ... Activated (December 22, 1994); did not play. ... Granted free agency (February 13, 1998). ... Re-signed by Lions (April 29, 1998). ... Released by Lions (February 4, 2000).
POST SEASON RECORDS: Shares NFL postseason career and single-game records for most two-point conversions—1 (December 30, 1995, vs. Philadelphia).
PRO STATISTICS: 1995—Caught one pass for five yards and recovered one fumble. 1997—Recovered one fumble.
SINGLE GAME HIGHS (regular season): Attempts—17 (September 19, 1999, vs. Green Bay); yards—96 (September 12, 1999, vs. Seattle); and rushing touchdowns—1 (November 22, 1998, vs. Tampa Bay).

			RUSHING				RECEIVING				KICKOFF RETURNS				TOTALS			
Year Team	G	GS	Att.	Yds.	Avg.	TD	No.	Yds.	Avg.	TD	No.	Yds.	Avg.	TD	TD	2pt.	Pts.	Fum.
1994—Detroit NFL						Did not play.												
1995—Detroit NFL	16	0	18	73	4.1	1	1	5	5.0	0	19	420	22.1	0	1	0	6	2
1996—Detroit NFL	15	0	19	86	4.5	0	2	28	14.0	0	1	8	8.0	0	0	0	0	0
1997—Detroit NFL	16	0	29	166	5.7	1	0	0	0.0	0	2	34	17.0	0	1	0	6	0
1998—Detroit NFL	15	0	19	102	5.4	1	3	58	19.3	0	2	15	7.5	0	1	0	6	0
1999—Detroit NFL	7	6	82	295	3.6	0	22	173	7.9	1	0	0	0.0	0	1	0	6	0
Pro totals (5 years)	69	6	167	722	4.3	3	28	264	9.4	1	24	477	19.9	0	4	0	24	2

ROAF, WILLIE   OT   SAINTS

PERSONAL: Born April 18, 1970, in Pine Bluff, Ark. ... 6-5/312. ... Full name: William Layton Roaf.
HIGH SCHOOL: Pine Bluff (Ark.).
COLLEGE: Louisiana Tech.
TRANSACTIONS/CAREER NOTES: Selected by New Orleans Saints in first round (eighth pick overall) of 1993 NFL draft. ... Signed by Saints (July 15, 1993). ... Designated by Saints as transition player (February 15, 1994).
PLAYING EXPERIENCE: New Orleans NFL, 1993-1999. ... Games/Games started: 1993 (16/16), 1994 (16/16), 1995 (16/16), 1996 (13/13), 1997 (16/16), 1998 (15/15), 1999 (16/16). Total: 108/108.
HONORS: Named offensive tackle on THE SPORTING NEWS college All-America second team (1992). ... Named offensive tackle on THE SPORTING NEWS NFL All-Pro team (1994-1996). ... Played in Pro Bowl (1994-1997 and 1999 seasons). ... Named to play in Pro Bowl (1998 season); replaced by Bob Whitfield due to injury.
PRO STATISTICS: 1994—Recovered one fumble. 1996—Recovered one fumble. 1999—Recovered one fumble.

ROAN, MICHAEL   TE   TITANS

PERSONAL: Born August 29, 1972, in Iowa City, Iowa. ... 6-3/250. ... Full name: Michael Phillip Roan.
HIGH SCHOOL: Iowa City (Iowa) High.
COLLEGE: Wisconsin.
TRANSACTIONS/CAREER NOTES: Selected by Houston Oilers in fourth round (101st pick overall) of 1995 NFL draft. ... Signed by Oilers (July 10, 1995). ... Oilers franchise moved to Tennessee for 1997 season. ... Oilers franchise renamed Tennessee Titans for 1999 season (December 26, 1998). ... On injured reserve with neck injury (January 14, 2000-remainder of playoffs).
PRO STATISTICS: 1995—Recovered one fumble. 1996—Returned one kickoff for 13 yards. 1997—Returned two kickoffs for 20 yards. 1998—Returned one kickoff for four yards and recovered one fumble in end zone for a touchdown.
SINGLE GAME HIGHS (regular season): Receptions—4 (December 6, 1998, vs. Baltimore); yards—51 (November 2, 1997, vs. Jacksonville); and touchdown receptions—1 (January 2, 2000, vs. Pittsburgh).

			RECEIVING				TOTALS			
Year Team	G	GS	No.	Yds.	Avg.	TD	TD	2pt.	Pts.	Fum.
1995—Houston NFL	5	2	8	46	5.8	0	0	0	0	1
1996—Houston NFL	15	1	0	0	0.0	0	0	0	0	0
1997—Tennessee NFL	14	13	12	159	13.3	0	0	0	0	0
1998—Tennessee NFL	16	1	13	93	7.2	0	1	0	6	1
1999—Tennessee NFL	11	1	9	93	10.3	3	3	0	18	0
Pro totals (5 years)	61	18	42	391	9.3	3	4	0	24	2

ROBBINS, AUSTIN   DT   RAIDERS

PERSONAL: Born March 1, 1971, in Washington, D.C. ... 6-6/290. ... Full name: Austin Dion Robbins.
HIGH SCHOOL: Howard D. Woodson (Washington, D.C.).
COLLEGE: North Carolina.
TRANSACTIONS/CAREER NOTES: Selected by Los Angeles Raiders in fourth round (120th pick overall) of 1994 NFL draft. ... Signed by Raiders (July 14, 1994). ... Raiders franchise moved to Oakland (July 21, 1995). ... Traded by Raiders to New Orleans Saints for undisclosed pick in 1997 draft (August 25, 1996). ... Granted free agency (February 14, 1997). ... Re-signed by Saints (June 7, 1997). ... Granted unconditional free agency (February 13, 1998). ... Re-signed by Saints (March 6, 1998). ... Granted unconditional free agency (February 11, 2000). ... Signed by Raiders (April 18, 2000).
PRO STATISTICS: 1995—Recovered two fumbles for six yards and one touchdown. 1998—Recovered one fumble in end zone for a touchdown. 1999—Recovered one fumble.

Year Team	G	GS	SACKS
1994—Los Angeles Raiders NFL	2	0	0.0
1995—Oakland NFL	16	0	2.0
1996—New Orleans NFL	15	7	1.0
1997—New Orleans NFL	12	0	0.0
1998—New Orleans NFL	16	1	1.0
1999—New Orleans NFL	14	3	2.0
Pro totals (6 years)	75	11	6.0

ROBBINS, BARRET   C   RAIDERS

PERSONAL: Born August 26, 1973, in Houston. ... 6-3/320.
HIGH SCHOOL: Sharpstown (Houston).
COLLEGE: Texas Christian.
TRANSACTIONS/CAREER NOTES: Selected by Los Angeles Raiders in second round (49th pick overall) of 1995 NFL draft. ... Signed by Raiders (June 20, 1995). ... Raiders franchise moved to Oakland (July 21, 1995).
PLAYING EXPERIENCE: Oakland NFL, 1995-1999. ... Games/Games started: 1995 (16/0), 1996 (14/14), 1997 (16/16), 1998 (16/16), 1999 (16/16). Total: 78/62.
PRO STATISTICS: 1996—Recovered one fumble.

ROBERSON, JAMES   DE

PERSONAL: Born May 3, 1971, in Bartow, Fla. ... 6-3/275. ... Full name: James Earl Roberson.
HIGH SCHOOL: Lake Wales (Fla.).
COLLEGE: Florida State.
TRANSACTIONS/CAREER NOTES: Signed as non-drafted free agent by New Orleans Saints (April 27, 1995). ... Claimed on waivers by Green Bay Packers (July 27, 1995). ... Released by Packers (August 21, 1995). ... Signed by Rhein Fire of World League (February 1996). ... Signed by Houston Oilers (July 20, 1996). ... Released by Oilers (August 25, 1996). ... Re-signed by Oilers to practice squad (August 26, 1996). ... Activated (September 6, 1996). ... Oilers franchise moved to Tennessee for 1997 season. ... Oilers franchise renamed Tennessee Titans for 1999 season (December 26, 1998). ... Granted free agency (February 12, 1999). ... Re-signed by Titans (May 3, 1999). ... Released by Titans (August 3, 1999). ... Signed by Jacksonville Jaguars (October 13, 1999). ... Released by Jaguars (November 29, 1999).
PRO STATISTICS: 1996—Recovered one fumble for four yards. 1997—Recovered one fumble.

Year Team	G	GS	SACKS
1996—Rhein W.L.	...	...	3.0
—Houston NFL	15	5	3.0
1997—Tennessee NFL	15	11	2.0
1998—Tennessee NFL	10	5	0.0
1999—Jacksonville NFL	2	0	1.0
W.L. totals (1 year)	...	...	3.0
NFL totals (4 years)	42	21	6.0
Pro totals (5 years)	...	...	9.0

ROBERTS, RAY   OT   LIONS

PERSONAL: Born June 3, 1969, in Asheville, N.C. ... 6-6/320. ... Full name: Richard Ray Roberts Jr.
HIGH SCHOOL: Asheville (N.C.).
COLLEGE: Virginia (degree in communication studies, 1991).
TRANSACTIONS/CAREER NOTES: Selected by Seattle Seahawks in first round (10th pick overall) of 1992 NFL draft. ... Signed by Seahawks (August 1, 1992). ... Designated by Seahawks as transition player (February 15, 1994). ... On injured reserve with ankle injury (December 11, 1994-remainder of season). ... Free agency status changed by Seahawks from transitional to unconditional (February 16, 1996). ... Signed by Detroit Lions (March 11, 1996). ... Granted unconditional free agency (February 13, 1998). ... Re-signed by Lions (February 19, 1998). ... On injured reserve with knee injury (December 22, 1999-remainder of season).
PLAYING EXPERIENCE: Seattle NFL, 1992-1995; Detroit NFL, 1996-1999. ... Games/Games started: 1992 (16/16), 1993 (16/16), 1994 (14/14), 1995 (11/0), 1996 (16/16), 1997 (14/14), 1998 (16/16), 1999 (14/14). Total: 117/106.
HONORS: Named offensive tackle on THE SPORTING NEWS college All-America second team (1991).
PRO STATISTICS: 1993—Caught one pass for four yards. 1996—Ran five yards with lateral from reception and recovered two fumbles. 1997—Recovered two fumbles for four yards. 1999—Recovered one fumble.

R

ROBERTSON, MARCUS   S   TITANS

PERSONAL: Born October 2, 1969, in Pasadena, Calif. ... 5-11/205. ... Full name: Marcus Aaron Robertson.
HIGH SCHOOL: John Muir (Pasadena, Calif.).
COLLEGE: Iowa State.
TRANSACTIONS/CAREER NOTES: Selected by Houston Oilers in fourth round (102nd pick overall) of 1991 NFL draft. ... Signed by Oilers (July 16, 1991). ... On injured reserve with knee injury (December 30, 1993-remainder of season). ... Granted free agency (February 17, 1994). ... Re-signed by Oilers (July 11, 1994). ... On injured reserve with knee injury (November 30, 1995-remainder of season). ... Oilers franchise moved to Tennessee for 1997 season. ... Oilers franchise renamed Tennessee Titans for 1999 season (December 26, 1998). ... Granted unconditional free agency (February 11, 2000). ... Re-signed by Titans (February 22, 2000).
CHAMPIONSHIP GAME EXPERIENCE: Played in AFC championship game (1999 season). ... Member of Titans for Super Bowl XXXIV (1999 season); inactive.
HONORS: Named free safety on THE SPORTING NEWS NFL All-Pro team (1993).
PRO STATISTICS: 1991—Credited with one sack, returned one punt for no yards and fumbled once. 1993—Recovered three fumbles for 107 yards and one touchdown. 1994—Returned one punt for no yards, fumbled once and recovered one fumble. 1996—Recovered one fumble for five yards. 1997—Returned one punt for no yards and recovered three fumbles for 67 yards and two touchdowns. 1999—Credited with $^{1}/_{2}$ sack.

			INTERCEPTIONS			
Year Team	G	GS	No.	Yds.	Avg.	TD
1991—Houston NFL	16	0	0	0	0.0	0
1992—Houston NFL	16	14	1	27	27.0	0
1993—Houston NFL	13	13	7	137	19.6	0
1994—Houston NFL	16	16	3	90	30.0	0
1995—Houston NFL	2	2	0	0	0.0	0
1996—Houston NFL	16	16	4	44	11.0	0
1997—Tennessee NFL	14	14	5	127	25.4	0
1998—Tennessee NFL	12	12	1	0	0.0	0
1999—Tennessee NFL	15	15	1	3	3.0	0
Pro totals (9 years)	120	102	22	428	19.5	0

ROBINSON, BRYAN   DL   BEARS

PERSONAL: Born June 22, 1974, in Toledo, Ohio. ... 6-4/295. ... Full name: Bryan Keith Robinson.
HIGH SCHOOL: Woodward (Cincinnati).
JUNIOR COLLEGE: College of the Desert (Palm Desert, Calif.).
COLLEGE: Fresno State.
TRANSACTIONS/CAREER NOTES: Signed as non-drafted free agent by St. Louis Rams (April 29, 1997). ... Claimed on waivers by Chicago Bears (August 31, 1998). ... Granted free agency (February 11, 2000). ... Re-signed by Bears (April 19, 2000).

Year Team	G	GS	SACKS
1997—St. Louis NFL	11	0	1.0
1998—Chicago NFL	10	5	0.5
1999—Chicago NFL	16	16	5.0
Pro totals (3 years)	37	21	6.5

ROBINSON, DAMIEN   S   BUCCANEERS

PERSONAL: Born December 22, 1973, in Dallas. ... 6-2/214. ... Full name: Damien Dion Robinson.
HIGH SCHOOL: Hillcrest (Dallas).
COLLEGE: Iowa.
TRANSACTIONS/CAREER NOTES: Selected by Philadelphia Eagles in fourth round (119th pick overall) of 1997 NFL draft. ... Signed by Eagles (June 4, 1997). ... Released by Eagles (August 25, 1997). ... Re-signed by Eagles to practice squad (August 27, 1997). ... Signed by Tampa Bay Buccaneers off Eagles practice squad (September 17, 1997). ... Inactive for 13 games (1997). ... On injured reserve with arm injury (October 27, 1998-remainder of season). ... Granted free agency (February 11, 2000). ... Re-signed by Buccaneers (May 15, 2000).
PLAYING EXPERIENCE: Tampa Bay NFL, 1998 and 1999. ... Games/Games started: 1998 (7/0), 1999 (16/16). Total: 23/16.
CHAMPIONSHIP GAME EXPERIENCE: Played in NFC championship game (1999 season).
PRO STATISTICS: 1999—Caught one pass for 17 yards, intercepted two passes for 36 yards, credited with $^{1}/_{2}$ sack and recovered two fumbles.

ROBINSON, EDDIE — LB — TITANS

PERSONAL: Born April 13, 1970, in New Orleans. ... 6-1/243. ... Full name: Eddie Joseph Robinson Jr.
HIGH SCHOOL: Brother Martin (New Orleans).
COLLEGE: Alabama State (degree in chemistry, 1993).
TRANSACTIONS/CAREER NOTES: Selected by Houston Oilers in second round (50th pick overall) of 1992 NFL draft. ... Signed by Oilers (Jul 16, 1992). ... Granted free agency (February 17, 1995). ... Re-signed by Oilers (July 1995). ... Granted unconditional free agency (February 16, 1996). ... Signed by Jacksonville Jaguars (March 1, 1996). ... Released by Jaguars (August 30, 1998). ... Signed by Tennessee Oiler (September 1, 1998). ... Oilers franchise renamed Tennessee Titans for 1999 season (December 26, 1998). ... Granted unconditional free agency (February 12, 1999). ... Re-signed by Titans (March 1, 1999).
CHAMPIONSHIP GAME EXPERIENCE: Played in AFC championship game (1996 and 1999 seasons). ... Played in Super Bowl XXXIV (199 season).
PRO STATISTICS: 1995—Intercepted one pass for 49 yards and a touchdown and recovered one fumble. 1996—Recovered one fumble 1997—Intercepted one pass for no yards and recovered two fumbles. 1998—Intercepted one pass for 11 yards. 1999—Recovered three fum bles for one yard.

Year Team	G	GS	SACKS
1992—Houston NFL	16	11	1.0
1993—Houston NFL	16	15	1.0
1994—Houston NFL	15	15	0.0
1995—Houston NFL	16	16	3.5
1996—Jacksonville NFL	16	15	1.0
1997—Jacksonville NFL	16	14	2.0
1998—Tennessee NFL	16	16	3.5
1999—Tennessee NFL	16	16	6.0
Pro totals (8 years)	127	118	18.0

ROBINSON, EUGENE — S

PERSONAL: Born May 28, 1963, in Hartford, Conn. ... 6-1/200. ... Full name: Eugene Keefe Robinson.
HIGH SCHOOL: Weaver (Hartford, Conn.).
COLLEGE: Colgate.
TRANSACTIONS/CAREER NOTES: Selected by New Jersey Generals in 1985 USFL territorial draft. ... Signed as non-drafted free agent b Seattle Seahawks (May 15, 1985). ... On injured reserve with Achilles' tendon injury (December 11, 1994-remainder of season). ... Traded b Seahawks to Green Bay Packers for LB Matt LaBounty (June 27, 1996). ... Granted unconditional free agency (February 13, 1998). ... Signe by Atlanta Falcons (March 6, 1998). ... Granted unconditional free agency (February 11, 2000).
CHAMPIONSHIP GAME EXPERIENCE: Played in NFC championship game (1996-1998 seasons). ... Member of Super Bowl championshi team (1996 season). ... Played in Super Bowl XXXII (1997 season) and Super Bowl XXXIII (1998 season).
HONORS: Played in Pro Bowl (1992, 1993 and 1998 seasons).
PRO STATISTICS: 1985—Returned one kickoff for 10 yards. 1986—Recovered three fumbles for six yards. 1987—Returned blocked pur eight yards for a touchdown and recovered one fumble. 1989—Fumbled once and recovered one fumble. 1990—Recovered four fumbles fo 16 yards and a touchdown. 1991—Recovered one fumble. 1992—Recovered one fumble. 1993—Recovered two fumbles for seven yards 1994—Recovered one fumble. 1995—Returned one punt for one yard and recovered one fumble. 1997—Fumbled once and recovered tw fumbles. 1998—Recovered two fumbles for 16 yards.
MISCELLANEOUS: Active NFL leader for career interceptions (56).

Year Team	G	GS	INTERCEPTIONS				SACKS
			No.	Yds.	Avg.	TD	No.
1985—Seattle NFL	16	0	2	47	23.5	0	0.0
1986—Seattle NFL	16	16	3	39	13.0	0	0.0
1987—Seattle NFL	12	12	3	75	25.0	0	0.0
1988—Seattle NFL	16	16	1	0	0.0	0	1.0
1989—Seattle NFL	16	14	5	24	4.8	0	0.0
1990—Seattle NFL	16	16	3	89	29.7	0	0.0
1991—Seattle NFL	16	16	5	56	11.2	0	1.0
1992—Seattle NFL	16	16	7	126	18.0	0	0.0
1993—Seattle NFL	16	16	†9	80	8.9	0	2.0
1994—Seattle NFL	14	14	3	18	6.0	0	1.0
1995—Seattle NFL	16	16	1	32	32.0	0	0.0
1996—Green Bay NFL	16	16	6	107	17.8	0	0.0
1997—Green Bay NFL	16	16	1	26	26.0	0	2.5
1998—Atlanta NFL	16	16	4	36	9.0	1	0.0
1999—Atlanta NFL	16	16	3	7	2.3	0	0.0
Pro totals (15 years)	234	216	56	762	13.6	1	7.5

ROBINSON, JEFF — TE — RAMS

PERSONAL: Born February 20, 1970, in Kennewick, Wash. ... 6-4/275. ... Full name: Jeffrey William Robinson.
HIGH SCHOOL: Joel E. Ferris (Spokane, Wash.).
COLLEGE: Idaho (degree in finance, 1992).
TRANSACTIONS/CAREER NOTES: Selected by Denver Broncos in fourth round (98th pick overall) of 1993 NFL draft. ... Signed by Bronco (July 13, 1993). ... Granted free agency (February 16, 1996). ... Re-signed by Broncos (March 28, 1996). ... Granted unconditional free agenc (February 14, 1997). ... Signed by St. Louis Rams (March 14, 1997).
CHAMPIONSHIP GAME EXPERIENCE: Played in NFC championship game (1999 season). ... Member of Super Bowl championship team (199 season).
PRO STATISTICS: 1993—Recovered one fumble for minus 10 yards. 1995—Returned one kickoff for 14 yards and recovered one fumble 1996—Recovered one fumble. 1998—Caught one pass for four yards and a touchdown. 1999—Caught six passes for 76 yards and tw touchdowns.

SINGLE GAME HIGHS (regular season): Receptions—2 (October 10, 1999, vs. San Francisco); yards—31 (October 10, 1999, vs. San Francisco); and touchdown receptions—1 (November 7, 1999, vs. Detroit).
MISCELLANEOUS: Played defensive line (1993-98).

Year Team	G	GS	SACKS
1993—Denver NFL	16	0	3.5
1994—Denver NFL	16	0	1.0
1995—Denver NFL	16	0	1.0
1996—Denver NFL	16	0	0.5
1997—St. Louis NFL	16	0	0.5
1998—St. Louis NFL	16	0	0.0
1999—St. Louis NFL	16	9	0.0
Pro totals (7 years)	112	9	6.5

ROBINSON, MARCUS   WR   BEARS

PERSONAL: Born February 27, 1975, in Fort Valley, Ga. ... 6-3/215.
HIGH SCHOOL: Peach County (Fort Valley, Ga.).
COLLEGE: South Carolina.
TRANSACTIONS/CAREER NOTES: Selected by Chicago Bears in fourth round (108th pick overall) of 1997 NFL draft. ... Signed by Bears (July 1, 1997). ... Inactive for four games (1997). ... On injured reserve with thumb injury (September 24, 1997-remainder of season). ... Assigned by Bears to Rhein Fire in 1998 NFL Europe enhancement allocation program (February 18, 1998).
SINGLE GAME HIGHS (regular season): Receptions—11 (December 19, 1999, vs. Detroit); yards—170 (December 19, 1999, vs. Detroit); and touchdown receptions—3 (December 19, 1999, vs. Detroit).
STATISTICAL PLATEAUS: 100-yard receiving games: 1999 (5).

Year Team	G	GS	No.	Yds.	Avg.	TD	TD	2pt.	Pts.	Fum.
				RECEIVING				TOTALS		
1997—Chicago NFL						Did not play.				
1998—Rhein NFLE	...	...	39	811	20.8	5	5	0	30	0
—Chicago NFL	3	0	4	44	11.0	1	1	0	6	0
1999—Chicago NFL	16	11	84	1400	16.7	9	9	0	54	0
NFL Europe totals (1 year)	...	...	39	811	20.8	5	5	0	30	0
NFL totals (1 year)	19	11	88	1444	16.4	10	10	0	60	0
Pro totals (2 years)	...	...	127	2255	17.8	15	15	0	90	0

RODENHAUSER, MARK   C

PERSONAL: Born June 1, 1961, in Elmhurst, Ill. ... 6-5/280. ... Full name: Mark Todd Rodenhauser. ... Name pronounced RO-den-how-ser.
HIGH SCHOOL: Addison (Ill.) Trail.
COLLEGE: Illinois State (degree in industrial technology).
TRANSACTIONS/CAREER NOTES: Signed as non-drafted free agent by Michigan Panthers of USFL (January 15, 1984). ... Released by Panthers (February 13, 1984). ... Signed by Memphis Showboats of USFL (December 3, 1984). ... Released by Showboats (January 22, 1985). ... Signed by Chicago Bruisers of Arena Football League (June 29, 1987). ... Granted free agency (August 15, 1987). ... Signed as replacement player by Chicago Bears (September 24, 1987). ... Left camp voluntarily (August 16, 1988). ... Released by Bears (August 17, 1988). ... Signed by Minnesota Vikings (March 16, 1989). ... Granted unconditional free agency (February 1, 1990). ... Signed by San Diego Chargers (March 1, 1990). ... Granted unconditional free agency (February 1-April 1, 1991). ... Re-signed by Chargers (April 5, 1991). ... On injured reserve with foot injury (November 13, 1991-remainder of season). ... Granted unconditional free agency (February 1, 1992). ... Signed by Bears (March 6, 1992). ... Released by Bears (December 18, 1992). ... Signed by Detroit Lions (April 30, 1993). ... Granted unconditional free agency (February 17, 1994). ... Re-signed by Lions (August 15, 1994). ... Selected by Carolina Panthers from Lions in NFL expansion draft (February 15, 1995). ... Granted unconditional free agency (February 16, 1996). ... Re-signed by Panthers (March 15, 1996). ... Granted unconditional free agency (February 14, 1997). ... Re-signed by Panthers (February 25, 1997). ... Granted unconditional free agency (February 13, 1998). ... Re-signed by Panthers (March 24, 1998). ... Released by Panthers (August 30, 1998). ... Signed by Pittsburgh Steelers (September 1, 1998). ... Released by Steelers (April 19, 1999). ... Signed by Seattle Seahawks (November 9, 1999). ... Granted unconditional free agency (February 11, 2000).
PLAYING EXPERIENCE: Chicago Bruisers Arena Football, 1987; Chicago NFL, 1987 and 1992; Minnesota NFL, 1989; San Diego NFL, 1990 and 1991; Detroit NFL, 1993 and 1994; Carolina NFL, 1995-1997; Pittsburgh NFL, 1998; Seattle NFL, 1999. ... Games/Games started: 1987 Arena Football (4/4), 1987 NFL (9/3), 1989 (16/0), 1990 (16/0), 1991 (10/0), 1992 (13/0), 1993 (16/0), 1994 (16/0), 1995 (16/0), 1996 (16/0), 1997 (16/0), 1998 (16/0), 1999 (8/0). Total Arena League: 4/4. Total NFL: 168/3. Total Pro: 172/7.
CHAMPIONSHIP GAME EXPERIENCE: Played in NFC championship game (1996 season).

RODGERS, DERRICK   LB   DOLPHINS

PERSONAL: Born October 14, 1971, in Memphis, Tenn. ... 6-1/230. ... Full name: Derrick Andre Rodgers.
HIGH SCHOOL: St. Augustine (New Orleans).
JUNIOR COLLEGE: Riverside (Calif.) Community College.
COLLEGE: Arizona State.
TRANSACTIONS/CAREER NOTES: Selected by Miami Dolphins in third round (92nd pick overall) of 1997 NFL draft. ... Signed by Dolphins (July 8, 1997). ... Granted free agency (February 11, 2000). ... Re-signed by Dolphins (April 28, 2000).
PRO STATISTICS: 1997—Recovered one fumble. 1999—Intercepted one pass for five yards and recovered two fumbles.

Year Team	G	GS	SACKS
1997—Miami NFL	15	14	5.0
1998—Miami NFL	16	16	2.5
1999—Miami NFL	16	15	0.0
Pro totals (3 years)	47	45	7.5

ROGERS, CHARLIE   RB   SEAHAWKS

PERSONAL: Born June 19, 1976, in Cliffwood, N.J. ... 5-9/179. ... Full name: John Edward Rogers.
HIGH SCHOOL: Matawan Regional (Aberdeen, N.J.).
COLLEGE: Georgia Tech.
TRANSACTIONS/CAREER NOTES: Selected by Seattle Seahawks in fifth round (152nd pick overall) of 1999 NFL draft. ... Signed by Seahawks (July 29, 1999).

			PUNT RETURNS				KICKOFF RETURNS				TOTALS		
Year Team	G	GS	No.	Yds.	Avg.	TD	No.	Yds.	Avg.	TD	TD	2pt.	Pts.	Fum.
1999—Seattle NFL	12	0	22	318	*14.5	1	18	465	25.8	0	1	0	6	3

ROGERS, CHRIS   CB   VIKINGS

PERSONAL: Born January 3, 1977, in Largo, Md. ... 5-10/192.
HIGH SCHOOL: Largo (Md.).
COLLEGE: Howard.
TRANSACTIONS/CAREER NOTES: Signed as non-drafted free agent by Minnesota Vikings (April 23, 1999). ... Released by Vikings (September 6, 1999). ... Re-signed by Vikings to practice squad (September 8, 1999). ... Released by Vikings (September 10, 1999). ... Re-signed by Vikings (September 22, 1999).
PLAYING EXPERIENCE: Minnesota NFL, 1999. ... Games/Games started: 1999 (10/4).

ROGERS, SAM   LB   BILLS

PERSONAL: Born May 30, 1970, in Pontiac, Mich. ... 6-3/245. ... Full name: Sammy Lee Rogers.
HIGH SCHOOL: Saint Mary's Preparatory (Orchard Lake, Mich.).
JUNIOR COLLEGE: West Hills College (Calif.), then West Los Angeles College.
COLLEGE: Colorado.
TRANSACTIONS/CAREER NOTES: Selected by Buffalo Bills in second round (64th pick overall) of 1994 NFL draft. ... Signed by Bills (July 12 1994). ... Granted free agency (February 14, 1997). ... Re-signed by Bills (June 12, 1997). ... Granted unconditional free agency (February 13 1998). ... Re-signed by Bills (February 15, 1998).
PRO STATISTICS: 1995—Recovered one fumble. 1996—Recovered two fumbles. 1999—Intercepted one pass for 24 yards and recovered two fumbles for seven yards.

Year Team	G	GS	SACKS
1994—Buffalo NFL	14	0	0.0
1995—Buffalo NFL	16	8	2.0
1996—Buffalo NFL	14	14	3.5
1997—Buffalo NFL	15	15	3.5
1998—Buffalo NFL	15	15	4.5
1999—Buffalo NFL	16	16	3.0
Pro totals (6 years)	90	68	16.5

ROGERS, TYRONE   DE   BROWNS

PERSONAL: Born October 11, 1976, in Montgomery, Ala. ... 6-5/240.
HIGH SCHOOL: Robert E. Lee (Montgomery, Ala.).
COLLEGE: Alabama State.
TRANSACTIONS/CAREER NOTES: Signed as non-drafted free agent by Cleveland Browns (April 23, 1999). ... Released by Browns (September 5, 1999). ... Re-signed by Browns to practice squad (September 6, 1999). ... Activated (November 23, 1999).
PLAYING EXPERIENCE: Cleveland NFL, 1999. ... Games/Games started: 1999 (3/0).

ROLLE, SAMARI   CB   TITANS

PERSONAL: Born August 10, 1976, in Miami. ... 6-0/175. ... Name pronounced suh-MARI ROLL.
HIGH SCHOOL: Miami Beach.
COLLEGE: Florida State.
TRANSACTIONS/CAREER NOTES: Selected by Tennessee Oilers in second round (46th pick overall) of 1998 NFL draft. ... Signed by Oilers (July 24, 1998). ... Oilers franchise renamed Tennessee Titans for 1999 season (December 26, 1998).
CHAMPIONSHIP GAME EXPERIENCE: Played in AFC championship game (1999 season). ... Played in Super Bowl XXXIV (1999 season).
PRO STATISTICS: 1999—Returned one punt for 23 yards, fumbled once and recovered one fumble for three yards.

			INTERCEPTIONS				SACKS
Year Team	G	GS	No.	Yds.	Avg.	TD	No.
1998—Tennessee NFL	15	1	0	0	0.0	0	2.0
1999—Tennessee NFL	16	16	4	65	16.3	0	3.0
Pro totals (2 years)	31	17	4	65	16.3	0	5.0

ROMANOWSKI, BILL   LB   BRONCOS

PERSONAL: Born April 2, 1966, in Vernon, Conn. ... 6-4/245. ... Full name: William Thomas Romanowski.
HIGH SCHOOL: Rockville (Vernon, Conn.).
COLLEGE: Boston College (degree in general management, 1988).
TRANSACTIONS/CAREER NOTES: Selected by San Francisco 49ers in third round (80th pick overall) of 1988 NFL draft. ... Signed by 49ers (July 15, 1988). ... Granted free agency (February 1, 1991). ... Re-signed by 49ers (July 17, 1991). ... Granted unconditional free agency

(March 1, 1993). ... Re-signed by 49ers (March 23, 1993). ... Traded by 49ers to Philadelphia Eagles for third-(traded to Los Angeles Rams) and sixth-round (traded to Green Bay) picks in 1994 draft (April 24, 1994). ... Granted unconditional free agency (February 16, 1996). ... Signed by Denver Broncos (February 23, 1996).

CHAMPIONSHIP GAME EXPERIENCE: Played in NFC championship game (1988-1990, 1992 and 1993 seasons). ... Member of Super Bowl championship team (1988, 1989, 1997 and 1998 seasons). ... Played in AFC championship game (1997 and 1998 seasons).

HONORS: Played in Pro Bowl (1996 and 1998 seasons).

PRO STATISTICS: 1988—Recovered one fumble. 1989—Returned one punt for no yards, fumbled once and recovered two fumbles. 1991—Recovered two fumbles. 1992—Recovered one fumble. 1993—Recovered one fumble. 1994—Recovered one fumble. 1995—Recovered one fumble. 1996—Recovered three fumbles. 1998—Recovered three fumbles. 1999—Fumbled once and recovered one fumble.

| | | | | INTERCEPTIONS | | | SACKS |
Year Team	G	GS	No.	Yds.	Avg.	TD	No.
1988—San Francisco NFL	16	8	0	0	0.0	0	0.0
1989—San Francisco NFL	16	4	1	13	13.0	∞1	1.0
1990—San Francisco NFL	16	16	0	0	0.0	0	1.0
1991—San Francisco NFL	16	16	1	7	7.0	0	1.0
1992—San Francisco NFL	16	16	0	0	0.0	0	1.0
1993—San Francisco NFL	16	16	0	0	0.0	0	3.0
1994—Philadelphia NFL	16	15	2	8	4.0	0	2.5
1995—Philadelphia NFL	16	16	2	5	2.5	0	1.0
1996—Denver NFL	16	16	3	1	0.3	0	3.0
1997—Denver NFL	16	16	1	7	7.0	0	2.0
1998—Denver NFL	16	16	2	22	11.0	0	7.5
1999—Denver NFL	16	16	3	35	11.7	1	0.0
Pro totals (12 years)	192	171	15	98	6.5	2	23.0

ROQUE, JUAN   OT   LIONS

PERSONAL: Born February 6, 1974, in San Diego. ... 6-8/332. ... Full name: Juan Armando Roque. ... Name pronounced row-KAY.

HIGH SCHOOL: Ontario (Calif.).

COLLEGE: Arizona State (degree in Latin American history).

TRANSACTIONS/CAREER NOTES: Selected by Detroit Lions in second round (35th pick overall) of 1997 NFL draft. ... Signed by Lions (July 13, 1997). ... On injured reserve with knee injury (December 2, 1997-remainder of season). ... On injured reserve with knee injury (August 31, 1998-entire season). ... Granted free agency (February 11, 2000). ... Re-signed by Lions (April 25, 2000).

PLAYING EXPERIENCE: Detroit NFL, 1997 and 1999. ... Games/Games started: 1997 (13/1), 1999 (4/2). Total: 17/3.

HONORS: Named offensive tackle on THE SPORTING NEWS college All-America second team (1996).

ROSENTHAL, MIKE   G   GIANTS

PERSONAL: Born June 10, 1977, in Pittsburgh. ... 6-7/315. ... Full name: Michael Paul Rosenthal.

HIGH SCHOOL: Penn (Mishawaka, Ind.).

COLLEGE: Notre Dame.

TRANSACTIONS/CAREER NOTES: Selected by New York Giants in fifth round (149th pick overall) of 1999 NFL draft. ... Signed by Giants (July 26, 1999).

PLAYING EXPERIENCE: New York Giants NFL, 1999. ... Games/Games started: 1999 (9/7).

ROSS, ADRIAN   LB   BENGALS

PERSONAL: Born February 19, 1975, in Santa Clara, Calif. ... 6-2/244. ... Full name: Adrian Lamont Ross.

HIGH SCHOOL: Elk Grove (Calif.).

COLLEGE: Colorado State.

TRANSACTIONS/CAREER NOTES: Signed as non-drafted free agent by Cincinnati Bengals (April 21, 1998).

PLAYING EXPERIENCE: Cincinnati NFL, 1998 and 1999. ... Games/Games started: 1998 (14/1), 1999 (16/10). Total: 30/11.

PRO STATISTICS: 1998—Intercepted one pass for 11 yards. 1999—Credited with one sack.

ROSSUM, ALLEN   CB/KR   EAGLES

PERSONAL: Born October 22, 1975, in Dallas. ... 5-8/178.

HIGH SCHOOL: Skyline (Dallas).

COLLEGE: Notre Dame.

TRANSACTIONS/CAREER NOTES: Selected by Philadelphia Eagles in third round (85th pick overall) of 1998 NFL draft. ... Signed by Eagles (July 14, 1998).

PRO STATISTICS: 1998—Credited with one sack and recovered three fumbles. 1999—Recovered two fumbles.

| | | | PUNT RETURNS | | | | KICKOFF RETURNS | | | | TOTALS | | |
Year Team	G	GS	No.	Yds.	Avg.	TD	No.	Yds.	Avg.	TD	TD	2pt.	Pts.	Fum.
1998—Philadelphia NFL	15	2	22	187	8.5	0	44	1080	24.5	0	0	0	0	4
1999—Philadelphia NFL	16	0	28	250	8.9	0	54	1347	24.9	1	1	0	6	6
Pro totals (2 years)	31	2	50	437	8.7	0	98	2427	24.8	1	1	0	6	10

ROUEN, TOM   P   BRONCOS

PERSONAL: Born June 9, 1968, in Hinsdale, Ill. ... 6-3/225. ... Full name: Thomas Francis Rouen Jr. ... Name pronounced RUIN.

HIGH SCHOOL: Heritage (Littleton, Colo.).

COLLEGE: Colorado State, then Colorado.

R

TRANSACTIONS/CAREER NOTES: Signed as non-drafted free agent by New York Giants (April 29, 1991). ... Released by Giants (August 19, 1991). ... Selected by Ohio Glory in fourth round (44th pick overall) of 1992 World League draft. ... Signed by Los Angeles Rams (July 1992). ... Released by Rams (August 24, 1992). ... Signed by Denver Broncos (April 29, 1993). ... Granted unconditional free agency (February 14, 1997). ... Re-signed by Broncos (March 6, 1997). ... Granted unconditional free agency (February 11, 2000). ... Re-signed by Broncos (February 24, 2000).

CHAMPIONSHIP GAME EXPERIENCE: Played in AFC championship game (1997 and 1998 seasons). ... Member of Super Bowl championship team (1997 and 1998 seasons).

HONORS: Named punter on THE SPORTING NEWS college All-America second team (1989).

PRO STATISTICS: 1993—Rushed once for no yards. 1998—Rushed once for no yards, missed one extra-point attempt and fumbled once for minus 15 yards. 1999—Rushed once for no yards and recovered one fumble.

				PUNTING			
Year Team	G	No.	Yds.	Avg.	Net avg.	In. 20	Blk.
1992—Ohio W.L.	10	48	1992	41.5	36.1	14	1
1993—Denver NFL	16	67	3017	45.0	37.1	17	1
1994—Denver NFL	16	76	3258	42.9	*37.1	23	0
1995—Denver NFL	16	52	2192	42.2	37.6	22	1
1996—Denver NFL	16	65	2714	41.8	36.2	16	0
1997—Denver NFL	16	60	2598	43.3	38.1	22	0
1998—Denver NFL	16	66	3097	46.9	37.6	14	1
1999—Denver NFL	16	84	3908	*46.5	35.6	19	0
W.L. totals (1 year)	10	48	1992	41.5	36.1	14	1
NFL totals (7 years)	112	470	20784	44.2	37.0	133	3
Pro totals (8 years)	122	518	22776	44.0	36.9	147	4

ROUNDTREE, RALEIGH   G/OT   CHARGERS

PERSONAL: Born August 31, 1975, in Augusta, Ga. ... 6-4/295. ... Full name: Raleigh Cito Roundtree.
HIGH SCHOOL: Josey (Augusta, Ga.).
COLLEGE: South Carolina State.
TRANSACTIONS/CAREER NOTES: Selected by San Diego Chargers in fourth round (109th pick overall) of 1997 NFL draft. ... Signed by Chargers (July 14, 1997). ... Inactive for all 16 games (1997). ... Granted free agency (February 11, 2000).
PLAYING EXPERIENCE: San Diego NFL, 1998 and 1999. ... Games/Games started: 1998 (15/5), 1999 (15/5). Total: 30/10.
PRO STATISTICS: 1998—Recovered one fumble.

ROYAL, ANDRE   LB

PERSONAL: Born December 1, 1972, in North Port, Ala. ... 6-1/220. ... Full name: Andre Tierre Royal.
HIGH SCHOOL: Tuscaloosa County (North Port, Ala.).
COLLEGE: Alabama.
TRANSACTIONS/CAREER NOTES: Signed as non-drafted free agent by Cleveland Browns (May 2, 1995). ... Released by Browns (August 21, 1995). ... Signed by Carolina Panthers to practice squad (August 30, 1995). ... Activated (September 26, 1995). ... Granted free agency (February 13, 1998). ... Tendered offer sheet by New Orleans Saints (March 19, 1998). ... Panthers declined to match offer (March 25, 1998). ... Traded by Saints to Indianapolis Colts for TE Scott Slutzker (August 30, 1998). ... On injured reserve with knee injury (December 24, 1998-remainder of season). ... Released by Colts (October 11, 1999).
PLAYING EXPERIENCE: Carolina NFL, 1995-1997; Indianapolis NFL, 1998 and 1999. ... Games/Games started: 1995 (12/0), 1996 (16/0), 1997 (16/13), 1998 (13/9), 1999 (3/3). Total: 60/25.
CHAMPIONSHIP GAME EXPERIENCE: Played in NFC championship game (1996 season).
PRO STATISTICS: 1996—Recovered one fumble. 1997—Credited with five sacks and recovered one fumble. 1999—Credited with one sack.

ROYALS, MARK   P   BUCCANEERS

PERSONAL: Born June 22, 1964, in Hampton, Va. ... 6-5/215. ... Full name: Mark Alan Royals.
HIGH SCHOOL: Mathews (Va.).
JUNIOR COLLEGE: Chowan College (N.C.).
COLLEGE: Appalachian State (degree in political science).
TRANSACTIONS/CAREER NOTES: Signed as non-drafted free agent by Dallas Cowboys (June 6, 1986). ... Released by Cowboys (August 8, 1986). ... Signed as replacement player by St. Louis Cardinals (September 30, 1987). ... Released by Cardinals (October 7, 1987). ... Signed as replacement player by Philadelphia Eagles (October 14, 1987). ... Released by Eagles (November 1987). ... Signed by Cardinals (December 12, 1987). ... Released by Cardinals (July 27, 1988). ... Signed by Miami Dolphins (May 2, 1989). ... Released by Dolphins (August 28, 1989). ... Signed by Tampa Bay Buccaneers (April 24, 1990). ... Granted unconditional free agency (February 1, 1992). ... Signed by Pittsburgh Steelers (March 15, 1992). ... Granted unconditional free agency (February 17, 1995). ... Signed by Detroit Lions (April 26, 1995). ... Granted free agency (February 16, 1996). ... Re-signed by Lions (June 19, 1996). ... Granted unconditional free agency (February 14, 1997). ... Signed by New Orleans Saints (April 25, 1997). ... Released by Saints (June 29, 1999). ... Signed by Buccaneers (August 4, 1999). ... Granted unconditional free agency (February 11, 2000). ... Re-signed by Buccaneers (March 24, 2000).
CHAMPIONSHIP GAME EXPERIENCE: Played in AFC championship game (1994 season). ... Played in NFC championship game (1999 season).
PRO STATISTICS: 1987—Had 23.3-yard net punting average. 1992—Completed only pass attempt for 44 yards. 1994—Rushed once for minus 13 yards. 1995—Rushed once for minus seven yards. 1996—Completed only pass attempt for minus eight yards and recovered one fumble. 1999—Attempted two passes with one completion for 17 yards.

				PUNTING			
Year Team	G	No.	Yds.	Avg.	Net avg.	In. 20	Blk.
1987—St. Louis NFL	1	6	222	37.0	.0	2	0
—Philadelphia NFL	1	5	209	41.8	.0	1	0
1988—				Did not play.			
1989—				Did not play.			
1990—Tampa Bay NFL	16	72	2902	40.3	34.0	8	0

1991—Tampa Bay NFL	16	84	3389	40.3	32.2	22	0
1992—Pittsburgh NFL	16	73	3119	42.7	35.6	22	1
1993—Pittsburgh NFL	16	89	3781	42.5	34.2	§28	0
1994—Pittsburgh NFL	16	§97	3849	39.7	35.7	†35	0
1995—Detroit NFL	16	57	2393	42.0	31.0	15	2
1996—Detroit NFL	16	69	3020	43.8	33.3	11	1
1997—New Orleans NFL	16	88	4038	*45.9	34.9	21	0
1998—New Orleans NFL	16	88	4017	‡45.6	36.0	26	0
1999—Tampa Bay NFL	16	90	3882	43.1	37.4	23	0
Pro totals (11 years)	162	818	34821	42.6	34.1	214	4

ROYE, ORPHEUS   DL   BROWNS

R

PERSONAL: Born January 21, 1974, in Miami. ... 6-4/288. ... Full name: Orpheus Michael Roye. ... Name pronounced OR-fee-us ROY.
HIGH SCHOOL: Miami Springs.
JUNIOR COLLEGE: Jones County Junior College (Miss.).
COLLEGE: Florida State.
TRANSACTIONS/CAREER NOTES: Selected by Pittsburgh Steelers in sixth round (200th pick overall) of 1996 NFL draft. ... Signed by Steelers July 16, 1996). ... Granted free agency (February 12, 1999). ... Re-signed by Steelers (April 23, 1999). ... Granted unconditional free agency (February 11, 2000). ... Signed by Cleveland Browns (February 12, 2000).
CHAMPIONSHIP GAME EXPERIENCE: Played in AFC championship game (1997 season).
PRO STATISTICS: 1996—Recovered one fumble. 1998—Returned one kickoff for no yards. 1999—Intercepted one pass for two yards and recovered one fumble.

Year Team	G	GS	SACKS
1996—Pittsburgh NFL	13	1	0.0
1997—Pittsburgh NFL	16	0	1.0
1998—Pittsburgh NFL	16	9	3.5
1999—Pittsburgh NFL	16	16	4.5
Pro totals (4 years)	61	26	9.0

RUBIO, ANGEL   DT   CARDINALS

PERSONAL: Born April 12, 1975, in Los Angeles. ... 6-2/298.
HIGH SCHOOL: Ceres (Calif.).
COLLEGE: Southwest Missouri State.
TRANSACTIONS/CAREER NOTES: Selected by Pittsburgh Steelers in seventh round (221st pick overall) of 1998 NFL draft. ... Signed by Steelers (May 20, 1998). ... Traded by Steelers to San Francisco 49ers for past considerations (August 24, 1998). ... Claimed on waivers by Cincinnati Bengals (September 23, 1998). ... Released by Bengals (September 30, 1998). ... Signed by 49ers to practice squad (October 1, 1998). ... Claimed on waivers by Arizona Cardinals (September 6, 1999).
PLAYING EXPERIENCE: Arizona NFL, 1999. ... Games/Games started: 1999 (2/0).

RUCCI, TODD   G   PATRIOTS

PERSONAL: Born July 14, 1970, in Upper Darby, Pa. ... 6-5/296. ... Full name: Todd L. Rucci. ... Name pronounced ROOCH-ee.
HIGH SCHOOL: Upper Darby (Drexel Hill, Pa.).
COLLEGE: Penn State.
TRANSACTIONS/CAREER NOTES: Selected by New England Patriots in second round (51st pick overall) of 1993 NFL draft. ... Signed by Patriots (July 22, 1993). ... On injured reserve with pectoral muscle injury (September 19, 1993-remainder of season). ... Granted unconditional free agency (February 13, 1998). ... Re-signed by Patriots (February 24, 1998).
PLAYING EXPERIENCE: New England NFL, 1993-1999. ... Games/Games started: 1993 (2/1), 1994 (13/10), 1995 (6/5), 1996 (16/12), 1997 (16/16), 1998 (16/16), 1999 (16/15). Total: 85/75.
CHAMPIONSHIP GAME EXPERIENCE: Played in AFC championship game (1996 season). ... Played in Super Bowl XXXI (1996 season).

RUCKER, MICHAEL   DE   PANTHERS

PERSONAL: Born February 28, 1975, in St. Joseph, Mo. ... 6-5/258. ... Full name: Michael Dean Rucker.
HIGH SCHOOL: Benton (St. Joseph, Mo.).
COLLEGE: Nebraska (degree in sociology).
TRANSACTIONS/CAREER NOTES: Selected by Carolina Panthers in second round (38th pick overall) of 1999 NFL draft. ... Signed by Panthers July 13, 1999).

Year Team	G	GS	SACKS
1999—Carolina NFL	16	0	3.0

RUDD, DWAYNE   LB   VIKINGS

PERSONAL: Born February 3, 1976, in Batesville, Miss. ... 6-2/233. ... Full name: Dwayne Dupree Rudd.
HIGH SCHOOL: South Panola (Batesville, Miss.).
COLLEGE: Alabama.
TRANSACTIONS/CAREER NOTES: Selected by Minnesota Vikings in first round (20th pick overall) of 1997 NFL draft. ... Signed by Vikings July 18, 1997).
CHAMPIONSHIP GAME EXPERIENCE: Played in NFC championship game (1998 season).
RECORDS: Shares NFL single-season records for most touchdowns by fumble recovery—2 (1998); most touchdowns by recovery of opponents' fumbles—2 (1998).

PRO STATISTICS: 1998—Recovered three fumbles for 157 yards and two touchdowns. 1999—Recovered one fumble.

Year Team	G	GS	SACKS
1997—Minnesota NFL	16	2	5.0
1998—Minnesota NFL	15	15	2.0
1999—Minnesota NFL	16	16	3.0
Pro totals (3 years)	47	33	10.0

RUDDY, TIM   C   DOLPHINS

PERSONAL: Born April 27, 1972, in Scranton, Pa. ... 6-3/300. ... Full name: Timothy Daniel Ruddy.
HIGH SCHOOL: Dunmore (Pa.).
COLLEGE: Notre Dame (degree in mechanical engineering).
TRANSACTIONS/CAREER NOTES: Selected by Miami Dolphins in second round (65th pick overall) of 1994 NFL draft. ... Signed by Dolphins (July 18, 1994). ... Granted unconditional free agency (February 11, 2000). ... Re-signed by Dolphins (February 24, 2000).
PLAYING EXPERIENCE: Miami NFL, 1994-1999. ... Games/Games started: 1994 (16/0), 1995 (16/16), 1996 (16/16), 1997 (15/15), 1998 (16/16), 1999 (16/16). Total: 95/79.
PRO STATISTICS: 1995—Fumbled once. 1996—Fumbled once for minus 14 yards. 1998—Fumbled once for minus three yards.

RUFF, ORLANDO   LB   CHARGERS

PERSONAL: Born September 28, 1976, in Charleston, S.C. ... 6-3/247. ... Full name: Orlando Bernarda Ruff.
HIGH SCHOOL: Fairfield Central (Winnsboro, S.C.).
COLLEGE: Furman.
TRANSACTIONS/CAREER NOTES: Signed as non-drafted free agent by San Diego Chargers (April 20, 1999).
PLAYING EXPERIENCE: San Diego NFL, 1999. ... Games/Games started: 1999 (14/0).

RUHMAN, CHRIS   OT   BROWNS

PERSONAL: Born December 19, 1974, in Houston. ... 6-5/321. ... Full name: Christopher Aamon Ruhman.
HIGH SCHOOL: Nimitz (Irving, Texas).
COLLEGE: Texas A&M.
TRANSACTIONS/CAREER NOTES: Selected by San Francisco 49ers in third round (89th pick overall) of 1998 NFL draft. ... Signed by 49ers (July 18, 1998). ... Released by 49ers (September 5, 1999). ... Signed by Cleveland Browns (September 20, 1999).
PLAYING EXPERIENCE: San Francisco NFL, 1998; Cleveland NFL, 1999. ... Games/Games started: 1998 (6/0), 1999 (5/2). Total: 11/2.
PRO STATISTICS: 1998—Recovered one fumble.

RUNYAN, JON   OT   EAGLES

PERSONAL: Born November 27, 1973, in Flint, Mich. ... 6-7/330. ... Full name: Jon Daniel Runyan.
HIGH SCHOOL: Carman-Ainsworth (Flint, Mich.).
COLLEGE: Michigan.
TRANSACTIONS/CAREER NOTES: Selected after junior season by Houston Oilers in fourth round (109th pick overall) of 1996 NFL draft. ... Signed by Oilers (July 20, 1996). ... Oilers franchise moved to Tennessee for 1997 season. ... Oilers franchise renamed Tennessee Titans for 1999 season (December 26, 1998). ... Granted free agency (February 12, 1999). ... Re-signed by Titans (June 23, 1999). ... Granted unconditional free agency (February 11, 2000). ... Signed by Philadelphia Eagles (February 14, 2000).
PLAYING EXPERIENCE: Houston NFL, 1996; Tennessee NFL, 1997-1999. ... Games/Games started: 1996 (10/0), 1997 (16/16), 1998 (16/16), 1999 (16/16). Total: 58/48.
CHAMPIONSHIP GAME EXPERIENCE: Played in AFC championship game (1999 season). ... Played in Super Bowl XXXIV (1999 season).
HONORS: Named offensive lineman on THE SPORTING NEWS college All-America second team (1995).

RUSK, REGGIE   S   CHARGERS

PERSONAL: Born December 19, 1972, in Texas City, Texas. ... 5-10/190. ... Full name: Reggie Leon Rusk.
HIGH SCHOOL: Texas City (Texas).
JUNIOR COLLEGE: City College of San Francisco.
COLLEGE: Kentucky.
TRANSACTIONS/CAREER NOTES: Selected by Tampa Bay Buccaneers in seventh round (221st pick overall) of 1996 NFL draft. ... Signed by Buccaneers (July 12, 1996). ... Released by Buccaneers (August 18, 1996). ... Re-signed by Buccaneers to practice squad (August 27, 1996). ... Activated (September 28, 1996). ... Released by Buccaneers (October 2, 1996). ... Re-signed by Buccaneers to practice squad (October 3, 1996). ... Assigned by Buccaneers to Scottish Claymores in 1997 World League enhancement allocation program (February 19, 1997). ... Released by Buccaneers (September 27, 1997). ... Re-signed by Buccaneers to practice squad (September 29, 1997). ... Signed by Seattle Seahawks off Buccaneers practice squad (December 5, 1997). ... Released by Seahawks (September 9, 1998). ... Signed by San Diego Chargers (December 22, 1998). ... Inactive for two games (1998). ... Released by Chargers (September 4, 1999). ... Re-signed by Chargers (November 3, 1999).
PLAYING EXPERIENCE: Tampa Bay NFL, 1996; Tampa Bay (4)-Seattle (2) NFL, 1997; San Diego NFL, 1999. ... Games/Games started: 1996 (1/0), 1997 (T.B.-4/0; Sea.-2/0; Total: 6/0), 1999 (9/0). Total: 16/0.

RUSS, BERNARD   LB   COWBOYS

PERSONAL: Born November 4, 1973, in Utica, N.Y. ... 6-1/238. ... Full name: Bernard Dion Russ.
HIGH SCHOOL: Collinwood (Cleveland).

JUNIOR COLLEGE: Arizona Western College.
COLLEGE: West Virginia.
TRANSACTIONS/CAREER NOTES: Signed as non-drafted free agent by Baltimore Ravens (April 25, 1997). ... Released by Ravens (August 24, 1997). ... Signed by New England Patriots to practice squad (August 27, 1997). ... Activated (December 9, 1997). ... On injured reserve with jaw injury (October 20, 1998-remainder of season). ... Assigned by Patriots to Scottish Claymores in 1999 NFL Europe enhancement allocation program (February 22, 1999). ... Released by Patriots (December 6, 1999). ... Signed by Dallas Cowboys (March 7, 2000).
PLAYING EXPERIENCE: New England NFL, 1997-1999; Scottish Claymores NFLE, 1999. ... Games/Games started: 1997 (2/0), 1998 (1/0), NFLE 1999 (games played unavailable), NFL 1999 (6/0). Total NFL: 9/0.

RUSS, STEVE — LB — BRONCOS

PERSONAL: Born September 16, 1972, in Stetsonville, Wis. ... 6-4/245.
HIGH SCHOOL: Stetsonville (Wis.).
COLLEGE: Air Force (degree in management).
TRANSACTIONS/CAREER NOTES: Selected by Denver Broncos in seventh round (218th pick overall) of 1995 NFL draft. ... Signed by Broncos for 1995 season. ... On reserved/military list entire 1995 season. ... On reserved/military list (August 13, 1996-entire season). ... On injured reserve with broken leg (August 11, 1998-entire season). ... Released by Broncos (September 5, 1999). ... Re-signed by Broncos (November , 1999).
PLAYING EXPERIENCE: Denver NFL, 1997 and 1999. ... Games/Games started: 1997 (14/0), 1999 (8/0). Total: 22/0.
CHAMPIONSHIP GAME EXPERIENCE: Member of Broncos for AFC championship game (1997 season); inactive. ... Member of Super Bowl championship team (1997 season); inactive.

RUSSELL, DARRELL — DT — RAIDERS

PERSONAL: Born May 27, 1976, in Pensacola, Fla. ... 6-5/325.
HIGH SCHOOL: St. Augustine (San Diego).
COLLEGE: Southern California.
TRANSACTIONS/CAREER NOTES: Selected by Oakland Raiders in first round (second pick overall) of 1997 NFL draft. ... Signed by Raiders July 23, 1997).
HONORS: Played in Pro Bowl (1998 and 1999 seasons). ... Named defensive tackle on THE SPORTING NEWS NFL All-Pro team (1999).
PRO STATISTICS: 1998—Recovered one fumble. 1999—Recovered one fumble.

Year Team	G	GS	SACKS
1997—Oakland NFL	16	10	3.5
1998—Oakland NFL	16	16	10.0
1999—Oakland NFL	16	16	9.5
Pro totals (3 years)	48	42	23.0

RUSSELL, TWAN — LB — DOLPHINS

PERSONAL: Born April 25, 1974, in Fort Lauderdale, Fla. ... 6-1/220. ... Full name: Twan Sanchez Russell.
HIGH SCHOOL: St. Thomas Aquinas (Fort Lauderdale, Fla.).
COLLEGE: Miami, Fla. (degree in broadcasting, 1996).
TRANSACTIONS/CAREER NOTES: Selected by Washington Redskins in fifth round (148th pick overall) of 1997 NFL draft. ... Signed by Redskins (May 9, 1997). ... On injured reserve with foot and knee injuries (September 23, 1998-remainder of season). ... On injured reserve with knee injury (November 16, 1999-remainder of season). ... Granted free agency (February 11, 2000). ... Signed by Miami Dolphins (March 3, 2000).
PLAYING EXPERIENCE: Washington NFL, 1997-1999. ... Games/Games started: 1997 (14/0), 1998 (3/0), 1999 (9/0). Total: 26/0.

RUTLEDGE, JOHNNY — LB — CARDINALS

PERSONAL: Born January 4, 1977, in Belle Glade, Fla. ... 6-3/242. ... Full name: Johnny Boykins Rutledge III.
HIGH SCHOOL: Glades Central (Belle Glade, Fla.).
COLLEGE: Florida.
TRANSACTIONS/CAREER NOTES: Selected by Arizona Cardinals in second round (51st pick overall) of 1999 NFL draft. ... Signed by Cardinals July 29, 1999).
PLAYING EXPERIENCE: Arizona NFL, 1999. ... Games/Games started: 1999 (6/0).

RUTLEDGE, ROD — TE — PATRIOTS

PERSONAL: Born August 12, 1975, in Birmingham, Ala. ... 6-5/262. ... Full name: Rodrick Almar Rutledge.
HIGH SCHOOL: Erwin (Birmingham, Ala.).
COLLEGE: Alabama.
TRANSACTIONS/CAREER NOTES: Selected by New England Patriots in second round (54th pick overall) of 1998 NFL draft. ... Signed by Patriots (June 15, 1998).
PLAYING EXPERIENCE: New England NFL, 1998 and 1999. ... Games/Games started: 1998 (16/4), 1999 (16/2). Total: 32/6.
PRO STATISTICS: 1999—Caught seven passes for 66 yards and fumbled once.
SINGLE GAME HIGHS (regular season): Receptions—1 (December 19, 1999, vs. Philadelphia); yards—13 (November 15, 1999, vs. New York Jets); and touchdown receptions—0.

R

SALAAM, EPHRAIM   OT   FALCONS

PERSONAL: Born June 19, 1976, in Chicago. ... 6-7/305. ... Full name: Ephraim Mateen Salaam. ... Name pronounced EFF-rum sah-LAHM.
HIGH SCHOOL: Florin (Sacramento).
COLLEGE: San Diego State.
TRANSACTIONS/CAREER NOTES: Selected by Atlanta Falcons in seventh round (199th pick overall) of 1998 NFL draft. ... Signed by Falcons (June 3, 1998).
PLAYING EXPERIENCE: Atlanta NFL, 1998 and 1999. ... Games/Games started: 1998 (16/16), 1999 (16/16). Total: 32/32.
CHAMPIONSHIP GAME EXPERIENCE: Played in NFC championship game (1998 season). ... Played in Super Bowl XXXIII (1998 season).

SALAAM, RASHAAN   RB

PERSONAL: Born October 8, 1974, in San Diego. ... 6-1/224. ... Full name: Rashaan Iman Salaam. ... Son of Sulton Salaam (formerly known as Teddy Washington), running back with Cincinnati Bengals of AFL (1968). ... Name pronounced raw-SHAWN saw-LAWM.
HIGH SCHOOL: La Jolla (Calif.) Country Day.
COLLEGE: Colorado.
TRANSACTIONS/CAREER NOTES: Selected after junior season by Chicago Bears in first round (21st pick overall) of 1995 NFL draft. ... Signed by Bears (August 3, 1995). ... On injured reserve with leg injury (September 23, 1997-remainder of season). ... Traded by Bears to Miami Dolphins for conditional pick in 1999 draft (April 22, 1998); trade later voided because Salaam failed physical (April 24, 1998). ... Released by Bears (August 12, 1998). ... Signed by Oakland Raiders (June 2, 1999). ... Released by Raiders (September 4, 1999). ... Signed by Cleveland Browns (September 28, 1999). ... Released by Browns (October 19, 1999). ... Signed by Green Bay Packers (December 29, 1999). ... Inactive for one game with Packers (1999). ... Granted free agency (February 11, 2000).
HONORS: Heisman Trophy winner (1994). ... Named College Football Player of the Year by THE SPORTING NEWS (1994). ... Doak Walker Award winner (1994). ... Named running back on THE SPORTING NEWS college All-America first team (1994).
PRO STATISTICS: 1995—Recovered one fumble. 1996—Recovered one fumble.
SINGLE GAME HIGHS (regular season): Attempts—30 (December 24, 1995, vs. Philadelphia); yards—134 (December 17, 1995, vs. Tampa Bay); and rushing touchdowns—3 (December 17, 1995, vs. Tampa Bay).
STATISTICAL PLATEAUS: 100-yard rushing games: 1995 (5), 1996 (1). Total: 6.

			RUSHING				RECEIVING				TOTALS			
Year Team	G	GS	Att.	Yds.	Avg.	TD	No.	Yds.	Avg.	TD	TD	2pt.	Pts.	Fum.
1995—Chicago NFL	16	12	296	1074	3.6	10	7	56	8.0	0	10	0	60	9
1996—Chicago NFL	12	6	143	496	3.5	3	7	44	6.3	1	4	0	24	3
1997—Chicago NFL	3	3	31	112	3.6	0	2	20	10.0	0	0	0	0	2
1998—						Did not play.								
1999—Cleveland NFL	2	0	1	2	2.0	0	0	0	0.0	0	0	0	0	0
Pro totals (4 years)	33	21	471	1684	3.6	13	16	120	7.5	1	14	0	84	14

SALAVE'A, JOE   DT   TITANS

PERSONAL: Born March 23, 1975, in Leone, American Samoa. ... 6-3/290. ... Full name: Joe Fagaone Salave'a. ... Name pronounced sala-VAY-uh.
HIGH SCHOOL: Oceanside (Calif.).
COLLEGE: Arizona (degree in sociology, 1997).
TRANSACTIONS/CAREER NOTES: Selected by Tennessee Oilers in fourth round (107th pick overall) of 1998 NFL draft. ... Signed by Oilers (June 30, 1998). ... Oilers franchise renamed Tennessee Titans for 1999 season (December 26, 1998).
PLAYING EXPERIENCE: Tennessee NFL, 1998 and 1999. ... Games/Games started: 1998 (13/0), 1999 (10/0). Total: 23/0.
CHAMPIONSHIP GAME EXPERIENCE: Played in AFC championship game (1999 season). ... Played in Super Bowl XXXIV (1999 season).
HONORS: Named defensive tackle on THE SPORTING NEWS college All-America third team (1997).
PRO STATISTICS: 1998—Credited with one sack.

SALEH, TAREK   FB/LB   BROWNS

PERSONAL: Born November 7, 1974, in Woodbridge, Conn. ... 6-0/240. ... Full name: Tarek Muhammad Saleh. ... Name pronounced TAR-ick sa-LAY.
HIGH SCHOOL: Notre Dame (West Haven, Conn.).
COLLEGE: Wisconsin.
TRANSACTIONS/CAREER NOTES: Selected by Carolina Panthers in fourth round (122nd pick overall) of 1997 NFL draft. ... Signed by Panthers for 1997 season. ... Selected by Cleveland Browns from Panthers in NFL expansion draft (February 9, 1999). ... Granted free agency (February 11, 2000). ... Re-signed by Browns (April 12, 2000)
PLAYING EXPERIENCE: Carolina NFL, 1997 and 1998; Cleveland NFL, 1999. ... Games/Games started: 1997 (3/0), 1998 (11/1), 1999 (16/0). Total: 30/1.
PRO STATISTICS: 1997—Credited with one sack. 1998—Returned one kickoff for eight yards. 1999—Returned five kickoffs for 43 yards and recovered one fumble.

SAMUEL, KHARI   LB   BEARS

PERSONAL: Born October 14, 1976, in New York. ... 6-3/242. ... Full name: Khari Iman Mitchell Samuel. ... Name pronounced CAR-ee.
HIGH SCHOOL: Framingham (Mass.).
COLLEGE: Massachusetts.
TRANSACTIONS/CAREER NOTES: Selected by Chicago Bears in fifth round (144th pick overall) of 1999 NFL draft. ... Signed by Bears (May 26, 1999).
PLAYING EXPERIENCE: Chicago NFL, 1999. ... Games/Games started: 1999 (13/1).
PRO STATISTICS: 1999—Recovered one fumble.

SANDERS, BRANDON — DB

PERSONAL: Born June 10, 1973, in San Diego. ... 5-9/185. ... Full name: Brandon Christopher Sanders.
HIGH SCHOOL: Helix (La Mesa, Calif.).
COLLEGE: Arizona.
TRANSACTIONS/CAREER NOTES: Signed as non-drafted free agent by Kansas City Chiefs (April 27, 1996). ... Released by Chiefs (August 20, 1996). ... Signed by New York Giants (March 10, 1997). ... Selected by Cleveland Browns from Giants in NFL expansion draft (February 9, 1999). ... Released by Browns (August 25, 1999). ... Signed by Giants (August 31, 1999). ... Released by Giants (September 1, 1999). ... Re-signed by Giants (October 26, 1999). ... Released by Giants (February 10, 2000).
PLAYING EXPERIENCE: New York Giants NFL, 1997-1999. ... Games/Games started: 1997 (12/0), 1998 (13/0), 1999 (9/2). Total: 34/2.

SANDERS, CHRIS — WR — TITANS

PERSONAL: Born May 8, 1972, in Denver. ... 6-1/188. ... Full name: Christopher Dwayne Sanders.
HIGH SCHOOL: Montbello (Denver).
COLLEGE: Ohio State.
TRANSACTIONS/CAREER NOTES: Selected by Houston Oilers in third round (67th pick overall) of 1995 NFL draft. ... Signed by Oilers (July 20, 1995). ... Oilers franchise moved to Tennessee for 1997 season. ... Oilers franchise renamed Tennessee Titans for 1999 season (December 26, 1998).
CHAMPIONSHIP GAME EXPERIENCE: Played in AFC championship game (1999 season). ... Played in Super Bowl XXXIV (1999 season).
PRO STATISTICS: 1995—Rushed twice for minus 19 yards. 1997—Rushed once for minus eight yards. 1998—Rushed once for minus nine yards.
SINGLE GAME HIGHS (regular season): Receptions—7 (December 14, 1997, vs. Baltimore); yards—147 (November 26, 1995, vs. Denver); and touchdown receptions—2 (October 26, 1997, vs. Arizona).
STATISTICAL PLATEAUS: 100-yard receiving games: 1995 (1), 1996 (3), 1997 (1), 1998 (1), 1999 (1). Total: 7.

			RECEIVING				TOTALS			
Year Team	G	GS	No.	Yds.	Avg.	TD	TD	2pt.	Pts.	Fum.
1995—Houston NFL	16	10	35	823	*23.5	9	9	0	54	0
1996—Houston NFL	16	15	48	882	§18.4	4	4	0	24	0
1997—Tennessee NFL	15	14	31	498	16.1	3	3	0	18	1
1998—Tennessee NFL	14	1	5	136	27.2	0	0	0	0	1
1999—Tennessee NFL	16	0	20	336	16.8	1	1	0	6	0
Pro totals (5 years)	77	40	139	2675	19.2	17	17	0	102	2

SANDERS, DEION — CB — REDSKINS

PERSONAL: Born August 9, 1967, in Fort Myers, Fla. ... 6-1/198. ... Full name: Deion Luwynn Sanders. ... Nickname: Prime Time.
HIGH SCHOOL: North Fort Myers (Fla.).
COLLEGE: Florida State.
TRANSACTIONS/CAREER NOTES: Selected by Atlanta Falcons in first round (fifth pick overall) of 1989 NFL draft. ... Signed by Falcons (September 7, 1989). ... On reserve/did not report list (July 27-August 13, 1990). ... Granted roster exemption for one game (September 1992). ... On reserve/did not report list (July 23-October 14, 1993). ... Designated by Falcons as transition player (February 15, 1994). ... Free agency status changed by Falcons from transitional to unconditional (April 28, 1994). ... Signed by San Francisco 49ers (September 15, 1994). ... Granted unconditional free agency (February 17, 1995). ... Signed by Dallas Cowboys (September 9, 1995). ... On reserve/did not report list (July 16-August 29, 1997). ... Released by Cowboys (June 2, 2000). ... Signed by Washington Redskins (June 5, 2000).
CHAMPIONSHIP GAME EXPERIENCE: Played in NFC championship game (1994 and 1995 seasons). ... Member of Super Bowl championship team (1994 and 1995 seasons).
HONORS: Named defensive back on THE SPORTING NEWS college All-America first team (1986-1988). ... Jim Thorpe Award winner (1988). ... Named cornerback on THE SPORTING NEWS NFL All-Pro team (1991-1999). ... Played in Pro Bowl (1991-1994 and 1998 seasons). ... Named kick returner on THE SPORTING NEWS NFL All-Pro team (1992). ... Named to play in Pro Bowl (1996 season); replaced by Darrell Green due to injury. ... Named to play in Pro Bowl (1997 season); replaced by Cris Dishman due to injury. ... Named to play in Pro Bowl (1999 season); replaced by Troy Vincent due to injury.
PRO STATISTICS: 1989—Fumbled twice and recovered one fumble. 1990—Fumbled four times and recovered two fumbles. 1991—Credited with a sack, fumbled once and recovered one fumble. 1992—Rushed once for minus four yards, fumbled three times and recovered two fumbles. 1993—Attempted one pass without a completion. 1994—Recovered one fumble. 1995—Rushed twice for nine yards. 1996—Rushed three times for two yards, fumbled twice and recovered three fumbles for 15 yards and one touchdown. 1997—Rushed once for minus 11 yards and fumbled once. 1998—Fumbled once and recovered one fumble. 1999—Attempted one pass without a completion and fumbled once.
MISCELLANEOUS: Only person in history to play in both the World Series (1992) and Super Bowl (1994 and 1995 seasons).

			INTERCEPTIONS				RECEIVING				PUNT RETURNS				KICKOFF RETURNS				TOTALS		
Year Team	G	GS	No.	Yds.	Avg.	TD	No.	Yds.	Avg.	TD	No.	Yds.	Avg.	TD	No.	Yds.	Avg.	TD	TD	2pt.	Pts.
1989—Atlanta NFL	15	10	5	52	10.4	0	1	-8	-8.0	0	28	307	11.0	†1	35	725	20.7	0	1	0	6
1990—Atlanta NFL	16	16	3	153	*51.0	2	0	0	0.0	0	29	250	8.6	†1	39	851	21.8	0	3	0	18
1991—Atlanta NFL	15	15	∞6	119	19.8	∞1	1	17	17.0	0	21	170	8.1	0	26	576	22.2	†1	2	0	12
1992—Atlanta NFL	13	12	3	105	‡35.0	0	3	45	15.0	1	13	41	3.2	0	40	*1067	‡26.7	*2	3	0	18
1993—Atlanta NFL	11	10	‡7	91	13.0	0	6	106	17.7	1	2	21	10.5	0	7	169	24.1	0	1	0	6
1994—San Fran. NFL	14	12	6	*303	*50.5	†3	0	0	0.0	0	0	0	0.0	0	0	0	0.0	0	3	0	18
1995—Dallas NFL	9	9	2	34	17.0	0	2	25	12.5	0	1	54	54.0	0	1	15	15.0	0	0	0	0
1996—Dallas NFL	16	15	2	3	1.5	0	36	475	13.2	1	1	4	4.0	0	0	0	0.0	0	2	0	12
1997—Dallas NFL	13	12	2	81	40.5	1	0	0	0.0	0	33	407	12.3	∞1	1	18	18.0	0	2	0	12
1998—Dallas NFL	11	11	5	153	30.6	1	7	100	14.3	0	24	375	*15.6	†2	1	16	16.0	0	3	0	18
1999—Dallas NFL	14	14	3	2	0.7	0	4	24	6.0	0	30	344	11.5	∞1	4	87	21.8	0	1	0	6
Pro totals (11 years)	147	136	44	1096	24.9	8	60	784	13.1	3	182	1973	10.8	6	154	3524	22.9	3	21	0	126

RECORD AS BASEBALL PLAYER

TRANSACTIONS/CAREER NOTES: Selected by Kansas City Royals organization in sixth round of free-agent draft (June 3, 1985); did not sign. ... Selected by New York Yankees organization in 30th round of free-agent draft (June 1, 1988). ... On disqualified list (August 1-September

24, 1990). ... Released by Yankees organization (September 24, 1990). ... Signed by Atlanta Braves (January 29, 1991). ... Placed on Richmond temporarily inactive list (August 1, 1991). ... On disqualified list (April 29-May 21, 1993). ... On disabled list (August 22-September 6, 1993). ... Traded by Braves to Cincinnati Reds for OF Roberto Kelly and P Roger Etheridge (May 29, 1994). ... On Cincinnati disabled list (June 1-July 16, 1995); included rehabilitation assignment to Chattanooga (July 12-14). ... Traded by Reds with P John Roper, P Ricky Pickett, P Scott Service and IF Dave McCarty to San Francisco Giants for OF Darren Lewis, P Mark Portugal and P Dave Burba (July 21, 1995). ... Granted free agency (December 21, 1995). ... Did not play baseball during 1996 season. ... Granted free agency (November 5, 1996). ... Re-signed by Reds (February 17, 1997). ... Granted free agency after 1997 season. ... Re-signed by Reds organization (January 8, 1998). ... Did not play baseball during 1998 season.

STATISTICAL NOTES: Led N.L. in caught stealing with 16 in 1994.

								BATTING							FIELDING		
Year Team (League)	Pos.	G	AB	R	H	2B	3B	HR	RBI	Avg.	BB	SO	SB	PO	A	E	Avg.
1988—GC Yankees (GCL)	OF	17	75	7	21	4	2	0	6	.280	2	10	11	33	1	2	.944
—Fort Lauderdale (FSL)	OF	6	21	5	9	2	0	0	2	.429	1	3	2	22	2	0	1.000
—Columbus (Int'l)	OF	5	20	3	3	1	0	0	0	.150	1	4	1	13	0	0	1.000
1989—Alb./Colon. (Eastern)	OF	33	119	28	34	2	2	1	6	.286	11	20	17	79	3	0	1.000
—New York (A.L.)	OF	14	47	7	11	2	0	2	7	.234	3	8	1	30	1	1	.969
—Columbus (Int'l)	OF	70	259	38	72	12	7	5	30	.278	22	46	16	165	0	4	.976
1990—New York (A.L.)	OF-DH	57	133	24	21	2	2	3	9	.158	13	27	8	69	2	2	.973
—Columbus (Int'l)	OF	22	84	21	27	7	1	2	10	.321	17	15	9	49	1	0	1.000
1991—Atlanta (N.L.)■	OF	54	110	16	21	1	2	4	13	.191	12	23	11	57	3	3	.952
—Richmond (Int'l)	OF	29	130	20	34	6	3	5	16	.262	10	28	12	73	1	1	.987
1992—Atlanta (N.L.)	OF	97	303	54	92	6	*14	8	28	.304	18	52	26	174	4	3	.983
1993—Atlanta (N.L.)	OF	95	272	42	75	18	6	6	28	.276	16	42	19	137	1	2	.986
1994—Atlanta (N.L.)	OF	46	191	32	55	10	0	4	21	.288	16	28	19	99	0	2	.980
—Cincinnati (N.L.)■	OF	46	184	26	51	7	4	0	7	.277	16	35	19	110	2	0	1.000
1995—Cincinnati (N.L.)	OF	33	129	19	31	2	3	1	10	.240	9	18	16	88	2	3	.968
—Chattanooga (Sou.)	OF	2	7	1	4	0	0	1	2	.571	0	1	1	3	1	0	1.000
—San Fran. (N.L.)■	OF	52	214	29	61	9	5	5	18	.285	18	42	8	127	0	2	.984
1996—								Did not play.									
1997—Cincinnati (N.L.)■	OF	115	465	53	127	13	7	5	23	.273	34	67	56	236	3	4	.984
1998—Cincinnati (N.L.)								Did not play.									
American League totals (2 years)		71	180	31	32	4	2	5	16	.178	16	35	9	99	3	3	.971
National League totals (6 years)		538	1868	271	513	66	41	33	148	.275	139	307	174	1028	15	19	.982
Major league totals (8 years)		609	2048	302	545	70	43	38	164	.266	155	342	183	1127	18	22	.981

CHAMPIONSHIP SERIES RECORD

								BATTING							FIELDING		
Year Team (League)	Pos.	G	AB	R	H	2B	3B	HR	RBI	Avg.	BB	SO	SB	PO	A	E	Avg.
1992—Atlanta (N.L.)	OF-PH	4	5	0	0	0	0	0	0	.000	0	3	0	1	0	0	1.000
1993—Atlanta (N.L.)	PH-OF-PR	5	3	0	0	0	0	0	0	.000	0	1	0	0	0	0	...
Championship series totals (2 years)		9	8	0	0	0	0	0	0	.000	0	4	0	1	0	0	1.000

WORLD SERIES RECORD

								BATTING							FIELDING		
Year Team (League)	Pos.	G	AB	R	H	2B	3B	HR	RBI	Avg.	BB	SO	SB	PO	A	E	Avg.
1992—Atlanta (N.L.)	OF	4	15	4	8	2	0	0	1	.533	2	1	5	5	1	0	1.000

SANDERS, FRANK   WR   CARDINALS

PERSONAL: Born February 17, 1973, in Fort Lauderdale, Fla.. ... 6-2/204. ... Full name: Frank Vondel Sanders.
HIGH SCHOOL: Dillard (Fort Lauderdale, Fla.).
COLLEGE: Auburn.
TRANSACTIONS/CAREER NOTES: Selected by Arizona Cardinals in second round (47th pick overall) of 1995 NFL draft. ... Signed by Cardinals (July 17, 1995). ... Granted free agency (February 13, 1998). ... Re-signed by Cardinals (March 13, 1998).
HONORS: Named wide receiver on THE SPORTING NEWS college All-America second team (1994).
PRO STATISTICS: 1995—Rushed once for one yard. 1996—Rushed twice for minus four yards and recovered one fumble. 1997—Attempted one pass with a completion for 26 yards and rushed once for five yards. 1998—Rushed four times for no yards and recovered two fumbles. 1999—Attempted one pass without a completion and recovered one fumble.
SINGLE GAME HIGHS (regular season): Receptions—13 (January 2, 2000, vs. Green Bay); yards—190 (November 15, 1998, vs. Dallas); touchdown receptions—2 (October 8, 1995, vs. New York Giants).
STATISTICAL PLATEAUS: 100-yard receiving games: 1995 (2), 1997 (2), 1998 (5), 1999 (2). Total: 11.

			RECEIVING				TOTALS			
Year Team	G	GS	No.	Yds.	Avg.	TD	TD	2pt.	Pts.	Fum.
1995—Arizona NFL	16	15	52	883	17.0	2	2	2	16	0
1996—Arizona NFL	16	16	69	813	11.8	4	4	0	24	1
1997—Arizona NFL	16	16	75	1017	13.6	4	4	1	26	3
1998—Arizona NFL	16	16	‡89	1145	12.9	3	3	0	18	3
1999—Arizona NFL	16	16	79	954	12.1	1	1	0	6	2
Pro totals (5 years)	80	79	364	4812	13.2	14	14	3	90	9

SANDERSON, SCOTT   G/OT   TITANS

PERSONAL: Born July 25, 1974, in Walnut Creek, Calif. ... 6-6/295. ... Full name: Scott Michael Sanderson.
HIGH SCHOOL: Clayton Valley (Concord, Calif.).
COLLEGE: Washington State.

TRANSACTIONS/CAREER NOTES: Selected by Houston Oilers in third round (81st pick overall) of 1997 NFL draft. ... Oilers franchise moved to Tennessee for 1997 season. ... Signed by Oilers (July 17, 1997). ... Oilers franchise renamed Tennessee Titans for 1999 season (December 26, 1998). ... On injured reserve with back injury (October 9, 1999-remainder of season). ... Granted free agency (February 11, 2000). ... Re-signed by Titans (March 24, 2000).
PLAYING EXPERIENCE: Tennessee NFL, 1997-1999. ... Games/Games started: 1997 (10/0), 1998 (15/3), 1999 (3/3). Total: 28/6.
HONORS: Named offensive tackle on The Sporting News college All-America first team (1996).

SANTIAGO, O.J. — TE — FALCONS

PERSONAL: Born April 4, 1974, in Whitby, Ont. ... 6-7/265. ... Full name: Otis Jason Santiago.
HIGH SCHOOL: St. Michael's (Toronto).
COLLEGE: Kent.
TRANSACTIONS/CAREER NOTES: Selected by Atlanta Falcons in third round (70th pick overall) of 1997 NFL draft. ... Signed by Falcons (July 11, 1997). ... On injured reserved with leg injury (November 20, 1997-remainder of season). ... Granted free agency (February 11, 2000).
CHAMPIONSHIP GAME EXPERIENCE: Played in NFC championship game (1998 season). ... Played in Super Bowl XXXIII (1998 season).
PRO STATISTICS: 1998—Recovered one fumble.
SINGLE GAME HIGHS (regular season): Reception—5 (September 14, 1997, vs. Oakland); yards—65 (December 27, 1998, vs. Miami); and touchdown receptions—2 (December 27, 1998, vs. Miami).

			RECEIVING				TOTALS			
Year Team	G	GS	No.	Yds.	Avg.	TD	TD	2pt.	Pts.	Fum.
1997—Atlanta NFL	11	11	17	217	12.8	2	2	0	12	1
1998—Atlanta NFL	16	16	27	428	15.9	5	5	0	30	1
1999—Atlanta NFL	14	14	15	174	11.6	0	0	0	0	0
Pro totals (3 years)	41	41	59	819	13.9	7	7	0	42	2

S

SAPP, PATRICK — LB

PERSONAL: Born May 11, 1973, in Jacksonville. ... 6-4/258. ... Full name: Patrick Zolley Sapp.
HIGH SCHOOL: Raines (Jacksonville).
COLLEGE: Clemson.
TRANSACTIONS/CAREER NOTES: Selected by San Diego Chargers in second round (50th pick overall) of 1996 NFL draft. ... Signed by Chargers for 1996 season. ... Traded by Chargers with first- (DE Andre Wadsworth) and second-round (CB Corey Chavous) picks in 1998 draft, first-round pick (WR David Boston) in 1999 draft and KR Eric Metcalf to Arizona Cardinals for first-round pick (QB Ryan Leaf) in 1998 draft (March 12, 1998). ... Granted free agency (February 12, 1999). ... Re-signed by Cardinals (June 9, 1999). ... Granted unconditional free agency (February 11, 2000).
PLAYING EXPERIENCE: San Diego NFL, 1996 and 1997; Arizona NFL, 1998 and 1999. ... Games/Games started: 1996 (16/0), 1997 (16/9), 1998 (16/1), 1999 (15/5). Total: 63/15.
PRO STATISTICS: 1998—Credited with one sack. 1999—Credited with one sack.

SAPP, WARREN — DT — BUCCANEERS

PERSONAL: Born December 19, 1972, in Orlando. ... 6-2/303. ... Full name: Warren Carlos Sapp.
HIGH SCHOOL: Apopka (Fla.).
COLLEGE: Miami (Fla.).
TRANSACTIONS/CAREER NOTES: Selected after junior season by Tampa Bay Buccaneers in first round (12th pick overall) of 1995 NFL draft. ... Signed by Buccaneers (April 27, 1995).
CHAMPIONSHIP GAME EXPERIENCE: Played in NFC championship game (1999 season).
HONORS: Lombardi Award winner (1994). ... Named defensive lineman on The Sporting News college All-America first team (1994). ... Played in Pro Bowl (1997-1999 seasons). ... Named defensive tackle on The Sporting News NFL All-Pro team (1999).
PRO STATISTICS: 1995—Intercepted one pass for five yards and a touchdown. 1996—Recovered one fumble. 1997—Recovered one fumble for 23 yards. 1998—Recovered one fumble. 1999—Recovered two fumbles.

Year Team	G	GS	SACKS
1995—Tampa Bay NFL	16	8	3.0
1996—Tampa Bay NFL	15	14	9.0
1997—Tampa Bay NFL	15	15	10.5
1998—Tampa Bay NFL	16	16	7.0
1999—Tampa Bay NFL	15	15	12.5
Pro totals (5 years)	77	68	42.0

SATURDAY, JEFF — OL — COLTS

PERSONAL: Born June 18, 1975, in Tucker, Ga. ... 6-2/295. ... Full name: Jeffrey Bryant Saturday.
HIGH SCHOOL: Shamrock (Tucker, Ga.).
COLLEGE: North Carolina.
TRANSACTIONS/CAREER NOTES: Signed as non-drafted free agent by Indianapolis Colts (January 7, 1999).
PLAYING EXPERIENCE: Indianapolis NFL, 1999. ... Games/Games started: 1999 (11/2).

SAUER, CRAIG — LB — VIKINGS

PERSONAL: Born December 13, 1972, in Sartell, Minn. ... 6-1/235.
HIGH SCHOOL: Sartell (Minn.).
COLLEGE: Minnesota.

TRANSACTIONS/CAREER NOTES: Selected by Atlanta Falcons in sixth round (188th pick overall) of 1996 NFL draft. ... Signed by Falcons (June 6, 1996). ... Granted unconditional free agency (February 11, 2000). ... Signed by Minnesota Vikings (February 23, 2000).
PLAYING EXPERIENCE: Atlanta NFL, 1996-1999. ... Games/Games started: 1996 (16/1), 1997 (16/1), 1998 (16/6), 1999 (16/3). Total: 64/11.
CHAMPIONSHIP GAME EXPERIENCE: Played in NFC championship game (1998 season). ... Played in Super Bowl XXXIII (1998 season).
PRO STATISTICS: 1997—Recovered one fumble. 1998—Intercepted one pass for no yards. 1999—Credited with one sack.

SAUERBRUN, TODD   P   CHIEFS

PERSONAL: Born January 4, 1973, in Setauket, N.Y. ... 5-10/204. ... Name pronounced SOUR-brun.
HIGH SCHOOL: Ward Melville (Setauket, N.Y.).
COLLEGE: West Virginia.
TRANSACTIONS/CAREER NOTES: Selected by Chicago Bears in second round (56th pick overall) of 1995 NFL draft. ... Signed by Bears (July 20, 1995). ... Granted free agency (February 13, 1998). ... Re-signed by Bears (May 19, 1998). ... On injured reserve with knee injury (September 23, 1998-remainder of season). ... Granted unconditional free agency (February 11, 2000). ... Signed by Kansas City Chiefs (March 27, 2000).
HONORS: Named punter on THE SPORTING NEWS college All-America first team (1994).
PRO STATISTICS: 1996—Rushed once for three yards, attempted two passes with two completions for 63 yards. 1997—Rushed twice for eight yards and fumbled once for minus nine yards. 1999—Rushed once for minus two yards and fumbled once.

| | | | | PUNTING | | | |
Year Team	G	No.	Yds.	Avg.	Net avg.	In. 20	Blk.
1995—Chicago NFL	15	55	2080	37.8	31.1	16	0
1996—Chicago NFL	16	78	3491	44.8	34.8	15	0
1997—Chicago NFL	16	95	4059	42.7	32.8	26	0
1998—Chicago NFL	3	15	741	49.4	42.1	6	0
1999—Chicago NFL	16	85	3478	40.9	35.4	20	0
Pro totals (5 years)	66	328	13849	42.2	34.1	83	0

SAWYER, COREY   CB

PERSONAL: Born October 4, 1971, in Key West, Fla. ... 5-11/177. ... Full name: Corey F. Sawyer.
HIGH SCHOOL: Key West (Fla.).
COLLEGE: Florida State.
TRANSACTIONS/CAREER NOTES: Selected after junior season by Cincinnati Bengals in fourth round (104th pick overall) of 1994 NFL draft. ... Signed by Bengals (July 22, 1994). ... On injured reserve with knee injury (September 23, 1998-remainder of season). ... Granted unconditional free agency (February 12, 1999). ... Re-signed by Bengals (May 11, 1999). ... Released by Bengals (September 6, 1999). ... Signed by New York Jets (September 14, 1999). ... Released by Jets (November 16, 1999).
HONORS: Named defensive back on THE SPORTING NEWS college All-America first team (1993).
PRO STATISTICS: 1994—Recovered one fumble. 1996—Recovered one fumble.

| | | | INTERCEPTIONS | | | | SACKS | PUNT RETURNS | | | | KICKOFF RETURNS | | | | TOTALS | | | |
Year Team	G	GS	No.	Yds.	Avg.	TD	No.	No.	Yds.	Avg.	TD	No.	Yds.	Avg.	TD	TD	2pt.	Pts.	Fum.
1994—Cincinnati NFL	15	0	2	0	0.0	0	0.0	26	307	11.8	1	1	14	14.0	0	1	0	6	2
1995—Cincinnati NFL	12	8	2	61	30.5	0	2.0	9	58	6.4	0	2	50	25.0	0	0	0	0	1
1996—Cincinnati NFL	15	2	2	0	0.0	0	1.5	15	117	7.8	0	12	241	20.1	0	0	0	0	2
1997—Cincinnati NFL	15	2	4	44	11.0	0	0.0	0	0	0.0	0	0	0	0.0	0	0	0	0	0
1998—Cincinnati NFL	3	0	1	58	58.0	1	0.0	0	0	0.0	0	0	0	0.0	0	1	0	6	0
1999—New York Jets NFL	5	0	0	0	0.0	0	0.0	4	25	6.3	0	0	0	0.0	0	0	0	0	0
Pro totals (6 years)	65	12	11	163	14.8	1	3.5	54	507	9.4	1	15	305	20.3	0	2	0	12	5

SAWYER, TALANCE   DE   VIKINGS

PERSONAL: Born June 14, 1976, in Bastrop, La. ... 6-2/272.
HIGH SCHOOL: Bastrop (La.).
COLLEGE: UNLV.
TRANSACTIONS/CAREER NOTES: Selected by Minnesota Vikings in sixth round (185th pick overall) of 1999 NFL draft. ... Signed by Vikings (June 4, 1999).
PLAYING EXPERIENCE: Minnesota NFL, 1999. ... Games/Games started: 1999 (2/0).

SCHAU, RYAN   G   EAGLES

PERSONAL: Born December 30, 1975, in Hammond, Ind. ... 6-6/300. ... Twin brother of Thomas Schau, center, New Orleans Saints.
HIGH SCHOOL: Bloomington (Ill.).
COLLEGE: Illinois.
TRANSACTIONS/CAREER NOTES: Signed as non-drafted free agent by Philadelphia Eagles (April 19, 1999).
PLAYING EXPERIENCE: Philadelphia NFL, 1999. ... Games/Games started: 1999 (1/0).

SCHLERETH, MARK   G   BRONCOS

PERSONAL: Born January 25, 1966, in Anchorage, Alaska. ... 6-3/287. ... Name pronounced SHLARE-eth.
HIGH SCHOOL: Robert Service (Anchorage, Alaska).
COLLEGE: Idaho.
TRANSACTIONS/CAREER NOTES: Selected by Washington Redskins in 10th round (263rd pick overall) of 1989 NFL draft. ... Signed by Redskins (July 23, 1989). ... On injured reserve with knee injury (September 5-November 11, 1989). ... On injured reserve with a nerve con-

dition known as Guillain-Barre Syndrome (November 16, 1993-remainder of season). ... Released by Redskins (September 2, 1994). ... Re-signed by Redskins (September 3, 1994). ... Granted unconditional free agency (February 17, 1995). ... Signed by Denver Broncos (March 27, 1995). ... Released by Broncos (February 14, 1997). ... Re-signed by Broncos (April 11, 1997). ... Granted unconditional free agency (February 13, 1998). ... Re-signed by Broncos (February 24, 1998).

PLAYING EXPERIENCE: Washington NFL, 1989-1994; Denver NFL, 1995-1999. ... Games/Games started: 1989 (6/6), 1990 (12/7), 1991 (16/16), 1992 (16/16), 1993 (9/8), 1994 (16/6), 1995 (16/16), 1996 (14/14), 1997 (11/11), 1998 (16/16), 1999 (16/16). Total: 148/132.

CHAMPIONSHIP GAME EXPERIENCE: Played in NFC championship game (1991 season). ... Member of Super Bowl championship team (1991, 1997 and 1998 seasons). ... Played in AFC championship game (1997 and 1998 seasons).

HONORS: Played in Pro Bowl (1991 and 1998 seasons).

PRO STATISTICS: 1989—Recovered one fumble. 1993—Recovered one fumble. 1997—Recovered one fumble.

SCHLESINGER, CORY FB LIONS

PERSONAL: Born June 23, 1972, in Columbus, Neb. ... 6-0/246.
HIGH SCHOOL: Columbus (Neb.).
COLLEGE: Nebraska (degree in indusrial technology education).
TRANSACTIONS/CAREER NOTES: Selected by Detroit Lions in sixth round (192nd pick overall) of 1995 NFL draft. ... Signed by Lions (July 19, 1995).
PRO STATISTICS: 1995—Recovered one fumble for 11 yards. 1999—Returned two kickoffs for 33 yards and recovered one fumble.
SINGLE GAME HIGHS (regular season): Attempts—10 (September 12, 1999, vs. Seattle); yards—50 (September 12, 1999, vs. Seattle); and rushing touchdowns—0.

			RUSHING				RECEIVING				TOTALS			
Year Team	G	GS	Att.	Yds.	Avg.	TD	No.	Yds.	Avg.	TD	TD	2pt.	Pts.	Fum.
1995—Detroit NFL	16	1	1	1	1.0	0	1	2	2.0	0	0	0	0	0
1996—Detroit NFL	16	1	0	0	0.0	0	0	0	0.0	0	0	0	0	0
1997—Detroit NFL	16	2	7	11	1.6	0	5	69	13.8	1	1	0	6	0
1998—Detroit NFL	15	2	5	17	3.4	0	3	16	5.3	1	1	0	6	0
1999—Detroit NFL	16	11	43	124	2.9	0	21	151	7.2	1	1	0	6	4
Pro totals (5 years)	79	17	56	153	2.7	0	30	238	7.9	3	3	0	18	4

SCHNECK, MIKE C STEELERS

PERSONAL: Born August 4, 1977, in Whitefish Bay, Wis. ... 6-0/242.
HIGH SCHOOL: Whitefish Bay (Wis.).
COLLEGE: Wisconsin.
TRANSACTIONS/CAREER NOTES: Signed as non-drafted free agent by Pittsburgh Steelers (April 23, 1999); contract voided by NFL because he did not meet eligibility requirements. ... Re-signed by Steelers (July 12, 1999).
PLAYING EXPERIENCE: Pittsburgh NFL, 1999. ... Games/Games started: 1999 (16/0).

SCHREIBER, ADAM C/G

PERSONAL: Born February 20, 1962, in Galveston, Texas. ... 6-4/295. ... Full name: Adam Blayne Schreiber.
HIGH SCHOOL: Butler (Huntsville, Ala.).
COLLEGE: Texas.
TRANSACTIONS/CAREER NOTES: Selected by Seattle Seahawks in ninth round (243rd pick overall) of 1984 NFL draft. ... Signed by Seahawks (June 20, 1984). ... Released by Seahawks (August 27, 1984). ... Re-signed by Seahawks (October 10, 1984). ... Released by Seahawks (August 29, 1985). ... Signed by New Orleans Saints (November 20, 1985). ... Released by Saints (September 1, 1986). ... Signed by Philadelphia Eagles (October 16, 1986). ... Claimed on waivers by New York Jets (October 19, 1988). ... Granted unconditional free agency (February 1, 1990). ... Signed by Minnesota Vikings (March 21, 1990). ... Granted unconditional free agency (February 1-April 1, 1992). ... Re-signed by Vikings for 1992 season. ... Granted unconditional free agency (March 1, 1993). ... Re-signed by Vikings (May 7, 1993). ... Released by Vikings (July 12, 1994). ... Signed by New York Giants (August 16, 1994). ... Granted unconditional free agency (February 17, 1995). ... Re-signed by Giants (May 8, 1995). ... Granted unconditional free agency (February 14, 1997). ... Signed by Atlanta Falcons (August 5, 1997). ... Granted unconditional free agency (February 12, 1999). ... Re-signed by Falcons (April 21, 1999). ... Released by Falcons (September 28, 1999).
PLAYING EXPERIENCE: Seattle NFL, 1984; New Orleans NFL, 1985; Philadelphia NFL, 1986 and 1987; Philadelphia (6)-New York Jets (7) NFL, 1988; New York Jets NFL, 1989; Minnesota NFL, 1990-1993; New York Giants NFL, 1994-1996; Atlanta NFL, 1997-1999. ... Games/Games started: 1984 (6/0), 1985 (1/0), 1986 (9/0), 1987 (12/12), 1988 (Phi.-6/0; N.Y. Jets-7/0; Total: 13/0), 1989 (16/0), 1990 (16/0), 1991 (15/0), 1992 (16/1), 1993 (16/16), 1994 (16/2), 1995 (16/0), 1996 (15/2), 1997 (16/0), 1998 (16/0), 1999 (3/0). Total: 202/33.
CHAMPIONSHIP GAME EXPERIENCE: Played in NFC championship game (1998 season). ... Played in Super Bowl XXXIII (1998 season).
PRO STATISTICS: 1990—Returned one kickoff for five yards. 1992—Recovered one fumble.

SCHROEDER, BILL WR PACKERS

PERSONAL: Born January 9, 1971, in Eau Claire, Wis. ... 6-3/205. ... Full name: William Fredrich Schroeder. ... Name pronounced SHRAY-der.
HIGH SCHOOL: Sheboygan (Wis.) South.
COLLEGE: Wisconsin-La Crosse (degree in physical education/teaching).
TRANSACTIONS/CAREER NOTES: Selected by Green Bay Packers in sixth round (181st pick overall) of 1994 NFL draft. ... Signed by Packers (May 10, 1994). ... Released by Packers (August 28, 1994). ... Re-signed by Packers to practice squad (August 30, 1994). ... Activated (December 29, 1994). ... Traded by Packers with TE Jeff Wilner to New England Patriots for C Mike Arthur (August 11, 1995). ... On injured reserve with foot injury (August 27, 1995-entire season). ... Released by Patriots (August 14, 1996). ... Signed by Packers to practice squad (August 28, 1996). ... Assigned by Packers to Rhein Fire in 1997 World League enhancement allocation program (February 19, 1997). ... On injured reserve with broken collarbone (December 9, 1998-remainder of season).
CHAMPIONSHIP GAME EXPERIENCE: Member of Packers for NFC championship game (1997 season); inactive. ... Member of Packers for Super Bowl XXXII (1997 season); inactive.

PRO STATISTICS: W.L.: 1997—Rushed twice of 18 yards. NFL: 1997—Recovered one fumble.
SINGLE GAME HIGHS (regular season): Receptions—7 (October 10, 1999, vs. Tampa Bay); yards—158 (October 10, 1999, vs. Tampa Bay), and touchdown receptions—2 (January 2, 2000, vs. Arizona).
STATISTICAL PLATEAUS: 100-yard receiving games: 1998 (1), 1999 (1). Total: 2.

				RECEIVING				PUNT RETURNS				KICKOFF RETURNS				TOTALS		
Year Team	G	GS	No.	Yds.	Avg.	TD	No.	Yds.	Avg.	TD	No.	Yds.	Avg.	TD	TD	2pt.	Pts.	Fum.
1994—Green Bay NFL									Did not play.									
1995—New England NFL									Did not play.									
1996—Green Bay NFL									Did not play.									
1997—Rhein W.L.	...	...	43	702	16.3	6	0	0	0.0	0	1	20	20.0	0	6	0	36	0
—Green Bay NFL	15	1	2	15	7.5	1	33	342	10.4	0	24	562	23.4	0	1	0	6	4
1998—Green Bay NFL	13	3	31	452	14.6	1	2	5	2.5	0	0	0	0.0	0	1	0	6	1
1999—Green Bay NFL	16	16	74	1051	14.2	5	0	0	0.0	0	1	10	10.0	0	5	0	30	3
W.L. totals (1 year)	...	...	43	702	16.3	6	0	0	0.0	0	1	20	20.0	0	6	0	36	0
NFL totals (2 years)	44	20	107	1518	14.2	7	35	347	9.9	0	25	572	22.9	0	7	0	42	8
Pro totals (3 years)	...	...	150	2220	14.8	13	35	347	9.9	0	26	592	22.8	0	13	0	78	8

SCHULTERS, LANCE S 49ERS

PERSONAL: Born May 27, 1975, in Brooklyn, N.Y. ... 6-2/195.
HIGH SCHOOL: Canarsie (Brooklyn, N.Y.).
JUNIOR COLLEGE: Nassau Community College (N.Y.).
COLLEGE: Hofstra.
TRANSACTIONS/CAREER NOTES: Selected by San Francisco 49ers in fourth round (119th pick overall) of 1998 NFL draft. ... Signed by 49ers (July 18, 1998).
HONORS: Played in Pro Bowl (1999 season).

			INTERCEPTIONS			
Year Team	G	GS	No.	Yds.	Avg.	TD
1998—San Francisco NFL	15	0	0	0	0.0	0
1999—San Francisco NFL	13	13	6	127	21.2	1
Pro totals (2 years)	28	13	6	127	21.2	1

SCHULZ, KURT S LIONS

PERSONAL: Born December 12, 1968, in Wenatchee, Wash. ... 6-1/208. ... Full name: Kurt Erich Schulz.
HIGH SCHOOL: Eisenhower (Yakima, Wash.).
COLLEGE: Eastern Washington.
TRANSACTIONS/CAREER NOTES: Selected by Buffalo Bills in seventh round (195th pick overall) of 1992 NFL draft. ... Signed by Bills (July 22, 1992). ... On injured reserve with knee injury (October 26-December 19, 1992). ... Granted unconditional free agency (February 11, 2000). ... Signed by Detroit Lions (February 18, 2000).
CHAMPIONSHIP GAME EXPERIENCE: Played in AFC championship game (1993 season). ... Member of Bills for Super Bowl XXVII (1992 season); inactive. ... Played in Super Bowl XXVIII (1993 season).
PRO STATISTICS: 1992—Recovered two fumbles. 1998—Recovered one fumble for nine yards. 1999—Recovered one fumble.

			INTERCEPTIONS			
Year Team	G	GS	No.	Yds.	Avg.	TD
1992—Buffalo NFL	8	1	0	0	0.0	0
1993—Buffalo NFL	12	0	0	0	0.0	0
1994—Buffalo NFL	16	0	0	0	0.0	0
1995—Buffalo NFL	13	13	6	48	8.0	▲1
1996—Buffalo NFL	15	15	4	24	6.0	0
1997—Buffalo NFL	15	14	2	23	11.5	0
1998—Buffalo NFL	12	12	6	48	8.0	0
1999—Buffalo NFL	16	16	3	26	8.7	0
Pro totals (8 years)	107	71	21	169	8.0	1

SCHWARTZ, BRYAN LB

PERSONAL: Born December 5, 1971, in St. Lawrence, S.D. ... 6-4/256. ... Full name: Bryan Lee Schwartz.
HIGH SCHOOL: Miller (S.D.).
COLLEGE: Augustana, S.D. (degree in biology, 1995).
TRANSACTIONS/CAREER NOTES: Selected by Jacksonville Jaguars in second round (64th pick overall) of 1995 NFL draft. ... Signed by Jaguars (June 1, 1995). ... On injured reserve with knee injury (September 24, 1996-remainder of season). ... Granted free agency (February 13, 1998). ... Re-signed by Jaguars (May 15, 1998). ... Granted unconditional free agency (February 12, 1999). ... Re-signed by Jaguars (April 20, 1999). ... On injured reserve with hamstring injury (January 3, 2000-remainder of playoffs). ... Granted unconditional free agency (February 11, 2000).
PLAYING EXPERIENCE: Jacksonville NFL, 1995-1999. ... Games/Games started: 1995 (14/9), 1996 (4/3), 1997 (16/16), 1998 (13/12), 1999 (8/0). Total: 55/40.
PRO STATISTICS: 1995—Recovered one fumble. 1997—Credited with 1/2 sack and recovered one fumble. 1998—Recovered four fumbles.

SCIOLI, BRAD DE COLTS

PERSONAL: Born September 6, 1976, in Bridgeport, Pa. ... 6-3/277. ... Full name: Brad Elliott Scioli. ... Name pronounced SHE-o-lee.
HIGH SCHOOL: Upper Merion (King of Prussia, Pa.).
COLLEGE: Penn State.

TRANSACTIONS/CAREER NOTES: Selected by Indianapolis Colts in fifth round (138th pick overall) of 1999 NFL draft. ... Signed by Colts (July 22, 1999).
PLAYING EXPERIENCE: Indianapolis NFL, 1999. ... Games/Games started: 1999 (10/0).

SCOTT, CHAD   DB   STEELERS

PERSONAL: Born September 6, 1974, in Washington, D.C. ... 6-1/192. ... Full name: Chad Oliver Scott.
HIGH SCHOOL: Suitland (Forestville, Md.).
COLLEGE: Towson State, then Maryland.
TRANSACTIONS/CAREER NOTES: Selected by Pittsburgh Steelers in first round (24th pick overall) of 1997 NFL draft. ... Signed by Steelers (July 16, 1997). ... On injured reserve with knee injury (July 20, 1998-entire season).
CHAMPIONSHIP GAME EXPERIENCE: Played in AFC championship game (1997 season).

			INTERCEPTIONS			
Year Team	G	GS	No.	Yds.	Avg.	TD
1997—Pittsburgh NFL	13	9	2	-4	-2.0	0
1998—Pittsburgh NFL			Did not play.			
1999—Pittsburgh NFL	13	12	1	16	16.0	0
Pro totals (2 years)	26	21	3	12	4.0	0

SCOTT, DARNAY   WR   BENGALS

PERSONAL: Born July 7, 1972, in St. Louis. ... 6-1/205.
HIGH SCHOOL: Kearny (San Diego).
COLLEGE: San Diego State.
TRANSACTIONS/CAREER NOTES: Selected after junior season by Cincinnati Bengals in second round (30th pick overall) of 1994 NFL draft. ... Signed by Bengals (July 18, 1994). ... Granted free agency (February 14, 1997). ... Re-signed by Bengals (June 16, 1997).
PRO STATISTICS: 1994—Completed only pass attempt for 53 yards.
SINGLE GAME HIGHS (regular season): Receptions—8 (October 10, 1999, vs. Cleveland); yards—157 (November 6, 1994, vs. Seattle); and touchdown receptions—2 (November 21, 1999, vs. Baltimore).
STATISTICAL PLATEAUS: 100-yard receiving games: 1994 (2), 1995 (1), 1996 (1), 1997 (2), 1998 (2), 1999 (2). Total: 10.

			RUSHING				RECEIVING				KICKOFF RETURNS				TOTALS			
Year Team	G	GS	Att.	Yds.	Avg.	TD	No.	Yds.	Avg.	TD	No.	Yds.	Avg.	TD	TD	2pt.	Pts.	Fum.
1994—Cincinnati NFL	16	12	10	106	10.6	0	46	866	§18.8	5	15	342	22.8	0	5	0	30	0
1995—Cincinnati NFL	16	16	5	11	2.2	0	52	821	15.8	5	0	0	0.0	0	5	0	30	0
1996—Cincinnati NFL	16	16	3	4	1.3	0	58	833	14.4	5	0	0	0.0	0	5	0	30	0
1997—Cincinnati NFL	16	15	1	6	6.0	0	54	797	14.8	5	0	0	0.0	0	5	0	30	0
1998—Cincinnati NFL	13	13	2	10	5.0	0	51	817	16.0	7	0	0	0.0	0	7	0	42	0
1999—Cincinnati NFL	16	16	0	0	0.0	0	68	1022	15.0	7	0	0	0.0	0	7	0	42	0
Pro totals (6 years)	93	88	21	137	6.5	0	329	5156	15.7	34	15	342	22.8	0	34	0	204	0

SCOTT, LANCE   C/G   PATRIOTS

PERSONAL: Born February 15, 1972, in Salt Lake City. ... 6-3/295.
HIGH SCHOOL: Taylorsville (Salt Lake City).
COLLEGE: Utah (degree in exercise and sports science).
TRANSACTIONS/CAREER NOTES: Selected by Arizona Cardinals in fifth round (165th pick overall) of 1995 NFL draft. ... Signed by Cardinals (July 24, 1995). ... Released by Cardinals (August 27, 1995). ... Re-signed by Cardinals to practice squad (October 2, 1995). ... Activated (November 14, 1995); did not play. ... Inactive for one game (1996). ... On injured reserve with shoulder injury (October 16, 1996-remainder of season). ... Released by Cardinals (August 19, 1997). ... Signed by New York Giants (August 25, 1997). ... Granted free agency (February 13, 1998). ... Re-signed by Giants (April 8, 1998). ... Granted unconditional free agency (February 12, 1999). ... Re-signed by Giants (May 11, 1999). ... On injured reserve with knee injury (September 6, 1999-entire season). ... Released by Giants (February 10, 2000). ... Signed by New England Patriots (April 10, 2000).
PLAYING EXPERIENCE: New York Giants NFL, 1997 and 1998. ... Games/Games started: 1997 (16/11), 1998 (16/16). Total: 32/27.
PRO STATISTICS: 1998—Fumbled once and recovered one fumble for minus one yard.

SCOTT, YUSUF   G   CARDINALS

PERSONAL: Born November 30, 1976 in La Porte, Texas ... 6-3/332. ... Full name: Yusuf Jamall Scott.
HIGH SCHOOL: La Porte (Texas).
COLLEGE: Arizona (degree in sociology).
TRANSACTIONS/CAREER NOTES: Selected after junior season by Arizona Cardinals in fifth round (168th pick overall) of 1999 NFL draft. ... Signed by Cardinals (June 18, 1999).
PLAYING EXPERIENCE: Arizona NFL, 1999. ... Games/Games started: 1999 (10/0).

SCROGGINS, TRACY   DE   LIONS

PERSONAL: Born September 11, 1969, in Checotah, Okla. ... 6-3/273.
HIGH SCHOOL: Checotah (Okla.).
JUNIOR COLLEGE: Coffeyville (Kan.) Community College.
COLLEGE: Tulsa.
TRANSACTIONS/CAREER NOTES: Selected by Detroit Lions in second round (53rd pick overall) of 1992 NFL draft. ... Signed by Lions (July 23, 1992). ... Granted free agency (February 17, 1995). ... Re-signed by Lions (May 17, 1995).

PRO STATISTICS: 1993—Intercepted one pass for no yards and recovered one fumble. 1994—Recovered one fumble. 1995—Recovered one fumble for 81 yards and a touchdown. 1996—Recovered one fumble. 1997—Recovered one fumble for 17 yards and a touchdown and credited with a safety. 1999—Recovered two fumbles for four yards.

Year Team	G	GS	SACKS
1992—Detroit NFL	16	7	7.5
1993—Detroit NFL	16	0	8.0
1994—Detroit NFL	16	9	2.5
1995—Detroit NFL	16	16	9.5
1996—Detroit NFL	6	6	2.0
1997—Detroit NFL	15	6	7.5
1998—Detroit NFL	11	3	6.5
1999—Detroit NFL	14	11	8.5
Pro totals (8 years)	110	58	52.0

SCURLOCK, MIKE　　　　　S

PERSONAL: Born February 26, 1972, in Tucson, Ariz. ... 5-10/200. ... Full name: Michael Lee Scurlock Jr. ... Cousin of Randy Robbins, safety with Denver Broncos (1984-91) and New England Patriots (1992).
HIGH SCHOOL: Sunnyside (Tucson, Ariz.), then Cholla (Tucson, Ariz.).
COLLEGE: Arizona.
TRANSACTIONS/CAREER NOTES: Selected by St. Louis Rams in fifth round (140th pick overall) of 1995 NFL draft. ... Signed by Rams (June 20, 1995). ... On injured reserve with sprained left knee (December 20, 1995-remainder of season). ... Released by Rams (August 24, 1997). ... Re-signed by Rams (November 4, 1997). ... Granted free agency (February 13, 1998). ... Re-signed by Rams (April 21, 1998). ... Granted unconditional free agency (February 12, 1999). ... Signed by Carolina Panthers (March 17, 1999). ... Released by Panthers (March 27, 2000).
PLAYING EXPERIENCE: St. Louis NFL, 1995-1998; Carolina NFL, 1999. ... Games/Games started: 1995 (14/1), 1996 (16/0), 1997 (5/0), 1998 (16/0), 1999 (14/0). Total: 65/1.
PRO STATISTICS: 1995—Intercepted one pass for 13 yards and recovered one fumble. 1999—Recovered one fumble.

SEARCY, LEON　　　　　OT　　　　　JAGUARS

PERSONAL: Born December 21, 1969, in Washington, D.C. ... 6-4/315. ... Full name: Leon Searcy Jr.
HIGH SCHOOL: Maynard Evans (Orlando).
COLLEGE: Miami, Fla. (degree in sociology, 1992).
TRANSACTIONS/CAREER NOTES: Selected by Pittsburgh Steelers in first round (11th pick overall) of 1992 NFL draft. ... Signed by Steelers (August 3, 1992). ... Granted unconditional free agency (February 16, 1996). ... Signed by Jacksonville Jaguars (February 18, 1996).
PLAYING EXPERIENCE: Pittsburgh NFL, 1992-1995; Jacksonville NFL, 1996-1999. ... Games/Games started: 1992 (15/0), 1993 (16/16), 1994 (16/16), 1995 (16/16), 1996 (16/16), 1997 (16/16), 1998 (15/15), 1999 (16/16). Total: 126/111.
CHAMPIONSHIP GAME EXPERIENCE: Played in AFC championship game (1994-1996 and 1999 seasons). ... Played in Super Bowl XXX (1995 season).
HONORS: Named offensive tackle on THE SPORTING NEWS college All-America second team (1991). ... Played in Pro Bowl (1999 season).
PRO STATISTICS: 1993—Recovered one fumble. 1995—Recovered one fumble. 1996—Recovered one fumble.

SEARS, COREY　　　　　DT　　　　　CARDINALS

PERSONAL: Born April 15, 1973, in San Antonio. ... 6-3/300. ... Full name: Corey Alexander Sears.
HIGH SCHOOL: Judson (Converse, Texas).
JUNIOR COLLEGE: Navarro College (Texas).
COLLEGE: Mississippi State.
TRANSACTIONS/CAREER NOTES: Signed as non-drafted free agent by Baltimore Ravens (April 29, 1996). ... On injured reserve (August 20-November 6, 1996). ... Released by Ravens (November 6, 1996). ... Signed by St. Louis Rams (April 24, 1998). ... Claimed on waivers by San Francisco 49ers (August 26, 1998). ... Released by 49ers (August 28, 1998). ... Signed by Rams to practice squad (September 1, 1998). ... Activated (November 30, 1998). ... Claimed on waivers by Arizona Cardinals (September 6, 1999).
PLAYING EXPERIENCE: St. Louis NFL, 1998; Arizona NFL, 1999. ... Games/Games started: 1998 (4/0), 1999 (9/1). Total: 13/1.

SEAU, JUNIOR　　　　　LB　　　　　CHARGERS

PERSONAL: Born January 19, 1969, in San Diego. ... 6-3/250. ... Full name: Tiaina Seau Jr. ... Name pronounced SAY-ow.
HIGH SCHOOL: Oceanside (Calif.).
COLLEGE: Southern California.
TRANSACTIONS/CAREER NOTES: Selected after junior season by San Diego Chargers in first round (fifth pick overall) of 1990 NFL draft. ... Signed by Chargers (August 27, 1990).
CHAMPIONSHIP GAME EXPERIENCE: Played in AFC championship game (1994 season). ... Played in Super Bowl XXIX (1994 season).
HONORS: Named linebacker on THE SPORTING NEWS college All-America first team (1989). ... Played in Pro Bowl (1991-1999 seasons). ... Named inside linebacker on THE SPORTING NEWS NFL All-Pro team (1992-1996 and 1998).
PRO STATISTICS: 1992—Recovered one fumble for 10 yards. 1993—Recovered one fumble for 21 yards. 1994—Recovered three fumbles. 1995—Recovered three fumbles for 30 yards and one touchdown. 1996—Recovered three fumbles. 1997—Fumbled once and recovered two fumbles for five yards. 1998—Recovered two fumbles. 1999—Caught two passes for eight yards and recovered one fumble.

Year Team	G	GS	INTERCEPTIONS				SACKS
			No.	Yds.	Avg.	TD	No.
1990—San Diego NFL	16	15	0	0	0.0	0	1.0
1991—San Diego NFL	16	16	0	0	0.0	0	7.0
1992—San Diego NFL	15	15	2	51	25.5	0	4.5
1993—San Diego NFL	16	16	2	58	29.0	0	0.0
1994—San Diego NFL	16	16	0	0	0.0	0	5.5

Year Team							
1995—San Diego NFL	16	16	2	5	2.5	0	2.0
1996—San Diego NFL	15	15	2	18	9.0	0	7.0
1997—San Diego NFL	15	15	2	33	16.5	0	7.0
1998—San Diego NFL	16	16	0	0	0.0	0	3.5
1999—San Diego NFL	14	14	1	16	16.0	0	3.5
Pro totals (10 years)	155	154	11	181	16.5	0	41.0

SEHORN, JASON   CB   GIANTS

PERSONAL: Born April 15, 1971, in Sacramento. ... 6-2/215.
HIGH SCHOOL: Mt. Shasta (Calif.).
JUNIOR COLLEGE: Shasta College (Calif.).
COLLEGE: Southern California.
TRANSACTIONS/CAREER NOTES: Selected by New York Giants in second round (59th pick overall) of 1994 NFL draft. ... Signed by Giants (July 17, 1994). ... Granted free agency (February 14, 1997). ... Re-signed by Giants (August 9, 1997). ... On injured reserve with knee injury (August 25, 1998-entire season).
PRO STATISTICS: 1996—Credited with three sacks, returned one punt for no yards, fumbled once and recovered one fumble. 1997—Credited with 1½ sacks and recovered one fumble for two yards. 1999—Fumbled once for minus one yard.

			INTERCEPTIONS			
Year Team	G	GS	No.	Yds.	Avg.	TD
1994—New York Giants NFL	8	0	0	0	0.0	0
1995—New York Giants NFL	14	0	0	0	0.0	0
1996—New York Giants NFL	16	15	5	61	12.2	1
1997—New York Giants NFL	16	16	6	74	12.3	1
1998—New York Giants NFL			Did not play.			
1999—New York Giants NFL	10	10	1	-4	-4.0	0
Pro totals (5 years)	64	41	12	131	10.9	2

RECORD AS BASEBALL PLAYER

TRANSACTIONS/CAREER NOTES: Threw right, batted right. ... Signed as non-drafted free agent by Chicago Cubs organization (July 24, 1989). ... Released by Cubs organization (April 4, 1991).

									BATTING						FIELDING		
Year Team (League)	Pos.	G	AB	R	H	2B	3B	HR	RBI	Avg.	BB	SO	SB	PO	A	E	Avg.
1990— Huntington (Appal.)....	OF	49	125	21	23	3	1	1	10	.184	8	52	9	82	3	5	.944

SELLERS, MIKE   FB   REDSKINS

PERSONAL: Born July 21, 1975, in Frankfurt, West Germany. ... 6-3/260.
HIGH SCHOOL: North Thurston (Lacey, Wash.).
JUNIOR COLLEGE: Walla Walla (Wash.) Community College.
TRANSACTIONS/CAREER NOTES: Signed by Edmonton Eskimos of CFL (March 21, 1995). ... Tranferred by Eskimos to reserve list (August 23, 1995). ... Transferred by Eskimos to injured list (October 12, 1995). ... Transferred by Eskimos to active roster (December 18, 1995). ... Signed as non-drafted free agent by Washington Redskins (February 11, 1998).
PRO STATISTICS: CFL: 1997—Rushed 40 times for 133 yards, returned one kickoff for 14 yards and recovered one fumble for 43 yards. 1998—Returned two kickoffs for 33 yards and recovered one fumble. 1999—Returned three kickoffs for 32 yards.
SINGLE GAME HIGHS (regular season): Receptions—3 (December 27, 1998, vs. Dallas); yards—18 (December 27, 1998, vs. Dallas); and touchdown receptions—0.

			RECEIVING				TOTALS			
Year Team	G	GS	No.	Yds.	Avg.	TD	TD	2pt.	Pts.	Fum.
1996—Edmonton CFL	17	...	0	0	0.0	0	0	0	0	0
1997—Edmonton CFL	16	...	0	0	0.0	0	0	0	0	0
1998—Washington NFL	14	1	3	18	6.0	0	0	0	0	0
1999—Washington NFL	16	2	7	105	15.0	2	2	0	12	1
CFL totals (2 years)	33	...	0	0	0.0	0	0	0	0	0
NFL totals (2 years)	30	3	10	123	12.3	2	2	0	12	1
Pro totals (4 years)	63	...	10	123	12.3	2	2	0	12	1

SEMPLE, TONY   G   LIONS

PERSONAL: Born December 20, 1970, in Springfield, Ill. ... 6-5/303. ... Full name: Anthony Lee Semple.
HIGH SCHOOL: Lincoln (Ill.) Community.
COLLEGE: Memphis State (degree in sports administration).
TRANSACTIONS/CAREER NOTES: Selected by Detroit Lions in fifth round (154th pick overall) of 1994 NFL draft. ... Signed by Lions (July 21, 1994). ... On injured reserve with knee injury (August 19, 1994-entire season). ... Granted free agency (February 14, 1997). ... Re-signed by Lions (June 13, 1997). ... Granted unconditional free agency (February 13, 1998). ... Re-signed by Lions (February 21, 1998).
PLAYING EXPERIENCE: Detroit NFL, 1995-1999. ... Games/Games started: 1995 (16/0), 1996 (15/1), 1997 (16/1), 1998 (16/3), 1999 (12/12). Total: 75/17.

SERWANGA, KATO   CB   PATRIOTS

PERSONAL: Born July 23, 1976, in Kampala, Uganda, Africa. ... 6-0/198. ... Twin brother of Wasswa Serwanga, cornerback, Kansas City Chiefs. ... Name pronounced kah-TOE sir-WAHN-guh.
HIGH SCHOOL: Sacramento (Calif.).

S

COLLEGE: Sacramento State, then Pacific, then California.
TRANSACTIONS/CAREER NOTES: Signed as non-drafted free agent by New England Patriots (April 24, 1998). ... Released by Patriots (August 30, 1998). ... Re-signed by Patriots to practice squad (August 31, 1998). ... Activated (December 12, 1998); did not play.
PRO STATISTICS: 1999—Credited with one sack and recovered one fumble.

			INTERCEPTIONS			
Year Team	G	GS	No.	Yds.	Avg.	TD
1998—New England NFL				Did not play.		
1999—New England NFL	16	3	3	2	0.7	0
Pro totals (1 years)	16	3	3	2	0.7	0

SERWANGA, WASSWA — CB — CHIEFS

PERSONAL: Born July 23, 1976, in Kampala, Uganda, Africa. ... 5-11/190. ... Full name: Wasswa Kenneth Serwanga. ... Twin brother of Kato Serwanga, cornerback, New England Patriots. ... Name pronounced ser-WAN-guh.
HIGH SCHOOL: Sacramento (Calif.).
COLLEGE: Sacramento State, then Pacific, then UCLA.
TRANSACTIONS/CAREER NOTES: Signed as non-drafted free agent by Chicago Bears (April 21, 1998). ... Released by Bears (August 21, 1998). ... Signed by San Francisco 49ers (April 23, 1999). ... Released by 49ers (September 5, 1999). ... Re-signed by 49ers to practice squad (September 7, 1999). ... Activated (October 12, 1999). ... Granted free agency (February 11, 2000). ... Selected by Amsterdam Admirals in 2000 NFL Europe draft (February 22, 2000). ... Signed by Kansas City Chiefs (April 24, 2000).
PLAYING EXPERIENCE: San Francisco NFL, 1999. ... Games/Games started: 1999 (9/0).

SHADE, SAM — S — REDSKINS

PERSONAL: Born June 14, 1973, in Birmingham, Ala. ... 6-1/201.
HIGH SCHOOL: Wenonah (Birmingham, Ala.).
COLLEGE: Alabama.
TRANSACTIONS/CAREER NOTES: Selected by Cincinnati Bengals in fourth round (102nd pick overall) of 1995 NFL draft. ... Signed by Bengals (July 18, 1995). ... Granted free agency (February 13, 1998). ... Re-signed by Bengals (June 15, 1998). ... Granted unconditional free agency (February 12, 1999). ... Signed by Washington Redskins (February 18, 1999).
PRO STATISTICS: 1997—Fumbled once and recovered one fumble. 1998—Recovered two fumbles for 55 yards and one touchdown. 1999—Recovered one fumble.

			INTERCEPTIONS				SACKS
Year Team	G	GS	No.	Yds.	Avg.	TD	No.
1995—Cincinnati NFL	16	2	0	0	0.0	0	0.0
1996—Cincinnati NFL	12	0	0	0	0.0	0	0.0
1997—Cincinnati NFL	16	12	1	21	21.0	0	4.0
1998—Cincinnati NFL	16	14	3	33	11.0	0	1.0
1999—Washington NFL	16	16	2	7	3.5	0	1.5
Pro totals (5 years)	76	44	6	61	10.2	0	6.5

SHANNON, LARRY — WR — RAIDERS

PERSONAL: Born February 2, 1975, in Gainesville, Fla. ... 6-4/210. ... Full name: Larry David Shannon.
HIGH SCHOOL: Bradford (Starke, Fla.).
COLLEGE: East Carolina.
TRANSACTIONS/CAREER NOTES: Selected by Miami Dolphins in third round (82nd pick overall) of 1998 NFL draft. ... Signed by Dolphins (July 22, 1998). ... On injured reserve with knee injury (August 24, 1998-entire season). ... Released by Dolphins (October 20, 1999). ... Re-signed by Dolphins to practice squad (October 21, 1999). ... Granted free agency following 1999 season. ... Signed by Oakland Raiders (March 14, 2000).
PLAYING EXPERIENCE: Miami NFL, 1999. ... Games/Games started: 1999 (2/0).

SHARPE, SHANNON — TE — RAVENS

PERSONAL: Born June 26, 1968, in Chicago. ... 6-2/230. ... Brother of Sterling Sharpe, wide receiver with Green Bay Packers (1988-94).
HIGH SCHOOL: Glennville (Ga.).
COLLEGE: Savannah (Ga.) State.
TRANSACTIONS/CAREER NOTES: Selected by Denver Broncos in seventh round (192nd pick overall) of 1990 NFL draft. ... Signed by Broncos (July 1990). ... Granted free agency (February 1, 1992). ... Re-signed by Broncos (July 31, 1992). ... Designated by Broncos as transition player (February 15, 1994). ... On injured reserve with broken collarbone (November 30, 1999-remainder of season). ... Granted unconditional free agency (February 11, 2000). ... Signed by Baltimore Ravens (February 16, 2000).
CHAMPIONSHIP GAME EXPERIENCE: Played in AFC championship game (1991, 1997 and 1998 seasons). ... Member of Super Bowl championship team (1997 and 1998 seasons).
HONORS: Played in Pro Bowl (1992, 1993 and 1995-1997 seasons). ... Named tight end on THE SPORTING NEWS NFL All-Pro team (1993 and 1996-1998). ... Named to play in Pro Bowl (1994 season); replaced by Eric Green due to injury. ... Named to play in Pro Bowl (1998 season); replaced by Frank Wycheck due to injury.
POST SEASON RECORDS: Shares NFL postseason single-game record for most receptions—13 (January 9, 1994, vs. Los Angeles Raiders).
PRO STATISTICS: 1991—Rushed once for 15 yards and recovered one fumble. 1992—Rushed twice for minus six yards. 1993—Returned one kickoff for no yards. 1995—Recovered one fumble.
SINGLE GAME HIGHS (regular season): Receptions—13 (October 6, 1996, vs. San Diego); yards—180 (September 3, 1995, vs. Buffalo); and touchdown receptions—3 (October 6, 1996, vs. San Diego).
STATISTICAL PLATEAUS: 100-yard receiving games: 1992 (2), 1993 (2), 1994 (1), 1995 (2), 1996 (3), 1997 (4). Total: 14.
MISCELLANEOUS: Holds Denver Broncos all-time records for most receiving yards (6,983) and most receptions (552). ... Shares Denver Broncos all-time record most touchdown receptions (44).

Year Team	G	GS	RECEIVING				TOTALS			
			No.	Yds.	Avg.	TD	TD	2pt.	Pts.	Fum.
1990—Denver NFL	16	2	7	99	14.1	1	1	0	6	1
1991—Denver NFL	16	9	22	322	14.6	1	1	0	6	0
1992—Denver NFL	16	11	53	640	12.1	2	2	0	12	1
1993—Denver NFL	16	12	81	995	12.3	§9	9	0	54	1
1994—Denver NFL	15	13	87	1010	11.6	4	4	2	28	1
1995—Denver NFL	13	12	63	756	12.0	4	4	0	24	1
1996—Denver NFL	15	15	80	1062	13.3	10	10	0	60	1
1997—Denver NFL	16	16	72	1107	15.4	3	3	1	20	1
1998—Denver NFL	16	16	64	768	12.0	▲10	10	0	60	1
1999—Denver NFL	5	5	23	224	9.7	0	0	0	0	0
Pro totals (10 years)	144	111	552	6983	12.7	44	44	3	270	7

SHARPER, DARREN   S   PACKERS

PERSONAL: Born November 3, 1975, in Richmond, Va. ... 6-2/210. ... Full name: Darren Mallory Sharper. ... Brother of Jamie Sharper, linebacker, Baltimore Ravens.
HIGH SCHOOL: Hermitage (Richmond, Va.).
COLLEGE: William & Mary.
TRANSACTIONS/CAREER NOTES: Selected by Green Bay Packers in second round (60th pick overall) of 1997 NFL draft. ... Signed by Packers (July 11, 1997).
CHAMPIONSHIP GAME EXPERIENCE: Played in NFC championship game (1997 season). ... Played in Super Bowl XXXII (1997 season).
PRO STATISTICS: 1997—Returned one kickoff for three yards and recovered one fumble for 34 yards and a touchdown. 1999—Returned one kickoff for four yards, credited with one sack and recovered one fumble for nine yards.

Year Team	G	GS	INTERCEPTIONS				PUNT RETURNS				TOTALS			
			No.	Yds.	Avg.	TD	No.	Yds.	Avg.	TD	TD	2pt.	Pts.	Fum.
1997—Green Bay NFL	14	0	2	70	35.0	∞2	7	32	4.6	0	3	0	18	1
1998—Green Bay NFL	16	16	0	0	0.0	0	0	0	0.0	0	0	0	0	0
1999—Green Bay NFL	16	16	3	12	4.0	0	0	0	0.0	0	0	0	0	0
Pro totals (3 years)	46	32	5	82	16.4	2	7	32	4.6	0	3	0	18	1

SHARPER, JAMIE   LB   RAVENS

PERSONAL: Born November 23, 1974, in Richmond, Va. ... 6-3/240. ... Full name: Harry Jamie Sharper Jr. ... Brother of Darren Sharper, safety, Green Bay Packers.
HIGH SCHOOL: Hermitage (Glen Allen, Va.).
COLLEGE: Virginia (degree in psychology, 1996).
TRANSACTIONS/CAREER NOTES: Selected by Baltimore Ravens in second round (34th pick overall) of 1997 NFL draft. ... Signed by Ravens (July 23, 1997). ... Granted free agency (February 11, 2000).
PRO STATISTICS: 1997—Intercepted one pass for four yards and fumbled once.

Year Team	G	GS	SACKS
1997—Baltimore NFL	16	15	3.0
1998—Baltimore NFL	16	16	1.0
1999—Baltimore NFL	16	16	4.0
Pro totals (3 years)	48	47	8.0

SHAW, BOBBY   WR   STEELERS

PERSONAL: Born April 23, 1975, in San Francisco. ... 6-0/186.
HIGH SCHOOL: Galileo (San Francisco).
COLLEGE: California.
TRANSACTIONS/CAREER NOTES: Selected by Seattle Seahawks in sixth round (169th pick overall) of 1998 NFL draft. ... Signed by Seahawks (June 5, 1998). ... Released by Seahawks (August 30, 1998). ... Re-signed by Seahawks to practice squad (August 31, 1998). ... Activated (November 4, 1998). ... Released by Seahawks (November 18, 1998). ... Signed by Pittsburgh Steelers (November 20, 1998).
HONORS: Named wide receiver on THE SPORTING NEWS college All-America first team (1997).
SINGLE GAME HIGHS (regular season): Receptions—7 (January 2, 2000, vs. Tennessee); yards—131 (January 2, 2000, vs. Tennessee); and touchdown receptions—1 (January 2, 2000, vs. Tennessee).
STATISTICAL PLATEAUS: 100-yard receiving games: 1999 (1).

Year Team	G	GS	RECEIVING				PUNT RETURNS				TOTALS			
			No.	Yds.	Avg.	TD	No.	Yds.	Avg.	TD	TD	2pt.	Pts.	Fum.
1998—Seattle NFL	1	1	0	0	0.0	0	0	0	0.0	0	0	0	0	0
1999—Pittsburgh NFL	15	1	28	387	13.8	3	4	53	13.3	0	3	0	18	0
Pro totals (2 years)	16	2	28	387	13.8	3	4	53	13.3	0	3	0	18	0

SHAW, HAROLD   FB   PATRIOTS

PERSONAL: Born September 3, 1974, in Magee, Miss. ... 6-0/228. ... Full name: Harold Lamar Shaw.
HIGH SCHOOL: Magee (Miss.).
COLLEGE: Southern Mississippi.
TRANSACTIONS/CAREER NOTES: Selected by New England Patriots in sixth round (176th pick overall) of 1998 NFL draft. ... Signed by Patriots (July 16, 1998).
PLAYING EXPERIENCE: New England NFL, 1998 and 1999. ... Games/Games started: 1998 (11/0), 1999 (8/0). Total: 19/0.
PRO STATISTICS: 1999—Rushed nine times for 23 yards and caught two passes for 31 yards.

SINGLE GAME HIGHS (regular season): Attempts—5 (January 2, 2000, vs. Baltimore); yards—17 (January 2, 2000, vs. Baltimore); and rushing touchdowns—0.

SHAW, SEDRICK   RB   BENGALS

PERSONAL: Born November 16, 1973, in Austin, Texas. ... 6-0/214.
HIGH SCHOOL: Lyndon B. Johnson (Johnson City, Texas).
COLLEGE: Iowa.
TRANSACTIONS/CAREER NOTES: Selected by New England Patriots in third round (61st pick overall) of 1997 NFL draft. ... Signed by Patriots (July 15, 1997). ... Traded by Patriots to Cleveland Browns for past considerations (April 22, 1999). ... Claimed on waivers by Cincinnati Bengals (September 29, 1999). ... Granted free agency (February 11, 2000). ... Re-signed by Bengals (April 19, 2000).
PRO STATISTICS: 1998—Returned one kickoff for 16 yards and recovered one fumble for minus seven yards.
SINGLE GAME HIGHS (regular season): Attempts—19 (October 11, 1998, vs. Kansas City); yards—81 (December 27, 1998, vs. New York Jets); and rushing touchdowns—1 (January 2, 2000, vs. Jacksonville).

Year Team	G	GS	Att.	Yds.	Avg.	TD	No.	Yds.	Avg.	TD	TD	2pt.	Pts.	Fum.
				RUSHING				RECEIVING				TOTALS		
1997—New England NFL	1	0	0	0	0.0	0	0	0	0.0	0	0	0	0	0
1998—New England NFL	13	1	48	236	4.9	0	6	30	5.0	0	0	0	0	2
1999—Cleveland NFL	3	0	3	2	0.7	0	2	8	4.0	0	0	0	0	1
—Cincinnati NFL	1	0	4	20	5.0	1	1	-4	-4.0	0	1	0	6	0
Pro totals (3 years)	18	1	55	258	4.7	1	9	34	3.8	0	1	0	6	3

SHAW, TERRANCE   CB

PERSONAL: Born November 11, 1973, in Marshall, Texas. ... 5-11/190. ... Full name: Terrance Bernard Shaw.
HIGH SCHOOL: Marshall (Texas).
COLLEGE: Stephen F. Austin State.
TRANSACTIONS/CAREER NOTES: Selected by San Diego Chargers in second round (34th pick overall) of 1995 NFL draft. ... Signed by Chargers (June 15, 1995). ... Released by Chargers (March 21, 2000).
PRO STATISTICS: 1997—Recovered one fumble.

Year Team	G	GS	No.	Yds.	Avg.	TD
			INTERCEPTIONS			
1995—San Diego NFL	16	14	1	31	31.0	0
1996—San Diego NFL	16	16	3	78	26.0	0
1997—San Diego NFL	16	16	1	11	11.0	0
1998—San Diego NFL	13	13	2	0	0.0	0
1999—San Diego NFL	8	8	0	0	0.0	0
Pro totals (5 years)	69	67	7	120	17.1	0

SHEDD, KENNY   WR   RAIDERS

PERSONAL: Born February 14, 1971, in Davenport, Iowa. ... 5-10/165.
HIGH SCHOOL: Davenport (Iowa) West.
COLLEGE: Northern Iowa.
TRANSACTIONS/CAREER NOTES: Selected by New York Jets in fifth round (129th pick overall) of 1993 NFL draft. ... Signed by Jets (July 13, 1993). ... Released by Jets (August 24, 1993). ... Re-signed by Jets to practice squad (September 1, 1993). ... Activated (December 31, 1993); did not play. ... Released by Jets (September 17, 1994). ... Re-signed by Jets to practice squad (September 21, 1994). ... Signed by Chicago Bears off Jets practice squad (October 25, 1994). ... Inactive for nine games (1994). ... Released by Bears (August 27, 1995). ... Selected by London Monarchs in 1996 World League draft (February 22, 1996). ... Signed by Barcelona Dragons of World League (May 23, 1996). ... Signed by Oakland Raiders (June 1996).
PRO STATISTICS: NFL: 1996—Credited with a safety and returned three kickoffs for 51 yards. 1997—Returned two kickoffs for 38 yards and recovered two fumbles for 25 yards and one touchdown. 1998—Returned two kickoffs for 32 yards and recovered two fumbles for four yards. 1999—Returned a blocked punt 20 yards for a touchdown.
SINGLE GAME HIGHS (regular season): Receptions—3 (September 21, 1997, vs. New York Jets); yards—51 (December 22, 1996, vs. Seattle); and touchdown receptions—1 (September 22, 1996, vs. San Diego).

Year Team	G	GS	No.	Yds.	Avg.	TD	TD	2pt.	Pts.	Fum.
			RECEIVING					TOTALS		
1993—New York Jets NFL						Did not play.				
1994—Chicago NFL						Did not play.				
1995—						Did not play.				
1996—Barcelona W.L.	...	...	14	328	23.4	1	1	0	6	0
—Oakland NFL	16	1	3	87	29.0	1	1	0	8	0
1997—Oakland NFL	16	0	10	115	11.5	0	1	0	6	0
1998—Oakland NFL	15	0	3	50	16.7	0	1	0	0	0
1999—Oakland NFL	12	0	0	0	0.0	0	1	0	6	0
W.L. totals (1 year)	...	...	14	328	23.4	1	1	0	6	0
NFL totals (4 years)	59	1	16	252	15.8	1	3	0	20	0
Pro totals (5 years)	...	...	30	580	19.3	2	4	0	26	0

SHEHEE, RASHAAN   RB   CHIEFS

PERSONAL: Born June 20, 1975, in Bakersfield, Calif. ... 5-10/210. ... Name pronounced ruh-SHAHN.
HIGH SCHOOL: Foothill (Bakersfield, Calif.).
COLLEGE: Washington.

TRANSACTIONS/CAREER NOTES: Selected by Kansas City Chiefs in third round (88th pick overall) of 1998 NFL draft. ... Signed by Chiefs (July 17, 1998).
SINGLE GAME HIGHS (regular season): Attempts—22 (October 3, 1999, vs. San Diego); yards—86 (October 3, 1999, vs. San Diego); and rushing touchdowns—1 (September 26, 1999, vs. Detroit).

			RUSHING				RECEIVING				KICKOFF RETURNS				TOTALS		
Year	Team	G	GS	Att.	Yds.	Avg.	TD	No.	Yds.	Avg.	TD	No.	Yds.	Avg.	TD	TD	2pt.	Pts.	Fum.
1998—Kansas City NFL..........	16	0	22	57	2.6	0	10	73	7.3	0	4	72	18.0	0	0	0	0	2
1999—Kansas City NFL..........	9	5	65	238	3.7	1	18	136	7.6	0	0	0	0.0	0	1	0	6	1
Pro totals (2 years)	25	5	87	295	3.4	1	28	209	7.5	0	4	72	18.0	0	1	0	6	3

SHELDON, MIKE   OT   DOLPHINS

PERSONAL: Born June 8, 1973, in Hinsdale, Ill. ... 6-4/305. ... Full name: Michael Joseph Sheldon.
HIGH SCHOOL: Willowbrook (Villa Park, Ill.).
COLLEGE: Grand Valley State (Mich.).
TRANSACTIONS/CAREER NOTES: Signed as non-drafted free agent by Buffalo Bills (April 1995). ... Released by Bills (August 27, 1995). ... Re-signed by Bills to practice squad (August 29, 1995). ... Released by Bills (August 20, 1996). ... Signed by Miami Dolphins to practice squad (August 27, 1996). ... Assigned by Dolphins to Rhein Fire in 1997 World League enhancement allocation program (February 17, 1997). ... Released by Dolphins (August 31, 1999). ... Re-signed by Dolphins (October 6, 1999). ... Released by Dolphins (October 18, 1999). ... Re-signed by Dolphins (November 2, 1999).
PLAYING EXPERIENCE: Rhein W.L., 1997; Miami NFL, 1997-1999. ... Games/Games started: W.L. 1997 (10/10), NFL 1997 (11/0), 1998 (9/2), 1999 (9/0). Total W.L.: 10/10. Total NFL: 29/2. Total Pro: 39/12.

SHELTON, DAIMON   FB   JAGUARS

PERSONAL: Born September 15, 1972, in Duarte, Calif. ... 6-0/254.
HIGH SCHOOL: Duarte (Calif.).
JUNIOR COLLEGE: Fresno (Calif.) City College.
COLLEGE: Cal State Sacramento.
TRANSACTIONS/CAREER NOTES: Selected by Jacksonville Jaguars in sixth round (184th pick overall) of 1997 NFL draft. ... Signed by Jaguars (May 23, 1997). ... Granted free agency (February 11, 2000). ... Re-signed by Jaguars (March 21, 2000).
CHAMPIONSHIP GAME EXPERIENCE: Played in AFC championship game (1999 season).
PRO STATISTICS: 1999—Returned one kickoff for no yards and recovered one fumble.
SINGLE GAME HIGHS (regular season): Attempts—13 (October 18, 1998, vs. Buffalo); yards —44 (October 18, 1998, vs. Buffalo); and rushing touchdowns—1 (November 1, 1998, vs. Baltimore).

			RUSHING				RECEIVING				TOTALS		
Year	Team	G	GS	Att.	Yds.	Avg.	TD	No.	Yds.	Avg.	TD	TD	2pt.	Pts.	Fum.
1997—Jacksonville NFL.................................	13	0	6	4	0.7	0	0	0	0.0	0	0	0	0	1
1998—Jacksonville NFL.................................	14	8	30	95	3.2	1	10	79	7.9	0	1	0	6	0
1999—Jacksonville NFL.................................	16	9	1	2	2.0	0	12	87	7.3	0	0	0	0	0
Pro totals (3 years)......................................	43	17	37	101	2.7	1	22	166	7.5	0	1	0	6	1

SHELTON, L.J.   OT   CARDINALS

PERSONAL: Born March 21, 1976, in Monrovia, Calif. ... 6-6/343. ... Full name: Lonnie Jewel Shelton. ... Son of Lonnie Shelton, forward with New York Knicks (1976-77 and 1977-78), Seattle SuperSonics (1978-79 through 1982-83) and Cleveland Cavaliers (1983-84 through 1985-86).
HIGH SCHOOL: Rochester (Rochester Hills, Mich.).
COLLEGE: Eastern Michigan.
TRANSACTIONS/CAREER NOTES: Selected by Arizona Cardinals in first round (21st pick overall) of 1999 NFL draft. ... Signed by Cardinals (September 24, 1999).
PLAYING EXPERIENCE: Arizona NFL, 1999. ... Games/Games started: 1999 (9/7).

SHEPHERD, LESLIE   WR

PERSONAL: Born November 3, 1969, in Washington, D.C. ... 5-11/186. ... Full name: Leslie Glenard Shepherd.
HIGH SCHOOL: Forestville (Md.).
COLLEGE: Temple.
TRANSACTIONS/CAREER NOTES: Signed as non-drafted free agent by Tampa Bay Buccaneers (May 2, 1992). ... Released by Buccaneers (August 31, 1992). ... Signed by Pittsburgh Steelers (March 17, 1993). ... Released by Steelers (August 24, 1993). ... Re-signed by Steelers to practice squad (August 31, 1993). ... Claimed on waivers by Washington Redskins (September 4, 1994). ... Released by Redskins (September 16, 1994). ... Re-signed by Redskins to practice squad (September 20, 1994). ... Activated (December 2, 1994). ... On injured reserve with elbow and wrist injuries (November 19, 1997-remainder of season). ... Granted unconditional free agency (February 12, 1999). ... Signed by Cleveland Browns (April 7, 1999). ... On injured reserve with knee injury (December 6, 1999-remainder of season). ... Granted unconditional free agency (February 11, 2000).
PRO STATISTICS: 1995—Returned three kickoffs for 85 yards and recovered one fumble. 1996—Recovered one fumble.
SINGLE GAME HIGHS (regular season): Receptions—7 (November 22, 1998, vs. Arizona); yards—135 (October 29, 1995, vs. New York Giants); and touchdown receptions—2 (September 28, 1997, vs. Jacksonville).
STATISTICAL PLATEAUS: 100-yard receiving games: 1995 (1), 1998 (1). Total: 2.

			RUSHING				RECEIVING				TOTALS		
Year	Team	G	GS	Att.	Yds.	Avg.	TD	No.	Yds.	Avg.	TD	TD	2pt.	Pts.	Fum.
1994—Washington NFL.................................	3	0	0	0	0.0	0	1	8	8.0	0	0	0	0	0
1995—Washington NFL.................................	14	4	7	63	9.0	1	29	486	16.8	2	3	0	18	0
1996—Washington NFL.................................	12	6	6	96	16.0	2	23	344	15.0	3	5	0	30	0

	G	GS	No.	Yds.	Avg.	TD	No.	Yds.	Avg.	TD					
1997—Washington NFL	11	9	4	27	6.8	0	29	562	19.4	5	5	0	30	0
1998—Washington NFL	16	16	6	91	15.2	1	43	712	16.6	8	9	1	56	0
1999—Cleveland NFL	9	8	1	5	5.0	0	23	274	11.9	0	0	0	0	0
Pro totals (6 years)	65	43	24	282	11.8	4	148	2386	16.1	18	22	1	134	0

SHIELDS, PAUL — RB — COLTS

PERSONAL: Born January 31, 1976, in Mesa, Ariz. ... 6-1/238. ... Full name: Paul L. Shields Jr.
HIGH SCHOOL: Camelback (Scottsdale, Ariz.).
JUNIOR COLLEGE: Scottsdale (Ariz.) Community College.
COLLEGE: Arizona.
TRANSACTIONS/CAREER NOTES: Signed as non-drafted free agent by Indianapolis Colts (April 22, 1999). ... Released by Colts (September 6, 1999). ... Re-signed by Colts to practice squad (September 7, 1999). ... Released by Colts (September 15, 1999). ... Re-signed by Colts (September 29, 1999).
PLAYING EXPERIENCE: Indianapolis NFL, 1999. ... Games/Games started: 1999 (13/3).
PRO STATISTICS: 1999—Caught four passes for 37 yards and returned one kickoff for three yards.

SHIELDS, SCOTT — S — STEELERS

PERSONAL: Born March 29, 1976, in San Diego. ... 6-4/228. ... Full name: Scott Paul Shields.
HIGH SCHOOL: Bonita Vista (Chula Vista, Calif.).
COLLEGE: Weber State.
TRANSACTIONS/CAREER NOTES: Selected by Pittsburgh Steelers in second round (59th pick overall) of 1999 NFL draft. ... Signed by Steelers (August 2, 1999).

			INTERCEPTIONS				SACKS
Year Team	G	GS	No.	Yds.	Avg.	TD	No.
1999—Pittsburgh NFL	16	1	4	75	18.8	0	1.0

SHIELDS, WILL — G — CHIEFS

PERSONAL: Born September 15, 1971, in Fort Riley, Kan. ... 6-3/321. ... Full name: Will Herthie Shields.
HIGH SCHOOL: Lawton (Okla.).
COLLEGE: Nebraska (degree in communications).
TRANSACTIONS/CAREER NOTES: Selected by Kansas City Chiefs in the third round (74th pick overall) of 1993 NFL draft. ... Signed by Chiefs (May 3, 1993). ... Designated by Chiefs as franchise player (February 11, 2000).
PLAYING EXPERIENCE: Kansas City NFL, 1993-1999. ... Games/Games started: 1993 (16/15), 1994 (16/16), 1995 (16/16), 1996 (16/16), 1997 (16/16), 1998 (16/16), 1999 (16/16). Total: 112/111.
CHAMPIONSHIP GAME EXPERIENCE: Played in AFC championship game (1993 season).
HONORS: Named guard on The Sporting News college All-America second team (1991). ... Named guard on The Sporting News college All-America first team (1992). ... Named guard on The Sporting News NFL All-Pro team (1999). ... Played in Pro Bowl (1995-1999 seasons).
PRO STATISTICS: 1993—Recovered two fumbles. 1994—Recovered one fumble. 1995—Recovered one fumble. 1998—Caught one pass for four yards and recovered one fumble. 1999—Recovered one fumble.

SIDNEY, DAINON — CB — TITANS

PERSONAL: Born May 30, 1975, in Atlanta. ... 6-0/188. ... Full name: Dainon Tarquinius Sidney. ... Name pronounced DAY-nun.
HIGH SCHOOL: Riverdale (Ga.).
COLLEGE: East Tennessee State, then Alabama-Birmingham.
TRANSACTIONS/CAREER NOTES: Selected by Tennessee Oilers in third round (77th pick overall) of 1998 NFL draft. ... Signed by Oilers (July 21, 1998). ... Oilers franchise renamed Tennessee Titans for 1999 season (December 26, 1998).
PLAYING EXPERIENCE: Tennessee NFL, 1998 and 1999. ... Games/Games started: 1998 (16/1), 1999 (16/2). Total: 32/3.
CHAMPIONSHIP GAME EXPERIENCE: Played in AFC championship game (1999 season). ... Played in Super Bowl XXXIV (1999 season).
PRO STATISTICS: 1999—Intercepted three passes for 12 yards and returned one punt for four yards.

SIMIEN, TRACY — LB

PERSONAL: Born May 21, 1967, in Bay City, Texas. ... 6-1/250. ... Full name: Tracy Anthony Simien. ... Cousin of Cedric Woodard, defensive tackle, Baltimore Ravens; related to Elmo Wright, wide receiver with Kansas City Chiefs (1971-74), Houston Oilers (1975) and New England Patriots (1975).
HIGH SCHOOL: Sweeny (Texas).
COLLEGE: Texas Christian.
TRANSACTIONS/CAREER NOTES: Signed as non-drafted free agent by Pittsburgh Steelers (May 3, 1989). ... Released by Steelers (September 5, 1989). ... Re-signed by Steelers to developmental squad (September 6, 1989). ... On developmental squad (September 6, 1989-January 5, 1990). ... Played in one playoff game with Steelers (1989 season). ... Granted unconditional free agency (February 1, 1990). ... Signed by New Orleans Saints (March 30, 1990). ... Released by Saints (September 3, 1990). ... Signed by Kansas City Chiefs to practice squad (November 30, 1990). ... Granted free agency after 1990 season. ... Re-signed by Chiefs (February 2, 1991). ... Assigned by Chiefs to Montreal Machine in 1991 WLAF enhancement allocation program (March 4, 1991). ... Granted unconditional free agency (February 13, 1998). ... Signed by San Diego Chargers (February 4, 1998). ... Released by Chargers (November 29, 1999).
CHAMPIONSHIP GAME EXPERIENCE: Played in AFC championship game (1993 season).
HONORS: Named outside linebacker on All-World League team (1991).
PRO STATISTICS: W.L.: 1991—Recovered one fumble for five yards. NFL: 1991—Recovered one fumble. 1994—Recovered two fumbles. 1995—Recovered three fumbles. 1996—Recovered one fumble. 1999—Recovered one fumble.

Year Team	G	GS	INTERCEPTIONS No.	Yds.	Avg.	TD	SACKS No.
1989—Pittsburgh NFL			Did not play.				
1990—Kansas City NFL			Did not play.				
1991—Montreal W.L.	10	10	0	0	0.0	0	5.0
—Kansas City NFL	15	12	0	0	0.0	0	2.0
1992—Kansas City NFL	15	15	3	18	6.0	0	1.0
1993—Kansas City NFL	16	14	0	0	0.0	0	0.0
1994—Kansas City NFL	15	15	0	0	0.0	0	0.0
1995—Kansas City NFL	16	16	0	0	0.0	0	1.0
1996—Kansas City NFL	16	13	1	2	2.0	0	0.0
1997—Kansas City NFL	16	0	0	0	0.0	0	0.0
1998—			Did not play.				
1999—San Diego NFL	8	4	1	4	4.0	0	1.0
W.L. totals (1 year)	10	10	0	0	0.0	0	5.0
NFL totals (7 years)	117	89	5	24	4.8	0	5.0
Pro totals (8 years)	127	99	5	24	4.8	0	10.0

SIMMONS, ANTHONY — LB — SEAHAWKS

PERSONAL: Born June 20, 1976, in Spartanburg, S.C. ... 6-0/230.
HIGH SCHOOL: Spartanburg (S.C.).
COLLEGE: Clemson (degree in marketing, 1998).
TRANSACTIONS/CAREER NOTES: Selected after junior season by Seattle Seahawks in first round (15th pick overall) of 1998 NFL draft. ... Signed by Seahawks (July 18, 1998).
PLAYING EXPERIENCE: Seattle NFL, 1998 and 1999. ... Games/Games started: 1998 (11/4), 1999 (16/16). Total: 27/20.
HONORS: Named inside linebacker on THE SPORTING NEWS college All-America first team (1996 and 1997).
PRO STATISTICS: 1998—Intercepted one pass for 36 yards and a touchdown.

SIMMONS, BRIAN — LB — BENGALS

PERSONAL: Born June 21, 1975, in New Bern, N.C. ... 6-3/248. ... Full name: Brian Eugene Simmons.
HIGH SCHOOL: New Bern (N.C.).
COLLEGE: North Carolina.
TRANSACTIONS/CAREER NOTES: Selected by Cincinnati Bengals in first round (17th pick overall) of 1998 NFL draft. ... Signed by Bengals (July 27, 1998).
HONORS: Named outside linebacker on THE SPORTING NEWS college All-America second team (1996). ... Named outside linebacker on THE SPORTING NEWS college All-America third team (1997).
PRO STATISTICS: 1998—Intercepted one pass for 18 yards and recovered one fumble for 22 yards. 1999—Recovered one fumble.

Year Team	G	GS	SACKS
1998—Cincinnati NFL	14	12	3.0
1999—Cincinnati NFL	16	16	3.0
Pro totals (2 years)	30	28	6.0

SIMMONS, CLYDE — DE — BEARS

PERSONAL: Born August 4, 1964, in Lanes, S.C. ... 6-5/292. ... Full name: Clyde Simmons Jr.
HIGH SCHOOL: New Hanover (Wilmington, N.C.).
COLLEGE: Western Carolina (degree in industrial distribution).
TRANSACTIONS/CAREER NOTES: Selected by Philadelphia Eagles in ninth round (233rd pick overall) of 1986 NFL draft. ... Signed by Eagles (July 3, 1986). ... Granted free agency (February 1, 1991). ... Re-signed by Eagles (August 28, 1991). ... Designated by Eagles as transition player (February 15, 1994). ... Signed by Phoenix Cardinals (March 17, 1994); Eagles received second-round pick (DB Brian Dawkins) in 1996 draft as compensation. ... Cardinals franchise renamed Arizona Cardinals for 1994 season. ... Released by Cardinals (August 19, 1996). ... Signed by Jacksonville Jaguars (August 23, 1996). ... Released by Jaguars (March 6, 1998). ... Signed by Cincinnati Bengals (May 13, 1998). ... Granted unconditional free agency (February 12, 1999). ... Signed by Chicago Bears (February 17, 1999).
CHAMPIONSHIP GAME EXPERIENCE: Played in AFC championship game (1996 season).
HONORS: Played in Pro Bowl (1991 and 1992 seasons). ... Named defensive end on THE SPORTING NEWS NFL All-Pro team (1991).
PRO STATISTICS: 1986—Returned one kickoff for no yards. 1987—Recovered one fumble. 1988—Credited with one safety, ran 15 yards with blocked field-goal attempt and recovered three fumbles. 1989—Intercepted one pass for 60 yards and a touchdown. 1990—Recovered two fumbles for 28 yards and one touchdown. 1991—Recovered three fumbles (including one in end zone for a touchdown). 1992—Recovered one fumble. 1993—Intercepted one pass for no yards. 1995—Intercepted one pass for 25 yards and a touchdown and recovered one fumble. 1996—Recovered one fumble. 1999—Recovered one fumble.

Year Team	G	GS	SACKS
1986—Philadelphia NFL	16	0	2.0
1987—Philadelphia NFL	12	12	6.0
1988—Philadelphia NFL	16	16	8.0
1989—Philadelphia NFL	16	16	15.5
1990—Philadelphia NFL	16	16	7.5
1991—Philadelphia NFL	16	16	13.0
1992—Philadelphia NFL	16	16	*19.0
1993—Philadelphia NFL	16	16	5.0
1994—Arizona NFL	16	16	6.0
1995—Arizona NFL	16	16	11.0
1996—Jacksonville NFL	16	14	7.5
1997—Jacksonville NFL	16	13	8.5
1998—Cincinnati NFL	16	16	5.0
1999—Chicago NFL	16	0	7.0
Pro totals (14 years)	220	183	121.0

SIMMONS, JASON   CB   STEELERS

PERSONAL: Born March 30, 1976, in Inglewood, Calif. ... 5-8/186. ... Full name: Jason Lawrence Simmons.
HIGH SCHOOL: Leuzinger (Lawndale, Calif.).
COLLEGE: Arizona State.
TRANSACTIONS/CAREER NOTES: Selected by Pittsburgh Steelers in fifth round (137th pick overall) of 1998 NFL draft. ... Signed by Steelers (July 14, 1998).
PLAYING EXPERIENCE: Pittsburgh NFL, 1998 and 1999. ... Games/Games started: 1998 (6/0), 1999 (16/0). Total: 22/0.
PRO STATISTICS: 1999—Recovered one fumble.

SIMMONS, TONY   WR   PATRIOTS

PERSONAL: Born December 8, 1974, in Galliapolis, Ohio. ... 6-1/206. ... Full name: Tony Angelo Simmons.
HIGH SCHOOL: St. Rita (Chicago).
COLLEGE: Wisconsin (degree in construction administration).
TRANSACTIONS/CAREER NOTES: Selected by New England Patriots in second round (52nd pick overall) of 1998 NFL draft. ... Signed by Patriots (July 18, 1998).
PRO STATISTICS: 1999—Returned six kickoffs for 132 yards.
SINGLE GAME HIGHS (regular season): Receptions—7 (October 10, 1999, vs. Kansas City); yards—109 (November 1, 1998, vs. Indianapolis); and touchdown receptions—1 (October 17, 1999, vs. Miami).
STATISTICAL PLATEAUS: 100-yard receiving games: 1998 (1), 1999 (1). Total: 2.

| | | | RECEIVING | | | | TOTALS | | | |
Year Team	G	GS	No.	Yds.	Avg.	TD	TD	2pt.	Pts.	Fum.
1998—New England NFL	11	6	23	474	20.6	3	3	0	18	0
1999—New England NFL	15	1	19	276	14.5	2	2	0	12	1
Pro totals (2 years)	26	7	42	750	17.9	5	5	0	30	1

SIMPSON, ANTOINE   DT   DOLPHINS

PERSONAL: Born December 2, 1976, in Gary, Ind. ... 6-2/310. ... Full name: Antoine Lagree Simpson.
HIGH SCHOOL: La Porte (Texas).
JUNIOR COLLEGE: Fort Scott (Kan.) Community College.
COLLEGE: Houston.
TRANSACTIONS/CAREER NOTES: Signed as non-drafted free agent by Miami Dolphins (April 23, 1998). ... Released Dolphins (August 25, 1998). ... Re-signed by Dolphins to practice squad (September 1, 1998). ... Released by Dolphins (September 8, 1998). ... Re-signed by Dolphins (February 3, 1999).
PLAYING EXPERIENCE: Miami NFL, 1999. ... Games/Games started: 1999 (3/0).

SIMS, BARRY   G/OT   RAIDERS

PERSONAL: Born December 1, 1974, in Park City, Utah. ... 6-5/295.
HIGH SCHOOL: Park City (Utah).
JUNIOR COLLEGE: Dixie College (Utah).
COLLEGE: Utah.
TRANSACTIONS/CAREER NOTES: Selected by Scottish Claymores in 1999 NFL Europe draft (February 23, 1999). ... Signed as non-drafted free agent by Oakland Raiders prior to 1999 season.
PLAYING EXPERIENCE: Scottish Claymores NFLE, 1999; Oakland NFL, 1999. ... Games/Games started: NFLE 1999 (games played unavailable), NFL 1999 (16/10).

SIMS, KEITH   G   REDSKINS

PERSONAL: Born June 17, 1967, in Baltimore. ... 6-3/318. ... Full name: Keith Alexander Sims.
HIGH SCHOOL: Watchung Hills Regional (Warren, N.J.).
COLLEGE: Iowa State (degree in industrial technology, 1989).
TRANSACTIONS/CAREER NOTES: Selected by Miami Dolphins in second round (39th pick overall) of 1990 NFL draft. ... Signed by Dolphins (July 30, 1990). ... On injured reserve with knee injury (October 12-November 18, 1991). ... Granted free agency (March 1, 1993). ... Re-signed by Dolphins (July 16, 1993). ... Granted unconditional free agency (February 16, 1996). ... Re-signed by Dolphins (March 8, 1996). ... Released by Dolphins (December 9, 1997). ... Signed by Washington Redskins (December 11, 1997). ... Inactive for two games with Redskins (1997). ... Granted unconditional free agency (February 13, 1998). ... Signed by Philadelphia Eagles (March 2, 1998). ... Released by Eagles (August 30, 1998). ... Signed by Washington Redskins (November 24, 1998). ... Granted unconditional free agency (February 12, 1999). ... Re-signed by Redskins (March 16, 1999). ... Granted unconditional free agency (February 23, 2000).
PLAYING EXPERIENCE: Miami NFL, 1990-1997; Washington NFL, 1998 and 1999. ... Games/Games started: 1990 (14/13), 1991 (12/12), 1992 (16/16), 1993 (16/16), 1994 (16/16), 1995 (16/16), 1996 (15/15), 1997 (8/4), 1998 (4/0), 1999 (12/12). Total: 129/120.
CHAMPIONSHIP GAME EXPERIENCE: Played in AFC championship game (1992 season).
HONORS: Played in Pro Bowl (1993-1995 seasons).
PRO STATISTICS: 1990—Returned one kickoff for nine yards and recovered one fumble. 1991—Caught one pass for nine yards. 1993—Recovered one fumble. 1994—Recovered two fumbles. 1995—Recovered one fumble.

SINCENO, KASEEM   TE   PACKERS

PERSONAL: Born March 26, 1976, in Bronx, N.Y. ... 6-4/259. ... Name pronounced sin-SEE-no.
HIGH SCHOOL: Liberty (N.Y.).

S

COLLEGE: Syracuse.

TRANSACTIONS/CAREER NOTES: Signed as non-drafted free agent by Phiadelphia Eagles (April 21, 1998). ... Released by Eagles (August 30, 1998). ... Re-signed by Eagles to practice squad (September 1, 1998). ... Activated (September 17, 1998). ... On injured reserve with ankle injury (December 1, 1998-remainder of season). ... On injured reserve with foot injury (September 5, 1999-entire season). ... Traded by Eagles to Green Bay Packers for TE Jeff Thomason (March 16, 2000).

PLAYING EXPERIENCE: Philadelphia NFL, 1998. ... Games/Games started: 1998 (10/0).

PRO STATISTICS: 1998—Caught three passes for 42 yards and one touchdown and fumbled once.

SINGLE GAME HIGHS (regular season): Receptions—1 (November 15, 1998, vs. Washington); yards—28 (September 27, 1998, vs. Kansas City); and touchdown receptions—1 (October 11, 1998, vs. Washington).

SINCLAIR, MICHAEL DE SEAHAWKS

PERSONAL: Born January 31, 1968, in Galveston, Texas. ... 6-4/275. ... Full name: Michael Glenn Sinclair.

HIGH SCHOOL: Charlton-Pollard (Beaumont, Texas).

COLLEGE: Eastern New Mexico (degree in physical education).

TRANSACTIONS/CAREER NOTES: Selected by Seattle Seahawks in sixth round (155th pick overall) of 1991 NFL draft. ... Signed by Seahawks (July 18, 1991). ... Released by Seahawks (August 26, 1991). ... Re-signed by Seahawks to practice squad (August 28, 1991). ... Activated (November 30, 1991). ... On injured reserve with back injury (December 14, 1991-remainder of season). ... Active for two games (1991); did not play. ... Assigned by Seahawks to Sacramento Surge in 1992 World League enhancement allocation program (February 20, 1992). ... On injured reserve with ankle injury (September 1-October 3, 1992). ... On injured reserve with thumb injury (November 10, 1993-remainder of season). ... Granted free agency (February 17, 1995). ... Re-signed by Seahawks (May 24, 1995). ... Granted unconditional free agency (February 16, 1996). ... Re-signed by Seahawks (February 17, 1996).

HONORS: Named defensive end on All-World League team (1992). ... Played in Pro Bowl (1996-1998 seasons).

PRO STATISTICS: W.L.: 1992—Recovered one fumble. NFL: 1995—Recovered two fumbles. 1997—Recovered one fumble in end zone for a touchdown. 1999—Recovered one fumble for 13 yards.

Year Team	G	GS	SACKS
1991—Seattle NFL	Did not play.		
1992—Sacramento W.L.	10	10	10.0
—Seattle NFL	12	1	1.0
1993—Seattle NFL	9	1	8.0
1994—Seattle NFL	12	2	4.5
1995—Seattle NFL	16	15	5.5
1996—Seattle NFL	16	16	13.0
1997—Seattle NFL	16	16	12.0
1998—Seattle NFL	16	16	*16.5
1999—Seattle NFL	15	15	6.0
W.L. totals (1 year)	10	10	10.0
NFL totals (7 years)	112	82	66.5
Pro totals (8 years)	122	92	76.5

SINGLETON, ALSHERMOND LB BUCCANEERS

PERSONAL: Born August 7, 1975, in Newark, N.J. ... 6-2/228. ... Full name: Alshermond Glendale Singleton.

HIGH SCHOOL: Irvington (N.J.).

COLLEGE: Temple (degree in sports recreation management).

TRANSACTIONS/CAREER NOTES: Selected by Tampa Bay Buccaneers in fourth round (128th pick overall) of 1997 NFL draft. ... Signed by Buccaneers (July 17, 1997).

PLAYING EXPERIENCE: Tampa Bay NFL, 1997-1999. ... Games/Games started: 1997 (12/0), 1998 (15/0), 1999 (15/0). Total: 42/0.

CHAMPIONSHIP GAME EXPERIENCE: Member of Buccaneers for NFC championship game (1999 season); inactive.

PRO STATISTICS: 1997—Returned blocked punt 28 yards for a touchdown. 1999—Intercepted one pass for seven yards and credited with $1/2$ sack.

SIRAGUSA, TONY DT RAVENS

PERSONAL: Born May 14, 1967, in Kenilworth, N.J. ... 6-3/340. ... Full name: Anthony Siragusa.

HIGH SCHOOL: David Brearley Regional (Kenilworth, N.J.).

COLLEGE: Pittsburgh.

TRANSACTIONS/CAREER NOTES: Signed as non-drafted free agent by Indianapolis Colts (April 30, 1990). ... Granted unconditional free agency (February 14, 1997). ... Signed by Baltimore Ravens (April 24, 1997).

CHAMPIONSHIP GAME EXPERIENCE: Played in AFC championship game (1995 season).

PRO STATISTICS: 1990—Recovered one fumble. 1991—Recovered one fumble for five yards. 1992—Recovered one fumble. 1994—Recovered one fumble. 1996—Recovered one fumble. 1997—Recovered one fumble for seven yards. 1998—Recovered one fumble. 1999—Recovered one fumble.

Year Team	G	GS	SACKS
1990—Indianapolis NFL	13	6	1.0
1991—Indianapolis NFL	13	6	2.0
1992—Indianapolis NFL	16	12	3.0
1993—Indianapolis NFL	14	14	1.5
1994—Indianapolis NFL	16	16	5.0
1995—Indianapolis NFL	14	14	2.0
1996—Indianapolis NFL	10	10	2.0
1997—Baltimore NFL	14	13	0.0
1998—Baltimore NFL	15	15	0.0
1999—Baltimore NFL	14	14	3.5
Pro totals (10 years)	139	120	20.0

S

SLADE, CHRIS   LB   PATRIOTS

PERSONAL: Born January 30, 1971, in Newport News, Va. ... 6-5/245. ... Full name: Christopher Carroll Slade. ... Cousin of Terry Kirby, running back, Cleveland Browns; and cousin of Wayne Kirby, outfielder, Baltimore Orioles organization.
HIGH SCHOOL: Tabb (Va.).
COLLEGE: Virginia.
TRANSACTIONS/CAREER NOTES: Selected by New England Patriots in second round (31st pick overall) of 1993 NFL draft. ... Signed by Patriots (July 24, 1993). ... Granted free agency (February 16, 1996). ... Re-signed by Patriots (May 28, 1996).
CHAMPIONSHIP GAME EXPERIENCE: Played in AFC championship game (1996 season). ... Played in Super Bowl XXXI (1996 season).
HONORS: Named defensive lineman on THE SPORTING NEWS college All-America first team (1992). ... Played in Pro Bowl (1997 season).
PRO STATISTICS: 1993—Recovered one fumble. 1995—Recovered two fumbles for 38 yards and one touchdown. 1996—Intercepted one pass for two yards and fumbled once. 1997—Intercepted one pass for one yard and a touchdown. 1999—Intercepted one pass for no yards.

Year Team	G	GS	SACKS
1993—New England NFL	16	5	9.0
1994—New England NFL	16	16	9.5
1995—New England NFL	16	16	4.0
1996—New England NFL	16	9	7.0
1997—New England NFL	16	16	9.0
1998—New England NFL	15	15	4.0
1999—New England NFL	16	16	4.5
Pro totals (7 years)	111	93	47.0

SLOAN, DAVID   TE   LIONS

PERSONAL: Born June 8, 1972, in Fresno, Calif. ... 6-6/260. ... Full name: David Lyle Sloan.
HIGH SCHOOL: Sierra Joint Union (Tollhouse, Calif.).
JUNIOR COLLEGE: Fresno (Calif.) City College.
COLLEGE: New Mexico.
TRANSACTIONS/CAREER NOTES: Selected by Detroit Lions in third round (70th pick overall) of 1995 NFL draft. ... Signed by Lions (July 20, 1995). ... Granted free agency (February 13, 1998). ... Re-signed by Lions (June 10, 1998). ... On physically unable to perform list with knee injury (August 25-October 23, 1998). ... Granted unconditional free agency (February 12, 1999). ... Re-signed by Lions (March 24, 1999).
HONORS: Played in Pro Bowl (1999 season).
PRO STATISTICS: 1995—Returned one kickoff for 14 yards. 1996—Recovered one fumble.
SINGLE GAME HIGHS (regular season): Receptions—7 (November 14, 1999, vs. Arizona); yards—88 (November 14, 1999, vs. Arizona); and touchdown receptions—1 (November 14, 1999, vs. Arizona).

Year Team	G	GS	RECEIVING No.	Yds.	Avg.	TD	TOTALS TD	2pt.	Pts.	Fum.
1995—Detroit NFL	16	8	17	184	10.8	1	1	0	6	0
1996—Detroit NFL	4	4	7	51	7.3	0	0	0	0	0
1997—Detroit NFL	14	12	29	264	9.1	0	0	0	0	0
1998—Detroit NFL	10	2	11	146	13.3	1	1	0	6	0
1999—Detroit NFL	16	15	47	591	12.6	4	4	0	24	0
Pro totals (5 years)	60	41	111	1236	11.1	6	6	0	36	0

SLUTZKER, SCOTT   TE

PERSONAL: Born December 20, 1972, in Hasbrouck Heights, N.J. ... 6-4/240.
HIGH SCHOOL: Hasbrouck Heights (N.J.).
COLLEGE: Iowa.
TRANSACTIONS/CAREER NOTES: Selected by Indianapolis Colts in third round (82nd pick overall) of 1996 NFL draft. ... Signed by Colts (July 11, 1996). ... On injured reserve with ankle injury (November 27, 1997-remainder of season). ... Traded by Colts to New Orleans Saints for LB Andre Royal (August 30, 1998). ... Granted free agency (February 12, 1999). ... Re-signed by Saints (April 14, 1999). ... On injured reserve with knee injury (December 24, 1999-remainder of season). ... Granted unconditional free agency (February 11, 2000).
PRO STATISTICS: 1997—Recovered two fumbles.
SINGLE GAME HIGHS (regular season): Receptions—4 (October 17, 1999, vs. Tennessee); yards—64 (November 21, 1999, vs. Jacksonville); and touchdown receptions—1 (October 17, 1999, vs. Tennessee).

Year Team	G	GS	RECEIVING No.	Yds.	Avg.	TD	TOTALS TD	2pt.	Pts.	Fum.
1996—Indianapolis NFL	15	0	0	0	0.0	0	0	0	0	0
1997—Indianapolis NFL	12	2	3	22	7.3	0	0	0	0	0
1998—New Orleans NFL	3	0	1	10	10.0	0	0	0	0	0
1999—New Orleans NFL	11	2	11	164	14.9	1	1	0	6	1
Pro totals (4 years)	41	4	15	196	13.1	1	1	0	6	1

SMALL, TORRANCE   WR   EAGLES

PERSONAL: Born September 4, 1970, in Tampa. ... 6-3/209. ... Full name: Torrance Ramon Small.
HIGH SCHOOL: Thomas Jefferson (Tampa).
COLLEGE: Alcorn State.
TRANSACTIONS/CAREER NOTES: Selected by New Orleans Saints in fifth round (138th pick overall) of 1992 NFL draft. ... Signed by Saints (July 15, 1992). ... Released by Saints (September 3, 1992). ... Re-signed by Saints to practice squad (September 4, 1992). ... Activated (September 19, 1992). ... Granted free agency (February 17, 1995). ... Tendered offer sheet by Seattle Seahawks (March 8, 1995). ... Offer matched by Saints (March 15, 1995). ... Released by Saints (May 28, 1997). ... Signed by St. Louis Rams (June 7, 1997). ... Granted unconditional free agency (February 13, 1998). ... Signed by Indianapolis Colts (April 15, 1998). ... Granted unconditional free agency (February 12, 1999). ... Signed by Philadelphia Eagles (February 16, 1999).

PRO STATISTICS: 1994—Recovered one fumble. 1995—Rushed six times for 75 yards and one touchdown and recovered one fumble. 1996—Rushed four times for 51 yards and one touchdown. 1998—Rushed once for two yards and attempted one pass without a completion. 1999—Attempted two passes without a completion.

SINGLE GAME HIGHS (regular season): Receptions—9 (November 29, 1998, vs. Baltimore); yards—200 (December 24, 1994, vs. Denver); and touchdown receptions—2 (December 19, 1999, vs. New England).

STATISTICAL PLATEAUS: 100-yard receiving games: 1994 (1), 1998 (2), 1999 (1). Total: 4.

				RECEIVING				TOTALS			
Year Team	G	GS	No.	Yds.	Avg.	TD	TD	2pt.	Pts.	Fum.
1992—New Orleans NFL	13	2	23	278	12.1	3	3	0	18	0
1993—New Orleans NFL	11	0	16	164	10.3	1	1	0	6	0
1994—New Orleans NFL	16	0	49	719	14.7	5	5	1	32	0
1995—New Orleans NFL	16	1	38	461	12.1	5	6	0	36	0
1996—New Orleans NFL	16	13	50	558	11.2	2	3	0	18	1
1997—St. Louis NFL	13	7	32	488	15.3	1	1	0	6	0
1998—Indianapolis NFL	16	4	45	681	15.1	7	7	0	42	0
1999—Philadelphia NFL	15	15	49	655	13.4	4	4	0	24	0
Pro totals (8 years)	116	42	302	4004	13.3	28	30	1	182	1

SMEDLEY, ERIC   DB

PERSONAL: Born July 23, 1973, in Charleston, W.Va. ... 5-11/199. ... Full name: Eric Alan Smedley.
HIGH SCHOOL: Capital (Chesterton, W.Va.).
COLLEGE: Indiana.
TRANSACTIONS/CAREER NOTES: Selected by Buffalo Bills in seventh round (249th pick overall) of 1996 NFL draft. ... Signed by Bills (July 2, 1996). ... Granted free agency (February 12, 1999). ... Re-signed by Bills (April 19, 1999). ... Released by Bills (September 4, 1999). ... Signed by Indianapolis Colts (October 12, 1999). ... Released by Colts (November 20, 1999). ... Re-signed by Colts (November 24, 1999). ... Granted unconditional free agency (February 11, 2000).
PLAYING EXPERIENCE: Buffalo NFL, 1996-1998; Indianapolis NFL, 1999. ... Games/Games started: 1996 (6/0), 1997 (13/1), 1998 (16/0), 1999 (7/0). Total: 42/1.
PRO STATISTICS: 1998—Credited with two sacks.

SMEENGE, JOEL   DE   JAGUARS

PERSONAL: Born April 1, 1968, in Holland, Mich. ... 6-6/265. ... Full name: Joel Andrew Smeenge. ... Name pronounced SMEN-ghee.
HIGH SCHOOL: Hudsonville (Mich.).
COLLEGE: Western Michigan.
TRANSACTIONS/CAREER NOTES: Selected by New Orleans Saints in third round (70th pick overall) of 1990 NFL draft. ... Signed by Saints (July 17, 1990). ... Granted free agency (March 1, 1993). ... Re-signed by Saints (July 9, 1993). ... Granted unconditional free agency (February 17, 1995). ... Signed by Jacksonville Jaguars (February 28, 1995). ... On injured reserve with broken jaw (November 12, 1996-remainder of season).
CHAMPIONSHIP GAME EXPERIENCE: Played in AFC championship game (1999 season).
PRO STATISTICS: 1991—Recovered one fumble. 1992—Recovered one fumble. 1995—Intercepted one pass for 12 yards and fumbled once. 1997—Recovered two fumbles for one yard. 1998—Recovered one fumble. 1999—Credited with a safety.

Year Team	G	GS	SACKS
1990—New Orleans NFL	15	0	0.0
1991—New Orleans NFL	14	0	0.0
1992—New Orleans NFL	11	0	0.5
1993—New Orleans NFL	16	2	1.0
1994—New Orleans NFL	16	2	0.0
1995—Jacksonville NFL	15	15	4.0
1996—Jacksonville NFL	10	10	5.0
1997—Jacksonville NFL	16	0	6.5
1998—Jacksonville NFL	16	14	7.5
1999—Jacksonville NFL	15	7	5.0
Pro totals (10 years)	144	50	29.5

SMITH, AARON   DE   STEELERS

PERSONAL: Born April 9, 1976, in Colorado Springs, Colo. ... 6-5/281. ... Full name: Aaron Douglas Smith.
HIGH SCHOOL: Sierra (Colorado Springs, Colo.).
COLLEGE: Northern Colorado.
TRANSACTIONS/CAREER NOTES: Selected by Pittsburgh Steelers in fourth round (109th pick overall) of 1999 NFL draft. ... Signed by Steelers (August 3, 1999).
PLAYING EXPERIENCE: Pittsburgh NFL, 1999. ... Games/Games started: 1999 (6/0).

SMITH, AKILI   QB   BENGALS

PERSONAL: Born August 21, 1975, in San Diego. ... 6-3/220. ... Full name: Kabisa Akili Maradu Smith. ... Cousin of Marquis Smith, defensive back, Cleveland Browns. ... Name pronounced uh-KEE-lee.
HIGH SCHOOL: Lincoln (San Diego).
JUNIOR COLLEGE: Grossmont College (Calif.).
COLLEGE: Oregon.
TRANSACTIONS/CAREER NOTES: Selected by Cincinnati Bengals in first round (third pick overall) of 1999 NFL draft. ... Signed by Bengals (August 24, 1999).
PRO STATISTICS: 1999—Caught one pass for six yards, fumbled four times and recovered one fumble for minus three yards.

SINGLE GAME HIGHS (regular season): Attempts—42 (October 10, 1999, vs. Cleveland); completions—25 (October 10, 1999, vs. Cleveland); passing yards—221 (October 10, 1999, vs. Cleveland); and touchdown passes—2 (October 10, 1999, vs. Cleveland).
MISCELLANEOUS: Regular-season record as starting NFL quarterback: 1-3 (.250).

				PASSING							RUSHING				TOTALS		
Year Team	G	GS	Att.	Cmp.	Pct.	Yds.	TD	Int.	Avg.	Rat.	Att.	Yds.	Avg.	TD	TD	2pt.	Pts.
1999—Cincinnati NFL.............	7	4	153	80	52.3	805	2	6	5.26	55.6	19	114	6.0	1	1	0	6

RECORD AS BASEBALL PLAYER

TRANSACTIONS/CAREER NOTES: Threw right, batted right. ... Selected by Pittsburgh Pirates organizaiton in seventh round of free-agent draft (June 3, 1993).

						BATTING									FIELDING		
Year Team (League)	Pos.	G	AB	R	H	2B	3B	HR	RBI	Avg.	BB	SO	SB	PO	A	E	Avg.
1993—GC Pirates (GCL)	OF	29	95	13	19	3	2	1	9	.200	10	18	1	31	2	4	.892
1994—GC Pirates (GCL).........	OF	19	69	10	12	3	0	2	10	.173	2	18	0	18	1	0	1.000
Totals (2 years)...................		48	164	23	31	6	2	3	19	.189	12	36	1	49	3	4	.929

SMITH, ANTOWAIN   RB   BILLS

PERSONAL: Born March 14, 1972, in Montgomery, Ala. ... 6-2/225. ... Full name: Antowain Drurell Smith. ... Name pronounced AN-twan.
HIGH SCHOOL: Elmore (Ala.).
JUNIOR COLLEGE: East Mississippi Junior College.
COLLEGE: Houston.
TRANSACTIONS/CAREER NOTES: Selected by Buffalo Bills in first round (23rd pick overall) of 1997 NFL draft. ... Signed by Bills (July 11, 1997).
PRO STATISTICS: 1998—Recovered two fumbles.
SINGLE GAME HIGHS (regular season): Attempts—31 (October 11, 1998, vs. Indianapolis); yards—130 (October 11, 1998, vs. Indianapolis); and rushing touchdowns—3 (September 21, 1997, vs. Indianapolis).
STATISTICAL PLATEAUS: 100-yard rushing games: 1997 (1), 1998 (3), 1999 (2). Total: 6.

			RUSHING				RECEIVING				TOTALS			
Year Team	G	GS	Att.	Yds.	Avg.	TD	No.	Yds.	Avg.	TD	TD	2pt.	Pts.	Fum.
1997—Buffalo NFL..............................	16	0	194	840	4.3	8	28	177	6.3	0	8	0	48	4
1998—Buffalo NFL..............................	16	14	300	1124	3.7	8	5	11	2.2	0	8	0	48	5
1999—Buffalo NFL..............................	14	11	165	614	3.7	6	2	32	16.0	0	6	0	36	4
Pro totals (3 years)............................	46	25	659	2578	3.9	22	35	220	6.3	0	22	0	132	13

SMITH, BRADY   DE   FALCONS

PERSONAL: Born June 5, 1973, in Royal Oak, Mich. ... 6-5/270. ... Full name: Brady McKay Smith. ... Son of Steve Smith, offensive tackle with four NFL teams (1966-74).
HIGH SCHOOL: Barrington (Ill.).
COLLEGE: Colorado State (degree in liberal arts).
TRANSACTIONS/CAREER NOTES: Selected by New Orleans Saints in third round (70th pick overall) of 1996 NFL draft. ... Signed by Saints (July 12, 1996). ... Granted free agency (February 12, 1999). ... Re-signed by Saints (April 14, 1999). ... Granted unconditional free agency (February 11, 2000). ... Signed by Atlanta Falcons (February 19, 2000).
PRO STATISTICS: 1996—Returned two kickoffs for 14 yards. 1999—Recovered two fumbles.

Year Team	G	GS	SACKS
1996—New Orleans NFL..	16	4	2.0
1997—New Orleans NFL..	16	2	5.0
1998—New Orleans NFL..	14	5	0.0
1999—New Orleans NFL..	16	16	6.0
Pro totals (4 years)...	62	27	13.0

SMITH, BRENT   OT   DOLPHINS

PERSONAL: Born November 21, 1973, in Dallas. ... 6-5/315. ... Full name: Gary Brent Smith.
HIGH SCHOOL: Pontotoc (Miss.).
COLLEGE: Mississippi State.
TRANSACTIONS/CAREER NOTES: Selected by Miami Dolphins in third round (96th pick overall) of 1997 NFL draft. ... Signed by Dolphins (July 8, 1997). ... Active for two games (1997); did not play. ... Granted free agency (February 11, 2000).
PLAYING EXPERIENCE: Miami NFL, 1998 and 1999. ... Games/Games started: 1998 (8/7), 1999 (13/4). Total: 21/11.

SMITH, BRUCE   DE   REDSKINS

PERSONAL: Born June 18, 1963, in Norfolk, Va. ... 6-4/279. ... Full name: Bruce Bernard Smith.
HIGH SCHOOL: Booker T. Washington (Norfolk, Va.).
COLLEGE: Virginia Tech.
TRANSACTIONS/CAREER NOTES: Selected by Baltimore Stars in 1985 USFL territorial draft. ... Signed by Buffalo Bills (February 28, 1985). ... Selected officially by Bills in first round (first pick overall) of 1985 NFL draft. ... On non-football injury list with substance abuse problem (September 2-28, 1988). ... Granted free agency (February 1, 1989). ... Tendered offer sheet by Denver Broncos (March 23, 1989). ... Offer matched by Bills (March 29, 1989). ... On injured reserve with knee injury (October 12-November 30, 1991). ... Released by Bills (February 10, 2000). ... Signed by Washington Redskins (February 12, 2000).
CHAMPIONSHIP GAME EXPERIENCE: Played in AFC championship game (1988 and 1990-1993 seasons). ... Played in Super Bowl XXV (1990 season), Super Bowl XXVI (1991 season), Super Bowl XXVII (1992 season) and Super Bowl XXVIII (1993 season).

HONORS: Named defensive lineman on THE SPORTING NEWS college All-America second team (1983 and 1984). ... Outland Trophy winner (1984). ... Named defensive end on THE SPORTING NEWS NFL All-Pro team (1987, 1988, 1990 and 1992-1997). ... Played in Pro Bowl (1987-1990, 1994, 1995, 1997 and 1998 seasons). ... Named Outstanding Player of Pro Bowl (1987 season). ... Named to play in Pro Bowl (1992 season); replaced by Howie Long due to injury. ... Named to play in Pro Bowl (1993 season); replaced by Sean Jones due to injury. ... Named to play in Pro Bowl (1996 season); replaced by Willie McGinest due to injury.

POST SEASON RECORDS: Shares Super Bowl single-game record for most safeties—1 (January 27, 1991, vs. New York Giants). ... Shares NFL postseason career record for most sacks—12. ... Shares NFL postseason single-game record for most safeties—1 (January 27, 1991, vs. New York Giants).

PRO STATISTICS: 1985—Rushed once for no yards and recovered four fumbles. 1987—Recovered two fumbles for 15 yards and one touchdown. 1988—Credited with one safety. 1993—Intercepted one pass for no yards and recovered one fumble. 1994—Intercepted one pass for no yards and recovered two fumbles. 1995—Recovered one fumble. 1996—Recovered one fumble. 1998—Recovered two fumbles for 18 yards. 1999—Recovered one fumble.

MISCELLANEOUS: Active NFL leader for career sacks (171). ... Holds Buffalo Bills all-time record for most sacks (171).

Year Team	G	GS	SACKS
1985—Buffalo NFL	16	13	6.5
1986—Buffalo NFL	16	15	15.0
1987—Buffalo NFL	12	12	12.0
1988—Buffalo NFL	12	12	11.0
1989—Buffalo NFL	16	16	13.0
1990—Buffalo NFL	16	16	19.0
1991—Buffalo NFL	5	5	1.5
1992—Buffalo NFL	15	15	14.0
1993—Buffalo NFL	16	16	14.0
1994—Buffalo NFL	15	15	10.5
1995—Buffalo NFL	15	15	10.5
1996—Buffalo NFL	16	16	▲13.5
1997—Buffalo NFL	16	16	§14.0
1998—Buffalo NFL	15	15	10.0
1999—Buffalo NFL	16	16	7.0
Pro totals (15 years)	217	213	171.0

SMITH, CHUCK   DE   PANTHERS

PERSONAL: Born December 21, 1969, in Athens, Ga. ... 6-2/262. ... Full name: Charles Henry Smith III.

HIGH SCHOOL: Clarke Central (Athens, Ga.).

COLLEGE: Northeastern Oklahoma A&M, then Tennessee.

TRANSACTIONS/CAREER NOTES: Selected by Atlanta Falcons in second round (51st pick overall) of 1992 NFL draft. ... Signed by Falcons (July 27, 1992). ... On suspended list (July 25-August 15, 1994). ... On injured reserve with knee injury (December 21, 1994-remainder of season). ... Granted free agency (February 17, 1995). ... Re-signed by Falcons (July 14, 1995). ... Granted unconditional free agency (February 16, 1996). ... Re-signed by Falcons (February 27, 1996). ... Granted unconditional free agency (February 11, 2000). ... Signed by Carolina Panthers (February 22, 2000).

CHAMPIONSHIP GAME EXPERIENCE: Played in NFC championship game (1998 season). ... Played in Super Bowl XXXIII (1998 season).

PRO STATISTICS: 1993—Recovered two fumbles. 1994—Intercepted one pass for 36 yards and a touchdown and recovered two fumbles. 1995—Recovered two fumbles. 1996—Intercepted one pass for 21 yards and recovered one fumble. 1997—Intercepted one pass for four yards. 1998—Recovered four fumbles for 71 yards and one touchdown. 1999—Recovered one fumble for 18 yards.

Year Team	G	GS	SACKS
1992—Atlanta NFL	16	0	2.0
1993—Atlanta NFL	15	1	3.5
1994—Atlanta NFL	15	10	11.0
1995—Atlanta NFL	14	13	5.5
1996—Atlanta NFL	15	15	6.0
1997—Atlanta NFL	16	15	12.0
1998—Atlanta NFL	16	16	8.5
1999—Atlanta NFL	16	16	10.0
Pro totals (8 years)	123	86	58.5

SMITH, DARRIN   LB

PERSONAL: Born April 15, 1970, in Miami. ... 6-1/230. ... Full name: Darrin Andrew Smith.

HIGH SCHOOL: Miami Norland.

COLLEGE: Miami, Fla. (degree in business management, 1991; master's degree in business administration, 1993).

TRANSACTIONS/CAREER NOTES: Selected by Dallas Cowboys in second round (54th pick overall) of 1993 NFL draft. ... Signed by Cowboys (July 21, 1993). ... On reserve/did not report list (July 20-October 14, 1995). ... Granted free agency (February 16, 1996). ... Re-signed by Cowboys (June 17, 1996). ... Granted unconditional free agency (February 14, 1997). ... Signed by Philadelphia Eagles (April 19, 1997). ... On injured reserve with ankle injury (November 19, 1997-remainder of season). ... Granted unconditional free agency (February 13, 1998). ... Signed by Seattle Seahawks (February 19, 1998). ... Released by Seahawks (February 10, 2000).

CHAMPIONSHIP GAME EXPERIENCE: Played in NFC championship game (1993 and 1995 seasons). ... Member of Super Bowl championship team (1993 and 1995 seasons).

PRO STATISTICS: 1993—Recovered one fumble. 1994—Recovered two fumbles for 11 yards. 1995—Recovered one fumble for 63 yards. 1997—Recovered one fumble. 1998—Recovered two fumbles.

Year Team	G	GS	INTERCEPTIONS No.	Yds.	Avg.	TD	SACKS No.
1993—Dallas NFL	16	13	0	0	0.0	0	1.0
1994—Dallas NFL	16	16	2	13	6.5	1	4.0
1995—Dallas NFL	9	9	0	0	0.0	0	3.0
1996—Dallas NFL	16	16	0	0	0.0	0	1.0
1997—Philadelphia NFL	7	7	0	0	0.0	0	1.0
1998—Seattle NFL	13	12	3	56	18.7	▲2	5.0

1999—Seattle NFL	15	15	1	0	0.0	0	1.0
Pro totals (7 years)	92	88	6	69	11.5	3	16.0

SMITH, DEREK   LB   REDSKINS

PERSONAL: Born January 18, 1975, in American Fork, Utah. ... 6-2/239. ... Full name: Derek Mecham Smith.
HIGH SCHOOL: American Fork (Utah).
JUNIOR COLLEGE: Snow College (Utah).
COLLEGE: Arizona State.
TRANSACTIONS/CAREER NOTES: Selected by Washington Redskins in third round (80th pick overall) of 1997 NFL draft. ... Signed by Redskins (July 11, 1997). ... Granted free agency (February 11, 2000). ... Re-signed by Redskins (April 11, 2000).
PRO STATISTICS: 1997—Recovered two fumbles for five yards. 1998—Recovered one fumble. 1999—Intercepted one pass for no yards and recovered one fumble.

Year Team	G	GS	SACKS
1997—Washington NFL	16	16	2.0
1998—Washington NFL	16	15	0.5
1999—Washington NFL	16	16	1.0
Pro totals (3 years)	48	47	3.5

SMITH, DETRON   FB   BRONCOS

S

PERSONAL: Born February 25, 1974, in Dallas. ... 5-10/230. ... Full name: Detron Negil Smith. ... Name pronounced DEE-tron.
HIGH SCHOOL: Lake Highlands (Dallas).
COLLEGE: Texas A&M.
TRANSACTIONS/CAREER NOTES: Selected by Denver Broncos in third round (65th pick overall) of 1996 NFL draft. ... Signed by Broncos (July 20, 1996).
PLAYING EXPERIENCE: Denver NFL, 1996-1999. ... Games/Games started: 1996 (13/0), 1997 (16/0), 1998 (15/2), 1999 (16/0). Total: 60/2.
CHAMPIONSHIP GAME EXPERIENCE: Played in AFC championship game (1997 and 1998 seasons). ... Member of Super Bowl championship team (1997 and 1998 seasons).
HONORS: Played in Pro Bowl (1999 season).
PRO STATISTICS: 1997—Rushed four times for 10 yards, caught four passes for 41 yards and one touchdown and returned one kickoff for no yards. 1998—Caught three passes for 24 yards and returned three kickoffs for 51 yards. 1999—Rushed once for seven yards, caught four passes for 23 yards, returned one kickoff for 12 yards and recovered one fumble.
SINGLE GAME HIGHS (regular season): Attempts—2 (December 21, 1997, vs. San Diego); yards—11 (December 21, 1997, vs. San Diego); and rushing touchdowns—0.

SMITH, ED   TE

PERSONAL: Born June 5, 1969, in Trenton, N.J. ... 6-4/253. ... Full name: Ed Martin Smith. ... Brother of Irv Smith, tight end with New Orleans Saints (1993-97), San Francisco 49ers (1998) and Cleveland Browns (1999).
HIGH SCHOOL: Pemberton (N.J.).
COLLEGE: None.
TRANSACTIONS/CAREER NOTES: Played for Frankfurt Galaxy of World League (1996). ... Signed as non-drafted free agent by St. Louis Rams (July 6, 1996). ... Released by Rams (August 20, 1996). ... Signed by Washington Redskins to practice squad (August 26, 1996). ... Granted free ageancy after 1996 season. ... Signed by Atlanta Falcons (March 3, 1997). ... Released by Falcons (August 24, 1997). ... Signed by Falcons to practice squad (August 26, 1997). ... Activated (November 20, 1997). ... Claimed on waivers by Cleveland Browns (April 22, 1999). ... Released by Browns (June 3, 1999). ... Signed by Detroit Lions (August 1, 1999). ... Released by Lions (September 5, 1999). ... Signed by Philadelphia Eagles (September 28, 1999). ... Released by Eagles (November 17, 1999). ... Signed by Detroit Lions (December 8, 1999). ... Released by Lions (February 10, 2000).
PLAYING EXPERIENCE: Atlanta NFL, 1997 and 1998; Philadelphia (7)-Detroit (3) NFL, 1999. ... Games/Games started: 1997 (5/1), 1998 (15/0), 1999 (Phi.-7/1; Det.-3/0; Total: 10/1). Total: 30/2.
CHAMPIONSHIP GAME EXPERIENCE: Played in NFC championship game (1998 season). ... Played in Super Bowl XXXIII (1998 season).
PRO STATISTICS: 1997—Caught one pass for two yards. 1999—Returned one kickoff for one yard.
SINGLE GAME HIGHS (regular season): Receptions—1 (November 30, 1997, vs. Seattle); yards—2 (November 30, 1997, vs. Seattle); and touchdown receptions—0.

RECORD AS BASEBALL PLAYER

TRANSACTIONS/CAREER NOTES: Batted right, threw right. ... Selected by Chicago White Sox organization in seventh round of free-agent draft (June 2, 1987). ... Traded by White Sox organization to Milwaukee Brewers organization for P Mike Hooper (June 13, 1991). ... Granted free agency after 1993 season. ... Signed by Chicago Cubs organization (November 5, 1993). ... Granted free agency after 1994 season. ... Signed by Cleveland Indians organization (December 9, 1994).
STATISTICAL NOTES: Led Gulf Coast League third basemen with nine double plays in 1987. ... Led Midwest League third basemen with 37 double plays in 1988. ... Led Midwest League third basemen with 40 errors in 1989.

						BATTING								FIELDING			
Year Team (League)	Pos.	G	AB	R	H	2B	3B	HR	RBI	Avg.	BB	SO	SB	PO	A	E	Avg.
1987— GC Whi. Sox (GCL)	3B	32	114	10	27	3	0	2	18	.237	6	28	3	31	73	12	.897
1988—South Bend (Mid.)	3B	130	462	51	107	14	1	3	46	.232	51	87	5	110	272	37	.912
1989—South Bend (Mid.)	3B-1B	115	382	52	94	20	2	8	49	.246	43	84	7	180	140	43	.882
1990—Sarasota (Fla. St.)	3B-1B	63	239	22	46	10	3	4	23	.192	11	61	0	91	97	17	.917
— Birmingham (Sou.)	3B-1B	72	247	22	61	14	3	1	23	.247	22	49	2	103	138	15	.941
1991—Sarasota (FSL)	1B-3B	54	198	27	43	7	0	3	27	.217	15	52	4	248	45	2	.993
— Beloit (Midwest)■	3B-1B	61	218	31	57	13	2	4	37	.261	21	41	5	64	112	10	.946
1992—Stockton (California)	3B-1B	99	355	57	93	21	4	11	57	.262	49	72	6	108	90	20	.908
— El Paso (Texas)	3B-1B	22	86	11	25	5	0	2	15	.291	8	20	0	104	43	7	.955

1993—El Paso (Texas).........	1B-OF-3B	118	419	64	123	23	6	8	69	.294	38	97	13	505	63	14	.976
1994—Orlando (South.)■....	3B-1B	115	401	51	104	17	5	16	60	.259	37	75	4	167	199	21	.946
1995—Buffalo (A.A.)■	3B-1B	13	31	4	10	0	1	3	9	.323	3	5	0	108	164	14	.951
—Cant./Akr. (Eastern) ..	OF-3B-1B	103	365	41	88	18	2	11	52	.241	36	93	0	13	1	3	.824

SMITH, EMMITT   RB   COWBOYS

PERSONAL: Born May 15, 1969, in Pensacola, Fla. ... 5-9/209. ... Full name: Emmitt J. Smith III.
HIGH SCHOOL: Escambia (Pensacola, Fla.).
COLLEGE: Florida (degree in public recreation, 1996).
TRANSACTIONS/CAREER NOTES: Selected after junior season by Dallas Cowboys in first round (17th pick overall) of 1990 NFL draft. ... Signed by Cowboys (September 4, 1990). ... Granted roster exemption (September 4-8, 1990). ... Granted free agency (March 1, 1993). ... Re-signed by Cowboys (September 16, 1993).
CHAMPIONSHIP GAME EXPERIENCE: Played in NFC championship game (1992-1995 seasons). ... Member of Super Bowl championship team (1992, 1993 and 1995 seasons).
HONORS: Named running back on THE SPORTING NEWS college All-America first team (1989). ... Played in Pro Bowl (1990-1992, 1995, 1998 and 1999 seasons). ... Named running back on THE SPORTING NEWS NFL All-Pro team (1992-1995). ... Named NFL Player of the Year by THE SPORTING NEWS (1993). ... Named Most Valuable Player of Super Bowl XXVIII (1993 season). ... Named to play in Pro Bowl (1993 season); replaced by Rodney Hampton due to injury. ... Named Sportsman of the Year by THE SPORTING NEWS (1994). ... Named to play in Pro Bowl (1994 season); replaced by Ricky Watters due to injury.
RECORDS: Holds NFL career record for most rushing touchdowns—136. ... Holds NFL single-season records for most touchdowns—25 (1995); and most rushing touchdowns—25 (1995).
POST SEASON RECORDS: Holds Super Bowl career record for most rushing touchdowns—5. ... Holds NFL postseason career record for most rushing touchdowns—18. ... Holds NFL postseason career record for most yards rushing—1,586. ... Shares NFL postseason career record for most games with 100 or more yards rushing—7. ... Shares NFL postseason career records for most points scored—126; and most touchdowns—21.
PRO STATISTICS: 1991—Recovered one fumble. 1992—Recovered one fumble. 1993—Recovered three fumbles. 1996—Recovered one fumble. 1997—Recovered one fumble. 1998—Recovered one fumble. 1999—Recovered one fumble.
SINGLE GAME HIGHS (regular season): Attempts—35 (November 7, 1994, vs. New York Giants); yards—237 (October 31, 1993, vs. Philadelphia); and rushing touchdowns—4 (September 4, 1995, vs. New York Giants).
STATISTICAL PLATEAUS: 100-yard rushing games: 1990 (3), 1991 (8), 1992 (7), 1993 (7), 1994 (6), 1995 (11), 1996 (4), 1997 (2), 1998 (7), 1999 (9). Total: 64. ... 100-yard receiving games: 1990 (1), 1993 (1). Total: 2.
MISCELLANEOUS: Active NFL leader for career rushing yards (13,963) and rushing touchdowns (136). ... Holds Dallas Cowboys all-time records for most yards rushing (13,963), most touchdowns (147) and most rushing touchdowns (136).

			RUSHING				RECEIVING				TOTALS			
Year Team	G	GS	Att.	Yds.	Avg.	TD	No.	Yds.	Avg.	TD	TD	2pt.	Pts.	Fum.
1990—Dallas NFL..............................	16	15	241	937	3.9	11	24	228	9.5	0	11	0	66	7
1991—Dallas NFL..............................	16	16	*365	*1563	4.3	12	49	258	5.3	1	13	0	78	8
1992—Dallas NFL..............................	16	16	‡373	*1713	4.6	*18	59	335	5.7	1	*19	0	114	4
1993—Dallas NFL..............................	14	13	283	*1486	*5.3	9	57	414	7.3	1	10	0	60	4
1994—Dallas NFL..............................	15	15	*368	1484	4.0	*21	50	341	6.8	1	*22	0	132	1
1995—Dallas NFL..............................	16	16	*377	*1773	4.7	*25	62	375	6.0	0	*25	0	*150	7
1996—Dallas NFL..............................	15	15	327	1204	3.7	12	47	249	5.3	3	15	0	90	5
1997—Dallas NFL..............................	16	16	261	1074	4.1	4	40	234	5.9	0	4	1	26	1
1998—Dallas NFL..............................	16	16	319	1332	4.2	13	27	175	6.5	2	15	0	90	3
1999—Dallas NFL..............................	15	15	‡329	1397	4.2	11	27	119	4.4	2	13	0	78	5
Pro totals (10 years)................................	155	153	3243	13963	4.3	136	442	2728	6.2	11	147	1	884	45

SMITH, FERNANDO   DE   VIKINGS

PERSONAL: Born August 2, 1971, in Flint, Mich. ... 6-6/287. ... Full name: Fernando Dewitt Smith. ... Brother of Robaire Smith, defensive end, Tennessee Titans.
HIGH SCHOOL: Northwestern Community (Flint, Mich.).
COLLEGE: Jackson State.
TRANSACTIONS/CAREER NOTES: Selected by Minnesota Vikings in second round (55th pick overall) of 1994 NFL draft. ... Signed by Vikings (July 15, 1994). ... Granted free agency (February 14, 1997). ... Re-signed by Vikings (February 20, 1997). ... Released by Vikings (July 28, 1998). ... Signed by Jacksonville Jaguars (August 13, 1998). ... Granted unconditional free agency (February 12, 1999). ... Signed by Baltimore Ravens (March 19, 1999). ... Granted unconditional free agency (February 11, 2000). ... Signed by Vikings (March 10, 2000).
PRO STATISTICS: 1996—Recovered two fumbles for four yards. 1997—Recovered one fumble for six yards. 1998—Recovered one fumble. 1999—Recovered three fumbles.

Year Team	G	GS	SACKS
1994—Minnesota NFL..............................	7	0	0.0
1995—Minnesota NFL..............................	12	1	2.5
1996—Minnesota NFL..............................	16	16	9.5
1997—Minnesota NFL..............................	12	11	4.0
1998—Jacksonville NFL..............................	14	0	2.0
1999—Baltimore NFL..............................	15	0	2.0
Pro totals (6 years)................................	76	28	20.0

SMITH, FRANKIE   S   BEARS

PERSONAL: Born October 8, 1968, in Groesbeck, Texas. ... 5-9/182. ... Full name: Frankie L. Smith.
HIGH SCHOOL: Groesbeck (Texas).
COLLEGE: Baylor.

S

TRANSACTIONS/CAREER NOTES: Selected by Atlanta Falcons in fourth round (104th pick overall) of 1992 NFL draft. ... Signed by Falcons (July 7, 1992). ... Released by Falcons (August 25, 1992). ... Signed by Miami Dolphins (March 17, 1993). ... Released by Dolphins (October 22, 1993). ... Re-signed by Dolphins to practice squad (October 23, 1993). ... Activated (November 29, 1993). ... Claimed on waivers by New England Patriots (February 27, 1996). ... Released by Patriots (August 17, 1996). ... Signed by San Francisco 49ers (September 12, 1996). ... Granted unconditional free agency (February 14, 1997). ... Re-signed by 49ers (March 26, 1997). ... Granted unconditional free agency (February 13, 1998). ... Signed by Chicago Bears (August 5, 1998). ... Granted unconditional free agency (February 12, 1999). ... Re-signed by Bears (March 26, 1999).

PLAYING EXPERIENCE: Miami NFL, 1993-1995; San Francisco NFL, 1996 and 1997; Chicago NFL, 1998 and 1999. ... Games/Games started: 1993 (5/1), 1994 (13/2), 1995 (11/1), 1996 (14/0), 1997 (16/0), 1998 (15/0), 1999 (15/0). Total: 89/4.

CHAMPIONSHIP GAME EXPERIENCE: Played in NFC championship game (1997 season).

PRO STATISTICS: 1994—Credited with one sack. 1997—Recovered one fumble. 1999—Credited with one sack and recovered one fumble.

SMITH, HUNTER · P · COLTS

PERSONAL: Born August 9, 1977, in Sherman, Texas. ... 6-2/212. ... Full name: Hunter Dwight Smith.
HIGH SCHOOL: Sherman (Texas).
COLLEGE: Notre Dame.
TRANSACTIONS/CAREER NOTES: Selected by Indianapolis Colts in seventh round (210th pick overall) of 1999 NFL draft. ... Signed by Colts (July 22, 1999).

			PUNTING				
Year Team	G	No.	Yds.	Avg.	Net avg.	In. 20	Blk.
1999—Indianapolis NFL	16	58	2467	42.5	30.6	16	†2

SMITH, IRV · TE

PERSONAL: Born October 13, 1971, in Trenton, N.J. ... 6-3/262. ... Full name: Irvin Martin Smith. ... Brother of Ed Smith, tight end with Atlanta Falcons (1997-98), Philadelphia Eagles (1999) and Detroit Lions (1999).
HIGH SCHOOL: Pemberton (N.J.).
COLLEGE: Notre Dame (degree in marketing).
TRANSACTIONS/CAREER NOTES: Selected by New Orleans Saints in first round (20th pick overall) of 1993 NFL draft. ... Signed by Saints (July 25, 1993). ... On physically unable to perform list with knee injury (July 14-29, 1996). ... On inactive list for six games (1996). ... On injured reserve with knee injury (December 14, 1996-remainder of season). ... Granted unconditional free agency (February 13, 1998). ... Signed by San Francisco 49ers (February 26, 1998). ... Traded by 49ers with DE Roy Barker to Cleveland Browns for past considerations (February 12, 1999). ... Granted unconditional free agency (February 11, 2000).
PRO STATISTICS: 1993—Recovered one fumble. 1994—Returned two kickoffs for 10 yards. 1995—Returned one kickoff for six yards. 1998—Returned two kickoffs for 35 yards. 1999—Returned three kickoffs for 15 yards.
SINGLE GAME HIGHS (regular season): Receptions—9 (November 12, 1995, vs. Indianapolis); yards—83 (November 12, 1995, vs. Indianapolis); and touchdown receptions—2 (December 10, 1995, vs. Atlanta).

			RECEIVING				TOTALS			
Year Team	G	GS	No.	Yds.	Avg.	TD	TD	2pt.	Pts.	Fum.
1993—New Orleans NFL	16	8	16	180	11.3	2	2	0	12	1
1994—New Orleans NFL	16	16	41	330	8.0	3	3	0	18	0
1995—New Orleans NFL	16	16	45	466	10.4	3	3	1	20	1
1996—New Orleans NFL	7	7	15	144	9.6	0	0	0	0	0
1997—New Orleans NFL	11	8	17	180	10.6	1	1	0	6	1
1998—San Francisco NFL	16	8	25	266	10.6	5	5	0	30	0
1999—Cleveland NFL	13	13	24	222	9.3	1	1	0	6	0
Pro totals (7 years)	95	76	183	1788	9.8	15	15	1	92	3

SMITH, JEFF · C/G · CHIEFS

PERSONAL: Born May 25, 1973, in Decatur, Tenn. ... 6-3/322. ... Full name: Jeffery Lee Smith.
HIGH SCHOOL: Meigs County (Decatur, Tenn.).
COLLEGE: Tennessee.
TRANSACTIONS/CAREER NOTES: Selected by Kansas City Chiefs in seventh round (241st pick overall) of 1996 NFL draft. ... Signed by Chiefs (July 24, 1996). ... Active for one game (1996); did not play. ... Assigned by Chiefs to Scottish Claymores in 1997 World League enhancement allocation program (February 19, 1997). ... Granted free agency (February 12, 1999). ... Re-signed by Chiefs (June 16, 1999). ... Granted unconditional free agency (February 11, 2000). ... Re-signed by Chiefs (March 21, 2000).
PLAYING EXPERIENCE: Scottish Claymores W.L., 1997; Kansas City NFL, 1997-1999. ... Games/Games started: W.L. 1997 (10/games started unavailable), NFL 1997 (3/0), 1998 (11/3), 1999 (15/2). Total: NFL 29/5.

SMITH, JERMAINE · DT · PACKERS

PERSONAL: Born February 3, 1972, in Augusta, Ga. ... 6-3/298. ... Full name: Matt Jermaine Smith.
HIGH SCHOOL: Laney (Augusta, Ga.).
JUNIOR COLLEGE: Georgia Military College.
COLLEGE: Georgia.
TRANSACTIONS/CAREER NOTES: Selected by Green Bay Packers in fourth round (126th pick overall) of 1997 NFL draft. ... Signed by Packers (July 9, 1997). ... On non-football injury list with injuries suffered in motorcycle accident (July 18, 1998-entire season).

CHAMPIONSHIP GAME EXPERIENCE: Member of Packers for NFC championship game (1997 season); inactive. ... Member of Packers for Super Bowl XXXII (1997 season); inactive.
PRO STATISTICS: 1999—Intercepted one pass for two yards and fumbled once.

Year	Team	G	GS	SACKS
1997—Green Bay NFL		9	0	1.0
1998—Green Bay NFL		Did not play.		
1999—Green Bay NFL		10	0	0.5
Pro totals (2 years)		19	0	1.5

SMITH, JIMMY   WR   JAGUARS

PERSONAL: Born February 9, 1969, in Detroit. ... 6-1/200. ... Full name: Jimmy Lee Smith Jr.
HIGH SCHOOL: Callaway (Jackson, Miss.).
COLLEGE: Jackson State (degree in business management, 1992).
TRANSACTIONS/CAREER NOTES: Selected by Dallas Cowboys in second round (36th pick overall) of 1992 NFL draft. ... Signed by Cowboys (April 26, 1992). ... On injured reserve with fibula injury (September 2-October 7, 1992); on practice squad (September 28-October 7, 1992). ... On non-football injury list with appendicitis (September 2, 1993-entire season). ... Released by Cowboys (July 11, 1994). ... Signed by Philadelphia Eagles (July 19, 1994). ... Released by Eagles (August 29, 1994). ... Signed by Jacksonville Jaguars (February 28, 1995). ... Granted free agency (February 16, 1996). ... Re-signed by Jaguars (May 28, 1996).
CHAMPIONSHIP GAME EXPERIENCE: Played in NFC championship game (1992 season). ... Member of Super Bowl championship team (1992 season). ... Played in AFC championship game (1996 and 1999 seasons).
HONORS: Played in Pro Bowl (1997-1999 seasons).
PRO STATISTICS: 1995—Recovered blocked punt in end zone for a touchdown and recovered one fumble. 1997—Recovered one fumble. 1998—Recovered two fumbles.
SINGLE GAME HIGHS (regular season): Receptions—14 (January 2, 2000, vs. Cincinnati); yards—220 (Novmeber 21, 1999, vs. New Orleans); and touchdown receptions—2 (August 31, 1997, vs. Baltimore).
STATISTICAL PLATEAUS: 100-yard receiving games: 1996 (4), 1997 (6), 1998 (5), 1999 (9). Total: 24.
MISCELLANEOUS: Holds Jacksonville Jaguars all-time record for most receptions (381), most yards receiving (5,674) and most touchdown receptions (28).

Year	Team	G	GS	RECEIVING No.	Yds.	Avg.	TD	KICKOFF RETURNS No.	Yds.	Avg.	TD	TOTALS TD	2pt.	Pts.	Fum.
1992—Dallas NFL		7	0	0	0	0.0	0	0	0	0.0	0	0	0	0	0
1993—Dallas NFL								Did not play.							
1994—								Did not play.							
1995—Jacksonville NFL		16	4	22	288	13.1	3	24	540	22.5	1	5	0	30	2
1996—Jacksonville NFL		16	9	83	§1244	15.0	7	2	49	24.5	0	7	0	42	1
1997—Jacksonville NFL		16	16	82	1324	16.1	4	0	0	0.0	0	4	0	24	1
1998—Jacksonville NFL		16	15	78	1182	15.2	8	0	0	0.0	0	8	0	48	2
1999—Jacksonville NFL		16	16	*116	1636	14.1	6	0	0	0.0	0	6	†1	38	1
Pro totals (6 years)		87	60	381	5674	14.9	28	26	589	22.7	1	30	1	182	7

SMITH, KEVIN   CB   COWBOYS

PERSONAL: Born April 7, 1970, in Orange, Texas. ... 5-11/190. ... Full name: Kevin Rey Smith.
HIGH SCHOOL: West Orange-Stark (Orange, Texas).
COLLEGE: Texas A&M.
TRANSACTIONS/CAREER NOTES: Selected by Dallas Cowboys in first round (17th pick overall) of 1992 NFL draft. ... Signed by Cowboys (April 26, 1992). ... On injured reserve with Achilles' tendon injury (September 22, 1995-remainder of season).
CHAMPIONSHIP GAME EXPERIENCE: Played in NFC championship game (1992-1994 seasons). ... Member of Super Bowl championship team (1992 and 1993 seasons).
HONORS: Named defensive back on THE SPORTING NEWS college All-America first team (1991).
PRO STATISTICS: 1992—Returned one punt for 17 yards and returned one kickoff for nine yards. 1993—Returned one kickoff for 33 yards and recovered one fumble for 14 yards. 1998—Returned one punt for 11 yards.

Year	Team	G	GS	INTERCEPTIONS No.	Yds.	Avg.	TD
1992—Dallas NFL		16	6	2	10	5.0	0
1993—Dallas NFL		16	16	6	56	9.3	1
1994—Dallas NFL		16	16	2	11	5.5	0
1995—Dallas NFL		1	1	0	0	0.0	0
1996—Dallas NFL		16	16	5	45	9.0	0
1997—Dallas NFL		16	16	1	21	21.0	0
1998—Dallas NFL		14	14	2	31	15.5	0
1999—Dallas NFL		8	8	1	16	16.0	0
Pro totals (8 years)		103	93	19	190	10.0	1

SMITH, LAMAR   RB   DOLPHINS

PERSONAL: Born November 29, 1970, in Fort Wayne, Ind. ... 5-11/225.
HIGH SCHOOL: South Side (Fort Wayne, Ind.).
COLLEGE: Houston.
TRANSACTIONS/CAREER NOTES: Selected by Seattle Seahawks in third round (73rd pick overall) of 1994 NFL draft. ... Signed by Seahawks (July 19, 1994). ... On non-football injury list with back injury (December 13, 1994-remainder of season). ... Granted free agency (February 14, 1997). ... Re-signed by Seahawks (February 1997). ... Granted unconditional free agency (February 13, 1998). ... Signed by New Orleans Saints (February 28, 1998). ... Released by Saints (February 24, 2000). ... Signed by Miami Dolphins (March 15, 2000).

PRO STATISTICS: 1995—Returned one kickoff for 20 yards. 1996—Recovered one fumble. 1997—Returned one kickoff for 14 yards. 1998—Attempted two passes with one completion for 20 yards and a touchdown. 1999—Attempted one pass without a completion.
SINGLE GAME HIGHS (regular season): Attempts—33 (November 17, 1996, vs. Detroit); yards—157 (September 27, 1998, vs. Indianapolis); and rushing touchdowns—2 (December 22, 1996, vs. Oakland).
STATISTICAL PLATEAUS: 100-yard rushing games: 1996 (1), 1998 (1). Total: 2.

			RUSHING				RECEIVING				TOTALS			
Year Team	G	GS	Att.	Yds.	Avg.	TD	No.	Yds.	Avg.	TD	TD	2pt.	Pts.	Fum.
1994—Seattle NFL	2	0	2	-1	-0.5	0	0	0	0.0	0	0	0	0	0
1995—Seattle NFL	13	0	36	215	6.0	0	1	10	10.0	0	0	0	0	1
1996—Seattle NFL	16	2	153	680	4.4	8	9	58	6.4	0	8	*3	54	4
1997—Seattle NFL	12	2	91	392	4.3	2	23	183	8.0	0	2	1	14	0
1998—New Orleans NFL	14	9	138	457	3.3	1	24	249	10.4	2	3	0	18	4
1999—New Orleans NFL	13	2	60	205	3.4	0	20	151	7.6	1	1	0	6	1
Pro totals (6 years)	70	15	480	1948	4.1	11	77	651	8.5	3	14	4	92	10

SMITH, LARRY — DT — JAGUARS

PERSONAL: Born December 4, 1974, in Kingsland, Ga. ... 6-5/282. ... Full name: Larry Smith Jr.
HIGH SCHOOL: Charlton County (Folkston, Ga.), then Valley Forge (Pa.).
COLLEGE: Florida State.
TRANSACTIONS/CAREER NOTES: Selected after junior season by Jacksonville Jaguars in second round (56th pick overall) of 1999 NFL draft. ... Signed by Jaguars (April 26, 1999).
CHAMPIONSHIP GAME EXPERIENCE: Played in AFC championship game (1999 season).

Year Team	G	GS	SACKS
1999—Jacksonville NFL	15	0	3.0

SMITH, MARK — DT — CARDINALS

PERSONAL: Born August 28, 1974, in Vicksburg, Miss. ... 6-4/294. ... Full name: Mark Anthony Smith.
HIGH SCHOOL: Vicksburg (Miss.).
JUNIOR COLLEGE: Navarro College (Texas), then Hinds Community College (Miss.).
COLLEGE: Auburn.
TRANSACTIONS/CAREER NOTES: Selected by Arizona Cardinals in seventh round (212th pick overall) of 1997 NFL draft. ... Signed by Cardinals (May 5, 1997). ... On injured reserve with knee injury (November 1, 1999-remainder of season). ... Granted free agency (February 11, 2000).
PRO STATISTICS: 1998—Recovered one fumble.

Year Team	G	GS	SACKS
1997—Arizona NFL	16	4	6.0
1998—Arizona NFL	14	13	9.0
1999—Arizona NFL	2	0	0.0
Pro totals (3 years)	32	17	15.0

SMITH, MARQUIS — DB — BROWNS

PERSONAL: Born January 13, 1975, in San Diego. ... 6-2/213. ... Cousin of Akili Smith, quarterback, Cincinnati Bengals. ... Name pronounced mar-KEYS.
HIGH SCHOOL: Patrick Henry (San Diego).
COLLEGE: California.
TRANSACTIONS/CAREER NOTES: Selected by Cleveland Browns in third round (76th pick overall) of 1999 NFL draft. ... Signed by Browns (July 15, 1999).
PLAYING EXPERIENCE: Cleveland NFL, 1999. ... Games/Games started: 1999 (16/2).

SMITH, NEIL — DE

PERSONAL: Born April 10, 1966, in New Orleans. ... 6-4/270.
HIGH SCHOOL: McDonogh 35 (New Orleans).
COLLEGE: Nebraska.
TRANSACTIONS/CAREER NOTES: Selected by Kansas City Chiefs in first round (second pick overall) of 1988 NFL draft. ... Signed by Chiefs (July 19, 1988). ... Designated by Chiefs as franchise player (February 25, 1993). ... Granted unconditional free agency (February 14, 1997). ... Signed by Denver Broncos (April 14, 1997). ... Granted unconditional free agency (February 13, 1998). ... Re-signed by Broncos (March 11, 1998). ... Released by Broncos (February 10, 2000).
CHAMPIONSHIP GAME EXPERIENCE: Played in AFC championship game (1993, 1997 and 1998 seasons). ... Member of Super Bowl championship team (1997 and 1998 season).
HONORS: Named defensive lineman on THE SPORTING NEWS college All-America first team (1987). ... Played in Pro Bowl (1991-1993, 1995 and 1997 seasons). ... Named to play in Pro Bowl (1994 season); replaced by Rob Burnett due to injury.
PRO STATISTICS: 1989—Recovered two fumbles for three yards and one touchdown. 1990—Recovered one fumble. 1991—Recovered two fumbles for 10 yards. 1992—Intercepted one pass for 22 yards and a touchdown and recovered two fumbles. 1993—Intercepted one pass for three yards and recovered three fumbles. 1994—Intercepted one pass for 41 yards and recovered one fumble for six yards. 1995—Recovered one fumble. 1998—Intercepted one pass for two yards.

Year Team	G	GS	SACKS
1988—Kansas City NFL	13	7	2.5
1989—Kansas City NFL	15	15	6.5
1990—Kansas City NFL	16	15	9.5
1991—Kansas City NFL	16	16	8.0
1992—Kansas City NFL	16	16	14.5
1993—Kansas City NFL	16	15	*15.0
1994—Kansas City NFL	14	13	11.5
1995—Kansas City NFL	16	14	12.0
1996—Kansas City NFL	16	16	6.0
1997—Denver NFL	14	13	8.5
1998—Denver NFL	14	14	4.0
1999—Denver NFL	15	8	6.5
Pro totals (12 years)	181	162	104.5

SMITH, OTIS CB JETS

PERSONAL: Born October 22, 1965, in New Orleans. ... 5-11/195. ... Full name: Otis Smith III.
HIGH SCHOOL: East Jefferson (Metairie, La.).
JUNIOR COLLEGE: Taft (Calif.) College.
COLLEGE: Missouri.
TRANSACTIONS/CAREER NOTES: Signed as non-drafted free agent by Philadelphia Eagles (April 25, 1990). ... On physically unable to per-form list with appendectomy (August 2, 1990-entire season). ... Granted free agency (February 1, 1992). ... Re-signed by Eagles (August 11, 1992). ... Granted unconditional free agency (February 17, 1994). ... Re-signed by Eagles (April 25, 1994). ... Released by Eagles (March 22, 1995). ... Signed by New York Jets (April 13, 1995). ... Released by Jets (September 24, 1996). ... Signed by New England Patriots (October 9, 1996). ... Granted unconditional free agency (February 14, 1997). ... Re-signed by Jets (May 20, 1997). ... Granted unconditional free agency (February 13, 1998). ... Re-signed by Jets (April 9, 1998). ... On injured reserve with broken collarbone (October 5, 1999-remainder of sea-son).
CHAMPIONSHIP GAME EXPERIENCE: Played in AFC championship game (1996 and 1998 seasons). ... Played in Super Bowl XXXI (1996 sea-son).
PRO STATISTICS: 1991—Recovered one fumble. 1994—Credited with one sack and returned one kickoff for 14 yards. 1995—Returned one kickoff for six yards. 1996—Credited with one sack. 1997—Recovered two fumbles for 40 yards.

			INTERCEPTIONS			
Year Team	G	GS	No.	Yds.	Avg.	TD
1990—Philadelphia NFL			Did not play.			
1991—Philadelphia NFL	15	1	2	74	37.0	∞1
1992—Philadelphia NFL	16	1	1	0	0.0	0
1993—Philadelphia NFL	15	0	1	0	0.0	0
1994—Philadelphia NFL	16	2	0	0	0.0	0
1995—New York Jets NFL	11	10	6	101	16.8	▲1
1996—New York Jets NFL	2	0	0	0	0.0	0
—New England NFL	11	6	2	20	10.0	0
1997—New York Jets NFL	16	16	6	158	26.3	†3
1998—New York Jets NFL	16	16	2	34	17.0	0
1999—New York Jets NFL	1	1	0	0	0.0	0
Pro totals (9 years)	119	53	20	387	19.4	5

SMITH, ROBERT RB VIKINGS

PERSONAL: Born March 4, 1972, in Euclid, Ohio. ... 6-2/210. ... Full name: Robert Scott Smith.
HIGH SCHOOL: Euclid (Ohio).
COLLEGE: Ohio State.
TRANSACTIONS/CAREER NOTES: Selected after sophomore season by Minnesota Vikings in first round (21st pick overall) of 1993 NFL draft. ... Signed by Vikings (July 16, 1993). ... On injured reserve with knee injury (December 7, 1993-remainder of season). ... On physically unable to perform list with knee injury (July 13-19, 1994). ... Granted free agency (February 16, 1996). ... Re-signed by Vikings (August 10, 1996). ... On injured reserve with knee injury (November 15, 1996-remainder of season). ... Granted unconditional free agency (February 14, 1997). ... Re-signed by Vikings (April 18, 1997). ... Designated by Vikings as franchise player (February 13, 1998). ... Free agency status changed from franchise to transitional (February 25, 1998). ... Re-signed by Vikings (March 4, 1998).
CHAMPIONSHIP GAME EXPERIENCE: Played in NFC championship game (1998 season).
PRO STATISTICS: 1993—Returned one punt for four yards. 1996—Recovered one fumble. 1997—Recovered one fumble.
SINGLE GAME HIGHS (regular season): Attempts—30 (September 8, 1996, vs. Atlanta); yards—179 (September 13, 1998, vs. St. Louis); and rushing touchdowns—2 (September 13, 1998, vs. St. Louis).
STATISTICAL PLATEAUS: 100-yard rushing games: 1993 (1), 1995 (2), 1996 (3), 1997 (6), 1998 (5), 1999 (4). Total: 21.

			RUSHING				RECEIVING				KICKOFF RETURNS				TOTALS			
Year Team	G	GS	Att.	Yds.	Avg.	TD	No.	Yds.	Avg.	TD	No.	Yds.	Avg.	TD	TD	2pt.	Pts.	Fum.
1993—Minnesota NFL	10	2	82	399	4.9	2	24	111	4.6	0	3	41	13.7	0	2	0	12	0
1994—Minnesota NFL	14	0	31	106	3.4	1	15	105	7.0	0	16	419	26.2	0	1	0	6	0
1995—Minnesota NFL	9	7	139	632	4.5	5	7	35	5.0	0	0	0	0.0	0	5	1	32	1
1996—Minnesota NFL	8	7	162	692	4.3	3	7	39	5.6	0	0	0	0.0	0	3	0	18	2
1997—Minnesota NFL	14	14	232	1266	5.5	6	37	197	5.3	1	0	0	0.0	0	7	0	42	0
1998—Minnesota NFL	14	14	249	1187	4.8	6	28	291	10.4	2	0	0	0.0	0	8	0	48	1
1999—Minnesota NFL	13	12	221	1015	4.6	2	24	166	6.9	0	0	0	0.0	0	2	0	12	1
Pro totals (7 years)	82	56	1116	5297	4.7	25	142	944	6.6	3	19	460	24.2	0	28	1	170	5

SMITH, ROD WR BRONCOS

PERSONAL: Born May 15, 1970, in Texarkana, Ark. ... 6-0/200.
HIGH SCHOOL: Arkansas (Texarkana, Ark.).
COLLEGE: Missouri Southern.
TRANSACTIONS/CAREER NOTES: Signed as non-drafted free agent by Denver Broncos (March 23, 1995).
CHAMPIONSHIP GAME EXPERIENCE: Played in AFC championship game (1997 and 1998 seasons). ... Member of Super Bowl championship team (1997 and 1998 seasons).
PRO STATISTICS: 1996—Rushed once for one yard. 1997—Rushed five times for 16 yards and recovered one fumble. 1998—Rushed six times for 63 yards, completed only pass attempt for 14 yards and recovered two fumbles for 11 yards and one touchdown. 1999—Attempted one pass without a completion.
SINGLE GAME HIGHS (regular season): Receptions—9 (January 2, 2000, vs. San Diego); yards—165 (December 6, 1998, vs. Kansas City); and touchdown receptions—2 (October 4, 1998, vs. Philadelphia).
STATISTICAL PLATEAUS: 100-yard receiving games: 1997 (6), 1998 (4), 1999 (3). Total: 13.

			RECEIVING				PUNT RETURNS				KICKOFF RETURNS				TOTALS			
Year Team	G	GS	No.	Yds.	Avg.	TD	No.	Yds.	Avg.	TD	No.	Yds.	Avg.	TD	TD	2pt.	Pts.	Fum.
1995—Denver NFL	16	1	6	152	25.3	1	0	0	0.0	0	4	54	13.5	0	1	0	6	0
1996—Denver NFL	10	1	16	237	14.8	2	23	283	12.3	0	1	29	29.0	0	2	0	12	1
1997—Denver NFL	16	16	70	1180	16.9 ▲12		1	12	12.0	0	0	0	0.0	0	12	0	72	3
1998—Denver NFL	16	16	86	1222	14.2	6	0	0	0.0	0	0	0	0.0	0	7	0	42	0
1999—Denver NFL	15	15	79	1020	12.9	4	0	0	0.0	0	1	10	10.0	0	4	0	24	1
Pro totals (5 years)	73	49	257	3811	14.8	25	24	295	12.3	0	6	93	15.5	0	26	0	156	5

S

SMITH, SHEVIN S BUCCANEERS

PERSONAL: Born June 17, 1975, in Miami. ... 5-11/204. ... Full name: Shevin Jamar Smith. ... Cousin of Derrick Thomas, linebacker with Kansas City Chiefs (1989-99); and cousin of Winston Moss, linebacker with Tampa Bay Buccaneers (1987-90), Los Angeles Raiders (1991-94) and Seattle Seahawks (1995-97).
HIGH SCHOOL: Miami Southridge.
COLLEGE: Florida State (degree in finance, 1998).
TRANSACTIONS/CAREER NOTES: Selected by Tampa Bay Buccaneers in sixth round (184th pick overall) of 1998 NFL draft. ... Signed by Buccaneers (June 4, 1998). ... Released by Buccaneers (August 25, 1998). ... Re-signed by Buccaneers to practice squad (August 31, 1998). ... Activated (November 11, 1998).
PLAYING EXPERIENCE: Tampa Bay NFL, 1998 and 1999. ... Games/Games started: 1998 (3/0), 1999 (16/0). Total: 19/0.
CHAMPIONSHIP GAME EXPERIENCE: Played in NFC championship game (1999 season).

SMITH, THOMAS CB BEARS

PERSONAL: Born December 5, 1970, in Gates, N.C. ... 5-11/190. ... Full name: Thomas Lee Smith Jr. ... Cousin of Sam Perkins, forward/center, Indiana Pacers.
HIGH SCHOOL: Gates County (Gatesville, N.C.).
COLLEGE: North Carolina.
TRANSACTIONS/CAREER NOTES: Selected by Buffalo Bills in first round (28th pick overall) of 1993 NFL draft. ... Signed by Bills (July 16, 1993). ... Granted free agency (February 16, 1996). ... Re-signed by Bills (February 27, 1996). ... Granted unconditional free agency (February 11, 2000). ... Signed by Chicago Bears (February 12, 2000).
PRO STATISTICS: 1993—Recovered one fumble. 1997—Fumbled once and recovered one fumble for one yard. 1998—Recovered one fumble. 1999—Recovered one fumble.

			INTERCEPTIONS			
Year Team	G	GS	No.	Yds.	Avg.	TD
1993—Buffalo NFL	16	1	0	0	0.0	0
1994—Buffalo NFL	16	16	1	4	4.0	0
1995—Buffalo NFL	16	16	2	23	11.5	0
1996—Buffalo NFL	16	16	1	0	0.0	0
1997—Buffalo NFL	16	16	0	0	0.0	0
1998—Buffalo NFL	14	14	1	0	0.0	0
1999—Buffalo NFL	16	16	1	29	29.0	0
Pro totals (7 years)	110	95	6	56	9.3	0

SMITH, TRAVIAN LB RAIDERS

PERSONAL: Born August 26, 1975, in Good Shepard, Texas. ... 6-4/240.
HIGH SCHOOL: Tatum (Texas).
COLLEGE: Oklahoma.
TRANSACTIONS/CAREER NOTES: Selected by Oakland Raiders in fifth round (152nd pick overall) of 1998 NFL draft. ... Signed by Raiders (July 6, 1998). ... Released by Raiders (August 26, 1998). ... Re-signed by Raiders to practice squad (August 31, 1998). ... Activated (December 15, 1998).
PLAYING EXPERIENCE: Oakland NFL, 1998 and 1999. ... Games/Games started: 1998 (2/0), 1999 (16/1). Total: 18/1.
PRO STATISTICS: 1999—Recovered one fumble for one yard.

SMITH, TROY WR EAGLES

PERSONAL: Born July 30, 1977, in Greenville, N.C. ... 6-2/193.
HIGH SCHOOL: Rose (Greenville, N.C.).

COLLEGE: East Carolina.
TRANSACTIONS/CAREER NOTES: Selected by Philadelphia Eagles in sixth round (201st pick overall) of 1999 NFL draft. ... Signed by Eagles (July 16, 1999). ... Released by Eagles (September 5, 1999). ... Re-signed by Eagles to practice squad (September 8, 1999). ... Activated (November 17, 1999).
PLAYING EXPERIENCE: Philadelphia NFL, 1999. ... Games/Games started: 1999 (1/0).
PRO STATISTICS: 1999—Caught one pass for 14 yards.
SINGLE GAME HIGHS (regular season): Receptions—1 (December 19, 1999, vs. New England); yards—14 (December 19, 1999, vs. New England); and touchdown receptions—0.

SMITH, VINSON — LB

PERSONAL: Born July 3, 1965, in Statesville, N.C. ... 6-2/247. ... Full name: Vinson Robert Smith.
HIGH SCHOOL: Statesville (N.C.).
COLLEGE: East Carolina (degree in communications, 1989).
TRANSACTIONS/CAREER NOTES: Signed as non-drafted free agent by Atlanta Falcons (May 2, 1988). ... On injured reserve with elbow injury (August 29-November 4, 1988). ... On injured reserve with knee injury (December 10, 1988-remainder of season). ... Granted unconditional free agency (February 1, 1989). ... Signed by Pittsburgh Steelers (February 28, 1989). ... On injured reserve with broken foot (August 29, 1989-entire season). ... Granted unconditional free agency (February 1, 1990). ... Signed by Dallas Cowboys (March 3, 1990). ... Granted free agency (February 1, 1992). ... Re-signed by Cowboys (August 4, 1992). ... Traded by Cowboys with LB Barry Minter and sixth-round pick (DE Carl Reeves) in 1995 draft to Chicago Bears for TE Kelly Blackwell, S Markus Paul and LB John Roper (August 17, 1993). ... Granted unconditional free agency (February 17, 1995). ... Re-signed by Bears (March 2, 1995). ... Granted unconditional free agency (February 14, 1997). ... Signed by Cowboys (July 19, 1997). ... Granted unconditional free agency (February 13, 1998). ... Signed by New Orleans Saints (September 9, 1998). ... Granted unconditional free agency (February 12, 1999). ... Re-signed by Saints (February 24, 1999). ... On injured reserve with ankle injury (December 16, 1999-remainder of season). ... Granted unconditional free agency (February 11, 2000).
CHAMPIONSHIP GAME EXPERIENCE: Played in NFC championship game (1992 season). ... Member of Super Bowl championship team (1992 season).
PRO STATISTICS: 1990—Recovered two fumbles. 1992—Recovered two fumbles. 1995—Fumbled once for two yards and recovered one fumble. 1996—Recovered two fumbles for 34 yards.

Year Team	G	GS	SACKS
1988—Atlanta NFL	3	0	0.0
1989—Pittsburgh NFL	Did not play.		
1990—Dallas NFL	16	1	0.0
1991—Dallas NFL	13	12	0.0
1992—Dallas NFL	16	13	1.0
1993—Chicago NFL	16	13	0.0
1994—Chicago NFL	12	10	1.0
1995—Chicago NFL	16	13	4.0
1996—Chicago NFL	15	12	1.0
1997—Dallas NFL	14	3	1.0
1998—New Orleans NFL	15	0	0.0
1999—New Orleans NFL	12	0	0.0
Pro totals (11 years)	148	77	8.0

SNIDER, MATT — FB — PACKERS

PERSONAL: Born January 26, 1976, in Des Moines, Iowa. ... 6-2/243. ... Full name: Matthew Kale Snider.
HIGH SCHOOL: Lower Merion (Wynnewood, Pa.).
COLLEGE: Richmond.
TRANSACTIONS/CAREER NOTES: Signed as non-drafted free agent by Carolina Panthers (April 27, 1999). ... Claimed on waivers by Green Bay Packers (July 1, 1999).
PLAYING EXPERIENCE: Green Bay NFL, 1999. ... Games/Games started: 1999 (8/0).

SOWELL, JERALD — FB — JETS

PERSONAL: Born January 21, 1974, in Baton Rouge, La. ... 6-0/245. ... Full name: Jerald Monye Sowell.
HIGH SCHOOL: Baker (La.).
COLLEGE: Tulane (degree in exercise science/kinesiology).
TRANSACTIONS/CAREER NOTES: Selected by Green Bay Packers in seventh round (231st pick overall) of 1997 NFL draft. ... Signed by Packers (July 10, 1997). ... Claimed on waivers by New York Jets (August 25, 1997). ... Granted free agency (February 11, 2000). ... Re-signed by Jets (April 25, 2000).
CHAMPIONSHIP GAME EXPERIENCE: Member of Jets for AFC championship game (1998 season); inactive.
PRO STATISTICS: 1999—Attempted one pass without a completion.
SINGLE GAME HIGHS (regular season): Attempts—14 (November 8, 1998, vs. Buffalo); yards—82 (September 20, 1998, vs. Indianapolis); and rushing touchdowns—0.

Year Team	G	GS	RUSHING Att.	Yds.	Avg.	TD	RECEIVING No.	Yds.	Avg.	TD	TOTALS TD	2pt.	Pts.	Fum.
1997—New York Jets NFL	9	0	7	35	5.0	0	1	8	8.0	0	0	0	0	0
1998—New York Jets NFL	16	2	40	164	4.1	0	10	59	5.9	0	0	0	0	2
1999—New York Jets NFL	16	0	3	5	1.7	0	0	0	0.0	0	0	0	0	0
Pro totals (3 years)	41	2	50	204	4.1	0	11	67	6.1	0	0	0	0	2

S

SPARKS, PHILLIPPI   CB

PERSONAL: Born April 15, 1969, in Oklahoma City. ... 5-11/195. ... Full name: Phillippi Dwaine Sparks. ... Name pronounced fuh-LEEP-ee.
HIGH SCHOOL: Maryvale (Phoenix).
JUNIOR COLLEGE: Glendale (Ariz.) Community College.
COLLEGE: Arizona State.
TRANSACTIONS/CAREER NOTES: Selected by New York Giants in second round (41st pick overall) of 1992 NFL draft. ... Signed by Giants (July 21, 1992). ... Granted free agency (February 17, 1995). ... Re-signed by Giants (May 8, 1995). ... Granted unconditional free agency (February 11, 2000).
PRO STATISTICS: 1992—Returned two kickoffs for 23 yards. 1997—Returned one kickoff for eight yards and credited with one sack. 1999—Recovered one fumble.

| | | | INTERCEPTIONS | | | |
Year Team	G	GS	No.	Yds.	Avg.	TD
1992—New York Giants NFL	16	2	1	0	0.0	0
1993—New York Giants NFL	5	3	0	0	0.0	0
1994—New York Giants NFL	11	11	3	4	1.3	0
1995—New York Giants NFL	16	16	5	11	2.2	0
1996—New York Giants NFL	14	14	3	23	7.7	0
1997—New York Giants NFL	13	13	5	72	14.4	0
1998—New York Giants NFL	13	13	4	25	6.3	0
1999—New York Giants NFL	11	11	1	28	28.0	0
Pro totals (8 years)	99	83	22	163	7.4	0

S

SPEARS, MARCUS   OT   CHIEFS

PERSONAL: Born September 28, 1971, in Baton Rouge, La. ... 6-4/320. ... Full name: Marcus DeWayne Spears.
HIGH SCHOOL: Belaire (Baton Rouge, La.).
COLLEGE: Northwestern State (La.).
TRANSACTIONS/CAREER NOTES: Selected by Chicago Bears in second round (39th pick overall) of 1994 NFL draft. ... Signed by Bears (July 16, 1994). ... Inactive for all 16 games (1994). ... Active for five games (1995); did not play. ... Assigned by Bears to Amsterdam Admirals in 1996 World League enhancement allocation program (February 19, 1996). ... Granted unconditional free agency (February 14, 1997). ... Signed by Green Bay Packers (March 12, 1997). ... Released by Packers (August 19, 1997). ... Signed by Kansas City Chiefs (September 16, 1997). ... On injured reserve with hand injury (December 9, 1998-remainder of season). ... Granted unconditional free agency (February 12, 1999). ... Re-signed by Chiefs (February 16, 1999).
PLAYING EXPERIENCE: Amsterdam W.L., 1996; Chicago NFL, 1996; Kansas City NFL, 1997-1999. ... Games/Games started: W.L. 1996 (games played unavailable), NFL 1996 (9/0), 1997 (3/0), 1998 (12/0), 1999 (10/2). Total NFL: 34/2.
HONORS: Named offensive lineman on THE SPORTING NEWS college All-America second team (1993).
PRO STATISTICS: 1996—Caught one pass for one yard and a touchdown. 1999—Recovered one fumble.

SPELLMAN, ALONZO   DL   COWBOYS

PERSONAL: Born September 27, 1971, in Mount Holly, N.J. ... 6-4/292. ... Full name: Alonzo Robert Spellman.
HIGH SCHOOL: Rancocas Valley Regional (Mount Holly, N.J.).
COLLEGE: Ohio State.
TRANSACTIONS/CAREER NOTES: Selected after junior season by Chicago Bears in first round (22nd pick overall) of 1992 NFL draft. ... Signed by Bears (July 13, 1992). ... Designated by Bears as transition player (February 16, 1996). ... Tendered offer sheet by Jacksonville Jaguars (February 17, 1996). ... Offer matched by Bears (February 23, 1996). ... Released by Bears (June 12, 1998). ... Signed by Dallas Cowboys (July 29, 1999). ... Granted unconditional free agency (February 11, 2000). ... Re-signed by Cowboys (March 21, 2000).
PRO STATISTICS: 1994—Intercepted one pass for 31 yards. 1995—Recovered one fumble. 1999—Recovered one fumble.

Year Team	G	GS	SACKS
1992—Chicago NFL	15	0	4.0
1993—Chicago NFL	16	0	2.5
1994—Chicago NFL	16	16	7.0
1995—Chicago NFL	16	16	8.5
1996—Chicago NFL	16	15	8.0
1997—Chicago NFL	7	5	2.0
1998—		Did not play.	
1999—Dallas NFL	16	16	5.0
Pro totals (7 years)	102	68	37.0

SPENCE, BLAKE   FB   JETS

PERSONAL: Born June 20, 1975, in Garden Grove, Calif. ... 6-4/249. ... Full name: Blake Andrew Spence.
HIGH SCHOOL: Capistrano Valley (San Juan Capistrano, Calif.).
COLLEGE: Oregon.
TRANSACTIONS/CAREER NOTES: Selected by New York Jets in fifth round (146th pick overall) of 1998 NFL draft. ... Signed by Jets (June 23, 1998).
PLAYING EXPERIENCE: New York Jets NFL, 1998 and 1999. ... Games/Games started: 1998 (5/0), 1999 (10/0). Total: 15/0.
CHAMPIONSHIP GAME EXPERIENCE: Played in AFC championship game (1998 season).
PRO STATISTICS: 1998—Caught one pass for five yards. 1999—Caught three passes for 15 yards and one touchdown.
SINGLE GAME HIGHS (regular season): Receptions—1 (October 25, 1998, vs. Atlanta); yards—5 (October 25, 1998, vs. Atlanta); and touchdown receptions—0.

SPENCER, JIMMY   CB   BRONCOS

PERSONAL: Born March 29, 1969, in Manning, S.C. ... 5-9/180. ... Full name: James Arthur Spencer Jr.
HIGH SCHOOL: Glades Central (Belle Glade, Fla.).
COLLEGE: Florida.
TRANSACTIONS/CAREER NOTES: Selected by Washington Redskins in eighth round (215th pick overall) of 1991 NFL draft. ... Signed by Redskins for 1991 season. ... Released by Redskins (August 26, 1991). ... Signed by New Orleans Saints (April 2, 1992). ... Granted unconditional free agency (February 16, 1996). ... Signed by Cincinnati Bengals (March 21, 1996). ... Released by Bengals (August 25, 1998). ... Signed by San Diego Chargers (September 1, 1998). ... Granted unconditional free agency (February 12, 1999). ... Re-signed by Chargers (April 7, 1999). ... On injured reserve with broken arm (December 20, 1999-remainder of season). ... Released by Chargers (February 10, 2000). ... Signed by Denver Broncos (March 6, 2000).
PRO STATISTICS: 1992—Recovered one fumble. 1993—Recovered three fumbles for 53 yards. 1994—Recovered one fumble. 1996—Recovered one fumble for 59 yards.

			INTERCEPTIONS			
Year Team	G	GS	No.	Yds.	Avg.	TD
1992—New Orleans NFL	16	4	0	0	0.0	0
1993—New Orleans NFL	16	3	0	0	0.0	0
1994—New Orleans NFL	16	16	5	24	4.8	0
1995—New Orleans NFL	16	15	4	11	2.8	0
1996—Cincinnati NFL	15	14	5	48	9.6	0
1997—Cincinnati NFL	16	9	1	-2	-2.0	0
1998—San Diego NFL	15	4	1	0	0.0	0
1999—San Diego NFL	14	7	4	1	0.3	0
Pro totals (8 years)	124	72	20	82	4.1	0

SPICER, PAUL   DE   LIONS

PERSONAL: Born August 18, 1975, in Indianapolis. ... 6-4/269.
HIGH SCHOOL: Northwestern (Indianapolis).
COLLEGE: College of DuPage (Ill.), then Saginaw Valley State (Mich.).
TRANSACTIONS/CAREER NOTES: Signed as non-drafted free agent by Seattle Seahawks (April 20, 1998). ... Released by Seahawks (August 24, 1998). ... Signed by Sasketchawan Roughriders of CFL (September 26, 1998). ... Signed by Detroit Lions (February 24, 1999). ... Released by Lions (September 5, 1999). ... Re-signed by Lions to practice squad (September 7, 1999). ... Activated (October 8, 1999). ... Released by Lions (November 6, 1999). ... Re-signed by Lions to practice squad (November 10, 1999).
PLAYING EXPERIENCE: Saskatchawan Roughriders CFL, 1998; Detroit NFL, 1999. ... Games/Games started: 1998 (7/games started unavailable), 1999 (2/0).

SPIKES, CAMERON   G   RAMS

PERSONAL: Born November 6, 1976, in Madisonville, Texas. ... 6-2/310. ... Full name: Cameron Wade Spikes.
HIGH SCHOOL: Bryan (Texas).
COLLEGE: Texas A&M.
TRANSACTIONS/CAREER NOTES: Selected by St. Louis Rams in fifth round (145th pick overall) of 1999 NFL draft. ... Signed by Rams (July 19, 1999).
PLAYING EXPERIENCE: St. Louis NFL, 1999. ... Games/Games started: 1999 (5/0).
CHAMPIONSHIP GAME EXPERIENCE: Member of Rams for NFC championship game (1999 season); inactive. ... Member of Super Bowl championship team (1999 season); inactive.

SPIKES, TAKEO   LB   BENGALS

PERSONAL: Born December 17, 1976, in Sandersville, Ga. ... 6-2/230. ... Full name: Takeo Gerard Spikes. ... Name pronounced tuh-KEE-oh.
HIGH SCHOOL: Washington County (Sandersville, Ga.).
COLLEGE: Auburn.
TRANSACTIONS/CAREER NOTES: Selected after junior season by Cincinnati Bengals in first round (13th pick overall) of 1998 NFL draft. ... Signed by Bengals (July 25, 1998).
HONORS: Named inside linebacker on The Sporting News college All-America first team (1997).
PRO STATISTICS: 1999—Intercepted two passes for seven yards and recovered four fumbles.

Year Team	G	GS	SACKS
1998—Cincinnati NFL	16	16	2.0
1999—Cincinnati NFL	16	16	3.0
Pro totals (2 years)	32	32	5.0

SPIRES, GREG   DE   PATRIOTS

PERSONAL: Born August 12, 1974, in Mariana, Fla. ... 6-1/265. ... Full name: Greg Tyrone Spires.
HIGH SCHOOL: Mariner (Cape Coral, Fla.).
COLLEGE: Florida State.
TRANSACTIONS/CAREER NOTES: Selected by New England Patriots in third round (83rd pick overall) of 1998 NFL draft. ... Signed by Patriots (July 16, 1998). ... On injured reserve with knee injury (December 15, 1999-remainder of season).

Year Team	G	GS	SACKS
1998—New England NFL	15	1	3.0
1999—New England NFL	11	0	0.5
Pro totals (2 years)	26	1	3.5

SPRIGGS, MARCUS   DT   BROWNS

PERSONAL: Born July 26, 1976, in Washington, D.C. ... 6-4/314.
HIGH SCHOOL: Woodson (Washington, D.C.).
COLLEGE: Ohio State, then Troy (Ala.) State.
TRANSACTIONS/CAREER NOTES: Selected by Cleveland Browns in sixth round (174th pick overall) of 1999 NFL draft. ... Signed by Browns (July 22, 1999). ... On injured reserve with shoulder injury (November 23, 1999-remainder of season).
PLAYING EXPERIENCE: Cleveland NFL, 1999. ... Games/Games started: 1999 (10/0).

SPRIGGS, MARCUS   OT   BILLS

PERSONAL: Born May 17, 1974, in Hattiesburg, Miss. ... 6-3/315. ... Full name: Thomas Marcus Spriggs.
HIGH SCHOOL: Byram (Jackson, Miss.).
JUNIOR COLLEGE: Hinds Community College (Miss.).
COLLEGE: Houston.
TRANSACTIONS/CAREER NOTES: Selected by Buffalo Bills in sixth round (185th pick overall) of 1997 NFL draft. ... Signed by Bills (June 13, 1997). ... Granted free agency (February 11, 2000). ... Re-signed by Bills (April 10, 2000).
PLAYING EXPERIENCE: Buffalo NFL, 1997-1999. ... Games/Games started: 1997 (2/0), 1998 (1/0), 1999 (11/2). Total: 14/2.

SPRINGS, SHAWN   CB   SEAHAWKS

PERSONAL: Born March 11, 1975, in Williamsburg, W.Va. ... 6-0/195. ... Son of Ron Springs, running back with Dallas Cowboys (1979-84) and Tampa Bay Buccaneers (1985 and 1986).
HIGH SCHOOL: Springbrook (Silver Spring, Md.).
COLLEGE: Ohio State.
TRANSACTIONS/CAREER NOTES: Selected by Seattle Seahawks in first round (third pick overall) of 1997 NFL draft. ... Signed by Seahawks (August 4, 1997).
HONORS: Named cornerback on THE SPORTING NEWS college All-America second team (1996). ... Played in Pro Bowl (1998 season).
PRO STATISTICS: 1998—Recovered two fumbles for 14 yards and one touchdown. 1999—Returned one kickoff for 15 yards, returned blocked field goal 61 yards for a touchdown and recovered one fumble.

			INTERCEPTIONS				TOTALS			
Year Team	G	GS	No.	Yds.	Avg.	TD	TD	2pt.	Pts.	Fum.
1997—Seattle NFL	10	10	1	0	0.0	0	0	0	0	0
1998—Seattle NFL	16	16	7	142	20.3	▲2	3	0	18	0
1999—Seattle NFL	16	16	5	77	15.4	0	1	0	6	0
Pro totals (3 years)	42	42	13	219	16.8	2	4	0	24	0

SPROTTE, JIMMY   LB

PERSONAL: Born October 2, 1974, in Olathe, Kan. ... 6-3/235. ... Full name: John Wild Sprotte. ... Name pronounced SPRAHT.
HIGH SCHOOL: Blue Ridge (Lakeside, Ariz.).
COLLEGE: Arizona.
TRANSACTIONS/CAREER NOTES: Selected by Tennessee Oilers in seventh round (205th pick overall) of 1998 NFL draft. ... Signed by Oilers (July 7, 1998). ... Released by Oilers (August 25, 1998). ... Re-signed by Oilers to practice squad (September 1, 1998). ... Signed by Cincinnati Bengals off Oilers practice squad (October 1, 1998). ... Released by Bengals (October 11, 1999). ... Re-signed by Bengals to practice squad (October 12, 1999). ... Released by Bengals (November 5, 1999). ... Selected by Frankfurt Galaxy in 2000 NFL Europe draft (February 22, 2000).
PLAYING EXPERIENCE: Cincinnati NFL, 1998 and 1999. ... Games/Games started: 1998 (5/0), 1999 (4/0). Total: 9/0.

STAAT, JEREMY   DE   STEELERS

PERSONAL: Born October 10, 1976, in Bakersfield, Calif. ... 6-5/300. ... Full name: Jeremy Ray Staat. ... Name pronounced STOHT.
HIGH SCHOOL: Bakersfield (Calif.).
JUNIOR COLLEGE: Bakersfield (Calif.) College.
COLLEGE: Arizona State.
TRANSACTIONS/CAREER NOTES: Selected by Pittsburgh Steelers in second round (41st pick overall) of 1998 NFL draft. ... Signed by Steelers (June 19, 1998).
PLAYING EXPERIENCE: Pittsburgh NFL, 1998 and 1999. ... Games/Games started: 1998 (5/0), 1999 (16/2). Total: 21/2.
HONORS: Named defensive tackle on THE SPORTING NEWS college All-America second team (1997).

STABLEIN, BRIAN   WR   LIONS

PERSONAL: Born April 14, 1970, in Erie, Pa. ... 6-1/194. ... Full name: Brian Patrick Stablein. ... Name pronounced STABE-line.
HIGH SCHOOL: McDowell (Erie, Pa.).
COLLEGE: Ohio State.
TRANSACTIONS/CAREER NOTES: Selected by Denver Broncos in eighth round (210nd pick overall) of 1993 NFL draft. ... Signed by Broncos (June 7, 1993). ... Released by Broncos (August 24, 1993). ... Signed by Indianapolis Colts to practice squad (September 7, 1993). ... Active for two games (1994); did not play. ... Granted free agency (February 14, 1997). ... Re-signed by Colts (June 10, 1997). ... Granted unconditional free agency (February 13, 1998). ... Signed by New England Patriots (March 19, 1998). ... Released by Patriots (August 30, 1998). ... Signed by Detroit Lions (September 1, 1998). ... Granted unconditional free agency (February 12, 1999). ... Re-signed by Lions (April 6, 1999).
CHAMPIONSHIP GAME EXPERIENCE: Played in AFC championship game (1995 season).
PRO STATISTICS: 1999—Recovered one fumble.

SINGLE GAME HIGHS (regular season): Receptions—5 (November 24, 1996, vs. New England); yards—48 (November 7, 1999, vs. St. Louis); and touchdown receptions—1 (October 24, 1999, vs. Carolina).

				RECEIVING			PUNT RETURNS				TOTALS		
Year Team	G	GS	No.	Yds.	Avg.	TD	No.	Yds.	Avg.	TD	TD	2pt.	Pts.	Fum.
1993—Indianapolis NFL								Did not play.						
1994—Indianapolis NFL								Did not play.						
1995—Indianapolis NFL	15	0	8	95	11.9	0	0	0	0.0	0	0	0	0	0
1996—Indianapolis NFL	16	0	18	192	10.7	1	6	56	9.3	0	1	0	6	0
1997—Indianapolis NFL	16	0	25	253	10.1	1	17	133	7.8	0	1	1	8	0
1998—Detroit NFL	10	0	7	80	11.4	0	0	0	0.0	0	0	0	0	0
1999—Detroit NFL	16	2	11	119	10.8	1	1	9	9.0	0	1	†1	8	1
Pro totals (5 years)	73	2	69	739	10.7	3	24	198	8.3	0	3	2	22	1

STAI, BRENDEN   G   CHIEFS

PERSONAL: Born March 30, 1972, in Phoenix. ... 6-4/310. ... Full name: Brenden Michael Stai. ... Name pronounced STY.
HIGH SCHOOL: Anaheim High.
COLLEGE: Nebraska.
TRANSACTIONS/CAREER NOTES: Selected by Pittsburgh Steelers in third round (91st pick overall) of 1995 NFL draft. ... Signed by Steelers (July 18, 1995). ... Granted free agency (February 13, 1998). ... Re-signed by Steelers (June 9, 1998). ... Released by Steelers (March 14, 2000). ... Signed by Kansas City Chiefs (May 4, 2000).
PLAYING EXPERIENCE: Pittsburgh NFL, 1995-1999. ... Games/Games started: 1995 (16/9), 1996 (9/9), 1997 (10/9), 1998 (16/16), 1999 (16/16). Total: 67/59.
CHAMPIONSHIP GAME EXPERIENCE: Played in AFC championship game (1995 and 1997 seasons). ... Played in Super Bowl XXX (1995 season).
HONORS: Named offensive lineman on THE SPORTING NEWS college All-America second team (1994).

STALEY, DUCE   RB   EAGLES

PERSONAL: Born February 27, 1975, in Columbia, S.C. ... 5-11/220. ... Name pronounced DEUCE.
HIGH SCHOOL: Airport (Columbia, S.C.).
JUNIOR COLLEGE: Itawamba Junior College (Miss.).
COLLEGE: South Carolina.
TRANSACTIONS/CAREER NOTES: Selected by Philadelphia Eagles in third round (71st pick overall) of 1997 NFL draft. ... Signed by Eagles (June 12, 1997).
PRO STATISTICS: 1997—Recovered one fumble. 1998—Recovered two fumbles. 1999—Recovered two fumbles.
SINGLE GAME HIGHS (regular season): Attempts—30 (December 13, 1998, vs. Arizona); yards—141 (December 13, 1998, vs. Arizona); and rushing touchdowns—2 (September 27, 1998, vs. Kansas City).
STATISTICAL PLATEAUS: 100-yard rushing games: 1998 (1), 1999 (5). Total: 6.

			RUSHING				RECEIVING				KICKOFF RETURNS				TOTALS		
Year Team	G	GS	Att.	Yds.	Avg.	TD	No.	Yds.	Avg.	TD	No.	Yds.	Avg.	TD	TD	2pt.	Pts.	Fum.
1997—Philadelphia NFL	16	0	7	29	4.1	0	2	22	11.0	0	47	1139	24.2	0	0	0	0	0
1998—Philadelphia NFL	16	13	258	1065	4.1	5	57	432	7.6	1	1	19	19.0	0	6	0	36	2
1999—Philadelphia NFL	16	16	325	1273	3.9	4	41	294	7.2	2	0	0	0.0	0	6	0	36	5
Pro totals (3 years)	48	29	590	2367	4.0	9	100	748	7.5	3	48	1158	24.1	0	12	0	72	7

STANLEY, CHAD   P   49ERS

PERSONAL: Born January 29, 1976, in Ore City, Texas. ... 6-3/205. ... Full name: Benjamin Chadwick Stanley.
HIGH SCHOOL: Ore City (Texas).
COLLEGE: Stephen F. Austin State.
TRANSACTIONS/CAREER NOTES: Signed as non-drafted free agent by San Francisco 49ers (April 23, 1999).
PRO STATISTICS: 1999—Rushed once for no yards and recovered one fumble.

				PUNTING			
Year Team	G	No.	Yds.	Avg.	Net avg.	In. 20	Blk.
1999—San Francisco NFL	16	69	2737	39.7	30.7	20	†2

STARKS, DUANE   CB   RAVENS

PERSONAL: Born May 23, 1974, in Miami. ... 5-10/170. ... Full name: Duane Lonell Starks.
HIGH SCHOOL: Miami Beach Senior.
JUNIOR COLLEGE: Holmes Junior College (Miss.).
COLLEGE: Miami (Fla.).
TRANSACTIONS/CAREER NOTES: Selected by Baltimore Ravens in first round (10th pick overall) of 1998 NFL draft. ... Signed by Ravens (August 5, 1998).

			INTERCEPTIONS			
Year Team	G	GS	No.	Yds.	Avg.	TD
1998—Baltimore NFL	16	8	5	3	0.6	0
1999—Baltimore NFL	16	5	5	59	11.8	1
Pro totals (2 years)	32	13	10	62	6.2	1

STEED, JOEL   NT   STEELERS

PERSONAL: Born February 17, 1969, in Frankfurt, West Germany. ... 6-2/308. ... Full name: Joel Edward Steed.
HIGH SCHOOL: W.C. Hinkley (Aurora, Colo.).
COLLEGE: Colorado (degree in sociology, 1991).
TRANSACTIONS/CAREER NOTES: Selected by Pittsburgh Steelers in third round (67th pick overall) of 1992 NFL draft. ... Signed by Steelers (July 27, 1992). ... On suspended list for violating league substance abuse policy (October 23-November 20, 1995). ... Granted unconditional free agency (February 13, 1998). ... Re-signed by Steelers (February 18, 1998).
CHAMPIONSHIP GAME EXPERIENCE: Played in AFC championship game (1994, 1995 and 1997 seasons). ... Played in Super Bowl XXX (1995 season).
HONORS: Named defensive lineman on THE SPORTING NEWS college All-America second team (1991). ... Played in Pro Bowl (1997 season).
PRO STATISTICS: 1993—Recovered one fumble. 1996—Recovered one fumble. 1997—Recovered one fumble. 1999—Recovered one fumble for four yards.

Year Team	G	GS	SACKS
1992—Pittsburgh NFL	11	4	0.0
1993—Pittsburgh NFL	14	12	1.5
1994—Pittsburgh NFL	16	16	2.0
1995—Pittsburgh NFL	12	11	1.0
1996—Pittsburgh NFL	16	14	0.0
1997—Pittsburgh NFL	16	16	1.0
1998—Pittsburgh NFL	16	16	1.0
1999—Pittsburgh NFL	14	14	3.0
Pro totals (8 years)	**115**	**103**	**9.5**

STEELE, GLEN   DE   BENGALS

PERSONAL: Born October 4, 1974, in Ligonier, Ind. ... 6-4/295. ... Full name: James Lendale Steele Jr.
HIGH SCHOOL: West Noble (Ligonier, Ind.).
COLLEGE: Michigan.
TRANSACTIONS/CAREER NOTES: Selected by Cincinnati Bengals in fourth round (105th pick overall) of 1998 NFL draft. ... Signed by Bengals (July 14, 1998). ... On injured reserve with ankle injury (December 15, 1998-remainder of season).
PLAYING EXPERIENCE: Cincinnati NFL, 1998 and 1999. ... Games/Games started: 1998 (10/0), 1999 (16/1). Total: 26/1.

STENSTROM, STEVE   QB   LIONS

PERSONAL: Born December 23, 1971, in El Toro, Calif. ... 6-2/202.
HIGH SCHOOL: El Toro (Calif.).
COLLEGE: Stanford (degree in public policy, 1994).
TRANSACTIONS/CAREER NOTES: Selected by Kansas City Chiefs in fourth round (134th pick overall) of 1995 NFL draft. ... Signed by Chiefs (September 11, 1995). ... Claimed on waivers by Chicago Bears (September 13, 1995). ... Activated (September 25, 1995). ... Active for 12 games (1995); did not play. ... Granted free agency (February 13, 1998). ... Re-signed by Bears (June 25, 1998). ... Granted unconditional free agency (February 12, 1999). ... Signed by San Francisco 49ers (July 1, 1999). ... Released by 49ers (February 7, 2000). ... Signed by Detroit Lions (February 21, 2000).
PRO STATISTICS: 1997—Fumbled once. 1998—Fumbled six times and recovered one fumble for minus nine yards. 1999—Caught one pass for nine yards and fumbled three times for minus one yard.
SINGLE GAME HIGHS (regular season): Attempts—42 (December 6, 1998, vs. Minnesota); completions—25 (December 6, 1998, vs. Minnesota); yards—303 (December 6, 1998, vs. Minnesota); and touchdown passes—1 (December 27, 1998, vs. Green Bay).
STATISTICAL PLATEAUS: 300-yard passing games: 1998 (1).
MISCELLANEOUS: Regular-season record as starting NFL quarterback: 1-9 (.100).

Year Team	G	GS	PASSING Att.	Cmp.	Pct.	Yds.	TD	Int.	Avg.	Rat.	RUSHING Att.	Yds.	Avg.	TD	TOTALS TD	2pt.	Pts.
1995—Chicago NFL								Did not play.									
1996—Chicago NFL	1	0	4	3	75.0	37	0	0	9.25	103.1	0	0	0.0	0	0	0	0
1997—Chicago NFL	3	0	14	8	57.1	70	0	2	5.00	31.0	1	6	6.0	0	0	0	0
1998—Chicago NFL	7	7	196	112	57.1	1252	4	6	6.39	70.4	18	79	4.4	2	2	0	12
1999—San Francisco NFL	6	3	100	54	54.0	536	0	4	5.36	52.8	3	15	5.0	0	0	0	0
Pro totals (4 years)	**17**	**10**	**314**	**177**	**56.4**	**1895**	**4**	**12**	**6.04**	**62.5**	**22**	**100**	**4.5**	**2**	**2**	**0**	**12**

STEPHENS, JAMAIN   OT   BENGALS

PERSONAL: Born January 9, 1974, in Lumberton, N.C. ... 6-5/330.
HIGH SCHOOL: Lumberton (N.C.).
COLLEGE: North Carolina A&T.
TRANSACTIONS/CAREER NOTES: Selected by Pittsburgh Steelers in first round (29th pick overall) of 1996 NFL draft. ... Signed by Steelers (July 17, 1996). ... Inactive for all 16 games (1996). ... Claimed on waivers by Cincinnati Bengals (August 3, 1999). ... On reserve/suspended list (September 5-October 11, 1999).
PLAYING EXPERIENCE: Pittsburgh NFL, 1997 and 1998; Cincinnati NFL, 1999. ... Games/Games started: 1997 (7/1), 1998 (11/10), 1999 (7/2). Total: 25/13.
CHAMPIONSHIP GAME EXPERIENCE: Member of Steelers for AFC championship game (1997 season); inactive.

STEPHENS, REGGIE   CB   GIANTS

PERSONAL: Born February 21, 1975, in Santa Cruz, Calif. ... 5-9/200.

HIGH SCHOOL: Santa Cruz (Calif.).
JUNIOR COLLEGE: Cabrillo College (Calif.).
COLLEGE: Rutgers.
TRANSACTIONS/CAREER NOTES: Signed as non-drafted free agent by New York Giants (April 27, 1999). ... Released by Giants (September 5, 1999). ... Re-signed by Giants to practice squad (November 16, 1999). ... Activated (December 10, 1999). ... Released by Giants (December 14, 1999). ... Re-signed by Giants to practice squad (December 15, 1999).
PLAYING EXPERIENCE: New York Giants NFL, 1999. ... Games/Games started: 1999 (1/0).

STEPHENS, TREMAYNE   RB   CHARGERS

PERSONAL: Born April 16, 1976, in Greenville, S.C. ... 5-11/206. ... Full name: Tremayne Raphael Stephens.
HIGH SCHOOL: Greer (S.C.) Senior.
COLLEGE: North Carolina State.
TRANSACTIONS/CAREER NOTES: Signed as non-drafted free agent by San Diego Chargers (April 20, 1998). ... Released by Chargers (September 11, 1999). ... Signed by Indianapolis Colts (September 15, 1999). ... Claimed on waivers by Chargers (September 20, 1999).
PRO STATISTICS: 1999—Recovered three fumbles.
SINGLE GAME HIGHS (regular season): Attempts—10 (December 27, 1998, vs. Arizona); yards—42 (December 27, 1998, vs. Arizona); and rushing touchdowns—2 (November 28, 1999, vs. Minnesota).

			RUSHING				RECEIVING				KICKOFF RETURNS				TOTALS		
Year Team	G	GS	Att.	Yds.	Avg.	TD	No.	Yds.	Avg.	TD	No.	Yds.	Avg.	TD	TD	2pt.	Pts. Fum.
1998—San Diego NFL	13	1	35	122	3.5	1	2	9	4.5	0	16	349	21.8	0	1	0	6 1
1999—San Diego NFL	11	2	24	61	2.5	3	18	133	7.4	1	18	335	18.6	0	4	0	24 2
Pro totals (2 years)	24	3	59	183	3.1	4	20	142	7.1	1	34	684	20.1	0	5	0	30 3

STEPNOSKI, MARK   C   COWBOYS

PERSONAL: Born January 20, 1967, in Erie, Pa. ... 6-2/265. ... Full name: Mark Matthew Stepnoski.
HIGH SCHOOL: Cathedral Prep (Erie, Pa.).
COLLEGE: Pittsburgh (degree in communications).
TRANSACTIONS/CAREER NOTES: Selected by Dallas Cowboys in third round (57th pick overall) of 1989 NFL draft. ... Signed by Cowboys (July 23, 1989). ... Granted free agency (February 1, 1992). ... Re-signed by Cowboys (September 5, 1992). ... Granted roster exemption (September 5-14, 1992). ... On injured reserve with knee injury (December 22, 1993-remainder of season). ... Granted unconditional free agency (February 17, 1994). ... Re-signed by Cowboys (June 29, 1994). ... Granted unconditional free agency (February 17, 1995). ... Signed by Houston Oilers (March 11, 1995). ... Oilers franchise moved to Tennessee for 1997 season. ... Granted unconditional free agency (February 12, 1999). ... Signed by Cowboys (April 13, 1999).
PLAYING EXPERIENCE: Dallas NFL, 1989-1994 and 1999; Houston NFL, 1995 and 1996; Tennessee NFL, 1997 and 1998. ... Games/Games started: 1989 (16/4), 1990 (16/16), 1991 (16/16), 1992 (14/14), 1993 (13/13), 1994 (16/16), 1995 (16/16), 1996 (16/16), 1997 (16/16), 1998 (13/13), 1999 (15/15). Total: 167/155.
CHAMPIONSHIP GAME EXPERIENCE: Played in NFC championship game (1992 and 1994 seasons). ... Member of Super Bowl championship team (1992 season).
HONORS: Named guard on The Sporting News college All-America first team (1988). ... Played in Pro Bowl (1992 and 1994-1996 seasons).
PRO STATISTICS: 1989—Recovered three fumbles. 1990—Returned one kickoff for 15 yards. 1992—Recovered one fumble. 1993—Fumbled once. 1994—Fumbled four times for minus three yards. 1997—Fumbled twice and recovered one fumble for minus seven yards. 1998—Rushed once for no yards, fumbled twice and recovered one fumble for minus six yards. 1999—Fumbled once and recovered one fumble for minus 26 yards.

STEUSSIE, TODD   OT   VIKINGS

PERSONAL: Born December 1, 1970, in Canoga Park, Calif. ... 6-6/308. ... Full name: Todd Edward Steussie. ... Name pronounced STEW-see.
HIGH SCHOOL: Agoura (Calif.).
COLLEGE: California.
TRANSACTIONS/CAREER NOTES: Selected by Minnesota Vikings in first round (19th pick overall) of 1994 NFL draft. ... Signed by Vikings (July 19, 1994).
PLAYING EXPERIENCE: Minnesota NFL, 1994-1999. ... Games/Games started: 1994 (16/16), 1995 (16/16), 1996 (16/16), 1997 (16/16), 1998 (15/15), 1999 (16/16). Total: 95/95.
CHAMPIONSHIP GAME EXPERIENCE: Played in NFC championship game (1998 season).
HONORS: Named offensive lineman on The Sporting News college All-America second team (1993). ... Played in Pro Bowl (1997 and 1998 seasons).
PRO STATISTICS: 1994—Recovered one fumble. 1996—Recovered one fumble. 1999—Recovered one fumble.

STEVENS, MATT   S

PERSONAL: Born June 15, 1973, in Chapel Hill, N.C. ... 6-0/206. ... Full name: Matthew Brian Stevens.
HIGH SCHOOL: Chapel Hill (N.C.).
COLLEGE: Appalachian State.
TRANSACTIONS/CAREER NOTES: Selected by Buffalo Bills in third round (87th pick overall) of 1996 NFL draft. ... Signed by Bills (July 15, 1996). ... Claimed on waivers by Philadelphia Eagles (August 25, 1997). ... On suspended list for anabolic steroid use (August 27-September 29, 1997). ... Claimed on waivers by Washington Redskins (December 8, 1998). ... Granted free agency (February 12, 1999). ... Re-signed by Redskins (April 23, 1999). ... Granted unconditional free agency (February 11, 2000).
PRO STATISTICS: 1996—Recovered one fumble. 1997—Recovered one fumble. 1999—Credited with one sack and recovered one fumble.

			INTERCEPTIONS			
Year Team	G	GS	No.	Yds.	Avg.	TD
1996—Buffalo NFL	13	11	2	0	0.0	0
1997—Philadelphia NFL	11	0	1	0	0.0	0

1998—Philadelphia NFL	7	1	0	0	0.0	0
—Washington NFL	3	0	0	0	0.0	0
1999—Washington NFL	15	1	6	61	10.2	0
Pro totals (4 years)	49	13	9	61	6.8	0

STEWART, JAMES RB LIONS

PERSONAL: Born December 27, 1971, in Morristown, Tenn. ... 6-1/226. ... Full name: James Ottis Stewart III.
HIGH SCHOOL: Morristown-Hamblen West (Morristown, Tenn.).
COLLEGE: Tennessee.
TRANSACTIONS/CAREER NOTES: Selected by Jacksonville Jaguars in first round (19th pick overall) of 1995 NFL draft. ... Signed by Jaguars (June 1, 1995). ... On injured reserve with knee injury (September 22, 1998-remainder of season). ... Granted unconditional free agency (February 11, 2000). ... Signed by Detroit Lions (February 14, 2000).
CHAMPIONSHIP GAME EXPERIENCE: Played in AFC championship game (1996 and 1999 seasons).
PRO STATISTICS: 1996—Recovered one fumble. 1999—Recovered one fumble.
SINGLE GAME HIGHS (regular season): Attempts—30 (December 2, 1999, vs. Pittsburgh); yards—145 (December 2, 1999, vs. Pittsburgh); and rushing touchdowns—5 (October 12, 1997, vs. Philadelphia).
STATISTICAL PLATEAUS: 100-yard rushing games: 1996 (1), 1997 (1), 1998 (2), 1999 (2). Total: 6.
MISCELLANEOUS: Holds Jacksonville Jaguars all-time records for most yards rushing (2,951), most touchdowns (38) and most rushing touchdowns (33).

			RUSHING				RECEIVING				TOTALS			
Year Team	G	GS	Att.	Yds.	Avg.	TD	No.	Yds.	Avg.	TD	TD	2pt.	Pts.	Fum.
1995—Jacksonville NFL	14	7	137	525	3.8	2	21	190	9.0	1	3	0	18	1
1996—Jacksonville NFL	13	11	190	723	3.8	8	30	177	5.9	2	10	0	60	2
1997—Jacksonville NFL	16	5	136	555	4.1	8	41	336	8.2	1	9	0	54	0
1998—Jacksonville NFL	3	3	53	217	4.1	2	6	42	7.0	1	3	0	18	2
1999—Jacksonville NFL	14	7	249	931	3.7	▲13	21	108	5.1	0	13	0	78	4
Pro totals (5 years)	60	33	765	2951	3.9	33	119	853	7.2	5	38	0	228	9

STEWART, KORDELL QB STEELERS

PERSONAL: Born October 16, 1972, in New Orleans. ... 6-1/211.
HIGH SCHOOL: John Ehret (Marrero, La.).
COLLEGE: Colorado.
TRANSACTIONS/CAREER NOTES: Selected by Pittsburgh Steelers in second round (60th pick overall) of 1995 NFL draft. ... Signed by Steelers (July 17, 1995).
CHAMPIONSHIP GAME EXPERIENCE: Played in AFC championship game (1995 and 1997 seasons). ... Played in Super Bowl XXX (1995 season).
PRO STATISTICS: 1995—Compiled a quarterback rating of 136.9. 1996—Compiled a quarterback rating of 18.8 and fumbled once. 1997—Compiled a quarterback rating of 75.2, fumbled six times and recovered one fumble for minus one yard. 1998—Compiled a quarterback rating of 62.9, punted once for 35 yards, fumbled three times and recovered two fumbles. 1999—Compiled a quarterback rating of 64.9, fumbled four times and recovered one fumble.
SINGLE GAME HIGHS (regular season): Attempts—48 (December 13, 1997, vs. New England); completions—26 (December 13, 1997, vs. New England); yards—317 (October 26, 1997, vs. Jacksonville); and touchdown passes—3 (December 7, 1997, vs. Denver).
STATISTICAL PLATEAUS: 300-yard passing games: 1997 (2). ... 100-yard rushing games: 1996 (1), 1998 (1). Total: 2.
MISCELLANEOUS: Regular-season record as starting NFL quarterback: 23-20 (.535). ... Postseason record as starting NFL quarterback: 1-1 (.500). ... Started two games at wide receiver (1995). ... Started two games at wide receiver (1996). ...Started one game at wide receiver (1999).

			PASSING						RUSHING				RECEIVING				TOTALS		
Year Team	G	GS	Att.	Cmp.	Pct.	Yds.	TD	Int.	Avg.	Att.	Yds.	Avg.	TD	No.	Yds.	Avg.	TD	TD	2pt.	Pts.
1995—Pittsburgh NFL	10	2	7	5	71.4	60	1	0	8.57	15	86	5.7	1	14	235	16.8	1	2	0	12
1996—Pittsburgh NFL	16	2	30	11	36.7	100	0	2	3.33	39	171	4.4	5	17	293	17.2	3	8	0	48
1997—Pittsburgh NFL	16	16	440	236	53.6	3020	21	§17	6.86	88	476	5.4	11	0	0	0.0	0	11	0	66
1998—Pittsburgh NFL	16	16	458	252	55.0	2560	11	18	5.59	81	406	5.0	2	1	17	17.0	0	2	0	12
1999—Pittsburgh NFL	16	12	275	160	58.2	1464	6	10	5.32	56	258	4.6	2	9	113	12.6	1	3	0	18
Pro totals (5 years)	74	48	1210	664	54.9	7204	39	47	5.95	279	1397	5.0	21	41	658	16.0	5	26	0	156

STEWART, RAYNA S JAGUARS

PERSONAL: Born June 18, 1973, in Oklahoma City. ... 5-10/198. ... Full name: Rayna Cottrell Stewart II. ... Name pronounced ruh-NAY.
HIGH SCHOOL: Chatsworth (Calif.).
COLLEGE: Northern Arizona (degree in advertising, 1995).
TRANSACTIONS/CAREER NOTES: Selected by Houston Oilers in fifth round (143rd pick overall) of 1996 NFL draft. ... Signed by Oilers (June 27, 1996). ... Oilers franchise moved to Tennessee for 1997 season. ... Released by Oilers (August 30, 1998). ... Signed by Miami Dolphins (September 15, 1998). ... Released by Dolphins (September 7, 1999). ... Signed by Jacksonville Jaguars (September 20, 1999). ... Granted unconditional free agency (February 11, 2000). ... Re-signed by Jaguars (February 25, 2000).
PLAYING EXPERIENCE: Houston NFL, 1996; Tennessee NFL, 1997; Miami NFL, 1998; Jacksonville NFL, 1999. ... Games/Games started: 1996 (15/0), 1997 (16/5), 1998 (14/0), 1999 (14/0). Total: 59/5.
CHAMPIONSHIP GAME EXPERIENCE: Played in AFC championship game (1999 season).
PRO STATISTICS: 1997—Credited with 1/2 sack and recovered one fumble. 1999—Recovered one fumble.

STEWART, RYAN S LIONS

PERSONAL: Born September 30, 1973, in Moncks Corner, S.C. ... 6-1/206.
HIGH SCHOOL: Berkeley (Moncks Corner, S.C.).

COLLEGE: Georgia Tech (degree in business management).
TRANSACTIONS/CAREER NOTES: Selected by Detroit Lions in third round (76th pick overall) of 1996 NFL draft. ... Signed by Lions (July 21, 1996). ... Released by Lions (August 24, 1997). ... Re-signed by Lions (October 30, 1997). ... Granted free agency (February 12, 1999). ... Re-signed by Lions (April 26, 1999). ... On injured reserve with groin injury (October 30, 1999-remainder of season). ... Granted unconditional free agency (February 11, 2000). ... Re-signed by Lions (April 11, 2000).
PLAYING EXPERIENCE: Detroit NFL, 1996-1999. ... Games/Games started: 1996 (14/2), 1997 (8/0), 1998 (16/0), 1999 (2/0). Total: 40/2.
PRO STATISTICS: 1996—Intercepted one pass for 14 yards. 1999—Credited with one sack.

STILL, BRYAN   WR   BEARS

PERSONAL: Born June 3, 1974, in Newport News, Va. ... 5-11/174. ... Full name: Bryan Andrei Still.
HIGH SCHOOL: Huguenot (Richmond, Va.).
COLLEGE: Virginia Tech.
TRANSACTIONS/CAREER NOTES: Selected by San Diego Chargers in second round (41st pick overall) of 1996 NFL draft. ... Signed by Chargers (June 25, 1996). ... Granted free agency (February 12, 1999). ... Re-signed by Chargers (July 22, 1999). ... Claimed on waivers by Atlanta Falcons (November 17, 1999). ... Released by Falcons (December 13, 1999). ... Signed by Dallas Cowboys (December 16, 1999). ... Inactive for one game with Cowboys (1999). ... Released by Cowboys (December 21, 1999). ... Signed by Chicago Bears (April 28, 2000).
PRO STATISTICS: 1996—Returned one punt for one yard and returned four kickoffs for 113 yards. 1999—Returned one kickoff for eight yards.
SINGLE GAME HIGHS (regular season): Receptions—8 (September 27, 1998, vs. New York Giants); yards—128 (September 6, 1998, vs. Buffalo); and touchdown receptions—1 (November 29, 1998, vs. Denver).
STATISTICAL PLATEAUS: 100-yard receiving games: 1998 (2).

| | | | RECEIVING | | | | TOTALS | | | |
Year Team	G	GS	No.	Yds.	Avg.	TD	TD	2pt.	Pts.	Fum.
1996—San Diego NFL	16	0	6	142	23.7	0	0	0	0	2
1997—San Diego NFL	15	4	24	324	13.5	0	0	0	0	0
1998—San Diego NFL	14	9	43	605	14.1	2	2	0	12	0
1999—San Diego NFL	4	0	8	96	12.0	0	0	0	0	0
—Atlanta NFL	3	1	2	14	7.0	0	0	0	0	0
Pro totals (4 years)	52	14	83	1181	14.2	2	2	0	12	2

STILLS, GARY   LB   CHIEFS

PERSONAL: Born July 11, 1974, in Trenton, N.J. ... 6-2/235.
HIGH SCHOOL: Valley Forge (Pa.) Military Academy.
COLLEGE: West Virginia.
TRANSACTIONS/CAREER NOTES: Selected by Kansas City Chiefs in third round (75th pick overall) of 1999 NFL draft. ... Signed by Chiefs (July 26, 1999).
PLAYING EXPERIENCE: Kansas City NFL, 1999. ... Games/Games started: 1999 (2/0).

STINCHCOMB, MATT   OT   RAIDERS

PERSONAL: Born June 3, 1977, in Lilburn, Ga. ... 6-6/310. ... Full name: Matthew Douglass Stinchcomb.
HIGH SCHOOL: Parkview (Lilburn, Ga.).
COLLEGE: Georgia.
TRANSACTIONS/CAREER NOTES: Selected by Oakland Raiders in first round (18th pick overall) of 1999 NFL draft. ... Signed by Raiders (July 22, 1999). ... On injured reserve with shoulder injury (October 1, 1999-remainder of season). ... Inactive for three games (1999).
HONORS: Named offensive tackle on THE SPORTING NEWS college All-America second team (1997 and 1998).

STOKES, J.J.   WR   49ERS

PERSONAL: Born October 6, 1972, in San Diego. ... 6-4/217. ... Full name: Jerel Jamal Stokes.
HIGH SCHOOL: Point Loma (San Diego).
COLLEGE: UCLA (degree in sociology, 1994).
TRANSACTIONS/CAREER NOTES: Selected by San Francisco 49ers in first round (10th pick overall) of 1995 NFL draft. ... Signed by 49ers (July 27, 1995). ... On injured reserve with wrist injury (October 26, 1996-remainder of season). ... Granted unconditional free agency (February 12, 1999). ... Re-signed by 49ers (March 8, 1999).
CHAMPIONSHIP GAME EXPERIENCE: Played in NFC championship game (1997 season).
HONORS: Named wide receiver on THE SPORTING NEWS college All-America first team (1993).
PRO STATISTICS: 1997—Recovered two fumbles. 1999—Recovered one fumble.
SINGLE GAME HIGHS (regular season): Receptions—9 (October 18, 1998, vs. Indianapolis); yards—130 (January 3, 2000, vs. Atlanta); and touchdown receptions—2 (December 6, 1998, vs. Carolina).
STATISTICAL PLATEAUS: 100-yard receiving games: 1995 (1), 1998 (2), 1999 (1). Total: 4.

| | | | RECEIVING | | | | TOTALS | | | |
Year Team	G	GS	No.	Yds.	Avg.	TD	TD	2pt.	Pts.	Fum.
1995—San Francisco NFL	12	2	38	517	13.6	4	4	0	24	0
1996—San Francisco NFL	6	6	18	249	13.8	0	0	0	0	0
1997—San Francisco NFL	16	16	58	733	12.6	4	4	0	24	1
1998—San Francisco NFL	16	13	63	770	12.2	8	8	0	48	0
1999—San Francisco NFL	16	7	34	429	12.6	3	3	†1	20	1
Pro totals (5 years)	66	44	211	2698	12.8	19	19	1	116	2

STOKLEY, BRANDON　　　　WR　　　　RAVENS

PERSONAL: Born June 23, 1976, in Blacksburg, Va. ... 5-11/197.
HIGH SCHOOL: Comeaux (Lafayette, La.).
COLLEGE: Southwestern Louisiana.
TRANSACTIONS/CAREER NOTES: Selected by Baltimore Ravens in fourth round (105th pick overall) of 1999 NFL draft. ... Signed by Ravens (July 28, 1999). ... On injured reserve with shoulder injury (October 25, 1999-remainder of season).
PLAYING EXPERIENCE: Baltimore NFL, 1999. ... Games/Games started: 1999 (2/0).
PRO STATISTICS: 1999—Caught one pass for 28 yards and a touchdown.
SINGLE GAME HIGHS (regular season): Receptions—1 (September 12, 1999, vs. St. Louis); yards—28 (September 12, 1999, vs. St. Louis); and touchdown receptions—1 (September 12, 1999, vs. St. Louis).

STOLTENBERG, BRYAN　　　　C　　　　PANTHERS

PERSONAL: Born August 25, 1972, in Kearney, Neb. ... 6-1/300. ... Full name: Bryan Douglas Stoltenberg. ... Name pronounced STOLL-ten-burg.
HIGH SCHOOL: Clements (Sugar Land, Texas).
COLLEGE: Colorado (degree in marketing).
TRANSACTIONS/CAREER NOTES: Selected by San Diego Chargers in sixth round (192nd pick overall) of 1996 NFL draft. ... Signed by Chargers (July 2, 1996). ... Released by Chargers (August 25, 1996). ... Re-signed by Chargers to practice squad (August 26, 1996). ... Activated (October 9, 1996). ... Released by Chargers (August 18, 1997). ... Signed by New York Giants (September 30, 1997). ... Granted free agency (February 13, 1998). ... Re-signed by Giants (May 4, 1998). ... Signed by Carolina Panthers (August 30, 1998). ... Granted free agency (February 12, 1999). ... Re-signed by Panthers (April 7, 1999).
PLAYING EXPERIENCE: San Diego NFL, 1996; New York Giants NFL, 1997; Carolina NFL, 1998 and 1999. ... Games/Games started: 1996 (9/0), 1997 (3/0), 1998 (14/10), 1999 (16/7). Total: 42/17.
HONORS: Named offensive lineman on THE SPORTING NEWS college All-America second team (1995).
PRO STATISTICS: 1997—Fumbled once.

S

STONE, DWIGHT　　　　WR/KR　　　　JETS

PERSONAL: Born January 28, 1964, in Florala, Ala. ... 6-0/195.
HIGH SCHOOL: Florala (Ala.).
JUNIOR COLLEGE: Marion (Ala.) Military Academy.
COLLEGE: Middle Tennessee State (degree in social work).
TRANSACTIONS/CAREER NOTES: Signed as non-drafted free agent by Pittsburgh Steelers (May 19, 1987). ... Crossed picket line during players strike (October 7, 1987). ... Granted free agency (February 1, 1992). ... Re-signed by Steelers (May 15, 1992). ... Released by Steelers (August 30, 1993). ... Re-signed by Steelers (August 31, 1993). ... Granted unconditional free agency (February 17, 1995). ... Signed by Carolina Panthers (May 16, 1995). ... Granted unconditional free agency (February 16, 1996). ... Re-signed by Panthers (March 19, 1996). ... Granted unconditional free agency (February 14, 1997). ... Re-signed by Panthers (July 17, 1997). ... Granted unconditional free agency (February 13, 1998). ... Re-signed by Panthers (March 24, 1998). ... Granted unconditional free agency (February 12, 1999). ... Signed by New York Jets (August 7, 1999). ... Granted unconditional free agency (February 11, 2000). ... Re-signed by Jets (May 25, 2000).
CHAMPIONSHIP GAME EXPERIENCE: Played in AFC championship game (1994 season). ... Played in NFC championship game (1996 season).
PRO STATISTICS: 1987—Recovered one fumble. 1989—Recovered one fumble. 1990—Recovered two fumbles. 1993—Recovered one fumble. 1997—Recovered one fumble and credited with a safety. 1998—Recovered a blocked punt in the end zone for a touchdown. 1999—Recovered two fumbles.
SINGLE GAME HIGHS (regular season): Receptions—6 (October 19, 1992, vs. Cincinnati); yards—124 (September 1, 1991, vs. San Diego); and touchdown receptions—2 (October 19, 1992, vs. Cincinnati).
STATISTICAL PLATEAUS: 100-yard receiving games: 1991 (1), 1992 (1), 1993 (1). Total: 3.

| | | | | RUSHING | | | | RECEIVING | | | | KICKOFF RETURNS | | | | TOTALS | | |
Year Team	G	GS	Att.	Yds.	Avg.	TD	No.	Yds.	Avg.	TD	No.	Yds.	Avg.	TD	TD	2pt.	Pts.	Fum.
1987—Pittsburgh NFL	14	0	17	135	7.9	0	1	22	22.0	0	28	568	20.3	0	0	0	0	0
1988—Pittsburgh NFL	16	6	40	127	3.2	0	11	196	17.8	1	29	610	21.0	†1	2	0	12	5
1989—Pittsburgh NFL	16	8	10	53	5.3	0	7	92	13.1	0	7	173	24.7	0	0	0	0	2
1990—Pittsburgh NFL	16	2	2	-6	-3.0	0	19	332	17.5	1	5	91	18.2	0	1	0	6	1
1991—Pittsburgh NFL	16	8	1	2	2.0	0	32	649	§20.3	5	6	75	12.5	0	5	0	30	0
1992—Pittsburgh NFL	15	12	12	118	9.8	0	34	501	14.7	3	12	219	18.3	0	3	0	18	0
1993—Pittsburgh NFL	16	15	12	121	10.1	1	41	587	14.3	2	11	168	15.3	0	3	0	18	2
1994—Pittsburgh NFL	15	1	2	7	3.5	0	7	81	11.6	0	11	182	16.5	0	0	1	2	0
1995—Carolina NFL	16	0	1	3	3.0	0	0	0	0.0	0	12	269	22.4	0	0	0	0	0
1996—Carolina NFL	16	0	1	6	6.0	0	1	11	11.0	0	0	0	0.0	0	0	0	0	0
1997—Carolina NFL	16	0	0	0	0.0	0	0	0	0.0	0	3	76	25.3	0	0	0	2	0
1998—Carolina NFL	16	0	0	0	0.0	0	1	7	7.0	0	9	252	28.0	0	1	0	6	0
1999—New York Jets NFL	16	0	2	27	13.5	0	0	0	0.0	0	28	689	24.6	0	0	0	0	3
Pro totals (13 years)	204	52	100	593	5.9	1	154	2478	16.1	12	161	3372	20.9	1	15	1	94	13

STONE, RON　　　　G　　　　GIANTS

PERSONAL: Born July 20, 1971, in West Roxbury, Mass. ... 6-5/320.
HIGH SCHOOL: West Roxbury (Mass.).
COLLEGE: Boston College.
TRANSACTIONS/CAREER NOTES: Selected by Dallas Cowboys in fourth round (96th pick overall) of 1993 NFL draft. ... Signed by Cowboys (July 16, 1993). ... Active for four games with Cowboys (1993); did not play. ... Granted free agency (February 16, 1996). ... Tendered offer sheet by New York Giants (March 1, 1996). ... Cowboys declined to match offer (March 7, 1996).

PLAYING EXPERIENCE: Dallas NFL, 1994 and 1995; New York Giants NFL, 1996-1999. ... Games/Games started: 1994 (16/0), 1995 (16/1), 1996 (16/16), 1997 (16/16), 1998 (14/14), 1999 (16/16). Total: 94/63.
CHAMPIONSHIP GAME EXPERIENCE: Member of Cowboys for NFC championship game (1993 season); inactive. ... Member of Super Bowl championship team (1993 and 1995 seasons). ... Played in NFC championship game (1994 and 1995 seasons).
PRO STATISTICS: 1994—Recovered one fumble. 1997—Recovered one fumble.

STORZ, ERIK   LB   JAGUARS

PERSONAL: Born June 24, 1975, in Rockaway, N.J. ... 6-2/240. ... Full name: Erik Erwin Storz.
HIGH SCHOOL: Morris Catholic (Denville, N.J.).
COLLEGE: Boston College (degree in marketing).
TRANSACTIONS/CAREER NOTES: Signed as non-drafted free agent by Cincinnati Bengals (April 21, 1998). ... Released by Bengals (July 25, 1998). ... Signed by Jacksonville Jaguars (August 19, 1998). ... Released by Jaguars (August 25, 1998). ... Re-signed by Jaguars to practice squad (November 25, 1998). ... Activated (December 25, 1998). ... On injured reserve with knee injury (November 2, 1999-remainder of season).
PLAYING EXPERIENCE: Jacksonville NFL, 1998 and 1999. ... Games/Games started: 1998 (1/0), 1999 (7/0). Total: 8/0.

STOUTMIRE, OMAR   S   JETS

PERSONAL: Born July 9, 1974, in Pensacola, Fla. ... 5-11/198.
HIGH SCHOOL: Polytechnic (Pasadena, Calif.).
COLLEGE: Fresno State.
TRANSACTIONS/CAREER NOTES: Selected by Dallas Cowboys in seventh round (224th pick overall) of 1997 NFL draft. ... Signed by Cowboys (July 14, 1997). ... Claimed on waivers by Cleveland Browns (September 6, 1999). ... Inactive for two games with Browns (1999). ... Released by Browns (September 21, 1999). ... Signed by New York Jets (October 6, 1999). ... Granted free agency (February 11, 2000). ... Re-signed by Jets (April 18, 2000).
PRO STATISTICS: 1997—Recovered one fumble. 1998—Recovered one fumble. 1999—Recovered one fumble.

| | | | INTERCEPTIONS | | | | SACKS |
Year	Team	G	GS	No.	Yds.	Avg.	TD	No.
1997—Dallas NFL		16	2	2	8	4.0	0	2.0
1998—Dallas NFL		16	12	0	0	0.0	0	1.0
1999—New York Jets NFL		12	5	2	97	48.5	1	1.0
Pro totals (3 years)		44	19	4	105	26.3	1	4.0

STOVER, MATT   K   RAVENS

PERSONAL: Born January 27, 1968, in Dallas. ... 5-11/178. ... Full name: John Matthew Stover.
HIGH SCHOOL: Lake Highlands (Dallas).
COLLEGE: Louisiana Tech (degree in marketing, 1991).
TRANSACTIONS/CAREER NOTES: Selected by New York Giants in 12th round (329th pick overall) of 1990 NFL draft. ... Signed by Giants (July 23, 1990). ... On injured reserve with leg injury (September 4, 1990-entire season). ... Granted unconditional free agency (February 1, 1991). ... Signed by Cleveland Browns (March 15, 1991). ... Granted free agency (March 1, 1993). ... Re-signed by Browns (July 24, 1993). ... Released by Browns (August 30, 1993). ... Re-signed by Browns (August 31, 1993). ... Granted unconditional free agency (February 17, 1994). ... Re-signed by Browns (March 4, 1994). ... Browns franchise moved to Baltimore and renamed Ravens for 1996 season (March 11, 1996).
PRO STATISTICS: 1992—Had only pass attempt intercepted.

| | | | KICKING | | | | | | |
Year	Team	G	XPM	XPA	FGM	FGA	Lg.	50+	Pts.
1990—New York Giants NFL					Did not play.				
1991—Cleveland NFL		16	33	34	16	22	§55	2-2	81
1992—Cleveland NFL		16	29	30	21	29	51	1-3	92
1993—Cleveland NFL		16	36	36	16	22	53	1-4	84
1994—Cleveland NFL		16	32	32	26	28	45	0-1	110
1995—Cleveland NFL		16	26	26	29	33	47	0-1	113
1996—Baltimore NFL		16	34	35	19	25	50	1-1	91
1997—Baltimore NFL		16	32	32	26	34	49	0-2	110
1998—Baltimore NFL		16	24	24	21	28	48	0-0	87
1999—Baltimore NFL		16	32	32	28	33	50	2-5	116
Pro totals (9 years)		144	278	281	202	254	55	7-19	884

STOYANOVICH, PETE   K   CHIEFS

PERSONAL: Born April 28, 1967, in Dearborn Heights, Mich. ... 5-11/194. ... Full name: Peter Stoyanovich. ... Name pronounced sto-YON-ovich.
HIGH SCHOOL: Crestwood (Dearborn Heights, Mich.).
COLLEGE: Indiana (degree in public affairs, 1989).
TRANSACTIONS/CAREER NOTES: Selected by Miami Dolphins in eighth round (203rd pick overall) of 1989 NFL draft. ... Signed by Dolphins (July 27, 1989). ... Granted free agency (February 1, 1991). ... Re-signed by Dolphins (September 6, 1991). ... Activated (September 13, 1991). ... Granted unconditional free agency (February 17, 1994). ... Re-signed by Dolphins (February 21, 1994). ... Traded by Dolphins to Kansas City Chiefs for fifth-round pick (DT Barron Tanner) in 1997 draft (August 21, 1996).
CHAMPIONSHIP GAME EXPERIENCE: Played in AFC championship game (1992 season).
HONORS: Named kicker on THE SPORTING NEWS college All-America second team (1988). ... Named kicker on THE SPORTING NEWS NFL All-Pro team (1992).
POST SEASON RECORDS: Holds NFL postseason record for longest field goal—58 yards (January 5, 1991, vs. Kansas City).

Year Team	G	No.	Yds.	PUNTING Avg.	Net avg.	In. 20	Blk.	XPM	XPA	KICKING FGM	FGA	Lg.	50+	Pts.
1989—Miami NFL	16	0	0	0.0	0	0	0	38	39	19	26	*59	1-3	95
1990—Miami NFL	16	0	0	0.0	0	0	0	37	37	21	25	53	2-3	100
1991—Miami NFL	14	2	85	42.5	38.5	1	0	28	29	*31	▲37	53	3-5	§121
1992—Miami NFL	16	2	90	45.0	45.0	0	0	34	36	†30	§37	53	3-8	*124
1993—Miami NFL	16	0	0	0.0	0	0	0	37	37	24	32	52	2-2	109
1994—Miami NFL	16	0	0	0.0	0	0	0	35	35	24	31	50	1-2	107
1995—Miami NFL	16	0	0	0.0	0	0	0	37	37	27	34	51	2-5	118
1996—Kansas City NFL	16	0	0	0.0	0	0	0	34	34	17	24	45	0-1	85
1997—Kansas City NFL	16	1	24	24.0	24.0	1	0	35	36	26	27	54	2-2	113
1998—Kansas City NFL	16	1	29	29.0	29.0	1	0	34	34	27	32	53	2-2	115
1999—Kansas City NFL	16	1	35	35.0	35.0	1	0	§45	§45	21	28	51	1-1	108
Pro totals (11 years)	174	7	263	37.6	36.4	4	0	394	399	267	333	59	19-34	1195

STRAHAN, MICHAEL   DE   GIANTS

PERSONAL: Born November 21, 1971, in Houston. ... 6-5/275. ... Full name: Michael Anthony Strahan. ... Nephew of Art Strahan, defensive tackle with Atlanta Falcons (1968). ... Name pronounced STRAY-han.
HIGH SCHOOL: Westbury (Houston), then Mannheim (West Germany) American.
COLLEGE: Texas Southern.
TRANSACTIONS/CAREER NOTES: Selected by New York Giants in second round (40th pick overall) of 1993 NFL draft. ... Signed by Giants (July 25, 1993). ... On injured reserve with foot injury (January 13, 1994-remainder of playoffs). ... Granted free agency (February 16, 1996). ... Re-signed by Giants (July 8, 1996).
HONORS: Named defensive end on THE SPORTING NEWS NFL All-Pro team (1997). ... Played in Pro Bowl (1997-1999 seasons).
PRO STATISTICS: 1995—Intercepted two passes for 56 yards. 1997—Recovered one fumble. 1998—Intercepted one pass for 24 yards and a touchdown. 1999—Intercepted one pass for 44 yards and a touchdown and recovered two fumbles.

Year Team	G	GS	SACKS
1993—New York Giants NFL	9	0	1.0
1994—New York Giants NFL	15	15	4.5
1995—New York Giants NFL	15	15	7.5
1996—New York Giants NFL	16	16	5.0
1997—New York Giants NFL	16	16	14.0
1998—New York Giants NFL	16	15	15.0
1999—New York Giants NFL	16	16	5.5
Pro totals (7 years)	103	93	52.5

STREETS, TAI   WR   49ERS

PERSONAL: Born April 20, 1977, in Matteson, Ill. ... 6-1/193.
HIGH SCHOOL: Thornton Township (Harvey, Ill.).
COLLEGE: Michigan.
TRANSACTIONS/CAREER NOTES: Selected by San Francisco 49ers in sixth round (171st pick overall) of 1999 NFL draft. ... Signed by 49ers (July 30, 1999). ... On non-football injury list with Achilles' tendon injury (July 30-November 30, 1999).
PLAYING EXPERIENCE: San Francisco NFL, 1999. ... Games/Games started: 1999 (2/0).
PRO STATISTICS: 1999—Caught two passes for 25 yards.
SINGLE GAME HIGHS (regular season): Receptions—2 (January 3, 2000, vs. Atlanta); yards—25 (January 3, 2000, vs. Atlanta); and touchdown receptions—0.

STRICKLAND, FRED   LB

PERSONAL: Born August 15, 1966, in Buffalo. ... 6-2/251. ... Full name: Fredrick William Strickland Jr.
HIGH SCHOOL: Lakeland Regional (Wanaque, N.J.).
COLLEGE: Purdue.
TRANSACTIONS/CAREER NOTES: Selected by Los Angeles Rams in second round (47th pick overall) of 1988 NFL draft. ... Signed by Rams (July 10, 1988). ... On injured reserve with foot injury (October 16, 1990-remainder of season). ... Granted free agency (February 1, 1991). ... Re-signed by Rams (August 13, 1991). ... Granted unconditional free agency (March 1, 1993). ... Signed by Minnesota Vikings (May 7, 1993). ... Granted unconditional free agency (February 17, 1994). ... Signed by Green Bay Packers (June 24, 1994). ... Granted unconditional free agency (February 16, 1996). ... Signed by Dallas Cowboys (March 11, 1996). ... Released by Cowboys (February 11, 1999). ... Signed by Washington Redskins (March 26, 1999). ... On injured reserve with knee injury (October 26, 1999-remainder of season). ... Granted unconditional free agency (February 11, 2000).
CHAMPIONSHIP GAME EXPERIENCE: Played in NFC championship game (1989 and 1995 seasons).
PRO STATISTICS: 1988—Recovered two fumbles. 1989—Recovered one fumble for minus three yards. 1993—Recovered four fumbles for four yards. 1994—Recovered one fumble. 1996—Recovered one fumble. 1997—Recovered two fumbles.

Year Team	G	GS	INTERCEPTIONS No.	Yds.	Avg.	TD	SACKS No.
1988—Los Angeles Rams NFL	16	0	0	0	0.0	0	4.0
1989—Los Angeles Rams NFL	12	12	2	56	28.0	0	2.0
1990—Los Angeles Rams NFL	5	5	0	0	0.0	0	0.0
1991—Los Angeles Rams NFL	14	10	0	0	0.0	0	1.0
1992—Los Angeles Rams NFL	16	0	0	0	0.0	0	0.0
1993—Minnesota NFL	16	15	0	0	0.0	0	0.0
1994—Green Bay NFL	16	14	1	7	7.0	0	0.0
1995—Green Bay NFL	14	10	0	0	0.0	0	0.0
1996—Dallas NFL	16	16	1	0	0.0	0	1.0
1997—Dallas NFL	15	14	0	0	0.0	0	0.5
1998—Dallas NFL	16	15	0	0	0.0	0	0.0

S

1999—Washington NFL	5	0	0	0	0.0	0	0.0
Pro totals (12 years)	161	111	4	63	15.8	0	8.5

STRINGER, KOREY — OT — VIKINGS

PERSONAL: Born May 8, 1974, in Warren, Ohio. ... 6-4/339.
HIGH SCHOOL: Harding (Warren, Ohio).
COLLEGE: Ohio State.
TRANSACTIONS/CAREER NOTES: Selected after junior season by Minnesota Vikings in first round (24th pick overall) of 1995 NFL draft. ... Signed by Vikings (July 22, 1995).
PLAYING EXPERIENCE: Minnesota NFL, 1995-1999. ... Games/Games started: 1995 (16/15), 1996 (16/15), 1997 (15/15), 1998 (14/14), 1999 (16/16). Total: 77/75.
CHAMPIONSHIP GAME EXPERIENCE: Played in NFC championship game (1998 season).
HONORS: Named offensive lineman on THE SPORTING NEWS college All-America second team (1993). ... Named offensive lineman on THE SPORTING NEWS college All-America first team (1994).
PRO STATISTICS: 1995—Caught one pass for minus one yard and recovered two fumbles.

STRONG, MACK — FB — SEAHAWKS

PERSONAL: Born September 11, 1971, in Fort Benning, Ga. ... 6-0/235.
HIGH SCHOOL: Brookstone (Columbus, Ga.).
COLLEGE: Georgia.
TRANSACTIONS/CAREER NOTES: Signed as non-drafted free agent by Seattle Seahawks (April 28, 1993). ... Released by Seahawks (September 4, 1993). ... Re-signed by Seahawks to practice squad (September 6, 1993). ... Released by Seahawks (February 10, 2000). ... Re-signed by Seahawks (February 14, 2000).
PRO STATISTICS: 1995—Returned four kickoffs for 65 yards and recovered one fumble. 1996—Recovered one fumble. 1997—Returned one kickoff for 16 yards and recovered one fumble. 1998—Recovered one fumble.
SINGLE GAME HIGHS (regular season): Attempts—10 (December 11, 1994, vs. Houston); yards—44 (December 11, 1994, vs. Houston); rushing touchdowns—1 (November 12, 1995, vs. Jacksonville).

			RUSHING				RECEIVING				TOTALS			
Year Team	G	GS	Att.	Yds.	Avg.	TD	No.	Yds.	Avg.	TD	TD	2pt.	Pts.	Fum.
1993—Seattle NFL							Did not play.							
1994—Seattle NFL	8	1	27	114	4.2	2	3	3	1.0	0	2	0	12	1
1995—Seattle NFL	16	1	8	23	2.9	1	12	117	9.8	3	4	0	24	2
1996—Seattle NFL	14	8	5	8	1.6	0	9	78	8.7	0	0	0	0	0
1997—Seattle NFL	16	10	4	8	2.0	0	13	91	7.0	2	2	0	12	0
1998—Seattle NFL	16	5	15	47	3.1	0	8	48	6.0	2	2	0	12	2
1999—Seattle NFL	14	1	1	0	0.0	0	1	5	5.0	0	0	0	0	0
Pro totals (6 years)	84	26	60	200	3.3	3	46	342	7.4	7	10	0	60	5

STRYZINSKI, DAN — P — FALCONS

PERSONAL: Born May 15, 1965, in Indianapolis. ... 6-2/205. ... Full name: Daniel Thomas Stryzinski. ... Name pronounced stra-ZIN-ski.
HIGH SCHOOL: Lincoln (Vincennes, Ind.).
COLLEGE: Indiana (bachelor of science degree in public finance and management, 1988).
TRANSACTIONS/CAREER NOTES: Signed as non-drafted free agent by Indianapolis Colts (July 1988). ... Released by Colts (August 23, 1988). ... Signed by Cleveland Browns (August 25, 1988). ... Released by Browns (August 30, 1988). ... Re-signed by Browns for 1989 season. ... Released by Browns (August 30, 1989). ... Signed by New Orleans Saints to developmental squad (October 11, 1989). ... Granted free agency after 1989 season. ... Signed by Pittsburgh Steelers (March 14, 1990). ... Granted unconditional free agency (February 1, 1992). ... Signed by Tampa Bay Buccaneers (February 21, 1992). ... Granted unconditional free agency (February 17, 1995). ... Signed by Atlanta Falcons (February 20, 1995).
CHAMPIONSHIP GAME EXPERIENCE: Played in NFC championship game (1998 season). ... Played in Super Bowl XXXIII (1998 season).
PRO STATISTICS: 1990—Rushed three times for 17 yards and recovered one fumble. 1991—Rushed four times for minus 11 yards, fumbled once and recovered two fumbles. 1992—Attempted two passes with two completions for 14 yards and rushed once for seven yards. 1994—Completed only pass attempt for 21 yards. 1995—Rushed once for no yards.

		PUNTING					
Year Team	G	No.	Yds.	Avg.	Net avg.	In. 20	Blk.
1990—Pittsburgh NFL	16	65	2454	37.8	34.1	18	1
1991—Pittsburgh NFL	16	74	2996	40.5	36.2	10	1
1992—Tampa Bay NFL	16	74	3015	40.7	36.2	15	0
1993—Tampa Bay NFL	16	*93	3772	40.6	35.2	24	1
1994—Tampa Bay NFL	16	72	2800	38.9	35.8	20	0
1995—Atlanta NFL	16	67	2759	41.2	36.2	21	0
1996—Atlanta NFL	16	75	3152	42.0	35.5	22	0
1997—Atlanta NFL	16	89	3498	39.3	36.7	20	0
1998—Atlanta NFL	16	74	2963	40.0	36.6	25	0
1999—Atlanta NFL	16	80	3163	39.5	37.1	27	0
Pro totals (10 years)	160	763	30572	40.1	36.0	202	3

STUBBLEFIELD, DANA — DT — REDSKINS

PERSONAL: Born November 14, 1970, in Cleves, Ohio. ... 6-2/315. ... Full name: Dana William Stubblefield.
HIGH SCHOOL: Taylor (North Bend, Ohio).
COLLEGE: Kansas.

TRANSACTIONS/CAREER NOTES: Selected by San Francisco 49ers in first round (26th pick overall) of 1993 NFL draft. ... Signed by 49ers (July 14, 1993). ... Granted unconditional free agency (February 13, 1998). ... Signed by Washington Redskins (February 23, 1998).
CHAMPIONSHIP GAME EXPERIENCE: Played in NFC championship game (1993, 1994 and 1997 seasons). ... Member of Super Bowl championship team (1994 season).
HONORS: Played in Pro Bowl (1994, 1995 and 1997 seasons). ... Named defensive tackle on THE SPORTING NEWS NFL All-Pro team (1997).
PRO STATISTICS: 1995—Intercepted one pass for 12 yards. 1996—Intercepted one pass for 15 yards and recovered one fumble. 1999—Recovered one fumble.

Year Team	G	GS	SACKS
1993—San Francisco NFL	16	14	10.5
1994—San Francisco NFL	14	14	8.5
1995—San Francisco NFL	16	16	4.5
1996—San Francisco NFL	15	15	1.0
1997—San Francisco NFL	16	16	15.0
1998—Washington NFL	7	7	1.5
1999—Washington NFL	16	16	3.0
Pro totals (7 years)	100	98	44.0

STYLES, LORENZO   LB   RAMS

PERSONAL: Born January 31, 1974, in Sharon, Pa. ... 6-1/245.
HIGH SCHOOL: Independence (Columbus, Ohio), then Farrell (Pa.).
COLLEGE: Ohio State.
TRANSACTIONS/CAREER NOTES: Selected after junior season by Atlanta Falcons in third round (77th pick overall) of 1995 NFL draft. ... Signed by Falcons (July 21, 1995). ... Released by Falcons (August 26, 1997). ... Signed by St. Louis Rams (November 4, 1997). ... On injured reserve with shoulder injury (December 9, 1997-remainder of season). ... Granted free agency (February 13, 1998). ... Re-signed by Rams (March 25, 1998). ... On injured reserve with shoulder injury (November 30, 1998-remainder of season). ... Released by Rams (May 5, 2000) ... Re-signed by Rams (June 4, 2000).
PLAYING EXPERIENCE: Atlanta NFL, 1995 and 1996; St. Louis NFL, 1997-1999. ... Games/Games started: 1995 (12/0), 1996 (16/0), 1997 (3/0), 1998 (7/3), 1999 (16/0). Total: 54/3.
CHAMPIONSHIP GAME EXPERIENCE: Played in NFC championship game (1999 season). ... Member of Super Bowl championship team (1999 season).
PRO STATISTICS: 1996—Returned one kickoff for 12 yards. 1999—Recovered one fumble.

SULLIVAN, CHRIS   DL   STEELERS

PERSONAL: Born March 14, 1973, in North Attleboro, Mass. ... 6-4/285. ... Full name: Christopher Patrick Sullivan.
HIGH SCHOOL: North Attleboro (Mass.).
COLLEGE: Boston College (degree in sociology, 1995).
TRANSACTIONS/CAREER NOTES: Selected by New England Patriots in fourth round (119th pick overall) of 1996 NFL draft. ... Signd by Patriots (July 12, 1996). ... Granted free agency (February 12, 1999). ... Re-signed by Patriots (June 1, 1999). ... Granted unconditional free agency (February 11, 2000). ... Signed by Pittsburgh Steelers (February 19, 2000).
PLAYING EXPERIENCE: New England NFL, 1996-1999. ... Games/Games started: 1996 (16/0), 1997 (16/10), 1998 (15/10), 1999 (16/0). Total: 63/20.
CHAMPIONSHIP GAME EXPERIENCE: Played in AFC championship game (1996 season). ... Played in Super Bowl XXXI (1996 season).
PRO STATISTICS: 1996—Recovered one fumble. 1998—Returned two kickoffs for 14 yards and credited with two sacks. 1999—Returned one kickoff for one yard and credited with one sack.

SUPERNAW, KYWIN   S   LIONS

PERSONAL: Born June 2, 1975, in Claremore, Okla. ... 6-1/207.
HIGH SCHOOL: Skiatook (Okla.).
COLLEGE: Northeastern Oklahoma A&M, then Indiana.
TRANSACTIONS/CAREER NOTES: Signed as non-drafted free agent by Detroit Lions (April 24, 1998). ... Released by Lions (August 30, 1998). ... Re-signed by Lions to practice squad (September 1, 1998). ... Activated (December 1, 1998). ... On injured reserve with ankle injury (October 14, 1999-remainder of season).
PLAYING EXPERIENCE: Detroit NFL, 1998 and 1999. ... Games/Games started: 1998 (2/0), 1999 (2/0). Total: 4/0.

SURTAIN, PATRICK   CB   DOLPHINS

PERSONAL: Born June 19, 1976, in New Orleans. ... 5-11/190. ... Full name: Patrick Frank Surtain. ... Name pronounced sir-TANE.
HIGH SCHOOL: Edna Karr (New Orleans).
COLLEGE: Southern Mississippi.
TRANSACTIONS/CAREER NOTES: Selected by Miami Dolphins in second round (44th pick overall) of 1998 NFL draft. ... Signed by Dolphins (July 21, 1998).
HONORS: Named cornerback on THE SPORTING NEWS college All-America second team (1997).
PRO STATISTICS: 1999—Credited with two sacks.

Year Team	G	GS	INTERCEPTIONS No.	Yds.	Avg.	TD
1998—Miami NFL	16	0	2	1	0.5	0
1999—Miami NFL	16	6	2	28	14.0	0
Pro totals (2 years)	32	6	4	29	7.3	0

SUTTLE, JASON   CB   BRONCOS

PERSONAL: Born December 2, 1974, in Minneapolis. ... 5-10/182. ... Full name: Jason John Suttle.
HIGH SCHOOL: Burnsville (Minn.).
COLLEGE: Wisconsin (degree in sociology).
TRANSACTIONS/CAREER NOTES: Signed as non-drafted free agent by San Diego Chargers (April 24, 1998). ... Released by Chargers (July 23, 1998). ... Signed by New England Patriots (August 4, 1998). ... Released by Patriots (August 24, 1998). ... Signed by Denver Broncos (March 9, 1999). ... Released by Broncos (September 5, 1999). ... Re-signed by Broncos to practice squad (September 6, 1999). ... Activated (September 18, 1999). ... Released by Broncos (November 9, 1999). ... Re-signed by Broncos to practice squad (November 10, 1999). ... Activated (December 31, 1999).
PLAYING EXPERIENCE: Denver NFL, 1999. ... Games/Games started: 1999 (5/0).

SWANN, ERIC   DT   CARDINALS

PERSONAL: Born August 16, 1970, in Pinehurst, N.C. ... 6-5/317. ... Full name: Eric Jerrod Swann.
HIGH SCHOOL: Western Harnett (Lillington, N.C.).
COLLEGE: Wake Technical College, N.C. (did not play football).
TRANSACTIONS/CAREER NOTES: Played with Bay State Titans of Minor League Football System (1990). ... Selected by Phoenix Cardinals in first round (sixth pick overall) of 1991 NFL draft. ... Signed by Cardinals (April 24, 1991). ... On injured reserve with knee injury (August 27-September 27, 1991). ... On injured reserve with knee injury (November 17, 1993-remainder of season). ... Cardinals franchise renamed Arizona Cardinals for 1994 season. ... Designated by Cardinals as franchise player (February 16, 1996). ... On injured reserve with dislocated finger (December 17, 1997-remainder of season). ... On injured reserve with knee injury (December 10, 1998-remainder of season).
HONORS: Named defensive tackle on THE SPORTING NEWS NFL All-Pro team (1995). ... Played in Pro Bowl (1995 and 1996 seasons).
PRO STATISTICS: 1992—Credited with one safety. 1993—Credited with one safety and recovered one fumble. 1994—Credited with one safety and recovered one fumble for 10 yards. 1995—Recovered two fumbles. 1996—Recovered three fumbles for 11 yards. 1997—Rushed once for no yards, fumbled once and recovered one fumble. 1999—Intercepted one pass for 42 yards and a touchdown.

Year Team	G	GS	SACKS
1991—Phoenix NFL	12	3	4.0
1992—Phoenix NFL	16	11	2.0
1993—Phoenix NFL	9	9	3.5
1994—Arizona NFL	16	16	7.0
1995—Arizona NFL	13	12	8.5
1996—Arizona NFL	16	15	5.0
1997—Arizona NFL	13	13	7.5
1998—Arizona NFL	7	5	4.0
1999—Arizona NFL	9	0	4.0
Pro totals (9 years)	111	84	45.5

SWAYDA, SHAWN   DE   FALCONS

PERSONAL: Born September 4, 1974, in Phoenix. ... 6-5/294. ... Full name: Shawn Gerald Swayda.
HIGH SCHOOL: Brophy Prep (Phoenix).
COLLEGE: Arizona State.
TRANSACTIONS/CAREER NOTES: Selected by Chicago Bears in sixth round (196th pick overall) of 1997 NFL draft. ... Signed by Bears (July 10, 1997). ... Released by Bears (August 18, 1997). ... Signed by Dallas Cowboys to practice squad (October 9, 1997). ... Released by Cowboys (November 4, 1997). ... Signed by Detroit Lions to practice squad (November 24, 1997). ... Granted free agency after 1997 season. ... Signed by Atlanta Falcons (March 24, 1998). ... Released by Falcons (September 14, 1999). ... Re-signed by Falcons (September 28, 1999).
PLAYING EXPERIENCE: Atlanta NFL, 1998 and 1999. ... Games/Games started: 1998 (5/0), 1999 (4/0). Total: 9/0.
CHAMPIONSHIP GAME EXPERIENCE: Member of Falcons for NFC championship game (1998 season); inactive. ... Member of Falcons for Super Bowl XXXIII (1998 season); inactive.

SWAYNE, HARRY   OT   RAVENS

PERSONAL: Born February 2, 1965, in Philadelphia. ... 6-5/295. ... Full name: Harry Vonray Swayne.
HIGH SCHOOL: Cardinal Dougherty (Philadelphia).
COLLEGE: Rutgers.
TRANSACTIONS/CAREER NOTES: Selected by Tampa Bay Buccaneers in seventh round (190th pick overall) of 1987 NFL draft. ... Signed by Buccaneers (July 18, 1987). ... On injured reserve with fractured hand (September 8-October 31, 1987). ... On injured reserve with neck injury (November 18, 1988-remainder of season). ... Granted free agency (February 1, 1990). ... Re-signed by Buccaneers (July 19, 1990). ... Granted unconditional free agency (February 1, 1991). ... Signed by San Diego Chargers (April 1, 1991). ... On injured reserve with fractured leg (November 26, 1991-remainder of season). ... Designated by Chargers as transition player (February 25, 1993). ... Tendered offer sheet by Phoenix Cardinals (April 9, 1993). ... Offer matched by Chargers (April 15, 1993). ... On physically unable to perform list (July 24-August 21, 1995). ... Free agency status changed by Chargers from transitional to unconditional (February 16, 1996). ... Re-signed by Chargers (July 24, 1996). ... Granted unconditional free agency (February 14, 1997). ... Signed by Denver Broncos (April 17, 1997). ... Granted unconditional free agency (February 12, 1999). ... Signed by Baltimore Ravens (February 26, 1999). ... On injured reserve with foot injury (November 10, 1999-remainder of season).
PLAYING EXPERIENCE: Tampa Bay NFL, 1987-1990; San Diego NFL, 1991-1996; Denver NFL, 1997 and 1998; Baltimore NFL, 1999. ... Games/Games started: 1987 (8/2), 1988 (10/1), 1989 (16/0), 1990 (10/0), 1991 (12/12), 1992 (16/16), 1993 (11/11), 1994 (16/16), 1995 (16/16), 1996 (16/3), 1997 (7/0), 1998 (16/16), 1999 (6/6). Total: 160/99.
CHAMPIONSHIP GAME EXPERIENCE: Played in AFC championship game (1994, 1997 and 1998 seasons). ... Played in Super Bowl XXIX (1994 season). ... Member of Super Bowl championship team (1997 and 1998 seasons).
PRO STATISTICS: 1998—Recovered one fumble.

S

SWEENEY, JIM   C/G

PERSONAL: Born August 8, 1962, in Pittsburgh. ... 6-4/297. ... Full name: James Joseph Sweeney.
HIGH SCHOOL: Seton-LaSalle (Pittsburgh).
COLLEGE: Pittsburgh (degree in administration of justice).
TRANSACTIONS/CAREER NOTES: Selected by Pittsburgh Maulers in 1984 USFL territorial draft. ... Selected by New York Jets in second round (37th pick overall) of 1984 NFL draft. ... Signed by Jets (July 12, 1984). ... Granted free agency (February 1, 1990). ... Re-signed by Jets (August 27, 1990). ... Released by Jets (August 30, 1993). ... Re-signed by Jets (August 31, 1993). ... Granted unconditional free agency (February 17, 1994). ... Re-signed by Jets (May 2, 1994). ... Granted unconditional free agency (February 17, 1995). ... Signed by Seattle Seahawks (March 23, 1995). ... Released by Seahawks (July 19, 1996). ... Signed by Pittsburgh Steelers (August 19, 1996). ... Granted unconditional free agency (February 11, 2000).
PLAYING EXPERIENCE: New York Jets NFL, 1984-1994; Seattle NFL, 1995; Pittsburgh NFL, 1996-1999. ... Games/Games started: 1984 (10/2), 1985 (16/16), 1986 (16/16), 1987 (12/12), 1988 (16/16), 1989 (16/16), 1990 (16/16), 1991 (16/16), 1992 (16/16), 1993 (16/16), 1994 (16/16), 1995 (16/16), 1996 (16/0), 1997 (16/1), 1998 (8/1), 1999 (6/0). Total: 228/176.
CHAMPIONSHIP GAME EXPERIENCE: Played in AFC championship game (1997 season).
HONORS: Named guard on THE SPORTING NEWS college All-America second team (1983).
PRO STATISTICS: 1990—Recovered one fumble. 1994—Recovered one fumble.

SWIFT, JUSTIN   TE   49ERS

PERSONAL: Born August 14, 1975, in Kansas City, Kan. ... 6-3/265. ... Full name: Justin Charles Swift.
HIGH SCHOOL: Blue Valley (Overland Park, Kan.).
COLLEGE: Kansas State.
TRANSACTIONS/CAREER NOTES: Selected by Denver Broncos in seventh round (238th pick overall) of 1999 NFL draft. ... Signed by Broncos (July 20, 1999). ... Released by Broncos (August 27, 1999). ... Signed by Philadelphia Eagles (September 14, 1999). ... Released by Eagles (September 28, 1999). ... Signed by Broncos to practice squad (October 19, 1999). ... Released by Broncos (November 2, 1999). ... Signed by San Francisco 49ers to practice squad (November 15, 1999). ... Released by 49ers (February 10, 2000). ... Re-signed by 49ers (February 18, 2000). ... Assigned by 49ers to Frankfurt Galaxy in 2000 NFL Europe enhancement allocation program (February 18, 2000).
PLAYING EXPERIENCE: Philadelphia NFL, 1999. ... Games/Games started: 1999 (1/0).

SWIFT, MICHAEL   CB

PERSONAL: Born February 28, 1974, in Dyersburg, Tenn. ... 5-10/165. ... Full name: Michael Aaron Swift.
HIGH SCHOOL: Lake County (Tiptonville, Tenn.).
COLLEGE: Austin Peay.
TRANSACTIONS/CAREER NOTES: Signed as non-drafted free agent by San Diego Chargers (April 26, 1996). ... Released by Chargers (August 25, 1996). ... Re-signed by Chargers to practice squad (October 14, 1996). ... Released by Chargers (November 24, 1996). ... Re-signed by Chargers to practice squad (November 27, 1996). ... Assigned by Chargers to Rhein Fire in 1997 World League enhancement allocation program (February 19, 1997). ... Released by Chargers (August 18, 1997). ... Re-signed by Chargers to practice squad (August 25, 1997). ... Activated (September 26, 1997). ... Granted free agency (February 13, 1998). ... Signed by Carolina Panthers (June 2, 1998). ... Inactive for four games (1998). ... On injured reserve with leg injury (October 7, 1998-remainder of season). ... On injured reserve with leg injury (December 28, 1999-remainder of season). ... Granted free agency (February 11, 2000).
PLAYING EXPERIENCE: Rhein W.L., 1997; San Diego NFL, 1997; Carolina NFL, 1999. ... Games/Games started: W.L. 1997 (games played unavailable), NFL 1997 (12/1), 1999 (15/0). Total NFL: 27/1.
PRO STATISTICS: W.L.: 1997—Intercepted one pass for eight yards. NFL: 1997—Recovered one fumble for six yards. 1999—Recovered one fumble.

SWINGER, RASHOD   DT   CARDINALS

PERSONAL: Born November 27, 1974, in Paterson, N.J. ... 6-3/316. ... Full name: Rashod Alexander Swinger.
HIGH SCHOOL: Manalapan (Englishtown, N.J.).
COLLEGE: Rutgers (degree in communications).
TRANSACTIONS/CAREER NOTES: Signed as non-drafted free agent by San Diego Chargers (April 21, 1997). ... Released by Chargers (August 25, 1997). ... Re-signed by Chargers to practice squad (August 26, 1997). ... Released by Chargers (September 2, 1997). ... Signed by Arizona Cardinals to practice squad (September 8, 1997). ... Activated (December 17, 1997). ... On injured reserve with knee injury (December 29, 1999-remainder of season).
PLAYING EXPERIENCE: Arizona NFL, 1997-1999. ... Games/Games started: 1997 (1/0), 1998 (16/11), 1999 (15/14). Total: 32/25.
PRO STATISTICS: 1999—Credited with one sack.

SWORD, SAM   LB   RAIDERS

PERSONAL: Born December 9, 1974, in Saginaw, Mich. ... 6-1/245.
HIGH SCHOOL: Arthur Hill (Saginaw, Mich.).
COLLEGE: Michigan.
TRANSACTIONS/CAREER NOTES: Signed as non-drafted free agent by Oakland Raiders (April 22, 1999).
PLAYING EXPERIENCE: Oakland NFL, 1999. ... Games/Games started: 1999 (10/5).
PRO STATISTICS: 1999—Credited with one sack.

SYVRUD, J.J.   LB   JETS

PERSONAL: Born May 10, 1977, in Rock Springs, Wyo. ... 6-3/255. ... Name pronounced SEV-rude.
HIGH SCHOOL: Rock Springs (Wyo.).

COLLEGE: Jamestown (N.D.) College.
TRANSACTIONS/CAREER NOTES: Selected by New York Jets in seventh round (235th pick overall) of 1999 NFL draft. ... Signed by Jets (June 18, 1999).
PLAYING EXPERIENCE: New York Jets NFL, 1999. ... Games/Games started: 1999 (1/0).

SZOTT, DAVE   G   CHIEFS

PERSONAL: Born December 12, 1967, in Passaic, N.J. ... 6-4/289. ... Full name: David Andrew Szott. ... Name pronounced ZOT.
HIGH SCHOOL: Clifton (N.J.).
COLLEGE: Penn State (degree in political science).
TRANSACTIONS/CAREER NOTES: Selected by Kansas City Chiefs in seventh round (180th pick overall) of 1990 NFL draft. ... Signed by Chiefs (July 25, 1990). ... Granted free agency (March 1, 1993). ... Re-signed by Chiefs for 1993 season. ... On injured reserve with arm injury (December 2, 1998-remainder of season).
PLAYING EXPERIENCE: Kansas City NFL, 1990-1999. ... Games/Games started: 1990 (16/11), 1991 (16/16), 1992 (16/16), 1993 (14/13), 1994 (16/16), 1995 (16/16), 1996 (16/16), 1997 (16/16), 1998 (1/1), 1999 (14/14). Total: 141/135.
CHAMPIONSHIP GAME EXPERIENCE: Played in AFC championship game (1993 season).
PRO STATISTICS: 1990—Recovered one fumble. 1991—Recovered one fumble. 1997—Recovered one fumble. 1999—Recovered one fumble.

TAIT, JOHN   OT   CHIEFS

PERSONAL: Born January 26, 1975, in Phoenix. ... 6-6/306.
HIGH SCHOOL: McClintock (Tempe, Ariz.).
COLLEGE: Brigham Young (degree in communications).
TRANSACTIONS/CAREER NOTES: Selected after junior season by Kansas City Chiefs in first round (14th pick overall) of 1999 NFL draft. ... Signed by Chiefs (September 9, 1999).
PLAYING EXPERIENCE: Kansas City NFL, 1999. ... Games/Games started: 1999 (12/3).

TALTON, TY   S   LIONS

PERSONAL: Born May 10, 1976, in Beloit, Wis. ... 5-11/201. ... Full name: Tyree Talton.
HIGH SCHOOL: Turner (Beloit, Wis.).
COLLEGE: Northern Iowa.
TRANSACTIONS/CAREER NOTES: Selected by Detroit Lions in fifth round (137th pick overall) of 1999 NFL draft. ... Signed by Lions (July 25, 1999). ... Claimed on waivers by Oakland Raiders (October 1, 1999). ... Inactive for two games with Raiders (1999). ... Released by Raiders (October 12, 1999). ... Signed by Lions (October 14, 1999).

			KICKOFF RETURNS				TOTALS			
Year Team	G	GS	No.	Yds.	Avg.	TD	TD	2pt.	Pts.	Fum.
1999—Detroit NFL	12	0	6	121	20.2	0	0	0	0	0

TAMM, RALPH   G/C

PERSONAL: Born March 11, 1966, in Philadelphia. ... 6-4/280. ... Full name: Ralph Earl Tamm.
HIGH SCHOOL: Bensalem (Pa.).
COLLEGE: West Chester (Pa.).
TRANSACTIONS/CAREER NOTES: Selected by New York Jets in ninth round (230th pick overall) of 1988 NFL draft. ... Signed by Jets for 1988 season. ... On injured reserve (August 29, 1988-entire season). ... Granted unconditional free agency (February 1, 1989). ... Signed by Washington Redskins for 1989 season. ... On injured reserve with shoulder injury (September 1, 1989-entire season). ... Granted unconditional free agency (February 1, 1990). ... Signed by Cleveland Browns (March 21, 1990). ... Released by Browns (September 5, 1991). ... Signed by Redskins (September 11, 1991). ... Released by Redskins (November 1991). ... Signed by Cincinnati Bengals (December 9, 1991). ... Granted unconditional free agency (February 1, 1992). ... Signed by San Francisco 49ers (March 29, 1992). ... On injured reserve with knee injury (December 15, 1992-January 16, 1993). ... Released by 49ers (May 5, 1995). ... Signed by Denver Broncos (June 7, 1995). ... Granted unconditional free agency (February 14, 1997). ... Signed by Kansas City Chiefs (June 9, 1997). ... Granted unconditional free agency (February 12, 1999). ... Re-signed by Chiefs (August 30, 1999). ... Granted free agency (February 11, 2000).
PLAYING EXPERIENCE: Cleveland NFL, 1990; Cleveland (1)-Washington (2)-Cincinnati (1) NFL, 1991; San Francisco NFL, 1992-1994; Denver NFL, 1995 and 1996; Kansas City NFL, 1997-1999. ... Games/Games started: 1990 (16/12), 1991 (Clev.-1/0; Wash.-2/0; Cin.-1/0; Total: 4/0), 1992 (14/1), 1993 (16/16), 1994 (1/1), 1995 (13/1), 1996 (9/0), 1997 (16/0), 1998 (16/0), 1999 (16/0). Total: 121/31.
CHAMPIONSHIP GAME EXPERIENCE: Played in NFC championship game (1992-1994 seasons). ... Member of Super Bowl championship team (1994 season).
PRO STATISTICS: 1993—Recovered one fumble in end zone for a touchdown. 1995—Recovered one fumble.

TANUVASA, MAA   DT   BRONCOS

PERSONAL: Born November 6, 1970, in America Samoa. ... 6-2/270. ... Full name: Maa Junior Tanuvasa. ... Name pronounced MAH-ah TAH-noo-VA-suh.
HIGH SCHOOL: Mililani (Wahiawa, Hawaii).
COLLEGE: Hawaii.
TRANSACTIONS/CAREER NOTES: Selected by Los Angeles Rams in eighth round (209th pick overall) of 1993 NFL draft. ... Signed by Rams for 1993 season. ... On injured reserve with knee injury (August 21, 1993-entire season). ... Released by Rams (August 23, 1994). ... Signed by Steelers to practice squad (December 1, 1994). ... Granted free agency after 1994 season. ... Signed by Denver Broncos (February 22, 1995). ... Released by Broncos (August 27, 1995). ... Re-signed by Broncos to practice squad (August 28, 1995). ... Activated (October 24, 1995). ... Granted free agency (February 14, 1997). ... Re-signed by Broncos (February 14, 1997).

CHAMPIONSHIP GAME EXPERIENCE: Played in AFC championship game (1997 and 1998 seasons). ... Member of Super Bowl championship team (1997 and 1998 seasons).
PRO STATISTICS: 1996—Recovered one fumble. 1998—Returned one kickoff for 13 yards and recovered two fumbles for minus one yard.

Year Team	G	GS	SACKS
1993—Los Angeles Rams NFL	Did not play.		
1994—Pittsburgh NFL	Did not play.		
1995—Denver NFL	1	0	0.0
1996—Denver NFL	16	1	5.0
1997—Denver NFL	15	5	8.5
1998—Denver NFL	16	16	8.5
1999—Denver NFL	16	16	7.0
Pro totals (5 years)	64	38	29.0

TATE, ROBERT — CB/KR — VIKINGS

PERSONAL: Born October 19, 1973, in Harrisburg, Pa. ... 5-10/192.
HIGH SCHOOL: John Harris (Harrisburg, Pa.), then Milford (Conn.) Academy.
COLLEGE: Cincinnati.
TRANSACTIONS/CAREER NOTES: Selected by Minnesota Vikings in sixth round (183rd pick overall) of 1997 NFL draft. ... Signed by Vikings (June 17, 1997). ... On injured reserve with ankle injury (October 8, 1997-remainder of season).
CHAMPIONSHIP GAME EXPERIENCE: Member of Vikings for NFC championship game (1998 season); inactive.
PRO STATISTICS: 1998—Caught one pass for 17 yards. 1999—Rushed once for four yards, caught one pass for three yards and intercepted one pass for 18 yards.
SINGLE GAME HIGHS (regular season): Receptions—1 (November 22, 1998, vs. Green Bay); yards—17 (November 22, 1998, vs Green Bay); and touchdown receptions—0.

			KICKOFF RETURNS				TOTALS			
Year Team	G	GS	No.	Yds.	Avg.	TD	TD	2pt.	Pts.	Fum.
1997—Minnesota NFL	4	0	10	196	19.6	0	0	0	0	0
1998—Minnesota NFL	15	1	2	43	21.5	0	0	0	0	0
1999—Minnesota NFL	16	1	25	627	25.1	1	1	0	6	1
Pro totals (3 years)	35	2	37	866	23.4	1	1	0	6	1

TAYLOR, AARON — G

PERSONAL: Born November 14, 1972, in San Francisco. ... 6-4/305. ... Full name: Aaron Matthew Taylor.
HIGH SCHOOL: De La Salle Catholic (Concord, Calif.).
COLLEGE: Notre Dame (degree in sociology, 1994).
TRANSACTIONS/CAREER NOTES: Selected by Green Bay Packers in first round (16th pick overall) of 1994 NFL draft . ... Signed by Packers (July 26, 1994). ... On physically unable to perform list with knee injury (August 25, 1994-entire season). ... On injured reserve with knee injury (January 11, 1996-remainder of playoffs). ... Granted unconditional free agency (February 13, 1998). ... Signed by San Diego Chargers (March 6, 1998). ... Announced retirement (February 10, 2000).
PLAYING EXPERIENCE: Green Bay NFL, 1995-1997; San Diego NFL, 1998 and 1999. ... Games/Games started: 1995 (16/16), 1996 (16/16), 1997 (14/14), 1998 (15/15), 1999 (14/14). Total: 75/75.
CHAMPIONSHIP GAME EXPERIENCE: Played in NFC championship game (1996 and 1997 seasons). ... Member of Super Bowl championship team (1996 season). ... Played in Super Bowl XXXII (1997 season).
HONORS: Named offensive lineman on THE SPORTING NEWS college All-America first team (1992 and 1993). ... Outland Award winner (1993). ... Lombardi Award winner (1993).
PRO STATISTICS: 1995—Recovered two fumbles. 1996—Recovered one fumble. 1998—Recovered one fumble.

TAYLOR, BOBBY — CB — EAGLES

PERSONAL: Born December 28, 1973, in Houston. ... 6-3/216. ... Full name: Robert Taylor. ... Son of Robert Taylor, silver medalist in 100-meter dash and member of gold-medal winning 400-meter relay team at 1972 Summer Olympics.
HIGH SCHOOL: Longview (Texas).
COLLEGE: Notre Dame.
TRANSACTIONS/CAREER NOTES: Selected after junior season by Philadelphia Eagles in second round (49th pick overall) of 1995 NFL draft. ... Signed by Eagles (July 19, 1995). ... On injured reserve with knee injury (October 17, 1997-remainder of season). ... Granted free agency (February 13, 1998). ... Re-signed by Eagles (June 11, 1998). ... On injured reserve with fractured jaw (December 28, 1999-remainder of season).
HONORS: Named defensive back on THE SPORTING NEWS college All-America first team (1993 and 1994).
PRO STATISTICS: 1996—Credited with one sack, fumbled once and recovered two fumbles for nine yards. 1997—Credited with two sacks. 1999—Recovered three fumbles.

			INTERCEPTIONS			
Year Team	G	GS	No.	Yds.	Avg.	TD
1995—Philadelphia NFL	16	12	2	52	26.0	0
1996—Philadelphia NFL	16	16	3	-1	-0.3	0
1997—Philadelphia NFL	6	5	0	0	0.0	0
1998—Philadelphia NFL	11	10	0	0	0.0	0
1999—Philadelphia NFL	15	14	4	59	14.8	1
Pro totals (5 years)	64	57	9	110	12.2	1

TAYLOR, CORDELL — CB — BEARS

PERSONAL: Born December 22, 1973, in Norfolk, Va. ... 6-0/190. ... Full name: Cordell Jerome Taylor.
HIGH SCHOOL: Booker T. Washington (Norfolk, Va.).

COLLEGE: Hampton (Va.).
TRANSACTIONS/CAREER NOTES: Selected by Jacksonville Jaguars in second round (57th pick overall) of 1998 NFL draft. ... Signed by Jaguars (May 26, 1998). ... Traded by Jaguars to Seattle Seahawks for conditional pick in 2000 draft (September 5, 1999). ... Released by Seahawks (October 5, 1999). ... Signed by Chicago Bears (December 28, 1999). ... Inactive for one game with Bears (1999).
PLAYING EXPERIENCE: Jacksonville NFL, 1998; Seattle NFL, 1999. ... Games/Games started: 1998 (10/0), 1999 (2/0). Total: 12/0.

TAYLOR, FRED   RB   JAGUARS

PERSONAL: Born June 27, 1976, in Pahokee, Fla. ... 6-1/227. ... Full name: Frederick Antwon Taylor.
HIGH SCHOOL: Glades Central (Belle Glade, Fla.).
COLLEGE: Florida.
TRANSACTIONS/CAREER NOTES: Selected by Jacksonville Jaguars in first round (ninth pick overall) of 1998 NFL draft. ... Signed by Jaguars (July 6, 1998).
CHAMPIONSHIP GAME EXPERIENCE: Played in AFC championship game (1999 season).
HONORS: Named running back on THE SPORTING NEWS college All-America third team (1997).
PRO STATISTICS: 1998—Recovered one fumble for nine yards.
SINGLE GAME HIGHS (regular season): Attempts—32 (December 6, 1998, vs. Detroit); yards—183 (December 6, 1998, vs. Detroit); and rushing touchdowns—3 (November 15, 1998, vs. Tampa Bay).
STATISTICAL PLATEAUS: 100-yard rushing games: 1998 (6), 1999 (3). Total: 9.

			RUSHING				RECEIVING				TOTALS			
Year Team	G	GS	Att.	Yds.	Avg.	TD	No.	Yds.	Avg.	TD	TD	2pt.	Pts.	Fum.
1998—Jacksonville NFL	15	12	264	1223	4.6	14	44	421	9.6	3	17	0	102	3
1999—Jacksonville NFL	10	9	159	732	4.6	6	10	83	8.3	0	6	0	36	0
Pro totals (2 years)	25	21	423	1955	4.6	20	54	504	9.3	3	23	0	138	3

TAYLOR, JASON   DE   DOLPHINS

PERSONAL: Born September 1, 1974, in Pittsburgh. ... 6-6/260. ... Full name: Jason Paul Taylor.
HIGH SCHOOL: Woodland Hills (Pittsburgh).
COLLEGE: Akron.
TRANSACTIONS/CAREER NOTES: Selected by Miami Dolphins in third round (73rd pick overall) of 1997 NFL draft. ... Signed by Dolphins (July 9, 1997). ... On injured reserve with broken collarbone (December 29, 1998-remainder of playoffs). ... Granted free agency (February 11, 2000). ... Re-signed by Dolphins (April 13, 2000).
PRO STATISTICS: 1997—Recovered two fumbles. 1999—Intercepted one pass for no yards and recovered two fumbles for four yards and one touchdown.

Year Team	G	GS	SACKS
1997—Miami NFL	13	11	5.0
1998—Miami NFL	16	15	9.0
1999—Miami NFL	15	15	2.5
Pro totals (3 years)	44	41	16.5

TEAGUE, GEORGE   S   COWBOYS

PERSONAL: Born February 18, 1971, in Lansing, Mich. ... 6-1/196. ... Full name: George Theo Teague. ... Name pronounced TEEG.
HIGH SCHOOL: Jefferson Davis (Montgomery, Ala.).
COLLEGE: Alabama.
TRANSACTIONS/CAREER NOTES: Selected by Green Bay Packers in first round (29th pick overall) of 1993 NFL draft. ... Signed by Packers (July 9, 1993). ... Granted free agency (February 16, 1996). ... Re-signed by Packers (April 12, 1996). ... Traded by Packers to Atlanta Falcons for conditional draft pick (July 16, 1996). ... Released by Falcons (August 17, 1996). ... Signed by Dallas Cowboys (August 23, 1996). ... Granted unconditional free agency (February 14, 1997). ... Signed by Miami Dolphins (March 20, 1997). ... Traded by Dolphins to Cowboys (May 6, 1998), as compensation for Dolphins signing free agent S Brock Marion (March 3, 1998). ... Granted unconditional free agency (February 11, 2000). ... Re-signed by Cowboys (March 13, 2000).
CHAMPIONSHIP GAME EXPERIENCE: Played in NFC championship game (1995 season).
POST SEASON RECORDS: Holds NFL postseason single-game record for longest interception return—101 yards, touchdown (January 8, 1994, at Detroit).
PRO STATISTICS: 1993—Returned one punt for minus one yard and recovered two fumbles. 1995—Recovered one fumble for four yards. 1998—Credited with two sacks. 1999—Recovered one fumble.

			INTERCEPTIONS			
Year Team	G	GS	No.	Yds.	Avg.	TD
1993—Green Bay NFL	16	12	1	22	22.0	0
1994—Green Bay NFL	16	16	3	33	11.0	0
1995—Green Bay NFL	15	15	2	100	50.0	0
1996—Dallas NFL	16	8	4	47	11.8	0
1997—Miami NFL	15	6	2	25	12.5	0
1998—Dallas NFL	16	5	0	0	0.0	0
1999—Dallas NFL	14	14	3	127	*42.3	†2
Pro totals (7 years)	108	76	15	354	23.6	2

TEAGUE, TREY   OT   BRONCOS

PERSONAL: Born December 27, 1974, in Jackson, Tenn. ... 6-5/285. ... Full name: Fred Everette Teague III. ... Name pronounced TEEG.
HIGH SCHOOL: University (Jackson, Tenn.).
COLLEGE: Tennessee.

TRANSACTIONS/CAREER NOTES: Selected by Denver Broncos in seventh round (200th pick overall) of 1998 NFL draft. ... Signed by Broncos (July 23, 1998). ... Inactive for all 16 games (1998).
PLAYING EXPERIENCE: Denver NFL, 1999. ... Games/Games started: 1999 (16/4).
CHAMPIONSHIP GAME EXPERIENCE: Member of Broncos for AFC championship game (1998 season); inactive. ... Member of Super Bowl championship team (1998 season); inactive.
PRO STATISTICS: 1999—Fumbled once for minus nine yards.

TERRELL, DARYL · OT · SAINTS

PERSONAL: Born January 25, 1975, in Vossburg, Miss. ... 6-5/296.
HIGH SCHOOL: Heidelberg (Miss.).
JUNIOR COLLEGE: Jones County Community College (Miss.).
COLLEGE: Southern Mississippi.
TRANSACTIONS/CAREER NOTES: Signed as non-drafted free agent by Baltimore Ravens (June 3, 1997). ... Released by Ravens (July 8, 1997). ... Signed by New Orleans Saints (April 27, 1998). ... Released by Saints (August 24, 1998). ... Re-signed by Saints to practice squad (September 2, 1998). ... Assigned by Saints to Amsterdam Admirals in 1999 NFL Europe enhancement allocation program (February 22, 1999).
PLAYING EXPERIENCE: Amsterdam Admirals NFLE, 1999; New Orleans NFL, 1999. ... Games/Games started: NFLE 1999 (games played unavailable), NFL 1999 (12/1).

TERRY, CHRIS · OT · PANTHERS

PERSONAL: Born August 8, 1975, in Jacksonville. ... 6-5/295. ... Full name: Christopher Alexander Terry.
HIGH SCHOOL: Jean Ribault (Jacksonville).
COLLEGE: Georgia.
TRANSACTIONS/CAREER NOTES: Selected by Carolina Panthers in second round (34th pick overall) of 1999 NFL draft. ... Signed by Panthers (May 24, 1999).
PLAYING EXPERIENCE: Carolina NFL, 1999. ... Games/Games started: 1999 (16/16).
PRO STATISTICS: 1999—Recovered two fumbles.

TERRY, COREY · LB · JAGUARS

PERSONAL: Born March 6, 1976, in Warrenton, N.C. ... 6-3/246. ... Full name: Corey TeWana Terry.
HIGH SCHOOL: Warren County (Warrenton, N.C.).
JUNIOR COLLEGE: Garden City (Kan.) Community College.
COLLEGE: Tennessee.
TRANSACTIONS/CAREER NOTES: Selected by Indianapolis Colts in seventh round (250th pick overall) of 1999 NFL draft. ... Signed by Colts (July 22, 1999). ... Released by Colts (August 30, 1999). ... Signed by Pittsburgh Steelers to practice squad (September 6, 1999). ... Signed by Jacksonville Jaguars off Steelers practice squad (November 2, 1999).
PLAYING EXPERIENCE: Jacksonville NFL, 1999. ... Games/Games started: 1999 (8/0).
CHAMPIONSHIP GAME EXPERIENCE: Played in AFC championship game (1999 season).

TERRY, RICK · DE

PERSONAL: Born April 5, 1974, in Lexington, N.C. ... 6-4/300. ... Full name: Richard Ross Terry Jr.
HIGH SCHOOL: Lexington (N.C.).
COLLEGE: North Carolina.
TRANSACTIONS/CAREER NOTES: Selected by New York Jets in second round (31st pick overall) of 1997 NFL draft. ... Signed by Jets (July 14, 1997). ... Inactive for four games with Jets (1998). ... Claimed on waivers by Carolina Panthers (October 7, 1998). ... Released by Panthers (December 28, 1999).

Year Team	G	GS	SACKS
1997—New York Jets NFL	14	0	2.0
1998—Carolina NFL	7	3	2.0
1999—Carolina NFL	8	0	0.0
Pro totals (3 years)	29	3	4.0

TESTAVERDE, VINNY · QB · JETS

PERSONAL: Born November 13, 1963, in Brooklyn, N.Y. ... 6-5/235. ... Full name: Vincent Frank Testaverde. ... Name pronounced TESS-tuh-VER-dee.
HIGH SCHOOL: Sewanhaka (Floral Park, N.Y.), then Fork Union (Va.) Military Academy.
COLLEGE: Miami (Fla.).
TRANSACTIONS/CAREER NOTES: Signed by Tampa Bay Buccaneers (April 3, 1987). ... Selected officially by Buccaneers in first round (first pick overall) of 1987 NFL draft. ... On injured reserve with ankle injury (December 20, 1989-remainder of season). ... Granted unconditional free agency (March 1, 1993). ... Signed by Cleveland Browns (March 31, 1993). ... Browns franchise moved to Baltimore and renamed Ravens for 1996 season (March 11, 1996). ... Released by Ravens (June 2, 1998). ... Signed by New York Jets (June 24, 1998). ... Granted free agency (February 12, 1999). ... Re-signed by Jets (March 1, 1999). ... On injured reserve with Achilles' tendon injury (September 13, 1999-remainder of season).
CHAMPIONSHIP GAME EXPERIENCE: Played in AFC championship game (1998 season).
HONORS: Named quarterback on THE SPORTING NEWS college All-America second team (1985). ... Heisman Trophy winner (1986). ... Named College Football Player of the Year by THE SPORTING NEWS (1986). ... Maxwell Award winner (1986). ... Davey O'Brien Award winner (1986). ... Named quarterback on THE SPORTING NEWS college All-America first team (1986). ... Played in Pro Bowl (1996 and 1998 seasons).

PRO STATISTICS: 1987—Fumbled seven times and recovered four fumbles for minus three yards. 1988—Fumbled eight times and recovered two fumbles. 1989—Fumbled four times and recovered two fumbles. 1990—Caught one pass for three yards, fumbled 10 times and recovered three fumbles. 1991—Fumbled five times and recovered three fumbles. 1992—Fumbled four times and recovered four fumbles for minus eight yards. 1993—Fumbled four times. 1994—Fumbled three times and recovered two fumbles for two yards. 1995—Caught one pass for seven yards and fumbled four times for minus four yards. 1996—Fumbled nine times for minus 11 yards. 1997—Caught one pass for minus four yards, fumbled 11 times and recovered five fumbles for minus nine yards. 1998—Fumbled seven times and recovered three fumbles for minus six yards.

SINGLE GAME HIGHS (regular season): Attempts—63 (December 6, 1998, vs. Seattle); completions—42 (December 6, 1998, vs. Seattle); yards—469 (October 16, 1988, vs. Indianapolis); and touchdown passes—4 (December 27, 1998, vs. New England).

STATISTICAL PLATEAUS: 300-yard passing games: 1987 (1), 1988 (4), 1989 (4), 1991 (1), 1992 (1), 1993 (1), 1995 (2), 1996 (5), 1997 (3), 1998 (1). Total: 23. ... 100-yard rushing games: 1990 (1).

MISCELLANEOUS: Regular-season record as starting NFL quarterback: 60-85-1 (.414). ... Postseason record as starting NFL quarterback: 2-2 (.500). ... Holds Tampa Bay Buccaneers all-time records for most yards passing (14,820) and most touchdown passes (77). ... Holds Baltimore Ravens all-time records for most yards passing (7,148) and most touchdown passes (51).

Year Team	G	GS	Att.	Cmp.	Pct.	Yds.	TD	Int.	Avg.	Rat.	Att.	Yds.	Avg.	TD	TD	2pt.	Pts.
1987—Tampa Bay NFL	6	4	165	71	43.0	1081	5	6	6.55	60.2	13	50	3.8	1	1	0	6
1988—Tampa Bay NFL	15	15	466	222	47.6	3240	13	*35	6.95	48.8	28	138	4.9	1	1	0	6
1989—Tampa Bay NFL	14	14	480	258	53.8	3133	20	†22	6.53	68.9	25	139	5.6	0	0	0	0
1990—Tampa Bay NFL	14	13	365	203	55.6	2818	17	∞18	7.72	75.6	38	280	7.4	1	1	0	6
1991—Tampa Bay NFL	13	12	326	166	50.9	1994	8	15	6.12	59.0	32	101	3.2	0	0	0	0
1992—Tampa Bay NFL	14	14	358	206	57.5	2554	14	16	7.13	74.2	36	197	5.5	2	2	0	12
1993—Cleveland NFL	10	6	230	130	56.5	1797	14	9	‡7.81	85.7	18	74	4.1	0	0	0	0
1994—Cleveland NFL	14	13	376	207	55.1	2575	16	18	6.85	70.7	21	37	1.8	2	2	0	12
1995—Cleveland NFL	13	12	392	241	61.5	2883	17	10	7.35	87.8	18	62	3.4	2	2	0	12
1996—Baltimore NFL	16	16	549	325	59.2	4177	§33	19	7.61	88.7	34	188	5.5	2	2	1	14
1997—Baltimore NFL	13	13	470	271	57.7	2971	18	15	6.32	75.9	34	138	4.1	0	0	0	0
1998—New York Jets NFL	14	13	421	259	61.5	3256	§29	7	7.73	§101.6	24	104	4.3	1	1	0	6
1999—New York Jets NFL	1	1	15	10	66.7	96	1	1	6.40	78.8	0	0	0.0	0	0	0	0
Pro totals (13 years)	157	146	4613	2569	55.7	32575	205	191	7.06	75.5	321	1508	4.7	12	12	1	74

THARPE, LARRY   OT   STEELERS

PERSONAL: Born November 19, 1970, in Macon, Ga. ... 6-4/305.
HIGH SCHOOL: Southwest (Macon, Ga.).
COLLEGE: Tennessee State.
TRANSACTIONS/CAREER NOTES: Selected by Detroit Lions in sixth round (145th pick overall) of 1992 NFL draft. ... Signed by Lions (July 23, 1992). ... On injured reserve with back and knee injuries (September 4-October 14, 1992). ... Inactive for 15 games (1994). ... Granted free agency (February 17, 1995). ... Signed by Arizona Cardinals (March 25, 1995). Lions received sixth-round pick (TE Kevin Hickman) in 1995 draft as compensation. ... Granted unconditional free agency (February 16, 1996). ... Signed by New England Patriots (April 29, 1996). ... Active for one game with Patriots (1996); did not play. ... Released by Patriots (October 23, 1996). ... Signed by Lions (February 21, 1997). ... Granted unconditional free agency (February 13, 1998). ... Re-signed by Lions (June 10, 1998). ... Granted unconditional free agency (February 12, 1999). ... Signed by Pittsburgh Steelers (April 4, 2000).
PLAYING EXPERIENCE: Detroit NFL, 1992, 1993, 1997 and 1998; Arizona NFL, 1995. ... Games/Games started: 1992 (11/0), 1993 (5/3), 1995 (16/16), 1997 (16/15), 1998 (16/9). Total: 64/43.

THIBODEAUX, KEITH   CB   VIKINGS

PERSONAL: Born May 16, 1974, in Opelousan, La. ... 5-11/189. ... Full name: Keith Trevis Thibodeaux. ... Name pronounced TEE-bo-do.
HIGH SCHOOL: Beau Chene (Opelousas, La.).
COLLEGE: Northwestern (La.) State.
TRANSACTIONS/CAREER NOTES: Selected by Washington Redskins in fifth round (140th pick overall) of 1997 NFL draft. ... Signed by Redskins (May 28, 1997). ... Released by Redskins (August 25, 1998). ... Signed by Atlanta Falcons (February 5, 1999). ... Released by Falcons (November 2, 1999). ... Signed by Minnesota Vikings (November 4, 1999). ... On injured reserve with shoulder injury (December 23, 1999-remainder of season).
PLAYING EXPERIENCE: Washington NFL, 1997; Atlanta (8)-Minnesota (3) NFL, 1999. ... Games/Games started: 1997 (15/0), 1999 (Atl.-8/0; Min.-3/0; Total: 11/0). Total: 26/0.

THIERRY, JOHN   DE   PACKERS

PERSONAL: Born September 4, 1971, in Opelousas, La. ... 6-4/260. ... Full name: John Fitzgerald Thierry. ... Name pronounced Theory.
HIGH SCHOOL: Plaisance (Opelousas, La.).
COLLEGE: Alcorn State.
TRANSACTIONS/CAREER NOTES: Selected by Chicago Bears in first round (11th pick overall) of 1994 NFL draft. ... Signed by Bears (June 21, 1994). ... On injured reserve with knee injury (November 5, 1997-remainder of season). ... Granted unconditional free agency (February 12, 1999). ... Signed by Cleveland Browns (February 26, 1999). ... Granted unconditional free agency (February 11, 2000). ... Signed by Green Bay Packers (February 17, 2000).
PRO STATISTICS: 1994—Returned one kickoff for no yards. 1995—Recovered four fumbles. 1998—Intercepted one pass for 14 yards and credited with a safety. 1999—Intercepted one pass for eight yards.

Year Team	G	GS	SACKS
1994—Chicago NFL	16	1	0.0
1995—Chicago NFL	16	7	4.0
1996—Chicago NFL	16	2	2.0
1997—Chicago NFL	9	9	3.0
1998—Chicago NFL	16	9	3.5
1999—Cleveland NFL	16	10	7.0
Pro totals (6 years)	89	38	19.5

THIGPEN, YANCEY   WR   TITANS

PERSONAL: Born August 15, 1969, in Tarboro, N.C. ... 6-1/203. ... Full name: Yancey Dirk Thigpen.
HIGH SCHOOL: Southwest Edgecombe (Tarboro, N.C.).
COLLEGE: Winston-Salem (N.C.) State.
TRANSACTIONS/CAREER NOTES: Selected by San Diego Chargers in fourth round (90th pick overall) of 1991 NFL draft. ... Signed by Chargers (July 15, 1991). ... Released by Chargers (August 26, 1991). ... Re-signed by Chargers to practice squad (August 28, 1991). ... Activated (September 20, 1991). ... Released by Chargers (September 26, 1991). ... Re-signed by Chargers to practice squad (September 28, 1991). ... Activated (December 7, 1991). ... Released by Chargers (August 31, 1992). ... Signed by Pittsburgh Steelers (October 5, 1992). ... On injured reserve with foot injury (January 3, 1997-remainder of playoffs). ... Granted unconditional free agency (February 13, 1998). ... Signed by Tennessee Oilers (February 14, 1998). ... Oilers franchise renamed Tennessee Titans for 1999 season (December 26, 1998).
CHAMPIONSHIP GAME EXPERIENCE: Played in AFC championship game (1994, 1995, 1997 and 1999 seasons). ... Played in Super Bowl XXX (1995 season). ... Member of Titans for Super Bowl XXXIV (1999 season); inactive.
HONORS: Played in Pro Bowl (1995 and 1997 seasons).
PRO STATISTICS: 1995—Rushed once for one yard. 1997—Rushed once for three yards and recovered one fumble. 1999—Returned one punt for 21 yards.
SINGLE GAME HIGHS (regular season): Receptions—11 (October 26, 1997, vs. Jacksonville); yards—196 (October 26, 1997, vs. Jacksonville); and touchdown receptions—3 (December 7, 1997, vs. Denver).
STATISTICAL PLATEAUS: 100-yard receiving games: 1995 (4), 1997 (6), 1998 (1), 1999 (1). Total: 12.

			RECEIVING				KICKOFF RETURNS				TOTALS			
Year Team	G	GS	No.	Yds.	Avg.	TD	No.	Yds.	Avg.	TD	TD	2pt.	Pts.	Fum.
1991—San Diego NFL	4	1	0	0	0.0	0	0	0	0.0	0	0	0	0	0
1992—Pittsburgh NFL	12	0	1	2	2.0	0	2	44	22.0	0	0	0	0	0
1993—Pittsburgh NFL	12	0	9	154	17.1	3	1	23	23.0	0	3	0	18	0
1994—Pittsburgh NFL	15	6	36	546	15.2	4	5	121	24.2	0	4	0	24	0
1995—Pittsburgh NFL	16	15	85	1307	15.4	5	0	0	0.0	0	5	0	30	1
1996—Pittsburgh NFL	6	2	12	244	20.3	2	0	0	0.0	0	2	0	12	0
1997—Pittsburgh NFL	16	15	79	1398	17.7	7	0	0	0.0	0	7	1	44	1
1998—Tennessee NFL	9	8	38	493	13.0	3	0	0	0.0	0	3	0	18	0
1999—Tennessee NFL	10	10	38	648	17.1	4	0	0	0.0	0	4	0	24	1
Pro totals (9 years)	100	57	298	4792	16.1	28	8	188	23.5	0	28	1	170	3

THOMAS, CHRIS   WR   VIKINGS

PERSONAL: Born July 16, 1971, in Ventura, Calif. ... 6-2/190. ... Full name: Chris Eric Thomas.
HIGH SCHOOL: Ventura (Calif.).
COLLEGE: Cal Poly-SLO (degree in English, 1994).
TRANSACTIONS/CAREER NOTES: Signed as non-drafted free agent by San Diego Chargers (May 6, 1993). ... Released by Chargers (August 30, 1993). ... Re-signed by Chargers to practice squad (September 1, 1993). ... Granted free agency after 1993 season. ... Signed by San Francisco 49ers (May 16, 1995). ... Released by 49ers (February 15, 1996). ... Re-signed by 49ers (May 15, 1996). ... Released by 49ers (August 20, 1996). ... Selected by Rhein Fire in 1997 World League draft (February 17, 1997). ... Signed by Washington Redskins (February 25, 1997). ... Released by Redskins (August 19, 1997). ... Re-signed by Redskins (August 21, 1997). ... Released by Redskins (August 23, 1997). ... Re-signed by Redskins (September 22, 1997). ... Granted free agency (February 12, 1999). ... Re-signed by Redskins (April 23, 1999). ... Released by Redskins (September 21, 1999). ... Signed by St. Louis Rams (October 20, 1999). ... Granted unconditional free agency (February 11, 2000). ... Signed by Minnesota Vikings (February 23, 2000).
CHAMPIONSHIP GAME EXPERIENCE: Member of Rams for NFC championship game (1999 season); inactive. ... Member of Super Bowl championship team (1999 season); inactive.
PRO STATISTICS: 1995—Returned one punt for 25 yards and returned three kickoffs for 49 yards. 1998—Recovered one fumble.
SINGLE GAME HIGHS (regular season): Receptions—4 (December 6, 1998, vs. San Diego); yards—62 (December 6, 1998, vs. San Diego); and touchdown receptions—0.

			RECEIVING				TOTALS			
Year Team	G	GS	No.	Yds.	Avg.	TD	TD	2pt.	Pts.	Fum.
1993—San Diego NFL						Did not play.				
1994—						Did not play.				
1995—San Francisco NFL	14	0	6	73	12.2	0	0	0	0	0
1996—						Did not play.				
1997—Washington NFL	13	0	11	93	8.5	0	0	0	0	0
1998—Washington NFL	14	0	14	173	12.4	0	0	0	0	0
1999—Washington NFL	2	0	0	0	0.0	0	0	0	0	0
—St. Louis NFL	6	0	1	6	6.0	0	0	0	0	0
Pro totals (4 years)	49	0	32	345	10.8	0	0	0	0	0

THOMAS, DAVE   CB   GIANTS

PERSONAL: Born August 25, 1968, in Miami. ... 6-3/218. ... Full name: Dave G. Thomas.
HIGH SCHOOL: Miami Beach.
JUNIOR COLLEGE: Butler County Community College (Kan.).
COLLEGE: Tennessee.
TRANSACTIONS/CAREER NOTES: Selected by Dallas Cowboys in eighth round (203rd pick overall) of 1993 NFL draft. ... Signed by Cowboys (July 15, 1993). ... Selected by Jacksonville Jaguars from Cowboys in NFL expansion draft (February 15, 1995). ... Granted free agency (February 16, 1996). ... Re-signed by Jaguars (June 3, 1996). ... On injured reserve with broken leg (October 29, 1996-remainder of season). ... Granted unconditional free agency (February 14, 1997). ... Re-signed by Jaguars (March 3, 1997). ... Granted unconditional free agency (February 11, 2000). ... Signed by New York Giants (April 10, 2000).
CHAMPIONSHIP GAME EXPERIENCE: Played in NFC championship game (1993 and 1994 seasons). ... Member of Super Bowl championship team (1993 season). ... Played in AFC championship game (1999 season).

PRO STATISTICS: 1995—Recovered one fumble. 1996—Returned one punt for one yard and fumbled once. 1997—Recovered one fumble. 1998—Recovered one fumble.

Year Team	G	GS	INTERCEPTIONS No.	Yds.	Avg.	TD
1993—Dallas NFL	12	0	0	0	0.0	0
1994—Dallas NFL	16	0	0	0	0.0	0
1995—Jacksonville NFL	15	2	0	0	0.0	0
1996—Jacksonville NFL	9	5	2	7	3.5	0
1997—Jacksonville NFL	16	15	2	34	17.0	0
1998—Jacksonville NFL	14	13	1	0	0.0	0
1999—Jacksonville NFL	15	0	2	36	18.0	0
Pro totals (7 years)	97	35	7	77	11.0	0

IN MEMORIAM — DERRICK THOMAS

PERSONAL: Born January 1, 1967, in Miami. ... Died February 8, 2000. ... 6-3/247. ... Full name: Derrick Vincent Thomas. ... Cousin of Shevin Smith, safety, Tampa Bay Buccaneers.
HIGH SCHOOL: South (Miami).
COLLEGE: Alabama.
TRANSACTIONS/CAREER NOTES: Selected by Kansas City Chiefs in first round (fourth pick overall) of 1989 NFL draft. ... Signed by Chiefs (August 24, 1989). ... Granted free agency (March 1, 1993). ... Re-signed by Chiefs (May 21, 1993). ... Granted unconditional free agency (February 14, 1997). ... Re-signed by Chiefs (March 26, 1997).
CHAMPIONSHIP GAME EXPERIENCE: Played in AFC championship game (1993 season).
HONORS: Named linebacker on THE SPORTING NEWS college All-America second team (1987). ... Butkus Award winner (1988). ... Named linebacker on THE SPORTING NEWS college All-America first team (1988). ... Played in Pro Bowl (1989-1997 seasons). ... Named outside linebacker on THE SPORTING NEWS NFL All-Pro team (1990-1992).
RECORDS: Holds NFL single-game record for most sacks—7 (November 11, 1990, vs. Seattle).
PRO STATISTICS: 1989—Recovered one fumble. 1990—Recovered two fumbles for 14 yards. 1991—Recovered four fumbles for 23 yards and one touchdown. 1992—Recovered three fumbles (including one in end zone for a touchdown). 1993—Recovered one fumble for 86 yards and a touchdown. 1994—Credited with one safety and recovered three fumbles for 11 yards. 1995—Recovered one fumble. 1996—Recovered one fumble. 1997—Credited with a safety. 1998—Recovered two fumbles for 27 yards and one touchdown and credited with a safety. 1999—Intercepted one pass for 20 yards and recovered one fumble.
MISCELLANEOUS: Holds Kansas City Chiefs all-time record for most sacks (126.5).

Year Team	G	GS	SACKS
1989—Kansas City NFL	16	16	10.0
1990—Kansas City NFL	15	15	*20.0
1991—Kansas City NFL	16	15	13.5
1992—Kansas City NFL	16	16	14.5
1993—Kansas City NFL	16	15	8.0
1994—Kansas City NFL	16	15	11.0
1995—Kansas City NFL	15	15	8.0
1996—Kansas City NFL	16	13	13.0
1997—Kansas City NFL	12	10	9.5
1998—Kansas City NFL	15	10	12.0
1999—Kansas City NFL	16	16	7.0
Pro totals (11 years)	169	156	126.5

THOMAS, FRED   CB   SAINTS

PERSONAL: Born September 11, 1973, in Bruce, Miss. ... 5-9/172.
HIGH SCHOOL: Bruce (Miss.).
JUNIOR COLLEGE: Northwest Mississippi Community College.
COLLEGE: Mississippi Valley State (did not play football), then Mississippi, then Tennessee-Martin.
TRANSACTIONS/CAREER NOTES: Selected by Seattle Seahawks in second round (47th pick overall) of 1996 NFL draft. ... Signed by Seahawks (July 19, 1996). ... Granted free agency (February 12, 1999). ... Re-signed by Seahawks (May 27, 1999). ... On injured reserve with broken leg (September 17, 1999-remainder of season). ... Granted unconditional free agency (February 11, 2000). ... Signed by New Orleans Saints (February 14, 2000).
PLAYING EXPERIENCE: Seattle NFL, 1996-1999. ... Games/Games started: 1996 (15/0), 1997 (16/3), 1998 (15/2), 1999 (1/0). Total: 47/5.
PRO STATISTICS: 1998—Recovered one fumble.

THOMAS, HENRY   DT   PATRIOTS

PERSONAL: Born January 12, 1965, in Houston. ... 6-2/277. ... Full name: Henry Lee Thomas Jr.
HIGH SCHOOL: Dwight D. Eisenhower (Houston).
COLLEGE: Louisiana Tech.
TRANSACTIONS/CAREER NOTES: Selected by Minnesota Vikings in third round (72nd pick overall) of 1987 NFL draft. ... Signed by Vikings (July 14, 1987). ... Designated by Vikings as transition player (February 25, 1993). ... Designated by Vikings as franchise player (February 15, 1994). ... Free agency status changed by Vikings from franchise to unconditional (February 15, 1995). ... Signed by Detroit Lions (February 27, 1995). ... Released by Lions (April 23, 1997). ... Signed by New England Patriots (June 12, 1997). ... Granted unconditional free agency (February 12, 1999). ... Re-signed by Patriots (February 16, 1999).
CHAMPIONSHIP GAME EXPERIENCE: Played in NFC championship game (1987 season).
HONORS: Named defensive lineman on THE SPORTING NEWS college All-America second team (1986). ... Played in Pro Bowl (1991 and 1992 seasons).
PRO STATISTICS: 1987—Intercepted one pass for no yards and recovered one fumble. 1988—Intercepted one pass for seven yards and recovered one fumble for two yards and a touchdown. 1989—Recovered three fumbles for 37 yards and one touchdown. 1990—Recovered one fumble. 1991—Recovered one fumble. 1993—Credited with a safety. 1994—Recovered one fumble. 1995—Recovered two fumbles.

1996—Recovered one fumble. 1997—Recovered one fumble. 1998—Intercepted one pass for 24 yards and a touchdown and recovered one fumble.

Year Team	G	GS	SACKS
1987—Minnesota NFL	12	12	2.5
1988—Minnesota NFL	15	15	6.0
1989—Minnesota NFL	14	14	9.0
1990—Minnesota NFL	16	16	8.5
1991—Minnesota NFL	16	15	8.0
71992—Minnesota NFL	16	16	6.0
1993—Minnesota NFL	13	13	9.0
1994—Minnesota NFL	16	16	7.0
1995—Detroit NFL	16	16	10.5
1996—Detroit NFL	15	15	6.0
1997—New England NFL	16	16	7.0
1998—New England NFL	16	15	6.5
1999—New England NFL	16	16	3.0
Pro totals (13 years)	197	195	89.0

THOMAS, HOLLIS — DT — EAGLES

PERSONAL: Born January 10, 1974, in Abilene, Texas. ... 6-0/306.
HIGH SCHOOL: Sumner (St. Louis).
COLLEGE: Northern Illinois.
TRANSACTIONS/CAREER NOTES: Signed as non-drafted free agent by Philadelphia Eagles (April 26, 1996). ... On injured reserve with arm/shoulder injury (December 2, 1998-remainder of season).
PRO STATISTICS: 1997—Recovered one fumble. 1998—Recovered one fumble. 1999—Recovered one fumble for two yards.

Year Team	G	GS	SACKS
1996—Philadelphia NFL	16	5	1.0
1997—Philadelphia NFL	16	16	2.5
1998—Philadelphia NFL	12	12	5.0
1999—Philadelphia NFL	16	16	1.0
Pro totals (4 years)	60	49	9.5

THOMAS, LAMAR — WR — DOLPHINS

PERSONAL: Born February 12, 1970, in Ocala, Fla. ... 6-1/170. ... Full name: Lamar Nathaniel Thomas.
HIGH SCHOOL: Buchholz (Gainesville, Fla.).
COLLEGE: Miami, Fla. (degree in sociology).
TRANSACTIONS/CAREER NOTES: Selected by Tampa Bay Buccaneers in third round (60th pick overall) of 1993 NFL draft. ... Signed by Buccaneers (July 14, 1993). ... Granted free agency (February 16, 1996). ... Re-signed by Buccaneers (May 16, 1996). ... Released by Buccaneers (July 17, 1996). ... Signed by Miami Dolphins (July 27, 1996). ... Granted unconditional free agency (February 14, 1997). ... Re-signed by Dolphins (March 11, 1997). ... On injured reserve with shoulder injury (September 5, 1999-entire season).
HONORS: Named wide receiver on THE SPORTING NEWS college All-America second team (1992).
PRO STATISTICS: 1995—Rushed once for five yards.
SINGLE GAME HIGHS (regular season): Receptions—6 (December 21, 1998, vs. Denver); yards—136 (December 21, 1998, vs. Denver); and touchdown receptions—3 (December 21, 1998, vs. Denver).
STATISTICAL PLATEAUS: 100-yard receiving games: 1998 (1).

Year Team	G	GS	RECEIVING No.	Yds.	Avg.	TD	TOTALS TD	2pt.	Pts.	Fum.
1993—Tampa Bay NFL	14	2	8	186	23.3	2	2	0	12	0
1994—Tampa Bay NFL	11	0	7	94	13.4	0	0	0	0	0
1995—Tampa Bay NFL	11	0	10	107	10.7	0	0	0	0	0
1996—Miami NFL	9	3	10	166	16.6	1	1	0	6	0
1997—Miami NFL	12	6	28	402	14.4	2	2	0	12	1
1998—Miami NFL	16	2	43	603	14.0	5	5	0	30	0
1999—Miami NFL					Did not play.					
Pro totals (6 years)	73	13	106	1558	14.7	10	10	0	60	1

THOMAS, MARK — DE — COLTS

PERSONAL: Born May 6, 1969, in Lilburn, Ga. ... 6-5/265. ... Full name: Mark Andrew Thomas.
HIGH SCHOOL: Lilburn (Ga.).
COLLEGE: North Carolina State.
TRANSACTIONS/CAREER NOTES: Selected by San Francisco 49ers in fourth round (89th pick overall) of 1992 NFL draft. ... Signed by 49ers (July 16, 1992). ... On injured reserve with ankle injury (September 1-October 7, 1992). ... On practice squad (October 7-November 11, 1992). ... On injured reserve (November 11, 1992-remainder of season). ... Selected by Carolina Panthers from 49ers in NFL expansion draft (February 15, 1995). ... Granted free agency (February 17, 1995). ... On injured reserve with thumb injury (November 27, 1995-remainder of season). ... Granted unconditional free agency (February 16, 1996). ... Re-signed by Panthers (February 20, 1996). ... Granted unconditional free agency (February 14, 1997). ... Signed by Chicago Bears (March 30, 1997). ... Claimed on waivers by Indianapolis Colts (December 2, 1998). ... Granted unconditional free agency (February 12, 1999). ... Re-signed by Colts (February 12, 1999).
CHAMPIONSHIP GAME EXPERIENCE: Member of 49ers for NFC championship game (1993 and 1994 seasons); inactive. ... Member of Super Bowl championship team (1994 season). ... Played in NFC championship game (1996 season).
PRO STATISTICS: 1993—Recovered one fumble. 1996—Recovered one fumble for 18 yards. 1997—Recovered one fumble. 1999—Recovered one fumble.

Year Team	G	GS	SACKS
1992—San Francisco NFL		Did not play.	
1993—San Francisco NFL	11	1	0.5
1994—San Francisco NFL	9	0	1.0
1995—Carolina NFL	10	0	2.0
1996—Carolina NFL	12	0	4.0
1997—Chicago NFL	16	7	4.5
1998—Chicago NFL	10	4	4.5
—Indianapolis NFL	4	1	1.0
1999—Indianapolis NFL	15	2	3.0
Pro totals (7 years)	87	15	20.5

THOMAS, MARK   TE   GIANTS

PERSONAL: Born May 26, 1975, in Smithfield, N.C. ... 6-4/258. ... Full name: Mark David Thomas.
HIGH SCHOOL: Smithfield-Selma (Smithfield, N.C.).
COLLEGE: North Carolina State.
TRANSACTIONS/CAREER NOTES: Signed as non-drafted free agent by Jacksonville Jaguars (April 23, 1998). ... Released by Jaguars (August 30, 1998). ... Re-signed by Jaguars to practice squad (September 7, 1998). ... Released by Jaguars (August 31, 1999). ... Signed by New York Giants to practice squad (December 22, 1999). ... Activated (December 24, 1999).
PLAYING EXPERIENCE: New York Giants NFL, 1999. ... Games/Games started: 1999 (2/0).

THOMAS, ORLANDO   S   VIKINGS

PERSONAL: Born October 21, 1972, in Crowley, La. ... 6-1/211.
HIGH SCHOOL: Crowley (La.).
COLLEGE: Southwestern Louisiana.
TRANSACTIONS/CAREER NOTES: Selected by Minnesota Vikings in second round (42nd pick overall) of 1995 NFL draft. ... Signed by Vikings (July 25, 1995). ... Granted unconditional free agency (February 12, 1999). ... Re-signed by Vikings (February 24, 1999). ... On injured reserve with shoulder injury (December 22, 1999-remainder of season).
CHAMPIONSHIP GAME EXPERIENCE: Played in NFC championship game (1998 season).
PRO STATISTICS: 1995—Fumbled once and recovered four fumbles for 19 yards and one touchdown. 1996—Recovered one fumble. 1997—Fumbled once and recovered two fumbles for 26 yards and one touchdown. 1998—Credited with $1/2$ sack. 1999—Recovered one fumble.

			INTERCEPTIONS				TOTALS			
Year Team	G	GS	No.	Yds.	Avg.	TD	TD	2pt.	Pts.	Fum.
1995—Minnesota NFL	16	11	*9	108	12.0	1	2	0	12	1
1996—Minnesota NFL	16	16	5	57	11.4	0	0	0	0	0
1997—Minnesota NFL	15	13	2	1	0.5	0	1	0	6	1
1998—Minnesota NFL	16	16	2	27	13.5	0	0	0	0	0
1999—Minnesota NFL	13	12	2	32	16.0	1	1	0	6	0
Pro totals (5 years)	76	68	20	225	11.3	2	4	0	24	2

THOMAS, RANDY   G   JETS

PERSONAL: Born January 19, 1976, in East Point, Ga. ... 6-4/301.
HIGH SCHOOL: Tri-Cities (East Point, Ga.).
JUNIOR COLLEGE: Copiah-Lincoln Junior College (Miss.).
COLLEGE: Mississippi State.
TRANSACTIONS/CAREER NOTES: Selected by New York Jets in second round (57th pick overall) of 1999 NFL draft. ... Signed by Jets (July 20, 1999).
PLAYING EXPERIENCE: New York Jets NFL, 1999. ... Games/Games started: 1999 (16/16).
HONORS: Named offensive guard on THE SPORTING NEWS college All-America second team (1998).

THOMAS, RATCLIFF   LB   COLTS

PERSONAL: Born January 2, 1974, in Alexandria, Va. ... 6-0/240.
HIGH SCHOOL: T.C. Williams (Alexandria, Va.).
COLLEGE: Maryland.
TRANSACTIONS/CAREER NOTES: Selected by Amsterdam Admirals in 1998 NFL Europe draft (February 18, 1998). ... Signed as non-drafted free agent by Indianapolis Colts (August 5, 1998). ... Released by Colts (September 9, 1998). ... Re-signed by Colts (September 29, 1998). ... Released by Colts (October 5, 1998). ... Re-signed by Colts (October 6, 1998). ... Released by Colts (November 25, 1998). ... Re-signed by Colts (January 19, 1999).
PLAYING EXPERIENCE: Indianapolis NFL, 1998 and 1999. ... Games/Games started: 1998 (5/0), 1999 (16/0). Total: 21/0.
PRO STATISTICS: 1999—Intercepted one pass for no yards.

THOMAS, ROBERT   FB   COWBOYS

PERSONAL: Born December 1, 1974, in Jacksonville, Ark. ... 6-1/252.
HIGH SCHOOL: Jacksonville (Ark.).
COLLEGE: Henderson State (Ark.).
TRANSACTIONS/CAREER NOTES: Signed as non-drafted free agent by Dallas Cowboys (February 24, 1998). ... Assigned by Cowboys to Rhein Fire in 1999 NFL Europe enhancement allocation program (February 22, 1999).

T

PLAYING EXPERIENCE: Dallas NFL, 1998 and 1999; Rhein NFLE, 1999. ... Games/Games started: 1998 (16/0), NFLE 1999 (games played unavailable), NFL 1999 (16/7). Total NFL: 32/7.
PRO STATISTICS: NFLE: 1999—Intercepted one pass for 13 yards. NFL: 1999—Rushed eight times for 35 yards and caught 10 passes for 64 yards.
SINGLE GAME HIGHS (regular season): Attempts—4 (December 19, 1999, vs. New York Jets); yards—22 (December 19, 1999, vs. New York Jets); and rushing touchdowns—0.
MISCELLANEOUS: Played linebacker (1998 and 1999).

THOMAS, RODNEY   RB   TITANS

PERSONAL: Born March 30, 1973, in Trinity, Texas. ... 5-10/210. ... Full name: Rodney Dejuane Thomas.
HIGH SCHOOL: Groveton (Texas).
COLLEGE: Texas A&M.
TRANSACTIONS/CAREER NOTES: Selected by Houston Oilers in third round (89th pick overall) of 1995 NFL draft. ... Signed by Oilers (August 1, 1995). ... Oilers franchise moved to Tennessee for 1997 season. ... Granted free agency (February 13, 1998). ... Re-signed by Oilers (June 2, 1998). ... Oilers franchise renamed Tennessee Titans for 1999 season (December 26, 1998).
CHAMPIONSHIP GAME EXPERIENCE: Played in AFC championship game (1999 season). ... Played in Super Bowl XXXIV (1999 season).
SINGLE GAME HIGHS (regular season): Attempts—25 (November 19, 1995 vs. Kansas City); yards—108 (November 5, 1995, vs. Cleveland); and rushing touchdowns—2 (December 24, 1995, vs. Buffalo).
STATISTICAL PLATEAUS: 100-yard rushing games: 1995 (2).

			RUSHING				RECEIVING				KICKOFF RETURNS				TOTALS			
Year Team	G	GS	Att.	Yds.	Avg.	TD	No.	Yds.	Avg.	TD	No.	Yds.	Avg.	TD	TD	2pt.	Pts.	Fum.
1995—Houston NFL	16	10	251	947	3.8	5	39	204	5.2	2	3	48	16.0	0	7	1	44	8
1996—Houston NFL	16	0	49	151	3.1	1	13	128	9.8	0	5	80	16.0	0	1	0	6	0
1997—Tennessee NFL	16	1	67	310	4.6	3	14	111	7.9	0	17	346	20.4	0	3	0	18	1
1998—Tennessee NFL	11	0	24	100	4.2	2	6	55	9.2	0	3	64	21.3	0	2	0	12	0
1999—Tennessee NFL	16	0	43	164	3.8	1	9	72	8.0	0	0	0	0.0	0	1	0	6	0
Pro totals (5 years)	75	11	434	1672	3.9	12	81	570	7.0	2	28	538	19.2	0	14	1	86	9

THOMAS, THURMAN   RB   DOLPHINS

T

PERSONAL: Born May 16, 1966, in Houston. ... 5-10/200. ... Full name: Thurman Lee Thomas.
HIGH SCHOOL: Willow Ridge (Sugar Land, Texas).
COLLEGE: Oklahoma State.
TRANSACTIONS/CAREER NOTES: Selected by Buffalo Bills in second round (40th pick overall) of 1988 NFL draft. ... Signed by Bills (July 14, 1988). ... Released by Bills (February 10, 2000). ... Signed by Miami Dolphins (March 6, 2000).
CHAMPIONSHIP GAME EXPERIENCE: Played in AFC championship game (1988 and 1990-1993 seasons). ... Played in Super Bowl XXV (1990 season), Super Bowl XXVI (1991 season), Super Bowl XXVII (1992 season) and Super Bowl XXVIII (1993 season).
HONORS: Named running back on THE SPORTING NEWS college All-America second team (1985). ... Played in Pro Bowl (1989-1991 and 1993 seasons). ... Named to play in Pro Bowl (1992 season); replaced by Ronnie Harmon due to injury. ... Named running back on THE SPORTING NEWS NFL All-Pro team (1990 and 1991). ... Named NFL Player of the Year by THE SPORTING NEWS (1991).
POST SEASON RECORDS: Holds NFL postseason career record for most yards gained—2,114. ... Holds NFL postseason record for most consecutive games with one or more touchdowns—9 (1992-1998). ... Shares NFL postseason single-game record for most receptions—13 (January 6, 1990, at Cleveland). ... Shares NFL postseason career records for most points scored—126; and most touchdowns—21.
PRO STATISTICS: 1988—Recovered one fumble. 1989—Recovered two fumbles. 1990—Recovered two fumbles. 1992—Recovered one fumble. 1993—Attempted one pass without a completion and recovered one fumble. 1994—Recovered two fumbles. 1996—Recovered one fumble.
SINGLE GAME HIGHS (regular season): Attempts—37 (November 8, 1992, vs. Pittsburgh); yards—214 (September 24, 1990, vs. New York Jets); and rushing touchdowns—3 (September 6, 1992, vs. Los Angeles Raiders).
STATISTICAL PLATEAUS: 100-yard rushing games: 1988 (2), 1989 (5), 1990 (5), 1991 (8), 1992 (9), 1993 (7), 1994 (4), 1995 (3), 1996 (2), 1997 (1). Total: 46. ... 100-yard receiving games: 1991 (2), 1996 (1). Total: 3.
MISCELLANEOUS: Active AFC leader for career rushing yards (11,938) and rushing touchdowns (65). ... Shares active AFC lead in touchdowns (87). ... Holds Buffalo Bills all-time record for most yards rushing (11,938) and most rushing touchdowns (65). ... Shares Buffalo Bills all-time record for most touchdowns (87).

			RUSHING				RECEIVING				TOTALS			
Year Team	G	GS	Att.	Yds.	Avg.	TD	No.	Yds.	Avg.	TD	TD	2pt.	Pts.	Fum.
1988—Buffalo NFL	15	15	207	881	4.3	2	18	208	11.6	0	2	0	12	9
1989—Buffalo NFL	16	16	298	1244	4.2	6	60	669	11.2	6	▲12	0	72	7
1990—Buffalo NFL	16	16	271	§1297	4.8	11	49	532	10.9	2	13	0	78	6
1991—Buffalo NFL	15	15	§288	§1407	*4.9	7	62	631	10.2	5	▲12	0	72	5
1992—Buffalo NFL	16	16	312	1487	§4.8	9	58	626	10.8	3	§12	0	72	6
1993—Buffalo NFL	16	16	*355	§1315	3.7	6	48	387	8.1	0	6	0	36	6
1994—Buffalo NFL	15	15	287	1093	3.8	7	50	349	7.0	2	9	0	54	1
1995—Buffalo NFL	14	14	267	1005	3.8	6	26	220	8.5	2	8	0	48	6
1996—Buffalo NFL	15	15	281	1033	3.7	8	26	254	9.8	0	8	0	48	1
1997—Buffalo NFL	16	16	154	643	4.2	1	30	208	6.9	0	1	0	6	2
1998—Buffalo NFL	14	3	93	381	4.1	2	26	220	8.5	1	3	0	18	0
1999—Buffalo NFL	5	3	36	152	4.2	0	3	37	12.3	1	1	0	6	0
Pro totals (12 years)	173	160	2849	11938	4.2	65	456	4341	9.5	22	87	0	522	49

THOMAS, TRA   OT   EAGLES

PERSONAL: Born November 20, 1974, in De Land, Fla. ... 6-7/349. ... Full name: William Thomas III. ... Name pronounced TRAY.
HIGH SCHOOL: De Land (Fla.).
COLLEGE: Florida State.

TRANSACTIONS/CAREER NOTES: Selected by Philadelphia Eagles in first round (11th pick overall) of 1998 NFL draft. ... Signed by Eagles June 19, 1998).

PLAYING EXPERIENCE: Philadelphia NFL, 1998 and 1999. ... Games/Games started: 1998 (16/16), 1999 (16/15). Total: 32/31.

PRO STATISTICS: 1998—Recovered one fumble. 1999—Recovered one fumble.

THOMAS, TRE   S

PERSONAL: Born September 12, 1975, in Houston. ... 6-1/211. ... Full name: Carl Grady Thomas III. ... Name pronounced TRAY.

HIGH SCHOOL: Kempner (Sugar Land, Texas).

COLLEGE: Texas.

TRANSACTIONS/CAREER NOTES: Signed as non-drafted free agent by Detroit Lions (March 25, 1997). ...Released by Lions (August 20, 1997). ... Signed by Jacksonville Jaguars (December 24, 1997). ... Released by Jaguars (August 25, 1998). ... Signed by Berlin Thunder of NFL Europe (May 13, 1999). ... Signed by New York Giants (June 23, 1999). ... Released by Giants (September 5, 1999). ... Re-signed by Giants to practice squad (October 26, 1999). ... Activated (November 10, 1999). ... Released by Giants (November 15, 1999). ... Re-signed by Giants to practice squad (November 17, 1999). ... Activated (November 27, 1999). ... Released by Giants (November 30, 1999). ... Re-signed by Giants to practice squad (December 1, 1999). ... Activated (December 4, 1999). ... Released by Giants (December 6, 1999). ... Re-signed by Giants to practice squad (December 8, 1999). ... Granted free agency (February 11, 2000).

PLAYING EXPERIENCE: Berlin NFLE, 1999; New York Giants NFL, 1999. ... Games/Games started: 1999 NFLE (6/6), 1999 NFL (2/0). Total Pro: 8/6).

THOMAS, WILLIAM   LB

PERSONAL: Born August 13, 1968, in Amarillo, Texas. ... 6-2/223. ... Full name: William Harrison Thomas Jr.

HIGH SCHOOL: Palo Duro (Amarillo, Texas).

COLLEGE: Texas A&M.

TRANSACTIONS/CAREER NOTES: Selected by Philadelphia Eagles in fourth round (105th pick overall) of 1991 NFL draft. ... Signed by Eagles July 17, 1991). ... Granted free agency (February 17, 1994). ... Re-signed by Eagles (July 23, 1994). ... Released by Eagles (March 23, 2000).

HONORS: Played in Pro Bowl (1995 and 1996 seasons).

POST SEASON RECORDS: Shares NFL postseason record for most touchdowns by interception return—1 (December 30, 1995, vs. Detroit).

PRO STATISTICS: 1991—Recovered one fumble. 1992—Recovered two fumbles for two yards. 1993—Recovered three fumbles. 1995—Recovered one fumble. 1996—Recovered one fumble for 23 yards and a touchdown. 1997—Recovered one fumble for 37 yards and a touchdown. 1998—Blocked a punt out of end zone for a safety. 1999—Recovered one fumble for nine yards.

			INTERCEPTIONS				SACKS
Year Team	G	GS	No.	Yds.	Avg.	TD	No.
1991—Philadelphia NFL	16	7	0	0	0.0	0	2.0
1992—Philadelphia NFL	16	15	2	4	2.0	0	1.5
1993—Philadelphia NFL	16	16	2	39	19.5	0	6.5
1994—Philadelphia NFL	16	16	1	7	7.0	0	6.0
1995—Philadelphia NFL	16	16	7	104	14.9	1	2.0
1996—Philadelphia NFL	16	16	3	47	15.7	0	5.5
1997—Philadelphia NFL	14	14	2	11	5.5	0	5.0
1998—Philadelphia NFL	16	16	1	21	21.0	0	2.0
1999—Philadelphia NFL	14	13	0	0	0.0	0	2.5
Pro totals (9 years)	140	129	18	233	12.9	1	33.0

THOMAS, ZACH   LB   DOLPHINS

PERSONAL: Born September 1, 1973, in Pampa, Texas. ... 5-11/235. ... Full name: Zach Michael Thomas.

HIGH SCHOOL: White Deer (Texas), then Pampa (Texas).

COLLEGE: Texas Tech.

TRANSACTIONS/CAREER NOTES: Selected by Miami Dolphins in fifth round (154th pick overall) of 1996 NFL draft. ... Signed by Dolphins July 10, 1996). ... Granted free agency (February 12, 1999). ... Re-signed by Dolphins (February 12, 1999).

HONORS: Named linebacker on THE SPORTING NEWS college All-America second team (1994). ... Named linebacker on THE SPORTING NEWS college All-America first team (1995). ... Played in Pro Bowl (1999 season).

PRO STATISTICS: 1996—Returned one kickoff for 17 yards and recovered two fumbles for seven yards. 1999—Returned one kickoff for 15 yards.

			INTERCEPTIONS				SACKS
Year Team	G	GS	No.	Yds.	Avg.	TD	No.
1996—Miami NFL	16	16	3	64	21.3	1	2.0
1997—Miami NFL	15	15	1	10	10.0	0	0.5
1998—Miami NFL	16	16	3	21	7.0	▲2	2.0
1999—Miami NFL	16	16	1	0	0.0	0	1.0
Pro totals (4 years)	63	63	8	95	11.9	3	5.5

THOMASON, JEFF   TE   EAGLES

PERSONAL: Born December 30, 1969, in San Diego. ... 6-5/255. ... Full name: Jeffrey David Thomason.

HIGH SCHOOL: Corona Del Mar (Newport Beach, Calif.).

COLLEGE: Oregon (degree in psychology).

TRANSACTIONS/CAREER NOTES: Signed as non-drafted free agent by Cincinnati Bengals (April 29, 1992). ... On injured reserve with sprained knee (September 1- December 5, 1992). ... Released by Bengals (August 30, 1993). ... Re-signed by Bengals (September 15, 1993). ... Claimed on waivers by Green Bay Packers (August 2, 1994). ... Released by Packers (August 21, 1994). ... Re-signed by Packers (January 20, 1995). ... Granted unconditional free agency (February 13, 1998). ... Re-signed by Packers (March 17, 1998). ... Traded by Packers to Philadelphia Eagles for TE Kaseem Sinceno (March 16, 2000).

CHAMPIONSHIP GAME EXPERIENCE: Played in NFC championship game (1995-1997 seasons). ... Member of Super Bowl championship team (1996 season). ... Played in Super Bowl XXXII (1997 season).
PRO STATISTICS: 1995—Returned one kickoff for 16 yards and recovered one fumble. 1996—Returned one kickoff for 20 yards.
SINGLE GAME HIGHS (regular season): Receptions—5 (September 1, 1997, vs. Chicago); yards—58 (September 1, 1997, vs. Chicago); and touchdown receptions—1 (December 20, 1999, vs. Minnesota).

				RECEIVING			TOTALS			
Year Team	G	GS	No.	Yds.	Avg.	TD	TD	2pt.	Pts.	Fum.
1992—Cincinnati NFL	4	0	2	14	7.0	0	0	0	0	0
1993—Cincinnati NFL	3	0	2	8	4.0	0	0	0	0	0
1994—					Did not play.					
1995—Green Bay NFL	16	1	3	32	10.7	0	0	0	0	0
1996—Green Bay NFL	16	1	3	45	15.0	0	0	0	0	0
1997—Green Bay NFL	13	1	9	115	12.8	1	1	0	6	1
1998—Green Bay NFL	16	2	9	89	9.9	0	0	0	0	0
1999—Green Bay NFL	14	2	14	140	10.0	2	2	0	12	0
Pro totals (7 years)	82	7	42	443	10.5	3	3	0	18	1

THOMPSON, BENNIE   S   RAVENS

PERSONAL: Born February 10, 1963, in New Orleans. ... 6-0/220.
HIGH SCHOOL: John McDonogh (New Orleans).
COLLEGE: Grambling State.
TRANSACTIONS/CAREER NOTES: Signed as non-drafted free agent by Kansas City Chiefs (May 9, 1985). ... Released by Chiefs (August 5 1985). ... Signed by Winnipeg Blue Bombers of CFL (April 21, 1986). ... Granted free agency (March 1, 1989). ... Signed by New Orleans Saints (April 12, 1989). ... Released by Saints (September 5, 1989). ... Re-signed by Saints to practice squad (September 6, 1989). ... Activated (December 15, 1989). ... Granted unconditional free agency (February 1-April 1, 1991). ... Re-signed by Saints for 1991 season. ... Granted unconditional free agency (February 1, 1992). ... Signed by Chiefs (March 28, 1992). ... Granted unconditional free agency (February 17 1994). ... Signed by Cleveland Browns (July 19, 1994). ... Browns franchise moved to Baltimore and renamed Ravens for 1996 season (March 11, 1996). ... Granted unconditional free agency (February 13, 1998). ... Re-signed by Ravens (March 10, 1998). ... Granted unconditional free agency (February 11, 2000). ... Re-signed by Ravens (May 1, 2000).
CHAMPIONSHIP GAME EXPERIENCE: Played in AFC championship game (1993 season).
HONORS: Played in Pro Bowl (1991 and 1998 seasons).
PRO STATISTICS: CFL: 1987—Recovered one fumble. 1988—Fumbled once and recovered two fumbles for two yards. NFL: 1991—Recovered two fumbles. 1994—Recovered one fumble. 1997—Recovered two fumbles. 1998—Returned one punt for 43 yards.

			INTERCEPTIONS				SACKS
Year Team	G	GS	No.	Yds.	Avg.	TD	No.
1986—Winnipeg CFL	9	...	2	49	24.5	0	0.0
1987—Winnipeg CFL	8	...	1	0	0.0	0	0.0
1988—Winnipeg CFL	18	...	4	58	14.5	0	0.0
1989—New Orleans NFL	2	0	0	0	0.0	0	0.0
1990—New Orleans NFL	16	2	2	0	0.0	0	0.0
1991—New Orleans NFL	16	0	1	14	14.0	0	0.0
1992—Kansas City NFL	16	0	4	26	6.5	0	1.5
1993—Kansas City NFL	16	0	0	0	0.0	0	0.5
1994—Cleveland NFL	16	0	0	0	0.0	0	1.0
1995—Cleveland NFL	13	0	0	0	0.0	0	0.0
1996—Baltimore NFL	16	0	0	0	0.0	0	3.0
1997—Baltimore NFL	16	1	0	0	0.0	0	0.0
1998—Baltimore NFL	16	0	0	0	0.0	0	0.0
1999—Baltimore NFL	16	0	0	0	0.0	0	0.0
CFL totals (3 years)	35	...	7	107	15.3	0	0.0
NFL totals (11 years)	159	3	7	40	5.7	0	6.0
Pro totals (14 years)	194	...	14	147	10.5	0	6.0

THOMPSON, DERRIUS   WR   REDSKINS

PERSONAL: Born July 5, 1977, in Cedar Hill, Texas ... 6-2/215. ... Cousin of Reyna Thompson, cornerback with Miami Dolphins (1986-88), New York Giants (1989-92) and New England Patriots (1993-94).
HIGH SCHOOL: Cedar Hill (Texas).
COLLEGE: Baylor.
TRANSACTIONS/CAREER NOTES: Signed as non-drafted free agent by Washington Redskins (April 21, 1999). ... Released by Redskins (September 4, 1999). ... Re-signed by Redskins to practice squad (September 6, 1999). ... Activated (November 16, 1999).
PLAYING EXPERIENCE: Washington NFL, 1999. ... Games/Games started: 1999 (1/0).

THOMPSON, MIKE   DT   BROWNS

PERSONAL: Born December 22, 1971, in Portage, Wis. ... 6-4/296. ... Full name: Michael John Thompson.
HIGH SCHOOL: Portage (Wis.).
COLLEGE: Wisconsin.
TRANSACTIONS/CAREER NOTES: Selected by Jacksonville Jaguars in fourth round (123rd pick overall) of 1995 NFL draft. ... Signed by Jaguars (June 1, 1995). ... Released by Jaguars (August 25, 1996). ... Signed by Green Bay Packers (January 2, 1997). ... Released by Packers (August 18, 1997). ... Signed by Kansas City Chiefs (August 21, 1997). ... Released by Chiefs (August 28, 1997). ... Signed by Cincinnati Bengals (December 15, 1997). ... Inactive for one game (1997). ... Selected by Cleveland Browns from Bengals in NFL expansion draft (February 9, 1999). ... Granted free agency (February 11, 2000). ... Re-signed by Browns (April 14, 2000).
PLAYING EXPERIENCE: Jacksonville NFL, 1995; Cincinnati NFL, 1998; Cleveland NFL, 1999. ... Games/Games started: 1995 (2/0), 1998 (9/0), 1999 (10/0). Total: 21/0.
PRO STATISTICS: 1998—Credited with $1/2$ sack. 1999—Recovered two fumbles.

THORNTON, JOHN   DT   TITANS

PERSONAL: Born October 2, 1976, in Philadelphia. ... 6-2/295. ... Full name: John Jason Thornton.
HIGH SCHOOL: Scotland (Pa.) School for Veterans' Children.
COLLEGE: West Virginia.
TRANSACTIONS/CAREER NOTES: Selected by Tennessee Titans in second round (52nd pick overall) of 1999 NFL draft. ... Signed by Titans July 26, 1999).
CHAMPIONSHIP GAME EXPERIENCE: Played in AFC championship game (1999 season). ... Played in Super Bowl XXXIV (1999 season).
PRO STATISTICS: 1999—Credited with a safety.

Year—Team	G	GS	SACKS
1999—Tennessee NFL	16	3	4.5

THRASH, JAMES   WR   REDSKINS

PERSONAL: Born April 28, 1975, in Denver. ... 6-0/200.
HIGH SCHOOL: Wewoka (Okla.).
COLLEGE: Missouri Southern.
TRANSACTIONS/CAREER NOTES: Signed as non-drafted free agent by Philadelphia Eagles (April 22, 1997). ... Released by Eagles (July 8, 1997). ... Signed by Washington Redskins (July 11, 1997). ... On injured reserve with shoulder injury (December 8, 1998-remainder of season). ... Granted free agency (February 11, 2000). ... Re-signed with Redskins (April 14, 2000).
PRO STATISTICS: 1999—Rushed once for 37 yards.
SINGLE GAME HIGHS (regular season): Receptions—4 (December 6, 1998, vs. San Diego); yards—66 (December 6, 1998, vs. San Diego); and touchdown receptions—1 (December 6, 1998, vs. San Diego).

			RECEIVING				KICKOFF RETURNS				TOTALS			
Year—Team	G	GS	No.	Yds.	Avg.	TD	No.	Yds.	Avg.	TD	TD	2pt.	Pts.	Fum.
1997—Washington NFL	4	0	2	24	12.0	0	0	0	0.0	0	0	0	0	0
1998—Washington NFL	10	1	10	163	16.3	1	6	129	21.5	0	1	0	6	0
1999—Washington NFL	16	0	3	44	14.7	0	14	355	25.4	1	1	0	6	0
Pro totals (3 years)	30	1	15	231	15.4	1	20	484	24.2	1	2	0	12	0

TILLMAN, PAT   S   CARDINALS

PERSONAL: Born November 6, 1976, in Fremont, Calif. ... 5-11/192. ... Full name: Patrick Daniel Tillman.
HIGH SCHOOL: Leland (San Jose, Calif.).
COLLEGE: Arizona State (degree in marketing, 1997).
TRANSACTIONS/CAREER NOTES: Selected by Arizona Cardinals in seventh round (226th pick overall) of 1998 NFL draft. ... Signed by Cardinals for 1998 season.
PLAYING EXPERIENCE: Arizona NFL, 1998 and 1999. ... Games/Games started: 1998 (16/10), 1999 (16/1). Total: 32/11.
HONORS: Named outside linebacker on THE SPORTING NEWS college All-America first team (1997).
PRO STATISTICS: 1998—Credited with one sack. 1999—Rushed once for four yards, intercepted two passes for seven yards, returned three kickoffs for 33 yards, fumbled once and recovered one fumble.

TIMMERMAN, ADAM   G   RAMS

PERSONAL: Born August 14, 1971, in Cherokee, Iowa. ... 6-4/300. ... Full name: Adam Larry Timmerman.
HIGH SCHOOL: Washington (Cherokee, Iowa).
COLLEGE: South Dakota State (degree in agriculture business).
TRANSACTIONS/CAREER NOTES: Selected by Green Bay Packers in seventh round (230th pick overall) of 1995 NFL draft. ... Signed by Packers (June 2, 1995). ... Granted free agency (February 13, 1998). ... Re-signed by Packers (April 15, 1998). ... Granted unconditional free agency (February 12, 1999). ... Signed by St. Louis Rams (February 15, 1999).
PLAYING EXPERIENCE: Green Bay NFL, 1995-1998; St. Louis NFL, 1999. ... Games/Games started: 1995 (13/0), 1996 (16/16), 1997 (16/16), 1998 (16/16), 1999 (16/16). Total: 77/64.
CHAMPIONSHIP GAME EXPERIENCE: Played in NFC championship game (1995-97 and 1999 seasons). ... Member of Super Bowl championship team (1996 and 1999 seasons). ... Played in Super Bowl XXXII (1997 season).
HONORS: Played in Pro Bowl (1999 season).
PRO STATISTICS: 1999—Recovered one fumble.

TOBECK, ROBBIE   C/G   SEAHAWKS

PERSONAL: Born March 6, 1970, in Tarpon Springs, Fla. ... 6-4/298. ... Full name: Robert L. Tobeck.
HIGH SCHOOL: New Port Richey (Fla.).
COLLEGE: Washington State.
TRANSACTIONS/CAREER NOTES: Signed as non-drafted free agent by Atlanta Falcons (May 7, 1993). ... Released by Falcons (August 30, 1993). ... Re-signed by Falcons to practice squad (August 31, 1993). ... Activated (January 1, 1994). ... Granted unconditional free agency (February 11, 2000). ... Signed by Seattle Seahawks (March 20, 2000).
PLAYING EXPERIENCE: Atlanta NFL, 1994-1999. ... Games/Games started: 1994 (5/0), 1995 (16/16), 1996 (16/16), 1997 (16/15), 1998 (16/16), 1999 (15/15). Total: 84/78.
CHAMPIONSHIP GAME EXPERIENCE: Played in NFC championship game (1998 season). ... Played in Super Bowl XXXIII (1998 season).
PRO STATISTICS: 1996—Caught two passes for 15 yards and a touchdown. 1997—Recovered one fumble. 1998—Recovered one fumble for one yard. 1999—Recovered one fumble.

TOLLIVER, BILLY JOE   QB   SAINTS

PERSONAL: Born February 7, 1966, in Dallas. ... 6-1/217. ... Full name: Billy Joe Tolliver.
HIGH SCHOOL: Boyd (Texas).
COLLEGE: Texas Tech.
TRANSACTIONS/CAREER NOTES: Selected by San Diego Chargers in second round (51st pick overall) of 1989 NFL draft. ... Signed by Chargers (July 30, 1989). ... On injured reserve with broken collarbone (September 5-October 18, 1989). ... On developmental squad (October 19-20, 1989). ... Traded by Chargers to Atlanta Falcons for fifth-round pick (LB Kevin Little) in 1992 draft (August 28, 1991). ... Granted free agency (March 1, 1993). ... Re-signed by Falcons (August 9, 1993). ... Granted unconditional free agency (February 17, 1994). ... Signed by Houston Oilers (September 7, 1994). ... Granted unconditional free agency (February 17, 1995). ... Signed by Falcons (October 23, 1996). ... Inactive for nine games (1996). ... Granted unconditional free agency (February 14, 1997). ... Re-signed by Falcons (March 19, 1997). ... Released by Falcons (October 27, 1997). ... Signed by Kansas City Chiefs (November 5, 1997). ... Released by Chiefs (August 25, 1998). ... Signed by New Orleans Saints (September 9, 1998).
PRO STATISTICS: 1989—Fumbled four times and recovered one fumble for minus six yards. 1990—Fumbled six times and recovered two fumbles. 1991—Fumbled three times. 1992—Fumbled five times. 1994—Fumbled seven times. 1997—Fumbled seven times and recovered two fumbles for minus one yard. 1998—Fumbled three times for minus 13 yards. 1999—Fumbled four times and recovered two fumbles for minus 24 yards.
SINGLE GAME HIGHS (regular season): Attempts—51 (December 16, 1990, vs. Denver); completions—28 (October 17, 1999, vs. Tennessee); yards—354 (October 17, 1999, vs. Tennessee); and touchdown passes—3 (December 27, 1998, vs. Buffalo).
STATISTICAL PLATEAUS: 300-yard passing games: 1989 (2), 1990 (1), 1998 (1), 1999 (1). Total: 5.
MISCELLANEOUS: Regular-season record as starting NFL quarterback: 15-32 (.319).

			PASSING								RUSHING				TOTALS		
Year Team	G	GS	Att.	Cmp.	Pct.	Yds.	TD	Int.	Avg.	Rat.	Att.	Yds.	Avg.	TD	TD	2pt.	Pts.
1989—San Diego NFL	5	5	185	89	48.1	1097	5	8	5.93	57.9	7	0	0.0	0	0	0	0
1990—San Diego NFL	15	14	410	216	52.7	2574	16	16	6.28	68.9	14	22	1.6	0	0	0	0
1991—Atlanta NFL	7	2	82	40	48.8	531	4	2	6.48	75.8	9	6	0.7	0	0	0	0
1992—Atlanta NFL	9	5	131	73	55.7	787	5	6	6.01	70.4	4	15	3.8	0	0	0	0
1993—Atlanta NFL	7	2	76	39	51.3	464	3	5	6.11	56.0	7	48	6.9	0	0	0	0
1994—Houston NFL	10	7	240	121	50.4	1287	6	7	5.36	62.6	12	37	3.1	2	2	0	12
1995—							Did not play.										
1996—Atlanta NFL							Did not play.										
1997—Atlanta NFL	6	1	115	63	54.8	685	5	1	5.96	83.4	7	8	1.1	0	0	0	0
—Kansas City NFL	3	0	1	1	100.0	-8	0	0	-8.00	79.2	2	-1	-0.5	0	0	0	0
1998—New Orleans NFL	7	4	199	110	55.3	1427	8	4	7.17	83.1	11	43	3.9	0	0	0	0
1999—New Orleans NFL	10	7	268	139	51.9	1916	7	16	7.15	58.9	26	142	5.5	3	3	0	18
Pro totals (9 years)	79	47	1707	891	52.2	10760	59	64	6.30	67.7	99	320	3.2	5	5	0	30

TOMCZAK, MIKE   QB   LIONS

PERSONAL: Born October 23, 1962, in Chicago ... 6-1/210. ... Full name: Michael John Tomczak. ... Name pronounced TOM-zak.
HIGH SCHOOL: Thornton Fractional North (Calumet City, Ill.).
COLLEGE: Ohio State (degree in communications).
TRANSACTIONS/CAREER NOTES: Selected by New Jersey Generals in 1985 USFL territorial draft. ... Signed as non-drafted free agent by Chicago Bears (May 9, 1985). ... Granted free agency (February 1, 1990). ... Re-signed by Bears (July 25, 1990). ... Granted unconditional free agency (February 1, 1991). ... Signed by Green Bay Packers (March 30, 1991). ... Granted free agency (February 1, 1992). ... Re-signed by Packers (August 19, 1992). ... Released by Packers (August 31, 1992). ... Signed by Cleveland Browns (September 16, 1992). ... Granted unconditional free agency (March 1, 1993). ... Signed by Pittsburgh Steelers (April 6, 1993). ... Granted unconditional free agency (February 14, 1997). ... Re-signed by Steelers (March 6, 1997). ... Granted unconditional free agency (February 11, 2000). ... Signed by Detroit Lions (March 3, 2000).
CHAMPIONSHIP GAME EXPERIENCE: Member of Bears for NFC championship game (1985 season); did not play. ... Member of Super Bowl championship team (1985 season). ... Played in NFC championship game (1988 season). ... Member of Steelers for AFC championship game (1994 and 1995 seasons); did not play. ... Member of Steelers for Super Bowl XXX (1995 season); did not play. ... Played in AFC championship game (1997 season).
PRO STATISTICS: 1985—Fumbled once and recovered one fumble for minus 13 yards. 1986—Fumbled twice. 1987—Fumbled six times and recovered one fumble. 1988—Fumbled once. 1989—Fumbled twice. 1990—Caught one pass for five yards and fumbled twice. 1991—Fumbled five times and recovered two fumbles for minus one yard. 1992—Fumbled five times. 1993—Fumbled twice and recovered one fumble. 1994—Fumbled twice. 1995—Fumbled twice and recovered one fumble. 1996—Fumbled seven times and recovered two fumbles. 1998—Fumbled twice. 1999—Fumbled three times for minus six yards.
SINGLE GAME HIGHS (regular season): Attempts—46 (December 18, 1999, vs. Kansas City); completions—26 (November 20, 1994, vs. Miami); yards—343 (November 20, 1994, vs. Miami); and touchdown passes—3 (December 1, 1991, vs. Atlanta).
STATISTICAL PLATEAUS: 300-yard passing games: 1989 (1), 1991 (1), 1992 (1), 1994 (1), 1996 (1), 1999 (1). Total: 6.
MISCELLANEOUS: Regular-season record as starting NFL quarterback: 42-31 (.575). ... Postseason record as starting NFL quarterback: 3-2 (.600).

			PASSING								RUSHING				TOTALS		
Year Team	G	GS	Att.	Cmp.	Pct.	Yds.	TD	Int.	Avg.	Rat.	Att.	Yds.	Avg.	TD	TD	2pt.	Pts.
1985—Chicago NFL	6	0	6	2	33.3	33	0	0	5.50	52.8	2	3	1.5	0	0	0	0
1986—Chicago NFL	13	7	151	74	49.0	1105	2	10	7.32	50.2	23	117	5.1	3	3	0	18
1987—Chicago NFL	12	6	178	97	54.5	1220	5	10	6.85	62.0	18	54	3.0	1	1	0	6
1988—Chicago NFL	14	5	170	86	50.6	1310	7	6	7.71	75.4	13	40	3.1	1	1	0	6
1989—Chicago NFL	16	11	306	156	51.0	2058	16	16	6.73	68.2	24	71	3.0	1	1	0	6
1990—Chicago NFL	16	2	104	39	37.5	521	3	5	5.01	43.8	12	41	3.4	2	2	0	12
1991—Green Bay NFL	12	7	238	128	53.8	1490	11	9	6.26	72.6	17	93	5.5	1	1	0	6
1992—Cleveland NFL	12	8	211	120	56.9	1693	7	7	8.02	80.1	24	39	1.6	0	0	0	0
1993—Pittsburgh NFL	7	1	54	29	53.7	398	2	5	7.37	51.3	5	-4	-0.8	0	0	0	0
1994—Pittsburgh NFL	6	2	93	54	58.1	804	4	5	8.65	100.8	4	22	5.5	0	0	0	0
1995—Pittsburgh NFL	7	4	113	65	57.5	666	1	9	5.89	44.3	11	25	2.3	0	0	0	0
1996—Pittsburgh NFL	16	15	401	222	55.4	2767	15	17	6.90	71.8	22	-7	-0.3	0	0	0	0
1997—Pittsburgh NFL	16	0	24	16	66.7	185	1	2	7.71	68.9	7	13	1.9	0	0	0	0

1998—Pittsburgh NFL............	16	0	30	21	70.0	204	2	2	6.80	83.2	0	0	0.0	0	0	0	0
1999—Pittsburgh NFL............	16	5	258	139	53.9	1625	12	8	6.30	75.8	16	19	1.2	0	0	0	0
Pro totals (15 years)	185	73	2337	1248	53.4	16079	88	106	6.88	68.9	198	526	2.7	9	9	0	54

TOMICH, JARED — DE — SAINTS

PERSONAL: Born April 24, 1974, in St. John, Ind. ... 6-2/272. ... Full name: Jared James Tomich.
HIGH SCHOOL: Lake Central (St. John, Ind.).
COLLEGE: Nebraska.
TRANSACTIONS/CAREER NOTES: Selected by New Orleans Saints in second round (39th pick overall) of 1997 NFL draft. ... Signed by Saints (July 17, 1997). ... On injured reserve with ankle injury (December 24, 1999-remainder of season). ... Granted free agency (February 11, 2000).
PRO STATISTICS: 1997—Returned one kickoff for no yards, fumbled once and recovered one fumble. 1998—Returned one kickoff for no yards and recovered one fumble.

Year Team	G	GS	SACKS
1997—New Orleans NFL..	16	1	1.0
1998—New Orleans NFL..	16	11	6.0
1999—New Orleans NFL..	8	6	3.0
Pro totals (3 years)...	40	18	10.0

TONGUE, REGGIE — S — SEAHAWKS

PERSONAL: Born April 11, 1973, in Baltimore. ... 6-0/206. ... Full name: Reginald Clinton Tongue.
HIGH SCHOOL: Lathrop (Fairbanks, Alaska).
COLLEGE: Oregon State.
TRANSACTIONS/CAREER NOTES: Selected by Kansas City Chiefs in second round (58th pick overall) of 1996 NFL draft. ... Signed by Chiefs (July 26, 1996). ... Granted unconditional free agency (February 11, 2000). ... Signed by Seattle Seahawks (February 22, 2000).
PRO STATISTICS: 1998—Recovered one fumble. 1999—Advanced a lateral from an intercepted pass 46 yards for a touchdown and recovered three fumbles for nine yards.

			INTERCEPTIONS				SACKS
Year Team	G	GS	No.	Yds.	Avg.	TD	No.
1996—Kansas City NFL..	16	0	0	0	0.0	0	0.0
1997—Kansas City NFL..	16	16	1	0	0.0	0	2.5
1998—Kansas City NFL..	15	15	0	0	0.0	0	2.0
1999—Kansas City NFL..	16	16	1	80	80.0	1	2.0
Pro totals (4 years)...	63	47	2	80	40.0	1	6.5

TOOMER, AMANI — WR — GIANTS

PERSONAL: Born September 8, 1974, in Berkely, Calif. ... 6-3/205. ... Name pronounced uh-MAHN-ee.
HIGH SCHOOL: De La Salle Catholic (Concord, Calif.).
COLLEGE: Michigan.
TRANSACTIONS/CAREER NOTES: Selected by New York Giants in second round (34th pick overall) of 1996 NFL draft. ... Signed by Giants (July 21, 1996). ... On injured reserve with knee injury (October 31, 1996-remainder of season). ... Granted free agency (February 12, 1999). ... Re-signed by Giants (July 31, 1999).
PRO STATISTICS: 1996—Recovered two fumbles. 1998—Attempted one pass without a completion. 1999—Rushed once for four yards.
SINGLE GAME HIGHS (regular season): Receptions—9 (December 26, 1999, vs. Minnesota); yards—181 (December 5, 1999, vs. New York Jets); and touchdown receptions—3 (December 5, 1999, vs. New York Jets).
STATISTICAL PLATEAUS: 100-yard receiving games: 1999 (4).

			RECEIVING				PUNT RETURNS				KICKOFF RETURNS				TOTALS			
Year Team	G	GS	No.	Yds.	Avg.	TD	No.	Yds.	Avg.	TD	No.	Yds.	Avg.	TD	TD	2pt.	Pts.	Fum.
1996—New York Giants NFL..	7	1	1	12	12.0	0	18	298	16.6	2	11	191	17.4	0	2	0	12	1
1997—New York Giants NFL..	16	0	16	263	16.4	1	47	455	9.7	∞1	0	0	0.0	0	2	0	12	0
1998—New York Giants NFL..	16	0	27	360	13.3	5	35	252	7.2	0	4	66	16.5	0	5	0	30	0
1999—New York Giants NFL..	16	16	79	1183	15.0	6	1	14	14.0	0	0	0	0.0	0	6	0	36	0
Pro totals (4 years)	55	17	123	1818	14.8	12	101	1019	10.1	3	15	257	17.1	0	15	0	90	1

TOVAR, STEVE — LB

PERSONAL: Born April 25, 1970, in Elyria, Ohio. ... 6-3/244. ... Full name: Steven Eric Tovar.
HIGH SCHOOL: West (Elyria, Ohio).
COLLEGE: Ohio State.
TRANSACTIONS/CAREER NOTES: Selected by the Cincinnati Bengals in third round (59th pick overall) of 1993 NFL draft. ... Signed by Bengals (July 19, 1993). ... Granted free agency (February 16, 1996). ... Re-signed by Bengals (April 15, 1996). ... On injured reserve with knee injury (December 2, 1996-remainder of season). ... Released by Bengals (August 21, 1998). ... Signed by San Diego Chargers (August 25, 1998). ... Granted unconditional free agency (February 12, 1999). ... Signed by Carolina Panthers (February 15, 1999). ... Released by Panthers (April 27, 2000).
PRO STATISTICS: 1993—Recovered one fumble. 1994—Returned one kickoff for eight yards and recovered two fumbles. 1996—Fumbled once.

			INTERCEPTIONS				SACKS
Year Team	G	GS	No.	Yds.	Avg.	TD	No.
1993—Cincinnati NFL...	16	9	1	0	0.0	0	0.0
1994—Cincinnati NFL...	16	16	1	14	14.0	0	3.0
1995—Cincinnati NFL...	14	13	1	13	13.0	0	1.0
1996—Cincinnati NFL...	13	13	4	42	10.5	0	3.0

T

1997—Cincinnati NFL	14	5	0	0	0.0	0	0.0
1998—San Diego NFL	16	2	0	0	0.0	0	1.0
1999—Carolina NFL	16	6	0	0	0.0	0	0.0
Pro totals (7 years)	105	64	7	69	9.9	0	8.0

TOWNSEND, DESHEA   CB   STEELERS

PERSONAL: Born September 8, 1975, in Batesville, Miss. ... 5-10/175. ... Full name: Trevor Deshea Townsend.
HIGH SCHOOL: South Panola (Batesville, Miss.).
COLLEGE: Alabama.
TRANSACTIONS/CAREER NOTES: Selected by Pittsburgh Steelers in fourth round (117th pick overall) of 1998 NFL draft. ... Signed by Steelers (July 6, 1998).
PLAYING EXPERIENCE: Pittsburgh NFL, 1998 and 1999. ... Games/Games started: 1998 (12/0), 1999 (16/4). Total: 28/4.

TRAPP, JAMES   CB   RAVENS

PERSONAL: Born December 28, 1969, in Greenville, S.C. ... 6-0/190. ... Full name: James Harold Trapp.
HIGH SCHOOL: Lawton (Okla.).
COLLEGE: Clemson.
TRANSACTIONS/CAREER NOTES: Selected by Los Angeles Raiders in third round (72nd pick overall) of 1993 NFL draft. ... Signed by Raiders (July 13, 1993). ... Raiders franchise moved to Oakland (July 21, 1995). ... Granted free agency (February 16, 1996). ... Re-signed by Raiders (March 30, 1996). ... Granted unconditional free agency (February 12, 1999). ... Signed by Baltimore Ravens (April 23, 1999). ... Granted unconditional free agency (February 11, 2000). ... Re-signed by Ravens (March 16, 2000).
PLAYING EXPERIENCE: Los Angeles Raiders NFL, 1993 and 1994; Oakland NFL, 1995-1998; Baltimore NFL, 1999. ... Games/Games started: 1993 (14/2), 1994 (16/2), 1995 (14/2), 1996 (12/4), 1997 (16/16), 1998 (16/0), 1999 (16/0). Total: 104/26.
PRO STATISTICS: 1993—Intercepted one pass for seven yards. 1994—Credited with one sack. 1995—Recovered one fumble. 1996—Intercepted one pass for 23 yards. 1997—Intercepted two passes for 24 yards and recovered two fumbles. 1999—Credited with one sack.

TRAYLOR, KEITH   DT   BRONCOS

PERSONAL: Born September 3, 1969, in Little Rock, Ark. ... 6-2/304. ... Full name: Byron Keith Traylor. ... Cousin of Isaac Davis, guard with San Diego Chargers (1994-97) and New Orleans Saints (1997).
HIGH SCHOOL: Malvern (Ark.).
JUNIOR COLLEGE: Coffeyville (Kan.) Community College.
COLLEGE: Oklahoma, then Central Oklahoma.
TRANSACTIONS/CAREER NOTES: Selected by Denver Broncos in third round (61st pick overall) of 1991 NFL draft. ... Signed by Broncos for 1991 season. ... Released by Broncos (June 7, 1993). ... Signed by Los Angeles Raiders (June 1993). ... Released by Raiders (August 30, 1993). ... Signed by Green Bay Packers (September 14, 1993). ... Released by Packers (November 9, 1993). ... Signed by Kansas City Chiefs (January 7, 1994). ... Released by Chiefs (January 14, 1994). ... Re-signed by Chiefs (May 18, 1994). ... Released by Chiefs (August 28, 1994). ... Re-signed by Chiefs (February 28, 1995). ... Granted unconditional free agency (February 14, 1997). ... Signed by Broncos (March 10, 1997).
CHAMPIONSHIP GAME EXPERIENCE: Played in AFC championship game (1991, 1997 and 1998 seasons). ... Member of Super Bowl championship team (1997 and 1998 seasons).
PRO STATISTICS: 1992—Returned one kickoff for 13 yards. 1995—Recovered one fumble. 1997—Intercepted one pass for 62 yards and a touchdown. 1998—Recovered one fumble.

Year Team	G	GS	SACKS
1991—Denver NFL	16	2	0.0
1992—Denver NFL	16	3	1.0
1993—Green Bay NFL	5	0	0.0
1994—	Did not play.		
1995—Barcelona W.L.	8	3	0.0
—Kansas City NFL	16	0	1.5
1996—Kansas City NFL	15	2	1.0
1997—Denver NFL	16	16	2.0
1998—Denver NFL	15	14	2.0
1999—Denver NFL	15	15	1.5
W.L. totals (1 year)	8	3	0.0
NFL totals (8 years)	114	52	9.0
Pro totals (9 years)	122	55	9.0

TREU, ADAM   C   RAIDERS

PERSONAL: Born June 24, 1974, in Lincoln, Neb. ... 6-5/300. ... Name pronounced TRUE.
HIGH SCHOOL: Pius X (Lincoln, Neb.).
COLLEGE: Nebraska.
TRANSACTIONS/CAREER NOTES: Selected by Oakland Raiders in third round (72nd pick overall) of 1997 NFL draft. ... Signed by Raiders for 1997 season.
PLAYING EXPERIENCE: Oakland NFL, 1997-1999. ... Games/Games started: 1997 (16/0), 1998 (16/0), 1999 (16/0). Total: 48/0.
PRO STATISTICS: 1999—Returned one kickoff for six yards and fumbled once.

TROTTER, JEREMIAH   LB   EAGLES

PERSONAL: Born January 20, 1977, in Hooks, Texas. ... 6-0/261.
HIGH SCHOOL: Hooks (Texas).

COLLEGE: Stephen F. Austin State.
TRANSACTIONS/CAREER NOTES: Selected after junior season by Philadelphia Eagles in third round (72nd pick overall) of 1998 NFL draft. ... Signed by Eagles (July 14, 1998).
PLAYING EXPERIENCE: Philadelphia NFL, 1998 and 1999. ... Games/Games started: 1998 (8/0), 1999 (16/16). Total: 24/16.
PRO STATISTICS: 1999—Intercepted two passes for 30 yards, credited with 2 1/2 sacks and recovered one fumble.

TUAOLO, ESERA   DT

PERSONAL: Born July 11, 1968, in Honolulu. ... 6-3/276. ... Full name: Esera Tavai Tuaolo. ... Name pronounced ess-ER-uh TOO-ah-OH-lo.
HIGH SCHOOL: Don Antonio Lugo (Chino, Calif.).
COLLEGE: Oregon State.
TRANSACTIONS/CAREER NOTES: Selected by Green Bay Packers in second round (35th pick overall) of 1991 NFL draft. ... Signed by Packers July 19, 1991). ... Released by Packers (October 1, 1992). ... Signed by Minnesota Vikings (November 24, 1992). ... Granted free agency February 17, 1994). ... Re-signed by Vikings (July 18, 1994). ... Granted unconditional free agency (February 17, 1995). ... Re-signed by Vikings (March 7, 1995). ... On physically unable to perform list with Achilles' tendon injury (July 22-August 26, 1996). ... Released by Vikings February 27, 1997). ... Signed by Buffalo Bills (June 25, 1997). ... Released by Bills (August 18, 1997). ... Signed by Jacksonville Jaguars November 4, 1997). ... Granted unconditional free agency (February 13, 1998). ... Signed by Atlanta Falcons (May 14, 1998). ... Granted unconditional free agency (February 12, 1999). ... Signed by Carolina Panthers (July 22, 1999). ... On injured reserve with groin injury December 7, 1999-remainder of season). ... Granted unconditional free agency (February 11, 2000).
CHAMPIONSHIP GAME EXPERIENCE: Played in NFC championship game (1998 season). ... Played in Super Bowl XXXIII (1998 season).
PRO STATISTICS: 1991—Intercepted one pass for 23 yards. 1995—Recovered two fumbles. 1998—Recovered one fumble. 1999—Recovered one fumble.

Year—Team	G	GS	SACKS
1991—Green Bay NFL	16	16	3.5
1992—Green Bay NFL	4	0	1.0
—Minnesota NFL	3	0	0.0
1993—Minnesota NFL	11	3	0.0
1994—Minnesota NFL	16	0	0.0
1995—Minnesota NFL	16	16	3.0
1996—Minnesota NFL	14	9	2.5
1997—Jacksonville NFL	6	1	1.0
1998—Atlanta NFL	13	1	0.0
1999—Carolina NFL	12	0	1.0
Pro totals (9 years)	111	46	12.0

TUBBS, WINFRED   LB   49ERS

PERSONAL: Born September 24, 1970, in Fairfield, Texas. ... 6-4/254. ... Full name: Winfred O'Neal Tubbs.
HIGH SCHOOL: Fairfield (Texas).
COLLEGE: Texas (degree in psychology, 1993).
TRANSACTIONS/CAREER NOTES: Selected by New Orleans Saints in third round (79th pick overall) of 1994 NFL draft. ... Signed by Saints July 20, 1994). ... On injured reserve with knee injury (December 22, 1995-remainder of season). ... Granted free agency (February 14, 1997). ... Re-signed by Saints (July 17, 1997). ... Granted unconditional free agency (February 13, 1998). ... Signed by San Francisco 49ers (February 18, 1998).
HONORS: Played in Pro Bowl (1998 season).
PRO STATISTICS: 1995—Recovered one fumble. 1996—Recovered one fumble. 1997—Recovered two fumbles. 1998—Recovered one fumble. 1999—Recovered one fumble.

			INTERCEPTIONS				SACKS
Year—Team	G	GS	No.	Yds.	Avg.	TD	No.
1994—New Orleans NFL	13	7	1	0	0.0	0	1.0
1995—New Orleans NFL	7	6	1	6	6.0	0	1.0
1996—New Orleans NFL	16	13	1	11	11.0	0	1.0
1997—New Orleans NFL	16	16	2	21	10.5	0	2.5
1998—San Francisco NFL	16	16	1	7	7.0	0	1.0
1999—San Francisco NFL	16	15	1	8	8.0	0	2.0
Pro totals (6 years)	84	73	7	53	7.6	0	8.5

TUCKER, JASON   WR   COWBOYS

PERSONAL: Born June 24, 1976, in Waco, Texas. ... 6-1/182.
HIGH SCHOOL: Robinson (Waco, Texas).
COLLEGE: Texas Christian.
TRANSACTIONS/CAREER NOTES: Selected after junior season by Cincinnati Bengals in sixth round (167th pick overall) of 1998 NFL draft. ... Signed by Bengals (July 19, 1998). ... Released by Bengals (August 19, 1998). ... Signed by Green Bay Packers to practice squad (October 28, 1998). ... Released by Packers (December 15, 1998). ... Signed by Dallas Cowboys (January 7, 1999). ... Assigned by Cowboys to Rhein Fire in 1999 NFL Europe enhancement allocation program (February 22, 1999).
PRO STATISTICS: NFL: 1999—Rushed once for eight yards and recovered one fumble.
SINGLE GAME HIGHS (regular season): Receptions—7 (December 24, 1999, vs. New Orleans); yards—128 (December 24, 1999, vs. New Orleans); and touchdown receptions—1 (January 2, 2000, vs. New York Giants).
STATISTICAL PLATEAUS: 100-yard receiving games: 1999 (2).

			RECEIVING				PUNT RETURNS				KICKOFF RETURNS				TOTALS			
Year—Team	G	GS	No.	Yds.	Avg.	TD	No.	Yds.	Avg.	TD	No.	Yds.	Avg.	TD	TD	2pt.	Pts.	Fum.
1999—Rhein NFLE	...	...	26	454	17.5	3	0	0	0.0	0	0	0	0.0	0	3	0	18	0
—Dallas NFL	15	4	23	439	19.1	2	4	52	13.0	0	22	613	27.9	0	2	0	12	1
NFL Europe totals (1 year)	...	...	26	454	17.5	3	0	0	0.0	0	0	0	0.0	0	3	0	18	0
NFL totals (1 year)	15	4	23	439	19.1	2	4	52	13.0	0	22	613	27.9	0	2	0	12	1
Pro totals (2 years)	...	...	49	893	18.2	5	4	52	13.0	0	22	613	27.9	0	5	0	30	1

TUCKER, REX   OL   BEARS

PERSONAL: Born December 20, 1976, in Midland, Texas ... 6-5/300. ... Full name: Rex Truman Tucker. ... Brother of Ryan Tucker, center, St
Louis Rams.
HIGH SCHOOL: Robert E. Lee (Midland, Texas).
COLLEGE: Texas A&M.
TRANSACTIONS/CAREER NOTES: Selected in third round by Chicago Bears (66th pick overall) of 1999 NFL draft. ... Signed by Bears (July
21, 1999).
PLAYING EXPERIENCE: Chicago NFL, 1999. ... Games/Games started: 1999 (2/1).

TUCKER, RYAN   C   RAMS

PERSONAL: Born June 12, 1975, in Midland, Texas. ... 6-5/305. ... Full name: Ryan Huey Tucker. ... Brother of Rex Tucker, offensive lineman
Chicago Bears.
HIGH SCHOOL: Robert E. Lee (Midland, Texas).
COLLEGE: Texas Christian.
TRANSACTIONS/CAREER NOTES: Selected by St. Louis Rams in fourth round (112th pick overall) of 1997 NFL draft. ... Signed by Rams (July
3, 1997). ... On physically unable to perform list with knee injury (August 19-October 29, 1997). ... Granted free agency (February 11, 2000)
... Tendered offer sheet by Miami Dolphins (February 17, 2000). ... Offer matched by Rams (February 22, 2000).
PLAYING EXPERIENCE: St. Louis NFL, 1997-1999. ... Games/Games started: 1997 (7/0), 1998 (4/0), 1999 (16/0). Total: 27/0.
CHAMPIONSHIP GAME EXPERIENCE: Played in NFC championship game (1999 season). ... Member of Super Bowl championship team (1999
season).
PRO STATISTICS: 1999—Caught one pass for two yards and a touchdown.

TUGGLE, JESSIE   LB   FALCONS

PERSONAL: Born April 4, 1965, in Spalding County, Ga. ... 5-11/232. ... Full name: Jessie Lloyd Tuggle Jr.
HIGH SCHOOL: Griffin (Ga.).
COLLEGE: Valdosta (Ga.) State.
TRANSACTIONS/CAREER NOTES: Signed as non-drafted free agent by Atlanta Falcons (May 2, 1987). ... Granted free agency (February 1
1991). ... Re-signed by Falcons (August 7, 1991). ... On reserve/did not report list (July 23-August 30, 1993). ... Granted roster exemption
(August 30-September 3, 1993). ... Granted unconditional free agency (February 11, 2000). ... Re-signed by Falcons (February 14, 2000).
CHAMPIONSHIP GAME EXPERIENCE: Played in NFC championship game (1998 season). ... Played in Super Bowl XXXIII (1998 season).
HONORS: Played in Pro Bowl (1992, 1994, 1995, 1997 and 1998 seasons).
RECORDS: Holds NFL career record for most touchdowns by recovery of opponents' fumbles—5; and most touchdowns by fumble recov-
ery—5.
PRO STATISTICS: 1988—Recovered one fumble for two yards and one touchdown. 1989—Recovered one fumble. 1990—Recovered two
fumbles for 65 yards and one touchdown. 1991—Recovered two fumbles for 18 yards and one touchdown. 1992—Recovered one fumble for
69 yards and one touchdown. 1993—Recovered one fumble. 1994—Recovered one fumble. 1998—Recovered one fumble for one yard and
a touchdown.

			INTERCEPTIONS				SACKS
Year Team	G	GS	No.	Yds.	Avg.	TD	No.
1987—Atlanta NFL	12	4	0	0	0.0	0	1.0
1988—Atlanta NFL	16	8	0	0	0.0	0	0.0
1989—Atlanta NFL	16	16	0	0	0.0	0	1.0
1990—Atlanta NFL	16	14	0	0	0.0	0	5.0
1991—Atlanta NFL	16	16	1	21	21.0	0	1.0
1992—Atlanta NFL	15	15	1	1	1.0	0	1.0
1993—Atlanta NFL	16	16	0	0	0.0	0	2.0
1994—Atlanta NFL	16	16	1	0	0.0	0	0.0
1995—Atlanta NFL	16	16	3	84	28.0	1	1.0
1996—Atlanta NFL	16	16	0	0	0.0	0	1.0
1997—Atlanta NFL	16	15	0	0	0.0	0	1.5
1998—Atlanta NFL	16	16	0	0	0.0	0	3.0
1999—Atlanta NFL	14	14	0	0	0.0	0	3.5
Pro totals (13 years)	201	182	6	106	17.7	1	21.0

TUINEI, VAN   DE   BEARS

PERSONAL: Born February 16, 1971, in Garden Grove, Calif. ... 6-4/275. ... Full name: Vaega Van Tuinei. ... Name pronounced TU-en-a.
HIGH SCHOOL: Westminster (Calif.).
JUNIOR COLLEGE: Golden West College (Calif.).
COLLEGE: Arizona.
TRANSACTIONS/CAREER NOTES: Signed as non-drafted free agent by San Diego Chargers (April 21, 1997). ... Released by Chargers (August
25, 1998). ... Re-signed by Chargers (August 27, 1998). ... Released by Chargers (August 30, 1998). ... Signed by Indianapolis Colts
(September 16, 1998). ... Claimed on waivers by Chicago Bears (September 6, 1999). ... Granted free agency (February 11, 2000). ... Re-
signed by Bears (April 26, 2000).
PLAYING EXPERIENCE: San Diego NFL, 1997; Indianapolis NFL, 1998; Chicago NFL, 1999. ... Games/Games started: 1997 (3/0), 1998 (12/0)
1999 (16/8). Total: 31/8.
PRO STATISTICS: 1998—Credited with two sacks and recovered one fumble. 1999—Returned one kickoff for no yards, credited with 2¹/₂
sacks and recovered two fumbles.

TUMAN, JERAME   TE   STEELERS

PERSONAL: Born March 24, 1976, in Liberal, Kan. ... 6-3/250. ... Full name: Jerame Dean Tuman. ... Name pronounced Jeremy TOO-man.
HIGH SCHOOL: Liberal (Kan.).
COLLEGE: Michigan.
TRANSACTIONS/CAREER NOTES: Selected by Pittsburgh Steelers in fifth round (136th pick overall) of 1999 NFL draft. ... Signed by Steelers July 19, 1999). ... On injured reserve with knee injury (October 27, 1999-remainder of season).
PLAYING EXPERIENCE: Pittsburgh NFL, 1999. ... Games/Games started: 1999 (7/0).
HONORS: Named tight end on THE SPORTING NEWS college All-America third team (1997).

TUPA, TOM   P/QB   JETS

PERSONAL: Born February 6, 1966, in Cleveland. ... 6-4/225. ... Full name: Thomas Joseph Tupa Jr.
HIGH SCHOOL: Brecksville (Broadview Heights, Ohio).
COLLEGE: Ohio State.
TRANSACTIONS/CAREER NOTES: Selected by Phoenix Cardinals in third round (68th pick overall) of 1988 NFL draft. ... Signed by Cardinals July 12, 1988). ... Granted free agency (February 1, 1991). ... Re-signed by Cardinals (July 17, 1991). ... Granted unconditional free agency February 1, 1992). ... Signed by Indianapolis Colts (March 31, 1992). ... Released by Colts (August 30, 1993). ... Signed by Cleveland Browns November 9, 1993). ... Released by Browns (November 24, 1993). ... Re-signed by Browns (March 30, 1994). ... Granted unconditional free agency (February 16, 1996). ... Signed by New England Patriots (March 15, 1996). ... Granted unconditional free agency (February 12, 1999). . Signed by New York Jets (February 15, 1999).
CHAMPIONSHIP GAME EXPERIENCE: Played in AFC championship game (1996 season). ... Played in Super Bowl XXXI (1996 season).
HONORS: Played in Pro Bowl (1999 season).
PRO STATISTICS: 1988—Attempted six passes with four completions for 49 yards. 1989—Rushed 15 times for 75 yards, attempted 134 passes with 65 completions for 973 yards (three touchdowns and nine interceptions), fumbled twice and recovered one fumble for minus six yards. 1990—Rushed once for no yards and fumbled once for minus seven yards. 1991—Rushed 28 times for 97 yards and a touchdown, attempted 315 passes with 165 completions for 2,053 yards (six touchdowns and 13 interceptions), fumbled eight times and recovered two fumbles. 1992—Rushed three times for nine yards, attempted 33 passes with 17 completions for 156 yards (one touchdwon and two inter- ceptions), fumbled once and recovered one fumble for minus one yard. 1995—Rushed once for nine yards, attempted one pass with a com- pletion for 25 yards. 1996—Attempted two passes without a completion. 1998—Rushed twice for minus two yards. 1999—Rushed twice for ight yards, attempted 11 passes with six completions for 165 yards and two touchdowns and fumbled once.
STATISTICAL PLATEAUS: 300-yard passing games: 1991 (1).
MISCELLANEOUS: Regular-season starting record as starting NFL quarterback: 4-9 (.308).

| | | | | PUNTING | | | |
Year Team	G	No.	Yds.	Avg.	Net avg.	In. 20	Blk.
1988—Phoenix NFL	2	0	0	0.0	.0	0	0
1989—Phoenix NFL	14	6	280	46.7	39.7	2	0
1990—Phoenix NFL	15	0	0	0.0	.0	0	0
1991—Phoenix NFL	11	0	0	0.0	.0	0	0
1992—Indianapolis NFL	3	0	0	0.0	.0	0	0
1993—Cleveland NFL				Did not play.			
1994—Cleveland NFL	16	80	3211	40.1	35.3	27	0
1995—Cleveland NFL	16	65	2831	43.6	36.2	18	0
1996—New England NFL	16	63	2739	43.5	36.0	14	0
1997—New England NFL	16	78	3569	§45.8	36.1	24	1
1998—New England NFL	16	74	3294	44.5	35.4	13	0
1999—New York Jets NFL	16	81	3659	45.2	38.2	25	0
Pro totals (11 years)	141	447	19583	43.8	36.3	123	1

TURK, DAN   C

PERSONAL: Born June 25, 1962, in Milwaukee. ... 6-4/290. ... Full name: Daniel Anthony Turk. ... Brother of Matt Turk, punter, Miami Dolphins.
HIGH SCHOOL: James Madison (Madison, Wis.).
COLLEGE: Drake, then Wisconsin.
TRANSACTIONS/CAREER NOTES: Selected by Jacksonville Bulls in USFL territorial draft. ... USFL rights traded by Bulls with rights to RB Marck Harrison and TE Ken Whisenhunt to Tampa Bay Bandits for rights to RB Cedric Jones, K Bobby Raymond and DB Eric Riley (January 8, 1985). ... Selected by Pittsburgh Steelers in fourth round (101st pick overall) of 1985 NFL draft. ... Signed by Steelers (July 19, 1985). ... On injured reserve with broken wrist (September 16, 1985-remainder of season). ... Traded by Steelers to Tampa Bay Buccaneers for sixth- round pick (DE Tim Johnson) in 1987 draft (April 13, 1987). ... Crossed picket line during players strike (October 14, 1987). ... On injured reserve with knee injury (October 18-November 18, 1988). ... Granted free agency (February 1, 1989). ... Rights relinquished by Buccaneers June 6, 1989). ... Signed by Los Angeles Raiders (June 21, 1989). ... Granted free agency (February 1, 1991). ... Re-signed by Raiders (July 2, 1991). ... Granted unconditional free agency (February 17, 1994). ... Re-signed by Raiders (February 23, 1994). ... Raiders franchise moved to Oakland (July 21, 1995). ... Granted unconditional free agency (February 14, 1997). ... Signed by Washington Redskins (July 10, 1997). ... Granted unconditional free agency (February 12, 1999). ... Re-signed by Redskins (June 2, 1999). ... Granted unconditional free agency February 11, 2000).
PLAYING EXPERIENCE: Pittsburgh NFL, 1985 and 1986; Tampa Bay NFL, 1987 and 1988; Los Angeles Raiders NFL, 1989-1994; Oakland NFL, 1995 and 1996; Washington NFL, 1997-1999. ... Games/Games started: 1985 (1/0), 1986 (16/4), 1987 (13/3), 1988 (12/10), 1989 (16/5), 1990 (16/0), 1991 (16/0), 1992 (16/0), 1993 (16/0), 1994 (16/0), 1995 (16/16), 1996 (16/2), 1997 (16/0), 1998 (16/0), 1999 (16/0). Total: 218/40.
CHAMPIONSHIP GAME EXPERIENCE: Played in AFC championship game (1990 season).
PRO STATISTICS: 1988—Fumbled once and recovered one fumble for minus 19 yards. 1989—Returned one kickoff for two yards and fum- bled once for minus eight yards. 1990—Returned one kickoff for seven yards. 1991—Returned one kickoff for no yards. 1992—Returned one kickoff for three yards. 1993—Returned one kickoff for no yards and recovered one fumble. 1996—Fumbled once and recovered one fumble or minus 29 yards. 1998—Fumbled once for minus four yards.

TURK, MATT   P   DOLPHINS

PERSONAL: Born June 16, 1968, in Greenfield, Wis. ... 6-5/235. ... Brother of Dan Turk, center with five NFL teams (1985-99).
HIGH SCHOOL: Greenfield (Wis.).
COLLEGE: Wisconsin-Whitewater.
TRANSACTIONS/CAREER NOTES: Signed as non-drafted free agent by Green Bay Packers (July 13, 1993). ... Released by Packers (August 4, 1993). ... Signed by Los Angeles Rams (April 1994). ... Released by Rams (August 22, 1994). ... Signed by Washington Redskins (April 5, 1995). ... Traded by Redskins to Miami Dolphins for conditional pick in 2001 draft (March 9, 2000).
HONORS: Played in Pro Bowl (1996-1998 seasons). ... Named punter on THE SPORTING NEWS NFL All-Pro team (1997).
PRO STATISTICS: 1996—Rushed once for no yards and fumbled once. 1997—Rushed once for no yards and fumbled once for minus 16 yards. 1998—Rushed twice for minus 12 yards and fumbled once. 1999—Fumbled once.

					PUNTING		
Year Team	G	No.	Yds.	Avg.	Net avg.	In. 20	Blk.
1995—Washington NFL	16	74	3140	42.4	37.7	†29	0
1996—Washington NFL	16	75	3386	*45.1	*39.2	25	0
1997—Washington NFL	16	84	3788	45.1	*39.2	32	1
1998—Washington NFL	16	93	4103	44.1	‡39.0	∞33	∞1
1999—Washington NFL	14	62	2564	41.4	35.6	16	0
Pro totals (5 years)	78	388	16981	43.8	38.3	135	2

TURLEY, KYLE   OT   SAINTS

PERSONAL: Born September 24, 1975, in Provo, Utah. ... 6-5/300. ... Full name: Kyle John Turley.
HIGH SCHOOL: Valley View (Moreno Valley, Calif.).
COLLEGE: San Diego State.
TRANSACTIONS/CAREER NOTES: Selected by New Orleans Saints in first round (seventh pick overall) of 1998 NFL draft. ... Signed by Saints (July 23, 1998).
PLAYING EXPERIENCE: New Orleans NFL, 1998 and 1999. ... Games/Games started: 1998 (15/15), 1999 (16/16). Total: 31/31.
HONORS: Named offensive tackle on THE SPORTING NEWS college All-America first team (1997).

IN MEMORIAM — ERIC TURNER

PERSONAL: Born September 20, 1968, in Ventura, Calif... Died May 28, 2000. ... 6-1/215. ... Full name: Eric Ray Turner.
HIGH SCHOOL: Ventura (Calif.).
COLLEGE: UCLA (degree in history, 1992).
TRANSACTIONS/CAREER NOTES: Selected by Cleveland Browns in first round (second pick overall) of 1991 NFL draft. ... Signed by Browns (July 14, 1991). ... On injured reserve with stress fracture in leg (August 28-November 2, 1991). ... Designated by Browns as transition player (February 25, 1993). ... Free agency status changed by Browns from transitional to franchise player (February 15, 1995). ... On injured reserve with back injury (December 15, 1995-remainder of season). ... Browns franchise moved to Baltimore and renamed Ravens for 1996 season (March 11, 1996). ... Released by Ravens (February 28, 1997). ... Signed by Oakland Raiders (April 24, 1997).
HONORS: Played in Pro Bowl (1994 and 1996 seasons).
PRO STATISTICS: 1991—Recovered one fumble. 1992—Credited with one sack and recovered two fumbles. 1994—Credited with one sack returned one punt for no yards and recovered one fumble. 1997—Fumbled once and recovered three fumbles for 65 yards and one touchdown. 1998—Credited with one sack. 1999—Recovered two fumbles for 34 yards.

			INTERCEPTIONS			
Year Team	G	GS	No.	Yds.	Avg.	TD
1991—Cleveland NFL	8	7	2	42	21.0	1
1992—Cleveland NFL	15	13	1	6	6.0	0
1993—Cleveland NFL	16	16	5	25	5.0	0
1994—Cleveland NFL	16	16	†9	199	22.1	1
1995—Cleveland NFL	8	8	0	0	0.0	0
1996—Baltimore NFL	14	14	5	1	0.2	0
1997—Oakland NFL	16	15	2	45	22.5	0
1998—Oakland NFL	6	6	3	108	*36.0	1
1999—Oakland NFL	10	10	3	43	14.3	0
Pro totals (9 years)	109	105	30	469	15.6	3

TURNER, KEVIN   FB

PERSONAL: Born June 12, 1969, in Prattville, Ala. ... 6-1/231. ... Full name: Paul Kevin Turner.
HIGH SCHOOL: Prattville (Ala.).
COLLEGE: Alabama.
TRANSACTIONS/CAREER NOTES: Selected by New England Patriots in third round (71st pick overall) of 1992 NFL draft. ... Signed by Patriots (July 21, 1992). ... Granted free agency (February 17, 1995). ... Tendered offer sheet by Philadelphia Eagles (February 26, 1995). ... Patriots declined to match offer (March 2, 1995). ... On injured reserve with knee injury (September 15, 1995-remainder of season). ... On injured reserve with neck injury (November 24, 1999-remainder of season). ... Granted unconditional free agency (February 11, 2000).
PRO STATISTICS: 1992—Returned one kickoff for 11 yards and recovered two fumbles. 1993—Attempted one pass without a completion and recovered two fumbles for six yards. 1994—Recovered two fumbles for minus three yards. 1997—Returned three kickoffs for 48 yards 1998—Returned one kickoff for 15 yards. 1999—Recovered one fumble.
SINGLE GAME HIGHS (regular season): Attempts—12 (October 24, 1993 vs. Seattle); yards—63 (December 19, 1993, vs. Cleveland); and rushing touchdowns—1 (September 4, 1994, vs. Miami).

			RUSHING				RECEIVING				TOTALS			
Year Team	G	GS	Att.	Yds.	Avg.	TD	No.	Yds.	Avg.	TD	TD	2pt.	Pts.	Fum.
1992—New England NFL	16	1	10	40	4.0	0	7	52	7.4	2	2	0	12	2

Year—Team													
1993—New England NFL	16	9	50	231	4.6	0	39	333	8.5	2	2	0	12	1
1994—New England NFL	16	9	36	111	3.1	1	52	471	9.1	2	3	0	18	4
1995—Philadelphia NFL	2	2	2	9	4.5	0	4	29	7.3	0	0	0	0	0
1996—Philadelphia NFL	16	12	18	39	2.2	0	43	409	9.5	1	1	0	6	1
1997—Philadelphia NFL	16	10	18	96	5.3	0	48	443	9.2	3	3	0	18	1
1998—Philadelphia NFL	16	15	20	94	4.7	0	34	232	6.8	0	0	0	0	1
1999—Philadelphia NFL	8	7	6	15	2.5	0	9	46	5.1	0	0	0	0	1
Pro totals (8 years)	106	65	160	635	4.0	1	236	2015	8.5	10	11	0	66	11

TURNER, SCOTT   CB   CHARGERS

PERSONAL: Born February 26, 1972, in Richardson, Texas. ... 5-10/180.
HIGH SCHOOL: J.J. Pearce (Richardson, Texas).
COLLEGE: Illinois (degree in speech communications, 1994).
TRANSACTIONS/CAREER NOTES: Selected by Washington Redskins in seventh round (226th pick overall) of 1995 NFL draft. ... Signed by Redskins (July 18, 1995). ... On injured reserve with ankle injury (December 11, 1997-remainder of season). ... Granted free agency (February 13, 1998). ... Re-signed by Redskins (April 30, 1998). ... Claimed on waivers by San Diego Chargers (August 31, 1998). ... Granted unconditional free agency (February 11, 2000). ... Re-signed by Chargers (April 3, 2000).
PRO STATISTICS: 1995—Returned one punt for no yards, credited with one sack, fumbled once and recovered one fumble. 1996—Recovered one fumble in end zone for a touchdown. 1998—Credited with one sack. 1999—Returned one punt for no yards and recovered one fumble.

			INTERCEPTIONS			
Year Team	G	GS	No.	Yds.	Avg.	TD
1995—Washington NFL	16	0	1	0	0.0	0
1996—Washington NFL	16	0	2	16	8.0	0
1997—Washington NFL	9	0	0	0	0.0	0
1998—San Diego NFL	16	1	1	0	0.0	0
1999—San Diego NFL	15	0	0	0	0.0	0
Pro totals (5 years)	72	1	4	16	4.0	0

TUTEN, MELVIN   OT   BRONCOS

PERSONAL: Born November 11, 1971, in Washington, D.C. ... 6-6/305. ... Full name: Melvin Eugene Tuten Jr.
HIGH SCHOOL: Woodrow Wilson (Washington, D.C.).
COLLEGE: Syracuse.
TRANSACTIONS/CAREER NOTES: Selected by Cincinnati Bengals in third round (69th pick overall) of 1995 NFL draft. ... Signed by Bengals (July 18, 1995). ... Released by Bengals (August 18, 1997). ... Signed by Denver Broncos (February 5, 1998). ... Released by Broncos (August 25, 1998). ... Re-signed by Broncos (December 30, 1998). ... Assigned by Broncos to Barcelona Dragons in 1999 NFL Europe enhancement allocation program (February 22, 1999). ... Released by Broncos (September 5, 1999). ... Re-signed by Broncos (November 10, 1999).
PLAYING EXPERIENCE: Cincinnati NFL, 1995 and 1996; Barcelona NFLE, 1999; Denver NFL, 1999. ... Games/Games started: 1995 (16/2), 1996 (16/7), NFLE 1999 (games played unavailable), NFL 1999 (2/0). Total NFL: 34/9.
PRO STATISTICS: 1995—Caught two passes for 12 yards and one touchdown.

TUTEN, RICK   P   RAMS

PERSONAL: Born January 5, 1965, in Perry, Fla. ... 6-2/221. ... Full name: Richard Lamar Tuten.
HIGH SCHOOL: Forest (Ocala, Fla.).
COLLEGE: Miami (Fla.), then Florida State (degree in economics, 1986).
TRANSACTIONS/CAREER NOTES: Signed as non-drafted free agent by San Diego Chargers (May 10, 1988). ... Released by Chargers (August 23, 1988). ... Signed by Washington Redskins (June 2, 1989). ... Released by Redskins (August 27, 1989). ... Signed by Philadelphia Eagles (December 13, 1989). ... Granted unconditional free agency (February 1, 1990). ... Signed by Buffalo Bills (March 28, 1990). ... Released by Bills (August 15, 1990). ... Re-signed by Bills (September 19, 1990). ... Granted unconditional free agency (February 1-April 1, 1991). ... Re-signed by Bills for 1991 season. ... Released by Bills (August 20, 1991). ... Signed by Green Bay Packers (August 27, 1991). ... Released by Packers (August 30, 1991). ... Signed by Seattle Seahawks (October 9, 1991). ... Granted unconditional free agency (February 1-April 1, 1992). ... Re-signed by Seahawks for 1992 season. ... Granted unconditional free agency (February 16, 1996). ... Re-signed by Seahawks (August 12, 1996). ... On injured reserve with pelvis injury (December 5, 1997-remainder of season). ... Granted unconditional free agency (February 13, 1998). ... Signed by St. Louis Rams (March 10, 1998). ... On injured reserve with thigh injury (November 10, 1999-remainder of season).
CHAMPIONSHIP GAME EXPERIENCE: Played in AFC championship game (1990 season). ... Played in Super Bowl XXV (1990 season).
HONORS: Played in Pro Bowl (1994 season).
PRO STATISTICS: 1992—Attempted one pass without a completion, rushed once for no yards, fumbled twice and recovered two fumbles for minus nine yards. 1993—Attempted one pass without a completion. 1994—Credited with a two-point conversion and attempted one pass without a completion. 1998—Attempted one pass without a completion.

		PUNTING					
Year Team	G	No.	Yds.	Avg.	Net avg.	In. 20	Blk.
1989—Philadelphia NFL	2	7	256	36.6	33.6	1	0
1990—Buffalo NFL	14	53	2107	39.8	34.2	12	0
1991—Seattle NFL	10	49	2106	43.0	36.8	8	0
1992—Seattle NFL	16	*108	*4760	44.1	38.7	*29	0
1993—Seattle NFL	16	▲90	*4007	44.5	37.2	21	1
1994—Seattle NFL	16	91	3905	42.9	36.7	33	0
1995—Seattle NFL	16	83	3735	*45.0	36.5	21	0
1996—Seattle NFL	16	85	3746	44.1	34.5	20	1
1997—Seattle NFL	11	48	2007	41.8	36.4	15	0
1998—St. Louis NFL	16	95	4202	44.2	35.3	16	0
1999—St. Louis NFL	8	32	1359	42.5	34.9	9	0
Pro totals (11 years)	141	741	32190	43.4	36.3	185	2

TYLSKI, RICH   G   STEELERS

PERSONAL: Born February 27, 1971, in San Diego. ... 6-5/308. ... Full name: Richard Lee Tylski. ... Name pronounced TILL-skee.
HIGH SCHOOL: Madison (San Diego).
COLLEGE: Utah State (degree in sociology, 1994).
TRANSACTIONS/CAREER NOTES: Signed as non-drafted free agent by New England Patriots (April 25, 1994). ... Released by Patriots (August 20, 1994). ... Re-signed by Patriots to practice squad (August 30, 1994). ... Claimed on waivers by Jacksonville Jaguars (July 26, 1995). ... Released by Jaguars (August 27, 1995). ... Re-signed by Jaguars to practice squad (August 28, 1995). ... Granted free agency (February 12, 1999). ... Re-signed by Jaguars (May 5, 1999). ... Granted unconditional free agency (February 11, 2000). ... Signed by Pittsburgh Steelers (February 28, 2000).
PLAYING EXPERIENCE: Jacksonville NFL, 1996-1999. ... Games/Games started: 1996 (16/7), 1997 (13/13), 1998 (11/8), 1999 (10/8). Total 50/36.
CHAMPIONSHIP GAME EXPERIENCE: Played in AFC championship game (1999 season).

ULMER, ARTIE   LB

PERSONAL: Born July 30, 1973, in Rincon, Ga. ... 6-3/247. ... Full name: Charles Artie Ulmer.
HIGH SCHOOL: Effingham County (Springfield, Ga.).
COLLEGE: Georgia Southern, then Valdosta (Ga.) State.
TRANSACTIONS/CAREER NOTES: Selected by Minnesota Vikings in seventh round (220th pick overall) of 1997 NFL draft. ... On suspended list for violating league substance abuse policy (August 19-September 23, 1997). ... Signed by Vikings (June 17, 1997). ... Assigned by Vikings to Frankfurt Galaxy in 1998 NFL Europe enhancement allocation program (February 18, 1998). ... Released by Vikings (August 24, 1998). ... Signed by Denver Broncos (January 14, 1999). ... On injured reserve with knee injury (November 4, 1999-remainder of season). ... Granted free agency (February 11, 2000).
PLAYING EXPERIENCE: Frankfurt NFLE, 1998; Denver NFL, 1999. ... Games/Games started: 1998 (games played unavailable), 1999 (7/0).
PRO STATISTICS: NFLE: 1998—Credited with three sacks.

UNUTOA, MORRIS   C   BUCCANEERS

PERSONAL: Born March 10, 1971, in Torrance, Calif. ... 6-1/284. ... Full name: Morris Taua Unutoa. ... Name pronounced oo-nuh-TOE-uh.
HIGH SCHOOL: Carson (Calif.).
COLLEGE: Brigham Young.
TRANSACTIONS/CAREER NOTES: Signed as non-drafted free agent by Philadelphia Eagles (April 26, 1996). ... Granted free agency (February 12, 1999). ... Re-signed by Eagles (March 24, 1999). ... Released by Eagles (September 8, 1999). ... Signed by Tampa Bay Buccaneers (October 5, 1999).
PLAYING EXPERIENCE: Philadelphia NFL, 1996-1998; Tampa Bay NFL, 1999. ... Games/Games started: 1996 (16/0), 1997 (16/0), 1998 (16/0) 1999 (12/0). Total: 60/0.
CHAMPIONSHIP GAME EXPERIENCE: Played in NFC championship game (1999 season).
PRO STATISTICS: 1996—Fumbled once.

UPSHAW, REGAN   DE   RAIDERS

PERSONAL: Born August 12, 1975, in Barrien Springs, Mich. ... 6-4/260. ... Full name: Regan Charles Upshaw.
HIGH SCHOOL: Pittsburg (Calif.).
COLLEGE: California.
TRANSACTIONS/CAREER NOTES: Selected after junior season by Tampa Bay Buccaneers in first round (12th pick overall) of 1996 NFL draft. ... Signed by Buccaneers (July 21, 1996). ... Traded by Buccaneers to Jacksonville Jaguars for undisclosed draft pick (October 19, 1999). ... Granted unconditional free agency (February 11, 2000). ... Signed by Oakland Raiders (February 28, 2000).
CHAMPIONSHIP GAME EXPERIENCE: Played in AFC championship game (1999 season).
PRO STATISTICS: 1996—Recovered one fumble. 1997—Recovered one fumble. 1998—Intercepted one pass for 26 yards.

Year Team	G	GS	SACKS
1996—Tampa Bay NFL	16	16	4.0
1997—Tampa Bay NFL	15	15	7.5
1998—Tampa Bay NFL	16	16	7.0
1999—Tampa Bay NFL	1	0	0.0
—Jacksonville NFL	6	0	0.0
Pro totals (4 years)	**54**	**47**	**18.5**

UWAEZUOKE, IHEANYI   WR

PERSONAL: Born July 24, 1973, in Lagos, Nigeria ... 6-2/198. ... Name pronounced ee-HAHN-ee oo-WAY-zoo-kay.
HIGH SCHOOL: Harvard (North Hollywood, Calif.).
COLLEGE: California (degree in political science, 1995).
TRANSACTIONS/CAREER NOTES: Selected by San Francisco 49ers in fifth round (160th pick overall) of 1996 NFL draft. ... Signed by 49ers (July 18, 1996). ... Claimed on waivers by Miami Dolphins (November 9, 1998). ... Granted free agency (February 12, 1999). ... Signed by Carolina Panthers (April 7, 1999). ... Released by Panthers (September 5, 1999). ... Signed by Detroit Lions (September 15, 1999). ... Granted unconditional free agency (February 11, 2000).
CHAMPIONSHIP GAME EXPERIENCE: Played in NFC championship game (1997 season).
PRO STATISTICS: 1997—Recovered two fumbles.
SINGLE GAME HIGHS (regular season): Receptions—3 (November 2, 1997, vs. Dallas); yards—41 (September 21, 1997, vs. Atlanta); and touchdown receptions—1 (November 10, 1996, vs. Dallas).

Year Team	G	GS	RECEIVING				PUNT RETURNS				KICKOFF RETURNS				TOTALS			
			No.	Yds.	Avg.	TD	No.	Yds.	Avg.	TD	No.	Yds.	Avg.	TD	TD	2pt.	Pts.	Fum.
1996—San Francisco NFL	14	0	7	91	13.0	1	0	0	0.0	0	1	21	21.0	0	1	0	6	0
1997—San Francisco NFL	14	0	14	165	11.8	0	34	373	11.0	0	6	131	21.8	0	0	0	0	4
1998—San Francisco NFL	7	0	3	67	22.3	0	0	0	0.0	0	0	0	0.0	0	0	0	0	0
—Miami NFL	4	0	0	0	0.0	0	0	0	0.0	0	0	0	0.0	0	0	0	0	0
1999—Detroit NFL	10	0	1	5	5.0	0	18	150	8.3	0	0	0	0.0	0	0	0	0	1
Pro totals (4 years)	49	0	25	328	13.1	1	52	523	10.1	0	7	152	21.7	0	1	0	6	5

VANCE, ERIC S CHARGERS

PERSONAL: Born July 14, 1975, in Tampa. ... 6-2/218.
HIGH SCHOOL: L.D. Bell (Hurst, Texas).
COLLEGE: Vanderbilt.
TRANSACTIONS/CAREER NOTES: Signed as non-drafted free agent by Carolina Panthers (April 25, 1997). ... Released by Panthers (September 1, 1997). ... Signed by San Diego Chargers to practice squad (December 3, 1997). ... Granted free agency after 1997 season. ... Signed by Tampa Bay Buccaneers (December 30, 1997). ... Released by Buccaneers (August 25, 1998). ... Signed by Indianapolis Colts to practice squad (August 31, 1998). ... Signed by Buccaneers off Colts practice squad (October 28, 1998). ... On injured reserve with foot injury (November 10-December 7, 1999). ... Released by Buccaneers (December 7, 1999). ... Signed by San Diego Chargers (February 22, 2000).
PLAYING EXPERIENCE: Tampa Bay NFL, 1998 and 1999. ... Games/Games started: 1998 (3/1), 1999 (6/0). Total: 9/1.

VANDERJAGT, MIKE K COLTS

PERSONAL: Born March 24, 1970, in Oakville, Ont. ... 6-5/210. ... Name pronounced vander-JAT.
HIGH SCHOOL: White Oaks (Ont.).
JUNIOR COLLEGE: Allan Hancock College (Calif.).
COLLEGE: West Virginia.
TRANSACTIONS/CAREER NOTES: Signed by Saskatchewan Roughriders prior to 1993 season. ... Signed by Toronto Argonauts of CFL (February 15, 1994). ... Released by Argonauts (June 13, 1994). ... Signed by Hamilton Tiger-Cats of CFL (June 24, 1994). ... Released by Tiger-Cats (July 11, 1994). ... Signed by Argonauts (March 16, 1995). ... Released by Argonauts (June 25, 1995). ... Re-signed by Argonauts of CFL (May 10, 1996). ... Signed as non-drafted free agent by Indianapolis Colts (March 4, 1998).
CHAMPIONSHIP GAME EXPERIENCE: Member of CFL championship team (1996 and 1997).
HONORS: Named Most Outstanding Canadian Player in Grey Cup (1996). ... Named to CFL All-Star team (1997).
PRO STATISTICS: CFL: 1996—Attempted two passes with one completion for 28 yards. 1997—Attempted one pass without a completion, rushed twice for 25 yards and fumbled once.

Year Team	G	PUNTING						KICKING						
		No.	Yds.	Avg.	Net avg.	In. 20	Blk.	XPM	XPA	FGM	FGA	Lg.	50+	Pts.
1993—Saskatchewan CFL	2	17	672	39.5	32.1	0	0	0	0	0	0	0	0-0	0
1994—								Did not play.						
1995—								Did not play.						
1996—Toronto CFL	18	103	4459	43.3	35.1	0	0	59	59	40	56	51	0-0	179
1997—Toronto CFL	18	118	5303	44.9	37.4	0	0	77	77	33	43	51	0-0	176
1998—Indianapolis NFL	14	0	0	0.0	.0	0	0	23	23	27	31	53	6-9	104
1999—Indianapolis NFL	16	0	0	0.0	0.0	0	0	43	43	34	38	53	1-2	*145
CFL totals (3 years)	38	238	10434	43.8	36.0	0	0	136	136	73	99	51	0-0	355
NFL totals (2 years)	30	0	0	0.0	0.0	0	0	66	66	61	69	53	7-11	249
Pro totals (5 years)	68	238	10434	43.8	36.0	0	0	202	202	134	168	53	7-0	604

VAN DYKE, ALEX WR EAGLES

PERSONAL: Born July 24, 1974, in Sacramento. ... 6-0/205. ... Full name: Franklin Alexander Van Dyke.
HIGH SCHOOL: Luther Burbank (Sacramento).
JUNIOR COLLEGE: Sacramento City College.
COLLEGE: Nevada.
TRANSACTIONS/CAREER NOTES: Selected by New York Jets in second round (31st pick overall) of 1996 NFL draft. ... Signed by Jets (July 15, 1996). ... Traded by Jets to Pittsburgh Steelers for sixth-round pick (LB Marc Megna) in 1999 draft (March 25, 1999). ... Released by Steelers (September 5, 1999). ... Signed by Philadelphia Eagles (October 12, 1999).
CHAMPIONSHIP GAME EXPERIENCE: Played in AFC championship game (1998 season).
HONORS: Named wide receiver on THE SPORTING NEWS college All-America second team (1995).
SINGLE GAME HIGHS (regular season): Receptions—4 (October 13, 1996, vs. Jacksonville); yards—35 (December 7, 1997, vs. Indianapolis); and touchdown receptions—2 (December 7, 1997, vs. Indianapolis).

Year Team	G	GS	RECEIVING				KICKOFF RETURNS				TOTALS			
			No.	Yds.	Avg.	TD	No.	Yds.	Avg.	TD	TD	2pt.	Pts.	Fum.
1996—New York Jets NFL	15	1	17	118	6.9	1	15	289	19.3	0	1	0	6	0
1997—New York Jets NFL	5	0	3	53	17.7	2	6	138	23.0	0	2	0	12	0
1998—New York Jets NFL	16	0	5	40	8.0	0	0	0	0.0	0	0	0	0	0
1999—Philadelphia NFL	2	0	0	0	0.0	0	0	0	0.0	0	0	0	0	0
Pro totals (4 years)	38	1	25	211	8.4	3	21	427	20.3	0	3	0	18	0

VANOVER, TAMARICK WR/KR

PERSONAL: Born February 25, 1974, in Tallahassee, Fla. ... 5-11/220. ... Name pronounced tom-ARE-ik.
HIGH SCHOOL: Leon (Tallahassee, Fla.).
COLLEGE: Florida State.

V

TRANSACTIONS/CAREER NOTES: Signed after sophomore season with Las Vegas Posse of CFL (February 13, 1994). ... Selected by Kansas City Chiefs in third round (81st pick overall) of 1995 NFL draft. ... Signed by Chiefs for 1995 season. ... Released by Chiefs (April 14, 2000).
HONORS: Named kick returner on THE SPORTING NEWS college All-America first team (1992). ... Named kick returner on THE SPORTING NEWS college All-America second team (1993).
PRO STATISTICS: CFL: 1994—Returned four unsuccessful field-goals for 31 yards, fumbled three times and recovered one fumble. NFL: 1996—Fumbled once. 1997—Fumbled six times and recovered one fumble. 1998—Fumbled twice. 1999—Fumbled three times and recovered one fumble.
SINGLE GAME HIGHS (regular season): Receptions—7 (September 1, 1996, vs. Houston); yards—85 (November 23, 1995, vs. Dallas); and touchdown receptions—1 (September 1, 1996, vs. Houston).

			RUSHING				RECEIVING				PUNT RETURNS				KICKOFF RETURNS				TOTALS		
Year Team	G	GS	Att.	Yds.	Avg.	TD	No.	Yds.	Avg.	TD	No.	Yds.	Avg.	TD	No.	Yds.	Avg.	TD	TD	2pt.	Pts.
1994—Las Vegas CFL	15	...	1	6	6.0	0	23	385	16.7	3	36	341	9.5	1	31	718	23.2	1	5	1	32
1995—Kansas City NFL..	15	0	6	31	5.2	0	11	231	21.0	2	§51	*540	10.6	†1	43	1095	25.5	†2	5	0	30
1996—Kansas City NFL..	13	6	4	6	1.5	0	21	241	11.5	1	17	116	6.8	0	33	854	§25.9	▲1	2	0	12
1997—Kansas City NFL..	16	0	5	50	10.0	0	7	92	13.1	0	35	383	10.9	1	51	1308	25.6	▲1	2	1	14
1998—Kansas City NFL..	12	0	2	1	0.5	0	0	0	0.0	0	27	264	9.8	0	41	956	23.3	0	0	0	0
1999—Kansas City NFL..	14	0	0	0	0.0	0	0	0	0.0	0	51	*627	12.3	†2	44	886	20.1	0	2	0	12
CFL totals (1 year)........	15	...	1	6	6.0	0	23	385	16.7	3	36	341	9.5	1	31	718	23.2	1	5	1	32
NFL totals (5 years).......	70	6	17	88	5.2	0	39	564	14.5	3	181	1930	10.7	4	212	5099	24.1	4	11	1	68
Pro totals (6 years)........	85	...	18	94	5.2	0	62	949	15.3	6	217	2271	10.5	5	243	5817	23.9	5	16	2	100

VAN PELT, ALEX   QB

PERSONAL: Born May 1, 1970, in Pittsburgh ... 6-0/220. ... Full name: Gregory Alexander Van Pelt.
HIGH SCHOOL: Grafton (W.Va.), then Winston Churchill (San Antonio).
COLLEGE: Pittsburgh.
TRANSACTIONS/CAREER NOTES: Selected by Pittsburgh Steelers in eighth round (216th pick overall) of 1993 NFL draft. ... Signed by Steelers for 1993 season. ... Released by Steelers (August 30, 1993). ... Signed by Kansas City Chiefs to practice squad (November 3, 1993). ... Activated (November 8, 1993); did not play. ... Released by Chiefs (November 17, 1993). ... Re-signed by Chiefs (May 18, 1994). ... Released by Chiefs (August 23, 1994). ... Signed by Buffalo Bills to practice squad (December 14, 1994). ... Activated (December 17, 1994); did not play. ... Granted unconditional free agency (February 11, 2000).
PRO STATISTICS: 1997—Fumbled three times and recovered three fumbles for minus seven yards.
SINGLE GAME HIGHS (regular season): Attempts—44 (December 20, 1997, vs. Green Bay); completions—23 (December 20, 1997, vs. Green Bay); yards—255 (December 20, 1997, vs. Green Bay); and touchdown passes—2 (October 26, 1997, vs. Denver).
MISCELLANEOUS: Regular-season record as starting NFL quarterback: 1-2 (.333).

			PASSING								RUSHING				TOTALS		
Year Team	G	GS	Att.	Cmp.	Pct.	Yds.	TD	Int.	Avg.	Rat.	Att.	Yds.	Avg.	TD	TD	2pt.	Pts.
1993—Kansas City NFL.........						Did not play.											
1994—Buffalo NFL................						Did not play.											
1995—Buffalo NFL................	1	0	18	10	55.6	106	2	0	5.89	110.0	0	0	0.0	0	0	0	0
1996—Buffalo NFL................	1	0	5	2	40.0	9	0	0	1.80	47.9	3	-5	-1.7	0	0	0	0
1997—Buffalo NFL................	6	3	124	60	48.4	684	2	10	5.52	37.2	11	33	3.0	1	1	0	6
1998—Buffalo NFL................	1	0	0	0	0.0	0	0	0	0.0	...	1	-1	-1.0	0	0	0	0
1999—Buffalo NFL................	1	0	1	1	100.0	9	0	0	9.00	104.2	1	-1	-1.0	0	0	0	0
Pro totals (5 years).............	10	3	148	73	49.3	808	4	10	5.46	46.8	16	26	1.6	1	1	0	6

VARDELL, TOMMY   FB

V

PERSONAL: Born February 20, 1969, in El Cajon, Calif. ... 6-2/234. ... Full name: Thomas Arthur Vardell.
HIGH SCHOOL: Granite Hills (El Cajon, Calif.).
COLLEGE: Stanford (degree in industrial engineering, 1992).
TRANSACTIONS/CAREER NOTES: Selected by Cleveland Browns in first round (ninth pick overall) of 1992 NFL draft. ... Signed by Browns (July 26, 1992). ... On injured reserve with calf injury (December 26, 1992-remainder of season). ... On injured reserve with knee injury (October 5, 1994-remainder of season). ... On physically unable to perform list with knee injury (July 17-23, 1995). ... Granted unconditional free agency (February 16, 1996). ... Signed by San Francisco 49ers (March 25, 1996). ... Released by 49ers (February 13, 1997). ... Signed by Detroit Lions (April 23, 1997). ... Granted unconditional free agency (February 12, 1999). ... Signed by 49ers (April 23, 1999). ... Announced retirement (February 4, 2000).
PRO STATISTICS: 1992—Returned two kickoffs for 14 yards. 1993—Returned four kickoffs for 58 yards. 1997—Returned one kickoff for 15 yards and recovered one fumble. 1998—Returned one kickoff for 23 yards.
SINGLE GAME HIGHS (regular season): Attempts—25 (October 17, 1993, vs. Cincinnati); yards—104 (September 19, 1993, vs. Los Angeles Raiders); and rushing touchdowns—3 (November 16, 1997, vs. Minnesota).
STATISTICAL PLATEAUS: 100-yard rushing games: 1993 (1).

			RUSHING				RECEIVING				TOTALS			
Year Team	G	GS	Att.	Yds.	Avg.	TD	No.	Yds.	Avg.	TD	TD	2pt.	Pts.	Fum.
1992—Cleveland NFL..................................	14	10	99	369	3.7	0	13	128	9.8	0	0	0	0	0
1993—Cleveland NFL..................................	16	12	171	644	3.8	3	19	151	7.9	1	4	0	24	3
1994—Cleveland NFL..................................	5	5	15	48	3.2	0	16	137	8.6	1	1	0	6	0
1995—Cleveland NFL..................................	5	0	4	9	2.3	0	6	18	3.0	0	0	0	0	0
1996—San Francisco NFL............................	11	7	58	192	3.3	2	28	179	6.4	0	2	0	12	0
1997—Detroit NFL.....................................	16	10	32	122	3.8	6	16	218	13.6	0	6	0	36	1
1998—Detroit NFL.....................................	14	9	18	37	2.1	6	14	143	10.2	1	7	0	42	1
1999—San Francisco NFL............................	6	4	6	6	1.0	1	7	36	5.1	0	1	0	6	0
Pro totals (8 years).................................	87	57	403	1427	3.5	18	119	1010	8.5	3	21	0	126	5

VERBA, ROSS   G/OT   PACKERS

PERSONAL: Born October 31, 1973, in Des Moines, Iowa. ... 6-4/308. ... Full name: Ross Robert Verba.
HIGH SCHOOL: Dowling (West Des Moines, Iowa).
COLLEGE: Iowa.
TRANSACTIONS/CAREER NOTES: Selected by Green Bay Packers in first round (30th pick overall) of 1997 NFL draft. ... Signed by Packers (July 31, 1997).
PLAYING EXPERIENCE: Green Bay NFL, 1997-1999. ... Games/Games started: 1997 (16/11), 1998 (16/16), 1999 (11/10). Total: 43/37.
CHAMPIONSHIP GAME EXPERIENCE: Played in NFC championship game (1997 season). ... Played in Super Bowl XXXII (1997 season).
PRO STATISTICS: 1999—Recovered one fumble for two yards.

VICKERS, KIPP   OL   RAVENS

PERSONAL: Born August 27, 1969, in Tarpon Springs, Fla. ... 6-2/298. ... Full name: Kipp Emmanuel Vickers.
HIGH SCHOOL: Tarpon Springs (Fla.).
COLLEGE: Miami (Fla.).
TRANSACTIONS/CAREER NOTES: Signed as non-drafted free agent by Indianapolis Colts (April 30, 1993). ... Released by Colts (August 30, 1993). ... Re-signed by Colts to practice squad (September 1, 1993). ... Activated (December 21, 1993); did not play. ... Released by Colts (August 28, 1994). ... Re-signed by Colts to practice squad (August 31, 1994). ... Released by Colts (November 1, 1994). ... Re-signed by Colts to practice squad (November 16, 1994). ... Activated (December 24, 1994); did not play. ... Assigned by Colts to Frankfurt Galaxy in 1995 World League enhancement allocation program (February 20, 1995). ... Released by Colts (February 4, 1997). ... Re-signed by Colts for 1997 season. ... Granted free agency (February 13, 1998). ... Re-signed by Colts (February 24, 1998). ... Released by Colts (August 24, 1998). ... Signed by Washington Redskins (November 24, 1998). ... Inactive for five games (1998). ... Granted free agency (February 12, 1999). ... Re-signed by Redskins (February 23, 1999). ... Granted unconditional free agency (February 11, 2000). ... Signed by Baltimore Ravens (February 17, 2000).
PLAYING EXPERIENCE: Frankfurt W. L., 1995; Indianapolis NFL, 1995-1997; Washington NFL, 1999. ... Games/Games started: W.L. 1995 (games played unavailable), NFL 1995 (9/10), 1996 (10/6), 1997 (9/0), 1999 (11/0). Total NFL: 39/6.
CHAMPIONSHIP GAME EXPERIENCE: Played in AFC championship game (1995 season).

VILLARRIAL, CHRIS   C   BEARS

PERSONAL: Born June 9, 1973, in Hummelstown, Pa. ... 6-4/310. ... Name pronounced vuh-LAR-ree-uhl.
HIGH SCHOOL: Hershey (Pa.).
COLLEGE: Indiana University (Pa.).
TRANSACTIONS/CAREER NOTES: Selected by Chicago Bears in fifth round (152nd pick overall) of 1996 NFL draft. ... Signed by Bears (July 11, 1996). ... Granted free agency (February 12, 1999). ... Re-signed by Bears (April 16, 1999).
PLAYING EXPERIENCE: Chicago NFL, 1996-1999. ... Games/Games started: 1996 (14/8), 1997 (11/11), 1998 (16/16), 1999 (15/15). Total: 56/50.
PRO STATISTICS: 1998—Recovered one fumble. 1999—Recovered two fumbles.

VINATIERI, ADAM   K   PATRIOTS

PERSONAL: Born December 28, 1972, in Yunkton, S.D. ... 6-0/200. ... Full name: Adam Matthew Vinatieri. ... Name pronounced VIN-a-TERRY.
HIGH SCHOOL: Rapid City (S.D.) Central.
COLLEGE: South Dakota State (degree in fitness and wellness).
TRANSACTIONS/CAREER NOTES: Signed by Amsterdam Admirals of World League for 1996 season. ... Signed as non-drafted free agent by New England Patriots (June 28, 1996). ... Granted free agency (February 12, 1999). ... Re-signed by Patriots (March 12, 1999).
CHAMPIONSHIP GAME EXPERIENCE: Played in AFC championship game (1996 season). ... Played in Super Bowl XXXI (1996 season).
PRO STATISTICS: 1996—Punted once for 27 yards. 1998—Credited with a two-point conversion.

		KICKING						
Year Team	G	XPM	XPA	FGM	FGA	Lg.	50+	Pts.
1996—Amsterdam W.L.	10	4	4	9	10	43	0-0	31
—New England NFL	16	39	42	27	35	50	1-2	120
1997—New England NFL	16	40	40	25	29	52	1-1	115
1998—New England NFL	16	32	32	31	39	55	2-2	127
1999—New England NFL	16	29	30	26	33	51	1-2	107
W.L. totals (1 year)	10	4	4	9	10	43	0-0	31
NFL totals (4 years)	64	140	144	109	136	55	5-7	469
Pro totals (5 years)	74	144	148	118	146	55	5-0	500

VINCENT, TROY   CB   EAGLES

PERSONAL: Born June 8, 1971, in Trenton, N.J. ... 6-1/200. ... Full name: Troy D. Vincent. ... Nephew of Steve Luke, safety with Green Bay Packers (1975-80).
HIGH SCHOOL: Pennsbury (Fairless Hills, Pa.).
COLLEGE: Wisconsin.
TRANSACTIONS/CAREER NOTES: Selected by Miami Dolphins in first round (seventh pick overall) of 1992 NFL draft. ... Signed by Dolphins (August 8, 1992). ... Designated by Dolphins as transition player (February 25, 1993). ... On injured reserve with knee injury (December 15, 1993-remainder of season). ... Tendered offer sheet by Philadelphia Eagles (February 24, 1996). ... Dolphins declined to match offer (March 3, 1996).
CHAMPIONSHIP GAME EXPERIENCE: Played in AFC championship game (1992 season).
HONORS: Named defensive back on THE SPORTING NEWS college All-America first team (1991). ... Played in Pro Bowl (1999 season).

RECORDS: Holds NFL record for longest interception return for a touchdown—104 yards (November 3, 1996; with lateral from LB James Willis).

PRO STATISTICS: 1992—Returned five punts for 16 yards and recovered two fumbles. 1993—Recovered one fumble. 1994—Ran 58 yards with lateral from interception for a touchdown. 1996—Ran minus two yards with lateral from punt return. 1997—Returned one punt for minus eight yards, fumbled once and recovered two fumbles for five yards. 1998—Credited with one sack. 1999—Credited with one sack.

				INTERCEPTIONS		
Year Team	G	GS	No.	Yds.	Avg.	TD
1992—Miami NFL	15	14	2	47	23.5	0
1993—Miami NFL	13	13	2	29	14.5	0
1994—Miami NFL	13	12	5	113	22.6	1
1995—Miami NFL	16	16	5	95	19.0	▲1
1996—Philadelphia NFL	16	16	3	144	*48.0	1
1997—Philadelphia NFL	16	16	3	14	4.7	0
1998—Philadelphia NFL	13	13	2	29	14.5	0
1999—Philadelphia NFL	14	14	†7	91	13.0	0
Pro totals (8 years)	116	114	29	562	19.4	3

VINSON, FRED   CB   SEAHAWKS

PERSONAL: Born April 2, 1977, in Aiken, S.C. ... 5-11/180. ... Full name: Fred Vinson Jr. ... Cousin of Corey Chavous, defensive back, Arizona Cardinals.
HIGH SCHOOL: North Augusta (S.C.).
COLLEGE: Vanderbilt (degree in engineering science and math).
TRANSACTIONS/CAREER NOTES: Selected by Green Bay Packers in second round (47th pick overall) of 1999 NFL draft. ... Signed by Packers (July 23, 1999). ... Traded by Packers with sixth-round pick (DT Tim Watson) in 2000 draft to Seattle Seahawks for RB Ahman Green and fifth-round pick (WR/KR Joey Jamison) in 2000 draft (April 14, 2000).
PRO STATISTICS: 1999—Credited with one sack.

				INTERCEPTIONS		
Year Team	G	GS	No.	Yds.	Avg.	TD
1999—Green Bay NFL	16	1	2	21	10.5	0

VINSON, TONY   RB

PERSONAL: Born March 13, 1971, in Frankfurt, West Germany ... 6-1/229. ... Full name: Anthony Cho Vinson.
HIGH SCHOOL: Denbigh (Newport News, Va.).
COLLEGE: Towson State.
TRANSACTIONS/CAREER NOTES: Selected by San Diego Chargers in fifth round (160th pick overall) of 1994 NFL draft. ... Signed by Chargers (July 14, 1994). ... Released by Chargers (August 22, 1994). ... Re-signed by Chargers to practice squad (August 29, 1994). ... Granted free agency after 1994 season. ... Signed by Atlanta Falcons (April 13, 1995). ... Released by Falcons (August 21, 1995). ... Re-signed by Falcons to practice squad (August 29, 1995). ... Assigned by Falcons to London Monarchs in 1996 World League enhancement allocation program (February 19, 1996). ... Released by Falcons (August 5, 1996). ... Signed by Baltimore Ravens (July 9, 1997). ... On injured reserve with shoulder injury (August 25, 1998-entire season). ... On injured reserve with shoulder injury (September 28, 1999-remainder of season). ... Granted free agency (February 11, 2000).
PLAYING EXPERIENCE: London W.L., 1996 and 1997; Baltimore NFL, 1997 and 1999. ... Games/Games started: 1996 (games played unavailable), W.L. 1997 (games played unavailable), NFL 1997 (13/0), 1999 (3/0). Total NFL: 16/0.
PRO STATISTICS: W.L.: 1996—Rushed 105 times for 516 yards and three touchdowns and caught 25 passes for 169 yards and two touchdowns. 1997—Rushed 67 times for 163 yards and one touchdown and caught three passes for minus five yards.

VON OELHOFFEN, KIMO   DL   STEELERS

PERSONAL: Born January 30, 1971, in Kaunakaki, Hawaii. ... 6-4/305. ... Full name: Kimo K. von Oelhoffen. ... Name pronounced KEE-moe von OHL-hoffen.
HIGH SCHOOL: Molokai (Hoolehua, Hawaii).
JUNIOR COLLEGE: Walla Walla (Wash.) Community College.
COLLEGE: Hawaii, then Boise State.
TRANSACTIONS/CAREER NOTES: Selected by Cincinnati Bengals in sixth round (162nd pick overall) of 1994 NFL draft. ... Signed by Bengals (May 9, 1994). ... Granted unconditional free agency (February 11, 2000). ... Signed by Pittsburgh Steelers (February 14, 2000).
PLAYING EXPERIENCE: Cincinnati NFL, 1994-1999. ... Games/Games started: 1994 (7/0), 1995 (16/0), 1996 (11/1), 1997 (13/12), 1998 (16/16), 1999 (16/5). Total: 79/34.
PRO STATISTICS: 1995—Returned one kickoff for 10 yards. 1996—Credited with one sack. 1999—Credited with four sacks and recovered one fumble.

VRABEL, MIKE   LB   STEELERS

PERSONAL: Born August 14, 1975, in Akron, Ohio. ... 6-4/250. ... Full name: Michael George Vrabel.
HIGH SCHOOL: Walsh Jesuit (Cuyahoga Falls, Ohio).
COLLEGE: Ohio State.
TRANSACTIONS/CAREER NOTES: Selected by Pittsburgh Steelers in third round (91st pick overall) of 1997 NFL draft. ... Signed by Steelers (July 15, 1997). ... Granted free agency (February 11, 2000). ... Re-signed by Steelers (April 20, 2000).
CHAMPIONSHIP GAME EXPERIENCE: Played in AFC championship game (1997 season).
PRO STATISTICS: 1997—Returned one kickoff for no yards and recovered one fumble. 1999—Returned one kickoff for six yards and recovered one fumble.

Year Team	G	GS	SACKS
1997—Pittsburgh NFL	15	0	1.5
1998—Pittsburgh NFL	11	0	2.5
1999—Pittsburgh NFL	10	0	2.0
Pro totals (3 years)	36	0	6.0

WADDY, JUDE   LB   PACKERS

PERSONAL: Born September 12, 1975, in Washington, D.C. ... 6-2/220. ... Full name: Jude Michael Waddy.
HIGH SCHOOL: Suitland (Forestville, Md.).
COLLEGE: William & Mary (degree in kinesiology).
TRANSACTIONS/CAREER NOTES: Signed as non-drafted free agent by Green Bay Packers (April 24, 1998). ... On suspended list for violating league substance abuse policy (December 23, 1998-September 20, 1999).
PLAYING EXPERIENCE: Green Bay NFL, 1998 and 1999. ... Games/Games started: 1998 (13/0), 1999 (14/8). Total: 27/8.
PRO STATISTICS: 1998—Credited with one sack. 1999—Credited with one sack.

WADE, JOHN   C   JAGUARS

PERSONAL: Born January 25, 1975, in Harrisonburg, Va. ... 6-5/294. ... Full name: John Robert Wade.
HIGH SCHOOL: Harrisonburg (Va.).
COLLEGE: Marshall (degree in business management, 1997).
TRANSACTIONS/CAREER NOTES: Selected by Jacksonville Jaguars in fifth round (148th pick overall) of 1998 NFL draft. ... Signed by Jaguars (June 1, 1998).
PLAYING EXPERIENCE: Jacksonville NFL, 1998 and 1999. ... Games/Games started: 1998 (4/0), 1999 (16/16). Total: 20/16.
CHAMPIONSHIP GAME EXPERIENCE: Played in AFC championship game (1999 season).
PRO STATISTICS: 1999—Fumbled once for minus 14 yards.

WADSWORTH, ANDRE   DE   CARDINALS

PERSONAL: Born October 19, 1974, in St. Croix, Virgin Islands (U.S.) ... 6-4/275.
HIGH SCHOOL: Florida Christian (Miami).
COLLEGE: Florida State (degree in marketing, 1997).
TRANSACTIONS/CAREER NOTES: Selected by Arizona Cardinals in first round (third pick overall) of 1998 NFL draft. ... Signed by Cardinals (September 5, 1998).
HONORS: Named defensive end on THE SPORTING NEWS college All-America first team (1997).
PRO STATISTICS: 1998—Recovered three fumbles. 1999—Intercepted one pass for 23 yards.

Year Team	G	GS	SACKS
1998—Arizona NFL	16	15	5.0
1999—Arizona NFL	11	7	2.0
Pro totals (2 years)	27	22	7.0

WAHLE, MIKE   OT   PACKERS

PERSONAL: Born March 29, 1977, in Portland, Ore. ... 6-6/306. ... Full name: Michael James Wahle. ... Name pronounced WALL.
HIGH SCHOOL: Rim of the World (Lake Arrowhead, Calif.).
COLLEGE: Navy.
TRANSACTIONS/CAREER NOTES: Selected by Green Bay Packers in second round of 1998 supplemental draft (July 9, 1998). ... Signed by Packers (August 6, 1998).
PLAYING EXPERIENCE: Green Bay NFL, 1998 and 1999. ... Games/Games started: 1998 (1/0), 1999 (16/13). Total: 17/13.
PRO STATISTICS: 1999—Recovered one fumble.

WAINRIGHT, FRANK   TE   RAVENS

PERSONAL: Born October 10, 1967, in Peoria, Ill. ... 6-3/255. ... Full name: Frank Wesley Wainright.
HIGH SCHOOL: Pomona (Arvada, Colo.).
COLLEGE: Northern Colorado.
TRANSACTIONS/CAREER NOTES: Selected by New Orleans Saints in eighth round (210th pick overall) of 1991 NFL draft. ... Signed by Saints (July 14, 1991). ... Released by Saints (August 26, 1991). ... Re-signed by Saints to practice squad (August 28, 1991). ... Activated (September 14, 1991). ... Granted unconditional free agency (February 1-April 1, 1992). ... Re-signed by Saints for 1992 season. ... On injured reserve with foot injury (August 23, 1994-entire season). ... Granted unconditional free agency (February 17, 1995). ... Signed by Denver Broncos (April 17, 1995). ... Released by Broncos (August 22, 1995). ... Signed by Philadelphia Eagles (August 29, 1995). ... Released by Eagles (October 25, 1995). ... Signed by Miami Dolphins (November 15, 1995). ... Granted unconditional free agency (February 16, 1996). ... Re-signed by Dolphins (March 5, 1996). ... Granted unconditional free agency (February 14, 1997). ... Re-signed by Dolphins (February 27, 1997). ... On injured reserve with chest injury (December 9, 1997-remainder of season). ... Granted unconditional free agency (February 12, 1999). ... Signed by Baltimore Ravens (February 25, 1999).
PRO STATISTICS: 1995—Recovered one fumble. 1996—Returned one kickoff for 10 yards.
SINGLE GAME HIGHS (regular season): Receptions—2 (December 3, 1992, vs. Atlanta); yards—42 (December 3, 1992, vs. Atlanta); and touchdown receptions—1 (September 15, 1996, vs. New York Jets).

Year Team	G	GS	RECEIVING				TOTALS			
			No.	Yds.	Avg.	TD	TD	2pt.	Pts.	Fum.
1991—New Orleans NFL	14	2	1	3	3.0	0	0	0	0	0
1992—New Orleans NFL	13	4	9	143	15.9	0	0	0	0	0
1993—New Orleans NFL	16	2	0	0	0.0	0	0	0	0	0

W

Year Team										
1994—New Orleans NFL	Did not play.									
1995—Philadelphia NFL	7	0	0	0	0.0	0	0	0	0	0
—Miami NFL	6	0	0	0	0.0	0	0	0	0	0
1996—Miami NFL	16	0	1	2	2.0	1	1	0	6	0
1997—Miami NFL	9	0	0	0	0.0	0	0	0	0	0
1998—Miami NFL	16	1	0	0	0.0	0	0	0	0	0
1999—Baltimore NFL	16	0	0	0	0.0	0	0	0	0	0
Pro totals (8 years)	113	9	11	148	13.5	1	1	0	6	0

WALKER, BRACEY   S   CHIEFS

PERSONAL: Born June 11, 1970, in Spring Lake, N.C. ... 6-0/204. ... Full name: Bracey Wordell Walker.
HIGH SCHOOL: Pine Forest (Fayetteville, N.C.).
COLLEGE: North Carolina.
TRANSACTIONS/CAREER NOTES: Selected by Kansas City Chiefs in fourth round (127th pick overall) of 1994 NFL draft. ... Signed by Chiefs (July 20, 1994). ... Claimed on waivers by Cincinnati Bengals (October 12, 1994). ... Granted free agency (February 14, 1997). ... Re-signed by Bengals (April 18, 1997). ... Claimed on waivers by Miami Dolphins (August 20, 1997). ... On injured reserve with leg injury (December 2, 1997-remainder of season). ... Granted unconditional free agency (February 13, 1998). ... Re-signed by Dolphins (April 27, 1998). ... Released by Dolphins (August 19, 1998). ... Signed by Chiefs (November 3, 1998). ... Granted unconditional free agency (February 11, 2000). ... Re-signed by Chiefs (February 24, 2000).
HONORS: Named defensive back on THE SPORTING NEWS college All-America second team (1993).
PRO STATISTICS: 1995—Recovered two fumbles. 1997—Recovered one fumble.

			INTERCEPTIONS			
Year Team	G	GS	No.	Yds.	Avg.	TD
1994—Kansas City NFL	2	0	0	0	0.0	0
—Cincinnati NFL	7	0	0	0	0.0	0
1995—Cincinnati NFL	14	14	4	56	14.0	0
1996—Cincinnati NFL	16	16	2	35	17.5	0
1997—Miami NFL	12	0	0	0	0.0	0
1998—Kansas City NFL	8	0	0	0	0.0	0
1999—Kansas City NFL	16	1	0	0	0.0	0
Pro totals (6 years)	75	31	6	91	15.2	0

WALKER, BRIAN   S   DOLPHINS

PERSONAL: Born May 31, 1972, in Colorado Springs, Colo. ... 6-1/200.
HIGH SCHOOL: Widefield (Colorado Springs, Colo.).
JUNIOR COLLEGE: Snow College (Utah).
COLLEGE: Washington State.
TRANSACTIONS/CAREER NOTES: Signed as non-drafted free agent by Washington Redskins (May 1, 1996). ... Released by Redskins (October 9, 1997). ... Signed by Miami Dolphins (December 9, 1997). ... Active for two games with Dolphins (1997); did not play. ... Claimed on waivers by Seattle Seahawks (September 6, 1999). ... Released by Seahawks (September 14, 1999). ... Re-signed by Seahawks (September 30, 1999). ... On injured reserve with hamstring injury (January 8, 2000-remainder of playoffs). ... Granted unconditional free agency (February 11, 2000). ... Signed by Dolphins (February 16, 2000).
PLAYING EXPERIENCE: Washington NFL, 1996 and 1997; Miami NFL, 1998; Seattle NFL, 1999. ... Games/Games started: 1996 (16/4), 1997 (5/0), 1998 (16/0), 1999 (5/0). Total: 42/4.
PRO STATISTICS: 1996—Credited with one sack. 1998—Intercepted four passes for 12 yards. 1999—Intercepted one pass for 21 yards and recovered one fumble.

WALKER, DARNELL   CB

PERSONAL: Born January 17, 1970, in St. Louis. ... 5-8/168. ... Full name: Darnell Robert Walker. ... Brother of Marquis Walker, defensive back, Oakland Raiders.
HIGH SCHOOL: Sumner (St. Louis).
JUNIOR COLLEGE: Coffeyville (Kan.) Community College.
COLLEGE: Oklahoma.
TRANSACTIONS/CAREER NOTES: Selected by Atlanta Falcons in seventh round (178th pick overall) of 1993 NFL draft. ... Signed by Falcons (July 14, 1993). ... Granted free agency (February 16, 1996). ... Re-signed by Falcons (June 12, 1996). ... Granted unconditional free agency (February 14, 1997). ... Signed by San Francisco 49ers (March 28, 1997). ... Released by 49ers (February 7, 2000).
CHAMPIONSHIP GAME EXPERIENCE: Played in NFC championship game (1997 season).
PRO STATISTICS: 1994—Credited with one sack. 1996—Recovered one fumble. 1997—Credited with one sack. 1999—Credited with one sack and recovered two fumbles for 71 yards and one touchdown.

W

			INTERCEPTIONS				TOTALS			
Year Team	G	GS	No.	Yds.	Avg.	TD	TD	2pt.	Pts.	Fum.
1993—Atlanta NFL	15	8	3	7	2.3	0	0	0	0	0
1994—Atlanta NFL	16	5	3	105	35.0	1	1	0	6	0
1995—Atlanta NFL	16	7	0	0	0.0	0	0	0	0	0
1996—Atlanta NFL	15	9	1	0	0.0	0	0	0	0	0
1997—San Francisco NFL	16	11	3	49	16.3	0	0	0	0	0
1998—San Francisco NFL	16	16	4	78	19.5	0	0	0	0	0
1999—San Francisco NFL	15	8	1	27	27.0	1	2	0	12	0
Pro totals (7 years)	109	64	15	266	17.7	2	3	0	18	0

WALKER, DENARD — CB — TITANS

PERSONAL: Born August 9, 1973, in Dallas. ... 6-1/190. ... Full name: Denard Antuan Walker.
HIGH SCHOOL: South Garland (Texas), than Harlingen (Texas) Military Institute.
COLLEGE: Louisiana State.
TRANSACTIONS/CAREER NOTES: Selected by Houston Oilers in third round (75th pick overall) of 1997 NFL draft. ... Oilers franchise moved to Tennessee for 1997 season. ... Signed by Oilers (July 18, 1997). ... Oilers franchise renamed Tennessee Titans for 1999 season (December 26, 1998). ... Granted free agency (February 11, 2000). ... Suspended two games by NFL for assault charges (March 14, 2000).
CHAMPIONSHIP GAME EXPERIENCE: Played in AFC championship game (1999 season). ... Played in Super Bowl XXXIV (1999 season).

			INTERCEPTIONS			
Year Team	G	GS	No.	Yds.	Avg.	TD
1997—Tennessee NFL	15	11	2	53	26.5	1
1998—Tennessee NFL	16	16	2	6	3.0	0
1999—Tennessee NFL	15	14	1	27	27.0	0
Pro totals (3 years)	46	41	5	86	17.2	1

WALKER, DERRICK — TE

PERSONAL: Born June 23, 1967, in Glenwood, Ill. ... 6-0/246. ... Full name: Derrick Norval Walker.
HIGH SCHOOL: Bloom (Chicago Heights, Ill.).
COLLEGE: Michigan (degree in communications).
TRANSACTIONS/CAREER NOTES: Selected by San Diego Chargers in sixth round (163rd pick overall) of 1990 NFL draft. ... Signed by Chargers (July 21, 1990). ... Granted free agency (March 1, 1993). ... Re-signed by Chargers for 1993 season. ... On injured reserve with knee injury (December 15, 1993-remainder of season). ... Released by Chargers (March 9, 1994). ... Signed by Kansas City Chiefs (August 29, 1994). ... Granted free agency (February 17, 1995). ... Tendered offer sheet by Washington Redskins (March 11, 1995). ... Offer matched by Chiefs (March 18, 1995). ... Released by Chiefs (February 13, 1998). ... Signed by Oakland Raiders (March 10, 1999). ... Released by Raiders (February 10, 2000).
PRO STATISTICS: 1991—Recovered one fumble. 1996—Recovered one fumble.
SINGLE GAME HIGHS (regular season): Receptions—8 (October 17, 1994, vs. Denver); yards—104 (October 25, 1992, vs. Denver); and touchdown receptions—1 (October 10, 1999, vs. Denver).
STATISTICAL PLATEAUS: 100-yard receiving games: 1992 (1).

			RECEIVING				TOTALS			
Year Team	G	GS	No.	Yds.	Avg.	TD	TD	2pt.	Pts.	Fum.
1990—San Diego NFL	16	13	23	240	10.4	1	1	0	6	1
1991—San Diego NFL	16	16	20	134	6.7	0	0	0	0	0
1992—San Diego NFL	16	16	34	393	11.6	2	2	0	12	0
1993—San Diego NFL	12	11	21	212	10.1	1	1	0	6	0
1994—Kansas City NFL	15	11	36	382	10.6	2	2	0	12	1
1995—Kansas City NFL	16	3	25	205	8.2	1	1	0	6	0
1996—Kansas City NFL	11	9	9	73	8.1	1	1	0	6	0
1997—Kansas City NFL	16	5	5	60	12.0	0	0	0	0	0
1998—					Did not play.					
1999—Oakland NFL	11	3	7	71	10.1	1	1	0	6	1
Pro totals (9 years)	129	87	180	1770	9.8	9	9	0	54	3

WALKER, GARY — DT — JAGUARS

PERSONAL: Born February 28, 1973, in Royston, Ga. ... 6-2/293. ... Full name: Gary Lamar Walker.
HIGH SCHOOL: Franklin County (Carnesville, Ga.).
JUNIOR COLLEGE: Hinds Community College (Miss.).
COLLEGE: Auburn.
TRANSACTIONS/CAREER NOTES: Selected by Houston Oilers in fifth round (159th pick overall) of 1995 NFL draft. ... Signed by Oilers (July 10, 1995). ... Oilers franchise moved to Tennessee for 1997 season. ... Granted free agency (February 13, 1998). ... Re-signed by Oilers (July 15, 1998). ... Granted unconditional free agency (February 12, 1999). ... Signed by Jacksonville Jaguars (February 15, 1999).
CHAMPIONSHIP GAME EXPERIENCE: Played in AFC championship game (1999 season).
PRO STATISTICS: 1996—Recovered one fumble.

Year Team	G	GS	SACKS
1995—Houston NFL	15	9	2.5
1996—Houston NFL	16	16	5.5
1997—Tennessee NFL	15	15	7.0
1998—Tennessee NFL	16	16	1.0
1999—Jacksonville NFL	16	16	10.0
Pro totals (5 years)	78	72	26.0

WALKER, MARQUIS — CB — RAIDERS

PERSONAL: Born July 6, 1972, in St. Louis. ... 5-10/175. ... Full name: Marquis Roshe Walker. ... Brother of Darnell Walker, cornerback with Atlanta Falcons (1993-96) and San Francisco 49ers (1997-99).
HIGH SCHOOL: Berkeley (St. Louis).
JUNIOR COLLEGE: Blinn College (Texas), then Cisco (Texas) Junior College.
COLLEGE: Southeast Missouri State.
TRANSACTIONS/CAREER NOTES: Signed as non-drafted free agent by St. Louis Rams (April 24, 1996). ... Released by Rams (September 4, 1996). ... Signed by Washington Redskins to practice squad (September 4, 1996). ... Signed by Rams off Redskins practice squad (November 6, 1996). ... Released by Rams (November 19, 1997). ... Selected by Frankfurt Galaxy in 1998 NFL Europe draft (February 18, 1998). ... Signed

W

by Oakland Raiders (May 5, 1998). ... Granted free agency (February 12, 1999). ... Re-signed by Raiders (March 5, 1999). ... Granted unconditional free agency (February 11, 2000). ... Re-signed by Raiders (April 25, 2000)
PLAYING EXPERIENCE: St. Louis (8)-Washington (1) NFL, 1996; St. Louis NFL, 1997; Oakland NFL, 1998 and 1999. ... Games/Games started: 1996 (St.L-8/4; Wash.-1/0; Total: 9/4), 1997 (10/0), 1998 (16/7), 1999 (16/0). Total: 51/11.
PRO STATISTICS: 1997—Recovered one fumble. 1998—Intercepted two passes for 28 yards and recovered one fumble for three yards. 1999—Intercepted one pass for no yards and credited with one sack.

WALLS, WESLEY   TE   PANTHERS

PERSONAL: Born February 26, 1966, in Pontotoc, Miss. ... 6-5/250. ... Full name: Charles Wesley Walls.
HIGH SCHOOL: Pontotoc (Miss.).
COLLEGE: Mississippi.
TRANSACTIONS/CAREER NOTES: Selected by San Francisco 49ers in second round (56th pick overall) of 1989 NFL draft. ... Signed by 49ers (July 26, 1989). ... Granted free agency (February 1, 1992). ... Re-signed by 49ers (July 18, 1992). ... On injured reserve with shoulder injury (September 1, 1992-January 16, 1993). ... On injured reserve with shoulder injury (October 27, 1993-remainder of season). ... Granted unconditional free agency (February 17, 1994). ... Signed by New Orleans Saints (April 27, 1994). ... Granted unconditional free agency (February 16, 1996). ... Signed by Carolina Panthers (February 21, 1996).
CHAMPIONSHIP GAME EXPERIENCE: Played in NFC championship game (1989, 1990 and 1996 seasons). ... Member of Super Bowl championship team (1989 season).
HONORS: Named tight end on The Sporting News college All-America second team (1988). ... Played in Pro Bowl (1996-1999 seasons).
PRO STATISTICS: 1989—Recovered one fumble. 1990—Returned one kickoff for 16 yards. 1993—Recovered one fumble. 1995—Returned one kickoff for six yards, fumbled once and recovered one fumble.
SINGLE GAME HIGHS (regular season): Receptions—8 (November 15, 1998, vs. Miami); yards—147 (September 7, 1997, vs. Atlanta); and touchdown receptions—2 (January 2, 2000, vs. New Orleans).
STATISTICAL PLATEAUS: 100-yard receiving games: 1997 (2).
MISCELLANEOUS: Holds Carolina Panthers all-time records for most receptions (231), most touchdown receptions (33) and most touchdowns (33).

			RECEIVING				TOTALS		
Year Team	G	GS	No.	Yds.	Avg.	TD	TD	2pt.	Pts.	Fum.
1989—San Francisco NFL	16	0	4	16	4.0	1	1	0	6	1
1990—San Francisco NFL	16	0	5	27	5.4	0	0	0	0	0
1991—San Francisco NFL	15	0	2	24	12.0	0	0	0	0	0
1992—San Francisco NFL					Did not play.					
1993—San Francisco NFL	6	0	0	0	0.0	0	0	0	0	0
1994—New Orleans NFL	15	7	38	406	10.7	4	4	1	26	0
1995—New Orleans NFL	16	10	57	694	12.2	4	4	1	26	1
1996—Carolina NFL	16	15	61	713	11.7	10	10	0	60	0
1997—Carolina NFL	15	15	58	746	12.9	6	6	0	36	0
1998—Carolina NFL	14	14	49	506	10.3	5	5	0	30	0
1999—Carolina NFL	16	16	63	822	13.0	12	12	0	72	1
Pro totals (10 years)	145	77	337	3954	11.7	42	42	2	256	3

WALSH, CHRIS   WR   VIKINGS

PERSONAL: Born December 12, 1968, in Cleveland. ... 6-1/199. ... Full name: Christopher Lee Walsh.
HIGH SCHOOL: Ygnacio Valley (Concord, Calif.).
COLLEGE: Stanford (degree in quantitative economics, 1991).
TRANSACTIONS/CAREER NOTES: Selected by Buffalo Bills in ninth round (251st pick overall) of 1992 NFL draft. ... Signed by Bills (July 22, 1992). ... Released by Bills (August 31, 1992). ... Re-signed by Bills to practice squad (September 1, 1992). ... Activated (September 19, 1992). ... Released by Bills (October 2, 1992). ... Re-signed by Bills to practice squad (October 2, 1992). ... Released by Bills (March 10, 1994). ... Signed by Minnesota Vikings (May 6, 1994). ... Granted unconditional free agency (February 16, 1996). ... Re-signed by Vikings (March 4, 1996). ... Granted unconditional free agency (February 13, 1998). ... Re-signed by Vikings (March 4, 1998).
CHAMPIONSHIP GAME EXPERIENCE: Member of Bills for AFC championship game (1993 season); inactive. ... Member of Bills for Super Bowl XXVIII (1993 season); inactive. ... Played in NFC championship game (1998 season).
PRO STATISTICS: 1994—Returned one kickoff for six yards. 1995—Returned three kickoffs for 42 yards. 1996—Attempted one pass without a completion and credited with one two-point conversion. 1997—Returned one kickoff for 10 yards.
SINGLE GAME HIGHS (regular season): Receptions—4 (October 22, 1995, vs. Green Bay); yards—31 (October 22, 1995, vs. Green Bay); and touchdown receptions—1 (October 10, 1999, vs. Chicago).

			RECEIVING				TOTALS		
Year Team	G	GS	No.	Yds.	Avg.	TD	TD	2pt.	Pts.	Fum.
1992—Buffalo NFL	2	0	0	0	0.0	0	0	0	0	0
1993—Buffalo NFL	3	0	0	0	0.0	0	0	0	0	0
1994—Minnesota NFL	10	0	0	0	0.0	0	0	0	0	0
1995—Minnesota NFL	16	0	7	66	9.4	0	0	0	0	0
1996—Minnesota NFL	15	0	4	39	9.8	1	1	1	8	0
1997—Minnesota NFL	14	0	11	114	10.4	1	1	0	6	0
1998—Minnesota NFL	15	0	2	46	23.0	0	0	0	0	0
1999—Minnesota NFL	16	1	2	24	12.0	1	1	0	6	0
Pro totals (8 years)	91	1	26	289	11.1	3	3	1	20	0

WALSH, STEVE   QB

PERSONAL: Born December 1, 1966, in St. Paul, Minn. ... 6-3/215. ... Full name: Stephen John Walsh.
HIGH SCHOOL: Cretin-Derham Hall (St. Paul, Minn.).
COLLEGE: Miami, Fla. (degree in finance).

W

TRANSACTIONS/CAREER NOTES: Selected by Dallas Cowboys in first round of 1989 NFL supplemental draft (July 7, 1989). ... Signed by Cowboys (July 29, 1989). ... Traded by Cowboys to New Orleans Saints for first- (traded to New England) and third-round (OT Erik Williams) picks in 1991 draft and second-round pick (traded to Cleveland) in 1992 draft (September 25, 1990). ... Active for two games (1992); did not play. ... Granted free agency (March 1, 1993). ... Re-signed by Saints (July 15, 1993). ... Released by Saints (April 23, 1994). ... Signed by Chicago Bears (April 26, 1994). ... Granted unconditional free agency (February 17, 1995). ... Re-signed by Bears (April 17, 1995). ... Granted unconditional free agency (February 16, 1996). ... Signed by St. Louis Rams (April 10, 1996). ... Granted unconditional free agency (February 14, 1997). ... Signed by Tampa Bay Buccaneers (April 16, 1997). ... Granted unconditional free agency (February 12, 1999). ... Signed by Indianapolis Colts (August 11, 1999). ... Released by Colts (February 8, 2000).

PRO STATISTICS: 1989—Fumbled three times and recovered two fumbles for minus 14 yards. 1990—Fumbled six times and recovered two fumbles. 1991—Fumbled three times and recovered one fumble for minus 20 yards. 1994—Fumbled seven times and recovered three fumbles for minus eight yards. 1996—Fumbled once and recovered one fumble. 1997—Fumbled once and recovered two fumbles.

SINGLE GAME HIGHS (regular season): Attempts—49 (October 29, 1989, vs. Phoenix); completions—26 (December 8, 1991, vs. Dallas); yards—317 (December 1, 1991, vs. San Francisco); and touchdown passes—3 (October 14, 1990, vs. Cleveland).

STATISTICAL PLATEAUS: 300-yard passing games: 1991 (1).

MISCELLANEOUS: Regular-season record as starting NFL quarterback: 20-18 (.526). ... Postseason record as starting NFL quarterback: 1-2 (.333).

| | | | PASSING | | | | | | | | RUSHING | | | | TOTALS | | |
Year Team	G	GS	Att.	Cmp.	Pct.	Yds.	TD	Int.	Avg.	Rat.	Att.	Yds.	Avg.	TD	TD	2pt.	Pts.
1989—Dallas NFL	8	5	219	110	50.2	1371	5	9	6.26	60.5	6	16	2.7	0	0	0	0
1990—Dallas NFL	1	0	9	4	44.4	40	0	0	4.44	57.6	1	0	0.0	0	0	0	0
—New Orleans NFL	12	11	327	175	53.5	1970	12	13	6.02	67.5	19	25	1.3	0	0	0	0
1991—New Orleans NFL	8	7	255	141	55.3	1638	11	6	6.42	79.5	8	0	0.0	0	0	0	0
1992—New Orleans NFL						Did not play.											
1993—New Orleans NFL	2	1	38	20	52.6	271	2	3	7.13	60.3	4	-4	-1.0	0	0	0	0
1994—Chicago NFL	12	11	343	208	60.6	2078	10	8	6.06	77.9	30	4	0.1	1	1	0	6
1995—Chicago NFL	1	0	0	0	0.0	0	0	0	0.0	...	0	0	0.0	0	0	0	0
1996—St. Louis NFL	3	3	77	33	42.9	344	0	5	4.47	29.4	6	10	1.7	0	0	0	0
1997—Tampa Bay NFL	13	0	17	6	35.3	58	0	1	3.41	21.2	6	-4	-0.7	0	0	0	0
1998—Tampa Bay NFL	5	0	19	9	47.4	58	0	3	3.05	14.7	0	0	0.0	0	0	0	0
1999—Indianapolis NFL	16	0	13	7	53.8	47	0	2	3.62	22.4	0	0	0.0	0	0	0	0
Pro totals (10 years)	81	38	1317	713	54.1	7875	40	50	5.98	66.4	80	47	0.6	1	1	0	6

WALTER, KEN   P   PANTHERS

PERSONAL: Born August 15, 1972, in Cleveland. ... 6-1/195. ... Full name: Kenneth Matthew Walter Jr.
HIGH SCHOOL: Euclid (Ohio).
COLLEGE: Kent.
TRANSACTIONS/CAREER NOTES: Signed as non-drafted free agent by Carolina Panthers (April 14, 1997).
PRO STATISTICS: 1997—Rushed once for minus five yards. 1998—Rushed three times for no yards, attempted one pass without a completion, fumbled twice and recovered two fumbles for minus 20 yards.

| | | PUNTING | | | | | |
Year Team	G	No.	Yds.	Avg.	Net avg.	In. 20	Blk.
1997—Carolina NFL	16	85	3604	42.4	36.4	29	0
1998—Carolina NFL	16	77	3131	40.7	38.1	20	0
1999—Carolina NFL	16	65	2562	39.4	36.7	18	0
Pro totals (3 years)	48	227	9297	41.0	37.1	67	0

WALZ, ZACK   LB   CARDINALS

PERSONAL: Born February 13, 1976, in Mountain View, Calif. ... 6-4/219. ... Full name: Zachary Christian Walz.
HIGH SCHOOL: Saint Francis (San Jose, Calif.).
COLLEGE: Dartmouth (degree in government and economics, 1998).
TRANSACTIONS/CAREER NOTES: Selected by Arizona Cardinals in sixth round (158th pick overall) of 1998 NFL draft. ... Signed by Cardinals (June 4, 1998). ... On injured reserve with knee injury (November 17, 1999-remainder of season).
PLAYING EXPERIENCE: Arizona NFL, 1998 and 1999. ... Games/Games started: 1998 (16/0), 1999 (9/9). Total: 25/9.
PRO STATISTICS: 1998—Recovered one fumble. 1999—Credited with one sack.

WARD, DEDRIC   WR/KR   JETS

PERSONAL: Born September 29, 1974, in Cedar Rapids, Iowa. ... 5-9/184. ... Full name: Dedric Lamar Ward. ... Name pronounced DEE-drick.
HIGH SCHOOL: Washington (Cedar Rapids, Iowa).
COLLEGE: Northern Iowa (degree in psychology).
TRANSACTIONS/CAREER NOTES: Selected by New York Jets in third round (88th pick overall) of 1997 NFL draft. ... Signed by Jets (July 17, 1997). ... Granted free agency (February 11, 2000). ... Re-signed by Jets (May 3, 2000).
CHAMPIONSHIP GAME EXPERIENCE: Played in AFC championship game (1998 season).
PRO STATISTICS: 1997—Rushed twice for 25 yards. 1998—Rushed twice for seven yards. 1999—Rushed once for minus one yard.
SINGLE GAME HIGHS (regular season): Receptions—6 (November 9, 1997, vs. Miami); yards—108 (November 9, 1997, vs. Miami); and touchdown receptions—1 (December 27, 1999, vs. Miami).
STATISTICAL PLATEAUS: 100-yard receiving games: 1997 (1).

| | | | RECEIVING | | | | PUNT RETURNS | | | | KICKOFF RETURNS | | | | TOTALS | | | |
Year Team	G	GS	No.	Yds.	Avg.	TD	No.	Yds.	Avg.	TD	No.	Yds.	Avg.	TD	TD	2pt.	Pts.	Fum.
1997—New York Jets NFL	11	1	18	212	11.8	1	8	55	6.9	0	2	10	5.0	0	1	0	6	1
1998—New York Jets NFL	16	2	25	477	19.1	4	8	72	9.0	0	3	60	20.0	0	4	0	24	0
1999—New York Jets NFL	16	10	22	325	14.8	3	38	288	7.6	0	0	0	0.0	0	3	0	18	2
Pro totals (3 years)	43	13	65	1014	15.6	8	54	415	7.7	0	5	70	14.0	0	8	0	48	3

W

WARD, HINES   WR   STEELERS

PERSONAL: Born March 8, 1976, in Forest Park, Ga. ... 6-0/197. ... Full name: Hines Ward Jr.
HIGH SCHOOL: Forest Park (Ga.).
COLLEGE: Georgia.
TRANSACTIONS/CAREER NOTES: Selected by Pittsburgh Steelers in third round (92nd pick overall) of 1998 NFL draft. ... Signed by Steelers (July 20, 1998).
PRO STATISTICS: 1998—Rushed once for 13 yards and attempted one pass with a completion for 17 yards. 1999—Rushed twice for minus two yards, returned one punt for two yards and returned one kickoff for 24 yards.
SINGLE GAME HIGHS (regular season): Receptions—7 (November 28, 1999, vs. Cincinnati); yards—89 (November 28, 1999, vs. Cincinnati); and touchdown receptions—1 (January 2, 2000, vs. Tennessee).

| | | | RECEIVING | | | | TOTALS | | |
Year Team	G	GS	No.	Yds.	Avg.	TD	TD	2pt.	Pts.	Fum.
1998—Pittsburgh NFL	16	0	15	246	16.4	0	0	0	0	0
1999—Pittsburgh NFL	16	14	61	638	10.5	7	7	†1	44	1
Pro totals (2 years)	32	14	76	884	11.6	7	7	1	44	1

WARFIELD, ERIC   CB   CHIEFS

PERSONAL: Born March 3, 1976, in Vicksburg, Miss. ... 6-0/195. ... Full name: Eric Andrew Warfield.
HIGH SCHOOL: Arkansas (Texarkana, Ark.).
COLLEGE: Nebraska.
TRANSACTIONS/CAREER NOTES: Selected by Kansas City Chiefs in seventh round (216th pick overall) of 1998 NFL draft. ... Signed by Chiefs (May 27, 1998).
PLAYING EXPERIENCE: Kansas City NFL, 1998 and 1999. ... Games/Games started: 1998 (12/0), 1999 (16/1). Total: 28/1.
PRO STATISTICS: 1999—Intercepted three passes for no yards.

WARNER, KURT   QB   RAMS

PERSONAL: Born June 22, 1971, in Burlington, Iowa. ... 6-2/220. ... Full name: Kurtis Eugene Warner.
HIGH SCHOOL: Regis (Cedar Rapids, Iowa).
COLLEGE: Northern Iowa (degree in communications).
TRANSACTIONS/CAREER NOTES: Signed as non-drafted free agent by Green Bay Packers (April 28, 1994). ... Released by Packers prior to 1994 season. ... Played for Iowa Barnstormers of Arena Football League (1995-97). ... Signed by St. Louis Rams (December 26, 1997). ... Assigned by Rams to Amsterdam Admirals in 1998 NFL Europe enhancement allocation program (February 18, 1998).
CHAMPIONSHIP GAME EXPERIENCE: Played in NFC championship game (1999 season). ... Member of Super Bowl championship team (1999 season).
HONORS: Named NFL Player of the Year by THE SPORTING NEWS (1999). ... Named quarterback on THE SPORTING NEWS NFL All-Pro team (1999). ... Named Most Valuable Player of Super Bowl XXXIV (1999 season). ... Played in Pro Bowl (1999 season).
RECORDS: Shares NFL single-season record for most games with 300 or more yards passing—9 (1999).
POST SEASON RECORDS: Holds Super Bowl single-game record for most yards passing—414 (January 30, 2000, vs. Tennessee).
PRO STATISTICS: 1999—Fumbled nine times for minus four yards.
SINGLE GAME HIGHS (regular season): Attempts—46 (October 31, 1999, vs. Tennessee); completions—29 (October 31, 1999, vs. Tennessee); yards—351 (December 5, 1999, vs. Carolina); and touchdown passes—5 (October 10, 1999, vs. San Francisco).
STATISTICAL PLATEAUS: 300-yard passing games: 1999 (9).
MISCELLANEOUS: Regular-season record as starting NFL quarterback: 13-3 (.813). ... Postseason record as starting NFL quarterback: 3-0 (1.000).

| | | | PASSING | | | | | | | RUSHING | | | | TOTALS | | |
Year Team	G	GS	Att.	Cmp.	Pct.	Yds.	TD	Int.	Avg.	Rat.	Att.	Yds.	Avg.	TD	TD	2pt.	Pts.
1998—Amsterdam NFLE	10	10	326	165	50.6	2101	15	6	6.44	78.8	19	17	0.9	1	1	0	6
—St. Louis NFL	1	0	11	4	36.4	39	0	0	3.55	47.2	0	0	0.0	0	0	0	0
1999—St. Louis NFL	16	16	499	325	*65.1	4353	*41	13	*8.72	*109.2	23	92	4.0	1	1	0	6
NFL Europe totals (1 year)	10	10	326	165	50.6	2101	15	6	6.44	78.8	19	17	0.9	1	1	0	6
NFL totals (2 years)	17	16	510	329	64.5	4392	41	13	8.61	107.9	23	92	4.0	1	1	0	6
Pro totals (3 years)	27	26	836	494	59.1	6493	56	19	7.77	96.5	42	109	2.6	2	2	0	12

W

WARREN, CHRIS   RB   COWBOYS

PERSONAL: Born January 24, 1968, in Silver Spring, Md. ... 6-2/227. ... Full name: Christopher Collins Warren Jr.
HIGH SCHOOL: Robinson Secondary (Fairfax, Va.).
COLLEGE: Virginia, then Ferrum, Va. (degree in psychology).
TRANSACTIONS/CAREER NOTES: Selected by Seattle Seahawks in fourth round (89th pick overall) of 1990 NFL draft. ... Signed by Seahawks (July 24, 1990). ... Granted free agency (March 1, 1993). ... Tendered offer sheet by New York Jets (April 23, 1993). ... Offer matched by Seahawks (April 23, 1993). ... Released by Seahawks (March 13, 1998). ... Signed by Dallas Cowboys (April 13, 1998).
HONORS: Played in Pro Bowl (1993-1995 seasons).
PRO STATISTICS: 1990—Fumbled three times and recovered one fumble. 1991—Fumbled three times and recovered one fumble. 1992—Fumbled twice and recovered two fumbles. 1993—Fumbled three times. 1994—Fumbled five times and recovered two fumbles. 1995—Fumbled five times and recovered two fumbles. 1996—Fumbled three times and recovered two fumbles for four yards. 1997—Fumbled twice. 1998—Recovered one fumble. 1999—Fumbled four times.
SINGLE GAME HIGHS (regular season): Attempts—36 (September 19, 1993, vs. New England); yards—185 (December 11, 1994, vs. Houston); and rushing touchdowns—3 (December 17, 1995, vs. Oakland).
STATISTICAL PLATEAUS: 100-yard rushing games: 1992 (3), 1993 (3), 1994 (7), 1995 (8), 1996 (3), 1998 (1). Total: 25.
MISCELLANEOUS: Holds Seattle Seahawks all-time record for most yards rushing (6,706).

Year Team	G	GS	RUSHING				RECEIVING				PUNT RETURNS				KICKOFF RETURNS				TOTALS		
			Att.	Yds.	Avg.	TD	No.	Yds.	Avg.	TD	No.	Yds.	Avg.	TD	No.	Yds.	Avg.	TD	TD	2pt.	Pts.
1990—Seattle NFL	16	0	6	11	1.8	1	0	0	0.0	0	28	269	9.6	0	23	478	20.8	0	1	0	6
1991—Seattle NFL	16	1	11	13	1.2	0	2	9	4.5	0	§32	298	9.3	▲1	32	792	24.8	0	1	0	6
1992—Seattle NFL	16	16	223	1017	4.6	3	16	134	8.4	0	34	252	7.4	0	28	524	18.7	0	3	0	18
1993—Seattle NFL	14	14	273	1072	3.9	7	15	99	6.6	0	0	0	0.0	0	0	0	0.0	0	7	0	42
1994—Seattle NFL	16	15	333	§1545	§4.6	9	41	323	7.9	2	0	0	0.0	0	0	0	0.0	0	11	1	68
1995—Seattle NFL	16	16	310	1346	4.3	§15	35	247	7.1	1	0	0	0.0	0	0	0	0.0	0	16	0	96
1996—Seattle NFL	14	14	203	855	4.2	5	40	273	6.8	0	0	0	0.0	0	0	0	0.0	0	5	1	32
1997—Seattle NFL	15	13	200	847	4.2	4	45	257	5.7	0	0	0	0.0	0	0	0	0.0	0	4	0	24
1998—Dallas NFL	9	0	59	291	4.9	4	13	66	5.1	1	2	11	5.5	0	5	90	18.0	0	5	0	30
1999—Dallas NFL	16	1	99	403	4.1	2	34	224	6.6	0	0	0	0.0	0	0	0	0.0	0	2	0	12
Pro totals (10 years)	148	90	1717	7400	4.3	50	241	1632	6.8	4	96	830	8.6	1	88	1884	21.4	0	55	2	334

WARREN, LAMONT   RB

PERSONAL: Born January 4, 1973, in Indianapolis. ... 5-11/202. ... Full name: Lamont Allen Warren.
HIGH SCHOOL: Dorsey (Los Angeles).
COLLEGE: Colorado.
TRANSACTIONS/CAREER NOTES: Selected after junior season by Indianapolis Colts in sixth round (164th pick overall) of 1994 NFL draft. ... Signed by Colts (July 13, 1994). ... Released by Colts (April 12, 1999). ... Signed by New England Patriots (April 17, 1999). ... Released by Patriots (February 22, 2000).
CHAMPIONSHIP GAME EXPERIENCE: Played in AFC championship game (1995 season).
PRO STATISTICS: 1994—Attempted one pass without a completion. 1996—Recovered one fumble. 1997—Attempted one pass without a completion and recovered one fumble.
SINGLE GAME HIGHS (regular season): Attempts—22 (December 23, 1995, vs. New England); yards—90 (December 23, 1995, vs. New England); and rushing touchdowns—1 (December 20, 1998, vs. Seattle).

Year Team	G	GS	RUSHING				RECEIVING				KICKOFF RETURNS				TOTALS			
			Att.	Yds.	Avg.	TD	No.	Yds.	Avg.	TD	No.	Yds.	Avg.	TD	TD	2pt.	Pts.	Fum.
1994—Indianapolis NFL	11	0	18	80	4.4	0	3	47	15.7	0	2	56	28.0	0	0	0	0	0
1995—Indianapolis NFL	12	1	47	152	3.2	1	17	159	9.4	0	15	315	21.0	0	1	0	6	1
1996—Indianapolis NFL	13	3	67	230	3.4	1	22	174	7.9	0	3	54	18.0	0	1	0	6	3
1997—Indianapolis NFL	13	0	28	80	2.9	2	20	192	9.6	0	1	19	19.0	0	2	0	12	0
1998—Indianapolis NFL	12	2	25	61	2.4	1	11	44	4.0	1	8	152	19.0	0	2	0	12	0
1999—New England NFL	16	2	35	120	3.4	0	29	262	9.0	1	2	25	12.5	0	1	0	6	0
Pro totals (6 years)	77	8	220	723	3.3	5	102	878	8.6	2	31	621	20.0	0	7	0	42	4

WASHINGTON, DEWAYNE   CB   STEELERS

PERSONAL: Born December 27, 1972, in Durham, N.C. ... 6-0/193. ... Full name: Dewayne Neron Washington.
HIGH SCHOOL: Northern (Durham, N.C.).
COLLEGE: North Carolina State.
TRANSACTIONS/CAREER NOTES: Selected by Minnesota Vikings in first round (18th pick overall) of 1994 NFL draft. ... Signed by Vikings (July 14, 1994). ... Granted unconditional free agency (February 13, 1998). ... Signed by Pittsburgh Steelers (February 25, 1998).
HONORS: Was a high school All-America selection by THE SPORTING NEWS (1989).
PRO STATISTICS: 1994—Recovered two fumbles for 17 yards and one touchdown. 1998—Recovered two fumbles.

			INTERCEPTIONS			
Year Team	G	GS	No.	Yds.	Avg.	TD
1994—Minnesota NFL	16	16	3	135	45.0	2
1995—Minnesota NFL	15	15	1	25	25.0	0
1996—Minnesota NFL	16	16	2	27	13.5	1
1997—Minnesota NFL	16	16	4	71	17.8	0
1998—Pittsburgh NFL	16	16	5	§178	35.6	▲2
1999—Pittsburgh NFL	16	16	4	1	0.3	0
Pro totals (6 years)	95	95	19	437	23.0	5

WASHINGTON, KEITH   DE   RAVENS

W

PERSONAL: Born December 18, 1972, in Dallas. ... 6-4/270. ... Full name: Keith L. Washington.
HIGH SCHOOL: Wilmer-Hutchins (Dallas).
COLLEGE: UNLV.
TRANSACTIONS/CAREER NOTES: Signed as non-drafted free agent by Minnesota Vikings (April 9, 1995). ... Released by Vikings (August 27, 1995). ... Re-signed by Vikings to practice squad (August 28, 1995). ... Activated (October 9, 1995); did not play. ... On injured reserve with ankle injury (November 15, 1995-remainder of season). ... Released by Vikings (August 25, 1996). ... Signed by Detroit Lions (August 26, 1996). ... Released by Lions (August 26, 1997). ... Signed by Baltimore Ravens (October 15, 1997). ... Granted free agency (February 13, 1998). ... Re-signed by Ravens (April 14, 1998). ... Granted unconditional free agency (February 11, 2000). ... Re-signed by Ravens (March 31, 2000).
PLAYING EXPERIENCE: Detroit NFL, 1996; Baltimore NFL, 1997-1999. ... Games/Games started: 1996 (12/0), 1997 (10/1), 1998 (16/0), 1999 (16/0). Total: 54/1.
PRO STATISTICS: 1996—Returned one kickoff for 14 yards. 1997—Credited with two sacks. 1998—Credited with one sack. 1999—Returned one kickoff for 12 yards, credited with one sack, fumbled once and recovered one fumble.

WASHINGTON, MARVIN   DE

PERSONAL: Born October 22, 1965, in Denver. ... 6-6/285. ... Full name: Marvin Andrew Washington. ... Cousin of Andrew Lang, center, New York Knicks.
HIGH SCHOOL: Justin F. Kimball (Dallas).
JUNIOR COLLEGE: Hinds Community College (Miss.).
COLLEGE: Texas-El Paso, then Idaho.
TRANSACTIONS/CAREER NOTES: Selected by New York Jets in sixth round (151st pick overall) of 1989 NFL draft. ... Signed by Jets (July 21, 1989). ... Granted free agency (February 1, 1991). ... Re-signed by Jets (May 5, 1991). ... Granted free agency (March 1, 1993). ... Tendered offer sheet by Seattle Seahawks (March 25, 1993). ... Offer matched by Jets (March 31, 1993). ... Released by Jets (August 11, 1997). ... Signed by San Francisco 49ers (August 21, 1997). ... On injured reserve with ankle injury (November 12, 1997-remainder of season). ... Granted unconditional free agency (February 13, 1998). ... Signed by Denver Broncos (March 2, 1998). ... Granted unconditional free agency (February 12, 1999). ... Signed by 49ers (April 1, 1999). ... On injured reserve with leg injury (October 12, 1999-remainder of season). ... Released by 49ers (February 9, 2000).
CHAMPIONSHIP GAME EXPERIENCE: Played in AFC championship game (1998 season). ... Member of Super Bowl championship team (1998 season).
PRO STATISTICS: 1989—Returned one kickoff for 11 yards and recovered one fumble. 1992—Credited with a safety. 1994—Intercepted one pass for seven yards, fumbled once and recovered one fumble. 1997—Recovered one fumble.

Year Team	G	GS	SACKS
1989—New York Jets NFL	16	0	1.5
1990—New York Jets NFL	16	0	4.5
1991—New York Jets NFL	15	15	6.0
1992—New York Jets NFL	16	14	8.5
1993—New York Jets NFL	16	16	5.5
1994—New York Jets NFL	15	15	3.0
1995—New York Jets NFL	16	16	6.0
1996—New York Jets NFL	14	14	2.5
1997—San Francisco NFL	10	1	1.0
1998—Denver NFL	16	0	2.0
1999—San Francisco NFL	5	5	0.0
Pro totals (11 years)	155	96	40.5

WASHINGTON, TED   NT   BILLS

PERSONAL: Born April 13, 1968, in Tampa. ... 6-5/330. ... Full name: Theodore Washington. ... Son of Ted Washington, linebacker with New York Jets (1973) and Houston Oilers (1974-82).
HIGH SCHOOL: Tampa Bay Vocational Tech Senior.
COLLEGE: Louisville.
TRANSACTIONS/CAREER NOTES: Selected by San Francisco 49ers in first round (25th pick overall) of 1991 NFL draft. ... Signed by 49ers (July 10, 1991). ... Traded by 49ers to Denver Broncos for fifth-round pick (traded to Green Bay) in 1994 draft (April 19, 1994). ... Granted unconditional free agency (February 17, 1995). ... Signed by Buffalo Bills (February 25, 1995). ... Designated by Bills as franchise player (February 13, 1998). ... Free agency status changed from franchise to transitional (February 27, 1998). ... Re-signed by Bills (March 2, 1998).
CHAMPIONSHIP GAME EXPERIENCE: Played in NFC championship game (1992 and 1993 seasons).
HONORS: Played in Pro Bowl (1997 and 1998 seasons).
PRO STATISTICS: 1993—Recovered one fumble. 1994—Intercepted one pass for five yards. 1997—Recovered one fumble. 1998—Intercepted one pass for no yards and credited with a safety.

Year Team	G	GS	SACKS
1991—San Francisco NFL	16	0	1.0
1992—San Francisco NFL	16	6	2.0
1993—San Francisco NFL	12	12	3.0
1994—Denver NFL	15	15	2.5
1995—Buffalo NFL	16	15	2.5
1996—Buffalo NFL	16	16	3.5
1997—Buffalo NFL	16	16	4.0
1998—Buffalo NFL	16	16	4.5
1999—Buffalo NFL	16	16	2.5
Pro totals (9 years)	139	112	25.5

WASHINGTON, TODD   C/G   BUCCANEERS

PERSONAL: Born July 19, 1976, in Nassawadox, Va. ... 6-3/324. ... Full name: Todd Page Washington.
HIGH SCHOOL: Nandua (Onley, Va.).
COLLEGE: Virginia Tech (degree in physical education and health, 1998).
TRANSACTIONS/CAREER NOTES: Selected by Tampa Bay Buccaneers in fourth round (104th pick overall) of 1998 NFL draft. ... Signed by Buccaneers (June 11, 1998).
PLAYING EXPERIENCE: Tampa Bay NFL, 1998 and 1999. ... Games/Games started: 1998 (4/0), 1999 (6/0). Total: 10/0.
CHAMPIONSHIP GAME EXPERIENCE: Played in NFC championship game (1999 season).

WATSON, CHRIS   CB   BRONCOS

PERSONAL: Born June 30, 1977, in Chicago. ... 6-1/192.
HIGH SCHOOL: Leo (Chicago).
COLLEGE: Eastern Illinois.
TRANSACTIONS/CAREER NOTES: Selected by Denver Broncos in third round (67th pick overall) of 1999 NFL draft. ... Signed by Broncos (June 15, 1999).

W

PRO STATISTICS: 1999—Recovered three fumbles.

				PUNT RETURNS				KICKOFF RETURNS				TOTALS		
Year Team	G	GS	No.	Yds.	Avg.	TD	No.	Yds.	Avg.	TD	TD	2pt.	Pts.	Fum.
1999—Denver NFL	14	1	44	334	7.6	1	48	1138	23.7	0	1	0	6	5

WATSON, EDWIN — RB — EAGLES

PERSONAL: Born September 29, 1976, in New Orleans. ... 6-0/225. ... Full name: Edwin David Watson II.
HIGH SCHOOL: Northern (Pontiac, Mich.).
COLLEGE: Purdue.
TRANSACTIONS/CAREER NOTES: Selected by Green Bay Packers in seventh round (218th pick overall) of 1998 NFL draft. ... Signed by Packers (June 8, 1998). ... On injured reserve with shoulder injury (August 6, 1998-entire season). ... Assigned by Packers to Berlin Thunder in 1999 NFL Europe enhancement allocation program (February 22, 1999). ... Released by Packers (September 4, 1999). ... Signed by Denver Broncos to practice squad (October 19, 1999). ... Signed by Philadelphia Eagles off Broncos practice squad (November 10, 1999).
SINGLE GAME HIGHS (regular season): Attempts—3 (December 19, 1999, vs. New England); yards—11 (December 19, 1999, vs. New England); and rushing touchdowns—0.

			RUSHING				RECEIVING				TOTALS			
Year Team	G	GS	Att.	Yds.	Avg.	TD	No.	Yds.	Avg.	TD	TD	2pt.	Pts.	Fum.
1998—Green Bay NFL							Did not play.							
1999—Berlin NFLE	10	9	117	503	4.3	3	7	64	9.1	0	3	0	18	0
—Philadelphia NFL	6	0	4	17	4.3	0	0	0	0.0	0	0	0	0	0
NFL Europe totals (1 year)	10	9	117	503	4.3	3	7	64	9.1	0	3	0	18	0
NFL totals (0 year)	6	0	4	17	4.3	0	0	0	0.0	0	0	0	0	0
Pro totals (1 years)	16	9	121	520	4.3	3	7	64	9.1	0	3	0	18	0

WATSON, JUSTIN — RB — RAMS

PERSONAL: Born January 1, 1975, in Bronx, N.Y. ... 6-0/225. ... Full name: Justin Sean Watson.
HIGH SCHOOL: Marshall (Pasadena, Calif.).
COLLEGE: San Diego State (degree in criminal justice).
TRANSACTIONS/CAREER NOTES: Signed as non-drafted free agent by San Diego Chargers (April 20, 1998). ... Released by Chargers (August 24, 1998). ... Re-signed by Chargers to practice squad (November 25, 1998). ... Assigned by Chargers to Berlin Thunder in 1999 NFL Europe enhancement allocation program (February 22, 1999). ... Released by Chargers (April 22, 1999). ... Signed by St. Louis Rams (July 1, 1999).
CHAMPIONSHIP GAME EXPERIENCE: Member of Rams for NFC championship game (1999 season); inactive. ... Member of Super Bowl championship team (1999 season); inactive.
SINGLE GAME HIGHS (regular season): Attempts—11 (December 26, 1999, vs. Chicago); yards—69 (October 24, 1999, vs. Cleveland); and rushing touchdowns—0.

			RUSHING				RECEIVING				TOTALS			
Year Team	G	GS	Att.	Yds.	Avg.	TD	No.	Yds.	Avg.	TD	TD	2pt.	Pts.	Fum.
1998—San Diego NFL							Did not play.							
1999—Berlin NFLE	...	...	81	333	4.1	2	18	188	10.4	1	3	0	18	0
—St. Louis NFL	8	0	47	179	3.8	0	0	0	0.0	0	0	0	0	2
NFL Europe totals (1 year)	...	...	81	333	4.1	2	18	188	10.4	1	3	0	18	0
NFL totals (0 year)	8	0	47	179	3.8	0	0	0	0.0	0	0	0	0	2
Pro totals (1 years)	...	...	128	512	4.0	2	18	188	10.4	1	3	0	18	2

WATTERS, RICKY — RB — SEAHAWKS

PERSONAL: Born April 7, 1969, in Harrisburg, Pa. ... 6-1/217. ... Full name: Richard James Watters.
HIGH SCHOOL: Bishop McDevitt (Harrisburg, Pa.).
COLLEGE: Notre Dame (degree in design, 1990).
TRANSACTIONS/CAREER NOTES: Selected by San Francisco 49ers in second round (45th pick overall) of 1991 NFL draft. ... Signed by 49ers (July 11, 1991). ... On injured reserve with foot injury (August 27, 1991-entire season). ... Designated by 49ers as transition player (February 15, 1994). ... Tendered offer sheet by Philadelphia Eagles (March 18, 1995). ... 49ers declined to match offer (March 25, 1995). ... Granted unconditional free agency (February 13, 1998). ... Signed by Seattle Seahawks (March 4, 1998).
CHAMPIONSHIP GAME EXPERIENCE: Played in NFC championship game (1992-1994 seasons). ... Member of Super Bowl championship team (1994 season).
HONORS: Played in Pro Bowl (1992-1996 seasons).
POST SEASON RECORDS: Shares Super Bowl single-game records for most points—18; and most touchdowns—3 (January 29, 1995, vs. San Diego). ... Holds NFL postseason single-game records for most points—30; most touchdowns—5; and most rushing touchdowns—5 (January 15, 1994, vs. New York Giants).
PRO STATISTICS: 1992—Attempted one pass without a completion and recovered one fumble. 1993—Recovered one fumble. 1994—Recovered two fumbles. 1997—Recovered one fumble. 1998—Completed only pass attempt for one yard and a touchdown and recovered one fumble.
SINGLE GAME HIGHS (regular season): Attempts—33 (December 10, 1995, vs. Dallas); yards—178 (December 20, 1998, vs. Indianapolis); rushing touchdowns—3 (December 5, 1993, vs. Cincinnati).
STATISTICAL PLATEAUS: 100-yard rushing games: 1992 (4), 1993 (3), 1994 (2), 1995 (4), 1996 (6), 1997 (2), 1998 (4), 1999 (4). Total: 29. ... 100-yard receiving games: 1994 (1).

			RUSHING				RECEIVING				TOTALS			
Year Team	G	GS	Att.	Yds.	Avg.	TD	No.	Yds.	Avg.	TD	TD	2pt.	Pts.	Fum.
1991—San Francisco NFL							Did not play.							
1992—San Francisco NFL	14	13	206	1013	4.9	9	43	405	9.4	2	11	0	66	2
1993—San Francisco NFL	13	13	208	950	4.6	‡10	31	326	10.5	1	11	0	66	5
1994—San Francisco NFL	16	16	239	877	3.7	6	66	719	10.9	5	11	0	66	8
1995—Philadelphia NFL	16	16	337	1273	3.8	11	62	434	7.0	1	12	0	72	6

W

Year Team	G	GS	Att.	Yds.	Avg.	TD	No.	Yds.	Avg.	TD	TD	2pt	Pts.	Fum.
1996—Philadelphia NFL	16	16	*353	1411	4.0	13	51	444	8.7	0	13	0	78	5
1997—Philadelphia NFL	16	16	285	1110	3.9	7	48	440	9.2	0	7	0	42	3
1998—Seattle NFL	16	16	319	1239	3.9	9	52	373	7.2	0	9	1	56	4
1999—Seattle NFL	16	16	325	1210	3.7	5	40	387	9.7	2	7	0	42	4
Pro totals (8 years)	123	122	2272	9083	4.0	70	393	3528	9.0	11	81	1	488	37

WAY, CHARLES FB

PERSONAL: Born December 27, 1972, in Philadelphia. ... 6-0/247. ... Full name: Charles Christopher Way.
HIGH SCHOOL: Northeast (Philadelphia).
COLLEGE: Virginia.
TRANSACTIONS/CAREER NOTES: Selected by New York Giants in sixth round (206th pick overall) of 1995 NFL draft. ... Signed by Giants (July 23, 1995). ... On injured reserve with knee injury (December 3, 1999-remainder of season). ... Announced retirement (June 2, 2000).
PRO STATISTICS: 1995—Returned one kickoff for eight yards. 1996—Returned two kickoffs for 19 yards and recovered three fumbles. 1997—Returned two kickoffs for 46 yards and recovered five fumbles. 1998—Recovered two fumbles.
SINGLE GAME HIGHS (regular season): Attempts—20 (October 26, 1997, vs. Cincinnati); yards—114 (November 16, 1997, vs. Arizona); and rushing touchdowns—2 (October 26, 1997, vs. Cincinnati).
STATISTICAL PLATEAUS: 100-yard rushing games: 1997 (1).

			RUSHING				RECEIVING				TOTALS			
Year Team	G	GS	Att.	Yds.	Avg.	TD	No.	Yds.	Avg.	TD	TD	2pt.	Pts.	Fum.
1995—New York Giants NFL	16	4	2	6	3.0	0	7	76	10.9	1	1	0	6	0
1996—New York Giants NFL	16	12	22	79	3.6	1	32	328	10.3	1	2	0	12	0
1997—New York Giants NFL	16	16	151	698	4.6	4	37	304	8.2	1	5	0	30	3
1998—New York Giants NFL	16	15	113	432	3.8	3	31	131	4.2	1	4	0	24	0
1999—New York Giants NFL	11	8	49	141	2.9	2	11	59	5.4	0	2	0	12	0
Pro totals (5 years)	75	55	337	1356	4.0	10	118	898	7.6	4	14	0	84	3

WAYNE, NATE LB BRONCOS

PERSONAL: Born January 12, 1975, in Chicago. ... 6-0/230.
HIGH SCHOOL: Noxubee County (Macon, Miss.).
COLLEGE: Mississippi.
TRANSACTIONS/CAREER NOTES: Selected by Denver Broncos in seventh round (219th pick overall) of 1998 NFL draft. ... Signed by Broncos (June 9, 1998). ... Assigned by Broncos to Barcelona Dragons in 1999 NFL Europe enhancement allocation program (February 22, 1999). ... Released by Broncos (September 19, 1999). ... Re-signed by Broncos to practice squad (September 21, 1999). ... Activated (September 22, 1999).
PLAYING EXPERIENCE: Denver NFL, 1998 and 1999; Barcelona NFLE, 1999. ... Games/Games started: 1998 (1/0), NFLE 1999 (games played unavailable); NFL 1999 (15/0). Total NFL: 16/0.
CHAMPIONSHIP GAME EXPERIENCE: Member of Broncos for AFC championship game (1998 season); inactive. ... Member of Super Bowl championship team (1998 season); inactive.
PRO STATISTICS: NFLE: 1999—Intercepted one pass for 31 yards and credited with one sack. NFL: 1999—Credited with two sacks.

WEARY, FRED CB SAINTS

PERSONAL: Born April 12, 1974, in Jacksonville. ... 5-10/181. ... Full name: Joseph Fredrick Weary.
HIGH SCHOOL: Mandarin (Jacksonville).
COLLEGE: Florida.
TRANSACTIONS/CAREER NOTES: Selected by New Orleans Saints in fourth round (97th pick overall) of 1998 NFL draft. ... Signed by Saints (July 10, 1998).
HONORS: Named cornerback on THE SPORTING NEWS college All-America first team (1997).
PRO STATISTICS: 1999—Recovered four fumbles for 60 yards.

			INTERCEPTIONS			
Year Team	G	GS	No.	Yds.	Avg.	TD
1998—New Orleans NFL	14	1	2	64	32.0	1
1999—New Orleans NFL	16	11	2	49	24.5	0
Pro totals (2 years)	30	12	4	113	28.3	1

W

WEATHERS, ANDRE CB GIANTS

PERSONAL: Born August 6, 1976, in Flint, Mich. ... 6-0/190. ... Full name: Andre Le'Melle Weathers.
HIGH SCHOOL: Flint (Mich.) Central.
COLLEGE: Michigan.
TRANSACTIONS/CAREER NOTES: Selected by New York Giants in sixth round (205th pick overall) of 1999 NFL draft. ... Signed by Giants (July 27, 1999). ... On injured reserve with knee injury (November 27, 1999-remainder of season).
PLAYING EXPERIENCE: New York Giants NFL, 1999. ... Games/Games started: 1999 (9/0).
PRO STATISTICS: 1999—Intercepted one pass for eight yards and a touchdown and recovered one fumble.

WEAVER, JED TE EAGLES

PERSONAL: Born August 11, 1976, in Bend, Ore. ... 6-4/246. ... Full name: Timothy Jed Weaver. ... Cousin of Jeff Weaver, pitcher, Detroit Tigers.
HIGH SCHOOL: Redmond (Ore.).
COLLEGE: Oregon.

TRANSACTIONS/CAREER NOTES: Selected by Philadelphia Eagles in seventh round (208th pick overall) of 1999 NFL draft. ... Signed by Eagles (July 16, 1999).
SINGLE GAME HIGHS (regular season): Receptions—4 (October 24, 1999, vs. Miami); yards—27 (October 24, 1999, vs. Miami); and touchdown receptions—0.

| | | | RECEIVING | | | | TOTALS | | | |
Year	Team	G	GS	No.	Yds.	Avg.	TD	TD	2pt.	Pts.	Fum.
1999—Philadelphia NFL		16	10	11	91	8.3	0	0	†1	2	0

WEBB, RICHMOND   OT   DOLPHINS

PERSONAL: Born January 11, 1967, in Dallas. ... 6-6/315. ... Full name: Richmond Jewel Webb Jr.
HIGH SCHOOL: Franklin D. Roosevelt (Dallas).
COLLEGE: Texas A&M (degree in industrial distribution).
TRANSACTIONS/CAREER NOTES: Selected by Miami Dolphins in first round (ninth pick overall) of 1990 NFL draft. ... Signed by Dolphins (July 27, 1990). ... Designated by Dolphins as franchise player (February 12, 1999). ... Designated by Dolphins as franchise player (February 11, 2000).
PLAYING EXPERIENCE: Miami NFL, 1990-1999. ... Games/Games started: 1990 (16/16), 1991 (14/14), 1992 (16/16), 1993 (16/16), 1994 (16/16), 1995 (16/16), 1996 (16/16), 1997 (16/16), 1998 (9/9), 1999 (15/14). Total: 150/149.
CHAMPIONSHIP GAME EXPERIENCE: Played in AFC championship game (1992 season).
HONORS: Named NFL Rookie of the Year by THE SPORTING NEWS (1990). ... Played in Pro Bowl (1990-1996 seasons). ... Named offensive tackle on THE SPORTING NEWS NFL All-Pro team (1992 and 1994).
PRO STATISTICS: 1995—Recovered one fumble.

WEBSTER, LARRY   DL   RAVENS

PERSONAL: Born January 18, 1969, in Elkton, Md. ... 6-5/305. ... Full name: Larry Melvin Webster Jr.
HIGH SCHOOL: Elkton (Md.).
COLLEGE: Maryland.
TRANSACTIONS/CAREER NOTES: Selected by Miami Dolphins in third round (70th pick overall) of 1992 NFL draft. ... Signed by Dolphins (July 10, 1992). ... Granted free agency (February 17, 1995). ... Signed by Cleveland Browns (May 4, 1995). ... On suspended list for violating league substance abuse policy (September 4-26, 1995). ... Browns franchise moved to Baltimore and renamed Ravens for 1996 season (March 11, 1996). ... On suspended list for violating league substance abuse policy (August 20, 1996-July 13, 1997). ... Granted unconditional free agency (February 13, 1998). ... Re-signed by Ravens (February 16, 1998). ... Granted unconditional free agency (February 11, 2000). ... Re-signed by Ravens (February 16, 2000). ... On suspended list for violating league substance abuse policy (April 11, 2000-present).
PLAYING EXPERIENCE: Miami NFL, 1992-1994; Cleveland NFL, 1995; Baltimore NFL, 1997-1999. ... Games/Games started: 1992 (16/0), 1993 (13/9), 1994 (16/7), 1995 (10/0), 1997 (16/3), 1998 (15/0), 1999 (16/16). Total: 102/35.
CHAMPIONSHIP GAME EXPERIENCE: Played in AFC championship game (1992 season).
PRO STATISTICS: 1992—Credited with 1$\frac{1}{2}$ sacks. 1993—Recovered one fumble. 1999—Credited with two sacks.

WEINER, TODD   OT   SEAHAWKS

PERSONAL: Born September 16, 1975, in Bristol, Pa. ... 6-4/300.
HIGH SCHOOL: Taravella (Coral Springs, Fla.).
COLLEGE: Kansas State.
TRANSACTIONS/CAREER NOTES: Selected by Seattle Seahawks in second round (47th pick overall) of 1998 NFL draft. ... Signed by Seahawks (July 15, 1998).
PLAYING EXPERIENCE: Seattle NFL, 1998 and 1999. ... Games/Games started: 1998 (6/0), 1999 (11/1). Total: 17/1.
HONORS: Named offensive tackle on THE SPORTING NEWS college All-America second team (1997).

WELBOURN, JOHN   G/OT   EAGLES

PERSONAL: Born March 30, 1976, in Torrance, Calif. ... 6-5/318.
HIGH SCHOOL: Palos Verdes Peninsula (Rolling Hills Estate, Calif.).
COLLEGE: California (degree in rhetoric).
TRANSACTIONS/CAREER NOTES: Selected by Philadelphia Eagles in fourth round (97th pick overall) of 1999 NFL draft. ... Signed by Eagles (July 25, 1999). ... On injured reserve with knee injury (September 13, 1999-remainder of season).
PLAYING EXPERIENCE: Philadelphia NFL, 1999. ... Games/Games started: 1999 (1/1).

W

WELDON, CASEY   QB

PERSONAL: Born February 3, 1969, in Americus, Ga. ... 6-1/206. ... Full name: William Casey Weldon.
HIGH SCHOOL: North Florida Christian (Tallahassee, Fla.).
COLLEGE: Florida State (degree in political science, 1991).
TRANSACTIONS/CAREER NOTES: Selected by Philadelphia Eagles in fourth round (102nd pick overall) of 1992 NFL draft. ... Signed by Eagles (July 26, 1992). ... On inactive list for all 16 games (1992). ... Claimed on waivers by Tampa Bay Buccaneers (September 1, 1993). ... Assigned by Buccaneers to Barcelona Dragons in 1995 World League enhancement allocation program (February 20, 1995). ... Granted unconditional free agency (February 14, 1997). ... Signed by San Diego Chargers (November 14, 1997). ... Inactive for six games during 1997 season. ... Granted unconditional free agency (February 13, 1998). ... Re-signed by Chargers (April 10, 1998). ... Released by Chargers (August 30, 1998). ... Signed by Washington Redskins (September 23, 1998). ... Inactive for 13 games (1998). ... Granted unconditional free agency (February 12, 1999). ... Re-signed by Redskins (March 4, 1999). ... Released by Redskins (April 21, 2000).
HONORS: Named quarterback on THE SPORTING NEWS college All-America second team (1991).
PRO STATISTICS: 1995—Fumbled four times. 1996—Fumbled once for minus one yard. 1999—Fumbled once and recovered one fumble for minus two yards.

SINGLE GAME HIGHS (regular season): Attempts—28 (December 23, 1995, vs. Detroit); completions—11 (December 23, 1995, vs. Detroit); yards—156 (October 1, 1995, vs. Carolina); and touchdown passes—1 (December 3, 1995, vs. Minnesota).

				PASSING							RUSHING				TOTALS		
Year—Team	G	GS	Att.	Cmp.	Pct.	Yds.	TD	Int.	Avg.	Rat.	Att.	Yds.	Avg.	TD	TD	2pt.	Pts.
1992—Philadelphia NFL								Did not play.									
1993—Tampa Bay NFL	3	0	11	6	54.5	55	0	1	5.00	30.5	0	0	0.0	0	0	0	0
1994—Tampa Bay NFL	2	0	9	7	77.8	63	0	0	7.00	95.8	0	0	0.0	0	0	0	0
1995—Barcelona W.L.	5	...	91	41	45.1	543	3	9	5.97	35.9	8	44	5.5	0	0	0	0
—Tampa Bay NFL	16	0	91	42	46.2	519	1	2	5.70	58.8	5	5	1.0	1	1	0	6
1996—Tampa Bay NFL	3	0	9	5	55.6	76	0	1	8.44	44.0	2	-1	-0.5	0	0	0	0
1997—San Diego NFL								Did not play.									
1998—Washington NFL								Did not play.									
1999—Washington NFL	2	0	0	0	0	0	0	0	0.0	...	5	-4	-0.8	0	0	0	0
W.L. totals (1 year)	5	...	91	41	45.1	543	3	9	5.97	35.9	8	44	5.5	0	0	0	0
NFL totals (5 years)	26	0	120	60	50.0	713	1	4	5.94	57.4	12	0	0.0	1	1	0	6
Pro totals (6 years)	31	...	211	101	47.9	1256	4	13	5.95	47.4	20	44	2.2	1	1	0	6

WELLS, DEAN   LB   PANTHERS

PERSONAL: Born July 20, 1970, in Louisville, Ky. ... 6-3/248. ... Full name: Donald Dean Wells.
HIGH SCHOOL: Holy Cross (Louisville, Ky.).
COLLEGE: Kentucky (degree in marketing, 1992).
TRANSACTIONS/CAREER NOTES: Selected by Seattle Seahawks in fourth round (85th pick overall) of 1993 NFL draft. ... Signed by Seahawks (July 13, 1993). ... Granted unconditional free agency (February 12, 1999). ... Signed by Carolina Panthers (April 7, 1999).
PLAYING EXPERIENCE: Seattle NFL, 1993-1998; Carolina NFL, 1999. ... Games/Games started: 1993 (14/1), 1994 (15/0), 1995 (14/10), 1996 (16/15), 1997 (16/16), 1998 (9/8), 1999 (16/10). Total: 100/60.
PRO STATISTICS: 1995—Recovered one fumble. 1996—Credited with one sack and recovered two fumbles. 1997—Credited with one sack and recovered one fumble. 1998—Intercepted one pass for 25 yards. 1999—Intercepted one pass for one yard and credited with ¹/₂ sack.

WELLS, MIKE   DT   BEARS

PERSONAL: Born January 6, 1971, in Arnold, Mo. ... 6-3/315. ... Full name: Mike Allan Wells.
HIGH SCHOOL: Fox (Arnold, Mo.).
COLLEGE: Iowa (degree in communication studies, 1994).
TRANSACTIONS/CAREER NOTES: Selected by Minnesota Vikings in fourth round (125th pick overall) of 1994 NFL draft. ... Signed by Vikings (June 24, 1994). ... Released by Vikings (August 28, 1994). ... Signed by Detroit Lions (August 29, 1994). ... Granted free agency (February 14, 1997). ... Re-signed by Lions (June 2, 1997). ... Granted unconditional free agency (February 13, 1998). ... Signed by Chicago Bears (February 17, 1998).
PLAYING EXPERIENCE: Detroit NFL, 1994-1997; Chicago NFL, 1998 and 1999. ... Games/Games started: 1994 (4/0), 1995 (15/0), 1996 (16/1), 1997 (16/16), 1998 (16/16), 1999 (16/16). Total: 83/49.
PRO STATISTICS: 1994—Credited with ¹/₂ sack. 1996—Recovered one fumble in end zone for a touchdown. 1997—Credited with one sack and recovered one fumble. 1998—Credited with three sacks. 1999—Credited with one sack and recovered one fumble.

WESLEY, JOE   LB   49ERS

PERSONAL: Born November 10, 1976, in Jackson, Miss. ... 6-1/229.
HIGH SCHOOL: Brookhaven (Miss.).
COLLEGE: Louisiana State.
TRANSACTIONS/CAREER NOTES: Signed as non-drafted free agent by San Francisco 49ers (April 23, 1999). ... Released by 49ers (September 5, 1999). ... Re-signed by 49ers to practice squad (September 6, 1999). ... Activated (September 15, 1999). ... On injured reserve with groin injury (December 8, 1999-remainder of season).
PLAYING EXPERIENCE: San Francisco NFL, 1999. ... Games/Games started: 1999 (8/0).

WEST, LYLE   S   GIANTS

PERSONAL: Born December 20, 1976, in Columbus, Ga. ... 6-0/215.
HIGH SCHOOL: Washington (Fremont, Calif.).
JUNIOR COLLEGE: Chabot College (Calif.).
COLLEGE: San Jose State.
TRANSACTIONS/CAREER NOTES: Selected by New York Giants in sixth round (189th pick overall) of 1999 NFL draft. ... Signed by Giants (July 29, 1999). ... On suspended list for violating league substance abuse policy (November 23-December 20, 1999).
PLAYING EXPERIENCE: New York Giants NFL, 1999. ... Games/Games started: 1999 (6/0).

WESTBROOK, BRYANT   CB   LIONS

PERSONAL: Born December 19, 1974, in Charlotte. ... 6-0/198. ... Full name: Bryant Antoine Westbrook.
HIGH SCHOOL: El Camino (Oceanside, Calif.).
COLLEGE: Texas.
TRANSACTIONS/CAREER NOTES: Selected by Detroit Lions in first round (fifth pick overall) of 1997 NFL draft. ... Signed by Lions (August 9, 1997).
PRO STATISTICS: 1999—Recovered one fumble.

W

Year Team	G	GS	INTERCEPTIONS No.	Yds.	Avg.	TD
1997—Detroit NFL	15	14	2	64	32.0	1
1998—Detroit NFL	16	16	3	49	16.3	1
1999—Detroit NFL	10	8	0	0	0.0	0
Pro totals (3 years)	41	38	5	113	22.6	2

WESTBROOK, MICHAEL   WR   REDSKINS

PERSONAL: Born July 7, 1972, in Detroit. ... 6-3/220.
HIGH SCHOOL: Chadsey (Detroit).
COLLEGE: Colorado.
TRANSACTIONS/CAREER NOTES: Selected by Washington Redskins in first round (fourth pick overall) of 1995 NFL draft. ... Signed by Redskins (August 14, 1995). ... On injured reserve with neck injury (December 8, 1998-remainder of season).
HONORS: Named wide receiver on THE SPORTING NEWS college All-America first team (1994).
PRO STATISTICS: 1999—Recovered one fumble.
SINGLE GAME HIGHS (regular season): Receptions—10 (November 22, 1998, vs. Arizona); yards—159 (September 12, 1999, vs. Dallas); and touchdown receptions—3 (November 22, 1998, vs. Arizona).
STATISTICAL PLATEAUS: 100-yard receiving games: 1996 (1), 1997 (1), 1998 (4), 1999 (5). Total: 11.

Year Team	G	GS	RUSHING Att.	Yds.	Avg.	TD	RECEIVING No.	Yds.	Avg.	TD	TOTALS TD	2pt.	Pts.	Fum.
1995—Washington NFL	11	9	6	114	19.0	1	34	522	15.4	1	2	0	12	0
1996—Washington NFL	11	6	2	2	1.0	0	34	505	14.9	1	1	0	6	0
1997—Washington NFL	13	9	3	-11	-3.7	0	34	559	16.4	3	3	0	18	0
1998—Washington NFL	11	10	1	11	11.0	0	44	736	16.7	6	6	0	36	0
1999—Washington NFL	16	16	7	35	5.0	0	65	1191	18.3	9	9	†1	56	3
Pro totals (5 years)	62	50	19	151	7.9	1	211	3513	16.6	20	21	1	128	3

WETNIGHT, RYAN   TE   BEARS

PERSONAL: Born November 5, 1970, in Fresno, Calif. ... 6-2/236. ... Full name: Ryan Scott Wetnight.
HIGH SCHOOL: Hoover (Fresno, Calif.).
JUNIOR COLLEGE: Fresno (Calif.) City College.
COLLEGE: Stanford.
TRANSACTIONS/CAREER NOTES: Signed as non-drafted free agent by Chicago Bears (April 29, 1993). ... Released by Bears (October 10, 1993). ... Re-signed by Bears to practice squad (October 11, 1993). ... Activated (October 29, 1993). ... Released by Bears (October 7, 1994). ... Re-signed by Bears (October 10, 1994). ... On injured reserve with knee injury (December 7, 1995-remainder of season). ... Granted unconditional free agency (February 14, 1997). ... Re-signed by Bears (April 2, 1997). ... Granted unconditional free agency (February 13, 1998). ... Re-signed by Bears (February 23, 1998).
PRO STATISTICS: 1997—Returned one kickoff for nine yards.
SINGLE GAME HIGHS (regular season): Receptions—6 (October 3, 1999, vs. New Orleans); yards—70 (December 7, 1997, vs. Buffalo); and touchdown receptions—1 (October 31, 1999, vs. Washington).

Year Team	G	GS	RECEIVING No.	Yds.	Avg.	TD	TOTALS TD	2pt.	Pts.	Fum.
1993—Chicago NFL	10	1	9	93	10.3	1	1	0	6	0
1994—Chicago NFL	11	0	11	104	9.5	1	1	0	6	0
1995—Chicago NFL	12	2	24	193	8.0	2	2	0	12	0
1996—Chicago NFL	11	5	21	223	10.6	1	1	0	6	0
1997—Chicago NFL	16	3	46	464	10.1	1	1	0	6	1
1998—Chicago NFL	15	3	23	168	7.3	2	2	0	12	1
1999—Chicago NFL	16	4	38	277	7.3	1	1	0	6	0
Pro totals (7 years)	91	18	172	1522	8.8	9	9	0	54	2

WHEATLEY, TYRONE   RB   RAIDERS

PERSONAL: Born January 19, 1972, in Inkster, Mich. ... 6-0/235.
HIGH SCHOOL: Robichaud (Dearborn Heights, Mich.).
COLLEGE: Michigan.
TRANSACTIONS/CAREER NOTES: Selected by New York Giants in first round (17th pick overall) of 1995 NFL draft. ... Signed by Giants (August 9, 1995). ... Traded by Giants to Miami Dolphins for seventh-round pick (LB O.J. Childress) in 1999 draft (February 12, 1999). ... Released by Dolphins (August 3, 1999). ... Signed by Oakland Raiders (August 4, 1999).
PRO STATISTICS: 1996—Completed only pass attempt for 24 yards and a touchdown and recovered one fumble for minus 18 yards. 1997—Recovered three fumbles. 1999—Recovered one fumble.
SINGLE GAME HIGHS (regular season): Attempts—25 (October 17, 1999, vs. Buffalo); yards—111 (December 19, 1999, vs. Tampa Bay); and rushing touchdowns—2 (December 19, 1999, vs. Tampa Bay).
STATISTICAL PLATEAUS: 100-yard rushing games: 1997 (1), 1999 (2). Total: 3.

Year Team	G	GS	RUSHING Att.	Yds.	Avg.	TD	RECEIVING No.	Yds.	Avg.	TD	KICKOFF RETURNS No.	Yds.	Avg.	TD	TOTALS TD	2pt.	Pts.	Fum.
1995—New York Giants NFL	13	1	78	245	3.1	3	5	27	5.4	0	10	186	18.6	0	3	0	18	2
1996—New York Giants NFL	14	0	112	400	3.6	1	12	51	4.3	2	23	503	21.9	0	3	0	18	6
1997—New York Giants NFL	14	7	152	583	3.8	4	16	140	8.8	0	0	0	0.0	0	4	0	24	3
1998—New York Giants NFL	5	0	14	52	3.7	0	0	0	0.0	0	1	16	16.0	0	0	0	0	0
1999—Oakland NFL	16	9	242	936	3.9	8	21	196	9.3	3	0	0	0.0	0	11	0	66	3
Pro totals (5 years)	62	17	598	2216	3.7	16	54	414	7.7	5	34	705	20.7	0	21	0	126	14

W

WHEATON, KENNY   S

PERSONAL: Born March 8, 1975, in Phoenix. ... 5-10/195. ... Full name: Kenneth Tyrone Wheaton.
HIGH SCHOOL: McClintock (Tempe, Ariz.).
COLLEGE: Oregon.
TRANSACTIONS/CAREER NOTES: Selected by Dallas Cowboys in third round (94th pick overall) of 1997 NFL draft. ... Signed by Cowboys (July 14, 1997). ... On injured reserve with knee injury (November 16, 1999-remainder of season). ... Granted free agency (February 11, 2000).
PLAYING EXPERIENCE: Dallas NFL, 1997-1999. ... Games/Games started: 1997 (2/0), 1998 (15/1), 1999 (5/0). Total: 22/1.
PRO STATISTICS: 1998—Intercepted one pass for 41 yards, credited with a safety and recovered two fumbles for 15 yards and one touchdown.

WHEELER, MARK   DT   EAGLES

PERSONAL: Born April 1, 1970, in San Marcos, Texas. ... 6-3/285. ... Full name: Mark Anthony Wheeler.
HIGH SCHOOL: San Marcos (Texas).
JUNIOR COLLEGE: Navarro College (Texas).
COLLEGE: Texas A&M.
TRANSACTIONS/CAREER NOTES: Selected by Tampa Bay Buccaneers in third round (59th pick overall) of 1992 NFL draft. ... Signed by Buccaneers (July 9, 1992). ... Granted unconditional free agency (February 16, 1996). ... Signed by New England Patriots (March 21, 1996). ... Granted unconditional free agency (February 12, 1999). ... Signed by Philadelphia Eagles (March 4, 1999).
CHAMPIONSHIP GAME EXPERIENCE: Played in AFC championship game (1996 season). ... Played in Super Bowl XXXI (1996 season).
PRO STATISTICS: 1996—Recovered one fumble. 1999—Recovered one fumble.

Year Team	G	GS	SACKS
1992—Tampa Bay NFL	16	16	5.0
1993—Tampa Bay NFL	10	10	2.0
1994—Tampa Bay NFL	15	8	3.0
1995—Tampa Bay NFL	14	12	1.0
1996—New England NFL	16	15	1.0
1997—New England NFL	14	14	4.0
1998—New England NFL	10	2	0.0
1999—Philadelphia NFL	13	0	0.0
Pro totals (8 years)	108	77	16.0

WHIGHAM, LARRY   S   PATRIOTS

PERSONAL: Born June 23, 1972, in Hattiesburg, Miss. ... 6-2/205. ... Full name: Larry Jerome Whigham.
HIGH SCHOOL: Hattiesburg (Miss.).
COLLEGE: Northeast Louisiana (degree in criminal justice).
TRANSACTIONS/CAREER NOTES: Selected by Seattle Seahawks in fourth round (110th pick overall) of 1994 NFL draft. ... Signed by Seahawks (June 9, 1994). ... Released by Seahawks (August 28, 1994). ... Re-signed by Seahawks to practice squad (August 29, 1994). ... Signed by New England Patriots off Seahawks practice squad (September 13, 1994). ... Granted free agency (February 14, 1997). ... Re-signed by Patriots (May 1, 1997). ... Granted unconditional free agency (February 12, 1999). ... Re-signed by Patriots (April 14, 1999).
CHAMPIONSHIP GAME EXPERIENCE: Played in AFC championship game (1996 season). ... Played in Super Bowl XXXI (1996 season).
HONORS: Played in Pro Bowl (1997 season).
PRO STATISTICS: 1994—Fumbled once. 1995—Recovered one fumble. 1996—Recovered one fumble. 1997—Credited with two sacks. 1998—Returned one kickoff for no yards. 1999—Credited with three sacks.

Year Team	G	GS	INTERCEPTIONS No.	Yds.	Avg.	TD
1994—New England NFL	12	0	1	21	21.0	0
1995—New England NFL	16	0	0	0	0.0	0
1996—New England NFL	16	1	0	0	0.0	0
1997—New England NFL	16	0	2	60	30.0	1
1998—New England NFL	16	0	1	0	0.0	0
1999—New England NFL	16	0	0	0	0.0	0
Pro totals (6 years)	92	1	4	81	20.3	1

WHITE, STEVE   DE   BUCCANEERS

W

PERSONAL: Born October 25, 1973, in Memphis, Tenn. ... 6-2/271. ... Full name: Stephen Gregory White.
HIGH SCHOOL: Westwood (Memphis, Tenn.).
COLLEGE: Tennessee (degree in psychology, 1996).
TRANSACTIONS/CAREER NOTES: Selected by Philadelphia Eagles in sixth round (194th pick overall) of 1996 NFL draft. ... Signed by Eagles (July 17, 1996). ... Released by Eagles (August 20, 1996). ... Signed by Tampa Bay Buccaneers to practice squad (August 27, 1996). ... Activated (October 15, 1996). ... Released by Buccaneers (November 9, 1996). ... Re-signed by Buccaneers (November 12, 1996).
PLAYING EXPERIENCE: Tampa Bay NFL, 1996-1999. ... Games/Games started: 1996 (4/0), 1997 (15/1), 1998 (16/0), 1999 (13/13). Total: 48/14.
CHAMPIONSHIP GAME EXPERIENCE: Played in NFC championship game (1999 season).
PRO STATISTICS: 1997—Returned one kickoff for no yards. 1998—Credited with two sacks and recovered one fumble. 1999—Credited with two sacks and recovered one fumble.

WHITEHEAD, WILLIE   DE   SAINTS

PERSONAL: Born January 26, 1973 in Tuskegee, Ala. ... 6-3/285. ... Full name: William Whitehead.
HIGH SCHOOL: Tuskegee (Ala.) Institute.

COLLEGE: Auburn.
TRANSACTIONS/CAREER NOTES: Signed as non-drafted free agent by San Fancisco 49ers (April 26, 1995). ... Released by 49ers (July 16, 1995). ... Signed by Baltimore Stallions of CFL (August 1995). ... Signed by Montreal Alouettes of CFL to practice squad (1996). ... Signed by Hamilton Tiger-Cats of CFL (May 14, 1997). ... Signed by Detroit Lions (February 11, 1998). ... Released by Lions (August 25, 1998). ... Signed by New Orleans Saints (January 27, 1999). ... Assigned by Saints to Frankfurt Galaxy in 1999 NFL Europe enhancement allocation program (February 22, 1999).
PRO STATISTICS: CFL: 1997-Recovered one fumble.

Year Team	G	GS	SACKS
1995—Baltimore CFL	1	...	0.0
1996—Montreal CFL		Did not play.	
1997—Hamilton CFL	15	...	13.0
1999—Frankfurt NFLE	...	...	2.0
—New Orleans NFL	16	3	7.0
CFL totals (3 years)	16	...	13.0
NFL Europe totals (1 year)	...	...	2.0
NFL totals (1 year)	16	3	7.0
Pro totals (5 years)	...	...	22.0

WHITFIELD, BOB   OT   FALCONS

PERSONAL: Born October 18, 1971, in Carson, Calif. ... 6-5/318. ... Full name: Bob Whitfield Jr.
HIGH SCHOOL: Banning (Los Angeles).
COLLEGE: Stanford.
TRANSACTIONS/CAREER NOTES: Selected after junior season by Atlanta Falcons in first round (eighth pick overall) of 1992 NFL draft. ... Signed by Falcons (September 4, 1992). ... Granted roster exemption for one game (September 1992).
PLAYING EXPERIENCE: Atlanta NFL, 1992-1999. ... Games/Games started: 1992 (11/0), 1993 (16/16), 1994 (16/16), 1995 (16/16), 1996 (16/16), 1997 (16/16), 1998 (16/16), 1999 (16/16). Total: 123/112.
CHAMPIONSHIP GAME EXPERIENCE: Played in NFC championship game (1998 season). ... Played in Super Bowl XXXIII (1998 season).
HONORS: Named offensive tackle on THE SPORTING NEWS college All-America first team (1991). ... Played in Pro Bowl (1998 season).
PRO STATISTICS: 1993—Recovered two fumbles. 1996—Recovered one fumble.

WHITING, BRANDON   DT/DE   EAGLES

PERSONAL: Born July 30, 1976, in Santa Rosa, Calif. ... 6-3/278. ... Name pronounced WHITE-ing.
HIGH SCHOOL: Polytechnic (Pasadena, Calif.).
COLLEGE: California.
TRANSACTIONS/CAREER NOTES: Selected by Philadelphia Eagles in fourth round (112th pick overall) of 1998 NFL draft. ... Signed by Eagles (July 14, 1998).
PRO STATISTICS: 1998—Recovered one fumble for 24 yards. 1999—Intercepted one pass for 22 yards and a touchdown and returned three kickoffs for 49 yards.

Year Team	G	GS	SACKS
1998—Philadelphia NFL	16	5	1.5
1999—Philadelphia NFL	13	2	1.0
Pro totals (2 years)	29	7	2.5

WHITTED, ALVIS   WR   JAGUARS

PERSONAL: Born September 4, 1974, in Durham, N.C. ... 6-0/186. ... Full name: Alvis James Whitted.
HIGH SCHOOL: Orange (Hillsborough, N.C.).
COLLEGE: North Carolina State.
TRANSACTIONS/CAREER NOTES: Selected by Jacksonville Jaguars in seventh round (192nd pick overall) of 1998 NFL draft. ... Signed by Jaguars (May 19, 1998).
CHAMPIONSHIP GAME EXPERIENCE: Played in AFC championship game (1999 season).
PRO STATISTICS: 1998—Returned a blocked punt 24 yards for a touchdown. 1999—Returned eight kickoffs for 187 yards and one touchdown.
SINGLE GAME HIGHS (regular season): Receptions—1 (November 22, 1998, vs. Pittsburgh); yards—55 (November 8, 1998, vs. Cincinnati); and touchdown receptions—0.

			RUSHING				RECEIVING				TOTALS			
Year Team	G	GS	Att.	Yds.	Avg.	TD	No.	Yds.	Avg.	TD	TD	2pt.	Pts.	Fum.
1998—Jacksonville NFL	16	0	3	13	4.3	0	2	61	30.5	0	1	0	6	0
1999—Jacksonville NFL	14	1	1	9	9.0	0	0	0	0.0	0	1	0	6	0
Pro totals (2 years)	30	1	4	22	5.5	0	2	61	30.5	0	2	0	12	0

WHITTINGTON, BERNARD   DE   COLTS

PERSONAL: Born August 20, 1971, in St. Louis. ... 6-5/280. ... Full name: Bernard Maurice Whittington.
HIGH SCHOOL: Hazelwood East (St. Louis).
COLLEGE: Indiana (degree in sports management).
TRANSACTIONS/CAREER NOTES: Signed as non-drafted free agent by Indianapolis Colts (May 5, 1994). ... Granted free agency (February 14, 1997). ... Re-signed by Colts (June 13, 1997).
CHAMPIONSHIP GAME EXPERIENCE: Played in AFC championship game (1995 season).
PRO STATISTICS: 1995—Recovered one fumble. 1998—Recovered two fumbles.

W

Year Team	G	GS	SACKS
1994—Indianapolis NFL	13	8	0.0
1995—Indianapolis NFL	16	13	2.0
1996—Indianapolis NFL	16	14	3.0
1997—Indianapolis NFL	15	6	0.0
1998—Indianapolis NFL	15	11	4.0
1999—Indianapolis NFL	15	15	1.0
Pro totals (6 years)	90	67	10.0

WHITTLE, JASON   G   GIANTS

PERSONAL: Born March 7, 1975, in Springfield, Mo. ... 6-4/305.
HIGH SCHOOL: Camdenton (Mo.).
COLLEGE: Southwest Missouri State.
TRANSACTIONS/CAREER NOTES: Signed as non-drafted free agent by New York Giants (April 24, 1998). ... Released by Giants (August 30, 1998). ... Re-signed by Giants to practice squad (September 1, 1998). ... Activated (December 16, 1998).
PLAYING EXPERIENCE: New York Giants NFL, 1998 and 1999. ... Games/Games started: 1998 (1/0), 1999 (16/1). Total: 17/1.

WIDMER, COREY   LB

PERSONAL: Born December 25, 1968, in Alexandria, Va. ... 6-3/255. ... Full name: Corey Edward Widmer.
HIGH SCHOOL: Bozeman (Mont.).
COLLEGE: Montana State.
TRANSACTIONS/CAREER NOTES: Selected by New York Giants in seventh round (180th pick overall) of 1992 NFL draft. ... Signed by Giants (July 21, 1992). ... On injured reserve with back injury (September 5-30, 1992). ... On practice squad (September 30-November 15, 1992). ... Granted free agency (February 17, 1995). ... Re-signed by Giants (April 18, 1995). ... Granted unconditional free agency (February 12, 1999). ... Re-signed by Giants (February 17, 1999). ... Released by Giants (June 5, 2000).
PRO STATISTICS: 1995—Returned one kickoff for no yards. 1996—Intercepted two passes for eight yards, fumbled once and recovered one fumble. 1997—Intercepted two passes for no yards. 1998—Recovered one fumble for four yards.

Year Team	G	GS	SACKS
1992—New York Giants NFL	8	0	0.0
1993—New York Giants NFL	11	0	0.0
1994—New York Giants NFL	16	5	1.0
1995—New York Giants NFL	16	0	0.0
1996—New York Giants NFL	16	16	2.0
1997—New York Giants NFL	16	15	1.5
1998—New York Giants NFL	16	15	0.0
1999—New York Giants NFL	15	13	3.0
Pro totals (8 years)	114	64	7.5

WIEGERT, ZACH   G   JAGUARS

PERSONAL: Born August 16, 1972, in Fremont, Neb. ... 6-5/310. ... Full name: Zach Allen Wiegert. ... Name pronounced WEE-gert.
HIGH SCHOOL: Fremont (Neb.) Bergan.
COLLEGE: Nebraska.
TRANSACTIONS/CAREER NOTES: Selected by St. Louis Rams in second round (38th pick overall) of 1995 NFL draft. ... Signed by Rams (July 18, 1995). ... Granted free agency (February 13, 1998). ... Re-signed by Rams (June 17, 1998). ... Designated by Rams as transition player (February 12, 1999). ... Re-signed by Rams (March 24, 1999). ... Released by Rams (April 28, 1999). ... Signed by Jacksonville Jaguars (May 5, 1999).
PLAYING EXPERIENCE: St. Louis NFL, 1995-1998; Jacksonville NFL, 1999. ... Games/Games started: 1995 (5/2), 1996 (16/16), 1997 (15/15), 1998 (13/13), 1999 (16/12). Total: 65/58.
CHAMPIONSHIP GAME EXPERIENCE: Played in AFC championship game (1999 season).
HONORS: Outland Trophy Award winner (1994). ... Named offensive lineman on THE SPORTING NEWS college All-America first team (1994).
PRO STATISTICS: 1996—Recovered two fumbles. 1997—Caught one pass for one yard and recovered four fumbles for no yards and one touchdown. 1998—Recovered one fumble. 1999—Caught one pass for minus three yards and recovered one fumble.

WIEGMANN, CASEY   C   BEARS

W

PERSONAL: Born July 20, 1973, in Parkersburg, Iowa. ... 6-3/295. ... Name pronounced WEG-man.
HIGH SCHOOL: Parkersburg (Iowa).
COLLEGE: Iowa.
TRANSACTIONS/CAREER NOTES: Signed as non-drafted free agent by Indianapolis Colts (April 26, 1996). ... Released by Colts (August 25, 1996). ... Re-signed by Colts to practice squad (August 27, 1996). ... Activated (September 10, 1996); did not play. ... Released by Colts (September 22, 1996). ... Re-signed by Colts to practice squad (September 23, 1996). ... Activated (October 15, 1996); did not play. ... Claimed on waivers by New York Jets (October 29, 1996). ... Released by Jets (September 21, 1997). ... Signed by Chicago Bears (September 24, 1997). ... Granted free agency (February 12, 1999). ... Tendered offer sheet by Miami Dolphins (April 5, 1999). ... Offer matched by Bears (April 8, 1999).
PLAYING EXPERIENCE: New York Jets (3)-Chicago (1) NFL, 1997; Chicago NFL, 1998 and 1999. ... Games/Games started: 1997 (NYJ-3/0; Chi.-1/0; Total: 4/0), 1998 (16/16), 1999 (16/0). Total: 36/16.
PRO STATISTICS: 1998—Returned one kickoff for eight yards, fumbled once and recovered one fumble for minus three yards. 1999—Returned one kickoff for two yards.

WILCOX, JOSH — FB

PERSONAL: Born June 5, 1974, in Junction City, Ore. ... 6-3/255.
HIGH SCHOOL: Junction City (Ore.).
COLLEGE: Oregon.
TRANSACTIONS/CAREER NOTES: Played for Amsterdam Admirals of World League (1997). ... Played for Amsterdam Admirals of NFL Europe (1998). ... Signed as non-drafted free agent by New Orleans Saints (July 24, 1998). ... Released by Saints (August 31, 1998). ... Re-signed by Saints to practice squad (September 1, 1998). ... Activated (December 9, 1998). ... Granted free agency (February 11, 2000).
PRO STATISTICS: NFLE: 1998—Returned one kickoff for 11 yards.
SINGLE GAME HIGHS (regular season): Receptions—3 (December 24, 1999, vs. Dallas); yards—30 (October 24, 1999, vs. New York Giants); and touchdown receptions—0.

| | | | RECEIVING | | | | TOTALS | | | |
Year Team	G	GS	No.	Yds.	Avg.	TD	TD	2pt.	Pts.	Fum.
1997—Amsterdam W.L.					Statistics unavailable.					
1998—Amsterdam NFLE	...	...	9	151	16.8	0	0	0	0	0
—New Orleans NFL	3	1	1	10	10.0	0	0	0	0	0
1999—New Orleans NFL	8	4	6	61	10.2	0	0	0	0	0
NFL Europe totals (1 year)	...	...	9	151	16.8	0	0	0	0	0
NFL totals (2 years)	11	5	7	71	10.1	0	0	0	0	0
Pro totals (3 years)	...	...	16	222	13.9	0	0	0	0	0

WILEY, CHUCK — DL — PANTHERS

PERSONAL: Born March 6, 1975, in Baton Rouge, La. ... 6-5/282. ... Full name: Samuel Charles Wiley Jr. ... Cousin of Doug Williams, quarterback with Tampa Bay Buccaneers (1978-82), Oklahoma Outlaws of USFL (1984), Arizona Outlaws of USFL (1985) and Washington Redskins (1986-89).
HIGH SCHOOL: Southern University Lab (Baton Rouge, La.).
COLLEGE: Louisiana State (degree in pre-physical therapy).
TRANSACTIONS/CAREER NOTES: Selected by Carolina Panthers in third round (62nd pick overall) of 1998 NFL draft. ... Signed by Panthers (June 10, 1998). ... On injured reserve with heel injury (August 30, 1998-entire season).
PLAYING EXPERIENCE: Carolina NFL, 1999. ... Games/Games started: 1999 (16/16).

WILEY, MARCELLUS — DE — BILLS

PERSONAL: Born November 30, 1974, in Compton, Calif. ... 6-4/275. ... Full name: Marcellus Vernon Wiley.
HIGH SCHOOL: Santa Monica (Calif.).
COLLEGE: Columbia (degree in sociology, 1997).
TRANSACTIONS/CAREER NOTES: Selected by Buffalo Bills in second round (52nd pick overall) of 1997 NFL draft. ... Signed by Bills (June 20, 1997).
PRO STATISTICS: 1997—Returned one kickoff for 12 yards, fumbled once and recovered two fumbles for 40 yards. 1998—Recovered one fumble for 15 yards. 1999—Intercepted one pass for 52 yards.

Year Team	G	GS	SACKS
1997—Buffalo NFL	16	0	0.0
1998—Buffalo NFL	16	3	3.5
1999—Buffalo NFL	16	1	5.0
Pro totals (3 years)	48	4	8.5

WILKINS, GABE — DE

PERSONAL: Born September 1, 1971, in Cowpens, S.C. ... 6-5/305. ... Full name: Gabriel Nicholas Wilkins.
HIGH SCHOOL: Gettis D. Broome (Spartanburg, S.C.).
COLLEGE: Gardner-Webb (N.C.).
TRANSACTIONS/CAREER NOTES: Selected by Green Bay Packers in fourth round (126th pick overall) of 1994 NFL draft. ... Signed by Packers (June 17, 1994). ... Granted free agency (February 14, 1997). ... Re-signed by Packers (April 28, 1997). ... Granted unconditional free agency (February 13, 1998). ... Signed by San Francisco 49ers (February 26, 1998). ... On physically unable to perform list with knee injury (July 18-November 7, 1998). ... Released by 49ers (June 6, 2000).
CHAMPIONSHIP GAME EXPERIENCE: Played in NFC championship game (1995-1997 seasons). ... Member of Super Bowl championship team (1996 season). ... Played in Super Bowl XXXII (1997 season).
PRO STATISTICS: 1997—Intercepted one pass for 77 yards and a touchdown and recovered three fumbles for one yard and one touchdown.

Year Team	G	GS	SACKS
1994—Green Bay NFL	15	0	1.0
1995—Green Bay NFL	13	8	3.0
1996—Green Bay NFL	16	1	3.0
1997—Green Bay NFL	16	16	5.5
1998—San Francisco NFL	8	4	0.0
1999—San Francisco NFL	16	15	1.0
Pro totals (6 years)	84	44	13.5

W

WILKINS, JEFF — K — RAMS

PERSONAL: Born April 19, 1972, in Youngstown, Ohio. ... 6-2/205. ... Full name: Jeff Allen Wilkins.
HIGH SCHOOL: Austintown Fitch (Youngstown, Ohio).
COLLEGE: Youngstown State (degree in communications, 1993).

TRANSACTIONS/CAREER NOTES: Signed as non-drafted free agent by Dallas Cowboys (April 28, 1994). ... Released by Cowboys (July 18, 1994). ... Signed by Philadelphia Eagles (November 14, 1994). ... Released by Eagles (August 14, 1995). ... Signed by San Francisco 49ers (November 8, 1995). ... Granted unconditional free agency (February 14, 1997). ... Signed by St. Louis Rams (March 6, 1997).
CHAMPIONSHIP GAME EXPERIENCE: Played in NFC championship game (1999 season). ... Member of Super Bowl championship team (1999 season).
PRO STATISTICS: 1999—Punted twice for 57 yards.

			KICKING						
Year Team	G	XPM	XPA	FGM	FGA	Lg.	50+	Pts.
1994—Philadelphia NFL	6	0	0	0	0	0	0-0	0
1995—San Francisco NFL	7	27	29	12	13	40	0-0	63
1996—San Francisco NFL	16	40	40	30	34	49	0-0	130
1997—St. Louis NFL	16	32	32	25	∞37	52	2-2	107
1998—St. Louis NFL	16	25	26	20	26	‡57	3-6	§85
1999—St. Louis NFL	16	*64	*64	20	28	51	1-4	‡124
Pro totals (6 years)	77	188	191	107	138	57	6-12	509

WILKINS, TERRENCE   WR/KR   COLTS

PERSONAL: Born July 29, 1975, in Washington, D.C. ... 5-8/179. ... Full name: Terrence Olondo Wilkins.
HIGH SCHOOL: Bishop Denis J O'Connell (Arlington, Va.).
COLLEGE: Virginia.
TRANSACTIONS/CAREER NOTES: Signed as non-drafted free agent by Indianapolis Colts (April 22, 1999).
PRO STATISTICS: 1999—Rushed once for two yards and recovered one fumble in end zone for a touchdown.
SINGLE GAME HIGHS (regular season): Receptions—5 (November 28, 1999, vs. New York Jets); yards—111 (November 21, 1999, vs. Philadelphia); and touchdown receptions—1 (December 5, 1999, vs. Miami).
STATISTICAL PLATEAUS: 100-yard receiving games: 1999 (1).

			RECEIVING			PUNT RETURNS				KICKOFF RETURNS				TOTALS			
Year Team	G	GS	No.	Yds.	Avg.	TD	No.	Yds.	Avg.	TD	No.	Yds.	Avg.	TD	TD	2pt.	Pts.	Fum.
1999—Indianapolis NFL	16	11	42	565	13.5	4	41	388	9.5	1	51	1134	22.2	▲1	7	0	42	3

WILKINSON, DAN   DT   REDSKINS

PERSONAL: Born March 13, 1973, in Dayton, Ohio. ... 6-5/313. ... Nickname: Big Daddy.
HIGH SCHOOL: Paul L. Dunbar (Dayton, Ohio).
COLLEGE: Ohio State.
TRANSACTIONS/CAREER NOTES: Selected after sophomore season by Cincinnati Bengals in first round (first pick overall) of 1994 NFL draft. ... Signed by Bengals (May 5, 1994). ... Designated by Bengals as franchise player (February 11, 1998). ... Tendered offer sheet by Washington Redskins (February 25, 1998). ... Bengals declined to match offer (February 26, 1998); Bengals received first-(LB Brian Simmons) and third-round (G Mike Goff) picks as compensation.
HONORS: Named defensive lineman on THE SPORTING NEWS college All-America first team (1993).
PRO STATISTICS: 1996—Intercepted one pass for seven yards, fumbled once and recovered one fumble. 1998—Intercepted one pass for four yards and recovered one fumble. 1999—Intercepted one pass for 88 yards and a touchdown and recovered one fumble.

Year Team	G	GS	SACKS
1994—Cincinnati NFL	16	14	5.5
1995—Cincinnati NFL	14	14	8.0
1996—Cincinnati NFL	16	16	6.5
1997—Cincinnati NFL	15	15	5.0
1998—Washington NFL	16	16	7.5
1999—Washington NFL	16	16	8.0
Pro totals (6 years)	93	91	40.5

WILLIAMS, AENEAS   CB   CARDINALS

PERSONAL: Born January 29, 1968, in New Orleans. ... 5-11/200. ... Full name: Aeneas Demetrius Williams. ... Name pronounced uh-NEE-us.
HIGH SCHOOL: Fortier (New Orleans).
COLLEGE: Southern (degree in accounting, 1990).
TRANSACTIONS/CAREER NOTES: Selected by Phoenix Cardinals in third round (59th pick overall) of 1991 NFL draft. ... Signed by Cardinals (July 26, 1991). ... Granted free agency (February 17, 1994). ... Cardinals franchise renamed Arizona Cardinals for 1994 season. ... Re-signed by Cardinals (June 1, 1994). ... Granted unconditional free agency (February 16, 1996). ... Re-signed by Cardinals (February 27, 1996).
HONORS: Named cornerback on THE SPORTING NEWS NFL All-Pro team (1995 and 1997). ... Played in Pro Bowl (1994-1999 seasons).
PRO STATISTICS: 1991—Fumbled once and recovered two fumbles for 10 yards. 1992—Recovered one fumble for 39 yards. 1993—Recovered two fumbles for 20 yards and a touchdown. 1994—Recovered one fumble. 1995—Fumbled once and recovered three fumbles. 1996—Credited with one sack and recovered one fumble. 1998—Credited with one sack. 1999—Recovered two fumbles.

			INTERCEPTIONS			
Year Team	G	GS	No.	Yds.	Avg.	TD
1991—Phoenix NFL	16	15	∞6	60	10.0	0
1992—Phoenix NFL	16	16	3	25	8.3	0
1993—Phoenix NFL	16	16	2	87	43.5	1
1994—Arizona NFL	16	16	†9	89	9.9	0
1995—Arizona NFL	16	16	6	86	14.3	†2
1996—Arizona NFL	16	16	6	89	14.8	1
1997—Arizona NFL	16	16	6	95	15.8	∞2
1998—Arizona NFL	16	16	1	15	15.0	0
1999—Arizona NFL	16	16	2	5	2.5	0
Pro totals (9 years)	144	143	41	551	13.4	6

W

WILLIAMS, ALFRED   DE

PERSONAL: Born November 6, 1968, in Houston. ... 6-6/265. ... Full name: Alfred Hamilton Williams.
HIGH SCHOOL: Jesse H. Jones Senior (Houston).
COLLEGE: Colorado.
TRANSACTIONS/CAREER NOTES: Selected by Cincinnati Bengals in first round (18th pick overall) of 1991 NFL draft. ... Signed by Bengals (July 18, 1991). ... Granted free agency (February 17, 1994). ... Re-signed by Bengals (June 15, 1994). ... Granted unconditional free agency (February 17, 1995). ... Signed by San Francisco 49ers (July 15, 1995). ... Granted unconditional free agency (February 16, 1996). ... Signed by Denver Broncos (February 27, 1996). ... On physically unable to perform list with tricep injury (August 25-October 23, 1998). ... On injured reserve with Achilles' tendon injury (November 2, 1999-remainder of season). ... Released by Broncos (February 10, 2000).
CHAMPIONSHIP GAME EXPERIENCE: Played in AFC championship game (1997 and 1998 seasons). ... Member of Super Bowl championship team (1997 and 1998 seasons).
HONORS: Named defensive end on THE SPORTING NEWS college All-America second team (1989). ... Butkus Award winner (1990). ... Named linebacker on THE SPORTING NEWS college All-America first team (1990). ... Named defensive end on THE SPORTING NEWS NFL All-Pro team (1996). ... Played in Pro Bowl (1996 season).
PRO STATISTICS: 1991—Recovered two fumbles for 24 yards. 1993—Credited with a safety. 1994—Credited with a safety and recovered one fumble. 1995—Recovered one fumble. 1996—Recovered one fumble. 1997—Recovered one fumble for 51 yards and a touchdown.

Year Team	G	GS	SACKS
1991—Cincinnati NFL	16	15	3.0
1992—Cincinnati NFL	15	6	10.0
1993—Cincinnati NFL	16	16	4.0
1994—Cincinnati NFL	16	16	9.5
1995—San Francisco NFL	16	0	4.5
1996—Denver NFL	16	16	13.0
1997—Denver NFL	16	16	8.5
1998—Denver NFL	10	0	3.0
1999—Denver NFL	7	6	4.0
Pro totals (9 years)	**128**	**91**	**59.5**

WILLIAMS, BEN   DE

PERSONAL: Born May 28, 1970, in Belzoni, Miss. ... 6-2/287.
HIGH SCHOOL: Humphreys County (Belzoni, Miss).
COLLEGE: Minnesota.
TRANSACTIONS/CAREER NOTES: Signed by Shreveport Pirates of CFL (May 1994). ... Signed as non-drafted free agent by Tampa Bay Buccaneers (July 30, 1996). ... Released by Buccaneers (August 18, 1996). ... Selected by England Monarchs in 1997 World League draft (February 1997). ... Signed by Arizona Cardinals (July 23, 1997). ... Released by Cardinals (August 19, 1997). ... Signed by Minnesota Vikings (June 15, 1998). ... Released by Vikings (August 30, 1998). ... Re-signed by Vikings to practice squad (August 31, 1998). ... Activated (December 8, 1998). ... On physically unable to perform list with hamstring injury (August 1-4, 1999). ... Released by Vikings (September 5, 1999). ... Signed by Philadelphia Eagles to practice squad (October 19, 1999). ... Activated (November 17, 1999). ... Released by Eagles (December 8, 1999).
PLAYING EXPERIENCE: Shreveport Pirates CFL, 1994 and 1995; England W.L., 1997; England NFLE, 1998; Minnesota NFL, 1998; Philadelphia NFL, 1999. ... Games/Games started: 1994 (16/games started unavailable), 1995 (18/-), 1997 (games played unavailable), NFLE 1998 (-), NFL 1998 (1/0), 1999 (3/0). Total CFL: 34/-. Total NFL: 4/0.
CHAMPIONSHIP GAME EXPERIENCE: Member of Vikings for NFC championship game (1998 season); inactive.
PRO STATISTICS: CFL: 1994—Credited with seven sacks and recovered one fumble. 1995—Credited with eight sacks and recovered two fumbles. W.L.: 1997—Credited with $3^1/_2$ sacks. NFLE: 1998—Credited with $5^1/_2$ sacks.

WILLIAMS, BRIAN   C

PERSONAL: Born June 8, 1966, in Mount Lebanon, Pa. ... 6-5/315. ... Full name: Brian Scott Williams.
HIGH SCHOOL: Mount Lebanon (Pittsburgh).
COLLEGE: Minnesota.
TRANSACTIONS/CAREER NOTES: Selected by New York Giants in first round (18th pick overall) of 1989 NFL draft. ... Signed by Giants (August 14, 1989). ... On injured reserve with knee injury (January 6, 1990-remainder of playoffs). ... On injured reserve with knee injury (December 6, 1992-remainder of season). ... Granted free agency (March 1, 1993). ... Re-signed by Giants (July 12, 1993). ... Granted unconditional free agency (February 17, 1994). ... Re-signed by Giants (March 1, 1994). ... Inactive for 13 games (1997). ... On injured reserve with eye injury (December 1, 1997-remainder of season). ... On physically unable to perform list with eye injury (July 25, 1998-entire season). ... Released by Giants (February 10, 2000).
PLAYING EXPERIENCE: New York Giants NFL, 1989-1996 and 1999. ... Games/Games started: 1989 (14/4), 1990 (16/1), 1991 (14/0), 1992 (13/1), 1993 (16/1), 1994 (14/14), 1995 (16/16), 1996 (14/14), 1999 (12/12). Total: 129/63.
CHAMPIONSHIP GAME EXPERIENCE: Played in NFC championship game (1990 season). ... Member of Super Bowl championship team (1990 season).
PRO STATISTICS: 1994—Fumbled twice for minus 34 yards and recovered one fumble.

WILLIAMS, BRIAN   LB   PACKERS

PERSONAL: Born December 17, 1972, in Dallas. ... 6-1/245. ... Full name: Brian Marcee Williams.
HIGH SCHOOL: Bishop Dunne (Dallas).
COLLEGE: Southern California (degree in public administration).
TRANSACTIONS/CAREER NOTES: Selected by Green Bay Packers in third round (73rd pick overall) of 1995 NFL draft. ... Signed by Packers (May 9, 1995). ... Granted free agency (February 13, 1998). ... Re-signed by Packers (February 17, 1998). ... On injured reserve with knee injury (November 9, 1999-remainder of season).
CHAMPIONSHIP GAME EXPERIENCE: Played in NFC championship game (1995-97 seasons). ... Member of Super Bowl championship team (1996 season). ... Played in Super Bowl XXXII (1997 season).

W

PRO STATISTICS: 1996—Recovered three fumbles. 1997—Intercepted two passes for 30 yards and recovered one fumble. 1999—Intercepted two passes for 60 yards and recovered one fumble.

Year Team	G	GS	SACKS
1995—Green Bay NFL	13	0	0.0
1996—Green Bay NFL	16	16	0.5
1997—Green Bay NFL	16	16	1.0
1998—Green Bay NFL	16	15	2.0
1999—Green Bay NFL	7	7	2.0
Pro totals (5 years)	68	54	5.5

WILLIAMS, CHARLIE   CB   COWBOYS

PERSONAL: Born February 2, 1972, in Detroit. ... 6-0/204.
HIGH SCHOOL: Henry Ford (Detroit).
COLLEGE: Bowling Green State.
TRANSACTIONS/CAREER NOTES: Selected by Dallas Cowboys in third round (92nd pick overall) of 1995 NFL draft. ... Signed by Cowboys (July 18, 1995). ... On physically unable to perform list with knee injury (July 18-November 8, 1996). ... Granted free agency (February 13, 1998). ... Re-signed by Cowboys (April 16, 1998). ... Granted unconditional free agency (February 11, 2000). ... Re-signed by Cowboys (May 1, 2000).
PLAYING EXPERIENCE: Dallas NFL, 1995-1999. ... Games/Games started: 1995 (16/0), 1996 (7/0), 1997 (16/0), 1998 (15/3), 1999 (16/8). Total: 70/11.
CHAMPIONSHIP GAME EXPERIENCE: Played in NFC championship game (1995 season). ... Member of Super Bowl championship team (1995 season).
PRO STATISTICS: 1996—Returned two kickoffs for 21 yards and fumbled once. 1997—Credited with two sacks. 1999—Recovered one fumble.

WILLIAMS, DAN   DE   CHIEFS

PERSONAL: Born December 15, 1969, in Ypsilanti, Mich. ... 6-4/293. ... Full name: Daniel Williams II. ... Brother of Lamanzer Williams, defensive end, Seattle Seahawks.
HIGH SCHOOL: Willow Run (Ypsilanti, Mich.).
COLLEGE: Tennessee State, then Toledo.
TRANSACTIONS/CAREER NOTES: Selected by Denver Broncos in first round (11th pick overall) of 1993 NFL draft. ... Signed by Broncos (July 19, 1993). ... On injured reserve with knee injury (December 19, 1995-remainder of season). ... Released by Broncos (July 18, 1997). ... Signed by Kansas City Chiefs (July 24, 1997). ... Designated by Chiefs as franchise player (February 13, 1998). ... Sat out 1998 season due to contract dispute. ... Granted unconditional free agency (February 12, 1999). ... Re-signed by Chiefs (February 16, 1999).
PRO STATISTICS: 1993—Recovered one fumble. 1994—Intercepted one pass for minus three yards. 1996—Recovered one fumble. 1997—Recovered two fumbles for two yards. 1999—Recovered two fumbles.

Year Team	G	GS	SACKS
1993—Denver NFL	13	11	1.0
1994—Denver NFL	12	7	0.0
1995—Denver NFL	6	6	2.0
1996—Denver NFL	15	15	1.0
1997—Kansas City NFL	15	6	10.5
1998—Kansas City NFL	Did not play.		
1999—Kansas City NFL	14	9	5.0
Pro totals (6 years)	75	54	19.5

WILLIAMS, DARRYL   S   BENGALS

PERSONAL: Born January 8, 1970, in Miami. ... 6-0/202. ... Full name: Darryl Edwin Williams.
HIGH SCHOOL: American (Hialeah, Fla.).
COLLEGE: Miami (Fla.).
TRANSACTIONS/CAREER NOTES: Selected after junior season by Cincinnati Bengals in first round (28th pick overall) of 1992 NFL draft. ... Signed by Bengals (July 25, 1992). ... Designated by Bengals as transition player (February 15, 1994). ... Free agency status changed by Bengals from transitional to unconditional (February 16, 1996). ... Signed by Seattle Seahawks (February 21, 1996). ... Released by Seahawks (March 1, 2000). ... Signed by Bengals (March 6, 2000).
HONORS: Named defensive back on THE SPORTING NEWS college All-America second team (1991). ... Played in Pro Bowl (1997 season).
RECORDS: Shares NFL single-game record for most opponents' fumbles recovered—3 (October 4, 1998, vs. Kansas City).
PRO STATISTICS: 1992—Recovered one fumble. 1993—Recovered two fumbles. 1994—Returned one punt for four yards and recovered two fumbles. 1995—Recovered three fumbles. 1996—Recovered one fumble for two yards. 1997—Recovered one fumble. 1998—Recovered three fumbles. 1999—Recovered one fumble.

Year Team	G	GS	INTERCEPTIONS No.	Yds.	Avg.	TD	SACKS No.
1992—Cincinnati NFL	16	12	4	65	16.3	0	2.0
1993—Cincinnati NFL	16	16	2	126	63.0	▲1	2.0
1994—Cincinnati NFL	16	16	2	45	22.5	0	1.0
1995—Cincinnati NFL	16	16	1	1	1.0	0	1.0
1996—Seattle NFL	16	16	5	148	29.6	1	0.0
1997—Seattle NFL	16	16	▲8	172	21.5	1	0.0
1998—Seattle NFL	16	16	3	41	13.7	0	0.0
1999—Seattle NFL	13	12	4	41	10.3	0	0.0
Pro totals (8 years)	125	120	29	639	22.0	3	6.0

W

WILLIAMS, ELIJAH   CB   FALCONS

PERSONAL: Born August 20, 1975, in Milton, Fla. ... 5-10/180. ... Full name: Elijah Elgebra Williams.
HIGH SCHOOL: Milton (Fla.).
COLLEGE: Florida.
TRANSACTIONS/CAREER NOTES: Selected by Atlanta Falcons in sixth round (166th pick overall) of 1998 NFL draft. ... Signed by Falcons (June 11, 1998).
PLAYING EXPERIENCE: Atlanta NFL, 1998 and 1999. ... Games/Games started: 1998 (15/0), 1999 (15/2). Total: 30/2.
CHAMPIONSHIP GAME EXPERIENCE: Played in NFC championship game (1998 season). ... Played in Super Bowl XXXIII (1998 season).
PRO STATISTICS: 1998—Rushed twice for minus two yards and returned seven kickoffs for 132 yards. 1999—Returned three kickoffs for 37 yards.

WILLIAMS, ERIK   OT   COWBOYS

PERSONAL: Born September 7, 1968, in Philadelphia. ... 6-6/311. ... Full name: Erik George Williams.
HIGH SCHOOL: John Bartram (Philadelphia).
COLLEGE: Central State (Ohio).
TRANSACTIONS/CAREER NOTES: Selected by Dallas Cowboys in third round (70th pick overall) of 1991 NFL draft. ... Signed by Cowboys (July 14, 1991). ... Designated by Cowboys as transition player (February 15, 1994). ... On non-football injury list with knee injury suffered in automobile accident (November 21, 1994-remainder of season).
PLAYING EXPERIENCE: Dallas NFL, 1991-1999. ... Games/Games started: 1991 (11/3), 1992 (16/16), 1993 (16/16), 1994 (7/7), 1995 (15/15), 1996 (16/16), 1997 (15/15), 1998 (15/15), 1999 (14/14). Total: 125/117.
CHAMPIONSHIP GAME EXPERIENCE: Played in NFC championship game (1992, 1993 and 1995 seasons). ... Member of Super Bowl championship team (1992, 1993 and 1995 seasons).
HONORS: Named offensive tackle on The Sporting News NFL All-Pro team (1993 and 1995). ... Played in Pro Bowl (1993, 1996, 1997 and 1999 seasons).
PRO STATISTICS: 1991—Recovered one fumble.

WILLIAMS, GENE   G

PERSONAL: Born October 14, 1968, in Blair, Neb. ... 6-2/320. ... Full name: Eugene Williams.
HIGH SCHOOL: Creighton Preparatory (Omaha, Neb.).
COLLEGE: Iowa State (degree in speech communications, 1991).
TRANSACTIONS/CAREER NOTES: Selected by Miami Dolphins in fifth round (121st pick overall) of 1991 NFL draft. ... Signed by Dolphins (July 11, 1991). ... Traded by Dolphins to Cleveland Browns for fourth-round pick (LB Ronnie Woolfork) in 1994 draft (July 12, 1993). ... Granted free agency (February 17, 1994). ... Re-signed by Browns for 1994 season. ... Traded by Browns to Atlanta Falcons for fifth-round pick (WR Jermaine Lewis) in 1996 draft (August 28, 1995). ... Granted unconditional free agency (February 11, 2000).
PLAYING EXPERIENCE: Miami NFL, 1991 and 1992; Cleveland NFL, 1993 and 1994; Atlanta NFL, 1995-1999. ... Games/Games started: 1991 (10/0), 1992 (5/0), 1993 (16/14), 1994 (15/9), 1995 (12/3), 1996 (10/0), 1997 (15/15), 1998 (16/16), 1999 (15/8). Total: 114/65.
CHAMPIONSHIP GAME EXPERIENCE: Played in NFC championship game (1998 season). ... Played in Super Bowl XXXIII (1998 season).
PRO STATISTICS: 1997—Recovered two fumbles. 1998—Recovered one fumble.

WILLIAMS, GEORGE   DT   GIANTS

PERSONAL: Born December 8, 1975, in Roseboro, N.C. ... 6-3/298.
HIGH SCHOOL: Rosewood (Goldsboro, N.C.).
COLLEGE: North Carolina State.
TRANSACTIONS/CAREER NOTES: Signed as non-drafted free agent by New York Giants (April 24, 1998).
PLAYING EXPERIENCE: New York Giants NFL, 1998 and 1999. ... Games/Games started: 1998 (2/0), 1999 (16/0). Total: 18/0.

WILLIAMS, GRANT   OT   PATRIOTS

PERSONAL: Born May 10, 1974, in Hattiesburg, Miss. ... 6-7/323.
HIGH SCHOOL: Clinton (Miss.).
JUNIOR COLLEGE: Hinds Community College (Miss.).
COLLEGE: Louisiana Tech (degree in biology, 1995).
TRANSACTIONS/CAREER NOTES: Signed as non-drafted free agent by Seattle Seahawks (April 22, 1996). ... Granted unconditional free agency (February 11, 2000). ... Signed by New England Patriots (March 17, 2000).
PLAYING EXPERIENCE: Seattle NFL, 1996-1999. ... Games/Games started: 1996 (8/0), 1997 (16/8), 1998 (16/0), 1999 (16/15). Total: 56/23.
PRO STATISTICS: 1997—Recovered two fumbles.

WILLIAMS, JAMAL   DT   CHARGERS

PERSONAL: Born April 28, 1976, in Washington, D.C. ... 6-3/305.
HIGH SCHOOL: Archbishop Carroll (Washington, D.C.).
COLLEGE: Oklahoma State.
TRANSACTIONS/CAREER NOTES: Selected by San Diego Chargers in second round of 1998 supplemental draft (July 9, 1998). ... Signed by Chargers (August 7, 1998).
PLAYING EXPERIENCE: San Diego NFL, 1998 and 1999. ... Games/Games started: 1998 (9/0), 1999 (16/2). Total: 25/2.
PRO STATISTICS: 1998—Intercepted one pass for 14 yards and a touchdown. 1999—Credited with one sack.

W

WILLIAMS, JAMEL   S

PERSONAL: Born December 22, 1973, in Gary, Ind. ... 5-11/205. ... Full name: Jamel Ishmael Williams. ... Name pronounced ja-MELL.
HIGH SCHOOL: Merrillville (Indiana).
COLLEGE: Nebraska.
TRANSACTIONS/CAREER NOTES: Selected by Washington Redskins in fifth round (132nd pick overall) of 1997 NFL draft. ... Signed by Redskins (June 2, 1997). ... Released by Redskins (September 27, 1999). ... Signed by Green Bay Packers (December 29, 1999). ... Inactive for one game with Packers (1999). ... Released by Packers (April 17, 2000).
PLAYING EXPERIENCE: Washington NFL, 1997-1999. ... Games/Games started: 1997 (16/0), 1998 (16/0), 1999 (3/0). Total: 35/0.

WILLIAMS, JAMES   LB

PERSONAL: Born October 10, 1968, in Natchez, Miss. ... 6-0/246. ... Full name: James Edward Williams.
HIGH SCHOOL: Natchez (Miss.).
COLLEGE: Mississippi State.
TRANSACTIONS/CAREER NOTES: Selected by New Orleans Saints in sixth round (158th pick overall) of 1990 NFL draft. ... Signed by Saints (May 9, 1990). ... Granted unconditional free agency (February 1-April 1, 1991). ... Re-signed by Saints for 1991 season. ... Granted unconditional free agency (February 17, 1994). ... Re-signed by Saints (March 18, 1994). ... Selected by Jacksonville Jaguars from Saints in NFL expansion draft (February 15, 1995). ... Released by Jaguars (December 5, 1995). ... Played with Amsterdam Admirals of World League (1996). ... Signed by Atlanta Falcons (May 9, 1996). ... On injured reserve with hamstring injury (August 20-22, 1996). ... Released by Falcons (August 22, 1996). ... Signed by New England Patriots (March 6, 1997). ... Released by Patriots (August 19, 1997). ... Signed by San Francisco 49ers (August 20, 1997). ... Granted unconditional free agency (February 13, 1998). ... Re-signed by 49ers (March 20, 1998). ... Selected by Cleveland Browns from 49ers in NFL expansion draft (February 9, 1999). ... Granted unconditional free agency (February 11, 2000).
CHAMPIONSHIP GAME EXPERIENCE: Played in NFC championship game (1997 season).
PRO STATISTICS: 1991—Recovered one fumble. 1994—Intercepted two passes for 42 yards and one touchdown. 1995—Intercepted two passes for 19 yards. 1997—Recovered one fumble. 1999—Recovered two fumbles.

Year Team	G	GS	SACKS
1990—New Orleans NFL	14	0	0.0
1991—New Orleans NFL	16	4	1.0
1992—New Orleans NFL	16	0	0.0
1993—New Orleans NFL	16	9	2.0
1994—New Orleans NFL	16	7	0.0
1995—Jacksonville NFL	12	6	0.0
1996—Amsterdam W.L.	...	...	1.0
1997—San Francisco NFL	16	0	0.0
1998—San Francisco NFL	15	0	0.0
1999—Cleveland NFL	16	0	0.0
W.L. totals (1 year)	...	...	1.0
NFL totals (9 years)	137	26	3.0
Pro totals (10 years)	...	...	4.0

WILLIAMS, JAMES   OT   BEARS

PERSONAL: Born March 29, 1968, in Pittsburgh. ... 6-7/340. ... Full name: James Otis Williams.
HIGH SCHOOL: Allderdice (Pittsburgh).
COLLEGE: Cheyney (Pa.) State.
TRANSACTIONS/CAREER NOTES: Signed as non-drafted free agent by Chicago Bears (April 25, 1991). ... Granted free agency (February 16, 1996). ... Re-signed by Bears (March 15, 1996).
PLAYING EXPERIENCE: Chicago NFL, 1991-1999. ... Games/Games started: 1991 (14/0), 1992 (5/0), 1993 (3/0), 1994 (16/15), 1995 (16/16), 1996 (16/16), 1997 (16/16), 1998 (16/16), 1999 (16/16). Total: 118/95.
PRO STATISTICS: 1991—Credited with one sack. 1996—Recovered two fumbles.
MISCELLANEOUS: Switched from defensive line to offensive line during the 1992 season.

WILLIAMS, JAY   DE   PANTHERS

PERSONAL: Born October 13, 1971, in Washington, D.C. ... 6-3/280. ... Full name: Jay Omar Williams.
HIGH SCHOOL: St. John's (Washington, D.C.).
COLLEGE: Wake Forest.
TRANSACTIONS/CAREER NOTES: Signed as non-drafted free agent by Miami Dolphins (April 28, 1994). ... Released by Dolphins (August 28, 1994). ... Signed by Los Angeles Rams to practice squad (September 27, 1994). ... Activated (December 7, 1994); did not play. ... Rams franchise moved from Los Angeles to St. Louis (April 12, 1995). ... On physically unable to perform list with forearm injury (July 31-November 18, 1996). ... Released by Rams (November 20, 1996). ... Re-signed by Rams (December 11, 1996). ... Granted free agency (February 12, 1999). ... Re-signed by Rams (May 4, 1999). ... Granted unconditional free agency (February 11, 2000). ... Signed by Carolina Panthers (February 16, 2000).
CHAMPIONSHIP GAME EXPERIENCE: Played in NFC championship game (1999 season). ... Member of Super Bowl championship team (1999 season).
PRO STATISTICS: 1997—Returned one kickoff for 10 yards.

Year Team	G	GS	SACKS
1994—Los Angeles Rams NFL	Did not play.		
1995—St. Louis NFL	6	0	0.0
1996—St. Louis NFL	2	0	0.0
1997—St. Louis NFL	16	2	1.0
1998—St. Louis NFL	16	1	1.0
1999—St. Louis NFL	16	0	4.0
Pro totals (5 years)	56	3	6.0

W

WILLIAMS, JERMAINE — RB — RAIDERS

PERSONAL: Born July 3, 1972, in Greenville, N.C. ... 6-0/235.
HIGH SCHOOL: J.H. Rose (Greenville, N.C.).
JUNIOR COLLEGE: Butler County Community College (Kan.).
COLLEGE: Houston.
TRANSACTIONS/CAREER NOTES: Signed as non-drafted free agent by Tampa Bay Buccaneers (April 25, 1997). ... Released by Buccaneers (August 4, 1997). ... Signed by Oakland Raiders (April 25, 1998). ... Released by Raiders (September 1, 1998). ... Re-signed by Raiders to practice squad (September 2, 1998). ... Activated (October 24, 1998).
PLAYING EXPERIENCE: Oakland NFL, 1998 and 1999. ... Games/Games started: 1998 (10/0), 1999 (15/0). Total: 25/0.
PRO STATISTICS: 1999—Caught one pass for 20 yards.

WILLIAMS, K.D. — LB — SAINTS

PERSONAL: Born April 21, 1973, in Tampa. ... 6-0/235. ... Full name: Kevin Williams. ... Cousin of Juran Bolden, cornerback with four NFL teams (1996-99).
HIGH SCHOOL: Jefferson (Tampa).
JUNIOR COLLEGE: Arizona West Junior College.
COLLEGE: Henderson State (Ark.).
TRANSACTIONS/CAREER NOTES: Signed by Winnipeg Blue Bombers of CFL (January 6, 1995). ... Traded by Blue Bombers of CFL with S Jason Mallett and DE Horace Morris to Sasketchewan Roughriders of CFL for LB Sheldon Benoit, CB Nick Ferguson and G John James (May 5, 1997). ... Traded by Roughriders of CFL with LB Lamar Griggs to Hamilton Tiger-Cats of CFL for second-round pick in 1998 CFL college draft and future considerations (September 4, 1997). ... Released by Tiger-Cats (October 9, 1997). ... Selected by Frankfurt Galaxy in 1998 NFL Europe draft (February 23, 1998). ... Signed as non-drafted free agent by Dallas Cowboys (July 21, 1998). ... Released by Cowboys (August 25, 1998). ... Signed by Kansas City Chiefs to practice squad (September 1, 1998). ... Released by Chiefs (Novmeber 3, 1998). ... Signed by Oakland Raiders (March 1999). ... Released by Raiders (December 14, 1999). ... Signed by New Orleans Saints (March 23, 2000).
PRO STATISTICS: CFL: 1995—Recovered three fumbles. 1996—Recovered two fumbles for seven yards. NFL: 1999—Recovered one fumble.

Year Team	G	GS	INTERCEPTIONS				SACKS
			No.	Yds.	Avg.	TD	No.
1995—Winnipeg CFL	15	0	1	0	0.0	0	5.0
1996—Winnipeg CFL	18	0	4	72	18.0	1	5.0
1997—Saskatchewan CFL	10	0	2	38	19.0	1	3.0
—Hamilton CFL	3	0	1	18	18.0	0	1.0
1998—Frankfurt NFLE	...	...	0	0	0.0	0	2.5
1999—Oakland NFL	9	8	1	14	14.0	0	1.0
NFL Europe totals (1 year)	...	...	0	0	0.0	0	2.5
CFL totals (3 years)	46	0	8	128	16.0	2	14.0
NFL totals (1 year)	9	8	1	14	14.0	0	1.0
Pro totals (5 years)	...	...	9	142	15.8	2	17.5

WILLIAMS, KARL — WR — BUCCANEERS

PERSONAL: Born April 10, 1971, in Albion, Mich. ... 5-10/177.
HIGH SCHOOL: Garland (Texas).
COLLEGE: Texas A&M-Kingsville.
TRANSACTIONS/CAREER NOTES: Signed as non-drafted free agent by Tampa Bay Buccaneers (April 23, 1996).
CHAMPIONSHIP GAME EXPERIENCE: Played in NFC championship game (1999 season).
PRO STATISTICS: 1996—Rushed once for minus three yards and recovered one fumble. 1997—Rushed once for five yards and recovered one fumble. 1999—Recovered one fumble.
SINGLE GAME HIGHS (regular season): Receptions—6 (September 13, 1998, vs. Green Bay); yards—87 (December 7, 1997, vs. Green Bay); and touchdown receptions—2 (November 2, 1997, vs. Indianapolis).

Year Team	G	GS	RECEIVING				PUNT RETURNS				KICKOFF RETURNS				TOTALS			
			No.	Yds.	Avg.	TD	No.	Yds.	Avg.	TD	No.	Yds.	Avg.	TD	TD	2pt.	Pts.	Fum.
1996—Tampa Bay NFL	16	0	22	246	11.2	0	13	274	21.1	1	14	383	27.4	0	1	0	6	2
1997—Tampa Bay NFL	16	8	33	486	14.7	4	46	‡597	13.0	∞1	15	277	18.5	0	5	0	30	5
1998—Tampa Bay NFL	13	6	21	252	12.0	1	10	83	8.3	0	0	0	0.0	0	1	0	6	0
1999—Tampa Bay NFL	13	4	21	176	8.4	0	20	153	7.7	0	1	15	15.0	0	0	0	0	2
Pro totals (4 years)	58	18	97	1160	12.0	5	89	1107	12.4	2	30	675	22.5	0	7	0	42	9

WILLIAMS, KEVIN — WR/KR

PERSONAL: Born January 25, 1971, in Dallas. ... 5-9/195. ... Full name: Kevin Ray Williams.
HIGH SCHOOL: Franklin D. Roosevelt (Dallas).
COLLEGE: Miami (Fla.).
TRANSACTIONS/CAREER NOTES: Selected after junior season by Dallas Cowboys in second round (46th overall) of 1993 NFL draft. ... Signed by Cowboys (April 29, 1993). ... Granted unconditional free agency (February 14, 1997). ... Signed by Arizona Cardinals (July 15, 1997). ... Granted unconditional free agency (February 13, 1998). ... Signed by Buffalo Bills (February 17, 1998). ... Released by Bills (April 14, 2000).
CHAMPIONSHIP GAME EXPERIENCE: Played in NFC championship game (1993-1995 seasons). ... Member of Super Bowl championship team (1993 and 1995 seasons).
PRO STATISTICS: 1993—Fumbled eight times and recovered four fumbles. 1994—Fumbled four times and recovered three fumbles. 1995—Fumbled three times. 1997—Fumbled three times and recovered one fumble. 1998—Fumbled three times and recovered two fumbles.
SINGLE GAME HIGHS (regular season): Receptions—9 (December 25, 1995, vs. Arizona); yards—203 (December 25, 1995, vs. Arizona); and touchdown receptions—2 (December 25, 1995, vs. Arizona).
STATISTICAL PLATEAUS: 100-yard receiving games: 1995 (1).

W

Year—Team	G	GS	RUSHING Att.	Yds.	Avg.	TD	RECEIVING No.	Yds.	Avg.	TD	PUNT RETURNS No.	Yds.	Avg.	TD	KICKOFF RETURNS No.	Yds.	Avg.	TD	TOTALS TD	2pt.	Pts.
1993—Dallas NFL..........	16	1	7	26	3.7	2	20	151	7.6	2	36	381	10.6	†2	31	689	22.2	0	6	0	36
1994—Dallas NFL..........	15	2	6	20	3.3	0	13	181	13.9	0	39	349	8.9	1	43	1148	26.7	1	2	0	12
1995—Dallas NFL..........	16	16	10	53	5.3	0	38	613	16.1	2	18	166	9.2	0	49	1108	22.6	0	2	0	12
1996—Dallas NFL..........	10	9	4	11	2.8	0	27	323	12.0	1	2	17	8.5	0	21	471	22.4	0	1	0	6
1997—Arizona NFL..........	16	0	1	-2	-2.0	0	20	273	13.7	1	40	462	11.6	0	‡59	*1458	24.7	0	1	0	6
1998—Buffalo NFL..........	16	0	5	46	9.2	0	29	392	13.5	1	37	369	10.0	0	47	1059	22.5	0	1	0	6
1999—Buffalo NFL........	16	0	1	13	13.0	0	31	381	12.3	0	33	331	10.0	0	42	840	20.0	0	0	0	0
Pro totals (7 years)	105	28	34	167	4.9	2	178	2314	13.0	7	205	2075	10.1	3	292	6773	23.2	1	13	0	78

WILLIAMS, KEVIN — CB/S — JETS

PERSONAL: Born August 4, 1975, in Pine Bluff, Ark. ... 6-0/190.
HIGH SCHOOL: Watson Chapel (Pine Bluff, Ark.).
COLLEGE: Oklahoma State.
TRANSACTIONS/CAREER NOTES: Selected by New York Jets in third round (87th pick overall) of 1998 NFL draft. ... Signed by Jets (July 20, 1998). ... On non-football illness list with viral infection (October 18, 1999-remainder of season).
CHAMPIONSHIP GAME EXPERIENCE: Played in AFC championship game (1998 season).
PRO STATISTICS: 1998—Intercepted one pass for 34 yards.

Year—Team	G	GS	KICKOFF RETURNS No.	Yds.	Avg.	TD	TOTALS TD	2pt.	Pts.	Fum.
1998—New York Jets NFL..............................	15	6	11	230	20.9	0	0	0	0	0
1999—New York Jets NFL..............................	4	0	6	166	27.7	0	0	0	0	1
Pro totals (2 years)	19	6	17	396	23.3	0	0	0	0	1

WILLIAMS, MOE — RB — VIKINGS

PERSONAL: Born July 26, 1974, in Columbus, Ga. ... 6-1/205. ... Full name: Maurice Jabari Williams.
HIGH SCHOOL: Spencer (Columbus, Ga.).
COLLEGE: Kentucky.
TRANSACTIONS/CAREER NOTES: Selected after junior season by Minnesota Vikings in third round (75th pick overall) of 1996 NFL draft. ... Signed by Vikings (July 22, 1996). ... On injured reserve with foot injury (December 8, 1998-remainder of season). ... Granted free agency (February 12, 1999). ... Re-signed by Vikings (April 30, 1999). ... Granted unconditional free agency (February 11, 2000). ... Re-signed by Vikings (March 10, 2000).
PRO STATISTICS: 1998—Recovered one fumble.
SINGLE GAME HIGHS (regular season): Attempts—19 (November 2, 1997, vs, New England); yards—43 (November 2, 1997, vs. New England); and rushing touchdowns—1 (October 24, 1999, vs. San Francisco).

Year—Team	G	GS	RUSHING Att.	Yds.	Avg.	TD	RECEIVING No.	Yds.	Avg.	TD	KICKOFF RETURNS No.	Yds.	Avg.	TD	TOTALS TD	2pt.	Pts.	Fum.
1996—Minnesota NFL..........	9	0	0	0	0.0	0	0	0	0.0	0	0	0	0.0	0	0	0	0	0
1997—Minnesota NFL..........	14	0	22	59	2.7	1	4	14	3.5	0	16	388	24.3	0	1	0	6	0
1998—Minnesota NFL..........	12	1	0	0	0.0	0	1	64	64.0	0	2	19	9.5	0	0	0	0	1
1999—Minnesota NFL..........	14	0	24	69	2.9	1	1	12	12.0	0	10	240	24.0	1	2	0	12	0
Pro totals (4 years)	49	1	46	128	2.8	2	6	90	15.0	0	28	647	23.1	1	3	0	18	1

WILLIAMS, NICK — FB — BENGALS

PERSONAL: Born March 30, 1977, in Farmington Hills, Mich. ... 6-1/267. ... Full name: James Nicolas Williams.
HIGH SCHOOL: Harrison (Farmington Hills, Mich.).
COLLEGE: Miami (Fla.).
TRANSACTIONS/CAREER NOTES: Selected by Cincinnati Bengals in fifth round (135th pick overall) of 1999 NFL draft. ... Signed by Bengals (May 19, 1999).
SINGLE GAME HIGHS (regular season): Attempts—4 (October 24, 1999, vs. Indianapolis); yards—18 (October 24, 1999, vs. Indianapolis); and rushing touchdowns—0.

Year—Team	G	GS	RUSHING Att.	Yds.	Avg.	TD	RECEIVING No.	Yds.	Avg.	TD	KICKOFF RETURNS No.	Yds.	Avg.	TD	TOTALS TD	2pt.	Pts.	Fum.
1999—Cincinnati NFL..........	11	0	10	30	3.0	0	10	96	9.6	0	8	109	13.6	0	0	0	0	1

W

WILLIAMS, PAT — DT — BILLS

PERSONAL: Born October 24, 1972, in Monroe, La. ... 6-3/310. ... Full name: Patrick Williams.
HIGH SCHOOL: Wossman (Monroe, La.).
JUNIOR COLLEGE: Navarro College (Texas).
COLLEGE: Northeast Oklahoma, then Texas A&M.
TRANSACTIONS/CAREER NOTES: Signed as non-drafted free agent by Buffalo Bills (April 25, 1997). ... Granted free agency (February 11, 2000). ... Re-signed by Bills (March 23, 2000).

Year—Team	G	GS	SACKS
1997—Buffalo NFL...	1	0	0.0
1998—Buffalo NFL...	14	0	3.5
1999—Buffalo NFL...	16	0	2.5
Pro totals (3 years)...	31	0	6.0

WILLIAMS, RICKY — RB — SAINTS

PERSONAL: Born May 21, 1977, in San Diego. ... 5-10/236. ... Full name: Errick Lynne Williams.
HIGH SCHOOL: Patrick Henry (San Diego).
COLLEGE: Texas.
TRANSACTIONS/CAREER NOTES: Selected by New Orleans Saints in first round (fifth pick overall) of 1999 NFL draft. ... Signed by Saints (May 14, 1999).
HONORS: Named running back on THE SPORTING NEWS college All-America first team (1997 and 1998). ... Doak Walker Award winner (1997 and 1998). ... Heisman Trophy winner (1998). ... Walter Camp Award winner (1998). ... Maxwell Award winner (1998). ... Named College Football Player of the Year by THE SPORTING NEWS (1998).
PRO STATISTICS: 1999—Attempted one pass without a completion and recovered one fumble.
SINGLE GAME HIGHS (regular season): Attempts—40 (October 31, 1999, vs. Cleveland); yards—179 (October 31, 1999, vs. Cleveland); and rushing touchdowns—2 (November 21, 1999, vs. Jacksonville).
STATISTICAL PLATEAUS: 100-yard rushing games: 1999 (2).

| | | | RUSHING | | | | RECEIVING | | | | TOTALS | | | |
Year Team	G	GS	Att.	Yds.	Avg.	TD	No.	Yds.	Avg.	TD	TD	2pt.	Pts.	Fum.
1999—New Orleans NFL	12	12	253	884	3.5	2	28	172	6.1	0	2	0	12	6

RECORD AS BASEBALL PLAYER

TRANSACTIONS/CAREER NOTES: Batted right, threw right. ... Selected by Philadelphia Phillies organization in eighth round of free-agent draft (June 1, 1995). ... Selected by Montreal Expos from Phillies organization in Rule 5 major league draft (December 14, 1998). ... Traded by Expos to Texas Rangers for cash considerations (December 15, 1998).

| | | | | | | BATTING | | | | | | | | FIELDING | | |
Year Team (League)	Pos.	G	AB	R	H	2B	3B	HR	RBI	Avg.	BB	SO	SB	PO	A	E	Avg.
1995—Martinsville (Appal.)....	OF	36	113	19	27	1	0	0	11	.239	6	32	13	51	5	3	.949
1996— Piedmont (S. Atl.)	OF	84	266	30	50	4	3	3	20	.188	18	87	17	117	9	9	.933
1997— Piedmont (S. Atl.)	OF	37	136	12	28	5	0	1	6	.206	9	44	10	58	5	3	.955
1998— Batavia (NY-Penn)	OF	13	53	7	15	0	0	0	3	.283	2	16	6	17	1	0	1.000

WILLIAMS, ROBERT — CB

PERSONAL: Born May 29, 1977, in Shelby, N.C. ... 5-10/177. ... Full name: Robert M. Williams.
HIGH SCHOOL: Shelby (N.C.).
COLLEGE: North Carolina.
TRANSACTIONS/CAREER NOTES: Selected after junior season by Kansas City Chiefs in fifth round (128th pick overall) of 1998 NFL draft. ... Signed by Chiefs (July 17, 1998). ... Traded by Chiefs to San Francisco 49ers for conditional seventh-round pick in 2000 draft (September 21, 1999). ... Inactive for one game with 49ers (1999). ... Claimed on waivers by Seattle Seahawks (October 6, 1999). ... Released by Seahawks (November 9, 1999). ... Re-signed by Seahawks (November 26, 1999). ... Claimed on waivers by New Orleans Saints (December 3, 1999). ... Inactive for five games with Saints (1999). ... Granted free agency (February 11, 2000).
PLAYING EXPERIENCE: Kansas City NFL, 1998; Kansas City (1)-Seattle (1) NFL, 1999. ... Games/Games started: 1998 (16/1), 1999 (K.C.-1/0; Sea.-1/0; Total: 2/0). Total: 18/1.
PRO STATISTICS: 1998—Credited with 1/2 sack. 1999—Recovered one fumble.

WILLIAMS, RODNEY — WR — RAIDERS

PERSONAL: Born August 15, 1973, in Los Angeles. ... 6-0/190.
HIGH SCHOOL: Palmdale (Calif.).
COLLEGE: Pierce College (Calif.), then Arizona.
TRANSACTIONS/CAREER NOTES: Signed as non-drafted free agent by Oakland Raiders (April 25, 1998). ... Assigned by Raiders to Barcelona Dragons in 2000 NFL Europe enhancement allocation program (February 18, 2000).
PLAYING EXPERIENCE: Oakland NFL, 1998 and 1999. ... Games/Games started: 1998 (1/0), 1999 (5/0). Total: 6/0.
PRO STATISTICS: 1998—Returned four kickoffs for 63 yards and fumbled once.

RECORD AS BASEBALL PLAYER

TRANSACTIONS/CAREER NOTES: Threw right, batted right. ... Selected by Kansas City Royals in 37th round of free-agent draft (June 3, 1991).

| | | | | | | BATTING | | | | | | | | FIELDING | | |
Year Team (League)	Pos.	G	AB	R	H	2B	3B	HR	RBI	Avg.	BB	SO	SB	PO	A	E	Avg.
1991— GC Royals (GCL)	OF	29	57	7	12	1	0	0	4	.211	6	20	4	13	4	1	.944
1992— Lethbridge (Pio.)	OF	34	114	7	19	1	0	0	5	.167	3	27	0	48	1	2	.961

WILLIAMS, ROLAND — TE — RAMS

W

PERSONAL: Born April 27, 1975, in Rochester, N.Y. ... 6-5/269. ... Full name: Roland Lamar Williams.
HIGH SCHOOL: East (Rochester, N.Y.).
COLLEGE: Syracuse (degree in speech communications, 1997).
TRANSACTIONS/CAREER NOTES: Selected by St. Louis Rams in fourth round (98th pick overall) of 1998 NFL draft. ... Signed by Rams (July 13, 1998).
CHAMPIONSHIP GAME EXPERIENCE: Played in NFC championship game (1999 season). ... Member of Super Bowl championship team (1999 season).
PRO STATISTICS: 1999—Recovered two fumbles.
SINGLE GAME HIGHS (regular season): Receptions—5 (October 24, 1999, vs. Cleveland); yards—50 (October 24, 1999, vs. Cleveland); and touchdown receptions—2 (October 24, 1999, vs. Cleveland).

Year Team	G	GS	No.	RECEIVING Yds.	Avg.	TD	TD	TOTALS 2pt.	Pts.	Fum.
1998—St. Louis NFL	13	9	15	144	9.6	1	1	0	6	0
1999—St. Louis NFL	16	15	25	226	9.0	6	6	0	36	0
Pro totals (2 years)	29	24	40	370	9.3	7	7	0	42	0

WILLIAMS, SAMMY   OL   RAVENS

PERSONAL: Born December 14, 1974, in Magnolia, Miss. ... 6-5/318.
HIGH SCHOOL: Thornton Township (Harvey, Ill.).
JUNIOR COLLEGE: Coffeyville (Kan.) Community College.
COLLEGE: Oklahoma.
TRANSACTIONS/CAREER NOTES: Selected by Baltimore Ravens in sixth round (164th pick overall) of 1998 NFL draft. ... Signed by Ravens (July 21, 1998). ... On injured reserve with knee and ankle injuries (August 30, 1998-entire season). ... Released by Ravens (September 4, 1999). ... Claimed on waivers by Kansas City Chiefs (September 6, 1999). ... Claimed on waivers by Ravens (November 10, 1999).
PLAYING EXPERIENCE: Kansas City NFL, 1999. ... Games/Games started: 1999 (1/0).

WILLIAMS, SHAUN   S   GIANTS

PERSONAL: Born October 10, 1976, in Los Angeles. ... 6-2/215. ... Full name: Shaun LeJon Williams.
HIGH SCHOOL: Crespi (Encino, Calif.).
COLLEGE: UCLA.
TRANSACTIONS/CAREER NOTES: Selected by New York Giants in first round (24th pick overall) of 1998 NFL draft. ... Signed by Giants (July 24, 1998).
PLAYING EXPERIENCE: New York Giants NFL, 1998 and 1999. ... Games/Games started: 1998 (13/0), 1999 (11/0). Total: 24/0.
HONORS: Named free safety on THE SPORTING NEWS college All-America second team (1997).
PRO STATISTICS: 1998—Intercepted two passes for six yards.

WILLIAMS, SHERMAN   RB

PERSONAL: Born August 13, 1973, in Mobile, Ala. ... 5-8/202.
HIGH SCHOOL: M.T. Blount (Prichard, Ala.).
COLLEGE: Alabama.
TRANSACTIONS/CAREER NOTES: Selected by Dallas Cowboys in second round (46th pick overall) of 1995 NFL draft. ... Signed by Cowboys (July 21, 1995). ... Released by Cowboys (July 10, 1998). ... Re-signed by Cowboys (September 1, 1998). ... Released by Cowboys (October 5, 1999).
CHAMPIONSHIP GAME EXPERIENCE: Played in NFC championship game (1995 season). ... Member of Super Bowl championship team (1995 season).
HONORS: Named running back on THE SPORTING NEWS college All-America second team (1994).
PRO STATISTICS: 1996—Attempted one pass without a completion. 1997—Recovered one fumble. 1998—Returned four kickoffs for 103 yards.
SINGLE GAME HIGHS (regular season): Attempts—23 (December 27, 1998, vs. Washington); yards—90 (December 27, 1998, vs. Washington); rushing touchdowns—1 (September 21, 1998, vs. New York Giants).

Year Team	G	GS	RUSHING Att.	Yds.	Avg.	TD	No.	RECEIVING Yds.	Avg.	TD	TD	TOTALS 2pt.	Pts.	Fum.
1995—Dallas NFL	11	0	48	205	4.3	1	3	28	9.3	0	1	0	6	2
1996—Dallas NFL	16	1	69	269	3.9	0	5	41	8.2	0	0	0	0	2
1997—Dallas NFL	16	0	121	468	3.9	2	21	159	7.6	0	2	0	12	5
1998—Dallas NFL	16	2	64	220	3.4	1	11	104	9.5	0	1	0	6	0
1999—Dallas NFL	1	0	0	0	0.0	0	0	0	0.0	0	0	0	0	0
Pro totals (5 years)	60	3	302	1162	3.8	4	40	332	8.3	0	4	0	24	9

WILLIAMS, TONY   DT   VIKINGS

PERSONAL: Born July 9, 1975, in Germantown, Tenn. ... 6-1/292. ... Full name: Anthony Demetric Williams.
HIGH SCHOOL: Oakhaven (Memphis, Tenn.), then Germantown (Tenn.).
COLLEGE: Memphis.
TRANSACTIONS/CAREER NOTES: Selected by Minnesota Vikings in fifth round (151st pick overall) of 1997 NFL draft. ... Signed by Vikings (June 17, 1997). ... Granted free agency (February 11, 2000).
PLAYING EXPERIENCE: Minnesota NFL, 1997-1999. ... Games/Games started: 1997 (6/2), 1998 (14/9), 1999 (16/12). Total: 36/23.
CHAMPIONSHIP GAME EXPERIENCE: Played in NFC championship game (1998 season).
PRO STATISTICS: 1998—Credited with one sack and recovered one fumble for six yards. 1999—Credited with five sacks and recovered one fumble.

W

WILLIAMS, TYRONE   CB   PACKERS

PERSONAL: Born May 31, 1973, in Bradenton, Fla. ... 5-11/195. ... Full name: Upton Tyrone Williams.
HIGH SCHOOL: Manatee (Bradenton, Fla.).
COLLEGE: Nebraska.
TRANSACTIONS/CAREER NOTES: Selected by Green Bay Packers in third round (93rd pick overall) of 1996 NFL draft. ... Signed by Packers (May 15, 1996). ... Granted free agency (February 12, 1999). ... Re-signed by Packers (May 17, 1999).
CHAMPIONSHIP GAME EXPERIENCE: Played in NFC championship game (1996 and 1997 seasons). ... Member of Super Bowl championship team (1996 season). ... Played in Super Bowl XXXII (1997 season).

PRO STATISTICS: 1996—Recovered one fumble. 1999—Fumbled once and recovered two fumbles for 12 yards.

				INTERCEPTIONS			
Year Team	G	GS	No.	Yds.	Avg.	TD	
1996—Green Bay NFL	16	0	0	0	0.0	0	
1997—Green Bay NFL	16	15	1	0	0.0	0	
1998—Green Bay NFL	16	16	5	40	8.0	0	
1999—Green Bay NFL	16	16	4	12	3.0	0	
Pro totals (4 years)	64	47	10	52	5.2	0	

WILLIAMS, TYRONE　　　DE　　　EAGLES

PERSONAL: Born October 22, 1972, in Philadelphia. ... 6-4/292. ... Full name: Tyrone M. Williams Jr.
HIGH SCHOOL: LaVista (Papillion, Neb.).
COLLEGE: Wyoming.
TRANSACTIONS/CAREER NOTES: Signed as non-drafted free agent by St. Louis Rams (July 25, 1996). ... Released by Rams (August 25, 1996). ... Re-signed by Rams to practice squad (August 26, 1996). ... Allocated by Rams to Rhein Fire in 1997 World League enhancement allocation program (February 19, 1997). ... Released by Rams (August 19, 1997). ... Signed by Chicago Bears to practice squad (August 27, 1997). ... Released by Bears (September 9, 1997). ... Re-signed by Rams to practice squad (September 25, 1997). ... Signed by Bears off Rams practice squad (October 29, 1997). ... Released by Bears (August 31, 1998). ... Signed by Philadelphia Eagles (July 6, 1999). ... Released by Eagles (September 4, 1999). ... Re-signed by Eagles (October 20, 1999).
PLAYING EXPERIENCE: Chicago NFL, 1997; Philadelphia NFL, 1999. ... Games/Games started: 1997 (3/0), 1999 (4/0). Total: 7/0.
PRO STATISTICS: 1999—Credited with three sacks and recovered one fumble.

WILLIAMS, WALLY　　　G/C　　　SAINTS

PERSONAL: Born February 19, 1971, in Tallahassee, Fla. ... 6-2/321. ... Full name: Wally James Williams Jr.
HIGH SCHOOL: James S. Rickards (Tallahassee, Fla.).
COLLEGE: Florida A&M.
TRANSACTIONS/CAREER NOTES: Signed as non-drafted free agent by Cleveland Browns (April 27, 1993). ... Browns franchise moved to Baltimore and renamed Ravens for 1996 season (March 11, 1996). ... Designated by Ravens as franchise player (February 13, 1998). ... Re-signed by Ravens (August 18, 1998). ... Granted unconditional free agency (February 12, 1999). ... Signed by New Orleans Saints (February 15, 1999). ... On injured reserve with neck injury (November 19, 1999-remainder of season).
PLAYING EXPERIENCE: Cleveland NFL, 1993-1995; Baltimore NFL, 1996-1998; New Orleans NFL, 1999. ... Games/Games started: 1993 (2/0), 1994 (11/7), 1995 (16/16), 1996 (15/13), 1997 (10/10), 1998 (13/13), 1999 (6/6). Total: 73/65.
PRO STATISTICS: 1994—Recovered one fumble. 1998—Recovered one fumble.

WILLIAMS, WILLIE　　　·　CB　　　SEAHAWKS

PERSONAL: Born December 26, 1970, in Columbia, S.C. ... 5-9/180. ... Full name: Willie James Williams Jr.
HIGH SCHOOL: Spring Valley (Columbia, S.C.).
COLLEGE: Western Carolina.
TRANSACTIONS/CAREER NOTES: Selected by Pittsburgh Steelers in sixth round (162nd pick overall) of 1993 NFL draft. ... Signed by Steelers (July 9, 1993). ... Granted free agency (February 16, 1996). ... Re-signed by Steelers (June 12, 1996). ... Granted unconditional free agency (February 14, 1997). ... Signed by Seattle Seahawks (February 18, 1997).
CHAMPIONSHIP GAME EXPERIENCE: Played in AFC championship game (1994 and 1995 seasons). ... Played in Super Bowl XXX (1995 season).
PRO STATISTICS: 1993—Returned one kickoff for 19 yards. 1996—Credited with one sack and recovered one fumble. 1998—Recovered one fumble.

				INTERCEPTIONS			
Year Team	G	GS	No.	Yds.	Avg.	TD	
1993—Pittsburgh NFL	16	0	0	0	0.0	0	
1994—Pittsburgh NFL	16	1	0	0	0.0	0	
1995—Pittsburgh NFL	16	15	§7	122	17.4	▲1	
1996—Pittsburgh NFL	15	14	1	1	1.0	0	
1997—Seattle NFL	16	16	1	0	0.0	0	
1998—Seattle NFL	14	14	2	36	18.0	1	
1999—Seattle NFL	15	14	5	43	8.6	1	
Pro totals (7 years)	108	74	16	202	12.6	3	

WILLIS, JAMES　　　LB

PERSONAL: Born September 2, 1972, in Huntsville, Ala. ... 6-2/237. ... Full name: James Edward Willis III.
HIGH SCHOOL: J.O. Johnson (Huntsville, Ala.).
COLLEGE: Auburn.
TRANSACTIONS/CAREER NOTES: Selected after junior season by Green Bay Packers in fifth round (119th pick overall) of 1993 NFL draft. ... Signed by Packers (May 21, 1993). ... On injured reserve with knee injury (December 23, 1993-remainder of season). ... Released by Packers (October 25, 1995). ... Signed by Philadelphia Eagles (October 31, 1995). ... Granted free agency (February 16, 1996). ... Re-signed by Eagles (March 1, 1996). ... Released by Eagles (June 8, 1999). ... Signed by Seattle Seahawks (June 25, 1999). ... Granted unconditional free agency (February 11, 2000).
PRO STATISTICS: 1993—Recovered one fumble. 1994—Fumbled once and recovered one fumble. 1997—Credited with two sacks and recovered two fumbles. 1998—Recovered one fumble.

				INTERCEPTIONS			
Year Team	G	GS	No.	Yds.	Avg.	TD	
1993—Green Bay NFL	13	0	0	0	0.0	0	

W

1994—Green Bay NFL	12	0	2	20	10.0	0
1995—Philadelphia NFL	5	0	0	0	0.0	0
1996—Philadelphia NFL	16	13	1	14	14.0	0
1997—Philadelphia NFL	15	15	1	0	0.0	0
1998—Philadelphia NFL	16	16	0	0	0.0	0
1999—Seattle NFL	16	0	0	0	0.0	0
Pro totals (7 years)	93	44	4	34	8.5	0

WILSON, AL — LB — BRONCOS

PERSONAL: Born June 21, 1977, in Jackson, Tenn. ... 6-0/240. ... Full name: Aldra Kauwa Wilson.
HIGH SCHOOL: Central Merry (Jackson, Tenn.).
COLLEGE: Tennessee.
TRANSACTIONS/CAREER NOTES: Selected by Denver Broncos in first round (31st pick overall) of NFL draft. ... Signed by Broncos (July 21, 1999).
PLAYING EXPERIENCE: Denver NFL, 1999. ... Games/Games started: 1999 (16/12).
HONORS: Named inside linebacker on THE SPORTING NEWS college All-America second team (1998).
PRO STATISTICS: 1999—Credited with one sack and recovered two fumbles.

WILSON, JAMIE — G/OT

PERSONAL: Born June 6, 1979, in Newport News, Va. ... 6-6/300. ... Full name: James Wesley Wilson.
HIGH SCHOOL: Gloucester (Va.).
COLLEGE: Marshall.
TRANSACTIONS/CAREER NOTES: Signed as non-drafted free agent by Carolina Panthers (April 12, 1997). ... Active for one game (1997); did not play. ... On injured reserve with neck injury (August 30, 1998-entire season). ... Traded by Carolina Panthers to Green Bay Packers for undisclosed draft pick (August 3, 1999). ... Claimed on waivers by Indianapolis Colts (August 12, 1999). ... Granted free agency (February 11, 2000).
PLAYING EXPERIENCE: Indianapolis NFL, 1999. ... Games/Games started: 1999 (5/0).

WILSON, JERRY — CB — DOLPHINS

PERSONAL: Born July 17, 1973, in Alexandria, La. ... 5-10/187. ... Full name: Jerry Lee Wilson Jr.
HIGH SCHOOL: La Grange (Lake Charles, La.).
COLLEGE: Southern (degree in rehabilitation counseling).
TRANSACTIONS/CAREER NOTES: Selected by Tampa Bay Buccaneers in fourth round (105th pick overall) of 1995 NFL draft. ... Signed by Buccaneers (May 9, 1995). ... On injured reserve with knee injury (August 31, 1995-entire season). ... Released by Buccaneers (August 20, 1996). ... Signed by Miami Dolphins to practice squad (October 29, 1996). ... Activated (November 5, 1996).
PLAYING EXPERIENCE: Miami NFL, 1996-1999. ... Games/Games started: 1996 (2/0), 1997 (16/0), 1998 (16/0), 1999 (16/1). Total: 50/1.
PRO STATISTICS: 1997—Credited with two sacks and recovered one fumble. 1998—Intercepted one pass for no yards. 1999—Intercepted one pass for 13 yards, returned three kickoffs for 50 yards and credited with three sacks.

WILSON, REINARD — LB — BENGALS

PERSONAL: Born December 17, 1973, in Lake City, Fla. ... 6-2/261. ... Name pronounced ruh-NARD.
HIGH SCHOOL: Columbia (Lake City, Fla.).
COLLEGE: Florida State.
TRANSACTIONS/CAREER NOTES: Selected by Cincinnati Bengals in first round (14th pick overall) of 1997 NFL draft. ... Signed by Bengals (July 18, 1997).
HONORS: Named defensive end on THE SPORTING NEWS college All-America second team (1996).

Year Team	G	GS	SACKS
1997—Cincinnati NFL	16	4	3.0
1998—Cincinnati NFL	16	15	6.0
1999—Cincinnati NFL	15	0	3.0
Pro totals (3 years)	47	19	12.0

WILSON, ROBERT — WR — SAINTS

PERSONAL: Born June 23, 1974, in Tallahassee, Fla. ... 5-11/176.
HIGH SCHOOL: Jefferson County (Monticello, Fla.).
COLLEGE: Florida A&M.
TRANSACTIONS/CAREER NOTES: Signed as non-drafted free agent by Seattle Seahawks (April 25, 1997). ... Released by Seahawks (August 18, 1997). ... Re-signed by Seahawks to practice squad (August 19, 1997). ... Activated (December 17, 1997); did not play. ... Released by Seahawks (September 6, 1999). ... Re-signed by Seahawks (October 20, 1999). ... Released by Seahawks (November 13, 1999). ... Signed by New Orleans Saints (March 6, 2000).
PLAYING EXPERIENCE: Seattle NFL, 1998 and 1999. ... Games/Games started: 1998 (16/0), 1999 (2/0). Total: 18/0.
PRO STATISTICS: 1998—Returned one kickoff for 16 yards.

WILSON, TROY — DE — SAINTS

PERSONAL: Born November 22, 1970, in Topeka, Kan. ... 6-4/257. ... Full name: Troy Ethan Wilson.
HIGH SCHOOL: Shawnee Heights (Tecumseh, Kan.).

W

COLLEGE: Pittsburg (Kan.) State (degree in business management, 1992).
TRANSACTIONS/CAREER NOTES: Selected by San Francisco 49ers in seventh round (194th pick overall) of 1993 NFL draft. ... Signed by 49ers (May 12, 1993). ... On non-football injury list with back injury (August 24-October 16, 1993). ... Released by 49ers (August 27, 1995). ... Signed by Denver Broncos (September 28, 1995). ... Released by Broncos (October 30, 1995). ... Signed by Kansas City Chiefs (April 1996). ... Released by Chiefs (August 20, 1996). ... Signed by St. Louis Rams (February 6, 1997). ... Released by Rams (August 19, 1997). ... Signed by 49ers (May 26, 1998). ... Claimed on waivers by New Orleans Saints (September 1, 1998). ... Granted free agency (February 12, 1999). ... Re-signed by Saints (May 17, 1999).
CHAMPIONSHIP GAME EXPERIENCE: Played in NFC championship game (1993 and 1994 seasons). ... Member of Super Bowl championship team (1994 season).

Year Team	G	GS	SACKS
1993—San Francisco NFL	10	0	5.5
1994—San Francisco NFL	11	0	2.0
1995—Denver NFL	3	0	0.5
1996—		Did not play.	
1997—		Did not play.	
1998—New Orleans NFL	15	0	1.0
1999—New Orleans NFL	16	4	5.5
Pro totals (5 years)	55	4	14.5

WILTZ, JASON   DT   JETS

PERSONAL: Born November 23, 1976, in New Orleans. ... 6-4/300.
HIGH SCHOOL: St. Augustine (New Orleans).
COLLEGE: Nebraska.
TRANSACTIONS/CAREER NOTES: Selected by New York Jets in fourth round (123rd pick overall) of 1999 NFL draft. ... Signed by Jets (July 29, 1999).
PLAYING EXPERIENCE: New York Jets NFL, 1999. ... Games/Games started: 1999 (12/1).
PRO STATISTICS: 1999—Intercepted two passes for five yards and credited with one sack.

WINFIELD, ANTOINE   CB   BILLS

PERSONAL: Born June 24, 1977, in Akron, Ohio. ... 5-8/180. ... Full name: Antoine D. Winfield.
HIGH SCHOOL: Garfield (Ohio).
COLLEGE: Ohio State.
TRANSACTIONS/CAREER NOTES: Selected by Buffalo Bills in first round (23rd pick overall) of 1999 NFL draft. ... Signed by Bills for 1999 season.
HONORS: Named cornerback on THE SPORTING NEWS college All-America second team (1997). ... Jim Thorpe Award winner (1998). ... Named cornerback on THE SPORTING NEWS college All-America first team (1998).

			INTERCEPTIONS			
Year Team	G	GS	No.	Yds.	Avg.	TD
1999—Buffalo NFL	16	2	2	13	6.5	0

WINTERS, FRANK   C   PACKERS

PERSONAL: Born January 23, 1964, in Hoboken, N.J. ... 6-3/305. ... Full name: Frank Mitchell Winters.
HIGH SCHOOL: Emerson (Union City, N.J.).
JUNIOR COLLEGE: College of Eastern Utah.
COLLEGE: Western Illinois (degree in political science administration, 1987).
TRANSACTIONS/CAREER NOTES: Selected by Cleveland Browns in 10th round (276th pick overall) of 1987 NFL draft. ... Signed by Browns (July 25, 1987). ... Granted unconditional free agency (February 1, 1989). ... Signed by New York Giants (March 17, 1989). ... Granted unconditional free agency (February 1, 1990). ... Signed by Kansas City Chiefs (March 26, 1990). ... Granted unconditional free agency (February 1, 1992). ... Signed by Green Bay Packers (March 17, 1992). ... Granted unconditional free agency (February 17, 1994). ... Re-signed by Packers (April 1, 1994). ... Granted unconditional free agency (February 14, 1997). ... Re-signed by Packers (March 26, 1997). ... On injured reserve with leg injury (December 16, 1998-remainder of season). ... Granted unconditional free agency (February 11, 2000). ... Re-signed by Packers (April 4, 2000).
PLAYING EXPERIENCE: Cleveland NFL, 1987 and 1988; New York Giants NFL, 1989; Kansas City NFL, 1990 and 1991; Green Bay NFL, 1992-1999. ... Games/Games started: 1987 (12/0), 1988 (16/0), 1989 (15/0), 1990 (16/6), 1991 (16/0), 1992 (16/11), 1993 (16/16), 1994 (16/16), 1995 (16/16), 1996 (16/16), 1997 (13/13), 1998 (13/13), 1999 (16/16). Total: 197/123.
CHAMPIONSHIP GAME EXPERIENCE: Played in AFC championship game (1987 season). ... Played in NFC championship game (1995-97 seasons). ... Member of Super Bowl championship team (1996 season). ... Played in Super Bowl XXXII (1997 season).
HONORS: Played in Pro Bowl (1996 season).
PRO STATISTICS: 1987—Fumbled once. 1990—Recovered two fumbles. 1992—Fumbled once. 1994—Fumbled once and recovered one fumble for minus two yards. 1996—Recovered one fumble. 1999—Recovered one fumble.

WISNE, JERRY   OT   BEARS

PERSONAL: Born July 28, 1976, in Rochester, Minn. ... 6-6/308. ... Full name: Gerald Edward Wisne. ... Name pronounced WHIZ-knee.
HIGH SCHOOL: Jenks (Tulsa, Okla.).
COLLEGE: Notre Dame.
TRANSACTIONS/CAREER NOTES: Selected by Chicago Bears in fifth round (143rd pick overall) of 1999 NFL draft. ... Signed by Bears (May 26, 1999).
PLAYING EXPERIENCE: Chicago NFL, 1999. ... Games/Games started: 1999 (7/1).

W

WISNIEWSKI, STEVE   G   RAIDERS

PERSONAL: Born April 7, 1967, in Rutland, Vt. ... 6-4/305. ... Full name: Stephen Adam Wisniewski. ... Brother of Leo Wisniewski, nose tackle with Baltimore/Indianapolis Colts (1982-84). ... Name pronounced wiz-NEWS-key.
HIGH SCHOOL: Westfield (Houston).
COLLEGE: Penn State.
TRANSACTIONS/CAREER NOTES: Selected by Dallas Cowboys in second round (29th pick overall) of 1989 NFL draft. ... Draft rights traded by Cowboys with sixth-round pick (LB Jeff Francis) in 1989 draft to Los Angeles Raiders for second-(RB Darryl Johnston), third-(DE Rhondy Weston) and fifth-round (LB Willis Crockett) picks in 1989 draft (April 23, 1989). ... Signed by Raiders (July 22, 1989). ... Granted free agency (March 1, 1993). ... Re-signed by Raiders for 1993 season. ... Raiders franchise moved to Oakland (July 21, 1995).
PLAYING EXPERIENCE: Los Angeles Raiders NFL, 1989-1994; Oakland NFL, 1995-1999. ... Games/Games started: 1989 (15/15), 1990 (16/16), 1991 (15/15), 1992 (16/16), 1993 (16/16), 1994 (16/16), 1995 (16/16), 1996 (16/16), 1997 (16/16), 1998 (16/16), 1999 (16/16). Total: 174/174.
CHAMPIONSHIP GAME EXPERIENCE: Played in AFC championship game (1990 season).
HONORS: Named guard on THE SPORTING NEWS college All-America first team (1987 and 1988). ... Named guard on THE SPORTING NEWS NFL All-Pro team (1990-1994). ... Played in Pro Bowl (1990, 1991, 1993 and 1995 seasons). ... Named to play in Pro Bowl (1992 season); replaced by Jim Ritcher due to injury.
PRO STATISTICS: 1989—Recovered three fumbles. 1995—Recovered one fumble.

WISTROM, GRANT   DE   RAMS

PERSONAL: Born July 3, 1976, in Webb City, Mo. ... 6-4/267. ... Full name: Grant Alden Wistrom.
HIGH SCHOOL: Webb City (Mo.).
COLLEGE: Nebraska.
TRANSACTIONS/CAREER NOTES: Selected by St. Louis Rams in first round (sixth pick overall) of 1998 NFL draft. ... Signed by Rams (July 18, 1998).
CHAMPIONSHIP GAME EXPERIENCE: Played in NFC championship game (1999 season). ... Member of Super Bowl championship team (1999 season).
HONORS: Named defensive end on THE SPORTING NEWS college All-America first team (1996 and 1997).
PRO STATISTICS: 1998—Recovered one fumble for four yards. 1999—Intercepted two passes for 131 yards and two touchdowns, fumbled once and recovered one fumble for 31 yards.

Year Team	G	GS	SACKS
1998—St. Louis NFL	13	0	3.0
1999—St. Louis NFL	16	16	6.5
Pro totals (2 years)	29	16	9.5

WITMAN, JON   FB   STEELERS

PERSONAL: Born June 1, 1972, in Wrightsville, Pa. ... 6-1/240. ... Full name: Jon Doyle Witman.
HIGH SCHOOL: Eastern York (Wrightsville, Pa.).
COLLEGE: Penn State.
TRANSACTIONS/CAREER NOTES: Selected by Pittsburgh Steelers in third round (92nd pick overall) of 1996 NFL draft. ... Signed by Steelers (July 16, 1996). ... Granted free agency (February 12, 1999). ... Re-signed by Steelers (March 10, 1999).
CHAMPIONSHIP GAME EXPERIENCE: Played in AFC championship game (1997).
PRO STATISTICS: 1996—Returned one kickoff for 20 yards.
SINGLE GAME HIGHS (regular season): Attempts—7 (November 3, 1996, vs. St. Louis); yards—33 (November 3, 1996, vs. St. Louis); and rushing touchdowns—0.

Year Team	G	GS	RUSHING				RECEIVING				TOTALS			
			Att.	Yds.	Avg.	TD	No.	Yds.	Avg.	TD	TD	2pt.	Pts.	Fum.
1996—Pittsburgh NFL	16	4	17	69	4.1	0	2	15	7.5	0	0	0	0	0
1997—Pittsburgh NFL	16	2	5	11	2.2	0	1	3	3.0	0	0	0	0	0
1998—Pittsburgh NFL	16	8	1	2	2.0	0	13	74	5.7	0	0	0	0	0
1999—Pittsburgh NFL	16	11	6	18	3.0	0	12	106	8.8	0	0	0	0	0
Pro totals (4 years)	64	25	29	100	3.4	0	28	198	7.1	0	0	0	0	0

WOHLABAUGH, DAVE   C   BROWNS

PERSONAL: Born April 13, 1972, in Hamburg, N.Y. ... 6-3/292. ... Full name: David Vincent Wohlabaugh. ... Name pronounced WOOL-uh-buh.
HIGH SCHOOL: Frontier (Hamburg, N.Y.).
COLLEGE: Syracuse.
TRANSACTIONS/CAREER NOTES: Selected by New England Patriots in fourth round (112th pick overall) of 1995 NFL draft. ... Signed by Patriots (June 26, 1995). ... Granted free agency (February 13, 1998). ... Re-signed by Patriots (May 28, 1998). ... Granted unconditional free agency (February 12, 1999). ... Signed by Cleveland Browns (February 16, 1999).
PLAYING EXPERIENCE: New England NFL, 1995-1998; Cleveland NFL, 1999. ... Games/Games started: 1995 (11/11), 1996 (16/16), 1997 (14/14), 1998 (16/16), 1999 (15/15). Total: 72/72.
CHAMPIONSHIP GAME EXPERIENCE: Played in AFC championship game (1996 season). ... Played in Super Bowl XXXI (1996 season).
PRO STATISTICS: 1995—Recovered one fumble. 1996—Recovered two fumbles for one yard.

WONG, KAILEE   LB   VIKINGS

PERSONAL: Born May 23, 1976, in Eugene, Ore. ... 6-2/247.
HIGH SCHOOL: North Eugene (Ore.).
COLLEGE: Stanford.

W

TRANSACTIONS/CAREER NOTES: Selected by Minnesota Vikings in second round (51st pick overall) of 1998 NFL draft. ... Signed by Vikings (July 25, 1998). ... On injured reserve with leg injury (December 31, 1998-remainder of season).
PLAYING EXPERIENCE: Minnesota NFL, 1998 and 1999. ... Games/Games started: 1998 (15/0), 1999 (13/8). Total: 28/8.
PRO STATISTICS: 1998—Credited with 1½ sacks. 1999—Recovered one fumble for four yards.

WOODALL, LEE   LB   PANTHERS

PERSONAL: Born October 31, 1969, in Carlisle, Pa. ... 6-1/230. ... Full name: Lee Artis Woodall.
HIGH SCHOOL: Carlisle (Pa.).
COLLEGE: West Chester (Pa.) University.
TRANSACTIONS/CAREER NOTES: Selected by San Francisco 49ers in sixth round (182nd pick overall) of 1994 NFL draft. ... Signed by 49ers (July 20, 1994). ... Released by 49ers (February 9, 2000). ... Signed by Carolina Panthers (March 22, 2000).
CHAMPIONSHIP GAME EXPERIENCE: Played in NFC championship game (1994 and 1997 seasons). ... Member of Super Bowl championship team (1994 season).
HONORS: Played in Pro Bowl (1995 and 1997 seasons).
PRO STATISTICS: 1994—Recovered one fumble. 1995—Recovered two fumbles for 98 yards and one touchdown.

			INTERCEPTIONS				SACKS
Year Team	G	GS	No.	Yds.	Avg.	TD	No.
1994—San Francisco NFL	15	13	0	0	0.0	0	1.0
1995—San Francisco NFL	16	16	2	0	0.0	0	3.0
1996—San Francisco NFL	16	13	0	0	0.0	0	2.5
1997—San Francisco NFL	16	16	2	55	27.5	0	0.0
1998—San Francisco NFL	15	15	1	4	4.0	0	0.0
1999—San Francisco NFL	16	16	0	0	0.0	0	2.5
Pro totals (6 years)	94	89	5	59	11.8	0	9.0

WOODEN, SHAWN   S   BEARS

PERSONAL: Born October 23, 1973, in Philadelphia. ... 5-11/205. ... Full name: Shawn Anthony Wooden.
HIGH SCHOOL: Abington (Pa.).
COLLEGE: Notre Dame (degree in computer science).
TRANSACTIONS/CAREER NOTES: Selected by Miami Dolphins in sixth round (189th pick overall) of 1996 NFL draft. ... Signed by Dolphins (July 10, 1996). ... On injured reserve with knee injury (September 15, 1998-remainder of season). ... Granted free agency (February 12, 1999). ... Re-signed by Dolphins (April 23, 1999). ... Granted unconditional free agency (February 11, 2000). ... Signed by Chicago Bears (March 6, 2000).
PRO STATISTICS: 1996—Recovered two fumbles. 1997—Fumbled once and recovered two fumbles. 1999—Recovered two fumbles.

			INTERCEPTIONS			
Year Team	G	GS	No.	Yds.	Avg.	TD
1996—Miami NFL	16	11	2	15	7.5	0
1997—Miami NFL	16	15	2	10	5.0	0
1998—Miami NFL	2	1	0	0	0.0	0
1999—Miami NFL	15	6	0	0	0.0	0
Pro totals (4 years)	49	33	4	25	6.3	0

WOODS, JEROME   S   CHIEFS

PERSONAL: Born March 17, 1973, in Memphis, Tenn. ... 6-2/202.
HIGH SCHOOL: Melrose (Memphis, Tenn.).
JUNIOR COLLEGE: Northeast Mississippi Community College.
COLLEGE: Memphis.
TRANSACTIONS/CAREER NOTES: Selected by Kansas City Chiefs in first round (28th pick overall) of 1996 NFL draft. ... Signed by Chiefs (August 12, 1996). ... Granted unconditional free agency (February 11, 2000). ... Re-signed by Chiefs (February 11, 2000).
PRO STATISTICS: 1996—Fumbled once and recovered one fumble. 1997—Credited with one sack and recovered two fumbles for 13 yards. 1999—Recovered one fumble for 19 yards.

			INTERCEPTIONS			
Year Team	G	GS	No.	Yds.	Avg.	TD
1996—Kansas City NFL	16	0	0	0	0.0	0
1997—Kansas City NFL	16	16	4	57	14.3	0
1998—Kansas City NFL	16	16	2	47	23.5	0
1999—Kansas City NFL	15	15	1	5	5.0	0
Pro totals (4 years)	63	47	7	109	15.6	0

W

WOODSON, CHARLES   DB   RAIDERS

PERSONAL: Born October 7, 1976, in Fremont, Ohio ... 6-1/205.
HIGH SCHOOL: Ross (Fremont, Ohio).
COLLEGE: Michigan.
TRANSACTIONS/CAREER NOTES: Selected after junior season by Oakland Raiders in first round (fourth pick overall) of 1998 NFL draft. ... Signed by Raiders (July 20, 1998).
HONORS: Named cornerback on THE SPORTING NEWS college All-America second team (1996). ... Heisman Trophy winner (1997). ... Jim Thorpe Award winner (1997). ... Maxwell Award winner (1997). ... Chuck Bednarik Award winner (1997). ... Named College Football Player of the Year by THE SPORTING NEWS (1997). ... Named cornerback on THE SPORTING NEWS college All-America first team (1997). ... Played in Pro Bowl (1998 and 1999 seasons).
PRO STATISTICS: 1999—Caught one pass for 19 yards and recovered one fumble for 24 yards.

Year Team	G	GS	INTERCEPTIONS No.	Yds.	Avg.	TD
1998—Oakland NFL	16	16	5	118	23.6	1
1999—Oakland NFL	16	16	1	15	15.0	1
Pro totals (2 years)	32	32	6	133	22.2	2

WOODSON, DARREN   S   COWBOYS

PERSONAL: Born April 25, 1969, in Phoenix. ... 6-1/219. ... Full name: Darren Ray Woodson.
HIGH SCHOOL: Maryvale (Phoenix).
COLLEGE: Arizona State (degree in criminal justice).
TRANSACTIONS/CAREER NOTES: Selected by Dallas Cowboys in second round (37th pick overall) of 1992 NFL draft. ... Signed by Cowboys (April 26, 1992).
CHAMPIONSHIP GAME EXPERIENCE: Played in NFC championship game (1992-1995 seasons). ... Member of Super Bowl championship team (1992, 1993 and 1995 seasons).
HONORS: Named strong safety on THE SPORTING NEWS NFL All-Pro team (1994-1996 and 1998). ... Played in Pro Bowl (1994-1996 and 1998 seasons). ... Named to play in Pro Bowl (1997 season); replaced by John Lynch due to injury.
PRO STATISTICS: 1993—Recovered three fumbles for three yards. 1994—Recovered one fumble. 1996—Fumbled once and recovered one fumble. 1997—Fumbled once and recovered two fumbles.

Year Team	G	GS	INTERCEPTIONS No.	Yds.	Avg.	TD	SACKS No.
1992—Dallas NFL	16	2	0	0	0.0	0	1.0
1993—Dallas NFL	16	15	0	0	0.0	0	0.0
1994—Dallas NFL	16	16	5	140	28.0	1	0.0
1995—Dallas NFL	16	16	2	46	23.0	1	0.0
1996—Dallas NFL	16	16	5	43	8.6	0	3.0
1997—Dallas NFL	14	14	1	14	14.0	0	2.0
1998—Dallas NFL	16	15	1	1	1.0	0	3.0
1999—Dallas NFL	15	15	2	5	2.5	0	1.0
Pro totals (8 years)	125	109	16	249	15.6	2	10.0

WOODSON, ROD   CB   RAVENS

PERSONAL: Born March 10, 1965, in Fort Wayne, Ind. ... 6-0/205. ... Full name: Roderick Kevin Woodson.
HIGH SCHOOL: R. Nelson Snider (Fort Wayne, Ind.).
COLLEGE: Purdue.
TRANSACTIONS/CAREER NOTES: Selected by Pittsburgh Steelers in first round (10th pick overall) of 1987 NFL draft. ... On reserve/unsigned list (August 31-October 27, 1987). ... Signed by Steelers (October 28, 1987). ... Granted roster exemption (October 28-November 7, 1987). ... Granted free agency (February 1, 1991). ... Re-signed by Steelers (August 22, 1991). ... Granted unconditional free agency (February 14, 1997). ... Signed by San Francisco 49ers (July 17, 1997). ... Released by 49ers (February 9, 1998). ... Signed by Baltimore Ravens (February 20, 1998).
CHAMPIONSHIP GAME EXPERIENCE: Played in AFC championship game (1994 season). ... Member of Steelers for AFC championship game (1995 season); inactive. ... Played in Super Bowl XXX (1995 season). ... Played in NFC championship game (1997 season).
HONORS: Named defensive back on THE SPORTING NEWS college All-America second team (1985). ... Named kick returner on THE SPORTING NEWS college All-America first team (1986). ... Named kick returner on THE SPORTING NEWS NFL All-Pro team (1989). ... Played in Pro Bowl (1989-1994, 1996 and 1999 seasons). ... Named cornerback on THE SPORTING NEWS NFL All-Pro team (1990 and 1992-1994).
RECORDS: Shares NFL career record for most touchdowns by interception return—9.
PRO STATISTICS: 1987—Recovered two fumbles. 1988—Recovered three fumbles for two yards. 1989—Recovered four fumbles for one yard. 1990—Recovered three fumbles. 1991—Recovered three fumbles for 15 yards. 1992—Recovered one fumble for nine yards. 1993—Rushed once for no yards and recovered one fumble. 1994—Recovered one fumble. 1996—Recovered three fumbles for 42 yards and a touchdown. 1997—Recovered one fumble. 1999—Recovered two fumbles.
MISCELLANEOUS: Active AFC leader for career interceptions (54). ... Holds Baltimore Ravens all-time record for most interceptions (13).

Year Team	G	GS	INTERCEPTIONS No.	Yds.	Avg.	TD	SACKS No.	PUNT RETURNS No.	Yds.	Avg.	TD	KICKOFF RETURNS No.	Yds.	Avg.	TD	TOTALS TD	2pt.	Pts.	Fum.
1987—Pittsburgh NFL	8	0	1	45	45.0	1	0.0	16	135	8.4	0	13	290	22.3	0	1	0	6	3
1988—Pittsburgh NFL	16	16	4	98	24.5	0	0.5	33	281	8.5	0	37	850	23.0	†1	1	0	6	3
1989—Pittsburgh NFL	15	14	3	39	13.0	0	0.0	29	207	7.1	0	§36	§982	*27.3	†1	1	0	6	3
1990—Pittsburgh NFL	16	16	5	67	13.4	0	0.0	§38	§398	10.5	†1	35	764	21.8	0	1	0	6	3
1991—Pittsburgh NFL	15	15	3	72	24.0	0	1.0	28	320	§11.4	0	*44	§880	20.0	0	0	0	0	3
1992—Pittsburgh NFL	16	16	4	90	22.5	0	6.0	32	364	§11.4	1	25	469	18.8	0	1	0	6	2
1993—Pittsburgh NFL	16	16	8	§138	17.3	▲1	2.0	42	338	8.0	0	15	294	19.6	0	1	0	6	2
1994—Pittsburgh NFL	15	15	4	109	27.3	2	3.0	39	319	8.2	0	15	365	24.3	0	2	0	12	2
1995—Pittsburgh NFL	1	1	0	0	0.0	0	0.0	0	0	0.0	0	0	0	0.0	0	0	0	0	0
1996—Pittsburgh NFL	16	16	6	121	20.2	1	1.0	0	0	0.0	0	0	0	0.0	0	2	0	12	1
1997—San Francisco NFL	14	14	3	81	27.0	0	0.0	1	0	0.0	0	0	0	0.0	0	0	0	0	0
1998—Baltimore NFL	16	16	6	108	18.0	▲2	0.0	0	0	0.0	0	0	0	0.0	0	2	0	12	0
1999—Baltimore NFL	16	16	†7	195	27.9	†2	0.0	2	0	0.0	0	0	0	0.0	0	2	0	12	1
Pro totals (13 years)	180	171	54	1163	21.5	9	13.5	260	2362	9.1	2	220	4894	22.2	2	14	0	84	23

WOODY, DAMIEN   C   PATRIOTS

PERSONAL: Born November 3, 1977, in Beaverdam, Va. ... 6-3/319. ... Full name: Damien Michael Woody.
HIGH SCHOOL: Patrick Henry (Beaverdam, Va.).
COLLEGE: Boston College.
TRANSACTIONS/CAREER NOTES: Selected after junior season by New England Patriots in first round (17th pick overall) of 1999 NFL draft. ... Signed by Patriots (July 30, 1999).

W

PLAYING EXPERIENCE: New England NFL, 1999. ... Games/Games started: 1999 (16/16).
PRO STATISTICS: 1999—Fumbled once and recovered one fumble for minus 10 yards.

WOOTEN, TITO　　　　S

PERSONAL: Born December 12, 1971, in Goldsboro, N.C. ... 6-0/195.
HIGH SCHOOL: Goldsboro (N.C.).
COLLEGE: North Carolina, then Northeast Louisiana.
TRANSACTIONS/CAREER NOTES: Selected by New York Giants in fourth round of 1994 NFL supplemental draft. ... Signed by Giants (July 22, 1994). ... Granted free agency (February 14, 1997). ... Re-signed by Giants for 1997 season. ... Granted unconditional free agency (February 13, 1998). ... Re-signed by Giants (February 13, 1998). ... Released by Giants (June 14, 1999). ... Signed by Indianapolis Colts (August 5, 1999). ... Released by Colts (December 20, 1999).
PRO STATISTICS: 1995—Recovered one fumble for one yard and a touchdown. 1996—Credited with a safety and recovered one fumble for 54 yards and a touchdown. 1997—Fumbled once and recovered one fumble. 1998—Credited with three sacks. 1999—Recovered two fumbles.

			INTERCEPTIONS			
Year　Team	G	GS	No.	Yds.	Avg.	TD
1994—New York Giants NFL	16	2	0	0	0.0	0
1995—New York Giants NFL	16	3	1	38	38.0	0
1996—New York Giants NFL	13	12	1	35	35.0	0
1997—New York Giants NFL	16	16	5	‡146	‡29.2	1
1998—New York Giants NFL	14	13	0	0	0.0	0
1999—Indianapolis NFL	8	1	1	4	4.0	0
Pro totals (6 years)	83	47	8	223	27.9	1

WORD, MARK　　　DE　　　CHIEFS

PERSONAL: Born November 23, 1975, in Miami. ... 6-4/270. ... Full name: Mark Bernard Word.
HIGH SCHOOL: Southridge (Miami).
JUNIOR COLLEGE: Hinds Community College (Miss.).
COLLEGE: Jacksonville State.
TRANSACTIONS/CAREER NOTES: Signed as non-drafted free agent by Kansas City Chiefs (April 20, 1999).
PLAYING EXPERIENCE: Kansas City NFL, 1999. ... Games/Games started: 1999 (5/0).

WORTHAM, BARRON　　　LB　　　COWBOYS

PERSONAL: Born November 1, 1969, in Fort Worth, Texas. ... 5-11/245. ... Full name: Barron Winfred Wortham.
HIGH SCHOOL: Everman (Texas).
COLLEGE: Texas-El Paso.
TRANSACTIONS/CAREER NOTES: Selected by Houston Oilers in sixth round (194th pick overall) of 1994 NFL draft. ... Signed by Oilers (July 12, 1994). ... Granted free agency (February 14, 1997). ... Oilers franchise moved to Tennessee for 1997 season. ... Re-signed by Oilers (July 9, 1997). ... Granted unconditional free agency (February 13, 1998). ... Re-signed by Oilers (February 23, 1998). ... Oilers franchise renamed Tennessee Titans for 1999 season (December 26, 1998). ... Released by Titans (April 25, 2000). ... Signed by Dallas Cowboys (May 4, 2000).
CHAMPIONSHIP GAME EXPERIENCE: Played in AFC championship game (1999 season). ... Played in Super Bowl XXXIV (1999 season).
HONORS: Named linebacker on The Sporting News college All-America second team (1993).
PRO STATISTICS: 1994—Recovered one fumble. 1995—Returned one kickoff for minus three yards. 1996—Recovered two fumbles. 1999—Recovered three fumbles for eight yards.

Year　Team	G	GS	SACKS
1994—Houston NFL	16	1	0.0
1995—Houston NFL	16	5	1.0
1996—Houston NFL	15	14	2.0
1997—Tennessee NFL	16	16	0.0
1998—Tennessee NFL	13	0	0.0
1999—Tennessee NFL	16	15	0.5
Pro totals (6 years)	92	51	3.5

WRIGHT, KENNY　　　CB　　　VIKINGS

PERSONAL: Born September 14, 1977, in Ruston, La. ... 6-1/196.
HIGH SCHOOL: Ruston (La.).
COLLEGE: Arkansas, then Northwestern (La.) State.
TRANSACTIONS/CAREER NOTES: Selected after junior season by Minnesota Vikings in fourth round (120th pick overall) of 1999 NFL draft. ... Signed by Vikings (July 21, 1999).
PLAYING EXPERIENCE: Minnesota NFL, 1999. ... Games/Games started: 1999 (16/12).
PRO STATISTICS: 1999—Intercepted one pass for 11 yards.

WRIGHT, LAWRENCE　　　S　　　BENGALS

PERSONAL: Born September 6, 1973, in Miami. ... 6-1/211. ... Full name: Lawrence D. Wright III.
HIGH SCHOOL: North Miami, then Valley Forge Military Academy (Wayne, Pa.).
COLLEGE: Florida.

W

TRANSACTIONS/CAREER NOTES: Signed as non-drafted free agent by Cincinnati Bengals (April 25, 1997). ... Released by Bengals (August 24, 1997). ... Re-signed by Bengals to practice squad (August 26, 1997). ... Activated (November 5, 1997). ... Released by Bengals (August 21, 1998). ... Re-signed by Bengals to practice squad (December 16, 1998).
PLAYING EXPERIENCE: Cincinnati NFL, 1997 and 1999. ... Games/Games started: 1997 (4/0), 1999 (14/0). Total: 18/0.
HONORS: Jim Thorpe Award winner (1996).
PRO STATISTICS: 1999—Recovered one fumble.

WRIGHT, TOBY — S

PERSONAL: Born November 19, 1970, in Phoenix. ... 5-11/212. ... Full name: Toby Lin Wright. ... Brother of Terry Wright, defensive back with Indianapolis Colts (1987-88) and Hamilton Tiger-Cats of CFL (1991-95).
HIGH SCHOOL: Dobson (Mesa, Ariz.).
JUNIOR COLLEGE: Phoenix College.
COLLEGE: Nebraska.
TRANSACTIONS/CAREER NOTES: Selected by Los Angeles Rams in second round (49th pick overall) of 1994 NFL draft. ... Signed by Rams (May 18, 1994). ... Rams franchise moved to St. Louis (April 12, 1995). ... On injured reserve with knee injury (November 30, 1998-remainder of season). ... Released by Rams (June 9, 1999). ... Signed by Washington Redskins (September 27, 1999). ... Released by Redskins (October 26, 1999).
PRO STATISTICS: 1994—Recovered one fumble for 98 yards and a touchdown. 1995—Rushed once for nine yards, recovered one fumble for 73 yards and a touchdown. 1997—Recovered one fumble for 34 yards. 1998—Credited with one sack.

			INTERCEPTIONS			
Year Team	G	GS	No.	Yds.	Avg.	TD
1994—Los Angeles Rams NFL	16	2	0	0	0.0	0
1995—St. Louis NFL	16	16	6	79	13.2	0
1996—St. Louis NFL	12	12	1	19	19.0	1
1997—St. Louis NFL	11	11	0	0	0.0	0
1998—St. Louis NFL	3	3	0	0	0.0	0
1999—Washington NFL	1	0	0	0	0.0	0
Pro totals (6 years)	59	44	7	98	14.0	1

WUERFFEL, DANNY — QB

PERSONAL: Born May 27, 1974, in Fort Walton Beach, Fla. ... 6-1/208. ... Full name: Daniel Carl Wuerffel. ... Name pronounced WER-ful.
HIGH SCHOOL: Fort Walton Beach (Fla.).
COLLEGE: Florida.
TRANSACTIONS/CAREER NOTES: Selected by New Orleans Saints in fourth round (99th pick overall) of 1997 NFL draft. ... Signed by Saints (July 17, 1997). ... Released by Saints (February 11, 2000).
HONORS: Davey O'Brien Award winner (1995 and 1996). ... Heisman Trophy winner (1996). ... Named College Player of the Year by THE SPORTING NEWS (1996). ... Named quarterback on THE SPORTING NEWS college All-America first team (1996).
PRO STATISTICS: 1997—Fumbled twice and recovered two fumbles. 1998—Fumbled once and recovered one fumble.
SINGLE GAME HIGHS (regular season): Attempts—47 (October 4, 1998, vs. New England); completions—25 (October 4, 1998, vs. New England); yards—278 (October 4, 1998, vs. New England); and touchdown passes—2 (October 4, 1998, vs. New England).
MISCELLANEOUS: Regular-season record as starting NFL quarterback: 2-4 (.333).

			PASSING								RUSHING				TOTALS		
Year Team	G	GS	Att.	Cmp.	Pct.	Yds.	TD	Int.	Avg.	Rat.	Att.	Yds.	Avg.	TD	TD	2pt.	Pts.
1997—New Orleans NFL	7	2	91	42	46.2	518	4	8	5.69	42.3	6	26	4.3	0	0	0	0
1998—New Orleans NFL	5	4	119	62	52.1	695	5	5	5.84	66.3	11	60	5.5	0	0	0	0
1999—New Orleans NFL	4	0	48	22	45.8	191	0	3	3.98	30.8	2	29	14.5	1	1	0	6
Pro totals (3 years)	16	6	258	126	48.8	1404	9	16	5.44	51.2	19	115	6.1	1	1	0	6

WUNSCH, JERRY — OT — BUCCANEERS

PERSONAL: Born January 21, 1974, in Eau Claire, Wis. ... 6-6/339. ... Full name: Gerald Wunsch. ... Name pronounced WUNCH.
HIGH SCHOOL: West (Wausau, Wis.).
COLLEGE: Wisconsin (degree in history).
TRANSACTIONS/CAREER NOTES: Selected by Tampa Bay Buccaneers in second round (37th pick overall) of 1997 NFL draft. ... Signed by Buccaneers (July 18, 1997).
PLAYING EXPERIENCE: Tampa Bay NFL, 1997-1999. ... Games/Games started: 1997 (16/0), 1998 (16/1), 1999 (16/13). Total: 48/14.
CHAMPIONSHIP GAME EXPERIENCE: Played in NFC championship game (1999 season).
PRO STATISTICS: 1997—Recovered one fumble.

W

WYCHECK, FRANK — TE — TITANS

PERSONAL: Born October 14, 1971, in Philadelphia. ... 6-3/250. ... Name pronounced WHY-check.
HIGH SCHOOL: Archbishop Ryan (Philadelphia).
COLLEGE: Maryland.
TRANSACTIONS/CAREER NOTES: Selected after junior season by Washington Redskins in sixth round (160th pick overall) of 1993 NFL draft. ... Signed by Redskins (July 15, 1993). ... On suspended list for anabolic steroid use (November 29, 1994-remainder of season). ... Released by Redskins (August 17, 1995). ... Signed by Houston Oilers (August 18, 1995). ... Granted free agency (February 16, 1996). ... Re-signed by Oilers (June 28, 1996). ... Oilers franchise moved to Tennessee for 1997 season. ... Oilers franchise renamed Tennessee Titans for 1999 season (December 26, 1998).
CHAMPIONSHIP GAME EXPERIENCE: Played in AFC championship game (1999 season). ... Played in Super Bowl XXXIV (1999 season).
HONORS: Played in Pro Bowl (1998 and 1999 seasons).

PRO STATISTICS: 1993—Recovered one fumble. 1995—Rushed once for one yard and a touchdown and recovered one fumble. 1996—Rushed twice for three yards. 1997—Recovered one fumble. 1998—Recovered two fumbles. 1999—Completed only pass attempt for 61 yards and a touchdown.

SINGLE GAME HIGHS (regular season): Receptions—10 (December 5, 1999, vs. Baltimore); yards—87 (December 5, 1999, vs. Baltimore); and touchdown receptions—2 (January 2, 2000, vs. Pittsburgh).

Year Team	G	GS	RECEIVING No.	Yds.	Avg.	TD	KICKOFF RETURNS No.	Yds.	Avg.	TD	TOTALS TD	2pt.	Pts.	Fum.
1993—Washington NFL	9	7	16	113	7.1	0	0	0	0.0	0	0	0	0	1
1994—Washington NFL	9	1	7	55	7.9	1	4	84	21.0	0	1	0	6	0
1995—Houston NFL	16	11	40	471	11.8	1	0	0	0.0	0	2	0	12	0
1996—Houston NFL	16	16	53	511	9.6	6	2	5	2.5	0	6	0	36	2
1997—Tennessee NFL	16	16	63	748	11.9	4	1	3	3.0	0	4	1	26	0
1998—Tennessee NFL	16	16	70	768	11.0	2	1	10	10.0	0	2	0	12	2
1999—Tennessee NFL	16	16	69	641	9.3	2	0	0	0.0	0	2	0	12	0
Pro totals (7 years)	**98**	**83**	**318**	**3307**	**10.4**	**16**	**8**	**102**	**12.8**	**0**	**17**	**1**	**104**	**5**

WYNN, RENALDO DE JAGUARS

PERSONAL: Born September 3, 1974, in Chicago. ... 6-3/280. ... Full name: Renaldo Levalle Wynn.
HIGH SCHOOL: De La Salle Institute (Chicago).
COLLEGE: Notre Dame (degree in sociology, 1996).
TRANSACTIONS/CAREER NOTES: Selected by Jacksonville Jaguars in first round (21st pick overall) of 1997 NFL draft. ... Signed by Jaguars (July 21, 1997). ... On injured reserve with groin injury (December 25, 1998-remainder of season).
CHAMPIONSHIP GAME EXPERIENCE: Played in AFC championship game (1999 season).
PRO STATISTICS: 1997—Recovered one fumble. 1998—Recovered one fumble. 1999—Recovered one fumble.

Year Team	G	GS	SACKS
1997—Jacksonville NFL	16	8	2.5
1998—Jacksonville NFL	15	15	1.0
1999—Jacksonville NFL	12	10	1.5
Pro totals (3 years)	**43**	**33**	**5.0**

YEAST, CRAIG WR BENGALS

PERSONAL: Born November 20, 1976, in Danville, Ky. ... 5-7/160. ... Full name: Craig Nelson Yeast.
HIGH SCHOOL: Harrodsburg (Ky.).
COLLEGE: Kentucky.
TRANSACTIONS/CAREER NOTES: Selected by Cincinnati Bengals in fourth round (98th pick overall) of 1999 NFL draft. ... Signed by Bengals (July 28, 1999).
PRO STATISTICS: 1999—Fumbled twice and recovered one fumble.
SINGLE GAME HIGHS (regular season): Receptions—3 (October 31, 1999, vs. Jacksonville); yards—20 (October 31, 1999, vs. Jacksonville); and touchdown receptions—0.

Year Team	G	GS	RUSHING Att.	Yds.	Avg.	TD	RECEIVING No.	Yds.	Avg.	TD	PUNT RETURNS No.	Yds.	Avg.	TD	KICKOFF RETURNS No.	Yds.	Avg.	TD	TOTALS TD	2pt.	Pts.
1999—Cincinnati NFL	9	0	2	-16	-8.0	0	3	20	6.7	0	10	209	20.9	†2	3	50	16.7	0	2	0	12

YOUNG, BRYANT DT 49ERS

PERSONAL: Born January 27, 1972, in Chicago Heights, Ill. ... 6-3/291. ... Full name: Bryant Colby Young.
HIGH SCHOOL: Bloom (Chicago Heights, Ill.).
COLLEGE: Notre Dame.
TRANSACTIONS/CAREER NOTES: Selected by San Francisco 49ers in first round (seventh pick overall) of 1994 NFL draft. ... Signed by 49ers (July 26, 1994). ... On injured reserve with broken leg (December 2, 1998-remainder of season). ... On physically unable to perform list with leg injury (July 30-August 10, 1999).
CHAMPIONSHIP GAME EXPERIENCE: Played in NFC championship game (1994 and 1997 seasons). ... Member of Super Bowl championship team (1994 season).
HONORS: Named defensive tackle on THE SPORTING NEWS NFL All-Pro team (1996 and 1998). ... Played in Pro Bowl (1996 and 1999 season).
PRO STATISTICS: 1994—Recovered one fumble. 1995—Recovered two fumbles. 1996—Recovered one fumble for 43 yards. 1998—Recovered one fumble. 1999—Credited with a safety.

Year Team	G	GS	SACKS
1994—San Francisco NFL	16	16	6.0
1995—San Francisco NFL	12	12	6.0
1996—San Francisco NFL	16	16	11.5
1997—San Francisco NFL	12	12	4.0
1998—San Francisco NFL	12	12	9.5
1999—San Francisco NFL	16	16	11.0
Pro totals (6 years)	**84**	**84**	**48.0**

W
Y

YOUNG, FLOYD CB BUCCANEERS

PERSONAL: Born November 23, 1975, in New Orleans. ... 6-0/179. ... Full name: Floyd Alexander Young.
HIGH SCHOOL: Clark (New Orleans).
JUNIOR COLLEGE: Scottsdale (Ariz.) Community College.
COLLEGE: Texas A&M-Kingsville.

TRANSACTIONS/CAREER NOTES: Signed as non-drafted free agent by Tampa Bay Buccaneers (May 5, 1997). ... Released by Buccaneers (July 18, 1997). ... Re-signed by Buccaneers (July 22, 1997). ... Released by Buccaneers (August 17, 1997). ... Re-signed by Buccaneers to practice squad (August 26, 1997). ... Activated (September 27, 1997). ... Granted free agency (February 11, 2000).
PLAYING EXPERIENCE: Tampa Bay NFL, 1997-1999. ... Games/Games started: 1997 (12/1), 1998 (11/0), 1999 (6/0). Total: 29/1.
CHAMPIONSHIP GAME EXPERIENCE: Played in NFC championship game (1999 season).
PRO STATISTICS: 1998—Recovered one fumble.

YOUNG, RYAN　　　　OT　　　　JETS

PERSONAL: Born June 28, 1976, in St. Louis. ... 6-5/320.
HIGH SCHOOL: Parkway Central (Chesterfield, Mo.).
COLLEGE: Kansas State.
TRANSACTIONS/CAREER NOTES: Selected by New York Jets in seventh round (223rd pick overall) of 1999 NFL draft. ... Signed by Jets (June 25, 1999).
PLAYING EXPERIENCE: New York Jets NFL, 1999. ... Games/Games started: 1999 (15/7).

YOUNG, STEVE　　　　QB

PERSONAL: Born October 11, 1961, in Salt Lake City. ... 6-2/215. ... Full name: Jon Steven Young.
HIGH SCHOOL: Greenwich (Conn.).
COLLEGE: Brigham Young (degree in law, 1994).
TRANSACTIONS/CAREER NOTES: Selected by Los Angeles Express in first round (10th pick overall) of 1984 USFL draft. ... Signed by Express (March 5, 1984). ... Granted roster exemption (March 5-30, 1984). ... Selected by Tampa Bay Buccaneers in first round (first pick overall) of 1984 NFL supplemental draft. ... On developmental squad (March 31-April 16, 1985). ... Released by Express (September 9, 1985). ... Signed by Buccaneers (September 10, 1985). ... Granted roster exemption (September 10-23, 1985). ... Traded by Buccaneers to San Francisco 49ers for second-round (LB Winston Moss) and fourth-round (WR Bruce Hill) picks in 1987 draft and cash (April 24, 1987). ... Granted free agency (February 1, 1991). ... Re-signed by 49ers (May 3, 1991). ... Designated by 49ers as franchise player (February 25, 1993). ... Announced retirement (June 12, 2000).
CHAMPIONSHIP GAME EXPERIENCE: Played in NFC championship game (1988-1990, 1992-1994 and 1997 seasons). ... Member of 49ers for Super Bowl XXIII (1988 season); did not play. ... Member of Super Bowl championship team (1989 and 1994 seasons).
HONORS: Davey O'Brien Award winner (1983). ... Named quarterback on THE SPORTING NEWS college All-America first team (1983). ... Named NFL Player of the Year by THE SPORTING NEWS (1992 and 1994). ... Named quarterback on THE SPORTING NEWS NFL All-Pro team (1992, 1994 and 1998). ... Played in Pro Bowl (1992-1995, 1997 and 1998 seasons). ... Named Most Valuable Player of Super Bowl XXIX (1994 season). ... Named to play in Pro Bowl (1996 season); replaced by Kerry Collins due to injury.
RECORDS: Holds NFL career records for highest completion percentage—64.3; highest passer rating—96.8; most seasons leading league in touchdown passes—4; and most consecutive seasons leading league in passer rating—4 (1991-1994). ... Holds NFL record for most consecutive games with 300 or more yards passing—6 (September 6-October 18, 1998). ... Holds NFL single-season record for highest passer rating—112.8 (1994).
POST SEASON RECORDS: Holds Super Bowl single-game record for most touchdown passes—6 (January 29, 1995, vs. San Diego). ... Shares Super Bowl single-game record for most passes attempted without an interception—36 (January 29, 1995, vs. San Diego). ... Shares NFL postseason single-game record for most touchdown passes—6 (January 29, 1995, vs. San Diego).
PRO STATISTICS: USFL: 1984—Fumbled seven times and recovered four fumbles. 1985—Fumbled seven times and recovered one fumble for minus 11 yards. NFL: 1985—Fumbled four times and recovered one fumble for minus one yard. 1986—Fumbled 11 times and recovered four fumbles for minus 24 yards. 1988—Fumbled five times and recovered two fumbles for minus 10 yards. 1989—Fumbled twice and recovered one fumble. 1990—Fumbled once. 1991—Fumbled three times and recovered one fumble for minus six yards. 1992—Fumbled nine times and recovered three fumbles for minus 13 yards. 1993—Caught two passes for two yards, fumbled eight times and recovered two fumbles for minus four yards. 1994—Fumbled four times and recovered one fumble for minus four yards. 1995—Fumbled three times. 1996—Fumbled three times and recovered one fumble. 1997—Fumbled four times and recovered two fumbles for minus 11 yards. 1998—Fumbled nine times and recovered one fumble. 1999—Fumbled twice.
SINGLE GAME HIGHS (regular season): Attempts—51 (October 18, 1998, vs. Indianapolis); completions—33 (October 18, 1998, vs. Indianapolis); yards—462 (November 28, 1993, vs. Los Angeles Rams); and touchdown passes—4 (November 22, 1998, vs. New Orleans).
STATISTICAL PLATEAUS: USFL: 300-yard passing games: 1984 (2). ... 100-yard rushing games: 1984 (1), 1985 (1). Total: 2. ... NFL: 300-yard passing games: 1991 (3), 1992 (3), 1993 (3), 1994 (5), 1995 (5), 1996 (1), 1997 (1), 1998 (7). Total: 28. ... 100-yard rushing games: 1990 (1).
MISCELLANEOUS: Active NFC leader for career passing yards (33,124) and career touchdown passes (232). ... Regular-season record as starting NFL quarterback: 94-49 (.657). ... Postseason record as starting NFL quarterback: 8-6 (.571).

Year	Team	G	GS	Att.	Cmp.	Pct.	Yds.	TD	Int.	Avg.	Rat.	Att.	Yds.	Avg.	TD	TD	2pt.	Pts.
						PASSING							**RUSHING**				**TOTALS**	
1984—Los Angeles USFL	12	12	310	179	57.7	2361	10	9	7.62	80.6	79	515	6.5	7	7	3	48
1985—Los Angeles USFL	13	0	250	137	54.8	1741	6	13	6.96	63.1	56	368	6.6	2	2	0	12
—Tampa Bay NFL	5	5	138	72	52.2	935	3	8	6.78	56.9	40	233	5.8	1	1	0	6
1986—Tampa Bay NFL	14	14	363	195	53.7	2282	8	13	6.29	65.5	74	425	5.7	5	5	0	30
1987—San Francisco NFL	8	3	69	37	53.6	570	10	0	8.26	120.8	26	190	7.3	1	1	0	6
1988—San Francisco NFL	11	3	101	54	53.5	680	3	3	6.73	72.2	27	184	6.8	1	1	0	6
1989—San Francisco NFL	10	3	92	64	69.6	1001	8	3	10.88	120.8	38	126	3.3	2	2	0	12
1990—San Francisco NFL	6	1	62	38	61.3	427	2	0	6.89	92.6	15	159	10.6	0	0	0	0
1991—San Francisco NFL	11	10	279	180	64.5	2517	17	8	*9.02	*101.8	66	415	6.3	4	4	0	24
1992—San Francisco NFL	16	16	402	268	*66.7	‡3465	*25	7	*8.62	*107.0	76	537	7.1	4	4	0	24
1993—San Francisco NFL	16	16	462	314	68.0	‡4023	*29	16	*8.71	*101.5	69	407	5.9	2	2	0	12
1994—San Francisco NFL	16	16	461	324	*70.3	3969	*35	10	*8.61	*112.8	58	293	5.1	7	7	0	42
1995—San Francisco NFL	11	11	447	299	*66.9	3200	20	11	7.16	92.3	50	250	5.0	3	3	0	18
1996—San Francisco NFL	12	12	316	214	*67.7	2410	14	6	‡7.63	*97.2	52	310	6.0	4	4	1	26
1997—San Francisco NFL	15	15	356	241	*67.7	3029	19	6	*8.51	*104.7	50	199	4.0	3	3	0	18
1998—San Francisco NFL	15	15	517	322	62.3	4170	*36	12	8.07	101.1	70	454	6.5	6	6	0	36
1999—San Francisco NFL	3	3	84	45	53.6	446	3	4	5.31	60.9	11	57	5.2	0	0	0	0
USFL totals (2 years)	25	...	560	316	56.4	4102	16	22	7.33	72.8	135	883	6.5	9	9	3	60
NFL totals (15 years)	169	143	4149	2667	64.3	33124	232	107	7.98	96.8	722	4239	5.9	43	43	1	260
Pro totals (17 years)	194	...	4709	2983	63.3	37226	248	129	7.91	94.0	857	5122	6.0	52	52	4	320

Y

ZAHURSKY, STEVE   G   BROWNS

PERSONAL: Born September 2, 1976, in Euclid, Ohio. ... 6-6/305. ... Name pronounced za-HER-ski.
HIGH SCHOOL: Euclid (Ohio).
COLLEGE: Kent.
TRANSACTIONS/CAREER NOTES: Signed as non-drafted free agent by Jacksonville Jaguars (April 23, 1998). ... Released by Jaguars (August 30, 1998). ... Signed by Philadelphia Eagles to practice squad (December 7, 1998). ... Granted free agency following 1998 season. ... Signed by Cleveland Browns (February 11, 1999).
PLAYING EXPERIENCE: Cleveland NFL, 1999. ... Games/Games started: 1999 (9/7).

ZEIER, ERIC   QB   BUCCANEERS

PERSONAL: Born September 6, 1972, in Pensacola, Fla. ... 6-1/214. ... Full name: Eric Royce Zeier. ... Name pronounced ZIRE.
HIGH SCHOOL: Heidelberg (West Germany), then Marietta (Ga.).
COLLEGE: Georgia.
TRANSACTIONS/CAREER NOTES: Selected by Cleveland Browns in third round (84th pick overall) of 1995 NFL draft. ... Signed by Browns (July 14, 1995). ... Browns franchise moved to Baltimore and renamed Ravens for 1996 season (March 11, 1996). ... Granted free agency (February 13, 1998). ... Tendered offer sheet by Atlanta Falcons (March 5, 1998). ... Offer matched by Ravens (March 10, 1998). ... Traded by Ravens to Tampa Bay Buccaneers for sixth-round pick (traded to Minnesota) in 1999 draft (April 17, 1999). ... Granted unconditional free agency (February 11, 2000). ... Re-signed by Buccaneers (March 2, 2000).
CHAMPIONSHIP GAME EXPERIENCE: Member of Buccaneers for NFC championship game (1999 season); did not play.
HONORS: Named quarterback on THE SPORTING NEWS college All-America second team (1994).
PRO STATISTICS: 1995—Fumbled three times. 1996—Fumbled twice and recovered one fumble. 1997—Fumbled three times for minus 14 yards. 1998—Fumbled twice and recovered one fumble. 1999—Fumbled once.
SINGLE GAME HIGHS (regular season): Attempts—54 (November 5, 1995, vs. Houston); completions—29 (October 31, 1999, vs. Detroit); yards—349 (December 21, 1997, vs. Cincinnati); and touchdown passes—3 (December 14, 1997, vs. Tennessee).
STATISTICAL PLATEAUS: 300-yard passing games: 1995 (1), 1997 (2). Total: 3.
MISCELLANEOUS: Regular-season record as starting NFL quarterback: 5-7 (.417).

					PASSING						RUSHING				TOTALS	
Year Team	G	GS	Att.	Cmp.	Pct.	Yds.	TD	Int.	Avg.	Rat.	Att.	Yds.	Avg.	TD	TD	2pt.	Pts.
1995—Cleveland NFL	7	4	161	82	50.9	864	4	9	5.37	51.9	15	80	5.3	0	0	1	2
1996—Baltimore NFL	1	0	21	10	47.6	97	1	1	4.62	57.0	2	8	4.0	0	0	0	0
1997—Baltimore NFL	5	3	116	67	57.8	958	7	1	8.26	101.1	10	17	1.7	0	0	0	0
1998—Baltimore NFL	10	4	181	107	59.1	1312	4	3	7.25	82.0	11	17	1.5	0	0	0	0
1999—Tampa Bay NFL	2	1	55	32	58.2	270	0	1	4.91	63.4	3	7	2.3	0	0	0	0
Pro totals (5 years)	25	12	534	298	55.8	3501	16	15	6.56	74.2	41	129	3.1	0	0	1	2

ZEIGLER, DUSTY   C   GIANTS

PERSONAL: Born September 27, 1973, in Savannah, Ga. ... 6-5/303. ... Full name: Curtis Dustin Zeigler. ... Name pronounced ZIG-ler.
HIGH SCHOOL: Effingham County (Springfield, Ga.).
COLLEGE: Notre Dame.
TRANSACTIONS/CAREER NOTES: Selected by Buffalo Bills in sixth round (202nd pick overall) of 1996 NFL draft. ... Signed by Bills (June 25, 1996). ... Granted free agency (February 12, 1999). ... Re-signed by Bills (April 15, 1999). ... Granted unconditional free agency (February 11, 2000). ... Signed by New York Giants (March 4, 2000).
PLAYING EXPERIENCE: Buffalo NFL, 1996-1999. ... Games/Games started: 1996 (2/0), 1997 (13/13), 1998 (16/16), 1999 (15/15). Total: 46/44.
PRO STATISTICS: 1997—Fumbled once and recovered one fumble for minus 12 yards. 1998—Fumbled three times for minus 19 yards.

ZELENKA, JOE   TE   REDSKINS

PERSONAL: Born March 9, 1976, in Cleveland. ... 6-3/280. ... Full name: Joseph John Zelenka.
HIGH SCHOOL: Benedictine (Cleveland).
COLLEGE: Wake Forest.
TRANSACTIONS/CAREER NOTES: Signed as non-drafted free agent by San Francisco 49ers (April 23, 1999). ... Traded by 49ers to Washington Redskins for conditional pick in 2001 draft (April 17, 2000).
PLAYING EXPERIENCE: San Francisco NFL, 1999. ... Games/Games started: 1999 (13/0).
PRO STATISTICS: 1999—Fumbled once and recovered one fumble for minus 15 yards.

ZELLNER, PEPPI   DE   COWBOYS

PERSONAL: Born March 14, 1975, in Forsythe, Ga. ... 6-5/257. ... Full name: Hundens Zellner.
HIGH SCHOOL: Mary Persons (Forsythe, Ga.).
JUNIOR COLLEGE: Georgia Military College.
COLLEGE: Fort Valley (Ga.) State.
TRANSACTIONS/CAREER NOTES: Selected by Dallas Cowboys in fourth round (132nd pick overall) of 1999 NFL draft. ... Signed by Cowboys (July 27, 1999).
PLAYING EXPERIENCE: Dallas NFL, 1999. ... Games/Games started: 1999 (13/0).
PRO STATISTICS: 1999—Credited with one sack.

ZEREOUE, AMOS   RB   STEELERS

PERSONAL: Born October 8, 1976, in Ivory Coast. ... 5-8/202. ... Name pronounced zer-O-way.
HIGH SCHOOL: W.C. Mepham (Hempstead, N.Y.).
COLLEGE: West Virginia.
TRANSACTIONS/CAREER NOTES: Selected after junior season by Pittsburgh Steelers in third round (95th pick overall) of 1999 NFL draft. ... Signed by Steelers (July 30, 1999).
HONORS: Named running back on THE SPORTING NEWS college All-America third team (1997).
SINGLE GAME HIGHS (regular season): Attempts—17 (September 12, 1999, vs. Cleveland); yards—44 (September 12, 1999, vs. Cleveland); and rushing touchdowns—0.

			RUSHING				RECEIVING				KICKOFF RETURNS				TOTALS			
Year Team	G	GS	Att.	Yds.	Avg.	TD	No.	Yds.	Avg.	TD	No.	Yds.	Avg.	TD	TD	2pt.	Pts. Fum.
1999—Pittsburgh NFL	8	0	18	48	2.7	0	2	17	8.5	0	7	169	24.1	0	0	0	0 0

ZGONINA, JEFF   DT   RAMS

PERSONAL: Born May 24, 1970, in Chicago. ... 6-2/300. ... Full name: Jeffrey Marc Zgonina. ... Name pronounced ska-KNEE-na.
HIGH SCHOOL: Mount Carmel (Chicago).
COLLEGE: Purdue (degree in community health promotion, 1992).
TRANSACTIONS/CAREER NOTES: Selected by Pittsburgh Steelers in seventh round (185th pick overall) of 1993 NFL draft. ... Signed by Steelers (July 16, 1993). ... Claimed on waivers by Carolina Panthers (August 28, 1995). ... Granted free agency (February 16, 1996). ... Re-signed by Panthers (April 11, 1996). ... Released by Panthers (August 19, 1996). ... Signed by Atlanta Falcons (October 8, 1996). ... Granted unconditional free agency (February 14, 1997). ... Signed by St. Louis Rams (March 17, 1997). ... Released by Rams (April 5, 1999). ... Signed by Oakland Raiders (October 13, 1998). ... Released by Raiders (October 18, 1998). ... Signed by Indianapolis Colts (November 25, 1998). ... Granted unconditional free agency (February 12, 1999). ... Signed by Rams (April 5, 1999).
PLAYING EXPERIENCE: Pittsburgh NFL, 1993 and 1994; Carolina NFL, 1995; Atlanta NFL, 1996; St. Louis NFL, 1997 and 1999; Indianapolis NFL, 1998. ... Games/Games started: 1993 (5/0), 1994 (16/0), 1995 (2/0), 1996 (8/0), 1997 (15/0), 1998 (2/0), 1999 (16/0). Total: 64/0.
CHAMPIONSHIP GAME EXPERIENCE: Played in AFC championship game (1994 season). ... Played in NFC championship game (1999 season). ... Member of Super Bowl championship team (1999 season).
PRO STATISTICS: 1993—Recovered one fumble. 1994—Returned two kickoffs for eight yards, fumbled once and recovered one fumble. 1996—Credited with one sack and recovered one fumble. 1997—Returned one kickoff for five yards and credited with two sacks. 1999—Credited with 4$\frac{1}{2}$ sacks.

ZOLAK, SCOTT   QB

PERSONAL: Born December 13, 1967, in Pittsburgh. ... 6-5/235. ... Full name: Scott David Zolak.
HIGH SCHOOL: Ringgold (Monongahela, Pa.).
COLLEGE: Maryland (degree in business administration).
TRANSACTIONS/CAREER NOTES: Selected by New England Patriots in fourth round (84th pick overall) of 1991 NFL draft. ... Inactive for all 16 games (1991). ... On injured reserve with ankle injury (December 18, 1992-remainder of season). ... Granted free agency (February 17, 1994). ... Re-signed by Patriots (April 2, 1994). ... Granted unconditional free agency (February 12, 1999). ... Signed by New York Jets (April 27, 1999). ... Released by Jets (August 22, 1999). ... Signed by Miami Dolphins (October 27, 1999). ... Released by Dolphins (May 22, 2000).
CHAMPIONSHIP GAME EXPERIENCE: Member of Patriots for AFC championship game (1996 season); inactive. ... Member of Patriots for Super Bowl XXXI (1996 season); inactive.
PRO STATISTICS: 1992—Fumbled five times and recovered three fumbles for minus 21 yards. 1995—Fumbled four times and recovered one fumble for minus two yards. 1998—Fumbled once.
SINGLE GAME HIGHS (regular season): Attempts—45 (October 1, 1995, vs. Atlanta); completions—24 (October 1, 1995, vs. Atlanta); yards—261 (November 15, 1992, vs. Indianapolis); and touchdown passes—2 (December 20, 1998, vs. San Francisco).
MISCELLANEOUS: Regular-season record as starting NFL quarterback: 3-4 (.429). ... Postseason record as starting NFL quarterback: 0-1.

			PASSING								RUSHING				TOTALS		
Year Team	G	GS	Att.	Cmp.	Pct.	Yds.	TD	Int.	Avg.	Rat.	Att.	Yds.	Avg.	TD	TD	2pt.	Pts.
1991—New England NFL								Did not play.									
1992—New England NFL	6	4	100	52	52.0	561	2	4	5.61	58.8	18	71	3.9	0	0	0	0
1993—New England NFL	3	0	2	0	0.0	0	0	0	0.0	39.6	1	0	0.0	0	0	0	0
1994—New England NFL	16	0	8	5	62.5	28	0	0	3.50	68.8	1	-1	-1.0	0	0	0	0
1995—New England NFL	16	1	49	28	57.1	282	1	0	5.76	80.5	4	19	4.8	0	0	0	0
1996—New England NFL	3	0	1	1	100.0	5	0	0	5.00	87.5	4	-3	-0.8	0	0	0	0
1997—New England NFL	4	0	9	6	66.7	67	2	0	7.44	128.2	3	-3	-1.0	0	0	0	0
1998—New England NFL	6	2	75	32	42.7	371	3	3	4.95	54.9	5	0	0.0	0	0	0	0
1999—Miami NFL	1	0	4	0	0.0	0	0	0	0.0	39.6	2	-2	-1.0	0	0	0	0
Pro totals (8 years)	55	7	248	124	50.0	1314	8	7	5.30	64.8	38	81	2.1	0	0	0	0

2000 DRAFT PICKS

ABRAHAM, JOHN — LB — JETS

PERSONAL: Born May 6, 1978, in Timmonsville, S.C. ... 6-4/250.
HIGH SCHOOL: Lamar (Timmonsville, S.C.).
COLLEGE: South Carolina.
TRANSACTIONS/CAREER NOTES: Selected by New York Jets in first round (13th pick overall) of 2000 NFL draft.
COLLEGE NOTES: Recovered one fumble for 24 yards (1999).

Year Team	G	SACKS
1996—South Carolina	11	4.0
1997—South Carolina	11	6.5
1998—South Carolina	10	7.0
1999—South Carolina	10	6.0
College totals (4 years)	42	23.5

ALEXANDER, SHAUN — RB — SEAHAWKS

PERSONAL: Born August 30, 1977, in Florence, Ky. ... 5-11/218.
HIGH SCHOOL: Boone County (Ky.).
COLLEGE: Alabama (degree in marketing, 1999).
TRANSACTIONS/CAREER NOTES: Selected by Seattle Seahawks in first round (19th pick overall) of 2000 NFL draft.
HONORS: Named running back on The Sporting News college All-America second team (1999).
COLLEGE NOTES: Attempted one pass without a completion (1996); returned two kickoffs for 90 yards and one touchdown (1999).

		RUSHING				RECEIVING				TOTALS	
Year Team	G	Att.	Yds.	Avg.	TD	No.	Yds.	Avg.	TD	TD	Pts.
1996—Alabama	11	77	589	7.6	6	7	53	7.6	0	6	36
1997—Alabama	9	90	415	4.6	3	4	37	9.3	0	3	18
1998—Alabama	11	258	1178	4.6	13	26	385	14.8	4	17	102
1999—Alabama	11	302	1383	4.6	19	24	322	13.4	4	24	144
College totals (4 years)	42	727	3565	4.9	41	61	797	13.1	8	50	300

ALFORD, DARNELL — OT — CHIEFS

PERSONAL: Born June 11, 1977, in Fredricksburg, Va. ... 6-4/334. ... Full name: Darnell LaShawn Alford.
HIGH SCHOOL: Chancellor (Fredricksburg, Va.).
COLLEGE: Boston College.
TRANSACTIONS/CAREER NOTES: Selected by Kansas City Chiefs in sixth round (188th pick overall) of 2000 NFL draft.
COLLEGE PLAYING EXPERIENCE: Boston College, 1995-1999. ... Games: 1995 (redshirted), 1996 (12), 1997 (did not play), 1998 (9), 1999 (12). Total: 33.

ANDERSON, MIKE — RB — BRONCOS

PERSONAL: Born September 21, 1973, in Winnsboro, S.C. ... 6-0/235.
HIGH SCHOOL: Winnsboro (S.C.).
JUNIOR COLLEGE: Mount San Jacinto Community College (Calif.).
COLLEGE: Utah.
TRANSACTIONS/CAREER NOTES: Selected by Denver Broncos in sixth round (189th pick overall) of 2000 NFL draft.

		RUSHING				TOTALS	
	G	Att.	Yds.	Avg.	TD	TD	Pts.
1996—Mt. San Jacinto CC	...	...	1511	...	...	...	...
1997—Mt. San Jacinto CC	...	...	1686	...	...	...	...
1998—Utah	11	244	1173	4.8	12	13	78
1999—Utah	9	95	977	10.3	10	11	66
Junior college totals (2 years)	...	...	3197	...	...	...	...
College totals (2 years)	20	339	2150	6.3	22	24	144

ANDERSON, RASHARD — DB — PANTHERS

PERSONAL: Born June 14, 1977, in Forest, Miss. ... 6-2/204.
HIGH SCHOOL: Forest (Miss.).
COLLEGE: Jackson State.
TRANSACTIONS/CAREER NOTES: Selected by Carolina Panthers in first round (23rd pick overall) of 2000 NFL draft.

		INTERCEPTIONS			
Year Team	G	No.	Yds.	Avg.	TD
1996—Jackson State		Did not play.			
1997—Jackson State	8	0	0	0.0	0
1998—Jackson State	11	4	44	11.0	0
1999—Jackson State	12	3	0	0.0	0
College totals (3 years)	31	7	44	6.3	0

ARRINGTON, LaVAR — LB — REDSKINS

PERSONAL: Born June 20, 1978, in Pittsburgh. ... 6-3/250. ... Full name: LaVar RaShad Arrington.
HIGH SCHOOL: North Hills (Pittsburgh).
COLLEGE: Penn State.
TRANSACTIONS/CAREER NOTES: Selected after junior season by Washington Redskins in first round (second pick overall) of 2000 NFL draft.
HONORS: Named linebacker on THE SPORTING NEWS college All-America first team (1998 and 1999). ... Butkus Award winner (1999). ... Chuck Bednarik Award winner (1999).
COLLEGE NOTES: Recovered one fumble for two yards and a touchdown (1999).

			INTERCEPTIONS			SACKS
Year Team	G	No.	Yds.	Avg.	TD	No.
1997—Penn State	11	0	0	0.0	0	2.0
1998—Penn State	11	2	16	8.0	0	7.0
1999—Penn State	11	1	27	27.0	0	9.0
College totals (3 years)	33	3	43	14.3	1	18.0

AUSTIN, REGGIE — CB — BEARS

PERSONAL: Born January 21, 1977, in Atlanta. ... 5-9/172.
HIGH SCHOOL: Harper (Atlanta).
COLLEGE: Wake Forest.
TRANSACTIONS/CAREER NOTES: Selected by Chicago Bears in fourth round (125th pick overall) of 2000 NFL draft.
COLLEGE NOTES: Credited with one sack (1997); returned one kickoff for 22 yards (1998).

			INTERCEPTIONS				PUNT RETURNS			TOTALS	
Year Team	G	No.	Yds.	Avg.	TD	No.	Yds.	Avg.	TD	TD	Pts.
1996—Wake Forest	8	1	0	0.0	0	1	7	7.0	0	0	0
1997—Wake Forest	11	2	16	8.0	0	18	93	5.2	0	0	0
1998—Wake Forest	11	4	45	11.3	0	21	158	7.5	0	0	0
1999—Wake Forest	11	2	1	0.5	0	31	329	10.6	0	0	0
College totals (4 years)	41	9	62	6.9	0	71	587	8.3	0	0	0

BANIEWICZ, MARK — OT — JAGUARS

PERSONAL: Born March 24, 1977, in Fairport, N.Y. ... 6-6/303. ... Full name: Mark J. Baniewicz. ... Name pronounced BAN-uh-wits.
HIGH SCHOOL: Penfield (Fairport, N.Y.).
COLLEGE: Syracuse (degree in finance, 1999).
TRANSACTIONS/CAREER NOTES: Selected by Jacksonville Jaguars in seventh round (247th pick overall) of 2000 NFL draft. ... Signed by Jaguars (May 24, 2000).
COLLEGE PLAYING EXPERIENCE: Syracuse, 1995-1999. ... Games: 1995 (redshirted), 1996 (6), 1997 (12), 1998 (11), 1999 (11). Total: 40.

BARNES, RASHIDI — DB — BROWNS

PERSONAL: Born June 26, 1978, in Berkeley, Calif. ... 5-11/205.
HIGH SCHOOL: Berkeley (Calif.).
COLLEGE: Colorado.
TRANSACTIONS/CAREER NOTES: Selected by Cleveland Browns in seventh round (225th pick overall) of 2000 NFL draft.

			INTERCEPTIONS			SACKS
Year Team	G	No.	Yds.	Avg.	TD	No.
1996—Colorado	9	0	0	0.0	0	0.5
1997—Colorado	11	1	26	26.0	0	2.0
1998—Colorado	6	1	3	3.0	0	0.0
1999—Colorado	11	1	0	0.0	0	3.0
College totals (4 years)	37	3	29	9.7	0	5.5

BARRETT, DAVID — CB — CARDINALS

PERSONAL: Born December 22, 1977, in Osceola, Ark. ... 5-10/195.
HIGH SCHOOL: Osceola (Ark.).
COLLEGE: Arkansas.
TRANSACTIONS/CAREER NOTES: Selected by Arizona Cardinals in fourth round (102nd pick overall) of 2000 NFL draft.

			INTERCEPTIONS			SACKS
Year Team	G	No.	Yds.	Avg.	TD	No.
1996—Arkansas	10	0	0	0.0	0	0.0
1997—Arkansas	11	1	-2	-2.0	0	3.0
1998—Arkansas	11	3	76	25.3	0	1.0
1999—Arkansas	11	3	45	15.0	1	1.0
College totals (4 years)	43	7	119	17.0	1	5.0

BARTEE, WILLIAM — CB — CHIEFS

PERSONAL: Born June 25, 1977, in Daytona Beach, Fla. ... 6-1/190.
HIGH SCHOOL: Atlantic (Daytona Beach, Fla.).

JUNIOR COLLEGE: Butler County Community College (Kan.).
COLLEGE: Oklahoma.
TRANSACTIONS/CAREER NOTES: Selected by Kansas City Chiefs in second round (54th pick overall) of 2000 NFL draft.
COLLEGE NOTES: Credited with one sack (1998).

		INTERCEPTIONS			
Year Team	G	No.	Yds.	Avg.	TD
1996—Butler County CC	11	0	0	0.0	0
1997—Butler County CC	11	4	...	...	1
1998—Oklahoma	6	1	-3	-3.0	0
1999—Oklahoma	11	1	0	0.0	0
Junior college totals (2 years)	22	4	...	...	1
College totals (2 years)	17	2	-3	-1.5	0

BEAN, ROBERT — CB — BENGALS

PERSONAL: Born January 6, 1978, in Atlanta. ... 5-10/178. ... Full name: Robert D. Bean Jr.
HIGH SCHOOL: Lakeside (Atlanta).
JUNIOR COLLEGE: Georgia Military College.
COLLEGE: Mississippi State.
TRANSACTIONS/CAREER NOTES: Selected by Cincinnati Bengals in fifth round (133rd pick overall) of 2000 NFL draft.
COLLEGE NOTES: Returned one punt for 33 yards and a touchdown (1998).

		INTERCEPTIONS			
Year Team	G	No.	Yds.	Avg.	TD
1996—Georgia Military College		Statistics unavailable.			
1997—Georgia Military College		Statistics unavailable.			
1998—Mississippi State	12	5	136	27.2	1
1999—Mississippi State	11	1	33	33.0	0
College totals (2 years)	23	6	169	28.2	1

BECHT, ANTHONY — TE — JETS

PERSONAL: Born August 8, 1977, in Drexel Hill, Pa. ... 6-5/267.
HIGH SCHOOL: Monsignor Bonner (Drexel Hill, Pa.).
COLLEGE: West Virginia (degree in business, 1999).
TRANSACTIONS/CAREER NOTES: Selected by New York Jets in first round (27th pick overall) of 2000 NFL draft. ... Signed by Jets (May 26, 2000).

		RECEIVING			
Year Team	G	No.	Yds.	Avg.	TD
1996—West Virginia	11	10	140	14.0	1
1997—West Virginia	12	9	135	15.0	1
1998—West Virginia	12	29	393	13.6	4
1999—West Virginia	11	35	510	14.6	5
College totals (4 years)	46	83	1178	14.2	11

BECKETT, ROGERS — S — CHARGERS

PERSONAL: Born January 31, 1977, in Apopka, Fla. ... 6-3/205.
HIGH SCHOOL: Apopka (Fla.).
COLLEGE: Marshall (degree in political science).
TRANSACTIONS/CAREER NOTES: Selected by San Diego Chargers in second round (43rd pick overall) of 2000 NFL draft.
COLLEGE NOTES: Returned one punt for six yards and returned one kickoff for 12 yards (1996).

		INTERCEPTIONS			
Year Team	G	No.	Yds.	Avg.	TD
1995—Marshall		Redshirted.			
1996—Marshall	...	1	0	0.0	0
1997—Marshall	...	3	0	0.0	0
1998—Marshall	12	3	2	0.7	0
1999—Marshall	10	4	20	5.0	1
College totals (4 years)	...	11	22	2.0	1

BEDELL, BRAD — OL — BROWNS

PERSONAL: Born February 12, 1977, in Arcadia, Calif. ... 6-4/299.
HIGH SCHOOL: Arcadia (Calif.).
JUNIOR COLLEGE: Mount San Antonio College (Calif.).
COLLEGE: Colorado.
TRANSACTIONS/CAREER NOTES: Selected by Cleveland Browns in sixth round (206th pick overall) of 2000 NFL draft.
COLLEGE PLAYING EXPERIENCE: Mount San Antonio College, 1995 and 1996; Colorado, 1997-1999. ... Games: 1995 (games played unavailable), 1996 (games played unavailable), 1997 (2), 1998 (11), 1999 (11). Total NCAA: 24.

BELL, MARCUS — LB — SEAHAWKS

PERSONAL: Born July 19, 1977, in St. John's, Ariz. ... 6-1/237. ... Full name: Marcus Udall Bell.
HIGH SCHOOL: St. John's (Ariz.).

2000 DRAFT PICKS

COLLEGE: Arizona.
TRANSACTIONS/CAREER NOTES: Selected by Seattle Seahawks in fourth round (116th pick overall) of 2000 NFL draft.
COLLEGE NOTES: Intercepted one pass (1999).

Year—Team	G	SACKS
1995—Arizona		Redshirted.
1996—Arizona	11	0.0
1997—Arizona	11	4.0
1998—Arizona	12	3.0
1999—Arizona	12	4.0
College totals (4 years)	46	11.0

BERRY, GARY — S — PACKERS

PERSONAL: Born October 24, 1977, in Worthington, Ohio. ... 5-11/199.
HIGH SCHOOL: DeSales (Worthington, Ohio).
COLLEGE: Ohio State.
TRANSACTIONS/CAREER NOTES: Selected by Green Bay Packers in fourth round (126th pick overall) of 2000 NFL draft.
COLLEGE NOTES: Returned three punts for 17 yards and one touchdown and returned three kickoffs for 59 yards (1997); returned 15 punts for 65 yards (1998).

		INTERCEPTIONS				SACKS
Year—Team	G	No.	Yds.	Avg.	TD	No.
1996—Ohio State	12	1	19	19.0	0	0.0
1997—Ohio State	13	5	136	27.2	1	1.0
1998—Ohio State	12	0	0	0.0	0	1.0
1999—Ohio State	10	1	12	12.0	0	1.0
College totals (4 years)	47	7	167	23.9	1	3.0

BLACK, AVION — WR — BILLS

PERSONAL: Born April 24, 1977, in Nashville. ... 5-11/181. ... Full name: Avion Carlos Black.
HIGH SCHOOL: Maplewood (Nashville).
COLLEGE: Tennessee State.
TRANSACTIONS/CAREER NOTES: Selected by Buffalo Bills in fourth round (121st pick overall) of 2000 NFL draft.
COLLEGE NOTES: Returned eight punts for 105 yards and rushed once for minus seven yards (1999).

		RECEIVING				KICKOFF RETURNS				TOTALS	
Year—Team	G	No.	Yds.	Avg.	TD	No.	Yds.	Avg.	TD	TD	Pts.
1996—Tennessee State						Redshirted.					
1997—Tennessee State	9	7	77	11.0	0	3	72	24.0	0	0	0
1998—Tennessee State	11	28	487	17.4	3	16	462	28.9	1	4	24
1999—Tennessee State	11	47	893	19.0	8	23	786	34.2	3	11	66
College totals (3 years)	31	82	1457	17.8	11	42	1320	31.4	4	15	90

BLACK, CLIFFTON — S — RAIDERS

PERSONAL: Born April 11, 1977, in Lubbock, Texas. ... 6-0/195.
HIGH SCHOOL: Monterrey (Lubbock, Texas).
COLLEGE: Southwest Texas State.
TRANSACTIONS/CAREER NOTES: Selected by Oakland Raiders in seventh round (231st pick overall) of 2000 NFL draft.

		INTERCEPTIONS				SACKS
Year—Team	G	No.	Yds.	Avg.	TD	No.
1995—Southwest Texas State	11	0	0	0.0	0	0.0
1996—Southwest Texas State	11	0	0	0.0	0	2.0
1997—Southwest Texas State	2	0	0	0.0	0	0.0
1998—Southwest Texas State	11	2	0	0.0	0	1.0
1999—Southwest Texas State	11	2	0	0.0	0	1.5
College totals (5 years)	46	4	0	0.0	0	4.5

BOIREAU, MICHAEL — DE — VIKINGS

PERSONAL: Born July 24, 1978, in Miami. ... 6-4/274. ... Full name: Michael Innocent Boireau.
HIGH SCHOOL: North Miami Beach.
JUNIOR COLLEGE: Northeast Mississippi Community College.
COLLEGE: Miami (Fla.).
TRANSACTIONS/CAREER NOTES: Selected by Minnesota Vikings in second round (56th pick overall) of 2000 NFL draft.
COLLEGE NOTES: Recovered one fumble (1999).

Year—Team	G	SACKS
1996—Northeast Mississippi JC	...	0.0
1997—Northeast Mississippi JC	...	8.5
1998—Miami (Fla.)	9	1.0
1999—Miami (Fla.)	13	3.5
Junior college totals (2 years)	...	8.5
College totals (2 years)	22	4.5

BOONE, ALFONSO — DT — LIONS

PERSONAL: Born January 11, 1976, in Saginaw, Mich. ... 6-3/305.
HIGH SCHOOL: Arthur Hill (Saginaw, Mich.).
JUNIOR COLLEGE: Mount San Antonio College (Calif.).
COLLEGE: None.
TRANSACTIONS/CAREER NOTES: Selected after sophomore season by Detroit Lions in seventh round (253rd pick overall) of 2000 NFL draft.

Year Team	G	SACKS
1998—Mt. San Antonio College	Statistics unavailable.	
1999—Mt. San Antonio College	10	8.5

BOWEN, MATT — S — RAMS

PERSONAL: Born November 12, 1976, in Glen Ellyn, Ill. ... 6-1/202.
HIGH SCHOOL: Glenbard West (Glen Ellyn, Ill.).
COLLEGE: Iowa.
TRANSACTIONS/CAREER NOTES: Selected by St. Louis Rams in sixth round (198th pick overall) of 2000 NFL draft.

		INTERCEPTIONS			
Year Team	G	No.	Yds.	Avg.	TD
1995—Iowa		Redshirted.			
1996—Iowa	11	0	0	0.0	0
1997—Iowa	12	2	126	63.0	1
1998—Iowa	11	2	0	0.0	0
1999—Iowa	11	1	0	0.0	0
College totals (4 years)	45	5	126	25.2	1

BRADY, TOM — QB — PATRIOTS

PERSONAL: Born August 3, 1977, in San Mateo, Calif. ... 6-4/211.
HIGH SCHOOL: Serra (San Mateo, Calif.).
COLLEGE: Michigan.
TRANSACTIONS/CAREER NOTES: Selected by New England Patriots in sixth round (199th pick overall) of 2000 NFL draft.

		PASSING								RUSHING				TOTALS	
Year Team	G	Att.	Cmp.	Pct.	Yds.	TD	Int.	Avg.	Rat.	Att.	Yds.	Avg.	TD	TD	Pts.
1995—Michigan						Redshirted.									
1996—Michigan	2	4	2	50.0	26	0	1	6.50	54.6	0	0	0.0	0	0	0
1997—Michigan	4	15	12	80.0	103	0	0	6.87	137.7	2	-14	-7.0	0	0	0
1998—Michigan	13	350	214	61.1	2636	15	12	7.53	131.7	59	-108	-1.8	2	2	12
1999—Michigan	12	341	214	62.8	2586	20	6	7.58	142.3	37	-47	-1.3	1	1	6
College totals (4 years)	31	710	442	62.3	5351	35	19	7.54	136.5	98	-169	-1.7	3	3	18

BROOKS, RODREGIS — CB — COLTS

PERSONAL: Born August 30, 1978, in Alexander City, Ala. ... 5-10/181. ... Full name: Rodregis A. Brooks.
HIGH SCHOOL: Dadeville (Ala.).
COLLEGE: Alabama-Birmingham.
TRANSACTIONS/CAREER NOTES: Selected after junior season by Indianapolis Colts in seventh round (238th pick overall) of 2000 NFL draft.
MISCELLANEOUS: Granted medical redshirt (1998).

		INTERCEPTIONS			
Year Team	G	No.	Yds.	Avg.	TD
1996—Alabama-Birmingham	11	2	0	0.0	0
1997—Alabama-Birmingham	11	3	0	0.0	0
1998—Alabama-Birmingham	2	0	0	0.0	0
1999—Alabama-Birmingham	11	9	152	16.9	1
College totals (4 years)	35	14	152	10.9	1

BROWN, COURTNEY — DE — BROWNS

PERSONAL: Born February 14, 1978, in Charleston, S.C. ... 6-4/266. ... Full name: Courtney Lanair Brown.
HIGH SCHOOL: Macedonia (Alvin, S.C.).
COLLEGE: Penn State.
TRANSACTIONS/CAREER NOTES: Selected by Cleveland Browns in first round (first pick overall) of 2000 NFL draft. ... Signed by Browns (May 10, 2000).
HONORS: Named defensive end on THE SPORTING NEWS college All-America first team (1999).
COLLEGE NOTES: Intercepted one pass for 25 yards (1999).

Year Team	G	SACKS
1996—Penn State	11	2.0
1997—Penn State	11	6.0
1998—Penn State	11	11.5
1999—Penn State	11	13.5
College totals (4 years)	44	33.0

BROWN, MIKE S BEARS

PERSONAL: Born February 13, 1978, in Scottsdale, Ariz. ... 5-10/202.
HIGH SCHOOL: Saguaro (Scottsdale, Ariz.).
COLLEGE: Nebraska.
TRANSACTIONS/CAREER NOTES: Selected by Chicago Bears in second round (39th pick overall) of 2000 NFL draft.
COLLEGE NOTES: Credited with two sacks (1999).

Year Team	G	INTERCEPTIONS No.	Yds.	Avg.	TD
1996—Nebraska	11	1	44	44.0	0
1997—Nebraska	12	2	26	13.0	0
1998—Nebraska	12	1	1	1.0	0
1999—Nebraska	12	5	40	8.0	0
College totals (4 years)	47	9	111	12.3	0

BROWN, RALPH CB GIANTS

PERSONAL: Born September 9, 1978, in Hacienda Heights, Calif. ... 5-10/178. ... Full name: Ralph Brown II.
HIGH SCHOOL: Bishop Amat (La Puente, Calif.).
COLLEGE: Nebraska.
TRANSACTIONS/CAREER NOTES: Selected by New York Giants in fifth round (140th pick overall) of 2000 NFL draft.
HONORS: Named cornerback on THE SPORTING NEWS college All-America first team (1999).
COLLEGE NOTES: Recovered one fumble for 74 yards and a touchdown (1998); recovered one fumble for 26 yards (1999).

Year Team	G	INTERCEPTIONS No.	Yds.	Avg.	TD
1996—Nebraska	12	4	83	20.8	1
1997—Nebraska	12	2	28	14.0	0
1998—Nebraska	12	2	60	30.0	0
1999—Nebraska	12	3	82	27.3	0
College totals (4 years)	48	11	253	23.0	1

BULGER, MARC QB SAINTS

PERSONAL: Born April 5, 1977, in Pittsburgh. ... 6-2/206.
HIGH SCHOOL: Central Catholic (Pittsburgh).
COLLEGE: West Virginia.
TRANSACTIONS/CAREER NOTES: Selected by New Orleans Saints in sixth round (168th pick overall) of 2000 NFL draft.

Year Team	G	PASSING Att.	Cmp.	Pct.	Yds.	TD	Int.	Avg.	Rat.	RUSHING Att.	Yds.	Avg.	TD	TOTALS TD	Pts.
1995—West Virginia						Redshirted.									
1996—West Virginia	6	42	19	45.2	352	3	1	8.38	134.4	3	-17	-5.7	0	0	0
1997—West Virginia	12	323	192	59.4	2465	14	10	7.63	131.7	53	-93	-1.8	2	2	12
1998—West Virginia	12	419	274	65.4	3607	31	10	8.61	157.3	33	-92	-2.8	0	0	0
1999—West Virginia	8	239	145	60.7	1729	11	13	7.23	125.7	19	-124	-6.5	0	0	0
College totals (4 years)	38	1023	630	61.6	8153	59	34	7.97	140.9	108	-326	-3.0	2	2	12

BULLUCK, KEITH LB TITANS

PERSONAL: Born April 4, 1977, in Suffern, N.Y. ... 6-3/232. ... Full name: Keith J. Bulluck.
HIGH SCHOOL: Clarkstown (New City, N.Y.).
COLLEGE: Syracuse.
TRANSACTIONS/CAREER NOTES: Selected by Tennessee Titans in first round (30th pick overall) of 2000 NFL draft.
COLLEGE NOTES: Intercepted three passes for no yards (1996).

Year Team	G	SACKS
1995—Syracuse		Redshirted.
1996—Syracuse	12	0.0
1997—Syracuse	12	1.0
1998—Syracuse	11	3.0
1999—Syracuse	10	2.0
College totals (4 years)	45	6.0

BURRESS, PLAXICO WR STEELERS

PERSONAL: Born August 12, 1977, in Norfolk, Va. ... 6-5/229.
HIGH SCHOOL: Green Run (Virginia Beach, Va.).
COLLEGE: Michigan State.
TRANSACTIONS/CAREER NOTES: Selected after junior season by Pittsburgh Steelers in first round (eighth pick overall) of 2000 NFL draft.

Year Team	G	RECEIVING No.	Yds.	Avg.	TD
1997—Michigan State		Did not play.			
1998—Michigan State	12	65	1013	15.6	8
1999—Michigan State	12	66	1142	17.3	12
College totals (2 years)	24	131	2155	16.5	20

CANIDATE, TRUNG — RB — RAMS

PERSONAL: Born March 3, 1977, in Phoenix. ... 5-11/192. ... Full name: Trung Jered Canidate.
HIGH SCHOOL: Central (Phoenix).
COLLEGE: Arizona.
TRANSACTIONS/CAREER NOTES: Selected by St. Louis Rams in first round (31st pick overall) of 2000 NFL draft.

Year Team	G	RUSHING				RECEIVING				TOTALS	
		Att.	Yds.	Avg.	TD	No.	Yds.	Avg.	TD	TD	Pts.
1995—Arizona						Redshirted.					
1996—Arizona	11	0	0	0.0	0	0	0	0.0	0	0	0
1997—Arizona	9	162	901	5.6	5	3	24	8.0	0	5	30
1998—Arizona	12	189	1321	7.0	10	9	191	21.2	0	10	60
1999—Arizona	12	253	1602	6.3	11	30	253	8.4	1	12	72
College totals (4 years)	44	604	3824	6.3	26	42	468	11.1	1	27	162

CARLISLE, COOPER — G/OT — BRONCOS

PERSONAL: Born August 11, 1977, in McComb, Miss. ... 6-5/300. ... Full name: Cooper Morrison Carlisle.
HIGH SCHOOL: McComb (Miss.).
COLLEGE: Florida.
TRANSACTIONS/CAREER NOTES: Selected by Denver Broncos in fourth round (112th pick overall) of 2000 NFL draft.
COLLEGE PLAYING EXPERIENCE: Florida, 1996-1999. ... Games: 1996 (11), 1997 (11), 1998 (11), 1999 (12). Total: 45.

CARMAZZI, GIOVANNI — QB — 49ERS

PERSONAL: Born April 14, 1977, in Sacramento. ... 6-3/224.
HIGH SCHOOL: Jesuit (Carmichael, Calif.).
COLLEGE: Pacific, then Hofstra.
TRANSACTIONS/CAREER NOTES: Selected by San Francisco 49ers in third round (65th pick overall) of 2000 NFL draft.
COLLEGE NOTES: Caught one pass for 23 yards and a touchdown (1997); caught one pass for minus seven yards (1999).

Year Team	G	PASSING								RUSHING				TOTALS	
		Att.	Cmp.	Pct.	Yds.	TD	Int.	Avg.	Rat.	Att.	Yds.	Avg.	TD	TD	Pts.
1995—Pacific University						Redshirted.									
1996—Hofstra	7	66	33	50.0	415	5	2	6.29	121.8	43	77	1.8	1	1	6
1997—Hofstra	11	408	288	70.6	3554	27	8	8.71	161.7	116	152	1.3	9	10	60
1998—Hofstra	11	367	227	61.9	2751	18	12	7.50	134.5	115	443	3.9	11	11	66
1999—Hofstra	11	346	216	62.4	2651	21	10	7.66	141.0	103	371	3.6	11	11	66
College totals (4 years)	40	1187	764	64.4	9371	71	32	7.89	145.0	377	1043	2.8	32	33	198

CARSON, LEONARDO — DT — CHARGERS

PERSONAL: Born February 11, 1977, in Mobile, Ala. ... 6-2/285. ... Full name: Leonardo Tremayne Carson.
HIGH SCHOOL: Shaw (Mobile, Ala.).
COLLEGE: Auburn.
TRANSACTIONS/CAREER NOTES: Selected by San Diego Chargers in fourth round (113th pick overall) of 2000 NFL draft.
COLLEGE NOTES: Intercepted one pass for 21 yards and a touchdown (1998); intercepted one pass for one yard (1999).

Year Team	G	SACKS
1996—Auburn	12	4.5
1997—Auburn	13	2.0
1998—Auburn	11	8.5
1999—Auburn	11	3.0
College totals (4 years)	47	18.0

CARTER, TYRONE — DB — VIKINGS

PERSONAL: Born March 31, 1976, in Pompano Beach, Fla. ... 5-8/190.
HIGH SCHOOL: Ely (Pompano Beach, Fla.).
COLLEGE: Minnesota.
TRANSACTIONS/CAREER NOTES: Selected by Minnesota Vikings in fourth round (118th pick overall) of 2000 NFL draft.
HONORS: Jim Thorpe Award winner (1999). ... Named strong safety on THE SPORTING NEWS college All-America first team (1999).
COLLEGE NOTES: Recovered two fumbles for 83 yards and two touchdowns (1996); recovered one fumble for five yards and a touchdown (1998); returned 30 punts for 356 yards (1999).

Year Team	G	INTERCEPTIONS				KICKOFF RETURNS				TOTALS	
		No.	Yds.	Avg.	TD	No.	Yds.	Avg.	TD	TD	Pts.
1996—Minnesota	11	1	0	0.0	0	19	357	18.8	0	2	12
1997—Minnesota	12	1	0	0.0	0	17	455	26.8	0	0	0
1998—Minnesota	11	1	8	8.0	0	13	347	26.7	1	2	12
1999—Minnesota	12	0	0	0.0	0	17	300	17.6	0	0	0
College totals (4 years)	46	3	8	2.7	0	66	1459	22.1	1	4	24

CHAMBERLIN, FRANK — LB — TITANS

PERSONAL: Born January 2, 1978, in Mahwah, N.J. ... 6-1/250. ... Full name: Frank Jacob Chamberlin.
HIGH SCHOOL: Mahwah (N.J.).

COLLEGE: Boston College.
TRANSACTIONS/CAREER NOTES: Selected by Tennessee Titans in fifth round (160th pick overall) of 2000 NFL draft.
COLLEGE NOTES: Played fullback (1997). ... Rushed seven times for 18 yards (1997); credited with two sacks (1998); intercepted one pass for 26 yards and credited with two sacks (1999).
COLLEGE PLAYING EXPERIENCE: Boston College, 1996-1999. ... Games: 1996 (11), 1997 (11), 1998 (11), 1999 (11). Total: 44.

CHANDLER, ERIC — DE — BROWNS

PERSONAL: Born June 6, 1977, in Starkville, Miss. ... 6-5/301.
HIGH SCHOOL: Starkville (Miss.).
COLLEGE: Jackson State.
TRANSACTIONS/CAREER NOTES: Selected by Cleveland Browns in seventh round (209th pick overall) of 2000 NFL draft.

Year Team	G	SACKS
1996—Jackson State	Did not play.	
1997—Jackson State	8	3.0
1998—Jackson State	9	4.0
1999—Jackson State	12	11.0
College totals (3 years)	29	18.0

CHAPMAN, DOUG — RB — VIKINGS

PERSONAL: Born August 22, 1977, in Chesterfield, Va. ... 5-10/215.
HIGH SCHOOL: Lloyd C. Bird (Chesterfield, Va.).
COLLEGE: Marshall.
TRANSACTIONS/CAREER NOTES: Selected by Minnesota Vikings in third round (88th pick overall) of 2000 NFL draft.

Year Team	G	RUSHING Att.	Yds.	Avg.	TD	RECEIVING No.	Yds.	Avg.	TD	TOTALS TD	Pts.
1995—Marshall					Redshirted.						
1996—Marshall	...	198	1238	6.3	15	15	155	10.3	1	16	96
1997—Marshall	...	176	1060	6.0	11	17	108	6.4	1	12	72
1998—Marshall	...	278	1265	4.6	17	26	279	10.7	3	20	120
1999—Marshall	11	164	686	4.2	12	24	321	13.4	1	13	78
College totals (4 years)	...	816	4249	5.2	55	82	863	10.5	6	61	366

CHAPMAN, LAMAR — DB — BROWNS

PERSONAL: Born November 6, 1976, in Liberal, Kan. ... 6-0/176.
HIGH SCHOOL: Liberal (Kan.).
COLLEGE: Kansas State.
TRANSACTIONS/CAREER NOTES: Selected by Cleveland Browns in fifth round (146th pick overall) of 2000 NFL draft.
HONORS: Named free safety on THE SPORTING NEWS college All-America second team (1999).
COLLEGE NOTES: Credited with $1/2$ sack (1999).

Year Team	G	INTERCEPTIONS No.	Yds.	Avg.	TD
1995—Kansas State			Redshirted.		
1996—Kansas State	9	1	30	30.0	0
1997—Kansas State	10	0	0	0.0	0
1998—Kansas State	12	1	17	17.0	0
1999—Kansas State	11	5	117	23.4	1
College totals (4 years)	42	7	164	23.4	1

CHARLTON, IKE — CB — SEAHAWKS

PERSONAL: Born October 6, 1977, in Orlando, Fla. ... 5-11/205. ... Full name: Isaac C. Charlton IV.
HIGH SCHOOL: Dr. Phillips (Orlando, Fla.).
COLLEGE: Virginia Tech.
TRANSACTIONS/CAREER NOTES: Selected after junior season by Seattle Seahawks in second round (52nd pick overall) of 2000 NFL draft.
COLLEGE NOTES: Rushed twice for 15 yards and caught one pass for 16 yards (1997); returned two punts for 17 yards (1998); recovered three fumbles for 62 yards and one touchdown (1999).

Year Team	G	INTERCEPTIONS No.	Yds.	Avg.	TD	KICKOFF RETURNS No.	Yds.	Avg.	TD	TOTALS TD	Pts.
1996—Virginia Tech					Redshirted.						
1997—Virginia Tech	11	2	28	14.0	0	18	373	20.7	0	0	0
1998—Virginia Tech	11	5	81	16.2	1	7	154	22.0	0	1	6
1999—Virginia Tech	11	1	37	37.0	0	0	0	0.0	0	1	6
College totals (3 years)	33	8	146	18.3	1	25	527	21.1	0	2	12

CHUSTZ, JOEY — OT — JAGUARS

PERSONAL: Born January 18, 1977, in Denham Springs, La. ... 6-7/304. ... Full name: Joseph Sim Chustz. ... Name pronounced SHOOTS.
HIGH SCHOOL: Denham Springs (La.).
COLLEGE: Louisiana Tech.

TRANSACTIONS/CAREER NOTES: Selected by Jacksonville Jaguars in fourth round (123rd pick overall) of 2000 NFL draft. ... Signed by Jaguars (May 16, 2000).
COLLEGE PLAYING EXPERIENCE: Louisiana Tech, 1995-1999. ... Games: 1995 (redshirted), 1996 (10), 1997 (12), 1998 (11), 1999 (11). Total: 44.

CLANCY, KENDRICK — DT — STEELERS

PERSONAL: Born September 17, 1978, in Tuscaloosa, Ala. ... 6-1/280.
HIGH SCHOOL: Holt (Tuscaloosa, Ala.).
JUNIOR COLLEGE: East Central Community College (Miss.).
COLLEGE: Mississippi.
TRANSACTIONS/CAREER NOTES: Selected by Pittsburgh Steelers in third round (72nd pick overall) of 2000 NFL draft.

Year Team	G	SACKS
1996—East Central CC	Statistics unavailable.	
1997—East Central CC	Statistics unavailable.	
1998—Mississippi	11	1.5
1999—Mississippi	11	7.0
College totals (2 years)	22	8.5

CLARIDGE, TRAVIS — OT — FALCONS

PERSONAL: Born March 23, 1978, in Detroit. ... 6-5/308.
HIGH SCHOOL: Fort Vancouver (Vancouver, Wash.).
COLLEGE: Southern California.
TRANSACTIONS/CAREER NOTES: Selected by Atlanta Falcons in second round (37th pick overall) of 2000 NFL draft. ... Signed by Falcons (May 16, 2000).
COLLEGE PLAYING EXPERIENCE: Southern California, 1996-1999. ... Games: 1996 (12), 1997 (11), 1998 (13), 1999 (12). Total: 48.

CLARK, DANNY — LB — JAGUARS

PERSONAL: Born May 9, 1977, in Country Club Hills, Ill. ... 6-2/230.
HIGH SCHOOL: Hillcrest (Ill.).
COLLEGE: Illinois.
TRANSACTIONS/CAREER NOTES: Selected by Jacksonville Jaguars in seventh round (245th pick overall) of 2000 NFL draft.

Year Team	G	INTERCEPTIONS				SACKS
		No.	Yds.	Avg.	TD	No.
1995—Illinois			Redshirted.			
1996—Illinois	11	0	0	0.0	0	0.0
1997—Illinois	11	1	0	0.0	0	5.0
1998—Illinois	11	2	24	12.0	0	0.0
1999—Illinois	11	1	0	0.0	0	3.0
College totals (4 years)	44	4	24	6.0	0	8.0

CLIFTON, CHAD — OT — PACKERS

PERSONAL: Born June 26, 1976, in Martin, Tenn. ... 6-5/329. ... Full name: Jeffrey Chad Clifton.
HIGH SCHOOL: Westview (Martin, Tenn.).
COLLEGE: Tennessee.
TRANSACTIONS/CAREER NOTES: Selected by Green Bay Packers in second round (44th pick overall) of 2000 NFL draft.
HONORS: Named offensive tackle on THE SPORTING NEWS college All-America second team (1999).
COLLEGE PLAYING EXPERIENCE: Tennessee, 1995-1999. ... Games: 1995 (redshirted), 1996 (12), 1997 (12), 1998 (12), 1999 (10). Total: 46.

COLE, CHRIS — WR — BRONCOS

PERSONAL: Born November 12, 1977, in Orange, Texas. ... 6-0/195. ... Full name: Charles Cole.
HIGH SCHOOL: West Orange-Stark (Orange, Texas).
COLLEGE: Texas A&M.
TRANSACTIONS/CAREER NOTES: Selected by Denver Broncos in third round (70th pick overall) of 2000 NFL draft.

Year Team	G	RECEIVING			
		No.	Yds.	Avg.	TD
1996—Texas A&M	6	0	0	0.0	0
1997—Texas A&M	12	25	333	13.3	3
1998—Texas A&M	13	38	667	17.6	5
1999—Texas A&M	11	22	363	16.5	0
College totals (4 years)	42	85	1363	16.0	8

COLE, GILES — TE — VIKINGS

PERSONAL: Born February 4, 1976, in Orange, Texas. ... 6-6/230.
HIGH SCHOOL: West Orange-Stark (Orange, Texas).
COLLEGE: Texas A&M-Kingsville.

2000 DRAFT PICKS

TRANSACTIONS/CAREER NOTES: Selected by Minnesota Vikings in seventh round (244th pick overall) of 2000 NFL draft.
COLLEGE NOTES: Caught six passes for 75 yards and one touchdown (1997); caught six passes for 64 yards (1998); caught one pass for two yards (1999).
COLLEGE PLAYING EXPERIENCE: Texas A&M-Kingsville, 1996-1999. ... Games: 1996 (did not play), 1997 (9), 1998 (8), 1999 (1). Total: 18.

COLEMAN, COSEY — G — BUCCANEERS

PERSONAL: Born October 27, 1978, in Clarkston, Ga. ... 6-4/322. ... Full name: Cosey Clinton Coleman.
HIGH SCHOOL: DeKalb (Clarkston, Ga.).
COLLEGE: Tennessee.
TRANSACTIONS/CAREER NOTES: Selected after junior season by Tampa Bay Buccaneers in second round (51st pick overall) of 2000 NFL draft.
COLLEGE PLAYING EXPERIENCE: Tennessee, 1997-1999. ... Games: 1997 (12), 1998 (12), 1999 (11). Total: 35.

COLES, LAVERANUES — WR — JETS

PERSONAL: Born December 29, 1977, in Jacksonville. ... 5-11/188.
HIGH SCHOOL: Jean Ribault (Jacksonville).
COLLEGE: Florida State.
TRANSACTIONS/CAREER NOTES: Selected by New York Jets in third round (78th pick overall) of 2000 NFL draft. ... Signed by Jets (May 1, 2000).

		RUSHING				RECEIVING				KICKOFF RETURNS				TOTALS	
Year Team	G	Att.	Yds.	Avg.	TD	No.	Yds.	Avg.	TD	No.	Yds.	Avg.	TD	TD	Pts.
1996—Florida State	9	14	91	6.5	0	10	104	10.4	2	5	124	24.8	0	2	12
1997—Florida State	11	6	41	6.8	0	21	384	18.3	1	8	169	21.1	0	1	6
1998—Florida State	11	15	128	8.5	1	19	397	20.9	3	13	369	28.4	1	5	30
1999—Florida State	4	0	0	0.0	0	12	179	14.9	1	6	154	25.7	0	1	6
College totals (4 years)	35	35	260	7.4	1	62	1064	17.2	7	32	816	25.5	1	9	54

COMBS, CHRIS — DE — STEELERS

PERSONAL: Born December 15, 1976, in Roanoke, Va. ... 6-4/284. ... Full name: Christopher Brandon Combs.
HIGH SCHOOL: Patrick Henry (Roanoke, Va.).
COLLEGE: Duke (degree in sociology).
TRANSACTIONS/CAREER NOTES: Selected by Pittsburgh Steelers in sixth round (173rd pick overall) of 2000 NFL draft.

Year Team	G	SACKS
1995—Duke	11	8.0
1996—Duke	Redshirted.	
1997—Duke	11	6.0
1998—Duke	11	4.0
1999—Duke	11	3.0
College totals (4 years)	44	21.0

COTTON, JAMES — DE — BEARS

PERSONAL: Born November 7, 1976, in Cleveland. ... 6-4/251.
HIGH SCHOOL: Collinwood (Cleveland).
JUNIOR COLLEGE: City College of San Francisco.
COLLEGE: Ohio State.
TRANSACTIONS/CAREER NOTES: Selected by Chicago Bears in seventh round (223rd pick overall) of 2000 NFL draft.

Year Team	G	SACKS
1996—City College of San Francisco	Statistics unavailable.	
1997—City College of San Francisco	...	8.0
1998—Ohio State	12	1.0
1999—Ohio State	12	5.0
Junior college totals (1 year)	...	8.0
College totals (2 years)	24	6.0

COWSETTE, DELBERT — DT — REDSKINS

PERSONAL: Born September 3, 1977, in Cleveland. ... 6-1/274. ... Full name: Delbert Ray Cowsette.
HIGH SCHOOL: Central Catholic (Cleveland).
COLLEGE: Maryland.
TRANSACTIONS/CAREER NOTES: Selected by Washington Redskins in seventh round (216th pick overall) of 2000 NFL draft. ... Signed by Redskins (May 18, 2000).

COLLEGE NOTES: Recovered one fumble for 54 yards and a touchdown (1996).

Year Team	G	SACKS
996—Maryland	11	2.0
997—Maryland	11	2.0
998—Maryland	11	3.0
999—Maryland	11	6.0
College totals (4 years)	44	13.0

DAWSON, JaJUAN — WR — BROWNS

PERSONAL: Born November 5, 1977, in Houston. ... 6-1/197. ... Full name: JaJuan LaTroy Dawson.
HIGH SCHOOL: H.L. Bourgeois (Gibson, La.).
COLLEGE: Tulane.
TRANSACTIONS/CAREER NOTES: Selected by Cleveland Browns in third round (79th pick overall) of 2000 NFL draft.
COLLEGE NOTES: Rushed once for three yards and returned 14 kickoffs for 328 yards (1999).

			RECEIVING		
Year Team	G	No.	Yds.	Avg.	TD
1995—Tulane			Redshirted.		
1996—Tulane	11	18	211	11.7	1
1997—Tulane	8	52	829	15.9	10
1998—Tulane	12	68	947	13.9	12
1999—Tulane	10	96	1051	10.9	8
College totals (4 years)	41	234	3038	13.0	31

DAYNE, RON — RB — GIANTS

PERSONAL: Born March 14, 1978, in Berlin, N.J. ... 5-10/253.
HIGH SCHOOL: Overbrook (Berlin, N.J.).
COLLEGE: Wisconsin.
TRANSACTIONS/CAREER NOTES: Selected by New York Giants in first round (11th pick overall) of 2000 NFL draft.
HONORS: Heisman Trophy winner (1999). ... Doak Walker Award winner (1999). ... Maxwell Award winner (1999). ... Named running back on THE SPORTING NEWS college All-America first team (1999). ... Named College Football Player of the Year by THE SPORTING NEWS (1999).

DENNIS, PAT — CB — CHIEFS

PERSONAL: Born June 3, 1978, in Shreveport, La. ... 6-0/202.
HIGH SCHOOL: Southwood (Shreveport, La.).
COLLEGE: Louisiana-Monroe.
TRANSACTIONS/CAREER NOTES: Selected after junior season by Kansas City Chiefs in fifth round (162nd pick overall) of 2000 NFL draft.

		INTERCEPTIONS				SACKS
Year Team	G	No.	Yds.	Avg.	TD	No.
1996—Louisiana-Monroe			Redshirted.			
1997—Louisiana-Monroe	12	3	0	0.0	0	1.0
1998—Louisiana-Monroe	11	7	196	28.0	2	1.0
1999—Louisiana-Monroe	11	3	14	4.7	0	0.0
College totals (3 years)	34	13	210	16.2	2	2.0

DIGGS, NA'IL — LB — PACKERS

PERSONAL: Born July 8, 1978, in Los Angeles. ... 6-4/226. ... Full name: Na'il Ronald Diggs.
HIGH SCHOOL: Dorsey (Los Angeles).
COLLEGE: Ohio State.
TRANSACTIONS/CAREER NOTES: Selected after junior season by Green Bay Packers in fourth round (98th pick overall) of 2000 NFL draft.
COLLEGE NOTES: Intercepted one pass for 18 yards and recovered one fumble for 47 yards and a touchdown (1998).

Year Team	G	SACKS
1996—Ohio State		Redshirted.
1997—Ohio State	13	6.0
1998—Ohio State	12	6.0
1999—Ohio State	12	6.0
College totals (3 years)	37	18.0

DIXON, RONALD — WR — GIANTS

PERSONAL: Born May 28, 1976, in Wildwood, Fla. ... 6-0/176.
HIGH SCHOOL: Wildwood (Fla.).
JUNIOR COLLEGE: Itawamba Community College (Miss.).
COLLEGE: West Georgia, then Lambuth University.
TRANSACTIONS/CAREER NOTES: Selected by New York Giants in third round (73rd pick overall) of 2000 NFL draft.
COLLEGE NOTES: Rushed once for 10 yards (1999).

		RECEIVING				PUNT RETURNS				KICKOFF RETURNS				TOTALS
Year Team	G	No.	Yds.	Avg.	TD	No.	Yds.	Avg.	TD	No.	Yds.	Avg.	TD	TD Pts.
1994—Itawamba CC							Statistics unavailable.							
1995—Itawamba CC							Statistics unavailable.							

Year—Team	G	Att.	Yds.	Avg.	TD	No.	Yds.	Avg.	TD	No.	Yds.	Avg.	TD	TD	Pts.
1996—West Georgia	12	45	874	19.4	11	0	0	0.0	0	1	23	23.0	0	11	66
1997—							Did not play.								
1998—							Did not play.								
1999—Lambuth University	11	89	1735	19.5	19	9	251	27.9	2	19	484	25.5	1	22	132
College totals (2 years)	23	134	2609	19.5	30	9	251	27.9	2	20	507	25.4	1	33	198

DROUGHNS, REUBEN — RB — LIONS

PERSONAL: Born August 21, 1978, in Chicago. ... 5-11/207.
HIGH SCHOOL: Anaheim (Calif.).
JUNIOR COLLEGE: Merced (Calif.) College.
COLLEGE: Oregon.
TRANSACTIONS/CAREER NOTES: Selected by Detroit Lions in third round (81st pick overall) of 2000 NFL draft.
COLLEGE NOTES: Returned four kickoffs for 66 yards (1997).

			RUSHING				RECEIVING				TOTALS	
Year Team	G	Att.	Yds.	Avg.	TD	No.	Yds.	Avg.	TD	TD	Pts.
1996—Merced College	11	211	1456	6.9	14	12	107	8.9	2	16	96
1997—Merced College	8	209	1611	7.7	12	22	308	14.0	2	14	84
1998—Oregon	5	112	844	7.5	9	3	44	14.7	2	11	66
1999—Oregon	11	277	1307	4.7	9	17	163	9.6	1	10	60
Junior college totals (2 years)	19	420	3067	7.3	26	34	415	12.2	4	30	180
College totals (2 years)	16	389	2151	5.5	18	20	207	10.4	3	21	126

DUGANS, RON — WR — BENGALS

PERSONAL: Born April 27, 1977, in Tallahassee, Fla. ... 6-1/205.
HIGH SCHOOL: Florida A&M University Develop Research (Tallahassee, Fla.).
COLLEGE: Florida State (degree in political science, 1999).
TRANSACTIONS/CAREER NOTES: Selected by Cincinnati Bengals in third round (66th pick overall) of 2000 NFL draft.
COLLEGE NOTES: Granted medical redshirt (1997).

		RECEIVING		
Year Team	G	No.	Yds.	Avg.	TD
1995—Florida State	11	14	157	11.2	0
1996—Florida State	11	7	66	9.4	1
1997—Florida State	2	3	37	12.3	0
1998—Florida State	12	38	616	16.2	3
1999—Florida State	10	43	644	15.0	3
College totals (5 years)	46	105	1520	14.5	7

DYER, DEON — FB — DOLPHINS

PERSONAL: Born October 2, 1977, in Chesapeake, Va. ... 6-0/264. ... Full name: Deon Joseph Dyer.
HIGH SCHOOL: Deep Creek (Chesapeake, Va.).
COLLEGE: North Carolina.
TRANSACTIONS/CAREER NOTES: Selected by Miami Dolphins in fourth round (117th pick overall) of 2000 NFL draft.

			RUSHING				RECEIVING				TOTALS	
Year Team	G	Att.	Yds.	Avg.	TD	No.	Yds.	Avg.	TD	TD	Pts.
1996—North Carolina	11	4	52	13.0	0	2	39	19.5	0	0	0
1997—North Carolina	0	25	90	3.6	1	5	31	6.2	0	1	6
1998—North Carolina	11	84	258	3.1	6	6	58	9.7	1	7	42
1999—North Carolina	11	73	233	3.2	2	7	55	7.9	1	3	18
College totals (4 years)	33	186	633	3.4	9	20	183	9.2	2	11	66

EDINGER, PAUL — K — BEARS

PERSONAL: Born January 17, 1978, in Frankfort, Mich. ... 5-10/169.
HIGH SCHOOL: Kathleen (Lakeland, Fla.).
COLLEGE: Michigan State.
TRANSACTIONS/CAREER NOTES: Selected by Chicago Bears in sixth round (174th pick overall) of 2000 NFL draft.

	PUNTING						KICKING					
	No.	Yds.	Avg.	Net avg.	In. 20	Blk.	XPM	XPA	FGM	FGA	Lg.	50+	Pts.
1996—Michigan State	55	2297	41.8	34.8	14	4	0	0	0	1	0	0-0	0
1997—Michigan State	54	2118	39.2	35.1	12	3	7	9	3	5	43	0-0	16
1998—Michigan State	5	146	29.2	23.4	1	0	28	31	22	26	49	0-0	94
1999—Michigan State	0	0	...	.0	0	0	40	41	21	26	55	0-0	103
College totals (4 years)	114	4561	40.0	34.4	27	7	75	81	46	58	55	0-0	213

EDWARDS, MARIO — CB — COWBOYS

PERSONAL: Born December 1, 1975, in Gautier, Miss. ... 6-0/191.
HIGH SCHOOL: Pascagoula (Miss.).
COLLEGE: Florida State.
TRANSACTIONS/CAREER NOTES: Selected by Dallas Cowboys in sixth round (180th pick overall) of 2000 NFL draft.

COLLEGE NOTES: Returned one blocked kick 24 yards and a touchdown (1995); intercepted six passes for 109 yards (1998).
COLLEGE PLAYING EXPERIENCE: Florida State, 1995-1999. ... Games: 1995 (7), 1996 (11), 1997 (redshirted), 1998 (12), 1999 (11). Total: 41.

ELLIS, SHAUN — DE — JETS

PERSONAL: Born June 24, 1977, in Anderson, S.C. ... 6-5/280. ... Full name: MeShaunda Pizarrur Ellis.
HIGH SCHOOL: Westside (Anderson, S.C.).
COLLEGE: Tennessee.
TRANSACTIONS/CAREER NOTES: Selected by New York Jets in first round (12th pick overall) of 2000 NFL draft.
COLLEGE NOTES: Recovered one fumble for 65 yards and intercepted one pass for 90 yards and a touchdown (1999).

Year Team	G	SACKS
1996—Tennessee	Did not play.	
1997—Tennessee	12	1.0
1998—Tennessee	12	1.0
1999—Tennessee	11	8.5
College totals (3 years)	35	10.5

ENGELBERGER, JOHN — DE — 49ERS

PERSONAL: Born October 18, 1976, in Heidelburg, Germany. ... 6-4/260. ... Full name: John Albert Engelberger.
HIGH SCHOOL: Robert E. Lee (Springfield, Va.).
COLLEGE: Virginia Tech.
TRANSACTIONS/CAREER NOTES: Selected by San Francisco 49ers in second round (35th pick overall) of 2000 NFL draft.
COLLEGE NOTES: Intercepted one pass for no yards (1997).

Year Team	G	SACKS
1995—Virginia Tech	Redshirted.	
1996—Virginia Tech	11	6.0
1997—Virginia Tech	10	6.0
1998—Virginia Tech	11	7.5
1999—Virginia Tech	11	7.0
College totals (4 years)	43	26.5

FARMER, DANNY — WR — STEELERS

PERSONAL: Born May 21, 1977, in Los Angeles. ... 6-3/217. ... Full name: Daniel Steven Farmer. ... Son of George Farmer, wide receiver with Chicago Bears (1970-75) and Detroit Lions (1975); nephew of Dave Farmer, running back with Tampa Bay Buccaneers (1978).
HIGH SCHOOL: Loyola (Los Angeles).
COLLEGE: UCLA.
TRANSACTIONS/CAREER NOTES: Selected by Pittsburgh Steelers in fourth round (103rd pick overall) of 2000 NFL draft.

Year Team	G	RECEIVING			
		No.	Yds.	Avg.	TD
1995—UCLA			Redshirted.		
1996—UCLA	11	31	524	16.9	4
1997—UCLA	12	41	649	15.8	3
1998—UCLA	12	58	1274	22.0	9
1999—UCLA	9	29	573	19.8	3
College totals (4 years)	44	159	3020	19.0	19

FIELDS, LEROY — WR — BRONCOS

PERSONAL: Born December 2, 1975, in Monroe, La. ... 6-3/205.
HIGH SCHOOL: West Monroe (Monroe, La.).
JUNIOR COLLEGE: Navarro College (Texas).
COLLEGE: Oklahoma, then Jackson State.
TRANSACTIONS/CAREER NOTES: Selected by Denver Broncos in seventh round (246th pick overall) of 2000 NFL draft. ... Signed by Broncos (May 16, 2000).
COLLEGE NOTES: Redshirted after two games in 1998.

Year Team	G	RECEIVING			
		No.	Yds.	Avg.	TD
1996—Oklahoma	10	41	910	22.2	9
1997—Jackson State	1	1	15	15.0	0
1998—Jackson State	2	2	37	18.5	0
1999—Jackson State	7	19	325	17.1	2
College totals (4 years)	20	63	1287	20.4	11

FLOWERS, ERIK — DE — BILLS

PERSONAL: Born March 1, 1978, in Oceanside, Calif. ... 6-4/248. ... Full name: Erik Mathews Flowers.
HIGH SCHOOL: Theodore Roosevelt (San Antonio, Texas).
JUNIOR COLLEGE: Trinity Valley Community College (Texas).
COLLEGE: Arizona State.
TRANSACTIONS/CAREER NOTES: Selected by Buffalo Bills in first round (26th pick overall) of 2000 NFL draft.

COLLEGE NOTES: Intercepted one pass for seven yards (1999).

Year Team	G	SACKS
1996—Trinity Valley CC	Statistics unavailable.	
1997—Trinity Valley CC	Statistics unavailable.	
1998—Arizona State	11	3.0
1999—Arizona State	12	10.0
College totals (2 years)	23	13.0

FRANK, JOHN   DE   EAGLES

PERSONAL: Born July 1, 1974, in Salt Lake City, Utah. ... 6-4/280.
HIGH SCHOOL: Skyline (Salt Lake City, Utah).
COLLEGE: Utah.
TRANSACTIONS/CAREER NOTES: Selected by Philadelphia Eagles in sixth round (178th pick overall) of 2000 NFL draft.
COLLEGE NOTES: Intercepted one pass (1999).

Year Team	G	SACKS
1995—Utah	Redshirted.	
1996—Utah	11	0.0
1997—Utah	8	4.0
1998—Utah	10	10.0
1999—Utah	11	13.0
College totals (4 years)	40	27.0

FRANKS, BUBBA   TE   PACKERS

PERSONAL: Born January 6, 1978, in Big Springs, Texas. ... 6-6/252. ... Full name: Daniel Lamont Franks.
HIGH SCHOOL: Big Springs (Texas).
COLLEGE: Miami (Fla.).
TRANSACTIONS/CAREER NOTES: Selected after junior season by Green Bay Packers in first round (14th pick overall) of 2000 NFL draft.
HONORS: Named tight end on THE SPORTING NEWS college All-America first team (1999).

Year Team	G	No.	Yds.	Avg.	TD
			RECEIVING		
1996—Miami (Fla.)			Redshirted.		
1997—Miami (Fla.)	11	19	294	15.5	4
1998—Miami (Fla.)	11	13	179	13.8	3
1999—Miami (Fla.)	12	45	565	12.6	5
College totals (3 years)	34	77	1038	13.5	12

FRANZ, TODD   DB   LIONS

PERSONAL: Born April 12, 1976, in Enid, Okla. ... 6-0/194. ... Full name: Stephen Todd Franz.
HIGH SCHOOL: Weatherford (Okla.).
COLLEGE: Tulsa.
TRANSACTIONS/CAREER NOTES: Selected by Detroit Lions in fifth round (145th pick overall) of 2000 NFL draft.
COLLEGE NOTES: Intercepted two passes for five yards and credited with one sack (1998); intercepted three passes for eight yards and credited with two sacks (1999).
COLLEGE PLAYING EXPERIENCE: Tulsa, 1996-1999. ... Games: 1996 (9), 1997 (9), 1998 (11), 1999 (11). Total: 40.

FREEMAN, ARTURO   S   DOLPHINS

PERSONAL: Born October 27, 1976, in Orangeburg, S.C. ... 6-0/196.
HIGH SCHOOL: Orangeburg-Wilkinson (Orangeburg, S.C.).
COLLEGE: South Carolina.
TRANSACTIONS/CAREER NOTES: Selected by Miami Dolphins in fifth round (152nd pick overall) of 2000 NFL draft.
COLLEGE NOTES: Credited with $1/2$ sack (1995); credited with one sack (1996); recovered one fumble for two yards (1997).

Year Team	G	No.	Yds.	Avg.	TD
			INTERCEPTIONS		
1995—South Carolina	11	1	0	0.0	0
1996—South Carolina	11	3	16	5.3	0
1997—South Carolina	11	6	95	15.8	1
1998—South Carolina			Redshirted.		
1999—South Carolina	9	0	0	0.0	0
College totals (4 years)	42	10	111	11.1	1

FRISCH, BYRON   DE   TITANS

PERSONAL: Born December 17, 1976, in Bonita, Calif. ... 6-5/267.
HIGH SCHOOL: Bonita Vista (Bonita, Calif.)
COLLEGE: Brigham Young.
TRANSACTIONS/CAREER NOTES: Selected by Tennessee Titans in third round (93rd pick overall) of 2000 NFL draft.

Year Team	G	SACKS
1995—Brigham Young	Redshirted.	

1996—Brigham Young	...	3.0
1997—Brigham Young	...	9.0
1998—Brigham Young	14	5.0
1999—Brigham Young	11	8.0
College totals (4 years)	...	25.0

FULCHER, MONDRIEL — TE — RAIDERS

PERSONAL: Born October 15, 1976, in Coffeyville, Kan. ... 6-3/250. ... Full name: Mondriel DeCarlos A. Fulcher.
HIGH SCHOOL: Field Kindley (Coffeyville, Kan.).
COLLEGE: Miami (Fla.).
TRANSACTIONS/CAREER NOTES: Selected by Oakland Raiders in seventh round (227th pick overall) of 2000 NFL draft.
COLLEGE NOTES: Rushed three times for 10 yards (1999).

		RECEIVING			
Year Team	**G**	**No.**	**Yds.**	**Avg.**	**TD**
1995—Miami (Fla.)		Redshirted.			
1996—Miami (Fla.)	11	12	149	12.4	2
1997—Miami (Fla.)	12	5	87	17.4	0
1998—Miami (Fla.)	11	17	289	17.0	1
1999—Miami (Fla.)	12	13	131	10.1	1
College totals (4 years)	46	47	656	14.0	4

GAVADZA, JASON — TE — STEELERS

PERSONAL: Born January 31, 1976, in Toronto. ... 6-3/247.
HIGH SCHOOL: Michael Power (Toronto).
COLLEGE: Kent.
TRANSACTIONS/CAREER NOTES: Selected by Pittsburgh Steelers in sixth round (204th pick overall) of 2000 NFL draft.

		RECEIVING			
Year Team	**G**	**No.**	**Yds.**	**Avg.**	**TD**
1995—Kent		Redshirted.			
1996—Kent	9	1	16	16.0	0
1997—Kent	11	19	382	20.1	4
1998—Kent	11	19	260	13.7	2
1999—Kent	11	47	654	13.9	7
College totals (4 years)	42	86	1312	15.3	13

GAYLOR, TREVOR — WR — CHARGERS

PERSONAL: Born November 3, 1977, in Hazelwood, Mo. ... 6-3/195.
HIGH SCHOOL: Hazelwood (Mo.) West.
COLLEGE: Miami of Ohio.
TRANSACTIONS/CAREER NOTES: Selected by San Diego Chargers in fourth round (111th pick overall) of 2000 NFL draft.
COLLEGE NOTES: Rushed five times for 40 yards and a touchdown and returned one punt for 16 yards (1998); rushed twice for seven yards and completed only pass attempt for 81 yards and a touchdown (1999).

		RECEIVING			
Year Team	**G**	**No.**	**Yds.**	**Avg.**	**TD**
1996—Miami of Ohio	5	8	75	9.4	0
1997—Miami of Ohio	11	29	375	12.9	4
1998—Miami of Ohio	11	38	653	17.2	5
1999—Miami of Ohio	11	53	1028	19.4	11
College totals (4 years)	38	128	2131	16.6	20

GBAJA-BIAMILA, KABEER — DE — PACKERS

PERSONAL: Born September 24, 1977, in Los Angeles. ... 6-4/244. ... Full name: Muhammed Kabeer Gbaja-Biamila.
HIGH SCHOOL: Crenshaw (Los Angeles).
COLLEGE: San Diego State.
TRANSACTIONS/CAREER NOTES: Selected by Green Bay Packers in fifth round (149th pick overall) of 2000 NFL draft.

Year Team	**G**	**SACKS**
1995—San Diego State	Redshirted.	
1996—San Diego State	11	2.0
1997—San Diego State	12	12.0
1998—San Diego State	11	7.0
1999—San Diego State	11	12.0
College totals (4 years)	45	33.0

GIBSON, DAVID — S — BUCCANEERS

PERSONAL: Born November 5, 1977, in Mission Viejo, Calif. ... 6-1/210.
HIGH SCHOOL: Mater Dei (Santa, Ana, Calif.).
COLLEGE: Southern California.
TRANSACTIONS/CAREER NOTES: Selected by Tampa Bay Buccaneers in sixth round (193rd pick overall) of 2000 NFL draft.
COLLEGE NOTES: Intercepted one pass for 16 yards and a touchdown (1998); intercepted three passes for one yard (1999).

Year Team	G	SACKS
1996—Southern California	9	0.0
1997—Southern California	11	6.0
1998—Southern California	13	3.0
1999—Southern California	12	0.0
College totals (4 years)	45	9.0

GIDEON, SHERROD — WR — SAINTS

PERSONAL: Born February 21, 1977, in Greenwood, Miss. ... 5-11/176.
HIGH SCHOOL: Greenwood (Miss.).
COLLEGE: Southern Mississippi.
TRANSACTIONS/CAREER NOTES: Selected by New Orleans Saints in sixth round (200th pick overall) of 2000 NFL draft.
COLLEGE NOTES: Returned 10 kickoffs for 252 yards (1996).

Year Team	G	RECEIVING				PUNT RETURNS				TOTALS	
		No.	Yds.	Avg.	TD	No.	Yds.	Avg.	TD	TD	Pts.
1995—Southern Mississippi		Redshirted.									
1996—Southern Mississippi	11	33	500	15.2	1	0	0	0.0	0	1	6
1997—Southern Mississippi	11	54	1008	18.7	9	33	347	10.5	0	9	54
1998—Southern Mississippi	11	66	1186	18.0	13	5	33	6.6	0	13	78
1999—Southern Mississippi	8	40	520	13.0	7	6	41	6.8	0	7	42
College totals (4 years)	41	193	3214	16.7	30	44	421	9.6	0	30	180

GOLD, IAN — LB — BRONCOS

PERSONAL: Born August 23, 1978, in Ann Arbor, Mich. ... 6-0/223. ... Full name: Ian Maurice Gold.
HIGH SCHOOL: Belleville (Mich.).
COLLEGE: Michigan.
TRANSACTIONS/CAREER NOTES: Selected by Denver Broncos in second round (40th pick overall) of 2000 NFL draft.
COLLEGE NOTES: Rushed four times for 13 yards (1996); rushed once for five yards and recovered one fumble (1999).

Year Team	G	INTERCEPTIONS				SACKS
		No.	Yds.	Avg.	TD	No.
1996—Michigan	8	0	0	0.0	0	0.0
1997—Michigan	12	0	0	0.0	0	0.0
1998—Michigan	9	1	46	46.0	1	2.0
1999—Michigan	12	1	17	17.0	0	4.0
College totals (4 years)	41	2	63	31.5	1	6.0

GOODRICH, DWAYNE — CB — COWBOYS

PERSONAL: Born May 29, 1978, in Oak Lawn, Ill. ... 5-11/198. ... Full name: Dwayne Lewis Goodrich.
HIGH SCHOOL: H.L. Richards (Oak Lawn, Ill.).
COLLEGE: Tennessee.
TRANSACTIONS/CAREER NOTES: Selected by Dallas Cowboys in second round (49th pick overall) of 2000 NFL draft.
COLLEGE NOTES: Recovered four fumbles (1996); recovered two fumbles (1997).

Year Team	G	INTERCEPTIONS				KICKOFF RETURNS				TOTALS	
		No.	Yds.	Avg.	TD	No.	Yds.	Avg.	TD	TD	Pts.
1996—Tennessee	10	2	45	22.5	1	0	0	0.0	0	1	6
1997—Tennessee	11	4	47	11.8	1	13	282	21.7	0	1	6
1998—Tennessee	12	3	14	4.7	0	1	26	26.0	0	0	0
1999—Tennessee	10	3	28	9.3	0	2	35	17.5	0	0	0
College totals (4 years)	43	12	134	11.2	2	16	343	21.4	0	2	12

GRANT, DEON — S — PANTHERS

PERSONAL: Born March 14, 1979, in Augusta, Ga. ... 6-1/207.
HIGH SCHOOL: Josey (Augusta, Ga.).
COLLEGE: Tennessee.
TRANSACTIONS/CAREER NOTES: Selected after junior season by Carolina Panthers in second round (57th pick overall) of 2000 NFL draft.
HONORS: Named free safety on THE SPORTING NEWS college All-America first team (1999).
COLLEGE NOTES: Recovered two fumbles and returned two punts for 11 yards (1998); returned one punt for one yard (1999).

Year Team	G	INTERCEPTIONS			
		No.	Yds.	Avg.	TD
1997—Tennessee	12	0	0	0.0	0
1998—Tennessee	12	5	79	15.8	0
1999—Tennessee	11	9	167	18.6	1
College totals (3 years)	35	14	246	17.6	1

GRANT, EARNEST — DT — DOLPHINS

PERSONAL: Born May 17, 1976, in Atlanta. ... 6-5/297.
HIGH SCHOOL: Forest (Atlanta).
COLLEGE: Arkansas-Pine Bluff.

TRANSACTIONS/CAREER NOTES: Selected by Miami Dolphins in sixth round (167th pick overall) of 2000 NFL draft.

Year Team	G	SACKS
1996—Arkansas-Pine Bluff	7	1.0
1997—Arkansas-Pine Bluff	11	2.5
1998—Arkansas-Pine Bluff	10	4.0
1999—Arkansas-Pine Bluff	10	3.0
College totals (4 years)	38	10.5

GRANT, ORANTES — LB — COWBOYS

PERSONAL: Born March 18, 1978, in Atlanta. ... 6-0/225.
HIGH SCHOOL: Dunwoody (Atlanta).
COLLEGE: Georgia.
TRANSACTIONS/CAREER NOTES: Selected by Dallas Cowboys in seventh round (219th pick overall) of 2000 NFL draft.

Year Team	G	SACKS
1996—Georgia	11	0.0
1997—Georgia	11	2.5
1998—Georgia	11	2.5
1999—Georgia	11	2.0
College totals (4 years)	44	7.0

GREEN, BARRETT — LB — LIONS

PERSONAL: Born October 29, 1977, in West Palm Beach, Fla. ... 6-0/217. ... Son of Joe Green, defensive back with New York Giants (1970 and 1971).
HIGH SCHOOL: Suncoast (West Palm Beach, Fla.).
COLLEGE: West Virginia.
TRANSACTIONS/CAREER NOTES: Selected by Detroit Lions in second round (50th pick overall) of 2000 NFL draft.
COLLEGE NOTES: Recovered one fumble (1997); recovered two fumbles (1998); recovered one fumble (1999).

Year Team	G	INTERCEPTIONS No.	Yds.	Avg.	TD	SACKS No.
1995—West Virginia				Redshirted.		
1996—West Virginia	11	0	0	0.0	0	0.0
1997—West Virginia	12	4	143	35.8	1	3.0
1998—West Virginia	12	1	11	11.0	0	0.0
1999—West Virginia	11	0	0	0.0	0	3.0
College totals (4 years)	46	5	154	30.8	1	6.0

GREEN, MIKE — S — BEARS

PERSONAL: Born December 6, 1976, in Ruston, La. ... 6-0/176.
HIGH SCHOOL: Ruston (La.).
COLLEGE: Louisiana-Lafayette.
TRANSACTIONS/CAREER NOTES: Selected by Chicago Bears in seventh round (254th pick overall) of 2000 NFL draft.
COLLEGE NOTES: Returned blocked punt one yard for a touchdown (1999).

Year Team	G	INTERCEPTIONS No.	Yds.	Avg.	TD
1996—Northwestern (La.) State			Did Not Play.		
1997—Northwestern (La.) State	8	0	0	0.0	0
1998—Northwestern (La.) State	11	2	0	0.0	0
1999—Louisiana-Lafayette	11	2	37	18.5	1
College totals (3 years)	30	4	37	9.3	1

GREEN, MIKE — RB — TITANS

PERSONAL: Born September 2, 1976, in Houston. ... 6-0/249.
HIGH SCHOOL: Klein (Houston).
JUNIOR COLLEGE: Blinn College (Texas).
COLLEGE: Houston.
TRANSACTIONS/CAREER NOTES: Selected by Tennessee Titans in seventh round (213th pick overall) of 2000 NFL draft.

Year Team	G	RUSHING Att.	Yds.	Avg.	TD	RECEIVING No.	Yds.	Avg.	TD	KICKOFF RETURNS No.	Yds.	Avg.	TD	TOTALS TD	Pts.
1996—Blinn College	10	155	1051	6.8	27	0	0	0.0	0	0	0	0.0	0	27	162
1997—Blinn College	7	120	414	3.5	5	0	0	0.0	0	0	0	0.0	0	5	30
1998—Houston	8	101	435	4.3	3	3	68	22.7	0	2	35	17.5	0	3	18
1999—Houston	10	142	838	5.9	8	6	46	7.7	0	3	62	20.7	0	8	48
Junior college totals (2 years)	17	275	1465	5.3	32	0	0	0.0	0	0	0	0.0	0	32	192
College totals (2 years)	18	243	1273	5.2	11	9	114	12.7	0	5	97	19.4	0	11	66

GRIFFIN, CORNELIUS — DT — GIANTS

PERSONAL: Born December 3, 1976, in Brundidge, Ala. ... 6-3/294.
HIGH SCHOOL: Pike County (Brundidge, Ala.).
JUNIOR COLLEGE: Pearl River Community College (Miss.).

COLLEGE: Alabama.
TRANSACTIONS/CAREER NOTES: Selected by New York Giants in second round (42nd pick overall) of 2000 NFL draft.

Year Team	G	SACKS
1995—Pearl River CC	10	0.0
1996—Pearl River CC	10	2.0
1997—	Did not play.	
1998—Alabama	12	1.0
1999—Alabama	11	5.5
Junior college totals (2 years)	20	2.0
College totals (2 years)	23	6.5

HADDAD, DREW　　　　　WR　　　　　BILLS

PERSONAL: Born August 15, 1978, in Westlake, Ohio. ... 5-11/184.
HIGH SCHOOL: St. Ignatius (Westlake, Ohio).
COLLEGE: Buffalo.
TRANSACTIONS/CAREER NOTES: Selected by Buffalo Bills in seventh round (233rd pick overall) of 2000 NFL draft.

Year Team	G	RECEIVING				PUNT RETURNS				KICKOFF RETURNS				TOTALS	
		No.	Yds.	Avg.	TD	No.	Yds.	Avg.	TD	No.	Yds.	Avg.	TD	TD	Pts.
1996—Buffalo	11	21	282	13.4	2	1	25	25.0	0	12	219	18.3	0	2	12
1997—Buffalo	10	67	1058	15.8	3	8	98	12.3	0	13	249	19.2	0	3	18
1998—Buffalo	11	67	911	13.6	5	23	410	17.8	2	3	52	17.3	0	7	42
1999—Buffalo	11	85	1158	13.6	6	21	254	12.1	0	0	0	0.0	0	6	36
College totals (4 years)	43	240	3409	14.2	16	53	787	14.8	2	28	520	18.6	0	18	108

HAGGANS, CLARK　　　　　DE　　　　　STEELERS

PERSONAL: Born January 10, 1977, in Torrance, Calif. ... 6-3/250. ... Full name: Clark Cromwell Haggans.
HIGH SCHOOL: Peninsula (Torrance, Calif.).
COLLEGE: Colorado State.
TRANSACTIONS/CAREER NOTES: Selected by Pittsburgh Steelers in fifth round (137th pick overall) of 2000 NFL draft.

Year Team	G	SACKS
1995—Colorado State	Redshirted.	
1996—Colorado State	12	11.0
1997—Colorado State	12	11.0
1998—Colorado State	12	4.0
1999—Colorado State	11	8.0
College totals (4 years)	47	34.0

HALL, DANTE　　　　　RB/KR　　　　　CHIEFS

PERSONAL: Born September 1, 1978, in Lufkin, Texas. ... 5-8/188. ... Full name: Damieon Dante Hall.
HIGH SCHOOL: Nimitz (Irving, Texas).
COLLEGE: Texas A&M.
TRANSACTIONS/CAREER NOTES: Selected by Kansas City Chiefs in fifth round (153rd pick overall) of 2000 NFL draft.
COLLEGE NOTES: Attempted one pass without a completion (1998).

Year Team	G	RUSHING				RECEIVING				PUNT RETURNS				KICKOFF RETURNS				TOTALS	
		Att.	Yds.	Avg.	TD	No.	Yds.	Avg.	TD	No.	Yds.	Avg.	TD	No.	Yds.	Avg.	TD	TD	Pts.
1996—Texas A&M	12	92	642	7.0	3	3	12	4.0	0	43	573	13.3	0	14	324	23.1	0	3	18
1997—Texas A&M	12	134	1010	7.5	9	8	97	12.1	0	17	208	12.2	1	7	156	22.3	0	10	60
1998—Texas A&M	13	243	1098	4.5	8	6	92	15.3	0	7	28	4.0	0	8	172	21.5	0	8	48
1999—Texas A&M	6	53	179	3.4	2	5	59	11.8	0	11	134	12.2	0	3	34	11.3	0	2	12
College totals (4 years)	43	522	2929	5.6	22	22	260	11.8	0	78	943	12.1	1	32	686	21.4	0	23	138

HAMILTON, JOE　　　　　QB　　　　　BUCCANEERS

PERSONAL: Born March 13, 1977, in Alvin, S.C. ... 5-10/190. ... Full name: Joseph Fitzgerald Hamilton.
HIGH SCHOOL: Macedonia (Alvin, S.C.).
COLLEGE: Georgia Tech.
TRANSACTIONS/CAREER NOTES: Selected by Tampa Bay Buccaneers in seventh round (234th pick overall) of 2000 NFL draft.
HONORS: Davey O'Brien Award winner (1999). ... Named quarterback on THE SPORTING NEWS college All-America second team (1999).

Year Team	G	PASSING								RUSHING				TOTALS	
		Att.	Cmp.	Pct.	Yds.	TD	Int.	Avg.	Rat.	Att.	Yds.	Avg.	TD	TD	Pts.
1996—Georgia Tech	10	188	108	57.4	1342	7	13	7.14	115.9	95	248	2.6	3	3	18
1997—Georgia Tech	11	268	173	64.6	2314	12	7	8.63	146.6	140	478	3.4	5	5	30
1998—Georgia Tech	11	259	145	56.0	2166	17	8	8.36	141.7	112	298	2.7	4	4	24
1999—Georgia Tech	11	305	203	66.6	3060	29	11	10.03	175.0	154	734	4.8	6	6	36
College totals (4 years)	43	1020	629	61.7	8882	65	39	8.71	148.2	501	1758	3.5	18	18	108

HAMNER, THOMAS　　　　　RB　　　　　EAGLES

PERSONAL: Born December 25, 1976, in Hamilton, Ohio. ... 6-0/197.
HIGH SCHOOL: Hamilton (Ohio).
COLLEGE: Minnesota.

2000 DRAFT PICKS

TRANSACTIONS/CAREER NOTES: Selected by Philadelphia Eagles in sixth round (171st pick overall) of 2000 NFL draft.

		RUSHING				RECEIVING				TOTALS	
Year Team	G	Att.	Yds.	Avg.	TD	No.	Yds.	Avg.	TD	TD	Pts.
1995—Minnesota						Redshirted.					
1996—Minnesota	11	195	883	4.5	3	15	81	5.4	0	3	18
1997—Minnesota	12	170	663	3.9	4	13	95	7.3	1	5	30
1998—Minnesota	11	209	838	4.0	4	13	72	5.5	0	4	24
1999—Minnesota	11	308	1426	4.6	10	21	305	14.5	3	13	78
College totals (4 years)	45	882	3810	4.3	21	62	553	8.9	4	25	150

HARRIS, ANTWAN — CB — PATRIOTS

PERSONAL: Born May 29, 1977, in Raleigh, N.C. ... 5-9/186. ... Full name: Melvin Antwan Harris.
HIGH SCHOOL: Ravenscroft (Raleigh, N.C.).
COLLEGE: Virginia.
TRANSACTIONS/CAREER NOTES: Selected by New England Patriots in sixth round (187th pick overall) of 2000 NFL draft.
COLLEGE NOTES: Returned one punt for 34 yards and a touchdown (1996).

		INTERCEPTIONS				KICKOFF RETURNS				TOTALS	
Year Team	G	No.	Yds.	Avg.	TD	No.	Yds.	Avg.	TD	TD	Pts.
1996—Virginia	9	2	95	47.5	1	6	94	15.7	0	2	12
1997—Virginia	9	0	0	0.0	0	7	146	20.9	0	0	0
1998—Virginia	9	2	0	0.0	0	0	0	0.0	0	0	0
1999—Virginia	7	0	0	0.0	0	0	0	0.0	0	0	0
College totals (4 years)	34	4	95	23.8	1	13	240	18.5	0	2	12

HARRIS, JEFF — CB — DOLPHINS

PERSONAL: Born July 19, 1977, in Jacksonville. ... 5-11/178. ... Full name: Jeffrey Terris Harris.
HIGH SCHOOL: Nease (St. Augustine, Fla.).
COLLEGE: Georgia.
TRANSACTIONS/CAREER NOTES: Selected by Miami Dolphins in seventh round (232nd pick overall) of 2000 NFL draft.

		INTERCEPTIONS			
Year Team	G	No.	Yds.	Avg.	TD
1995—Georgia			Redshirted.		
1996—Georgia			Did not play.		
1997—Georgia	11	0	0	0.0	0
1998—Georgia	11	4	0	0.0	0
1999—Georgia	10	2	9	4.5	0
College totals (3 years)	32	6	9	1.5	0

HARRISON, LLOYD — CB — REDSKINS

PERSONAL: Born June 21, 1977, in Jamiaca. ... 5-10/190.
HIGH SCHOOL: Sewanhaka (Floral Park, N.Y.).
COLLEGE: North Carolina State.
TRANSACTIONS/CAREER NOTES: Selected by Washington Redskins in third round (64th pick overall) of 2000 NFL draft.
COLLEGE NOTES: Recovered three fumbles (1999).

		INTERCEPTIONS			
Year Team	G	No.	Yds.	Avg.	TD
1995—North Carolina State			Redshirted.		
1996—North Carolina State	8	0	0	0.0	0
1997—North Carolina State	11	0	0	0.0	0
1998—North Carolina State	11	7	51	7.3	0
1999—North Carolina State	12	5	0	0.0	0
College totals (4 years)	42	12	51	4.3	0

HAWTHORNE, MICHAEL — CB — SAINTS

PERSONAL: Born January 26, 1975, in Sarasota, Fla. ... 6-3/196. ... Full name: Michael Seneca Hawthorne.
HIGH SCHOOL: Booker (Sarasota, Fla.).
COLLEGE: Purdue.
TRANSACTIONS/CAREER NOTES: Selected by New Orleans Saints in sixth round (195th pick overall) of 2000 NFL draft.
COLLEGE NOTES: Credited with one sack (1999).

		INTERCEPTIONS			
Year Team	G	No.	Yds.	Avg.	TD
1995—Purdue			Redshirted.		
1996—Purdue	9	0	0	0.0	0
1997—Purdue	12	2	45	22.5	0
1998—Purdue	4	2	0	0.0	0
1999—Purdue	8	0	0	0.0	0
College totals (4 years)	33	4	45	11.3	0

HAYES, WINDRELL — WR — JETS

PERSONAL: Born December 14, 1976, in Stockton, Calif. ... 5-11/204.
HIGH SCHOOL: Franklin (Stockton, Calif.).

JUNIOR COLLEGE: San Joaquin Delta College, Calif. (did not play football).
COLLEGE: San Jose State, then Southern California.
TRANSACTIONS/CAREER NOTES: Selected by New York Jets in fifth round (143rd pick overall) of 2000 NFL draft. ... Signed by Jets (May 24, 2000).

			RECEIVING			
Year Team	G	No.	Yds.	Avg.	TD	
1995—San Jose State	11	39	535	13.7	5	
1996—San Jose State	11	58	848	14.6	4	
1997—San Joaquin Delta College			Did not play.			
1998—Southern California	12	24	340	14.2	2	
1999—Southern California	10	55	720	13.1	4	
COLLEGE totals (2 years)	22	97	1383	14.3	9	
College totals (2 years)	22	79	1060	13.4	6	

HILLIARD, JOHN — DT — SEAHAWKS

PERSONAL: Born April 16, 1976, in Shreveport, La. ... 6-2/285. ... Full name: John Edward Hilliard.
HIGH SCHOOL: Sterling (Houston).
COLLEGE: Mississippi State.
TRANSACTIONS/CAREER NOTES: Selected by Seattle Seahawks in sixth round (190th pick overall) of 2000 NFL draft.
COLLEGE NOTES: Redshirted after two games (1996).

Year Team	G	SACKS
1995—Mississippi State	10	1.0
1996—Mississippi State	2	0.0
1997—Mississippi State	11	0.0
1998—Mississippi State	11	3.0
1999—Mississippi State	11	2.0
College totals (5 years)	45	6.0

HOUSER, KEVIN — FB — SAINTS

PERSONAL: Born August 23, 1972, in Westlake, Ohio. ... 6-2/250.
HIGH SCHOOL: Westlake (Ohio).
COLLEGE: Ohio State.
TRANSACTIONS/CAREER NOTES: Selected by New Orleans Saints in seventh round (228th pick overall) of 2000 NFL draft.
COLLEGE NOTES: Caught one pass for 10 yards (1998); caught six passes for 55 yards and two touchdowns (1999).
COLLEGE PLAYING EXPERIENCE: Ohio State, 1996-1999. ... Games: 1996 (11), 1997 (13), 1998 (12), 1999 (12). Total: 48.

HOVAN, CHRIS — DT — VIKINGS

PERSONAL: Born May 12, 1978, in Rocky River, Ohio. ... 6-2/305. ... Full name: Christopher James Hovan.
HIGH SCHOOL: St. Ignatius (Rocky River, Ohio).
COLLEGE: Boston College.
TRANSACTIONS/CAREER NOTES: Selected by Minnesota Vikings in first round (25th pick overall) of 2000 NFL draft.

Year Team	G	SACKS
1996—Boston College	12	0.0
1997—Boston College	11	4.0
1998—Boston College	11	5.5
1999—Boston College	11	11.0
College totals (4 years)	45	20.5

HOWARD, DARREN — DE — SAINTS

PERSONAL: Born November 19, 1976, in St. Petersburg, Fla. ... 6-3/281.
HIGH SCHOOL: Boca Ciega (Fla.).
COLLEGE: Kansas State.
TRANSACTIONS/CAREER NOTES: Selected by New Orleans Saints in second round (33rd pick overall) of 2000 NFL draft.
COLLEGE NOTES: Recovered one fumble for four yards (1997); recovered one fumble for four yards (1998); intercepted two passes for 35 yards and one touchdown (1999).

Year Team	G	SACKS
1995—Kansas State		Redshirted.
1996—Kansas State	9	2.5
1997—Kansas State	11	11.0
1998—Kansas State	12	10.5
1999—Kansas State	11	5.5
College totals (4 years)	43	29.5

HOWELL, ETHAN — WR — REDSKINS

PERSONAL: Born October 14, 1977, in Monroe, La. ... 5-11/178.
HIGH SCHOOL: Monroe (La.).
COLLEGE: Grambling State, then Oklahoma State.

TRANSACTIONS/CAREER NOTES: Selected by Washington Redskins in seventh round (250th pick overall) of 2000 NFL draft. ... Signed by Redskins (May 19, 2000).
COLLEGE NOTES: Returned three kickoffs for 37 yards (1999).

			RECEIVING		
Year Team	G	No.	Yds.	Avg.	TD
1995—Grambling State			Redshirted.		
1996—Oklahoma State			Did not play.		
1997—Oklahoma State	3	0	0	0.0	0
1998—Oklahoma State	11	11	351	31.9	3
1999—Oklahoma State	11	32	496	15.5	3
College totals (3 years)	25	43	847	19.7	6

HUSAK, TODD — QB — REDSKINS

PERSONAL: Born July 6, 1978, in Long Beach, Calif. ... 6-3/216.
HIGH SCHOOL: St. John Bosco (Bellflower, Calif.).
COLLEGE: Stanford.
TRANSACTIONS/CAREER NOTES: Selected by Washington Redskins in sixth round (202nd pick overall) of 2000 NFL draft.

				PASSING							RUSHING				TOTALS	
Year Team	G	Att.	Cmp.	Pct.	Yds.	TD	Int.	Avg.	Rat.	Att.	Yds.	Avg.	TD	TD	Pts.
1996—Stanford	4	39	19	48.7	202	1	2	5.18	90.4	0	0	0.0	0	0	0
1997—Stanford	6	78	37	47.4	582	4	5	7.46	114.2	12	-30	-2.5	0	0	0
1998—Stanford	11	447	233	52.1	3092	17	7	6.92	119.6	48	-66	-1.4	0	0	0
1999—Stanford	10	308	176	57.1	2688	18	11	8.73	142.6	30	3	0.1	3	3	18
College totals (4 years)	31	872	465	53.3	6564	40	25	7.53	126.0	90	-93	-1.0	3	3	18

IOANE, JUNIOR — DT — RAIDERS

PERSONAL: Born July 21, 1977, in American Samoa. ... 6-4/320. ... Full name: Junior Burton Ioane.
HIGH SCHOOL: North Sanpete (Mount Pleasant, Utah).
JUNIOR COLLEGE: Snow College (Utah).
COLLEGE: Arizona State.
TRANSACTIONS/CAREER NOTES: Selected by Oakland Raiders in fourth round (107th pick overall) of 2000 NFL draft.

Year Team	G	SACKS
1996—Snow Junior College	...	0.0
1997—Snow Junior College	...	11.0
1998—Arizona State	11	4.0
1999—Arizona State	7	1.5
Junior college totals (2 years)	...	11.0
College totals (2 years)	18	5.5

ISSA, JABARI — DT/DE — CARDINALS

PERSONAL: Born April 18, 1978, in Foster City, Calif. ... 6-5/296.
HIGH SCHOOL: San Mateo (Calif.).
COLLEGE: Washington.
TRANSACTIONS/CAREER NOTES: Selected by Arizona Cardinals in sixth round (176th pick overall) of 2000 NFL draft.

Year Team	G	SACKS
1996—Washington	10	0.0
1997—Washington	11	1.0
1998—Washington	11	9.0
1999—Washington	11	2.0
College totals (4 years)	43	12.0

JACKSON, DARRELL — WR — SEAHAWKS

PERSONAL: Born December 6, 1978, in Dayton, Ohio. ... 6-0/197. ... Full name: Darrell Lamont Jackson.
HIGH SCHOOL: Tampa Catholic.
COLLEGE: Florida.
TRANSACTIONS/CAREER NOTES: Selected after junior season by Seattle Seahawks in third round (80th pick overall) of 2000 NFL draft.
COLLEGE NOTES: Rushed once for 12 yards (1998); rushed twice for 14 yards and returned eight punts for 69 yards (1999).

			RECEIVING		
Year Team	G	No.	Yds.	Avg.	TD
1997—Florida	9	4	53	13.3	1
1998—Florida	11	26	292	11.2	4
1999—Florida	12	67	1156	17.3	9
College totals (3 years)	32	97	1501	15.5	14

JACKSON, JARIOUS — QB — BRONCOS

PERSONAL: Born May 3, 1977, in Tupelo, Miss. ... 6-0/228. ... Full name: Jarious K. Jackson.
HIGH SCHOOL: Tupelo (Miss.).
COLLEGE: Notre Dame.
TRANSACTIONS/CAREER NOTES: Selected by Denver Broncos in seventh round (214th pick overall) of 2000 NFL draft.

Year Team	G	PASSING								RUSHING				TOTALS	
		Att.	Cmp.	Pct.	Yds.	TD	Int.	Avg.	Rat.	Att.	Yds.	Avg.	TD	TD	Pts.
1996—Notre Dame	6	15	10	66.7	181	3	0	12.07	234.0	11	16	1.5	0	0	0
1997—Notre Dame	9	17	8	47.1	146	1	1	8.59	126.8	8	36	4.5	3	3	18
1998—Notre Dame	10	188	104	55.3	1740	13	6	9.26	149.5	92	361	3.9	3	3	18
1999—Notre Dame	12	316	184	58.2	2753	17	14	8.71	140.3	140	464	3.3	7	7	42
College totals (4 years)	37	536	306	57.1	4820	34	21	8.99	145.7	251	877	3.5	13	13	78

JAMES, JENO   G   PANTHERS

PERSONAL: Born January 12, 1977, in Montgomery, Ala. ... 6-3/292. ... Full name: Jenorris James.
HIGH SCHOOL: Sidney Lanier (Montgomery, Ala.).
COLLEGE: Auburn.
TRANSACTIONS/CAREER NOTES: Selected by Carolina Panthers in sixth round (182nd pick overall) of 2000 NFL draft.
COLLEGE PLAYING EXPERIENCE: Auburn, 1995-1999. ... Games: 1995 (redshirted), 1996 (12), 1997 (13), 1998 (11), 1999 (11). Total: 47.

JAMISON, JOEY   WR/KR   PACKERS

PERSONAL: Born October 12, 1978, in Jacksonville. ... 5-9/170.
HIGH SCHOOL: Wolfson (Jacksonville).
COLLEGE: Texas Southern.
TRANSACTIONS/CAREER NOTES: Selected by Green Bay Packers in fifth round (151st pick overall) of 2000 NFL draft.
COLLEGE NOTES: Rushed twice for minus one yard (1998); rushed 23 times for 145 yards and one touchdown (1999).

Year Team	G	RECEIVING				PUNT RETURNS				KICKOFF RETURNS				TOTALS	
		No.	Yds.	Avg.	TD	No.	Yds.	Avg.	TD	No.	Yds.	Avg.	TD	TD	Pts.
1996—Texas Southern								Did not play.							
1997—Texas Southern	...	0	0	0.0	0	0	0	0.0	0	0	0	0.0	0	0	0
1998—Texas Southern	...	4	92	23.0	1	28	474	16.9	1	11	399	36.3	1	3	18
1999—Texas Southern	11	6	136	22.7	1	38	583	15.3	2	0	0	0.0	0	4	24
College totals (3 years)	...	10	228	22.8	2	66	1057	16.0	3	11	399	36.3	1	7	42

JANIKOWSKI, SEBASTIAN   K   RAIDERS

PERSONAL: Born March 2, 1978, in Poland. ... 6-1/255.
HIGH SCHOOL: Seabreeze (Daytona, Fla.).
COLLEGE: Florida State.
TRANSACTIONS/CAREER NOTES: Selected after junior season by Oakland Raiders in first round (17th pick overall) of 2000 NFL draft.
HONORS: Named kicker on THE SPORTING NEWS college All-America first team (1998 and 1999). ... Lou Groza Award winner (1998 and 1999).

Year Team	KICKING						
	XPM	XPA	FGM	FGA	Lg.	50+	Pts.
1997—Florida State	37	39	16	21	56	1-1	85
1998—Florida State	42	43	27	32	53	2-1	123
1999—Florida State	47	47	23	30	54	5-2	116
College totals (3 years)	126	129	66	83	56	8-4	324

JENNINGS, BRIAN   TE   49ERS

PERSONAL: Born October 14, 1976, in Mesa, Ariz. ... 6-5/238. ... Full name: Brian Lewis Jennings.
HIGH SCHOOL: Red Mountain (Mesa, Ariz.).
COLLEGE: Arizona State.
TRANSACTIONS/CAREER NOTES: Selected by San Francisco 49ers in seventh round (230th pick overall) of 2000 NFL draft.

Year Team	G	RECEIVING			
		No.	Yds.	Avg.	TD
1996—Arizona State				Did not play.	
1997—Arizona State	11	0	0	0.0	0
1998—Arizona State	10	0	0	0.0	0
1999—Arizona State	12	4	46	11.5	1
College totals (3 years)	33	4	46	11.5	1

JOHNSON, JERRY   DT   BRONCOS

PERSONAL: Born July 11, 1977, in Fort Pierce, Fla. ... 6-0/292.
HIGH SCHOOL: Central (Fort Pierce, Fla.).
COLLEGE: Florida State.
TRANSACTIONS/CAREER NOTES: Selected by Denver Broncos in fourth round (101st pick overall) of 2000 NFL draft.

Year Team	G	SACKS
1995—Florida State		Redshirted.

1996—Florida State	11	4.0
1997—Florida State	12	3.0
1998—Florida State	12	3.0
1999—Florida State	11	1.0
College totals (4 years)	46	11.0

JOHNSON, MATT G COLTS

PERSONAL: Born September 24, 1973, in Roanoke, Ind. ... 6-4/332.
HIGH SCHOOL: North Bend (Ore.).
JUNIOR COLLEGE: Ricks College (Idaho).
COLLEGE: Brigham Young.
TRANSACTIONS/CAREER NOTES: Selected by Indianapolis Colts in fifth round (138th pick overall) of 2000 NFL draft.
COLLEGE PLAYING EXPERIENCE: Ricks College, 1993 and 1996; Brigham Young, 1997-1999. ... Games: 1993 (games played unavailable), 1994 (Mormon mission), 1995 (Mormon mission), 1996 (10), 1997 (redshirted), 1998 (14), 1999 (11). Total NCAA: 25.

JONES, DHANI LB GIANTS

PERSONAL: Born February 22, 1978, in San Diego. ... 6-1/235. ... Full name: Dhani Makalani Jones.
HIGH SCHOOL: Winston Churchill (Potomac, Md.).
COLLEGE: Michigan.
TRANSACTIONS/CAREER NOTES: Selected by New York Giants in sixth round (177th pick overall) of 2000 NFL draft.
COLLEGE NOTES: Intercepted one pass for 17 yards (1997).

Year Team	G	SACKS
1996—Michigan	11	0.0
1997—Michigan	12	4.0
1998—Michigan	12	3.0
1999—Michigan	12	3.0
College totals (4 years)	47	10.0

JONES, THOMAS RB CARDINALS

PERSONAL: Born August 19, 1978, in Big Stone Gap, Va. ... 5-10/205. ... Full name: Thomas Quinn Jones.
HIGH SCHOOL: Powell Valley (Big Stone Gap, Va.).
COLLEGE: Virginia (degree in psychology, 1999).
TRANSACTIONS/CAREER NOTES: Selected by Arizona Cardinals in first round (seventh pick overall) of 2000 NFL draft.
HONORS: Named running back on THE SPORTING NEWS college All-America first team (1999).

		RUSHING				RECEIVING				PUNT RETURNS				KICKOFF RETURNS				TOTALS	
Year Team	G	Att.	Yds.	Avg.	TD	No.	Yds.	Avg.	TD	No.	Yds.	Avg.	TD	No.	Yds.	Avg.	TD	TD	Pts.
1996—Virginia	11	36	205	5.7	3	4	26	6.5	0	1	11	11.0	0	0	0	0.0	0	3	18
1997—Virginia	11	201	692	3.4	4	17	127	7.5	1	3	41	13.7	0	1	20	20.0	0	5	30
1998—Virginia	11	238	1303	5.5	13	28	179	6.4	2	1	13	13.0	0	1	27	27.0	0	15	90
1999—Virginia	11	334	1798	5.4	16	22	239	10.9	1	2	17	8.5	0	0	0	0.0	0	17	102
College totals (4 years)	44	809	3998	4.9	36	71	571	8.0	4	7	82	11.7	0	2	47	23.5	0	40	240

JORDAN, LEANDER G PANTHERS

PERSONAL: Born September 15, 1977, in Pittsburgh. ... 6-3/333.
HIGH SCHOOL: Garfield (Pittsburgh), then Peabody (Pittsburgh), then Brashear (Pittsburgh).
COLLEGE: Indiana University (Pa.).
TRANSACTIONS/CAREER NOTES: Selected by Carolina Panthers in third round (82nd pick overall) of 2000 NFL draft.
COLLEGE PLAYING EXPERIENCE: Indiana (Pa.), 1996-1999. ... Games: 1996 (11), 1997 (9), 1998 (11), 1999 (11). Total: 42.

KACYVENSKI, ISAIAH LB SEAHAWKS

PERSONAL: Born October 3, 1977, in Endicott, N.Y. ... 6-1/250. ... Name pronounced kaz-uh-VEN-skee.
HIGH SCHOOL: Union Endicott (N.Y.).
COLLEGE: Harvard.
TRANSACTIONS/CAREER NOTES: Selected by Seattle Seahawks in fourth round (119th pick overall) of 2000 NFL draft.

		INTERCEPTIONS				SACKS
Year Team	G	No.	Yds.	Avg.	TD	No.
1996—Harvard	10	4	0	0.0	0	0.0
1997—Harvard	10	0	0	0.0	0	1.5
1998—Harvard	10	2	0	0.0	0	1.0
1999—Harvard	10	5	52	10.4	0	2.0
College totals (4 years)	40	11	52	4.7	0	4.5

KEATON, CURTIS RB BENGALS

PERSONAL: Born October 18, 1976, in Columbus, Ohio. ... 5-10/210. ... Full name: Curtis Isaiah Keaton.
HIGH SCHOOL: Beechcroft (Columbus, Ohio).
COLLEGE: West Virginia, then James Madison.

TRANSACTIONS/CAREER NOTES: Selected by Cincinnati Bengals in fourth round (97th pick overall) of 2000 NFL draft.
COLLEGE NOTES: Returned nine kickoffs for 179 yards (1997); returned nine kickoffs for 242 yards (1999).

Year Team	G	RUSHING				RECEIVING				TOTALS	
		Att.	Yds.	Avg.	TD	No.	Yds.	Avg.	TD	TD	Pts.
1995—West Virginia	7	28	136	4.9	0	0	0	0.0	0	0	0
1996—West Virginia					Medical redshirt.						
1997—West Virginia	12	60	268	4.5	3	0	0	0.0	0	3	18
1998—James Madison	11	223	1064	4.8	10	10	32	3.2	0	10	60
1999—James Madison	12	314	1719	5.5	20	7	63	9.0	1	21	126
College totals (4 years)	42	625	3187	5.1	33	17	95	5.6	1	34	204

KEITH, JOHN · S · 49ERS

PERSONAL: Born February 4, 1977, in Newman, Ga. ... 6-0/207. ... Full name: John Martin Keith.
HIGH SCHOOL: East Coweta (Ga.).
COLLEGE: Furman.
TRANSACTIONS/CAREER NOTES: Selected by San Francisco 49ers in fourth round (108th pick overall) of 2000 NFL draft.
COLLEGE NOTES: Recovered one fumble for three yards (1998).

Year Team	G	INTERCEPTIONS			
		No.	Yds.	Avg.	TD
1995—Furman			Redshirted.		
1996—Furman	13	2	0	0.0	0
1997—Furman	11	4	0	0.0	0
1998—Furman	7	2	20	10.0	0
1999—Furman	12	3	0	0.0	0
College totals (4 years)	43	11	20	1.8	0

KELLY, BEN · CB · DOLPHINS

PERSONAL: Born September 15, 1978, in Cleveland. ... 5-10/191.
HIGH SCHOOL: Mentor Lake (Cleveland).
COLLEGE: Colorado.
TRANSACTIONS/CAREER NOTES: Selected after junior season by Miami Dolphins in third round (84th pick overall) of 2000 NFL draft.
COLLEGE NOTES: Recovered two fumbles for 134 yards and two touchdowns (1999).

Year Team	G	INTERCEPTIONS				PUNT RETURNS				KICKOFF RETURNS				TOTALS	
		No.	Yds.	Avg.	TD	No.	Yds.	Avg.	TD	No.	Yds.	Avg.	TD	TD	Pts.
1996—Colorado								Redshirted.							
1997—Colorado	11	2	47	23.5	0	0	0	0.0	0	25	777	31.1	1	1	6
1998—Colorado	11	4	1	0.3	0	11	229	20.8	2	20	474	23.7	0	2	12
1999—Colorado	11	5	49	9.8	0	28	166	5.9	0	19	547	28.8	2	4	24
College totals (3 years)	33	11	97	8.8	0	39	395	10.1	2	64	1798	28.1	3	7	42

KELLY, LEWIS · G · VIKINGS

PERSONAL: Born April 21, 1977, in Lithonia, Ga. ... 6-4/272.
HIGH SCHOOL: Henderson (Lithonia, Ga.).
COLLEGE: South Carolina State.
TRANSACTIONS/CAREER NOTES: Selected by Minnesota Vikings in seventh round (248th pick overall) of 2000 NFL draft.
COLLEGE PLAYING EXPERIENCE: South Carolina State, 1995-1999. ... Games: 1995 (redshirted), 1996 (10), 1997 (11), 1998 (11), 1999 (8). Total: 40.

KENNEDY, KENOY · S · BRONCOS

PERSONAL: Born November 15, 1977, in Terrell, Texas. ... 6-1/203.
HIGH SCHOOL: Terrell (Texas).
COLLEGE: Arkansas.
TRANSACTIONS/CAREER NOTES: Selected by Denver Broncos in second round (45th pick overall) of 2000 NFL draft.
COLLEGE NOTES: Advanced lateral three yards and recovered one fumble for 12 yards (1997); credited with two sacks (1998); recovered two fumbles for 64 yards (1999).

Year Team	G	INTERCEPTIONS			
		No.	Yds.	Avg.	TD
1996—Arkansas	10	0	0	0.0	0
1997—Arkansas	11	0	0	0.0	0
1998—Arkansas	11	2	90	45.0	0
1999—Arkansas	11	3	97	32.3	0
College totals (4 years)	43	5	187	37.4	0

KINNEY, ERRON · TE · TITANS

PERSONAL: Born July 28, 1977, in Ashland, Va. ... 6-5/272. ... Full name: Erron Quincy Kinney.
HIGH SCHOOL: Patrick Henry (Ashland, Va.).
COLLEGE: Florida.
TRANSACTIONS/CAREER NOTES: Selected by Tennessee Titans in third round (68th pick overall) of 2000 NFL draft.

Year	Team	G	No.	Yds.	Avg.	TD
1995—Florida				Redshirted.		
1996—Florida		11	3	40	13.3	0
1997—Florida		11	12	162	13.5	1
1998—Florida		11	8	79	9.9	3
1999—Florida		11	16	226	14.1	1
College totals (4 years)		44	39	507	13.0	5

KITCHINGS, DESMOND — WR/KR — CHIEFS

PERSONAL: Born July 19, 1978, in Columbia, S.C. ... 5-9/175. ... Full name: Louis Desmond Kitchings.
HIGH SCHOOL: Wagener-Salley (Wagener, S.C.).
COLLEGE: Furman.
TRANSACTIONS/CAREER NOTES: Selected by Kansas City Chiefs in seventh round (208th pick overall) of 2000 NFL draft.
COLLEGE NOTES: Rushed six times for 75 yards and one touchdown (1997); rushed 12 times for 130 yards and one touchdown (1998); rushed 35 times for 361 yards and four touchdowns (1999).

Year	Team	G	RECEIVING No.	Yds.	Avg.	TD	KICKOFF RETURNS No.	Yds.	Avg.	TD	TOTALS TD	Pts.
1996—Furman		11	5	136	27.2	1	1	20	20.0	0	1	6
1997—Furman		11	30	354	11.8	3	9	266	29.6	1	5	30
1998—Furman		11	35	560	16.0	3	11	241	21.9	0	4	24
1999—Furman		11	48	911	19.0	5	15	527	35.1	3	12	72
College totals (4 years)		44	118	1961	16.6	12	36	1054	29.3	4	22	132

KLEMM, ADRIAN — OT — PATRIOTS

PERSONAL: Born May 21, 1977, in Inglewood, Calif. ... 6-3/308.
HIGH SCHOOL: Santa Monica (Calif.).
COLLEGE: Hawaii.
TRANSACTIONS/CAREER NOTES: Selected by New England Patriots in second round (46th pick overall) of 2000 NFL draft.
COLLEGE NOTES: Hawaii, 1995-1999. ... Games: 1995 (redshirted), 1996 (4), 1997 (12), 1998 (12), 1999 (12). Total: 40.

KLINE, ANDREW — G — RAMS

PERSONAL: Born October 5, 1976 ... 6-2/303. ... Full name: Andrew William Kline.
HIGH SCHOOL: Beverly Hills (Calif.).
COLLEGE: San Diego State.
TRANSACTIONS/CAREER NOTES: Selected by St. Louis Rams in seventh round (220th pick overall) of 2000 NFL draft.
COLLEGE PLAYING EXPERIENCE: San Diego State, 1995-1999. ... Games: 1995 (redshirted), 1996 (games played unavailable), 1997 (7), 1998 (11), 1999 (11).

LARRIMORE, KAREEM — CB — COWBOYS

PERSONAL: Born April 21, 1976, in Los Angeles. ... 5-11/190. ... Full name: Kareem Maktrel Larrimore.
HIGH SCHOOL: Alain Locke Senior (Los Angeles).
JUNIOR COLLEGE: Cerritos College (Calif.).
COLLEGE: West Texas A&M.
TRANSACTIONS/CAREER NOTES: Selected by Dallas Cowboys in fourth round (109th pick overall) of 2000 NFL draft.
COLLEGE NOTES: Returned one punt for 77 yards and a touchdown (1997); returned four punts for six yards (1998); returned one punt for minus one yard (1999).

Year	Team	G	INTERCEPTIONS No.	Yds.	Avg.	TD	KICKOFF RETURNS No.	Yds.	Avg.	TD	TOTALS TD	Pts.
1996—Cerritos College		5	0	0	0.0	0	0	0	0.0	0	0	0
1997—Cerritos College		10	5	65	13.0	0	0	0	0.0	0	1	6
1998—West Texas A&M		11	2	90	45.0	1	20	532	26.6	1	2	12
1999—West Texas A&M		10	5	109	21.8	1	15	318	21.2	0	1	6
Junior college totals (2 years)		15	5	65	13.0	0	0	0	0.0	0	1	6
College totals (2 years)		21	7	199	28.4	2	35	850	24.3	1	3	18

LARSON, LEIF — DT — BILLS

PERSONAL: Born April 3, 1975, in Oslo, Norway. ... 6-4/300. ... Name pronounced LIFE.
HIGH SCHOOL: St. Halluard U.G.S. (Tofte, Norway).
COLLEGE: Texas-El Paso.
TRANSACTIONS/CAREER NOTES: Selected by Buffalo Bills in sixth round (194th pick overall) of 2000 NFL draft.

Year	Team	G	SACKS
1996—Texas-El Paso		8	1.0
1997—Texas-El Paso		11	2.0
1998—Texas-El Paso		11	2.5
1999—Texas-El Paso		9	0.0
College totals (4 years)		39	5.5

LECHLER, SHANE   P   RAIDERS

PERSONAL: Born August 7, 1976, in Sealy, Texas. ... 6-2/230. ... Full name: Edward Shane Lechler.
HIGH SCHOOL: East Bernard (Texas).
COLLEGE: Texas A&M.

TRANSACTIONS/CAREER NOTES: Selected by Oakland Raiders in fifth round (142nd pick overall) of 2000 NFL draft.
HONORS: Named punter on THE SPORTING NEWS college All-America second team (1997). ... Named punter on THE SPORTING NEWS college All-America first team (1998).

Year Team	No.	Yds.	Avg.	Net Avg.	In 20	Blk.
1995—Texas A&M				Redshirted		
1996—Texas A&M	72	3074	42.7	39.6	...	...
1997—Texas A&M	56	2631	47.0	41.3	...	...
1998—Texas A&M	80	3485	43.6	39.2	...	...
1999—Texas A&M	60	2787	46.5	42.6	...	...
College totals (4 years)	268	11977	44.7	40.7	...	...

LEE, CHARLES   WR   PACKERS

PERSONAL: Born November 19, 1977, in Miami. ... 6-2/202.
HIGH SCHOOL: Homestead (Fla.).
COLLEGE: Central Florida.
TRANSACTIONS/CAREER NOTES: Selected by Green Bay Packers in seventh round (242nd pick overall) of 2000 NFL draft.

		RECEIVING			
Year Team	G	No.	Yds.	Avg.	TD
1996—Central Florida			Did not play.		
1997—Central Florida	11	29	460	15.9	6
1998—Central Florida	11	46	656	14.3	3
1999—Central Florida	11	87	1133	13.0	5
College totals (3 years)	33	162	2249	13.9	14

LEWIS, JAMAL   RB   RAVENS

PERSONAL: Born August 28, 1979, in Atlanta. ... 5-11/231. ... Full name: Jamal Lafitte Lewis.
HIGH SCHOOL: Douglass (Atlanta).
COLLEGE: Tennessee.
TRANSACTIONS/CAREER NOTES: Selected after junior season by Baltimore Ravens in first round (fifth pick overall) of 2000 NFL draft.
HONORS: Named College Football Freshman of the Year by THE SPORTING NEWS (1997).

		RUSHING				RECEIVING				TOTALS	
Year Team	G	Att.	Yds.	Avg.	TD	No.	Yds.	Avg.	TD	TD	Pts.
1997—Tennessee	12	232	1364	5.9	7	23	275	12.0	2	9	63
1998—Tennessee	4	73	497	6.8	3	1	16	16.0	1	4	24
1999—Tennessee	10	182	816	4.5	7	15	193	12.9	1	8	48
College totals (3 years)	26	487	2677	5.5	17	39	484	12.4	4	21	135

LUCAS, ANTHONY   WR   PACKERS

PERSONAL: Born November 20, 1976, in Tallulah, La. ... 6-3/192. ... Full name: Anthony Wayne Lucas.
HIGH SCHOOL: McCall (Tallulah, La.).
COLLEGE: Arkansas (degree in social work).
TRANSACTIONS/CAREER NOTES: Selected by Green Bay Packers in fourth round (114th pick overall) of 2000 NFL draft.
COLLEGE NOTES: Granted medical redshirt (1996). ... Rushed once for three yards (1997).

		RECEIVING			
Year Team	G	No.	Yds.	Avg.	TD
1995—Arkansas	11	27	526	19.5	4
1996—Arkansas	1	3	32	10.7	0
1997—Arkansas	11	27	495	18.3	4
1998—Arkansas	10	43	1004	23.3	10
1999—Arkansas	10	37	822	22.2	5
College totals (5 years)	43	137	2879	21.0	23

LYMAN, DUSTIN   TE   BEARS

PERSONAL: Born August 5, 1976, in Boulder, Colo. ... 6-4/254.
HIGH SCHOOL: Fairview (Boulder, Colo.).
COLLEGE: Wake Forest.
TRANSACTIONS/CAREER NOTES: Selected by Chicago Bears in third round (87th pick overall) of 2000 NFL draft.
COLLEGE NOTES: Intercepted one pass for 41 yards and a touchdown (1997).

Year Team	G	SACKS
1995—Wake Forest		Redshirted.

996—Wake Forest	10	1.0
997—Wake Forest	11	7.0
998—Wake Forest	5	1.0
999—Wake Forest	9	2.0
ollege totals (4 years)	35	11.0

MACKLIN, DAVID — DB — COLTS

ERSONAL: Born July 14, 1978, in Newport News, Va. ... 5-9/195. ... Full name: David Thurman Macklin.
IGH SCHOOL: Menchville (Newport News, Va.).
OLLEGE: Penn State.
RANSACTIONS/CAREER NOTES: Selected by Indianapolis Colts in third round (91st pick overall) of 2000 NFL draft.
OLLEGE NOTES: Returned two punts for 18 yards (1996).

		INTERCEPTIONS			
ear Team	G	No.	Yds.	Avg.	TD
996—Penn State	13	0	0	0.0	0
997—Penn State	11	1	0	0.0	0
998—Penn State	11	6	120	20.0	1
999—Penn State	12	1	0	0.0	0
ollege totals (4 years)	47	8	120	15.0	1

MALANO, MIKE — OL — VIKINGS

ERSONAL: Born October 16, 1976, in Delta, Colo. ... 6-2/307. ... Full name: Michael James Malano.
IGH SCHOOL: Horizon (Scottsdale, Ariz.).
OLLEGE: San Diego State.
RANSACTIONS/CAREER NOTES: Selected by Minnesota Vikings in seventh round (240th pick overall) of 2000 NFL draft.
ONORS: Named center on THE SPORTING NEWS college All-America second team (1999).
OLLEGE PLAYING EXPERIENCE: San Diego State, 1995-1999. ... Games: 1995 (redshirted), 1996 (11), 1997 (11), 1998 (11), 1999 (11).
otal: 44.

MALBROUGH, ANTHONY — DB — BROWNS

ERSONAL: Born December 9, 1976, in Beaumont, Texas. ... 5-8/178.
IGH SCHOOL: Westbrook (Texas).
OLLEGE: Texas Tech.
RANSACTIONS/CAREER NOTES: Selected by Cleveland Browns in fifth round (130th pick overall) of 2000 NFL draft.
OLLEGE NOTES: Played running back (1997). ... Rushed eight times for 37 yards (1997).

		INTERCEPTIONS			
Year Team	G	No.	Yds.	Avg.	TD
1995—Texas Tech		Did not play.			
1996—Texas Tech		Redshirted.			
1997—Texas Tech	5	0	0	0.0	0
1998—Texas Tech	11	1	0	0.0	0
1999—Texas Tech	11	1	3	3.0	0
College totals (3 years)	27	2	3	1.5	0

MARRIOTT, JEFF — DT — PATRIOTS

PERSONAL: Born March 3, 1977, in Chillicothe, Mo. ... 6-4/301.
HIGH SCHOOL: Chillicothe (Mo.).
COLLEGE: Missouri.
TRANSACTIONS/CAREER NOTES: Selected by New England Patriots in fifth round (161st pick overall) of 2000 NFL draft.

Year Team	G	SACKS
1995—Missouri		Redshirted.
1996—Missouri	11	1.0
1997—Missouri	11	0.0
1998—Missouri	11	2.0
1999—Missouri	11	4.0
College totals (4 years)	44	7.0

MARTIN, TEE — QB — STEELERS

PERSONAL: Born July 25, 1978, in Mobile, Ala. ... 6-1/221. ... Full name: Tamaurice Nigel Martin.
HIGH SCHOOL: Williamson (Mobile, Ala.).
COLLEGE: Tennessee.
TRANSACTIONS/CAREER NOTES: Selected by Pittsburgh Steelers in fifth round (163rd pick overall) of 2000 NFL draft.

		PASSING								RUSHING				TOTALS	
Year Team	G	Att.	Cmp.	Pct.	Yds.	TD	Int.	Avg.	Rat.	Att.	Yds.	Avg.	TD	TD	Pts.
1996—Tennessee	5	4	2	50.0	24	0	0	6.00	100.4	12	14	1.2	0	0	0
1997—Tennessee	5	12	6	50.0	87	1	1	7.25	121.7	8	-4	-0.5	0	0	0
1998—Tennessee	12	267	153	57.3	2164	19	6	8.10	144.4	103	287	2.8	7	7	42
1999—Tennessee	11	305	165	54.1	2317	12	9	7.60	125.0	81	317	3.9	9	9	54
College totals (4 years)	33	588	326	55.4	4592	32	16	7.81	133.6	204	614	3.0	16	16	96

McCASLIN, EUGENE   LB   PACKERS

PERSONAL: Born July 12, 1977, in Tampa. ... 6-1/221. ... Full name: Eugene William McCaslin Jr.
HIGH SCHOOL: Chamberlain (Tampa).
COLLEGE: Florida.
TRANSACTIONS/CAREER NOTES: Selected by Green Bay Packers in seventh round (249th pick overall) of 2000 NFL draft.
COLLEGE NOTES: Played running back (1996-1998). ... Rushed 41 times for 290 yards and four touchdowns and caught two passes for 24 yards (1996); rushed 24 times for 93 yards and one touchdown and caught three passes for 34 yards (1997); rushed 69 times for 321 yards and one touchdown and caught four passes for 29 yards (1998); credited with six sacks (1999).
COLLEGE PLAYING EXPERIENCE: Florida, 1995-1999. ... Games: 1995 (redshirted), 1996 (9), 1997 (9), 1998 (8), 1999 (11). Total: 37.

McDOUGLE, STOCKAR   G   LIONS

PERSONAL: Born January 11, 1977, in Deerfield Beach, Fla. ... 6-6/350.
HIGH SCHOOL: Deerfield Beach (Fla.).
JUNIOR COLLEGE: Navarro College (Texas).
COLLEGE: Oklahoma.
TRANSACTIONS/CAREER NOTES: Selected by Detroit Lions in first round (20th pick overall) of 2000 NFL draft.
COLLEGE PLAYING EXPERIENCE: Navarro College, 1996 and 1997; Oklahoma 1998 and 1999. ... Games: 1996 (games played unavailable), 1997 (games played unavailable), 1998 (11), 1999 (12). Total NCAA: 23.

McINTOSH, CHRIS   OT   SEAHAWKS

PERSONAL: Born February 20, 1977, in Pewaukee, Wis. ... 6-6/315.
HIGH SCHOOL: Pewaukee (Wis.).
COLLEGE: Wisconsin.
TRANSACTIONS/CAREER NOTES: Selected by Seattle Seahawks in first round (22nd pick overall) of 2000 NFL draft.
HONORS: Named offensive tackle on THE SPORTING NEWS college All-America first team (1999).
COLLEGE NOTES: Wisconsin, 1995-1999. ... Games: 1995 (redshirted), 1996 (13), 1997 (13), 1998 (12), 1999 (12). Total: 50.

McINTOSH, DAMION   OT   CHARGERS

PERSONAL: Born March 25, 1977, in Kingston, Jamaica. ... 6-4/325.
HIGH SCHOOL: McArthur (Hollywood, Fla.).
COLLEGE: Kansas State.
TRANSACTIONS/CAREER NOTES: Selected by San Diego Chargers in third round (83rd pick overall) of 2000 NFL draft.
COLLEGE PLAYING EXPERIENCE: Kansas State, 1995-1999. ... Games: 1995 (redshirted), 1996 (9), 1997 (10), 1998 (12), 1999 (11). ... Played defensive tackle and offensive tackle (1996-1998). ... Credited with two sacks (1996); credited with 4 1/2 sacks (1997); credited with one sack and recovered three fumbles (1998).

McKINLEY, ALVIN   DT   PANTHERS

PERSONAL: Born June 9, 1978, in Kosciusko, Miss. ... 6-3/292. ... Full name: Alvin Jerome McKinley.
HIGH SCHOOL: Weir (Miss.).
JUNIOR COLLEGE: Holmes Junior College (Miss.).
COLLEGE: Mississippi State.
TRANSACTIONS/CAREER NOTES: Selected by Carolina Panthers in fourth round (120th pick overall) of 2000 NFL draft.

Year—Team	G	SACKS
1996—Holmes JC	11	2.0
1997—Holmes JC	10	1.0
1998—Mississippi State	12	0.0
1999—Mississippi State	11	2.0
Junior college totals (2 years)	21	3.0
College totals (2 years)	23	2.0

MEALEY, RONDELL   RB   PACKERS

PERSONAL: Born February 24, 1977, in New Orleans. ... 6-0/206.
HIGH SCHOOL: Destrehan (La.).
COLLEGE: Louisiana State.
TRANSACTIONS/CAREER NOTES: Selected by Green Bay Packers in seventh round (252nd pick overall) of 2000 NFL draft.

		RUSHING				RECEIVING				KICKOFF RETURNS				TOTALS	
Year—Team	G	Att.	Yds.	Avg.	TD	No.	Yds.	Avg.	TD	No.	Yds.	Avg.	TD	TD	Pts.
1995—Louisiana State					Redshirted.										
1996—Louisiana State	11	103	603	5.9	10	8	86	10.8	1	12	260	21.7	0	11	66
1997—Louisiana State	11	112	664	5.9	7	7	60	8.6	0	6	107	17.8	0	7	42
1998—Louisiana State	11	68	334	4.9	4	2	9	4.5	2	11	273	24.8	0	6	36
1999—Louisiana State	11	170	637	3.7	8	16	147	9.2	1	0	0	0.0	0	9	54
College totals (4 years)	44	453	2238	4.9	29	33	302	9.2	4	29	640	22.1	0	33	198

MEESTER, BRAD — G/C — JAGUARS

PERSONAL: Born March 23, 1977, in Parkersburg, Iowa. ... 6-3/298.
HIGH SCHOOL: Aplington-Parkersburg (Aplington, Iowa).
COLLEGE: Northern Iowa.
TRANSACTIONS/CAREER NOTES: Selected by Jacksonville Jaguars in second round (60th pick overall) of 2000 NFL draft. ... Signed by Jaguars (May 16, 2000).
COLLEGE PLAYING EXPERIENCE: Northern Iowa, 1995-1999. ... Games: 1995 (reshirted), 1996 (14), 1997 (11), 1998 (11), 1999 (11). Total: 47.

MEIER, ROB — DE — JAGUARS

PERSONAL: Born August 29, 1977, in West Vancouver, B.C. ... 6-5/282. ... Full name: Robert Jack Daniel Meier.
HIGH SCHOOL: Sentinel (West Vancouver, B.C.).
COLLEGE: Washington State.
TRANSACTIONS/CAREER NOTES: Selected by Jacksonville Jaguars in seventh round (241st pick overall) of 2000 NFL draft. ... Signed by Jaguars (May 17, 2000).

Year Team	G	SACKS
1995—Washington State	Redshirted.	
1996—Washington State	11	0.0
1997—Washington State	12	0.0
1998—Washington State	11	2.0
1999—Washington State	11	2.0
College totals (4 years)	45	4.0

MERCIER, RICHARD — G — RAVENS

PERSONAL: Born May 13, 1975, in Montreal. ... 6-3/295. ... Full name: Richard Marc Mercier.
HIGH SCHOOL: Vanier (Quebec).
COLLEGE: Miami (Fla.).
TRANSACTIONS/CAREER NOTES: Selected by Baltimore Ravens in fifth round (148th pick overall) of 2000 NFL draft.
HONORS: Named guard on THE SPORTING NEWS college All-America first team (1999).
COLLEGE PLAYING EXPERIENCE: Miami, Fla., 1995-1999. ... Games: 1995 (10), 1996 (12), 1997 (medical redshirt), 1998 (11), 1999 (11). Total: 44.

MIDGET, ANTHONY — CB — FALCONS

PERSONAL: Born February 22, 1978, in Clewiston, Fla. ... 5-11/193. ... Full name: Anthony Queen Midget.
HIGH SCHOOL: Clewiston (Fla.).
COLLEGE: Virginia Tech.
TRANSACTIONS/CAREER NOTES: Selected by Atlanta Falcons in fifth round (134th pick overall) of 2000 NFL draft. ... Signed by Falcons (May 9, 2000).
COLLEGE NOTES: Credited with one sack and intercepted one pass (1996); intercepted four passes for five yards (1999).
COLLEGE PLAYING EXPERIENCE: Virginia Tech, 1996-1999. ... Games: 1996 (11), 1997 (10), 1998 (11), 1999 (11). Total: 44.

MILEM, JOHN — DE — 49ERS

PERSONAL: Born June 9, 1975, in Concord, N.C. ... 6-7/290.
HIGH SCHOOL: Rowan College (Salisbury, N.C.).
COLLEGE: Lenoir-Rhyne College (N.C.).
TRANSACTIONS/CAREER NOTES: Selected by San Francisco 49ers in fifth round (150th pick overall) of 2000 NFL draft.

Year Team	G	SACKS
1997—Lenoir-Rhyne College	11	2.0
1998—Lenoir-Rhyne College	Redshirted.	
1999—Lenoir-Rhyne College	11	14.0
College totals (2 years)	22	16.0

MOORE, COREY — LB — BILLS

PERSONAL: Born March 20, 1977, in Brownsville, Tenn. ... 5-11/213. ... Full name: Corey Antonio Moore.
HIGH SCHOOL: Haywood (Brownsville, Tenn.).
JUNIOR COLLEGE: Holmes Junior College (Miss.).
COLLEGE: Virginia Tech.
TRANSACTIONS/CAREER NOTES: Selected by Buffalo Bills in third round (89th pick overall) of 2000 NFL draft.
HONORS: Named defensive end on THE SPORTING NEWS college All-America second team (1998). ... Lombardi Award winner (1999). ... Bronko Nagurski Award winner (1999). ... Named defensive end on THE SPORTING NEWS college All-America first team (1999).
COLLEGE NOTES: Recovered two fumbles for 27 yards and one touchdown (1995); recovered one fumble for two yards (1998); recovered one fumble for 32 yards (1999).

Year Team	G	SACKS
1995—Holmes JC	10	4.0
1996—Virginia Tech	Redshirted.	

1997—Virginia Tech	11	4.5
1998—Virginia Tech	11	13.5
1999—Virginia Tech	11	17.0
Junior college totals (1 year)	10	4.0
College totals (3 years)	33	35.0

MOORE, MICHAEL　　　　　G　　　　　REDSKINS

PERSONAL: Born November 1, 1976, in Fayette, Ark. ... 6-3/320.
HIGH SCHOOL: Fayette (Ark.) County.
COLLEGE: Alabama, then Troy (Ala.) State.
TRANSACTIONS/CAREER NOTES: Selected by Washington Redskins in fourth round (129th pick overall) of 2000 NFL draft.
COLLEGE PLAYING EXPERIENCE: Alabama, 1995-1998. Troy State, 1999. ... Games: 1995 (redshirted), 1996 (6), 1997 (11), 1998 (5), 1999 (11). Total: 33.

MOORE, MUNEER　　　　　WR　　　　　BRONCOS

PERSONAL: Born March 15, 1977, in Yonkers, N.Y. ... 6-1/200.
HIGH SCHOOL: Northampton (Eastville, Va.).
COLLEGE: Richmond.
TRANSACTIONS/CAREER NOTES: Selected by Denver Broncos in fifth round (154th pick overall) of 2000 NFL draft.

		RECEIVING			
Year　Team	G	No.	Yds.	Avg.	TD
1995—Richmond			Redshirted.		
1996—Richmond	11	22	337	15.3	3
1997—Richmond	11	29	326	11.2	1
1998—Richmond	12	41	613	15.0	1
1999—Richmond	11	52	769	14.8	7
College totals (4 years)	45	144	2045	14.2	12

MOORE, RON　　　　　DT　　　　　PACKERS

PERSONAL: Born August 10, 1977, in Sanford, Fla. ... 6-2/316. ... Full name: Ronald Moore.
JUNIOR COLLEGE: Hinds Community College (Miss.).
COLLEGE: Northwestern Oklahoma State.
TRANSACTIONS/CAREER NOTES: Selected by Green Bay Packers in seventh round (229th pick overall) of 2000 NFL draft.

Year　Team	G	SACKS
1996—Hinds CC	...	3.0
1997—Hinds CC	...	3.0
1998—Northwestern Oklahoma State	10	9.0
1999—Northwestern Oklahoma State	9	5.0
Junior college totals (2 years)	...	6.0
College totals (2 years)	19	14.0

MOREAU, FRANK　　　　　RB　　　　　CHIEFS

PERSONAL: Born September 9, 1976, in Elizabethtown, Ky. ... 6-0/224.
HIGH SCHOOL: Central Hardin (Elizabethtown, Ky.).
COLLEGE: Louisville (degree in justice administration).
TRANSACTIONS/CAREER NOTES: Selected by Kansas City Chiefs in fourth round (115th pick overall) of 2000 NFL draft.
COLLEGE NOTES: Granted medical redshirt (1996).

		RUSHING				RECEIVING				TOTALS	
Year　Team	G	Att.	Yds.	Avg.	TD	No.	Yds.	Avg.	TD	TD	Pts.
1995—Louisville	6	96	416	4.3	2	0	0	0.0	0	2	12
1996—Louisville	1	7	14	2.0	0	1	0	0.0	0	0	0
1997—Louisville	11	120	573	4.8	5	10	45	4.5	0	5	30
1998—Louisville	11	43	307	7.1	3	5	39	7.8	0	3	18
1999—Louisville	10	233	1289	5.5	17	38	285	7.5	0	17	102
College totals (5 years)	39	499	2599	5.2	27	54	369	6.8	0	27	162

MORRIS, ARIC　　　　　S　　　　　TITANS

PERSONAL: Born July 22, 1977, in Oak Park, Mich. ... 5-10/208.
HIGH SCHOOL: Berkley (Mich.).
COLLEGE: Michigan State.
TRANSACTIONS/CAREER NOTES: Selected by Tennessee Titans in fifth round (135th pick overall) of 2000 NFL draft.
COLLEGE NOTES: Recovered one fumble and returned four kickoffs for 50 yards (1996); recovered one fumble (1997); recovered two fumbles and rushed once for 21 yards (1998).

		INTERCEPTIONS			
Year　Team	G	No.	Yds.	Avg.	TD
1996—Michigan State	11	0	0	0.0	0
1997—Michigan State	12	1	18	18.0	0
1998—Michigan State	12	3	9	3.0	0
1999—Michigan State	12	2	93	46.5	1

College totals (4 years) 47 6 120 20.0 1

MORRIS, ROB — LB — COLTS

PERSONAL: Born January 18, 1975, in Nampa, Idaho. ... 6-2/250.
HIGH SCHOOL: Nampa (Idaho).
COLLEGE: Brigham Young.
TRANSACTIONS/CAREER NOTES: Selected by Indianapolis Colts in first round (28th pick overall) of 2000 NFL draft.
HONORS: Named linebacker on THE SPORTING NEWS college All-America second team (1999).
COLLEGE NOTES: Played fullback and linebacker (1993). ... Caught one pass for 27 yards (1993); intercepted one pass for 51 yards and a touchdown (1998).

Year Team	G	SACKS
1993—Brigham Young	...	0.0
1994—Brigham Young	Mormon mission.	
1995—Brigham Young	Mormon mission.	
1996—Brigham Young	Redshirted.	
1997—Brigham Young	...	1.0
1998—Brigham Young	14	6.0
1999—Brigham Young	7	6.0
College totals (4 years)	...	13.0

MORRIS, SAMMY — RB — BILLS

PERSONAL: Born March 23, 1977, in San Antonio. ... 6-0/228.
HIGH SCHOOL: John Jay (San Antonio).
COLLEGE: Texas Tech.
TRANSACTIONS/CAREER NOTES: Selected by Buffalo Bills in fifth round (156th pick overall) of 2000 NFL draft.

		RUSHING				RECEIVING				TOTALS	
Year Team	G	Att.	Yds.	Avg.	TD	No.	Yds.	Avg.	TD	TD	Pts.
1995—Texas Tech						Redshirted.					
1996—Texas Tech	8	29	226	7.8	4	13	221	17.0	2	6	36
1997—Texas Tech						Did not play.					
1998—Texas Tech						Did not play.					
1999—Texas Tech	9	140	562	4.0	3	23	386	16.8	2	5	30
College totals (2 years)	17	169	788	4.7	7	36	607	16.9	4	11	66

MORRIS, SYLVESTER — WR — CHIEFS

PERSONAL: Born October 6, 1977, in New Orleans. ... 6-3/208.
HIGH SCHOOL: McDonogh (New Orleans).
COLLEGE: Jackson State.
TRANSACTIONS/CAREER NOTES: Selected by Kansas City Chiefs in first round (21st pick overall) of 2000 NFL draft.
COLLEGE NOTES: Rushed twice for 33 yards (1998); rushed five times for 100 yards and two touchdowns (1999).

		RECEIVING			
Year Team	G	No.	Yds.	Avg.	TD
1995—Jackson State		Redshirted.			
1996—Jackson State	8	4	52	13.0	0
1997—Jackson State	11	46	739	16.1	4
1998—Jackson State	11	62	1258	20.3	17
1999—Jackson State	11	63	1139	18.1	13
College totals (4 years)	41	175	3188	18.2	34

MORTON, CHAD — RB — SAINTS

PERSONAL: Born April 4, 1977, in Torrance, Calif. ... 5-8/186. ... Brother of Johnnie Morton, wide receiver, Detroit Lions; and half brother of Michael Morton, running back with Tampa Bay Buccaneers (1982-84), Washington Redskins (1985) and Seattle Seahawks (1987).
HIGH SCHOOL: South Torrance (Calif.).
COLLEGE: Southern California.
TRANSACTIONS/CAREER NOTES: Selected by New Orleans Saints in fifth round (166th pick overall) of 2000 NFL draft.
COLLEGE NOTES: Played cornerback and running back (1996 and 1997). ... Intercepted two passes for 32 yards and credited with one sack (1997).

		RUSHING				RECEIVING				PUNT RETURNS				KICKOFF RETURNS				TOTALS	
Year Team	G	Att.	Yds.	Avg.	TD	No.	Yds.	Avg.	TD	No.	Yds.	Avg.	TD	No.	Yds.	Avg.	TD	TD	Pts.
1995—Southern California							Redshirted.												
1996—Southern California	12	26	171	6.6	2	2	24	12.0	0	16	149	9.3	0	0	0	0.0	0	2	12
1997—Southern California	11	30	214	7.1	1	1	17	17.0	0	21	168	8.0	0	0	0	0.0	0	1	6
1998—Southern California	11	199	985	4.9	6	181	136	0.8	1	4	21	5.3	0	2	116	58.0	1	8	48
1999—Southern California	12	262	1141	4.4	15	17	79	4.6	0	7	52	7.4	0	19	341	17.9	0	15	90
College totals (4 years)	46	517	2511	4.9	24	201	256	1.3	1	48	390	8.1	0	21	457	21.8	1	26	156

MURPHY, FRANK — RB — BEARS

PERSONAL: Born February 11, 1977, in Callahan, Fla. ... 6-0/206.
HIGH SCHOOL: West Nassau (Callahan, Fla.).

JUNIOR COLLEGE: Itawamba Community College (Miss.), then Garden City (Kan.) Commmunity College.
COLLEGE: Kansas State.
TRANSACTIONS/CAREER NOTES: Selected by Chicago Bears in sixth round (170th pick overall) of 2000 NFL draft.

Year Team	G	RUSHING				RECEIVING				KICKOFF RETURNS				TOTALS	
		Att.	Yds.	Avg.	TD	No.	Yds.	Avg.	TD	No.	Yds.	Avg.	TD	TD	Pts.
1995—Itawamba CC							Statistics unavailable.								
1996—							Did not play.								
1997—Garden City CC	10	210	1370	6.5	26	17	266	15.6	4	0	0	0.0	0	30	180
1998—Kansas State	8	55	257	4.7	5	3	91	30.3	1	8	210	26.3	0	6	30
1999—Kansas State	7	97	541	5.6	6	6	39	6.5	0	7	199	28.4	0	6	36
Junior college totals (1 year)	10	210	1370	6.5	26	17	266	15.6	4	0	0	0.0	0	30	180
College totals (2 years)	15	152	798	5.3	11	9	130	14.4	1	15	409	27.3	0	12	66

MYERS, BOBBY　　　　　S　　　　　TITANS

PERSONAL: Born October 11, 1976, in Hamden, Conn. ... 6-1/189.
HIGH SCHOOL: Hamden (Conn.).
COLLEGE: Wisconsin.
TRANSACTIONS/CAREER NOTES: Selected by Tennessee Titans in fourth round (124th pick overall) of 2000 NFL draft.
COLLEGE NOTES: Credited with two sacks (1998); credited with two sacks (1999).

Year Team	G	INTERCEPTIONS			
		No.	Yds.	Avg.	TD
1995—Wisconsin			Redshirted.		
1996—Wisconsin	9	0	0	0.0	0
1997—Wisconsin	13	1	0	0.0	0
1998—Wisconsin	12	2	0	0.0	0
1999—Wisconsin	12	4	54	13.5	0
College totals (4 years)	46	7	54	7.7	0

NOA, KAULANA　　　　　OT　　　　　RAMS

PERSONAL: Born December 29, 1976, in Honokaa, Hawaii. ... 6-3/307.
HIGH SCHOOL: Honokaa (Hawaii).
COLLEGE: Hawaii.
TRANSACTIONS/CAREER NOTES: Selected by St. Louis Rams in fourth round (104th pick overall) of 2000 NFL draft.
COLLEGE PLAYING EXPERIENCE: Hawaii, 1995-1999. ... Games: 1995 (redshirted), 1996 (12), 1997 (12), 1998 (12), 1999 (12). Total: 48.

NORTHCUTT, DENNIS　　　　　WR　　　　　BROWNS

PERSONAL: Born December 22, 1977, in Los Angeles. ... 5-10/167.
HIGH SCHOOL: Dorsey (Los Angeles).
COLLEGE: Arizona.
TRANSACTIONS/CAREER NOTES: Selected by Cleveland Browns in second round (32nd pick overall) of 2000 NFL draft.
HONORS: Named wide receiver on THE SPORTING NEWS college All-America second team (1999).
COLLEGE NOTES: Played wide receiver and cornerback (1996). ... Intercepted two passes for 62 yards and rushed five times for eight yards (1996); rushed eight times for 130 yards and one touchdown (1997); rushed 10 times for 54 yards (1998); rushed 14 times for 200 yards and one touchdown (1999).

Year Team	G	RECEIVING				PUNT RETURNS				KICKOFF RETURNS				TOTALS	
		No.	Yds.	Avg.	TD	No.	Yds.	Avg.	TD	No.	Yds.	Avg.	TD	TD	Pts.
1995—Arizona								Redshirted.							
1996—Arizona	11	8	75	9.4	1	4	32	8.0	0	1	23	23.0	0	1	6
1997—Arizona	12	60	786	13.1	9	3	6	2.0	0	12	280	23.3	0	10	60
1998—Arizona	13	67	969	14.5	6	41	461	11.2	0	13	256	19.7	0	6	36
1999—Arizona	12	88	1422	16.2	8	23	436	19.0	2	9	191	21.2	0	11	66
College totals (4 years)	48	223	3252	14.6	24	71	935	13.2	2	35	750	21.4	0	28	168

NUGENT, DAVID　　　　　DL　　　　　PATRIOTS

PERSONAL: Born October 27, 1975, in Collierville, Tenn. ... 6-4/303. ... Full name: David Michael Nugent.
HIGH SCHOOL: Germantown (Tenn.).
COLLEGE: Purdue.
TRANSACTIONS/CAREER NOTES: Selected by New England Patriots in sixth round (201st pick overall) of 2000 NFL draft.
COLLEGE NOTES: Intercepted one pass (1997); credited with one sack (1998); credited with two sacks and recovered one fumble for 12 yards and a touchdown (1999).
COLLEGE PLAYING EXPERIENCE: Purdue, 1996-1999. ... Games: 1996 (9), 1997 (12), 1998 (13), 1999 (11). Total: 45.

O'NEAL, DELTHA　　　　　CB　　　　　BRONCOS

PERSONAL: Born January 30, 1977, in Stanford, Calif. ... 5-10/196. ... Full name: Deltha Lee O'Neal III.
HIGH SCHOOL: West (Milpitas, Calif.).
COLLEGE: California.
TRANSACTIONS/CAREER NOTES: Selected by Denver Broncos in first round (15th pick overall) of 2000 NFL draft.

HONORS: Named kick returner on THE SPORTING NEWS college All-America first team (1999). ... Named cornerback on THE SPORTING NEWS college All-America second team (1999).
COLLEGE NOTES: Played running back (1996 and 1997). ... Rushed 102 times for 496 yards and one touchdown and caught six passes for 60 yards and one touchdown (1996); rushed 36 times for 172 yards and one touchdown and caught 18 passes for 223 yards and one touchdown (1997); rushed twice for eight yards and caught five passes for 52 yards (1998); rushed once for minus three yards (1999).

Year Team	G	INTERCEPTIONS				PUNT RETURNS				KICKOFF RETURNS				TOTALS	
		No.	Yds.	Avg.	TD	No.	Yds.	Avg.	TD	No.	Yds.	Avg.	TD	TD	Pts.
1995—California								Did not play.							
1996—California	12	0	0	0.0	0	5	38	7.6	0	28	647	23.1	1	3	18
1997—California	11	0	0	0.0	0	25	256	10.2	0	30	646	21.5	0	2	12
1998—California	11	2	76	38.0	1	38	447	11.8	0	22	624	28.4	0	1	6
1999—California	11	9	280	31.1	4	42	428	10.2	1	19	555	29.2	1	5	30
College totals (4 years)	45	11	356	32.4	5	110	1169	10.6	1	99	2472	25.0	2	11	66

OLSON, ERIK   S   JAGUARS

PERSONAL: Born January 4, 1977, in Ventura, Calif. ... 6-1/215. ... Full name: Erik James Olson.
HIGH SCHOOL: Ventura (Calif.).
COLLEGE: Colorado State.
TRANSACTIONS/CAREER NOTES: Selected by Jacksonville Jaguars in seventh round (236th pick overall) of 2000 NFL draft. ... Signed by Jaguars (May 19, 2000).

Year Team	G	INTERCEPTIONS				SACKS
		No.	Yds.	Avg.	TD	No.
1995—Colorado State				Redshirted.		
1996—Colorado State	12	3	0	0.0	0	0.0
1997—Colorado State	12	1	20	20.0	0	0.0
1998—Colorado State	10	1	0	0.0	0	1.0
1999—Colorado State	9	6	93	15.5	1	0.0
College totals (4 years)	43	11	113	10.3	1	1.0

PARKER, JEREMIAH   DE   GIANTS

PERSONAL: Born November 15, 1977, in Franklin, La. ... 6-5/275.
HIGH SCHOOL: DeAnza (Richmond, Va.).
COLLEGE: California.
TRANSACTIONS/CAREER NOTES: Selected by New York Giants in seventh round (217th pick overall) of 2000 NFL draft.
COLLEGE NOTES: Recovered one fumble (1999).

Year Team	G	SACKS
1996—California	7	0.0
1997—California	10	1.0
1998—California	11	2.0
1999—California	11	4.5
College totals (4 years)	39	7.5

PASS, PATRICK   RB   PATRIOTS

PERSONAL: Born December 31, 1977, in Tucker, Ga. ... 5-10/208.
HIGH SCHOOL: Tucker (Ga.).
COLLEGE: Georgia.
TRANSACTIONS/CAREER NOTES: Selected by New England Patriots in seventh round (239th pick overall) of 2000 NFL draft.
COLLEGE NOTES: Returned 10 kickoffs for 217 yards (1999).
MISCELLANEOUS: Selected by Florida Marlins organization in 44th round of free-agent draft (June 4, 1996).

Year Team	G	RUSHING				RECEIVING				TOTALS	
		Att.	Yds.	Avg.	TD	No.	Yds.	Avg.	TD	TD	Pts.
1996—Georgia	10	69	354	5.1	2	4	10	2.5	0	2	12
1997—Georgia	11	64	232	3.6	1	12	175	14.6	1	2	12
1998—Georgia	9	26	101	3.9	0	0	0	0.0	0	0	0
1999—Georgia	11	62	335	5.4	2	19	250	13.2	1	3	18
College totals (4 years)	41	221	1022	4.6	5	35	435	12.4	2	7	42

RECORD AS BASEBALL PLAYER

TRANSACTIONS/CAREER NOTES: Selected by Florida Marlins organization in 44th round of free-agent draft (June 4, 1996).

Year Team (League)	Pos.	G	AB	R	H	2B	3B	HR	RBI	Avg.	BB	SO	SB	PO	A	E	Avg.
1996— GC Marlins (GCL)	OF	29	90	14	22	4	0	0	8	.244	15	27	5	27	0	2	.931

PENNINGTON, CHAD   QB   JETS

PERSONAL: Born June 26, 1976, in Knoxville, Tenn. ... 6-3/229. ... Full name: James Chad Pennington.
HIGH SCHOOL: Webb (Knoxville, Tenn.).
COLLEGE: Marshall.
TRANSACTIONS/CAREER NOTES: Selected by New York Jets in first round (18th pick overall) of 2000 NFL draft.

2000 DRAFT PICKS

Year—Team	G	Att.	Cmp.	Pct.	PASSING Yds.	TD	Int.	Avg.	Rat.	RUSHING Att.	Yds.	Avg.	TD	TOTALS TD	Pts.
1995—Marshall	14	354	219	61.9	2445	15	15	6.91	125.4	68	-113	-1.7	0	0	0
1996—Marshall							Did not play.								
1997—Marshall	13	469	276	58.8	3817	42	12	8.14	151.6	57	-50	-0.9	1	1	6
1998—Marshall	13	456	297	65.1	3830	28	7	8.40	152.9	55	8	0.1	1	1	6
1999—Marshall	13	433	292	67.4	4006	38	12	9.25	168.6	64	93	1.5	2	2	12
College totals (4 years)	53	1712	1084	63.3	14098	123	46	8.23	150.8	244	-62	-0.3	4	4	24

PETERSON, JULIAN — LB — 49ERS

PERSONAL: Born July 28, 1978, in Hillcrest Heights, Md. ... 6-3/235.
HIGH SCHOOL: Crossland (Temple Hills, Md.).
JUNIOR COLLEGE: Valley Forge Junior College (Pa.).
COLLEGE: Michigan State.
TRANSACTIONS/CAREER NOTES: Selected by San Francisco 49ers in first round (16th pick overall) of 2000 NFL draft.
COLLEGE NOTES: Recovered two fumbles for 40 yards and one touchdown and intercepted one pass for 23 yards and a touchdown (1998).

Year—Team	G	SACKS
1996—Valley Forge J.C.	...	19.5
1997—Valley Forge J.C.	...	20.5
1998—Michigan State	12	10.0
1999—Michigan State	12	15.0
Junior college totals (2 years)	...	40.0
College totals (2 years)	24	25.0

PHILYAW, MARENO — WR — FALCONS

PERSONAL: Born December 19, 1977, in Atlanta. ... 6-2/208.
HIGH SCHOOL: North Clayton (College Park, Ga.).
COLLEGE: Troy (Ala.) State.
TRANSACTIONS/CAREER NOTES: Selected by Atlanta Falcons in sixth round (172nd pick overall) of 2000 NFL draft. ... Signed by Falcons (May 23, 2000).
COLLEGE NOTES: Played quarterback and running back (1997). ... Attempted 39 passes with 13 completions for 146 yards and one interception (1997); returned one punt for eight yards (1999).

Year—Team	G	RUSHING Att.	Yds.	Avg.	TD	RECEIVING No.	Yds.	Avg.	TD	KICKOFF RETURNS No.	Yds.	Avg.	TD	TOTALS TD	Pts.
1996—Troy State	11	3	104	34.7	1	3	42	14.0	0	1	13	13.0	0	1	6
1997—Troy State	11	97	459	4.7	4	0	0	0.0	0	0	0	0.0	0	4	24
1998—Troy State	11	4	39	9.8	1	18	343	19.1	3	16	432	27.0	0	4	24
1999—Troy State	11	9	122	13.6	3	32	632	19.8	4	16	371	23.2	0	7	42
College totals (4 years)	44	113	724	6.4	9	53	1017	19.2	7	33	816	24.7	0	16	96

PINKSTON, TODD — WR — EAGLES

PERSONAL: Born April 23, 1977, in Forest, Miss. ... 6-2/170.
HIGH SCHOOL: Forest (Miss.).
COLLEGE: Southern Mississippi.
TRANSACTIONS/CAREER NOTES: Selected by Philadelphia Eagles in second round (36th pick overall) of 2000 NFL draft.

Year—Team	G	RECEIVING No.	Yds.	Avg.	TD
1995—Southern Mississippi			Redshirted.		
1996—Southern Mississippi	11	11	181	16.5	1
1997—Southern Mississippi	11	38	360	9.5	3
1998—Southern Mississippi	11	52	848	16.3	7
1999—Southern Mississippi	11	48	977	20.4	11
College totals (4 years)	44	149	2366	15.9	22

PLUMMER, AHMED — CB — 49ERS

PERSONAL: Born March 26, 1976, in Wyoming, Ohio. ... 5-11/191. ... Full name: Ahmed Kamil Plummer.
HIGH SCHOOL: Wyoming (Ohio).
COLLEGE: Ohio State.
TRANSACTIONS/CAREER NOTES: Selected by San Francisco 49ers in first round (24th pick overall) of 2000 NFL draft.
COLLEGE NOTES: Credited with one sack (1997).

Year—Team	G	INTERCEPTIONS No.	Yds.	Avg.	TD
1995—Ohio State			Redshirted.		
1996—Ohio State	10	0	0	0.0	0
1997—Ohio State	13	5	83	16.6	1
1998—Ohio State	12	4	2	0.5	0
1999—Ohio State	12	5	64	12.8	0
College totals (4 years)	47	14	149	10.6	1

POLK, DaSHON — LB — BILLS

PERSONAL: Born March 13, 1977, in Pacoima, Calif. ... 6-1/221. ... Full name: DaShon Lamor Polk.
HIGH SCHOOL: Taft (Pacoima, Calif.).
COLLEGE: Arizona.
TRANSACTIONS/CAREER NOTES: Selected by Buffalo Bills in seventh round (251st pick overall) of 2000 NFL draft.

Year Team	G	SACKS
1995—Arizona	9	0.0
1996—Arizona	Redshirted.	
1997—Arizona	12	0.0
1998—Arizona	13	5.5
1999—Arizona	11	3.0
College totals (4 years)	45	8.5

PORTER, JERRY — WR — RAIDERS

PERSONAL: Born July 14, 1978, in Washington, D.C. ... 6-2/220.
HIGH SCHOOL: Coolidge (Washington, D.C.).
COLLEGE: West Virginia.
TRANSACTIONS/CAREER NOTES: Selected by Oakland Raiders in second round (47th pick overall) of 2000 NFL draft.
COLLEGE NOTES: Played wide receiver and free safety (1997-1999). ... Intercepted five passes for 57 yards and returned two punts for three yards (1998); intercepted one pass for 68 yards and a touchdown, rushed six times for 52 yards and attempted six passes with three completions for 20 yards (1999).

		RECEIVING				KICKOFF RETURNS				TOTALS	
Year Team	G	No.	Yds.	Avg.	TD	No.	Yds.	Avg.	TD	TD	Pts.
1996—West Virginia				Did not play.							
1997—West Virginia	12	13	280	21.5	0	1	25	25.0	0	3	18
1998—West Virginia	12	0	0	0.0	0	8	129	16.1	0	0	0
1999—West Virginia	11	15	311	20.7	4	1	16	16.0	0	5	30
College totals (3 years)	35	28	591	21.1	4	10	170	17.0	0	8	48

POTEAT, HANK — CB — STEELERS

PERSONAL: Born August 30, 1977, in Harrisburg, Pa. ... 5-10/190. ... Full name: Henry Major Poteat.
HIGH SCHOOL: Harrisburg (Pa.).
COLLEGE: Pittsburgh.
TRANSACTIONS/CAREER NOTES: Selected by Pittsburgh Steelers in third round (77th pick overall) of 2000 NFL draft.
COLLEGE NOTES: Played running back and cornerback (1996 and 1997). ... Rushed 20 times for 88 yards and caught six passes for 47 yards (1996); rushed seven times for two yards and caught four passes for 48 yards (1997).

		INTERCEPTIONS				PUNT RETURNS				KICKOFF RETURNS				TOTALS	
Year Team	G	No.	Yds.	Avg.	TD	No.	Yds.	Avg.	TD	No.	Yds.	Avg.	TD	TD	Pts.
1996—Pittsburgh	8	0	0	0.0	0	3	18	6.0	0	17	445	26.2	0	0	0
1997—Pittsburgh	11	1	42	42.0	0	6	43	7.2	0	11	307	27.9	0	0	0
1998—Pittsburgh	10	6	53	8.8	0	16	131	8.2	0	36	764	21.2	0	0	0
1999—Pittsburgh	11	3	56	18.7	0	19	307	16.2	1	17	401	23.6	0	1	6
College totals (4 years)	40	10	151	15.1	0	44	499	11.3	1	81	1917	23.7	0	1	6

PRENTICE, TRAVIS — RB — BROWNS

PERSONAL: Born December 8, 1976, in Louisville, Ky. ... 5-11/221. ... Full name: Travis Jason Prentice.
HIGH SCHOOL: Manual (Louisville, Ky.).
COLLEGE: Miami of Ohio.
TRANSACTIONS/CAREER NOTES: Selected by Cleveland Browns in third round (63rd pick overall) of 2000 NFL draft.
HONORS: Named running back on THE SPORTING NEWS college All-America second team (1998 and 1999).

		RUSHING				RECEIVING				TOTALS	
Year Team	G	Att.	Yds.	Avg.	TD	No.	Yds.	Avg.	TD	TD	Pts.
1995—Miami of Ohio				Redshirted.							
1996—Miami of Ohio	11	123	601	4.9	12	1	7	7.0	0	12	72
1997—Miami of Ohio	11	296	1549	5.2	25	23	138	6.0	0	25	150
1998—Miami of Ohio	11	365	1787	4.9	19	11	107	9.7	1	20	120
1999—Miami of Ohio	11	354	1659	4.7	17	19	270	14.2	4	21	126
College totals (4 years)	44	1138	5596	4.9	73	54	522	9.7	5	78	468

RACKERS, NEIL — K — BENGALS

PERSONAL: Born August 16, 1976, in Florissant, Mo. ... 6-0/200.
HIGH SCHOOL: Aquinas-Mercy (Florissant, Mo.).
COLLEGE: Illinois.
TRANSACTIONS/CAREER NOTES: Selected by Cincinnati Bengals in sixth round (169th pick overall) of 2000 NFL draft.
COLLEGE NOTES: Caught one pass for 18 yards and a touchdown (1999).

			KICKING				
Year Team	XPM	XPA	FGM	FGA	Lg.	50+	Pts.
1995—Illinois			Redshirted.				

1996—Illinois	18	18	2	5	42	0-0	24
1997—Illinois	10	11	5	10	41	0-0	25
1998—Illinois	14	16	7	10	46	0-0	35
1999—Illinois	44	44	20	26	50	0-0	104
College totals (4 years)	86	89	34	51	50	0-0	188

RATTAY, TIM — QB — 49ERS

PERSONAL: Born March 15, 1977, in Elyria, Ohio. ... 6-0/215.
HIGH SCHOOL: Phoenix Christian.
JUNIOR COLLEGE: Scottsdale (Ariz.) Community College.
COLLEGE: Louisiana Tech.
TRANSACTIONS/CAREER NOTES: Selected by San Francisco 49ers in seventh round (212th pick overall) of 2000 NFL draft.

		PASSING								RUSHING				TOTALS	
Year Team	G	Att.	Cmp.	Pct.	Yds.	TD	Int.	Avg.	Rat.	Att.	Yds.	Avg.	TD	TD	Pts.
1995—Scottsdale (Ariz.) CC	...	...	...	...	3256	28	...	...	...	...	...	...	...	...	...
1996—Louisiana Tech							Redshirted.								
1997—Louisiana Tech	11	477	293	61.4	3881	34	10	8.14	149.1	64	87	1.4	1	1	6
1998—Louisiana Tech	12	559	380	68.0	4943	46	13	8.84	164.8	43	-78	-1.8	1	1	6
1999—Louisiana Tech	10	516	342	66.3	3922	35	12	7.60	147.9	46	-112	-2.4	0	0	0
Junior college totals (1 year)	...	...	...	...	3256	28	...	...	...	...	...	...	...	...	...
College totals (3 years)	33	1552	1015	65.4	12746	115	35	8.21	154.3	153	-103	-0.7	2	2	12

REDMAN, CHRIS — QB — RAVENS

PERSONAL: Born July 7, 1977, in Louisville, Ky. ... 6-3/223.
HIGH SCHOOL: Male (Louisville, Ky.).
COLLEGE: Louisville.
TRANSACTIONS/CAREER NOTES: Selected by Baltimore Ravens in third round (75th pick overall) of 2000 NFL draft.

		PASSING								RUSHING				TOTALS	
Year Team	G	Att.	Cmp.	Pct.	Yds.	TD	Int.	Avg.	Rat.	Att.	Yds.	Avg.	TD	TD	Pts.
1995—Louisville							Redshirted.								
1996—Louisville	10	272	144	52.9	1773	8	9	6.52	110.8	37	-148	-4.0	0	0	0
1997—Louisville	11	445	261	58.7	3079	18	14	6.92	123.8	47	-121	-2.6	0	0	0
1998—Louisville	10	473	309	65.3	4042	29	15	8.55	151.0	40	-33	-0.8	2	2	12
1999—Louisville	11	489	317	64.8	3647	29	13	7.46	141.7	43	-110	-2.6	1	1	6
College totals (4 years)	42	1679	1031	61.4	12541	84	51	7.47	134.6	167	-412	-2.5	3	3	18

REDMOND, J.R. — RB — PATRIOTS

PERSONAL: Born September 28, 1977, in Carson, Calif. ... 5-11/216. ... Full name: Joseph Robert Redmond.
HIGH SCHOOL: Carson (Calif.).
COLLEGE: Arizona State.
TRANSACTIONS/CAREER NOTES: Selected by New England Patriots in third round (76th pick overall) of 2000 NFL draft.

		RUSHING				RECEIVING				PUNT RETURNS				KICKOFF RETURNS				TOTALS	
Year Team	G	Att.	Yds.	Avg.	TD	No.	Yds.	Avg.	TD	No.	Yds.	Avg.	TD	No.	Yds.	Avg.	TD	TD	Pts.
1996—Arizona State	11	71	327	4.6	2	10	211	21.1	2	35	286	8.2	0	2	83	41.5	0	4	24
1997—Arizona State	11	155	915	5.9	7	15	186	12.4	1	27	259	9.6	0	15	323	21.5	0	8	48
1998—Arizona State	10	166	883	5.3	11	22	194	8.8	0	18	246	13.7	1	10	235	23.5	0	12	72
1999—Arizona State	10	224	1085	4.8	12	12	97	8.1	1	26	192	7.4	0	0	0	0.0	0	13	78
College totals (4 years)	42	616	3210	5.2	32	59	688	11.7	4	106	983	9.3	1	27	641	23.7	0	37	222

REESE, QUINTON — DE — LIONS

PERSONAL: Born August 26, 1977, in Birmingham, Ala. ... 6-4/252. ... Full name: Quinton Jarrod Reese.
HIGH SCHOOL: West End (Birmingham, Ala.).
COLLEGE: Auburn.
TRANSACTIONS/CAREER NOTES: Selected by Detroit Lions in sixth round (181st pick overall) of 2000 NFL draft.

Year Team	G	SACKS
1995—Auburn		Did not play.
1996—Auburn	12	4.5
1997—Auburn	12	4.5
1998—Auburn	11	2.5
1999—Auburn	11	3.0
College totals (4 years)	46	14.5

RENES, ROB — DT — COLTS

PERSONAL: Born March 28, 1977, in Holland, Mich. ... 6-1/308.
HIGH SCHOOL: West Ottawa (Holland, Mich.).
COLLEGE: Michigan.
TRANSACTIONS/CAREER NOTES: Selected by Indianapolis Colts in seventh round (235th pick overall) of 2000 NFL draft.
HONORS: Named defensive tackle on THE SPORTING NEWS college All-America first team (1999).

Year Team	G	SACKS
1995—Michigan	Redshirted.	
1996—Michigan	9	0.0
1997—Michigan	12	4.0
1998—Michigan	13	0.0
1999—Michigan	12	1.0
College totals (4 years)	46	5.0

REYES, TUTAN — OT — SAINTS

PERSONAL: Born October 28, 1977, in Queens, N.Y. ... 6-3/299.
HIGH SCHOOL: August Martin (Queens, N.Y.).
COLLEGE: Mississippi.
TRANSACTIONS/CAREER NOTES: Selected by New Orleans Saints in fifth round (131st pick overall) of 2000 NFL draft.
COLLEGE PLAYING EXPERIENCE: Mississippi, 1995-1999. ... Games: 1995 (redshirted), 1996 (11), 1997 (12), 1998 (12), 1999 (11). Total: 46.

ROBBINS, FRED — DT — VIKINGS

PERSONAL: Born March 25, 1977, in Pensacola, Fla. ... 6-4/312. ... Full name: Fredrick Robbins.
HIGH SCHOOL: Gonzalez (Pensacola, Fla.).
COLLEGE: Wake Forest.
TRANSACTIONS/CAREER NOTES: Selected by Minnesota Vikings in second round (55th pick overall) of 2000 NFL draft.
COLLEGE NOTES: Recovered one fumble (1999).

Year Team	G	SACKS
1995—Wake Forest	Redshirted.	
1996—Wake Forest	11	3.0
1997—Wake Forest	11	4.0
1998—Wake Forest	11	3.0
1999—Wake Forest	11	5.0
College totals (4 years)	44	15.0

ROBINSON-RANDALL, GREG — OT — PATRIOTS

PERSONAL: Born June 23, 1978, in Hitchcock, Texas. ... 6-5/339.
HIGH SCHOOL: La Marque (Texas).
JUNIOR COLLEGE: Coffeyville (Kan.) Community College.
COLLEGE: Michigan State.
TRANSACTIONS/CAREER NOTES: Selected by New England Patriots in fourth round (127th pick overall) of 2000 NFL draft.
COLLEGE PLAYING EXPERIENCE: Coffeyville Community College, 1996 and 1997; Michigan State, 1998 and 1999. ... Games: 1996 (11), 1997 (11), 1998 (12), 1999 (12). Total Junior College: 22. Total NCAA: 24.

ROMAN, MARK — CB — BENGALS

PERSONAL: Born March 26, 1977, in New Iberia, La. ... 5-11/188. ... Full name: Mark Emery Roman.
HIGH SCHOOL: New Iberia (La.).
COLLEGE: Louisiana State.
TRANSACTIONS/CAREER NOTES: Selected by Cincinnati Bengals in second round (34th pick overall) of 2000 NFL draft.
COLLEGE NOTES: Credited with one sack (1998).

Year Team	G	INTERCEPTIONS			
		No.	Yds.	Avg.	TD
1996—Louisiana State	11	4	116	29.0	1
1997—Louisiana State	9	1	5	5.0	0
1998—Louisiana State	11	3	59	19.7	1
1999—Louisiana State	6	2	83	41.5	1
College totals (4 years)	37	10	263	26.3	3

ROMERO, JOHN — C — EAGLES

PERSONAL: Born October 3, 1976, in San Leandro, Calif. ... 6-3/326.
HIGH SCHOOL: St. Mary's (Stockton, Calif.).
COLLEGE: California.
TRANSACTIONS/CAREER NOTES: Selected by Philadelphia Eagles in sixth round (192nd pick overall) of 2000 NFL draft.
COLLEGE NOTES: Played defensive tackle (1996).
COLLEGE PLAYING EXPERIENCE: California, 1995-1999. ... Games: 1995 (redshirted), 1996 (3), 1997 (7), 1998 (11), 1999 (8). Total: 29.

SAMUELS, CHRIS — OT — REDSKINS

PERSONAL: Born July 28, 1977, in Mobile, Ala. ... 6-5/325.
HIGH SCHOOL: Shaw (Mobile, Ala.).
COLLEGE: Alabama.
TRANSACTIONS/CAREER NOTES: Selected by Washington Redskins in first round (third pick overall) of 2000 NFL draft.

HONORS: Outland Trophy winner (1999). ... Named offensive tackle on THE SPORTING NEWS college All-America first team (1999).
COLLEGE PLAYING EXPERIENCE: Alabama, 1995-1999. ... Games: 1995 (redshirted), 1996 (11), 1997 (11), 1998 (11), 1999 (12). Total: 45.

SANDERS, LEWIS — S — BROWNS

PERSONAL: Born June 22, 1978, in Staten Island, N.Y. ... 6-0/200. ... Full name: Lewis Lindell Sanders.
HIGH SCHOOL: St. Peter's (Staten Island, N.Y.).
COLLEGE: Maryland.
TRANSACTIONS/CAREER NOTES: Selected after junior season by Cleveland Browns in fourth round (95th pick overall) of 2000 NFL draft.
COLLEGE NOTES: Recovered one fumble for 28 yards and a touchdown (1999).

Year Team		INTERCEPTIONS				KICKOFF RETURNS				TOTALS	
	G	No.	Yds.	Avg.	TD	No.	Yds.	Avg.	TD	TD	Pts.
1996—Maryland	11	0	0	0.0	0	2	14	7.0	0	0	0
1997—Maryland	10	4	99	24.8	0	19	460	24.2	1	1	6
1998—Maryland						Medical redshirt.					
1999—Maryland	11	6	37	6.2	0	18	482	26.8	1	2	12
College totals (3 years)	32	10	136	13.6	0	39	956	24.5	2	3	18

SANDERS, QUINCY — S — REDSKINS

PERSONAL: Born April 8, 1977, in Rockford, Ill. ... 6-1/204.
HIGH SCHOOL: Reed (Sparks, Nev.).
COLLEGE: UNLV.
TRANSACTIONS/CAREER NOTES: Selected by Washington Redskins in fifth round (155th pick overall) of 2000 NFL draft.
COLLEGE NOTES: Intercepted two passes (1997); intercepted one pass for 34 yards and a touchdown (1999). ... Granted medical redshirt (1998).
COLLEGE PLAYING EXPERIENCE: UNLV, 1995-1999. ... Games: 1995 (7), 1996 (8), 1997 (11), 1998 (2), 1999 (11). Total: 39.

SANYIKA, SEKOU — LB — CARDINALS

PERSONAL: Born March 17, 1978, in New Orleans. ... 6-4/237.
HIGH SCHOOL: R.L. Stevenson (Hercules, Calif.).
COLLEGE: California.
TRANSACTIONS/CAREER NOTES: Selected by Arizona Cardinals in seventh round (215th pick overall) of 2000 NFL draft.
COLLEGE NOTES: Intercepted two passes for 34 yards (1999).

Year Team	G	SACKS
1995—California		Redshirted.
1996—California	9	3.0
1997—California	11	3.0
1998—California	11	7.0
1999—California	11	6.5
College totals (4 years)	42	19.5

SAVEA, MANUIA — OL — BROWNS

PERSONAL: Born February 22, 1975, in Auto, American Samoa. ... 6-2/306. ... Full name: Manuia J. Savea.
HIGH SCHOOL: Fagaitua (American Samoa).
JUNIOR COLLEGE: City College of San Francisco (Calif.).
COLLEGE: Arizona.
TRANSACTIONS/CAREER NOTES: Selected by Cleveland Browns in seventh round (207th pick overall) of 2000 NFL draft.
COLLEGE PLAYING EXPERIENCE: City College of San Francisco, 1997; Arizona, 1998 and 1999. ... Games: 1997 (games played unavailable), 1998 (13), 1999 (12). Total NCAA: 25.

SCOTT, GARI — WR — EAGLES

PERSONAL: Born June 2, 1978, in Lake Park, Fla. ... 6-0/191.
HIGH SCHOOL: Suncoast (Riviera Beach, Fla.).
COLLEGE: Michigan State.
TRANSACTIONS/CAREER NOTES: Selected by Philadelphia Eagles in fourth round (99th pick overall) of 2000 NFL draft.
COLLEGE NOTES: Rushed once for minus eight yards (1999).

Year Team		RECEIVING				PUNT RETURNS				KICKOFF RETURNS				TOTALS	
	G	No.	Yds.	Avg.	TD	No.	Yds.	Avg.	TD	No.	Yds.	Avg.	TD	TD	Pts.
1996—Michigan State	10	5	89	17.8	1	0	0	0.0	0	1	22	22.0	0	1	6
1997—Michigan State	12	41	680	16.6	7	15	160	10.7	0	11	283	25.7	0	7	42
1998—Michigan State	12	58	843	14.5	4	32	440	13.8	0	18	354	19.7	0	4	24
1999—Michigan State	11	30	483	16.1	6	37	488	13.2	1	7	137	19.6	0	7	42
College totals (4 years)	45	134	2095	15.6	18	84	1088	13.0	1	37	796	21.5	0	19	114

SCOTT, TONY — CB — JETS

PERSONAL: Born October 3, 1976, in Lawndale, N.C. ... 5-10/193.
HIGH SCHOOL: Lawndale (N.C.).

2000 DRAFT PICKS

COLLEGE: North Carolina State.
TRANSACTIONS/CAREER NOTES: Selected by New York Jets in sixth round (179th pick overall) of 2000 NFL draft. ... Signed by Jets (May 9, 2000).
COLLEGE NOTES: Credited with one sack (1999).

		INTERCEPTIONS			PUNT RETURNS				TOTALS	
Year Team	G	No.	Yds.	Avg.	TD	No.	Yds.	Avg.	TD	TD	Pts.
1996—North Carolina State	11	1	30	30.0	0	17	165	9.7	0	0	0
1997—North Carolina State	11	1	0	0.0	0	6	26	4.3	0	0	0
1998—North Carolina State	11	2	36	18.0	0	0	0	0.0	0	0	0
1999—North Carolina State	11	4	38	9.5	0	1	25	25.0	1	1	6
College totals (4 years)	44	8	104	13.0	0	24	216	9.0	1	1	6

SEALS, RICHARD — DT — JETS

PERSONAL: Born March 18, 1976, in Houston. ... 6-2/316.
HIGH SCHOOL: James Madison (Houston).
COLLEGE: Utah.
TRANSACTIONS/CAREER NOTES: Selected by New York Jets in seventh round (218th pick overall) of 2000 NFL draft. ... Signed by Jets (May 17, 2000).

Year Team	G	SACKS
1995—Utah		Redshirted.
1996—Utah	12	2.0
1997—Utah	1	0.0
1998—Utah	9	2.5
1999—Utah	11	8.0
College totals (4 years)	33	12.5

SEIDER, JA JUAN — QB — CHARGERS

PERSONAL: Born April 16, 1977, in Belle Glade, Fla. ... 6-1/230.
HIGH SCHOOL: Belle Glade (Fla.).
COLLEGE: West Virginia, then Florida A&M.
TRANSACTIONS/CAREER NOTES: Selected by San Diego Chargers in sixth round (205th pick overall) of 2000 NFL draft.

		PASSING								RUSHING				TOTALS	
Year Team	G	Att.	Cmp.	Pct.	Yds.	TD	Int.	Avg.	Rat.	Att.	Yds.	Avg.	TD	TD	Pts.
1996—West Virginia	1	1	0	0.0	0	0	0	0.0	0.0	0	0	0.0	0	0	0
1997—West Virginia	4	14	6	42.9	101	0	0	7.21	103.5	13	-3	-0.2	0	0	0
1998—West Virginia	2	1	1	100.0	32	0	0	32.00	368.8	0	0	0.0	0	0	0
1999—Florida A&M	10	252	149	59.1	2048	23	2	8.13	155.9	106	587	5.5	10	10	60
College totals (4 years)	17	268	156	58.2	2181	23	2	8.14	153.4	119	584	4.9	10	10	60

SHEA, AARON — TE/FB — BROWNS

PERSONAL: Born December 5, 1976, in Ottawa, Ill. ... 6-3/244.
HIGH SCHOOL: Ottawa (Ill.).
COLLEGE: Michigan.
TRANSACTIONS/CAREER NOTES: Selected by Cleveland Browns in fourth round (110th pick overall) of 2000 NFL draft.

		RUSHING				RECEIVING				TOTALS	
Year Team	G	Att.	Yds.	Avg.	TD	No.	Yds.	Avg.	TD	TD	Pts.
1995—Michigan				Redshirted.							
1996—Michigan	12	0	0	0.0	0	5	46	9.2	1	1	6
1997—Michigan	12	0	0	0.0	0	9	85	9.4	0	0	0
1998—Michigan	11	16	73	4.6	0	16	154	9.6	1	1	6
1999—Michigan	12	11	31	2.8	0	38	289	7.6	3	3	18
College totals (4 years)	47	27	104	3.9	0	68	574	8.4	5	5	30

SHEPHERD, JACOBY — CB — RAMS

PERSONAL: Born August 31, 1979, in Lufkin, Texas. ... 6-1/195. ... Full name: Jacoby Lamar Shepherd.
HIGH SCHOOL: Lufkin (Texas).
JUNIOR COLLEGE: Tyler (Texas) Junior College, then Cloud County Community College, Kan. (did not play football).
COLLEGE: Oklahoma State.
TRANSACTIONS/CAREER NOTES: Selected after junior season by St. Louis Rams in second round (62nd pick overall) of 2000 NFL draft.

		INTERCEPTIONS			
Year Team	G	No.	Yds.	Avg.	TD
1996—Tyler JC			Statistics unavailable.		
1997—Tyler JC			Statistics unavailable.		
1998—			Did not play.		
1999—Oklahoma State	11	2	0	0.0	0
College totals (1 years)	11	2	0	0.0	0

SHIVERS, WES — OT — TITANS

PERSONAL: Born March 8, 1977, in Jackson, Miss. ... 6-5/318. ... Full name: Wesley Davis Shivers.

2000 DRAFT PICKS

HIGH SCHOOL: Brandon (Miss.), then Benton (Miss.) Academy.
JUNIOR COLLEGE: Hinds Community College (Miss.).
COLLEGE: Mississippi State.
TRANSACTIONS/CAREER NOTES: Selected by Tennessee Titans in seventh round (238th pick overall) of 2000 NFL draft.
COLLEGE PLAYING EXPERIENCE: Hinds Community College, 1996 and 1997; Mississippi State, 1998 and 1999. ... Games: 1996, (games played unavailable), 1997 (games played unavailable), 1998 (12), 1999 (12). Total NCAA: 24.

SHORT, BRANDON LB GIANTS

PERSONAL: Born July 11, 1977, in McKeesport, Pa. ... 6-3/253. ... Full name: Brandon Darnell Short.
HIGH SCHOOL: McKeesport (Pa.).
COLLEGE: Penn State.
TRANSACTIONS/CAREER NOTES: Selected by New York Giants in fourth round (105th pick overall) of 2000 NFL draft.
HONORS: Named linebacker on THE SPORTING NEWS college All-America second team (1999).
COLLEGE NOTES: Granted medical redshirt (1995).

Year Team	G	SACKS
1995—Penn State	1	0.0
1996—Penn State	12	3.5
1997—Penn State	11	2.5
1998—Penn State	11	5.5
1999—Penn State	12	5.0
College totals (5 years)	47	16.5

SIMON, COREY DT EAGLES

PERSONAL: Born March 2, 1977, in Pompano Beach, Fla. ... 6-2/293.
HIGH SCHOOL: Ely (Pompano Beach, Fla.).
COLLEGE: Florida State.
TRANSACTIONS/CAREER NOTES: Selected by Philadelphia Eagles in first round (sixth pick overall) of 2000 NFL draft.
HONORS: Named defensive tackle on THE SPORTING NEWS college All-America first team (1999).
COLLEGE NOTES: Recovered two fumbles (1997); recovered one fumble and intercepted one pass (1999).

Year Team	G	SACKS
1996—Florida State	3	0.0
1997—Florida State	10	2.0
1998—Florida State	12	5.0
1999—Florida State	11	4.0
College totals (4 years)	36	11.0

SIMONEAU, MARK LB FALCONS

PERSONAL: Born January 16, 1977, in Phillipsburg, Kan. ... 6-0/233.
HIGH SCHOOL: Smith Center (Kan.).
COLLEGE: Kansas State.
TRANSACTIONS/CAREER NOTES: Selected by Atlanta Falcons in third round (67th pick overall) of 2000 NFL draft. ... Signed by Falcons (May 17, 2000).
COLLEGE NOTES: Named linebacker on THE SPORTING NEWS college All-America first team (1999).

Year Team	G	INTERCEPTIONS No.	Yds.	Avg.	TD	SACKS No.
1995—Kansas State			Redshirted.			
1996—Kansas State	11	0	0	0.0	0	3.5
1997—Kansas State	11	0	0	0.0	0	4.0
1998—Kansas State	11	2	0	0.0	0	1.5
1999—Kansas State	11	2	61	30.5	1	6.5
College totals (4 years)	44	4	61	15.3	1	15.5

SIRMON, PETER LB TITANS

PERSONAL: Born February 18, 1977, in Wenatchee, Wash. ... 6-2/246. ... Full name: Peter Anton Sirmon.
HIGH SCHOOL: Walla Walla (Wash.).
COLLEGE: Oregon.
TRANSACTIONS/CAREER NOTES: Selected by Tennessee Titans in fourth round (128th pick overall) of 2000 NFL draft.
COLLEGE NOTES: Intercepted two passes (1997); intercepted two passes for 28 yards (1999).

Year Team	G	SACKS
1995—Oregon		Redshirted.
1996—Oregon	11	0.0
1997—Oregon	12	4.5
1998—Oregon	3	1.0
1999—Oregon	12	2.5
College totals (4 years)	38	8.0

SLAUGHTER, T.J. LB JAGUARS

PERSONAL: Born February 20, 1977, in Birmingham, Ala. ... 6-0/247.
HIGH SCHOOL: John Carroll (Birmingham, Ala.).

COLLEGE: Southern Mississippi.
TRANSACTIONS/CAREER NOTES: Selected by Jacksonville Jaguars in third round (92nd pick overall) of 2000 NFL draft. ... Signed by Jaguars (May 16, 2000).
COLLEGE NOTES: Granted medical redshirt (1997).

Year Team	G	SACKS
1995—Southern Mississippi	11	1.0
1996—Southern Mississippi	10	4.5
1997—Southern Mississippi	2	0.0
1998—Southern Mississippi	11	3.0
1999—Southern Mississippi	11	3.5
College totals (5 years)	45	12.0

SMITH, EMANUEL — WR — JAGUARS

PERSONAL: Born February 3, 1976, in Clinton, Miss. ... 6-1/219.
HIGH SCHOOL: Clinton (Miss.).
COLLEGE: Arkansas.
TRANSACTIONS/CAREER NOTES: Selected by Jacksonville Jaguars in sixth round (196th pick overall) of 2000 NFL draft.
COLLEGE NOTES: Returned four kickoffs for 77 yards (1998).

Year Team	G	RECEIVING			
		No.	Yds.	Avg.	TD
1996—Arkansas	10	16	152	9.5	0
1997—Arkansas	11	28	380	13.6	1
1998—Arkansas	11	25	372	14.9	2
1999—Arkansas	11	32	331	10.3	1
College totals (4 years)	43	101	1235	12.2	4

SMITH, MARVEL — OT — STEELERS

PERSONAL: Born August 6, 1978, in Oakland. ... 6-5/320. ... Full name: Marvel Amos Smith.
HIGH SCHOOL: Skyline (Oakland).
COLLEGE: Arizona State.
TRANSACTIONS/CAREER NOTES: Selected after junior season by Pittsburgh Steelers in second round (38th pick overall) of 2000 NFL draft.
COLLEGE PLAYING EXPERIENCE: Arizona State, 1997-1999. ... Games: 1997 (10), 1998 (11), 1999 (12). Total: 33.

SMITH, PAUL — RB — 49ERS

PERSONAL: Born January 31, 1978, in El Paso, Texas. ... 5-11/234.
HIGH SCHOOL: Andress (El Paso, Texas).
COLLEGE: Texas-El Paso.
TRANSACTIONS/CAREER NOTES: Selected by San Francisco 49ers in fifth round (132nd pick overall) of 2000 NFL draft.

Year Team	G	RUSHING				RECEIVING				TOTALS	
		Att.	Yds.	Avg.	TD	No.	Yds.	Avg.	TD	TD	Pts.
1996—Texas-El Paso	11	67	189	2.8	0	2	-1	-0.5	0	0	0
1997—Texas-El Paso	11	115	432	3.8	2	8	84	10.5	0	2	12
1998—Texas-El Paso	10	149	660	4.4	2	13	179	13.8	0	2	12
1999—Texas-El Paso	11	272	1258	4.6	12	7	84	12.0	1	13	78
College totals (4 years)	43	603	2539	4.2	16	30	346	11.5	1	17	102

SMITH, ROBAIRE — DE/DT — TITANS

PERSONAL: Born November 15, 1977, in Flint, Mich. ... 6-4/271. ... Brother of Fernando Smith, defensive end, Minnesota Vikings.
HIGH SCHOOL: Flint (Mich.).
COLLEGE: Michigan State.
TRANSACTIONS/CAREER NOTES: Selected by Tennessee Titans in sixth round (197th pick overall) of 2000 NFL draft.
HONORS: Named defensive end on THE SPORTING NEWS college All-America second team (1999).
COLLEGE NOTES: Recovered one fumble for 37 yards and a touchdown (1997).

Year Team	G	SACKS
1996—Michigan State	Did not play.	
1997—Michigan State	12	12.0
1998—Michigan State	9	2.0
1999—Michigan State	12	8.0
College totals (3 years)	33	22.0

SMITH, TERRELLE — FB — SAINTS

PERSONAL: Born March 12, 1978, in West Covina, Calif. ... 6-0/246.
HIGH SCHOOL: Canyon Springs (Moreno Valley, Calif.).
COLLEGE: Arizona State.
TRANSACTIONS/CAREER NOTES: Selected by New Orleans Saints in fourth round (96th pick overall) of 2000 NFL draft.
COLLEGE NOTES: Played linebacker (1997 and 1998).

Year Team	G	RUSHING				RECEIVING				TOTALS	
		Att.	Yds.	Avg.	TD	No.	Yds.	Avg.	TD	TD	Pts.
1996—Arizona State					Did not play.						
1997—Arizona State	3	0	0	0.0	0	0	0	0.0	0	0	0
1998—Arizona State	10	0	0	0.0	0	0	0	0.0	0	0	0
1999—Arizona State	11	21	127	6.0	1	9	88	9.8	0	1	6
College totals (3 years)	24	21	127	6.0	1	9	88	9.8	0	1	6

SOWARD, R. JAY — WR — JAGUARS

PERSONAL: Born January 16, 1978, in Rialto, Calif. ... 5-11/177. ... Full name: Rodney Jay Soward.
HIGH SCHOOL: Eisenhower (Rialto, Calif.).
COLLEGE: Southern California.
TRANSACTIONS/CAREER NOTES: Selected by Jacksonville Jaguars in first round (29th pick overall) of 2000 NFL draft

Year Team	G	RECEIVING				PUNT RETURNS				KICKOFF RETURNS				TOTALS	
		No.	Yds.	Avg.	TD	No.	Yds.	Avg.	TD	No.	Yds.	Avg.	TD	TD	Pts.
1996—Southern California	12	18	507	28.2	5	1	-1	-1.0	0	14	440	31.4	2	7	42
1997—Southern California	11	48	831	17.3	8	5	37	7.4	0	15	394	26.3	1	9	54
1998—Southern California	11	44	679	15.4	6	7	202	28.9	2	16	344	21.5	0	8	48
1999—Southern California	11	51	655	12.8	4	18	218	12.1	1	11	236	21.5	0	5	30
College totals (4 years)	45	161	2672	16.6	23	31	456	14.7	3	56	1414	25.3	3	29	174

ST. CLAIR, JOHN — C — RAMS

PERSONAL: Born July 15, 1977, in Roanoke, Va. ... 6-4/293. ... Full name: John Bradley St. Clair.
HIGH SCHOOL: William Fleming (Roanoke, Va.).
COLLEGE: Virginia.
TRANSACTIONS/CAREER NOTES: Selected by St. Louis Rams in third round (94th pick overall) of 2000 NFL draft.
COLLEGE NOTES: Played tight end (1996).
COLLEGE PLAYING EXPERIENCE: Virginia, 1995-1999. ... Games: 1995 (redshirted), 1996 (8), 1997 (11), 1998 (10), 1999 (11). Total: 40.

ST. LOUIS, BRAD — TE — BENGALS

PERSONAL: Born August 19, 1976, in Waverly, Mo. ... 6-3/240. ... Full name: Brad Allen St. Louis.
HIGH SCHOOL: Belton (Mo.).
COLLEGE: Southwest Missouri State.
TRANSACTIONS/CAREER NOTES: Selected by Cincinnati Bengals in seventh round (210th pick overall) of 2000 NFL draft.

Year Team	G	RECEIVING			
		No.	Yds.	Avg.	TD
1996—Southwest Missouri State	8	5	72	14.4	0
1997—Southwest Missouri State	11	30	349	11.6	3
1998—Southwest Missouri State	11	26	282	10.8	0
1999—Southwest Missouri State	11	32	371	11.6	4
College totals (4 years)	41	93	1074	11.5	7

STACHELSKI, DAVE — TE — PATRIOTS

PERSONAL: Born March 1, 1977, in Marysville, Wash. ... 6-3/250.
HIGH SCHOOL: Marysville-Pilchuck (Marysville, Wash.).
COLLEGE: Boise State.
TRANSACTIONS/CAREER NOTES: Selected by New England Patriots in fifth round (141st pick overall) of 2000 NFL draft.

Year Team	G	RECEIVING			
		No.	Yds.	Avg.	TD
1995—Boise State			Redshirted.		
1996—Boise State	3	2	14	7.0	0
1997—Boise State	5	0	0	0.0	0
1998—Boise State	8	2	6	3.0	0
1999—Boise State	12	31	453	14.6	6
College totals (4 years)	28	93	467	13.5	6

STITH, SHYRONE — RB — JAGUARS

PERSONAL: Born April 2, 1978, in Portsmouth, Va. ... 5-7/203. ... Full name: Shyrone Orenthal Stith.
HIGH SCHOOL: Western Branch (Chesapeake, Va.).
COLLEGE: Virginia Tech.
TRANSACTIONS/CAREER NOTES: Selected after junior season by Jacksonville Jaguars in seventh round (243rd pick overall) of 2000 NFL draft. ... Signed by Jaguars (May 17, 2000).

Year Team	G	RUSHING				RECEIVING				KICKOFF RETURNS				TOTALS	
		Att.	Yds.	Avg.	TD	No.	Yds.	Avg.	TD	No.	Yds.	Avg.	TD	TD	Pts.
1996—Virginia Tech	11	89	474	5.3	5	4	26	6.5	0	0	0	0.0	0	5	30
1997—Virginia Tech									Redshirted.						
1998—Virginia Tech	11	133	699	5.3	3	5	42	8.4	0	14	282	20.1	0	3	18
1999—Virginia Tech	11	226	1119	5.0	13	4	48	12.0	0	15	387	25.8	0	13	78
College totals (3 years)	33	448	2292	5.1	21	13	116	8.9	0	29	669	23.1	0	21	126

TANT, JAY   TE   CARDINALS

PERSONAL: Born December 4, 1977, in Kettering, Ohio. ... 6-3/252. ... Full name: Jay William Tant.
HIGH SCHOOL: Alter (Kettering, Ohio).
COLLEGE: Northwestern.
TRANSACTIONS/CAREER NOTES: Selected by Arizona Cardinals in fifth round (164th pick overall) of 2000 NFL draft.

RECEIVING

Year Team	G	No.	Yds.	Avg.	TD
1996—Northwestern	9	2	9	4.5	0
1997—Northwestern	11	10	106	10.6	0
1998—Northwestern	12	30	327	10.9	2
1999—Northwestern	10	17	203	11.9	0
College totals (4 years)	42	59	645	10.9	2

TAUSCHER, MARK   OT   PACKERS

PERSONAL: Born June 17, 1977, in Auburndale, Wis. ... 6-3/314.
HIGH SCHOOL: Auburndale (Wis.).
COLLEGE: Wisconsin.
TRANSACTIONS/CAREER NOTES: Selected by Green Bay Packers in seventh round (224th pick overall) of 2000 NFL draft.
COLLEGE PLAYING EXPERIENCE: Wisconsin, 1995-1999. ... Games: 1995 (redshirted), 1996 (did not play), 1997 (games played unavailable), 1998 (games played unavailable), 1999 (12).

TAYLOR, SHANNON   LB   CHARGERS

PERSONAL: Born February 16, 1975, in Roanoke, Va. ... 6-3/247. ... Full name: Shannon A. Taylor.
HIGH SCHOOL: Patrick Henry (Roanoke, Va.).
COLLEGE: Virginia.
TRANSACTIONS/CAREER NOTES: Selected by San Diego Chargers in sixth round (184th pick overall) of 2000 NFL draft.
COLLEGE NOTES: Intercepted one pass for four yards and returned two kickoffs for 22 yards (1996).

Year Team	G	SACKS
1996—Virginia	11	2.0
1997—Virginia	11	2.0
1998—Virginia	Did not play.	
1999—Virginia	11	6.0
College totals (3 years)	33	10.0

TAYLOR, TRAVIS   WR   RAVENS

PERSONAL: Born March 30, 1978, in Jacksonville. ... 6-1/200. ... Full name: Travis Lamont Taylor.
HIGH SCHOOL: Camden County (Ga.), then Jean Ribault (Jacksonville).
COLLEGE: Florida.
TRANSACTIONS/CAREER NOTES: Selected after junior season by Baltimore Ravens in first round (10th pick overall) of 2000 NFL draft.

Year Team	G	No.	Yds.	Avg.	TD
1997—Florida	7	1	11	11.0	0
1998—Florida	11	37	676	18.3	9
1999—Florida	9	34	463	13.6	6
College totals (3 years)	27	72	1150	16.0	15

THOMAS, ADALIUS   DE   RAVENS

PERSONAL: Born August 18, 1977, in Equality, Ala. ... 6-2/270.
HIGH SCHOOL: Central Coosa (Equality, Ala.).
COLLEGE: Southern Mississippi.
TRANSACTIONS/CAREER NOTES: Selected by Baltimore Ravens in sixth round (186th pick overall) of 2000 NFL draft.
HONORS: Named defensive end on THE SPORTING NEWS college All-America second team (1999).
COLLEGE NOTES: Intercepted one pass (1997).

Year Team	G	SACKS
1995—Southern Mississippi	Redshirted.	
1996—Southern Mississippi	11	4.0
1997—Southern Mississippi	11	9.0
1998—Southern Mississippi	11	12.5
1999—Southern Mississippi	11	9.0
College totals (4 years)	44	34.5

THOMAS, JASON   G   CHARGERS

PERSONAL: Born June 10, 1977, in Savannah, Ga. ... 6-3/300.
HIGH SCHOOL: A.E. Beach (Savannah, Ga.).
COLLEGE: South Carolina, then Hampton.
TRANSACTIONS/CAREER NOTES: Selected by San Diego Chargers in seventh round (222nd pick overall) of 2000 NFL draft.

COLLEGE PLAYING EXPERIENCE: South Carolina, 1995 and 1996; Hampton, 1997-1999. ... Games: 1995 (redshirted), 1996 (2), 1997 (11), 1998 (11), 1999 (11). Total: 35.

THOMAS, KIWAUKEE   CB   JAGUARS

PERSONAL: Born June 19, 1977, in Warner Robins, Ga. ... 5-11/186. ... Full name: Kiwaukee Sanchez Thomas. ... Name pronounced kee-WA-kee.
HIGH SCHOOL: Perry (Ga.).
COLLEGE: Georgia Southern.
TRANSACTIONS/CAREER NOTES: Selected by Jacksonville Jaguars in fifth round (159th pick overall) of 2000 NFL draft. ... Signed by Jaguars (May 25, 2000).
COLLEGE NOTES: Intercepted one pass for 21 yards (1999).
COLLEGE PLAYING EXPERIENCE: Georgia Southern, 1996-1999. ... Games: 1996 (9), 1997 (11), 1998 (11), 1999 (10). Total: 41.

THOMPSON, MICHAEL   OT   FALCONS

PERSONAL: Born February 11, 1977, in Savannah, Ga. ... 6-4/318. ... Full name: Michael Anthony Thompson.
HIGH SCHOOL: Windsor Forest (Savannah, Ga.).
COLLEGE: Tennessee State.
TRANSACTIONS/CAREER NOTES: Selected by Atlanta Falcons in fourth round (100th pick overall) of 2000 NFL draft. ... Signed by Falcons (May 16, 2000).
COLLEGE NOTES: Played defensive tackle (1995). ... Played tight end (1996). ... Credited with two sacks (1995); caught six passes for 71 yards (1996).
COLLEGE PLAYING EXPERIENCE: Tennessee State, 1995-1999. ... Games: 1995 (11), 1996 (10), 1997 (medical redshirt), 1998 (11), 1999 (11). Total: 43.

THOMPSON, RAYNOCH   LB   CARDINALS

PERSONAL: Born November 21, 1977, in New Orleans. ... 6-3/220. ... Full name: Raynoch Joseph Thompson.
HIGH SCHOOL: St. Augustine (New Orleans).
COLLEGE: Tennessee.
TRANSACTIONS/CAREER NOTES: Selected by Arizona Cardinals in second round (41st pick overall) of 2000 NFL draft.
COLLEGE NOTES: Intercepted one pass for five yards (1997); intercepted three passes for 64 yards (1999).

Year Team	G	SACKS
1996—Tennessee	Did not play.	
1997—Tennessee	12	1.0
1998—Tennessee	12	2.0
1999—Tennessee	12	1.0
College totals (3 years)	36	4.0

TILLMAN, TRAVARES   S   BILLS

PERSONAL: Born October 8, 1977, in Lyons, Ga. ... 6-1/189. ... Full name: Travares Arastius Tillman.
HIGH SCHOOL: Toombs County (Lyons, Ga.).
COLLEGE: Georgia Tech.
TRANSACTIONS/CAREER NOTES: Selected by Buffalo Bills in second round (58th pick overall) of 2000 NFL draft.
COLLEGE NOTES: Returned blocked punt 30 yards for a touchdown (1997).

Year Team	G	INTERCEPTIONS No.	Yds.	Avg.	TD
1996—Georgia Tech	9	1	0	0.0	0
1997—Georgia Tech	11	4	32	8.0	0
1998—Georgia Tech	11	1	0	0.0	0
1999—Georgia Tech	9	1	9	9.0	0
College totals (4 years)	40	7	41	5.9	0

TISDALE, CASEY   DE/LB   PATRIOTS

PERSONAL: Born June 18, 1976, in Oakland. ... 6-4/258.
HIGH SCHOOL: University (San Diego).
JUNIOR COLLEGE: San Diego Mesa College.
COLLEGE: New Mexico.
TRANSACTIONS/CAREER NOTES: Selected by New England Patriots in seventh round (226th pick overall) of 2000 NFL draft.
COLLEGE NOTES: Intercepted one pass for nine yards (1999).

Year Team	G	SACKS
1995—San Diego Mesa College	Statistics unavailable.	
1996—San Diego Mesa College	Statistics unavailable.	
1997—New Mexico	Redshirted.	
1998—New Mexico	12	3.0
1999—New Mexico	11	6.5
College totals (2 years)	23	9.5

TOSI, MAO — DE/DT — CARDINALS

PERSONAL: Born December 12, 1976, in Anchorage, Alaska. ... 6-5/291.
HIGH SCHOOL: East Anchorage (Alaska).
JUNIOR COLLEGE: Butler County Community College (Kan.).
COLLEGE: Idaho.
TRANSACTIONS/CAREER NOTES: Selected by Arizona Cardinals in fifth round (136th pick overall) of 2000 NFL draft.
COLLEGE NOTES: Recovered one fumble and intercepted one pass (1999).

Year Team	G	SACKS
1996—Butler County CC	Statistics unavailable.	
1997—Butler County CC	Statistics unavailable.	
1998—Idaho	12	4.0
1999—Idaho	9	7.5
College totals (2 years)	21	11.5

TOWNS, LESTER — LB — PANTHERS

PERSONAL: Born August 28, 1977, in Pasadena, Calif. ... 6-1/252.
HIGH SCHOOL: Pasadena (Calif.).
COLLEGE: Washington.
TRANSACTIONS/CAREER NOTES: Selected by Carolina Panthers in seventh round (221st pick overall) of 2000 NFL draft.

Year Team	G	SACKS
1996—Washington	11	1.5
1997—Washington	11	5.0
1998—Washington	10	4.5
1999—Washington	11	0.0
College totals (4 years)	43	11.0

ULBRICH, JEFF — LB — 49ERS

PERSONAL: Born February 17, 1977, in San Jose, Calif. ... 6-0/249.
HIGH SCHOOL: Live Oak (Morgan Hill, Calif.).
JUNIOR COLLEGE: Gavilan College (Calif.).
COLLEGE: San Jose State, then Hawaii.
TRANSACTIONS/CAREER NOTES: Selected by San Francisco 49ers in third round (86th pick overall) of 2000 NFL draft.

Year Team	G	SACKS
1995—San Jose State	Redshirted.	
1996—Gavilan College	Statistics unavailable.	
1997—Hawaii	Did not play.	
1998—Hawaii	7	1.0
1999—Hawaii	12	8.0
College totals (2 years)	19	9.0

URLACHER, BRIAN — LB — BEARS

PERSONAL: Born May 25, 1978, in Pasco, Wash. ... 6-3/249. ... Full name: Brian Keith Urlacher.
HIGH SCHOOL: Lovington (N.M.).
COLLEGE: New Mexico.
TRANSACTIONS/CAREER NOTES: Selected by Chicago Bears in first round (ninth pick overall) of 2000 NFL draft.
HONORS: Named strong safety on THE SPORTING NEWS college All-America second team (1999).
COLLEGE NOTES: Played strong safety and linebacker (1996-1999). ... Returned two kickoffs for 15 yards (1997); returned three punts for 38 yards (1998); returned three kickoffs for 79 yards, returned 10 punts for 158 yards, caught seven passes for 61 yards and recovered three fumbles for 115 yards and one touchdown (1999).

Year Team	G	INTERCEPTIONS No.	Yds.	Avg.	TD	SACKS No.
1996—New Mexico	10	0	0	0.0	0	0.0
1997—New Mexico	12	2	15	7.5	0	2.0
1998—New Mexico	12	0	0	0.0	0	2.0
1999—New Mexico	11	1	1	1.0	0	1.0
College totals (4 years)	45	3	16	5.3	0	5.0

VAUGHN, DARRICK — CB — FALCONS

PERSONAL: Born October 2, 1978, in Houston. ... 5-11/190.
HIGH SCHOOL: Aldine Nimitz (Houston).
COLLEGE: Southwest Texas State.
TRANSACTIONS/CAREER NOTES: Selected by Atlanta Falcons in seventh round (211th pick overall) of 2000 NFL draft. ... Signed by Falcons (May 17, 2000).
COLLEGE NOTES: Credited with 1/2 sack (1997); returned eight punts for 116 yards and one touchdown (1999).

Year Team	G	INTERCEPTIONS No.	Yds.	Avg.	TD
1996—Southwest Texas State	7	0	0	0.0	0
1997—Southwest Texas State	11	1	0	0.0	0
1998—Southwest Texas State	11	3	0	0.0	0

1999—Southwest Texas State	11	4	0	0.0	0
College totals (4 years)	40	8	0	0.0	0

WADE, TODD OT DOLPHINS

PERSONAL: Born October 30, 1976, in Jackson, Miss. ... 6-8/319.
HIGH SCHOOL: Jackson (Miss.) Prep.
COLLEGE: Mississippi.
TRANSACTIONS/CAREER NOTES: Selected by Miami Dolphins in second round (53rd pick overall) of 2000 NFL draft.
COLLEGE NOTES: Mississippi, 1995-1999. ... Games: 1995 (redshirted), 1996 (11), 1997 (11), 1998 (11), 1999 (11). Total: 44.

WALKER, DARWIN DT CARDINALS

PERSONAL: Born June 15, 1977, in Walterboro, S.C. ... 6-1/280. ... Full name: Darwin Jamar Walker.
HIGH SCHOOL: Walterboro (S.C.).
COLLEGE: North Carolina State, then Tennessee.
TRANSACTIONS/CAREER NOTES: Selected by Arizona Cardinals in third round (71st pick overall) of 2000 NFL draft.
HONORS: Named defensive tackle on The Sporting News college All-America second team (1999).

Year Team	G	SACKS
1995—North Carolina State	9	1.0
1996—Tennessee	Redshirted.	
1997—Tennessee	13	1.0
1998—Tennessee	13	6.0
1999—Tennessee	11	7.0
College totals (4 years)	46	15.0

WALTERS, TROY WR VIKINGS

PERSONAL: Born December 15, 1976, in College Station, Texas. ... 5-7/171.
HIGH SCHOOL: A&M Consolidated (College Station, Texas).
COLLEGE: Stanford.
TRANSACTIONS/CAREER NOTES: Selected by Minnesota Vikings in fifth round (165th pick overall) of 2000 NFL draft.
HONORS: Named wide receiver on The Sporting News college All-America first team (1999). ... Fred Biletnikoff Award winner (1999).
COLLEGE NOTES: Rushed twice for six yards and returned 15 kickoffs for 284 yards (1999).

Year Team	G	RECEIVING No.	Yds.	Avg.	TD	PUNT RETURNS No.	Yds.	Avg.	TD	TOTALS TD	Pts.
1995—Stanford						Redshirted.					
1996—Stanford	11	32	444	13.9	3	24	268	11.2	1	4	24
1997—Stanford	11	86	1206	14.0	8	30	424	14.1	2	10	60
1998—Stanford	9	52	880	16.9	5	13	87	6.7	0	5	30
1999—Stanford	11	74	1456	19.7	10	19	131	6.9	0	10	60
College totals (4 years)	42	244	3986	16.3	26	86	910	10.6	3	29	174

WARREN, STEVE DT PACKERS

PERSONAL: Born January 22, 1978, in Springfield, Mo. ... 6-1/307.
HIGH SCHOOL: Kickapoo (Springfield, Mo.).
COLLEGE: Nebraska.
TRANSACTIONS/CAREER NOTES: Selected by Green Bay Packers in third round (74th pick overall) of 2000 NFL draft.

Year Team	G	SACKS
1996—Nebraska	8	0.5
1997—Nebraska	12	1.0
1998—Nebraska	10	0.0
1999—Nebraska	12	7.0
College totals (4 years)	42	8.5

WARRICK, PETER WR BENGALS

PERSONAL: Born June 19, 1977, in Bradenton, Fla. ... 5-11/195.
HIGH SCHOOL: Southeast (Bradenton, Fla.).
COLLEGE: Florida State.
TRANSACTIONS/CAREER NOTES: Selected by Cincinnati Bengals in first round (fourth pick overall) of 2000 NFL draft.
HONORS: Named wide receiver on The Sporting News college All-America first team (1998 and 1999).
COLLEGE NOTES: Rushed eight times for 20 yards (1996); rushed three times for minus 16 yards (1997); rushed 13 times for 85 yards and a touchdown and attempted four passes with two completions for 60 yards and one touchdown (1998); rushed 16 times for 96 yards and three touchdowns and attempted three passes with one completion for 35 yards and a touchdown (1999).

Year Team	G	RECEIVING No.	Yds.	Avg.	TD	PUNT RETURNS No.	Yds.	Avg.	TD	KICKOFF RETURNS No.	Yds.	Avg.	TD	TOTALS TD	Pts.
1995—Florida State							Redshirted.								
1996—Florida State	11	22	467	21.2	4	10	114	11.4	0	9	188	20.9	0	4	24
1997—Florida State	11	53	884	16.7	8	29	388	13.4	1	1	23	23.0	0	9	54
1998—Florida State	12	61	1232	20.2	12	15	208	13.9	0	0	0	0.0	0	13	78
1999—Florida State	9	71	934	13.2	8	18	227	12.6	1	0	0	0.0	0	12	72

| College totals (4 years) | 43 | 207 | 3517 | 17.0 | 32 | | 72 | 937 | 13.0 | 2 | | 10 | 211 | 21.1 | 0 | | 38 | 228 |

WASHINGTON, MARCUS — LB — COLTS

PERSONAL: Born October 17, 1977, in Auburn, Ala. ... 6-3/247. ... Full name: Marcus Cornelius Washington.
HIGH SCHOOL: Auburn (Ala.).
COLLEGE: Auburn.
TRANSACTIONS/CAREER NOTES: Selected by Indianapolis Colts in second round (59th pick overall) of 2000 NFL draft.

Year Team	G	SACKS
1996—Auburn	12	2.0
1997—Auburn	13	3.0
1998—Auburn	11	4.0
1999—Auburn	11	7.0
College totals (4 years)	47	16.0

WATSON, TIM — DT — SEAHAWKS

PERSONAL: Born December 23, 1974, in Williamstown, N.J. ... 6-4/290.
HIGH SCHOOL: Mainland Republic (N.J.).
COLLEGE: Maryland, then Rowan College (N.J.).
TRANSACTIONS/CAREER NOTES: Selected by Seattle Seahawks in sixth round (185th pick overall) of 2000 NFL draft.
COLLEGE NOTES: Recovered one fumble for 33 yards and a touchdown (1999).

Year Team	G	SACKS
1993—Maryland	7	0.0
1994—Maryland		Redshirted.
1995—Maryland	11	2.0
1996—Maryland	11	3.0
1997—		Did not play.
1998—		Did not play.
1999—Rowan College	14	11.0
College totals (4 years)	43	16.0

WEBSTER, JASON — CB — 49ERS

PERSONAL: Born September 8, 1977, in Houston. ... 5-9/180.
HIGH SCHOOL: Willowridge (Houston).
COLLEGE: Texas A&M.
TRANSACTIONS/CAREER NOTES: Selected by San Francisco 49ers in second round (48th pick overall) of 2000 NFL draft.
COLLEGE NOTES: Returned three punts for 97 yards and recovered two fumbles (1998); returned 12 punts for 75 yards, reutrned five kick-offs for 103 yards and recovered two fumbles (1999).

		INTERCEPTIONS			
Year Team	G	No.	Yds.	Avg.	TD
1996—Texas A&M	12	1	6	6.0	0
1997—Texas A&M	12	0	0	0.0	0
1998—Texas A&M	12	2	49	24.5	0
1999—Texas A&M	11	4	14	3.5	0
College totals (4 years)	47	7	69	9.9	0

WEBSTER, NATE — LB — BUCCANEERS

PERSONAL: Born November 29, 1977, in Miami. ... 5-11/225. ... Full name: Nathaniel Webster Jr.
HIGH SCHOOL: Northwestern (Miami).
COLLEGE: Miami (Fla.).
TRANSACTIONS/CAREER NOTES: Selected after junior season by Tampa Bay Buccaneers in third round (90th pick overall) of 2000 NFL draft.
HONORS: Named linebacker on THE SPORTING NEWS college All-America second team (1999).
COLLEGE NOTES: Intercepted three passes (1999).

Year Team	G	SACKS
1997—Miami (Fla.)	6	0.0
1998—Miami (Fla.)	10	3.0
1999—Miami (Fla.)	12	4.0
College totals (3 years)	28	7.0

WESLEY, GREG — S — CHIEFS

PERSONAL: Born March 19, 1976, in England, Ark. ... 6-2/214. ... Full name: Gregory Wesley.
HIGH SCHOOL: England (Ark.).
COLLEGE: Arkansas-Pine Bluff.
TRANSACTIONS/CAREER NOTES: Selected by Kansas City Chiefs in third round (85th pick overall) of 2000 NFL draft.
COLLEGE NOTES: Credited with one sack (1997).

		INTERCEPTIONS			
Year Team	G	No.	Yds.	Avg.	TD
1996—Arkansas-Pine Bluff		Did not play.			
1997—Arkansas-Pine Bluff	9	0	0	0.0	0

	G	No.	Yds.	Avg.	TD
1998—Arkansas-Pine Bluff	11	3	17	5.7	0
1999—Arkansas-Pine Bluff	11	4	68	17.0	0
College totals (3 years)	31	7	85	12.1	0

WHALEN, JAMES   TE   BUCCANEERS

PERSONAL: Born December 11, 1977, in Portland, Ore. ... 6-2/228. ... Full name: James Patrick Whalen Jr.
HIGH SCHOOL: La Salle (Portland, Ore.).
JUNIOR COLLEGE: Shasta College (Calif.).
COLLEGE: Kentucky.
TRANSACTIONS/CAREER NOTES: Selected by Tampa Bay Buccaneers in fifth round (157th pick overall) of 2000 NFL draft.

		RECEIVING			
Year Team	G	No.	Yds.	Avg.	TD
1996—Shasta College	...	17	257	15.1	5
1997—Kentucky	11	7	66	9.4	0
1998—Kentucky	11	23	239	10.4	3
1999—Kentucky	11	90	1019	11.3	10
Junior college totals (1 year)	...	17	257	15.1	5
College totals (3 years)	33	120	1324	11.0	13

WHEATLEY, AUSTIN   TE   SAINTS

PERSONAL: Born November 16, 1977, in Milan, Ill. ... 6-5/254.
HIGH SCHOOL: Rock Island (Ill.).
COLLEGE: Iowa.
TRANSACTIONS/CAREER NOTES: Selected by New Orleans Saints in fifth round (158th pick overall) of 2000 NFL draft.
COLLEGE NOTES: Punted five times for 205 yards (1997).

		RECEIVING			
Year Team	G	No.	Yds.	Avg.	TD
1995—Iowa			Redshirted.		
1996—Iowa	11	0	0	0.0	0
1997—Iowa	12	7	108	15.4	1
1998—Iowa	11	9	137	15.2	0
1999—Iowa	11	9	103	11.4	0
College totals (4 years)	45	25	348	13.9	1

WHEELER, DAMEN   CB   CHARGERS

PERSONAL: Born September 3, 1977, in Sacramento. ... 5-9/170.
HIGH SCHOOL: Valley (Sacramento).
COLLEGE: Colorado.
TRANSACTIONS/CAREER NOTES: Selected by San Diego Chargers in sixth round (203rd pick overall) of 2000 NFL draft.
COLLEGE NOTES: Returned seven kickoffs for 91 yards and two punts for 33 yards (1997); returned five punts for 67 yards (1999).

		INTERCEPTIONS			
Year Team	G	No.	Yds.	Avg.	TD
1996—Colorado	7	2	26	13.0	0
1997—Colorado	11	1	0	0.0	0
1998—Colorado	11	1	38	38.0	0
1999—Colorado	11	4	40	10.0	1
College totals (4 years)	40	8	104	13.0	1

WHITE, DEZ   WR   BEARS

PERSONAL: Born August 23, 1979, in Orange Park, Fla. ... 6-0/219. ... Full name: Edward Dezmon White. ... Nephew of Adrian White, defensive back with New York Giants (1987-89 and 1991), Green Bay Packers (1992) and New England Patriots (1993).
HIGH SCHOOL: Bolles (Orange Park, Fla.).
COLLEGE: Georgia Tech.
TRANSACTIONS/CAREER NOTES: Selected after junior season by Chicago Bears in third round (69th pick overall) of 2000 NFL draft.
COLLEGE NOTES: Rushed 11 times for 67 yards (1999).

		RECEIVING				KICKOFF RETURNS				TOTALS	
Year Team	G	No.	Yds.	Avg.	TD	No.	Yds.	Avg.	TD	TD	Pts.
1997—Georgia Tech	10	0	0	0.0	0	14	330	23.6	1	1	6
1998—Georgia Tech	11	46	973	21.2	9	26	682	26.2	1	10	60
1999—Georgia Tech	11	44	860	19.5	5	29	689	23.8	0	5	30
College totals (3 years)	32	90	1833	20.4	14	69	1701	24.7	2	16	96

WILEY, MICHAEL   WR   COWBOYS

PERSONAL: Born January 5, 1978, in Spring Valley, Calif. ... 5-11/189.
HIGH SCHOOL: Monte Vista (Spring Valley, Calif.).
COLLEGE: Ohio State.
TRANSACTIONS/CAREER NOTES: Selected by Dallas Cowboys in fifth round (143rd pick overall) of 2000 NFL draft.
COLLEGE NOTES: Attempted four passes with three completions for 69 yards and one touchdown (1997); attempted two passes with two completions for 33 yards (1998); attempted five passes with five completions for 123 yards and one touchdown (1999).

			RUSHING				RECEIVING				KICKOFF RETURNS				TOTALS	
Year	Team	G	Att.	Yds.	Avg.	TD	No.	Yds.	Avg.	TD	No.	Yds.	Avg.	TD	TD	Pts.
1996—Ohio State		10	23	176	7.7	1	6	194	32.3	3	1	12	12.0	0	4	24
1997—Ohio State		13	105	588	5.6	6	9	83	9.2	0	13	344	26.5	1	7	42
1998—Ohio State		12	198	1235	6.2	10	27	200	7.4	1	6	143	23.8	0	11	66
1999—Ohio State		12	183	952	5.2	10	14	153	10.9	1	8	114	14.3	0	11	66
College totals (4 years)		47	509	2951	5.8	27	56	630	11.3	5	28	613	21.9	1	33	198

WILLIAMS, BOBBY — G — EAGLES

PERSONAL: Born September 25, 1976, in Jefferson, Texas. ... 6-3/320.
HIGH SCHOOL: Jefferson (Texas).
COLLEGE: Arkansas.
TRANSACTIONS/CAREER NOTES: Selected by Philadelphia Eagles in second round (61st pick overall) of 2000 NFL draft.
COLLEGE NOTES: Arkansas, 1995-1999. ... Games: 1995 (redshirted), 1996 (9), 1997 (11), 1998 (11), 1999 (11). Total: 42.

WILLIAMS, JAMES — WR — SEAHAWKS

PERSONAL: Born March 6, 1978, in Raymond, Miss. ... 5-10/180.
HIGH SCHOOL: Warren Central (Vicksburg, Miss.).
JUNIOR COLLEGE: Hinds Community College (Miss.).
COLLEGE: Marshall.
TRANSACTIONS/CAREER NOTES: Selected by Seattle Seahawks in sixth round (175th pick overall) of 2000 NFL draft.
COLLEGE NOTES: Returned 12 kickoffs for 302 yards (1998); returned 15 kickoffs for 494 yards and one touchdown (1999).

			RECEIVING			
Year	Team	G	No.	Yds.	Avg.	TD
1996—Hinds CC		...	17	326	19.2	3
1997—Hinds CC		...	30	463	15.4	3
1998—Marshall		12	26	591	22.7	4
1999—Marshall		...	47	880	18.7	13
Junior college totals (2 years)		...	47	789	16.8	6
College totals (2 years)		...	73	1471	20.2	17

WILLIAMS, JOSH — DT — COLTS

PERSONAL: Born August 9, 1976, in Houston. ... 6-3/284.
HIGH SCHOOL: Cypress Creek (Houston).
COLLEGE: Michigan.
TRANSACTIONS/CAREER NOTES: Selected by Indianapolis Colts in fourth round (122nd pick overall) of 2000 NFL draft.

Year	Team	G	SACKS
1995—Michigan		Redshirted.	
1996—Michigan		11	0.0
1997—Michigan		12	7.0
1998—Michigan		13	1.0
1999—Michigan		12	3.0
College totals (4 years)		48	11.0

WILSON, ANTONIO — LB — VIKINGS

PERSONAL: Born December 29, 1977, in Seagoville, Texas. ... 6-2/244.
HIGH SCHOOL: Skyline (Dallas).
COLLEGE: Texas A&M-Commerce.
TRANSACTIONS/CAREER NOTES: Selected by Minnesota Vikings in fourth round (106th pick overall) of 2000 NFL draft.
COLLEGE NOTES: Intercepted one pass for 18 yards (1997); Intercepted one pass and recovered two fumbles for 65 yards and one touchdown (1998); intercepted one pass (1999).

Year	Team	G	SACKS
1995—Texas A&M-Commerce		Redshirted.	
1996—Texas A&M-Commerce		11	2.0
1997—Texas A&M-Commerce		11	2.5
1998—Texas A&M-Commerce		11	2.0
1999—Texas A&M-Commerce		11	9.0
College totals (4 years)		44	15.5

WILSON, GILLIS — DE — PANTHERS

PERSONAL: Born October 15, 1977, in Morgan City, La. ... 6-2/282. ... Full name: Gillis R. Wilson III.
HIGH SCHOOL: Patterson (La.).
COLLEGE: Southern.
TRANSACTIONS/CAREER NOTES: Selected by Carolina Panthers in seventh round (147th pick overall) of 2000 NFL draft.

Year	Team	G	SACKS
1996—Southern		Statistics unavailable.	

1997—Southern	4	0.0
1998—Southern	11	1.0
1999—Southern	12	8.0
College totals (3 years)	27	9.0

WOODARD, CEDRIC — DT — RAVENS

PERSONAL: Born September 5, 1977, in Bay City, Texas. ... 6-2/290. ... Full name: Cedric Darnell Woodard. ... Cousin of Tracy Simien, linebacker with Pittsbrugh Steelers (1989), Kansas City Chiefs (1991-97) and San Diego Chargers (1999); and cousin of Elmo Wright, wide receiver with Kansas City Chiefs (1971-74), Houston Oilers (1975) and New England Patriots (1975).
HIGH SCHOOL: Sweeny (Texas).
COLLEGE: Texas.
TRANSACTIONS/CAREER NOTES: Selected by Baltimore Ravens in sixth round (191st pick overall) of 2000 NFL draft.

Year Team	G	SACKS
1996—Texas	12	10.0
1997—Texas	11	1.0
1998—Texas	11	6.0
1999—Texas	13	4.0
College totals (4 years)	47	21.0

WYNN, SPERGON — QB — BROWNS

PERSONAL: Born August 10, 1978, in Houston. ... 6-3/226.
HIGH SCHOOL: Episcopal (Bellaire, Texas).
COLLEGE: Minnesota, then Southwest Texas State.
TRANSACTIONS/CAREER NOTES: Selected by Cleveland Browns in sixth round (183rd pick overall) of 2000 NFL draft.

Year Team	G	PASSING								RUSHING				TOTALS	
		Att.	Cmp.	Pct.	Yds.	TD	Int.	Avg.	Rat.	Att.	Yds.	Avg.	TD	TD	Pts.
1995—Minnesota					Redshirted.										
1996—Minnesota	2	1	0	0.0	0	0	1	0.0	-200.0	3	8	2.7	0	0	0
1997—Minnesota					Did not play.										
1998—Southwest Texas State	11	284	173	60.9	1851	10	6	6.52	123.1	127	-196	-1.5	2	2	12
1999—Southwest Texas State	11	323	161	49.8	1646	14	13	5.10	98.9	94	-49	-0.5	3	3	18
College totals (3 years)	24	608	334	54.9	3497	24	20	5.75	109.7	224	-237	-1.1	5	5	30

YOUNG, BRIAN — DE — RAMS

PERSONAL: Born July 8, 1977, in Lawton, Okla. ... 6-2/278.
HIGH SCHOOL: Andress (El Paso, Texas).
COLLEGE: Texas-El Paso.
TRANSACTIONS/CAREER NOTES: Selected by St. Louis Rams in fifth round (139th pick overall) of 2000 NFL draft.

Year Team	G	SACKS
1995—Texas-El Paso	8	1.5
1996—Texas-El Paso		Redshirted.
1997—Texas-El Paso	11	3.0
1998—Texas-El Paso	11	3.5
1999—Texas-El Paso	12	8.0
College totals (4 years)	42	16.0

2000 DRAFT PICKS

BELICHICK, BILL — PATRIOTS

PERSONAL: Born April 16, 1952, in Nashville. ... Full name: William Stephen Belichick. ... Son of Steve Belichick, fullback with Detroit Lions (1941); head coach at Hiram (Ohio) College (1946-49); assistant coach, Vanderbilt (1949-53); assistant coach, North Carolina (1953-56); assistant coach, Navy (1956-83); and administrative assistant, Navy (1983-89).
HIGH SCHOOL: Annapolis (Md.) and Phillips Academy (Andover, Mass.).
COLLEGE: Wesleyan University (degree in economics, 1975).

HEAD COACHING RECORD

BACKGROUND: Assistant special teams coach, Baltimore Colts NFL (1975). ... Assistant special teams coach, Detroit Lions NFL (1976 and 1977). ... Assistant special teams coach/assistant to defensive coordinator, Denver Broncos NFL (1978). ... Special teams coach, New York Giants NFL (1979 and 1980). ... Linebackers coach, Giants (1981 and 1982). ... Defensive coordinator/linebackers coach, Giants (1983-1988). ... Defensive coordinator/secondary coach, Giants (1989 and 90). ... Assistant head coach/secondary coach, New England Patriots NFL (1996). ... Assistant head coach/secondary coach, New York Jets NFL (1997-1999).

			REGULAR SEASON			POST-SEASON	
	W	L	T	Pct.	Finish	W	L
1991—Cleveland NFL	6	10	0	.375	3rd/AFC Central Division	—	—
1992—Cleveland NFL	7	9	0	.438	3rd/AFC Central Division	—	—
1993—Cleveland NFL	7	9	0	.438	3rd/AFC Central Division	—	—
1994—Cleveland NFL	11	5	0	.688	2nd/AFC Central Division	1	1
1995—Cleveland NFL	5	11	0	.313	4th/AFC Central Division	—	—
Pro totals (5 years)	36	44	0	.450	**Pro totals (5 years)**	1	1

NOTES:
1994—Defeated New England, 20-13, in first-round playoff game; lost to Pittsburgh, 29-9, in conference playoff game.

BILLICK, BRIAN — RAVENS

PERSONAL: Born February 28, 1954, in Fairborn, Ohio. ... Full name: Brian Harold Billick. ... Played tight end.
HIGH SCHOOL: Redlands (Calif.).
COLLEGE: Air Force, then Brigham Young.
TRANSACTIONS/CAREER NOTES: Selected by San Francisco 49ers in 11th round of 1977 NFL draft. ... Signed by 49ers for 1977 season. ... Released by 49ers (August 30, 1977). ... Signed by Dallas Cowboys (May 1978). ... Released by Cowboys before 1978 season.

HEAD COACHING RECORD

BACKGROUND: Assistant coach, University of Redlands (1977). ... Graduate assistant, Brigham Young (1978). ... Assistant public relations director, San Francisco 49ers NFL (1979 and 1980). ... Assistant coach and recruiting coordinator, San Diego State (1981-1985). ... Offensive coordinator, Utah State (1986-1988). ... Assistant coach, Stanford (1989-1991). ... Tight ends coach, Minnesota Vikings (1992). ... Offensive coordinator, Minnesota Vikings (1993-1998).

			REGULAR SEASON			POST-SEASON	
	W	L	T	Pct.	Finish	W	L
1999—Baltimore NFL	8	8	0	.500	3rd/AFC Central Division	—	—

CAMPO, DAVE — COWBOYS

PERSONAL: Born July 18, 1947, in New London, Conn. ... Full name: David Cross Campo.
HIGH SCHOOL: Robert E. Fitch (Groton, Conn.).
COLLEGE: Central Connecticut State.

HEAD COACHING RECORD

BACKGROUND: Coach, Central Connecticut State (1971 and 1972). ... Coach, Albany State (1973). ... Coach, Bridgeport (1974). ... Coach, University of Pittsburgh (1975). ... Coach, Washington State (1976). ... Coach, Boise State (1977-1979). ... Coach, Oregon State (1980). ... Coach, Weber State (1981 and 1982). ... Coach, Iowa State (1983). ... Coach, Syracuse (1984-1986). ... Secondary coach, Miami, Fla. (1987 and 1988). ... Secondary coach, Dallas Cowboys NFL (1989-1994). ... Defensive coordinator, Cowboys (1995-1999).

COSLET, BRUCE — BENGALS

PERSONAL: Born August 5, 1946, in Oakdale, Calif. ... Full name: Bruce Noel Coslet. ... Played tight end.
HIGH SCHOOL: Joint Union (Oakdale, Calif.).
COLLEGE: Pacific (degrees in history and psychology).
TRANSACTIONS/CAREER NOTES: Signed as non-drafted free agent by Cincinnati Bengals (1969).
PRO STATISTICS: 1973—Returned one kickoff for no yards and recovered one fumble. 1975—Rushed once for one yard and recovered two fumbles for two yards. 1976—Recovered two fumbles.

		RECEIVING				TOTALS			
Year Team	G	No.	Yds.	Avg.	TD	TD	2pt.	Pts.	Fum.
1969—Cincinnati AFL	8	1	39	39.0	1	1	...	6	0
1970—Cincinnati NFL	14	8	97	12.1	1	1	...	6	0
1971—Cincinnati NFL	14	21	356	17.0	4	4	...	24	3
1972—Cincinnati NFL	10	5	48	9.6	1	1	...	6	0
1973—Cincinnati NFL	13	9	123	13.7	0	0	...	0	0
1974—Cincinnati NFL	14	2	24	12.0	0	0	...	0	0

1975—Cincinnati NFL	14	10	117	11.7	0	0	...	0	0
1976—Cincinnati NFL	14	5	73	14.6	2	2	...	12	0
AFL totals (1 year)	8	1	39	39.0	1	1	...	6	0
NFL totals (7 years)	93	60	838	14.0	8	8	...	48	3
Pro totals (8 years)	101	61	877	14.4	9	9	...	54	3

HEAD COACHING RECORD

BACKGROUND: Special teams/tight ends coach, San Francisco 49ers NFL (1980). ... Special teams/tight ends coach, Cincinnati Bengals NFL (1981-1983). ... Wide receivers coach, Bengals (1984 and 1985). ... Offensive coordinator, Bengals (1986-1989 and 1994-October 21, 1996).

		REGULAR SEASON				POST-SEASON	
	W	L	T	Pct.	Finish	W	L
1990—New York Jets NFL	6	10	0	.375	4th/AFC Eastern Division	—	—
1991—New York Jets NFL	8	8	0	.500	T2nd/AFC Eastern Division	0	1
1992—New York Jets NFL	4	12	0	.250	4th/AFC Eastern Division	—	—
1993—New York Jets NFL	8	8	0	.500	3rd/AFC Eastern Division	—	—
1996—Cincinnati NFL	7	2	0	.778	T3rd/AFC Central Division	—	—
1997—Cincinnati NFL	7	9	0	.438	4th/AFC Central Division	—	—
1998—Cincinnati NFL	3	13	0	.188	5th/AFC Central Division	—	—
1999—Cincinnati NFL	4	12	0	.250	5th/AFC Central Division	—	—
Pro totals (8 years)	47	74	0	.388	**Pro totals (2 years)**	0	1

NOTES:

1991—Lost to Houston, 17-10, in first-round playoff game.
1996—Replaced Dave Shula as head coach (October 21), with 1-6 record and club in fifth place.

COUGHLIN, TOM — JAGUARS

PERSONAL: Born August 31, 1946, in Waterloo, N.Y. ... Full name: Thomas Richard Coughlin.
HIGH SCHOOL: Waterloo (N.Y.) Central.
COLLEGE: Syracuse (bachelor's degree in education, 1968; master's degree in education, 1969).

HEAD COACHING RECORD

BACKGROUND: Graduate assistant, Syracuse (1969). ... Quarterbacks/offensive backfield coach, Syracuse (1974-1976). ... Offensive coordinator, Syracuse (1977-1980). ... Quarterbacks coach, Boston College (1980-1983). ... Receivers coach, Philadelphia Eagles NFL (1984 and 1985). ... Receivers coach, Green Bay Packers NFL (1986 and 1987). ... Receivers coach, New York Giants NFL (1988-1990).

		REGULAR SEASON				POST-SEASON	
	W	L	T	Pct.	Finish	W	L
1970—Rochester Tech	4	3	0	.571	Eastern College Athletic Conference	—	—
1971—Rochester Tech	5	2	1	.688	Eastern College Athletic Conference	—	—
1972—Rochester Tech	4	5	0	.444	Eastern College Athletic Conference	—	—
1973—Rochester Tech	3	5	1	.389	Eastern College Athletic Conference	—	—
1991—Boston College	4	7	0	.364	7th/Big East Conference	—	—
1992—Boston College	8	2	1	.773	3rd/Big East Conference	0	1
1993—Boston College	8	3	0	.727	3rd/Big East Conference	1	0
1995—Jacksonville NFL	4	12	0	.250	5th/AFC Central Division	—	—
1996—Jacksonville NFL	9	7	0	.563	2nd/AFC Central Division	2	1
1997—Jacksonville NFL	11	5	0	.688	T1st/AFC Central Division	0	1
1998—Jacksonville NFL	11	5	0	.688	1st/AFC Central Division	1	1
1999—Jacksonville NFL	14	2	0	.875	1st/AFC Central Division	1	1
College totals (7 years)	36	27	3	.568	**College totals (2 years)**	1	1
Pro totals (5 years)	49	31	0	.613	**Pro totals (4 years)**	4	4

NOTES:

1992—Lost to Tennessee, 38-23, in Hall of Fame Bowl.
1993—Defeated Virginia, 31-13, in CarQuest Bowl.
1996—Defeated Buffalo, 30-27, in first-round playoff game; defeated Denver, 30-27, in conference playoff game; lost to New England, 20-6, in AFC championship game.
1997—Lost to Denver, 42-17, in first-round playoff game.
1998—Defeated New England, 25-10, in first-round playoff game; lost to New York Jets, 34-24, in conference playoff game.
1999—Defeated Miami, 62-7, in conference playoff game; lost to Tennessee, 33-14, in AFC championship game.

COWHER, BILL — STEELERS

PERSONAL: Born May 8, 1957, in Pittsburgh. ... Full name: William Laird Cowher. ... Played linebacker.
HIGH SCHOOL: Carlynton (Carnegie, Pa.).
COLLEGE: North Carolina State (bachelor of science degree in education, 1979).
TRANSACTIONS/CAREER NOTES: Signed as non-drafted free agent by Philadelphia Eagles (May 8, 1979). ... Released by Eagles (August 14, 1979). ... Signed by Cleveland Browns (February 27, 1980). ... On injured reserve with knee injury (August 20, 1981-entire season). ... Traded by Browns to Eagles for ninth-round pick (WR Don Jones) in 1984 draft (August 21, 1983). ... On injured reserve with knee injury (September 25, 1984-remainder of season).
PLAYING EXPERIENCE: Cleveland NFL, 1980 and 1982; Philadelphia NFL, 1983 and 1984. ... Games: 1980 (16), 1982 (9), 1983 (16), 1984 (4). Total: 45.
PRO STATISTICS: 1983—Recovered one fumble.

HEAD COACHING RECORD

BACKGROUND: Special teams coach, Cleveland Browns NFL (1985 and 1986). ... Defensive backs coach, Browns (1987 and 1988). ... Defensive coordinator, Kansas City Chiefs NFL (1989-1991).

HONORS: Named NFL Coach of the Year by THE SPORTING NEWS (1992).

	W	L	T	Pct.	REGULAR SEASON Finish	POST-SEASON W	L
1992—Pittsburgh NFL	11	5	0	.688	1st/AFC Central Division	0	1
1993—Pittsburgh NFL	9	7	0	.563	2nd/AFC Central Division	0	1
1994—Pittsburgh NFL	12	4	0	.750	1st/AFC Central Division	1	1
1995—Pittsburgh NFL	11	5	0	.688	1st/AFC Central Division	2	1
1996—Pittsburgh NFL	10	6	0	.625	1st/AFC Central Division	1	1
1997—Pittsburgh NFL	11	5	0	.688	T1st/AFC Central Division	1	1
1998—Pittsburgh NFL	7	9	0	.438	3rd/AFC Central Division	—	—
1999—Pittsburgh NFL	6	10	0	.375	4th/AFC Central Division	—	—
Pro totals (8 years)	**77**	**51**	**0**	**.602**	**Pro totals (7 years)**	**5**	**6**

NOTES:
1992—Lost to Buffalo, 24-3, in conference playoff game.
1993—Lost to Kansas City, 27-24 (OT), in first-round playoff game.
1994—Defeated Cleveland, 29-9, in conference playoff game; lost to San Diego, 17-13, in AFC championship game.
1995—Defeated Buffalo, 40-21, in conference playoff game; defeated Indianapolis, 20-16, in AFC championship game; lost to Dallas, 27-17, in Super Bowl XXX.
1996—Defeated Indianapolis, 42-14, in first-round playoff game; lost to New England, 28-3, in conference playoff game.
1997—Defeated New England, 7-6, in conference playoff game; lost to Denver, 24-21, in AFC championship game.

CUNNINGHAM, GUNTHER — CHIEFS

PERSONAL: Born June 19, 1949, in Munich, Germany. ... Full name: Gunther Manfred Cunningham.
HIGH SCHOOL: Lompoc (Calif.).
JUNIOR COLLEGE: Allan Hancock College (Calif.).
COLLEGE: Oregon.

HEAD COACHING RECORD

BACKGROUND: Defensive line coach, Oregon (1969-1971). ... Defensive line coach, Arkansas (1972). ... Assistant offensive line coach/head coach freshman team, Stanford (1973). ... Defensive line coach, Stanford (1974-1976). ... Secondary coach, University of California (1977). ... Linebackers coach, University of California (1978). ... Defensive coordinator/defensive line coach, University of California (1979 and 1980). ... Defensive line/linebackers coach, Hamilton Tiger-Cats of CFL (1981). ... Defensive line coach, Baltimore Colts NFL (1982-1984). ... Defensive line coach, San Diego Chargers NFL (1985-1990). ... Linebackers coach, Oakland Raiders NFL (1991). ... Defensive coordinator, Raiders (1992 and 1993). ... Defensive line coach, Raiders (1994). ... Defensive coordinator, Kansas City Chiefs NFL (1995-1998).

	W	L	T	Pct.	REGULAR SEASON Finish	POST-SEASON W	L
1999—Kansas City NFL	9	7	0	.563	T1st/AFC Western Division	—	—

DUNGY, TONY — BUCCANEERS

PERSONAL: Born October 6, 1955, in Jackson, Mich. ... Full name: Anthony Kevin Dungy. ... Played defensive back and quarterback. ... Name pronounced DUN-gee.
HIGH SCHOOL: Parkside (Jackson, Mich.).
COLLEGE: Minnesota (degree in business administration, 1978).
TRANSACTIONS/CAREER NOTES: Signed as non-drafted free agent by Pittsburgh Steelers (May 1977). ... Traded by Steelers to San Francisco 49ers for 10th-round pick in 1980 draft (August 21, 1979). ... Traded by 49ers with RB Mike Hogan to New York Giants for WR Jimmy Robinson and CB Ray Rhodes (March 27, 1980).
CHAMPIONSHIP GAME EXPERIENCE: Played in AFC championship game (1978 season). ... Played in Super Bowl XIII (1978 season).
PRO STATISTICS: 1977—Attempted eight passes with three completions for 43 yards and two interceptions, rushed three times for eight yards and fumbled once. 1978—Recovered two fumbles for eight yards. 1979—Recovered two fumbles.

Year Team	G	INTERCEPTIONS No.	Yds.	Avg.	TD
1977—Pittsburgh NFL	14	3	37	12.3	0
1978—Pittsburgh NFL	16	6	95	15.8	0
1979—San Francisco NFL	15	0	0	...	0
Pro totals (3 years)	**45**	**9**	**132**	**14.7**	**0**

HEAD COACHING RECORD

BACKGROUND: Defensive backs coach, University of Minnesota (1980). ... Defensive assistant, Pittsburgh Steelers NFL (1981). ... Defensive backs coach, Steelers (1982 and 1983). ... Defensive coordinator, Steelers (1984-1988). ... Defensive backs coach, Kansas City Chiefs NFL (1989-1991). ... Defensive coordinator, Minnesota Vikings NFL (1992-1995).

	W	L	T	Pct.	REGULAR SEASON Finish	POST-SEASON W	L
1996—Tampa Bay NFL	6	10	0	.375	4th/NFC Central Division	—	—
1997—Tampa Bay NFL	10	6	0	.625	2nd/NFC Central Division	1	1
1998—Tampa Bay NFL	8	8	0	.500	3rd/NFC Central Division	—	—
1999—Tampa Bay NFL	11	5	0	.688	1st/NFC Central Division	1	1
Pro totals (4 years)	**35**	**29**	**0**	**.547**	**Pro totals (2 years)**	**2**	**2**

NOTES:
1997—Defeated Detroit, 20-10, in first-round playoff game; lost to Green Bay, 21-7, in conference playoff game.
1999—Defeated Washington, 14-13, in conference playoff game; lost to St. Louis, 11-6, in NFC championship game.

FASSEL, JIM   GIANTS

PERSONAL: Born August 31, 1949, in Anaheim. ... Full name: James Fassel. ... Played quarterback.
HIGH SCHOOL: Anaheim (Calif.) High.
JUNIOR COLLEGE: Fullerton (Calif.) College.
COLLEGE: Southern California, then Long Beach State (degree in physical education, 1972).
TRANSACTIONS/CAREER NOTES: Selected by Chicago Bears in seventh round of 1972 NFL draft.

HEAD COACHING RECORD

BACKGROUND: Coach, Fullerton College (1973). ... Player/coach, Hawaii Hawaiians WFL (1974). ... Quarterbacks/receivers coach, Utah (1976). ... Offensive coordinator, Weber State (1977 and 1978). ... Offensive coordinator, Stanford (1979-1983). ... Offensive coordinator, New Orleans Breakers USFL (1984) ... Quarterbacks coach, New York Giants NFL (1991). ... Offensive coordinator, Giants (1992) ... Assistant head coach/offensive coordinator, Denver Broncos NFL (1993 and 1994). ... Quarterbacks coach, Oakland Raiders NFL (1995). ... Offensive coordinator/quarterbacks coach, Arizona Cardinals NFL (1996).
HONORS: Named NFL Coach of the Year by THE SPORTING NEWS (1997).

				REGULAR SEASON		POST-SEASON	
	W	L	T	Pct.	Finish	W	L
1985—Utah	8	4	0	.667	2nd/Western Athletic Conference	—	—
1986—Utah	2	9	0	.182	9th/Western Athletic Conference	—	—
1987—Utah	5	7	0	.417	7th/Western Athletic Conference	—	—
1988—Utah	6	5	0	.545	4th/Western Athletic Conference	—	—
1989—Utah	4	8	0	.333	7th/Western Athletic Conference	—	—
1997—New York Giants NFL	10	5	1	.656	1st/NFC Eastern Division	0	1
1998—New York Giants NFL	8	8	0	.500	3rd/NFC Eastern Division	—	—
1999—New York Giants NFL	7	9	0	.438	3rd/NFC Eastern Division	—	—
College totals (5 years)	25	33	0	.431			
Pro totals (3 years)	25	22	1	.531	Pro totals (2 years)	0	1

NOTES:
1997—Lost to Minnesota, 23-22, in first-round playoff game.

FISHER, JEFF   TITANS

PERSONAL: Born February 25, 1958, in Culver City, Calif. ... Full name: Jeffrey Michael Fisher. ... Played safety.
HIGH SCHOOL: Taft (Woodland Hills, Calif.).
COLLEGE: Southern California (degree in public administration, 1981).
TRANSACTIONS/CAREER NOTES: Selected by Chicago Bears in seventh round (177th pick overall) of 1981 NFL draft. ... On injured reserve with broken leg (October 24, 1983-remainder of season). ... On injured reserve with ankle injury entire 1985 season.
CHAMPIONSHIP GAME EXPERIENCE: Played in NFC championship game (1984 season).
PRO STATISTICS: 1981—Recovered one fumble. 1984—Recovered one fumble.

Year Team	G	INTERCEPTIONS				PUNT RETURNS				KICKOFF RETURNS				TOTALS			
		No.	Yds.	Avg.	TD	No.	Yds.	Avg.	TD	No.	Yds.	Avg.	TD	TD	2pt.	Pts.	Fum.
1981—Chicago NFL	16	2	3	1.5	0	43	509	11.8	1	7	102	14.6	0	1	...	6	3
1982—Chicago NFL	9	3	19	6.3	0	7	53	7.6	0	7	102	14.6	0	0	...	0	2
1983—Chicago NFL	8	0	0	...	0	13	71	5.5	0	0	0	...	0	0	...	0	0
1984—Chicago NFL	16	0	0	...	0	57	492	8.6	0	0	0	...	0	0	...	0	4
1985—Chicago NFL							Did not play.										
Pro totals (4 years)	49	5	22	4.4	0	120	1125	9.4	1	14	204	14.6	0	1	0	6	9

HEAD COACHING RECORD

BACKGROUND: Defensive backs coach, Philadelphia Eagles NFL (1986-1988). ... Defensive coordinator, Eagles (1989 and 1990). ... Defensive coordinator, Los Angeles Rams NFL (1991). ... Defensive backs coach, San Francisco 49ers NFL (1992 and 1993). ... Defensive coordinator, Houston Oilers NFL (February 9-November 14, 1994). ... Oilers franchise moved to Tennessee for 1997 season.

				REGULAR SEASON		POST-SEASON	
	W	L	T	Pct.	Finish	W	L
1994—Houston NFL	1	5	0	.167	4th/AFC Central Division	—	—
1995—Houston NFL	7	9	0	.438	T2nd/AFC Central Division	—	—
1996—Houston NFL	8	8	0	.500	T3rd/AFC Central Division	—	—
1997—Tennessee NFL	8	8	0	.500	3rd/AFC Central Division	—	—
1998—Tennessee NFL	8	8	0	.500	2nd/AFC Central Division	—	—
1999—Tennessee NFL	13	3	0	.813	2nd/AFC Central Division	3	1
Pro totals (6 years)	45	41	0	.523	Pro totals (1 year)	3	1

NOTES:
1994—Replaced Jack Pardee as head coach (November 14) with 1-9 record and club in fourth place.
1999—Defeated Buffalo, 22-16, in first-round playoff game; defeated Indianapolis, 19-16, in conference playoff game; defeated Jacksonville, 33-14, in AFC championship game; lost to St. Louis, 23-16, in Super Bowl XXXIV.

GREEN, DENNIS   VIKINGS

PERSONAL: Born February 17, 1949, in Harrisburg, Pa.
HIGH SCHOOL: John Harris (Harrisburg, Pa.).
COLLEGE: Iowa (degree in recreation education, 1971).

HEAD COACHING RECORD

BACKGROUND: Graduate assistant, University of Iowa (1972). ... Running backs/receivers coach, Dayton (1973). ... Running backs/receivers coach, Iowa (1974-1976). ... Running backs coach, Stanford (1977 and 1978). ... Special teams coach, San Francisco 49ers NFL (1979). ... Offensive coordinator, Stanford (1980). ... Receivers coach, 49ers (1986-1988).

				REGULAR SEASON		POST-SEASON	
	W	L	T	Pct.	Finish	W	L
1981—Northwestern	0	11	0	.000	10th/Big Ten Conference	—	—
1982—Northwestern	3	8	0	.273	T8th/Big Ten Conference	—	—
1983—Northwestern	2	9	0	.182	T8th/Big Ten Conference	—	—
1984—Northwestern	2	9	0	.182	9th/Big Ten Conference	—	—
1985—Northwestern	3	8	0	.273	T9th/Big Ten Conference	—	—
1989—Stanford	3	8	0	.273	T7th/Pacific-10 Conference	—	—
1990—Stanford	5	6	0	.455	T6th/Pacific-10 Conference	—	—
1991—Stanford	8	3	0	.727	T2nd/Pacific-10 Conference	0	1
1992—Minnesota NFL	11	5	0	.688	1st/NFC Central Division	0	1
1993—Minnesota NFL	9	7	0	.563	2nd/NFC Central Division	0	1
1994—Minnesota NFL	10	6	0	.625	1st/NFC Central Division	0	1
1995—Minnesota NFL	8	8	0	.500	4th/NFC Central Division	—	—
1996—Minnesota NFL	9	7	0	.563	2nd/NFC Central Division	0	1
1997—Minnesota NFL	9	7	0	.563	T3rd/NFC Central Division	1	1
1998—Minnesota NFL	15	1	0	.938	1st/NFC Central Division	1	1
1999—Minnesota NFL	10	6	0	.625	2nd/NFC Central Division	1	1
College totals (8 years)	26	62	0	.295	**College totals (1 year)**	0	1
Pro totals (8 years)	81	47	0	.633	**Pro totals (7 years)**	3	7

NOTES:
1991—Lost to Georgia Tech, 18-17, in Aloha Bowl.
1992—Lost to Washington, 24-7, in first-round playoff game.
1993—Lost to New York Giants, 17-10, in first-round playoff game.
1994—Lost to Chicago, 35-18, in first-round playoff game.
1996—Lost to Dallas, 40-15, in first-round playoff game.
1997—Defeated New York Giants, 23-22, in first-round playoff game; lost to San Francisco, 38-22, in conference playoff game.
1998—Defeated Arizona, 41-21, in conference playoff game; lost to Atlanta, 30-27, in NFC championship game.
1999—Defeated Dallas, 27-10, in first-round playoff game; lost to St. Louis, 49-37, in conference playoff game.

GROH, AL   JETS

PERSONAL: Born July 13, 1944, in New York.
HIGH SCHOOL: Chaminade (Manhasset, N.Y.).
COLLEGE: Virginia (degree in commerce, 1967).

HEAD COACHING RECORD

BACKGROUND: Coach, Albemarle High School, Charlottesville, Va. (1967). ... Defensive coach, Army freshman team (1968 and 1969). ... Head coach, Virginia freshman team (1970-1972). ... Defensive line coach, Virginia (1971 and 1972). ... Linebackers coach, North Carolina (1973-1977). ... Defensive coordinator, Air Force (1978-1979). ... Defensive coordinator, Texas Tech (1980). ... Special teams coach/tight ends coach, Atlanta Falcons NFL (1987). ... Offensive coordinator, South Carolina (1988). ... Linebackers coach, New York Giants NFL (1989 and 1990). ... Defensive coordinator, Giants (1991). ... Linebackers coach, Cleveland Browns NFL (1992). ... Defensive coordinator/linebackers coach, New England Patriots NFL (1993-1996). ... Linebackers coach, New York Jets NFL (1997-1999).

				REGULAR SEASON		POST-SEASON	
	W	L	T	Pct.	Finish	W	L
1981—Wake Forest	4	7	0	.364	6th/Atlantic Coast Conference	—	—
1982—Wake Forest	3	8	0	.273	7th/Atlantic Coast Conference	—	—
1983—Wake Forest	4	7	0	.364	7th/Atlantic Coast Conference	—	—
1984—Wake Forest	6	5	0	.545	4th/Atlantic Coast Conference	—	—
1985—Wake Forest	4	7	0	.364	8th/Atlantic Coast Conference	—	—
1986—Wake Forest	5	6	0	.455	8th/Atlantic Coast Conference	—	—
College totals (6 years)	26	40	0	.394			

GRUDEN, JON   RAIDERS

PERSONAL: Born August 17, 1963, in Sandusky, Ohio. ... Son of Jim Gruden, scout, San Francisco 49ers; and brother of Jay Gruden, quarterback with Tampa Bay Storm of Arena League (1991-96) and current head coach, Orlando Predators of Arena League.
HIGH SCHOOL: Clay (South Bend, Ind.).
COLLEGE: Dayton, then Tennessee (degree in communications, 1985).

HEAD COACHING RECORD

BACKGROUND: Graduate assistant, Tennessee (1986 and 1987). ... Passing game coordinator, Southeast Missouri State (1988). ... Wide receivers coach, Pacific (1989). ... Assistant coach, San Francisco 49ers NFL (1990) ... Wide receivers coach, University of Pittsburgh (1991). ... Offensive/quality control coach, Green Bay Packers NFL (1992). ... Wide receivers coach, Packers (1993 and 1994). ... Offensive coordinator, Philadelphia Eagles NFL (1995-1997).

	REGULAR SEASON					POST-SEASON	
	W	L	T	Pct.	Finish	W	L
1998—Oakland NFL	8	8	0	.500	T2nd/AFC Western Division	—	—
1999—Oakland NFL	8	8	0	.500	T3rd/AFC Western Division	—	—
Pro totals (2 years)	16	16	0	.500			

HASLETT, JIM   SAINTS

PERSONAL: Born December 9, 1957, in Pittsburgh. ... Full name: James Donald Haslett. ... Cousin of Hal Stringert, defensive back with San Diego Chargers (1974-80). ... Played linebacker.
HIGH SCHOOL: Avalon (Pittsburgh).
COLLEGE: Indiana University, Pa. (degree in elementary education).
TRANSACTIONS/CAREER NOTES: Selected by Buffalo Bills in second round (51st pick overall) of 1979 NFL draft. ... On injured reserve with back injury (September 13-November 17, 1983). ... On injured reserve with broken leg (September 1, 1986-entire season). ... Released by Bills (September 7, 1987). ... Signed by New York Jets as replacement player (September 30, 1987). ... On injured reserve with back injury (October 20, 1987-remainder of season).
HONORS: Played in Pro Bowl (1980 and 1981 seasons).
PRO STATISTICS: 1979—Recovered two fumbles. 1980—Recovered one fumble. 1982—Recovered one fumble and caught one pass for four yards. 1984—Recovered three fumbles for ten yards. 1985—Recovered three fumbles and fumbled once. 1987—Recovered one fumble.

		INTERCEPTIONS			
Year Team	G	No.	Yds.	Avg.	TD
1979—Buffalo NFL	16	2	15	7.5	0
1980—Buffalo NFL	16	2	30	15.0	0
1981—Buffalo NFL	16	0	0	...	0
1982—Buffalo NFL	6	0	0	...	0
1983—Buffalo NFL	5	0	0	...	0
1984—Buffalo NFL	15	0	0	...	0
1985—Buffalo NFL	16	1	40	40.0	0
1986—Buffalo NFL		Did not play.			
1987—New York Jets NFL	3	1	9	9.0	0
Pro totals (8 years)	93	6	94	15.7	0

HEAD COACHING RECORD

BACKGROUND: Linebackers coach, University of Buffalo (1988). ... Defensive coordinator, University of Buffalo (1989 and 1990). ... Defensive coordinator, Sacramento Surge W.L. (1991 and 1992). ... Linebackers coach, Oakland Raiders NFL (1993 and 1994). ... Linebackers coach, New Orleans Saints NFL (1995). ... Defensive coordinator, Saints (1996). ... Defensive coordinator, Pittsburgh Steelers NFL (1997-1999).

HOLMGREN, MIKE   SEAHAWKS

PERSONAL: Born June 15, 1948, in San Francisco. ... Full name: Michael George Holmgren. ... Played quarterback.
HIGH SCHOOL: Lincoln (San Francisco).
COLLEGE: Southern California (degree in business finance, 1970).
TRANSACTIONS/CAREER NOTES: Selected by St. Louis Cardinals in eighth round of 1970 NFL draft. ... Released by Cardinals (1970).

HEAD COACHING RECORD

BACKGROUND: Assistant coach, Sacred Heart Cathedral Prep School, San Francisco (1972 and 1973). ... Assistant coach, Oak Grove High School, San Jose, Calif. (1975-1980). ... Offensive coordinator/quarterbacks coach, San Francisco State (1981). ... Quarterbacks coach, Brigham Young (1982-1985). ... Quarterbacks coach, San Francisco 49ers NFL (1986-1988). ... Offensive coordinator, 49ers (1989-1991).

	REGULAR SEASON					POST-SEASON	
	W	L	T	Pct.	Finish	W	L
1992—Green Bay NFL	9	7	0	.563	2nd/NFC Central Division	—	—
1993—Green Bay NFL	9	7	0	.563	T2nd/NFC Central Division	1	1
1994—Green Bay NFL	9	7	0	.563	T2nd/NFC Central Division	1	1
1995—Green Bay NFL	11	5	0	.688	1st/NFC Central Division	2	1
1996—Green Bay NFL	13	3	0	.813	1st/NFC Central Division	3	0
1997—Green Bay NFL	13	3	0	.813	1st/NFC Central Division	2	1
1998—Green Bay NFL	11	5	0	.688	2nd/NFC/Central Division	0	1
1999—Seattle NFL	9	7	0	.563	T1st/AFC Western Division	0	1
Pro totals (8 years)	84	44	0	.656	**Pro totals (7 years)**	9	6

NOTES:
1993—Defeated Detroit, 28-24, in first-round playoff game; lost to Dallas 27-17, in conference playoff game.
1994—Defeated Detroit, 16-12, in first-round playoff game; lost to Dallas, 35-9, in conference playoff game.
1995—Defeated Atlanta, 37-20, in first-round playoff game; defeated San Francisco, 27-17, in conference playoff game; lost to Dallas, 38-27, in NFC championship game.
1996—Defeated San Francisco, 35-14, in conference playoff game; defeated Carolina, 30-13, in NFC championship game; defeated New England, 35-21, in Super Bowl XXXI.
1997—Defeated Tampa Bay, 21-7, in conference playoff game; defeated San Francisco, 23-10, in NFC championship game; lost to Denver, 31-24, in Super Bowl XXXII.
1998—Lost to San Francisco, 30-27, in first-round playoff game.
1999—Lost to Miami, 20-17, in first-round playoff game.

HEAD COACHES

JAURON, DICK — BEARS

PERSONAL: Born October 7, 1950, in Swampscott, Mass. ... Full name: Richard Manuel Jauron. ... Played defensive back.
COLLEGE: Yale (degree in history).
TRANSACTIONS/CAREER NOTES: Selected by Detroit Lions in fourth round of 1973 NFL draft. ... Released by Lions (August 23, 1978). ... Signed by Cincinnati Bengals (August 29, 1978). ... On injured reserve with knee injury (November 12, 1980-remainder of season).
HONORS: Played in Pro Bowl (1974 season).

Year Team	G	INTERCEPTIONS				PUNT RETURNS				KICKOFF RETURNS				TOTALS			
		No.	Yds.	Avg.	TD	No.	Yds.	Avg.	TD	No.	Yds.	Avg.	TD	TD	2pt.	Pts.	Fum.
1973—Detroit NFL	14	4	208	52.0	1	6	49	8.2	0	17	405	23.8	0	1	...	6	0
1974—Detroit NFL	14	1	26	26.0	0	17	286	16.8	0	2	21	10.5	0	0	...	0	0
1975—Detroit NFL	10	4	39	9.8	0	6	29	4.8	0	0	0	...	0	0	...	0	0
1976—Detroit NFL	6	2	0	0.0	0	0	0	...	0	0	0	...	0	0	...	0	0
1977—Detroit NFL	14	3	55	18.3	0	11	41	3.7	0	0	0	...	0	0	...	0	0
1978—Cincinnati NFL	16	4	52	13.0	1	3	32	10.7	0	0	0	...	0	1	...	6	0
1979—Cincinnati NFL	16	6	41	6.8	0	1	10	10.0	0	0	0	...	0	0	...	0	0
1980—Cincinnati NFL	10	1	11	11.0	0	0	0	...	0	0	0	...	0	0	...	0	0
Pro totals (8 years)	100	25	432	17.3	2	44	447	10.2	0	19	426	22.4	0	2	...	12	0

HEAD COACHING RECORD

BACKGROUND: Secondary coach, Buffalo Bills NFL (1985). ... Defensive backs coach, Green Bay Packers NFL (1986-94). ... Defensive coordinator, Jacksonville Jaguars NFL (1995-1998).

	REGULAR SEASON					POST-SEASON	
	W	L	T	Pct.	Finish	W	L
1999—Chicago NFL	6	10	0	.375	5th/NFC Central Division	—	—

MARIUCCI, STEVE — 49ERS

PERSONAL: Born November 4, 1955, in Iron Mountain, Mich. ... Full name: Steven Mariucci. ... Played quarterback.
HIGH SCHOOL: Iron Mountain (Mich.).
COLLEGE: Northern Michigan.
TRANSACTIONS/CAREER NOTES: Signed with Hamilton Tiger-Cats of CFL for 1978 season.

HEAD COACHING RECORD

BACKGROUND: Quarterbacks/running backs coach, Northern Michigan (1978 and 1979). ... Quarterbacks/special teams coordinator, Cal State Fullerton (1980-1982). ... Assistant head coach, Louisville (1983 and 1984). ... Receivers coach, Orlando Renegades USFL (1985). ... Quality control coach, Los Angeles Rams NFL (fall 1985). ... Wide receivers/special teams coach, University of California (1987-1989). ... Offensive coordinator/quarterbacks coach, University of California (1990 and 1991). ... Quarterbacks coach, Green Bay Packers NFL (1992-1995).

	REGULAR SEASON					POST-SEASON	
	W	L	T	Pct.	Finish	W	L
1996—California	6	6	0	.500	T5th/Pacific-10 Conference	0	1
1997—San Francisco NFL	13	3	0	.813	1st/NFC Western Division	1	1
1998—San Francisco NFL	12	4	0	.750	2nd/NFC Western Division	1	1
1999—San Francisco NFL	4	12	0	.250	4th/NFC Western Division	—	—
College totals (1 year)	6	6	0	.500	**College totals (1 year)**	0	1
Pro totals (3 years)	29	19	0	.604	**Pro totals (3 years)**	2	2

NOTES:
1996—Lost to Navy, 42-38, in Aloha Bowl.
1997—Defeated Minnesota, 38-22, in conference playoff game; lost to Green Bay, 23-10, in NFC championship game.
1998—Defeated Green Bay, 30-27, in first-round playoff game; lost to Atlanta, 20-18, in conference playoff game.

MARTZ, MIKE — RAMS

PERSONAL: Born May 13, 1951, in Sioux Falls, S.D.
HIGH SCHOOL: Madison (San Diego).
JUNIOR COLLEGE: San Diego Mesa Community College.
COLLEGE: UC Santa Barbara, then Fresno State.

HEAD COACHING RECORD

BACKGROUND: Coach, Bullard High School, Fresno, Calif. (1973). ... Coach, San Diego Mesa Community College (1974, 1976 and 1977). ... Coach, San Jose State (1975). ... Coach, Santa Ana College (1978). ... Coach, Fresno State (1979). ... Coach, Pacific University (1980 and 1981). ... Running backs coach, University of Minnesota (1982). ... Quarterbacks/receivers coach, Arizona State (1983-1987). ... Offensive coordinator, Arizona State (1984 and 1988-1991). ... Offensive assistant, Los Angeles Rams NFL (1992-1994). ... Offensive assistant, St. Louis Rams NFL (1995 and 1996). ... Quarterbacks coach, Washington Redskins NFL (1997 and 1998). ... Offensive coordinator, Rams (1999).

MORA, JIM — COLTS

PERSONAL: Born May 24, 1935, in Los Angeles. ... Full name: James Ernest Mora.
HIGH SCHOOL: University (Los Angeles).
COLLEGE: Occidental College (bachelor degree in physical education, 1957), then Southern California (master's degree in education, 1967).
MISCELLANEOUS: Played for U.S. Marines at Quantico (1957) and Camp Lejeune (1958 and 1959).

HEAD COACHING RECORD

BACKGROUND: Assistant coach, Occidental College (1960-1963). ... Linebackers coach, Stanford (1967). ... Defensive assistant, University of Colorado (1967-1973). ... Linebackers coach, UCLA (1974). ... Defensive coordinator, University of Washington (1975-1977). ... Defensive line coach, Seattle Seahawks NFL (1978-1981). ... Defensive coordinator, New England Patriots NFL (1982).
HONORS: Named USFL Coach of the Year by THE SPORTING NEWS (1984). ... Named NFL Coach of the Year by THE SPORTING NEWS (1987).

					REGULAR SEASON		POST-SEASON	
	W	L	T	Pct.	Finish		W	L
1964—Occidental	5	4	0	.556	3rd/Southern Calif. Intercollegiate Conference		—	—
1965—Occidental	8	1	0	.889	1st/Southern Calif. Intercollegiate Conference		—	—
1966—Occidental	5	4	0	.556	4th/Southern Calif. Intercollegiate Conference		—	—
1983—Philadelphia USFL	15	3	0	.833	1st/Atlantic Division		1	1
1984—Philadelphia USFL	16	2	0	.889	1st/Eastern Conference Atlantic Division		3	0
1985—Baltimore USFL	10	7	1	.583	4th/Eastern Conference		3	0
1986—New Orleans NFL	7	9	0	.438	4th/Western Division		—	—
1987—New Orleans NFL	12	3	0	.800	2nd/Western Division		0	1
1988—New Orleans NFL	10	6	0	.625	T1st/Western Division		—	—
1989—New Orleans NFL	9	7	0	.563	3rd/Western Division		—	—
1990—New Orleans NFL	8	8	0	.500	2nd/Western Division		0	1
1991—New Orleans NFL	11	5	0	.688	1st/Western Division		0	1
1992—New Orleans NFL	12	4	0	.750	2nd/Western Division		0	1
1993—New Orleans NFL	8	8	0	.500	2nd/Western Division		—	—
1994—New Orleans NFL	7	9	0	.438	T2nd/Western Division		—	—
1995—New Orleans NFL	7	9	0	.438	T3rd/Western Division		—	—
1998—Indianapolis NFL	3	13	0	.188	5th/AFCWestern Division		—	—
1999—Indianapolis NFL	13	3	0	.813	1st/AFC Eastern Division		0	1
College totals (3 years)	18	9	0	.667				
USFL totals (3 years)	41	12	1	.769	**USFL totals (3 years)**		7	1
NFL totals (12 years)	107	84	0	.560	**NFL totals (5 years)**		0	5
Pro totals (15 years)	148	96	1	.606	**Pro totals (8 years)**		7	6

NOTES:
1983—Defeated Chicago, 44-38 (OT), in divisional playoff game; lost to Michigan, 24-22, in USFL championship game.
1984—Defeated New Jersey, 28-7, in conference playoff game; defeated Birmingham, 20-10, in conference championship game; defeated Arizona, 23-3, in USFL championship game.
1985—Defeated New Jersey, 20-17, in conference playoff game; defeated Birmingham, 28-14, in conference championship game; defeated Oakland, 28-24, in USFL championship game.
1987—Lost to Minnesota, 44-10, in wild-card playoff game.
1990—Lost to Chicago, 16-6, in conference playoff game.
1991—Lost to Atlanta, 27-20, in first-round playoff game.
1992—Lost to Philadelphia, 36-20, in first-round playoff game.
1999—Lost to Tennessee, 19-16, in conference playoff game.

PALMER, CHRIS — BROWNS

PERSONAL: Born September 23, 1949, in Brewster, N.Y. ... Full name: Christopher J. Palmer.
COLLEGE: Southern Connecticut State.

HEAD COACHING RECORD

BACKGROUND: Wide receivers/defensive line coach, University of Connecticut (1972-1975). ... Wide receivers coach, Lehigh University (1975). ... Offensive coordinator, Colgate University (1976-1982). ... Offensive line coach, Montreal Concordes CFL (1983). ... Wide receivers coach, New Jersey Generals USFL (1984). ... Quaterbacks coach/offensive coordinator, New Jersey Generals USFL (1985). ... Wide receivers coach, Houston Oilers NFL (1990-1992). ... Wide receivers coach, New England Patriots NFL (1993-1995). ... Quarterbacks coach, Patriots (1996). ... Offensive coordinator, Jacksonville Jaguars NFL (1997 and 1998).

					REGULAR SEASON		POST-SEASON	
	W	L	T	Pct.	Finish		W	L
1986—New Haven	8	2	0	.800	Independent		—	—
1987—New Haven	8	2	0	.800	Independent		—	—
1988—Boston University	4	7	0	.364	T7th/Yankee Conference		—	—
1989—Boston University	4	7	0	.364	6th/Yankee Conference		—	—
1999—Cleveland NFL	2	14	0	.125	6th/AFC Central Division		—	—
College totals (4 years)	24	18	0	.571				

PHILLIPS, WADE — BILLS

PERSONAL: Born June 21, 1947, in Orange, Texas. ... Son of O.A. (Bum) Phillips, head coach with Houston Oilers (1975-80) and New Orleans Saints (1981-85).
HIGH SCHOOL: Port Neches-Groves (Neches, Texas).
COLLEGE: Houston (degrees in physical education and speech).

HEAD COACHING RECORD

BACKGROUND: Assistant coach, University of Houston (1969). ... Head coach, Orange (Texas) High School (1970-1972). ... Assistant coach, Oklahoma State (1973 and 1974). ... Assistant coach, Kansas (1975). ... Assistant coach, Houston Oilers NFL (1976-1980). ... Assistant coach, New Orleans Saints NFL (1981-November 25, 1985). ... Assistant coach, Philadelphia Eagles NFL (1986-1988). ... Defensive coordinator, Denver Broncos NFL (1989-January 25, 1993). ... Defensive coordinator, Buffalo Bills NFL (1995-1997).

			REGULAR SEASON				POST-SEASON	
	W	L	T	Pct.	Finish		W	L
1985—New Orleans NFL................	1	3	0	.250	3rd/NFC Western Division		—	—
1993—Denver NFL	9	7	0	.563	3rd/AFC Western Division		0	1
1994—Denver NFL	7	9	0	.438	4th/AFC Western Division			
1998—Buffalo NFL	10	6	0	.625	T2nd/AFC Eastern Division		0	1
1999—Buffalo NFL	11	5	0	.688	2nd/AFC Eastern Division		0	1
Pro totals (5 years)	**38**	**30**	**0**	**.559**	**Pro totals (3 years)**		**0**	**3**

NOTES:
1993—Lost to Los Angeles Raiders, 42-24, in first-round playoff game.
1998—Lost to Miami, 24-17, in first-round playoff game.
1999—Lost to Tennessee, 22-16, in first-round playoff game.

REEVES, DAN   FALCONS

PERSONAL: Born January 19, 1944, in Rome, Ga. ... Full name: Daniel Edward Reeves. ... Played running back.
HIGH SCHOOL: Americus (Ga.).
COLLEGE: South Carolina.
TRANSACTIONS/CAREER NOTES: Signed as non-drafted free agent by Dallas Cowboys for 1965 season.
CHAMPIONSHIP GAME EXPERIENCE: Played in NFL championship game (1966 and 1967 seasons). ... Played in NFC championship game (1970 and 1971 seasons). ... Played in Super Bowl V (1970 season). ... Member of Super Bowl championship team (1971 season).
HONORS: Named halfback on THE SPORTING NEWS NFL Eastern Conference All-Star team (1966).
PRO STATISTICS: 1965—Returned two kickoffs for 45 yards. 1966—Returned two punts for minus one yard, returned three kickoffs for 56 yards and fumbled six times. 1967—Fumbled seven times. 1969—Fumbled twice. 1970—Fumbled four times. 1971—Fumbled once.

			PASSING						RUSHING				RECEIVING				TOTALS		
Year Team	G	GS	Att.	Cmp.	Pct.	Yds.	TD	Int.	Avg.	Att.	Yds.	Avg.	TD	No.	Yds.	Avg.	TD	TD	2pt.	Pts.
1965—Dallas NFL..........	13	...	2	1	50.0	11	0	0	5.50	33	102	3.1	2	9	210	23.3	1	3	...	18
1966—Dallas NFL..........	14	...	6	3	50.0	48	0	0	8.00	175	757	4.3	8	41	557	13.6	8	16	...	96
1967—Dallas NFL..........	14	...	7	4	57.1	195	2	1	27.86	173	603	3.5	5	39	490	12.6	6	11	...	66
1968—Dallas NFL..........	4	...	4	2	50.0	43	0	0	10.75	40	178	4.5	4	7	84	12.0	1	5	...	30
1969—Dallas NFL..........	13	...	3	1	33.3	35	0	1	11.67	59	173	2.9	4	18	187	10.4	1	5	...	30
1970—Dallas NFL..........	14	...	3	1	33.3	14	0	1	4.67	35	84	2.4	2	12	140	11.7	0	2	...	12
1971—Dallas NFL..........	14	...	5	2	40.0	24	0	1	4.80	17	79	4.6	0	3	25	8.3	0	0	...	0
1972—Dallas NFL..........	14	...	2	0	0.0	0	0	0	...	3	14	4.7	0	0	0	...	0	0	...	0
Pro totals (8 years)	100	...	32	14	43.8	370	2	4	11.56	535	1990	3.7	25	129	1693	13.1	17	42	...	252

HEAD COACHING RECORD

BACKGROUND: Player/coach, Dallas Cowboys NFL (1970 and 1971). ... Offensive backs coach, Cowboys (1972 and 1974-1976). ... Offensive coordinator, Cowboys (1977-1980).
HONORS: Named NFL Coach of the Year by THE SPORTING NEWS (1993 and 1998).

			REGULAR SEASON				POST-SEASON	
	W	L	T	Pct.	Finish		W	L
1981—Denver NFL	10	6	0	.625	T1st/AFC Western Division		—	—
1982—Denver NFL	2	7	0	.222	12th/AFC		—	—
1983—Denver NFL	9	7	0	.563	T2nd/AFC Western Division		0	1
1984—Denver NFL	13	3	0	.813	1st/AFC Western Division		0	1
1985—Denver NFL	11	5	0	.688	2nd/AFC Western Division		—	—
1986—Denver NFL	11	5	0	.688	1st/AFC Western Division		2	1
1987—Denver NFL	10	4	1	.700	1st/AFC Western Division		2	1
1988—Denver NFL	8	8	0	.500	2nd/AFC Western Division		—	—
1989—Denver NFL	11	5	0	.688	1st/AFC Western Division		2	1
1990—Denver NFL	5	11	0	.313	5th/AFC Western Division		—	—
1991—Denver NFL	12	4	0	.750	1st/AFC Western Division		1	1
1992—Denver NFL	8	8	0	.500	3rd/AFC Western Division		—	—
1993—New York Giants NFL	11	5	0	.688	2nd/NFC Eastern Division		1	1
1994—New York Giants NFL	9	7	0	.563	2nd/NFC Eastern Division		—	—
1995—New York Giants NFL	5	11	0	.313	4th/NFC Eastern Division		—	—
1996—New York Giants NFL	6	10	0	.375	5th/NFC Eastern Division		—	—
1997—Atlanta NFL.........................	7	9	0	.438	T2nd/NFC Western Division		—	—
1998—Atlanta NFL.........................	14	2	0	.875	1st/NFC Western Division		2	1
1999—Atlanta NFL.........................	5	11	0	.313	3rd/NFC Western Division		—	—
Pro totals (19 years)	**167**	**128**	**1**	**.566**	**Pro totals (9 years)**		**10**	**8**

NOTES:
1983—Lost to Seattle, 31-7, in wild-card playoff game.
1984—Lost to Pittsburgh, 24-17, in conference playoff game.
1986—Defeated New England, 22-17, in conference playoff game; defeated Cleveland, 23-20 (OT), in AFC championship game; lost to New York Giants, 39-20, in Super Bowl XXI.
1987—Defeated Houston, 34-10, in conference playoff game; defeated Cleveland, 38-33, in AFC championship game; lost to Washington, 42-10, in Super Bowl XXII.
1989—Defeated Pittsburgh, 24-23, in conference playoff game; defeated Cleveland, 37-21, in AFC championship game; lost to San Francisco, 55-10, in Super Bowl XXIV.
1991—Defeated Houston, 26-24, in conference playoff game; lost to Buffalo, 10-7, in AFC championship game.
1993—Defeated Minnesota, 17-10, in first-round playoff game; lost to San Francisco, 44-3, in conference playoff game.
1998—Defeated San Francisco, 20-18, in conference playoff game; defeated Minnesota, 30-27, in NFC championship game; lost to Denver, 34-19, in Super Bowl XXXIII.

REID, ANDY   EAGLES

PERSONAL: Born March 19, 1958, in Los Angeles. ... Full name: Andrew Walter Reid.
HIGH SCHOOL: John Marshall (Los Angeles).
COLLEGE: Brigham Young (bachelor's degree in physical education; master's degree in professional leadership, physical education and athletics).

HEAD COACHING RECORD
BACKGROUND: Graduate assistant, Brigham Young University (1982). ... Offensive coordinator, San Francisco State (1983-1985). ... Offensive line coach, Northern Arizona University (1986). ... Offensive line coach, University of Texas-El Paso (1987 and 1988). ... Offensive line coach, University of Missouri (1989-1992). ... Tight ends coach, Green Bay Packers NFL (1993-1996). ... Quarterbacks coach, Packers (1997 and 1998).

	REGULAR SEASON					POST-SEASON	
	W	L	T	Pct.	Finish	W	L
1999—Philadelphia NFL	5	11	0	.313	5th/NFC Eastern Division	—	—

RILEY, MIKE   CHARGERS

PERSONAL: Born July 6, 1953, in Wallace, Idaho ... Full name: Michael Joseph Riley.
HIGH SCHOOL: Corvallis (Ore.).
COLLEGE: Alabama (degree in social science), then Whitworth College, Wash. (master's degree).
HONORS: Named CFL Coach of the Year (1988 and 1990).

HEAD COACHING RECORD
BACKGROUND: Graduate assistant, University of California (1975). ... Graduate assistant, Whitworth College (1976). ... Defensive coordinator/secondary, Linfield College (1977-1982). ... Secondary coach, Winnipeg Blue Bombers of CFL (1983-1985). ... Defensive coordinator, Northern Colorado University (1986). ... Offensive coordinator/quarterbacks coach, University of Southern California (1993-1996).

	REGULAR SEASON					POST-SEASON	
	W	L	T	Pct.	Finish	W	L
1987—Winnipeg CFL	12	6	0	.667	1st/Eastern Division	0	1
1988—Winnipeg CFL	9	9	0	.500	2nd/Eastern Division	3	0
1989—Winnipeg CFL	7	11	0	.389	3rd/Eastern Division	1	1
1990—Winnipeg CFL	12	6	0	.667	1st/Eastern Division	2	0
1991—San Antonio W.L.	4	6	0	.400	—		
1992—San Antonio W.L.	7	3	0	.700	—	—	—
1997—Oregon State	3	8	0	.273	10th/Pacific 10 Conference	—	—
1998—Oregon State	5	6	0	.455	T8th/Pacific 10 Conference	—	—
1999—San Diego NFL	8	8	0	.500	T3rd/AFC Western Division	—	—
College totals (2 years)	8	14	0	.364			
W.L. totals (2 years)	11	9	0	.550			
CFL totals (4 years)	40	32	0	.556	**CFL totals (4 years)**	6	2
NFL totals (1 years)	8	8	0	.500			
Pro totals (7 years)	59	49	0	.546	**Pro totals (5 years)**	6	2

NOTES:
1987—Lost to Toronto Argonauts, 19-3, in Divisional Finals of Grey Cup.
1988—Defeated Hamilton, 35-28, in Divisional Semi-finals of Grey Cup; defeated Toronto, 27-11, in Divisional Finals of Grey Cup; defeated B.C., 22-21, in Grey Cup Finals.
1989—Defeated Toronto, 30-7, in Divisional Semifinals of Grey Cup; lost to Hamilton, 14-10, in Divisional Finals of Grey Cup.
1990—Defeated Toronto, 20-17, in Divisional Finals of Grey Cup; defeated Edmonton, 50-11, in Grey Cup finals.

ROSS, BOBBY   LIONS

PERSONAL: Born December 23, 1936, in Richmond, Va. ... Full name: Robert Joseph Ross.
HIGH SCHOOL: Benedictine (Richmond, Va.).
COLLEGE: Virginia Military Institute (degrees in English and history, 1959).

HEAD COACHING RECORD
BACKGROUND: Head coach, Benedictine High School, Richmond, Va. (1959; record: 1-8-1). ... Served in military (1960-1962). ... Assistant coach, Colonial Heights (Va.) High School (1962). ... Head coach, Colonial Heights (Va.) High School (1963 and 1964). ... Freshman coach, Virginia Military Institute (1965). ... Defensive backs coach, VMI (1966). ... Offensive backs coach, William & Mary (1967 and 1968). ... Defensive backs coach, William & Mary (1969). ... Defensive coordinator, William & Mary (1970). ... Linebackers coach, Rice (1971). ... Linebackers coach, Maryland (1972). ... Special teams coach, Kansas City Chiefs NFL (1978 and 1979). ... Offensive backs coach, Chiefs (1980 and 1981).
HONORS: Named College Football Coach of the Year by THE SPORTING NEWS (1990).

	REGULAR SEASON					POST-SEASON	
	W	L	T	Pct.	Finish	W	L
1973—The Citadel	3	8	0	.273	T7th/Southern Conference	—	—
1974—The Citadel	4	7	0	.364	5th/Southern Conference	—	—
1975—The Citadel	6	5	0	.545	4th/Southern Conference	—	—
1976—The Citadel	6	5	0	.545	6th/Southern Conference	—	—
1977—The Citadel	5	6	0	.455	T3rd/Southern Conference	—	—
1982—Maryland	8	3	0	.727	2nd/Atlantic Coast Conference	0	1
1983—Maryland	8	3	0	.727	1st/Atlantic Coast Conference	0	1
1984—Maryland	8	3	0	.727	1st/Atlantic Coast Conference	1	0

HEAD COACHES

	W	L	T	Pct.	Finish	Post-season W	Post-season L
1985—Maryland	8	3	0	.727	1st/Atlantic Coast Conference	1	0
1986—Maryland	5	5	1	.500	5th/Atlantic Coast Conference	—	—
1987—Georgia Tech	2	9	0	.182	8th/Atlantic Coast Conference	—	—
1988—Georgia Tech	3	8	0	.273	8th/Atlantic Coast Conference	—	—
1989—Georgia Tech	7	4	0	.636	T4th/Atlantic Coast Conference	—	—
1990—Georgia Tech	10	0	1	.955	1st/Atlantic Coast Conference	1	0
1991—Georgia Tech	7	5	0	.583	T2nd/Atlantic Coast Conference	1	0
1992—San Diego NFL	11	5	0	.688	1st/AFC Western Division	1	1
1993—San Diego NFL	8	8	0	.500	4th/AFC Western Division	—	—
1994—San Diego NFL	11	5	0	.688	1st/AFC Western Division	2	1
1995—San Diego NFL	9	7	0	.563	2nd/AFC Western Division	0	1
1996—San Diego NFL	8	8	0	.500	3rd/AFC Western Division	—	—
1997—Detroit NFL	9	7	0	.563	T3rd/NFC Central Division	0	1
1998—Detroit NFL	5	11	0	.313	4th/NFC Central Division	—	—
1999—Detroit NFL	8	8	0	.500	T3rd/NFC Central Division	0	1
College totals (15 years)	90	74	2	.548	**College totals (6 years)**	4	2
Pro totals (8 years)	69	59	0	.539	**Pro totals (5 years)**	3	5

NOTES:

1982—Lost to Washington, 21-10, in Aloha Bowl.
1983—Lost to Tennessee, 30-23, in Florida Citrus Bowl.
1984—Defeated Tennessee, 28-27, in Sun Bowl.
1985—Defeated Syracuse, 35-18, in Cherry Bowl.
1990—Defeated Nebraska, 45-21, in Florida Citrus Bowl.
1991—Defeated Stanford, 18-17, in Aloha Bowl.
1992—Defeated Kansas City, 17-0, in first-round playoff game; lost to Miami, 31-0, in conference playoff game.
1994—Defeated Miami, 22-21, in conference playoff game; defeated Pittsburgh, 17-13, in AFC championship game; lost to San Francisco, 49-26, in Super Bowl XXIX.
1995—Lost to Indianapolis, 35-20, in first-round playoff game.
1997—Lost to Tampa Bay, 20-10, in first-round playoff game.
1999—Lost to Washington, 27-13, in first-round playoff game.

SEIFERT, GEORGE — PANTHERS

PERSONAL: Born January 22, 1940, in San Francisco. ... Full name: George Gerald Seifert. ... Name pronounced SEE-fert.
HIGH SCHOOL: Polytechnic (Pasadena, Calif.).
COLLEGE: Utah (bachelor's degree in zoology, 1963; master's degree in physical education, 1966).
MISCELLANEOUS: Served six months in U.S. Army after college.

HEAD COACHING RECORD

BACKGROUND: Graduate assistant, Utah (1964). ... Assistant coach, Iowa (1966). ... Defensive backs coach, Oregon (1967-1971). ... Defensive backs coach, Stanford (1972-1974 and 1977-1979). ... Defensive backs coach, San Francisco 49ers NFL (1980-1982). ... Defensive coordinator, 49ers (1983-1988).
HONORS: Named NFL Coach of the Year by The Sporting News (1990 and 1994).

	W	L	T	Pct.	Finish	Post-season W	Post-season L
1965—Westminster College (Utah)	3	3	0	.500	Independent	—	—
1975—Cornell	1	8	0	.111	8th/Ivy League	—	—
1976—Cornell	2	7	0	.222	T7th/Ivy League	—	—
1989—San Francisco NFL	14	2	0	.875	1st/NFC Western Division	3	0
1990—San Francisco NFL	14	2	0	.875	1st/NFC Western Division	1	1
1991—San Francisco NFL	10	6	0	.625	T2nd/NFC Western Division	—	—
1992—San Francisco NFL	14	2	0	.875	1st/NFC Western Division	1	1
1993—San Francisco NFL	10	6	0	.625	1st/NFC Western Division	1	1
1994—San Francisco NFL	13	3	0	.813	1st/NFC Western Division	3	0
1995—San Francisco NFL	11	5	0	.688	1st/NFC Western Division	0	1
1996—San Francisco NFL	12	4	0	.750	T1st/NFC Western Division	1	1
1999—Carolina NFL	8	8	0	.500	2nd/NFC Western Division	—	—
College totals (3 years)	6	18	0	.250			
Pro totals (9 years)	106	38	0	.736	**Pro totals (8 years)**	10	5

NOTES:

1989—Defeated Minnesota, 41-13, in conference playoff game; defeated Los Angeles Rams, 30-3, in NFC championship game; defeated Denver, 55-10, in Super Bowl XXIV.
1990—Defeated Washington, 28-10, in conference playoff game; lost to New York Giants, 15-13, in NFC championship game.
1992—Defeated Washington, 20-13, in conference playoff game; lost to Dallas 30-20 in NFC championship game.
1993—Defeated New York Giants, 44-3, in conference playoff game; lost to Dallas 38-21, in NFC championship game.
1994—Defeated Chicago, 44-15, in conference playoff game; defeated Dallas, 38-28, in NFC championship game; defeated San Diego, 49-26, in Super Bowl XXIX.
1995—Lost to Green Bay, 27-17, in conference playoff game.
1996—Defeated Philadelphia; 14-0, in first-round playoff game; lost to Green Bay, 35-14, in conference playoff game.

SHANAHAN, MIKE — BRONCOS

PERSONAL: Born August 24, 1952, in Oak Park, Ill. ... Full name: Michael Edward Shanahan.
HIGH SCHOOL: Franklin Park (East Leyden, Ill.).
COLLEGE: Eastern Illinois (bachelor's degree in physical education, 1974; master's degree in education, 1975).

HEAD COACHING RECORD

BACKGROUND: Graduate assistant, Eastern Illinois (1973 and 1974). ... Running backs/wide receivers coach, Oklahoma (1975 and 1976). ... Backfield coach, Northern Arizona (1977). ... Offensive coordinator, Eastern Illinois (1978). ... Offensive coordinator, University of Minnesota (1979). ... Offensive coordinator, University of Florida (1980-1983). ... Quarterbacks coach, Denver Broncos NFL (1984, 1989 and 1990). ... Offensive coordinator, Broncos (1985-1987 and 1991). ... Offensive coordinator, San Francisco 49ers NFL (1992-1994).

		REGULAR SEASON				POST-SEASON	
	W	L	T	Pct.	Finish	W	L
1988—Los Angeles Raiders NFL	7	9	0	.438	3rd/AFC Western Division	—	—
1989—Los Angeles Raiders NFL	1	3	0	.250	—	—	—
1995—Denver NFL	8	8	0	.500	T3rd/AFC Western Division	—	—
1996—Denver NFL	13	3	0	.813	1st/AFC Western Division	0	1
1997—Denver NFL	12	4	0	.750	2nd/AFC Western Conference	4	0
1998—Denver NFL	14	2	0	.875	1st/AFC Western Division	3	0
1999—Denver NFL	6	10	0	.375	5th/AFC Western Division	—	—
Pro totals (7 years)	**61**	**39**	**0**	**.610**	**Pro totals (5 years)**	**7**	**1**

NOTES:

1989—Replaced as Raiders coach by Art Shell (October 3) with club tied for fourth place.

1996—Lost to Jacksonville, 30-27, in conference playoff game.

1997—Defeated Jacksonville, 42-17, in first-round playoff game; defeated Kansas City, 14-10, in conference playoff game; defeated Pittsburgh, 24-21, in AFC championship game; defeated Green Bay, 31-24, in Super Bowl XXXII.

1998—Defeated Miami, 38-3, in conference playoff game; defeated New York Jets, 23-10, in AFC championship game; defeated Atlanta, 34-19, in Super Bowl XXXIII

SHERMAN, MIKE — PACKERS

PERSONAL: Born December 19, 1954, in Norwood, Mass.
COLLEGE: Central Connecticut State.

HEAD COACHING RECORD

BACKGROUND: Head coach, Stamford High School, Stamford, Conn. (1979 and 1980). ... Coach, University of Pittsburgh (1981 and 1982). ... Coach, Tulane (1983 and 1984). ... Offensive coordinator, Holy Cross (1985-1988). ... Offensive line coach, Texas A&M (1989-1993). ... Offensive line coach, UCLA (1994). ... Offensive line coach, Texas A&M (1995-1996). ... Tight ends coach, Green Bay Packers NFL (1997-1998). ... Offensive coordinator/tight ends coach, Seattle Seahawks NFL (1999).

TOBIN, VINCE — CARDINALS

PERSONAL: Born September 29, 1943, in Burlington Junction, Mo.
HIGH SCHOOL: Maryville (Mo.).
COLLEGE: Missouri (bachelor's degree in physical education, 1965; master's degree in guidance and counseling, 1966).

HEAD COACHING RECORD

BACKGROUND: Graduate assistant, University of Missouri (1965 and 1966). ... Defensive ends coach, Missouri (1967-1970). ... Defensive coordinator, Missouri (1971-1976). ... Defensive coordinator, British Columbia Lions of CFL (1977-1982). ... Defensive coordinator, Philadelphia/Baltimore Stars USFL (1983-1985). ... Defensive coordinator, Chicago Bears NFL (1986-1992). ... Defensive coordinator, Indianapolis Colts NFL (1994 and 1995).

		REGULAR SEASON				POST-SEASON	
	W	L	T	Pct.	Finish	W	L
1996—Arizona NFL........................	7	9	0	.438	4th/NFC Eastern Division	—	—
1997—Arizona NFL........................	4	12	0	.250	5th/NFC Eastern Division	—	—
1998—Arizona NFL........................	9	7	0	.563	2nd/NFC Eastern Division	1	1
1999—Arizona NFL........................	6	10	0	.375	4th/NFC Eastern Division	—	—
Pro totals (4 years)	**26**	**38**	**0**	**.406**	**Pro totals (2 years)**	**1**	**1**

NOTES:

1998—Defeated Dallas, 20-7, in first-round playoff game; lost to Minnesota, 41-21, in conference playoff game.

TURNER, NORV — REDSKINS

PERSONAL: Born May 17, 1952, in LeJeune, N.C. ... Full name: Norval Eugene Turner. ... Brother of Ron Turner, head coach, University of Illinois.
HIGH SCHOOL: Alhambra (Calif.).
COLLEGE: Oregon (degree in history, 1975).

HEAD COACHING RECORD

BACKGROUND: Graduate assistant, Oregon (1975). ... Receivers coach, Southern California (1976-1979). ... Defensive backs coach, USC (1980). ... Quarterbacks coach, USC (1981-1983). ... Offensive coordinator, USC (1984). ... Receivers coach, Los Angeles Rams NFL (1985-1990). ... Offensive coordinator, Dallas Cowboys NFL (1991-1993).

		REGULAR SEASON				POST-SEASON	
	W	L	T	Pct.	Finish	W	L
1994—Washington NFL..................	3	13	0	.188	5th/NFC Eastern Division	—	—
1995—Washington NFL..................	6	10	0	.375	3rd/NFC Eastern Division	—	—
1996—Washington NFL..................	9	7	0	.563	3rd/NFC Eastern Division	—	—

997—Washington NFL	8	7	1	.531	2nd/NFC Eastern Division	—	—
998—Washington NFL	6	10	0	.375	4th/NFC Eastern Division	—	—
999—Washington NFL	10	6	0	.625	1st/NFC Eastern Division	1	1
Pro totals (6 years)	**42**	**53**	**1**	**.443**	**Pro totals (1 year)**	**1**	**1**

NOTES:
1999—Defeated Detroit, 27-13, in first-round playoff game; lost to Tampa Bay, 14-13, in conference playoff game.

WANNSTEDT, DAVE — DOLPHINS

PERSONAL: Born May 21, 1952, in Pittsburgh. ... Full name: David Raymond Wannstedt.
HIGH SCHOOL: Baldwin (Pittsburgh).
COLLEGE: Pittsburgh (bachelor of science degree in physical education, 1974; master's degree in education, 1975).
TRANSACTIONS/CAREER NOTES: Selected by Green Bay Packers in 15th round (376th pick overall) of 1974 NFL draft. ... On injured reserve with neck injury entire 1974 season.

HEAD COACHING RECORD

BACKGROUND: Graduate assistant, University of Pittsburgh (1975). ... Defensive line coach, Pittsburgh (1976-1978). ... Defensive line coach, Oklahoma State (1979 and 1980). ... Defensive coordinator, Oklahoma State (1981 and 1982). ... Defensive line coach, Southern California (1983-1985). ... Defensive coordinator, Miami, Fla. (1986-1988). ... Defensive coordinator, Dallas Cowboys NFL (1989-1992). ... Assistant head coach, Miami Dolphins NFL (1999).

	REGULAR SEASON					POST-SEASON	
	W	L	T	Pct.	Finish	W	L
1993—Chicago NFL	7	9	0	.438	4th/NFC Central Division	—	—
1994—Chicago NFL	9	7	0	.563	T2nd/NFC Central Division	1	1
1995—Chicago NFL	9	7	0	.563	3rd/NFC Central Division	—	—
1996—Chicago NFL	7	9	0	.438	3rd/NFC Central Division	—	—
1997—Chicago NFL	4	12	0	.250	5th/NFC Central Division	—	—
1998—Chicago NFL	4	12	0	.250	5th/NFC Central Division	—	—
Pro totals (6 years)	**40**	**56**	**0**	**.417**	**Pro totals (1 year)**	**1**	**1**

NOTES:
1994—Defeated Minnesota, 35-18, in first-round playoff game; lost to San Francisco, 44-15, in conference playoff game.